PHILOSOPHY · POETRY · HISTORY

PHILOSOPHY
POETRY · HISTORY

AN ANTHOLOGY OF ESSAYS
BY
BENEDETTO CROCE

Translated and Introduced
by Cecil Sprigge

LONDON
OXFORD UNIVERSITY PRESS
NEW YORK · TORONTO
1966

Oxford University Press, Ely House, London W. 1

GLASGOW NEW YORK TORONTO MELBOURNE WELLINGTON
CAPE TOWN SALISBURY IBADAN NAIROBI LUSAKA ADDIS ABABA
BOMBAY CALCUTTA MADRAS KARACHI LAHORE DACCA
KUALA LUMPUR HONG KONG

★

FILOSOFIA · POESIA · STORIA was first published in Italy
by Riccardo Ricciardi, Milan–Naples, 1951.

195
C 937p
117163

PRINTED IN ITALY
BY STAMPERIA VALDONEGA · VERONA

CONTENTS

III

AESTHETICS: THE PHILOSOPHY OF ART
AND LANGUAGE

IV

THE THEORY OF HISTORY

V
ECONOMICS AND ETHICS

VI
ESSAYS IN CRITICISM AND LITERARY HISTORY

VII
MORAL AND POLITICAL HISTORY

decade of Croce's birth, the ancient monarchy of Naples collapsed, the Pope was stripped of his domains, Austria was chased out of Italy; Benedetto was four years old when the Piedmontese King marched into Rome. The old formulae of legitimacy and the old hierarchies of a religiously directed culture were challenged and defeated. The extreme school of innovators had wanted a people's republic, not a national monarchy, and protested noisily against the middling solution. On the other side fallen princes and outraged ecclesiastics foretold the early doom of a settlement obtained by the guile of an apostate Court exploiting (and cheating) the forces of disorder.

Men of enthusiastic temperament suffered humiliation from the disproportion between recent dreams and their first realization. Foreign poets were no longer writing odes to Italy. The thin schematism of the Piedmontese liberal monarchy could provide a single administrative apparatus for Italy but not a focus for the sentiments of local societies, separated from each other by centuries of history, deeply divided in their feelings about the discomfiture of the Church, and linguistically hardly able to understand each other.

In the Kingdom of Naples the Piedmontese found a foreign and mysterious country, ready to cheer the new King – for many dynasties had been and gone – and ready even to invest him with a certain poetic halo for deeds done in the far North. Much less did the Neapolitans like his taxgathering officials and the hard bargaining business men in their wake. But if the Southern Kingdom had simply crumbled under the joint impact of Garibaldi's seaborne partisans and the Piedmontese Army, a wing of the Neapolitan gentry was rightly associated in the triumph. From the days of Napoleon this group had repeatedly risked its life in agitations to extort a liberal constitution from the Bourbons. The boldest had tasted the royal gaols or exile or both. The highly bred Neapolitan exiles had thronged Turin in the fifties, and these were not the first from Naples to help build up a tradition of common Italian patriotism which enabled the Piedmontese to march upon the South in 1860 in the guise of liberators. The exiles finally returning triumphantly to Naples included Francesco De Sanctis, one of the most ardent philosophic minds of his generation, and the two brothers Spaventa, all fired with German idealistic philosophy. Soon De Sanctis was to produce his *History of Italian Literature*, often described as the only existing worthy history of the Italian nation. His writings struck a deep chord in the boy Croce.

Amid these stresses the household of Croce's parents attended strictly to family business, drawing on themselves the scorn of their patriot cousins, the Spaventas. In the Croce household, quietly traditional, it was remembered with pain that Bertrando Spaventa, the formidable patriot professor of philosophy, was not only an ex-priest but had said mass in the Croce family chapel. Here was much material for self-questioning by a young boy with a singular urge for making up his mind. Naples and Italy, Papalism and Liberalism, venerable custom and quickening innovation – the dialectic of these divergent loyalties, recollected from boyhood, underlies Croce's successive histories of Naples, of United Italy, and of Modern Europe which have been "best sellers" among his vastly various works. The History of Naples is the most delicately traced of these narratives. An elegiac leave-taking from the ancient throne served by Croce's family, rounds off the story of the necessary resolution of Naples into the "larger and keener" life of the united nation.

In the seventies, "good society" in Naples felt the stress of divergent sentiments, but no agonizing conflict. For, at least on the surface of affairs, Northern and Southern Italy, suddenly thrown together by the diplomatic genius of Cavour, were finding their respective levels and functions. North Italy brought wealth, enterprise, and technical capacity; though the manner often offended, and the exploitation of the South by Northern capitalism became a permanent bitter accusation on the national political stage. As individuals, however, the Southerners displayed on that stage a striking capacity for parliamentary debate, administration, police work, and the law, their alertness and subtlety carrying them to the heads of their professions. Silvio Spaventa became a powerful Minister. Parliamentary majorities in the new Rome were based upon combinations of notables in the South. For the alertness and subtlety of the Southerner as an individual were balanced by the traditionalism of Southern social relations.

Sure of his status and his influence in a society whose surface was merely rippled by political change, the representative man of the South displayed a mastery of principle which awed the more restless and experimental Northerner. In Croce's lifetime no heady or windy "movement" has had its origin or best fortunes in the South; a fact which, if on the one hand it reflects the long survival of feudal servitudes, checking the impulse of righteous protest against inhuman neglect and exploitation, on the other hand brings into evidence the strong virtue of resignation which, together with courage, constitutes, as Croce says, man's only serious equipment for life.

One primacy of the South the political events of the nineteenth century did nothing to impair. As in previous ages, the South continued to be the breeding place of Italy's speculative philosophers.

II

Life and Fortunes of a Philosopher

Three Neapolitan thinkers have in the modern age achieved the status of national educators for the whole Italian-speaking family: the oldest in time, Giambattista Vico, about a century after his death in 1744; the second, Francesco De Sanctis (1817-1883), in his late prime; while Benedetto Croce has been a commanding figure throughout the greater part of a long life in which, with unflagging argumentative zeal, he has afforded neither his followers nor his adversaries a moment's rest. All the three great Neapolitan thinkers have left sketches of their youth and mental development; the two elders, both of whom Croce deeply venerates as predecessors and inspirers, accompanied their self-portraits with an agreeable wealth of reference to the city background – the teeming alleys between high gaunt palaces, the warm, fluent unfolding of young minds in a disputatiousness bridging the social gulfs between princes, prelates, and humble men. These adornments are absent from Croce's sketch. Croce emphatically disclaims for his *Contribution to the Criticism of Myself* the character of a Confession or Memoir, giving to the brief review of the events of his early life the restrained quality of an Introduction to a classic, or, one might almost say, of an obituary notice. The style of the Sketch greatly disappointed an English critic, Mr. Middleton Murry, who asked a quarter of a century ago: "Can it be that there is a fundamental aridity in the Philosopher of the Spirit?"

The restraint which that romantic critic found so forbidding does in fact characteristically reflect one of Croce's most steadily observed principles, which has given rise in Italy to complaints about Croce's "inhuman" treatment of the many poets and thinkers on whom he has left a whole library of brilliantly polished monographs. The study of men, for Croce, is that of their works or acts. What lies "behind" or "beneath" is disregarded as the no longer relevant refuse of a process whose sole value lay in the creative climax, the result. Hence an almost obsessive refusal to seek, in the stanzas of a poet, the reflection of some biographical experience, some love story with a recognizable name. Hence a horror of the pursuit of psychological origins for intellectual or moral attitudes.

This exclusive valuation of the work, the act, is at first sight disconcerting because, from the very outset, Croce's philosophy proclaims the supremacy of "the individual". But the quality of individuality is habitually attributed by Croce to a thought, an act, an intuition, entities to which he ascribes a fully real character; whereas the empirical individuality behind the thought, act, or intuition ranks, as he once wrote, merely as "an appearance fixed by a name". We shall have much to say later upon Croce's view of human personality, but enough has been said here to show that the 'aridity' of the *Contribution* is deliberate. The reader of that brief austere document, if he comes to it as one who has sympathetically made himself familiar with some side of the philosopher's work, is likely to find it full of "human interest", for all the theory; and Croce's works include some biographical sketches of other personalities glowing with a restrained admiration and sympathy. The lines of the self-portrait are austere, but they are firm and shapely. The net consequence of Croce's theoretical abasement of the personality is not really to dissolve his portrayal of a human life, his own or that of others, into an evanescent blur upon the film of historical process, but rather to reveal the essential history of a man as the unfolding from out of him of an indestructible, but not static, reality. Croce's basic philosophical works can hardly be studied without a growing awareness that the whole system is, in a sense, an autobiography, and the *Philosophy of Practice*, in which the first person scarcely makes a grammatical appearance at all, was found by a Catholic critic many years ago to recall the *Confessions* of Saint Augustine.

Born not in Naples itself but in the mountainous Abruzzi region, where both parents sprang from wealthy landowners, Benedetto spent his early childhood in the family mansion in Naples. His paternal grandfather had been a high magistrate of the Neapolitan Kingdom and Benedetto's father held aloof from Italian politics, diligently absorbed in the affairs of the various family estates. At nine years of age Benedetto and a brother (who in later life followed the father's model, devoting himself exclusively to estate management) were sent to a boarding school in Naples, run by priests for the nobility and gentry. Encouraged by his gentle and cultivated mother, Benedetto was a tireless reader of novels, notably those of Walter Scott. He was, however, a pugnacious as well as a bookish child. Later he began to pore upon religious problems, and after struggling with doctrinal doubts and forming tearful resolutions to embrace the devout life, he "lost interest, carried along by life, no more asking myself whether I believed or no, continuing, by force of habit and conformity, some religious practices till little by little I dropped those also, and one day I remarked and said to myself clearly that I was altogether quit of religious beliefs".

This adolescent crisis was past, and Benedetto had begun turning his hand to occasional literary journalism, when in his seventeenth year the family, visiting the island of Ischia, were caught by an earthquake. Both parents, and the only daughter, were killed: Benedetto, buried for more than twelve hours in debris, was finally rescued. He had suffered severe injuries, with diffused but lasting effects upon his organism, and the two young brothers were now wealthy orphans. They were invited to Rome by their father's cousin Silvio Spaventa, and took up residence in this powerful statesman's house. For three years Benedetto lived in deep depression, out of tune with the political society which filled the house, wholly uninspired by the law faculty at Rome University where he was studying with a vague view to the career of diplomacy. "These were my saddest and darkest years, the only ones in which often, as I laid my head on the pillow, I keenly desired never to wake again, and even had notions of suicide. I had no friends, no diversions, I never once saw Rome by night." In 1886 he withdrew from the University without a degree and returned to Naples. He attended, though without enthusiasm, to the business of the family estate, and for the rest spent his time in the study of local Neapolitan folklore and municipal history.

A failure, from the point of view of his guardian, the youthful Croce, master of his time and movements, worked assiduously for several years in the fields of local Neapolitan culture. He promoted and directed periodical publications devoted to the history and folklore of Naples, financed and organized the reprint of old Neapolitan books, and visited Spain to study the interpenetration of Spanish and Neapolitan literature and learning in the centuries of Spanish greatness (early and sustained Spanish studies have never, however, led Croce to accept Spain as a compeer in the creative work of European civilization with Italy, France, England, and Germany). Before he was thirty, the learned world of Naples, and indeed of Italy, was recognizing in Benedetto Croce an outstanding master of historical and philological research.

The student years in Rome had apparently yielded him nothing but melancholy memories of a distasteful scene, nothing except one friendship which now proved to have gone deep. This friendship, unexpectedly revived, became bound up with the sudden development of new imperious interests. The Neapolitan holder of the Rome Chair of Moral Philosophy, Antonio Labriola, in his austere lectures on Duty, but perhaps still more in his brilliant table talk as a guest at Spaventa's house, had appealed to that strain of ethical severity which in Benedetto Croce has always been interwoven with a pugnacious gusto for the give and take of naive living and feeling. Labriola's influence was now rekindled as he revealed to Croce his own decision to throw himself into the Socialist movement.

In 1893 Croce had lived through a period of doubt and uneasy conscience regarding the pursuit of pure erudition. What was the purpose of this precise scholarship, what was its meaning for human destiny? On a day of intense self-questioning he wrote a brief essay entitled *The Inclusion of History under the General Idea of Art*, but turned back, after this rapid catharsis, to his usual studies. The doubts, however, were revived in 1895, when Labriola, having declared himself a Socialist, sought help from Croce for the publication of his newly composed essays on the teachings of Karl Marx:

"I read and reread them," says Croce "and my mind was fired anew. I could not detach myself from these thoughts and problems which took root and branched out in me." He plunged into the study of economics and of German and Italian Socialist publications 'with a strange sense of novelty like a man in love for the first time when no longer young'. The flame of this new enthusiasm "burned away my abstract moralism, and I learned that the course of history has the right to drag along and to crush individuals; I gained faith and hope from the vision of the rebirth of humanity redeemed by labour". But, adds Croce in the *Contribution* from which these extracts are taken, "that political enthusiasm, that faith, did not last".

For a year or two Croce did indeed take part in the intellectual discussions of higher European Socialism, contributing articles on the revisions required in the Marxist economic theory to such reviews as the Paris *Le Devenir*, corresponding intensively with the French syndical theorist Georges Sorel, and earning in print, at least once, the appellation "Comrade Croce". But the final conclusion of these Marxist studies was the judgement which Croce has never modified: that the Marxian doctrine was without philosophical significance and was fraught with errors in its economic deductions, admitting at the same time that Marx was a notable political figure and that the theory of economic materialism opened valuable new perspectives to the historian (following here only the external course of Croce's activities, we shall leave to the next chapter the study of this "Marxist crisis" as a step towards the formation of Croce's mature philosophy).

It was now, towards the turn of the century, and between his thirtieth and fortieth year, that Croce, obeying his "true nature as a man of study and of thought", set himself wholeheartedly to the elaboration of a complete formal doctrine of philosophy. This complete doctrine is sketched in outline in the *Aesthetic* (1902), where the nature of Art is developed by distinguishing its sphere from, and relating it to, the spheres of Thought and Practice. With the three further volumes on *Logic*, *Practice* (Economics and Ethics), and *Historiography*, and the monumental monographs on *Vico* and *Hegel*, Croce fully stated his philosophical position in the years preceding the first world war, at which time the philosopher's eminence was nationally recognized by the conferment of a Life Senatorship in 1910. No comparable attempt had been made in modern times to bring into a comprehensive and fully interconnected pattern the entire range of human intellectual, or, to use Croce's own term, spiritual activity: indeed, by inference, the whole range of human experience and behaviour. The response in Italy, to what seemed the authoritative delineation of the frontiers of art and science, religion and technical progress, was powerful, and was quickly echoed abroad. Yet some of Croce's success must be ascribed to a hasty or disingenuous misreading of his "lyrical" theory of aesthetics as giving a licence to throw over all severe standards in art.

The architecture of this philosophic "system" (a word carefully avoided by Croce) was conceived by its author as providing a base for sallies and campaigns in many directions, not as a peaceful citadel, and still less as an ivory tower. In fact, almost simultaneously with the publication of the *Aesthetic*, Croce initiated the review *La Critica*, which was to appear without interruption on the

fifteenth day of alternate months from 1902 up to 1943 when the
events of a real war, not unconnected with the war of ideas fought
in the pages of *La Critica*, brought about a British military occupation of the publishing offices at Bari which defeated even Croce's
indomitable efficiency. The publication of *La Critica*, however,
was quickly resumed, and it still appears at irregular intervals,
slightly changed in size and character.

A note of combativeness, even of provocation, was sounded in
the opening page of *La Critica* in 1902: "We intend to fight for a
determinate order of ideas. Nothing is more harmful to healthy
learning than a mistaken sentiment of tolerance, or, to put it
more clearly, of indifference and scepticism. . . . Liberty is better
served by presenting a clear target to one's opponents than by
joining with them in an insincere and useless brotherliness." The
Editor went on to proclaim the necessity for "a general reawakening of the philosophic spirit . . ., a well-weighed return to traditions of thought which were unhappily interrupted after the
Italian Revolution in 1860". The editorial manifesto bristled with
warnings to various groups to which the Review "will give no
quarter", to the "pseudo-naturalistic contemners of philosophic
thought", the "mystico-reactionaries", the "Jesuitico-Voltairians",
"those who want to put the world into knickers and induce adults
to become children", and other allusively described cliques whose
identity was clear to readers at the time. But beyond the proposal
to tackle and to put in their due place the current authors, foreign
as well as Italian, of works of philosophy, history, and general
literature, *La Critica* set itself the task of sorting out and appraising
the entire intellectual production of Italy in the second half of the
nineteenth century.

The programme was too vast for single-handed execution, and
before launching *La Critica* Croce enlisted the co-operation of a
still younger philosopher with whom he had developed a warm
intimacy as a fellow investigator in the field of Marxism, the
Sicilian, Giovanni Gentile. It was Gentile, in fact, who undertook
the cold-blooded overhauling, author by author, work by work,
of the Italian philosophical production of the previous half-century,

while Croce applied himself to a critical inventory of the general literature of Italy since the unification. *La Critica*, in its first decade, was the merciless castigator of academic philosophers, but what mainly brought notoriety was its summary dismissal of the contemporary literary idols of Italy. Among the younger authors severely handled by Croce were Gabriele D'Annunzio, Giovanni Pascoli, and Antonio Fogazzaro – planets of diverse shape and radiance who were all alike weighed in the balance of a single well-defined criterion and found wanting in their various and contrasting ways.

But *La Critica*, so battlesome towards the literary world at large, failed to maintain its own internal peace under the joint leadership of two young philosophers, mutually indebted – at first Croce was perhaps the greater debtor – but singularly different in temperament and range of interests: for Croce moved in the atmosphere of an altogether wider world. Croce was the owner of *La Critica* and Gentile withdrew.

The breach between Croce and Gentile would require close attention, in a more detailed examination of Croce's mental development, than can here be attempted. But its consequences spread far beyond the philosophic ground on which a divergence became increasingly apparent between the Neapolitan thinker's finely modulated thought, restrained from fanatical excess by wide literary culture and social worldly wisdom, and the Sicilian's prophetic ardour concentrated in a cult of technical elaboration and exactitude. In December 1913 the contestants arraigned each other in a published *Discussion between Philosophic Friends* – seldom can friendship have been more coolly attested than on Croce's side. The quarrel, on which Croce maintains silence in his autobiographical sketch, left deep traces not only in the world of Italian letters but in that of politics: and at this stage in the description of Croce's external career, politics now for the first time become important. As a Senator he was in touch with the political masters of the land, and his philosophic quarrel foreshadowed the intense political antagonisms of the next thirty years.

In 1915 Italy was wracked by conflicting sympathies in the Euro-

pean War. Everything predisposed Croce to stand with those who
wished to preserve Italy's neutrality. His philosophic affinities were
with the classical German school. The Positivists whom *La Critica*
had mercilessly flayed looked to France as their spiritual home. If
Croce needed a further impetus towards association with the Neutralists, one of whose strongholds lay in the literary circles of
Naples, there was the spectacle of the apostle of decadent luxury,
Gabriele D'Annunzio, emerging in shining armour as the arch-
propagandist of war. Then amid scenes of public turbulence and
crass overriding of parliamentary opinion, the monarchy guided
Italy into war at the side of the West. At that stage Croce made a
public declaration of complete loyalty to the national cause. His
neutralism had sprung from distrust of the "new and better world"
gospel preached with varying grades of sincerity by the war party.
Croce had not waited until 1915 to show dislike of the Prussian
nationalists and imperialists. But in Germany he saw much else
besides – the *Gründlichkeit* which generations of earnest Italians
had so much admired when in despair over their own happy-go-
lucky political improvisations. He loyally accepted war at the side
of the West, but he bluntly rejected invitations to recognize the
war as a contest between higher and lower civilizations. In the
pages of *La Critica*, by persistently attending to German literature,
he went almost so far as to recognize in the enemy an abiding
cultural superiority, and fiercely attacked the phalanx of Italian
professors, mostly of radical and Socialist colour, who attempted
to idealize Italy's war as a crusade for higher values.

This attitude to the war, like the antagonism towards D'Annunzio and the breach with Gentile, foreshadowed the political attitude
which Croce was to assume in the impending Fascist era. Before
that, Croce acquired a personal experience of politics. In 1920, at a
moment of bitter revulsion from the wartime mood and of alarming internal weakness, Italy recalled to the helm the aged and experienced Giovanni Giolitti, leader of the Neutralists in 1915.
Giolitti invited Croce, who as a Senator had the necessary parliamentary qualification, to join the Cabinet as Minister of Education.
The Ministry lasted a year, in circumstances which did not allow

Croce to make a mark as an educational reformer, but gave scope
for a display of energy and severity in coping with indiscipline
and laxity. He induced Giolitti to take firm measures against a
strike movement in the civil service. Life as a hard-pressed Minister
confirmed Croce in his scorn for political rhetoric. For Giolitti,
the patient, astute, flexible, pointedly prosaic dominator of the
Italian Parliaments of 1900-1915, Croce conceived a fervent admiration though the old politician's attempt to regain control of a
rapidly changing Italy after the war proved futile. This sympathy
became a dominating note in Croce's subsequent writings on
modern Italian history – their true hero is Giolitti – and an inspiration when the development of events much later thrust Croce
himself into the momentary position of a political personage of
the first rank.

Giolitti's failure in 1921 was soon followed by the dictatorship of
Mussolini, who named as his Minister of Education none other
than Giovanni Gentile. At this time, like Giolitti himself, Croce
favoured the formation of Mussolini's Government as an adventurous remedy for a disastrous disorder. Some years before, he
had seen hope for all Europe in the decision of the German Socialists to vote the Kaiser's military credits and thus to bring their
rebellious energies into the stream of a coherent national policy.
In the emergence of Mussolini, recently the leader of the most
extreme Socialist faction, as an ostensible spokesman of Italian
patriotism, armed with a programme of reinforcement for the
institutions of the State, Croce at first saw the hope of an end to
the sterile "anti-national" disaffection of the working classes. The
inwardly lawless character of Mussolini's régime – which at the
outset took the form of a broadly based coalition imposing its
will by decrees for the limited period of an emergency – became
generally evident in 1923 to 1924; but Croce was late to perceive
it. He voted for a motion of confidence in the Government, even
after the murder in 1924 of the Socialist leader Matteotti had been
ascribed, with evidence satisfying to many moderate and critical
men, to a terroristic group nestling close to the apex of power. It
was only in 1925 that Croce clearly branded the dictatorship as

lawless and immoral. For this Gentile gave the signal. Precisely when Mussolini threw off the mask of constitutional scruple, Gentile proclaimed his unlimited approval, and composed in praise of the "régime" a *Manifesto of the Fascist Intellectuals*. To this document Croce wrote an immediate retort, signed by the most eminent men of letters of the country.

Fascism was in Croce's Manifesto described as "an incoherent and bizarre mixture of appeals to authority and demagogy, of professions of reverence for the laws, ultramodern concepts and moth-eaten bric-à-brac, absolutism and Bolshevism, unbelief and toadying to the Catholic Church, flight from culture and sterile reachings towards a culture without a basis, mystical languors and cynicism". This was language which it was possible to print in Italy early in 1925 when for some months the "régime" appeared to be tottering under the shame of the Matteotti outrage. Croce also entered into personal controversy with Mussolini, for Mussolini having publicly boasted "I have never read a page of Croce", Croce retorted that he had been quoted by Mussolini, "but of course what he says may be true, for his writings are written for him by others". Croce had become a major enemy of the régime, a fact which about this time was acknowledged by Fascist roughs breaking into the Croce library in Naples and doing much damage. Croce never ceased to display hostility to Mussolini's policy, attending the Senate on the chief occasions and joining with a handful of men of his generation in speaking and voting against the Government. Thus he delivered the only speech against the Lateran Pacts of 1929, which obtained an official reconciliation of the Roman Church with the Kingdom of Italy at the price of restoring to the Pope a token territorial sovereignty. Such speeches were delivered to a lowering House, and were of course kept far from the columns of the controlled Press (Gentile also, it should be mentioned, opposed the Pacts in the internal counsels of the Fascist Party).

In the aftermath of the affair of the Manifestos, Croce officially joined the Italian Liberal Party. The fact that this entity scarcely existed – all the pre-Mussolinian Governments having been implicitly Liberal as heirs of the nineteenth-century revolutions – did not deprive the gesture of importance for the future. The explicit repudiation of all liberal ideas by Fascism incited a few men of conscience to give a formal frame to Italian liberalism which was soon engulfed in the general suppression of all political bodies outside the Fascist circle. But Croce's adherence was no passing episode. He has even described the entire purport of his ethical and political writing of later years as the laying of foundations for the resurrection of a Liberal Party.

The Fascists retorted by isolating Croce from the educational and social currents of the country. His books, cancelled from scholastic curricula, were partly replaced by those of Gentile. It became dangerous for anyone's career to be marked as visitor to Palazzo Filomarino, the spacious, challengingly unmodern dwelling of the philosopher in Naples, with its vast courtyard and endless lengths of booklined wall. Nevertheless – and this circumstance deserves attention – Croce was able to continue to publish *La Critica* and his books, though prudent booksellers kept them in the background.

The political status of Croce in the years from 1926 to the fall of Fascism in 1943 – his name being banned from public mention yet his books being allowed to appear – was much debated in Italian and foreign intellectual circles at the time, and more recently has formed the argument of a whole series of Communist publications seeking to interpret the relative half-tolerance extended to a bitter opponent of the régime in the light of Croce's even greater bitterness against Communism. It is suggested, not without adroit arguments, that Croce enjoyed a semi-official licence to indulge without personal danger in a muffled criticism of the régime. Fascism, say the Communists, was a terroristic police system and method of mystification employed by the decaying Italian capitalist bourgeoisie to roll back the vital impetus of Communism. Mussolini and his lieutenants were little more than "marionettes worked by plutocratic strings". The Communists have argued that the same dark forces maintained Croce, and minor figures of a similar complexion, as a second line of anti-Communist defence against the day when the Fascist façade – too superlatively favourable to last for ever – should crumble. A less abstract representation of the phenomenon of Fascism may help us to see clearer into this business. Croce's own behaviour shows that Italian Fascism for a time drew its strength from a show of effort to restore civil and social discipline in a politically paralysed country. Only in its final exasperation did it completely flout the sensibilities of morally responsible men in the professions, the civil service, and the armed forces.

If this is recognized, we may extract this element of truth from the Communist thesis of a special and interested tolerance accorded to Croce by the "forces behind Fascism". Mussolini was never able, indeed could never attempt, to choke completely the circulation of ideas of a liberal complexion. He could not risk wholly estranging the liberal-minded elements in the Italian middle classes, whose passive support, given to Fascism in the belief that it was a safeguard against upheavals, he still needed. This is perhaps another way of saying that Fascism never very thoroughly conquered the society for which it administered the State, and in the face of a social eminence such as Croce's, it sought a *modus vivendi*, rather than the suppression of the enemy.

In Fascist times the Palazzo Filomarino, previously thronged with callers, was abandoned by the prudent, for contacts with Croce were fatal to official or academic careers. On summer visits to Piedmont, Croce could, with less anxiety for the consequences, collect round him a few young persons. All direct reference to Italian politics disappeared from *La Critica*. But discerning readers found in the derisory accounts of the regimentation of culture by the Soviet régime, or in the contemptuous exposures of German racialist theories, a transparent comment upon events nearer home. The daily press carried no mention of Croce or of any of his writings, but the adjective "Crocian" (printed, according to Italian practice, without a capital) appeared in literary and learned publications. Some learned academies, which Croce and his friends had used as platforms or vehicles of publicity, were wound up by Governmental decree.

Neither public occupations nor isolation in any way affected Croce's assiduity in his literary tasks, or deflected him from functioning (according to his own description) as "the perfect employee of myself". Even while Croce was Minister of Education *La Critica* had appeared punctually, consisting in the main of writings of his own. When it was suggested that for a Minister he was diverting too much energy to a private task, he replied that the year's programme for the review had been worked out long before and the contributions themselves largely written, so that he had only to give them the finishing touches.

Throughout his life Croce has planned his researches and his compositions some years ahead, and has stuck indomitably to the timetable. In the period of his exclusion from public life he completed and published the historical trilogy: *History of Naples, History of Italy from the Unification to the European War*, and *History of Europe in the Nineteenth Century*, together with the less organic *History of the Baroque Age*, and a score of volumes equally distributed between theoretical philosophy, literary criticism, and historico-cultural erudition. The volumes of Croce comprised in the uniform edition of Laterza – a publisher of Bari who rose to eminence by a discerning association of fortunes with Croce – numbered twenty-seven in 1922 (the first year of Fascism), forty-eight in 1942 (the last year), and fifty-five in 1950, exluding a considerable number of brief monographs, and political pamphlets published by Laterza or others. Through the rich variety of these works, but more explicitly through the historical volumes, ran the purpose of shaping the mind of a new governing class in Italy to resume the direction of the country after the "parenthesis" of Fascism. The word is here deliberately brought to notice. It is one of the standing reproaches levelled against Croce's historical vision that he regards periods rich in headlines for the newspapers, wars or dictatorships, as parentheses: thus his historical works have habitually had for their themes periods between wars, and his personal political activity, as though by a psychological choice, skipped the period of Italy's greatest prominence in world affairs. This attraction towards the calmer periods of history cannot possibly be ascribed

to a languor in Croce's notoriously polemical temperament, but
rather to an appetite for the fine shades and subtle tendencies in
human affairs which public excitements obscure. It may be compared with the distaste of an ardent and accomplished duellist for
a swordsmen's brawl in the dark.

The fruits of Croce's long solitude and patient penetration of the
thoughtful minds of Italy during the Fascist régime were shown
when, on the abrupt collapse of Fascism through Badoglio's Palace
Revolution in 1943, Crocian Liberalism at once became the favoured doctrine of all the major newspapers; and Croce's aid was
entreated for buttressing the monarchical institutions in the hour
of their discredit. There followed rapidly the Eisenhower-Badoglio
Armistice, the Allied landings in South Italy, the German occupation of Rome and of North Italy. During these events Croce
was at Sorrento, a "no man's land" at about an hour's motoring
drive from the battlefields of Salerno. It was believed in Allied
Intelligence quarters that Croce might have been seized by the
Germans, and on September 15th an Italian launch under British
orders ran into Sorrento harbour and carried the philosopher to
safety in the island of Capri.

For the following nine months Croce was at the centre of the
embittered political scene in South Italy. The resuscitation of the
Liberal Party, which Croce declared to have been the inspiring
purpose of his own historical writings during the dictatorship, was
effected, and Croce became its official leader. Marshal Badoglio,
with King Victor Emmanuel, had set up a nominal Italian Government under Allied control in Brindisi. Croce agreed with Count
Sforza and with the principal non-Fascist notables then in South
Italy, to refuse office or co-operation in a Government serving
King Victor Emmanuel, whom they held responsible for the
national disaster. But while demanding abdication of the obstinate
monarch whom he tellingly characterized as "a man who was all
prose", Croce withstood the Republican agitation of the other
"secular" parties – Radicals, Socialists, and Communists; he urged
the formation of a Regency to rule in the name of an infant prince.
The attitude of the Communists after some oscillation took the

opposite bend. Contemptuous of the Monarchy as such, they were perfectly ready to serve Victor Emmanuel for the moment. A middle course in this question and in social policy was steered by a new and ephemeral movement, the Action Party. The "Actionist" episode ranks high among the vexations of Croce's later years.

The Actionist movement had grown up, during the last phase of Fascism, largely in his own close family and familiar circle, inspired by the ideal of renewing or integrating old-fashioned liberalism with a "social content". Like many other Italian movements of the twentieth century, not excluding Communism, it had drawn largely upon Croce's own teaching. Many years earlier, Croce had established the distinction between liberal politics and individualist economics. He had also declared that nothing in the liberal tradition stood against even the most drastic social reform. But the Action Party, grounded upon these dicta, was from the outset condemned by Croce as a romantic aberration. It was not among these fervent intellectuals, fed by the milk of his own word, that Croce in the 1943 crisis discovered a political affinity. The philosopher-historian who had withstood the Lateran Treaties, and seen all his own works (with Gentile's) placed upon the Index Expurgatorius of the Church, found it much easier to work with the political Catholics. He had himself prepared the way for a Liberal-Catholic understanding by publishing, during the agonies of Fascism, one of his most brilliant pamphlets (analysed in a later chapter), *Why we cannot but call ourselves Christians*. The subsequent triumph of the Christian Democrats in Italy, and the small influence exercised by the resuscitated Liberals, have not induced Croce to deflect his fire, in any large measure, from the Marxists to the Clericals.

At this point we may turn back for a moment to Gentile. The Sicilian philosopher had long lost the political eminence which he had won in the first years of the dictatorship. He had retained important posts with a considerable scope for patronage, but this patronage he had in many cases used humanely. But as Fascism precipitated towards its agony, its directors turned once again to the man who in 1925 had propounded the first philosophical defence of the system. In the summer of 1943, with the Allies already on Sicilian soil and plots for Mussolini's overthrow thickening at the Court and among the party chieftains themselves, Gentile was summoned to deliver, on the Roman Capitol, in the presence of the high authorities, a discourse to the nation, identifying the Fascist war cause with Christian civilization and the great Italian and European tradition. A few weeks later Gentile threw in his lot with the fanatical last-ditchers of the Fascist Social Republic. He was assassinated in Florence, by anti-Fascist conspirators, in April 1944. Tears were shed in the Croce household, by the womenfolk who remembered old days, while Croce in his diary recorded that he had hoped "in memory of our early friendship, to ensure his personal safety, and to guide him back to the studies which he had deserted".

In South Italy, the first political assembly to be sanctioned by the Allies elected Croce as its first and principal spokesman. With all the respect and reticence called for by Italy's position as an occupied and contested country, Croce demanded with firm dignity the right for Italy to be heard by the United Nations and to be allowed to solve her internal problems, first of all the dismissal of an unworthy King. The monarchical issue in fact, for several months, totally frustrated all attempts to form a political Government for liberated Italy. A formula was at last devised, in deep secrecy, by Croce and Enrico De Nicola. It provided for King Victor Emmanuel, who stubbornly refused to abdicate, to withdraw into private life. With this political achievement to his credit, and the shortly ensuing liberation of Rome which brought many new political forces into play, the political episode in Croce's life practically drew to an end. He refused several suggestions that he should himself head a Government, or, as was later suggested, that he should become President of the new Republic. Public office – local or national – has never been sought by Croce or accepted by him save as a call in an emergency. In the diary of these recent events which he published after the war, Croce expresses – with a diffidence coming from the heart – doubt of his own fittedness to cope with practical political problems. Friends

and adversaries have understood what it cost the scholar and
thinker to throw himself in his old age into the national affairs of
a country on the edge of disintegration. A unique national status
has been the reward of this sacrifice, as well as of sheer might of
intellect.

In 1946 Benedetto Croce fulfilled a long-standing intention by
founding and endowing with the assignment of his vast private
library in the Palazzo Filomarino, Naples, a school of historical
studies for postgraduates. Making good the loss inflicted upon him
by the Fascist régime in isolating him from the young generation,
Croce has in extreme old age taken on the task of communicating
his teachings by word of mouth, each lecture being however immediately published in *La Critica* and forming part of the copious
further elucidations of the theory of history which have made up
the bulk, but by no means the totality, of seven large volumes
added to the Laterza edition since 1944.

Last Essays was the title given by Croce to a volume published
in his seventieth year. Its purport was disbelieved, and would not
easily be believed even now that he is eighty-five.

III
Encounter with Science

Croce has expounded his philosophy with such sustained clarity in
the *Aesthetic*, the *Logic*, and other major volumes, that one might
here go forward, it would seem, with the statement of a creed in
his own terms, showing the timeless passage of the universal Spirit
through the necessary, eternal, organically related aspects or forms
of the Beautiful, the True, the Useful or Vital, and the Good – an
ideal history which would be as the motif underlying the infinite
fugues of real occurrence. But such a proceeding would not only
ill befit the present undidactic essay; it would also run counter to
the evolution of Croce's own thought which eschews such guides
or maps to other thinkers' philosophic systems.

The maturest works of Croce do not disregard, and certainly do
not disclaim, the principles which he enounced early in the century

in the volumes of the *Philosophy of the Spirit*. But they present a profusion of meditation branching forth ever more boldly from the original centre. Or rather they deny that any part of philosophy can in an absolute sense be central. "Every particular truth is instrinsically systematic and either expressly or implicitly refers to all the others," Croce wrote in 1941. The biographical sketch, the book review, the notebook entry, the diary, the letter to friends on current affairs, have provided what has been most appreciated by the later generations of Croce's readers. In these the utterance has been liveliest and most convincing. But Croce's canons of criticism also deter us from the ambition of trying to sum up and present any author in his material entirety. An author's thought, he repeatedly reminds us, is nothing if not the answer to a special problem. To string together a number of answers in a creed, instead of eliciting them from particular questions, may serve some mnemonic purpose, but does not generate understanding.

There is also this consideration. To be a mere and sheer philosopher is far from being Croce's boast. He has been very untender in his own handling of the specialists of pure thought. He has inveighed against the all too philosophic, and has paid tribute to the unphilosophic. A man who has expressed himself so freely about everything must expect to be appraised not only by those who pit their philosophic culture against his own and, however humbly, share his responsibilities to the philosophic tradition, but also by the writer for the general reader.

Yet we should be missing the particular flavour of Croce's work if we merely analysed his popular books – histories, essays on human conduct, appreciations of poets, denunciations of Fascists, Marxists, and Clericals. The particular flavour comes from Croce's attempt to keep each of his immensely various activities running in explicit relation to the others. Inevitably therefore we shall have to draw together the main lines of his philosophy, but shall try to do so in the course of enquiries into particular issues, not by way of a creed or a tidy compendium of doctrine.

We will seek access to a major wing of Croce's thought by recollecting the retirement of the young diplomat *manqué* to Naples, in 1887, to join the long line of cultivated gentlemen in the Italian South who have devoted, and still devote, their lives to the pursuit of local history and erudition. He diligently prepares and publishes introductions to documents of folklore, civic tradition, and linguistics – the status of local dialect literature is naturally an important interest in a territory which so recently lost its autonomy. Then we see Croce's scholarly routine suddenly broken in upon by the composition and appearance of a writing of quite a different order – *History Brought within the General Concept of Art*. Croce in his maturity could look back to this as the embryonic attempt to clarify History and Art as articulations in a general philosophic scheme. But at the age of twenty-six, he did not yet recognize the signal. He was in fact, by the standards of the early maturing South Italian intellect, a late-comer to philosophical thought.

True, this first philosophical composition "brought me", Croce recorded later in the *Contribution*, "a revelation of myself . . . astonishing me by the facility and warmth with which I wrote it, as something coming from the heart". The theme pointed to his future teaching; not that the inclusion of History in Art remained as an article in his faith, but the essence of the essay lay more in what it rejected. Croce, investigator of historical detail, rejected an idolization of scientific method which sought to include History under the concept of Science. This gives an important clue. Croce's first philosophical declaration was a refusal to ground his historical studies on the methods of Science – a notion which later on we must scrutinize carefully.

Early in the nineteenth century, after Napoleon, Philosophy had been the magic word in Europe. We find Hegel smilingly noting the appearance of a treatise on philosophical hairdressing. Now there was a different vogue, and every branch of learning and skill aspired to dignity as 'scientific'. The fashion invaded Italy rather belatedly, but with vehemence. Although England was not fully involved in the changes of intellectual weather experienced by the continental nations, as for instance by South Italy in particular sympathy with Germany, it was yet from Victorian England that the wind of scientific enthusiasm blew down upon Naples and

Rome, rich with the renown of the Utilitarian school and of the clear-spoken Herbert Spencer. From France descended the banners of Auguste Comte and Hippolyte Taine proudly flying in the same winds. And similar influences came from Germany, clothed in Gothic print which commanded a peculiar respect. Ponderous German tributes to the cosmic claims of Science strove to inherit the prestige still enjoyed, in conservative Naples, by the Hegelian school. It was in the spirit of the earlier German tradition, familiar to all cultivated Neapolitans and paralleled by the still earlier teachings of their own Vico, that Croce withstood the pretensions of the new "scientific" philosophy. There was something in this reaction akin to the coolness with which families like the Croces, though not bigoted Papists or enemies of political change, had viewed the noisier type of neo-Italian democrat in the middle of the century.

After finding expression in the 1893 essay, Croce's vein of philosophy appeared to be exhausted. He returned to his erudition, though with a sense of privation. He published valuable books but: "no sooner had I published the most conspicuous of my works, receiving congratulations, praise, and encouragement from many sides . . . than distaste and repugnance for these studies invaded me . . . I wearied of acquiring disconnected and inanimate information with effort, but without a constructive urge".

The trains of thought sketched in 1893, and then neglected, came to life again under a quite new stimulus and by a circuitous route which at first seemed to go in the opposite direction. For what gave the stimulus was Marxist Socialism, a doctrine which was often interpreted as the logical culmination of the cult of Science, tidying up all social reality in terms of a scientific absolute, the concept of historical materialism. On the other hand, the Marxist school in question claimed to develop its theory of matter not in the blunt terms of a merely mechanistic science, but sublimely ascribing to this primordial stuff the agility, ascribed by the Hegelians to Mind, of creatively contradicting itself. We have seen that Croce's philosophic maturity was preceded and prepared by a Marxist phase of heightened emotional colour. But for "Marxist" phase it is better, in reviewing Croce's intellectual development, to substitute "economic" phase. For in exercising his mind on Marxism, Croce plunged for some years into a fervent study of general economics. Close familiarity with British, French, German, and Italian economic classics accounts perhaps better than anything else for the matter-of-fact clarity, the unportentousness of Croce's expositions, so different in this respect from those of his philosophical contemporary and fellow pioneer, Gentile.

Let us pause to consider this economic phase, with an eye for the singularity of this circumstance that a philosopher who, at least outside Italy, has been famous almost exclusively for his theory of artistic values, spent several years in an intense preoccupation with the theory of economic value. This bestriding of seldom associated spheres bespeaks at once what, save for the contamination of the word, one would call a totalitarian ambition. Doubtless any speculative philosophy must seek, in the words of Whitehead, "to frame a coherent, logical, necessary set of ideas in terms of which every element of our experience can be interpreted". But some philosophies are marked out by a universal coherence achieved at the price of genuine sensitivity for the distinctions between the things which are to cohere. Such a fine critic as the English philosopher Bernard Bosanquet felt this forcing of coherence in Croce's work so strongly as to speak of Croce's "masterful and almost unscrupulous genius", and of the work as dominated deleteriously by the "lure of singleness". But Bosanquet perhaps knew nothing of Croce's work anterior to the *Aesthetic*, and may have missed the key to the meaning of Croce's ardour for single-minded utterance, necessitated by the dangers of a more exposed position than that of the English idealist.

The work of Croce, philosophical, literary, and political, takes on a full meaning only when the vast scope of its unity is discovered. The Aesthetician is profoundly at one with the scrutinizer of politics. True enough, Croce's systematic works are built up from uncompromising assertions, unsoftened by the admission of the reader into the intimacy of precedent perplexity, which humanizes the pages of English philosophers from Locke and Hume to

Bradley. But Croce's work is not to be known intimately by poring over the *Aesthetic*, *Logic*, and other systematic works. Croce must be heard also in the intimate communications of books like the *Ethical Fragments*, where he reviews the great concerns of humanity, marriage, death, friendship, love, sickness, despair, at an ambling pace, with the reins of coherence held lightly, but never thrown to the wind. In these informal excursions Croce responds to his inspiration with a freshness which reassures us that he is not, as has been said, "a terrible intellectual machine producing endless series of flashing thoughts" but a man who has chosen to forge himself a coherent outlook sooner than surrender to disruptive tendencies glimpsed in his own mind as in a mirror of civilization. Close students of the work of Croce as a whole know that it is alive with qualifications, explanatory admissions, anxious adjustments of that which has to be said "by way of metaphor" or "for the necessity of discourse" to that which is meant to be pronounced as truth; and then again rich in the resolution of the ostensibly dogmatic into fine and modest weighing of particular questions.

But to resume the study of a time when these characteristics were but latent, the years of Croce's economic phase were marked by turmoils like those, says Croce, of a man experiencing first love late in life. He struggled with the idea of dramatically changing his style of life, renouncing his social privilege, inherited sentiment and taste, and taking upon himself the cross of the oppressed classes.

That the torments and consolations of love, in the literal sense, entered somehow into the matter, is perhaps not unfairly inferred from Croce's old-age fantasy on the life of Hegel, permeated, one feels, with self-portraiture, and suggesting with an admirable delicacy the reflections of early love in Hegel's work.

But the turmoils died down, and the redemptive enthusiasm with which for a while Antonio Labriola, sincere and gifted votary of the Communist Manifesto, infected his former pupil, were in the long run not to convert a thinker into a social mystic, but to extend Croce's range of intellectual enquiry and to build up a method of coherence capable of extension from social science to studies more intimately akin to his temperament.

The study of Karl Marx, to which Croce devoted months of concentrated reading and writing, led on to the study of the economists whom Marx had tried to chase out of court. The study of the economists brought Croce into correspondence with the renowned Vilfredo Pareto, and a debate between the two men (Pareto older by a score of years) on the first principles of this science – and then to the question, crucial in this story, in what sense is it a science?

First Croce examined with growing scepticism the contentions of *Das Kapital*. He became convinced that the labour theory of value and the derivative theory of surplus value were not conceptions inferred or deduced from observation. They were arrived at by first advancing an imaginary hypothesis – the functional society – and then describing the failure of a particular social reality – the society of the late nineteenth century – to conform to this hypothesis. He turned to the "orthodox" economists and found in them theories which, at first by contrast, appeared to him to be inferred from observation of reality: the marginal theory of value and the general analysis of competitive markets.

But now, looking closer, Croce suspected that the current theories of competitive economics rested in their turn upon a contamination of reason with "sectarian superstitions". Here was the beginning of a conviction that economics, whether initiated with a presupposition of a type of society or a type of man, could not serve to arrive at the truth. Before passing to the broader consequences of such a conviction, one may remark that it is beset by dangers of its own; above all by the danger of breeding total indifference to economic formulations of any kind, and the readiness to dismiss them as suspect instruments of which politics can make use according to the varying problems of the hour. In the political convulsions of 1920 a generation of Italians, nourished upon facile interpretations of Croce's doctrine, were perhaps too much disinclined to take the economists' warnings seriously. The economists have not yet wholly forgiven him.

In his correspondence with Pareto, Croce pressed for the definition of a starting point for economics. He pursued the reluctant
economist and sociologist down the avenues of the utilitarian pain
and pleasure calculus, and extorted from him a definition of the
buyer's and seller's *choice* as the fundamental economic fact. Croce
pressed further. To choose is to choose something, to perform an
act of will. What then is the relation of the economic choice of
buyer and seller to the moral choice between good and evil? The
controversy reached no conclusion. Croce ended by offering as the
basis or starting point of economics this definition: "economic fact
is the practical activity of man, independent of any moral or immoral direction". Pareto was uninterested. "My problem", he said,
is "whether the phenomena of production and exchange present
any uniformities, and if so which?"

Croce was driven to the conclusion that he and his disputant had
been seeking a basis for two quite different edifices, one for a
system of abstracted uniformities, the other for an aspect of total
reality. And hence Croce inferred, firstly that the science of economics was not engaged in pursuing truth, but secondly – and
significantly – that truth about human conduct cannot be told
without a permanent regard for the economic principle as a "practical activity independent of any moral or immoral direction", or,
as he has finally come to call it, vitality. The words "about human
conduct" could be omitted. For Croce the economic principle is
universal, and its coequal inclusion in philosophy with the good,
the true, the beautiful, is perhaps Croce's most striking innovation
in philosophical doctrine.

Let us turn back for a moment, from the work to the author.
What is the significance of this anxious hunt of the young thinker
for the primal economic fact and of the importance given by him
to his conclusion? The triumphant discovery of the economic
principle as anterior to morals corresponds to Croce's youthful
uprising against a strain of moral tyranny which he turned inwards
upon himself with grim resolution, we may feel, in the grievous
period after his family disaster. Following his life we can feel,
rather than read in the documents, the search for liberation from a

sense of duty so morbidly swollen as to expel all vivacity from the conduct of life. The consolation of organized religion, the momentary recapture of innocence through penitence, did not come into question for a spirit firmly pledged to the dignity and integrity of the intellect. It was to the real and rational world – to what was going on around him – that Croce turned, seeking an impulse to live, and scenting out invitations to an activity not weighed down by moral implications. Such an impulse he at first described as "economic", but has since found for it wider terms like "vitality". Croce has claimed the right to "spiritualize" this primal vivacity which he makes precedent – not in time but in the spirit – to the moral choice. This is not immoralism, for Croce finally makes morals, like vitality, all-pervasive. But at every instant morality is summoned to crown the vitality which a man brings into play for its own sake.

Such was the ultimate and positive consequence for Croce's philosophy of his incursion into economics, and his debate with the spokesmen of the economic science. Yet truly they reach further, for it is a parallel liberation which Croce seeks in his presentation of Art as ideally anterior to Thought. A Vitality not duty-bound, and an Art not thought-bound are his principal legacies to the framers of philosophic theory. And the broadest conclusion of his economic enquiry was a clear recapture of the ancient philosophical disco-ordination between the pure "knowledge" of philosophy and the mere "exactness" of Science.

One is forcibly struck by the fact that the particular science which Croce stringently discriminated from philosophy, afterwards attributing to all sciences a similar non-logical character, is one which is hardly recognized by the builders of general scientific systems. A fuller account would have to show that Croce has in fact elaborated the difference between a science which tends, like economics, to resolve its data into the abstract universals of mathematics and thus resembles philosophy in its universality, and on the other hand a science which sorts things into classes, like biology, and resembles philosophy in its concreteness. Croce, moreover, has later read deeply the literature of general scientific method and first principles. The numeratory and the classificatory sciences have been given different labels. But they are lumped together in their exclusion from the realm of the concrete-universal, that is, from philosophy. Croce balances this by spontaneously proclaiming the total incompetence of philosophical thought in Science. He acknowledges, from across the gulf, the dignity of Science; there is nothing he will not concede to it, except an ability or an honest desire to intuit, to think, to express, to judge. "Thank you for very little," the scientists have retorted. But Croce refuses to recognize the legitimacy of the grievance.

We have some later light from Croce himself on the original development of these ideas. Re-publishing his *Logic* in 1916, he wrote: "The first edition of this book was generally taken to be a spirited attack upon Science.... But the detachment of Philosophy from Science which is here effected, is not a detachment from the real knowledge contained in Science – its historical and real elements – but only from the schematic form in which these are compressed, mutilated, and altered." Much later he wrote to a gifted young critic: "It is most true and most essential that at first I did not distinguish between Science and Philosophy and strove to philosophize Science and to render Philosophy scientific, until I became aware of the diversity of the two orders of problems and their two logics."

It is no part of this small book to attempt to expound general philosophical positions, especially if they are not peculiar to Croce. But some enlargement upon the "two logics" seems necessary. The argument for regarding Science as basically unlogical (or having its own pseudo-logic) can be illustrated as follows. A primitive scientist utters generalizations about fish, calling "fish" whatever swims in the sea. But a more refined observer excludes whales because they suckle their young and must go with the mammals. But however refined the observer, however deep he goes in selecting abiding and organic characteristics, instead of obvious resemblances, to serve as ticket of admission to a class, there remain always, at least potentially, marginal beings whose inclusion or exclusion must be decided by arbitrary choice. Even the atoms grouped in their billions are only abstractly considered as indifferent units by disregarding differences which we have not the strength to investigate. But philosophy seeks knowledge of the whole.

Let us not make too much of the words. The English philosopher Locke wrote over two centuries ago: "Natural philosophy is not capable of being made a Science." His meaning in modern English parlance is "Natural Science is not capable of being made a Philosophy", which is much what we have heard Croce saying. In Italy the change of nomenclature has been less complete, and *Scienza*, like the German *Wissenschaft*, is not a word practically monopolized by those working by experiment and calculation; the title of Vico's eighteenth-century philosophical masterpiece *Scienza Nuova* would in itself offer some resistance to this.

The atmosphere of words is not without influence upon events. The almost exclusively technical connotation of the word Science in modern English usage has diminished the temptation of scientists to identify their findings with knowledge in general. A similarly exclusive sense in Italian would perhaps have deterred Croce from publishing his first major works with the provocative titles *Aesthetic as the Science of Expression* and *Logic as the Science of the Concept*. We shall here however use the word "Science" as Croce has often done, in the colloquial English sense.

In his study of Marx, economics drove Croce to define his conception of Science; but meanwhile there was also the question of the Marxian claim to Hegel's philosophic heritage. Had Marx, by transplanting the Hegelian triad of thesis, antithesis, and synthesis from the operations of Mind to the sensible world (an operation already, in fact, effected on a gigantic scale by Hegel himself in his luckless *Philosophy of Nature*), really set a topsy-turvy philosophy on its feet? Croce joined with the young Sicilian philosopher Giovanni Gentile in overhauling the early Hegelian investigations of Marx and Engels the conclusion of which had been taken for granted in *Das Kapital*. The two young southerners became close friends and allies, and it was from Gentile that Croce first heard the formula which could crown his emancipation of Philosophy from Science. Philosophy, said Gentile, was identical with History, or, as Croce later put it, was the "methodology" of History. It can never, like Science, disregard all that is irrelevant to the uniformities which Science espies as the raw material of its "laws". Science, in fact, is practical. Science's "truths" are wilful arrangements. They are elaborately disciplined versions of the actions which we are all perpetually performing in order to live, but cannot perform if we try to judge them in the light of full rationality, of theoretical coherence. It was this coherence that Croce sought, though the more we look into his invitation to quicken ourselves by coherent thought, the less shall we find in it an offer of tranquil contemplation. The comfortable words of abstraction, the rich storehouse of exemplars, types, quantities, whether or not dignified as scientific terminology, to which we perpetually resort in order to subordinate our experience to ready-made categories, are in philosophy banished by a suspense of the will. This, in itself, is vigorous action; and if Croce is leading us aright, through the limpidity of an intuition of things in their uniqueness we gain the arduous privilege of a thought which is by necessity radically original.

IV
A Christian Philosophy?

A very simple example of the use made by Croce of his severance of Philosophy from Science may be found in a review of the Italian translation of Alfred Russell Wallace's *Place of Man in the Universe*, published in 1906. Croce quotes paragraphs in which the British naturalist argues that the universe is a unit, the number of the stars not infinite, and the earth near to the centre. Wallace's reason is that a universe of infinite variety would be monotonous, and the emergence of Man with his intellectual and moral faculties would be degraded by appearing to be a process realizable in this, that, or the other of numerous worlds, instead of as something unique. But this, says Croce, is speculative reasoning, which has nothing whatever to do with physics, astronomy, or natural science. He

objects to the utterance of such views from a throne of scientific
eminence as though they could derive prestige from the voice of
a man justly renowned as a scientific classifier.

But these reproofs to physical and natural scientists are comparatively rare. The "scientists" strongly assailed by Croce were much
more often those who advertised a scientific method in the investigation of Croce's own preferred field. Such were the professors of
linguistics in their search for the laws of the development of languages, and for "origins" of speech in onomatopœic imitation of
noises, or deliberate symbolism, who met from Croce the same
treatment as Pareto in the field of economics. For Croce's *Aesthetic
as the Science of Expression and General Linguistics* sought to fix a
starting point for the philosophy of language, artistic intuition
independent of any judgement about reality or unreality, in close
symmetry with what we have already heard him define as the
philosophic starting point for *Filosofia Economica*, practical activity
of man independent of any moral direction. He set similar limits
upon the sphere of linguistic *science* as upon that of economic
science.

We will not linger long over Croce's aesthetic theory. In its
original and cruder form it was lucidly though disapprovingly
expounded for English readers by Bernard Bosanquet in his communication to the British Academy in 1919. Bosanquet, already
quoted, analysed the doctrine with high professional skill, but
without the advantage of knowing the origin of Croce's particular
impulses. In a later and subtler form Croce's own contribution to
the Encyclopaedia Britannica (14th edition, *Aesthetics*) expounds it
with full authority. Here we will merely quote from the original
Aesthetic the paragraph which affirms that Art or Language (the
terms with Croce are almost interchangeable) is the operation of
the theorizing spirit which disregards reality just as the economic
or vital operation disregards morality: "Awareness of reality is
founded upon a distinction of real from unreal images which in
the initial stage (i.e. that of Art) does not occur. The intuitions of
Art, therefore, are not intuitions of reality or unreality, not perceptions, but pure intuitions."

What Croce is trying to do is to affirm that when in logic we come to distinguish something as real, the something is not an atomic impression or sensation passively received and measurable perhaps by the psychologist-scientist, but is an awareness of something in its wholeness, innocent, as yet, of the choice between reality and unreality; just as our ethical decisions crown an already achieved "economic" act of will, and are not responses to a passively registered lure to maximum advantage, even of the greatest number. This precedent something, which is Art, is also Expression, and also Language. With this glance we must, at least for the moment, relinquish consideration of a highly contended feature of Croce's philosophy, its refusal of any logical character to Art, after noting its careful symmetry with the severance of the economic or vital from the ethical in practical life.

A digression was needed to illustrate one of the major campaigns waged by Croce in his early career – that of the philosophic aesthetician against the scientific incursion into the field of art history and criticism. It is necessary, though somewhat tedious, to avoid here a confusion. The scientists who, in the heyday of European Positivism, approached art problems with a battery of classifications and calculations, offering mathematical formulae for perfect beauty or seeking causal relations between colour effect and artistic force, were not quite identical with the peccant philosophers who sought logical truth in art. In the Crocian pattern there is an outer exclusion of art criticism from the sphere of science and an inner exclusion from that of logic or history, symmetrical with the major severance of the Philosophy of Economy, or Vitality, from Economic Science, and its distinction, inside the Philosophy of Practice, from Ethics. These doctrinal points are here mentioned not so much in the hope of rendering them intelligible in a brief schematic paragraph, as to illustrate the hot pursuit of symmetry running right through Croce's thought. Carried over into the work of disciples who, not having themselves forged these distinctions for specific purposes, are unable to disregard them with Croce's authoritative *insouciance*, the symmetrical armour seems sheerly burdensome. It is the proof of

Croce's genius that in his many freely flowing narratives the pattern remains in the background like an invisible garrison.

In recounting Croce's search for a principle of knowledge to pit against the crass simplifications of late nineteenth-century science, there has been no mention of religion. Croce's attention in his formative period was in fact entirely turned away from the inherited religious views of Italy and from their professors, smarting under the political disasters of the Holy See. The inferiority of Catholic culture, its merely defensive position in the face of the burgeoning of modern thought, has been steadily presupposed by Croce, and he is far from having sounded a retreat on this ground. But this abasement of Catholic culture has never prevented Croce from cordially appreciating the working servitors of organized religion, practical men who keep an immense organization in running order. In this chapter we shall see him completely justifying the organization as an historical product, and we might feel tempted to say that he regards the earnest priest as in his own sphere equally indispensable for the living of life with the strenuous scientist. But this would be going too far. Croce has never taught that Philosophy could supersede Science, render it unnecessary, but he has taught that it could supersede Religion in the sense of cult. Croce has ended by claiming the name of Christian, but has not wavered from the hope that a Religion of Liberty, superseding the Churches in their present form, will give a fresh development to the heritage of Christianity. A Protestant? In his search for a religious ethic springing immediately from the conscience he might appear so. One of Croce's most moving compositions is a short life of the one great Neapolitan Calvinist, V. di Caracciolo. But Croce's references to the Protestant Churches are seldom complimentary. Many years ago he wrote: "Protestantism today stands like a tiresome child between an adult, Modern Thought, and a still robust old man, Catholicism. Children should not get in the way."

What is this Modern Thought? Certainly not, as we have seen, the pretensions of Science. It is essentially Thought uncontaminated by Myth. Myth is the keyword used by Croce to repel religious dogma from an invasion of the Philosophy of the Spirit, the scheme of intellectual coherence. But Myth is by no means found only in the formularies of Churches. Let us, on the contrary, at once see how Croce discerns and condemns a mythical corruption in the two very thinkers whom he regards as his own principal models and forerunners. Giambattista Vico (1668-1744) enjoys Croce's quite particular affection and admiration; the first editions of his works are placed on a sort of altar in Croce's study. This lonely Neapolitan at the height of the European mathematico-scientific Enlightenment offered in opposition to Descartes his "New Science" (science in the older sense) in which the sequence of the forms of the Spirit, and not the "clear and distinct ideas" of the seventeenth century, was placed at the base and at the apex of knowledge. And poetic utterance, or Art, was shown as more fundamental than logical utterance. We see the first outlines of Croce's own philosophy.

But this priority of the Aesthetic, as Croce constantly seeks to bring home to us, is extratemporal. Thought, he says, is inexplicable save as what follows upon artistic intuition, but we are always, and not in some limited time or place, intuiting, and also always thinking. Attempts to collocate the operations of intuition, thought (or indeed will) here rather than there, now rather than then, create myths. Thus it is a Vicoesque myth that the "poetic" epochs of the Trojan war, or the Middle Ages, preceded the ensuing ages of reason. Vico's observation of how the Homeric age gave way to an age of historical and logical meditation, and of how, similarly, the Poetic age of Dante gave way to that of the coldly reasoning, prose-writing school of Machiavelli, was acute: but his thought became contaminated with myth when he traced a chronologically necessary sequence as an effect of the sequence of the forms of the Spirit. There can be no cause in history, says Croce, scientific or metaphysical. What happens, happens for its own sake.

Hegel, likewise, was myth-building when, having traced the ideal development of social man from servitude to freedom, or of logical thought from a mutual exclusion of positive and negative to an ultimate synthesis, he passed on to *apply* these successions as ruling the process of events. Thus Orient, Classical Antiquity, and Christendom he presented as reflexes, in time, of the spiritual process of liberation, and he presented Heraclitus, Plato, and Aristotle as incarnations of the growth of Logic. But the sequence of the forms of the Spirit, the development towards freedom, the progressive attainment of the Idea, are anterior to the construction of time-space. The spontaneity of Art, the clarity of thought, the affirmation of freedom are the tale of universal history in its whole palpitation, and not of arbitrarily severed temporo-spatial blocks.

The question what is really meant by a sequence or series which is *not* temporo-spatial, is one which the critic has to address to the whole idealistic school of philosophy, and not to Croce alone. But of Croce one may reasonably enquire, "What is it that you, the historian, are engaged in doing if not to label events, periods, and personalities with such universal and ideal designations as poetic, free, rational and so forth?" By what right does Croce as an aesthetic critic proclaim the artistic genius of Shakespeare and the splendour of the sacrifice of Thermopylae, and yet challenge the authority of Vico and Hegel to designate epochs as poetic or particular persons as incarnations of logical phases?

The answer which we arrive at in studying Croce is that for him, in strictness, the individual act is the sole reality. It is only the act that can be affirmed to be beautiful, logical, useful, or good (or whatever other words do service in diverse contexts for these ruling concepts). Even this must be qualified by the consideration that the act is always all these things and, in judging it, we note the accentuation of one of the aspects of the Spirit (even this distinction of accent was thrown overboard by Gentile, in whom Croce has had the advantage of studying his own idealist ruthlessness pushed to still more comfortless extremes). The individual names used in historic writing are according to Croce symbolic. Historical judgements are pure apprehensions of the spiritual act. The act is, in the case of art, not the "communication" of beauty by speech or colours or sound, but the intuition by which individuality or clarity is, so to speak, seized and lifted out of the turbulence of volition. From all this Bosanquet, himself an Idealist, would appear justified in charging Croce with rejecting the reality of the external world. Texts would not be wanting. Yet a prolonged immersion in Croce's thought leaves one convinced that his last word is not a denial of the external world (he would not concede this distinction of "external" from "internal") but an affirmation of it in terms refined to an unbearable purity from contradiction; a purity which he himself is the first to declare must be perpetually violated by the universal practical tendency of life. In fact, in Croce's own writing his canons of judgement hardly figure as more than an aspiration, a tendency; were they pressed harder they would silence him.

We have involved ourselves, momentarily, in great perplexities which this is no place to attempt to unravel. But enough has perhaps been said to indicate in what sense Croce outlaws as "mythical" both the creeds of dogmatic religions, and also the metaphysical first causes of philosophers. The creeds ascribe absolute value to events, persons, places and they forbid the scrutiny of these sacred preserves by the mind vowed to ruthless enquiry.

How does Croce approach the sacred preserves? It is fitting at this point to look back at what he tells us of his boyish loss of religious faith. In the *Contribution* he traces it not to intellectual difficulties but to a psychological impediment – his inability to fulfil the instruction to "love God". The image of this God whom Croce could bring himself to fear, but not to love, recurs often in swift allusion in Croce's pages, a Being not so much oppressive as capricious, whose arbitrary interventions and determinations, did one believe in them, would vitiate any reasonableness or harmony that one might discern in existence, and deprive tragedy itself of dignity, mocking the sufferer with awareness of a hidden puller of strings behind the phantasms against which he was pitting his powers.

But if this God vanishes as one term in the impossible love relationship, the other term, the individual Soul, must also vanish. In fact we find Croce also recoiling always with distaste from the spectacle of a "Self", a monad capriciously revealed in unfathom-

able impulses. What is the way of release? To withdraw all reverence from what was imagined to exist as a mystery: to put faith in
what shines back intelligibly when the mind throws its beams:
in the Rational Spirit immanent in events, not in an arbitrary
manipulator behind them, and in the activity which a man knows
himself to develop, not in a Soul hovering in mysterious depths.
The detachment of God and the Soul as mysteriously special
entities transcending the range of critical knowledge, with their
histories walled off from the universality of History: this is the
great Myth which Croce rejects in the name of Modern Thought.
For honest believers in it he shows a tenderness which turns to
scorn if men capable of intellectual adventure and originality seize
upon the myths and laws of an institution as an alibi to evade the
responsibilities of conviction and conscience.

Throughout his writings Croce has interpreted religion as a
philosophy arrested in its development by the materialization of
concepts into myths. But he has made notable shifts in the accent
of his criticism. In 1906 we find Croce using military metaphors
for the conflict between religion and philosophy. But in the fullness
of time he has claimed a specific Christian character for his
thought. The challenge has not been withdrawn, but we find an
altogether more generous comprehension for the opponent. This
he developed at length in the essay *Why we cannot but call ourselves
Christians*, published in 1943. We shall now analyse this at some
length; for it is an excellent example of Croce's presentation of
historical thought as a contribution to the problems of the hour.

The hour was that – in 1943 – of the imminent collapse of the
Fascist régime and of its war front, threatening chaos to the nation;
an hour in which Liberals and Catholics anxiously sought the
ground for a common effort to consolidate a new national unity.
The air was thick, too, with talk of revolution.

Christianity, Croce's argument starts, has been the greatest revolution in history, so great that understandably it has appeared as
something miraculous. For the Christian Revolution operated in
the intimacy of the moral conscience, and man's conscience or
consciousness (one word in Italian) seemed thereby to have

achieved a new spiritual quality. Yet this was not really a miracle irrupting from without into history: it was the most solemn of crises in the sphere of human historical development. The awakened conscience saw reality dawning in a new light, no longer in the object but in the subject, and saw God no longer as an undifferentiated unity but as one and distinct, unity and trinity. Then the Christian Faith in its advance clothed itself in myths and discordant ideas, but still did not lose its original sense. To understand it we must attend to its success in preserving its purity, not to its incidental succumbing to infections. We read Homer for his poem and not for his slips, Croce remarks.

But the formative process of Christianity had to reach a provisional resting place and to gain stability. The fixation and institutionalization of Christianity is often blamed, says Croce, as a decadence. But the same happens with studies and sciences. The flow of criticism is arrested and frozen in catechisms and manuals. Human existence cannot skip this stage in which a pause is given to thought and it "dies beautifully in action". The Church developed its sacraments and its laws, educated the barbarian peoples to their use, beneficially held Eastern pessimisms at arm's length, and asserted the superiority of moral to political law. The author of a book has to cease improving and correcting it. He has not perfected his task, yet he sends his manuscript to the printer. And although the work of such geniuses as St. John and St. Paul still remained rich in potentialities for new form, the Church provisionally stabilized the acquired results.

It is not just, Croce continues, to denounce the Catholic Church for corruptions which later became rampant also, in shabbier form, in those reformed churches which cried out against Rome. When corruption threatened to overwhelm her, and the new philosophic thought was rendering her scholastic thought obsolete, the Catholic Church reformed herself and scored fresh triumphs in the New World. "An institution does not die for its incidental defects . . . but because it no longer satisfies a need" (but whether the Church is approaching that situation, Croce will not in this context discuss).

In later ages, the men of the Renaissance who understood the virtue of poetry, art, and politics, and asserted their human character in the face of supernaturalism and asceticism, were truly carrying the Christian spirit forward to new realizations. The Church of Rome was necessarily concerned to defend its institutions and stability, and was therefore obliged to condemn and persecute these renovators and enlargers, though without having any vigorous culture of its own to pit against the mathematicians, the teachers of natural law, the philosophers of the spirit, all in their way developers of the Christian spirit. It was obliged to deny the name of Christian to those workers who, with their labour and sacrifice and blood, were causing the truths proclaimed by Jesus to fructify. "For these, like every other work of the mind, are a sketch calling for continual enrichment with new lines and shades." The Church cannot recognize that there are Christians outside itself, "but we", while comprehending the Churchman's position, "must claim the name". The claim of a Christian character for actors in fields outside the Church is fortified by the consideration that art and literature have always refrained from portraying Jesus with the light touch of innocent mockery which they allow themselves in all other contexts, and also by the observation that secular movements fall back upon the Christian phraseology of martyrdom and revelation when solemnizing their own sentiments.

"None can say whether another revelation or religion, of equal or higher rank, will light upon humanity in a future of which we now discern no glimmer. But evidently in our present time we are in no sense outside the limits of Christianity." The essay ends with a fervent assertion that the life of the philosophy of the Spirit is the life of Christian devotion although God has ceased to be for the philosopher an intellectual mystery and has become limpid truth seen by the light of a logic "which may well call itself divine".

This essay shows Croce developing his thought in a simple form as a contribution to the rescue of the nation from a particular stress and anguish. He lifts himself high above Party. His conservative strain comes out strongly in a full comprehension for the necessities of holding an institution together by the sacrifice of perfection to order. As a dialectician Croce surveys the stress and anguish in a human drama in which the guardians of order necessarily face the champions of progress and development, each giving to the other his cue. But we are not left with an unresolved duality. A clear position emerges for action. Croce chooses the part of an innovator within the strong stream of inspiration still springing from "the Christian Revolution".

This position may be assailed from two sides. It may be said that the innovations proposed by Croce do not really carry forward the Spirit with the power and breadth called for in our situation, and that a far greater Revolution is in fact called for, one which, reversing the direction of the search for reality back again from Subject to Object, subordinates Conscience to calculated purpose, perhaps on the grandiose scale of an organization of humanity for the conquest of nature. This, in reality, is the claim of the nineteenth-century "Religion of Science" once again, and we have shown Croce's total rejection of it, because he had seen through to the covert negation, implicit in this religion, of art, history, and morality, although, in the Positivist Age, this cruel faith was still uncruel.

Or it may be said from the other side that in fact Croce's innovation itself delivers a mortal blow to Christianity, leaving no right to claim a Christian character. Gone, it seems, is the God to whom Christians pray, gone is the praying soul, and the drama of the Incarnation and Redemption is merged in the flux of occurrence. Heaven and Earth and their link pass away into a universal monotony, gratuitously termed spiritual. To this charge the student of Croce is obliged to seek an answer. If the replacement of God and the Soul by the spiritual act is found to signify not the mournful death of these concepts, but their liberation from images which have become obstructions; if the withdrawal of the prestige of mystery from the deepest and richest memories of the race leaves them standing forth in natural majesty, and no longer assailable by facile doubts, then Croce has made good his claim, or the claim of the thought which he sums up. But the Crocian philosophy renounces in its theoretical vision, as in its ethics, the image of a resting place to be won by perfect acceptance of truths and codes. Such a resting place would be the suicide of history, of wide-awake life. A tranquillity or serenity is indeed immanent in history as the holding of energies in reserve when the struggle calls for other energies.

Carrying our question "is this a Christian philosophy?" to Croce in his function as a moral educator, we meet once more the repudiation of a dualism. As Croce's religious thought rejects a separate or transcendent supernatural, his ethics reject asceticism, the sovereignty of "soul" over "body", and the authority of all laws which elaborate that distinction.

For Croce, the ethical activity is not the conquest of sinful physical appetite by the virtuous soul, but the crowning of a strong intention ("the economic act of the spirit") by a universal or moral intention. This distinction in the acts of the Will ("economic" and "ethical") corresponds to the necessity in the thinking Mind for a clear representation ("the aesthetic form") to precede true (logical) judgement. The two "earlier" forms (though Croce wants the earliness to be considered as non-temporal), the Aesthetic and the Economic, have been grouped by Croce under the provocative title "the two worldly sciences". They enjoy his special affection as the means by which modern thought, in the sphere of theory, dethrones dogmatic religion without selling the pass to scientific rationalism, and in the sphere of practice dethrones the ascetic ideal without surrendering morality to the sway of a utility calculus. As from the artistic intuition the mind passes on to a spiritual but untheological vision, not narrowed to a particular strip of "sacred" history, so from the economic volition the will passes on to the pursuit of universal purpose, not of some narrowly classified virtues. The good man has to do something far more difficult than to stick to rules.

There is a whole series of ethical essays, or lay sermons, in which Croce discusses what, in given circumstances, he does have to do. Croce the moralist has forsworn moral regulations or laws, at any rate in their claim to be clear or sufficient, but he is no relativist or agnostic in this or any sphere. There is for him a rightness in action as much as there is a truth in history. The *Ethical Fragments*, one of the books most valued by a wide circle of Italian readers, point to typical problems of anxious humanity, moral quandaries which yield, in cheerful or melancholy vein, but always decorously, to the fine handling of the exquisite discriminator. Here, if he has been successful, Croce has brought the casuistry of the confessional into an air no longer cloyed by hope of rewards or murky with fears of punishment. The problems, we feel, have been thrown up sometimes by personal experience, sometimes by reading, sometimes by some street scene witnessed during the philosopher's evening walks.

One is unhappy, ill employed, or ill wedded, and one puts a brave face on it and carries through one's duty. One rejects any ignoble expedient of escape or release. But may one not innocently indulge in the imaginations of an existence eased by a change in these circumstances? No, comes the answer, there are no indifferent external circumstances. If I wander in thought to the advantage I would have from my enemy's accidental death, I am weakening my will to withstand or to reconcile myself to him in the one given reality.

Another case: recalling that whatever I love is destined to change, I want to steel myself against loss by according only a limited love, as Montaigne advises. But Montaigne is wrong. True love accepts without any reserve its conjunction with pain. "The purpose which sages or philosophers have sought to achieve by weakening the energy of love is not to be won this way. . . . It is only to be won by loving with such elevation of spirit as to attain the strength to stand up to grief, the possibility of surpassing it in a new love."

Sexual love contends with our moral life, our work, our business. How are we to compose the conflict? By weaving over love an ideology of soul-comradeship, constancy, purity? But the senses are not constant, the fancy is fickle. Perhaps then by uprooting our natural inclinations? The attempt has a certain grandeur but it smacks of insanity. By analysing them scientifically? This would be an insanity without grandeur, for love can no more be split into component parts than a work of art. The solution is to involve love in the ethical implications of marriage ("the tomb of a merely wild love") or in other ethical activity. "The good rule of education is this: not to withstand the natural tendency which leads to the follies of love, but to plant and develop other spiritual interests capable of limiting and if necessary subduing these."

Lying is repugnant to the moral spirit. But is it not charity to spare a patient by hiding the facts of his illness? Is not a brutal revelation of fact often a consummate villainy? Yes. For there is really no such thing as telling the whole truth. The truth is Thought and the "telling" of it is the use of verbal stimulants to obtain the alliance of another mind in Thought. The obligation of truth is not to administer stimulants regardless of occasion, but to radiate thought to promote the ends of life.

Delight in evil. . . . How can man delight in evil which is the negation of all values? Yet poets like Poe and Baudelaire portray this delight. In reality, Croce answers, what is termed delight in evil is often simply a satisfaction in winning "forbidden fruit" against the injunctions of law. Now, morality can never be truly represented by law, and therefore the satisfaction given when the will overcomes the obstacle of law is simply that of surmounting an obstacle. This is not a delight in evil.

How do these ethical counsels, of which a handful have here been summarized, stand to Christian ethical teaching? In those quoted there is for example no exaltation of loves or loyalties carried forward to an after-life, no praise of chastity or of verbal veracity, no veneration of a sacrosanct law, no flight to the absolute good (which if ever suggested by Croce is never portrayed as a haven of peace) from the powers of darkness (which are nothing more terrifying than the eclipse of one aspect of the spirit by another). But there is no note of indulgence or laxity. Croce refers all moral problems to a creative conscience stricter than any lawgiver and innocent of any calculation of advantage. Conscience will not listen to advantage even if extended to comprise the greatest good of the greatest number to all eternity, for such a quantitative extension could never attain universality, never define an absolute "great event" as the criterion for the value of acts moving towards it or away from it.

But it will be asked: is not this moral conscience, stripped of legal scaffolding and indifferent to any scientific justification, simply the arbitrary, just the helplessly evanescent sentiment of an individual, or rather (since we are denied belief even in ourselves except as a conventional continuity) of an imperceptible phantasm in the boundless sea of existence? The same anguish meets us here as in the aesthetic and logical spheres where Croce has seemed to sweep aside all orientations for the intuition of the beautiful, all tests for the cognition of the true, dissolving them in the flux of the spirit.

There can be no answer except Croce's own portrayal of the beautiful, the true, the vital, the good.

The refinement of logic and ethics which we have traced must rank at lowest valuation as a valiant effort to heal the split mind of the modern European. If the system itself seems in certain lights to be held in place only by masterful simplifications and verbal licences, let us at least allow that the business of a coherency is to cohere, and let the attempt be measured against other speculative essays in coherency. There is no need to claim that coherency is the fullest or highest endeavour of man. Croce has had the modesty to declare that his outlook is essentially the restricted one of the man of letters. But even in this range Croce is aware how little has been achieved. Christianity, liberated from myth and asceticism, has but touched the mind of our times. "Far from having penetrated the convictions and judgements of the people at large," Croce has written, "the religion of liberty has not yet even been intellectually developed so as to establish the intellectual classes in secure possession of it." But a penetration to the people, he says, "must come even if the religion of liberty has to clothe itself in myth" (an aspiration, or admission, to which we will refer again).

It sometimes seems to the student of Croce that the expulsion of the Transcendental Absolute from the core of his thought has been like a grave surgical operation followed by an inpouring of healing influences, not merely restoring equilibrium but promising new health and growth. His Ethic disclaims the war of soul against body, only to discover the triumph of spiritual will over the utilitarian craving for quiescence whether in fleshly pleasures, rationalistic formulae, or the religious imagination.

The healing influences restore to us, through reverence for continuity, the confidence in personal identity which in the logical scheme had been sacrificed to the pre-eminent, indeed sole, reality of spiritual acts. They revivify nature, which seemed to have withered up in the piercing light of an intuition, sole creator of all the beauty perceived and expressed. Religious myth, science, and the laws prove to have been dragged from their tyrannical dominance only to take up more honourable and useful functions as guides to probability. What function indeed could be more exalted than to guide us towards probability in spheres where certainty would signify stagnation, that death of enquiry and endeavour – of History – which with Croce always stands for ultimate absurdity?

V
Croce and the Secular Myths

Croce has severed the living from the dead in Christian tradition by discerning the vitiation of Thought by Myth. The myth, in one of Croce's descriptions, is the hybridization of the artistic fancy with the logical concept, so that an intuition or representation (let us say the vision of Jesus as God or of the labourers of Europe as guiltless of oppression and pregnant with fully social energy) is presented as a definition. Or a concept like Morality is petrified into a divine table of laws. Those who pursue intuition and concept through the corridors of Croce's philosophy and history will find these ghostly playmates often taking a broad and bewildering licence to use each others' language and vesture "for the convenience of discourse". But it is not difficult to see the broad sense in which for Croce religious dogma and Hegelian metaphysic alike pervert truth into myth, and the same is done, brutally or crassly, by such doctrines as the racialism of Hitler's Germany and the Communism of Marx.

What then of a "totalitarianism" nearer home, Italian Fascism? Whether from contempt, or prudence, or as some will assert because its tenets, if distortedly, reflected his own teachings, Croce has had no occasion to argue on a theoretical level with the make-shift assortment of doctrines which it was attempted to combine in a 'Fascist Philosophy'. Not all of the tendencies which converged into Fascism were distasteful to Croce. We have seen him in an earlier chapter in sympathy with aspirations for a strongly administered State, which should be respectful of national traditions and uninhibited by any economic orthodoxies. A family of European corporative States, with Trade Unions converted from sentimental internationalism to national loyalties, seems to have been Croce's hope before the first European War. There was a line of descent from these ideas to the Fascist movement. But there were other ultimately triumphant trends originating in quarters which he detested. Croce had for years denounced D'Annunzio's luxurious aestheticism which infected the middle class youth of Italy with a desperate resolve to draw attention to itself in rhetorical posturings. Later it fell to Croce to condemn also the close colleague and co-operator of his first philosophic decade, Giovanni Gentile. Brief mention has been made of the theoretical aspect of the dispute, and we cannot go into this further, but it is remarkable to find in Croce's arraignment of Gentile in the placid atmosphere of 1913 these warnings:

"What troubles me above all in your thought is its tendency to weaken the awareness of conflict in the conscience. I am troubled by the acquiescence in the accomplished fact and the deed done which is induced by your attenuation of error and evil to wholly unreal shadows. . . . The complete scoundrel is not only innocent for you but is good in the immediacy of his conscience. . . . I fear that you and your friends are on the way back to an attitude of moral and ethical indifference, not perhaps as men, but certainly as theorists, and this theory will bear or is already bearing the fruit which theories do bear."

The fruit which they bore in Fascism was, however, in Croce's final judgement contemptible rather than terrible. After the fall of Fascism in Italy he wrote: "There was an intimate and profound difference between Nazism and Fascism. The former was a terrible crisis that had been brewing for centuries in German history. The latter was an outgrowth extraneous to Italy's long history and repugnant to recent Italian traditions. The former had a diabolic and tragic aspect. The latter, even amid crimes, destructions, and ruins, could not rid itself of a carnival air."

Croce's awareness of the terrible German crisis was not tardy. Anticipations of his recoil from the Nazi racial mysticism could be quoted from works written in the heyday of Croce's prominence as a lover of Germany. In 1943 he recapitulated his scattered judgements in a brief volume *The Spiritual Quarrel of Germany with Europe*. We have seen Croce's forebodings about Italian Fascism foreshadowed in a theoretical dissension with Gentile, and we can trace a foreboding of the maniacal character of German nationalism in Croce's criticisms of classical German logic. Croce's whole philosophic system under one aspect may be viewed as the attempt to purge the idealistic tradition from Hegel's mythical elaborations. He sensed disease in Hegel's regimentation of the logical pattern in a time pattern. Croce wished the forms of the spirit to pervade reality at a deeper level than its analysis into time and space. But Hegel had frozen the distinct forms of art, logic, and nature, into fragments of temporo-spatial reality. Arbitrarily selected eras, peoples, races, or individuals were erected into incarnations of liberty, art, justice, or virility, not as symbols freely standing for those distinctions but as mythical or corpulent concepts, worshipped or abhorred with fanaticism.

Croce recapitulates some of these forebodings in an article written in 1936: "The history of the elevation of the racial sentiment to a scientific doctrine has its mental origins in the particular persistence in Germany of the tradition of the succession of the kingdoms, along with the Biblical idea of the chosen people and the Augustinian idea of predestination. In the eighteenth century these ideas became secularized and assumed a philosophical vesture as can be seen in Hegel's classical *Philosophy of History*. . . . There was introduced into the vision of the one history of humanity a cleft between the 'Germanic' and the 'non-Germanic', splitting asunder even the sphere of poetry and art. . . . As time went on, the assignment by philosophers to the various peoples of characters and missions which were interpreted in philosophical terms ceased. But the materialistic school maintained the same distinctions and divisions, merely materializing them into the zoological concept of races, which were accordingly designated as some superior and some inferior, some strong and some weak, some masterful and some servile." In the light of this kink in German thought (which will be recognized as the "mythical" error of Hegel, expounded popularly) Croce traces the infection by it of European culture in general.

By constantly analysing in pungent terms the German racialist theory as its vogue spread after the first war, Croce did much to keep the intelligent Italian public ashamed of the cynical adoption of racialism by the Italian régime in 1938, though sense of humour, natural courtesy, and the disapproval of the Church in any case greatly mitigated them in the application. Although Croce in the first decades of the century had kept close links with Germany, it may be remarked that he then already scented danger in the Kaiser's attempted spokesmanship for the white races. And incidentally, he showed disgust for the sacking of the treasures of the Chinese palaces by the German-led European expedition against the Boxer insurgents – one of the rather rare cases of a turning of Croce's attention to the Eastern cultures; though one also finds him, in those relatively placid times, giving a fleeting inspection to the Indian systems of Logic (Croce's *Aesthetic* in its first fame was actually translated into Japanese).

The ideology of class conflict radiated from Moscow is for Croce another cult originating in a similar falsification of thought. For fifty-five years Croce has watched the developments of Socialism and Communism on the theoretical and the practical plane. From the beginning (after his own Marxist phase)[1] we find him wholly

1. Senator Benedetto Croce, some years ago, took exception to an entry in the index – not the text – of my book *The Development of Modern Italy* in which he was described in youth as having "embraced Socialism". No more was meant than that he had passed through a period when the writings of his friend Labriola, the pioneer of Italian Marxism, had, in Croce's own words, "set his mind aflame". Croce never joined a Marxist party, but Labriola evidently, for a time, hoped to have his young friend's company in a political crusade.

denying the presence of any authentic philosophic inspiration in
Marxism. "It was the constant habit of Marx and Engels to seek
out in the philosophers precisely what is not philosophical, their
practical tendencies, their social and class feelings. . . . Hegelism
strengthened Marx in his action and his social observation, and the
dialectic in his hands was a powerful instrument, vigorously
wielded, but unknown to him in its intimate logical constitution"
(1909). Croce has always maintained that as a movement of
thought Marxism perished after it had stimulated historical writers
to take a new range of problems into their ken. There might
seem, on the other hand, to have been an unacknowledged change
in Croce's verdict upon Marxism as a political movement. In 1909
he regarded Marxist Socialism as decaying on the political plane
for want of a revolutionary impulse. He is speaking (in that year)
of the "revolutionary" part played by the Italian bourgeoisie in its
achievement of the unification of Italy. "If the Italian bourgeois
revolutionaries had come to terms with the old Governments (of
the separate Italian States), moderating their demands and negotiat-
ing for reforms and compromises, Italy would never have been
unified. . . . If the proletariat really wants to imitate the bourgeoisie in overthrowing an old society, it must find the strength
and capacity to imitate it also in the stern work of demolition and
reconstruction." This complaint of a deficiency in revolutionary
spirit might seem to be singularly far removed from the attitude of
one who has mercilessly mocked the Social Revolutionaries of the
second post-war period. But Croce has not been asleep. He has
retained a piercing memory for his numberless pronouncements,
and in 1947 powerfully defended his claim to consistency. But we
cannot follow him here into that intricate political polemic.

After the war, Croce, as the most illustrious adversary of fallen
Fascism, was at the height of national fame at that moment when
the well-organized Communist Party manoeuvred strenuously to
capture the vacant citadels of power. A Marxist cultural front was
desired to accompany the political front of the workers and
peasants. Here Croce's influence barred the way. No small part of
the Communist literary output of these years was devoted to

probing the defences of Croce's uncompromisingly negative
judgement upon the entire movement. Croce retorted with zeal
and pungency.

Karl Marx, he argued, inherited and transported into his doctrines just those mechanical and decadent elements in the Hegelian system which derived from Hegel's unconscious servitude to
theological myth, clad in metaphysical terminology. Hegel had
localized the spiritual essence of liberty in the post-Napoleonic
Prussian Constitutional Monarchy. But Marx, with a far cruder
obtuseness, had equated the balance of universal history, in its
aspect of unceasing strain and alternation of fortunes, with the
conflict of social classes. But what reality pertains to these "classes"?
They are assortments of human material, made in the pursuit of
ends which are vital in politics. But they have nothing to do with
the concepts by which the mind explains historical reality. What
are the "classless State", the "realm of freedom", and the other
ideals to which the Marxist turns his hopes? Simply the theological
heaven in new vesture; to set hopes upon them, instead of coping
with the real world, is to yield to weariness, to the vain desires of
the somnolent and inferior personality which we carry around
with us, the shadow-side of our spiritual life. And what is this
"Matter" of the materialists but an empirical classification borrowed
from the world of Physics, and offered to superstition as an incarnation of the essence which eludes all dimensions?

The attempted proclamation of a "new" culture, the call for a
"new directing class", offends the philosopher for whom newness
can be nothing more than a particular emphasis upon one of the
aspects of eternal history. In Croce's vision a leadership of mankind,
marked out by its sensitivity to these ever-changing aspects, is
always present, and is always facing new circumstances. At one
time it gathers strength in patient expectation, at another, in some
happy but fleeting season, it can celebrate the apparent achievement of liberty and distribute its fruits among some neglected
groups of society.

The most impressive study of Croce as an historical figure is a
fragmentary work, composed in prison between 1929 and 1935, by

the principal founder of the Italian Communist Party, the late Antonio Gramsci. Gramsci attributes to Croce such a commanding
position in the development of modern Italy that he regards an
immersion in Crocian thought as one of the primary necessities for
a Communist education. In a development foreseen by Gramsci,
Croce was to serve as the starting point for a new Italian florescence
of Marxist thought, just as Hegel had provided a starting point for
Marx himself. Croce's thought was to be liberated from its literary
and contemplative seclusion and launched into the world of action.
For Gramsci, Croce is the symbolic figure of the high Italian
culture which in its intimate conscience had already freed itself
from the myths of the Church centuries ago, but in doing so lost
touch with its own people, the workers and peasants of Italy,
because the minds of ordinary people can only be awakened and
held by doctrine clad in myth. Clearly, Gramsci accepts Croce's
own valuation of the slogans of Communism as illusory, but he
would say that they are a *vital* illusion. Somewhat remarkably, we
have found Croce himself conceding the need for vital myth in
words already quoted: the Religion of Liberty will have to penetrate to the people, he has said, "even if it has to clothe itself in a
Myth".

In Italy, more perhaps than elsewhere in Europe, high culture
thinks its thought on one side of the road, and the people cultivate
their myth on the other. The precarious and brittle nature of the
united Italian State which came into being through the "bourgeois
revolutions" of 1848-1870 itself bore testimony to the perilous cleft.
The nobler figures of Italian Communism, like Gramsci, may have
sincerely striven to bridge it, but the course of politics has driven
them into a mythicism so crass as to be self-defeating. Sane but
simple minds have preferred the old myths.

If Benedetto Croce has in a lifetime been steadily writing for an
élite, and not for the people, the people – first and foremost his
own Neapolitans – have appreciated the frank and shrewd character of "Don Benedetto", this energetic, loquacious ornament of
his city, who likes to bring out his anecdotage and repartee in the
popular dialect, as he wanders through its massive mouldering

architecture and tinsel gaieties, an old farmer in from the country, one might suppose, save for the small sensitive hands and the fine pensive eyes.

VI

Conclusion

Few of the critics of Croce's life-work fail to employ the word "Olympian" to express sometimes their admiration, but more often their dissatisfaction, with the lessons conveyed by it. Such critics do homage to the clarity and elegance of Croce's systematic thought and to the intricate workmanship which has bound together, as in a vast scheme of mental fortifications, the glacis of dialectic, the high ground of morals, and the moving waters of history and politics. But what then?

Croce stands ceaselessly observant upon his mountain top, countering every external threat by fresh dispositions of his own forces. The whole system is mobile and in constant war trim. Yet does it not wholly lack an impetus to carry the struggle forward to a conclusion? In its identification of Truth and Reality with the systole and diastole of history does it not renounce the highest of human quests? Does it not disconsolately cry halt to the eternal effort to surpass the relative and the provisional, either in the achievement of some satisfying Divine Embrace or by the discovery of an infallible measure of Progress to dominate the deserts of Eternity? Many are the students of Croce who after experiencing an initial liberation through the harmonious fullness of his philosophy have come to bewail a sense of emptiness at the core, as though for the sake of an unfailing serenity amid transient experience the great hope of outstripping transience itself had been mortified.

Croce, in this small book, has been considered primarily as a contributor to the discussions and issues of his times. It is, so to speak, a discussion of the public relations of his philosophy. We shall conclude therefore by listening to voices of protest raised in the arena, rather than to the still small voice of an intimate criticism, whose

plaint is that we find in this delicate moralist, so sensitive to historical pathos, so reverent to the marks and relics of human achievement and failure, a deficiency in the vision which forgets itself in
impressions effortlessly receivable, and finds a satisfaction in the
precision of their givenness. The "natural history" to which Croce
does homage as the reality masked by the abstractions of Science,
elicits from him only a rudimentary sentiment, and no one perhaps
has ever closed a book of Croce (as he might have done after
reading Locke) with a heightened appreciation of our natural
setting. Yet this is, in the main, a complaint against Croce the
young and masterful synthetist; and the sense of living nature seems
to streak some of his more recent pages. "Every philosopher", he
himself wrote long ago, "at the end of his enquiry perceives the
first faint lines of another."

But let us take Croce for what he has principally been, the
spokesman of an anti-mystical and anti-utopian Humanism. There
is a striking coincidence of the dissatisfactions expressed from the
two great institutional camps in modern Europe, the Catholic
which in Croce's self-liquidating historicism perceives no issue
towards a redemptive divine Otherness, and the Marxian which
sees no issue towards a revolutionary dynamism blazing the trail
through the unknowable.

From the point of view of transcendental religion which feels the
need to pass on from intellectual clarity to an intense immolation
and, in fact, to the attainment of spiritual "results", it is complained
that "in all Croce's works there is wanting the real element, the
true drama. . . . The drama of man towards God, in whom Croce
does not believe, is missing: so is the drama of man towards the
mystery of life. Therefore all is resolved, all is finished, all is concluded in that which is. And in the absence of the drama of the
Spirit, all that which is, is dull reality, irrelevance." And further,
"the struggle, the human conflict, the battle between flesh and
spirit, all this would (in Croce's view of life) be finished, non-
existent. How could it be otherwise, given a conception in which
Reason is confounded with the individual himself? How could the
conquest of a new and higher spiritual level signify a victory, if

Reason, meeting no dualism in the individual, but wholly identified with him, finds no obstacle to throw down, no difficulty to
surmount?" (Antonio Lombardi in *La Filosofia di Benedetto Croce*,
Rome 1946.)

The desolation felt by religious critics at the lack of a culminating reference, in the Crocian philosophy, to a divine Reality,
approachable or conquerable by steps of mystic intellection and
exercise, is paralleled by the impatience of those who feel the lack
of a culminating reference to a human crusade for the regeneration
of human society. Let us again quote some sentences from the
prison notebooks of the founder of the Italian Communist Party,
who spent so much of his long sentence time meditating on Croce's
theory of history.

"To view historical development like a game with an umpire and
rules to be loyally respected, is to lay down a pattern for history
in which the ideology is grounded not upon the political *content* but
upon the *form and method* of the struggle. This is an ideology which
tends to blunt the antithesis, to distribute it through a long series of
moments, to reduce the dialectic to a process of reformist evolution, of revolution-restoration in which only the second term
of this combination is really valid.... Vitality and expansive
power are precluded from a philosophy that is not at the same
time an actual policy, closely related to the preponderant activity
of the popular classes, which is work, and not presented as being,
within certain limits, necessarily involved with Science.... It is
this latter conception which links man to nature by means of skills,
maintains his superiority, and advances it by creative work; and
thereby exalts his spirit and history." (Antonio Gramsci in *Il Materialismo Storico e la Filosofia di Benedetto Croce*, Rome 1948.)

Both the Catholic and the Marxist critic give expression to a
feeling of frustration in face of a philosophy which seems to them
to be orientated towards equilibrium in an accepted reality, when
they would have it directed along a route for the surpassing of
reality as known at any moment. The Catholic convicts Croce of
refusal to tackle the road of methodic religious exercise and cult, the
Communist of a proud rejection of the evangelism of political zeal.

In a convulsed world, protests the Catholic, in which codes of conduct venerated only yesterday, filial obedience, chastity, submission to hierarchy, are loudly and overtly flouted, is it not a frivolous desertion to weaken reverence for the formularies and traditional wisdom of solid time-tested institutions? Must not the young man or woman of good will, in this predicament, make a clean sweep of the subtleties and sensibilities cultivated by the complacent introspection of recent comfortable centuries, in order to discover, in obedience to the never silenced, explicit voice of transcendant religion, a clear-cut course of duty commensurate with the danger of the times?

Not altogether otherwise is the case stated from the Marxist platform. The old world, the old society, it is said, is breaking down. Its thoughts, its institutions, its culture litter the floor of our existence in decaying masses. Hypocrisy courses through our professions and actions, tainting every intention with insincere concessions to established but obsolescent authority. What attitude can there be worthy of resolute youth if not to devote oneself to a cause propounding the radical renovation of our system of ideas and loyalties, so that, however painful the work of demolition and the loss of familiar landmarks, there may be provided a clean foundation for the erection of a rational order of being, owing nothing of its prestige to antique mystery, but attracting by the clear prophecy of an honest and simple world on the other side of mighty struggles?

What substitute for a manly enrolment in the service of ancient sanctified values, asks the Catholic; what substitute for militancy in the cause of a bright and clear new order, asks the Communist, can be offered by the Crocian "Religion of Liberty"? Never unburdening the individual from the distracting pursuit for well-fitting convictions in a relentlessly flowing world, this Crocian philosophy, it is said, withholds from him both the chrism of a peculiar consecration through humble service to a uniquely divine order, and also the exhilaration of a "scientific" faith, poised, in a determined fusion of the will and the understanding, towards the emergence of future historical perfections.

To operate in the turmoils of the present world with no better orientations than what the philosophically sensitized and tremulously suspended intimate conscience can determine from moment to moment or (a mere quantitative difference) from period to period, is this not to accept so weak an equipment that in practice the religionist of freedom will consult merely his own safety and comfort, and lie, lulled in the crystalline coils of Croce's dialectic, as an effective absentee from the harsh but fruitful struggles of his kind? Such are the protests against Croce's cultural hegemony in Italy, which in different forms have accompanied it throughout a half-century, but have taken sharper outlines as the philosopher himself, in an old age of matchless activity, has worked and re-worked his ideas in a veritable library of books, and has won for his own person the deference which is paid to great institutions.

In such criticisms one may detect the implicit presumption that spiritual culture is self-regarding, that its pursuit concerns what one does with one's loneliness, and subtracts from society the energies which a full manner of life pours into the vital human drama. It is indeed true that spiritual culture recognizes a quality of loneliness in the dignity of the individual. Wherein would lie the value and richness of society itself were not the individual ploughing and mining in the remoter ranges of his consciousness a wealth which is perpetually brought to society as a fresh and unique contribution? But the loneliness is in the research, not in the disposal of the harvest; and if the individual should seek to hoard it for himself, he would merely lose his own individuality.

Groundless also is the apprehension that a philosophy of quality and of individuality deadens the stimuli which should incite a man to a wide and generous participation in public affairs. It is true that, while fortifying him for the pursuit of those interests and duties for which his personality appears best suited, it will discourage him from the bravado of an attempt to reverse the currents which have made him what he is; to attempt, for example, the role of a hero if he finds in himself the soul of an entertainer; or the role of a champion of righteous revolt if his understanding casts him for that of a mediator. Or if sometimes the call must come for a great change in the emphasis of a human life, the philosophy which we are considering will encourage a man not to quit his natural path in anxious scruple lest perhaps he should have misconstrued his destiny, but only – if ever – because a new note has been added and the old cadence is now imperatively felt to be tending towards an unsuspected resolution. Only a tyrannical propensity, scorning and secretly fearing what is free in men, sees in the lighthearted-ness of the liberal sense of duty, in its comprehension of the duties of adversaries even if these threaten one's own cause or task to the death, a culpable frivolousness. As if the grim set countenance or ecstatic prostration of the fanatic were the necessary patent of "seriousness" on the part of a contributor to the human struggle.

But neither is it in reality true that the liberal, by contrast with the adepts of transcendant dogma or world-conquering ideology, lacks institutions or cults by which he may fortify himself, or sacrifice himself to fortify them. It might even be said that the liberal sense of institution and of cult invests too much of life to be compressed into a department, even a sovereign department. Awareness of the human condition in a living universe is an exercise so immense that we may feel impatience at the solemnity with which religious and ideological groups claim election for special destinies beyond the grave, or upon peculiar peaks of history. The spectacle of nature, the sensible human form, and the organization of consciousness are themselves institutions which in the broadest sweep of our awareness we are entitled to view as the matrices and last resting places of the most majestic systems and codes. Yet such a breadth of view would be degraded if enlisted to justify an emancipation from immediate concerns. The contests of life are fought on the ground of present fact, and the liberal mind, challenging the pretensions of static coagulations of power in Churches, States, Parties, Classes, and Societies, is itself forced to assume the best but necessarily defective and perishable armour that it can find.

It must fight for liberty by associating if and where necessary with tyranny, and it must combat dogmatism with weapons forged in the armouries of dogma. Thus there can be no final answer to a question such as this: "Should we force men to be free by depriving them of the freedom to be unfree?" There can but be piecemeal answers thrown up in the hurly-burly of polemics or politics. Nor can there be a final retort to such a protest as this: "The philosophy which you offer in replacement of authoritarian creeds is itself rooted in the authority of generations of men who, not as disembodied absolute intelligences, and not without appetites for power and regimentation, nor yet without arbitrary embellishment or truncations of discourse which had got out of rational control, have bound their successors in a tradition which must be obeyed before it is criticized."

This is true, and we find Benedetto Croce himself observing: "In philosophical argument, the opponent's philosophy is often charged with being more or less mythological. Thus there is talk of a mythology of Atoms, Chance, Ether, the Two Substances, Monads, the Blind Will, the Unconscious; and, for that matter, also of a mythology of the Immanent Spirit, for such accusations have not been lacking against the philosophy upheld by myself, or some versions of it" (*Logica*, 3rd edn., p. 301). But characteristic of Croce's long philosophic career has been not the achievement of an unassailable rational immaculacy in the form of the presentation of his thought, but an unflagging alacrity to put his conceptual pattern of coherence to the test as a critical organ in wide and various fields of knowledge.

A student who has accompanied him through long stretches of this career will feel that the progressive elaboration of the philosophy has been elicited by the challenge of facts, and not by a sheltered proliferation of images. Throughout the thinker's career runs a manly confidence in the survival of truth through the eternal accretion and shedding of illusions. Its earnestness seems however to be tempered by the recollection that if life is man's only field for work and thought, it is also the only playground for fancy and make-believe which are the devices by which Truth makes felt the need of her presence.

The philosophy of Croce offers no encouragement to the hope of achieving serenity by the artificial resuscitation, by however exquisite a process, of outworn beliefs. For it attributes the peace which men have indeed, in their day, found in these, to the absorbing and rewarding labour which they then devoted to refining and purifying those beliefs into the more freely flowing forms of thought which are now natural to our society; and that fine rapture of other times cannot now be recaptured with conscious care. The thought which we have inherited is to be accepted reverently, but as an element in the living tissue, growing and developing by an incalculable fecundity for fresh pattern. Therefore, we are warned against the illusion that we may eternalize the crystallizations of design which in thought, as in life itself, mark the settlement of exhausted stresses.

This philosophy warns against the vanity of the worship of an embalmed past, but equally it forbids us to applaud the insolently floodlit perspectives upon the future, inferred from a quantitative prolongation (no matter with what pseudo-qualitative refinements of acceleration or pendulum movement) of the tendencies which we see operating around us. These tendencies the free mind deems to be visible only in respect of some present urgency, and for the rest opaque with all the vital illusions of such beings as ourselves. We live, indeed, by projecting the abstracted schemes of present experience into the future, but spiritual culture enables us to know that these motions of the will are life-promoting only when integrated in a spirit open to the ever fresh in-streaming of beauty and truth. Thus while we free ourselves perpetually from the grasp of what is dead in the past, we are no less bold in facing the claims of what pretends to hold the secrets of the future. When the will seeks to command thought, its orders, however lusty and resonant, have about them a hint of the death rattle.

The voice of Benedetto Croce, charged so richly with individual experience, recalls not only to Italy but to every society which has received the forms of Western culture and the warmth of the Christian hope, how free devotion, rendered with a mind adventurously flexible but not frivolously mobile, is the very stuff of history, that is of significant human life, whether our special propensity be for the role of preserver or of renovator. Such an embracing of contrary values and aspirations in a desperately catholic vision of what ennobles the spectacle of life, is rashly represented by mere conservatives or mere revolutionaries as a degenerate incapacity for deep feeling or for whole-hearted participation in necessary struggle. More subtly it has been argued that the catholicity of Croce's historico-political embrace extends only to adversaries within a privy circle (such as the "high bourgeoisie" of Italy) between whom political contests have little more than a sporting character. Implacable hatreds, and exclusions from the glory of history, are, it is implied, kept for the real or class enemy. It may well be that the social standards of his upbringing, insufficiently modernized in the light of the material capacities of modern society, have left dead deposits in the stream of Croce's thought. There appears to be no justification for supposing Croce to be blinded by malignancy against the class of manual worker, in his vigorous assaults against Marxism in his advanced old age. If there is any final word for the times in the philosophy of which, with eyes on its illustrious teacher, we have tried to convey not the formulae but the feeling, it is surely that the drama of history has room for all its actors: that we are cast for diverse and conflicting parts to perform which to the best of our abilities itself is virtue and blessedness. But *si tratta di vincere non di stravincere*, to win victories, not to annihilate the opponent; and of virtue as of all else the best measure is not the infinite but the sufficient.

POSTSCRIPT

Benedetto Croce has honoured the author by reading this essay in proof. I am indebted to him not only for some small rectifications on details of his life which it has been possible to include in the text, but also for an observation upon the circumstances of the severe judgements which he passed early in the century upon his contemporaries D'Annunzio, Pascoli, and Fogazzaro. These, he now writes, are to be interpreted in the light of his "admiration and esteem for the healthy and manly tone of the preceding phase of Italian literature represented by men like Carducci and Verga".

His criticism of the younger authors, Croce says, "implicitly" measured them against their predecessors. It should, in fact, be clear to the reader of this small book that Croce, for all his controversial verve, has not been idly quarrelsome: a negation of value on a certain side is normally, in his mouth, equivalent to an affirmation of value on another side even if this, for some motive of tactics, sentiment or delicacy, remains unmentioned (just as in some of his words of praise there may be readily recognized a shaft of unspoken reproof against persons unnamed).

However, an inference which has been drawn by dialectical casuists from Croce's denunciations of Communist doctrine published during Fascism, namely that these expressed an implied support for Fascism, is rejected indignantly by Croce, who, defining his practical policy at that time, writes to the author that he "regarded the Communists as allies of the Liberals in the opposition against Fascism, and always maintained courteous relations with them". On his own treatment by the Fascists, Croce stresses that the nocturnal assault on his library by Fascist roughs occasioned much damage. The assailants were driven off by the fury of the philosopher "and his courageous wife". The freedom of publication which he nevertheless enjoyed under Fascism Croce explains partly by the vanity of Mussolini, who shunned the imputation of underestimating a known and established author, and partly by the dictator's desire to have a retort ready when foreigners declared that literature was muzzled in Fascist Italy.   C. S.

C ·IOICA XXII ZZ

Mantegna's LOGIC, page 111

I

THE LOGIC OF PHILOSOPHY

I

CONCERNING MY PHILOSOPHICAL WORK

I HAVE never complied with requests for a brief or popular exposition of My Philosophy: for two reasons. Philosophy like every other work of man can be truly understood only by those of the craft. And the possessive "My" displeases me: the craftsman who takes over the work of his fellow and predecessor, to better it, calls it not "my" work but, at the most, "ours". However, at the age which I have now reached I am not unwilling to pause for a moment and to meet the request so far as may be done reasonably and discreetly. For at this (my present) age (said the poet Giovanni Prati) "the profound melancholy of the fleeting days" invades the soul. Fortunate poet! He tasted such melancholy, but he was spared the cruel sadness of an evening of life set amid the ruin and destruction of what was dearest and holiest in our world. At this age one views one's life as a Whole which has become visible to the backward-looking eye. One discerns one's place in history, and – putting the matter bluntly – looks upon oneself as though already dead.

The philosopher's task being thus viewed as a collaboration, no room remains for the claim or the dream that his work or his "system" can unveil once and for all the so-called "mystery of reality", proclaiming truth in its wholeness and finality, bringing a quietus to thought and to the thinker himself – for what were there left in life for him had he no longer to labour thoughtfully in order to live manfully?

Man's thought and man's doubt can never cease, and he could not think did he not live in the truth, the light of God. But in this unceasing process he is brought up, from time to time, against obstacles of a more general sort, clouds, mists, perplexities, which must be dissipated if he is to go forward in the way of judgement and right action. The special title of philosopher goes to him who shifts some such obstacle, great or small, dispels a cloud, pierces a gloom, with swift or slow, but in any case sure effects in heightening the tone of culture and of the moral life.

It is foolish, then, to regard philosophies as a sort of far-fetched ingenious invention, or a spinning of fancies apt to awaken enthusiasms and fanaticisms and to command belief, only to fall, each in its turn, as each philosopher contradicts and replaces his forerunner. Only to the levity and ignorance of the gaping and indifferent herd does it appear so. But the truths defined by philosophers do not thus abase each other. The one is added to and completes the other, and thus they dominate thought and life, unknown to the herd which is unknowingly itself dominated. That truth which Socrates bequeathed to mankind when, in argument against the scepticism, the rhetorical and literary amateurishness of the Sophists, he exalted the force of logic, the concept, the definition of the concept – when was it laid low? Or that truth of Descartes, who placed man in direct contact with thought as the sole vindicator of his own real existence? Or that truth of Vico who bound Thinking to Doing and affirmed that man could know his history because he had himself made it? Or the truth of Emmanuel Kant? When was Kant's discovery of the a priori synthesis laid low? – his new theory of judgement showing the category to be empty if divorced from intuition, and intuition to be blind if divorced from the category? – a truth which finally overcame sensism and abstract intellectualism? Who laid low or uprooted the truth proclaimed by Hegel that the principle of contradiction superficially imbibed in the formula "A is A and not not-A" must be profoundly reformed because a living and developing reality demands the contrasting principle "A is also not-A"; and the logic of mere intellect must yield its supremacy to the dialectical logic?

My work as a philosopher is on one side consequent upon this requirement so forcefully expressed and developed by Hegel. I could not feign a different and unreal history in the place of the history which really happened and which gives me my starting point. My work, like that of any other philosopher, major or minor, must needs be accomplished in correlation and connexion with the work that went before.

Now Hegel was the latest great speculative genius known to the history of philosophy, a genius equal to Plato, Aristotle, Descartes, Vico, Kant. After him there had been only minor spirits, or mere *epigoni* who do not count. But as to Hegel I felt piercingly and saw clearly that like Catullus in regard to his beloved Lesbia I was unable to live with him or without him. Certainly not without him, well though I know how his philosophy had been rebelliously assailed right through the nineteenth century and accused of systematic waywardness, contempt of fact, playful sophistry, visionary folly even, or, still worse, charlatanism. Meanwhile Hegel's criticism of traditional logic had not been refuted by anyone; Trendelenburg and his like had made feeble and wretched attempts, after which it was quietly assumed that the battle was won. Far from this, the substantial truth of Hegel's dialectic had entered into the sap and blood of the century. The cult of historical thought, promoted by Hegel, reigned in the spirit of the age, so that natural sciences themselves took on a kind of historical character in the language of evolution, and to be a philosophy of evolution was the claim of the new Positivism. The politics of the age had abandoned the eighteenth-century belief in intellectualistic rationalism, enlightenment, and Jacobin radicalism, and so the newly dawning revolutionary urge of Socialism or Communism claimed a scientific status, thanks to its adoption and interested adaptation of Hegel's Historicism.

Even today – in Russia – these doctrines are dressed up or masked in Hegelian weeds.

But on the other side there were the orthodox Hegelians, numerous, distinguished, and respectable in Italy. They clung to Hegel's books as to a Bible. In their hands his philosophy became a religion with catechisms, dogmas, and superstitions, and the school a congregation of devout believers. Not from them could come any criticism or rectification of the word of the Master, nor any encouragement to such an undertaking. Thus frozen and solidified, this word had lost its original virtue. The real Hegel had long struggled with himself, and had died still in the throes of inner doubt and stress. Against the Hegel of the orthodox

Hegelians I was myself a rebel by reason of my love for history, by them neglected or regulated according to an a priori dialectic (instead of the dialectic which arises genuinely out of memory and the reliving of transmitted records). And I was a rebel also by reason of my love of poetry which I saw these orthodox Hegelians, in the manner of old Baumgarten, defining as a confused perception, an imaginous manipulation of concepts and conceptual stresses, an inchoate philosophizing; and because I could not mentally digest those dialectic progressions which are affirmed by Hegel, as, for example, the advance from the Idea to Nature, from Nature to the Spirit, and thence back again to the fresh possession of the Idea, and together with these rejected almost the whole of that apparatus of triads which Hegel was continually propounding and resolving and with their aid illegitimately conferring upon the whole system an apparent logical solidity and coherence.

None the less there was no progress to be made without first settling accounts with Hegel. I lacked the boldness to emulate Tommaso Campanella (in the poem of Alessandro Poerio) with his proud defiance of Aristotle:

"Seated upon his age-old throne
The Stagyrite could not silence my cry: – I challenge thee!"

My opposition on this side was therefore circumspect and even timid. I felt uneasily that a hidden truth underlay the waywardness of the Hegelian system. Useless, then, to try and wash one's hands of this truth, or even of these wayward features, by dismissing the system contemptuously without discerning the component strains and comprehending the reason of their association. At last, when my thought had ripened, I caught sight of Hegel's logic standing forth powerful, irresistible, luminous, from the murky maze – the dialectic or logic of philosophy created by Hegel – while at the same time there fell away the distortions and perversions of that mighty thought derived from the theological, academic, and political traditions of Hegel's place and time, and from his own eagerness to announce a new and final philosophy and to sum up universal history. Having thus understood the human, all too human fate that had overtaken Hegel's almost

divine genius, I turned refreshed to unravel patiently the skein
that bound together Hegel the philosopher, the rediscoverer of
dialectic, the robust and profound thinker, and Hegel the man,
passionate and practical, not yet or no longer a philosopher,
constructor of a closed system, all too facile piecer together of
triads. The result was my notorious book: What is Living and
What is Dead in Hegel's Philosophy (1906).

I need not recount the objections raised by the surviving
Hegelians and their last pupils and parrots to my speculative
method which they blamed for its very attempt to distinguish
the living and the dead, the true and the false, in a system;
whereas, said they, echoing Hegel, a system is the working out of
a particular principle which can and must be criticized and bettered
in its compact unity, in virtue of a different and superior principle,
not by division and criticism of its single parts. But I deliberately
denied the compact unity of philosophical systems, espying behind
their apparent unity the reality of a problem or series or complex
of particular problems, some properly solved and others not,
such settlements being never more than provisional and liable to
be reopened (necessarily, sooner or later) with the growth of
experience and the inevitable arising of fresh problems, in a word
with the movement of history. I did not, then, recognize
this working out of a new and particular principle to its final
conclusions in each system. In my view the only principle in
thought and philosophy was thought itself, in its eternal and
universal nature. Similarly I rejected their admonitions to deduce
or develop the forms of the spirit or categories progressively one
out of the other by demonstrating the logical contradictions
inherent in each. For to admit such a development, such a
wearisome procession and succession of logical contradictions
leading up to a final repose in a last and ultimate category was
precisely that doctrine of Panlogism which had weakened and
discredited Hegel's work and estranged me myself. For myself,
having settled my accounts with Hegel, I turned with a good
conscience to make use of his great truths, which I had preserved
for the help which they would give me in tackling on new lines

the problems which he had furnished with hasty and fictitious solutions.

Thus I introduced and supported solutions quite different from those given by Hegel for the problems of aesthetics, of the theory of language and ethics, of economy and law, and so forth. In the domain of logic itself I saw the relations between the natural sciences, history, and philosophy, in a light which caused me to reject outright the two imaginary sciences framed and developed by Hegel (the Philosophy of Nature and the Philosophy of History), and to modify and rectify his "Phenomenology of the Spirit" – reshaping it into a "Phenomenology of Error" (and at the same time of the Search for Truth) – and likewise in regard to the History of Philosophy which Hegel had raised to a new dignity, I was moved to reject its pretension to display the categories successively emerging into history, but to preserve the unity, indeed the identity, of the History of Philosophy with Philosophy itself.

As I turned over and over in my mind the Dialectic which I recognized, in Hegel's logic, to have a substantial value, I perceived none the less – and this was the crucial point – that the Dialectic itself was overlaid and spoiled by the outworn relics, smacking of theology, academic disputation, and traditional Metaphysics, and by mental habits carried forward from abstract Logic. Hence the arbitrariness of his treatment of particular problems, in contrast with the powerful lights of his great mind, his experience, his penetration into human affairs. Hegel had a severe and manly but at the same time broad vision of morality; and yet his fondness for his triads and his unpolitical, submissive, and (in this respect) typically German temperament caused him to subordinate morality to the State, particularly the Prussian State, which represented for him the perfect product of the art of politics. Hegel had a knowledge and love of poetry, music, and the figurative arts rare among philosophers, yet in his critical work he introduced non-aesthetic (that is logical, cultural, and social) considerations, thus blinding himself to the naivety of Art. More thoroughly than other philosophers of his time he has marked the contrast between the proceedings of the intellect in the sciences and those of the reason in philosophy. But then he went on to bind these two together as anticipation and realization in a single homogeneous process. A realist, he often denied the clear evidence of reality. A keen immanentist, he reopened the door to the transcendent. Thus the systematic machine which he had started up pushed and dragged him, crushing the seeds of his best thought.

In what manner did Hegel conceive the form of the opposition which gives to dialectic its meaning and motion? Hegel's starting point is not invincible Zoroastrian or Manichean dualism but an opposition which tends to a conciliation. How did he come upon it? I reached this conviction. If one philosophically investigates the genesis of the opposites, one comes to the irresistible conclusion that opposition can only arise out of the soil of distinction. It has its birth in the ascent from one form to another, from one act of the spirit to another, from a distinct to a distinct. What is fundamental is the distinction within the unity of the spirit. Indeed this unity is itself nothing else than the process of the distinctions, for an undistinguished unity would be abstract, immobile, and dead, mathematical, not organic and vital. But Hegel, I saw, had grasped and stuck to mere opposition, making this his foundation and origin of reality. This doctrine blurred his consciousness of the complex dialectic of the spirit in its different forms, so that he abased and denied these, taking them one and all to be mere strivings for the attainment of philosophic truth in a sort of mysticism of the Idea. This initial aberration ran like a serious fault through his entire construction. For all that, the principle of opposition, wondrously glimpsed in antiquity by Heraclitus the Obscure, reawakened and sharpened by Hegel, and felt now to be a necessary instrument for the progress of modern thought constitutes Hegel's immortal glory as a regenerator of philosophy, imperfect and insufficiently argued as his enunciation of it might be.

This force of opposition, this conservation and elevation by way of supersession, is perceptible on every hand in my own new construction, new in its foundations and arranged in its parts on a considerably different design from that bequeathed by Hegel.

Without that principle modern thought could build nothing. As to the arrangement of the edifice which I have planned and decorated, my own interior, the Spirit and Nature are no longer two compartments linked by God or the Idea. Instead, the Spirit is made to shape from out of its own unity – and for its own ends – the concept of Nature and the External World. Thus the door is firmly closed against the Transcendent. The triptych of "Rational", "Real", and (connecting these two) "Metaphysical" Philosophy which originated with the Stoics and centuries later was still preserved in the Wolffian system has vanished (Hegel's Philosophy of the Spirit, Philosophy of Nature, and Metaphysical Logic). There remains alone, having absorbed the others, the Philosophy of the Spirit, affirming the absolute spirituality of reality. In place of the various forms of the Spirit, all logical, but with a logic becoming perfect only in the last of the series which thus remains void of reference to the others which it has absorbed and superseded, we have now the eternal circle of the eternal forms or values or categories of the Spirit, each of which presupposes the other, each necessary, none marked out as superior because the circle itself, the Spirit in its totality, alone has superiority.

Objections and censures and rather silly satires have been launched against my "four" categories (as if the true, the beautiful, the good, and the useful were personal excogitations of mine: they are the spiritual forces and ideals invoked by man at every instant, and not in vain). I have constantly been urged to unify them *à la Hegel*, in other words to sacrifice and destroy them, which I have not dreamed of doing. In my conception poetry is poetry and not philosophy; practice and morality are themselves, not poetry or philosophy; philosophy is philosophy and not one of those others, though nourishing and nourished by them all. Morality itself, while being in a certain sense the unifying power of the Spirit, has this character only when appearing among the others as their equal, moderating and steering them, exercising empire, not tyranny, because respecting their autonomies.

And historical knowledge, or History, which formerly was kept like an inferior at a distance from Philosophy, is now recog-

nized to be itself the concreteness of Philosophy. When the Kantian
definition of the judgement is refined and deepened, it is History
that pronounces the sole judgement which is a judgement of
truth, and includes in itself Philosophy which lives only in history
and as history. Having then to give a name to my construction,
sooner than the vague and ambiguous one (as it has become)
of Idealism, I have chosen that of "Absolute Historicism".

An equation of the philosophy which I have thus broadly
described with that of Hegel, or with an "Italian neo-Hegelism",
cannot be allowed to pass. One should indeed always avoid such
attributions of thought to schools, revivals, resurrections and the
like. Instead, if it really is thought, one should attribute it firmly
to the thinker, or better still to the moment of history in which
it has originated, understanding that thought is always original,
reducible to nothing other than itself, and similarly underivable
from anything else, and universal only on these terms. If thoughts
are dealt with in any other way, their truth and their character
are ignored in favour of a causal and determinist treatment of them
as material entities, wholly illegitimate in philosophy.[1] Need I say
that this argument is in no way inspired by the *laudum immensa
cupido* which sometimes leads to a silly vain reluctance to recognize
indebtedness to a master? What can be sweeter and more tran-
quillizing than the feeling of trust and faithfulness towards the
person and the authority of a master? Who, at least in youth, has
not desired this and wished that it might endure for ever, as one
always longs for the one supremely faithful heart upon which one
might rest in perfect reliance? I too have felt this sweetness, and
remember with what yearning and delight I first awaited and
then enjoyed the presence and the words of those who could dispel
my doubts and enlighten me – my masters to whose level I reached
up to identify and dissolve myself therein. But if even in love
and moral friendship an undisturbed continuity of relations is a
rare and fleeting good fortune enjoyed by the few – experience
is always supervening to warn us against looking for that faithful

1. On "neo-"philosophies see my *Discorsi di varia Filosofia* 1, 107-15.

heart elsewhere than in ourselves – we can never expect permanence in our relation to the master of our intellectual life. For it is they themselves who help our thought to attain freedom and an independent productivity in the new situations arising for it. Thus, often without realizing it or wishing to do so, they shape us differently from themselves, to become their opponents or confuters. Such was my own experience with the philosophy of Hegel. I never cease to venerate him as one of my greatest teachers in philosophy, but I should be a poor sort of disciple if I had not, whenever, and then in the full measure that this seemed necessary to me, developed and corrected his theories, completed and replaced them, revising the very structure of the system and indeed opposing to Hegel's conception of a definitive system that of a system not definitive but in motion, offering provisional and dynamic solutions – the conception which it would have behoved Hegel himself to adopt.

What will be the future fortunes then of "my" philosophy? Like all others, to be an instant in the history of thought, superseded – as I myself have repeatedly superseded it and shall further do so as long as I live and think – in the course of the growth and expansion of the human spirit, *unda quae supervenit undam*. Yet the truths which it has been able to rediscover and to establish are abiding, which is all that a thinker, major or minor, can ask for.

[1945]

PHILOSOPHY AS ABSOLUTE HISTORICISM

WHAT I intend is to expound briefly (but without neglecting any of the essential links and progressions, nor yet omitting some pertinent historical illustrations), the arguments which lead me to regard the resolution of Philosophy into History ("Absolute Historicism") as *temporis partus masculus*, the ripe product of the history of thought in its development up to our times. The description was coined by Francis Bacon to fit a not dissimilar case. That the parturition should have tarried until our times, that the conclusion should have been drawn now and not earlier, results from the recentness of the termination, only in the course of the 19th century, of the travail of thought in establishing the logical premises in virtue of which this free act could wear the stamp of necessity. At that point it became henceforth impermissible to linger or to turn backwards to a different outlook; to do so would be just a lazy acquiescence in the ideas of the past.

Simply for didactic clarity I divide the argument into two parts: (1) Philosophy can only be, and in reality has always only been, Philosophy of the Spirit; (2) Philosophy of the Spirit can in the concrete only be, and has in effect always only been, historical thought, or History, representing the moment when historical thought (in conditions themselves historically determined) reflects upon its own method – a moment now strongly and now weakly emphasized, and susceptible of separate literary and didactic exposition, but intrinsically inseparable from the total process.

In the history of Philosophy, that is of Thought, critical knowledge or the Philosophy of the Spirit wages a ceaseless, varying contest against two other modes for satisfying the soul's aspiration for the light of truth. The former of these modes was mistaken by Plato for Poetry. But Poetry in its naivety cannot come into conflict with Thought.

What does so is the Myth or Revealed Truth of Religion. This is not a simple ideal or lyrical image, like Poetry's, but an image doing service for conceptual truth, for an explanation of things and happenings, logically inconceivable and undemonstrable but nevertheless getting belief for its claims on the strength of dreams, visions, oracles, fanciful interpretations of events, misunderstood language, utterances of men deceived or deceiving; and on the strength also of the tradition which preserves and consecrates it. Theology elaborates it logically and doctrinally, but only within the limits of the revelation which in the last resort must be venerated and accepted. The latter of the two modes opposed to critical thought is Metaphysic. Customarily Metaphysic follows upon Myth and ousts it, or sometimes lives alongside of it. Its nature must now be more closely investigated.

The breeding place of Metaphysic is in the distance at which the mind holds myth and revealed truth when it sets forth on the discovery of the categories for the cognition of reality. In the early stage of this withdrawal and research, the mind, still unsure of its own path, tries, though necessarily in vain, to follow the track of the natural or experimental sciences, since these offer the model of an approach which is not mythical but scientific. Hence an effort to grasp at something which shall have the character both of entity and of philosophic category, concepts both empirical and also pure, objects or forces both material and also spiritual and logical, in a word hybrid mental figures or combinations which, try as one will, one cannot think out properly. The naturalistic aspect of these metaphysical notions transpires clearly in their attempt to assign a *cause* or causes to reality. (The causal principle pertains entirely to the natural sciences.) The categorial aspect transpires in the "ultimate" or "final" character ascribed to such a cause or causes – a contradiction in terms; for causes are never ultimate or final, being just relations between particular facts and having outside this context neither use nor sense. The very term Metaphysic, in which the significance of the *meta* shifts from *post* to *trans*, expresses a vain attempt to rise from a world of objects to a world of being, of supreme objects which are not objects – inviting and pushing one along the path of the Transcendent from which the critical spirit ever turns away, scenting the nearness of a crash into the void. Metaphysic thus makes a bad attempt to surpass the conceptions of naturalism, and wantonly abases and discredits true Philosophy, by claiming for itself the higher rank of "First Philosophy" or "General Philosophy", treating consciousness as a psychological or naturalistic fact, and assigning to the enquiries of the Philosophy of the Spirit (Logic, Ethic, and so forth), the lower rank of "particular" or "secondary" philosophies in common with the natural sciences. (This is the old and not yet extinct threefold classification – Metaphysic, or Ontology, and at a lower level the "Real" and "Rational" Philosophies.) From the point of view of Metaphysic all the problems of the life of the Spirit, which with their ceaseless proliferation and mutual reference weave the single web of philosophic thought, do not attain the philosophic dignity which is reserved for the supreme problem or problems; supreme, but empty.

And Metaphysic makes also an ill-conceived attempt to get beyond History and to attain a world outside or above history by dint of enclosing itself in a system proudly indicated to be definitive. But this brings ill fame and discredit upon the genuine need of the human mind for a systematicity, that is for a continuous and progressive systematizing of historical experience wholly inside the range of history.

Thus the entities of the Metaphysicians reveal, under analysis, the mixture of their component parts as being derived variously from the problems of History and Philosophy and from the schemes of the natural sciences. But on the other hand these entities tend to resume the character of Myths, those myths from which Metaphysic had in the first place represented a withdrawal, a rejection of them. Not infrequently the myths of the Religions have been translated into pseudo-rational entities only for these to be translated back into revealed truths of the Religions. And not infrequently the assertors of the metaphysical entities have recourse to a vaunted super-rational faculty, called ecstasy or intellectual intuition or sentiment (by which nothing else can seriously be meant than a rapt and impassioned imagination) as the means whereby these shine and reveal themselves to men.

Almost any metaphysical construct can be taken to exemplify the nature of this mental process – or rather, mental blockage. The "water" of Thales, which in the general run of histories of philosophy opens the series of metaphysical entities, may or may not derive from oriental notions or from the myth of the Ocean. But it is supposed to be not a deity but a concept, and not the concept of water, a thing among things, but a generating and explicatory principle of all things. But though it may have been obscurely understood or interpreted as "that which flows" or "that which generates", it is not truly a spiritual category, but stands perpetually on the brink of rebecoming Father, Ocean. The Hegelian "Idea", which if it does not close the long series is certainly one of its highlights, is not the Spirit, or a form of the Spirit, but an entity proclaimed in its transcendent purity in the resolutory act of issuing forth from itself, becoming nature, and rejoining itself by way of the advance of the Spirit in man. In this sort of theophany the Idea is in perpetual danger of reconverting itself into the old Judaeo-Christian God, and in fact underwent that conversion if not expressly in the work of Hegel, yet certainly in the theism of many of his pupils. Such a naturalistic yet at the same time more than naturalistic construction is evident in the "atoms" of Democritus, the "ideas" of Plato, the "monads" of Leibniz, various as is the content and origin of these. The fabular mode of exposition is found in Plato's myths and in the oriental and Neo-Platonic emanationists (for example in the theory of beauty as a ray of spiritual light shining through matter, where light, matter, and ray are not physical, but not logical terms either). More than once the German idealist philosophy was charged with the use of a narrative (*erzählend*) type of exposition akin to the first chapter of Genesis. When the construction culminates in a negative, the "Unknowable", this is an entity just like the others and like them suggests an attitude of devotion (compare Goethe's "das Unerforschliche ruhig zu verehren") and seems to call for an altar like that in Athens "to the unknown God" which was seen by Paul.

The naturalistic character of Metaphysic, prominent even in Hegel with his establishment of a continuity between the work of Science and its elevation to Philosophy, became a pre-eminent demand or claim in the dim and heavy metaphysical essays of the Positivists, and ended by being openly professed by belated Idealist metaphysicians like Hartmann who pretended to have arrived at his speculative conclusions by the "inductive method of the Sciences". Schelling's assignment to Poetry of the office of a true and proper metaphysical organ may suffice to exemplify one such kind of recourse to revelation. For Poetry, thus distorted in its nature, is no longer Poetry but a self-revelation of the Absolute in contempt for the channels of thought and logic. These enraptured metaphysicians continue however to believe that they speak in conformity with critical reason *per sapientiam* while they often do speak, as the Apostle claimed to do, *per stultitiam predicationis*.

No less than Metaphysic, the Philosophy of the Spirit refuses any association with Myth and Revealed Truths. But whereas Metaphysic adopts a method tainted by naturalism and stumbles again headlong into myth and revelation, the Philosophy of the Spirit – that is Philosophy – has never ceased to produce all those concepts thanks to which humanity attains a progressively clear, sure, and broad judgement and understanding of life and reality.

Even though sometimes it may be pursued in less than full awareness, and perhaps in a terminology still smacking of metaphysics and religion, the method of the Philosophy of the Spirit has never been abstraction and generalization but always understanding of the universal immanent in the individual. The Philosophy of the Spirit does not pile up universals alongside of other universals but traces the relations between the component universals in the Whole. It does not sort out particular facts into classes but understands particular facts as the concrete realization of the universal itself. It develops pure and speculative, not physical and mathematical concepts. Sentimental attitudes and the constructs of the imagination are excluded from its purely critical proceedings. Since the ancient Greeks, we may say, this Philosophy, delving profoundly and pursuing its problems along the tracks of logical necessity, has elaborated what have come to be known as the theories of logic, ethics, politics, economy, aesthetics, and the other innumerable departments and specializations of thought which serve men for the interpretation of their lives and for coping actively with the future, little though they may be aware of the instruments they are using or of the work that has gone into their construction. All true Philosophers, in their philosophic labours, not in the metaphysical notions which they have worked up or taken over, have been founders or improvers of this mental arsenal. When in philosophy we speak of Socrates we think how he established and fixed Concept and Definition, and promoted the analysis of morality. Speaking of Saint Augustine we recall his forceful admonition to look not outwards but inwards into the inner man, where is the sole seat of truth. Kant means for us the a priori synthesis which at one stroke dismissed, on either hand, the one-sided contentions of the Sensists and the Intellectualists, and Kant means too the critique of any heteronomous view of morality, and the assertion of the original character of the aesthetic judgement. Vico means the doctrine of the *conversio veri et facti*[1] and the conception of the spirit as "eternal ideal history". Hegel stands for the dialectical form of thought, Pascal for the liberation of the moral conscience from the snares of casuistry, Machiavelli for the law and the necessary place of power and of political conflict. And so forth for all the infinite aspects of spiritual activity which we must at every moment discern and qualify and restore into the harmony of the Whole by virtue of our thought linked to the thoughts of preceding thinkers and following up their critical and theoretical work.

This is the true and genuine history of philosophy: nothing in it gets lost and we see the chain reaching to ourselves to receive new links. But no such chain of development can be formed by successive revealed truths or by successive metaphysical notions: this is precluded by their aforesaid character as the hybrid and sterile offspring of imagination and thought. Where they appear to display a line of movement and progress, a closer observation

1. Vico's principle will at this first stage be more easily recognized in its Latin form than in an attempted English rendering from the Italian. – Translator.

shows this movement and progress as pertaining really to the critical thought, the philosophy of the spirit, wrapped up in those forms and working inside them. The principle of their history, then, is outside themselves in that sole and eternal mover, the Reason. In this sense one may speak of a progress from the crude discernment of the divine by primitive religions which locate it in the elves inhabiting fountains and trees, to monotheism which is in its way a unification of the real in one concept: or a progress from the barbaric god of the Israelites to a just and beneficent God, from the resurrection of the flesh to the immortality of the soul, from desolate Hades or the triumphant reign of the Messiah to the Christian Paradise, from the good and evil powers of the Parsee doctrine to the version of these in Christian theology, from the legalities of the Mosaic law to the justification by faith in Christ, from the return of the seasons celebrated in harvest festivals to the idea of spiritual renewal by redemption and salvation, from the triads of deities in Eastern and antique religion to the Christian Trinity which seems to capture and symbolize the dialectic rhythm of mind and reality.

If the Modernists had succeeded in speeding up the "Evolution of Dogma" through the refinements which they advocated, the result would have been the total dissolution of the dogmas into the concepts of philosophy. Similarly although all the metaphysical constructs as such are of the same order, the water of Thales and the Idea of Hegel being natural and also more-than-natural notions, yet there certainly is a vast distance and difference in the intellectual wealth and energy of the thoughts which they envelop. Even in antiquity Anaxagoras, who instead of a physical thing proposed Mind (albeit conceived physically) as the Principle, appeared "sober" by contrast with his "drunken" predecessors. And if we compare Spinoza's two "Attributes" with Descartes' "Res Cogitans" and "Res Extensa", both the pairs are indeed forms of the spirit which are not mediated and resolved into the concrete spiritual process but projected outside the spirit into the metaphysical field. Yet Spinoza marks an advance on Descartes and there is a further advance from Spinoza's Substance to Leibniz's

Monad. For the latter, though in metaphysical guise, stands for an absolute Spiritualism in which nature and matter lose their former solidity as real things and parallel attributes.

But when facile critics display and mock at the diversity of the various philosophic systems and of their explicatory principles, reviewing the jumbled and often bizarre constructions erected by the metaphysicians each only to tumble upon the next (water, fire, atom, monad, substance, absolute, idea, will, and so forth), these critics not only confound Philosophy with Metaphysic, but obscure from themselves that true progress of thought which does transpire from the succession of the metaphysical systems themselves. On the other hand, the often heard statement that the myths of the religions and the entities of the metaphysicians serve to stimulate the growth and advancement of Philosophy needs this qualification. Philosophical problems and concepts are stimulated not by the external influence of these fanciful and arbitrary shapes but by the motion of life and history providing the conditions and setting up the demand for new philosophic expressions which often start by assuming such disguises.

In this way Religion and Metaphysic must always reappear, and it is the eternal task of criticism to release from their envelope what there is of philosophic bud and sprout, and to help the latter to completion and development according a proper field of satisfaction to the new requirements.

Considered in their logical form, seventeenth-century "Natural Law" and "Social Contract"; eighteenth-century "Reason", preached by the Enlightenment; and "Popular Sovereignty" were all myths and metaphysical constructs, but by understanding the aspirations, the moral and political passions, which conduced to those imaginative representations, and by purifying these from fleeting elements, it was possible for critical thought to infer from the first two the affirmation that humanity bears in itself its own law and does not receive it from another world or a God, and from the third the notion of the power exercised by Reason, or Thought, (even if at first these were wrongly equated with more intellect and ratiocination), to reform and renew individual and social life; and to transform the last notion (of popular sovereignty) into the more correct concept of sovereign liberty. When in our own times we criticize those perverted notions "class", "race", and "Stateless society" we are naturally inclined to describe them as "myths" and such they are. But such perverted notions, due to the heat of passion and to consequent impassioned sophistry, do none the less include in themselves questions regarding the forces behind mankind and its history, and at times hint at true concepts. For example Fichte, in his passionate exaltation of Germanity, assigned moral purposes to this, and came near to dissolving this Germanic image into the high ideal of humanity itself. Again, the Marxist conception of history as class struggle, which with this coarse myth revived the dialectical mode of thought in the writing of history.

Philosophy, then, in its life and action, its useful and durable work, has always been the Philosophy of the Spirit, or of human concerns, and has always resisted and restrained religious and metaphysical Transcendence, or with instinctive repugnance has left this on one side and has attended solely to its own work. But this attitude of distinction and opposition has not always been fully conscious. Sometimes the indifference and impatience of the philosopher has been expressed in verbal shafts like that of Shaftesbury against Mock Philosophy as contrasted with Home Philosophy (the philosophy which is of use in our home, the human home) or Pope's "proper study of mankind is man", or other quips of the Enlightenment against the speculations of *méta-physique*. But awareness concerning this relation has been more or less fully attained only recently, by what historical process and by what mode of reasoning and with what precise formulation it will be useful to illustrate. And in philosophy, as in all human activity, the clear awareness of the nature of the work one is doing is moral strength, getting the better of vacillations and guarding against distractions.

No doubt the attitude of Philosophy towards the religion, whose revealed truths it has ever sought to exchange for truths validated by experience, thought, reason, has been accompanied by more self-awareness. The history of Philosophy is marked by the persecution of philosophers, martyrs of Reason, at the hands of the priests. Yet usually the relation has taken the calmer shape of an illogical but naively accepted distinction of spheres, Philosophy recognizing the authority of the religions, respecting their sacred preserves, and claiming for itself the freedom to study mere human affairs, *Weltweisheit*, worldly wisdom, without prejudice to the existence and superiority of *Gottweisheit*, the truth of the revealed faith and of theological knowledge. Another device for eluding the contrast between religion and Philosophy, which brought a certain security for several centuries, was the doctrine of the "double truth" (of philosophy and of revelation respectively). Socrates discoursed of man but refrained from speculating about the cosmos, Vico claimed for the mind of man knowledge of the history which is the work of men, while renouncing the study of Nature, this being God's work known only to the Divine Mind. The men of the Enlightenment, the Encyclopedists, fought a fierce war against the religions but remained Deists. Even the Neo-critical and Positivist thinkers of the 19th century found a place for the "Beyond Reason" and honoured it with garlands of sentiment and hope. In all of these different instances we discern the tradition of the division of tasks. The motive for observing it was by no means always a politic caution for the avoidance of trouble with ecclesiastical authority and its secular arm. Where there was a total denial of the religions and of the mythical God, its mouthpieces were most frequently popular and superficial writers, Naturists and Sensists, unaware and ignorant of the gravity and difficulty of unresolved problems concerning matter and nature, scientific classification and speculative thought. The deeper thinkers, on the other hand, stopped short of difficulties which they could not resolve and which as they sometimes resignedly supposed could never be resolved by the mind of man. None the less they were often, and rightly, accused or suspected of atheism, meaning in this context the denial of the very foundation of the religions, the Revelation. Such a denial was logically comprised in the very affirmation of a philosophical truth, for this, if it is indeed truth, must by right be the adjudicator in every problem of truth and cannot tolerate a superior or a rival. Even today, when all the traditional religions have by internal weakening lost all prospect of doing more than to maintain, or possibly to extend, a superficial dominion over flocks not conspicuous for intellectual vigour, Philosophy seldom proclaims frankly and proudly its concern with this world, but usually displays some residuary attachment to the Transcendent, the consequence of an enduring metaphysical infection which ever and anon reopens the way to myths and revelations and seems to stand surety for their respectability.

The most impressive and noble of the modern philosophies, the one which put Mind at the centre of its pattern and called itself Idealism, itself ran aground on the metaphysical rocks. Though combating the old Metaphysic, it forced and suppressed and almost suffocated its own brilliant theories, befitting a philosophy of the spirit, in a new metaphysic, presented and extolled as a "metaphysic of mind" by contrast with the "metaphysic of the object". But this distinction did not avail to extirpate the rejected and discredited metaphysic of the object as it was taught by Wolff and his disciples, late lingerers in the eighteenth century. The construction of a metaphysic of the mind was itself enough to debase the mind to an object, and thus a transcendent and mythical entity. Hence the spectacle of the Ego, the Absolute, the Idea, the Will, the Fancy, and, last of the bunch, the Unconscious, being made to generate the non-Ego as something for the Ego to exercise its morality upon; or to descend into nature and man or exercise themselves in leaps into the sensible; or to become natural in order to repossess themselves as spiritual; or to generate consciousness in order to deny themselves in the aspect of will, and to annihilate life – and so forth. In the book of nature there were written no longer the mathematical signs familiar to Galileo, but symbols of logical and dialectical transitions whose terms, however, instead of being categories and mental positions, were physical forces and natural classes. In history, it was sought to track down and to illustrate a concealed sub-history, a design of the gods or of God hidden from men and revealed to the metaphysician, – small matter

whether the divinity called itself Hegel's Idea or by preference
Matter and Economics. Things have not changed either in the
latest presentations of an Idealism conceived as a Metaphysic of
Mind. The actor may have changed his clothes and assumed another name. But the persistence of the old game is shown in the
very fact of the maintenance of two logics, one for the use of
men in reasoning about the affairs of the world, called abstract,
and the other for the use of the metaphysician, called concrete.
(When it opens its lips, however, it cannot avoid saying just the
same as the other one.) But there is only one Logic, implicit in
every judgement that is uttered, always concrete. The Philosophy
of the Spirit traces its theory, distinguishing it from the utterances
of sentiment and from the abstractions and artifices of calculation
and of empirical classifications. By contrast Metaphysic, in making
and sustaining its constructions, is constantly obliged to return,
openly or covertly, to the excogitation of a so-called higher logic,
hovering between nature and beyond-nature.

There were reactions against Idealism, with the war-cry "No
more metaphysics". But these brought no effective liberation,
because what they offered in place was not genuine philosophy
but the ideal of natural science, and it is well known what happens
when this is advanced outside its own proper domain. No wonder
the Positivist school invented new entities like Evolution and the
aforementioned Unknowable, which were not logically demonstrated but affirmed with an act of faith as a sort of revelation.
The counterreaction against Positivism, represented by the so-
called Philosophy of Values (that is to say of the forms of the
spirit, though this was not acknowledged), had not the strength
or courage to develop these forms so as to embrace the whole
matter of philosophy, but limited itself to describing them and
classifying them (like objects of a natural science), leaving a world
of nature alongside of the world of values, two worlds which
like the *res cogitans* and the *res extensa* seemed to be waiting for
God, Substance, or the Absolute to provide them with a common
unifying foundation.

What with the cults of science and nature and, in their train, a

Metaphysic verbally rejected but in fact incautiously introduced and entertained, rarely had Philosophy been in such a poor, feeble, and unaware condition, or so forgetful of its recent and best tradition, as in the second half of the 19th century. In this tradition itself, however, and notably in the treasures concealed beneath the metaphysical mailcoat of Hegel's thought, there were waiting ready to be put in order and utilized two arguments strong enough for a successful demolition of the obstacles blocking the way to the determination and definition and self-recognition of the Philosophy of the Spirit as total philosophy.

These obstacles lay in a couple of linked dualisms, the dualism of inner and outer reality, or body and soul, and the dualism of values, of being and not-being, life and death, good and evil, and other such aspects. Whenever the spirit, in its innerness, feels itself confronting something outer, body, matter, or the object, it feels forced to acknowledge a second reality, a *res extensa*, obeying laws which are not the spirit's own laws but are devised by the natural sciences. And hereupon it feels the need for some transcendent unity to embrace both. Similarly whenever the good, the beautiful, the true, the vital are ranged against evil, ugliness, falsehood, death as if the latter series were real like the former, one is led to imagine outside and above the two series, and free from their antinomies, a world of values, of pure truth, goodness, beauty, and deathless life – in a word, the transcendent.

In Hegel's thought, which gathered and potentiated the efforts of earlier philosophers, this duality of opposites had been overcome by the dialectic which, establishing their unity, demonstrated the division of being from not-being to be nought but the abstraction and arbitrary proceeding of the intellect, as was also the cutting in twain of the terms of the real which placed one term outside the other. With Hegel, the second terms of the dualisms were welded to the first which thus, with the dissolution of the abstraction, gained rightful concreteness. The principle of contradiction of the old logicians (a thing cannot simultaneously be and not be) was replaced – and shown up as contradictory and inadequate – by a higher principle of contradiction.

Neither Hegel's philosophy nor those of his contemporaries and predecessors (the author of the Critique of Pure Reason and his British forerunner) appreciated that the criticism of the abstractions of the intellect, and of the abusive incursion of physical scientific method in philosophy, was going to break up and dissolve the very conception of a Nature in opposition to the Spirit, and was going to make of nature just a product of the spirit, indeed of the abstracting spirit. Hence their unfriendliness to Berkeley's logical volatilization of matter, and their clinging to the idea or project of a "philosophy of nature". Nor did they clearly perceive that if the arbitrary proceedings and abstractions devised by the "intellect" (*Verstand*) and discarded by "reason" (*Vernunft*) in the sphere of pure knowledge are indispensable to the construction of the grand pattern of the sciences with their laws and mathematical formulations, then the justification which has been withheld from them in the realm of theoretical and speculative reason had to be made good to them in that of practical reason, thus restoring to them their legitimacy and dignity and providing a firm base for their operations. The critical analyses of these thinkers pointed to such a conclusion, but they did not embrace it or draw its strict consequences, and therefore they continued improperly to devise appeasements and politic alliances of philosophy with the sciences, and sharings out of the sections of a supposed single task.

Yet from the camp of the sciences itself, some scientists given to reflection upon the method of their operations and, more or less consciously, seeking a philosophic ground, raised their voice to give warning that the character of the sciences had been misunderstood, being truly concerned not with knowing but with doing, with utility. This was the origin of the theory which came to be called the "economic" theory of the construction of the sciences.

Once nature has been resolved into a form or product of the spirit, and similarly the negative into the positive, and evil into good (evil is the very life of good), the philosophy of the spirit is no longer liable to collide with an impenetrable Other, an Opposite, alien and heteronomous, but can open its boundaries and receive in them all that is thinkable – the secular problems of Metaphysic itself, one and many, subject and object, being and knowing, finite and infinite, universal and individual, freedom and necessity, immanence and transcendence, God and immortality, and as many more as there may be, none excluded. None excluded – but all brought back to their proper sphere, criticized where they have gone awry, rephrased in the proper terms and thus soluble and solved. Philosophy thereby becomes "Absolute Spiritualism", a much better name really than "Idealism" or "New Idealism" because this word has come historically to carry a strong flavour of the now defunct Metaphysic of the Idea.

However, even this conception of philosophy as Philosophy of the Spirit and Absolute Spiritualism remains obscured by the shadow as it were of a scruple or residue of transcendence and metaphysic, unless a further dualism, rising out of the eclipse of those others, is also resolved. Aside or athwart the truth of philosophy or the universal, there stands another truth, that of individuality, historical truth. If these two are left in this juxtaposition as two different orders of truth – distinguished in the traditional schools as "truths of reason" and "truths of fact", – each would be, once again, transcendent in respect of the other. It is worse than a useless attempt to solve the difficulty, to follow the haughty example of the scholastic and academic philosophers who abased and despised factual or "historical" truth. Real knowing and doing has its raw material in those factual truths, the nourishment of decision and action. To despise them, moreover, is an offence against the ever stronger sense of history characteristic of modern times, which triumphed in the nineteenth century and is still today in a lively phase of development.

But now, if those two orders of truth have appeared to be theoretically independent, or at most related as coordinates and parallels, yet in their actuality they reveal a mutual connexion or embryonic unification. For one can see that historical composition in all ages depends more or less directly upon the contemporary state of thought. In the narratives and explanations of facts and events given by history, we perceive the concepts (with their attendant limitations and errors) of the philosophy of the spirit as understood in the writer's time – we become aware of obscurities due to belief in metaphysical entities, of incoherences due to clinging religious myths, and at the same time of the bright rays of the critical thought which is beginning to dispel or reshape them. This is the only way of comprehending the history of historical composition from its earliest and humblest beginnings. For it is entirely mistaken to suppose that philosophy commences to play a part only when, as in the 18th century, there is much talk about it, or when, as early in the next century, it develops (and sometimes abuses) its strength. The "historical sense" which then seemed a new acquisition was nothing more than the growth and deepening and sharpening of philosophic concepts which had been forming in the minds not of self-styled philosophers alone but in the philosophic intelligence of men who thought of themselves as just historians.

If, however, philosophy be conceived as standing to history in the relation of guide to guided, light-bringer to the lightless, form to matter, then undeniably a form of transcendence is perpetuated or reintroduced with the assignment of a primacy or sovereignty to philosophy over history similar to that claimed by the metaphysical entities over experienced reality. There is only one way to avoid this dressing up of the spirit as a metaphysical and transcendent entity. It is to conceive of philosophy as being dependent upon history in the same measure as history is upon philosophy. But since Spirit and History are not concepts in natural science, their relation cannot be summed up in the scientific formula of the reciprocal action of forces, but must be interpreted as a synthetic or dialectical unity.

The doctrine of the oneness of history and philosophy is commonly ascribed to Hegel (usually in the course of attempts to refute it). But to be precise Hegel offers only the formula of the oneness of philosophy with the history of philosophy. Even so he does not so much identify the one with the other as suggest a double character in the philosophic process, what is first thought in idea reappearing, in the second place, as historical realization, in which the eternal categories become temporalized and follow each other in an appropriate adaptation to determined chronological epochs. No wonder the historians rebelled against the abasement of history to this task of allegorical illustration of doctrinal truths.

Now there was to be found both in Hegel and Kant a concept which when developed and deepened showed the way to a true and proper definition of the oneness of history and philosophy. In Kant there was the a priori synthesis of concept and intuition, declared inseparable on pain of the concept being rendered empty and the intuition blind. In Hegel there was the new formula of the a priori synthesis, the concept of the concept or idea, as unity of the logos and the representation, the universal and the individual. But Kant, immersed in the problem of the physical sciences, was hardly aware of the problems of history, while Hegel, though he started by affirming the identity of the real and the rational, went on to disidentify them by acknowledging the irrational and accidental as a sort of waste product of the real. And while he affirmed philosophy to be the spirit of an epoch contemplating itself, he never plumbed the truly historical quality of philosophic activity, which is concerned not with the abstract general character of an epoch but with the individual passional and moral urges which stir and inspire every thinker. Had he done so, his place in the history of philosophy would have been more varied and rich, and he would have rid himself of the burdensome metaphysical-religious supposition of an "eternal gospel" waiting to be proclaimed to mankind, and of a definitive and final philosophy.

The demonstration of the oneness of philosophy and history must be understood and developed in another way. Since the historical judgement combines individual with universal, subject with predicate, representation with concept, it must be demonstrated that there is no genuine and concrete judgement whatever other than the historical, and thus the solutions and definitions of philosophy are historical, referring to the particular historical situation of the thinker at the moment. And the situation which gives rise to the mental problem in question is, in the act of

solution and definition of that problem, itself historically illumined, represented, and judged. Real and genuine philosophy, far
removed from the bloodless disquisitions and teachings of the
schools, pulsates with the passional and moral life which it gathers
into itself and appeases by removing the mental tangles which
tormented it, presenting the historical situation in its genuine
truth, and making the way clear for a completer satisfaction in
ensuing practical activity. Thus Philosophy, far from resting content with a sterile contemplation and adoration of the divine life
in the universe, as described and exalted by the rhetoricians who
exercise themselves, they too, in her fields, and far from offering
a liberation from the travail of life, travails herself to create
continuously an ever new world. This theory is fully supported
by the history of philosophy which includes no concept or doctrine that has not actively operated in life, nor any that can be
understood without taking into account the affections and practical
needs of the various epochs, or rather of the thinkers who in the
various epochs pondered over their experience and their practical,
passional, and moral life. The first rule for interpreting a philosophic proposition is to ask against whom or what it has been
argumentatively developed, what "anguish" it has stilled or sought
to still. Without such a serious historical interpretation the theories
of the philosophers take on the same appearance as the metaphysical systems – of a string of meaningless interconflicting assertions
(which is just how they do appear to the profane, those who fail
to accompany with their own thought the process of thought
they have passed through). Scepticism then takes its seat upon the
heap of ruins, with its witless smile.

When philosophy has been intimately united and welded to
historical composition, and the spirit to its own history, what
remains as thinkable, always and exclusively, is the individuality
of acts, which cannot be transcended even by the thought of the
spirit in and for itself. For, as said, the Spirit is never in and for
itself, but always in history. And though there is a habit and
a necessity of composing didactic treatises of "Pure Philosophy",
giving definitions and arrangements of the spiritual categories,

these works of general and abstract and historically indifferent appearance none the less always push down their roots into the soil of history whence the sap rises into all their ramifications. The assignment to didactic philosophy of the function of "methodology of history" (to quote my definition of many years ago) shuts the door against any metaphysical interpretation of the Philosophy of the Spirit and of Absolute Spiritualism and indicates as a still better description "Absolute Historicism".

[1939]

III

THE VEIL OF MYSTERY

Reality identified with History, and Philosophy with Absolute Historicism, excite two seemingly sentimental reactions – "too much" and "too little".

On the one hand repugnance is felt against the idea that spirit, as manifested in man, can be so great and powerful as to be held identical and coextensive with the whole of a wholly spiritual reality and enthroned on the seat of God and the Absolute. Mistakenly, it is supposed that this high place is being impiously invaded and occupied by a particular man in all his particularity and abstractness. The feelings of religious reverence and awe arise to repel the invasion, with the result that courage fails and there is a return to the customary and coarse conception of a nature existing on its own, independent of its opposite number, the spirit, and a God or an Absolute overtopping both. In the preceding essay an answer was given to the theoretic formulation of this protest.

On the other hand there is the feeling of "too little" as of one who is disappointed at receiving less than his expectation and his due, so that he remains in suspense and desire for something precious, and as this is not forthcoming, retreats and envelops himself in the wisdom of ignorance, the veil of mystery, which, including apparently all that something extra which men long for, seems to give better comfort than the glaring light of philosophy and history. This feeling merits to be probed in its theoretical reflection, its supporting concept of "mystery", or rather in its manner of representing and understanding that concept.

In its correct and proper sense mystery is simply a moment which unceasingly and unfailingly recurs in the process of spirit and thought, the moment in which the mind struggles to assimilate the invading new flood of life and passion, to convert this strong undiscriminating pressure, this sharp blind goading, into the logical formulation of a problem and its simultaneous resolution in the truth of a judgement. In the stress of this struggle, reality ever wears the face of a sphinx and utters enigmatic sounds, and the clouds, which will in time be dissipated and dispelled, for the moment keep thickening and induce perplexity and dismay. On the ordinary level of swift action and thought all this happens in a flash, and the moment of doubt and mystery, though unfailingly present, is almost unfelt, unnoticed. But there are occasions when this travail, sharp and grievous, lengthens out over whole phases and periods of a lifetime. This is what becomes spoken of as impenetrable mystery, impenetrable at least for the time being, compelling us to pore over it unceasingly and not to cease until we have seen light. If life and reality ceased to throw up mysteries this would mean that the forces of generation and novelty were extinct, and the world close to its end. If our Thought, as soon as it has converted the current mysteries into problems and thus solved them, did not forthwith find others in its path, then the light of truth would be extinguished, for it is a light which shines only in the reflections which it excites as the shadows perpetually gather against it and are perpetually dissipated.

Pertinent to the conception of mystery is the mysterious halo which seems to surround poetry and all beautiful works of art. It is not that poetry and art are caught up in the travail of thought and suffer from their encounter with the impediment. Quite the contrary. Art and poetry being disengaged from this process make no distinctions, pass no judgements, but spontaneously and unreflectingly create images expressive of life in action, life the sphinx. The naivety and innocence of art and poetry lie in their ignorance that mystery is mysterious, in their flowering which ripens no fruits on the tree of knowledge. (Mysteries are known only in the process of formulating and solving them.)

Mystery, logically considered, is not, then, that which eludes penetration and solution by thought, but on the contrary what by definition can be and is continually penetrated and resolved. Otherwise it would be not mystery but urge, unreality, vain imagination, mere vocal cry. The history of thought and life is simply the history of mysteries encountered and solved. The sum

3

of these solutions makes up man's heritage of truth, in course of continuous enrichment.

Poetry, from time to time, itself becomes the object of critical thought, of philosophy, which, by distinguishing and judging its lyrical content, formulates and solves the mystery of poetry.

But if mystery is thus properly not that which is other than thought, but a moment in thought itself, whence arises the strange notion of mystery for its own sake, impenetrable by thought, hope and promise of a truth transcending man's small and imperfect discussions and conclusions, his finite, prosaic, anguished, blind life? Since it cannot be traced or located in the positive forms in which the spirit develops its activity, might its place be found in the phenomenology of consciousness, in the ranks of those pro-visional and imperfect solutions of speculative problems which critical philosophy has identified and confuted under such de-scriptions as "empiricism", "intellectualism", "transcendentism", "materialism", and so forth. But no, it is not there, nor yet, strictly speaking, is it to be found in the habitations of religious transcendence, where there is so much talk of "the mysteries of the faith". For revealed truths have the attributions of the utmost lucidity and certainty, and are mysterious only to human intel-ligence and reason which cannot of itself attain or demonstrate them but must receive them from on high. Mysticism likewise denies that Being, Reality, God can be any better conceived by the method of induction and deduction employed by the sciences, than by the speculative method of philosophy. And for mysticism Being, Reality, God are really so unmysterious that it embraces and possesses them in the plenitude of silent feeling, a silence which then proceeds to commit the great offence of talking and reasoning about itself.

Where this dazzling darkness, now agreeably luminous among the shades, now disturbing and frightening, really has its origin, is in the unsatisfied and restless cravings in its depth. This feeble assertion of Mystery, like the correspondingly sterile attitude of those for whom it is "too much" to surrender the notions of the transcendent, always in some degree springs from a weakness of

the intelligence and the will, preventing emancipation from traditional and crude methods, putting its questions badly and uncritically, and for want of vigour and courage resorting to the facile
conclusion that what is not known cannot be known, falling into
an inert slumber sooner than face the strain of a higher climb.
Hence all those philosophies which crown their apex with the
Unknowable, hence the acknowledgment of insoluble "riddles of
the universe" (of which the naturalistic Dubois-Reymond counted
up precisely seven), hence these anxious queries whence we come
and whither we go, why and when the world was created, why
there is life, – and that mechanical and insincere refrain that mystery
surrounds us on every hand. Yet the complaint of "too little", the
unsatisfied craving, are an index of something more than mere
mental laziness and levity. They have a deeper, more hidden root
in the thirst for the impossible, for absolute happiness, beatitude, or
whatever it may be.

"Absolute" we say to distinguish it from what modestly passes
for happiness, the state of wellbeing and calm and bearable conditions which everyone tries to enjoy, and of hope and trust in the
future which everyone elicits or tries to elicit from the moving
world, attaining them, missing them, losing them, rediscovering
and then again losing them, without ever really knowing whether
to win them was truly well for us, or to lose them truly ill, for
this life of ours, our human doings, prospers with comfort and
wellbeing but is also weakened by them, is downcast by misfortune,
suffering, and sadness but takes nourishment and new strength
from them. So treatises on "the art of happiness" can never do
more than suggest conduct in particular cases. But in the bosom
of mankind there springs ever anew the ideal of a constant,
absolute happiness, something far beyond such precarious and
mutable satisfaction. This fills men with a wan desire, which, not
being appeased by the momentary pleasure of the imagination
found in brief and shifting dreams, seeks an issue along the way
of theory. This it was that formed the theme of the practical
philosophy of the Greeks, when it enquired in what consisted
eudaemonia and how to win it, and sometimes identified this with

pure griefless pleasure, sometimes with the reduction of human needs to a minimum, or with apathy, ataraxia, or calm contemplation quit of all affection and passion. Christianity put it outside the range of earthly life, then it was brought back to earth in the image of the perfected republic, the faultless state of reason, in which all needs would be satisfied and appeased, science would direct and govern men's minds with its certain light, justice, peace, and goodness would triumph, and there would be no more occasion for the tempests of the heart. Such, even today, is the ideal cherished by simple souls under the name of "Communism", naively understood, the purpose of which would be to resolve "the social question", in other words (since the question of society is the question of history itself, which the course of history everlastingly solves and reproposes) to overcome history, or, as it is put, to pass from the realm of struggle and necessity to that of liberty, which last word in this context symbolizes precisely the emptiness of non-history, the exhaustion and superannuation of life, of the reality which is one with life. There are many, indeed innumerable other forms assumed and assumable by this ideal, notably ecstasy in beauty, ravishment in love, drunkenness with power, exaltation of the self in an encircling and immortalizing glory. But pure pleasure is never attained in the impure and travailed fortunes of life; there is no calm unperturbed by the threats and assaults of the passions; the promise of paradise fails under the breath of doubt and criticism which dissolve its shape; the perfect state eludes the hand stretched out to grasp it, and in its place is found a state which is new because everything in history is new, but substantially like the old in being composed of the same elements and subject to the same inevitable relations; love brings often disappointment, always pain and grief; beauty is a rapid vision of real life as it pauses but does not tarry; power and glory do not confer personal happiness or the aspired beatitude. Therefore upon the optimism of this ideal there follows without fail the pessimism which lurks in its depths, and which, while seeking the contrary, it may but excite and aggravate, and certainly cannot appease and dominate. For that there is required an ideal other than that of absolute happiness and blessedness.

Such an ideal is born and becomes operative in the practical spirit of men of moral sensibility even before and without the help of a philosophy which grounds it upon the teaching that life stands above pleasure and pain because it includes both terms and denies their separate and detached existence. It is the ideal of workmanship, of self identification and immolation with and in the work that one has taken in hand, whether this be a work on the grand scale, as the imagination immediately suggests, for example the work of the poet, philosopher, scientist, social reformer; or, not less, any other work promoting the ends of life, the mother's upbringing of her children, the help and encouragement of friend to friend, the sweat of the peasant who loves the land, humble offices rendered disinterestedly by those who are thereby not humiliated but exalted, and differ from their superiors not in rank but only in the different quality of their aptitudes and circumstances. Thus viewed, pain is the sacrifice called for by the work, pleasure is the self-awareness of laborious purposive accomplishment, and takes on an objective character. Our dearest and tenderest affections become purified and elevated. The transports of love, the anxious fear of losing our loved ones, the anguish of actually losing them, is converted into a discovery and possession of the imperishable, a union with it. Even the interruption and suspense of work through the force of events are made good by the confidence that what was achieved or attempted was not in vain, and will be taken up by other hands. The fleetingness of hedonistic pleasure is really overcome by eternity, because work which enters into the world process and lives in it is necessarily eternal. Glory is released from personal limits, purged of "vainglory", and becomes one with immortality as we have now come to conceive it, the immortality of souls being seen as the immortality of works which no force and no occurrence can cancel, works which are really "souls", or spiritual forces, embracing each other in that Ideal which is the Real. In fact, a man worthy the name – though he may imagine and express it differently – studies always not himself but his work, which is his only true "self", the object of all his cares, his hopes, his joy. On the brink of death he thinks not of his person but of his work, and nothing so much troubles him as the thought of leaving it unfinished or exposed to danger, so that he puts all his zeal into care for its preservation and continuation. The saying "après moi le déluge" is not only the most cowardly but in its forced cynicism the falsest ever spoken.

Now works are the product not of passivity (symbolized by forced, servile, and mechanical labour), but of activity, and this explains the identification of the moral ideal with the ideal of freedom, without which men's powers cannot be deployed in harmony with the intimate moral aspiration peculiar to each yet substantially the same for all. The many theories of liberty that have been built upon the utilitarian principle, or upon that of nature (struggle for life, survival of the strongest or the fittest), ill become their object. They debase and outrage and corrupt the essence of liberty which is moral, and in our sense religious. Wellbeing, justice, equality, and all those other aspirations and recommended goals do not carry their justification in themselves but have to be measured solely by their aptitude for maintaining and promoting and enriching liberty, by which is meant man's creative power in truth, goodness, beauty. What a contrast to those conceptions which set the end of social and political order in "human happiness" or (refining this expression by an illicit resort to arithmetic) "the greatest good of the greatest number". The numerical reference is so absurdly placed in the definition of this ideal as to render criticism or condemnation superfluous. What is absurd is non-existent and cannot even be convicted of baseness.

As against the hedonistic and utilitarian conception, the morality of laborious activity may be termed an "heroic" morality provided that the term be purged of all suggestion of excessive solemnity or swashbuckling prowess, so as simply to connote an elevation above pleasure and pain, a resolute renunciation of the will-o'-wisp of personal beatitude, a contentment in the plain joy of a greater or smaller participation in the continuous creativity of the world. Its message can be summed up in the exclamation "Courage!", which, more than any other, the active man repeats to himself through all the length of his working day. Courage in the face of distressful partings, of passions wildly resurgent which fasten their grip upon the shifting circumstances which disappoint our loves and hopes, of the griefs which must be supported and accepted and borne with and taken for the severe accompaniments of our moral life. All that is human: and it is human also to hesitate and fall and succumb to the effort, and this calls for judgement in the spirit of human fairness and pity. For the life of a man who has distinguished himself from the anxious herd of petty pleasure-seekers by opening himself and vibrating to the universal, is to be viewed as is the most beautiful poem, not in its incidental weaknesses and little defects, but in its beautiful dominant line and its successfulness. The just man sins seven times daily, and is just because he continually returns to his cherished task. And then, apart from the particular errings and strayings into which for all our care we are always falling back again, there comes sometimes an imperious rebellion of the feelings, driving us to the search and experiment of a different and contrasting conception of the world. For the active man, the "hero", finds at his side or in his breast another man, a poor fellow who keeps on hankering for happiness, beatitude, contradicting his own better self, falling short of the faith which inspired and still inspires his work. No need to cite what daily experience illustrates: torments of desolation and despair which will not be quieted in what we love and in our work, lacerations which seemingly cannot be healed, insufficient pondering and preparation for the seemingly fearful idea of death. Let me recall that a supreme philosopher, Emmanuel Kant, so severe a moralist, so strong an antagonist to the doctrine of eudaemonism, yielded none the less when at a certain point in his teachings he postulated the union of virtue with happiness in a higher and supersensible sphere. And a supreme poet, Wolfgang Goethe, after celebrating his hero's ceaseless effort of ascent and self-redemption in strenuous work, fell prey to the insidiously returning sentiment of beatitude and crowned the drama of Faust with the erotic notion of the eternal female opening the way to Paradise.

This lower but ever rekindled craving for perfect and absolute happiness is the strongest and most direct support of the idea of mystery, conceived as essence and existence. Whatever else is asked, philosophy has for it or can have for it an answer and a satisfaction: but not for this. Those who seek a "something", those who are dissatisfied with real life, those who think that reality is oppressive for them and wish to emerge or escape from its limits – how can there be provided for them a reservoir of confused, contradictory, and empty hopes, unthinkable thoughts, hollow mists, restless shades? Where nothing is experienced there is no problem and philosophy has nothing to say. They then appease or think to appease their whimsy by placing it beyond the philosophic sphere, in the distant glimmering realm of Mystery, where it is possible to prolong the vague hope of beatitude, but not to gain release from suspense and fear of the dreadful unknown, nor even an imaginative consolation and comfort as in the Christian paradise of harmonious sound and sight, or the German warrior's Valhalla, or the lawns and sparkling streamlets of the fair garden of Islam.

Our interpretation of Mystery is confirmed by the importance of this idea in the Romantic Age, to which it seems properly to belong, for before that there were no more than hints of it. The ancients' plan or desire was to realize happiness or beatitude in this world, and on becoming convinced of the intrinsic impossibility of this, their reaction was that of the Cyrenaic philosopher Hegesias, counsellor of death. The Christians knew that "ultima felicitas hominis non est in hac vita", and since they had a clear revelation of the other world, they had no need to devise an outlet for their search after happiness in the supposition of a world of mystery. But when rationalism (the merely intellectualistic rationalism and also the deeper dialectical rationalism) had turned a critical eye on the Christian beliefs, and the world appeared empty of God and bereft of the hope that had for centuries inspired it, then in default of the rediscovery of God in the depths of personal being, or of a reflowering of hope through faith in human activity, or of strength to welcome and embrace the unconfessional conception of the world variously delineated by the philosophies then ripening, a strange and sometimes crazy assortment of ideals took hold of men's imaginations, wreaking havoc in their minds – ideals of a return to the distant primitive and barbaric past, to the theocratic and feudal middle age, to old religions, the Catholic in all its ponderousness, the Pagan, the old Eastern; ideals of personal blessedness through religiously sublimated love, or through life lived as a brilliant poetic inebriation, or through poetry cultivated as the spasm of pleasure, and so forth.[1] But not one of these ideals, when it was sought to realize them, brought rest and peace, all fell asunder when they seemed about to facilitate an ascent to heaven. But then in default of the will and the ability to abandon these enormous pseudo-poetic dreams for the seemingly narrow and prosaic reality of life, all ended with the attempt to probe and interrogate the mystery, as something which, if incomprehensible, was anyway existent, indeed all that there was of existent.

Today, at the tail end of romanticism and of its decadent perversions, the idea of mystery lingers on and provides a number of authors of philosophic books with a way of escape from their difficulties. But it seems to have lost its former force and together with that the marks of the not ignoble malady which it exhibited in the romantic age. The world, it seems, is no longer seeking painfully to recapture its lost God and Paradise Lost, as when that travail led to the assertion of the mystery of the universe. Something else it is that travails the world, a sense of being dragged down to animality, sheer vitality seeking to take the place of the spirit. (For some German philosophers of today the "spirit" is the enemy of the "soul" or the "life" elaborated in their theories and programmes.) Yet the world struggles in horror against this descent into the abyss, for the immortal conscience still summons it to turn away from this evil idolatry, this impulsive embrace and forced cult of bestiality, and to renew the simple faith in civilization and humanity.

[1939]

1. See the characterization of Romanticism in my *History of Europe in the 19th century*, Chapter III.

IV

PRIMACY OF THE ACTIVE LIFE[1]

I<small>T</small> is now fairly generally agreed, though with a diversity of practical inferences, that the modern age is distinguished from the mediaeval by its reaffirmation of the value of the life of this world as contrasted with a life "beyond this world". The practical inferences differ because one side wishes to prolong and intensify this historical trend while the other aspires in various ways to return to the mediaeval conception and discipline. For sure, what has happened in the last five centuries does not encourage this aspiration, for they have been centuries of triumph for the mundane ideal. The fleeting counter-successes of the ultramundane ideal (for example with the Counter-Reformation in the sixteenth century and the Restoration in the nineteenth, and again between the world wars in part of Europe) have been unaccompanied by the strong and simple religious faith which characterized the middle ages. Their prevailing character has been patently political and mundane. The masses of men above whose head is hoisted the standard of the old beliefs are not earnestly religious but concerned with their own advantage. This significant and easily perceived character is rendered particularly evident by the deficiency of creative thought and of art in this political-social movement. Its spokesmen repeat the outworn doctrines of mediaeval scholasticism without succeeding in confuting or critically improving upon those fresh but mature doctrines which have been formed in five centuries of experiment and uninhibited meditation. They show no susceptibility to the inner conflict in which thought is turned over and surpassed; worse still, its self-proclaimed artists and poets frequently dally with the unhealthy sensualism of these times,

---

1. Literally "Primacy of Doing". The translator is faced here with the impossibility of conveying, at all events in an appropriately dignified English, the brief forcefulness of the Italian infinitive used as a noun. A single word must therefore in general cover Croce's *Fare* and *Attività*, which are in fact in this essay used as virtual synonyms. – Translator.

thus excluding themselves both from the sphere of poetry and
art and from that of Christianity.

Though feeling it pertinent to recall this state of affairs, I will
here say no more of it, for I am now intent not upon a political
argument but upon defining the fundamental character of the
revolution in philosophy, and first and foremost in the theory
of knowledge, which occurred during those centuries and is still
in full development.

This revolution springs, one might say, from the contrast between the active and the contemplative life, in which is rooted
the opposition between the modern and the middle age, the
mundane and the ultramundane conception of life. For the ultramundane conception the True and the Good is located in static
perfection in the highest heaven to be passively contemplated
there, whereas for the active life the search for truth (no less than
the performance of tasks) proceeds without pause, knowing no
terminus but making of every point of arrival a new point of
departure.

This conception, for which the infinity of truth is balanced by the
no less infinite potentiality of the search for truth, is the very
contrary of scepticism. There is no need for it, then, to elude
scepticism by hiding itself in that sublime *asylum ignorantiae* of an
ascription of primacy to the practical reason. The practical reason
is practical, not theoretic, and it does not offer truths that may
be intuited and demonstrated. The "primacy" of which we are
speaking here is not that of a particular form of the spirit over the
others, but that of the principle which regulated them all alike.
This is the principle of "doing" (for greater clearness, of ποιεῖν
and ποίησις as contrasted with πράσσειν and πρᾶξις), of activity
against contemplative passivity, and activity not limited to useful and moral action, but extended to embrace all the forms of
"doing" which are also forms of "knowing", from poetry to
philosophy and history.[1]

1. The word "poetry", from ποιεῖν, in the sense of a "doing" distinct
from the "doing" covered by the word πράσσειν, has well guarded the active
and creative character of the concept of poetry, while at the same time

The problem was to provide a philosophical foundation, a theory of knowledge, for the activity or "doing" which permeated the whole range of modern life; so as not to leave this in company with a philosophy which contradicted and was contradicted by it, making for darkness and perplexity along the inevitable way forward, and for vain exploration of blind alleys better left on one side. An arduous problem of profound speculation, in air too high and pure to be breathed at first save by a few minds. The task was, by trying and trying again, to light upon the new mental thread, fine and strong, binding together the new facts and the new truths which they proclaimed or suggested piecemeal. This search has been the inner striving, the hidden spring of the philosophical development of the modern age. One who now points to it and throws light upon it seems to others, and to himself, to be the revealer of a secret previously kept hidden, but truth to tell the reason why it was left unspoken before lay in the long and exhausting travail of the research.

That the difficulty of the research was equal to its importance can well be briefly illustrated by drawing a comparison with what

somewhat dimmed its other necessary and essential character as a form of "knowing". Hence a tendency to assimilate poetry to the practical "doing", ethical or hedonistic, or to regard it as a middle term between knowledge and operation, truth and morality. All this is proved by the history of aesthetic doctrine, but would merit a particular enquiry and exposition elsewhere. The indeterminateness of the concept ποιεῖν has brought it about that what has been more or less recognized in the case of poetry has been recognized inadequately or not at all, or has been definitely denied, in the case of cognitive, intellectual, or philosophic activity, perhaps as a precaution against admixtures of fancy or poetry with thought. Such admixtures are certainly improper and to be carefully guarded against. But far from being improper, it is a deepening of understanding to perceive and affirm clearly that philosophy, like poetry or art, like all the aspects of the spirit, is "doing" and not contemplation and acceptance of the given. Greek philosophy distinguishes ποιεῖν and πράσσειν but naturally this does not help with our problem which arises from the premises of modern philosophy. For Aristotle ποιεῖν signifies more or less technique, while πράσσειν is the work of moral wisdom. In Plotinus the former is internal activity, contemplation, the latter is external activity through the instrumentality of the body, and therefore inferior and impoverished. See the careful examination of René Arnou in Πρᾶξις et Θεωρια, Étude de détail sur le vocabulaire et la pensée des Ennéades de Plotin (Paris, Alcan, 1921).

is called "Pragmatism", the main contribution of America to the philosophy of Europe. That doctrine rightly affirms that pure thought in the sense of useless thought does not exist, that truth is not a copy of a transcendent and absolute reality, that propositions differ in respect not of their relation to the supposed objective reality but in respect of their differing practical ends, that the true is a value like the beautiful and the good, that the criterion of true and false is in the consequences which they engender, and so on.[1] These are all true propositions or at least can be given a true interpretation, but they are not linked in the unity of the spirit so as to render them strong and coherent. Such a systematization and demonstration the Pragmatists refuse to provide. Great is their abhorrence for what they call "organic" philosophy, meaning, historically, the so-called idealistic tradition of Kant and Hegel. By thus indulging in the tasteless pleasure of viewing the imperishable major philosophic geniuses of the human race as foolish or misguided, by thus cutting themselves off from the history of thought, they weaken the force of those truths which they do perceive or glimpse, leaving them truncated and obscure. It is curious to watch the Pragmatist authors, for all their intelligence and quickness, digging themselves with whimsical obstinacy into this negative attitude.[2] If there were no "organic philosophy" we should make shift with books of "stray thoughts" the value of which is limited precisely by a more or less total lack of organic quality, which leaves even their meaning uncertain.[3] What could be purer pragmatism than Goethe's solemn line "Was fruchtbar ist allein ist wahr" (only the fruitful is true)?[4] Yet Goethe lacks a

1. For convenience I have availed myself of the meaty sketch of Pragmatism in the *Encyclopaedia Britannica*, XIV Edition.
2. See the remarks in my *Discorsi di varia filosofia*, II, pages 112-19 on Dewey and his aesthetic theory, which accepts all the concepts elaborated by myself concerning art, but rejects what holds them together; and this without offering any alternative nexus because if he did so the author's conscience would be pricked and scandalized by such a sinful relapse into "organic philosophy".
3. See my observations on Goethe's maxims, reflections, and opinions in my *Goethe*, 4th edn., Bari 1946, II, 205-10).
4. *Vermächtnis* (in the series *Gott und Welt*).

philosophy in the strict sense, and the meaning of this very verse is disputable.

The labours of modern thought in the last and culminating period (from the 18th century to our present time) to attain by the speculative method a philosophy of "doing" as contrasted with "contemplating" have now been intelligently examined, constructed, and expounded, in a work of Professor Manlio Ciardo to which I wish the luck and still more the attention which it deserves.[1]

The book is entitled "The Four Epochs of Historicism". It leads off with the epoch of Vico. It is high time that Vico, chronologically anterior to Kant, should be accorded a place of honour in the great philosophy of modern times, a place grudged him by those historians of philosophy who have not yet made the basic discovery that the history of philosophy, like that of any other aspect of the spirit, needs to be rearranged, viewed in fresh perspective, extended in its scope, to match the self-deepening process of thought. Vico, when in the theory of knowledge advanced in his *De Antiquissima* he confronted the idol of his century, exact and mathematical science, saw and affirmed that this was an artificial truth, a *fictio* shaped by the spirit of man, and with his critical formula *verum facimus*, he reached forward to Kant. Jacobi, one of the handful who saw and studied the Italian thinker's book, noted and clearly stated this. But in Vico's subsequent *Scienza Nuova* the doctrine of the convertibility of fact with truth took on this different and much more fruitful meaning: Man has a full knowledge of History because it is his own work, just as God knows Nature because that is His creation. And with this the whole world of humanity and history was won for knowledge and truth. The world of nature remained excluded. Vico could not, in his unsympathetic and unripe age, attain to the inference that nature is not an external reality but that the concept nature is the concept of the external devised by man for his own practical ends and accordingly, since that concept is his own work,

1. *Le quattro epoche dello storicismo* (Bari, Laterza, 1947).

nature can be known by man. (Religious prudence would in any case have impeded Vico from making such a statement.) It is Vico's resolute opposition and clear antithesis to Descartes which indicates the direction that was to be taken by philosophy. Contrary to what is conventionally asserted by idealists hovering between the old and the new, Descartes symbolizes not the starting point of the new philosophy but the last, and in truth most refined form of the philosophy of contemplation, its critical moment, if you will. Descartes' canon of evidence, and of its ultimate confirmation in faith, was still deeply scholastic, whence the interpretation given to his thought in our days is once again hesitating and discordant. Vico's confutation of Descartes was well described by De Sanctis as "complete – the last word of criticism".[1]

The second epoch is opened by Kant. The *cogito* of Descartes, accepted by Vico as symbol of consciousness, but not of science, was by Kant replaced with the activist a priori synthesis. This fuses Intuition with Category in Judgement. The a priori synthesis had an extended applicability, and thus an universal validity, which Kant's eye failed to measure, though that he had an inkling of it is shown by his awareness of having made a revolutionary discovery comparable with the astronomical theory of Copernicus. The a priori synthesis consolidated the convertibility of fact with truth in one of its further aspects and problems. But Kant, in propounding it, was thinking of its reference to physico-mathematical science. This led him to proclaim that thought is impotent to resolve the antinomies of philosophic problems, or to demonstrate the supreme concepts, God, Freedom, Immortality, which he therefore relegated to the class of postulates of the practical reason. His absorption with physico-mathematical science prevented Kant from achieving, like Vico, a passage, progress, and elevation from the *fictiones* of mathematical science to the *realitates* of history, which would have permitted him to recognize in the a priori synthesis the true and real organ of historical thought, and so to attain the further conclusion (so remote from his own habit

1. *Storia della letteratura italiana*, ed. Croce (Bari, 1925) II, 291.

of thought) of the oneness of philosophy with history and of spiritualism as absolute historicism.

With Hegel there enters into philosophy not indeed absolute historicism, but the concept of the primary importance of the logic of history. Hegel understood the breadth and universality of the a priori synthesis, which received from him an adequate logical form in the universal concrete, synthesis of universal and particular, and in the Idea, synthesis of knowing and willing, theory and practice; and in the dialectic which by surpassing them unifies opposite terms, overcoming the dualism of positive and negative, good and evil, true and false.

But Hegel, in the inebriation of his dialectical vision, in his impatience with the intellectualistic and arbitrary distinctions which everyday thought takes to be real and speculative, threw overboard, in company with these, also those other distinctions which were not intellectualistic and arbitrary, subjecting them all to resolution in the dialectic of opposites. He never paused to think that opposition and dialectic themselves cannot arise without distinction, which is their point of reference, and they its obverse side. It happened to Hegel, therefore, that conceiving the development of the spirit, and of history, as a thronging succession of mere oppositions and overcomings, he was obliged to devise an end and meaning for his process by fixing a final point – thereby contradicting law and the logic of the process itself, crowning its *numquam quiescere* with an absolute *quiescere*, a retirement, once and for all, of action and thought and of all history, to bask in the vision of the Idea. Hegel's system therefore took on the lineaments of a theology in which the God Idea determined to create the world of nature, and in which man raised himself from this, and in bestriding the course of a definite ideal and historical development, redeemed himself and returned to God – a journey in which starting point and point of arrival were equally inconceivable. It seems at first puzzling that this systematic and theological Hegel, who in good faith and with full conviction considered Christianity as the "absolute" religion beyond which it was not given to go – nor did he himself wish to go further than to understand its truth as if by the light of a *fides quaerens intellectum* – this Hegel, who reduced historical knowledge itself to a phantom by superimposing a philosophy of history on the model of the theological schools, should not have been welcomed and utilized by church circles. Something of that sort was indeed attempted in Italy by Gioberti with his "Ens" creator of the Existent and his Existent returning to the "Ens", a doctrine much favoured in its day by those wishing to be Catholics and Idealists at the same time, just as in politics they were Catholics and Liberals.

But a closer consideration explains the suspicion, aversion, fear, abhorrence aroused by that philosophy of the universal concrete, of dialectic, of historical interpretation. For these were mighty and demonic forces penetrating into the world of thought and able to carry the day boldly for an immanentist and activist conception of human life. And thus it was that they operated autonomously outside and beyond the system, which they rejected and forgot, using other words and images, and the spirit of Hegel thus throughout the nineteenth century overhung those who despised and rejected him and often made of them unwitting Hegelian disciples.

At the turn of the nineteenth and beginning of the twentieth century the fourth epoch of historicism opened, and the setting was in Italy. Suitably to the proclivities of the Italian spirit, the way lay through the domain of poetry and art. Hegel's Aesthetic attracted the minds of the Italians by its assignment of a high rank to art in the life of the spirit and by showing a broad understanding for the different forms and periods of art history. On the other hand repugnance was felt (and this was still more emphatic) for its doctrine of the resolution and dissolution of art into philosophy, (with a shaky definition of beauty as the sensible manifestation of the Idea, which Idea was sometimes presented as the whole of reality, sometimes just as logical thought and the concept; and from this was inferred, displeasingly for the Italians, that art must die if indeed it had not already died in the final triumph of speculative thought). Displeasing also was the Hegelian reverence for the empirically discriminated *genres* in art, and epochs in history to

4

which that philosophy gave the rank of philosophically distinguished moments. These repugnances gave rise to the counter-
assertion of the autonomy of art, proclaimed in the teeth of
sensism and materialism and positivism on the one side, but no
less of the Hegelian school on the other side; and to the formulation
of the moment of Distinction in opposition to the Hegelian
abuse of the dialectical method.

But the logical correction first inspired by the love of poetry
and beauty proved to require to be extended also to the other
sides of the Hegelian philosophy: to the Hegelian ethic, in which
the dialectical method had corrected Kant's intransigent doctrine,
but also, by an abuse, betrayed it; and to the Hegelian theory of
history, which had audaciously contrived a philosophic super-
history (in truth, history itself, born in union with philosophy,
is philosophy, and cannot be further philosophized); and to the
Hegelian theory of the natural sciences, originally by Hegel
discerningly qualified as abstractions or wilful proceedings of the
intellect, but subsequently subjected by him to a "Philosophy of
Nature", charged with the impossible task of philosophizing the
products of the intellect; and finally to the Hegelian Logic itself,
in which it was necessary to show up critically the mechanical (and
conversely mythological) handling of the dialectical principle.

This critical operation led to the attainment of the conception of
Absolute Historicism, unique form of Knowing, which respects
the mathematical and natural sciences in their proper instrumental
or practical function, and includes philosophy itself not as sovereign, but as that one among the various parts of the unique reality
of history which is concerned with the understanding of method.
Whereas for Hegel Knowledge after having arrived at the fullness
of ultimate truth resumed a character of motionless contemplation, it now had restored to it the character of activity already
recognized in Vico's principle of the convertibility of fact with
truth, and in Kant's a priori synthesis, the character required by
the whole modern conception of life. And thereby historical
knowledge became firmly knitted to the moral activity of man,
its eternal premiss and eternal sequel. The *cogito* of Descartes, who

vainly attempted to attain to the spiritual and creative *sum*, the active and practical *sum*, leaving intact the *res* which he accepted so believingly, by faith, has herewith been converted into a "doing" – the active thought which engenders fresh action out of the understanding of past action, in the ideal and historical circle of reality.

[1946]

V

THEORY OF DISTINCTION
AND OF THE FOUR SPIRITUAL CATEGORIES

A MAN, a worker, whose days have been prolonged until the age when the scope of his work can be surveyed as a whole, yet has retained strength enough to continue labouring at it in a manner which he feels to be not useless, is somewhat in the position of the manager of an enterprise who still puts in some personal work but is disposed to impart hints and counsels to those who are about to take over from him. Francesco Gaeta concluded a lyric with the prayer to sister Death to open for him "the feigned window wrought in the hard solidity of nothingness". This striking and beautiful poetic image is not, however, true moral doctrine, for one who has not wasted his powers will at the close of his life see open before his eyes the world of the future for which he always lived, and those younger – whom he ever desired should also be better – than himself, he sees taking up with fresh energy the work beside which he himself now stands, tired but content.

As is widely known and understood, the *leitmotif* of my mental labours has been a sturdy defence of the concept of "distinction". All philosophers, all men, indeed, think only in as far as they distinguish, so that this defence might seem superfluous or arrogant were it not justified by the general character of the age in which my life has been and is passed, an age which, torn between romanticism, positivism, naturalism, activism, mysticism, and the like, blunted the edge and weakened or impaired the virtue of distinctions in philosophy and morals. Not that I consciously and deliberately set myself against the tendency of my times. Thank heavens I was spared from indulgence in such "gladiatorial" attitudes if not by modesty yet at all events by my lively Neapolitan sense of the ridiculous. So if I accept the current appraisal of my own work, this is because now that I can look back and recall its development, it seems to me to be the right one and to give an opening for profitable comment.

There were two principal arguments involved in that "defence", one against the sensists, psychologists, associationists, naturalists, and materialists who used and indeed proliferated distinctions at every point, but held them all to be equally empirical and conventional and in an absolute sense valueless; and the other against the idealists of the leading speculative school of the nineteenth century, the Hegelians, who, after affirming the principle of dialectic, made use of it to treat distinctions in a light-handed way as partialities or successive steps towards logical maturity, and therefore resolving or annihilating all distinctions in the Logos or Idea when in fullness of time this was attained.

I found no great difficulty in coping with the former schools. In all justice, even the most celebrated among them were men of small understanding. If not to themselves, at least to men of understanding I made it clear that an empirical or conventional distinction cannot be established without the backing of an absolute and real distinction, much as paper money can only circulate upon the basis of real exchanges of goods and services, and counterfeit money presupposes money which is genuine. On that side the argument was soon as good as won.

The other confutation was necessarily more difficult and subtle. The dialectical principle was in all truth a great renewal and even revolution which Hegel had the outstanding merit of introducing and utilizing in modern thought. There could be no question of turning back to the old metaphysic of Being with a sacrifice of that logic of Becoming which having entered the world of thought was no more to be expelled from it. Although the error of the panlogistic conception in the Hegelian and derivative systems was plainly discernible, yet this gave no ground for regarding that logic as erroneous, but only for suspecting a grave imperfection in the concept, that is in its theoretical elaboration. My confutation, then, started with an enquiry for a theory of opposition, bringing in its train conciliation and the rise to a higher level without loss of the already attained, arising within the unity of the spirit, so as to avoid both a Manichaean dualism and also an engulfment in oppositionless, immobile unity. The demonstration which I gave was this. Opposition is not the starting point of logic but itself presupposes distinction within the spiritual unity, and this unity calls for a more concrete and philosophic concept of itself as organic and living, not abstract mathematical unity; that is to say as unity-distinction, each of these terms being defined by and identical with the other. It is only in the passage from one distinct to the other, from one to another form or category of reality or the spirit, that there comes about opposition, the travail of working that passage across the ground contested between new and old, positive and negative. Single distinctions are not then steps leading towards the One in which all come to be merged and surpassed, but are the energy of unity passing perpetually from one form to another, weaving the web of history in indefatigable freshness. The process of reality can in its fullness only be thought of historically, where history, however, is free motion, not – as with Hegel – enchained in a system claimed itself to be the goal and conclusion of history. Only the logic of the historical understanding measures up to Thought, and this means the abandonment of definite systems in favour of historical systematizations which have to be – in correspondence with life itself – perpetually amplified and enriched.

The forms or categories of reality and the spirit, the supreme values, had by a kind of *consensus gentium* in the course of the centuries been summed up in the triad True, Good, Beautiful, but I felt the need, for completeness, of a fourth term, the Useful, Economic, Vital (or whatever other word is preferred), something illogically despised and calumniated and dubbed materialistic by philosophers who dared not rebel against the almost unconsciously absorbed but speculatively indefensible educational tradition of the Triad – those same philosophers who in other circumstances combated the theory of the creative efficacy of the passions.

The introduction of the fourth term, changing the triad to a tetrad, necessitated a somewhat different but much more realistic pattern for the order and relations of the forms of the spirit. It helped to put an end to the pseudodialectic proliferation of triads (in the old game of triadism all distinctions were emptied of significance). But the introduction of the new category was required also as a preparation and help for the resolution of the duality spirit-nature, soul-body, internal reality-external reality, the unveiling of that mystery which man constructs for himself when he allows imagination to get the better of thought and to lead him into the inertia or delirium of the transcendent, one of those mysteries which, as Goethe remarked in a similar context, remains mysterious only because *niemand hört's gerne*, none likes to hear the simple explanation and to abandon illusions and foolish hopes.

For the same motive let us watch and beware lest an hierarchical division of high and low, superior and inferior (easily introduced from common ways of speech where Bergson's distinction between *parler le monde* and *penser le monde* is overlooked) gain currency in respect of the four forms of the spirit. The forms of the spirit, being all necessary, are all necessarily of equal rank, and can be arranged only in an order of succession and implication, and not of rank, for in the circularity or circulation of spiritual life none constitutes an absolute beginning or an absolute end. To which form, in fact, does everyday thought incline to assign the lowest rank? Undoubtedly to the form of vitality, utility, economy, which expresses its joy and affirms its value in the deployment of the physiological forces, whence it comes easily to receive the metaphorical attribute of materiality and animality. But its true definition is this: the form of pure individuality creating and main-taining itself and upholding its own right along with the others in the dialectic and unity of the spirit. Suffice it to recall what hap-pened when that form was for a long time depressed and decried and downtrodden, and with what force and power it recovered to overwhelm mediaeval asceticism with antique and modern light in the great age known as the Renaissance.

I cannot recall any further resistances against the enlargement of the triad of values to a tetrad, bringing in its train a new philosophy of the spirit and a simplified, deepened interpretation of the famous ten categories of the venerable Aristotelian table. I may disregard some tasteless witticisms against what were offensively

termed "Croce's four words" as if these universally visible flags
pointing the way throughout the life and history of the human
race had been some bumptious invention of mine. I may disregard
also the frivolous remark that the categories are not these all
too modest four but that, luxuriant and infinite in number, they
coincide with the infinite affections of the human soul, a luxuriance
and infinity swimming and splashing in which one may sink into
the gloom of mysticism and of the so-called undifferentiated "Pure
Act"; and together with this I disregard the seemingly serious
logical objection that if the categories are four the numerical series
could and should be continued, which overlooks that this "four"
is not an arithmetical number but the symbol of a speculative
relation. This should not be a difficult notion for minds accustomed
to the logical exposition of the famous "sacred numbers", first
and foremost of the triad, the triunity or Most Holy Trinity.
Vain attempts are still occasionally being made to cancel the
fourth category of the tetrad by resolving it in one of the other
three or redistributing it among these, but there have been no
further attempts to make additions to the four except one, outside
Italy, not long pursued, to add a category of "nature", and a logically ingenuous proposal to round off the series with the category "religion" – whereas really if religion fails to permeate the
whole four, *infusa per artus*, no place can be found for it beside or
above them or in any way attached to them from outside.

But while at least for the present attempts to alter the tetrad by
addition or subtraction have been suspended, there have been demands and suggestions for a widening of the scope of the categories by specialization within the tetrad, that is by distinguishing
in each category sub-forms or steps to mark and explain the
passage from one to the other. Some have held that I myself
in fact recognize such sub-forms, though without providing an
adequate internal and spiritual explanation of them, displaying
them instead as the product of casual or mechanical occasions. As
one example they have cited my theory of "literature" as something
distinct from "poetry" yet tempering with poetic expression the
modes of rhetoric, prose, and didactic exposition. An alternative

arrangement has been suggested: the recognition of literary expression as a "pre-poetic" grade of the spirit "situated at the terminal boundary of affective or sentimental expression, where dying whiteness has not yet given way to blackness, that is, where the surge of the feelings having already become in its way harmonious, germinally musical, is prepared and fitted for the approach of the divine melancholy of Poetry".[1] There has been a similar proposal to remove the concept of "mythology" from the Phenomenology of Errors where I had carefully placed it and to make of it instead a grade of the poetic or aesthetic form.

I will not develop at length the obvious difficulties of method which would attend the introduction of these supposed transitional grades, these tints between black and white which self-evidently cannot have a categorical character, cannot, that is, serve as the ground and utterance of judgements but can at most only be understood as psychological and empirical classes and thus serve empirical purposes. True and proper categorical judgements have to be clear-cut, with no "almost" or "more or less" in them. An expression is or is not poetry, an act is or is not moral. For brevity, I will simply take up here once again my argument about literary expression, to show that in my theory this in no wise derives from mechanical occasions but is fully recognized as a fine product of the practical spirit, the practical "tact" (or "touch") exercised in given conditions upon a given material.

How in practice does a literary page illustrating a philosophical proposition come into being? Say that I have worked for some hours, days, or even years to resolve a philosophical difficulty and now at last have or seem to have achieved it. *Eureka!* As a thinker I am satisfied and my satisfaction is registered, conformably to my present state of mind, either in some formula of scholastic jargon, or in some stroke of the pen, or in some poet's verse or whatever it may be that I adopt to symbolize my thought. My philosophical task with myself is finished. But another task confronts me, that of communicating the truth which I have thought out for the use of

1. See the notable work of A. ATTISANI, *Cosmicità ed eternità dell'Arte* (Milan, Principato, 1946).

other men (and in a sense for my own use), presenting and preserving it in the most easily receivable and most impressive guise. The mark or formula which I used to express my discovery will now be of no use save in the particular case of men initiated into my hieroglyphics or my slang of the moment. I now have need of modes of expression current in society or literature, pleasing or anyway not displeasing to aesthetically refined readers of poetry and novels who dislike slang and call for a more ingratiating approach. Emerging, then, from my exclusive philosophic meditation, and surveying the world around me for which and to which I want to speak, I am invaded by a crowd of feelings stirred up by that philosophic truth – waves of enthusiasm for the announcement and triumphant assertion of that truth, recollection of imagination of other similar experiences rousing human interest, spasms of irritation, resentment, contempt for the opposition which I foresee, retorts, satirical remarks, irony and quips, even, which come to the mind as apt to parry and overcome the attacks, desire to illuminate and persuade whoever is well disposed, zeal to cite examples and to provide a methodic exposition, and so forth. For all these and other feelings and desires I want to find an aesthetic form which will also be a suitable form for the expression and inculcation of a truth. Evidently if one of those feelings inspired me poetically and absorbed me, then from my inner experience there would be born a song, a story, a comedy, a tragedy, not a didactic exposition which is what is now needed, and needed incidentally by myself since I will be more fully in possession of my truth when I have given it a literary embodiment, less likely to confound or change it, to more or less forget it, and able to rediscover it in its precise expressiveness even should I ever come to forget it totally. So here I am, no longer chewing the cud of that logical problem which I have already solved or seemed to solve, but engaged with the new problem of expression, and requiring, as for any aesthetic operation whether of poetry, painting, or music, a unifying and generating impulse to embrace, order, coordinate, arrange, measure out, and bring into proportion all the single parts, all the expressions which must go to make a page of prose. Every writer knows the stage at which this rumination duly produces the first words, the words of the beginning, which would not be a beginning were it not accompanied by the vision of the whole, still tightly packed like thread in a ball from which in due course the hand will draw it out. There will be founderings, partial or total revisions, changes of mind, corrections, touching up of the page to get the single expressions more in keeping with each other or better differentiated; all which is a labour just like that of the poet and the artist, save that here in every part and at every stage the prevailing purpose is didactic. A pure and simple poet, who took it upon himself to pass judgement upon the page without adapting eye and mind to the logic of the prose-writer's labour will say that it is all contaminated by non-poetical purpose, but the prose-writer's honour and commitment is to work in that way, and he feels that if he departed from that purpose he might perhaps sacrifice what he had begun and drop his task in favour of the quite different one of composing a poem, but that if he went on trying to do both at once he would write a page of inharmonious prose, including some poetic fragment which would be thus relegated to a place where no one would look for it, causing perhaps an agreeable astonishment to some readers, but perhaps to some an irritation such as is felt when things are out of their proper place.

A complete understanding of the difference between poetic and literary work (implying no disregard for the latter, or lowering of its rank), and a training in the often subtle and delicate task of distinguishing between them, is indispensable for anyone who takes up certain important problems of artistic history and criticism. For example, in reading certain facile refutations of my judgement on the character of Manzoni's romance *I Promessi Sposi*, I feel that not only the crux of the question but the first terms of it have been ignored. Otherwise, instead of a refutation, there would have come a recognition that my judgement and the theoretical considerations leading to it did but set forth rationally the universal feeling about that much loved and most beautiful book.

In the process of literary composition just described where are to be found the alleged mechanical or eclectic combination, the thrusting together of two forms and two different principles in an arbitrary and wilful compromise, leading to a loss of unity in the work? The motive in play is one and one only, the sense of the appropriate, the search for *sermo opportunus qui est optimus*, the practical necessity of the case, the attainment of a beauty which will lend itself to the service of truth, thus renouncing its independence in order here to be no longer pure beauty but an instrument and a portion of a practical work, though the breath of beauty no more ceases here than does the physical breathing of a horse which the rider puts through its paces.[1]

There is an analogous case to this of literature in its relation to and differentiation from poetry, in the natural or "positive" sciences. To understand these there is no need for a new category of the spirit in addition to the categories of philosophic-historic truth and practical utility. The sciences derive the body of their

---

1. The tracing back of literature to "taste" or better "tact", to the alert and active sense of the appropriate (as πρέπον this was one of the capital concepts of the Rhetoric of antiquity), is found by Fubini (in a very notable essay "Arte, Linguaggio, Letteratura", published in the Florence Review *Belfagor*, III, 2, of July 1948) not entirely satisfactory. He would prefer to view literature as "aesthetic activity itself in such form as is permitted by the prevalence of another purpose; appropriateness, as the ruling purpose, being here considered as the aspect assumed in this case by the law of poetry with a renunciation of overt poetical fashions for the sake of preserving the intimate harmony of the discourse" (page 404). But if indeed the "prevailing purpose" is "other" then aesthetic, and its rulings are directed to "appropriateness" and not beauty, Fubini really confirms my conclusion that literature results from the moderating function exercised over all the energies of the spirit, in the interest of conservation and harmony, by the practical form of the spirit. The practical form prevents two opposite excesses: the tendency of the content, be it philosophic, scientific, passional, or in one of many ways oratorical, to violate and ignore the aesthetic sense and the cult of beauty, in its struggle to overcome dumbness and to express itself; and the tendency of the aesthetic form to smother the extra-aesthetic content, present and operating, the consequence of thwarting which is an output not of good literature but of weak and graceless "literary poetry" rejected equally by poetic taste and literary taste. The difficulties experienced in receiving my theory come principally perhaps from a failure to conceive speculatively, in its purity and depth and universality, the practical (economic and ethical) form, ridding it of the empirical notions attached to it by everyday mental associations.

knowledge from historic-philosophic truth (observation, description, and recording of fact) and they derive their abstracting, generalizing, classifying, law-giving form from the practical and economic process applied to summarizing and preserving the known facts in readiness for the various necessary uses. Analogously to what happens with literary composition, if the spirit of "pure knowledge", the sheer philosophic urge (like the poetic impetus in the other case) breaks into their midst, their work falls asunder and perishes. And unless this destruction is compensated by the accidental discovery of some philosophic truth, the work perishes in the extravagant hybridism of some so-called Philosophy of Nature, such as are neither sciences nor philosophies. Or some doctrine is produced like that of the Aristotelian "Simplicius" banished long ago by Galileo from the world of physics.

In the case of the sciences, too, there was an attempt by philosophers, including Hegel, to treat them as a "pre-philosophy" or preparation for philosophy, and much labour was required to restore to them their due and necessary autonomy and by this fair deal to guarantee a proper autonomy to philosophy itself.

[1946]

VI

IDENTITY OF THE DEFINITION WITH THE INDIVIDUAL (OR HISTORICAL) JUDGEMENT[1]

THE distinction between the definitory judgement on the one hand, the individual judgement on the other, is generally allowed. It can, as I have said,[2] be traced in one at least of the senses given to the terms analytic and synthetic judgement, but it is expressed even more clearly in the well-known distinctions between truth of reason and truth of fact, truths necessary and contingent, a priori and a posteriori, affirmations in logic and affirmations in history. Indeed only in virtue of such a distinction would it seem possible to find meaning in the logical doctrine which asserts that propositions may be formally true yet materially false. Otherwise it is inadmissible ever to distinguish formal truth from effective truth – presuming of course that "formal" refers to philosophic form and not to a formalistic logic which wilfully traces forms which are in themselves neither true nor false. It is inadmissible that a proposition should be true in one respect and false in another, as if judgement could ever be passed on a proposition save in respect of its unequivocal meaning and value. If, however, the distinction between truth of reason and truth of fact is given, then it must be acknowledged that a single verbal proposition might incorporate affirmations of both sorts, the one true and the other false. "Cambronne's saying that the Guard will die but will never surrender is a sublime saying": this proposition is formally (rationally) true and materially (factually) false, because Cambronne never said that. "Guerrazzi's novel *L'Assedio di Firenze* is a most beautiful

---

1. Editor's Note. In the pages which follow, Logic accomplishes a decisive step forward, surpassing the scholastic division between truth of fact and truth of reason, and showing that all definitions are at the same time historical judgements, while all judgements of fact are also judgements of value and vice versa. The way is thus thrown open for Vico's *conversio veri et facti*, for Hegel's identification of the real with the rational, and for Croce's definition of philosophy as the methodology of history.

2. In previous chapter of Croce's *Logic*. – Translator.

book for it inflamed many young minds with patriotism" may be materially (factually) true, but is formally (rationally) false because the effect in question is no proof of the beauty of a book, for this does not consist in its practical and persuasive efficacy.

But despite the prestige seemingly pertaining to the distinction between definitory and individual judgement, rational and factual truth, with its secular tradition confirmed by general assent and common usage, this distinction encounters a serious difficulty.

To understand this difficulty it is necessary to start by determining exactly what is affirmed when definitory judgement or rational truth is said to be followed by individual judgement or factual truth. We are already familiar with a distinction of this sort between intuition and concept, and have become aware that we were thereby distinguishing two fundamental forms of the spirit, the representative or fanciful, and the logical. Distinguishing now between definitory judgement and individual judgement, are we making an analogous affirmation whereby the logical form (concept, definition) is distinguished from another form which is no longer logical though containing in itself, absorbed and subordinate, the quality of logic, just as the concept so contains in itself the intuition? In other words, is the individual judgement ultralogical? For sure, it is asserted to be not mere definition, but can it be asserted not to be logic?

Now in the individual judgement the subject is indeed a representation, yet this representation does not here play the same part as in aesthetic contemplation. It is here as the subject of judgement, not, then, as pure and simple representation, but as a representation which one *thinks*, that is to say, as logicity. Hegel has often remarked that the unity of individual and universal can only be questioned by those who have never paid attention to the judgements which they themselves are continually uttering, as when, with use of the copulative verb, they boldly state Peter *is* Man.[1] (That is to say the individual (subject) *is* the universal

---

1. In English of course they would say "is a man" but for this argument it is better to omit an article which Italian, like Latin, can dispense with. – Translator.

(predicate) – not something different, a piece or fragment, but just that, the universal.) And then, are not truths of fact also truths of reason? Would it not be irrational to think that a fact was other than it was? Is the existence of Caesar or Napoleon less rational than that of quality and becoming? Are not so-called contingent things as necessary as so-called necessary things? We properly make fun of those who insist upon thinking that things might have happened otherwise than as they did, and in truth Caesar and Napoleon are as necessary as quality and becoming.

Examples could easily be multiplied and would provide ever surer evidence that the individual judgement is no less logical than the definitory judgement, while factual, contingent, a posteriori truths are as logical as rational, necessary, a priori truths. If it is still, however, desired to keep a distinction between the two forms, this must cease to be viewed as a distinction between forms of the spirit. It would be one of those sub-distinctions within the logical form which at the outset we have ruled out. Once again we have to ask ourselves, how can logical thought which thinks the universal think doubly, once in this and once in that way, be universal thought of the universal on one side and universal thought of the individual on the other? The distinction between intuition and concept is that between individual and universal. But that universal should be distinguished from universal by the introduction of individuality as the differentiating elements is inconceivable.

Equally inconceivable and impossible is it that we should abandon the conclusion which we had already reached that individual judgement is possible only on the basis of a presupposed concept or definitory judgement. We cannot in fact get rid of that presupposition and return to the old fashion of regarding the individual or perceptive judgement as anterior to the concept, void of logical character, mere assertion of fact unillumined by the universal. Every attempt to do this breaks down. Our difficulty has now become more arduous, for if we cannot accept a duality of logical forms, still less can we regard the individual judgement as non-logical and sub-logical.

The only issue from these difficulties seems to be to hold fast to our earlier conclusion that the definitory judgement is necessarily presupposed by the individual judgement, but at the same time to affirm that the individual is necessarily presupposed by the definitory. Let us take this as an hypothesis, to see where it would lead us and what would be the consequences for this enquiry.

If each of these two judgements presupposes the other, reciprocally, we could no longer speak of a distinction between the two judgements, but of a correlation or unity within which distinction could be introduced only by abstraction and an arbitrary proceeding, dividing the necessarily indivisible. On the other hand such a confessedly arbitrary distinction could still serve as a good help for the teacher in expounding the full nature of the logical act, so as to justify both our previous proceeding of developing first the concept and definitory judgement and then the individual judgement, and also our steady warning as to the provisional nature of that distinction, whence arose the further question of the unity of the act, which we are now exploring. With this hypothesis there would fall to the ground all the difficulties originating in the appearance of a duality of logical forms. Definitions and individual judgements, rational and factual truths, truths necessary and contingent, a priori and a posteriori, would be revealed as all one act, all one truth. But at the same time it would be shown to be legitimate in practice to talk of them as distinct acts, in so far as in expressing the one truth, the one judgement, one may verbally or stylistically emphasize now the definition and now the assertion of fact, now the subject and now the predicate.

But this highly advantageous and genuine way of issue from our difficulties would seem to be forbidden to us by the absence, in the definitions, of any trace of the individual judgement which we want to see contained in them and all one with them. "The Will is the Practical Form of the Spirit." "Virtue is the habit of moral actions." Where, it will be asked, can we espy in such sayings the individual judgement and the representative element? Of course they show the expressive and representative verbal form without which the concept could not concretely exist. But what we sought was an affirmation of fact, and this is missing. So the proposed hypothesis, however ingenious and advantageous, having failed to stand up to our examination, must, it seems, be dismissed, leaving us obliged to think out some better one, or, if that fails, to despair and give up all hope of a solution.

But let us not be precipitate. It has been mentioned in passing that the verbal or literary form may throw emphasis upon one phase of the judgement almost to the extent of relegating the other to oblivion, without, however, actually suppressing it. Let us attend to this detail and remember also the inverse case of perceptive or factual judgements which, particularly when they are such as we have called purely existential or such as are called impersonal, seemed at first to exhibit no trace of any concept, and yet when analysis has passed beyond mere appearance and has examined what is expressed and implied (implication also being a mode of expression) in the verbal forms, it has discovered the concepts present there, proving once more that no judgement is possible save on a basis of concept. In reality a definition does not float in the air in the way that appearances suggest when we consider the examples given in treatises shorn of any reference to the where and the when and the who and all the material setting in which the definition was uttered. When a definition is so sketchily presented we seek in vain for a representative element and an individual judgement. But then the definition in question has been mutilated, rendered abstract and indeterminate, and will become determinate only with the attribution of a meaning by the hearer. When instead we consider the definition in its concrete reality, a careful search will always discover the representative element and the individual judgement.

Every definition is the answer to a question, the solution of a problem, and there would be no call to pronounce it save for the asking of questions and the setting of problems. Why otherwise should we bestir ourselves, and to what end? Like every act of the spirit, definition is born in a contrast, a travail, a conflict requiring settlement, a darkness seeking light, or, as we have put it, a question wanting an answer. Not only does the answer presuppose the question, but such as the answer is, such must have been the question. The answer, if it did not fit the question, would be not an answer but a get-out. All this simply means that the nature of the question gives its own colour to the answer, and a definition, concretely considered, receives its determination from the problem which gives rise to it. A variation of the problem varies the definitory act.

Now a question, a problem, a doubt, is always individually conditioned. A child's doubt is not that of an adult, nor an unlettered man's that of a man of letters, nor a novice's that of an expert, nor an Italian's that of a German, nor an early nineteenth-century German's that of a German a hundred years before, nor even is that of an individual at one moment the same doubt as that which he formulates immediately after. For simplicity's sake we say that just the same question has been asked by many men in different times and places, but this is, as remarked, a simplification, an abstraction. In reality, every question differs from every other, and every definition, though its sound embodied in certain determinate words seems to be constant, in reality represents a difference, for the same seemingly identical material words really differ with the spiritual differences of those who pronounce them, individuals who ever find themselves in new and individual circumstances. "Virtue is the habit of moral actions" is a formula which has perhaps been uttered thousands of times, but if each time it has been meant seriously as the definition of virtue, it corresponds to a similar number of more or less diverse psychological situations and is really not one definition but many thousands.

Yes, it will be said, but through them all the concept always remains the same, just as a man who changes his clothes yet remains always the same man. But apart from the consideration that the man who changes his clothes does not remain quite the same, the relation between concept and definition is not the relation between man and clothes. A concept only exists by being thought and embodied in words, that is to say defined, and if the definitions vary the concept varies. True the definitions are themselves variants of the Concept, of that which has identity *par excellence*. They are the life of the concept, not of the representation. But the concept does not exist outside its own life, and the thinking of it is, each time, a phase of its life and never a final reckoning with it. The longest swim, the highest flight, cannot land you beyond water and air.

If we admit that every conceptual thought, every definition, is thus individually and historically conditioned (in these conditions lying the origin of the doubt, the problem, the question to which the definition furnishes an answer), we must go on to admit that the definition which holds the answer and affirms the concept, in doing so throws light upon the individual and historical conditions, the group of facts whence itself emerges. It throws light, that is to say it reveals the condition in its reality, takes it for a subject and caps it with a predicate, passes judgement upon it. And since fact is always individual, this which it frames is an individual judgement. In other words every definition is also an individual judgement. But that is precisely the hypothesis which we had advanced. What seemed a disputable assumption now proves true: namely that truth of reason distinguished from truth of fact, analytic distinguished from synthetic judgement, definitory distinguished from individual judgement, are abstractions. The logical act, the thought of the pure concept, stands alone, and in it definition is identical with individual judgement.

This theory undoubtedly disturbs the common manner of thinking (which for that matter is itself disturbed by implicit contradictions). But even common thought can be brought to familiarize itself with it by dwelling upon the phases which occur in our pronouncement of definitory judgements. Our definitions are always aimed against some adversary. They change with time and circumstances. Definitions which we gave at one stage of our mental development we no longer give at another, not because we judge them erroneous but because they have come to seem superficial or for some reason inopportune and inept. Such modifications and changes cannot but result from the continual operation of our judgement upon particular factual situations.

One may try to locate the acts of judgement either before or after each act of definition, but really they occur simultaneously, or, still more truly, we may say that they are coincidental and identical with them.

Suppose that someone attains to a conceptual truth, as, for example, some theory of art or morals. He will at once be aware that in forming those concepts he has come to know better not merely the realm of concepts but also the realm of things, and that a concept, as soon as it becomes clear, *ipso facto* clarifies those things from the medley and maelstrom of which itself springs. One who looks at heaven and forgets earth may be an astronomer but is certainly no philosopher, for in the act of thought, the world of ideas, heaven and earth are all one and a clear view of heaven brings clearness into the outlines of earth.

We have illustrated the identity of definition and individual judgement by what are commonly called negative, hypothetical, observational, inductive methods, but the result can also be confirmed "deductively". If conceptual thought is superior to pure representation, and a superior spiritual grade necessarily includes in itself the inferior, then in the concept there needs must be found, together with the conceptual element, also the representative element, so joined and fused that they can be distinguished only by an abstraction. And indeed the logical act is verbally expressed, is represented, is individuated. But if we cleave it asunder, not as a merely empirical distinction but as a supposedly real distinction, into concept and individual judgement, the result is two monsters, a concept which is not individuated and therefore lacks concrete existence, and a judgement void of thought, and therefore, as a judgement, non-existent.

Our distinction between definition and individual judgement was provisional, and equally provisional must be considered the partial justification which, on that basis, we allowed to propositions formally (logically) true and materially (individually or historically) false. The latter distinction may be currently useful for indicating certain types of error or mental habits as contrasted with others, but it is inadmissible in strict logic, for in every error of fact there is always some conceptual obscurity, and in every conceptual obscurity some obscurity in the judgement of fact. Similarly, in empirical usage, we may allow some validity to the notion that factual errors may arise through the use or misuse of pure concepts. But this can have no validity in logic, where the opposite notion must prevail that every deepening and refinement of concepts contributes to the better knowledge of facts. There is a current contrast drawn between Platonists who attend to the cult of ideas and Aristotelians whose cult is that of facts. But the Platonists, if they seriously attend to ideas, are Aristotelians, because they attend also to facts, and the Aristotelians, if serious, are conversely Platonists. The difference between them is indeed superficial. One is often amazed at the singular penetration and insight of "devotees of ideas" into factual situations, and at the deep philosophy manifested by "devotees of facts".

There is no need for pedantic condemnation of every phrase which uses the metaphor "application of concepts". Metaphors in themselves are harmless. But that metaphor, if taken for a doctrine, gives rise to a grave error in logical science, and against this it behoves us to insist that the concept is not applied to the intuition since never for an instant is it separate from this. And judgement is the immediate act of the spirit, is indeed the logical spirit itself.

It is advantageous to investigate the circumstances of the origin of the erroneous doctrine of the application of the concepts to the intuition. We shall discover forthwith that its origin cannot lie with the empirical concepts. The construction of an empirical concept is an inductive operation, a pronouncement that objects a, b, c, d, etc. belong to a determined class. The construction of the class and the classificatory judgement are really one and the same act though for convenience we have treated them in succession. The origin of the doctrine of application lies really with the abstract concepts, void of representative content, useless in themselves for the production of individual judgements, so that they can only be applied to individual judgements after these have, as previously described, been elaborated with the aid of the concept

of homogeneity into pseudo-judgements. Not merely the doctrine of application, but also the distinctions between analytic and
synthetic judgements, definitions and perceptions, truths rational
and factual, necessary and contingent, have their basis in the
abstract concepts, and here too is the origin of the theory of propositions which are formally true and materially false. (Thus –
two unicorns plus three unicorns makes five unicorns, is formally
true because two and three make five, but materially false because
unicorns do not exist.) Rational, necessary, a priori truths, analytic
judgements, and pure definitions would here be a proper description of numerals and their laws, while factual, contingent, a
posteriori truths, synthetic and individual judgements, would
describe the truths derived from experience. But if this is admissible in the realm of abstraction where veritable thought and truth
exercise no sway, in the realm of truth and thought, on the contrary, the terms of each series exist in the corresponding terms of
the other, and analysis apart from synthesis is equally unthinkable
with synthesis apart from analysis. In the same way, in the practical
spirit, intention and action may be empirically distinguished, but
pure intention apart from effective action is really not intention at
all, but nullity, just like action apart from and void from intention.
The theoretic spirit and the practical spirit, here once again, are in
perfect correspondency.

[1909]

VII

THE MYTH OF SENSATION

THE Philosophy of the Spirit now barely mentions the once much discussed and important "Sensation", supposed reaction of that which is within to a stimulus from without, primal act of the psychic life, celebrated for centuries and millenaries in the theories of philosophy. There is still, indeed, mention of motions of the soul, tendencies of dread or of desire or of aspiration, and so forth, and of intuitions which throw light upon them, form them into images and express them, and of judgements which discern and assess them, and of abstracting and generalizing processes which order and classify them, and of volitions and actions matured by this travail, and of the unfailing new crop of tendencies, desires, dreads, springing forth from the maturity of action, and of the closing and coincident reopening of the circle, spiritual life viewed as eternal circularity, unceasing development and enrichment of itself in itself. But of "sensation" there is no talk because it is found nowhere in the spiritual field.

How should that which formerly appeared poised at the threshold of the spirit now be found nowhere? For the simple reason that the spiritual act which it is meant to mark does not exist and therefore cannot be reached by thought and treated as reality. All that can be done is to investigate how that elusive and unknowable concept had its origin and lasted so long.

The search will gradually reveal that sensation has the character of a myth, a myth dependent upon and forming a necessary part of a greater myth, that of the dualism of spirit and nature, inner and outer, soul and body, and of the relations engaged between these.

Once these terms have been established and dualistically viewed as pairs of entities or things, it results that when they are brought into contact and launched on a life in common, their first meeting takes the aspect of a stimulus evoking a reaction. Nature, the body, the external, in giving the stimulus appear active, but as the object of the ensuing reaction are passive, while the spirit, the soul, that which is within, in receiving the stimulus are passive, but become active in facing up to it, altering their own dispositions in self-defence. In the oldest Greek philosophies the commerce between the two series is actually represented by effluxes from things which penetrate into the organs of the senses, little shapes detaching themselves from things and entering into the soul. This doctrine flourished on in the *species sensibiles* of the scholastics as also in such images of the poets of the *stil nuovo*, as the sprites issuing from the poetic person of the lady-love. But apart from these fanciful representations, the dualistic conception of stimulus and reaction, passive and active, body and soul lingers on in various degrees in all the philosophers, even in a Fichte when he struggles to interpret the Non-Self as a position of the Self, or in a Herbart when as a way of escape from dualism he invokes a concurrence of the soul with the other metaphysical "reals".[1] And like Aristotle, who sought to emphasize the spirituality of the intrinsically immaterial sensation by comparing it to wax which received the imprint of the seal without retaining any metallic ingredient,[2] so Hegel resorts to conceptually inadequate comparisons and images when he describes sensation as the awakening of the spirit out of "slumbering nature" and, again, as the form of the "dim agitation of the spirit in its individuality void of consciousness and intellection, whose content is limited and transitory because it belongs to natural and immediate Being".[3]

The history of the theory of sensation is tedious whether the same words be found repeated over and over again, or the same things in somewhat differing words. The myth attained to a maximum of pretension when Weber invested it with an air of scientific strictness, carried still further by Fechner. The law of Sensation, we were told, was "logarithmically progressive response to the stimulus" – one of the chief if not the chiefmost "discovery" of so-called Psychophysics, a branch of learning whose glories are

1. See VOLKMANN'S *Lehrbuch der Psychologie* (Cöthen, 1884), I, 218.
2. *De Anima*, II, 12, 494 a.
3. *Encyclopaedia*, paras. 399-400.

adequately indicated in the amorous combination of incompatibles in its name.

For all that, amid hesitations and contradictions one sometimes comes upon a confession that sensation has no reality at all. For example in the *Psychologie* of Münsterberg we read that its existence is not even a hypothesis capable of experimental verification or negation, but is a conceptual expedient ("ein Hülfsbegriff") without any corresponding object, but serving a logical need.[1] And in the *Vocabulaire de la Philosophie* of the French Philosophical Society it is thus described: "Un phénomène psychique, presque impossible à saisir dans sa pureté, mais dont on s'approche comme d'une limite : ce serait l'état brut et immédiat conditionné par une excitation physiologique susceptible de produire une modification consciente ; en d'autres termes ce qui resterait d'une perception actuelle, si l'on en retirait tout ce qu'y ajoutent la mémoire, l'habitude, l'entendement, la raison, et si l'on rétablissait tout ce que l'abstraction en écarte, notamment le ton affectif, l'aspect dynamogénique ou inhibitoire qu'elle présente"[2] But these half-admissions stopped short of a due acknowledgement that the concept of sensation is a myth, depending upon that other myth of external reality or nature or whatever term be used. We will not here explicitly trace the origin of that major myth, beyond recalling that it is to be found in the vice, common both to everyday thought and to philosophic theorization, of confounding the justified and appropriate exteriorization of living reality by the physico-mathematical sciences in their mechanical constructions, with the truth of poetry and thought.

A further proof of the unreality of sensation is that whenever some distinction or philosophic discourse takes its start from this, as soon as the argument gets into the sphere of effective reality it transpires that what was meant was not really sensation but something else, or several other things, presented under that name. Aristotle was the first among many to recognize in sensation a double aspect or element, theoretical and practical, cognitive and

---

1. HUGO MÜNSTERBERG, *Grundzüge der Psychologie* (Leipzig, 1900), p. 313.
2. Edited by Lalande (Paris, 1926), II, 755.

appetitive, or to point out that it includes imaginative and intellectual elements, memories and presentiments, and so on. In these observations sensation has been unwittingly ousted from the centre of attention, and the object under consideration is really the whole activity of the spirit in a compressed and pregnant form, or it may be in a confused, tangled, and defective form. Similarly when it appears that certain philosophic trends of undoubted importance in the history of thought (like so-called Sensism and Sensualism) have their origin or basis in the concept of sensation, a closer inspection shows that it was not this inexistent concept that was in question, but some truly existent form and force of the human spirit.

The logical structure of the "Sensist" doctrine does not essentially differ from that of the Intuitionists, Aesthetists, and the like, though emerging from a different historical milieu and bearing a different emphasis. The concept of sensation really only affords support to this school when what is meant by it is intuition, albeit a small and slight and unclear intuition, by contrast with the sensation of a single pure colour or a single pure sound or any other of those equally empty abstractions which are trotted out in books of psychology. Every concrete and real sensation is always a complete intuitive organism. When this is recognized, it is clear that the error into which the Sensists fell, and thereby merited philosophic confutation, was akin to that of the Intuitionists: they stop short at what they call sensation and pretend to deduce from this the further development of the act of knowing. But this, in truth, is not a repetition or dilation or refinement of the intuition but is the critical operation by which intuition is transfigured into the subject of a predicate, that is, into a judgement. And it is clear why Sensism was a beneficial current in the history of thought. Like Intuitionism it carried a protest against rationalism or intellectualism of a mathematical type, which, wholly absorbed in itself, desiccates reality, contorting it and evaporating it in its bloodless patterns. Sensism, like Intuitionism, was therefore not only efficacious in its negative task of rousing a stronger awareness of what thought and the criticism of thought are, but was also efficacious in the positive work of bringing out the then neglected and rejected virtue of sense, that is of intuition, and therewith of fancy, poetry, art, and the whole aesthetic world. "Aesthetic" is a word derived from "aisthesis", sense, and the definition given by its first formulator to this science was *Scientia cognitionis sensitivae*, while Vico ascribed to the poets "the sensitivity of the human race".

The "Sensualists", who in their various shades are theorists of the practical sphere, quite evidently are not concerned with sensation, that indefinable something, but, when they are hedonists, with pleasure, and when they are utilitarians, with utility. The two concepts really coincide, for the useful is pleasurable and conversely. Their error then and now is and will always be a failure or refusal to recognize, when considering the pleasurable and the useful, the reality and originality of the moral conscience, and how the will and action, surpassing utility and pleasure, encompass and regulate them towards new and higher ends. Much like that of Sensism in the theoretic sphere, Sensualism (or hedonism or utilitarianism) serves in the sphere of the Philosophy of Practice to withstand absurd ascetic teachings tending to suppress vitality and sensibility, in which moral life is necessarily rooted, and against the empty moralists who ask for nothing more than words and formulas.

In the history of philosophy, then, the concept of sensation evaporates as soon as it is handled, and unless in its place there is found an effective spiritual act, theoretic or practical, aesthetic or logical, what remains is simply the myth of which we have explained the origin.

[1942]

VIII

CHARACTER AND MEANING
OF THE NEW PHILOSOPHY OF THE SPIRIT

It might seem a toying with trifles, and in poor taste too, to discuss whether to symbolize the life of the spirit by a "pinnacle" or a "circle". Yet the question implies problems and solutions of much importance, errors and truths of great weight.

The image of the pinnacle suggests a grouping of the forms of the spirit like the foundations, the steps, the slopes which arise towards a summit; or, dropping metaphor, like a series of more or less incomplete forms, of progressively improving approximations, tending towards a final and perfect form in which there would be realized a full and unmixed satisfaction, the culminating beatitude.

An objection at once occurs against the concept of incomplete activities, and it is this. A form of activity can never in itself, in its inner being, be incomplete. If it were, it could rank neither as activity nor as form, for this rank involves positive function and autonomy. Incompleteness can never reside in a particular form or category. It can occur only phenomenologically in the process of a single act, theoretical or practical, in its effort to realize its own end, in the resulting struggle, in its partial retreat or backward tendency towards the ground from which it has pushed forward, a ground where it could not stand firm and where it cannot return for all the anguish and peril ahead. Incomplete it can be said to be only in reference to the next stage to be attained. To say that the aesthetic form is incomplete by the standard of logic, or (as has also been suggested) that logic is incomplete by the standard of aesthetics, or that the action directed towards utility is incomplete by the measure of morality, is meaningless. Meaningless also is the more specious variant which groups the spiritual activities as higher and lower, nobler and humbler. For given that all are necessary and fulfil a necessary function none is humbler and none higher than another. Higher and lower are terms which can be used reasonably in the quite different sense of an indication of the order of succession of forms which are all necessary and thus all equal.

And another objection occurs against the idea of a perfect and completely final form. For if every form finds its material in the preceding form, and in turn becomes itself the material of the succeeding form, then an absolute, perfect form would violate the law of the spirit. It would rise upon the material basis humbly constituted by the others, but would not proffer a similar service in its turn, marking by that failure the exhaustion and death of the spiritual process. If this completed form were taken for "supreme" and "definitive" truth, what sort of a truth would this be, which would not open the way to new action, new struggles, passions, pathos, nor initiate a new phase of human history, but would stand aside, cold, sterile, inert? If the completed form were taken for a practical issue, what sort of practicality would this be which was not energized by the travail of a search for self-knowledge and self-surpassing? Or if the completed form were, as in other prescriptions, a truth that was not logical and conceptual, but aesthetic and intuitional, what sort of an intuition would be one which did not prepare and require and call for concept and judgement, and what sort of an art would be one whose soil did not nourish the shoots of criticism? Finally, if the completed form were conceived as a mystical state, a melting into the ineffability of immediate contact with the divine, there must yet be some way of issue from this moltenness, this ineffability, for to linger too long in it would be idleness and tedium, such tedium as is distilled by the very idea of beatitude and paradise and the passive contemplation of God.

A third objection which occurs is that the attainment of the perfect and absolute form, after all others had been assayed and found wanting, would constitute a liberation from the world which is made up of those forms and of the life which they breathe. Now life is certainly a continuous self-liberation from the travail of the passions, a continuous purification and catharsis. This conception found its first formulation in aesthetic theory, but is no less true of every form of spiritual activity, since activity means precisely liberation from, rejection of, passivity. It is this that brings the full joy which is known in the accomplishment of work of any kind, in the making of beauty or the thinking of truth, the production of new economic wealth or of new moral wealth, in love which brings new buds to life or in sacrifice of life for an idea or for the creation of immortal life. But this liberation, which is a vital act, nay *the* vital act, cannot be a liberation *from* life, by way of a leap into the transcendent such as it is easy to proclaim with empty words, but impossible for thought to execute – thought which is entirely a thinking in the terms of life and the world. True it is that ever and anon one cannot but pine and sigh for such a transcendent liberation, but that is human weakness, comprehensible to thought as a psychic event of hedonistic character, but not to be taken into account as a logical event.

Let us add this objection from the side of history. (For the idea of the spirit and its forms should not be considered solely as the articulation of reality in the logic of development, but as being the foundation, indeed the very existence, of that logic by the light of which all reality and all history have to be interpreted, and as thus being itself an "ideal eternal history".) Ideal eternal history, as it has been called, has but to be affirmed, and therewith every notion of an effective history beginning at a point in time and running on to a "culmination" or an "end in time", that is to a definite and completed triumph crowning a series of conations, is rejected and confuted. In reality history has no beginning and no end. We are in history and we are ourselves history – history with its eternal categories, its dialectical process, its returns of grief and joy. History is the drama which is not subject to time but devises and utilizes time for its own requirements, as a map plotted to indicate the way through the pressing flood of reality, that is, our own unceasing activity. This means that we must not wait upon the future or upon another life for our meeting with the eternal, the infinite, but effect it in the present, as is alone possible. At every instant it is open to us to be worthy to ascend to heaven.

And yet the vision of the spirit and of history as of a climb

to a pinnacle, or ultimate peak of perfection, was accepted and
worked up in the major philosophic systems of the nineteenth
century, not only in those styling themselves idealist or spiritualist,
but also in some which boasted of being materialistic. It may
suffice to recall how in the greatest of all, the Hegelian system, the
Idea issues forth from itself and becomes nature, in order to provide
a first rung or series of rungs by which to climb through the
realms of nature and thus to attain the rung, or to climb the series
of rungs of the life of the spirit and finally to possess itself in fully
deployed consciousness. From the lowest and almost animal rung
of the sentient soul ascent is made to consciousness, perception,
intellect, appetite, cognitive and general self-consciousness, and so
to the wholeness of the theoretical spirit, intuition and thought
leading on to the further ascent of the practical spirit by way of
sentiment, impulse, wilful choice, happiness, and liberty, which is
the completion of the stage of subjectivity. But then comes the
ascent of and by subjectivity itself which realizes itself as objectivity, practice, by way of law, morality, the State, the history of
the world. Yet this too is not yet the apex, but a grade or ledge of
a pyramid having its pinnacle in the absolute spirit, the sphere of
religion. But inside the pinnacle are more steps: art, or incomplete
religiosity, revealed religion, also incomplete, and it is only with
the attainment of finally perfected religiosity that the spirit wins
its peace in Philosophy, where the owl of Minerva, the fully-
understanding Mind, takes its flight above a world now fully
created and therefore to be created no more. It is in correspondence
with this scheme that Hegel develops the history of art, of revealed
religion, and of philosophy, and in the history of philosophy
places the categories of logic as philosophical moments or epochs.
And there is an analogous development of objective or practical
history, or the history of the State, in which the idea takes shape
as liberty and passes through the three epochs or three worlds, the
oriental, in which only One is free, the Graeco-Roman, in which
a Number are free, and the Germanic world in which All are
free, and strife is placated or on the way to placation.

For the building of this historic-philosophic machine, in all its vastness and complexity, Hegel needed an instrument, and he unfortunately forged it by mishandling the great truth which he had established in the world of thought, that is the speculative or dialectical logic, thereby compromising that truth itself, though not, of course, silencing it, for, once uttered, a truth cannot be silenced. The instrument in question was his arrangement of the forms of the spirit as dialectical opposites, each and every one being regarded as unstable in its unilaterality and abstractness, and revealing a corresponding weakness, save only the last, the Idea, the concrete fulfilment. The stuff of this scheme Hegel found in the historical and scientific literature of his time, many parts of which, especially the historical writings, he penetrated with his profound historical acumen, but satisfied himself in regard to other parts, and to the entire field viewed as a whole, with a triadic patterning which bore the appearance but lacked the reality of deep speculation.

In this philosophic and historical construction Hegel figured grandiosely as the last heir of those historical-cosmical visions of the Orient, which exercised their influence in the last phases of Greek philosophy, and then flowed into the cleansing stream of Christianity, to be cherished and further elaborated by the early fathers, the scholastics, and the mediaeval historians. Hegel's *Encyclopaedia*, for all its wealth of original and true thought, displays a basic outline which was already traceable in such a work as the *Itinerarium mentis in Deum* of Bonaventura of Bagnorea, which describes the ascent from animality and sensuality to the spirit and from the spirit to the mind, God being present in all the stages but in the first showing himself only in hints, in the second in reflections and enigmas, and in the third alone fully revealed. The same outline underlies Dante's Divine Comedy (or drama with a happy ending). Only Dante's genius hides it beneath the potency of his poetic inspiration. Religious mythology is, in the Hegelian system, transported into philosophy and into secular historical interpretation, as, for example, in the trisection of Christian-Germanic (that is, mediaeval and modern) history into the reigns of the Father, Son, and Holy Ghost, corresponding respectively to the confused, tumultuous epoch of the Germanic invasions, the epoch of the struggles between Church and State, and the epoch of the Protestant Reformation. (There is here an echo of the "Eternal Gospel" of Joachim da Fiore, never quite forgotten by the Protestants.) To sum up, these depictions of the life of the spirit as an ascent to a pinnacle stand for or reveal clinging survivals of theological or theosophical conceptions in modern philosophy.

Such artificial and even monstrous elaborations fall down and can be swept away with the substitution for the image of the "pinnacle" of that of the "circle". For with the latter, each of the spiritual forms regains that positivity, self-sufficiency, *perfectio*, which it could not have in a conception which viewed each single form as a halting place, at different stages of the ascent, save only that final culmination, so that the initiation and progress of the spiritual process could be viewed only as a climbing through successive imperfections. In the circular conception the process is placed in the relation of each form to every other, conformably to its own nature which determines its office and its situation in the circle. Poetry is poetry in as much as it is neither logicality nor practical action, and the poetry is pure in proportion to its freedom from the attitudes of those other forms. Such being its quality and its office, it is antecedent to logic, to thought, just as this is in turn antecedent to practice, to action; and it cannot be shifted from this location to another. Logical judgement presupposes the antecedent work of intuition in forming the subject which is to be promoted as predicate: it cannot therefore make its appearance save when furnished with its premiss and its material, which is poetry, and this it cannot generate of itself.

Each form, then, has its own function, and its own place in the order of succession, and each is in turn the form of a precedent material and the material of a succeeding form. It follows that none is, in an absolute sense, first or last. The use in such a connexion of words like first, second, third, last, must be understood as a mere didactic convenience. The circle revolves for ever on itself, and to say that it has recommenced its gyration by regaining the "first" point is a conventional, not a real pronouncement. All

controversies and competitions concerning the rank of one form
compared with another (claims that the active is higher than the
contemplative, the aesthetic higher than the logical, the useful
higher than the moral, and so forth) prove to be quite vain. Each
has need of every other, and all of each. Secondly, it proves to be
a meaningless problem to seek to merge the single forms in a unity.
The problem grew out of a supposition that one of the forms
must be that which unified all, so it was sought to determine which.
Did this primacy belong, it was asked, to the logos, the ethos, the
fancy, or what? But the problem was an empty one, for the unity
lies nowhere else than in the distinction of the forms one from
another in their distinct qualities and functions. And thirdly, since
the circle leaves no room for a "higher world" (or super-circle),
suited to meet the customary hankering for a breach of circular
continuity and for an evasion from the circular law, it is herewith
recognized to be impossible to free onself from life and life's duty
of passing eternally from form to form, from activity to activity.
Yes, one may protest against this and sigh for the impossible, but
even this psychic behaviour is, in the final analysis, an act of life,
of life at its weakest, an expedient, in default of any other, for
alleviating the torment. And the last achievement of the circular
conception of the spirit which we will point out is this: it leaves
no place for so-called universal history. This last, as soon as it
seeks to be more than a *chronica mundi*, and to take organic shape,
must inevitably offer a "philosophy of history", that is a transcendent and of course arbitrary unification of all history from
the creation to the dissolution of the world. Now in the circular
conception all history is particular history, and is universal only
in as much as the universal resides in the particular and nowhere
else. Man, in his individuality, needs individuated history and
historical knowledge, not a pretentious universal history which is
really only a pale, vague ghost of something unreal and imaginary.

The image of the spirit and of history visualized as a climb to
a pinnacle is reflected in almost the whole of the output of that
idealistic and spiritualistic philosophy which was still enveloped in
more or less theological conceptions. By contrast, the circular

vision is reflected, in the field of philosophy, by only one conspicuous but very complex and circuitous thinker, Vico, remembered chiefly for his theory of "courses and recourses". But, if this is remembered, it is seldom understood in all its depth. Only recently has it been remarked that Vico's theory, unlike the theories of the ancient political writers on the different forms of the State and on the order of succession in which they occur, arises not from a superficial sociological classification, but from an original and profound inspection of the forms of the spirit, and that it provides a canon of interpretation for the facts of history, serving, incidentally, to correct what is exaggerated and over-simplified in Vico's own essays in historical interpretation. Modern enquiry has, however, lighted upon a limitation and a lacuna in the thought of that philosopher who himself somewhat confusedly felt that this thought was highly original and important, but could not discern just where the novelty and the originality lay. The truth is that Vico's circular conception of the spirit and of history found no room for the concept of "progress" which precisely in his own age attained to such popularity and roused so much faith and such great hopes in the world. This limitation in Vico may be assigned to his own psychological condition, and we will not go into that question. But the lacuna was such that it needed not to be made good by the introduction of additional concepts for it sufficed, as a remedy, to see clearly into the logic of the circle; according to which, and in which, each form in each of its moments has before itself and in itself all the work of the spirit concerning the problem which engages it, and therefore its fresh work is not simply other than what preceded it, but richer, and so progressive. A new technical discovery is in its form just what technical discoveries have always been, but concretely it contains in itself the former discoveries, and, in addition, what is new.

A new philosophical concept receives the concepts of the past into itself, modifying and enriching them. A new poetry of genius, – uttered, let us say, in our own time – though formally it only rivals that of Homer, and does not surpass it, nevertheless surpasses it by enshrining in images and words the experience of post-

Homeric humanity. No need, then, to reject or to upset Vico's circular theory. Enough to explore it more thoroughly in this part, and in the others to persevere in the never-ending task of enriching the concepts of the single forms by noting the incessant and ever fresh problems which come to birth in their train.

The importance which was felt to pertain to Vico's vision of the spirit and of history found no clear formulation either among those whom this repelled or among those whom it attracted. But the former, if they failed fully to assess the revolutionary force concealed in his enunciation, as the guiding principle of his theory of knowledge, of "the conversion of truth and fact", at any rate perceived that this theory was dangerously contrary to the teachings of the Church: indeed, not only did it clash with the Holy Scriptures and the views of the Fathers, but its pattern of "courses and recourses" went against the whole Christian conception of history as a triumphal progress from the creation of the world to the redemption and the unending life of the Church.

Those favourably disposed to Vico, on the other hand, failed to see the full implications of his thought: how by attributing an energetic and productive character to those forms which were considered unlogical and irrational (fancy, myth, right of the strong and the strength of the right), and by tracing a "course" of human history in its passage from those forms to the forms of pure mind and morality, followed by a "recourse" or refreshing and rejuvenating return to the earlier forms, it opened the way to a fully immanentist view of reality. And this Vico himself would perhaps have denied with a shudder. It is not the materialists, positivists, sceptics, pessimists, and similar negators, with their much ado about nothing, who have entered upon the way opened by Vico, but the painstaking and subtle investigators into the folds and the recesses of the human mind, where from time to time may be found keys to unlock the doors of the seeming mysteries through which men stray into the inviting but flimsy purlieus of the transcendent.

[1945]

IX

ON THE SURVIVALS
OF THEOLOGIZING PHILOSOPHY

I

PROBLEMS WHICH DO AND PROBLEMS WHICH DO NOT ARISE

In philosophical enquiry, the principle that the problem is one with its solution should never be forgotten, which is to say that a problem wins its character as a problem only with its solution. Common sense says much the same when it remarks that a problem well defined is as good as solved, or that well begun is in this case more than half done.

Indeed, how could a problem be formulated without being in the same act resolved? To formulate a problem is to define its terms, and this implies simultaneously defining the relation of the terms to each other and to the whole. Without this, the terms would be left vague and uncertain, and so would the problem, which would not, accordingly, be formulated. But to define the terms and their relation amounts to solving the problem: for after this what more would remain to be done? What was the problem set for if not to get these made clear?

What happens on the hither side of a solution is not a formulation, a precise interrogation, but at the most only a dim stirring, a sense of discomfort, a pain, the well recognized symptom of the growth and ripening of a problem which life is now ready to present to thought. It pertains to the human condition to know this sort of travail, painful not for the difficulty of finding an answer to a question, but for the effort needed in dragging to the light a question together with its answer. The question has not yet or not fully been framed, it is not so much expressed as implicit in the unexpressed, stammering for defect of expressive power. Yet under the hard soil, as yet barely cracking, there presses a thought which will end by coming to the light. For the moment one glimpses its outline only to lose it again. This happens to the scientist as he ponders, and, no differently, to the poet or, for that matter, the man of action, who feels a grip on his practical problem only at the moment of tackling it, while the vague urge which as yet stops short of action is for him not a labour or a problem but a discomfort perhaps signalling the imminence of a problem, but meanwhile holding him up in an inertia which he strives to overcome.

But this simple truth, concurred in by philosophy and everyday experience or common sense, comes up against everyone's awareness of problems said to have been set but not solved, or formulated at one time and solved only a long time after. As there is no possible logical confutation of what we said before, it must be that those which we have just spoken of are not, in fact, problems, but merely alleged or nominal problems. We all know poems which rebel against the law of beauty, of poetry, which means not that the law is invalid but that the alleged poems are not poems. This is a similar case.

In the case of "poems" which are not really poems we feel obliged to designate them as something else which they really are, and now we have a similar obligation to clear up the nature of these alleged "problems", and how they arise. What they are is quickly said: they are aggregates of representations, purporting to be concepts, or amalgamations of representation and concept, which can be and are expressed in words, but in words void of logical meaning, or meaningless empty sounds, or words of merely sentimental and fanciful significance. Nor is it hard to say how these alleged problems arise. They arise from the assumption that certain words and certain representations are concepts, and have the character of hypothesized or hypothetic problems, in which there is an implicit "if" which it is always possible to render explicit.

Let us take an example at random, the problem whether the soul is mortal or immortal, a good case of a problem which seems to be real and also insoluble, or needing a long time for solution. What remained indeterminate in this problem was the meaning of "soul", of "mortal", and of "immortal".

The soul was not thought out as a pure concept but represented as a thing, or better as a breath, a pneuma. And "immortal" was far from being thought out as a concept, since it was distinguished from and counterposed to "mortal", whereas these terms, which it was improper to sunder, are really a single concept, it being impossible to conceive life without death or death without life. Was this, then, a problem? Yes, on the assumption that those terms had a meaning. But once caught up in assumptions and conditionals there is no way forward. The problem was itself hypothetic, alleged, and ineffectual, and that was why it seemed divorced from its solution, which either failed to turn up, or, if it turned up, fell short of expectations.

Take another example, a particularly frivolous enquiry picked at random in the field of erudite argument. "Was Gemma Donati a good wife to Dante Alighieri?" The more prudent Dantists, though they think this an important problem, despair of solving it. Many have pored over it, their foreheads wrinkled (though not with thought). Suppose now that we could produce some intimate correspondence between Dante and Gemma, or Dante and a close friend. Then, indeed, out of the study of that correspondence there would suddenly arise a problem of knowledge of the relations between Dante and his wife. But since we have no such correspondence, and no other documents to take its place, the question is meaningless, or rather would have a meaning *if* we possessed the documents needed to solve it. Its meaning is therefore hypothetical, not concrete and actual, and the question being insoluble is not a question but an alleged question.

Towards such false problems there are three possible attitudes known to experience. First, one may turn them over and over again, always vainly, excogitating mutually destructive and ever unsatisfying solutions. Thus philosophers and schoolmen have for centuries turned over the problem of the soul, and others of a likeness. The less content such problems have the more majestic and sublime do they seem, and they are dubbed the "ultimate", "fundamental", or "eternal" problems. It availed little that Emmanuel Kant collected a number of them from the hands of his philosophic predecessors and contemporaries and threw them aside in a bundle as insoluble and absurd questions. They sprouted up again in similar or different form, and are the great pasture of philosophical careerists, composers of theses for a doctorate, or for an academic competition, or a review article or a lecture: people who would have nothing to do if they could not settle down to the "eternal problems" which derive so much substance and importance from themselves (for anyone's means of subsistence are substantial and important, even unsubstantial problems). Men of pure learning have their own set of "eternal problems", unchanging or changing little, on which floods of ink are expended, and likewise those inactive men of action who for ever pore over the "great questions" (the "social question", the question of "alliance between the peoples", "feminist question", "question of perpetual peace", and so on) which get in the way of practical business, encourage idleness, but at the same time give it a spice of excitement, making it seem almost like work.

The second attitude consists in furnishing a solution to the problems of the only sort that can be devised in view of the way in which they arise, namely an imaginative solution. Thus we are offered, in philosophy, a rapid succession of "metaphysics" and "systems", well groomed and admirably coherent, but with a coherence that is not logical, not critical. In pure learning we get brilliant and lucid explanations which lack nothing except supporting evidence. In the world of affairs we get proposals, schemes, utopias, whose only defect is that they cannot be and are not put into effect. Around all these rages the hottest controversy waged in the fields of non-thought and non-action, of merely passional faith, of excited partisanship for attractive combinations of words and images. For here there is no possibility of reaching an understanding with the opponent, or at any rate a mutual respect, as there is in the domain of criticism and labour where the debate concerns true problems of effective thought and action. In this latter debate all the participants are at the same time confident and doubtful, courageous and aware of the difficulties, and thus the genuine thinker, while perhaps feeling a certain contempt for wordy and fanatical associates and followers, feels on the contrary a high esteem for those who think on different and conflicting lines, for in his heart of hearts he knows that the difference and conflict is serious, rooted in the nature of the problems, and thus the contestants are making by various routes for a new and broader way. Thus too the man of action despises the horde of followers whom he must needs gather in his wake, but admires his eminent rival, and would sometimes gladly have a heart to heart talk with him, feeling sure they would find much to agree about, including perhaps their duty to go on disagreeing about much else.

The third and last attitude which may be and very often is adopted in face of the sham problems is what is called scepticism or agnosticism. This attitude is not a frank recognition that the problems in question do not arise. It is on the contrary an obstinate reaffirmation that they do arise, coupled with the conclusion that nevertheless they are insoluble, whether, as it sometimes seems, for the general reason of the limitations of the human mind, or, as is at other times held, for the particular reason that intellects capable of resolving them are not at the moment available. So agnosticism may be absolute, proclaiming frontiers wholly impassable by humankind, or it may be relative, waiting upon the emergence of a great man, revealer, redeemer, and the coming of a more fortunate age. Thus an exemption from the hard work of subjecting the insoluble problem to critical enquiry is purchased at the cost of decrying man's thought and will, as though these forces of humanity and reality were all too fragile instruments, or at the cost of humiliating one's own manhood by throwing the task upon "him who is to to come". (If he does come, he will himself be no more than a man.)

What the quite different attitude of the thinker is, towards those insoluble problems, we have already hinted at in stressing the obligation to criticize the problems themselves. This means discovering how and why these vain gropings, unreal as problems but real as a cross between imagination and thought, a medley of will and whim, do arise at all. Until this discovery is made, in the ripeness of time, critical minds and severely disciplined intellects hold aloof from them. Not being personally stirred by them, they feel no need to take them into account, or indeed they carry their disinterest to the point of accepting some imaginary solution in the same spirit as an artist or scientist who for the time being accepts any form of government, any trend of affairs, if only he be left free to follow his heart's devices and to fulfil his own personal mission. But as they proceed with their critical and critically constructive task there comes a moment when, turning their attention to some insoluble problems previously left to the labours of others (whose conclusions they had themselves perhaps accepted as a matter of routine), of a sudden they rapidly break down their pretended character as problems rectify the terms, and in the place of the unreal and insoluble problems thus construct problems which are real and soluble, and by their emergence explain what was the origin of those others, since *verum index sui et falsi*.

II

A PROBLEM WHICH DOES NOT ARISE:
THE KNOWABLENESS OF REALITY

A notable case of a problem which does not arise is that of the knowableness of the real, the relation between "thought" and "being", that is the problem whether thought does or does not apprehend being, and how, and how much. In this problem "being" and "thought" are terms which have not really been thought out, thus remaining vague and uncertain. And the history of philosophy shows that what has been described above as happening in general where problems are misconceived and therefore insoluble, has happened in this case.

It is needless, in so familiar a matter, to quote names of books and philosophers to show that this problem often found an issue in scepticism and agnosticism. Sometimes, on the plea of present ignorance, it was hoped that the future progress of philosophic study would produce some light. Sometimes human ignorance was taken to be quite invincible, and it was trusted that in a future life we should get some answer to our curious questioning whether the thoughts of this life are reality or dream, or in what measure compounded of both. Or there was desolate weeping, or bitterly mocking laughter, at the idea that truth could never be known here or hereafter. Everyone knows how the question has been dragged and is still dragged from one hypothesis to another, through endless and fruitless arguments. We will here simply point to some attempts at a positive solution, for no other purpose than to indicate how such solutions have always been imaginative, not logical, mythical, not speculative.

The two terms Thought and Being were ranged opposite each other and treated as two entities or two things, and thence sprang the question whether one fitted in with the other, and of what kind and degree might be their agreement and disagreement. But as neither of these things "Thought" and "Being" offered a measure for comparing them together, there was nothing for it but to hunt out a third thing, a third entity, and this hunt was pushed into the domain of sheer imagination, myth-building. It matters little what various shapes the mythology assumed; displaying, in one example, a God who had arranged thought and being in such wise that to the former the latter was always transparent, and even the divine Creator was transparent to it too; in another example God and the world known to thought only partially, or known through a veil; or in another example, taking the place of God as third term, Matter, it being said that thought and being were forms of matter, one as material as the other (this Matter was itself really conceived as a God). Then there was the mythology of the Logos, the Absolute Thought which creates the world of being imprinting its own forms in this, and then above it raises the spirit, humanity, which knows the world of being because it finds in it, as in itself, the forms of the Logos which produced spirit and nature, and thus rejoins the Logos, the absolute Thought.

All these shapes, some crude and some refined, are equally mythological, and their significance is always in the provision of a *Deus ex machina* transcending the reality which needs to be explained, and offering in lieu of an explanation a fable or Platonic "myth".

Being mythological and therefore transcendental, these conceptions are religious, and in this lies the reason of the great and passionate interest which at all times they have aroused. The terms of the problem precluded a pursuit of it on immanentist lines, and opened the doors to the transcendent, the Hegelian Logos being actually identified by an important branch of that school with the personal God. With the presentation of Being and Thought as two things, two finites, there had inevitably to be introduced an infinite, an infinite *thing*, an Ens, a God. And the discussion wandered off into particular modes of conceiving or rather of imagining God. It no longer sounds paradoxical to say that the materialists were themselves theologians of a particularly narrow, fanatical, and rabid sort.

But while this insoluble problem was being debated on the stage among philosophers, and appeared to the philosophic herd to be philosophy's prime business, other thinkers in the back room (or may be the same thinkers, even though they lacked resolution to cut loose wholly from the insoluble argument on the front stage) were proposing and solving properly formulated and precise problems. They were enquiring by what methods the mind constructs natural science, mathematics, and geometry, how it produces poetry and art, what are the laws which hold sway in practical and moral life, what is the scope of the speculative urge as it sweeps forward beyond the range of usefulness of the positive sciences, and what are ideas and philosophic concepts as distinguished from natural and mathematical concepts, and so on. Enquiries of this sort, not unfamiliar to antiquity and the Middle Ages, have been the particular glory of modern thought since Descartes, Vico, and Leibniz. One who has looked deeply into them so as for their sake to forget the great problem of the world and of God, of thought and being, neglecting metaphysics (he will be told) for psychology and the theory of knowledge, will find with astonishment on returning to contemplate the obsessive problem upon which he had turned his back that it dissolves beneath his gaze, as in the poem of Keats the ghost of the lady dissolves under the keen gaze of the Sophist.

The exploring mind, well versed in the forms of the human spirit, will never in its long researches have encountered things or entities, accompanied by thoughts to mirror their shapes more or less faithfully. The thinker will on the contrary only have encountered forms of activity, forms of doing, and among these forms of doing forms of "knowing" which he will have discovered to be itself a "doing" not less real than any other. Never anywhere has he found ready-made objects, but only objects in course of becoming, that is of making themselves, by dint of willing and thinking, so that these "objects" are really "subjects", or rather they are a unique Subject of which the objects or single subjects are but its own abstracted aspects. He has heard talk of the Ideals which shine down upon men requiring their reverence and obedience, only to discover that those ideals were simply the reality and necessity of human life and work. And of an Art which men brought into being by imitating nature or ideal models of beauty: and this art turned out to be a creation drawn forth by man himself out of his own being. And of a Space and Time enframing reality, which space and time he found to be constructions of the human spirit, along with number and geometric form. And of the unchanging Laws of Nature, discovered now to be laws promulgated and imposed by man himself in his invention of nature. And of the eternal Ideas contemplated by philosophy, only to find that these are metaphors for the categories or forms in which the human spirit expends and regathers itself eternally.

His mind being thus strengthened by new discipline and equipped with the results of critical judgement which accordingly rank for him as unfailing convictions, how can this question whether "thought" reflects "being", and in what manner and measure, have any meaning for him? He now no longer sees before him these two things, thought and being, but only recognizes within himself forms of doing, forms of creating. The question whether one of these mirrors or copies or imitates the other, sounds to him as though born and spoken in ignorance. For that which is merely mirrored, copied, and imitated would be an action that was not active, a nonsense.

But it will not be enough to thus deny the old and absurd and insoluble problem. His widened experience permits him to discern how that problem was born in the past and how it is perpetually reborn in the lower reaches of mental development. It is born and reborn because among the forms of spiritual doing there is included what is called the abstracting form which has its own duty and performs due services. The abstracting form, cutting out the product from its unity with the producer, and fashioning it, for its own purposes, into an entity, induces unwary minds to believe that the resulting fiction has a more than fictional existence, as though one could treat characters on the stage as real and build up relations with them off the stage. The critic, however, will not regard these proceedings of the unwary as useless, for without such mistaken strivings there would be no stimulus to the search for new truth, and the critical mind itself, in coping with them, adds new truths to its store.

III

THE PROBLEM OF BEING AND KNOWING IN ITS OVERLAPPING
WITH THE PROBLEM OF THE UNITY OF THE SPIRIT

Although the problem of the knowableness of reality and of the relations between being and thought is to be regarded as antiquated (despite which it is and will be still amply debated), it yet deserves attention from another angle, inasmuch as its mode of presentation, with the mythological solutions which we have described, has a lingering impact upon another and much more effective problem, that of the unity of the spirit or the unity of the real.

The distinction of the various forms of the spirit, that great labour of modern philosophy which has brought such important advances in the conception and judgement of life and history, sprang from a new concept of unity, a concept which was variously described as "synthesis", "relation", and "dialectic", but under each and all of these names it combats the old concept of an immobile, indifferent, unrelated unity. Hegel made this new concept of unity coincide with the concept of a lively and active opposition, mediating itself in such wise that for him concrete unity and opposition were mutually definitory terms. A more careful enquiry, necessitated by the obvious artificiality and mistakenness of the conclusions to which this method led Hegel and his school in their philosophic teachings, has arrived not at a rejection of the concept of opposition, but at a deeper inspection of it, revealing how the Hegelians confounded with it that of distinction, and in their attention to opposition overlooked distinction. But distinction is not only unsusceptible of resolution into opposition, but is the true foundation from which distinction can arise, the condition or spring which originates opposition, explains the life of reality, and confirms its dialectic unity.

To define concrete unity as distinction (concrete and, in Hegel's phrasing, "restless" distinction which is entirely at one with the unitary process) is to exclude entirely the conception of distinction as a multiplicity of which the terms stand outside each other and transcend each other. For each term of the distinction, each form of the spirit, we may describe as conditioning and conditioned by every other. Each element is at the same time a resultant. Therefore the spiritual forms for which Hegel devised the triangular or triadic symbol of thesis, antithesis, and synthesis, of affirmation, negation, and mediation, of positive abstract, negative abstract, and positive concrete (two abstracts facing a concrete which, coming last, is also in truth first), are here instead symbolized by the circle, the geometrical figure richest in geometrical irrationality. (The "squaring of the circle" has long been a proverbially discredited operation. In our image this "square" or figure of lineal geometry would stand for a merely intellectualistic logic.)

Now concrete distinction, being all one with concrete unity, in no wise partakes of unrelated multiplicity. The generation of abstract distinction, that unrelated multiplicity in which indeed each term stands outside every other and all are bound together abstractly by their homogeneity (the proceeding known in formalistic logic and in the logic of the natural sciences as classification) can only be explained as a process issuing forth from the concrete distinction. Classification is nothing else but the projection into space (and consequent falsification) of the unity-distinction, the restless process of the spirit. In this projection one term comes to stand forth from among the terms and to this the other terms become subordinated, unable, however, to link up with each other, and placed in a mere immobile juxtaposition.

This classification, this distinction rendered static instead of speculative and dialectical, has often been felt to carry a sort of memory and yearning directed towards something else. Hence sprang a singular attempt to correct its immobility, unrelatedness, abstractness, by a transference from space into time, a conversion of natural concepts into chronological epochs. The attempt took shape in some parts of the philosophy of Schelling, was very notable in Hegel, and was variously elaborated by the Positivists with their erection of the categories of formalistic and (natural) scientific logic into "epochs" of the history of philosophy, and of psychological classes into "epochs" of human history.

This transference from space into time has almost the air of a symbolic ceremony in honour of the unknown God, foreshadowing a real act which is yearned for and dimly divined, not realized and effectuated. The effectuation, in truth, cannot be achieved by a transference from an external to an external, but only by drawing the external or abstract back into the internal or concrete from which it takes its origin or, as we may say, by drawing chronological time back into ideal time, the mythological history of the spirit into the ideal eternal history which Vico dimly saw to be the law of the spirit.

This ideal eternal history, this distinction which is itself the process of unity, and itself is concrete unity, has no need for any external agency to buttress the unitary compactness which is its own internal character. To the thinking mind it can never take on an appearance of unity extraneous to variety or of variety extraneous to unity. But minds running on the track of outworn Metaphysic, familiar with those antiquated solutions of the problem of being and knowing which we have called metaphysical (and which as we have seen all need the buttress of a transcendent unity), are not so easily satisfied with the simple truth expounded here.

Devoured by a frenzy of unificatory zeal, they fail to recognize in
the forms of the spirit the real unity which is nothing else but
their own active distinction, and misreading the terms of the one
relation as a multiplicity, they espy dualisms and rush forward
to surmount an obstacle that has already been left behind, to
unify that which already has all the unity it needs and asks no
more.

The mind thus bewitched by the old metaphysical reasoning,
in its zealous striving to possess what one Italian philosopher,
Spaventa, actually invoked as a "brain above brain", runs perforce
into one of two blind alleys, the first being, so to speak, a hunt for
unity on the hither side of the process of distinction, and the
second a hunt on the yonder side. In the first one, the forms of the
spirit have the appearance of being generated by a single principle,
it matters little what one, whether, for example, by one of the
forms themselves (logical thought, will, fancy, and so forth) elevated to be the generator of the others, whose appearance of
distinction from it is then said to be merely empirical, or else some
new and hermaphroditic form, like the Hegelian Idea, union of
cognition and volition, which is called in to perform the duty and
is able to recognize an effective distinction in the particular forms
solely because such a distinction is already implicit in its own confusion. The error here lies not in the particular choice of the unitary
principle introduced, but in the introduction of any principle on
a footing of superiority to the real process, in which position its
affinity with the Transcendent God and the Unmoved Mover is
plainly apparent.

In the second blind alley unity is sought and found in an indistinction of the forms, an indistinction out of which it is supposed
that the process of distinction develops by way of abstraction and
transcendence, whereas the indistinction is really nothing else
than the process of distinction when it is not known to thought,
but merely vitally experienced in an immediacy which is itself, at
bottom, an abstraction: for concretely there is no immediacy
which does not mediate itself in action, in fancy, in thought.

This effort, then, pursued along the first blind alley, leads to metaphysic and mythologism, and if refuge be then sought in the second blind alley, one is back in the arms of mysticism.

What critical urge, that is to say what need for a better judgement and understanding of life and history, inspired the effort? It is hard to see, and in fact the answer is, none at all. And if indeed we agreed to bring in mysticism as a corrector and integrator, all critical or historical problems would therewith be reduced to mere appearance, thought-spinning, arbitrariness by the measure of mystical feeling. Or, making the other choice, we would have a mythological or allegorical explanation of reality, ineffectual as regards individual problems and judgements unless to rename them in sacred and solemn terminology. In either case when judging the way of the world, science, morality, art, or any other human concernment, one would go on employing the concepts which the critique of the spiritual forms offers in progressive refinement, even should one want to mount the high chair of myth and mysticism to declare that such profane distinctions merit no more than toleration.

11 7 / 63

In fact it is no historical or critical urge that foments this zealous hunt for unity, but the incessant religious urge for an escape, a beatification, a pacification in a mythical image or mystical sensation of God. No irreverence is here intended towards this urge which has and will always have its place as a moment in the dialectic of the spirit. But whoever holds firm to the recognition of life itself as the sole divinity, contents himself with the unity which this offers to him, the "restless" unity which is all one with variety, and he resigns himself uncomplainingly to the impossibility of an appeasement, knowing that to sink to rest – even in the bosom of God – is contrary to life.

[1918]

X

PHILOSOPHY AND NON-PHILOSOPHY

WHAT is the problem of Philosophy? There can be only one brief and substantial answer to this question. It is the same as the problem of the religions: the knowledge of the good and its struggle against evil; and of salvation. Or, in the past and present language of the religions, the struggle of light against darkness, God against the devil, the spirit against the flesh; redemption from sin. There is no difference, then, in the essence of the problems. Philosophy can never without self-contradiction deny God, the spirit, immortality. But it is bound to think out these terms in a conceptual purity which forbids the helping-out and adulteration of thought by the imagination, and forbids the fixation of an eternal process in a particular moment of time and space under the description of "revelation".

Now the struggle of the positive against the negative would be inconceivable if the protagonist were an abstract, mechanical, and mathematical unity, and not a concrete and living unity struggling against death. Life, in fact, consists in a multiplicity of functions and a harmony between them. The positive, which we have compendiously described as the good, turns out when attentively considered to be a good which is truth, a good which is beauty, a good which is the practical or useful, a good which is morality or the religious or however we choose to term it. Long before methodical philosophy had established and reasoned out the distinctions between these forms (or, as sometimes happened, confounded or denied or anyway thrown doubt upon them) the human mind recognized them and proclaimed them under innumerable terms of language. These forms are harmonious each with each, not in a static harmony which would submerge them all but in a dynamic harmony which is for ever being attained and then missed for the sake of a reattainment on a higher level. As in Dante's verse, "the lower foot stays firm" while the other one moves painfully to reach a higher foothold, or to put the matter philosophically, the spirit, which is an incessant progress and surpassing of the achieved by new action, contains in itself the moment of opposition to progress; and the dialectic of thought is one with the dialectic of reality.

The process of distinction brings into being also something which is useful for the vital activity of knowledge. This Useful is not the True, but is inconceivable without truth as its basis, and must necessarily be conjoined with it. We are speaking of that which is known as Science or Technique, a formation necessary for the spirit, to despise and reject which would be as rash as to despise and reject philosophy. The great thing is not to be betrayed into mistaking the one for the other, to the disadvantage of philosophy and of science itself, as happened when the Aristotelians of the time faced the attacks of Galileo. When science (for example the science of psychology which is indeed science and is not philosophy) offers its results, which are truly, according to a happy saying, well fitted *pour parler le monde*, to seek to make a different use of them, elaborating them as though they were speculative categories, is a sterile and interminable undertaking, the only clear and intelligent conclusion of which will be an absolute scepticism like that of David Hume. And by propounding this, Hume, as is well known, prepared the way for Kant's critical philosophy of the a priori synthesis. In fact, in the setting of psychological argument, the primal truths lose that energy and vitality which belongs to them as protagonists in the struggle between good and evil, as values, for in the psychological setting, or any scientific setting, they figure as mere crude "facts".

I set forth these thoughts not because *repetita juvant* but as the introduction to a recommendation which I have myself followed steadily in my philosophical meditations and enquiries. This is, never to take for a starting point the superficial and empirical concepts of psychology, but always the categories of the Philosophy of the Spirit; and never the study of impressions, sensations, perceptions (internal and external), desires, habits, conscious and unconscious acts, and so forth, but instead the study of Logic, Utility, Ethics, Aesthetics, the study of the way in which the true, the good, the useful, the beautiful come into existence, face each other, and get the better of their opposites. Having followed this rule, it will then be possible to discriminate among the empirical concepts of psychology, and (after getting rid of some altogether, or allowing them to persist merely as words of common usage)[1] to work over them so as to rediscover in them a significance for truth. The approach to reality in its fullness and concreteness necessarily lies by way of the ideality which is the measure of it, the sole criterion in every judgement by which reality can be effectively known.[2]

Another counsel which I should like to give, in connexion with the preceding, and which is important in its bearing upon tuition, is this: never surrender to the illusion that the starting point of philosophizing should be or ever is a study of the texts of the philosophers of various ages, or a memorizing of the history of philosophy. This, on the contrary, leads to the extinction of any spontaneous start which there might have been and to the boredom and disappointment of the learners, even when the histories of philosophy given to them are worthy of the philosophers of the past in being themselves philosophical, and not as often happens soulless chronicles and handbooks. The teaching of a history of philosophy in which all philosophy is set forth on a single level of indifference is the principal origin of the discredit in which philosophy is held, by the inexpert, as being a vain succession of opinions contradicting each other and leaving the mind empty; which it truly is when it is expounded in dull histories or imbibed in

---

1. An example of a psychological concept to be dropped because altogether indeterminate and vague, is that of "sensation", despite its age-long importance in philosophy. I have explained why in *The Myth of Sensation* (pp. 72-76 in this volume).

2. Along with the wretchedly sophistical passage of the Idea (logos) to Nature, another flagrant example of arbitrary construction in the Hegelian system is the passage of the Philosophy of the spirit from subjective to objective and then absolute spirit, retracing its steps several times and now swelling empirical concepts to speculative rank, now reducing the speculative concepts to empirical. Yet the profound thought of Hegel makes its voice heard somehow amid this unangelic choir of discordant voices.

a dull spirit. But just as poetry has its starting point not in the reading of poets or of critics and historians of poetry, but in the sufferings and loves of the soul (these are not themselves poetry but there is no poetry without them), so the starting point of philosophy is some tangle in the experience of life which calls to be unravelled. It may be objected: "Blessed are they who do not land themselves in these internal twists but live by the light of common sense and traditional truths and even proverbs, like Sancho Panza." Certainly there is something to be said for that condition of simplicity and innocence, narrow though the range of such a felicity must be. But it is a felicity not given to all, and which anyway comes and goes, and the normal state of mind of the nobler and more active part of human society is, on the contrary, a restless and anxious search for the light. True, it is impossible to practise philosophy without making contact with the history of this activity, but the distinction between thinking philosophically and developing the history of philosophy (or between new thought and the thought which went before) holds good only on the ideal plane. Concretely they are one, each being a function of the other, and every serious thinker in the very act of thinking constructs his own history of philosophy. The truth of this is attested by our impatience and maladjustment in listening to lectures and perusing books which do not grip our mind. For the time being, at least, we remain detached from them, even if one day they may grip the mind and be gripped by it. But then, after long waiting, we have the joy of unexpected and sudden intimacies, coming like grace from on high to lighten our path, as we discover the book and the teacher of whose history our own is to be the continuation. A first knot has been untied, our philosophic life has begun, and thereby we are helped and encouraged to untie others that are in our path, to widen the scope of our history of philosophy ever further towards the frontier of the whole thought of all times, until this gradually ceases to appear as something extraneous to ourselves, becoming instead a domestic, fraternal history of likes and unlikes, of disagreement and collaboration between brothers.

My third recommendation is to remember always that philosophy does not engender philosophy any more than poetry engenders poetry (a poet, my friend, used to tell me that the word *poet* lacked a plural). This is the reason for the nullity of academic philosophy and academic poetry and of the schools which turn out "poets" and "philosophers" wanting not only in the wit which comes from nature alone, but also in the stimulating experience of pain, the only stimulus they know being whim and vanity. The philosophic process consists always in the solving of a problem which in that very act of solution is rendered clear and determinate. The process is rounded off by a doctrinal formulation, after which the author of the formula figures not (as he did in the creative process) as philosopher but as possessor of his formula. The formula can of itself never reanimate him, nor he it, to philosophic life, until, undertaking a new problem, stimulated by a new pain, he initiates the process afresh and reattaching himself to the formula, strengthens and rectifies it, modifies and expands it. Until he has done this the author stands in no position of privilege over the readers or possible readers of his doctrinal formulation, and actually becomes their historical inferior should it happen, as it has more than once in the history of thought, that some reader understands the truth which he has (in common parlance) discovered, better than he himself, making of it a link in the chain of new truth. In that way Fichte and Schelling surpassed Kant, but above all this was done by Hegel with his conversion of Kant's a priori synthesis into the Idea, the dialectic.

And what is this stimulus, this pain which is necessary for one who would embark upon the work of philosophy, and necessary for one who would continue in it? Nothing else than the freshness of a thought which dismisses preconceptions, which is held for ever in contact with reality, with experience, and which utters what experience, being dumb, cannot say, but being imperious, requires should be uttered in its presence by thought. But philosophers who meditate upon things are a rarity. Most "philosophers" think only about formulas, combining them, squeezing them, scrambling them without, however, extracting a dram of new truth from them. But whatever is greatly valuable in reality is rare, and if reality seems to dole it out parsimoniously, instead of in great quantities, there is some real reason for this.

[1948]

XI

POPULAR THOUGHT AND TRUE THOUGHT

POPULAR thought is commonly despised. Now what do we mean
by the term? Certainly not the thought of the ordinary people,
or of the humblest individual. Precisely what is meant by a term
fluently used with apparent certainty as to its meaning, is in fact
never explicitly stated.

Well, I shall try to do so, and never mind if my definition at
first sounds paradoxical. This popular or commonplace thought,
I say, consists in the ascription of full reality to genus, species,
class, and so on , as though these were existing things. It is reasoning (so-called), in the currency of words, clichés, prejudices, repeated from hearsay. By contrast true thought is a thinking with
one's own mind, a looking with one's own eyes, a discernment of
the particular and singular in things, that which is proper to them,
a possession of the lively sense of individuality.

Individuality is, however, always in reference to universality,
and there is here a difficulty, for it seems that philosophy is now
being called for and a requirement advanced that everyone should
practise professional philosophy. But if we are not afraid to think
we shall see that this is not really meant, and the difficulty will be
overcome.

For sure, thinking which is not commonplace has always the
work of philosophy behind it, but philosophy is natural to man
and is at work even when he is unaware of it. If philosophy alone
tells us the truth, it is inconceivable that there should be another
truth to challenge it: the only truth anyone ever enunciates, other
than popular truth, needs must be philosophical. This is implied
when people say that common sense or good sense is worth all
the philosophy there is. But as there is no reason to deny the
possession of such common or good sense by the professional
philosopher, it must be admitted that he partakes of the common
thinking of humanity and is by this very token a philosopher.
It seems to, but does not really, constitute a strong objection to

this that the works even of great philosophers contain much that is contrary to good sense. So much we must admit, recognizing that it could hardly be otherwise. For though a philosopher may take in hand the refutation of certain manifestations of popular thought, and succeed in the task, yet many other such thoughts will remain at large, even in the mind of the philosopher who has accomplished the liberation. Were it not so happiness would be plethoric, would indeed be unhappy, because if no error remained and if there were no creation of new errors at the heels of the new truths, there would be no thinking. Take the case of Hegel, who conferred upon philosophical culture the concept of dialectic. Forthwith, in a grandiose deployment of system, he put his seal upon innumerable distinctions current in popular thought, most illicitly inferring them by the very dialectic which should have ruled them out. Not only did he preserve the triad of Logos or God, Spirit, and Nature, but he developed dialectically the five senses and the five parts of the globe. Consequently modern thinkers are continually occupied with stripping Hegel of a spurious wealth, and leaving him with nothing but the concept of dialectic, naked, but with the nakedness of truth or, I should say, of holiness.

To reason truthfully, it behoves us to abandon all the distinctions of genus, species, class, and so on, these being properly termed *empirical* distinctions because formed with the aid of the imagination, and to hold firm to those distinctions, and those only, which spring from the universal and are the concrete form of universality – the so-called *categories*. The philosopher and the man of good sense agree in this, but the former is steadily aware and the latter only intermittently aware of what he is doing.

To speak of my own experience, this thought used to grip and worry me even before I could grasp it. I was a mere beginner when I first noticed that we can only philosophize about that which we possess historically in its particularity and singularity. My first philosophical study, the Aesthetic, was flanked by a work upon Italian literature in almost all its departments and on most of the major departments of the literatures of other countries and of antiquity. It was work not of an amateurish sort but such as called for scholarly precision. It was the particular problem that used to rouse me and enable me to state the universal problem with propriety, and to resolve it. Thus the growth of my Aesthetic was bound up with that of my literary criticism and history, and such has always been and will be its development *usque dum vivam*. I have dealt similarly with the practical and moral aspects of spiritual life, and with philosophy itself, always supplying historical reviews of the various departments, histories of philosophy and monographs on individual philosophers, and what I have called ethico-political histories of peoples and periods. And where I felt my own competence for discussion reaching its limits, in the field of natural science, I limited my attention in the main to such of the natural sciences as were obviously founded upon spiritual problems, like linguistics and economics. For the rest I have felt myself strengthened by the conviction that in a world so full of life there cannot be non-living things, cannot be an *ens* like "Matter", nor can the world be divided into two worlds, one of them closed to experience and thus an impossible subject for thought.

As I am here writing about myself, let me say that the welcome accorded early in the century in Italy and elsewhere to my philosophical work was largely due to this concrete character; due above all to my strong distaste for the philosophical jargon which often masks uncertainty and obscurity of thought and my preference on the contrary for a maximum possible use of common language; and then to the defence which I raised against merely generic objections by mobilizing a host of factual proofs too daunting for the objectors, so as to expose plainly the airy character of their objections. An attempt was made to rescue a certain rival philosophy, which had, in its opposition to mine, abandoned the principle of the inseparability of universal and particular, by inventing a pure act of thought affirmed in virtue of a superior logic, while the world in its particularity and singularity was left to the attention of an inferior logic, of confessedly false character. This really meant installing a muddled mysticism in the upper region while allowing popular thought to rule unchecked everywhere else. The philosophy in question is now dead, never having really come to life (if it had it would survive in some modification of itself), but I should like it to linger on just as it is so as to serve for a long time to warn philosophers not to shirk the duty of using their wits to understand things.

It happened as it often happens in the world of literature: the new way of thought attracted some serious young thinkers and at the same time many amateurs interested simply in following the fashion. Consequently those who were at a loss how to contradict me found a way out in girding at the "pupils" whom the "sinless father of sinful sons" was supposed to have begotten. The supposed master of these pupils watched the spectacle, truth to tell, in ironic detachment, and once upon a time answered those foolish conventional complaints against them with the quip that, as a wetnurse had told him, the first milk is always a bit thin – let them just wait and see.

Well, it turns out that the fabric of this philosophical work, continually being enlarged, has survived two wars, and the one-time pupils are no more pupils but original investigators and thinkers. And towards the philosophy itself new and strange attitudes have developed, having in common a way of saying that one cannot quite see how to oppose or to replace it, but replaced it must be because it cannot give satisfaction. It is as if a disease were observed, but its origin unknown and therefore attributed now to this and now to that chance circumstance. What is overlooked is that in the process of enquiry and recuperation there may descend from the heights or spring up from the depths the grace of an illumination whereby what did not satisfy because it was not understood becomes at last understood. There is another and much harsher objection: it is said that it is this philosophy which prevents Italy from embracing "Marxist culture" and is thus the real and the great enemy of progress and truth. What is wrong in this remarkable charge is that it gives the title "Marxist culture" to an ignorance of all the philosophy of all the ages, to which for better or for worse mine is conjoined, and that it honours as philosophy

a way of life based on the maxim that the business is not to know
the world but to change it.

It is not to be denied that the attempt may have some sort of
success. The reiteration of that demand as a truth calling for
obedience may, even though it cannot destroy philosophy, or,
otherwise described, thought, nevertheless lead to a frightful mental degeneration in human society. But even in that case we
should not yield to perplexity, because truth must be defended to
the very last, and even if events should fall out against it, it cannot
by any exercise of might be extirpated, but will always send out
new and fresh shoots carrying in them all the truths that ever were
known in the past, enriched by an increment of new thought.

[1950]

XII

MANTEGNA'S PLAYING CARDS:
A PORTRAYAL OF "LOGIC"

SOME REMARKS AND EXCURSIONS

In the celebrated playing cards for the game of Taroc attributed to Mantegna I am attracted specially by the one which portrays "Logic". The figure is of a curly-headed woman holding in her left hand, and fixedly regarding, a dragon enmeshed in a veil.

It is now generally recognized that these are not cards really intended for use in play, but are "instruction cards", that is various series of pictures making up a little illustrated encyclopaedia for the pleasure and instruction of children. And although for convenience they still go under the name of Mantegna's cards, following the attribution of Lanzi, there have been great discussions about their real author or his school. The conjecture of an origin in Umbria-Tuscany or in Florence at the time of Botticelli is no longer much spoken for. The modern preferences are for a Venetian artist like Bartolomeo Vivarini or Crivelli, or for a Ferrarese, either, as Adolfo Venturi suggests, Galasso, or, following Hind, who is supported also by Berenson, someone from the circle of Francesco Cossa.[1] There is discussion also about the relationship between the two considerably different packs known to us.[2] And then, which of the two is the original, or is each independently derived from an original? However, the question has no great importance for me, for it is of one only of the two unidentical portrayals of "Logic" that I wish to speak: that belonging to the

1. Of the many writings on the subject I will quote only: ADOLFO VENTURI, *Arte ferrarese nel Rinascimento* (in *Arte*, XXVIII, 1925, pp. 89-109); R. LONGHI, *Officina ferrarese* (Rome, ed. d'Italia, 1934, note to page 162); A. DE WITT, I *"tarocchi di Mantegna"* (in *Arte*, N. S. 1936, pp. 213-36); A. M. HIND, *Early Italian Engraving. A critical catalogue with complete reproduction of all the prints described* (London, Quaritch, 1938), I (text), pp. 221-240; bibliography pp. 233-4; *Die Tarocchi, zwei italienische Kupferstichfolgen* (Berlin, Cassirer, 1910; published by the *Graphische Gesellschaft*), with preface by P. Kristeller.

2. Both packs are fully reproduced in the volume of the *Graphische Gesellschaft*.

pack designated by the letter E, which Hind considers to be the
earlier in date, not later, in fact, than 1467. I prefer it to the less
dramatic corresponding card in the pack designated S. Hind recognizes that the delineations in the pack S are better drawn and
more natural than those in E, which have, he says, a formal, tense,
and somehow contracted character. But he adds that these last
have an impressive dignity by contrast with the softer, prettier
manner, as he puts it, of the former.

I go back to the figure on the card in front of me: a young
woman, bare-armed, sleeves rolled right back, gown flowing
down to the feet, with an expression at once of fear, of absorption,
and of sorrow, yet at the same time piercingly alert, gazes upon
the unpleasant monster which, the better to watch it, she has with
her left hand lifted up, wrapped in a transparent veil, to the level
of her eyes. With the outstretched fingers of the disengaged right
hand she makes the instinctive gesture for warding off a repulsive
object. The right foot and leg, indeed the whole body, are preparing a retreat.

This figure, with its conventional curly hair and the dragon, is
one of those of which the tradition went back through many
generations of the Middle Ages to the book *De nuptiis Philologiae
et Mercurii* whose author living in the first half of the fifth century
was the African Martianus Capella. Among the Seven Arts whom
(as recounted in that book) the bride receives as a wedding gift,
one is Dialectic, a lady of pale complexion but alert expression,
her eyes for ever darting hither and thither, hair massed and curled
in elegant ringlets. She wears the Athenian pallium and robe, in her
left hand she grasps a snake winding enormous coils, in her right
hand some writings upon wax tablets, and a concealed fishhook.
To all and sundry she offered the captious argument.[1]

The artists who in the Middle Ages and on into the Renaissance
furnished a portrayal of Dialectic in a series of the Liberal Arts,
stuck fairly closely to the canon fixed by Martianus Capella. Let us

1. From the commentary of Rémy d'Auxerre reproduced in P. D'AN-
CONA, *Le rappresentazioni allegoriche delle Arti liberali nel medioevo e nel
Rinascimento* (Rome, 1903; extract from *Arte*, vol. v), pp. 13-14 of the extract.

ignore the literary portrayals and mention a few only of the innumerable examples in the plastic arts. In the thirteenth-century
cathedral of Chartres a sculptured figure of Dialectic holds in the
right hand a winged dragon and in the left a sceptre. In the Tri-
vulzio candelabra of the same or next century the figure conceals
a snake in a pallium apparently pulling it away from a monkey-
headed man who is advancing. In the fountain of Perugia Dialectic
holds the snake in her hand, in the base of the pulpit of Siena she
holds two snakes, as also in the pulpit of Giovanni Pisano in Pisa.
Depicted in the "Cappella degli Spagnuoli"[1] she lifts a sprig in her
left hand while with the right she grasps a snake seeking to hide
itself in the folds of her robe. In the fresco of Giusto dei Menabuoi
in the Eremitani chapel in Padua she tries to set two serpents, held
in either hand, against one another. Portrayed in a miniature in a
magnificent codex in the San Marco library she clasps the serpent
in the left hand and in the right hand lifts an implement adorned
with figures. In the frescoes by Antonazzo in the castle of Bracciano
we come once again on the youthful, blonde, and curly-headed
personage, bare-armed, with the snake hidden in the veil. In
Filippino Lippi's painting in the Carafa chapel in Santa Maria sopra
Minerva she carries the snake coiled round her arm. In Pinturicchio's in the Borgia rooms she sits enthroned in stately robes, a
small snake in each hand. In Freiburg cathedral, however, Dialectic
counts numbers on her fingers, a gesture assigned by Martianus
Capella to Arithmetic, while it is Philosophy who, at Freiburg,
has the dragon, crushing it with her heel. This transposition can
also be found among other places on the tomb of King Robert in
the church of Santa Chiara in Naples, where Dialectic appears to
be counting on her fingers the arguments to be used in the contest.
On the campanile of Santa Maria del Fiore she appears with the
wholly different symbolism of a huge pair of scissors in her
right hand, and elsewhere sometimes (for example on the pulpit
of Nicola Pisano) in the likeness of an old woman plunged in
meditation. There are some Renaissance portrayals from which
the antique and mediaeval symbolism has wholly disappeared. In

1. Santa Maria Novella, Florence (Translator's note).

8

the Malatesta temple the noble figure of a woman, erect between two fluted columns joined by festoons of flowers and fruit, appears to be presiding over the union of two children engaged in the conferment of a ring. In the paintings of Justus of Ghent for the palace of Urbino, Dialectic, enthroned, presents a book to the kneeling figure of Federigo di Montefeltro, while in those of the palace of Schifanoia, Dialectic and the other Liberal Arts look like handsome pagan goddesses.[1]

About allegorical concepts and second meanings in works of art (painting, sculpture, music, architecture, or poetry – the case is always the same) it is well known how their attachment can only be obtained by an outward device: they cannot be melted or merged into the lineaments of the artistic creations which exist and live for themselves. The reason commonly given is that only bodies and not souls can be depicted, but the truth is the reverse. Art depicts and sculpts souls, souls in their bodies, and these cannot put up with the presence of something above them claiming to amplify or to deform their self-sufficient life, spinner of its own web. The utmost that these commanded second meanings can achieve is to bring to one's mind ideas and tendencies which were cherished by certain men or certain ages and thereby won faculty of entry and of dominion in regions not proper to them. The curiosity so aroused must be appeased not by cross-questioning the paintings, sculptures, poetry, or musical compositions, for these do not, nor could they, answer such enquiries (they just persist in radiating colourful, linear, verbal, or orchestral harmonies); but by seeking out any papers, books, and documents which there may be attesting the allegorical intentions. Surveying with the single eye of the artist those numerous mediaeval and Renaissance portrayals of the seven Liberal Arts, we can soon eliminate the mere inferior aggregates of imagery lacking a synthesis

1. These details have been taken from the already mentioned work of D'Ancona, which gives a number of pictorial illustrations. I have also used A. FILANGIERI DI CANDIDA's *Marciano Capella e la rappresentazione delle "Arti liberali" nel Medio evo e nel Rinascimento* (Naples, 1900, reprinted from the review *Flegrea*).

or poetically synthetic principle – these never rise to artistic form but remain hieroglyphics requiring for their interpretation the possession or discovery of a key – but we then linger over the others, few or many, having their own life into whose inner warmth and rapture they can draw us. They may all be designated by the same name, but between one and another there are such differences as those differentiating the Dialectic of the Siena pulpit from that of the bas-reliefs of St. Francis of Rimini, that of the Borgia Apartments from that – to recall only some of the examples already mentioned – of the palace of Urbino. Which is as much as to say the difference that lies between the soul of a Giovanni Pisano and an Agostino di Duccio (or whoever it was that worked for Malatesta), the soul of a Pinturicchio and a Justus of Ghent.

To return to our educational playing-card design: this figure of "Logic" like the others speaks to us for itself, of itself, and in its own way – the way already described. We witness the drama of a painful astonishment (be the object of this what it may) and a resolute firmness, a horror at the touch or the nearness of something evil, and a contest engaged for its repression or destruction. More than this the artist, as an artist, could not and did not give. But what he has given has a unity of artistic expression and a vitality lacking in many of the designs on the pattern laid down by Martianus Capella.

We cannot with any certainty decide whether the artist had in his mind any logical concept of the "Logic" of which the design bears his name. Did he accept or reject the bad reputation borne for centuries by what was taken for the Art of laying snares and pitfalls and achieving the triumph of error over truth? Thus had Logic been portrayed by Martianus Capella, and a sluggish tradition, almost unconsciously perpetuated throughout the Middle Ages, had reviled such an Art as being one that worked towards no noble end (this was still said in the early days of the Renaissance), but was good simply for triumphing in disputation, like that other loud-mouthed and coarse-gestured Art of Rhetoric.[1]

1. D'ANCONA in op. cit. gives examples from Sicco Polentone and the *Paradiso degli Alberti*.

Much more probably our author was utterly ignorant of such judgements, reflections, and controversies. He may very well have understood nothing of the symbolism elaborated by Martianus Capella. Perhaps he just followed his own feelings in interpreting the foul monster wrapped in the veil, which he will have found in many a designer's manual with accompanying instructions, and its relation to the woman who grasps it in her hand, holds it up aloft, and gazes fixedly upon it.[1] The artist has not informed us and it is not in our power to give information concerning his intentions and secret thoughts. But the figure which he has drawn speaks to us in that language of art which is the instigator of infinite suggestion. It is permissible and customary for anyone who hears it to give it a meaning adapted to the most various situations of his own life, the most various phases of his own actions and feelings. And so, among the many possible particular dramas, I am glad to enlist its significance for one to which the very name of "Logic" and my own affection for philosophical study leads me. Such is my right, in virtue of my sentiment, my imagination, nor does its exercise harm anyone or anything while I respect the work of art for what it is on the level of human universality.

Well then, the drama which I call upon this representation to suggest is that of Truth and the struggle against Error carried on by Logic. And Logic, for me at least, far from being the malign maker of traps and sophistries of that old Carthaginian's imagination – poor Martianus Capella, he knew no better or could invent no better – is a beneficent power ever ready to take on the hard task of unravelling tangled skeins of sophistry, dispelling irrational combinations which had received an appearance of genuineness through some outburst of wrongful passion, dissolving

<hr>

1. In a French *Art du blason* said to be of the year 1424 we find the following description closely corresponding in its material details to the design of our artist: "Une femme jeune, les cheveux crispés, les bras tous nudz hault recoursez d'une chemise jusques aux pieds, es mammelles et au nombril troussée: porte de gueules une serpent volant d'or enveloppée d'un drap d'argent". (The whole passage concerning the liberal arts is printed in *Catalogue of early Italian paintings preserved in the department of prints and drawings in the British Museum* by ARTHUR M. HIND, London, 1910, pp. 220-21 *n*.)

obstacles placed by superstition in the path of free research. Often, at the first hint of such distortions and falsifications, we feel perplexity, almost fear, come over us, as though we too were being treacherously assailed, and might find our spirits entangled, contaminated, overcome, rendered subservient to their dominion: and often, too, some weariness and diffidence at the unceasing reappearance of ancient errors in novel garb. But we hear the voice of conscience and rouse ourselves to obey the prohibition of tolerance of offences against the purity of truth. And we arise in firm resolution to fulfil our task, following the lead of our figure of Logic who meets and transfixes with her intrepid gaze the monster for all the pride of its hideousness and the mocking defiance with which it meets every comer.

Woe if there should be a slackening in this labour of defence and counter-attack. Woe to men and societies who do not feel the influence of strict logic in all their living motions. A statesman of the good old times, Bernardo Tanucci, used to sum up the vices and defects of the men around him under the single head "want of syllogism". And in fact where knowledge of the syllogism is wanting or weak the way lies open for confused sensation and ignoble desire to let loose those heady streams of imagination which conduce to frenzied and destructive behaviour. In what manner have such phantasms gathered so as now to fill the skies not of Europe only but the two hemispheres! Logic neither quenches nor replaces the spontaneity of active endeavour, but upholds and defends it against the distortions superinduced upon it by a crude convulsive vitality flaunting an appearance of energy, but in essence weak and monstrous. I for my part being devoted to Logic have framed and hung on my study wall this "playing card of Mantegna" as it were the likeness of a Saint to whom I appeal to keep me ever under her strict and benevolent attention.

[1941]

II
PHILOSOPHICAL CRITICISM

I

THE PHILOSOPHICAL CONCEPT
OF THE HISTORY OF PHILOSOPHY

WHAT at first sounds like the evident truth, that the history of philosophy ought to be expounded objectively, proves, on further consideration, to be both very true and very untrue. This perplexed oscillation between appearances of total truth and of total untruth, arises out of a confusion in the meaning that is given to objectivity in its relation to subjectivity.

A prohibition which is widely but erroneously endorsed, forbids the introduction of any "personal" judgement into the exposition of concepts and systems. In other words it is held to be inadmissible to pass judgement upon a philosophy in terms of another philosophy which the judge holds to be true. It is not denied that, in principle, a man of philosophic mind, a conceptual thinker, may, when he passes to the task of history, impose upon himself a rigorous impartiality and reservation of his own opinions, yet it is thought generally prudent not to require this almost impossible degree of discipline from a philosopher, but to seek a safer guarantee by confiding the task of writing the history of philosophy to men who are definitely not philosophers. These will be quite out of temptation's way, incapable of yielding to it, having their minds unencumbered, empty, nay barred against any irruption of that disturbing passion and presumptuous faith. Ideas of this sort explain the distrust which has surrounded philosophers who have composed histories of philosophy, "systematists" they have been called, and further it explains the inclination to rule out at once their interpretations, all biased as they are held to be by their philosophic tendency. Not even Aristotle's famous historical remarks on the thinkers who preceded him have been spared such strictures, while they have been positively heaped upon that modern Aristotle, Hegel. As an historical exposition, the matter-of-fact and unintelligent records of Diogenes Laertius are almost preferred, as impartial, to the over-intelligent records of Aristotle.

If, in this manner, every right of judgement, every mental re-elaboration of philosophic thought is to be forbidden to the historians of it, one might as well conclude that the only genuine history of thought consists in textual editions of works edited by skilful scholars. Nevertheless, educational necessity, the need for gradual preparation, for aid to reading and study, sets up a demand for extracts, compendiums, full and detailed expositions, backed up by chronological and biographical information about the authors, and for rearrangement in panoramic patterns of the contents of the works of the authors in question. Excellent arrangements of this sort have been produced and are still produced, in rough correspondence with the ideal of a history free of the element of judgement. Sometimes one remains astonished at the clearness and precision of such expositions provided by authors who would not be capable of tackling any philosophical problem on their own, nor yet pretend to any such originality, or have any desire to get involved in such a task. Well, although in such works there may be little or next to no speculative energy, yet literary taste, coupled with an acquaintance with the vocabulary, the style, the references of authors to their contemporaries or predecessors, has enabled their compilers to follow the rhythm and the accentuation of the texts which they present, to bring into prominence the salient parts, to illustrate their relations to one another, and so to present them with substantial fidelity albeit without understanding and appreciation, to readers who for their part may or may not understand them. The work in question is to be compared with that of good translators, which is estimable and useful within its due limits.

However, it must be remarked that expositions of this sort do not truly fulfil the office of history, because the listing of the facts (the 'facts' in our present context are concepts and systems) is not integrated by explanations of their origin, descriptions of their particularities and qualities, tracing of their logical reasons, or, in naturalistic language, their "causes". For this could not be done without bringing them into relation with other concepts and systems and passing judgement. The strong determination not to

infringe the already mentioned prohibition by introducing judgement into the philosophic field, leads, however, to an inclination
to introduce it instead into the psychological field, and to furnish
explanations stemming from the dispositions, habits, and experiences of the philosophers or of the age and the society to which
they belonged. "Psychology" in this case, though the word betokens a branch of natural science, really betokens nothing more
than the practical, social, political, moral, nay physiological and
pathological history of the philosophers, and this, even if the facts
about it be available and deserving of investigation and narration,
can never give birth to a history of philosophy, which is an original
activity of the spirit, differentiating itself from practical life,
transcending it, and being nothing but itself. To attempt to replace
the history of philosophy by that of the practical is tantamount to
denying philosophy in its essence, treating it as mere interest and
practicality, and this was not, in fact, very far from the minds of
the attempters, despairing and sceptical as they were as to the
labours and potentialities of philosophy.

Now when such an attempt to shift the discussion on to psychological or sociological ground proves vain and fruitless, there is
nothing for it but to seek for a criterion of judgement in the field
of theory. As, however, the prohibition against historians of philosophy getting involved in doctrines and systems, in pure philosophy, in fact, is still supposed to be valid (so that concrete philosophical discussion appears to be both compromising and unworthy
of a serious scholar) resort is had to the singular scheme of excluding from the scope of attention and operation everything else
except the testing of every doctrine and system as to its logical
coherency or incoherency. Now logical coherency, in the deepest
sense, is nothing less than truth itself. There cannot be incoherent
and inconsistent truths: truths, if inconsistent, would be inexistent, and therefore the test as to coherency is indistinguishable
from judgement as to concrete and definite truth. To judge as to
the coherency of a teaching there is, then, nothing for it but to
get involved in the details of truth in the particular. Aesthetic
coherency is, in the same way, nothing other than beauty and

poetry: aesthetic judgement is the discernment of the beautiful from the ugly in poetry. There is, however, a different, unphilosophical sort of (so-called) coherency, the logical chain or calculus of a series of propositions, bound each to each, and all dependent from one premiss, which may be either true or false. But this is a mere appearance of coherency, within which a substantial and effective incoherency may prevail. It had and has its due place in the exercises of scholastic logic, the formal art of debate, but none at all in philosophy and the history of philosophy. The restriction of attention by historians of philosophy to everything else except this apparent coherency, would signify nothing more nor less than the exclusion from it of truth. For the palm for coherency might well go to the feeblest reasoner, and blame fall upon the greatest philosophers. For sometimes it is the schoolboy minds which can give an appearance of complete clarity, smoothness, fluency, consequence, until indeed one looks into the depths of their thought which they themselves are unable to fathom. And by contrast it is sometimes the case that great speculative thinkers, shaken by the very grandeur of their thought, allow obscurity, incoherences, contradictions, roughnesses, to persist, although they themselves have laid down the principles making for clearness and smoothness. Vico was given to quoting the ancient maxim of the writer of *On the Sublime*: "In matters of the greatest importance it is better to forget the virtue of diligence which lingers over minute details." There are also among works of poetry or would-be poetry many in which no defect can be observed save the fundamental defect of their essential nullity, while works of genius, powerful and brilliant, are riddled with defects.

The notion, then, of finding a guiding principle of judgement in the presence or absence of a formal coherency in the teachings under examination, must fall to the ground. Those who propose it as the right method for the History of Philosophy (names, here omitted, could be furnished of authors in whose books of philosophical history each of the attitudes which we are investigating is propounded or upheld, with chapter and verse) believed that it afforded them a way of avoiding the error of a psychological or practical conception of the history of philosophy. But they may be found once again falling back into that very error when, giving a new turn to their teaching, they contend that in addition to the test of more or less perfect consequentiality, of which we have just been speaking, there should be applied a test of greater or lesser "fecundity" in the systems which the history of philosophy sets out to investigate. Yet the "fecundity" of a concept or philosophic doctrine proves also, when rightly considered, to coincide with its truth. Truth is always fecund, even when lodged in the mind of the few, or of one solitary thinker, even when it seems to lie for centuries motionless in a manuscript, or is generally rejected and derided. And to discover authentically whether a concept is fecund, there is no other way than by passing judgement on whether it is true, in other words exerting that very faculty of philosophical judgement which it is desired to avoid and fear of which inspires these anxious disclaimers. If however "spiritual fecundity" be a euphemism for the popularization of the philosophers, their exploitation to provide dogmatic premises, their conversion into accepted faiths, their consolidation and fixation in schools or churches (we may recall the case of the sway of Aristotelian doctrine from the late Middle Ages until the Renaissance and the rebellion of the physicists and natural scientists), the generation of modes of action out of their theories (we may recall Cartesian rationalism and mathematicism, the eighteenth-century Enlightenment and the French Revolution), why then we are talking no more of the history of philosophy but of practical, political, and moral history, actuated by the feelings and volitions of men; a history which not only does not coincide with but is not even chronologically parallel with that of philosophy.

The various methodologies described above have been attempts to win a solid footing in the history of philosophy in order to expel and to replace the Hegelian type of such history. But this last has, instead, triumphed over them all, immune to all their attempts against it, thanks to its possession of a principle of truth, while the lack of such a principle to support them causes the others to stumble blindly, unable to discover a sure balance. The principle in question

affirms that the history of philosophy is philosophy, philosophy
that has become fully aware of itself and so aware of the way in
which its own development and formation was accomplished, and
in this awareness recalls the various stages through which it has
passed, judging and defining them. In virtue of his assertion of
this principle Hegel is entitled to be considered the true founder of
the historiography of philosophy. Indeed all are agreed in recognizing this title, even, somewhat strangely or absurdly, those very
writers who deny his principle and wish to promote a history
without judgement or with a biased and foreign sort of judgement.
(Really they here ought to consider Hegel not as a founder but as
a corruptor.)

There is nevertheless undeniably something in Hegel's method
which conveys a feeling of forced artificiality, and rouses suspicion
lest a licence be thereby given to the introduction of distortions
into the pure truth and objectivity of history. There is in fact, in
part, a real justification for these feelings, arising out of what we
have called Hegel's persistent metaphysical garb, and the mytho-
logizing tendency in him which is therewith associated. The very
truths which he pronounces wear what has been called an "archaic"
appearance to our eyes. In arranging and developing the history
of philosophy, Hegel takes for his standpoint not the particular
historical moment and conditions of his own teaching, and its
relations with the teachings current in his time, but an imaginary
position marking the arrival of Philosophy at its highest, unsurpas-
sable, completest fulfilment, beyond which there can arise no new
philosophy but only details and applications. At such a point philosophy would be able to survey its own entire past history (future
history there will be none) in every stage from its first beginning
to its ultimate end. Now in reality there is no ultimate end, no
definitive system, and equally no Beginning-in-Itself from which
all other stages draw their origin. The Beginning lies, in every
case, there where the mental interest of any one of us reaches back
to, in relation to the problem occupying it at the moment: this may
be a very short time or a very long time, so long in fact that
ancient Greece, Egypt, or the East stand towards it as mere indi-

cations of the measureless ranges of pre-history. The position accorded to the Beginning, in correspondency with the first category of Logic-Metaphysics, exemplifies that mythological process which disturbs and disfigures truth in the mind of Hegel, by inducing him to assimilate two abstractions, the logico-metaphysical categories on the one hand, the chronological epochs on the other, an arbitrary systematic pattern and an arbitrary chopping up of the gradualities of historical development. He thus comes to see all the teachings of the philosophers not in the light of the individuality and variety of the problems to which each one refers, but as a succession of progressively fuller solutions to one and the same problem, culminating and finding quiescence in the total fulfilment of the all-sided and definitive solution.

When we divest the discussion of this heavy archaic mantle, and envisage the relation between philosophy and history of philosophy as that of the only philosophic activity that there is, that of the philosophic act in its perpetually individual and ever various accomplishment, distinguishing and at the same time uniting the subject and the object, we can at last pronounce an unequivocal differentiation between the subjective and the objective. These two unseverable moments of the one unity only become severed and so falsified, when the subjective is mistaken for the arbitrariness of practice, for caprice, while the objective is wrongly identified with something supposedly external to our spirit and our thought. But as we can now see it, the subjective is my thought, where "I" am considered as the living and practically operating man, while the historically objective is the very concreteness and integrity of this thought, in its relation with the other thoughts which it encounters and raises to a higher level; in its relation, in fact, with its own history. If we analyse one of our acts of thought, we always find, in the culminating judgement, reference to other judgements which become justified and historicized in this very elaboration. And so it is from a single stem that we gather the one flower of philosophy which is the history of philosophy and of history of philosophy which is philosophy. Is not this truth quite commonly recognized with the saying that a philosophical problem can only be understood and handled in its historical terms, in terms of which the historical meaning is defined? And so only the true philosopher is able to discern the distinguishing features of an act of thought, a concept, a doctrine, a past system of thought, conferring objectivity upon it by the very process of differentiating it, within the unity, from his own new, personal, subjective thought. It is an historical error to falsify the teachings of the past by confounding them with our own, but it is that just because it is also a philosophical error, to assert that two judgements born of different conditions, premisses, and experiences are identical. For this is impossible and unthinkable: they could never be more than identical in one respect and different in another. For the same reason it is an historical as well as a philosophical error to reject past teachings absolutely as being strange and alien to us: even what is proclaimed strange and alien lives on within our truth, is an essential element of it, and has become ours. Any proposition claiming to be new and disclaiming or not revealing this identity-diversity in respect to the teachings and systems of the past, misses historical rank, reducing itself to a vain repetition and clumsy combination of past thoughts, or at the very best showing itself to be a new but still troublously immature and haltingly diffident concept. This indissoluble unity of the historical with the philosophical judgement has for consequence that there can never be an exhaustive history of the philosophy of the past as a whole, nay, not even of any single thinker or system, for new aspects will always become discernible in the light of the never ceasing development of thought.

We have now arrived at a total rejection of the supposition which we set out to consider, of an objectivity eschewing philosophy and judgement, by showing that true objectivity lies in judging, in philosophizing. The figure of the historian eschewing philosophy yields to the very different one of the philosopher who in virtue of his own thought is a historian, the sole worthy historian of human thought. We had seen philosophy made over into the supposedly pure and blameless hands of the non-philosophers, people who knew not what philosophy was, and raised childish or even barbarous objections to philosophic proceedings: now we have established that whoever would judge the philosophers must himself be of philosophic rank. And truly no one who has not himself procured some advance in the field of thought can understand the historical series of efforts which made that advance possible. He who presumes to pass general judgement upon a great philosopher, Vico, Kant, or Hegel, should have raised himself up to and beyond the level of the object of judgement, bringing the whole complex of the problems which that philosopher had raised and the solutions which he had formulated somewhat forward. This of course is the work not of a single individual but of the mental efforts and experiences of the whole intervening age, summed up and concentrated sometimes in individuals. How could it be supposed that the thinkers aimed their sentences at assiduous textual critics, schoolmaster authors of manuals, literary academicians fearful of ever crossing the frontiers of convention, lukewarm spectators of philosophic truth, sceptical unbelievers in it – of such is composed the majority of those "historians of philosophy" among whom flourished the opinion, particularly during the heyday of Positivism in my youth, that the agreeable object of knowledge is not that endless conflict of views called philosophy, but the history of it. They implied, though they did not always say it outright, that this was the history of a malady of the human brain that positivist science was now gradually eliminating.

To be judged by one's peers is, in truth, the only sort of judgement that there is, and every sort of history is alike in that respect, differing only in respect of the sphere of spiritual activity presenting itself for judgement. Where the sphere in question is philosophy, the historian must be required to be a philosopher on his own account, one who has won his way somewhat ahead of the philosopher, the teaching, the concept which he undertakes to weigh and to interpret. Where it is poetry, the critic and historian must be a poet who relives the poet's travail in poetic union with him, yet is different and distinct from him, surpassing him in that judgement which is necessary at the more highly developed level of aesthetic thought. Where the sphere is that of politics, or that of morals, the historian feels in his breast aspirations and impediments, hopes and fears, similar and conjoined to those which actuated the man of action, yet superior to those, or more complex, because pertaining to a superior and more complex age; and in reflecting upon that past history, he opens the way for new history, in which the subject of his narration, or other subjects, will go forward. The idea that poetry can be judged by those insensitive to it, or political and ethical history be composed by men who are in a practical and personal sense spineless and unfeeling, is just as absurd as the idea that the history of philosophy can be written by non-philosophers, or, even, by those who despise philosophy's labours as futile.

Following the rule which applies equally to all sorts of historical composition as to the setting of problems and the observance of method, it is necessary, for historians of philosophy, to discriminate as rigorously as historians of other spiritual activities are wont to do, between history and pseudo-history, history and the accumulation of facts. The Graeco-Roman world, when it distinguished between "history" and "annals" or "chronicles", was already aware of a difference which later ages repeatedly brought out and stressed. But the distinction was usually drawn chiefly with an eye to external literary forms. And annals and chronicles being often dressed up in the solemn weeds of history, though lacking any internal coherency, there was no true and substantial criterion for establishing the distinction until the historical interpretation of facts came to be defined as that which answers the needs and requirements of intellectual, aesthetic, economic, political, and generally speaking moral progress. Any exposition of facts which is not unified and inspired by that aim remains more or less at the level of mere chronicle and anecdote. It is interesting to observe that the ancient Greeks and Romans, and all those who for centuries afterwards echoed them, assigned to history the task of education and incitement to goodness, while later times, up to the modern age, carefully divested history of that external and superimposed finality in order to recognize a finality proper and natural to history – that of simply understanding what has happened. Yet by dint of probing this proper and natural finality of history, it has come to be seen that understanding is itself not to be attained without a stirring of the passion for a moral end. This is a typical example of a process following the pattern of thesis, antithesis, and synthesis, ending up with a truth similar to, yet profoundly different from that which was the starting point.

The foregoing considerations permit one now to express a feeling of dissatisfaction, annoyance, tedium, at seeing the perpetual outpouring by literary and publishing enterprises of works of "universal" history, history of "the nations", and so forth, purporting to furnish a history starting with the origins or the prehistory of things and reaching to our own days – facts being accumulated on facts, events on events, with no glimpse of a logical or moral design, nothing to indicate the why or for what end of all this happening, so as to induce weariness and distaste in the reader. (There are readers of these works, and readers who are prepared to put up with a lot.) But such compilations serve at the very most, when carefully and precisely executed, as reference books for looking up some details of an event which it is opportune to recall in some genuine historical enquiry. How different is the appearance and the effect upon minds and hearts of historical narrations inspired by passion, disciplined by conscientious research into the documents, and executed in the service of a faith and for the sake of shedding light upon tasks ahead. How different, too, from those general histories of the literary art, pieced together out of superficial, excerpted, stunted judgements on the poets, are the critical essays devoted to a single poet or poetical work, born of a felt need to dispel impediments to the understanding of this, and to re-establish historic truth: such criticism brings the critic and the reader, reinvigorated by the clarification, to the direct intuition and enjoyment of the poetry.

The greater part of the histories of philosophy on our bookshelves conform to the vulgar, partly conventional and partly commercial type of political and literary-artistic histories of which we have spoken. All the more necessary is it to put on one side and apart the small number of works of an altogether different and more powerful nature, starting with the first book of Aristotle's Metaphysics and with Hegel's introduction to his Encyclopaedia. The authentic manner of history of thought is in such works found not only in the prologues and epilogues of books of strictly philosophical appearance which open and close with a survey of the teachings of previous thinkers, but also in the introductions to social, moral, and political histories where we find, for example, discussions on the significance of words like Renaissance or Romanticism, and where, by dint of an improved theoretical elaboration, the definitions of earlier writers are reviewed in an orderly dialectical argument which comes to constitute a history of the problem. In the case of essays in literary criticism, for instance essays of interpretation concerning Dante or Shakespeare, we may find similarly, along with the new interpretation, a history of earlier criticism ranged not as an arbitrary succession of opinions but as a continuous progressive dialogue.

Some approach is made towards a more concrete and less unsatisfactory history of philosophy when side by side with the serial treatment of the philosophers, or involved in this, we are given a history of problems: as for example of the problem of the nature of knowledge, or the ethical, political, historical, aesthetic problem or whatever it may be. But though this may afford some glimpse of truth, here too we have an abstract attitude the deficiency of which lies in want of a clear and precise rational understanding that only such a problem as is well determined and individuated, and leads up to a new and well individuated problem of which the enquirer seeks the origin and precedents in it, can properly be the object of historical treatment. The monographic literary form symbolizes in this field of the history of philosophy, as in every other historical field, the genuine form of history, while the encyclopaedic or more or less "universal" form remains appropriate to an enquiry which is not critical or scientific but merely sums up in broad terms the results obtained by various monographically conducted enquiries.

The second half of the nineteenth century was much admired as the great age of study of the history of philosophy. Never before had it been so broadly and fully cultivated. But that abundant output betokened not a love and a zeal for philosophy, but rather a dislike and a coolness. Philosophy had decayed into a sheer matter of diligence, learned cataloguing, philological ingenuity. The need is now for a historiography less laboriously extensive, more intensive, and complementary to true and original philosophic thought, integrating this and being integrated by it.

Such being the authentic form of the history of philosophy, its relation to the work of philosophy itself needs to be thought out anew. The demand commonly made that a good knowledge of past philosophy should be the preliminary to any contemporary and new philosophizing should be taken in a considerably different sense from the obvious and commonly current. For if the historical interpretation of philosophy can only come about relatedly to fresh philosophic activity, and in union with it, as one of its aspects or moments, then clearly such interpretation cannot precede that activity, or be its starting point, or exist in itself precedently to it. Accordingly, if any plausible meaning is to be given to the claim that philosophical history should come first and furnish a necessary link to philosophical thought, it must be attained by using the term "history" in the sense of mere extrinsic and philological learning, able to give just a general orientation and information about philosophical documents and texts useful for the pursuit of the study, by contrast with that living and true history of philosophy which is born simultaneously with the act of philosophizing. The necessity of acquiring, as a preliminary, such extrinsic information, is a wise mode of warning off the crude and ignorant, so far as this is possible, from entering the lists of philosophy without first submitting themselves to some cultivation. But it is something quite other than a true and concrete demonstration of what has been achieved in philosophy and what remains to be achieved, or a statement of the conditions and programme of future philosophizing. Mere learning cannot fulfil this function, for which it is quite unequipped. A new philosophic thought is preceded by an obscure urge to win freedom from mental difficulties in which one feels oneself involved without yet being able to name or define them. This urge converts the anguish into the terms of a problem and with this the solution is already given. No less than poetry, philosophical thought arises out of an unforeseeable and necessary creative inspiration, and, as has been said of poetry, it retains the "smell of earth", that is of the feelings and passions which conveyed the obscure urge and were thereby placated and clarified even in its ideal form.

What a contrast to such a birth of philosophic thought do those numberless works and volumes present, which, dignified by the description of histories of philosophy, are, philosophically, null and void, like numberless similar or analogous volumes in the field of poetry and art. In either case such works are designated "non-original" works, an inexact or, at best, metaphorical and comparative designation, for whatever a man does is original, and those works too have their own particular originality, though lying not in the realm of the history of truth or beauty, but in the very different realm of the history of "mechanical" operations, and more particularly of practical exercises utilizing the formulae or rather the dry and empty husks of the philosophies conceived and the poems or artistic achievements created by others. The smell which they have about them is not that of the wild and fruitful earth, but that of written and printed paper. Their origin and their originality derive from practical needs which may be multiple and various: impatient speed to patch up nascent doubts with any old solution permitting one then to bask in the belief that one has attained a firm theoretical conviction; vain aspiration to cut a certain figure in the world of philosophy and art; or it may be just economic necessity, pressing one to accept any employment that the market offers, and the one which it offers is that of the philosophic or poetic pot-boiler. These works are not to be chased off the face of the earth, for they are, in their way, legitimate. The impatience, the playing-about, the illusion are in their way legitimate, for by yielding to them and trying them out one is in the long run led and forced to the discovery of the real and serious self. Legitimate, too, is the earning of a livelihood from any trade. The philosopher who ponders over the history of philosophy, the art critic meditating on the history of art, are in duty bound to ban such works from their respective confines, indeed they are anyway in the course of social existence periodically consigned to oblivion, being replaced by other works of the same quality but with more appeal to new fashions, inclinations, or market demand. Sometimes I muse as in a nightmare upon the vast and monstrous library which would result if some book-collector should want to withstand those purges, and should preserve all the philosophic volumes and articles published albeit only in the last century or half century. The very few among them endowed with intellectual vigour would, no doubt, be highly unpopular in that bad company, nay would be drowned and lost in it, and the stupidly repetitive, the eclectically facile, the academically pompous, would flaunt their pride over them. Fortunately, while there are collectors who assemble all the volumes of verse, mostly bad, published in a given age, no one as far as I know has thought of collecting philosophical publications in the same way. This is perhaps because, as Seneca noted mournfully, "satis ipsum nomen philosophiae invidiosum est", lacking attraction for curious and jaded imaginations. Or it may be that the pseudo-philosophic output of scholastic manuals, theses, or dissertations to earn honours for professorial authors is so vast and unwieldy, far exceeding that of bad verses (which serve no such practical purpose), as to discourage the thought of collecting them. It would take an incredibly simple and credulous novice to embark trustfully upon the accumulation and ordering of such heaps of shallow works, and the enterprise would kill him.

It is further to be hoped that the authors of more or less comprehensive panoramas of the history of philosophy will cease to give their main attention to those cumbrous works which impose upon the simple by their appearance as well-rounded systems of philosophy, and will correspondingly give more attention and prominence to effective philosophic thought wherever this is to be found, whether embedded in systems or outside them, and maybe presented in volumes which are not considered to be philosophical at all. (It is greatly to be hoped and legitimately to be expected that historians of poetry and art will similarly thin down their material, as is so necessary, and accept fresh material only after such thinning, so that space and air may be afforded for the enjoyment of works of genuine inspiration hitherto overgrown and concealed by heavy, luxuriant, maybe cleverly conceived work.)

This advice aims at winning attention chiefly for what we will call the more inventive moment of the concept rather than for the reasoning and systematic moment. Only a rough validity is claimed for the distinction between these two moments. It is in the second of them that the particular virtue of philosophic thought is commonly held to reside, but if the first were lacking the second could not occur or would fall into nullity. When a concept of fresh content finds utterance, or when an old concept, found to be applicable with a new scope, is thereby renewed, this initiates a philosophical process in the course of which either the inventors of the concept or their successors will discover, amplify, and finally render altogether systematic the demonstrations which the concept or concepts call for. One has but to think of the century-long phases lying between the Pauline affirmation of justification by faith in Christ and Kant's doctrine of the autonomy of the pure moral conscience; or between Machiavelli's intimations that politics consitutes an original force, and the systematization of this teaching by Vico with his doctrine of the "course" and "recourse" of the human mind; or between the inkling of certain seventeenth-century critics of the concept of taste or judgement (neither sense nor sheer intellect but an "unarguing" discernment of beautiful and unbeautiful in poetry and the arts) and the systematic solutions propounded by modern aesthetics. St. Paul, Machiavellí, Ludovico Zuccolo, and the like were men of religion or politics or letters, not philosophers in the academic sense, because they composed no systems; but truly they were philosophers inasmuch as they were discoverers and enunciators of new concepts who accordingly have a full right to be celebrated in the history of thought and philosophy. The inventive moment may have been lacking in systematic coherence, but were there no such moment there would be no new and progressively elaborate systematizations: there would be nothing but cumbrous purely mechanical systems such as we have spoken of earlier. The new concepts may seem to us and may be confused, but they show their speculative energy in the very insistence with which they are announced and upheld, in express or implied polemics against whoever would deny or disregard them. There is about them an awareness of a systematization to come, which they herald.

It follows from all that has been said that the serious study of philosophy calls for abandonment of the traditional study of "schools" or in older terminology "sects" of philosophers, just as such methods are being dropped also in the history of poetry and art. The works of a "school" either have something individual and original about them and thus do not belong to a school, or else they have no such thing and therefore do not belong at all to the sphere of thought and fantasy, but merely to that of culture and practical life, in which it is pertinent to enquire into the wider or narrower diffusion of this or that teaching in these or those circumstances.[1]

It is on the lines that have been suggested above, that the history of philosophy may be a living history of what was and always will be eternally alive.

[1940]

---

1. See *Conversazioni critiche*, Bari, 1939, v, 243-45.

II

VICO AND THE SUBSEQUENT DEVELOPMENT
OF PHILOSOPHIC AND HISTORICAL THOUGHT

It is impossible to write about Vico without feeling impelled to
survey the ensuing age and to note similarities and analogies between his teachings and those of authors fifty or a hundred years
later. This is because Vico in his own age was considered an ec-
centric and was always a solitary; the development of thought in
the succeeding age was scarcely influenced by him; nay even today,
while restricted circles are familiar enough with him, he has not
secured the place in the general history of thought which is due to
him. Now what simpler manner could there be of demonstrating
that his teachings, whether true or false, answered deep spiritual
needs, than the recollection of similar ideas and explorations which
at a later time flourished so copiously and intensely as to set a
mark upon the entire philosophical and historical labour of a
century? Such an appeal to subsequent events may, it is true, seem,
after our examination of the substance of Vico's thought, superfluous, but inasmuch as this like every other discourse ought to
conclude on a rhetorical note, let the peroration consist in a rapid
outline of the philosophy and scholarship of later times in their
relation to the thought of Vico. No other peroration could suggest
itself more spontaneously.

Indeed, it would be possible to follow Vico's own method of
comparing the second barbarian age with the first, and to present
the subsequent history of thought as a "recourse" or recurrence of
Vico's ideas. For there was indeed a recurrence of the criticism to
which he had subjected Descartes' theory of immediate knowledge;
a recurrence of Vico's canon of the *conversio veri et facti*: the recurrence lay in the speculative movement which went from Kant to
Hegel, culminating in the thesis of the identity of truth with fact,
of thought with being. Vico's unification of philosophy and philology recurred in the rehabilitation of history against the scepticism and intellectualism of the eighteenth century, the offspring of

Descartes; in the Kantian a priori synthesis which reconciled the ideal with the real, category with experience; and in the historical philosophy of Hegel, the culminating point of nineteenth-century historicism. Vico's occasional forcible and erroneous commingling of methods to procure the unification of philosophy and philology recurred also in works of the Hegelian school. The defect in question might rightly be called "Vico-ism". Vico had assigned only a limited value to mathematics and the exact sciences, and had criticized the mathematical-naturalistic conception of philosophy. These attitudes recurred in the criticism to which Jacobi subjected Spinoza's determinism, and in Hegel's critique of the abstract intellect, while the fact that the force of mathematics resides not in postulates but in definitions was reiterated by Dugald Stewart and others, so that Vico's *fictiones* have now entered into the ordinary vocabulary of the theory of mathematical and natural science. What Vico called poetic logic or the science of fancy became that Aesthetic Science which German philosophers, scholars, and artists eagerly pursued in the eighteenth century, till Kant carried it decisively further forward by his critique of intuition viewed as the confused concept (the Leibnizian doctrine), and Schelling and Hegel accomplished another great advance by comprehending art among the pure forms of the spirit, which brought them close to the doctrine of Vico. German (but not only German) Romanticism echoed Vico in the formulation of its theories, when it celebrated the fantasy as original creative power. There was too a recurrence of Vico's teachings on language, his interpretation of it not (in the intellectualist fashion) as an artificial system of signs but (as in Herder and Humboldt) as the free and poetic creation of the spirit. The interpretation of religion and myth in terms of allegory and deception gave way, in the teachings of David Hume, to the view of religion as a natural process corresponding to the initial stages of human life, all passion and imagination; Heyne then taught that myth is a *"sermo symbolicus"*, the product not of whim but of want and poverty, of *"sermonis egestas"*, reduced to expressing itself *"per rerum jam tum notarum similitudines"*; and O. Müller that it is impossible to understand myth without pene-

trating deeply enough into the human soul to perceive how it
necessarily and spontaneously arises. Religion thus ceased to be
viewed as extraneous and hostile to philosophy, a foolishness or
else a snare by which the cunning entrap the simple-minded. It
was, instead, viewed as Vico suggested, as a rudimentary philosophy thanks to which what was somehow present in poetic and
religious metaphysic survives in a rational metaphysic. By the
same token, poetry and history were no longer held asunder or
marshalled for mutual attack. On the contrary, one of the great
inspirers of the new German literature, Hamann (no match for
Vico as a thinker, but similar to him in temperament), had uttered
the prophetic warning: "If our poetry is no good, our history too
will be leaner than Pharaoh's kine." And a breath of poetry came
to freshen the historical writing of the nineteenth century, restoring to it colour and warmth. The utilitarism of Hobbes, Locke,
and the like came under fire, while the doctrine of the moral
conscience as a native sensitiveness, an altogether unreflective
judgement, reappeared, clad in new armour, in the *Critique of
Practical Reason*, and the fight against social atomism and the
contractualism which followed in its wake was pursued in Hegel's
Philosophy of Right. Freedom of conscience and religious indif-
ferentism as taught and inculcated by the seventeenth-century
publicists was repudiated at the level of philosophical doctrine,
and Hegel held just like Vico that a people without a deity was a
fond invention of the chroniclers of voyages in unknown or little
known regions, but altogether unevidenced in history.

The idealist school of German philosophy, carrying a stage
further the labours of the Reformation (which Vico had no occasion to know and still less to judge accurately), aimed not at
excising religion from the tissues of life, but at clothing philosophy
itself with the spiritual value of religion, which was thus confirmed
in a more refined form. That rugged *certitude* which Vico distinguished from the truth of law, was pondered over by thinkers
from Tomasio to Kant and Fichte, and then by the later moderns,
who sought, even if they did not find, the distinguishing criterion,
and all, or nearly all, showed lively awareness of the element of

"force" or "compulsion" which had been overlooked in the out-worn and superficial rhetoric of the moralizing school. It fell to the historical school of jurists, in their reaction against eighteenth-century revolutionary and abstractly reforming doctrine, to pick up the threads of Vico's other controversy, his resistance to the Platonic and Grotian notion of an ideal republic or a natural law, outside and above history, and to recognize, with Vico, that law is correlative to the entire social life of a people at a given historical moment, only in the context of which can law be critically comprehended, law, which is something as lively and plastic and changeable as language itself. And Vico's "Providence", Rationality and Objectivity of History, having a logic other than that which the individual's imagination and illusion project into it, took on with Hegel another and more prosaic description, "the cunning of history", wittily but absurdly transmuted by Schopenhauer into the celebrated cunning of the species, and unwittily but with insight by Wundt into the "law" of "heterogenesis of ends".

Thus almost all the capital ideas of the idealistic philosophy of the nineteenth century can be considered recurrences of Vico's teachings. Not quite all: for there are some which were not so much anticipated or prepared, as left room for by Vico, who felt the need of them, so that their enunciation is not a recurrence but a nineteenth-century advance upon him, accompanied by discordant warnings and reproofs at his expense. Later philosophy did not accept Vico's distinction between two worlds, those of the spirit and of nature, to both of which (so he held) was applicable the criterion of the interconvertibility of truth and fact, but applicable as regards the first by man, since that world was made by man and can be known by him, and as regards the second by God the creator alone, never by man. For the later, the new philosophy, out-Vicoing Vico, elevated the human demigod to divine status, the human mind to the status of Universal Spirit or Idea, and, spiritualizing and idealizing Nature, tried to embrace nature also as a comprehensible work of the Spirit in "The Philosophy of Nature". Every residue of a doctrine of Transcendency was thus eliminated, and the concept of Progress, ignored by Vico, though glimpsed and proclaimed in superficial rationalistic style by the Cartesians and their eighteenth-century successors, shone forth.

In this sphere, then, Vico's anticipation of the nineteenth century was incomplete. It was, by contrast, as complete as possible in the spheres where Vico's historical "discoveries" were echoed by the history and criticism of the later century. First and foremost in that of method: his scepticism about the tales of the ancient historians, his valuation of documents and monuments as more important than narratives, his exploration of languages as treasuries of primitive ideas and customs, his social interpretations of myths, his higher esteem for that which has developed spontaneously than for that which has been called forth by the contact of civilization, his warnings against reading the psychology of a modern age into primitive minds: all this and much more was echoed by the later thinkers. They echoed also his actual solutions of historical problems, affirming, as he had done, the archaic and barbaric character of the primitive Greek and Roman civilizations, the aristocratic and feudal nature of the primitive Greek and Roman political constitutions. To them also the ceremonial of ancient justice appeared as a dramatic poem evoking the circumstances of primitive war-making. So too after the French Jacobins and their Italian imitators nobody else visualized the Roman heroes as democratic heroes; and Homer was held to be a poet all the greater for his lack of polish. The history of Rome was reconstructed primarily upon the basis of Roman law, the names of the seven kings were read as symbols of institutions, and the tales of the origin of Rome were understood to be late Greek inventions or imitations of a Greek model. The substance of Roman history was found in the economic and juridical contest between the patricians and the plebeians (descendants, these, of the famuli or clients); and the class struggle, which Vico had been the first to draw into the limelight, was accepted as a widely valid canon of interpretation for the history of all times and for the understanding of the great historical upheavals. The Middle Ages, as they had attracted Vico, attracted the thinkers of the new age, especially during the post-Napoleonic restoration period, and were viewed, in accordance with Vico's theory, as the religious, aristocratic, and poetic period, the youthful age of modern Europe, by contrast with a rationalistic and bourgeois state of society. Italy rediscovered the greatness of her Dante. De Sanctis was the successor to Vico's initiation of the critical study of Dante, just as Niebuhr and Mommsen were heirs to his Roman historiography, Wolf, and then O. Müller and others, to his Homeric theory, Cornewall Lewis, Pais, and Lambert to his analogous theory concerning the twelve tables, Heyne, Müller, and Bachofen to his interpretation of myths, Grimm and other scholars to his ambition of reconstructing primitive life with the help of etymologies, Savigny and the historical school to his study of the spontaneous development of law, with preference for the customary over the codified, the Frenchmen Thierry and Fustel de Coulanges, the Italian Troya, and a legion of German scholars to his conception of the Middle Ages and of feudalism, Marx and Sorel to his idea of the class struggle and the rejuvenation of society by a return to primitive feeling, recurrences of barbarism: nay even Nietzsche's Superman is in some ways an echo of the Hero as portrayed by Vico. These are just a few names chosen and cited almost at random: to recall them all in their due place would mean writing the entire history of the most modern European thought. And this has not yet run its full course, even if under the description "positivism" we experienced a parenthesis of partial return to the abstract and materialistic thought of the eighteenth century. But the parenthesis now appears to be finally closed.

This multiple recurrence of the work of an individual in the work of many generations, this matching of a man with a century, justifies the conferment upon Vico, in the light of what happened after him, of the description "the nineteenth century in embryo". This will indicate the sort of place that he ought to hold in the history of modern thought. He should be placed alongside of Leibniz, with whom he has often been compared, and not because he is really, as has been mistakenly or superficially demonstrated, like him, but because he is so unlike as to be almost his opposite. Leibniz carried the doctrines of Descartes to their richest potentialities. For all his theory of "little perceptions" and "confused knowledge" he is an intellectualist; for all his dynamism (perhaps more imaginative than truly philosophical) he is a mechanical mind; for all his vast historical erudition, anti-historical; for all his life-long preoccupation with language, incapable of seeing into the nature of language; for all his attempt to explain the evil in the universe, an anti-dialectical thinker. Towards subsequent idealism the philosophy of Leibniz stands as the most perfect form of the old metaphysic which had to be superseded, whereas that of Vico stands as the first sketch of the new metaphysic, awaiting its development and definition. Leibniz addressed himself to his own century which rallied round him and gave immediate resonance to his utterance. Vico addressed himself to a coming century and around him found silence and the desert. But resonance or silence, the crowd or the desert, neither add to nor detract from the inner quality of thought.

[1910]

III

CONSIDERATIONS ON THE PHILOSOPHY
OF JACOBI

Jacobi's philosophy is pretty generally assessed in the histories of philosophical thought as the work of an amateur, dealing with only some single points of philosophy, impotent to compass the sublimities of a system, and attaining instead of this to a mere personal pattern of feeling or mysticism, of no theoretical value. Accordingly, the tone of comment upon him is usually condescending, perhaps indulgent, as befitting a good and well-intentioned soul who should not be blamed merely for not having achieved what his modest powers were incapable of achieving. We find much the same valuation and tone of comment on Jacobi in the fullest and most widely known monograph on the subject in a neo-Latin tongue, that of Lévy-Bruhl,[1] and wherever it is found it moves those of a better understanding to resentment at such an offence to truth, or to annoyance at the way in which narrow minds, all unaware of their inferiority, presume to measure themselves against their superiors. Thus Lévy-Bruhl treats Jacobi as little better than a psychopath and warns us not to "séparer la doctrine de l'homme" inasmuch as if we seek of him "une doctrine qui fasse corps, qui se défende ou qui s'impose" such a doctrine "n'échappe plus à une condamnation rigoureuse".[2] Such attitudes and judgements are typical among professional philosophers, just as among professional men of letters the praise of their own peers, makers of verse and prose which conform to the rules, and the sharp censure of poets and writers who follow an inner inspiration and detach themselves from the throng, are habitual. Very different was the attitude towards Jacobi of great philosophers who were his adversaries: Fichte, who took pains to obtain from Jacobi a recognition that they were really in agreement and afterwards declared that the particular disagreements which had divided them

1. *La philosophie de Jacobi* (Paris, 1894).
2. Ibid., 259-62 (the conclusion).

did not prevent him from still regarding him as "one of the first men of his age, one of the few links in the chain of true philosophic profundity";[1] Hegel, who having in his youth criticized him sharply, in his maturity repented of the first judgement and assigned him a high place in the construction of the logic of philosophy;[2] Schelling, who at first went for him in bitter controversial vein, but came to declare him "the most instructive personality in the whole of modern philosophy";[3] Herbart (belonging to a very different school), who numbered Jacobi "among the most eminent of his time"; admiring for example the help he had given to the reconstruction of the idea of reality, so badly spoiled by the Aristotelian distinction of matter and form, and his conception of cause detached from temporal conditions;[4] and finally of course Hamann and Herder, who, although authors of new truths, could also well, by those same critics, be dismissed as amateur philosophers (by critics, that is to say, who have never discovered any truth for themselves, but most scrupulously repeat, water down, dissect, and eclectically recombine, the discoveries of inspired philosophers).

Jacobi's philosophy, far from being "amateurish" in the bad sense of the word, serves as a most pure and serious example of the spontaneous generation of honest and fruitful philosophic thought. Jacobi did not study to be a philosopher; for many years he devoted himself to business and trade; and his philosophy was assuredly personal in the sense of being non-imitative, personal, that is, like the work of the poet whose universality is all one with his personality. As he himself said, it arose not out of any desire to

1. In his work of 1801: *Friedrich Nicolais Leben und sonderbare Meinungen*, in a note to Chapter VI (*Werke*, Leipzig, 1910, III, 678).

2. In the dissertation of 1802: *Glauben und Wissen oder die Reflektionsphilosophie der Subjektivität* (in *Erste Druckschriften*, ed. Lasson, Leipzig, 1928; specially pp. 262-273) as contrasted with the review (1817) of the third volume of the works of Jacobi (in *Werke*, XVII, 3-37); and in the introduction to the *Logica* in the *Encyclopaedia*.

3. *Münchener Vorlesungen zur Geschichte der neueren Philosophie*, ed. Drews (Leipzig, 1906), p. 167.

4. See the note to par. 155 in the *Introduction to Philosophy* (Italian translation by Vidossich, Bari, 1908) which he removed in the last editions.

elaborate a professorial system or any such chance occasion for a cold and lifeless labour, but out of a higher and irresistible impetus. It was directed towards the discovery not of truth in general, which is an absurdity like existence or reality in general, but of certain truths, required for the setting of his mind and heart at rest.[1] The crisis which brought to Jacobi self-awareness and self-confidence, opening "a new epoch" in his life, was marked by a conversation with the teacher and philosopher Lesage, to whom he frankly confessed that he could not understand philosophical literature and was tormented by the slightness and weakness of his own intelligence. The other answered him smilingly "Vous êtes malin", and assured him that most of the contents of the philosophical books he was reading either meant nothing or were erroneous.[2] From then onwards his effort to obey his inner voice without forcing it or betraying its purity was so scrupulous as to make him distrustful of subsequent reflection as being liable often to spoil what had been created in the first ardour, and which was to him as to poets is the sacred mystery that has been celebrated in their moment of inspiration. He remained tenaciously attached to his own thoughts, indefatigable in proclaiming and defending them as long as he lived. At the end of his life in his last discourse he repeated what he had said in the first.[3] He was sure that he was working for the "invisible church", and at the end of his long struggle he held that he had participated in the best and most useful of all tasks, and having lived enough was entitled to ask the Lord to let him depart in peace according to his deserts. But in his eagerness for truth, his effort to attain sureness, he did not shut himself up in the assured pride of a visionary, but sought out the reason of the errors of others, and that positive element which lay

1. *Spinoza's Teachings: Letters to Mendelssohn* (Italian translation by Capra, Bari, 1914) pp. 4, 18. Let me point out that as Jacobi continually presented his favourite thoughts in new literary forms, the few quotations which I give in this essay suffice for a short documentation, but do not pretend to offer, in the references, a *concordantia jacobiana*.

2. *David Hume über den Glauben, oder Idealismus und Realismus* (*Werke*, II, 180-5).

3. *Spinoza's Teachings*, p. 19.

in those errors, striving to find his way sympathetically into their way of thought, erroneous though it might be.[1]

The blame which has also fallen upon Jacobi for his incapacity to achieve a systematic construction has its root in the ordinary, and I would add vulgar concept of system. It behoves us to rid ourselves of this, to change profoundly the meaning which we give to "system". We should in fact maintain on the one hand that every single truth is essentially systematic, linking itself expressly or implicitly to all other philosophic truths, in default of which it would not be truth at all; but on the other hand, and no less strongly, that the closed and definitive system is a Utopian aspiration. Truth is the history of truth, and in history any one personage plays his part and cannot play that of all others, present and future; nay, he cannot even play his own future part in its development towards that end which death alone will seal. It was in view of just such considerations that I myself offered the sublimation of the concept of system into that of systematizations, systematizations understood to be at one and the same time complete and incomplete, already made and still to be made. But this concept of systematizations is dynamic, and if it is, instead, taken to be static, the consequence must be that a character of historical wholeness will be attributed to a moment of history, in a vain effort to exhaust the inexhaustible motion of thought. Philosophical encyclopaedias may in their way be useful enough, no denial is here intended of this, but they should be taken for what they really are, namely total expositions of a moment of thought, themselves, accordingly, caught up in history, and not, what would be something else, total achievements of thought. The source of effective philosophy is life itself, not the scholastic encyclopaedia; such philosophy is, as Jacobi insisted, particular and determinate, a contribution to the warm process of thought, not an end or conclusion of it. It happens that certain thinkers, after treading for a certain time in the conventional ruts of formulae and problems, at a certain point of their lives break free and attain to effective phi-

1. *Werke*, II, 186.

losophic activity, so winning immortal fruits. At other times they, or some other thinker, will be misled by the dream of a perfectly rounded and final system, into loading upon their own works of creative genius some additional feature which springs not from free and authentic thought but from bookish or artificial study. In any case, thinkers belong to the history of thought solely in virtue of their fortunate moments, their discoveries of particular truths. At the threshold of the temple of philosophy they must lay down all the rest of their heavy luggage, purge themselves of all the waste matter that has become attached to them. Here the work of the critics comes in, distinguishing what is living from what – having given rise to new problems and suitable solutions in other thinkers' minds, or in the mind of the critic himself (who to be a true critic must be a philosopher, an original philosopher) – is dead. It is just so that in the poets, even the greatest of them, poetic and unpoetic passages are found side by side, the latter seldom being absent or negligible. Jacobi, who belonged to the company of simple and uncontaminated philosophers, holding fast to his own living experience, avoiding the artificial and the spectacular, did but seldom pretend to see beyond the limits of his field of vision, or indulge in vague and confused utterance. He preferred to leave his system open rather than to close it with masonry which others would then have to demolish in order to readmit the fresh air of life. Jacobi once said of Montesquieu that whatever defects he exhibited nevertheless "he truly promoted mental enlightenment by adding to the total of distinct concepts, this being the true criterion of merit in a philosophic writer – the rest is gone with the wind".[1] This tribute may be fittingly paid to Jacobi himself. The form which he gave to his literary expressions, shaping them on the spur of the moment and resorting at first to the naive devices of the philosophical tale, was a protest against the academic chair-holders of his time, who with their conviction that "what is not right for the class-room is not right for humanity"[2] were bound to be outraged by the ap-

1. In the review (1783) of *Des lettres de cachet* (by Linguet) in *Werke* III,, 434.
2. *Spinoza's Teachings*, p. 19.

pearance of his work in such an irregular and unacademic guise.

Let us now turn to yet another charge which is made against Jacobi: that which stresses his sentimentalism or mysticism. Now while it is true that no satisfying philosophical conclusions can be elicited from this source, nevertheless it is a necessary moment of the human spirit, the moment of "self-feeling" as yet indeterminate and depending for its philosophical value upon what went before and what came after it. What went before it was a practical act whereby certain unsatisfactory theoretical assertions, dazzling and distorting rather than light-bringing, were rejected in favour of a re-entry into oneself, a retreat to a resting-place in the shade. What came after was a theoretical criticism of those assertions, those fallacious, inadequate, or ill-digested theories, and with this a new philosophical truth. The pure, strict, and abstract mystic is simply not to be found in the world, those who so describe themselves being either foolish souls or the weary who have lingered too long in that shadowy retreat from which they should have come forth rested and reinvigorated. Now Jacobi's mystical moment was preceded by a grievous discomfort in face of the philosophical ideal of his time, materialism, naturalism, determinism, intellectualism, logicism, exaltation of the exact science of nature to the status of metaphysic, introduction of this metaphysic into the field of philosophical truth. It was followed by the reasoned criticism of that ideal, the sense of need for a new logic of philosophy, activated by what Jacobi first called "feeling" or "immediate knowing", but later renamed "reason", therewith heralding a new and deeper rationalism.[1] Jacobi was thus far from being a sheer abstract mystic. His was a critical thought, positive and negative alike, as is all serious and permanently valuable critical thought.

We should carefully note the nature of Jacobi's criticism of what he variously terms "Spinozism", "Fatalism", "Atheism", and also

[1]. Jacobi ended by calling himself and his disciples "realists of the true and original reason", saying that the academic philosophers had wrongly foisted on them the description "Philosophers of sentiment or Gemüt" (*Werke, Einleitung* to Vol. II, 12).

(showing that his rejection of system usually betokens simply a rejection of deterministic intellectualism) "Systematism", by all of which he means philosophy developed along the causal and deterministic pattern of the physico-mathematical science of nature. Jacobi himself enunciated this criticism with the greatest clearness in all his works from the first to the last, while it has been only very approximately and roughly potted in the relevant chapters of the histories of philosophy. Jacobi sincerely admired the philosophy of Spinoza as the most logical and coherent of all developments of the principle of Cause, in which the Teleological principle was wholly and radically banned, while at the starting point of the chain of causes and effects Spinoza placed an immaterial void (but this was really thoroughly material, however much the lack of material definition was emphasized), a God (in reality not a God at all, being neither spirit nor person, but thing, divine thing, *das* and not[1] *der Gott*), to which he illicitly attributed infinite other realities and perfections over and above the extensiveness which was its only legitimate attribute.[2] It is so to speak the interest of physico-mathematical science – the model for Spinoza's construction – that there should be no God: God is indifferent to its purposes and rightly goes unsought by it.[3] The principle of causality has no sway beyond nature, the total sphere of the finite, and indeed its analysis leads to the recognition that there is no totality, the concept of nature, when severed from the supernatural, turning out to be fictitious.[4] The principle of cause, which becomes absurd when carried into the realm of theory and truth, has its origin in the fact that man is not solely an intuitive and believing being, but also one who acts. Cause is nothing else than this acting, living, free, personal force, the producer of every effect. We experience this in our own selves, nor could we otherwise arrive at this arbitrary representation of cause and effect or apply it in equally arbitrary fashion.[5] The mathematical elements such as point, line, surface, would be *mauvaises plaisanteries* if we conceived them as being anterior to reality. They are but an abstraction derived from and

1. *Einleitung*, in *Werke*, II, 83.   2. *Spinoza's Teachings*, p. 14.
3. Ibid., p. 9.   4. Ibid., p. 11.   5. *Werke*, II, 200-201.

constructed upon reality, a system of symbols and signs having a distant relation with reality and seeming wholly intelligible only because shaped by ourselves. Indeed for this reason what lies outside of the system seems unintelligible.[1] But what lies outside it is art, philosophy, virtue, all that moves and uplifts us in Homer, Sophocles, Pheidias, Socrates, Epaminondas, and the reason of whose moving and uplifting power is not to be explored. A disciple of Newton may feel delight in contemplating the starry heaven, but if asked why he feels it he will answer that it springs from his ignorance.[2] But this deterministic and fatalistic view is abhorred by human feeling which seeks out what the other ignores and finds in it the highest value for its own sake in the mode of immediate knowledge.[3]

The emphasis placed by Jacobi upon such immediacy of knowing is entirely legitimate. For, as he used to say, all of us are born in and all must remain in the faith "just as we are all born and must remain in society, unable to reach out towards certainty unless that certainty has already been granted to us, granted, that is, in terms of something already known for certain, not requiring and not admitting proof, but carrying its own ground in itself, whereas what is known by proof is but second-hand knowledge".[4] And Jacobi uttered the warning that whoever, unlike himself, was not invaded by the sense of liberty, could never be won round to his views, which would remain for such an one sheer nothingness, and their author a nobody.[5] Pointless is therefore the customary objection that Jacobi's philosophy "is wanting in genuine and objective demonstration, being a purely personal philosophy".[6] One might with as much justice assent to a demand for a demonstration of the affirmation that a certain poem or picture is beautiful, which would undermine one of the most sure results of Kant's *Critique of Judgement* – the grounding of aesthetic judgement in

1. *Werke*, II, 178-9, IV, part II, p. 132.
2. *Einleitung* in *Werke*, II, 54-55.
3. Ibid., p. 48.
4. *Spinoza's Teachings*, p. 123.
5. Ibid., p. 7.
6. For example by ÜBERWEG-HEINZE, 9th edn., III, 379.

immediate taste. Taste, it was there said, was theirs who possessed it: those who do not possess it should try to awaken it if they can, and to cultivate its gradual growth, but cannot possibly demand that it should be demonstrated to them by a sort of mathematical operation. Where the aesthetic valuation is worked out in logical terms such a rational development presupposes the priority of an immediate spiritual act: it has issued forth from the sphere of immediate knowledge into that of intellectual argument. Hegel himself praised Jacobi for his clear and vigorous insistence upon the supreme importance of the immediacy of the knowledge of God, the God who is Life, Spirit, and Eternal Love, and who, discerning himself in himself, is his own self-knowledge.[1] Now Kant, in the *Critique of Pure Reason*, had himself pointed out the limits of physico-mathematical natural science, confuting the metaphysics constructed upon that basis. Kant was pursuing the train of thought of the *De Antiquissima*, ignorant of its existence, though Jacobi at a certain point of his work was on the contrary aware of it, and was the first to spot the link of Vico's famous saying "Geometrica ideo demonstramus quia facimus: physica si demonstrare possemus, faceremus" with Kant's *Critique of Pure Reason*.[2] Now Kant had distinguished the *Verstand* or Intellect from the *Vernunft*, or Reason, and had shown how abusive are the methods of the former when applied to the problems of the supra-sensible. But he had not been brave enough to declare the science of the intellect to be non-truth, non-science, by contrast with the sole true science and philosophy which is that of the Reason. On the contrary he had held the former to be the sole and true science, the only science given to mankind, introducing thereupon a veritable confusion of tongues, in that while explicitly subordinating Reason to Intellect he implicitly subordinated Intellect to Reason. Thus the deepest needs of the human spirit, instead of being satisfied, were but hinted at in the postulates of the practical Reason, and judged irreducible to the fullness of knowledge. Jacobi

1. In the notice already quoted, *Vermischte Schriften*, II, 9.
2. In Chapter III of the *De Antiquissima*: compare JACOBI, *Von den göttlichen Dingen und ihrer Offenbarung*, composed in 1811 (*Werke*, III, 351-54).

was more radical and more inspired than Kant in his treatment
of the problem, for having given to Caesar, that is the Intellect,
the things which were Caesar's, all that pertains to its sphere of
work, he gave to no element of this the rank of truth, but reserved
the awareness of truth to the "feeling" which we have seen he also
called "Reason".

The superiority of this position of Jacobi to that of Kant was
recognized openly by Hegel in the preface to the Logic in his
Encyclopaedia. Hegel enumerated in the order of their progressive
perfection the "three positions of thought in regard to objectivity":
first the naive position of the old intellectualistic-dogmatic philosophy, corresponding more or less to the conclusions of Wolff
and the empiricists (whose system-building appears to conflict
with but is really akin to that philosophy); secondly the Kantian
critical position; thirdly, and furthest ahead in the line of progress,
Jacobi's theory of immediate knowledge.[1] It was Hegel's further
opinion that Jacobi in his critique of Kantian philosophy had not
just pushed forward his own differing conception without arguing
the matter out, but had treated it in the most authentic, that is to
say in the dialectical manner. On the other hand in dealing with
the philosophy of Fichte, technically formulated in a manner
which would have facilitated a dialectical confutation, Jacobi had
contented himself with assailing the underlying Fichtean principle
of the abstract, unilateral, and unmoved Ego with the weapon of
his own keen intuition of the absolute concreteness of the spiritual.[2]

But Hegel, while feeling that Jacobi's insistence upon the concrete brought him close to his own way of thought, could not
rest content with the concept of an immediate Knowing which
was not itself a mediation. The mediation in question would
indeed be something quite different from the ratiocinative intellect:
it would be a mediation surpassing the Reason which Jacobi
called by the various terms "feeling", "insight", "assurance", "intellectual intuition", "faith", "irresistible certainty", dangerous terms

1. *Encyclopaedia*, §§ 61-78.
2. See besides these paragraphs of the *Encyclopaedia* the already quoted
review in *Vermischte Schriften*, pp. 15-21.

which could serve to introduce sheer occurrence, the caprice of
individual opinion and assertion, imagination and superstition, and
who knows what else. Faith and intuition when elevated by Jacobi
to such exalted status were not, Hegel pointed out, something
different from Thought; and there was in Jacobi's discussion too
much of the *aut-aut*, amounting to a relapse into the *principium
exclusi tertii*, or that very "intellect" as envisaged in the old metaphysics which he had criticized. And if, said Hegel, the intuition
of the Absolute is intellectual, having for its content not the rigid
Substance but the Spirit, it would likewise behove us to reject any
mere form of substantive knowledge, tantamount to an immediacy
of knowing. Hegel accordingly indicated to Jacobi the proper
goal, the new dialectical mode of thought for which his theory of
the anti-intellectualistic immediate knowledge had been the preparation and the summons. And he recalled a letter written by
Jacobi to his brother of September 5th 1787 in which, expounding
the opinions of Hamann, he had pointed out how Hamann disliked the principle of contradiction and of the excluded middle and
aimed with an insistent though only in part realizable desire at the
attainment of Bruno's *coincidentia oppositorum*, that distant light
which shone ever more strongly for him. It was to be hoped,
then, said Hegel, that Jacobi, who had shown such insight into
the mind of Hamann, would himself come to terms with a mode
of knowledge which expressed awareness of the coincidence of
opposites, and rescued from the category of impenetrable mysteries
and prodigies the ideas of Personality, Freedom, and God.[1]

In all of this, Hegel was right. There was a provisional character,
a sort of allusiveness pointing to a concealed and privy nucleus, in
Jacobi's propositions that Reason is intuition, sentiment, tendency,
and instinct;[2] that it does not, like the intellect, create concepts, or
construct systems, or even pass judgements, but that, on the
contrary, it does but make positive revelations and announcements,
alike, in this, to the exterior senses;[3] that this revelation is properly

1. See quoted paragraphs, *passim*, and Review, pp. 12, 26-37.
2. *Jacobi an Fichte* in *Werke*, III, 32, and *passim*.
3. *Werke*, II, 58, *Einleitung*.

to be termed miraculous;[1] that faith is the reflection of the divine
knowledge and will in the infinite spirit of man, and that if man
presumed to convert it into knowledge, this would fulfil the
promise of the Serpent to Eve in the Garden: man would become
as God;[2] together with numerous other sayings of the same sort
all tending in one direction. This concealed nucleus required to be
brought out into the light and set to work. There is, indeed, a
moment of the immediacy of truth, but this moment is referrable
and complementary to a mediation. Truth is an inner vital experience of men who in the very act of that experience seek it
out, defend it, dispute logically to possess it. Truth is (and indeed
mankind is) History, in being and in development, and is what it
is by developing, and develops by being what it is. Jacobi, however, remained distrustful of all invitations to accomplish that
final step, turning a deaf ear. Why so distrustful? Why so stubborn?
Truth to tell, Jacobi too had his good reasons. In the position into
which Hegel was trying to thrust him he felt the presence of a
danger. There seemed somehow to him, and not altogether
wrongly, to be a trap in the proffered replacement of the liv-
ingly concrete real by the conceptual abstractions and fictions of
the intellect. That formula – said to sum up Jacobi's theory – of
the inverse relation between reality and intelligibility, so that in
a limiting case the perfectly intelligible is unreal and the perfectly
real unintelligible,[3] was only apparently paradoxical and astounding. As he meant it, it had a character of full truth. He spied out
the "idealism" lurking in the various and rival doctrines of the
Spinozian philosophers; an idealism which according to the original
sense of that word in the controversies of the times held truth, or as
much of truth as is accessible to men, to lie in the abstractions of
physico-mathematical science or of a metaphysical causal-deter-
minism modelled thereupon. He, by contrast, claimed to be a
"realist" and nothing else, vigilant against every interference by or
recourse to the intellect, because, he said, the realist who wanders

1. *Werke*, II, 167.   2. *Werke*, II, 55-56, *Einleitung*.
3. Lévy-Bruhl, op. cit., p. 79.

along that path is bound to tumble into the snares set for him by the idealist.[1] For him Kant too was an idealist, even though, in the spirit of realism, he posited a thing-in-itself which, for all his beliefs and opinions, he was not in a position to posit or to relate and articulate in any manner with the constructs of science, there being no transition from the one to the other. Still more obviously was Fichte an idealist, with his dissolution of everything into a fluid *menstruum* with not so much as a *caput mortuum* of *non-Ego* left unmelted.[2] As for Hegel, he might indeed be compassing emancipation from Spinozism with his philosophy of freedom, but in Jacobi's view he was sticking to the method of science and gaining the progress which he made by a straining of the intellect. Jacobi justified his own repugnance for the notion of Dialectic by pointing to the reappearance which this must needs evoke of necessity, system, the substitution of the general and abstract for the individual and concrete.[3] And in truth, important and fruitful as was the dialectical doctrine at which Hegel had arrived, a logic having its home in philosophy and history, yet by a kind of compromise with the Hellenic and Scholastic tradition and with Cartesian and Spinozian rationalism, he left standing the constructs of the Intellect, merely undertaking to correct and elevate and complete them by the agency of the Dialectic, which, when used for this purpose, necessarily became something extrinsic. The result was that he preserved many of the patterns of the old metaphysics, albeit filling them with a content of new thought which should logically have burst and dispersed them. Hence Hegel's inadmissible philosophizations of mechanics, physics, chemistry, physiology, zoology, and the whole range of natural and psychological disciplines together with the empirical classifications practised upon the moral and juridical sciences, and the formalized versions of aesthetics and logic. Hence, too, arose Hegel's antiquat-

1. *Werke*, II, 172-73.
2. *Werke*, III, 22.
3. Letter to Neeb of May 30 1817 about Hegel's review article, in ROTH, *Jacobi's Briefwechsel*, II, 466-8, here cited according to the summary given by Lévy-Bruhl (op. cit., p. 258).

ed tripartition of philosophy into a logical-metaphysical department, a philosophy of nature, and a philosophy of mind, or spirit,
and his grave compromising of his own profound conception of
the historical nature of the real, by treating it naturalistically,
tricking it out with abstract dialectics and imprisoning it in a
definitive totality in his philosophy or metaphysics of history. And
it was this that brought about that consequent anti-metaphysical
rebellion which undermined philosophy itself and opened the way
to positivism and other nineteenth-century mental adventures.

   Therefore it was that Jacobi would not be won round by the
deference his censor and contradictor was now showing to him
or by the good will with which he was exhorted to accompany
Hegel along the common path. The essential truth to which Jacobi
clung so tightly was recognized even by his other much more
censorious censor, Schelling, whom Jacobi had on his side accused
not only of "idealism" but of "idealmaterialism".[1] Schelling, having in the second phase of his thought shaken off (or so he imagined) his inherited idealism, had now taken up a position against
Hegel, and in doing so paid tribute to Jacobi as the man who had
all along rightly stood up to Hegel and his like, maintaining that
logic (the intellectualistic logic, that is) does not coincide with
reality, and that to want to deduce the existent is sheer vanity.[2]
This shows the strength and the weight of Jacobi's supposed
obstinacy in rejecting any theory of knowledge which might have
caught him up in the nets of intellectualism, an obstinacy which
some have mistakenly represented as poverty, logical incapacity,
the confession of impotence.[3]

   But in what way was it possible to accept the great principle of
dialectical thinking as proclaimed by Hegel, without getting
caught up in those nets and artifices? Correlatively, how was it
possible to preserve and maintain the salutary lessons of the critique
directed against causal determinism and the systems of abstrac-

   1. *Werke*, III, 354.
   2. *Münchener Vorlesungen*, p. 133, n. 2.
   3. Among them LÉVY-BRUHL, op. cit., *passim*, esp. the conclusion, pp.
247-54.

tions, and yet to advance a stage beyond the provisional form of immediate, alogical thought? How to exorcize the ghost of "idealism" in that pejorative sense as equivalent to phenomenism and illusionism, engendering the monster solipsism. How to reacquire faith in the truth and reality of knowledge by retracing the way from outwardness to inwardness, from nature to spirit, from perception to self-awareness? This was a problem that neither Hegel nor Jacobi could tackle, but only their successors. It is our present and living problem. Useless to enquire how Hegel and Jacobi solved it or would have solved it, for they neither could nor did propound it in these right terms. However, to throw light upon that problem is to justify and to understand their teachings, for philosophers are to be understood not by statically halting by their side, but by dynamically overtaking them.

Jacobi opposed to the "idealism" which, however unwillingly, remains tied to the idea of knowledge as *Verstand* and to the schemes of the natural sciences, no matter how much it tries to improve upon them by the dialectical method, the unspoiled truth of things seen or felt and uncontaminated by abstraction. To the abstract deductions of the ideas of God, freedom, personality, the values of the spirit, he opposed the knowledge of these ideas by feeling or immediate knowing, admitting a "rational intuition" with a "sensible intuition" to match it.[1] But he made no particular enquiry why and how the intellectualistic knowledge of the *Verstand* came about. He even thought that the *Verstand* could make an appearance without the necessary premiss of the *Vernunft* which alone can afford the conditions for its practical origin.[2] Above all, he omitted to enquire whether the spirit can ever know things if it has not produced them itself: too easily he renounced any explanation and rested content with the word Wonder. As already mentioned he had knowledge of Vico's *De Antiquissima* and very intelligently spotted in Vico's *Verum-Factum* the germ of the Kantian a priori synthesis and the agnosticism that went with it. But he did not know Vico's *Scienza Nuova*, in

1. *Spinoza's Teachings*, p. 6; *Einleitung* in *Werke*, II, 59.
2. *Einleitung*, p. 110.

which that scepticism is laid aside, and the *Verum-Factum* principle
is raised to the higher level of a contemplation of truth, inasmuch
as "man knows his own history because he himself made it". That
the spirit and philosophy are historical was a doctrine outside his
range of vision. Once, it is true, he mentions it, saying that philosophy cannot create its own material, this being always part and
parcel of present or past history; but he does not develop or deepen
this statement, which, indeed, he appears to mean in the relativistic
sense of a dependence of philosophy upon the changing passions
of the times.[1] But the failure to pursue those hints further, the
limits which he laid upon himself, the uncertainties which made
him pause, do not annul the truth of his observations on scientific
method, his criticism of the devices of deterministic metaphysics,
the prominence into which he drew the immediacy of knowing
in the workings of the human soul, and other points which he
clearly established. (Of course, like all the conclusions of philosophy, these are conclusions only in the sense of being starting
points for further progress.) A philosopher takes up his place in the
history of thought in virtue solely of those truths which he
positively enunciated: the truths which others say that he ought
to have enunciated belong not to him but to those others, and his
errors, whether great or small, do not count. History, unlike
schoolmasters in junior forms, does not give bad marks, but only
good ones.

No less important are the truths which Jacobi enunciated and
upheld in the sphere of moral philosophy. It behoves us in the
first place to recognize the value of his affirmation of a personal
God counterposed to that impersonal God which he saw enthroned
at the apex of the intellectualistic philosophies, a composition of
nothingness, a concept of pure negation, of material immateriality,
however much dressed up as the Unconditioned, the Absolute,
the Unity-Totality, the Idea, and so forth, without independence
or consciousness, in its very appearance no more than an empty
shadow, vainly invested with an atmosphere of rigid religious

---

1. *Spinoza's Teachings*, p. 137.

devotion; a God that could in no way be proclaimed, being a mere insoluble residue of deterministic science, one of the postulates or *foci imaginarii* of the practical reason.[1] "Man", he protests, "is thus made out to be a compost of the illusion of the sense and of the illusion of the reason, of optical illusions and ideal illusions. On one side is nature, a dream, on the other side God, a dream, and in betwixt an Intellect which ends by revealing to this Misbeing (*Unwesen*), Man, how his dream of truth is the truth of a dream that is necessary, eternal, and universal, and from which there is no awakening save into a general nothingness."[2] Jacobi repeatedly demonstrated, and it is therefore hardly necessary to labour the point, that he did not identify his Personal God with the God of any positive or revealed religion, or with any mythical form,[3] though it must perhaps be recognized that this, like his other limiting concepts, was not arrived at by dint of speculative, albeit anti-intellectualistic thought, but hailed as a miracle. Yet in regard to this affirmation-negation we may once again say that Jacobi proffered it in response to a deep challenge or, as it might be put, by way of revolt against the confounding of concept with reality. Just as the concept of poetry is not poetry and cannot raise the feelings which are raised by the living individuality of poems, or be made the object of a loving cult (how tiresome we most of us find the aesthete worshippers and priests of an indescribable pure and abstract beauty!), so the reality of God can only be living reality, "personality" and not abstraction, independence and a-wareness, not their opposites. Yet Jacobi, having rejected the God of the positive religions and other similar mythical forms, was unable to conceive Deity, as he would have desired, as being external to man, or as some sort of theistic or pantheistic essence partaking of Being. He must perforce direct his critical thought, just like Hegel, to that very contradictory concept of "Being", and so pass on to the conception of a Becoming which surpasses

1. *Einleitung*, 78-82; *Werke*, III, 201, 341-46, 382-88.
2. *Werke*, III, 229-31.
3. Hence the irony of LÉVY-BRUHL who finds Jacobi's mysticism "singulièrement timide et réservé, bien discret" etc. (op. cit., 242-43).

Being and Not-Being, and eludes the stranglehold of the *aut-aut*, "either God external to man or man himself as God",[1] by holding both the terms thus defined to be mythical entities: by contrast with which only the becoming, the divine which produces itself in its own works and history, truly *is*. With a slight modification we could here repeat what Fichte said of the Ego: "My solution, the solution of my reason, is not Ego, Myself, but more than Myself, better than Myself, something wholly different."[2]

But much neater and clearer than this was the argument which Jacobi conducted in a different direction against another confusion, and its serious practical consequences, the confusion of moral reality with laws and institutions, outward things. This serious argument reveals itself on examination to be analogous to Jacobi's own criticism of the abstract concepts when these are made to usurp the place of the realistic intuition of truth. Jacobi accordingly was the adversary of every sort of law-imposed morality. He was even dissatisfied with Kant's doctrine and contrary to his concept of duty and formula of the universal law with all the other particulars deduced or imagined by Kant to be deducible therefrom. What alone counts for Jacobi is the voice of the heart, the inner urge, the moral conscience, sure and lasting source of all goodness in human works. It is this that stands above all law, indeed as occasion requires transforms the eternal law, or replaces it by the originality of action, or even breaks up, with violence, the tables of the laws.[3] In a famous page[4] Jacobi approves and celebrates the mendacity of the dying Desdemona, the ruse of Pylades, Timoleon's fratricide (his brother was the tyrant), the violation of oaths and laws by Epaminondas and John de Witt, David's rape of the treasures of the Temple, the suicide of Otho, and the plucking of ears of corn on the sabbath: for the law is made for man not man for the law, and man's sovereign right, his divine nature, is his

1. *Werke*, III, 48-49.
2. *Werke*, III, 35.
3. Especially in the novel *Woldemar* this theme is developed with warm and clear eloquence.
4. Letter to Fichte, *Werke*, III, 37.

principium aggratiandi against the mere letter of the law. This marked the conclusion of the reign of casuistry, of Jesuitical morality,
and the justification of the criticism directed against it, albeit in
heavy legal trappings, by the Jansenists. It led the way, one may
say, for Schleiermacher's celebrated memorial on the subject of
the "permissive". Jacobi starts from a comparison which is truly
something more than a comparison, being the index of a common
spiritual principle. He starts, that is, from recalling how in the
sphere of poetry and beauty Taste has a full and absolute right;
nothing can flourish without taste, and the knowledge and pronouncement of taste are uttered without recourse to the intellect
or to demonstrations, for it is a law unto itself.[1] Jacobi feels keenly
the link of virtue with the life of the passions: he dislikes the
Kantian categorical imperative, "stiff and dead";[2] he sees clearly
that without sensations, appetitions, passions, there is no issue for
the human reason; that true morality does indeed master passion,
but preserves the form of passion, fine and noble feelings being
engendered solely by fine and noble impulses;[3] and that morality
can be incited only by persuasive example, not by calculations and
maxims. Not all the subtleties of transcendental philosophy could
avail to dislodge his heart from his breast to make room for the
mere urge of the abstract, nor would he free himself from dependence upon love in order to bask in the delights of pride.[4]

Hegel, while acknowledging the justice of Jacobi's criticism of
the Kantian law and his rightful defence of the omnipotent, pure,
and universal negativity of the will against the assertions of the
determinate, nevertheless considered that Jacobi had overshot the
mark when he passed on from challenging determinate laws to
challenging the very idea of law and its particularization into the
rights, duties, and rules which form the content of the ethical
sphere. Hegel feared that this attitude was coloured by a remnant
of the vain and capricious morality of the Romantics, a tendency
to rate magnanimity higher than rectitude, nobility higher than
morality. These, in his view, were ethics of presumption, and an

1. *Woldemar* (*Werke*, v), 78-108.   2. *Werke*, III, 37-39, 41.
3. *Woldemar*, 191-94.   4. *Werke*, III, 40-41.

inflation of the sentiment.[1] Yet in truth Jacobi did not deny the laws and their usefulness. He held them to be indispensable supports of virtue, a sort of crutch or artificial limb which may at the right moment take on the attributes of life. True, he sometimes called them a "necessary evil". But not only does the "necessary" assign to them a rightful place: there is a further explanation given by Jacobi. Being devices, he says, not for promoting the good but for preventing the bad, they easily take on the nature of evil. The conscience cannot be ruled by them but, on the contrary, they are subject to the conscience. The method of the stick and the carrot is most suitable treatment for beasts, but liberty, unconstrained judgement, self-determination are the character of man: indeed among the animals the tiger and the lion are more akin to him than beasts of burden or fattened flocks.[2] In his moral simplicity and uprightness Jacobi in fact exhibits no trace of the whims and caprices of the Romantics. He himself utters warnings against that sort of egoism which is generated in the struggles against social laws.[3] Romantic sickliness is quite absent, and in *Woldemar*, the unfinished novel which celebrates the ideal of a pure love between man and woman, warning is given of the real and serious danger of friendship passing over into erotic bewitchment; of the enslavement to something outside ourselves and our inner life which is threatened by the allurements of a mortal countenance fully occupying our senses and robbing us of our selves.[4]

Jacobi does not merit Hegel's adverse criticism. Indeed this criticism, with its zealous championship of laws and institutions, shows up the great fault in Hegelian ethics, the fault which led Hegel to conceive morality as an abstract, imperfect, inferior moment, with the final, concrete, and superior sphere of the ethical, the sphere of the State, of historically given institutions, raised

1. See review article already quoted, pp. 22-27, and *Encyclopaedia* (quoted paragraphs).
2. *Woldemar*, 86-87, 445-6, and passim.
3. Ibid., 445-6.
4. Ibid., 309, 360-1, 465, and passim.

above it. This may properly be called a historicism of bad quality, calculated to depress and oppress the moral conscience and the creative urges. Hegel may indeed have had good reason to inveigh against the sentimentalism, the unbridled licence of the passions, the feigned nobility of feeling, the anarchism of the Romantics. But this gave him no right to exalt his day-to-day controversial arguments as a moralist and publicist to the level of philosophical principle, distorting the truth and in practice introducing errors and favouring various abuses including those directly opposite to what he was combating – for example, in his campaign against sentimentalism and softness, opening the way to harshness, and in his campaign against the impulse of the passions inculcating servile obedience; and demolishing anarchy only to introduce tyranny. This was no merely individual and self-regarding error on the part of Hegel; it was at large in the conceptions and way of life of his nation. Even today we see its strength in the theories and the fanatical cult of the State there prevailing, and moreover we recognize what underlies the supposedly "ethical" nature of that State – something far from pleasant.

Jacobi made freedom the centre of the soul. Lacking freedom, a man could never become aware of limits or break the bounds of those limits to soar to the unlimited and suprasensible.[1] He called freedom the "root of virtue" and also the "fruit of virtue".[2] Now Jacobi was a resolute and constant upholder of political liberty, finding himself called upon to defend it against adverse fashions and factions of every sort. In this way he stood up against two hostile assaults from the two foes of freedom standing at opposite extremes in the eighteenth century: absolutism and Jacobinism, Joseph II and Robespierre. In both of these, no doubt, there was elevated feeling and warm faith in the Reason, but both of them desired to impose the good, as they saw it, by exercising authority forcefully upon the will. But such violent use of force is at one and the same time an imposition of law and a flouting of law by the imposer. As such it is sterile, or, as history teaches us, fruitful only

1. *Introduction*, as quoted, pp. 80–81.
2. *Woldemar*, p. 447.

through exciting a reaction on the part of the forces of freedom against the obstacles placed in its way. Far from creating those forces it encounters their hostility. If it brings with it some advantages of detail, these are of no account, in their pettiness and fleetingness, by comparison with the dreadful effects produced. Military victories and reinforcement against enemies are no adequate compensations. The internal enemy, who in annihilating the sense of liberty annihilates also the sense of the fatherland, is far worse than the external enemy. Nor can or should any political constitution have virtue for its immediate object, since virtue can never be engendered out of something other than itself.[1] And Jacobi likewise enjoins Robespierre and the Jacobins to appreciate that *la raison* in which they place such faith was not Reason, but a mistakenly and wrongly conceived sort of abstract intellect, not, indeed, peculiar to the French legislators but in truth the "erreur du siècle". This had been encouraged by the rapid progress of the exact sciences, giving rise to the idea of a "manière fixe" in government founded upon sheer "raison". This amounted to a confounding of impressions received in experience with the real principles which are antecedent to all experience; a levelling of the differences and contrasts among men to an abstraction of humanity and of "natural law"; a waiting upon the operation of "raison" to supply that lively impulse to Society and the State which only the affections can convey.[2] Herewith Jacobi, stressing his anti-intellectualism even in the political field, declared against the Enlightenment. But this really meant that he was a man of the Enlightenment in the better and deeper sense, as attested incidentally by his vigorous maintenance of the essential value of culture. He stressed the emergence from culture, and from no other breeding ground, of all truly great men of action, and their reliance upon the support of culture; men of ancient and of modern history. In this, he considered, lay the difference between Protestantism and

1. In *Etwas das Lessing gesagt hat: ein Commentar zu den Reisen der Päpste* (*Werke*, II, 77).

2. Open letter (in French) to Laharpe, Pempelfort, May 5 1790, in *Werke*, II, 513-44.

Catholicism, for Jacobi rightly placed the origins of the Reformation in the Humanism which preceded it.[1]

He too had shared in the great and noble sentiments unleashed by that rebirth of mankind which, at the beginning, the French Revolution seemed to be. And to Laharpe he wrote: "Jamais il n'y a eu un moment d'espérance plus beau pour nous que celui de la convocation de vos états généraux" when, at the sight of a people united around a virtuous king "nos coeurs se précipitaient tous vers le trône de Louis XVI, devenu celui de l'humanité triomphante, devenu le siège de la majesté réelle, qui, ayant une fois apparu sur la terre, devait en faire disparaître toutes les fausses images".[2] Which meant, in more political terms, that his historical ideal was that which flourished and prevailed in the following century, of constitutional and popular monarchy. As early as 1777 he had indignantly dismissed the theory expounded by Wieland that the right of the strongest was, *jure divino*, the source of the power of government, which right was allegedly all one with "natural necessity" and was a "right rooted in the nature of things". But for Jacobi there could be no right where there was no mention of "choice" and "moral law", but of necessity pure and simple (as contrasted with "that which is morally necessary"), and where *Unrecht* or wrong was equated with the impossible in general rather than with the "morally impossible", and the ultimate source of morality in human freedom was overlooked. Jacobi recalled to Wieland that Spinoza, who had agreed with him in making right coincide with force, disagreed with him in drawing from this coincidence of security or peace, which the Dutch phi-

---

1. *Woldemar*, pp. 206-15: "Wahre Erleuchtung die Menschen unter allen Umständen auch bessert und darum selbst die geringste Verbesserung der Erziehung und des Unterrichts von unendlichen guten Folgen seyn muss." This shows how out of place is the surprise of Lévy-Bruhl (op. cit., pp. 136) when, on observing that Jacobi "reste un libéral" he adds "pourtant il n'aurait jamais dû l'être", on the grounds that Jacobi was against the ideas of the eighteenth century and the Enlightenment. He ignores the fact that Liberalism was born of a critical attitude, not merely negative, but, as serious criticism always is, positive and constructive, in regard to Enlightenment and Jacobinism.

2. See letter as quoted, pp. 524-25.

losopher had described as being, taken in itself as an ultimate aim
in lieu of Reason, the most miserable of human conclusions.[1] By
contrast, he said, Wieland kept all his praises for the power of
usurpation, pouring contempt upon the Republic of Athens and
the constitution of England.[2] And although Jacobi admired Burke,
and felt the importance of the past and of tradition, yet he did not
believe it possible to return to the forms of the past, though one
could return to the moral feelings which those forms had stood
for.[3] He disliked also the reactionary and conservative ideals of
those who in their hatred of abstract rationalism called for "liberties" – the privileged liberties of classes and ranks – instead of
for liberty. The chief exponent of this last current of thought, so
influential in German policy of the following century and in the
ideology of German romanticism (whereas Italian romanticism
was of a deeply liberal colour), was at that time Möser, an historian
and writer much esteemed by Jacobi and cited by him with approval in many contexts, but not this one.[4] Jacobi's view of those
"liberties" in the plural appears clearly in his reflection upon the
popular outbreak in Flanders to the tune of "Nous ne voulons pas
être libres, c'est notre ancienne constitution que nous voulons".
In which connexion he recalled the French aristocrat who left the
Hall of Hercules exclaiming "C'est une si belle chose que la

1. "At experientia contra docere videtur, pacis et concordiae interesse,
ut omnis potestas ad unum conferatur. Nam nullum imperium tamdiu
absque ulla notabili mutatione stetit quam Turcarum, et contra nulla
minus diuturna quam popularia seu democratica fuerunt, nec ulla ubi
tot seditiones moverentur. Sed si servitium, barbaries et solitudo pax ap-
pellanda est, nihil hominibus pace miserius. Plures sane acerbiores contentiones inter parentes et liberos, quam inter dominos et servos moveri
solent, nec tamen Oeconomiae interest, ius paternum in dominium mutare,
et liberos perinde ac servos habere. Servitutis igitur, non pacis, interest,
omnem potestatem ad unum transferre: nam pax, ut iam diximus, non
in belli privatione, sed in animorum unione sive concordia consistit"
(*Tractatus politicus*, c. VI, § 4).
2. See *Über Recht und Gewalt, oder philosophische Erwägung eines Aufsatzes
von Wieland über das göttliche Recht der Obrigkeit* (*Werke*, VI, 419-64).
3. *Werke*, VI, 198, a Reflection of 1776.
4. For Möser see A. GERBI, *La Politica del Romanticismo*, Bari, 1932, 21-63;
A. OMODEO, in *Critica*, XXXVIII, 227-34; and C. ANTONI in *Studî germanici*,
IV, 219-53.

liberté, qu'on veut avoir la sienne et celle des autres".[1] Is it possible for a people to reject true liberty, to reject equality of rights and duties and submission to the rules of accurate justice? "Hélas, oui, il le pourra. Il le pourra puisqu' il n'y a rien que les hommes en général haïssent autant que l'égalité, rien qu'ils aiment autant que de primer, d'opprimer, de régner."[2] The reference here was to equality before the law, juridical equality, not an abstract material equality: for this last he himself rejected actually in favour of the opposed principle of inequality, just as he rejected abstract tolera- tion as a feigned homage to freedom which was really the very opposite of that – a mask for indifference and idleness. The truly tolerant man is he who allows to other men the same faculty of intolerance which he permits to himself.[3] Like all serious political and moral thinkers Jacobi always kept in sight the truth that war is of the nature of existence, that containment and defence are impossible without attack, and that non-resistance is nullity.[4] Even to his death he remained a liberal, after Leipzig and Waterloo, in the age of the Restoration. A liberal: yet ever aware of the great dangers against which even liberal constitutions could not guaran- tee modern society, but only a strong feeling and demonstration of faith, a resolute affirmation and negation. "Whoever has no reli- gion had best procure one," he said.[5]

Such was Jacobi, a man of that wonderful late seventeenth- century Germany which was so European and cosmopolitan, so free of heart and mind and fancy, so brilliant and original, the Germany of Goethe and Kant – a thinker usually consigned to a humble or at best secondary position in the history of philosophy who is, on the contrary, worthy of a prominent place, as I have here sought to show.

[1941]

1. Letter to Laharpe, 514-15.
2. Letter, p. 515.
3. *Werke*, III, 314-15.
4. *Werke*, III, 314-15; VI, 231.
5. *Werke*, I, 268: see L. MATHIAS in the little anthology *Die Schriften F. H. J.* (Berlin, 1926), pp. 46-47.

IV

AN UNKNOWN PAGE FROM THE LAST MONTHS
OF THE LIFE OF HEGEL

Professor Hegel looked up from his large study table covered
with books and papers and asked the maidservant what it was.
He had heard a knock on the front door just before she came in.
"There's a foreign gentleman asking if he can come in and have a
word. His name is on this card." The name written was: "Francesco
Sanseverino of Naples". Professor Hegel at once recalled the
young Neapolitan who had visited him in Berlin about seven
years earlier, in the Spring of 1824, with a letter of introduction
from an Austrian general and diplomatist then in Italy.

Sanseverino had first been in Germany in 1812-13 as an officer in
one of the Neapolitan regiments which took part in Napoleon's
invasion of Russia and in the subsequent armed clashes on German
soil. The intelligent and studious youth had been struck and attracted by the vigorous and original intellectual life which he
found around him, and, back in Naples, had continued to obtain
and read German books and to meditate a return to Germany in
order to get in closer touch with its new culture and philosophy.
When in 1819 he was able to visit Berlin again, his arrival coincided with the rise to fame of Hegel. He heard echoes of the solemn
inaugural lecture with which his course had opened the previous
year, naming the German people as "God's chosen people in philosophy". Sanseverino had noticed the convergence, in Hegel, of
a drive towards philosophical greatness and leadership with a
surge of confidence in the new might of the Prussian State after
the war of liberation. In 1824, before setting out on his third
visit, he had carefully read and deeply pondered all of Hegel's
published works, the *Phenomenology*, the bulky *Logic*, the concise
Encyclopaedia, and lastly the *Philosophy of Right*, besides some of
the scattered review articles. But he was still in the stage of learning
and digesting what he learned; more eager to hear than to talk.
He paid a respectful visit to Hegel, telling him of the ardour and

zeal with which he was following his work, and of the hope which he cherished of finding *himself* in that pursuit. The Professor had been attracted by the simplicity and straightforwardness of these remarks, as well as by a touch of Neapolitan irony, that viewing of oneself as if from the outside, with understanding but not without a smile. Sanseverino attended Hegel's lectures in the University, met and talked with some of his leading pupils – Marheineke, Gans, Henning, Hotho, and Michelet, the faithful band of his disciples at that time, but refrained from entering into argument with them either. He told Hegel that he hoped to come back and see him once again a year or two later, and got encouragement to do so. And when he got home, to Naples, he pursued his researches and meditations, studying the greatly enlarged and improved *Encyclopaedia* of 1827. He was not too much concerned at not being able to follow those lectures of Hegel which the pupils were subsequently to publish. Useful as these would be as expositions (especially the lectures on the history of philosophy and on aesthetics) the arguments – in principle and general form – were already covered *in nuce* in the published works.

It was towards the end of the summer of 1831 that Sanseverino returned once more to Germany. He was told that Professor Hegel had just come back from the country where he had taken his family when the cholera epidemic, affecting Germany as well as other countries, was reaching its height. He was received by Hegel with the politeness natural in a wellbred man untouched by the ostentatious boorishness then fashionable in Germany. He told Hegel the course of his studies up to date, avoiding mention, incidentally, of his participation in the Neapolitan constitutional revolution of 1820-21, for he was aware of Hegel's political attitude and of his opinion that such revolutions and convulsions were a "weakness of the Latin peoples". Only when the Professor asked him what were the conclusions which he had reached in the course of those studies did he come to the point of his visit.

Sanseverino asked to be allowed to recount in some detail the reasons of his particular affection for Prof. Hegel's philosophy, that is for his philosophical attitude. This, it seemed to him, had its

root in far richer and more modern strivings of the intellect than
those even of the revolutionary Kant. Kant, Severino went on,
was attracted to the physico-mathematical sciences, which seemed
to him to be the authentic field of human knowledge. He had
indeed taken a direct hand in them. But he neglected, nay, almost
ignored the history of mankind, and even his knowledge of the
history of philosophy showed large gaps and misunderstandings.
He had little feeling for poetry (his favourite poets were Horace
and Pope) and no experience at all of the other arts, save perhaps
of music, called by him "the indiscreet art" because one could be
forced to hear it against one's will. True, by a miracle of critical
acumen, hearing the new talk that was going on concerning
problems of taste, he succeeded in uttering some profound although negative truths about beauty; but he stopped short of
identifying beauty with art. For he conceived art to be a combined play of intellect and imagination, not far differently from
the tradition which sees in art an imaginous envelope to render
attractive some teaching that it is desired to dispense. Want of
historical sense weakened his political theories, want of poetic
sense weakened his religious conceptions; his ethic was austere,
but abstract and rather inhuman. Revolutionary though Kant
was, his culture was still that of the eighteenth century. He was
one of the Romantics in his a priori synthesis, his conception of
the beautiful, his postulates of the practical, but he had the
rationalistic formation of the Classicals. Now your philosophy,
Professor, is quite different, tending not towards the natural
and mathematical sciences but towards poetry – of which it is the
complement – , towards religion – in which it brings clarity – and
towards history, where it discovers its concreteness and actuality.
It has therefore the sort of range of interests which best corresponds
to the nature of philosophy and the moral requirements of the
modern age.

Sanseverino went on: There is another aspect in your philosophy which I find pleasing. In spite of its didactic severity and even
aridity, I feel in it the presence of a passionate being, a man who
has lived and loved. I cannot imagine Kant being able to write

those pages of your "Philosophy of Right" which define and celebrate the married estate in which the natural link of the flesh loses its importance in favour of a spiritual and substantial link, indissoluble, superior to the accidents of the passions and the pleasures. I won't repeat bachelor Kant's definition of marriage, which was, for him, just a contract. Nor can I imagine Kant delighting like yourself, Professor, in the depictions of the penitent Magdalen by Italian painters, and giving a kind, indulgent interpretation to the life and feelings of the object of the portrait on the grounds (as though, almost, you yourself had yielded to the allurements of the frail creature) that a beauty so full of feeling could not have loved but nobly and deeply, and that her fault, if any, must be the touching fault of an excessive grief and repentance. And then, your mocking disdain for the ascetic devotees of personal moral perfection, tormenting themselves with scruples as they anxiously pursue it. I recall the words: "What use to the world is your laboured and studied perfection, with the touch of egotism and vanity in all those worryings? What the world wants and is waiting for is effective work. You have sinned. Very well, then, don't dwell on it overmuch but redeem yourselves in work." And then I like the impatience that sometimes peeps from behind the philosopher, as when treating of Newton as the symbolic figure of the mechanical conception of reality, and of the discovery which he made thanks to an apple falling from a tree, you could not refrain from the caustic comment that apples have always been of ill omen for mankind, for Eve's apple cost man paradise, the apple of Paris caused the Trojan war, and now there is Newton's apple. And then there was your remark about your admirable colleague Schleiermacher's reduction of religion to a "feeling of dependency" – "The dog, then, must be the best of all Christians."

Hegel smiled at these recollections of his satirical quips, specially those which recalled to him his life and loves and the natural son he had begotten, and the little occasions for jealousy that he gave sometimes with his courting of the ladies of the opera to his still young and much loved and revered wife.

And now, continued Sanseverino, having proclaimed what you
will perhaps allow me to call my feelings of sympathy for your
philosophical work and its outward features, my next task must
be to indicate what seem to me to be the great truths which you
have introduced into philosophy, truths which, as the reserves
and revulsions of your present adversaries already show, may
indeed be misrepresented, denied, or rated cheaply, but can never
be plucked out by the roots – they will always flower anew. But
I must ask leave once again to take a liberty. It cannot be for me
to pronounce these truths in your own manner and words, or
with the ordered derivations, consequences, relations as set forth
by you. It would be better for me to say nothing than to attempt
it. Of course, reading the works of a poet I may and should sink
my attention in his words, his sounds and rhythms, attaining a
unity of soul with him, inactive in all else save my sharing of his
whole activity as a poet. But a philosophical opinion has to be
encountered with thought; one thought has to welcome the other;
and this can only be done in an embrace of envelopment; only in
the process of critical elaboration can understanding be afforded.

Hegel here interposed: I have in fact become rather impatient
of the many repeaters of my formulas. Some time ago a Hungarian
took to visiting me and demonstrating his mastery of my philosophy by reciting page upon page of my works learned by
memory. I had to tell him that this was heroic and wonderful,
but no proof of speculative capacity. The excellent Signor Cousin
is another who affords me small comfort. He is much interested
in my philosophy but with an "Ah! que c'est difficile tout ça",
burying his head in his hands, when one of my pupils tries to
give him the required explanations, he renounces all attempts to
understand it, as being something too high and distant for him.
He wrote to me that he was waiting impatiently for the new
edition of the *Encyclopaedia* "[pour] en attraper quelque chose . . .
ajuster à sa taille quelques lambeaux de mes grandes pensées". But
even my own pupils somewhat annoy me with their excessive
faithfulness, tending to render static what I feel in myself to be still
dynamic. I am rather afraid of the sort of approval in which trust

in the master, and, by reflection, one-sidedness and fanaticism of the scholars, counts for so much. I too desire and have hitherto waited in vain to see my thought rendered back to me through the agency of another mind understanding and fathoming it – someone who as you say understands it critically and will put it into other words. So I wait with much interest to know what these truths of mine will be which you will set forth in your own way.

– Well then, they are these: First and foremost, the way you make a clean sweep of the absurd envisagement of philosophical concepts as detached from facts, and, thus detached, as being thinkable in themselves; and then equally you dismiss the similarly absurd envisagement of facts as being susceptible of affirmation by themselves without the presence of concepts. The concept, or Idea, or Universal-Concrete, or whatever we call it, is the union of the universal and the individual judgement in action. The new Concept of the philosophical concept springs from Kant's a priori synthesis; but it is you who have emancipated this from the limitation of Kant's special reference to physico-mathematical science, and given it its full significance as the law of knowledge, or more properly speaking of the Spirit, in all its forms. And you have envisaged true judgement not as an empirical classification or proposition but as categorical judgement, valuation. Now once we have grasped the concept of the universal concrete, we can dismiss the distinction between rational and factual truths, finding every rational truth to be at the same time factual. And, something which is of the greatest importance, we may do away with the separation of, nay with the very distinction between history and philosophy. Every historical proposition contains a philosophical affirmation and every philosophical proposition an historical affirmation. History is redeemed from the age-long contempt in which it has been held as a mere collection of facts, and philosophy from the vacuity and uselessness with which it has been and is so often charged. However, if on the one hand you implicitly heal that breach and proclaim that identification, with a change from customary ways of thought which is of the highest intellectual importance, on the other hand, by a no less important originality on your part, two mental forms which have been improperly harnessed together, and in a forced unity have alternatingly taken on each other's shape, fall asunder – philosophy and science. For, as you point out, the concepts of the sciences are products of the intellect, not of the reason; they are arbitrary and not necessary; they obey ends which are not philosophical but practical. Consequently philosophy and science can now enjoy complete autonomy, for the problems of each are no concern of the other. Your third great truth I take to be the definite resolution of the dualism of positive and negative, good and evil, light and darkness, Ormuzd and Ariman, by dint of your demonstration that the negation stands, not over against, but inside the affirmation, evil not over against but inside good, nothingness not over against being but in being, so that true being is becoming. The moment of negativity is not a reality apart, but is reality itself when discerned in the process of its becoming, in the effort of detachment from and outranging of one form and entry into possession of another. The form which is to be surpassed, and which more or less successfully resists that change, in so doing takes on the air of negativity, evil, error, ugliness, death. From this dialectic is derived the solemn aphorism 'the real is rational and the rational is real', meaning that history and the past have a sacred or divine character, as having been willed by God. The past is the platform on which we build or the starting point from which we go forward, not to be denied or condemned without therewith denying and condemning the entire enchainment of history and reality. But the irresistible truth of that aphorism seems sometimes to founder under the impact of a present and overwhelming evil that has to be encountered. For that reason it behoves us to add that although historical thought annuls the dualism between the rational and the real, the practical and moral conscience must continually restore and uphold it. For *Sein* and *Sollen*, the terms not of theoretical truth but of practice and morality, require it. This surely will set at rest all those who are haunted by some kind of fear that morality is being chased out of the world, evil being put on a level with good, brute fact being installed in the rightful place of moral judgement and action.

Here Hegel remarked: On the whole I recognize my own thought in this interpretation which you are giving of it. But I have never asserted, and I could not, I think, bring myself to assert the identity of philosophy with history. Nor have I asserted that the character of the natural sciences is practical, or that the relation of the rational to the real is one thing in the reality of history and another thing in the sphere of practice and morality. And then, in your exposition, I miss a great deal of additional matter which I regard as essential in my system.

For that very reason – answered the Neapolitan – I felt bound to start by telling you that my summary exposition of your thought could only be of so much as I myself had found true or had verified through the workings of my own mind, including inferences never drawn by yourself and excluding other inferences and elaborations of yours which I myself cannot make out to be true. May I ask you to tolerate a further observation, attributing it not to arrogance but solely to the sense that genius has, as a foil to its divine side, also its human side? I want to say that when I pass from the great and fruitful principles to the detailed elaboration of them in your system, it often seems to me as though some hostile factor had operated to deflect those principles from their logical consequences, constraining you to accept what was intimately extraneous and contradictory; and what was worse, to apply the dialectic where it was inapplicable, and worst of all, thereby to debase the dialectic in a superficial and mechanical employment. How that has happened I cannot say. Truth is its own justification and rational exposition, but error cannot explain its own origin in non-truth without unmasking and confessing its own erring character. The critic or the self-criticizing author may well define the consistency of an error, but not exactly how the error came into the world. As to this, there can be only more or less abstract and psychological speculation, apart from such generic pronouncements as that all error has its origin elsewhere than in pure thought, in some impulse proceeding from a basis of interest of one kind or another. Thus I might opine that in your case the error sprang from allowing yourself to be dominated by traditional religious conceptions or traditional scholastic teachings, classifications, and methods. But I could not in this way explain the inexplicable – how it came about that your powerful genius, in rebelling successfully against so many secular convictions and preconceptions, nevertheless in other cases gave in to them, failing to complete the task of confutation. But truth to say there can be no giving of reasons for a failure to do something. An error is in the last analysis a concept that has not been realized, but taken for granted, not thought out, and thus, not brought into existence.

Well, then, said Hegel, let us forget about the search for reasons of error. I agree that such a search must be indefinite – perhaps the problem itself is non-existent. Tell me rather what it is in my system that you find inexplicable. Bring in a formal bill of charges against me – I shall gladly listen to it as an excellent antidote not only to the insipid criticisms which I see in various reviews and pamphlets, but also to the excessive praises and endorsements of my own milieu. I see you are not one of those numerous all too doughty disputants who wear one out with useless and empty contradiction, but a self-possessed and thoughtful enquirer who contradicts only in the course of and for the purposes of the enquiry.

Then, as you kindly allow it, I will indeed propound what you call a Bill of Charges. That will make for clearness in the enunciation of criticisms, by a brisk procedure which will serve your ends (for your time is precious) as well as my own. It will be, in any case, a briskness of literary form and not a token of disrespect. Well, then, to begin with: whatever gave you the right to think out and to compose a Philosophy of Nature after you had already designated the *Verstand*, or abstract intellect, operating by conventions and arbitrary divisions of the indivisible, as being, when the veils are stripped off, the parent of natural science? For surely this led to the implicit though maybe unspoken conclusion that Nature being "external" has no reality outside of this natural science with which it is wholly coincident. Accordingly it is impermissible to speak of nature as a form or degree of reality or as "Otherness in itself" by contraposition to Spirit or Mind. For by a simple logical analysis you had already unmasked the mystery of nature. Notwithstanding which you continued to recognize a reality in nature and a superscience or philosophy thereof called "Philosophy of Nature" in which you resurrected outworn Aristotelian doctrine and semi-mythical natural philosophies of the Renaissance – those doctrines for the sake of and against which Galileo constructed a physico-mathematical and experimental science. But you took over the antiquated Philosophy of Nature from your young friend Schelling, worked it up, and appropriated it, forgetting the danger which would lurk in such a gift from the hands of a quick and agile but far from solid thinker whose speculative standing you must have recognized for inferior to your own. Nor would this have mattered nearly so much if this Philosophy of Nature had merely been superadded to your system beyond and on top of Natural Science like a sort of allegory or fancy to be accepted or rejected at choice, but altogether unlinked with it. But on the contrary you have linked it up with Natural Science, teaching that the concepts of science "stretch forward", as you put it, preparing for the ulterior labours of Philosophy. Whereas surely those concepts, having their origin in the conventional and the arbitrary, cannot be accepted in philosophy either as a preliminary or as a collateral aid, but have to be swept out of the way as being useless even for building purposes. Thus in practice you have denied that logical theory of the natural sciences which was one of the most important principles, a curative principle, affirmed by yourself. And to make matters worse, there now crops up yet another philosophical science in another field, your "Philosophy of History", which is the very negation of the unity of philosophy with history. For if these two are one in the unity of the universal concrete, there is no room whatever for a philosophy to render history philosophic (which it is already in and of itself). But with your Philosophy of History you have destroyed this intimate unity of the two. This is in part the fruit of the contempt you have always felt for historians as narrators of facts unconcerned with thought. A more attentive probing would have shown you that as long as a composition is history, by contrast with mere chronicling, thought must enter into it to interpret, qualify, and spiritualize the narrative, which will indeed itself be valuable in proportion to the depth and richness and excellence of the thought. There can be no question, then, of breaking into the single and continuous process of the composition in order to find an aperture for insertion of philosophic thought: that thought was already there from the beginning. Really there is no call in this connexion for anything more than an instructional hint. The historians should be encouraged to give greater depth and elaboration and precision to the philosophy which already they implicitly employ, and to drop their phobia of philosophizing, while the philosophers should be advised to drop their ignorance and contempt of historical matters, and to devise a philosophy of a higher order than that which they hitherto practised, that is, one more concerned with the knowledge of mankind, of history. The "Philosophy of History", not unknown to the schools of the Jewish prophets and the Christian theologians, had almost wholly disappeared from Renaissance historiography, but persisted in the theological schools of the Protestant Universities, whence it reappeared in the works of the post-Kantian thinkers, winning your own authoritative support, although really it is neither history nor philosophy but a betwixt-and-between direction distracting to both of them. Even in the History of Philosophy which you have so meritoriously improved both with your new and original interpretations of the great philosophers whom you could view from the level of an equal genius, and by rising superior to mere erudition, mere advocacy of certain points of view, or mere neutral eclecticism – even in this, as a fruit of the method of Philosophy of History, you have introduced the predetermined pattern of a single problem supposedly propounded by philosophy at the beginning, and then, through the ages, ever more thoroughly investigated, until finally it is resolved and therewith the history of philosophy itself comes to an end. The same or something similar happens with the history of art and religion, which thanks to that doctrine of a super-history find themselves wedged into Procrustean beds from which they struggle to free themselves into a freer, more truly philosophical position, exempt from the artificial preconceived pattern of that arbitrary and not genuinely philosophical reduplication.

Hegel listened attentively to the charges, especially that concerning the alleged infiltration of a disturbing element into his courses on the history of philosophy, art, religion, and the State, which were then enjoying great popularity. But he said nothing, and Sanseverino continued: Nor am I able to understand why you determined to preserve the triple division of philosophy into a foreground of Logic and Metaphysic and, behind and beyond this, the constructions of Philosophy of Nature and Philosophy of Spirit. This triple scheme was current in the German eighteenth century and had indeed a long history reaching back to the Stoics of antiquity. But if, for the reasons I have set forth, the Philosophy of Nature be ruled out, it would seem to me that, Logic and Philosophy of Spirit being left together in the field, the former will at once be seen as really belonging to and ready to be absorbed in the latter. There can be no solidity about a Philosophy of Spirit in which the logical spirit cannot develop its full play. Indeed, Logic, as you expound it, is itself partly a Philosophy of Spirit, for it embraces the cognitive spirit, and the practical spirit, together with the absolute or dialectical spirit which is the very nerve of philosophy, and with these also the anti-dialectical, dividing, abstracting "intellect" from the operations of which derive the sciences – all of which shows that your categories are at least partly conceived as Forms of Spirit, although not all of these are covered, while sometimes the categories have the differing character of a catalogue of concepts requiring explanation. I will not now examine in detail your theories of Law, Politics, Art, Religion, the Absolute Spirit. But I must remark that the Logic which crowns your system is made, as in the old academic systems, to figure as the organ serving to construct the system, whereas in a thorough-going Philosophy of Spirit Logic is made

– in the act of building itself – to build up the Whole, that is the Entire Concept of Spirit, which, if it does not do, it cannot even build itself. However, it is less the subdivisions in the system, and the placing therein of the various doctrines, which seem to offend against the great logical principles set forth above, than rather, above all, the end towards which it is directed and the method employed. What is aimed at is clearly a history of the world and of its creation, nay, a history of God from before the creation of the world – of God having at His disposal all the categories required for such a creation which when the time came He resolved to effect, issuing forth from Himself, making Himself *Other*, making Himself Nature, to emerge then out of that nature which had come to life by His divine breath, into Man. And dwelling in Man's consciousness and spirit God becomes progressively Subjective or Cognitive Spirit, and thereafter Objective or Practical Spirit, creating the world of Law, Morality, Economy, Politics, History. From History God finally returns into Himself as Absolute Spirit, firstly in the two progressive but inadequate essays of Art and Religion, and lastly as Pure Idea, with entire and definitive satisfaction and self-enjoyment. Such is the framework of your philosophy: it is a history of the cosmos, a history on a set theme moving to a predetermined end along a chain of solutions of diminishing but persistent imperfection – persistent, that is, until the final phase of all which marks the end of the world and the entry into the kingdom of heaven. But how came it that a philosophy which by developing the concept of the Universal Concrete had liberated mankind from the obsession of Nature, showing this to be a construction of the human will (which does not mean something merely wilful, since it well serves certain ends), and had provided in its place the boundless field of history, perpetual becoming, infinite creation of ever new forms, should at the last fall back into a conception of religious transcendence, with the consequence that among the scholars attending your lectures one hears talk of a revived theism and a renewed and illuminating Christian theology?

Professor Hegel had listened motionless to this criticism and denunciation. And now Sanseverino by way of conclusion added this corollary to his argument:

And what, Sir, about the method? Is not the method which is given out as being dialectical and should be such, in point of fact destructive of the very idea of dialectic, if a great truth once firmly enunciated could be destroyed? Sir, it was not in your power to destroy it. It is as though you had pierced a mountain wall by which a stream had been confined: now the waters have sprung out into the open and nobody, not even he who revealed and released them, can remove or reverse or abate a flow which has never been in your power, and will, whatever you do, continue on its own course. In other words that current of thought will by its own strength and in its own right exercise a function of authority and criticism and correction, and if you yourself after having served it in so signal and ever memorable a fashion wish to do so no more, it will seek out and find other, more willing instruments. Or is it inability rather than unwillingness that you now experience? – Whichever it be, it is the destiny of the exceptional man to come into the world with a task to perform, knowing however that the labours of human thought extend to infinity so that, accomplishing his task, he must resign himself to a transference of the torch into other hands. A great philosopher of Naples whom you have perhaps not yet read or anyway been able to study properly (though his chief work has lately been translated into German), I mean Giambattista Vico, a genius in whom you might see not merely a forerunner but the fulfiller of some gaps left in your own work and one who though a Catholic by profession was less bound by ancient religious conceptions than yourself, wrote a sonnet to celebrate the personal aspect of the end of the composition and revision of his masterpiece: "My trembling hand now lays the pen aside; the treasure of my thoughts has now been spent." He felt that after more than once recasting his great book, he had nothing left to accomplish in the world.

But to return to the Dialectic. What was its origin? And what became of it? Its origin was, surely, an effort to break those dualisms of positive and negative, truth and error, life and death, good and evil. Its equipment for that purpose lay in the forms, the categories, the values of the Spirit, the True, Beautiful, Good, Useful, and their contraries. Thus it was in one and the same moment of its activity the distinction between these forms and the passage from one to another, the becoming of them in a transit through the purgatory or hell of Nothing (or however else we choose to describe the negative strength-weakness of Being), the manner whereby every man at every moment attains the Good, the Beautiful, the Useful, the True, and risks at every moment losing his gain unless, as his spiritual nature requires, he goes on to make a new acquisition. But you, Sir, lost sight of the character of the category and of the distinction which is implicit in the dialectic, so much absorbed were you in the construction of the system: you introduced Dialectic where it had no right to be, in the realm of empirical concepts and collective historical process. There, the dialectical operation could only be arbitrary and formal. And this you did because you accepted and held yourself bound by a historical-theological pattern which you strove to display. That pattern, exhibiting a history rendered painful by continual disappointment, never allows the contemplator to utter the summons of Faust to the flying moment – "Stay, for thou art so fair" – but leaves him for ever face to face with an act which lacks that instant of satisfaction and repose; for being never at unity with itself it harbours an inner contradiction and an inner urge to break the contradiction. Indeed Good and Evil here lose their contours: Good which is never realized is converted into perpetual Evil, perpetual, that is to say, until the final and conclusive moment. Unfortunately it is the world itself that disappears at that moment, the world in which we live and which Philosophy should teach us to know and to experience worthily.

Hegel had listened in silent attention, never interrupting Sanseverino. It would have been improper and maladroit, he felt, to enter into an argument with one who had long studied his works and had come frankly to pour out to him, in a communion of mind and of feeling, the conclusions reached in a labour of long duration. These conclusions merited long pondering before it would be fitting to contradict them, demur at them, or even express more or less agreement with them. Nor, for that matter, did Sanseverino expect an answer, well knowing as he did that a serious thinker cannot merely acquiesce in objections of that order: all he can do is to weigh and reweigh them in due season and see whether they will afford some new stimulus and direction to his thought as it pursues its own course. Hegel, therefore, after listening in silence, made no philosophical rejoinder, but took his companion's arm and led him to a window of his study. It was a small house on the Kupfergraben, overlooking a stretch of the Spree, close to the town but away from town noises. He pointed out the Montbijou castle just opposite and the adjoining buildings of the great Museums. Then with simple cordiality he asked Sanseverino what he meant to do on returning to Naples.

I mean, said the other, to remain your conscientious, grateful, and devoted disciple, and never to forget how much I learned from you or how you led me to the upper reaches of thought, freed from the torments of doubt and conflict, in a position to despise the popular and superficial thought of the majority. The task which I shall in particular choose for myself will be to sketch out what I believe to be the logical consequences of your own profound logical discoveries and to give them systematic form – consequences different from those which a German background and tradition have led you to proclaim. The system will be secular, not theological like yours, and simple, flexible, rather than complicated and ponderous. The concept of the Universal Concrete leads, though you would not and will not admit it, to that of the unity of Philosophy with History. In that case what really occupied and fills the whole field of knowledge is History. (This is shown by the fact that men desire to know, not ideas for their own sake, but facts, concrete reality, for which ideas are the necessary means but no more than the means.) What, then, will be the form of Philosophy? That, surely, of a Logic of History, an illustration of the concepts used in the interpretation of history. But that Logic or Methodology is not to be rated cheaply: it is nothing more nor less than a complete Philosophy of the Spirit, a philosophy not to be completely summed up in any book, because it is in continual process of growth, and the motion of history, presenting ever new problems to the mind, ensures that the growth will never stop short. Philosophy is never final, its systems are never static but are ever in motion – indeed they would be better described as provisional systematizations, pauses (so to speak) giving an occasion for taking breath as at the end of a well-rounded paragraph. No problem that has ever been propounded in philosophy is alien to this philosophy of the Spirit. Each and all of them it accepts, and by shaping them into problems of Spirit resolves them: on no other plane can they, if they are genuinely significant problems, be resolved. There is no reason then for those respectable gentlemen the Professors of Philosophy to fear that the conception of Philosophy as *method* will impoverish philosophy. On the contrary it stands for an enrichment, and calls for rather more alert minds, truth to tell, than those of Professors passing their time over outworn, inconclusive, sterile problems. Within the range of this philosophy of the Spirit the theory of Art, Aesthetics, must be worked out anew, liberating it from clinging remnants of the old-fashioned Rhetoric and Poetic, and also from newfangled psychologism. The aesthetic principle must be understood in its originality, free of either panlogistical or hedonistic contamination. Another need is that there must be instituted a philosophy of Vitality or Utility as one may prefer to call it, drawn together out of the theories of politics, economics, the passions, and so on. And there must be a theory of the writing of History, including the critique and history of the theory itself. I could go on mentioning yet further needs. Now Naples, the city upon which the alert minds of South Italy converge, seems ready and suited for such a studious task. Naples has in the past provided almost all the serious philosophers of Italy, and while alive to sublime speculations, is kept on the firm ground of the concrete and historical by an unfailing realism. Herder, Hamann, and even Goethe observed or sensed this robust aptitude of Naples for philosophy. A young King has come to the throne, there is a feeling of fresh air, of hope and confidence, private study circles are springing up, voluntary universities, as it were, outside the official university, formed by eager men of study. Foreign literature passes from hand to hand and reviews of a serious character are appearing with contributions by competent authors. All this draws me back to Naples. Your own philosophy is coming to be known. But I am far from satisfied with the way in which your interpreters have represented your thought as a sort of rationalized religion, and themselves take on the air and accents of a priesthood, and we begin to see the formation of a sort of Hegelian Church. We must stop that.

In conversation of this sort the two passed away the evening, and the meeting of their minds developed into a meeting of hearts, because even a clash of thoughts induces a sort of brotherly closeness. So when Sanseverino took his leave Hegel said to him, with a certain pressingness of affection, that he counted upon his early return to Berlin.

In the ensuing days Hegel never ceased to remeditate that conversation, turning over in his mind his own theories in the light of the objections proffered by the Neapolitan gentleman, debating with himself how to defeat them, coping with doubts that had sometimes before come to him though never with the present force. Hegel had conceived a philosophy to set forth the grounds of the universe and to set a conclusion to history: it summed up, ordered, and completed the philosophical work of thousands of years, recognizing the contribution rendered by each other system, and justifying all of them with a powerful final act of correction and synthesis. After that, the history of mankind had (in the terms of that philosophy) attained its fullness: the end was linked to the beginning, and none could see whence a further stimulus, a further scope for human labour, should arise. To devise such a philosophy would have seemed a piece of colossal presumption, had it not been the consequence of adopting, as model for the philosophical pattern, the pattern of the traditional religious history of creation, of the laborious process of earthly life, and of its ultimate resolution in the life of the other world. And because it had followed that model, its author had shown no sign of overweening self-importance, expectation of present applause and future triumph, in this unlike Tommaso Campanella, proclaimer – not without fanaticism – of the City of the Sun, and of the perfection which the world would therewith attain before Chaos rendered all things to the One. Hegel was far from being intoxicated by his primacy of the past ten years, still fully maintained, among philosophers. Nor did he seem to be satisfied with his achievement, or sure of it. His son Carl had heard him cry out "What God doomed me to be a philosopher?" and his wife had often heard him murmur at his desk "I shall never be able to see it through". And there is truth in what Thaulow said, that Hegel may have thought that philosophy would only begin after him, certainly not that it would end with him.

But now he could not get out of his mind the clear and incisive objection that he had heard critically expounded by his visitor from abroad with whom, nevertheless, he had felt so much at home. "The guiding thought is magnificent, but the System, far from giving it strength, dilutes and weakens and compromises it." All the same, his life of thought had, by dint of long study, taken firm shape in that rich system, even could he acquiesce in the criticism now proffered by one who was no adversary but a disinterested, unprejudiced, affectionate reader and disciple, this would have meant . . . It would have meant retracing the course he had followed for over forty years of intense labour, changing the route he had plotted, arriving at a point different from what he had believed to be his point of destination. And this line of direction had served for the orientation and development of that vast network of teachings which had become, by this time, an aspect of the political mission of Prussia. The thought of having to revise it, if it arose in his mind, overwhelmed and almost frightened him. Where would he have found the required strength, which must be not only intellectual strength but ability to concentrate all the powers of a human being, the so-called physical powers, passion, enthusiasm, dedication, sacrifice, as though nothing else existed in the world, or rather, everything were summed up in that single purpose in the service of which alone he could physically breathe and live? In time past he had known such concentration, above all in the great mental crisis marking the end of his youth. He had known it as pain of hell and divine joy, the voluptuous abandonment to a work of sorrow and love, when he was composing the "Phenomenology" and put the manuscript under his arm while the guns of Jena were still firing. But how should that power have flowed back into his veins, and if it could do so would not this be not merely marvellous but a marvel contrary to nature, monstrous?

So a feeling of humility and renunciation sprang up in him. It seemed now to him that the work he had achieved, its truth and its error, had proceeded not merely from himself but from inspiration and necessity, from the best that there was within him albeit marked and limited by human weakness. And it seemed best to retain its presentation to the world in this form corresponding to the stage of history which the world had now entered into. It would thus be a lesson, an experiment, and a warning in virtue, on the one hand of its merits and of what there was in it that would be imperishable, and, on the other hand, of its defects, contradictions, insufficiencies, the purging and rectification and revision of which would mean fresh labours, new creative work, another philosopher. In a mood that was in a way both heroic and paternal he conceived of people saying of this successor "the son is stronger than the father", as Hector desired they should say it some day of his infant son. Then he murmured to himself verses by old Giambattista Vico which Sanseverino had just brought to his notice – verses about the treasure of thought that had long been open to him, but was now closed and would in time be open to another. In humility, now, he was waiting for his "departure in peace", calmly aware, at the same time that he had been "the Lord's servant", one who on the altar of the Lord could place the work that he had been assigned and allowed to accomplish within divinely set limitations.

All this was true, and the conclusion was just. Nevertheless when a man of thought is told, and made actually to suspect, that

error had crept into the thought which had served him as Truth
and afforded him a place of repose, how can the prick of remorse
be blunted, how can he settle down to live with that error unexa-
mined, uncorrected, unconfuted? How can he be expected to
remain cold and indifferent towards what has been the purpose of
his life, that whose immaculate purity he feels it to be his moral
duty to procure and to protect?

Unrest and anguish of this sort Hegel could not chase out of
his mind so as wholly to recover faith in his life's work, the
nourishment he conveyed in the Berlin university lecture hall to
his eager audience. Full of mental energy he still was: that very
year, touched off by the noise of revolutionary happenings in
France, he had given vent to his robust conservative convictions,
his suspicion of *hommes de principe* in rebellion against *hommes
d'état*, in a long article against the English Reform Bill. He was
always weaving into his lectures arguments suggested by the latest
events. Accordingly it would be impossible for him to obey the
wise counsel to let what's done be done – impossible once the
thing done had lost for him the certainty that pertains to truth
acquired and possessed.

Such was Hegel's state of mind at a moment when the cholera
epidemic which had been dying down in Berlin suddenly was
wafted back, and suddenly struck down on November 14 1831
the greatest philosopher of those times. His loving and faithful
pupils, undertaking the publication of a dozen volumes of his
lectures as a supplement to his written works, stressed, with increasing emphasis, the formal outlines of the system as they had
been built up and worked out in the course of university tuition.
Little or nothing was then remembered of the prehistory of the
system, the history of the travailed formation of Hegel's thought.
Only about a century later could this be recaptured by research
into unpublished early works. And it was about a century later
that the thesis expounded by the Neapolitan scholar to Hegel in
the foregoing conversation was pursued. Then, and not till then,
was the contrast developed between Hegel the philosopher and
Hegel the system-builder, "The Living and the Dead Hegel" as

a book-title had it. It was not just in Naples, where Hegel was much studied in the nineteenth century, retaining disciples even in the age of Positivism, but in Italy at large, that the Hegelian crisis matured. From that moment, in Italy, the thought of Hegel the philosopher has recovered potency in a systematization altogether different from that chosen by Hegel himself, in which consequences are drawn which he never intended, while theories which he had taken over from his forerunners, but which could not be retained, have been entirely reshapen. The very name of the systematization has been changed. "Absolute Idealism" no longer fitted the case or underlined the fundamental feature of it: and spontaneously the appropriate term came into being – "Absolute Historicism". Be that as it may, Hegel now belongs to us: he cannot be all in all to us if only because his belonging to us, our possession of him, can only be of value (as the possession of any thought can only be of value) when it incites new life, new thought.[1]

[1948]

1. Need I remark that this "Unknown Page from the last Months of the Life of Hegel" is a product of my fancy? This caprice occurred to me during a sleepless night and was put down on paper the morning after. Should the reader ask me in the terms of the classic enquiry of Cardinal Ippolito where I got it from, I should answer that the material came to me by way of my intimate acquaintance with Hegel's thought, and the all too many inner dialogues in which, within my own mind, I was mentally addressing him. For the rest, it cannot be said that an historical basis for the caprice is entirely lacking. Traces of a constructively critical attitude towards Hegel's philosophy were really to be found in nineteenth-century Naples, if not as early as 1830, at any rate towards the middle of the century. They are to be found, however, not among the orthodox Hegelians, not even in the severest and most thoughtful of them, Bertrando Spaventa, but in the fresh and uninhibited mind of one who without formally professing philosophy had a clearer and more genuine vein of it than the professors — Francesco De Sanctis. Among the few references to Hegel that he left here is one to be found in a lecture of 1879 on Zola: "At the time when Hegel reigned supreme I expressed my hesitations about his a-priorism, his triad, his formulas. But then there are in Hegel two principles which stand at the base of the whole contemporary movement— the principle of Becoming, basis of Evolution, and the principle of Existence, basis of Realism. His system has fallen to pieces, but these two principles give Hegel a standing in respect of the future".

V

GIOBERTI AS PHILOSOPHER

I HAVE never had much use for Gioberti as a philosopher – he has always seemed to me lacking in critical acumen and devoid of speculative originality. This aversion of mine has been explained by a contrast of temperaments,[1] but really it results wholly from the reasons I have just stated: what is called my temperamental intolerance simply reflects these reasons. One dislikes an ugly poem for its ugliness, not for a contrast between one's temperament and the poet's.

Gioberti's philosophical writings are full of Jewish, Christian, and Catholic myths, which he embraces with explicit recognition as an integral and indeed dominating feature of his thought. We should not simply on this account dismiss his philosophy with an adverse judgement. Two cases are conceivable in which a thinker's activity, though cramped or obscured by mythical images, could preserve and maintain its vitality and produce new and robust philosophical truths.

The first would be the case in which there was an internal struggle in the thinker's mental process between the traditional beliefs by which he is moved to sentiments of awe and reverence, and, on the other hand, the critical spirit in him which, operating apparently within the bounds set by those beliefs, nevertheless desists from drawing its own full conclusions, so that these two tendencies in him become intermingled, but not confounded. The second case would arise if a thinker for some political end and calculation makes a profession of certain beliefs so as to mask ideas which in reality corrode and destroy them. The former of the two cases is usually recognized as illustrating sincerity, simplicity, good faith, the second of them as betokening insincerity, astuteness. Gioberti's

1. "Croce has always shown some hostility to Gioberti, deriving, really, from a deep diversity of philosophical temper, not from failure to understand" (S. CARAMELLA, *La formazione della filosofia giobertiana*, Genoa, 1927, pp. 24-25). But something more than a clash of temperaments is needed to explain why I do *not* understand!

case would seem to be nearer the second than the first, or perhaps at different times of his life, or at one and the same time, he hovered from the one to the other, thanks to want of clarity or to the ease with which he was accustomed to run off in pursuit of ratiocinations which were really concoctions of the imagination – however that may be, it is always difficult to find one's way amid those labyrinths of partly conscious and partly unconscious play-acting in which the author himself sometimes loses the way. There is an example in Giambattista Vico, who was formerly reckoned to belong to the order of the wholly sincere and straightforward, but whom recent biographical studies display in a rather different light, so that we may perhaps now attribute to him less frankness, more awareness, and a circumspect care to show himself behind a veil which his humble station in life and his natural timidity rendered advisable. Fortunately no philosophical necessity constrains us to resolve these insoluble or only quite empirically soluble problems. For in either of the two cases mentioned what matters is not the sincerity or otherwise of the thinker, but the existence, if any, and the nature of the philosophical thought. Thus Gioberti may or may not be serious when he appeals to the "Prime Biblical" and to Genesis, or when he defines the Catholic Church as "the successive reorganization of the human race sundered by sin, reunited by grace", the Papal authority as "the elective spiritual fatherhood required to seal the unity of the great human family", or again Italy as being for sure "the mother nation of the human race" because containing in itself "the principle of the moral unity of the world" and so on, but in any case we can just relax our attention and let him talk on until we observe that he has begun to say something of philosophical significance.[1]

The worst of it is that even so Gioberti gives us little or nothing, for consider his major philosophical proposition, his famous "ideal Formula" which (it is he himself who celebrates this *eureka*) "came like a flash of light revealing, albeit confusedly, the solution of

1. See the abundant anthology of the *Nuova Protologia*, ed. Gentile (Bari, 1912), which more than suffices for a knowledge of the thought and method of Gioberti; vol. I, 176, 183; cf. also *Primato*, II, 178 and following.

all those difficulties which had tormented him, seeming wellnigh insuperable", but which, when he had once grasped it in its proper terms, "he tried out, applying it on the one hand to all the questions of philosophy and on the other hand to all the systems of the said science, finding that it could solve the problems and explain the systems not only much better than had been possible before, but more fully and precisely than could in such a case have been expected, for an exactness and stringency were achieved in the speculative sphere equal to that which is achieved in mathematics". Thanks to this formula there could be discovered "a new and wonderful accord between speculation and faith, nature and grace, reason and revelation, philosophy and theology"[1] – and so on, for our author is nothing if not copious, and I propose to cite from him the minimum necessary, thus sparing fatigue to myself and the reader. What, then, is this Formula? "That which is creates the existent, and the existent returns to that which is": that is, God or the Spirit creates the world which then in the course of its evolution returns to the creator. And is this, then, a philosophical principle, apt to dispel confusions and errors and to open up a previously unattainable understanding of some real order of things or of the order of the world? Rather, it is a fable born of a biblical-Christian or indeed neo-platonic inspiration, and while you remain in its limits you will get nothing out of it except the description contained in its words: a creator, a creature, and the return of the creature to the creator's embrace.

The use which Gioberti made of this Formula was not – and could not be, seeing that it was a mere fable – to criticize and to confute what he called the two great philosophical errors and horrors in philosophy, "pantheism" and "psychologism", but merely to reject and denigrate them. By these terms he did not mean in the one case the naturalistic pantheism which is indeed highly questionable, and in the other case the equally questionable psychological philosophy of the empiricists, the associationists, and so forth: he meant, by the first, the immanent conception of the

1. *Nuova Protologia*, I, 74-77.

deity in any form, and by the second the philosophy of the Spirit, which is as much as to say any genuine philosophy, for at least since the time of Socrates there has been none such that was not the study of the human spirit. What Gioberti propounded in lieu of these two was Christian Theism and Ontologism, not however by the critical arguments whereby other ontologists and theists have sought or managed to rouse some interest even in their opponents' minds, but by displays of the imagination. The Formula became for him a key to open all doors, giving him, as we have heard him declare in the quotation, a solution to the most various problems, great and small, with a facility which he himself found astonishing. Thus: What is this principle of causality ("every effect has a cause") and what its relation with the principle of finality ("every action has its end")? Well, the former concerns the first creative cycle, the latter concerns the second, for "finality is the law of the human spirit".[1] Again: What is the Good? it is "*Ens*, Being, which by the exercise of choice, creates the Good". In its first cycle "the judgement, in making its choice, gives preference to law before feeling and thereby produces virtue". In the second cycle, "virtue reconciling the feelings to the law, creates blessedness", and thus grasps the two divine realms, Church and Paradise, in perfect correspondency with the two creative cycles which aim at "perfect realization of the universal cycle through time and space, earth and heaven".[2] Again: What is the rational form of the marvellous in the two aesthetic forms in which it makes its appearance, the mysterious and the praeternatural?

The ideal Formula furnishes the logical ground, in that its first member, the Absolute Intelligible, having reached, in virtue of the interposed movement of creation, the final term, sheds forth upon all things a light "which from our point of view is surrounded by darkness", thus giving rise to the "Subjective Super-Intelligible". Meanwhile the second member of the Formula gives rise to the concept of the "Super-Natural".[3] What is Sovereignty,

1. *Nuova Protologia*, II, 193.
2. *Del buono e del bello* (ed. Le Monnier), 121-22.
3. Ibid., 413-14.

what is the people, and what is the relation between them, or
otherwise expressed what is the relation in the duality of Authority and Liberty? Perfectly simple: Being creates the existent, to
wit Sovereignty, and the existent, to wit the People, returns to
Being, acquiring sovereignty by the play of the politically capable
and the electorate.[1] What are those three principal forms into
which poetry falls divided, ode, drama, and epic? They are "the
reproduction of the two generative cycles" showing the "correspondency of poesy and cosmology".[2] And then, how to solve
the difficult logical problems of the character of the various intellectual fashions which are commonly all lumped together as
"Science"? Once again by recourse to the ideal Formula. Being is
concerned with a parcel containing the First Philosophy, Ontology, Rational Theology, and Revealed Theology. A second parcel,
which contains as its miscellaneous contents Arithmetic (Time),
Geometry (Space), Logic (Truth), Morality (the Good), belongs
to the Copula. The third parcel, holding no less strange a medley
than Psychology, Cosmology, Aesthetics, Politics, and the Physical
and Natural Sciences, is the concern of the Existent.[3]

Enough said of these tricks or enchantments of the Formula. But
Gioberti shows no better capacity when he turns to define more
directly the particular concepts, the very substance one should
suppose of his philosophy. Here too we have at the outset a concept all important for Gioberti (and it is certainly all important
in the theory of knowledge): the intuiting faculty, or Intuition,
and its relations with what he calls Reflection, that is with
Thought, Judgement. Now the importance and fruitfulness of
that concept depends upon the framing and fixing of a weighty
distinction between Intuition and Thought-Judgement. Only a
clear distinction of this sort can lead to an understanding of how,
by an act of negation, Thought or Judgement arises as the second,
higher stage of the theoretical operation. But in Gioberti there is
no such distinction. Intuition is for him at one time Involution,

---

1. *Introduzione allo studio della filosofia*, 2nd edn., 1844, II, 108.
2. Ibid., III, 55.   3. Ibid., III, 3-17.

the imperfect form of Thought itself, a confused concept or confusion of concepts which "offers us all the truths, twisted and twined together so as to appear one truth, much as a group of mountains seen from afar may look like one mountain". At another time it is the first act of thought – but then again it is not active but passive – in fact, a "mystery". In any case it is not dialectically expounded with the introduction of a counterposition, a negation.[1] For Gioberti Dialectic means simply the harmonization of opposites and this too in a necessarily imperfect manner. For it is only in the infinite that opposites become identified in God, in whom there is no opposition just as there is no evil, no dialectical process either, for this, says Gioberti "is a solely psychological event within us, but a cosmological event outside us". (He thus rejects the teaching of Hegel, who located opposition and dialectical movement within the Logos, and stained reality itself, if stained be the right term, with evil.)[2] The categories, being for Gioberti nothing but "the most general ideas", have for him no truly creative potency, for "in God they form a single idea which then falls asunder and passes, by the medium of creative action, from the condition of intelligible absolute to that of relative intelligible".[3]

In the same way the essential distinction between intellect and reason, outlined in Kant and in Hegel assuming the importance of a mental revolution, is in Gioberti denied as a distinction of mental forms and transferred instead to the "object" (as though the object were not itself conceived and posited by the mind), on the ground that "the intellect applies itself to that which exists, not to that which is (*ens*).[4] After which, small wonder that Gioberti "asks leave to smile at what modern philosophers and scholars call 'the spontaneous development of the human spirit'" (the expression offends him, and he can hardly bring himself to pronounce it, so inelegant it seems to him). He smiles at it for the fine reason that

1. *Nuova Protologia*, II, 200, 270, and elsewhere.
2. Ibid., II, 267, 270, 313, 434; cf. *Del buono*, p. 18.
3. *Nuova Protologia*, II, 381.
4. Ibid., II, 387.

"all development must presuppose some previously present seeds which could not develop and fructify without the aid of reason and language"[1] – as if the concept of development, which is all one with that of history, negated reason and language and were identified with that of the absurdity of a machine or a stuff moving and growing blindly and mutely. Gioberti, however, was de-demonstrably ignorant of the true character and problematicity of history, just as he was ignorant of the meaning of the high esteem into which history had come in his own times. He explained this by merely academic considerations: "The historical sciences are in vogue today partly because there is a greater supply than in the past of archaeological and philological materials, partly because, being concerned with matters of fact, they seem in an age given over to doubt and chimaera to be less airy than the prevailing concernment with ideas, and appeal to the more solid minds which in this dearth of sound doctrine still refuse to be nourished upon vapour and wind."[2] But even while he accepts the view that the feeling for history is "healthy" he observes in it "an occasional weakness" of a sort that impairs the dignity of history itself: "for keen minds are usually disinclined to linger overlong amid phenomena, since they are able to wander and range with swift and sure feet in the world of the rational as in that of the sensuous". In other words, Gioberti displays his ignorance of the theory, well advanced in his time, of the immanence of the rational in the factual, and of the concreteness of the universal which thereby becomes individual. Instead, he clings to the old scholastic notion of the superiority of concept to judgement and philosophy to history – as though, forsooth, a philosopher could ever think without his thought therewith arriving at an historical truth. He also showed a preference for biography, saying that this "surpasses history in beauty, importance, usefulness, depth, and precision". Comment is unnecessary.

What, now, has Gioberti to say about the concepts of ethics? He can only give the following tautological, highly vague, and

1. *Del buono*, p. 136.   2. *Nuova Protologia*, I, 225.

yet mistaken definition of moral activity: the Good is "a divine perfection in which rational and free creatures may imperfectly participate through informedness as to the absolute law, and the choice of a conformity of the will to it". He insists particularly that "human liberty is a force which does not contain in itself its own law" – a "force", then, so forceful that it has to get a law imposed upon it from outside. That the law of liberty should be discovered in the bosom of liberty itself seems to him a blasphemy: he shrinks from it, imagining that at that rate virtues and vices, shameful misdeeds and heroic actions, "Heliogabalus and Plato", would all come to the same thing. In the moral act he finds an analogy for intuition and reflection in the "affection" and the "exercise of the will".[1] The latter of these two selects "from among the tangled mass of the affectivities a special object towards which freedom tends". On the other hand the affection is implanted by God in man in order to "serve as a help and stimulus in the production of the Good and as a supplement to the Good itself"[2] – a curious sort of aid and stimulus, one must think, if it does not operate in virtue of its own quality as affection, and may take the form of an unhealthy urge which tends to vitiate the will. In all this Gioberti shows complete ignorance of that theory of the passions which the thought of the modern age had held in great account, and complete ignorance of that passion above the passions, dominating and transfiguring them, which was progressively individuated as "the moral sense", "the moral conscience", "the awareness of liberty". He persists in placing the concept of liberty on the one side, and on the other side the norm or system of norms controlling liberty. Indeed he is wholly unaware of the underlying motive of the rebellion against casuistic theory, that is against the normative, legalistic conception of morality. The theories of laxism have in his eyes the character of an accidental phenomenon, "the excess of certain authors", and of casuism he loosely judges that "it may, when employed very cautiously and carefully, serve the useful end of breaking in the novice in the

1. Italian, *arbitrio* – Translator.   2. *Del buono*, 11, 91, 93, 103, 106.

science of conduct to the application of the rules and the conversion of his speculative enunciations into practical judgements".[1] Gioberti, far from recognizing the great advance registered by moral philosophy with the drawing of a precise distinction between politics and ethics, expresses horror at this "absolute divorce". He congratulates the ancients on having known nothing of such a distinction and attributes the blame for introducing it to "the school of Machiavelli, the rise of which coincided with the eclipse of the civil constitution of the Middle Age, and the substitution, for the catholic liberty and unity of foregoing centuries, of religious schism and monarchical despotism".[2] His view of war was no less superficial. He deemed it necessary, "provided it be just, moderate, and constructive – not sheerly destructive",[3] which is as much as to say that he did not at all understand the nature of the necessity of war, which springs from that of life itself, nor how, when war is undertaken, it can never heed counsels or submit to limitations alien to its nature, but must always, from the point of view of each combatant, be both destructive and constructive.

That Gioberti should have liberated himself from false notions of the "origin" of language in which his contemporaries were for the most part still involved would be too much to expect. He for his part was glad enough to argue that since language could not have been invented by "the first man, ignorant of all truth and wholly inarticulate", it must therefore have had a divine origin. Just how this was to be understood he expounded at different times in different ways, sometimes making an anthropomorphic God personally communicate language to man, but sometimes indicating the emergence of language by natural spontaneity.[4] But he remained utterly impervious to the fanciful, aesthetic, and musical nature of human utterance, such utterance ranking in his view

1. *Del buono*, 42-43.
2. Ibid., 39.
3. *Nuova Protologia*, II, 268.
4. Ibid., I, 104 seqq.: but compare other remarks in the *Introduction* and the *Protologia*.

as a contrivance, a *pis aller*, a "narrow frame where the Idea, which
brooks no term, finds itself confined and has to accustom itself to
the narrow apprehension which is all that reflex cognition can
afford, much as the eye of the astronomer can find scope and pleasure in contemplating the grandeur of the heavens through a small
aperture and a slender lens". Whenever he encountered the problems of aesthetics he showed the same want of understanding, as,
for example, in the very definition which he gives of the beautiful: "the individual union of an intelligible type with an element
of fancy, procured by the aesthetic imagination". Of the imagination which performs that task he has nothing to say but that
it is "that faculty which, transforming intelligible types into phantasms, and conferring a mental life upon the images which it has
conceived, creates the beautiful".[1] He thus discourses in a circle. It
is in vain that he strives to think out this unthinkable business of
the intelligibles being rendered sensible and vice versa: all that he
can do is to give an imaginous description of the curious process
by which "The Sensibles are mentally drawn forth out of the
material in which they inhere, and are, so to speak, pressed and
rolled into the thinnest and finest sheet or film, like a geometrical
surface in its want of thickness, but unlike it in being no abstraction
but on the contrary retaining shape, colour, and other external
concrete appearances together with an addition conferred by the
fancy – something vague, indefinite, mobile, mysterious." "Conversely", Gioberti continues, "the Intelligibles take on a bodily
form, shedding, when they enter the confined room and assume
finite shapes like real things, those endowments of eternity, universality, necessity, which invested them in the sphere of reason" –
and so on.[2] In the same mythic vein he explains the cosmic birth
of the beautiful out of the sublime which creates and contains it
in its receptacle, time and space. Sublime is that creative power,
beautiful the effect of the creation, as in the words of Genesis
admired by Longinus: "the *Fiat* sublime and the light beautiful,
prime condition for the visual expression of the beauty that is

1. *Del buono e del bello*, pp. 351, 370.
2. Ibid., p. 371.

diffused in the grand breadth of cosmic space, the ocean-bed, as it were, of light".[1] Still in this mythical vein he resolves the difficult problem of so-called "natural" beauty (the beauty, that is, which in virtue of a highly complicated internal process, and thanks to a particular mode of exteriorization of the phantasm, in truth turns out to be one with the unique beauty which is intuition, spiritual expression – in other words with the beauty of Art). For Gioberti it is all simple enough: perfect natural beauty pertains to the beginning of the world when those natures which had just emerged all fresh and new from the divine creation "could not but duly express their own eternal model". The proper moment of this perfection was "the second period of the primordial age, described in detail by Moses in his six days of creation . . . when he makes the Creator repeat at every stage in that divine progress that He saw that the work of His hands was good". But then, along with moral evil, there crept into the world ugliness, or aesthetic evil. Then it was that the beauty of art came in "to help out, in some degree, the beauty of nature". But the former remains for Gioberti ever inferior to the latter because, as he declares in sharp express contradiction of Hegel, the spirit is not superior to nature but part of it. For nature is the art of God, and human art the mere offspring of this.[2] We will not pursue Gioberti in his further theoretical exercises, for example his characterization of the arts, in which music "working upon number" is denominated "the arithmetic of aesthetic mathematics", architecture the geometry thereof, acting and dancing the mechanics of the same system, white poetry and eloquence "having all the genres open to them" rank as "universal and encyclopaedic".[3]

Such being Gioberti's manner of handling the concepts – often, seemingly, in a verbal drunkenness, and without any logical demonstration of the process – what wonder if his philosophical style be slipshod, with abundant resort to all those phrases which philosophy, as the strict and categorical determination of concepts,

1. *Del buono e del bello*, p. 397.
2. Ibid., pp. 431, 434-35, 438, 442, 443.
3. Ibid., p. 374.

must eschew – "mainly", "largely", "almost", "more or less", and so on; as in these samples: "Aesthetics mainly concerns the concepts of the sublime and the beautiful" – "the beautiful is mainly covered in the third term of the formula" – "the two generative cycles are reproduced more or less in the three main forms of poetry" – "languages having been more or less adulterated by men are defective by comparison with the primitive language created by God, being largely the product of human wit" – "moral evil, when it is serious, annihilates the second generative cycle for him who commits it, imprisoning that man in himself" – "the time and space of the fancy or aesthetic time and space are pretty well halfway between the two species" – "the union of sensible and intelligible in the beautiful is as great as it can be without erasing the distinction" – "the prevalence, like a sort of hegemony of the soul over the body, of the intelligible in the fancy, must not exceed a certain degree nor so overwhelm the sensible as to impair or annul it".[1] We will not linger, either, over Gioberti's historical digressions, into which he poured a copious but invariably second-hand erudition, never attempting to go back to the sources or to perform a critical function. In his interpretation of events and epochs he allowed himself a still greater liberty than in his speculative arguments. Consider, for example, his conception of philosophical epochs as progressive stages of decadence, from the age of the Fathers of the Church, through Renaissance and Reformation, down to the modern age inaugurated by the outrageous corruptor Descartes.[2] The Middle Age is characterized as the age which begins everything and concludes nothing, and is made to correspond with cosmic time, "which is itself the preliminary sketch of Olympus" and may conversely be called "the Middle Age of the tellurian world": the Modern Age is "arrangement of rebirth" in such wise that "modern man, generally speaking, has much less grasp of Christian than the educated man in ancient times had of Pagan civilization".[3] What, then, of the account of

1. *Introduzione*, III, 52, 54, 55; *Del buono e del bello*, 320, 344, 365, 373.
2. *Nuova Protologia*, II, 187.
3. *Del buono e del bello*, p. 13.

the various moralities of the various peoples in the book *Del buono* or of poetry and the various arts in *Del bello*? What indeed of the whole staggering construction of *Il Primato d'Italia*, scene of the most wonderful exercises of his historical talent? The very few who today open or try to read that book remain stunned. In truth Gioberti's proceeding was that of the preacher, seeking to shake and astound his hearers with seemingly triumphant argument, to heap upon them piles of uncritically collected facts, rather than to teach and educate their minds, let alone to seek truth and promote knowledge. His was indeed a preacher's style, diffuse and wordy and not unmixed with self-satisfaction at his skilful use of the Italian language, the study of which the purist school had restored to honour in his time.

If we would see Gioberti's "philosophy" (in spite of all we have said we will continue to call it so for want of a better name) in historical perspective, we should without doubt view it as related to the German philosophy of the first half of the nineteenth century, being one of the numerous productions of the *epigoni* of the great thinkers Fichte, Schelling, and above all Hegel. It is no disproof of this that Gioberti was always giving himself airs as the critic and overtaker of "the German school". He himself from youth always exalted that school above the others of modern times, not only for its having demolished and put out of court the doctrine of Sensism, but for having freed itself of the psychologism of the Kantian as well as the Cartesian tradition, seeking instead with sustained and subtle efforts to recapture the lost Idea, to rise to the Absolute, the *Ens*, and indeed its masters desired "to rank as Christians – indeed sometimes they smacked a little of Catholicism", for "the divine fire will not easily die out in these late-born sons of the Orient". That he was nevertheless dissatisfied with, and opposed to, them, he explained by their not "succeeding in recomposing the ideal formula", not rising superior to Pantheism.[1] But this was itself less of a difference than he imagined, for there were notoriously some theistic interpretations of Hegel and some

1. *Nuova Protologia*, I, 207-208.

declared theists among the Hegelians, indeed, in the copious crop of systems all showing a family likeness there were Catholic and catholicizing specimens. Conversely Gioberti's own philosophy, in despite of his sincere or politic professions of orthodoxy and exaltations of the papacy, was always held in suspicion and mistrust by the Catholic Church and by strict believers, on account of the hint or scent which they discerned in it of that very pantheism of which he so zealously accused others. In our view the real and substantial difference was of another, a philosophical order: what Gioberti had in common with Hegel, his metaphysics or theologizing philosophy with his *Ens* creating the Existent and Existent making its return to the *Ens* – modelled undoubtedly upon the Hegelian Idea, with its resolve to issue forth from itself and to create Nature in order to reconcentrate itself in the Spirit, was the dead or moribund side of Hegel's thought by contrast with the vital element in Hegel, the power whereby his dialectic demolished false divisions and distinctions which had been noxious in every field of learning, making room for the concept of Becoming and thereby for the historical envisagement of reality. Gioberti, the looseness of whose concepts we have illustrated, was not only void of the speculative wealth offered by Hegel, but wholly lacking in mental energy and originality.

For all that, Gioberti's philosophical works were much admired and discussed in Italy, and gave rise to a school which lasted for twenty or thirty years between 1840 and 1870. This success cannot be ascribed simply to the fervour and nobility of their author's own character, apostle of Italian nationality, independence, and liberty, so popular at that time among Catholics who shared his political views and were trying to harmonize them with loyalty towards religion, church, and papacy. There was in addition some genuine philosophical interest due partly to the fact of the reaction against eighteenth-century thought, partly to the feeling that Gioberti might be a substitute for the German idealism towards which many were attracted although there was as yet little direct or detailed knowledge of it in Italy.

When by the efforts of scholars such knowledge began to be

available, one of the first to absorb it and profit deeply by it, Bertrando Spaventa, passed a highly adverse judgement upon Gioberti, writing to his brother in one of the clandestine letters on philosophical topics which were smuggled through to him in the gaol of Santo Stefano: "I had not for ten years read Gioberti. I never liked him, and now he seems to me to be simply beating the big drum. Of philosophy I find in him nothing, nothing whatever: no broad view, no historical criterion, no penetrating insight into systems, no understanding of his own time or of the human spirit. Just endless chatter and perpetual fantasticality."[1] And some months later he said that after renewed study he liked him less than ever, because "of philosophy he offers nothing whatsoever except a heap of stuff always found in every philosophical system and even in religious presentations". Despite the confutations of Descartes and Spinoza he found in him a total absence of the concepts of Spirit and Creation.[2]

But strangely enough Spaventa, after further study particularly of Gioberti's posthumous works which had been meanwhile published by Massari, greatly changed his first judgement, praising where he had blamed and admiring where he had previously yawned. It was the study of the same posthumous works which changed the views also of Ausonio Franchi. In 1852 he had laid against Gioberti the serious charge of treating the truth not as an end, but as a means for subserving diplomatically certain personal and political ends, and had proclaimed that his prestige in Italy was in total eclipse. But after reading the posthumous works he recanted, and announced the restoration of Gioberti's former prestige, heightened and purified, on the grounds that in these works he had "finally shaken off the Roman dogmatic yoke, and had recognized in every revelation and religion a phenomenon, process, natural law of the human spirit", passing like himself (Ausonio Franchi was an ex-monk) "to the cause of rationalism

---

1. See Silvio Spaventa, *Dal 1848 al 1861* (Essays, letters, and documents edited by B. Croce), 2nd edn., Bari, 1923, p. 244.
2. Ibid., p. 248.

and humanism".[1] Spaventa came to the same conclusion, having in mind the Hegelian form of rationalism and humanism, for in a further letter to his brother in September 1858 he announced the surprising new discoveries he had made in his reading of Gioberti: "I have somewhat come round to him. In his last, posthumous, writings he has eliminated many imperfections which I found in the first form of his system. It is curious to note how the development of his thought has taken the form of a sort of self-criticism. There was some seed of novelty in the first form, but hidden and repressed. His great defect is want of science. He proceeds by way of aphorisms. But there is much good in him, for the inwardness of his work is profoundly speculative. What is needful is to express his thought in its true form showing that certain terminological externals, which he himself came largely to abandon, are in contradiction to his own speculative principles." Thus without overlooking the confusion, the contradiction, and the error to be found even in the posthumous works, Spaventa reiterated that there was good stuff in them: "Often enough Gioberti seems to be practising irony at his own expense. He introduces you over and over again to the same old principle of the *Ens* creating the Existent: but 'create' is given a quasi-Hegelian meaning, with finite and infinite drawn together, finite figuring as potential infinite."[2] Now Spaventa was firmly convinced that Hegel had with his system touched the supreme truth, and he saw the importance of the German philosopher as lying principally in that part of his work which for us must rank as the most traditional, aged, and least solid part: but this was the part which was significant for the inner stresses of the seeker after a system to refine upon and replace Christian and Catholic religion – Spaventa himself, after all, had studied theology and been a churchman. So, while continuing to remark upon the "want of science" in those works, yet he "came round to" their author. This want of science we ourselves have called want of critical and logical power and of all true

1. See *La filosofia delle scuole italiane* (2nd edn., Florence, Le Monnier, 1863), pp. 23-24, 81-82.
2. *Dal 1848 al 1861*, pp. 362-64.

speculative capacity. Fundamental as this defect really was, Spaventa more and more lost sight of it, and from accepting and esteeming Gioberti he passed to exalting him with the dedication to his philosophy of a long and laborious study. In his lectures and lessons of the year 1860-61, developing a view of the history of Italian philosophy which he had arrived at under the inspiration of a moderate yet, for all its moderation, not wholly justified nationalism, Spaventa saluted in Gioberti "the limit so far reached by our (Italian) speculation". He had, in fact, come to find in Gioberti "the reproduction, though perfected and resolved into a higher principle, of the realism of Bruno; furthermore the basis laid for the new metaphysic invoked by Vico; and with this the satisfaction of the religious requirements of Campanella, Galuppi, and Rosmini, faith and knowledge being not separated but reconciled in the unity of the Ideal Science". This philosophy was such that "it alone corresponds to the spirit of the age, it alone sums up all the most glorious moments of Italian philosophy, reintroduces our philosophy into the common life of European philosophy, and can, as no other can, restore to Italian speculative thought the freedom and glory due to it so that it becomes a national philosophy".[1] I will not here repeat the criticism I have passed elsewhere upon such schematic and arbitrary modes of conceiving the history of thought. I will only remark that the enthusiasm which flamed up for a time does not seem to have lasted, for of the bulky monograph on Gioberti he never printed more than the part which he had written in the later years of his exile.[2] He never published, and perhaps he never wrote, the second and final volume. After that he never returned to the subject, and about the influence which Gioberti was going to exert in imparting a fresh direction to Italian philosophy there is no word in Spaventa's later writings. Spaventa devoted himself to expounding

1. See *Carattere e sviluppo della filosofia italiana* (1860): in *Scritti filosofici* edited by Gentile, Naples, 1900, pp. 115-52); further the lesson included in *La filosofia italiana nei suoi rapporti con la filosofia europea* (Naples, 1861-2, 3rd edn., Bari, 1926, pp. 160-89).
2. *La filosofia del Gioberti*, vol. 1 (Naples, 1863).

and commenting upon the difficult text of Hegel, and then, in his
last years, strove to save whatever of conceptual and speculative
thought could be saved when the new antispeculative barbarism
called Positivism surged around him.

Meanwhile in the same University, of Naples, where Spaventa
was teaching, his contemporary and old fellow-exile Francesco
De Sanctis, who had passed through the same mental experiences
as a warm admirer of Hegel and had already, before 1848, passed
criticisms on Gioberti,[1] – De Sanctis, that literary critic whose
rare philosophical pronouncements are almost always packed
with truth – said, in his memorable lessons of 1872 on the Italian
Moderates of the nineteenth century, all that there was to say
about Gioberti: what that was seemed to his clear intelligence to
brook no doubt. Gioberti (he said amiably) in assailing Sensism
had followed the trend of the times; his philosophical activity
was largely an echo of European philosophy; the objection which
Gioberti raised against Hegel's identification of knowing with
being, and his implicit humanism, were nothing at all new, and
there had been no need for the appeal to Pythagoras, the ancient
wisdom of the Italians, Plotinus, Bruno, and Vico, because the
whole matter was contained in that versicle in the first chapter of
Genesis "God created the heaven and the earth". He added that
Gioberti was lacking in any "powerful reasoning capacity or logical
vigour", that he "would not come down on to concrete ground",
and that his synthesis, far from being a synthesis, was "just one
side of an unanalysed idea"; and that the "immense stock of facts"
collected and displayed by him "did not add up to a serious
culture". He would not allow the comparison of Gioberti with
Vico because Vico, in spite of his erroneous conception of an
historical development proceeding one-sidedly by way of "course"
and "recourse", possessed a solid knowledge of history and had
discoveries to his credit in the field of Roman law as well as a
remarkable power of analysis, while unlike Gioberti he had an

1. For his critical exposition of both these thinkers' aesthetic theories see
the lessons anterior to 1848 in *Teoria e storia della letteratura*, ed. Croce, II,
61-130.

aptitude misunderstood and despised as mere psychology by the other, which enabled him to enunciate those axioms or dignities which, De Sanctis remarks, are "masterpieces". He adds that Vico was continually discovering something new wherever he passed, thus "opening the way to the many branches of learning which have blossomed since his time". Gioberti, who was less philosopher than "orator", achieved nothing similar.[1]

And in the Italian philosophical revival after the positivist period, Gioberti's philosophy, despite those old predictions and godspeeds of Spaventa's, exerted no stimulating influence. The revival came in other ways and reached other harbours – mainly by the way of meditation upon the problems of historical composition, utterly unknown to Gioberti. True, some appearance of interest in his work was furnished by some pupils of Spaventa's own pupils, who, having failed to understand that their master's tenderness for Gioberti had been but occasional and transitory, deemed it their duty to resuscitate and to endorse the testimonials of esteem and admiration which as we have seen he had let fall. Moreover, the routine of university life encourages the production of academic dissertations and theses on any and every subject whether important and interesting or tedious. Several such were written about Gioberti (some, like Saitta's monograph, conducted with an accuracy and acumen worthy of a less boring subject), while unpublished writings of his were printed and plans laid for a reprint of his complete works. I believe that this project, unsolicited, unwanted, unnecessary, is in hand, unattended by the smallest interest. Some too took delight in finding to their astonishment in Gioberti's phrases anticipations of all the latest and most futuristic thoughts, a task made easy by the vague and contradictory character of the only thoughts contained there. All this would have little importance save for the persistence of an antiquated notion of philosophy, that which I have called "theologizing philosophy".

According to that notion the philosopher is the sublime perso-

1. *La letteratura italiana nel secolo XIX* (Croce's edn., Naples, 1897, pp. 301-15).

nage who is bent wholly upon resolving the metaphysical problem, that insoluble problem lying halfway between the naturalistic and the mythological. The insoluble character of this problem, and the profusion of images with which, in the guise of critical conclusions, the claim to have solved it is usually advanced, are surely responsible for the frequent or common charge that philosophy is useless: no such charge is made against any other human activity. The "philosopher" in question deems himself exempt from the obligation to master any detail of historical reality, or any of the philosophical sciences which he calls "particular", sweeping these aside with the description of "empirical" or "psychological", in patent ignorance of what psychologism and empiricism really are. Worse still, he may deign to take part in their labours, contributing mere formulas and generalities which experts in the problems of those sciences at once recognize as cheap tricks or refusals to take the matter seriously. So too he will stand aside from all practical political or moral endeavour on the fields of human contests, enveloping himself in an odious pretended serenity, really coldness and indifference. Unless indeed from time to time he puts in an appearance to proffer generic and obvious precepts having an ambiguous bearing upon the necessities of the struggle. Or else, by ill luck, he decides more or less naively to resort to those elaborate subtle trickeries which seem to him the very consummation of ability, as if to prove to himself and others that although an idealist in philosophy he can be a great realist in practical life.

Gioberti is for sure well suited to serve as an ideal for philosophers of that sort. He could do so also in the field of politics, in which, while no doubt sincerely and tirelessly working for the political and moral renewal of Italy, he went too far in the use of obscure manoeuvres and sly combinations which then fell asunder in his hands.[1] We have lately seen and heard his attitudes and

1. Concerning Gioberti as a politician a fresh and persuasive estimate is given by OMODEO in *Vincenzo Gioberti e la sua evoluzione politica* (Turin, Einaudi, 1941). Omodeo rightly remarks that in Gioberti's books we see "the tenacious pursuit of an ideal in the sadness of a double exile, in a nobly

gestures and words repeated among us, and his favourite terminology of "mimesis" and "methexis" and suchlike formulas absurdly applied to the not very noble political affairs of the passing
moment. It may be that this contemporary exhibition of Gioberti in pseudo-philosophy and malpractice is what has induced
me to turn my mind to a philosophy which I had long forgotten,
and to define its qualities and deny altogether the one of speculative greatness or grandeur which an old tradition and a new
fancifulness would still reverently attribute to it.

[1942]

endured poverty, an absolute disinterestedness: an ideal of free and ascending
progress restlessly seeking clarity in the terms of philosophy and politics".
But Omodeo also remarks that it is needful to recall to the resuscitators of
an inferior neo-Guelfism, a neo-Giobertianism giving itself airs of cleverness, that Gioberti's experiment is not reproducible, not to be given a simple
linear extension, for Gioberti's active heritage was taken up and merged
by Cavour in the sanity of his own policy. He adds: "The so-called realism
of Gioberti, like the pretended realism of many contemporary philosophers
who have tried to tread in his footsteps, consists not in gearing his own creative activity to the situations in which it has to work, but in a sort of passive
contemplation of a providential order revealed to contemplation in signs
and presages" (pp. 96-97).

III
AESTHETICS: THE PHILOSOPHY
OF ART AND LANGUAGE

I

AESTHETICA IN NUCE[1]

WHEREIN CONSISTS ART OR POETRY. – If one examines some poetical work with the intent of arriving at what it is that makes us
describe it as poetical, two elements are immediately recognized
as being constant and necessary in a poem: a complex of images,
and a feeling which inspires this. Let us recall, for example, a passage of Virgil's Aeneid which we will have learned by heart at
school (III. 294...). Aeneas recounts how on learning that the ruler
of the place where he had landed was the Trojan Helenus with
Andromache as his consort, he in his wonder and surprise became
inflamed with a strong desire to see that surviving son of Priam
and to learn of the mighty events that had overtaken him. He
meets Andromache outside the city walls, near the waters of a
stream renamed Simoens, celebrating funeral rites before the green
turf of an empty grave, and two altars placed there in honour of
Hector and Astyanax. She is astounded at the sight of him, stumbles, and in broken words asks him if he be a living man or a
shade; and not less shaken is the questioner Aeneas than she, in her
grief and abashment, as she recalls how she survived battle and
outrage, was cast for by lot and assigned as slave and concubine to
Pyrrhus, then rejected by Pyrrhus and allotted by him to be the
slave bride of the slave Helenus, after which Pyrrhus was slain by
the hand of Orestes and Helenus, liberated, became king. Then
Aeneas with his men enters the city and is welcomed by the son of
Priam in that little Troy, that miniature Pergamus, built in the
likeness of the great one, beside a new Xanthus; and there Aeneas
kisses the lintel of a new Scaean gate. All these, and further episodes
here omitted, are images of persons, things, attitudes, gestures,
sayings, mere images which are nowise offered as history, historical
judgement, nor are taken or considered as such. But through

1. I borrow this title which Hamann once used for an Essay. The present
piece was written as the article on *Aesthetics* in the *Encyclopaedia Britannica*,
XIV edn.

them all runs a feeling which is ours as much as that of the poet, a human feeling of poignant memories, shuddering horror, melancholy, homesickness, tender-heartedness, indeed of something both puerile and pious which transpires in that pointless reconstruction of things lost, those toys of religious piety, the *parva Troia, Pergama simulata magnis, arens Xanti cognomine rivus*: something not to be expressed in logical terms, but which poetry, and poetry alone, can, in its own way, fully recount. Here then, in the first and abstract analysis are two elements, but they are not to be thought of as two strands, not even as two closely interwoven strands, because in effect the feeling has been wholly converted into images, the complex of images which we have recalled; it is a feeling which has been contemplated and therewith resolved and surpassed. Poetry, then, is neither feeling, nor image, nor the sum of these two, but is "contemplation of feeling", "lyrical intuition", or, what comes to the same, "pure intuition", pure, that is to say, of any historical or critical assessment of the reality or unreality of the images entering into the fabric, pure palpitation of life as ideal quality. Doubtless in poetry other things can be found besides these two elements or moments and their synthesis, but such other things are either intermingled but extraneous elements, (reflections, exhortations, controversies, allegories etc.), or else they are just these very feelings and images, or feeling-images, released from the link which connected them, taken materially, reconstituted as they were previously to the poetic creation. In the first eventuality they are non-poetic elements which have simply been introduced and superadded, in the second they are elements which have been unpoeticized by an unpoetic or no longer poetic reader who has caused the poetry to evaporate, either because he could not abide in poetry's ideal sphere, or because he was engaged upon the legitimate business of historical investigation, or else upon some other practical concerns for the purpose of which poetry is reduced to, or rather employed as, a document or instrument.

What has here been said of "poetry" can be said equally of all the other "arts" as customarily enumerated, painting, sculpture,

architecture, music. Whenever the question is that of the eligibility
of some spiritual production to be considered as art, the dilemma
will arise: either this is a lyrical intuition, or else it is something
else, maybe very respectable, but not art. If, as some theorists
have had it, the art of painting is an imitation or reproduction of
objects, data, then it would be not art but something mechanical
and practical. If, following other theories, the painter's task were
to blend lines and lights and colours with a zealous pursuit of
novelty of effect, then he would be not an artist but a technical
inventor. If music consisted similarly in combinations of tones,
then Leibniz's and Father Kircher's paradox could be put into
effect (the composition of musical scores by the unmusical), and
the fears expressed by Proudhon in regard to poetry and by Stuart
Mill in regard to music, lest, the totality of possible combinations
of words or notes having been exhausted, the poetical and the
musical should lose their place in the world, would have a basis.
Undoubtedly, both in poetry and in these other arts, extraneous
elements obtain an entrance, whether *a parte objecti* or *a parte
subjecti*, whether, that is, in faulty execution or in the aesthetically
defective appreciation of works by those who view them or hear
them; whence it comes that the critics of those arts advise us to
rule out or give no heed to what they call the "literary" elements
in painting, sculpture, and music, and the critic of poetry demands our attention for the "poetry" and frowns upon the allurements of mere literature. Now he who has an understanding
for poetry makes straight for the poetical heart of the poem, and
feels its rhythm vibrate in his own heart, or else, if he fails to hear
such a heartbeat, he denies the presence of poetry, no matter how
much else that is admirable for skill and wit, for nobility of
intention, quickness of intelligence, agreeableness of effects, may
be found standing in the work in its stead. He who has no understanding of poetry follows the lure of these things, and his error
is not that he admires them, but that he admires them as poetry.

THE DISTINCTION OF ART FROM NON-ART. – Defined as lyrical
or pure intuition, art is implicitly distinguished from all the other

forms of spiritual production. The distinctions in question are made explicit in the following negations:

1. Art is not philosophy. For philosophy is the logical understanding of the universal categories of being, but art is the unreflective intuition of being. Philosophy surpasses and resolves the image, while art abides within the sphere of image and has here its reign. But art, it will be said, may not behave irrationally nor disregard logic. Quite right; art is neither irrational nor illogical; yet the reason and logic of art are quite other than dialectical or conceptual reason and logic. It was to draw attention to this peculiarity and originality that the names "Logica Sensitiva" and "Aesthetica" were coined. As often as a "logical" character is claimed for art, there is either a play of words confounding the conceptual with the aesthetic logic, or a use of the former to symbolize the latter.

2. Art is not history. History must critically distinguish between reality and unreality, between factual reality and imagined reality, between the reality of action and that of desire. But art does not reach to such distinctions, remaining, as we said, in the sphere of pure image. Whether Helenus, Andromache, Aeneas had historical existence is of no significance for the poetic quality of the Aeneid. However, the historical criterion, it has been objected, is not extraneous to art, seeing that art observes the law of verisimilitude. We answer that this last word is here no better than a metaphor enlisted, rather clumsily, to denote the coherency of images with one another. For if the images were not thus coherent, they could not exert their power as images (any more than the *delphinus in silvis* and the *aper in fluctibus* of Horace), unless perhaps as a quaint eccentricity of the imagination.

3. Art is not natural science, nor is it mathematics. For natural science is an abstracting classification exerted upon historical reality, while mathematics is an operation with abstractions, not a contemplation. If a likeness has sometimes been traced between the works of mathematicians and of poets, this rests merely upon an outward and generic analogy, while the mathematic or geometric element sometimes alleged to be harboured in the inner

essence of the arts is an unconscious metaphor for the constructive, cohesive, unifying power of the poetic spirit as it fashions for itself a body of images.

4. Art is not the play of the imagination, passing on from image to image under the spur of desire for variety, relaxation, distraction, or for entertainment by the interesting appearances of things agreeable, moving, or pathetic. In art, the imagination is disciplined by the single task of converting tumultuous feeling into clear intuition. Indeed there have been various proposals to abandon here the word "imagination" in favour of (poetic or creative) "fancy". For imagination is in itself alien to poetry: witness the unpoetical character of the works of Anne Redcliffe or Dumas père.

5. Art is not immediacy of feeling. Andromache at the sight of Aeneas becomes *amens – diriguit visu in medio – labitur – longo vix tandem tempore fatur*. As she speaks, *longos ciebat incassum fletus.* But it is not the poet who thus raves, gazes fixedly, stumbles, struggles to utter hard-found words, breaks into long lament. The poet, having made of these commotions the argument of his poem, utters harmonious verses. Doubtless the feelings in their immediacy are, as it is commonly said, "expressed". If they were not expressed, if they were not (besides all else) sensible and bodily facts or, as the positivists and the neo-critical school used to say, "psychophysical phenomena", they would not be concrete things, would not exist. Andromache, after all, expressed herself in the manner described. But such "expression", albeit conscious, can rank as expression only by metaphorical licence, when compared with the spiritual or aesthetic expression which alone truly expresses, that is to say gives to the feeling a theoretical form and converts it into language, song, shape. It is in the difference between feeling as contemplated (poetry, in fact), and feeling as enacted or undergone, that lies the catharsis, the liberation from the affections, the calming property which has been attributed to art; and to this corresponds the aesthetic condemnation of works of art if or in so far as immediate feeling breaks into them or uses them as an outlet. The same difference accounts for that other

character (once again, properly speaking, synonymous with poetic expressiveness), the "infinity" of art which differentiates it from feeling or immediate passion which are finite, and this is also described as the "universal" or "cosmic" character of poetry. For when feeling, instead of entering in its travail into the living of life, is held in contemplation, it becomes thereby diffused far and wide through the domain of the soul, the domain of the world. And infinite then are its resonances: joy and grief, pleasure and pain, effort and relaxation, gravity and lightness, and all the rest, find in it their link each with the other, and pass by delicate shades each into the other, so that each feeling, though keeping its individual features, its original and dominant motive, yet eludes restriction or exhaustion in this. An image of comedy, if the comedy be poetic, has about it something that is not comic, as we see with Don Quixote or Falstaff, while an image of dreadfulness is never, in poetry, lacking in some comforting elevation, some goodness and love.

6. Art is not didactic and rhetorical, for these words betoken the art which has been overtaken and subdued and limited by a practical purpose, whatever that may be – whether, didactically, to implant in minds a certain philosophic, historical, or scientific truth, or, rhetorically, to sway minds to feel and by consequence to act in a certain particular manner. In oratory, expression loses its "infinity" and independence, and becoming the means to an end, is dissolved into that end. That is how Schiller is led to speak of the "non-determinant" character of art by contrast with the office of oratory which is to "determine" or to "move". Here we have an explanation of the quite proper distrust which is felt for "political poetry", sometimes described as necessarily bad poetry, though this is true only if it fails to rise above the "political" level to a poetic serenity and humanity.

7. If art is not to be confounded with that form of practical action which seems nearest to it, the didactic and rhetorical, still less is it to be confounded with other forms of action designed to produce certain effects of pleasure, sensual delight, or convenience, or for that matter of virtuousness or pious uplift. It behoves art to

exclude the meretricious, but also the well-intentioned, as being both, in their different ways, unaesthetic and indigestible for the poetic mind. Flaubert remarked that obscene books are deficient in *vérité*, but Voltaire used his wit upon certain *Poésies sacrées*, so called because *"personne n'y touche"*.

ART IN ITS RELATIONS. – The foregoing explicitly formulated "negations" are, as it will be easily understood, equally well formulated as "relations", it being impossible to conceive of the various and distinct forms of spiritual activity as separate, operating in isolation, providing each one solely for itself. There is no call for us to develop here a complete systematic exposition of the forms or spiritual categories in their order and dialectic. But limiting our remarks to art, we will simply say that the category of art, like any other, implies, and is implied by, conditions, and is conditioned by all the others in their turn. How could the aesthetic synthesis of poetry take place without a precedent disturbance of the mind? (*Si vis me flere dolendum est*: et cetera.) And that precedent state of mind which we have called feeling, what else is it if not the spirit which has thought, willed, acted, and which thinks, desires, suffers, rejoices, labours within itself? Poetry is as a ray of sunshine clothing that mist with its light, outlining the hidden features of things. For that reason, it is no task for empty spirits, closed minds; and those artists who in their mistaken devotion to pure art, art for art's sake, shut out the stir of life and the throes of thought, turn out to be altogether unproductive of anything more than imitations or incoherent impressionism.

The foundation of all poetry is therefore the human personality, and since the human personality fulfils itself morally, the foundation of all poetry is the moral conscience. This does not mean that the artist requires to be a deep thinker and an acute critic, nor that he must be a moral paragon or hero. It means that he must be sufficiently a participant in the world of thought and of action, by way either of personal experience or of sympathy with the experience of others, to live the human drama in its fullness. As a practical man he may err, he may stain his purity and incur blame.

But he must needs have alive in him, in some form or other, the sentiment of purity and impurity, righteousness and guilt, good and evil. He may not be endowed with marked courage as a man of action, he may even show himself wavering and timid, but he must at any rate be sensitive to the dignity of courage. Many artistic inspirations spring not from the artist's practical personality but from his feeling for what he is not but ought to be, what he admires when he sees it, and would fain be himself. Many, and those perhaps the finest, of the pages of heroic and warlike poetry, are the work of authors who could never have learned to wield an arm.

By this we do not mean that a moral personality is sufficient equipment for the poet and artist. To be *vir bonus* is not sufficient equipment even for oratory: the orator must be also *dicendi peritus*. There can be no poetry without the poetic art, that form of theoretical synthesis which was defined above, the gift without which all the rest is no more than a pile of logs which cannot be set aflame for want of a torch. And yet the figure of the pure poet, pure artist, cultivator of pure beauty, untouched by human concerns, is not a figure but a caricature.

What demonstrates that poetry both implies and is implied by the other forms of the spirit, both conditions and is conditioned by them, is the fact that logical thought cannot subsist without the help of the poetic fancy in giving a contemplative form to the travail of the feelings, an intuitive expression to dim impressions, itself becoming representation and language (a language of which the words may be speech, song, colour, or some other medium). Logical thought is not itself language, but is never without language, of which language it is poetry that has been the creator. Logical thought by the use of concepts sorts out the representations of poetry, dominates them, which would be impossible were they not already there as its potential subjects. Likewise, save for the critical discernments of thought there could be no action, nor consequently any goodness of action, as conscience and duty. No man, however seemingly absorbed in logical and critical and scientific study, or in practical interests, or the fulfilment of duty, lacks his little fund of fancy and poetry deep in his heart. Even the pedant Wagner, *famulus* to Faust, confessed that he too often went through *grillenhafte Stunden*. Indeed without such a fund one would not be a man, a thinking and acting agent, at all. But, disregarding such an extreme and therefore absurd hypothesis, it suffices to say that where the fund is scanty, there is proportionate superficiality and aridity in thought, and proportionate coldness in action.

THE AESTHETIC SCIENCE, OR SCIENCE OF ART, AND ITS PHILOSOPHICAL CHARACTER. – The concept of Art expounded above is, in a way, the common concept, as it appears with more or less clarity in current discussion, serving as a point of reference, more or less explicit, in all such discussions, which perpetually gravitate back to it. It performs this service not only in our own times, but in all times, as a collection of the sayings of writers, poets, artists, laymen, and even of the common man, if properly interpreted, could easily show. In spite of this it is necessary to dispel any mistaken supposition that this concept Exists as an innate idea. It is not an innate idea, but it is an operative *a priori*. Such an *a priori* is not something in itself, but has its being solely in the single productions which it generates. Just as the *a priori* of Art, Poetry, Beauty has no existence as an idea to be perceived and admired in itself in some region beyond the skies, but is present solely in the numberless works of poetry, art, beauty which it has shapen and still shapes, so too, similarly, the logical *a priori* of Art is to be found nowhere else than in the particular judgements which it has formed and for ever forms, the confutations, demonstrations, theories wrought by it, the problems and groups of problems resolved. All the definitions, distinctions, negations, relations expounded above have their history, all have been elaborated in the course of the centuries, and have come to us as the product of that slow, varied, and laborious process. The Aesthetic Science, or Science of Art, has not for its task, then, as sometimes appears from the pages of educational handbooks, the fixation, once for all, of a definition of art, to be developed with a fully exhaustive wealth of attendant concepts, but has simply to provide a continuously renewed and improved systematization of the problems which from age to age arise out of men's ponderings on art. This is precisely equivalent to saying that the task is to resolve difficulties, to criticize errors, out of which errors there thus comes the stimulus and the material for a perpetual progress of thought.

From this it is evident that no exposition of Aesthetics, and least of all a summary exposition like the present, can pretend to treat exhaustively the infinite problems thrown up, or henceforth to be thrown up, in the history of Aesthetics. It can only recall and deal with certain ones, first and foremost those which even now persist stubbornly in the discussions of ordinary educated people. What is here said implies an "etcetera" printed at the conclusion, to send the reader on a continuance of the exploration on the lines suggested to him, whether he chooses to pore over the discussions of past times, or to attend to the more or less novel debates of the present, which almost every hour branch out and proliferate in aspects of fresh appearance.

Another observation will not be out of place. Aesthetics is indeed a particular philosophic discipline having for its origin a particular and distinct category of the spirit. But as a philosophical discipline it can never detach itself from the main stem of philosophy. For its problems are those of the relation between art and the other spiritual forms, problems of difference and of identity. It is, in reality, the whole of philosophy displayed with a more special emphasis on the side of art. The cry has often gone up for an Aesthetic which should be able to stand on its own, uninvolved in any general philosophic conception, fitting in equally well with various general conceptions or with all: but this is a contradictory and therefore an impracticable demand. Those too who have proclaimed some non-philosophical doctrine of aesthetics, whether naturalistic, inductive, physical, physiological, or psychological, when they began to put their programme into execution, surreptitiously introduced a general philosophical conception, which might be positivism, naturalism, or even materialism. Whoever regards these as fallacious or outworn philosophies, can spare himself the trouble of confuting the aesthetic or pseudo-aesthetic doctrines built upon them (and in turn serving them as foundations). He will not regard the problems pertinent to them as being still open and calling for discussion, or anyway for close discussion. To take an example: if the doctrine of psychological association (which put mechanical workings in the place of the a priori synthesis) has spent its force, this brings with it not only the demise of logical associationism, but also that of aesthetic associationism with its association of "content" and "form" or of "two representations", which by contrast with what Campanella called the *tactus intrinsecus* making its contact *cum magna suavitate*, stood for a *tactus extrinsecus* in which the terms, as soon as they had touched, *discedebant*. Similarly, with the obsolescence of biological and evolutionist explanations of logical and ethical values, the analogous derivation of aesthetic values fell to the ground. The demonstration that empirical methods cannot help towards an understanding of reality, brings with it that of the hopelessness of an attempt to build an Aesthetic on the classification of aesthetic data and the deduction of laws therefrom.

INTUITION AND EXPRESSION. – If we start with defining a work of art as a "lyrical image", the problem quickly presents itself: What is the relation of "intuition" to "expression", and what is the mode of passage from the one to the other. Substantially this is the same problem which makes an appearance, in other parts of philosophy, as that of the relation between inward and outward, spirit and matter, soul and body, or again, in the Philosophy of Practice, between intention and will, will and action, and so forth.

In such terms the problem is insoluble, for once inward is severed from outward, spirit from body, will from action, intuition from expression, there is no way of passing from the former terms to the latter save by reuniting them in a third term, which has sometimes been called God, sometimes the Unknowable. The dualism must needs lead either to a Transcendence or to an Agnosticism. Now when problems prove insoluble in the terms in which they are propounded, the only course is to criticize the term themselves, to look into how they have originated and into the logical justification of that origin. Our enquiry will lead to this conclusion: these terms have their origin not as derivations from a philosophic principle, but as the effect of an empirical and naturalistic classification which formed these two classes of inward and outward (disregarding the fact that the inward must always be also outward, while the outward is inconceivable without its inwardness), and similarly the classes of souls and bodies, images and expressions. But notoriously things which have been distinguished empirically and materially, and not philosophically, or formally, can never be brought together in a higher synthesis. The soul is the soul inasmuch as it is the body, the will is will inasmuch as it moves legs and arms, thus becoming action. Intuition is, in its very operation, expression. An image not expressed as word, song, line, colouring, sculpture, architecture – or at the very least as a word murmured, a song hummed to oneself, a line, a colour viewed in fancy so as to give its tone to the whole soul, the organism – is a non-existent image, of which the existence may indeed be asserted, but cannot be affirmed, since an affirmation would necessarily have to be supported by the demonstration that it was somehow embodied and expressed.

The penetrating philosophical doctrine of the identity of intuition and expression is, moreover, at one with ordinary common sense, which mocks at those who say they have thoughts but cannot express them, or claim to have conceived a great pictorial work of art which they cannot put on the canvas. *Rem tene verba sequentur*: if the *verba* are lacking, the *res* too must be wanting.

The identity of which we are speaking is discoverable in all the spheres of the spirit, but is perhaps, in the sphere of art, specially conspicuous. To watch the creation of a work of art is to watch, as it were, the mystery of the creation of the world: hence the influence exerted by the aesthetic science upon philosophy as a whole, which it guides towards the conception of Unity-Totality. Aesthetics, when it rejects abstract spiritualism, and the dualism resulting from that abstraction, in the life of art, bases itself upon (but at the same time lays the basis for) idealism or absolute spiritualism.

EXPRESSION AND COMMUNICATION. – Such objections as are raised against the identification of intuition with expression usually arise out of a psychological illusion. It appears to us that we are perpetually in possession of a vast wealth of lively and concrete images, when all that we possess is but signs and names. Or they may arise from a faulty analysis of certain cases, as when it is thought that some artists achieve merely a fragmentary expression of a whole world of images which they possess in their soul, whereas in truth they have nothing more in their soul than just those fragments, accompanied not by the supposed world of images but at the most by an aspiration or confused effort to attain it, to attain, that is, a larger and grander image, in which they may or may not be successful.

But another origin for such objections lies in the confounding of expression with something which really is distinct from the image and its expression: with communication. Communication is the business of fixing the intuition-expression in an object which we will allow ourselves to call, metaphorically, material or physical, even though in reality we have to deal not with the material and physical but with a spiritual operation. We will take this liberty because the demonstration that the so-called physical is unreal, and has to be resolved into the spiritual, is of prime importance for philosophy as a whole, but touches only indirectly upon the elucidation of aesthetic problems. For brevity's sake, then, we will here use this metaphor or symbol of matter and nature.

The poem, we must see, is there already in its entirety when the poet has expressed it in words uttered to himself. When he goes on to raise his voice to utter it to others, or procures that others shall commit it to memory and chant it to each other as in a *schola cantorum*, or shall record it in writing and printing, this is a new stage of great social and cultural importance having not an aesthetic but a practical character. Likewise with the painter, who paints upon canvas or upon wood, but could not paint at all, did not the intuited image, the line and colour as they have taken shape in the fancy, precede, at every stage of the work, from the first stroke of the brush or sketch of the outline to the finishing touches, these manual actions. And when it happens that some stroke of the brush runs ahead of the image, then the artist, in his final revision, erases and corrects it.

It is, no doubt, very difficult to perceive the frontier between expression and communication in actual fact, for the two processes usually alternate rapidly and are almost intermingled. But the distinction is ideally clear and must be strongly maintained. Neglect of it, or wavering inattention, are at the origin of confusions between art and technics. The technical does not enter into art, but pertains to the concept of communication. By it, generally speaking, we signify a cognition or complex of cognitions suited and arranged for the uses of practical action, meaning, in the case of art, that practical action which constructs means and instruments for recording and communicating works of art: cognitions concerning the preparation of canvases, panels, wall surfaces, pigments, varnishes, or concerning the acquisition of good pronunciation or vocal delivery, and so on. Books on such technical cognitions are not books on Aesthetics and cannot constitute parts or sections of them, if the concepts are thought out in full consequentiality and the words properly used in correspondence with them. For we need not pause to argue about the mere word, when "technique" is used, for example, in the sense of "inner technique" and thus as a synonym for the work of the artist, the formation of the intuition-expression, or in the sense of "discipline", the indispensable continuity with the historical tradition from which no one may sever himself though no one may rest satisfied by simple attachment to it. The confounding of art and the technical, the substitution of the technical for the artistic, is a frequent recourse of impotent artists who hope by dint of the practical, that is of practical devices and inventions, to discover the strength and reliance which they cannot muster in themselves.

ARTISTIC OBJECTS: THE THEORY OF THE PARTICULAR ARTS AND OF NATURAL BEAUTY. – Thus, guided by technical skill, the work of communication, devoted to the preservation and publication of artistic images, produces the material objects which, meta-phorically, we call "artistic" or "works of art": paintings, sculptures, buildings, and on a more complex level literary and musical scripts, and nowadays gramophones with their records, whereby it is possible to reproduce voices and sounds. But these voices and sounds, these pictorial, sculptural, architectural signs, are works of art which exist nowhere else than in the souls which create or recreate them.

The impression of a paradox in this truth as to the non-existence of objects or things of beauty, may be lessened by recalling the analogous case of Economics. It is well known that there are no commodities which naturally and physically possess utility. There are needs, and there is labour, and the adjective 'useful' is drawn from these and metaphorically applied, in economics, to physical things. An economist who sought to deduce the economic value of things from their physical qualities would commit a crude *ignoratio elenchi*.

However crude, the fallacy has been committed, and in Aesthet-ics the error still flourishes as a doctrine of the particular arts and of their respective limits, that is, of the aesthetic character proper to each. The limits so set upon the arts are merely technical or physical, corresponding to the consistency of the artistic objects: sounds and tones, objects coloured, carved, and sculptured, objects constructed without apparent reference to natural bodies (whence poetry, music, painting, sculpture, architecture, and so on). The question as to the artistic character of each of these arts, as to each one's potentiality and the confines of this, as to what sort of images can be expressed in sounds, what in tones, colours, lines, and so forth, is like a question put to the economist as to which physically constituted things should be priced and which should go unpriced, and what should be the ratio of the prices, whereas it is clear that physical constitution enters not into the matter at all, and that each thing may be wanted and sought and marked with the higher or the highest price according to needs and circumstances.

Having rashly ventured on this slippery surface, even the great Lessing was driven to such strange conclusions as that poetry is concerned with "actions" and sculpture with "bodies", and no less a man than Richard Wagner talked irresponsibly of an all-embracing art, the Opera, which would aggregate the potentialities of the single arts. But the artistically sensitive man will in a poet's single line discover the musical, the pictorial, the sculptural, the architectonic, and in a picture too he will find all this, for a picture is always of the soul, not merely of the eyes, and in the soul it is present not only as colour but also as sound, as word, nay even as silence (which is in its way sound and word). When one seeks to grasp the musical, the picturesque, or whatever quality it may be, in isolation, they become elusive and shade into one another, merging in unity. And thus, no matter how common be the current usage of those separate words, it becomes evident that there is one Art, and it is not divided into arts. Though one, it is infinitely various, but varying not with the technical concepts of the arts, but with the infinite variety of artistic personalities and their states of mind.

The problem of natural beauty arises with the confusion between artistic creations and the instruments of communication or "artistic things". Let us ignore the question raised by some theorists whether there be in nature other poetic and artistic beings besides men – it should in any case be answered in the affirmative, both out of due regard for the songbirds, and also, still more, in virtue of the idealist conception of the world as all life and spirituality, though we, as in the fairy story, have lost that blade of grass which, held in the mouth, gave the power of understanding the speech of beasts and plants. The real meaning of "natural beauty" is that certain persons, things, places are, by the effect which they exert upon one, comparable with poetry, painting, sculpture, and the other arts. And there is no difficulty about admitting these "natural artistic things", for the process of poetic communication can be conducted by means of naturally given objects as well as by means of artificially produced objects. It is the fancy of the lover that creates the woman who is for him beautiful, and personifies her in Laura. It is the pilgrim's fancy that creates a sublime or enchanting landscape and fixes it in the scenery of a lake or mountain. These poetic creations are sometimes diffused throughout a more or less wide social circle, whence those female "professional beauties" admired by all, and the "views" at the sight of which everyone displays a more or a less sincere rapture. True, such formations are impermanent. Sometimes a witticism dispels the enchantment, or people get tired of them, or fashion changes capriciously. Unlike works of art, they are unsusceptible of authoritative interpretation. The Gulf of Naples, viewed from one of the finest villas on the Vomero, once acquired by a Russian lady, was described by that same lady after some years of inescapable familiarity with it, as *une cuvette bleue*. She came so to hate that blueness rimmed with green, that she sold the villa. The image of the *cuvette bleue* was incidentally a poetic creation. We will not argue with it.

LITERARY AND ARTISTIC GENRES AND AESTHETIC CATEGORIES. – Broader and worse consequences in literary and artistic criticism and history have followed from a theory of different but analogous origin, the theory of the literary and artistic kinds or *genres*. Once again, a classification, in itself legitimate and useful, is made to serve as a foundation. The theory we have just been discussing was founded on the technical or physical assortment of artistic objects; that which we are now discussing is founded upon the classification of works of art, according to their content or sentimental motive, into tragic, comic, lyric, heroic, amorous, idyllic, romantic, and such divisions and subdivisions. There is indeed a practical utility, when preparing an edition of the works of a poet, in grouping the lyrical pieces in one volume, the dramas in a second, longer poems in a third, narratives in a fourth and so on, and it is positively unavoidable when talking and writing about those works to recall them, or groups of them, by such labels. Illegitimate, on the other hand, we must once again declare to be any inference from these classificatory expedients to the aesthetic

laws of composition or the aesthetic criteria of judgement. We
thereby rule out such arguments as those which infer from the
classifications in question that a tragedy may or may not legitimately have such and such a theme, or set of characters, or mode
of development, or scope – all those arguments which instead of
seeking out and pronouncing upon the poetic essence of a work,
enquire whether it is a tragedy or a poem, and whether it conforms
to the "laws" of one or of another such "genre". Criterions of this
latter sort held the criticism of the Renaissance and of the French
classical age in a bondage (witness the disputes of those times about
the *Commedia* of Dante, the poems of Ariosto and Tasso, the
Pastor Fido of Guarini, the *Cid* of Corneille, the dramas of Lope
de Vega), liberation from which was largely accountable for the
great advance of literary criticism in the nineteenth century. The
decay of these mistaken criteria has not to the same extent profited the artists. Irrespectively of how they are viewed in theory, in
practice the artistically gifted man experiences the chains of this
bondage, and indeed forges them into an instrument of power,
while the ungifted find means of converting their very freedom
into a new sort of servitude.

Some have thought that, of these literary classifications, one
series at least deserved to be retained and given philosophic rank,
namely the differentiation of "lyric", "epic", and "dramatic" which
they proposed to interpret as three moments in the process of
objectivization; the outpouring of the *ego* in the lyric being followed by the detachment of feeling which the *ego* effects in epic
narration, and, further on, by the *ego*'s generation of its own
mouthpieces, the *dramatis personae*, in drama. But the lyric is no
such outpouring: it is not a cry or a wail but is precisely the
objectivization whereby the *ego* contemplates, narrates, dramatizes
itself for itself, and the lyrical spirit forms the poetry of the epic
and the dramatic work, the three being distinguishable only by
exterior characteristics. A wholly poetical work like *Macbeth* or
Antony and Cleopatra is verily a lyric in which the characters and
scenes constitute its various tones and consecutive strophes.

In the old-fashioned systems of Aesthetic, and in present-day works on the same model, much is made of the "categories of the beautiful", the sublime, the tragic, the comic, the pleasing, the humorous, and so on, which merely psychological and empirical concepts the philosophers, particularly the Germans, proceeded to treat as philosophical concepts. Indeed, they developed them by that dialectical method which is suitable to pure or speculative concepts and to those alone, tracing a fanciful course of development which culminated now in the Beautiful, now in the Tragic, now in the Humorous – an idle game. Let us instead take those concepts for what they have already been shown to be. We will then remark how they substantially correspond to the concepts or the literary and artistic genres, from which origin, indeed, principally through the agency of the treatises known as "Institutions in the Art of Letters", they found their way into philosophy. As psychological and empirical concepts they have no part in Aesthetics. Taken as a whole, they stand simply for the totality of the feelings which are the perpetual material of artistic intuition, arranged in empirical groups and assortments.

RHETORIC, GRAMMAR, AND THE PHILOSOPHY OF LANGUAGE. – Errors can always be shown to have sprung out of some aspect of truth, through the arbitrary combination of things which taken in themselves were legitimate. This will once again become evident when we proceed to examine certain other erroneous doctrines which have played an important part in the past and still play some part. In teaching the art of letters, it is perfectly legitimate to make use of differentiations between the simple and the figurative style, between direct and metaphorical, or different sorts of metaphorical utterance. It is perfectly legitimate to observe that in such a place plain utterance and in such another metaphorical utterance is suitable, that elsewhere a given metaphor is incoherent or over-elaborate, and that here the figure of "preterition" is called for, there that of "hyperbole" or "irony". But the merely didactic and practical origin of these distinctions gets forgotten; there arises a philosophic theory of form as distinguishable into "plain" and "ornate", "logical" and "affective", or what-

ever it may be, whereby Rhetoric gets transported into the field
of Aesthetic and the genuine concept of expression is vitiated. In
reality, expression is never logical but always affective, lyrical,
fanciful, and always (but one can equally say, never) metaphorical,
and always proper. It is never plain so as to be in need of covering
and never ornate so as to be in need of liberation from the extraneous, but is always *simplex munditiis*, bright with its own light.
Logical thought, or science, too, in expressing itself, becomes
feeling and fancy, whence a work of philosophy, history, science,
may be beautiful as well as true, and is in any case judged by
aesthetic as well as logical standards; and sometimes a book is
said to be erroneous as theory, criticism, or historical assertion,
yet, by reason of the feeling which animates and is expressed by it,
of value as a work of art. The ferment of truth which was at work
in the distinction between logical and metaphorical form, between
the dialectical and the rhetorical, was the need for constructing a
science of Aesthetics alongside of the science of Logic. But it was
a mistake to try and distinguish the two sciences in the field of
expression, which belongs solely to one of them.

No less legitimately, in the sphere of linguistic instruction, the
practice developed in antiquity of differentiating expressions as
periods, propositions, and words, and words themselves as belonging to different classes, each of these being analysed in their in-
flections and composition out of roots and suffixes, syllables and
sounds or letters. Here is the origin of alphabets, grammars, and
vocabularies, and analogously, of the metrical arts for the use of
poetry, and of grammars of music and painting for music and the
figurative and architectonic arts. Antiquity itself, however, failed
to prevent an illicit transference *ab intellectu ad rem*, one of those
shifts from the level of abstractions and the empirical to reality
and the philosophical, which we have observed in other cases.
Thus it was that language came to be conceived as the aggregation
of words, words as the aggregation of syllables, roots, suffixes:
whereas it is the *continuum* of speech (one might say the organism)
which is the *prius*, and words, syllables, roots, are the anatomical
lay-out, the product of the abstracting intellect, not the original

and real fact of the matter, but a *posterius*. But when Grammar, like Rhetoric, had been introduced into the bosom of Aesthetics, then "expression" had to share the ground with the "means" of expression, and this was a mere duplication, because the means of expression are expression itself, dissected by the grammarians. From this error, and from the associated error as to "plain" form and "ornate" form, derives a mistaken view about the Philosophy of Language. For the Philosophy of Language is not, as is misleadingly suggested, a philosophical Grammar, but stands above grammar, nor can it give philosophical shape to the classifications of the grammarians, but on the contrary, when these get in the way, it eliminates them. It is all one with the Philosophy of poetry and art, the science of intuition-expression, or Aesthetics, and it embraces language in its whole scope, including phonic and articulate language in its integral reality as lively and complete expression.

THE CLASSIC AND THE ROMANTIC. – The problems which we have recalled belong rather to the past (a past of many centuries) than to the present. For those misjudged positions and faulty solutions survive nowadays rather as things mechanically repeated in school books than as opinions current in general discourse and culture. Yet from the old roots new shoots push forth ever and anon, and must be carefully pruned and excised, such as that theory of styles which is applied by Wölfflin and others in the history of art, and extended by Strich and others to the history of poetry, a veritable new invasion of rhetorical abstractions in the field of aesthetic judgement and history.

But the principal contemporary problem which Aesthetics must take in hand is one which harks back to the crisis in art and art criticism which occurred in the romantic age. It is possible indeed to point to certain precedents and parallels in earlier ages, for instance to Hellenistic art, late Roman literature, and in more modern times the Baroque art and poetry which followed on those of the Renaissance. There was however a particular origination, a particular configuration and grandiosity about the crisis of the romantic age with its contrapositions of naive poetry and sentimental poetry and of classical art and romantic art, dividing, by the use of these concepts, the one and only Art into two inwardly diverse arts, and taking sides with the latter term as that which in consonance with modern times upheld the primacy, in art, of sentiment, passion, imagination. This, on one side, was a well-justified reaction against the satirical or frivolous, unfeeling, unfanciful, poetically shallow literature composed to the prescription of the French rationalists and classicists. Yet on another side Romanticism was a revolt not against Classicism but against the classic, against the idea of calm and infinity in the artistic image, against the catharsis of art, and in favour of the turmoil of passion, in its very resistance to the processes of purification. This was well understood by Goethe, who was at once a poet of passion and of serenity, and thus classical in his poet-hood. Goethe pronounced against the romantic poetry, describing it as "hospital poetry". Later, it was supposed that the illness had run its course and that Romanticism had expired. But it was only certain forms, and certain contents, and not the soul of Romanticism, not the over-forcing of art into an immediate expression of the passions and the impressions, which had expired. Changing its name to "realism", "verism", "symbolism", "artistic style", "impressionism", "sensualism", "imaginism", "decadentism", and, in the extreme forms of the present day, "expressionism" or "futurism", the same thing went on and flourished. The concept of art itself is in these doctrines disturbed and confounded with one or other of the concepts of non-art. They are in fact directed against art, as is shown by the detestation of the extreme wing of the school in question for museums, for libraries, for the whole art of the past, for the very idea of an art the existence of which is bound up in the art which in the course of history has come into being. It is easy to see the links binding the movement in its present guise with industrialism and with the psychology which is encouraged by this. Its art seeks not to express and thereby to rise superior to the practical life of modern times, which is non-art, into the infinity and universality of contemplation, but to be the shouting, gesticulating, polychromatic side of this life itself. Meanwhile, of course, the true poets and artists, as rare now as they always were, carry on working on the old, the one and only artistic principle, expressing what they feel in harmonious form, while the appreciators of art, who (they too) are rarer than is commonly thought, continue to judge by that principle. The inclination to destroy the idea of art is however specially characteristic of our times, taking its origin from the *proton pseudos* which confounds spiritual or aesthetic expression with natural or practical expression. Whereas the beautiful creation which art elaborates, builds, traces, colours, and moulds is altogether different from that which throngs and breaks out from the passages of the senses, tumultuously. The present task of Aesthetics is the restoration and defence of the classical against the romantic; of the synthetic, formal, and theoretical moment which is of the essence of art, against that affective moment which it is art's business to resolve into itself, but which in our days is in rebellion against art seeking itself to occupy the throne. For sure, *portae Inferi non praevalebunt* against the inexhaustible energy of the creative spirit. Nevertheless the effort of these "gates of Hell" to prevail disturbs the aesthetic judgement, the life of art, and, accordingly, thought and morality.

CRITICISM AND HISTORY OF ART AND LITERATURE. – There is another group of questions which, though there is a convenience in their being commonly included in treatises of Aesthetics, belong essentially to logic and the theory of history – those which concern aesthetic judgement and the history of poetry and the arts. The demonstration rendered by Aesthetics that the aesthetic activity, or art, is one of the forms of the spirit, a value, a category, and not as various schools have had it, an empirical concept applicable to certain orders of utilitarian or miscellaneous facts, has, by thus fixing the autonomy of aesthetic value, firmly demonstrated that the aesthetic is the predicate of a special judgement, the aesthetic judgement, and is the argument of a special history, the history of poetry and the arts.

The questions which arise concerning the aesthetic judgement and the history of art and literature, are substantially those same questions as to method which are found in all the fields of history, though here assuming the special form of problems of art. Thus it is asked whether the aesthetic judgement is absolute or relative. But every historical judgement, the aesthetic – which affirms the reality and the quality of aesthetic facts – as much as any other, is at the same time both absolute and relative. It is absolute in its employment of a category of universal truth, but relative in that its construct is historically conditioned. In the historical judgement the category thus becomes individualized while the individual becomes absolute. The sensistic, hedonistic, and utilitarian aestheticists who used to deny the absoluteness of the aesthetic judgement were in fact denying the quality, the reality, the autonomy of art. Again, it is asked whether the knowledge of past ages, of the whole history of a given moment, is needful for the passing of an aesthetic judgement. Certainly it is necessary; poetic creation has to presuppose all the other spirit which it converts into lyrical image, and the single aesthetic creation must presuppose all the other creations, such as passions, sentiments, customs, of a given historical moment. Both the "historicists" who advocate a merely historical judgement of art and the "aestheticists" who in contrast with these advocate a merely aesthetic judgement are evidently at fault, the former when they wish to see in art all the other histories (those for example of social conditions, or of the life of the author) without seeing, pre-eminent among these, that of art itself; and the second in wanting to judge the work of art outside of history, depriving it of its genuine meaning and substituting for this a work of fancy or of arbitrary comparison. Finally there is a sort of scepticism as to the very possibility of entering into a relation of understanding with the art of the past, a scepticism which if allowed at all ought to extend itself to every other part of history (intellectual, political, religious, moral), but can be confuted by a *reductio ad absurdum*, in that even so-called modern or contemporary art and history are of the "past" along with those of remoter times; and none can be rendered "present" save in the soul which responds to them, the intelligence which understands them. That there should be artistic works and epochs which remain obscure to us means only that at this moment there are wanting the conditions for experiencing them anew in our souls and understanding them – which is no less true in respect of the ideas, customs, and actions of countless peoples and ages. Humanity, just like an individual, remembers a few things and forgets many others, but may revive the memory of these when the course of spiritual development requires it.

And there is one more question as to the form which is suitable for the history of art and literature. Today the prevailing form is still that which was mainly devised by the romantic age – the exposition of the history of works of art in terms of the social ideas and aspirations of an epoch, so that the work of art appears as the aesthetic expression of these. Art is thus brought into close relation with social history, whence comes a tendency to overlook and almost to suffocate the peculiar and individual accent of any work of art, that which renders it clearly different from any other. All art comes thus to be viewed as social documentation. True, in practice this method is tempered by what might be called the method of "individualization", or emphasis upon the particular character of single works. But the combination of the two methods has the defects inseparable from eclecticism. To get clear of these there is really no other way than to follow out the individualizing method to the very end: to treat works of art not in relation to social history but as being each one a world in itself, each one, in its hour, receiving the inflow of the whole of history, transfigured and elevated by the power of fancy into the individuality of the work of art which is a creation, not a reflection, and a monument, not a document. As a document of the Middle Ages the work of Dante is equalled or outclassed by many works of poor poetry or non-poetry, and so too the work of Shakespeare as a document of the Elizabethan age. Some have objected that the history of art and literature would, if this advice were followed, be resolved into a disconnected series of essays and monographs. But connectedness is ensured by the whole of human history, of which poetic personalities are a part, a very conspicuous part. The appearance of Shakespeare's poetry is no less important than the Reformation or the French Revolution. Just because they are a part of it, poetic personalities should not be merged and lost to sight in history, that is in the other parts of history, but should retain their own proper and original outline and character.

HISTORY OF AESTHETICS. – From our demonstration that Aesthetics is a philosophical science, it follows that its history cannot be separated from that of the remainder of Philosophy, to which it brings and from which it receives light. The "subjectivist" turn which philosophy took with Descartes, by encouraging enquiry into the creative power of the spirit, indirectly encouraged also the enquiry into the power of the aesthetic faculty. To illustrate an influence which worked conversely, being exerted by Aesthetics upon philosophy as a whole, one may recall how a growing awareness of the creative fancy and of the logic of poetry helped to free the logic of philosophy from intellectualistic and formalistic traditions, and thus, communicating something of the speed of poetry to the motions of thought, helped to birth the higher speculative or dialectical logic of Schelling and Hegel. But if the history of Aesthetics ought properly to be worked into the total history of philosophy, this latter ought to be extended beyond the customary confines within which it is limited to the study of the works of so-called professional philosophers and of the didactic treatises known as "systems of philosophy". For new philosophic thought, or the seeds of it, is found often to be alive and active in books of authors who are not professional philosophers, and do not give them the outward form of systems. Ethical thought is found in ascetic and religious works, political thought in those of the historians, aesthetic in the works of art critics and so on. And then, strictly speaking, the subject of the history of Aesthetics is not a single and lone problem of the definition of art nor can it be exhausted in the attainment of such a definition now or henceforth, but it includes the numberless problems which grow up around art and in which, rendered particular and concrete, the single problem of the definition of art has its sole true existence. Subject to these warnings, which should not be forgotten, one may trace a general outline of the history of Aesthetics, to serve as a preliminary indication, without running the risk of its being interpreted in too rigid and simplifying a manner.

We may here accept as not merely a useful indication but an historical truth, the common observation that Aesthetics is a modern science. Graeco-Roman antiquity speculated not at all, or very little, about art, being much more interested in producing treatises of artistic instruction or, as we might say, in producing an empirical science, as contrasted with a philosophy, of art. The ancient treatises bearing the descriptions of Grammar, Rhetoric, Institutions of Oratory, Architecture, Music, Painting, Sculpture, were the basis of all subsequent educational literature including that of the present day, for if by now the arguments have been simplified and are taken *cum grano salis* they have by no means been, in fact could not be, wholly abandoned. The philosophy of art could not find favourable conditions or stimulations of its enquiries in ancient philosophy, the great concern of which was with "physics" and "metaphysics", while "psychology" (or as we should more precisely put it, the philosophy of the spirit) was but a secondary and occasional interest. Among occasional hints of a treatment of the philosophical problems of Aesthetics may be mentioned the Platonic negation of the value of poetry, the Aristotelian counter-affirmation, which came to the defence with an attempt to assign to poetry a sphere of its own between those of history and of philosophy, and, from another angle, the specula-tions of Plotinus who for the first time joined and united the two previously unrelated concepts of "art" and "the beautiful". Other notable notions of antiquity were: the assignment to poetry of *mythos* and the refusal to it of *logos*, and the discrimination of the "semantic", rhetorical, and embryonically poetical expressions in propositions, from the "apophantic" or logical expressions. Recently there has been talk of yet another vein of Greek Aesthetics running through the Epicurean teachings expounded by Philodemus, where an almost romantic emphasis seems to be placed on the fancy. However that may be, the hints in question remained sterile, and the keen and confident judgement of the ancients in the matter of art was never deepened and shaped into a genuine philosophic science, owing to the limits set by the generally objectivist or naturalistic character of ancient philosophy. It was Christianity which, by exalting the problems of the soul and setting them in the centre of observation, began to stir up the forces which were to sweep aside those limits.

At the outset, however, Christian philosophy itself, owing to the prevalence of transcendence, mysticism, and asceticism, and also owing to the scholastic form inherited from ancient philosophy, even while it treated moral problems with heightened urgency and with a new delicacy, none the less eschewed the problems of fancy and of taste, neither observing them nor exploring them, just as it eschewed such corresponding problems in the practical sphere as those of passion, interest, utility, policy, economy. The political and the economic were considered solely in a moral light, and correspondingly art was subordinated to the purpose of an allegorical illustration of things moral and religious. The hints of a doctrine of art which lay scattered in the works of Greek and Roman writers were ignored or read superficially. The philosophy of the Renaissance, which itself partook of naturalism, brought back into circulation, with its own commentaries and adaptations, the treatises of the ancients on art and rhetoric. But for all the effort that was then put into enquiries into the "true", the "lifelike", "imitation", "idea", "beauty", the mysterious aspect of beauty and love, the "catharsis" or purging of the passions, and the perplexities involved in the old and the new classifications of literary genres, all this never amounted to the discovery of a genuine aesthetic principle. There was no thinker able to do for poetry and art what Machiavelli had done for politics, no one yet who could energetically assert and expound, and not just admit, in some transient observation, art's original and autonomous character.

A much greater part was taken in the attainment of such a conclusion by the thought of the late Renaissance, known in Italy under the names of *secentismo*, baroquism, or literary and artistic decadence. For it was this age which got into the regular habit of distinguishing, alongside of and apart from the intellect, the *inge-*

nium (in Italian *genio* or *ingegno*) as the veritable generator of art, and corresponding to this, a critical faculty – which came to be known as "taste" – differing from the ratiocinative or logical judgement in that it judged "without discourse", or "without concept". Resort was had also to the description *nescio quid*, an expression much used in Italian conversation (*non so che*), seeming to stand for a mysterious something, not reducible to logical terms; and this exercised a suggestion also on foreign minds. Then too it became the fashion to exalt the "fancy", that fascinating enchantress, the "sensible" or "sensuous" in the images of poetry, and the miracles of "colour" in the art of painting, by contrast with "design", which seemed to have about it something coldly logical. This way of thought, which tended to be unclear and troublous, was from time to time brought to clarity in reasoned theories such as that of Zuccolo (1623), who criticized the idea of "the metrical", and put in its place what he called the judgement of sense, which was not a measurement by eye or ear but the judgement of "a higher faculty united to the senses", or that of Mascardi (1636), who refuted the objective and rhetorical labelling of styles, interpreting style as being instead the particular and individual manner proper to each one's particular genius, so that there are as many styles as there are writers; or that of Pallavicino (1644), who criticized the notion of the verisimilar or lifelike, taking instead the "first apprehensions" or fancies, "neither true nor false", to be the true domain of poetry; or yet again that of Tesauro (1654), who sought to elaborate a rhetorical logic, distinct from dialectical logic, and extended the domain of the rhetorical forms to include not only verbal, but pictorial and plastic expressions.

The philosophy of Descartes and of his immediate followers breathed some hostility to poetry and the fancy, but nevertheless, as already remarked, by its enquiries into the subjective, the spiritual, it helped on the consolidation of the preceding tentative suggestions into systematic form, the search for a principle underlying the arts. Once again it was Italian thinkers who took advantage of the methods of Descartes without accepting the Frenchman's rigid intellectualism or his disdain for poetry. Such writers as Calopreso (1691), Gravina (1692, 1708), Muratori (1704) composed the first treatises on Poetry in which the concept of Fancy had an important or leading part. They in turn considerably influenced Bodmer and the Swiss school, and through them the German and other European critical and aesthetic schools. Recently Robertson has pointed to the "Italian origins of the Aesthetics of Romanticism".

The thinker in whom the work of these minor theorists culminated, G. B. Vico, in his *Scienza Nuova* (1725, 1730) set forth a "logic of poetry" which he distinguished from the logic of the intellect. Poetry in his view was a mode of knowledge, a theoretical form, preceding the reasoning and philosophical form. Its sole principle he found to be the Fancy, the Fancy which is strong in proportion to its freedom from that ratiocination which challenges and destroys it. Father and prince of all poets was, according to Vico, the barbaric Homer, and next to him (though his poetry is infected by theological and scholastic culture) the semi-barbaric Dante. Vico gazed from a distance at the tragic poetry of England, without being able to see its outlines clearly, but had it been possible for him to discern Shakespeare, then that English tragedian, whose name remained unknown to him, would certainly have ranked with him as the third great barbaric poet. Neither as teacher of Aesthetics, nor in any other of his activities did Vico originate a school. He was too far ahead of his time, and his teaching was wrapped up in a sort of historical symbolism. The success of the doctrine of the "logic of poetry" had for its medium the much shallower but more suitably presented work of the systematizer of the rather hybrid aesthetic doctrines of Leibniz, the *Meditationes* (1735) and *Aesthetica* (1750-58) of Baumgarten, who gave to this "logic" the various names of *ars analogi rationis, scientia cognitionis sensitivae, gnoseologia inferior,* and (the name which has stuck) *Aesthetica.*

The school of Baumgarten, which now distinguished but now confounded the forms of the fancy and of the intellect, describing the fancy as *cognitio confusa,* but ascribing to it its own *perfectio,* combined with the English investigators and analysts of the aesthetic, Shaftesbury, Hutcheson, Hume, Home, Gerard, Burke, Alison, with the many other authors of essays on beauty and taste in that period, and with the theoretical and historical labours of Lessing and Winckelmann, to influence, whether as models or as deterrents, the emergence of the other great aesthetic treatise of the eighteenth century, the *Critique of Judgement* of Emmanuel Kant (1790). Kant in his earlier *Critique* had thrown doubts upon it, but in the later work he saw that art and the beautiful form the matter for a particular philosophic science. In other words he discovered the autonomy of aesthetic activity. Kant demonstrated against the utilitarians that the delight given by beauty is "disinterested" (having no utilitarian interest). Against the intellectualists he showed that it is "non-conceptual". Against both utilitarians and intellectualists he showed that it "has the form of finality without the representation of the end". Against the hedonists he showed that it is the "object of a universal pleasure". Kant did not really advance beyond this negative and generic formulation of the concept of the beautiful. (In the same way in the *Critique of Practical Reason*, after insuring the integrity of the moral law, he contented himself with a generic formulation of Duty.) But what he established remains established for ever. After the *Critique of Judgement* it was still no doubt possible to fall back upon hedonistic and utilitarian explanations of art and beauty, but only for those who did not know or understand Kant's demonstrations. There should have been no occasion either for a relapse into the Leibniz-Baumgarten theory of art as a confused imaginous concept, had Kant succeeded in linking his theory of the beautiful as that which pleases without concept, and that which is finality without the representation of the end, to Vico's highly imperfect and very unsteady, yet powerful theory of the logic of the fancy. This theory was at the time finding some sort of expression in the writings of Hamann and Herder. Kant himself, however, encouraged the relapse into the theory of the "confused concept" when he attributed to genius the gift of combining the intellect and the imagination, and distinguished art from "pure beauty" under the appellation "adherent beauty".

In post-Kantian philosophy there is in fact a relapse into the tradition of Baumgarten, poetry and art being considered once again a form of knowledge of the Absolute or the Idea, whether equal to the philosophic form, or inferior and precedent to it, or, as in Schelling's philosophy of 1800, superior, the very organ of the Absolute. In the richest and most notable work of this school, Hegel's *Lectures on Aesthetics* (1818 . . .), art is together with religion and philosophy transferred into the "sphere of the absolute spirit" in which the spirit becomes emancipated from empirical knowledge and practical operations, and finds beatitude in the thought of God or the Idea. It remains doubtful whether in the triad so constituted the prior moment is art or religion. Hegel gave differing accounts of his own doctrine on this point. Certain it is, however, that both art and religion are seen by Hegel as fading out, their work being now accomplished, in the final synthesis, which is philosophy. In other words art is treated as an inferior or imperfect philosophy, an imaginous philosophy, contradictory in the inadequacy of its form to its content, philosophy alone being able to dissolve the contradiction. Hegel, who inclined to identify the philosophic system and dialectic of the categories with real history, arrived in this manner at his famous paradox which asserts the mortality of art as a form no longer satisfying to the highest mental interest of the modern age.

This conception of art as philosophy, intuitive philosophy, symbol of philosophy and so forth can be found throughout the idealistic writings on aesthetics of the first half of the nineteenth century. The contrary case of Schleiermacher in his lectures on Aesthetics (1825, 1832-33), which have reached us in sketchy form, is a rare exception. For all the high level of the treatises in question, informed by such great enthusiasm for poetry and art, the all too artificial principle on which they were based was one of the motifs of the reaction in the second half of the century, itself part and parcel of the general reaction against the idealistic philosophy of the great post-Kantian systems. That antiphilosophical tendency had doubtless its own significance as a sign of discontent and of the need for seeking out new ways, but no new aesthetic theory came into being with it to correct the errors of what had gone before or to show the way of further progress. What happened was on the one hand a breach of continuity in the tradition of thought, and on the other hand a desperate attempt to resolve the problems of aesthetics, which are speculative problems, by the methods of the empirical sciences (as in the case of Fechner), and yet again the return to a hedonistic and utilitarian aesthetics, the utilitarian theory being translated by such a writer as Spencer into associationism, evolutionism, and the biological doctrine of heredity. No work of value was done by the latter-day idealists like Vischer, Schasler, Carrière, Lotze, nor by the representatives of the other schools of the first half of the century, the "formalistic" Herbartians (Zimmermann), the eclectics and psychologists, all of whom worked in terms of two abstractions, "content" and "form", whence they were called "formalists" or "contentists", but sometimes sought out methods for welding the two unrealities together, without noticing that they thereby produced just a third unreality. The best thought on art in that period was to be found in the pages not of the professional philosophers or aestheticians but in those of the critics of poetry and art, De Sanctis in Italy, Baudelaire and Flaubert in France, Pater in England, Hanslick and Fiedler in Germany, Julius Lange in Holland, and many others. Their work was the sole compensation for the aesthetic trivialities of the positivist philosophers and the tedious vacuity of the so-called idealists.

Aesthetics fared better in the first part of the twentieth century thanks to the general reawakening of speculative thought. Specially worthy of note is the developing unification of Aesthetics with the Philosophy of Language, helped on by the crisis which has overtaken the linguistic science of naturalistic and positivistic type, with its enquiries into phonetic laws and similar abstractions. But such recent work in aesthetics is too fresh and growing to be as yet summed up and assigned a place in history.

[1928]

II

THE PHILOSOPHY OF LANGUAGE

The writings of that indefatigable scholar Bertoni, who is the representative Italian specialist in the theory of language, seem to me to have introduced confusion and contradiction into concepts which for my part I had taken great care to put forward and to develop with exactness, and which called indeed for a continuation, elaboration, enrichment, prolongation, or what you will, but not surely for a mutilation and mishandling such as has now been administered, certainly unwittingly, by one endeavouring to improve upon them.

I am therefore constrained to take up once again an argument which I had long since laid aside when I felt satisfied that the branch of enquiry in question was proceeding now on the right lines (and I still feel so, generally speaking). I trust that my present criticism, having its origin in entirely objective considerations, may be taken in that spirit by Italian scholars, and even, if that be at all possible, by that very author whom I feel it my duty to criticize.

In the first place, the leading concept in the argument, that of Language, has in these new theories suffered the misadventure of which I have already spoken, losing the clear outline which I had given to it without acquiring any other. The result is a wavering between on the one hand an implicit negation of the original nature of language, and, on the other hand, a maze of maldeterminations, some generic and vague, some plainly erroneous, some muddled and strained.

In the theory which I worked out some forty years ago, I did not merely affirm, against the then flourishing professors of naturalistic, positivist, and psychological theories of language, that language is a spiritual and creative act. Still less did I sit back idly enjoying the vision of the spirituality in question or spending time in exalting its virtues like certain contemporary rhetoricians of idealism. Indeed I could not and cannot see what there is to admire and gape at in the fact that reality and thought are reality and thought, that life is life, and the poet's activity the writing of poetry. Instead, I went straight for the particular philosophic problem which had to be faced and solved, namely, that of which peculiar act of spirituality the linguistic act is. In the course of the enquiry I had come to the conclusion that the linguistic act is not the expression of thought and of the logical, but of fancy, that is to say of passion elevated and transfigured into image, and is accordingly identical and synonymous with the activity of poetry. "Language" is here to be understood in its genuine natural purity, which for that matter it retains even when, in the service of thought and logic, it is employed as the sign for the concept. It could not execute this office did it not retain its own identity. And thus even in the language which is called unpoetical, prosaic, there has always been felt to be present something irreducible to logic. Of this nature is the metaphor, which is but the live word which is always metaphor because it is always the product of the fancy. And of such a nature is the harmony and sweetness and virtue of the sound, the spell of the music which abides even in the language of prose, governing the phrases, words, and syllables, all the parts of the discourse. One can as it were actually feel the necessity for a theory of language distinct and different from the theory of logic, in the presence of these elements which are so distinct and different from anything logical. Intellectualistic theories, philosophical grammars, have not succeeded in explaining those elements. At very best they have been able to ignore them, closing their eyes to shut out the view of them although unable really to chase them off. And what are these elements? They are nothing else than the fancy which creates its images, sings with the voice of poetry. From the standpoint of logic they may seem merely a secondary and ornamental addition, but from that of language they are primary and essential, indeed they are everything, they are language itself.[1] After reaching this conclusion it

1. Note for example my observations on Schleiermacher's theory of language, and the contradictions he fell into when trying to explain the relation between language and poetry. See my *Ultimi Saggi* (Bari, 1935), pp. 177-8. The same philosopher's perplexities, which have in any case the

was easy for me to identify poetic language with all those other languages from which it is, albeit only empirically, distinguished, the languages of music, painting, sculpture, architecture, and to identify the theory of language with that of Art, or "Aesthetics".[1]

Doubtless, it is difficult to understand and fully master the theory which resolves and crowns the concept of language in that of poetry. Like every other philosophical theory it carries a continuous reference back to philosophy as a whole. But the good scholar at whom the present criticism is levelled has not merely failed to understand the theory in its foundations, he has in addition been so wrong as to try and improve upon it with the help of what calls itself "actual idealism", the work of a writer on philosophical subjects who is notorious for his complete obtusity in regard to the concerns of poetry and art, which he confounds sometimes with crude feeling, sometimes with thought engaged in defining feeling, he being quite incapable of conceiving the fancy in its autonomous and creative function. Accordingly, we hear this new theoretician or reformer of the philosophy of language proclaiming that "language is spirit or thought",[2] and that "the concrete expression, the true and pulsating reality" is "incarnation of thought" or "revelation of thought",[3] and again that "the history of language is identical with the history of thought, because language is, in the last resort, thought itself",[4] and yet again that "we are now after long and strenuous enquiries and discussions in a position to identify the history of language with the history of thought".[5] This should mean, if anything, that we have now

merit of drawing attention to the importance of the problem, have been further explored by A. CORSANO in *La psicologia del linguaggio in F. S.* (*Giorn. Crit. d. filos. ital.*, Nov.-Dec. 1940, pp. 385-97).

1. See besides the familiar chapters of *Estetica*, also *Problemi di Estetica* (3rd edn., Bari, 1940), pp. 141-230, including a note on "The Crisis in Linguistics" on pp. 205-10, and further, *Conversazioni critiche*, I, 87-113, and *La poesia* (Bari, 1936).

2. *Programma di filologia romanza come scienza idealistica* (Geneva, 1923), p. 11.

3. *Lingua e cultura*, Studies in language (Florence, 1939), pp. 7, 15.

4. *Lingua e poesia*, Essays in literary criticism (Florence, 1937), pp. 8-9.

5. *Lingua e pensiero*, Studies and essays on language (Florence, 1932), p. 5.

returned to the philosophic grammars and the logical theories of language. But really for this there was no need of the many and heavy labours of which he speaks. It would have sufficed to remain keeping company with those seventeenth-century theorists who in their time deserved all respect for having gone beyond the merely empirical lore of the grammarians and attempted a scientific treatment of language.

Now if our author, in re-echoing the teachings of the unaesthetic philosopher to whom I have alluded, had really accepted them in their full weight and measure, and upheld them resolutely as his own doctrines, such a tenacious grasp and defence of this antiquated and absurd position would have a certain character and would serve a certain purpose. The absurd has its place and function in studious pursuits, serving as an excitant and as a counter-irritant. But to qualify for that role our author ought to accept fully all those consequences which the unaesthetic philosopher has been enabled by his own obtuseness to draw. First and foremost he should bravely and loyally renounce all claim to judge of the expressions of language, recognizing, like his guide and master, that discernment between the beautiful and the ugly is an empty pretence, therefore void of truth, and that aesthetic criticism is nonsense, seeing that the act of thought is everything, and is perpetually falling away into the condition of fact, outside of which alternation of condition there is simply no subject for discourse.

But our author lacks an alert and uncompromising faith in the principle which he echoes. Accordingly he seeks out eclectic combinations such as that art "according to our (his) view resides in the energy of the spirit: the artist is he who bears a major imprint of the spirit, whether he be philosophizing, composing verses, or composing scientific works. Language, which is energy, is art . . . true and great art", or "if the spiritual spark be feeble, it is mere expression and inferior art".[1] This is quite the customary way of escape sought by those who are incapable of dialectically elaborating, distinguishing, and unifying concepts, and

---

1. *Programma*, cit., pp. 15-16.

therefore think to tone them down and harmonize them, arranging them in an apparent comprehensive unification. And one is left in curiosity as to the measure by which to distinguish the very great, great, middling, or small grade of "energy" which determines whether poetry is or is not present. But, behold, we are given a variant of this energy thanks to which poetry is poetry: "The work of art is the whole thought of the author, for it is his language; but in lyrical form, that is having the warmth of love, love which is feeling, passion, thrill, exaltation, and more besides(?). Everything, even scientific prose, becomes poetry and art, when it is dictated by love and when the poet testifies to his internal inspiration: the work of art is in fact a 'huge' word in which the voice of love echoes with peculiar resonance; and the artist who can boast of the greatest flow of feeling can by the same token boast of a richer and more energetic spirit, the source of a plenitude of beauty in his work, a miracle worthy of a divine creator."[1] Now this is certainly not the sort of writing we expect from a man of clear ideas and high standards of learning. In other passages, however, we find the aesthetic moment brought back into prominence and claiming pre-eminence, sometimes rather shyly, as when we are warned that language, as the concrete expression and revelation of thought, can be "studied in itself, in its own pregnant life, and with due regard for all the elements entering into it", or that "we may examine primarily the aesthetic moment which, though in different empirical versions and degrees, characterizes all works of poetry",[2] or yet again that "in the language of poetry there lurk the fundamental problems of the science of language interpreted as a spiritual science".[3] But sometimes the claim is open and bold, albeit contradictory of the author's own premiss: "We hold that language is man in his wholeness (man, who is not solely a creator of poetry), but we recognize that language in its essential character derives from the fancy."[4] In this discussion of language, the reader will notice how frequently our author seeks to help out these clumsy and confused explanations with some symptomatic word

1. *Programma*, cit., p. 31.   2. *Lingua e cultura*, cit., p. 15.
3. Ibid., p. 296.   4. *Lingua e poesia*, cit., p. 12.

like "really" or "fundamentally". Far from his having in any way carried forward my theoretical expositions to fresh conclusions, I have to confess that upon comparing his formulas with mine, I have the impression of looking at an illustrated school book in which the idle pupil has amused himself by furnishing a female figure with moustaches and eyeglass, so that the frontispiece has lost its previous coherence without acquiring any other. This comparison is meant to be not offensive but vividly clear.

I for my part, having identified the theory of language with the theory of poetry, and established the point that linguistic expressions are to be interpreted, appreciated, judged, and accounted solely as poetical expressions within the indefeasible unification of form and content in the aesthetic synthesis (and outside of this they have no reality), then went on to cope with the further question, what such study of language as is undertaken, not by critics and historians of poetry and literature, but by the investigators of meanings and sounds, etymologists and phoneticians, must be taken to be.[1] Naturally it did not for a moment occur to me to deny their right to pursue those studies. I was only trying to see clearly into the nature and theoretical justification of these. And my line of thought was this: – That which, when the production, contemplation, and criticism of the expressive (in a single term, the aesthetic) is left out of consideration, is called "language", cannot indeed be language since this term belongs to just what is here left out of consideration. Nor can it be described as the "matter" (*qua talis*) of language. The term "Matter" is significant solely as correlative to the "Form" which possesses and resolves it into itself. It is, philosophically speaking, an ideal moment. What I am considering must then be something quite different, something entering into the moral life of man among his appetites, desires, volitions, actions, habits, flights of imagination, modes of behaviour (including that behaviour which gives this or that meaning to articulated sounds, and articulates them in this or that manner); all of which is indeed "matter" by reference to the synthesis of

1. See my remarks on VOSSLER's *Die Sprache als Schöpfung und Entwicklung* (1905), in *Conversazioni Critiche*, I, 91-97.

poetry, of the word, but is in itself not "matter" but practice. It is in fact impossible to reconstruct human society in its full integrity without taking account, among other institutes and habits, of the institute and habit of talking, the waves of language which are born, or rather come into view and win prevalence, the new or resuscitated words, structure of sentences, tones of speech, tricks of pronunciation, and then the retreat and submergence of those waves, their relegation from among "living" to among "dead" languages. If the enquirers into languages are not forthwith reckoned among the historians of civilization and culture, that is because their work is normally confined to the level of philological scholarship, the collection and interpretation of factual data, dispersedly, profusely, sometimes rather mechanically, tacitly provided for the use of the scholar himself or for others at such time as they have to undertake a task of a more properly historical order. Let me take an example which happens to be near at hand. The philologists have etymological dictionaries and historical grammars of the Spanish language, they have traced the story of many words in that language, they have made lists of Spanish turns of phrase that have been taken into Italian or other languages. I myself have contributed to these labours. But it was only when in one of my early books (I happen now to be correcting the proofs for a new edition of this) I wished to build upon those researches, examining the manner of life introduced by the Spaniards into Italy, the imitations to which this gave rise, the reactions against it, the changes which it underwent, that those investigations into the Spanish language became relevant and took their due place among all the other investigations which threw light on the politics, soldiery, religion, business, sports, amours of the Spaniards in Italy, and more broadly on Italian manners at the turn of the fifteenth and sixteenth centuries. Linguistic studies become history only when they are fused in the history of culture and civilization. Where an effort is made to maintain them as a sort of history in its own right, with words and phrases as its protagonists, evidently this fusion has not been fully effected. Unless indeed we have to do simply with a literary device intended to brighten up the exposition, without any idea of allowing the reader to take these metaphors for logical and serious definitions.

I still believe in that reasoning. I still hold that the way to establish (or, if that be necessary, to re-establish) good relations between the two orders of studies is to hold fast to the notion that there can be no other critique or history of language save that which is conformable to its nature, namely the aesthetic, while it must be made clear that what is studied outside the aesthetic sphere is therefore not language but things, practical facts. But the writer I am now dealing with failed to understand my distinction between the history of poetry and the history of civilization and culture. He therefore had recourse to the fount of authority already mentioned from whom he had derived the false idea of language in which he has become entangled, being unable either to define it appropriately or to make effective use of the idea in the criticism and history of poetry. The authority has next provided him with another ill-devised device, the distinction between Act and Fact. The aim of this is to cause the object to disappear with extreme rapidity into the subject, and similarly nature into thought. But the proceeding is illusory. Nature remains, refusing to be digested in this manner. A far less poverty-stricken philosophy of the spirit, a far richer dialectic, is needed to make nature – we will not say "disappear", but take its place in the spirit itself, a form among the forms of the spirit. The distinction between Act and Fact has now by our theorizer been translated for his own purposes into the more particular distinction between *lingua*, tongue, and *linguaggio*, language. Now of Fact, abstracted from Act, there can be no philosophy or history, and our new theorist is unable to furnish any account of the history to which the students of language outside the aesthetic sphere are contributing. His concept of "tongue" (I myself would call it *praxis*, or a part of *praxis*) is vague and confused, almost chaotic. It is (he says) "what we call culture, doctrine, technique, premiss, source, scheme, paradigm, grammar",[1] or again it is "the objective moment, the (in particular)

1. *Lingua e pensiero*, p. 5.

tongue of culture, the instrumental tongue, the tongue which is at the disposal of all and can be studied in various ways, as physical fact, social fact, or means of communication".[1] But then our author ends by admitting that this "tongue" differentiated from language is an unreality, an abstraction. "An attempt to maintain it rigorously in its abstraction would doubtless reveal that it could not stand up to a genuine historical examination." "Try as one will, one must understand the tongue in order to be able to talk about it, one must meditate it in order to be able in any sense at all to study it." "Thus willy-nilly one ends by working at language, for better or for worse, even when one believes oneself to be working at 'tongue'."[2] According to our author, then, either the studies of the linguistic experts are mistaken, or they must be brought within the scope of the aesthetic study of language. It is not I who said this, for in the first place it is against common sense, in the second place it is untrue. It is altogether right that "objective" language should be pursued by linguistic research, for it is real, and not abstract, finding its reality in a particular form of the spirit and in the history corresponding to this.

The identification of language with poetical expression substitutes a simple and fruitful concept for the complicated but sterile concepts to be found in so many treatises and debates on language. In the first place it dismisses the outmoded problem of the origin of language, that is to say of its origin as an institution supposedly coming into existence at some point or contingency of history. It shows on the contrary that language, since it coincides with a spiritual category, is not itself born in history but is the premiss of what is born in history. It frees the mind from those theories which sought an origin for language in onomatopoeic utterance, in interjections, conventional signs, divine or quasi-divine communications. It liberates us also from intellectualistic or rationalistic definitions of the parts of speech, distinctions between proper and metaphorical speech and so on. Logically, therefore, it puts an end to all such naturalistic or positivistic inventions as "phonetic

1. *Lingua e cultura*, p. 15.   2. *Lingua e pensiero*, pp. 13-14.

laws", with the accompanying physiological explanations. All those "causes" of linguistic changes to the multiplication of which there was no end, now yield to a single formative principle which Gilliéron, writing without any philosophic pretensions, has discovered to consist in the need for clarity. Unknown to himself he uses that same word *claritas* which right from the beginning of modern speculation upon art has been used to designate distinctively the aesthetic mode of knowledge.

The mysterious veil has also been lifted from the problem of the reciprocal understanding of the users of speech. This has been referred back to the concept of the spirit as universal-individual, itself constituting the communication and mutual society of beings, without which there would be no historical occurrence, no world.[1] This theory of language has rendered its liberating service by converting what used to be known as "the science of general linguistics" into "the philosophy of language", and further into "the philosophy of poetry and art". These effects are to be seen copiously in such works of the first years of this century as those, in Germany, of Vossler and his school and of Spitzer,[2] to mention no other names than these. Its efficacy has perhaps been less among professional philosophers, in part because of the continued tendency among them to diverge towards one of the opposite but equally debased extremes of intellectualism and empiricism, in part because of their ignorance and inexperience of these problems of language and of the old and new controversies that have arisen around them. An Italian philosophic congress which recently included among its themes that of the nature of language, testifies distressingly to my remarks.[3] One is however easily consoled for the want of support on the part of the professional philosophers by the feeling that one is in accord with the spirit of Giambattista Vico, whose advice to "seek the origins of the languages in the origins of

1. See my *Poesia*, cit., pp. 65-86 and especially 78-80.
2. VOSSLER, *Positivismo e idealismo nella scienza del linguaggio* (Italian trans., Bari, 1908) and *Gesammelte Aufsätze zur Sprachphilosohie* (Munich, 1925). SPITZER, *Stilstudien* (Munich, 1928) and *Stil und Literaturstudien* (Marburg, 1931).
3. *Pagine Sparse* (Naples, 1943), III, 112.

17

poetry" remained for so long disregarded.[1] There have also been excellent essays, particularly those of Vossler and Spitzer, analysing the language of poets and other writers from the aesthetic standpoint. And here it will be well to observe that if poetry and language are not two but one, there can be no study of poetry without an express or implied perpetual attention to the language of the poet, and no study of language apart from poetry, nor yet is it right to distinguish two parts of the study, as for instance a general and a particular, or a part referring to the lyrical impetus of poetry and a part referring to the language in which this takes concrete form. Whenever poetry is or has been spoken of it is on the language that the discourse turns, the language which does not accompany poetry but is poetry, from which poetry cannot be severed and which cannot be added to poetry. (How ridiculous then are the claims of modern schools of poetry to have discovered this truth when what they have really done was to misunderstand it.) In tuition, or in argument, there may indeed be more or less emphasis on the lyrical impetus or on the single expressions. The proportion will depend on circumstances and on the starting point of the enquiry, and this cannot be fixed by general rules; it is a matter for the tact and the taste, the discretion and the intelligence of the critic.

The conception of linguistic studies as having an historical character, but within the range of the history of culture and civilization, has given to such enquiries a breadth and flexibility which they did not before possess, oppressed as they were by a naturalist school cherishing the ideal or the will-o'-the-wisp of converting live and concrete history into abstract sociology, and claiming to have won a marvellous and certain discovery in the "science of linguistics" with its apparatus of phonetic laws.[2] Yet precisely in this sphere great and almost clamorous results have followed upon the promulgation of different ideas and a different

1. *La filosofia di G. B. Vico* (3rd edn., Bari, 1933, pp. 50-54).
2. Labriola believed mistakenly that this science of linguistics should serve as a model for all branches of history (see CROCE, *Problemi di Estetica*, 4th edn., Bari, 1949, p. 206).

example. The methodology which I propounded in my first essay, "Aesthetics as the Science of Expression and as General Linguistics",[1] found allies, in the first place, among such of the ever more troubled and disquieted professors of that discipline (for example Schuchardt) as were led by alert observation and historical sense to feel doubts about the phonetic laws and about the neo-grammarians who proclaimed them. There followed, in complete independence from the already mentioned philosophical critique, the brilliant reformation initiated by Gilliéron with his preface to the *Atlas Linguistique de la France* (1902) and later his *Faillite de l'étymologie phonétique* (1919), which offered a history of words (that is, of the human spirit which perpetually creates words even then when it appears to be repeating them unchangingly) previously smothered and hidden under the largely fictitious construction of a history furnishing explanations by application of the phonetic laws. The way opened by Gilliéron was and is followed also in Italy (by Bartoli,[2] Bertoldi,[3] Pellis, and others) and a linguistic atlas was in preparation: I do not know whether it is to be completed. How impossible it is for the mind engaged in civil and cultural history to treat the words which have come into existence separately from other existent things of a political, moral, economic, and social order, is well illustrated in some of these "linguistic atlases" when they designate certain objects by words which can themselves only be clearly understood by reference to changes in the objects. The new mode of language study has mitigated the excessively sharp differentiations previously drawn between national, international, and professional languages, dialects, slangs, and the like, all these being now recognized to be rough divisions with shifting limits.

1. Reprint edited by ATTISANI, *La Prima Forma dell'Estetica e della Logica* (Messina, Principato, 1924).
2. *Introduzione alla neolinguistica, principî, scopi, metodi* (Geneva, Olschki, 1925).
3. "To look through and beyond the history of words to the history of culture is now so widely felt to be a necessity that I should unhesitatingly regard it as one of the most typical and fruitful tasks of modern linguistics" (V. BERTOLDI, *Questioni di metodo nella linguistica storica*, Naples, 1938, p. 171).

But the new mode of language study does not affect dictionaries and grammars. Doubtless these too feel the wind of the transformation of the history of language into aesthetic history, and of the history of words into social history, and are thereby refreshed and revived and above all made better aware of the right limits of their scope. But they cannot ever shed that abstract and naturalistic character which belongs to and determines them. Attempts to give philosophical character or form to such books result in a mere play of words, a forgetfulness of what they are about. Grammars and dictionaries are aids to learning languages and learning them well. The method of grammars is declension and syntax, that of dictionaries is definition, exemplification, translation. Their office is to assist but not actually to bring about a full and lively understanding and expression, for this last is the office of the aesthetic synthesis and of it alone. They assist by means of abstractions which, working as abstractions, bring about, by a reaction, the concreteness which can immediately dispense with the instruments which were useful to it and will be useful again as often as the educative and formative process has to be resumed.

[1941]

III

THE TOTALITY OF ARTISTIC EXPRESSION

Artistic representation embraces the whole, and reflects in itself the cosmos, though in utterly individual form. This has already been said here many times. Indeed it is by this test that we are accustomed to distinguish profound, vigorous, perfect art, from art which in one or another way falls short. The older Aesthetics had however a somewhat unfortunate way of expounding this character of art, namely the familiar way of relating it closely to religion and philosophy as having the same end as these – the knowledge of ultimate reality – which Art was said to attain either in competition with them, or by preparing the way and holding the fort for their supreme and definitive attainment, or, finally, by itself constituting this supreme and definitive point of arrival.

This teaching had a double failing. Firstly it conceived the process of Knowing in all too simplified a manner, without differences and antitheses, seeing it now as purely intuitional, now as purely logical, now as purely mystical. Secondly it conceived it as the discovery of a static and consequently transcendent truth. In this way artistic representation was indeed recognized as having a cosmic and total character, but at the cost of a failure to recognize what is original in art, a failure which weakened spiritual productivity in general.

An attempt was made to evade the second of these errors, and to obtain some degree of reconciliation with the intimate and irresistible quality of modern thought as immanentism and absolute spiritualism, by viewing art no longer as the awareness of an immobile concept, but as the unending formation of the concept in its developing identity with judgement. This could well suffice to explain its character as totality, for all judgement is judgement of the universal. Art, accordingly, would be not mere representation but critical representation, and would in a single act determine the place and the value of things, penetrating them with the light of the universal. It is a theory which runs up against a single difficulty, but one so solid that the collision is fatal. The difficulty is this: that critical representation is something beyond art, it is historical judgement or history. Unless indeed one should stick to that outmoded but still widely prevalent view of history as a mere and sheer recital of facts, but in that case judgement or critical representation should be identified with philosophy, with so-called "philosophy of history", and not with art. The theory of art as judgement does indeed evade the faults of immobility and transcendence, but only to run into that other fault of an excessively simplified view of knowledge, taking here the shape of an exclusive logicism, and perhaps tending towards a new and more recondite transcendence; in any case, denying to art that which is the sole function of art.

For Art is pure intuition or pure expression, not Schellingian intellectual intuition, not Hegelian logicism, not the judgement of historical reflection, but intuition wholly pure of concept and judgement, the dawn of knowledge, without which the further and more complex forms of knowledge are inconceivable. And its character of totality can be understood without our having ever needed to issue forth from the limits of pure intuition, or to undertake readjustments or, still worse, eclectic additions. We have remained inside the limits of intuition, scrutinizing them, indeed, with ever closer attention, and within those limits exploring at ever deeper levels the inexhaustible riches of the intuitional principle.

We are at present placed much as we were on that previous occasion when we replied to teachings which would have identified art not with intuition but with feeling, or with intuition and feeling, for pure intuition seemed (to those who opposed that doctrine) too cold. We replied by demonstrating that pure intuition, precisely because it is free of intellectualistic and logical taint, is full of feeling and passion. It confers intuitive and expressive form on nothing else save upon a state of mind, and therefore, under that apparent coldness, there is warmth, and a true creation of art is pure intuition precisely in virtue of being purely lyrical. When therefore we have seen certain theorists recently, by changeful and tortuous routes, arriving finally at the conclusion that art is intuition and feeling, we have felt that they were saying nothing very new; were in fact merely repeating the words of innumerable aphorisms pronounced by artists and critics. Moreover, with their "and" or "also" (how rightly Hegel abhorred this conjunction in philosophy), they kept well outside the range of truly scientific formulation, failing to provide a unified explanation of their aesthetic doctrine, but merely aggregating or soldering together two terms which require on the contrary to be identified and discovered one in the other.

The universal or cosmic character which is rightly recognized in artistic representation (never better expounded, surely, than in W. von Humboldt's essay[1] on *Hermann und Dorothea*) stands forth when we attentively consider what we have just enunciated. What is a feeling or a state of mind? Is it something that can be detached from the universe to live a life of its own? Can the part and the whole, the individual and the cosmos, the finite and the infinite have reality the one apart from the other and outside the other? It will be admitted that whenever we detach or isolate one term of the relation from the other, the result will be the work of abstraction, in which alone abstract individuality and finitude, abstract unity and infinity, have their being. Pure intuition or artistic representation on the other hand is utterly resistant to abstraction, or rather, thanks to its own character as naive or "dawning" knowledge, utterly ignores it. In intuition, the single pulsates with the life of the whole, and the whole is in the life of the single. Every genuine artistic representation is itself and is the universe, the universe in *that* individual form and *that* individual form as the universe. In every utterance, every fanciful creation, of the poet, there lies the whole of human destiny, all human hopes, illusions, griefs, joys, human grandeurs and miseries, the whole drama of reality perpetually evolving and growing out of itself in suffering and joy.

1. See particularly §§ IV-IX of that essay (pp. 129-40 of vol. II in the Prussian Academy's edition of *Gesamm. Schriften*).

Inconceivable, therefore, would be the presence in artistic representation of the mere particular, the abstract individual, the finite in its finitude. Where there is an appearance, and perhaps even a sort of reality, of such a presence, the representation cannot be wholly, if it is at all, artistic. There will have been a halfway halt in the difficult passage from immediate feeling to its mediation and resolution in art, and in the passage from passion to contemplation, from practical desire, yearning, will, to aesthetic knowledge; a halt at the point where the white is giving way, but has not yet given way to the black, and where there can be no stopping save by some more or less conscious arbitrary decision. When artists allow themselves to enlist art not solely to serve as a contemplation and appeasement of their own passion, but to be itself passion and passionate outburst, then, into the representation which they elaborate, they admit the wailing and shrieking of their own lusts, anguishes, mental upheavals, and the atmosphere becomes thereby close, privy, finite; qualities which derive not from the feeling (which, like every form or act of reality, is at once individual and universal), nor yet from the intuition (likewise at once individual and universal), but from feeling which is no longer merely feeling and representation which is not yet purely intuition. Hence as has often been said the inferior artist provides a much better documentation than the superior artist for enquiries into his own life and the life of his times. The superior artists rise above their times, their environment, their own private lives. Hence that sort of turmoil into which we are thrown by works which are atremble with passion but fall short of that idealization of passion in pure intuitive form in which the property of art consists.

For this reason I long ago, as a young man, uttered a warning in my *Estetica* against the confounding of aesthetic expression, identified in my theory with intuition, and established as the principle of art, with that practical expression which is indeed termed expression but is nothing else than desire, craving, will, action, in its immediacy; and is then adopted as a concept of the natural sciences, the index of a real psychic condition, as for instance in Darwin's enquiries into the expression of feeling in man and in the animals. I illustrated the difference by contrasting a man in the throes of wrath who by giving vent to it gradually dissipates the passion, and an artist or actor who portrays wrath and masters the tempest of the feelings, throwing over it the rainbow of aesthetic expression. Indeed artistic expression is so profoundly different from the impulse of practical life, that this difference suggested to Edmond de Goncourt the theme for that celebrated and appalling scene in one of his novels in which an actress standing at the bedside of her dying lover cannot resist the urge of her own genius to imitate the contraction of the man's features in his agony.

To give artistic form to a content of feeling means, then, impressing upon it the character of totality, breathing into it the breath of the cosmos. Thus understood, universality and artistic form are not two things but one. Rhythm and metre, balance and rhyme, metaphors and the subjects embedded in them, blendings of colour and tone, symmetry, harmony, all of these proceedings which the rhetorical art studies all too abstractly, and thus under a guise of externality, chanciness, distortion, are but so many synonyms of the artistic form which, even while it individualizes, harmonizes individuality with universality and thus in the same act universalizes. Correspondingly, those theories which made their appearance at the dawning of modern aesthetics (and indeed were heralded in antiquity by the difficult Aristotelian theory of the *catharsis*), the theory of the *Interesselosigkeit* (Kant's term) of art, its disinterestedness or rather emancipation from all practical interests, are to be understood as defences against the introduction or retention in art of immediate feeling, a food not digested by the organism and thus turning to poison. They are thus by no means to be understood as affirming the indifference of art, its reduction to the level of an idle game. Not thus did Schiller himself, to whom is due the unfortunate introduction of the word and concept "play" into aesthetic discussions, mean it, though this was what the theory came to when the extreme German romantic school propounded their "irony", celebrated by Friedrich Schlegel as "agility", and by Ludwig Tieck as "not surrender-

ing wholly to one's subject but exercising oneself upon it", the
end of all which was an artistic clownery or the imposition upon
the vast world of art of one dominating ideal, the clownish-
grotesque. In memory Heinrich Heine thus addressed this earnestly pursued and treasured ideal of his youth:

> *Wahnsinn, der sich klug gebärdet!*
> *Weisheit, welche überschnappt!*
> *Sterbeseufzer, welche plötzlich*
> *Sich verwandeln in Gelächter! . . .*

Such art offered a signal example of the invasion of the pure
artistic vision by the practical individuality of the poet, reaching
a peak in what was known as "humorous art", and giving Hegel
a powerful inducement to pronounce art to be in a condition of
dissolution, and to predict its disappearance in the modern world.
If a more direct illustration be desired of what is meant by the
emancipation of art from practical interest, let us say that it means
not the suppression of those interests but rather the joint presence
and efficacy of all of them in the representation, whereby alone
the individual representation, sloughing off its particularity and
acquiring the value of totality, becomes concretely individual.

What is irreconcilable with the principle of pure intuition is not
universality, but the intellectualist and transcendentist transformation of universality introduced into art in the form of allegory
or symbol, or in the semi-religious form of a revelation of hidden
deity, or, again, in a logical form which, distinguishing and reuniting the subject and the predicate, breaks the charm of art, for
whose idealism and naive apparitions it respectively substitutes
realism and critical perception or historical enquiry. With this
there is irreconcilability not only because art, on such terms,
would lose its efficacity, but also because a desperate theoretical
expedient of that sort uselessly clutters up that doctrine of pure
intuition according to which the representation, following as it
does upon cosmic feeling, conveys a purely intuitive universality,
formally different from any logical and critical category of universality.

But those who resort to such expedients are moved primarily by moral considerations, or what they take for such. At one time they are rightly disquieted by certain manifestations of false art, at another time they are wrongly alarmed by wholly innocent manifestations of true art. Now it is only by upholding the principle of pure intuition, emancipated even from moral interests, that we can both help them in their rightful protests and also dispel their mistaken alarms. Only with the aid of that principle can we effectively free art from immorality without falling into a foolish moralism. Any other course will land us in some paraphrase of the famous sentence of the Paris magistrates against the author of *Madame Bovary* in 1858: "Attendu que la mission de la littérature doit être d'orner et de récréer l'esprit en élevant l'intelligence et en épurant les moeurs . . .; attendu que pour accomplir le bien qu'elle est appelée à produire, ne doit pas seulement être chaste e pure dans sa forme et dans son expression . . .", a sentence which might have been signed by one of the characters of the novel itself, the chemist Homais. But they are men of little faith who think that morality has to be artificially cultivated and propped up in the course of human life and, with the same devices, carried into art. If the ethical principle is a cosmic force (as it certainly is) and queen of the world, the world of liberty, she reigns in her own right, while art, in proportion to the purity with which she re-enacts and expresses the motions of reality, is herself perfect. The more undiluted the art, the better the portrayal of the morality which is in things themselves. That a man should resort to art in order to vent his feelings of hatred and bile, this is a small thing. If he is a true artist, then out of his very representation will come a motion of love to supersede his hatred, and he will be justified in despite of himself. What matters it that others will wish to abuse his poetry to minister to their own sensuality and luxury? In the course of his work his aesthetic conscience will have bidden him to unify what has been dispersed in sensuality, to clarify the troubled stream of lust, and will have brought to his lips an involuntary note of pain or sadness. It may happen to an artist, to emphasize for his own private purposes some particular, to colour some episode, place the accent upon some word. But the logic of his work, its aesthetic coherency, will constrain him to undo what he has thus misdone. The aesthetic conscience has no need to borrow from morality its sense of modesty, it has in itself its own aesthetic modesty and chastity, and knows where the sole permitted form of expression must be silence. And when an artist violates this modesty and his own aesthetic conscience, admitting into the field of art something unborn of artistic conviction, then, no matter how noble his zeal and his intentions, he is both artistically false and morally reprehensible, having fallen short of his duty as an artist which was his first and nearest duty. The introduction of the obscene and sensual into art, which so greatly scandalizes the timid, is only one case of such immorality, and not necessarily or always the worst of such cases, for to me at least the foolish intrusion of virtue, calculated to render virtue itself ridiculous, is still worse.

Aesthetic activity in the exercise of this office of self-balance, self-limitation, is commonly called Taste, and is something which according to the well-known saying improves with the years in those who are true artists and true knowers of art. In other words, youth generally appreciates only the somewhat exuberant and glutinous sort of passional art which is well stocked with amorous, rebellious, patriotic, humanitarian, or such other directly emotive and practical expressions. Little by little such easy enthusiasms give way to satiety and nausea, and more and more we come to appreciate such art or poetry or fragments thereof as have attained purity of form, beauty that never wearies or cloys. The artist now becomes increasingly severe towards his own work, difficult to please, and likewise the critic in his judgements, but at the same time the admiration, where it can be given, is ever warmer and deeper.

This train of thought leads me on to say that the philosophy of art, or Aesthetics, is like any other science in that it does not live outside time, outside historical conditions. And as the times demand, it turns now to one and now to another of the problems which concern its own object. In the Renaissance, when poetry

THE TOTALITY OF ARTISTIC EXPRESSION 269

and art were following new paths leading them away from the rough heartiness of the Middle Ages, aesthetic teaching concentrated on the problems of symmetry, design, language, style, reconstructing a discipline of form on the model of antiquity. But when in the course of three centuries this discipline had frozen into a pedantry which mortified feeling and fancy in art, so that all Europe, over-intellectualized, lost its poetic vein, until the Romantic reaction set in and actually endeavoured to re-establish the Middle Ages, then it was time for Aesthetics to involve itself in the problems of fancy, genius, enthusiasm, to break down and to remould rules and classifications, to study the value of inspiration and spontaneous execution. Now, however, after a century and a half of Romanticism, may it not perhaps be well that Aesthetics should throw light rather upon the cosmic or integral character of artistic truth, the purification from particular inclinations, immediate forms of feeling and passion, which this calls for? In France, and occasionally elsewhere, we now hear talk of a "return to the classic", that is to the precepts of Boileau and to the literature of the century of the great Louis – a rather frivolous ambition, for this return is no more possible than the desire of the Renaissance and of the Romantic movement to return respectively to antiquity and to the Middle Ages. Moreover it seems to me that these preachers of classicism are still more infected by the poetry of passion and the senses than are those whom they attack, these being often enough simple souls susceptible of guidance and of transformation into artists of the classical type. Yet be that as it may, the present historical conditions do broadly justify the trend in question.

Modern literature of the last century and a half wears the general air, it has often been remarked, of a great Confession. The *Confessions* of the thinker of Geneva are indeed the progenitor of a line of books. Characteristic of the confessional style is an abundance of personal, particular, practical, and autobiographical outpourings such as I have already contrasted with "Expression", all this being matched by a relatively weak relation to integral truth, and thus by weakness or absence of what is called style. About the reasons for the ever greater share in literature taken by women (as to which the German aestheticist Borinski has argued that modern society in its intentness on politics and business increasingly delegates the poetical functions to its women, much as primitive warlike societies delegated them to druidesses and the like) many views have been advanced, but my own is that it has to do with the aforesaid "confessional" character of our modern writing, which has thrown open the doors to women, those beings so rich in feeling and in practicality who, when reading poetry, are apt to underline the passages which accord with their own personal sentimental successes and failures, and are never at a loss when invited to unburden their souls, and care little whether they are or are not mistresses of style. (It has been wittily remarked: *"Le style, ce n'est pas la femme."*) But if women thus run riot in modern literature, this is because the men themselves are, aesthetically, somewhat feminized, as shown in the shamelessness with which they wash their personal linen in public, and that frenzy of sincerity which just because it is a frenzy is not sincerity but more or less astute deception winning credence by its cynicism. The example was given by Rousseau. Now just as the victims of grave diseases hanker after remedies which, under colour of alleviating, in truth aggravate the sickness; so we have had through the last century, up to our days, the offer of one cure after another for restoring form and style, dignity, serenity and impassiveness in art, pure beauty: but the attempt to come by these deliberately did but make the malady, observed but uncured, more evident. That other endeavour to get the better of Romanticism, by way of realism and *verismo*, and with the help of the natural sciences and of the attitude which they encourage, was indeed more manly, but the romantic exaggeration of emphasis upon the particular as such, and upon the mass of particulars, was enhanced rather than attenuated in this school, itself romantic in origin and character. Other well-known literary programmes arose out of the same exaggeration, the "artistic writing" advocated and practised particularly by the Goncourts, and, at the other end of the scale, the spasmodic efforts of the Italian Pascoli to attain a realistic representation of immediate impressions, in virtue of which he may be considered a precursor of futurism and of the music of "noise".

The nature of the malady affecting the great body of modern literature was early diagnosed, and by great artists, the greatest in Europe. Almost in the same words, while knowing nothing of one another, Wolfgang Goethe and Giacomo Leopardi compared and contrasted the ancients and the moderns. The ancients, said the German poet, "represented existence, but we are wont to represent effect. They depicted the fearful, we depict fearfully; they the agreeable, we agreeably ... whence our exaggeration, mannerism, false prettiness, inflation, for when you work to produce effect, and for effect, you never believe that you have wrung the feelings sufficiently." The Italian poet praised the "simplicity" and "naturalness" of the ancients: "... they did not, like the moderns, run after the details of things, displaying the art of the writer who speaks and describes not as nature suggests but with a laborious subtleness, circumstantial precision, expansion and subdivision of the description for the sake of effect, whereby the intention is laid bare, natural easiness and artlessness are lost, affectation and artifice are made evident, and, in the poem, it is the poet who speaks rather than the subject". And as a consequence, with the ancients, "the impression of the poem or work of art was infinite", but "with the modern it is finite". Goethe too plumed himself on a pungent term for the work of the Romantics. He called it "hospital poetry", constrasting this with the "Tyrtaean poetry" which for him was not only the poetry of battle songs but all poetry which "arms men with courage to stand up to the battle of life". Oscar Wilde protested against the coupling of the words "morbid" and "art", but the protest, coming from him of all people, confirms its appropriateness.

The "general character" of a literature or an art cannot be applied directly as a description, still less as a critical valuation, of the poetical output of the literature or art in question. As we know, such a general character betokens no truly aesthetic or artistic value, but simply a practical tendency to be discerned in the elements which are not strictly speaking artistic: the matter, and sometimes even the faults of a literature. Need it be said that the artists of genius, the authentic poets, the great works and the great portions of works – which is all that counts in the history of poetry – are not subject to the malady or the general tendency. There is a sphere of light which is the gathering-place for the great poets and artists of every place and time. They have right of citizenship and enjoy mutual fraternity whether they belong to the eighth century before Christ or the twentieth after, whether they wear the Greek *peplos*, the Florentine *lucco*, the English *doublet*, or the white linen of the Orientals. All are classics in the best sense of the word which for me signifies a particular fusion of the primitive and the inspired with the cultivated and traditional. It must not however be thought that the outlining of the thought, feeling, and culture of an age is of no use for the study of poetry. In the first place it sharpens and substantiates that criterion by which the art of the true artists can be distinguished from that of the semi-artists, non-artists, and mere craftsmen. In the second place it helps us to know the great artists themselves, enabling us to discern the difficulties which they had to surmount, the victories which they scored over the resistent material which they chose for their work, transforming it into an artistic content, and finally (for even the great artists partake of mortality) it helps to explain their occasional deficiencies.

Furthermore the outlining of the prevailing tendency or general character also serves as a warning to artists to beware of that adversary who lurks in the very conditions in which they must work, and against whom criticism can furnish no aid save such a general warning. Yet such a general warning may be put into this particular form: not to listen to those who now or at any time have spoken of the state of mind of which we are speaking as pertaining to a particular people or race, and then conveyed to other peoples by a physical contagion. It may be true that raw, violent, unmediated expression is frequently found in the Germanic peoples, who have had a relatively brief experience of social refinement, but such a disposition is in reality rooted in human nature and ever apt to break out, and has indeed been historically displayed as a "mass phenomenon" of great intensity in every part of Europe since the end of the eighteenth century, in correspondence with common and general philosophical, religious, and moral conditions. This very fact that the tendency in question is primarily and directly of a philosophical religious and moral order, and only indirectly a literary tendency, makes it impossible to get the better of it by application of aesthetic formularies, as though the fault lay in an error of rhetoric or technique. The malady will decline and almost cease when a new faith springs up in the mind of Europeans as the fruit of so many ardours and endurances, so much spilling of blood. In like manner it has been and may be resisted and overcome in the case of individual artists by dint of the healthy development of their philosophic, ethical, religious character, in other words their personality, which stands at the base of art as of all else. If the malady does not diminish, if it now grows and takes on fresh complications, this will mean that our much tried and much trying human society must still face a yet longer test. Even so, true artists will always find their way to integral truth and classical form as, in the course of the nineteenth century, for all the infections in the air, the great figures of modern literature were able to do, Goethe, Foscolo, Manzoni, Leopardi, Tolstoi, Maupassant, Ibsen, Carducci.

[1917]

EXPRESSION PURE AND OTHERWISE

THE SENTIMENTAL OR IMMEDIATE EXPRESSION

W E commonly mean by "expression" an expression which is sentimental or immediate; but neither practically nor theoretically is this really "expression". The very fact that it is immediate, precludes it from being an active and creative, that is an authentic expression. We are really here using the word in the same way as when we describe thirty-eight degrees centigrade as the "expression" of a fever, a cloudy sky as the "expression" of rain to come, an appreciation of foreign exchange as "expression" of the diminished purchasing power of the home currency, a blush as the "expression" of modesty, a flush as the "expression" of anger. In all of these cases the particulars which are singled out serve to indicate certain facts, but in reality they are part and parcel of the facts. And in just the same way, that expression of feeling or passion which issues forth in articulate sound is indeed the symptom of a sentiment or passion, yet is for him who experiences it, the feeling, the passion itself, of which the "expression" is inseparably part and parcel.

If we reduce sentimental expression to its simplest and most elementary form, its cell, this is found to consist in an exclamation – "Oh", "Ah", "Oh", "Oow", and so on; not the sort of interjection which rings out in poetry, and is by the grammarians abstractly treated as one of their "parts of speech", and has become a theoretical expression, a word, but what might be called a "natural" interjection, exploding from the chest or larynx of one in the grip of wonder, joy, grief, displeasure, fear; feelings which as they agitate him, pass into articulated language. When in the interests of prudence or of good manners we seek to inhibit these vocal ejaculations, we can at the utmost repress them, and the repressed feeling opens for itself another channel, that is it undergoes a change into other more or less kindred shades of feeling expressed in gesture, mimicry, the play of the facial muscles: this happens, more or less visibly, by dint of the inhibitory effort itself. And from the lips there may burst forth not only rapid interjections such as those of which we have just given some examples, but torrents of language, swelling and tumbling more voluminously than those which the lady Julia in Byron's *Don Juan* let fall in a whole series of flowing stanzas feigning indignation when her husband caught her in bed. These deluges of articulate sound can also discharge themselves in writing, filling volume upon volume. Nevertheless if the origin is an agitation of the feelings, all this out-pouring will be nothing but interjection, and by the same token feeling, and not, therefore, the theoretical expression of feeling which involves a new spiritual act, a new form of consciousness. Charles Darwin, though a naturalist, did not hesitate to stress the difference between two things confounded under a single name. He had hoped, when embarking upon his study of the expression of the feelings in men and in animals, to win help from the study of painting and sculpture, but he won nothing or almost nothing of the kind, no doubt (as he himself wrote) because "in works of art the principal aim is beauty, and the violent contraction of the facial muscles is incompatible with beauty".

The confusion of sentimental, natural expression (or rather, non-expression) with poetical expression, was a favourite error of the Romantics, in those theories and judgements of theirs which if they did not always match their own effective works, matched their illusions. Certain post-romantic, modern schools have fallen into it anew, with this difference, that the passion and feeling which these latter display has less of nobility and of deeply stirred humanity than that of their predecessors. In Italy, Giosue Carducci was the interpreter of the reaction of the pure poetic conscience against such idolatry of "the heart" as the very genius of poetry. We all remember the sarcasm and invective launched by him against that *vil muscolo nocivo alla grand'arte pura* (vile muscle, he called it, harmful to the purity of great art). In France the interpret-ers were Baudelaire and Flaubert, the latter of whom went too far in propounding the doctrinal paradox of the "impersonality" of art. But these are only one or two names and episodes to recall a long and mighty struggle. Recalling other far from insignificant men who were by their own sublime or delicate sensibilities led to forget or to rebel against the discipline of art, the severity of poetry, the ideal of beauty, and in that discussion sometimes argued the case for the passions, the feelings, the heart, one feels sometimes a certain shame or vexation on hearing that same equation of poetry with feeling blurted out in the form of wretchedly pedantic and professorial sophisms by men lacking any sense of art and ignorant of the historical development of aesthetic doctrine. And when they advance the argument that feeling, sentiment, is not a mere formless matter, but has form, self-expression, this is a preaching to the converted. For we have clearly recognized that feeling, like every other act and fact (indeed like poetic intuition itself, which is never unaccompanied by expression), is not a spirit without a body; but, on the contrary, soul and body, internal and external, though divided by the abstract schemes of natural science, are all one in that reality in which the word is made flesh. But there is something which their teaching can never reveal, for it can never grasp it: the expression of poetry in its utter differentiation from the pseudo-expression of the feelings. The great William Shakespeare, who passed at one time for the very symbol of unconfined passion in art, not only belied this notion in the making of his own poetry, but when occasionally he let fall some hint of his own theories of art, instead of stressing feeling and passion he defined poetry as a kind of magic, thanks to which the poet, rolling his eye from heaven to earth and from earth to heaven, gives shape, local habitation, and name, to "aery nothings". And he bade poets – far from giving vent to violence – to maintain "temperance" and "smoothness" even in the midst of the tempest and whirlwind of the affections.

But feeling ceases to be form and becomes matter when taken in relation to the poetic expression which follows upon it and at the moment of that following. So it must be, by virtue of that law of the spirit according to which, in the living dialectic of the spirit, that which in a preceding grade was form, becomes, in a succeeding grade, mere matter ready to receive the imprint of other form. Passion, which attains to form in passionate man, becomes mere matter when that man becomes reflective, having the passion for the object of the reflection. It need perhaps hardly be said that the relation between form and matter is not that of cause and effect, as in a natural science, nor even is so to be described in a deliberate over-statement. It is more necessary to point out that neither is it that relation of original and copy, which seems to be suggested by the metaphors of common discourse, which have words "rendering" or "representing" feeling, and have art "imaging" or "mimicking" or "imitating" nature and reality. That all too simple theory which takes knowledge to be a copy, *Abbild*, constitutes the elevation of such metaphors to logical rank. On the philosophical level the theory is easily confuted by the observation that it substitutes for the act of knowledge a useless duplication of the object of knowledge. And it has for ages been confuted in the field of art by the popular recognition that coloured wax figures, which may actually be mistaken for reality, are neither painting nor sculpture, any more than that trick of exactly imitating the mewing or roaring of animals is poetry or art. Poetry cannot copy or imitate feeling, because feeling, which in its own sphere has form, is in the presence of art formless, indeterminate, chaos, and so, since chaos is a mere negative moment, nothingness. Like every other spiritual activity, poetry, which creates the solution, creates therewith the problem, creates along with the form also the content as not formless but formed matter. Until the poetic spark is kindled there are not figures picked out in light and shade but darkness. It is this spark which sheds light, that light in virtue of which the arrival of Homer has been compared to sunrise upon the earth. The "Homeric clarity" is still today the attribute of all true poetry.

Darkness, however, is not non-existence, and nothingness is not nothingness but is, as we have said, a negative moment taking its origin from a positive. Were the formless feeling not backed by such a positive then poetry would not come to birth, for neither is the spirit an abstract nor are the forms of the spirit unrelated one to another: *nulla ars in se tota versatur*. Each form lives by the life of all the others. The defence is carried beyond legitimate lengths by the critics and poets and fine connoisseurs of art who affirm that poetry is creation of beauty but has no content and no meaning. They fail to see that beauty is the transfiguration of feeling, in which as in that other transfiguration described by Saint Mark: *Resplendet facies sicut sol, vestimenta facta sunt alba ut nix*.

If ignorance about what art and poetry are were not so talkative as it is; if the notion that knowledge is a copy and spiritual creation a creation in the abstract were not so persistent; there would be no urgent need to argue and demonstrate that poetry is distinct from feeling, having feeling as its necessary material, and being the transfiguration of feeling. For these statements would pass unchallenged. Any one of us may observe in himself the genesis of poetical expressions: however tenuous these may be, they arise always out of an emotive experience which takes shape and attains self-recognition only in the word. And each of us is led by such experiences to suppose that the same happens to those who are in a specialized and pre-eminent sense poets. We may not know the passions which compose their life, but this very ignorance leads us on to construct by a facile work of the imagination dramas of love and heroism, disasters and afflictions, enacted or suffered by artists and poets, imaginatively embroidered links between the feeling and the fancy. Goethe never tired of repeating that all poetry is "occasional" poetry, drawing its "incentive" and its "matter" from reality. And he even described his own vast and various output of lyrical verse, tragedies, idylls, poems, tales, as being in his own eyes "fragments of a general confession". He said that he liberated and cleansed himself of what pleased or tormented or otherwise engaged him by transforming it into an "image", that is by means of that theoretical act which in regard to the office of poetry as the cleanser of passion has been called "catharsis".

II
POETIC EXPRESSION

What is, then, the poetic expression which calms and transfigures the feelings? This expression, we have said, differs from feeling, in being a theoretical proceeding, a knowing. Feeling cleaves to the particular: however high and noble be its source, it cannot quit the ground of biased passion, of the antinomy of good and evil, of the urgency of pleasure and pain. By contrast poetry reattaches the particular to the universal, accepts equally (and rises above) both pleasure and pain; and above the clash of parties, above discordancy, above the narrowness of the finite, it discovers the vision of the parts embraced in the whole, it discovers harmony, it discovers the sweep of the infinite. To confer this stamp of universality, totality, is its character, and where there appear to be images, but that stamp is feeble and defective, we say that the image lacks fullness, that there is a deficiency of "the supreme imagination", creative fancy, inner poetry. Now, as in every phase of spiritual life, so in the case of poetry, there can be no achievement without an internal struggle within the spirit, which here will be the struggle of poetry against that feeling which provides the matter, but at the same time renders this heavy and resistant. Therefore that victory whereby the resistant matter is converted into the image, is signalized by recovered calm, still tremulous, maybe, with the tears which that smile has come to banish, and signalized too by the new and cleansing feeling of delight in beauty.

To the ancient Greeks the operation of poetry appeared so wonderful, so miraculous, as it were, that they deemed it a sacred afflatus, an enthusiasm, a rage, a divine madness, and severed the bards from other mortals, honouring them as mouthpieces of the Gods, beloved pupils of the Muse, singers whose song reaches the broad heaven. Such tributes have not been wholly withheld from the poets by the modern age, which often envelops its poets with a chorus of praise and a kind of reverent protection, and to them, mainly if not exclusively, attributes the privilege of "inspiration" and the quality of "genius". Strictly speaking inspiration and genius, the *quid divinum*, are present in every human being and work: without them these would not be authentically human. What gives the appearance of a special presence of these characters in poetic creation, is that elevation of the individual to the universal, of the finite to the infinite, which is not to be found, at all events in the same way, in praxis and passion, where indeed the inverse process obtains, and is to be found, but only as a secondary characteristic, mediated by poetry, in thought and philosophy. The knowing of poetry seemed to be different from the knowing of philosophy. More than a knowing it seemed to be a producing, a shaping, moulding, or ποιεῖν, whence the name it has in the modern languages. It was to poetic knowledge that for the first time the recognition was accorded that its knowing is a making and not, as commonly conceived, a mere receiving.

However, lest this universality, divinity, cosmic quality which we attribute to poetry be misunderstood and materialized in a restriction to one particular tone of poetry; lest, by a worse error of which examples have been and are still seen, or glimpsed, this attribution be erected into a programme for the production of a type of poetry or of a school for producing the same, it will be well to translate those words into others less liable to be misunderstood. Well then, the universality (or any such similar term) is simply the whole and undivided humanity of poetry's vision. Wherever a vision of this sort takes shape (no matter what its particular content), in that content will be found universality, without there being any need for the infinite, the cosmos, the deity to put in an appearance in direct images such as are found in the psalm "The heavens declare the glory of God" or in the *Laudes Creaturarum*. The attempt to distinguish matter for poetry from what is not matter for poetry, whether on these or on other lines (the vain labour of philosophers and essayists of past times, which fortunately nobody in our times even attempts to renew), resolves itself into an attempt to discover in the matter of poetry that poetical quality which cannot possibly reside elsewhere than in the poetry itself. There is nothing exclusively poetical about a Hector, an Ajax, an Antigone, a Dido, a Francesca, a Gretchen, a

Macbeth, a Lear, for Falstaff, Don Quixote, Sancho Panza are equally poetical, nor about a Cordelia, a Desdemona, an Andromache, for so too is a Manon Lescaut, a Madame Bovary, or the Countess and her Cherubino in "Figaro". Not only the sentiments of a Foscolo, a De Vigny, a Keats, but also those of a Villon are poetic, and poetic are not only the hexameters of Virgil but also the macaronic hexameters of Merlin Cocai with their beautifully human traits, and likewise alongside of the sonnets of Petrarch those of the burlesque pedant Fidenzio Glottocrisio. The humblest popular song, if lit up by a ray of humanity, is poetry which can hold up its head to any poetry, however sublime. There is a solemn snobbery which resists the recognition of the poetic character of works in which gaiety and laughter have their place, while all too readily recognizing it wherever there is concentrated gravity, gloom, tragedy, terror. Yet not infrequently works of this last sort prove to be stiff, raw, violent, unpoetic, while closer acquaintance with the others shows the gaiety and laughter to be close to tears and informed by human understanding.

The impression left in the mind by poetry has suggested the word "melancholy" and truly the conciliation of those contraries whose strife is alone the breath of life, the fading out of passions which have brought pain but at the same time a strange and pleasurable warmth, the adieu said to that heart and home, for which we fiercely fight, but in which also we have our enjoyment, our suffering, our dreams, this poetic elevation to heavenwards is at the same time a backward glance, unregretting yet somehow regretful. Poetry has been seen as the sister of love and has been conjoined and fused with love in a single semblance partaking of them both. But poetry is more truly the sunset of the love passion which has burned up all reality, a sunset, a death, rendered bearable by memory. A veil of sadness seems to envelop beauty, and in truth it is no veil but beauty's very countenance.

III
THE EXPRESSION OF PROSE

To poetry is attributed the sphere of the imagination, of dream, of unreality. Such is the generally accepted view, but we cannot merely accept this as it stands. By dint of revision and correction we must show that poetry precedes the distinction between real and unreal, and accordingly must not be labelled as belonging to either of these two categories. The sphere of poetry is that of sheer quality lacking the predicate of existence; void, therefore, of the thought and criticism which distinguish and thereby convert the world of fancy into the world of reality. The expression of prose is distinguished from the expression of poetry purely and simply, as fancy, poesy, are distinguished from thought, philosophy. Any different criterion of distinction, based upon physical distinctions of articulated sounds, the order and series of sounds, the rhythms and metres, is doomed to fruitlessness in the case of the form of expression which we are now studying, and equally in the others which call for our inspection. All of them, viewed from outside, display the same sounds, the same or but fleetingly and deceptively distinguished forms of phonic order and series. The argument as to the difference between prosaic and poetic expression may be said to have been settled when Aristotle pointed out its pointlessness with his remark that there are rhymed philosophical utterances and there are poems in prose. Modern attempts to reopen it have met with no better success.

In the light of the relation which we have recognized between poetry and philosophy, there is something at first sight almost astonishing in the great mistake of those theories which, even if they stop short of actually identifying these two, subordinate poetry to philosophy as receiving from it its final direction and the rational ordering of its parts. Not only has philosophy no authority whatever over poetry (as the saying went, *Sorbonae nullum jus in Parnasso*), for poetry has its birth unhelped by and prior to philosophy, but the approach of philosophy, far from engendering or strengthening poetry, brings death to it, it being death for the world of poetry when it expires into the world of poetry and reality. Yet like all other errors (provided that they do not become fossilized in the hands of academicians and professors as mere mechanical repetitions of formulae) this one too contains lively elements of truth – in the first place, a proper assertion, against the wild deliverance of the passions, against sensual and sentimental dissipation, of the ideal and theoretical character of poetry, of poetry's theoretical operativeness. Close observation but improper definition are combined in the affirmation that perfection and beauty would be unattainable were not the critical spirit at work within poetry and that therefore it must be so at work. It is not noticed that the word "critical" is here employed metaphorically, and that, as in other cases which we have come or shall come across, the metaphor becomes a blunder when confounded with the concept from which it is derived, meaning, in our present case, when confounded with that strictly so termed *critical* operation having for its task the differentiation of the real from the unreal, thereby, as we have seen, bringing about the death of poetry. What was meant by "critical" in the metaphor was, on the contrary, nothing else than the quality of poetry itself. Poetry cannot do its work without self-government, without reining in itself (*sibi imperiosa*, as Horace says), without receiving and rejecting, trying and testing, operating *tacito quodam sensu* until it finds satisfaction in the image expressed by the sound. It is alike in this to every task of mankind which is never without the sense of what is propitious and what is harmful. We are not expected to describe as "utilitarian criticism and theory" the process by which when sitting down one shifts until one finds the right position in the chair and then having found it makes oneself comfortable. The efforts and pauses and renewed efforts of the woman in labour are not necessarily described as "obstetrical criticism" – this last comparison is deliberate because the 'birth-pangs of genius' is a common enough association of words. True poets, for sure, bring forth not without pain. It is no good sign with them when everything translates itself with prompt facility into verse. Ovid's confession, *piget corrigere et longi ferre laboris onus*, was not honourable for himself.

Judgements rightly and properly so-called may, it is true, interrupt the course, or let us rather say may occur in the suspensions and intervals of poetic labour. As reflections and judgements they will have their utility as counteractors of theoretical prejudices, yet poetically they will remain sterile, for the generative power resides solely in a sensible balance and self-correction which we will not, as others have done, call unconscious and instinctive (whereas it is active and conscious), true though it be that it is not *self*-conscious and logically discriminating as is the critical judgement. Therefore do we on the one hand reject the superfluous and futile interference of the critical spirit in poetic creativity, because not even "a thousand Romes, a thousand Athens" can put poetry on lips to which nature has denied it. But on the other hand we reject also the concept of a genius uninformed by taste as one against which, though allowing always, of course, for the fact that genius may be intermittent or of varying strength, we must reassert the unity and identity of genius and taste.

Further support for that specious attachment of poetry to philosophy was found in the conception of philosophy as a contemplation of pure ideas, which, handed on by the abstracting to the imagining faculty, took on the aspects of deities composing a sort of mythology, more subtle but in substance not less fanciful than the earlier and more popular mythology. That fanciful superhuman world of ideal essences took on the appearance of a world of human beings, with human attitudes and motions, in a new Olympus recalling that of Homer's gods. And this seemed to offer itself to the purposes of poetry as well as any other natural reality, indeed, as its contemplators and visionaries held, with a peculiarly apt worthiness and elevation. But serious thought, philosophy, is something far other than that abstract or mythological contemplation, it is the exercise of judgement, exercised, most certainly, upon ideas, categories, concepts, but solely for the judgement of facts, which judgement consists in making the qualifying distinction, beyond the reach or the ambition of poetry which has its own sufficient sphere, between the real and the unreal. Whoever knows of any other definition of thought and philosophy is requested to communicate it for the correction and amplification of the present author's horizon which for the time being remains enclosed by these (for him) impassable limits. Pending that, we hold to the view that no other thought is conceivable save the exercise of judgement, and no other judgement save that which is brought to bear upon real, historical existence. Even when thought bears upon pure ideas, pure categories of judgement (real and unreal, being and not-being, true and false, good and evil, and so on by way of distinction and subdistinction), these are not to be thought of otherwise than as individuated in facts. When we undertake and achieve the solution of the problems which have historically risen around these ideas, they themselves are still nothing else but Thought, which is always the subject and never the object of knowing.

If, now, thought has no other office than to distinguish the images of the real from those of the unreal, and has itself nothing to do with the creation of the images which fancy, poetry, offers to it to be its material, then the expression of prose, unlike poetic expression, which expresses the feelings and affections, must express the definitions of thought, consisting accordingly not in images but in symbols or signs of concepts.

This character is very plain in the prose of the abstract sciences, particularly so in the mathematics, little less in physics, chemistry, and the classifications of the natural sciences, but also in specialized philosophical treatises where for purely didactic reasons the philosophy is severed from the facts on which it rests. Yet this character pertains not less truly also to historical prose, and this is the fundamental case since it covers the prime act of judgement in its concreteness and entirety, and in it the signs seem to lie concealed beneath a thick growth of images. So much impressed were the old rhetoricians by this that they held history to be differentiated both from oratory and from the other sorts of prose as "proxima poetis et quodammodo carmen solutum", something composed "verbis ferme poetarum".

If we compare a page of a novel with a page of history we find in each the same or much the same vocabulary, syntax, rhythms, and evocations of images. Between the one and the other there seems to be no important difference. Yet in the novel the images stand and move of themselves in the intuitive unity which has given this form to a particular tone of feeling, while in the page of history they are held on their course by an invisible thread, a thread of thought and known to thought, and from this, not from the intuition, the fancy, they take their coherency, their unity. They have the appearance of images, but they are realizations of concepts, signs of those categories which are at work incarnated and diversified in the personages and actions of history, encountering each other and having their dialectical development. In the novel there is a warmth which spreads into all its parts. In the history there is a watchful coldness, ready to extinguish or damp down any incipient poetic inflammation, or to save from such peril the mental threads which are tied and untied, stretched and relaxed, in the service of history.

This too is, in its way, a drama, the drama of thought, the dialectical drama. That coldness is a secret ardour which seems cold only because it wards off an ardour of a different sort. More than one of the old-fashioned aestheticists, devisers of graduatory systems of the various arts, could not bring themselves to exclude Dialectics altogether from the realm of Beauty which they were engaged in describing but, to cite the case of our own Tari, found room for it "at the frontier.... Like a sun which has set yet leaves on the horizon a pallid, subdued, yet consoling afterglow". The truth is that the soul of prose is altogether other than the soul of poetry. Prose inclines to precisely contrary attitudes. The ideal of the prose writer lies in the direction not of sense value in the image, but of restraint in the sign. More than once, indeed, the said ideal has been carried to the length of an impracticable attempt to reduce the expressions of prose to mathematical symbolism. Not only have such philosophers as Spinoza written in the geometric style or attempted a resort to calculus, but there have been historians (no less a man than Vincenzo Cuoco among them), who played with the notion of substituting for the names of persons in a historical narration, the letters of the alphabet. Such attempts were impracticable, utopian, because names, numerals, alphabetical letters are all alike placed in discourse as signs, and there is no way of properly or usefully introducing the signs appropriate for one discipline into another.

In its character as symbol or sign, prose expression is not properly speaking language, any more than the natural manifestation of feeling is language, the only true language or word being poetic utterance, whence the deep truth in those old sayings that poetry is the mother tongue of humanity, and that "poets came into the world earlier than prose-writers". Poetry is language in its genuineness. Exploration in depth of the problem of the nature of language, even when undertaken in the semi-mythological terms of a research into the historical origins of language (as if language could possibly have had a dated origin), has always been found to involve the successive rejection of the superficial doctrines which explained language as interjection (passion and feeling), as onomatopoeia (the copying or imitation of things), as social convention (the fixing of signs), or as the work of reflective thought (logical analysis) in favour of the explanatory principle offered by poetry. Thus came Vico to proclaim "within poetry lies the origin of languages", and others, like Herder, to describe the process of poetic creation when they sought to represent dramatically the utterance by the first man of the first word, which was no word to be found in a dictionary but an expression complete in itself, the budding, as it were, of the first poem. The notion was that thereafter the first poetic language decayed and misgrew into workaday language, of merely instrumental usefulness, and only from time to time was it by the miracle of genius rediscovered by some few who were able to awaken the bright stream anew and cause it to sparkle in the sunshine. In reality, language has never so misgrown, has never, by what would have been an unnatural process, lost its own poetic nature. That supposed merely instrumental language is merely an imagined assemblage of all the unpoetical expressions, the expressions of the feelings, of prose, of oratory also (the subject of our next chapter). In everyday expression and converse we may if we listen attentively discern how in its lively flow there is a never-failing renewal and invention of imaginous language and a flowering of poetry severe and sublime, or tender, or gracious and smiling.

IV

ORATORICAL EXPRESSION

Practical activity makes use of articulated sounds in order to excite certain states of minds: such expression we call oratorical. Let us consider this in its most primitive form. Just as we illustrated the expression of the feelings by exclamatory syllables, so we can illustrate oratorical expression by imperatives like "Come on!" "Quick!" "Away!" "Down!" and the like. These are used not as words or conceptual signs but as sounds. It is often said that oratorical expression bends or subdues words and poetic images to its own end. There is no great harm in saying this, but it is not strictly correct.

The importance of noting this lies in the fact that old-fashioned treatises of aesthetics and theory of art postulated a class of "unfree" arts, arts, that is, serving extraneous ends. Among these, alongside of the curiously termed "unfree arts of perception" (in which there figured such objects and utensils as the house, the garden, the chalice, the necklace, as being doubly valuable for utility on the one hand, beauty on the other), there were placed the "unfree arts of the fancy", the arts of the word, or oratory, the art of bending poetic images to the service of practical utility. There was an unconscious and involuntary violation of the spirit in this recognition and philosophical justification of a kind of enslavement of the fancy and the judgement, which can never be enslaved or enslave themselves, never silence or muffle their own voice, but can at the most give utterance to a false and feigning voice, only however to render the true voice more resonant when the falsehood gives way to a heightened remorse.

Oratorical expression is in its essence practical, and it differs from other practicality only outwardly, not substantially. It is almost comical to see Quintilian's embarrassment when he attempts a rigorous differentiation. First of all he tries to find it in the function of oratory to "persuade", but at the same moment he perceives that persuasion can be exerted equally well by means very different from verbal articulation. "Verum et pecunia persuadet et gratia et auctoritas dicentis et dignitas, postremo aspectus etiam ipse sine voce, quo vel recordatio meritorum cuiusque vel facies aliqua miserabilis vel formae pulcritudo sententiam dictat." For an example he cites Hyperides baring the beautiful breast of Phryne, and, again, Antonius tearing away the clothing of Aquilius to discover the scars of his glorious wounds. Nor yet can Quintilian satisfy himself with the definition of oratory as a persuasion exerted "dicendo". For "persuadent dicendo ... vel ducunt in id quod volunt alii quoque ut, meretrices, adulatores, corruptores" – classes with which the severe and dignified orator desired no connexion. In truth, no more than an outward distinction can be drawn between persuasion by word and gesture, and pressure upon the will of others by main force. The two gods Peitho and Anankaia, Persuasion and Force, whom Themistocles conducted in his train in order, he said, that the men of Andros might pay the tribute, were in substance one and the same god, who, whether by words or by main force, could do no more than try to arouse in the men of Andros a state of mind, it being impossible to plant in them persuasion and will, these being acts of freedom which are accomplished by each one solely in a state of freedom. But the attempt to prepare and to provoke acts of will is an unjustifiably narrow field in which to circumscribe the work of the oratorical expression. The inducement of states of mind of any and every sort belongs to it, as will here be further set forth.

For did not the ancient rhetoricians prescribe to the orator, besides *persuadere*, also *docere* and *delectare*? Sometimes, it is true, the "docere" in question was expounded as being not a true and strictly theoretical "docere" but in its essence a "persuadere" by means of practical allurements and appeal to positive beliefs. The "delectare" was similarly for the most part expounded as a subordinate of persuasion. At other times, however, no such subordination was understood, but, on the contrary, an independent and self-regarding status was recognized. And this is correct. We should, in fact, make room for another particular practical sphere alongside of the practical sphere which is wholly concerned in the preparation of volitions. This other practical sphere should be so defined as to embrace the stirring of the motions of the soul for purposes of entertainment, motions of all sorts, unpleasant as well as pleasant, for the very fact that the purpose of the stirring is entertainment confers the pleasurableness which is here in question. This sphere corresponds to a need of the human spirit which (as is less properly said of nature) abhors a vacuum, and can never remain unoccupied. For when a man will not or cannot pursue some task, then he turns at once to some other which is of readier access or easier execution, or else, to keep himself in training as a human being, he generates fancies, reviewing a succession of human situations accompanied by appropriate motions of the soul, these too the work of fancy, and not proceeding from action and reality. It is this enjoyment of the stir of motions in themselves, and not for their particular content, which distinguishes the act of Entertainment from the pleasure of the imagination, and distinguishes it on another side from the act of Play with which it has often been confounded. (Indeed art and poetry have themselves in consequence been blasphemously confounded with play.) Play is a broader concept, not attached to any particular behaviour but to the change-over from one thing to another in order to find relief from the weariness occasioned by the first. One may point to the choice of pastimes by hard-working men. They habitually choose something useful to do and in some measure fulfil the injunction of the hardworking Muratori who in a sonnet prescribed to himself, and he fully observed the prescription, no other refreshment from his task but a change of task. "Non la quiete, ma il mutar fatica – alla fatica sia solo ristoro." The need for entertainment is hedonistic, utilitarian, economic: use which word you will. The moral conscience has nothing to say against it, but does from time to time issue a reproof when entertainment passes from being a necessary relaxation to being a waste of time, momentary or habitual: a reproof which is also in place when the change-over from a harder to an easier task involves a dereliction of duty.

If we thus enlarge the field of oratory to include besides the functions of persuasion, those also of entertainment, then we place alongside of the orator of parliaments and law-courts those who devise the means of entertainment, from the gravest and most tragic devices for stirring the motions of the soul to the lightest and gayest, from the sacred to the profane, from the elevated to the debased, from the healthy to the unhealthy, degenerate, licentious, and libidinous: playwrights, novelists, actors, mimes, film stars, histrions, buffoons, tightrope walkers, acrobats, athletes, runners; in fact a rather mixed company, but certainly no worse a one than those courtesans and pandars of whom the good Quintilian could not think how to rid himself. Companions all, and rivals: for not infrequently the non-writers among those soul-stirrers triumph over the writers, as was the experience of Terence who three times saw the theatre where his fine comedy *Hecyra* was being played emptied by the counter-attraction of tightrope-walkers, boxers, and gladiators, respectively. (This shows that the pushing into the background of art and letters in our days by the triumphant rivalry of sport, rather distressing for those all over the world who were accustomed to a different respective valuation, might take on additional lustre as constituting a renewal of similar triumphs in past centuries if the sportsmen were interested in such historical glories!) The two-sided attitude of poets and men of letters towards the theatre, their distrust and dislike of it on the one hand, and admiration for it on the other, arises out of their fear of being mastered by something unpoetic, anti-literary, histrionic, and their desire, nevertheless, to triumph also in that field, to triumph there as champions of poetry and literature.

The rhetoricians of antiquity rightly maintained that the value of oratory was not to be gauged *ab eventu*, by its success in gaining in a particular case the effect of persuasion at which it was aimed. It was, they said, with the orator as with the doctor, who is valued according to his ability, not according as his patient recovers or dies. Works of entertainment, too, are to be judged solely by the use which they make of the means available to them, not by the effect achieved. If the work has been properly done, the author is not to be blamed if the audience remains unmoved or bored, or if, uncontented with mere entertainment, it passes from the stirring of the fancy to a further phase such as stoning the actor who plays the part of the villain, as has happened more than once at popular performances, and as Don Quixote himself did, revealing in that act all his generous impulsiveness. But the oratorical art, in all this wide sense, is a practical and not an aesthetic art, and for this reason it has to proportion itself to the quality of those to whom it appeals. The orator for the so-called masses, formerly called the plebs, may reasonably employ language and gestures which in context would be a perpetual outrage to dignity. Indeed in that context a decorous and dignified speaker would be a bad orator, bringing no advantage to the cause which it was his duty to uphold. Similarly, since there is a public which fastens on to images of rough design and crude colour, paying to them a ready tribute of tears, laughter, and excitement, this public will find admirable entertainment in the works of Anne Radcliffe, Eugène Sue, Paul de Kock, Gaboriau, Ohnet, Montépin, and similar authors of rattling tales, thrillers, mammoth dramas, and so forth. It is related that Pope Gregory XVI put the question to an illustrious French visitor as soon as he entered the room: "What has Monsieur Paul de Kock on hand now?". The Pope was in fact a passionate reader of that author. But such artless productions have had a great fascination not only for a Pope (who was a good simple friar), but – maybe by dint of sheer contrast – for highly cultivated writers. Madame de Sévigné was drawn by an irresistible attraction to the novels of La Calprenède, though she judged them to be "detestable". Some generations later, with a different public on the scene, it becomes hard indeed to understand how such books could rouse excitement and enthusiasm, how *Calloandro Fedele* and *Le Juif errant* could run into repeated editions and translations. Yet if we observe the tastes of the young or of the humble classes we may find that they still win the rapture of some readers.

In the minds of the ancient rhetoricians (to whose authority we gladly appeal, for never since was that art so carefully and nobly studied and expounded) the practical character of the oratorical art was a firmly established truth. Therefore it was that they excluded from consideration the "quaestiones infinitae", or merely theoretical and scientific questions, to concentrate their readers' attention upon "hypotheses", "quaestiones finitae", and "contentiones causarum", such as had given the first impulse and furnished the principal and most conspicuous argument to their treatises. While noting some affinities between the orators and the poets they repeatedly inculcated a distrust of the reading and imitation of poetry, as tending to introduce extraneous interests at the expense of the practical interest. Cicero had said that the poets spoke "aliam quandam linguam" and Quintilian confirmed that poets and orators are harmful to one another if they fail to remember that "sua cuique proposita est lex, suus cuique decor". Their attention was too much fixed upon the practical aspect for them to give more than secondary attention to the theory of the form of speech and of elocution. Only by slow stages – and not completely until modern times – did this come to win the status of a distinct branch of study. By contrast, the ancient rhetoricians had much to say, and said it in great detail, about the "customs" and "affections" of humanity which it behoved the orator to know, and here theory was enlisted to assist experience.

The oratory of entertainment has had enemies who not only denounced this or that feature, but denied its right to exist at all. Ever memorable are the persecutions of the theatre by the Church, which actually denied Christian burial to actors. And the oratory of persuasion has also had from ancient times its denouncers who regarded it as "fallendi ars" inspired not by "bona conscientia" but by the pursuit of "victoria litigantis". A great thinker like Emmanuel Kant expressed his total disregard for an art which profited by the weaknesses of men, this being inexcusable even when the intention and the effect are good. He said that the triumphs of oratory coincided with the decadence of the States and of the patriotic virtues in Athens and Rome. He contrasted the art of the rhetorician with the utterance of a man equipped with clear and sure knowledge of affairs, warm-hearted and upright, speaking without art but to good effect. In defence of the oratory of entertainment we have already cited an argument which amounts to the same, really, as the traditional wisdom about the overstretched bow. It may suffice to add the remark that the Church when it anathematized the theatre found it necessary to initiate or to licence theatres of its own for the exhibition of thrilling mysteries, sacred representations, edifying dramas, "autos", and lives of saints, in which inevitably there was a considerable intermixture of the profane. There is moreover a close link between the theatre and the liturgical drama, the holy mass with its single actor supported and answered by the young acolyte acting as server. But the oratory of persuasion cannot be adequately justified by the plea of the moral obligations, "omnes animi virtutes", which Cicero and Quintilian required in the orator. For this form of oratory, as for the other, a justification must be elicited out of its own essence, its own end, which is, of course, the end of utility, prudence, policy, a spiritual-practical form which Kant, with austere obstinacy, steadily neglected and avoided, thus leaving a dangerous gap in his promised "inventory of the human spirit". Like Kant, many other philosophers have declined to look closely upon or to explore thoroughly the form in question, either for want of experience or for want of an appropriate stimulus. Like politics, the oratory of persuasion, which belongs really to the sphere of persuasion, may be verbally forsworn, but in fact imposes itself upon those who would forswear it. The Christian writers who began by showing abhorrence for the schools of the rhetoricians, ended by going to school with them, and soon boasted their Basils, their Gregory Nazianzens, their John Chrysostoms. Tolstoi says in his Diary that "for women language is simply a means for gaining an end, and they strip it of its fundamental sense, the expression of truth". If that were so, then all men would earn the description of women, for all men, when necessary, use language as oratorical expression, or rather, in doing so, it is not truly language, truth-speaking words, that they use, but articulate sounds constituting actions: yet not for that can they be charged with falsehood or lying. It happened once to Maurice Barrès, who had perhaps never before reflected on the nature of such expressions, to receive sudden illumination when seeking in vain for the logical meaning of a famous slogan of Gambetta. And he wrote: "But is it necessary that combinations of words like this should have a meaning? Is it not enough that they were suitable for producing the impression which was produced?". For sure, it was not in order to convey a logical meaning or a poetical meaning, that commanders in the heat of war and battle uttered certain famous articulate sounds, like the Greek captain's retort to one telling him of the enemy's superior numbers, that what was needed was to know where the enemy could be found and fought, not how numerous he was; or Frederick II of Prussia's shout to the fleeing soldiers of his army, did they mean to live for ever?, which halted them and made it possible to re-form them against the enemy, or that word which General Cambronne, when he had been accepted into good society and had married an English wife, would never openly acknowledge that he had spoken at Waterloo.

[1935]

V

POETRY, THE WORK OF TRUTH:
LITERATURE, THE WORK OF CIVILIZATION

You might suppose that the argument of this lecture,[1] the relation between poetry and literature, is destined for those of you who are pursuing the vocation of literary and artistic history and criticism, and that it is of small interest to students of political and moral history. I will not pause to remind you of the grand principle that all truths coexist in a relation of mutual demonstration, support, clarification, or to recall the advice of Plato to his faithful but unpolished disciple Xenocrates to "sacrifice to the Graces", which in our case might mean to cultivate poetry and literature as necessities for the historian worthy of that name. I will only say now that you will receive in this lecture some new information on a concept which is bound to interest you historians: the concept of civilization.

In the distant age of Greek antiquity poetry and literature were already being studied theoretically, giving rise to two separate branches of learning, exemplified in Aristotle's *Poetics* and *Rhetoric*, of which the former is partly and the latter wholly preserved for us. Treatises on Rhetoric had the nature of textbooks for lawyers and for public men in general. You may be interested to know why in Italian we can write not only Retorica but also, in defiance of etymology, Rettorica. The reason is that in the eleventh and twelfth centuries this branch of learning was considered necessary for the "rectors" or magistrates entrusted with the *rettoria*, rectorship or governorship of lands, as I myself learned some time ago from an appendix to a book by the French scholar Pézard on Brunetto Latini's role in the Inferno of Dante. I read it in manuscript and as far as I know it has not yet been published, so that this curious piece of information may constitute an indiscretion, for which the author will surely pardon me.

1. From the lectures given in 1949 to the Naples School of Historical Studies, then published in *Quaderni della Critica*.

The *Poetics* and the *Rhetoric* were linked by the fact that the latter part of this second branch of learning, concerned with the Art of Speech (περὶ τῆς λέξεως), began in later times to be detached and to form, nearer to our own age, a separate body which came to be regarded as a sequel and conclusion of the *Poetics*, this last being concerned with the literary genres or kinds, while the Art of Speech was supposed to lay down the rules of fair speech just as grammar gave those of correct speech. Thus all the concepts of Rhetoric came to flow into the Poetic: the distinctions between *content* and *form*, between the *nude* and the *ornate* style, between *proper* and *metaphorical* discourse, and further the various modes of metaphors and figures, and the general law governing the use of all those distinctions, which was the concept of the πρέπον or suitable.

When I set to work to elaborate afresh the doctrine of Aesthetics, among other ingredients which I rejected, such as the "literary genres", the theory of the "modifications of the beautiful", and that of the "divisions of the arts", I expelled, from the field of poetry and the arts, "Rhetoric", and did so with particular ruthlessness, because I thought I discerned in every one of its lineaments a disregard of and an offence against the true nature of poetry.

Take for instance the distinction and separation of content from form. Wherever, I asked, is there in poetry a content distinct from the poetical form? No doubt there is a pre-existing *matter* for poetry, namely men's feelings. But this matter receives poetic form, and he who would pronounce upon the character of poetry has no other course open to him than to read or repeat the poem without losing a syllable, a comma, an accent, because all these and other elements are conjoined in determining its character. For instructional purposes we may stress this or that particular, but neither jointly nor severally can these ever avail to make us know the poem and trace its true and individual physiognomy. For this nothing else will serve except direct vision or intuition. Content and form are in poetry fused indistinguishably as in a single act. Were it otherwise, poetry would be not truth but the allegorical disguise of truth, that is, not poetry. The word of poetry is not a garment donned by poetry, it is poetry's own self. I mean here the spiritual word, not that abstract physical sound which aroused the strange and perhaps jocular admiration of Gautier for "Minos et Pasiphaë", and gave rise to the unhappy charlatanries of Mallarmé and other decadents. Again, what is "adorned" or "naked" expression? How, if an expression is expressive, can it be naked, and how, on the other hand, can it be adorned, if this means laden with something over and above and extraneous to the expression? How can "proper" words be distinguished from those which are "metaphorical" or imaginous? Poetic expression is always both proper and imaginous, the image being the work of the creative fancy. What is this πρέπον, this "aptness" or "suitability" to which is committed the value of the expressive form, the standard of judgement, whereas the sole value and standard of poetry is beauty? Now beauty is a mental brightness, while suitability is a practical matter, as in the question whether a shoe fits or whether certain behaviour is helpful in producing a desired effect. In fact, whoever wishes to deny poetry has but to recite, giving them out for attributes of poetry, all the qualities of rhetorical and literary expression. This will be the death of poetry. If, on the contrary, one wishes to give a true account of poetry, it suffices to attribute to it the very opposite of such qualities.

After I had thus reclaimed poetry from the attachments of rhetoric or literature, rescuing and safeguarding what was dear to me, I gave little further heed to "literature", which was then for me a secondary interest. This is the usual way with philosophical enquiries. They proceed from pause to pause, and the next pause is interrupted, the task resumed, only when a new problem arises in us to excite our intellect. Such a new problem means a new torment, but also a new pleasure, a "sweet love" as Saint Thomas says in the poem when announcing to Dante the next point of doctrine which he is going to unravel:

> ... Quando l'una paglia è trita,
> quando la sua semenza è già riposta
> a batter l'altra dolce amor m'invita.

In truth, I had rolled back the invasions and usurpations of the rhetorical or literary theory of expression in the field of the theory of poetry, little recking if I had at the same time rolled back literature and even a theory which, however false in relation to poetry, might well not be false in another sphere. But the rejection of literature itself required a denial of positivity, of value, an affirmation of an intrinsic negativity in literature, the treatment ot the concept of literature as the concept of an error. It is true thaf in my youth the word "literature" was often used in a pejorative sense (compare: "Et tout le reste est littérature"). But this did not and could not mean anything else than that poetry is not literature but is music ("De la musique avant toute chose"), that is, pure art. There was talk also of "bad literature" and this implied that there was also a literature which is good. For that matter everyone of us does his best to turn out works consisting of the most adequate literature that his skill, his deliberate studies, his constant efforts, his repeated corrections of first drafts, enable him to provide. Nobody, in fact, likes being called unlettered, barbaric, awkward, tasteless. The respectability and the claims of literature are thus beyond all question. Rhetoric too had got itself a bad name, specially from the Romantics, who for that matter endowed the world with a Rhetoric of their own, less careful and less useful than that of Quintilian, to mention for example one who might with advantage still be read and studied in our schools. Alessandro Manzoni, the classical, the Virgilian Manzoni, made fun of the rhetoric of his "Seventeenth-Century Anonymous Author" and of his strings of conceits and metaphors, yet he too acknowledged that a touch of rhetoric, "discreet, subtle, tasteful", is indispensable.

Our present question is rather different and may for convenience be divided into the three queries: 1. what need is met by literature; 2. how does literature originate; 3. what form of the spirit is it which fashions it? I have discussed this subject in a book designed as an introduction to the study of literature and poetry (*La Poesia*), and I return to it now, not only for the sake of expounding it to you, but also in order to add to the argument of the book some thoughts which had not then occurred to me. Like all those who feel a responsibility for the work they perform, I am accustomed to turn back to what I have already written and published, to dip into my own books to see whether I discover errors or deficiencies and whether there are suggestions which could be further developed. With some surprise I have sometimes found myself accused in consequence of that scrupulous re-examination and correction of my works, of contradicting myself and failing in coherence. Does coherence, then, consist in standing still, or does it not consist in advancing by movement towards an ever richer coherency? A proverb of Naples has it that man is not born a master of his trade, he does not start with the knowledge which has to be acquired in the course of life. I would add that man does not even die a perfectly accomplished master. Let me recall how long ago a Neapolitan surgeon whom I knew as a fellow member of the Senate suddenly felt himself mortally stricken while performing an operation: his dying gesture was to pass the lancet to his assistant saying "Now you carry on".

Well then, as to the first query I will say that the human soul being poetical, musical, or however we express this responsiveness to the power of harmony and beauty, feels the need to extend the domain of beauty as widely as possible, and to expel or to modify whatever by its presence detracts from or disturbs and offends beauty. This is not always actually possible. Suffering, when not extreme, may find an appropriate utterance, but great suffering is either silent or finds an outlet in rough language and gestures. In the heat of the battle the leader, as Parini puts it, "shouts insupportably for ears refined". Only in the pages of the historians of antiquity, who delighted in such ornaments, does he deliver a well-phrased harangue. He who is in the grip of violent feelings would be ashamed, even were he able, to work up a beautiful expression which would tame what is to him the sacred rage of his passion. One pressing eagerly to attain his end will not pause to discover a wealth of words in which to clothe his demand and his ideal. Even the thinker, when an idea dawns in his mind, must often resign himself to renouncing the search for a fine and adequate expression, in favour of some sign, mark, line, scratch, or even conventional word with which to fix it in his mind so that in due season it may flash forth again when he is at ease and in a suitable frame of mind. In these cases we yield to obstacles just as we yield to an illness, not as welcoming and cultivating it, but with sighs and groans, vowing to get rid of it all as soon as possible, so as to be able to array one's feelings and volitions and thoughts in the light which poetry has kindled in one's soul – an immortal light! That light which has arrayed or will array them, softens them, eliminates all that is barbarous, renders them urbane or, as the Greeks said, citizenly (ἀστεῖοι). Literature, which performs this office, civilizing those expressions which are immediate or natural, is in itself a large part of what we call "Civilization".

We pass on to the second query. What has hitherto been said cannot be doubted: the existence of our faculties of letters itself attests it. But the manner in which Literature accomplishes this office is not so clear, and as far as I know the theorists keep silent about it, and perhaps few have ever considered this with attention or sought to formulate it. The civilizing effect we are speaking of is evidently not procured by the intervention or requested mediation of the spirit or genius of poetry. This cannot strictly speaking be bent or turned to any use, being, like the love of Carmen, *un oiseau sauvage que l'on ne peut apprivoiser*. When it intervenes, it does so by its own impulse, drawing and resolving into itself every affection, every volition, every thought. We needs must, then, ascribe to the practical activity of the spirit the adoption – for the use of that which in itself is unpoetic – of poetic or aesthetic form, abstracted from poetry. Is that possible? And, to start with, is there any other example outside the aesthetic field of a similar or analogous operation, by which we may explain and justify such a transference of formal or more accurately speaking formalistic character?

There is such an example, and I marvel that it has not been thought of before. In the field of logic there exists besides the deep and substantial logic whereby the universal is conceived in the individual, a logic which we might call superficial, a purely

syllogistic and formalistic logic which may clothe with itself affirmations that are untrue, indeed not only tolerates but sometimes
requires that this should happen, for the sake of an abbreviation
of argument and an easier arrival, by the critical method, at an
establishment or re-establishment of the truth; or at the very least,
as happens in practical affairs, secures a pseudo-logical, lawyerish
agreement bringing to a temporary or final end a dispute which
was dragging on harmfully – a better occasion will arise some day
for a proper solution. Such is that *logica utens* which European
civilization owes mainly to the Aristotelian *Organon* and to the
great use and enrichment of this by the mediaeval scholastics. It is
no doubt an ill, maybe even a great ill calling for correction, when
a truth has been left unspoken or an error has been spoken. But
worse still is it when an error is presented in confused, disordered,
incorrect, and perpetually contradictory shape, wrapped up at
every point in the language of the passions, so that the critic or corrector loses heart, unable to cope with the constancy and violence
of such ignorance, and turns his back without having overcome it,
leaving it to its own fate. By comparison it is better that the error
should remain provisionally in command of the argument, if only
it be consecutively set forth, set forth, in fact, with such stringency
that this very stringency will at a given moment halt and arrest
and execute it at the conclusion of that well-spun argument which
will have rendered the original fallacy transparent, bringing it to
a confession of its fault. The education in "formal" reasoning
which during two thousand years Europe received first from the
Greek sophists and philosophers and later from the Catholic universities of the Middle Ages, and finally from the secular schools
and universities, has not always been appraised at its full value,
whether because advantages which have become common property are always undervalued, or because minds which were turned
to that other speculative, dialectical, profound logic, turned away
from the periodical distractions and unfair competition of the
formalistic logic. However, where the want of the formal discipline
was obvious and harmful, this did not pass unnoticed. I remember
the Russian Chadaiev, in 1828, noted this as a deficiency in the

Russian people, remarking sadly, "Le syllogisme de l'Occident nous est inconnu."

Now this function of formalistic logic which arrays the truth and renders it more easily communicable, but similarly arrays error, rendering it more limpid and therefore easier to see through – so that both truth and error are left intact beneath the veil of logical method whose benefits are conferred impartially, maintaining the argument at a rational level and excluding recourse to the stirring of feelings or other irrelevancies – this or the same sort of function is performed analogously by that aesthetic formalism which treats matters of judgement and philosophy, of history, of science, and matters too of exhortation, menace, flattery, love, pain – in a word the whole range of the intrinsically non-poetic – as though they were poetic, attending to harmony of diction, rhythm, melody, coherence, and proportion of images, in a word to all those details and all those minutiae which are needful in good prose, that is good literature. Should it happen that suddenly an inspiration of true poetry should spring out of this, the heart will rejoice, but will at the same time withdraw and ward it off like a temptation or defer it: this not being a permitted occasion for poetry. The man of literature or prose has no wish to compose poetry, feeling indeed that the mere touch of this adversary would undo the web that he has skilfully woven. Yet he wants to adopt for his own use the "idea" of poetry, or as one might say the "Aestheticity" without the "poeticity", its depthless surface, its form which, in being severed from the content, is severed from itself, is no more itself but an external vesture, utilizable as such, a coat of all those colours and shades which may from time to time be suited to the spirit of the man of literature, of prose, according as his mood is austere, calm, solemn, conversational, or gay. Sometimes it happens that he despises or thinks he despises literature, proclaiming that he means to write just those words which come to his lips, the words of common and popular speech. Do not believe him. Not that he is a liar, but he certainly deceives himself. Just on such an occasion he is likely to be more of a man of letters than ever. Good literature will have become a second nature to him, so that the more subtle and shy and aristocratic his art, the more he will seem to himself to be borne on the current of the natural and popular. At other times he may show disdain and haughtiness towards poetry as being by comparison with literature a frivolity. Had I time, I might quote examples of this attitude. It has been remarked that the Greeks and Romans strictly practised the separation of the writers of poetry from the writers of prose. We have no knowledge of prose works of Sophocles or Euripides, of Virgil or Lucretius or Propertius, while the verses composed by the supreme man of prose and literature, Cicero, became proverbial as ridiculous attempts, *ridenda poëmata*. The modern poets have been more versatile composing, as they still do, worthy and important prose works. I merely remark on this fact in passing, and do not draw any consequences from it, though it may be worth someone else's attention. Instead I will observe that in the sphere of the pictorial and plastic arts, and of music and architecture, as well as in that of the "spoken word" or articulated utterance, there are to be found "literary" works. Connoisseurs and critics recognize these at once, but are wrong in despising them, for they have their own value and serve their purpose excellently.

I come to the third query. Whose handiwork is this prose or literature? We must of course discard the suggestion that it is the joint work of the poet and the non-poet when they *coniurent amice*. Such an agreement is not strictly speaking possible, and, were it, the products of the collaboration would be feeble in the extreme, the result of a series of transactions and mis-tones. But neither may we attribute it to the poet alone, for we have already delineated his impatient and tempestuous, domineering and disdainful treatment of any content which resists and holds its own ground. And here the content, whether of philosophic and historic thought, of scientific construction, of deliberate effort to induce in others a state of mind propitious to some action, or of utterance for the relief of one's own mental turmoil, has to be fully respected in all its weightiness and precision. Indeed if the satisfaction of the aesthetic urge is accomplished in a measure exceeding what is felt to be the complement and perfection of the thought or the excitement of the feelings which is at stake, then the content resists assimilation to an aesthetic form which flies asunder like an ill-fitting garment. Indeed a true fit can be accomplished only by dint of a long training in that, as it were, diplomatic capacity to accord two wills in such manner that neither abases itself but each finds in the other some interest common to both, the energy of natural expression sacrificing as much of itself as does not help on the purpose in hand, and acquiring a brightness of beauty which shines not for its own sake but for the help which it can render. Such "practical tact" plays in literature the same sort of role as the "aesthetic taste" plays in poetical composition. Its part is not that of the creative genius operating with *quodam sensu sine ratione et arte*, but is an operation with a calculating and selective adroitness, as in the handling of a technical instrument. The author of this handiwork is, then, the practical mind, which works identically in every practical business save for the variations called for in the different tasks presented to it: in our case, then, not the practical spirit of the engineer building a machine, the chemist compounding a drug, the soldier planning a bombardment or an air-raid, but that of the man who would present in fine array, and at the same time in the fullness of their being, the results of his efforts as a philosopher, historian, scientist, orator, politician, or maybe simply his agitations, his affections, his feelings.

So now the present lecturer, that old foe of Rhetoric, which he once abhorred for having penetrated or having been introduced into the sacred precincts of poetry, takes up such an attitude as one of the poets of the Italian Risorgimento advised his countrymen to take up towards the Germans: once they had been driven back across the Alps they should be treated again as brothers. Having expelled Rhetoric from those precincts, I feel it my duty and pleasure to make peace and to suggest to my former foe lines of defence which were not previously available. I will observe that Rhetoric unwittingly tended to provide a theory, not of poetry, but of literature, offering or furnishing to this end the concepts proper to Rhetoric, first and foremost the fundamental practical concept of the πρέπον, the suitable or appropriate. Not without reason Rhetoric then went on to distinguish in literature form and content, the raiment and the body which it clothed, calling the former the ornament. And I will not now be too strait-laced or severe about that description of a "proper" or "naked" expression contrasted with the ornate or metaphorical expression, but will understand it as meaning the natural, savage, or barbarian expression which not having undergone an aesthetic elaboration and clarification remains in its previous condition as non-aesthetic fact.

Before closing this lecture, let me dwell again for a moment on the concept of civilization as the process of redemption of humanity from barbarism, a process in which the formation and progress of literary expression is, as we have said, an important factor. Truth to tell, the radiation of poetic or aesthetic virtue works not only at one point but throughout the body of civilization. From it come all those customs and relations in human societies which we call gentle and gallant, and thus (to take perhaps the most striking and imaginatively convincing example), those ceremonial features of capital executions, in ancient if not in modern times, according to which the executor of high purposes (for by such a title was his function ennobled), before seizing upon the condemned, went down on his knees to him to ask pardon since what he was about to do was done not in hatred but in obedience to the guardians of the law. In one of my essays I have attributed to Aesthetics (considered by professorial philosophers to be a specialized science of secondary importance, not to be taken too seriously) an outstanding importance for all the other branches of philosophy, for their problems have analogues and correspondences with those of aesthetics the solution of which can help on the solution of their own. To this I must now add an affirmation of the importance of poetry and art, not in their theory but in their concreteness, for the social, political, and moral institutions of men. I should be sorry if this efficacy which I attribute to the philosophy of art, in the field of theory, and to art itself in the field of practice, were regarded as a paradox in which I indulge merely because I have myself delighted in those studies. Let me say then that this idea, far from being paradoxical, lives already in the ancient conception of the poet as the teacher of peoples whom he drew forward out of a condition of barbarism and set to build their city to the tune of his lyre.

Speaking of this powerful efficacy of poetry in the origination of literature and of civilized behaviour, I may here appropriately comment upon an important observation of Goethe. I have mentioned it on another occasion, but it still remains little known and unutilized even in France, where it should have roused much attention seeing that it refers directly to a particular aspect of the French spirit. As far as I know the only critic to mention it was Sainte-Beuve in his *Tableau de la poésie française au XVI siècle*, though he read it and took his version from a French translation fantastic rather than incomprehensible, the work of two ignoramuses – hence the passage is in France as good as unknown. It is a note to a German edition of Diderot's *Neveu de Rameau* entitled *Geschmack* (taste). Goethe points out that in France, especially since Louis XIV, "the various kinds of poetry were treated as if they were various grades of society, each one having its own code of manners", much as there are different conventions according as one is in exclusively male or in mixed or in highly distinguished company. Now the *convenances* which prevail in such a well-ordered society were transferred to tragedy, comedy, odes, and other literary types, and according to a supposed code of manners certain images and words were admitted or excluded in each class. Hence *goût* in French came to have an altogether different and almost opposite significance to that of *Geschmack* in German, which meant poetic taste. Now such an application of the rules of good society to poetry was doubtless still more absurd and harmful than those mistaken but practically inoffensive distinctions prescribed by Rhetoric. For they were the torment of the great poets and the comfort of the minor and feeble. But it was the fact that both sets of rules, those of literature and those of good behaviour in society, came from the same source, that is from the aesthetic formalistic adornment both of immediate, natural expression, and of social relations, which facilitated such an application in France of drawing-room conventions to poetry. This remark of Goethe on French *goût* I have chosen for the conclusion of my talk today in the course of which I have been obliged to insist upon a number of difficult because highly unaccustomed distinctions, knowing well that I could not and cannot implant my solutions in your minds unless for your part, by dint of meditating these problems and theories, you discover them for yourselves, or for that matter discover better ones to pass beyond them and take their place.

[1948]

VI

THE HISTORIC-AESTHETIC CRITERION

Scepticism in the aesthetic field has the same ground as other scepticisms. It springs from the imagination that on the one hand there are things, and on the other hand there are men with their ever-changing feelings, which they, poor dupes, give out for thoughts and judgements, whereas being in reality unable ever to break the boundaries of feeling, they can in fact never attain to truth about things. However, reality is not really composed in that way, of things and of feelings. It is wholly composed of acts. Thought is act, fancy is act. There are no acts which do not attain to themselves, and by following their own nature, achieve their own end, whatever that may be. The supposed variance among men in respect of their concepts and judgements, moral ideas, discriminations of the beautiful from the ugly, that variance which scepticism mounts so gaily as its favourite war horse, may indeed have some appearance of reality, and may be allowed to pass as a subject of careless conversation, but strictly speaking it has no real existence. If we look closely at this variance in the field which we are now attending to, that of poetry, our analysis will show us no variance at all but a diversity of acts which do not clash with one another. Take that little poem of Catullus, "Vivamus, mea Lesbia, atque amemus". Let us say that in a crowd of men some say that this poem is beautiful, others the opposite. Let us now first make a distinction in the crowd. Some or many of the speakers have not really felt any impression of beauty or of ugliness. They are simply repeating the words of others or saying what first comes into their head in order to have an air of intelligence and knowledge, or of enthusiasm or superiority. They represent no variance of feeling but are mere vociferators, and daily experience tells us what a large part they play in the realm of babble, where vanity fair deals in poetry just as in philosophy, politics, and all else. Too much honour is done to these in terming them opponents. In practice the honour is withheld and they are either left alone to get on with their chatterings, their admirations, their condemnations, or are passed by with a smile. The two remaining cases must now be investigated. There are on the one hand – in the crowd – those who have genuinely experienced a feeling of agreement and pleasure, on the other hand those who have genuinely experienced the opposite feeling. Now, if that poem is beautiful, the soul which entered into relation with that beauty needs must have become a participator in and proclaimer of that joy. As to the others it needs must be supposed – by the same token – that they entered into a relation, not with the poetry as poetry, but with the matter of the poem which (to continue with our example of the poem of Catullus) they may have mistaken for information about a moral act; for having judged this act reprehensible, they judge the poem to be ugly since it is a celebration of sensual delight, an invitation to oceans of kisses, hundreds upon hundreds, sufficient to drown that recollection of the Four Last Things which is the one perpetual guarantee against falling into sin. What we are here saying is confirmed by the frequent experience that when the condemning judges are made to listen to the beauties of the poem which they condemn as ugly, and when such a recital succeeds in touching their aesthetic sensitiveness, they will often retort: "Yes, as form it is beautiful, but as poetry it is ugly", or the like. Those who feel in this way, whose arguments and answers are of this sort, are, like those of whom we spoke earlier, legion. We will not concede to these, either, the status of opponents. They are, we will say, moralists, incapable of breaking the bounds of their one and only passion, dry of heart and of fancy. We are left with only one case, that of those who feel the beauty of what is beautiful: the spectacle of contrasting feelings about works of poetry vanishes like a bad dream.

But truly, without recourse to such methodic demonstration, the "auctoritas humani generis" sufficed to show it up for a waking dream. We can look back upon an age-long, lively discussion at work on the arguments of poetry and beauty, a keen and unflagging meditation on the principles underlying them, and then (which even alone might impress us) that vast, ever growing, ever improving mass of scholarly labour devoted to their service, from the Alexandrine grammarians' work – or, to go further back in time, from that of the editors of the age of Pisistratus – to that of the Italian school of the Renaissance, that of the French, Dutch, English, German, modern European, and modern American schools. Work of this sort was not disdained by men like Poliziano who were themselves poets. As author of the *Miscellanea* he took part in it and promoted it. Surely so broad, multiple, and severe a task (as this enquiry into art and beauty) would never have been shouldered and sustained by the human race (which as a whole avoids wasting its time) if the aim had been an impossible one like that of reproducing pleasures of a practical order, as, for example, reconstituting conditions of the palate and the stomach such as to allow of enjoying and digesting the acorns and raw flesh which were so tasty to our remote ancestors, or the "black broth" of the Spartans, or to render pleasurable a variation of our modern cuisine with those mediaeval recipes, or even those of the sixteenth and seventeenth centuries which seem so fearful when we read them in ancient cookery books. Heaven knows what it would be like to have to "relive" those experiences. We should certainly fare no better than the guests of Madame Dacier to whom, according to the legend or the anecdote, she served up the aforesaid "black broth". For the learned lady had, it seems, by dint of scholarly researches discovered the ingredients and the mode of cooking that dish, forgetting only to provide the Academicians whom she had invited with ancient Spartan stomachs.

* *
*

There is, then, no getting rid of that vicious circle, without getting rid at the same time of the very idea of poetry, and no other course remains for us save to heighten our attention to a degree at which it will at last become clear that the circle is not vicious at all, but is rather, if we like so to regard it, magical. The magic is that same by dint of which each of us at every moment penetrates the other, so that we live and think only thanks to the concurrent life and thought of others, and are thus at one stroke personal and social, individual and universal, human beings and humanity. In virtue of such magic there occurs the daily miracle of the learning of foreign languages: without it, it would not suffice to have presented to our senses and our intelligences the objects, customs, events, persons, about which propositions are framed in those languages, nor to know the broad and abstract correspondences of meaning between the foreign articulated sounds and the abstract articulated sounds of our own familiar tongue. All the highly useful information which linguistic scholarship gives us would remain dispersed and inert, save for the fundamental and essential fact that we are speaking beings and that our foreign conversationalist is also a speaking being, so that his and our vibrations are of the same sort, vibrations of our common humanity, so that consent and sympathy end by making our utterances mutually comprehensible.

It is not really only those which we call new and foreign languages that are such, but, to speak strictly and logically, every word that we hear is a new and foreign language, never before uttered, unidentifiable with any of those ever uttered before. And if thus hearing it for the first time we yet understand it, we do so by one of those acts of consent and sympathy which we have described as fundamental and essential. These acts of consent are always preceded by efforts, by some "philological preparation" greater or smaller, obvious, concealed, or almost invisible, learned from books or supplied by one's memory, slow and difficult or easy and lightning-quick in such degree as to make the solemn description "philological" seem rather grotesque. But in fact all poetic creation, and re-creation of poetry in ourselves, is simply an expression of new language, it being an illusion, which we will not here pause to confute, that poets, and, in general, speaking men make use of articulated sounds as they might of ready-made tickets which it is their part merely to dispose or redispose in some arrangement – an illusion sprung from the mythology of grammarians and lexicographers. But indeed the statement that all new poetry is new language is attested by common experience and reflection. It is a disaster when poetry proves to be old language, the mechanical combination of forms already fixed, words already spoken. When it is not the poet with his creative inspiration but the language, or sum of expressions already coined, which dictates the poem, the product or outcrop is either a mere toy, though perhaps a very dazzling one, or a mere accident, like that legendary sponge of Apelles.

What happens is that with the articulate sound there enters into the soul of the listener or reader the image which was expressed in that sound and was that sound. If reception and understanding are impeded by some obscurity, some hiatus, it will be necessary to apply and wait for new aids from "philological scholarship" (in the broad and yet precise sense in which we have used this term). These will illuminate the obscurity and fill in the hiatus, a process in which any personal imagination on our part would be out of place. A feeling of repugnance against the introduction of any such extraneous influence accompanies the re-creation of a poem, and is one and the same as the feeling of reverence for the poem. For in the presence of the poem one should behave, it has been said, as in the presence of a man of importance, hat in hand, listening to what he says without interrupting him.

What is achieved in this process is an historical interpretation, but this is not to be understood in the sense of an origination of the judgement proper to the historian (for that would carry us outside the sphere of poetry into that of reflective thought). Nor yet must the achievement be viewed as one of sheer scholarship, for scholarship is in itself not historical, and performs here, in any case, a merely instrumental office. What we here mean by an historical interpretation is the re-creation, as against the creation, of a poem which, since it already exists, must necessarily exist in history (there is no existence outside history). There is nothing new about the fact of such historical interpretation, which must needs always have been so. But the clear affirmation of this point of theory, the inference from it of a particularized historical method, has been a triumph of that deeper conception of history which gradually matured throughout the eighteenth century, was progressively, though interruptedly, elaborated in the nineteenth, and is still fighting its way forward. Its adversaries are relativists, contingentists, phenomenists, actualists. In the particular field of poetry and art they assume the guise of hedonists.

The affirmation of the historical character of the interpretation of poetry brings into evidence something which this has in common with the interpretation of all those other sorts of "expression" which we have analysed and defined – the expressions of prose, oratory, literary entertainment, literary outpouring of feelings. None of these is comprehensible, in itself, until with the aid of philological scholarship it has been felt and understood in its historical existence. Even that immediate expression which is a non-expression requires such an historical interpretation, being, as we know, a piece of evidence which it is incorrect to integrate with the play of the imagination, but correct to integrate with observation and penetration of the reality to which the evidence testifies. (The proceeding is like that of the medical man in making his diagnosis.) Poetry is an historical fact, but one which has its own particular quality, different from that of other historical facts. It is like all of these in that it originates in the existing reality, and issues forth (as they all do) beyond the limit set by that reality. But its manner of issuing forth is peculiar to itself, consisting in the intuitive conjunction and fusion of the particular with the universal, the individual with the cosmos, so that, as Goethe once said of art in general, its point of departure is the "characteristic", but its result is "beauty". The historical interpretation of poetry is then at one and the same time also its aesthetic interpretation, this latter being neither a negation nor an extension of its historical character, but being that historical character itself. It is all one whether we call it "historical" interpretation, letting this adjective stand for a re-ference to the "history of poetry", or alternatively "aesthetic inter-pretation", letting this other adjective stand for a reference to the "poetry which is historically existent". It is for clearness of ex-position, and not from a taste for eclectic combination of terms, that we have written the term "historic-aesthetic", rather than sought to invent a term to express more vigorously the fusion of the two elements – two, when viewed in abstract analysis, but in reality constituting a single act.

We are now in a position to understand what is reasonable and what is unreasonable in the contentions of each of the two rival schools of poetic interpretation, which have challenged one another so fiercely in Italy, especially in those early years of the present century which were so rich in intellectual vigour. Their contest was not useless, for, exhausted by what was illogical in its own contentions, each one relinquished the field when there appeared a force, opposed to both, proclaiming that one and only true and legitimate doctrine of interpretation which is expounded above. One school boasted the description "historical", but should really at best have been described as "historicistical", with a note of disapproval in the term, for it set out to interpret poetry not as poetry but as prose, oratory, and so forth. Such characters could indeed be found in some poems, constituting their extraneous and unpoetical portion. In others they could not be found, but were introduced by the work of the imagination which misunderstood and distorted the poetic elements themselves. But usually the school treated poems simply as documents of non-poetical history, useful in the construction of biographies of authors and as portrayals of the life of certain ages or races. The second school boasted the description "aesthetic" but should have been disapprovingly termed "aestheticizing". For it met the first school's pseudo-historical interpretation of poetry with a similarly caricaturish pseudo-aesthetic canon of interpretation. In fact both these schools appeared like caricatures; both the grave, ponderous, yet simple-minded interpreters of poetry as non-poetry, and the less simple-minded, indeed rather fraudulent, cheerful upholders of their own semi-poetry at the expense of the genuine poetry of the poets. This contest has been forgotten in Italy. The former school now counts few adherents and has lost its importance. The adherents of the latter seem wholly to have vanished. In Italy, then, there is no longer the same degree of confusion. But in other countries of high culture the same seems not to be true. They have not experienced such a debate, or not in all its depth and intensity, and have accordingly made a smaller and less sure progress.

Yet if these exaggeratedly historical and aesthetic doctrines may be said to belong to the past in Italy, and to form, themselves, a subject of historical enquiry, this gives no ground for a feeling of immunity from the tendencies in question, the tendency to historicize poetry in a mistaken manner, and the tendency to put in the place of poetry new and personal products of the imagination, two erroneous and perilous doctrines apt to mislead even those who in theory profess the true doctrine and endeavour to frame judgements conformable to it.

Here are two examples of the errors which can result from such ways of thought. The first is taken from the argument on the right way of interpreting ancient poetry. By this term is meant Graeco-Roman poetry, though in truth there is no poetry which is not more or less ancient, which does not belong to the past, being as such both detached from us and linked to us, with a possible exception for poetry freshly created at this very moment of speaking, which accordingly has no need of interpretation. Those warnings which we hear, that ancient poetry should on no account be interpreted in the light of contemporary and modern ideas and feelings, are not superfluous. Should we ignore them the result would really be, not an interpretation at all, but a new act of the fancy. Homer, in Cesarotti's version, thus took on the guise of a bewigged and besworded eighteenth-century gentleman in flowered waistcoat – today, perhaps, the temptation would be rather to portray him as a twentieth-century decadent. In this way we should fall back into that sort of aestheticism which we have already disposed of. However, if starting with the rejection of aestheticism we should go on to require an interpretation of Graeco-Roman poetry in the light of Graeco-Roman feelings, we should be falling into the contrary error of historicism, forgetting that those ideas and feelings and the reality of which they were part were transfigured in the poetry, shedding their historical particularity in order to take on a human universality. The episode of Hector and Andromache, or that of Nausicaa and the Phaeacian islanders, belong not to Greece or any particular locality or date, but to an ideal clime, an eternal season. Mastery of the Greek language, knowledge of historical events and of customs, and all those aids which are procured to us by scholarship, what are they but the ladder set up for climbing to a region where, when we have arrived, ladders are no more of use, the earth having faded out in that heaven? For a confirmation of this truth, I suggest reading Homer in one of those editions which are illustrated with figures reproduced from Greek vases, gems, paintings and sculptures, figures of warriors in their chariots, archaic deities, filleted priests, sea-farers embarked on ships of ancient type. The result is not merely displeasing but disgusting. What have these manikins, these barbaric idols, these harnesses of war and navigation to do with Achilles and Ajax, Athena and Aphrodite, the battle scenes of the Iliad, the seascapes of the Odyssey? Another lesson may be learned from the distaste which poets – real poets, not poetasters – always feel when asked to prefix their own portraits as the frontispiece to their poetical works, matched by the disappointment of readers who in such realistic portraits fail to find the likeness of the poets dear to them, whence the resort to ideal portraits (the poetasters themselves often arrange to be portrayed with tumbling locks and eyes raised to heaven for the reception of inspiration). Poets, it is well known, seek to draw a veil over the identity of persons and occasions which have given rise to and suggested their poems. And it is well known how stupid and odious are the revelations which scholars make when they unveil such circumstances with the design of throwing light upon the poetry. Goethe was greatly indignant when in his own lifetime he was subjected to such nuisances purporting to give a foretaste of his immortality. How should we gain or what comfort receive by making the personal acquaintance of Lesbia and Cynthia, Beatrice and Laura, Charlotte, Fanny, Aspasia, Nerina, Silvia, the "dark lady", the "veiled lady"? We could but measure once again the distance which as we so well know separates amorous imagining from factual reality and that still wider distance between amorous desire and poetry. Might we even discover as some writer (whose identity I forget) wrote, that all those women were ugly, and in feelings, language, and behaviour little different from serving wenches?

The second example of the dangers of such a way of thought

which I will cite is the obstinate research which goes on concerning the aims and the theories of the poets, without an understanding of which it is said to be impossible to understand their poems. But if this be so let us in the first place, with great clearness, ask how it is that we can understand the poetry of poets who set before themselves no aim, and had no theory about the feelings of which they rendered a lively representation. For surely no one will maintain that aims and theories – the appurtenances of the orator and the philosopher – are indispensable to the poet, as a superaddition of another or of two other functions to his own? The truth is that even those poets who are orators and philosophers besides, and thus dispose of aims and of theories, cannot express poetically that which is only expressible in oratory and prose. And therefore, in their creative operations, they put them on one side, take distance from them, or retain them simply as particular tones of feeling, redeemed from all conceptual coldness or purposive crudity. Only by an optical illusion do we espy in Greek tragedy the idea of Fate or in the work of a Christian poet the idea of Providence. Fate and Providence are concepts which can be thought but cannot be represented, and the representation in question can never be other or more than that of a feeling of fear and resignation (to which is given the name of fate), or that of a feeling of trust and hope (to which is given the name of providence) – lights and shadows, not concepts. To the question what they think of fate and providence, of justice and injustice, of the laws of Gods and men, and the implied accusation of impiety in such matters, the poets should make the same answer as Paolo Veronese when charged before the judges of the Inquisition of having introduced into his picture a figure not warranted by the account in the scriptures: he painted, he said, "by such standards as were within the measure of his understanding", and he had introduced the figure in question "for purposes of decoration, as the custom is", because a certain colour or shade was necessary for his purposes irrespective of the sacred narrative. Painters, said Veronese, "take the same licence in such matters as do poets and madmen".

[1936]

VII

THE INDULGENCE DUE TO TRUE POETS

He who, reading a poem, identifies himself with its author, elevating and conforming his own spirit to the spirit of the poet, raises himself, like the poet, above particular interests and affections incidental to the given circumstances, and like the poet cleanses himself in a catharsis and opens himself to the delight of beauty.

Altogether different is his experience when he meets with pseudo-poetry, works offering themselves with poetic pretension and appearance but discovered to be, when one seeks to re-create them in oneself and to savour them, simply utilitarian productions, which are called, in virtue of such deception and disappointment, "ugly". This discovery occasions distaste and displeasure, but the producer of the work in question experienced enjoyment.

Yes, he experienced enjoyment, for in thus producing things which to others appear ugly, he cultivates the belief and the illusion that he is bringing forth works of beauty, and therein he satisfies his own ambition, flatters his own vanity, as of one appearing in his own and others' eyes to be a brilliant man, an artist, a creator. The bad poet "gaudet in se et se ipse miratur", and thanks to this self-satisfaction often cuts in society an agreeable and amiable figure, like that Suffenus portrayed by Catullus, "venustus et dicax et urbanus", who, however, in his verse writing "unus caprimulgus aut fossor videtur". As a verse-writer he is a butcher, a tormentor of the ear and of the fancy: the man of culture therefore avoids and flees him, only, however, to be pursued by Suffenus with praises, flatteries, caresses dispensed in the hope of eliciting compliments to feed his illusion and appease his vanity. By dint of satire and comedy revenge may be wrought against the bad poet, but can any revenge equal the torment which he is wont to inflict with a greater display of enterprise and tenacity than any buzzing and biting insect?

If the really bad poets are less disliked than the mediocre or the baddish, this is because they are more easily spotted by all, and put out of harm's way. Little odium is reserved for those who openly and frankly traffic in ugliness, for they do no harm to anyone who refrains from seeking them out. Indeed for the most part they are well aware of the true value of their work, and tell you sensibly and modestly: "Don't read my novel, it's not meant for the likes of you", or even emulate the rudely frank stage-manager of "Nanà" who protested: "Don't talk to me about my theatre, call it my brothel."

Our detestation of the ugly should in any case not be carried to such lengths as to constitute an "odium auctoris" prejudicing the enjoyment of poetry where it may be found. For poetry, which sometimes flowers in loneliness on the arid rocks of the intellect, sometimes also flourishes in the midst of ugliness. Said Boileau: "Parmi son fatras obscur, souvent Brébeuf étincelle", and Francesco Petrarca, with a different intent: "Tardi non fur mai grazie divine" – "The divine graces never came too late" –, and some there are who, after producing for years on end inferior literature, of a sudden, all unexpectedly, come out with a powerfully conceived story or drama. There are poets, as we all know, remembered for a single fine sonnet.

Suffenus is self-satisfied, but not Virgil. Virgil is for ever aware of the imperfections of his own work, and not only aware, but zealous to eliminate them; sometimes in vain, so that, dying, he ordered the destruction of the manuscript of the Aeneid. It is not the ugly work that exhibits imperfections. It was, from birth, unpoetical, and its life, such as it is, is of another order. Imperfections are displayed by work which was, from birth, poetical, a heavenly creation bearing the marks, on its vesture, of its earthly travel. The poet (akin in this to the moral man who suffers from those stains of impurity which are never absent from any of his actions) suffers from the faults which he sees in his work and which, even to the smallest of them, he would fain wash out, so that he might send the work on its way through the world, robed in white as the King of France would send his daughter, his beloved and sole heir (the image is that of Jacopone for the Soul), to be admired in that whiteness wherever her way should lie. But poetry comes into men's minds with the suddenness of lightning, and men labour after in the wake of poetry, charmed and striving to retain all that they can from the visitation, which they would fain prolong in order to obtain a clear and detailed vision. But as they look it is gone, possibly to return anew, less fleetingly, but possibly not, so that the poet is left with his words, those which are illumined and those which remain opaque, while he awaits and invokes, with or without success, some new ray to shine on them. Thus Virgil, anxious not to lose the whole for the sake of a part or a particle, the maximum for the minimum, and not to let slip the happy moment, was accustomed, his biographer tells us, to jot down imperfect or provisional verses ("dum scriberet, ne quid impetum moraretur, quaedam imperfecta reliquit, alia laevissimis versis veluti fulsit"), and comforted himself and his friends with a humorous comparison of those verses to *tibicines* able to sustain the construction until solid columns could be substituted for them. The poet suffers from such imperfections, yearns to amend them, yet a sort of mystic reverence for the experience which he has undergone often deters him from the risks of the attempt, for the cold intellect is not the warm fancy, and the instrument with which one seeks to "polire" may (as Quintilian says) "exterere", that is carry away what is most valuable. Nothing then remains save to ask indulgence, as Dante implicitly asked it when he confessed that the form often failed to fit the intention of art through the unresponsiveness of the matter, "perché a risponder la materia è sorda", and as Goethe asked it explicitly with his request that no one stretch out a correcting and warning hand and thereby stop the poet's mill in its rotations, for, said Goethe, whoever understands knows also how to pardon.

Men of penetrating taste, the large-minded and generous-hearted, are always ready to make such allowances, in the domain of poetry as in that of morals, for what they look at is the substance of a work, an action, a life, leaving it to such as Zoilus (men of the breed of those valets for whom no man is a great man, the close inspectors of every hair espied on their master's coat) to display unbending severity. Such are those commentators who painstakingly enumerate the imperfections, negligences, errors of the poet, and then, when they would fain praise, provide a counter-catalogue of beauties and merits. What they never can understand is that the defects are incidental to the merits, that hesitations or errors of detail result from the impetuous power which invests the whole, and that the starting point for criticism is the centre and not the outskirts of the work. In Alfieri there is much harshness and abstract rationalization, but with all that he is much more of a poet than the smooth, nay in his way perfect Metastasio. Manzoni's *Cinque Maggio* has often been censured verse by verse, sentence by sentence, not wholly without reason, yet it is great lyrical poetry. In the presence of interpreters proclaimed and self-proclaimed as exquisite and subtle, exhibiting as glorious discoveries of their own sensitiveness and acumen the imperfections and weak points of the poets, the poetical reader, the man of serious taste, is moved to impatience and resentment. He feels inclined to say: Do you think I didn't notice these things myself, before you? – but unlike you I did not feel called upon or inclined to point them out or underline them.

Besides such imperfections in poetry as are by their nature susceptible of correction and are in fact for the most part corrected in the course of the work or when the creative mood returns, there is also the unpoetic element which is incapable of correction. The author felt neither dislike nor guilt when he penned the passage, nor does the reader when he reads it, but views it with a sort of indifference. Such are the structural parts, the conventional features, in every poetical work, sometimes barely visible but at other times highly evident, expecially in works of great extension and complexity. Well known are what the French call *chevilles*, the Italians *zeppe*, or, as Galileo called such props and fillings, the *intarsiature*, while Gino Capponi described them as the "mathematical" parts of a work embedded among the poetical. Foscolo said that no poetic genius could avail to render them superfluous: they were humanly unavoidable faults. This, incidentally, is as much as to say that they are not faults at all, for otherwise they would be remediable. From whence then do they really arise?

From the need to maintain the rhythmic unity of the expression even at the cost of a partial sacrifice of coherent image to sound. Yet sound is itself an image evoked by the poetic motive. Think of those four admirable lines in which Ariosto shows Fiordiligi overcome by dismay and distress when the two barons, Brandi-marte's comrades in the fight that has just concluded, enter her presence silently and without him:

> Tosto che entrâro, ed ella loro il viso
> Vide di gaudio in tal vittoria privo,
> Senz'altro annunzio sa, senz'altro avviso,
> Che Brandimarte suo non è più vivo! . . .

In the third verse the two words *annunzio* and *avviso* are syn-onyms and perhaps neither fits the case perfectly. The word *avviso* was chosen for the sake of the rhyme. Yet that accelerated rhythm which results from the succession of the two words, severed and linked at once by the intervening caesura, echoes the rapid heart-beat of Fiordiligi, creating a higher poetic image, and the rhyme at the end seems to arrest that heart-beat in dismay at the sight of the two men only, and of their features unlit by any joy despite the victory.

It is customary to put the blame for such alleged failures on the seduction and corruptions of "rhyme", for the future avoidance of whose dangerous temptations it is proposed to do away with rhyme, to write blank verse, or occasionally rhyming verse in which the rhymes may turn up at sweet will and not in any fixed place. But then at other times blame is put upon the metre, the measured strophe, and the use is recommended of "free verse", exempt from the regularities of scansion and recurring stanza. Yet if those blank verses, those unmeasured stanzas, unregulated lines, are really the product of poetic inspiration, and if they accordingly carry in themselves their own necessity and law, they will always, perforce, have to make use of some sort of props or fillings or whichever of the above-mentioned terms we use for these. But if, as so often is the case especially with compositions in free verse, they are just spiritless excogitations, then they will likewise be helped out with fillings, only they will be ugly fillings of ugly material, on which nobody will ever, as happens with works of true poets, smile indulgently, nay almost approvingly, terming them "amiable defects". The fillings used by true poets for the sake of harmonious expression are, truth to say, neither beautiful nor ugly, but are simple props for the upholding of poetical effect.

In writing about these delicate matters, one recalls that saying of Master Eckhart when he was almost frightened by his own profound but potentially heretical statement that the eye of God is the same eye with which man sees God; that if God were not, man would not be, but neither would God be if man were not. Eckhart makes haste to remark: "But such things it is not necessary to know, for they are easily misunderstood and can only be rightly understood in conception." What we are here saying must be known to the philosopher, the interpreter, the critic, but the poets do better not to know them, or not to linger over them, but rather to abide in their blessed simplicity as unsatisfiable strivers for perfection who none the less, when needs must, set to work on the humble task of filling in gaps for the sake of that very perfection. The critics do well to treat them with the same sort of good manners which restrains us from calling attention to the fact that some man, though he is alive and moving, requires glasses to see his way and a stick to lean on while walking.

Conventional or structural devices have also and analogously to be brought into play for the linking of two pieces of poetry together. As I have already quoted one of Ariosto's loveliest stanzas, so, as a small example of this latter type of resort to conventional expedient, I will quote Dante in one of his most poetic episodes, that in which, after Francesca da Rimini has recounted her love, hers and his, and the tragedy which led both of them to one death, ending her words with a curse against the killer, the fratricide, to her in turn the pilgrim of the dark regions tells how her story has moved him, and asks her how in the hour of gentle sighs love had granted occasion for unlawful desires.

> Ma dimmi: al tempo de' dolci sospiri,
> A che e come concedette amore
> Che conosceste i dubbiosi desiri?

Why this abrupt question? A matter of petty and improper curiosity? Hardly. The question stands there merely to link the first piece of poetry with the second in which Francesca, in a sorrowing rapture, will relate the occasion of their possession and overwhelming by passion. Those verses are like a wooden bridge giving passage from one green bank to the other. From contemplation of one bank each passes at once to contemplating the other with an attention which quite ignores the bridge. The conventional or structural aid serves to afford a full presentation of the poetry of Francesca which Dante could present in no other way, in a poem woven from the tale of encounters and queryings between souls.

These lines of Dante belong, then, to the class which includes the informative and annotative passages of poems, dramas, novels; also, for the most part, the descriptions of past events which are put into the mouth of some character, the information vouchsafed by a messenger about events happening off the stage, and in part also the reflections and comments of the Chorus in Greek tragedy, the reviews and genealogies in epic poems, psychological explanations in novels, and the introduction into any of these sorts of poetic work of characters required simply to get the plot going, and incapable, therefore, of attaining a poetic intensity. To mention one such case – If the "pius Aeneas" of Virgil never grips our fancy, our heart, as does the Dido whom he abandons, this is not, as is said, a consequence of his "piety", his being shaped for moral and religious ends, nor is it that the betrayers of love make no appeal to the poetic heart (one might reasonably affirm the contrary). It is because Aeneas was conceived to personify and celebrate the history of Rome, and his abandonment of the passionate Carthaginian queen is necessitated simply by the purpose of introducing into the poem the origin of the long enmity and war of Rome against Carthage. Goffredo, in Tasso's poem, is also pious, yet he is poetic, or anyway more poetic than the more artificial Aeneas. There is no need to multiply examples of such artifice, such joining and cementing of elements. They are easy enough to see on every hand. All that need be said is that although they have nothing poetic about them, such devices are by good poets provided with grace and charm, whereas the bad poets obtrude them gracelessly.

As before, these expedients are adopted to the end of permitting the stream of poetry to flow fully and abundantly without such loss of the higher harmony of the whole, or of the principal parts, as would occur if the stream were allowed to break up into streamlets and rills and pools. The explanation given by Chateaubriand that from time to time weariness overcomes the poet, inducing him to take a rest and to give a rest to his readers – also supposedly wearied by a too vigorous and sustained poetic pleasure – is not quite adequate. Chateaubriand added that for his part he could not wish to have the fine passages of *Le Cid* and *Horace* cemented together by "des harmonies élégantes ou travaillées" rather than by the unpretentious connexions actually provided. And anthologies of poetic "beauties" although useful for educational purposes do not wholly satisfy lovers of poetry just because they present the "beauties" in a detachment, which is somehow inappropriate, from the "structural" framework.

However, a proper regard for such "structural elements" should not be exaggerated into a mistaken and perverted attribution of poetical value to them. Such is the error committed by unskilful interpreters who either let themselves be overawed by the fame of a great poet (though truly they do him no honour in attributing the same rank to his artifice as to his poetry) or, as is so often the case, are simply lacking in poetic understanding and sensibility. I have elsewhere compared their behaviour to that of those Trojans who, after eating the food placed before them, still hungry, consumed also the farinaceous "tables" on which it was served: but food is one thing and tables are another, nor do hooks and hangers form part of a picture. But such is the import of the praise given to Corneille, Calderón, Apostolo Zeno, and others for having, it is said, devised a structure and mechanism for French tragedy, Spanish comedy, Italian melodrama, or other types of work, for the benefit of their successors whether poets or non-poets. Of the same order is the praise to Aeschylus for introducing a second actor in Greek tragedy, and to the inventors of the sonnet and the introducers of those forms into the various literatures. This misestimation of the structural element leads to a view of poetry as a succession of conventions and artifices, and of poets as the inventors of such things, whence the various inventions and devices, nay the very tricks and turns which they are supposed to have played, are made the subject of respectful and admiring specialized researches.

The indiscriminate assimilation of both the digestible and the indigestible elements has had for its consequence a reaction towards another equally fallacious theory which recognizes no right of existence for any other element in poetry than the poetic. This is an additional reason for banning the former theory. The latter theory, to which by reaction the former gives rise, can take two forms. The first of these affirms that only short poems which can be read at one stretch of, say, at the most a quarter of an hour's duration, can be poetic, and not tragedies which take several hours or poems and novels which take several days to read. The second form has it that poetry exists only in stretches or fragments, all which remains being an inert mass in or upon which the fragments or pieces are embedded or applied (so that now we have to disembed or detach them). In the first form lies the gross logical error of introducing the concept of time into an ideal process, overlooking the truth that the composition or study of a poem, whether it lasts a matter of minutes or of years, takes place in an ideal rhythm which transports the author and reader outside the realm of time. Besides, in actual fact, the poetry which is present in long poems, dramas, novels, always provided that these are poetically inspired, is not located in a few choice places but circulates through the whole. There are works from which no portion can be detached and committed to an anthology as a beauty, yet they are recognizably suffused and pervaded by poetry. This consideration rules out also the second form. It is perhaps barely worth noticing that the second form has stimulated a school of so-called Fragmentists who deliberately compose fragments in order to be sure of producing solely poetry, pure of all extraneous props and links. It may be imagined what foolishness has in fact resulted from such an attempt.

There is a further, a third case worth looking into, of the relation between structure and poetry. This is the case of a poet making use of a traditional or it may be of a newly invented tale, not in order to absorb it into his poem, transfigured into an image of his feeling, but because it is agreeable to himself or his readers, exciting in those who are predisposed to it actions and passions which are evoked by that plot, those characters, those names. The tale serves him, in fact, as a pattern on which to embroider his poetry, a pattern which is sometimes covered and virtually annulled by the embroidery, but sometimes is left partly uncovered to display itself more or less conspicuously. Even when this happens, the poetic interpreter should show indifference for the pattern and exclusive interest for the embroidery. But unskilled and un-poetic readers fall into confusion here too, confounding pattern with embroidery and poring over the former as though it had in itself the substance or breath of poetry. Hence spring all those dissertations which have been published on the right way to handle or the differing ways in which authors have handled the tales of Prometheus, Orestes, Lucretia, Sophonisba, Faust, Don Juan, and so on and so on. But evidently the poet is never caught up in such plots and characters: he has his being in the personal and the universal which he infuses into or adds to them. Shakespeare himself, who often took his highest flights from a light foothold in some popular tale or fable, yet sometimes worked upon patterns of the sort we have been mentioning. This has been made the basis for pertinacious discussions about incongruities, contradictions, and puerilities in Shakespeare, one of the most recent of such criticisms coming from Leo Tolstoi, who failed to distinguish between the plot and the poetry of King Lear.

There is finally a variant of this third case which calls not only for mention but for close attention since it concerns two at least of the great poets of our time, not indeed Homer or Shakespeare, but Dante and Goethe, each of whom was not only an outstanding poetic temperament or *Natur* (to use Goethe's description of Dante), but also a powerful thinker employing the forms of thought, and a man of warm religious and moral sensibility,

THE INDULGENCE DUE TO TRUE POETS 329

solicitous for the fate of mankind and for man's control of his life.
In their minds they harboured both the phantom shapes of poetry
and also those other concepts and motions. And they poured all of
this into their poetry and would fain have rendered it all poetical.
But actually they could render poetical only what had, in themselves, become sheer feeling, and not what had taken and kept,
in their mind and their disposition, a conceptual form, as science
and philosophy, or a practical form, as oratory, satire, and so on.
Thus Dante in the *Divine Comedy* and Goethe in *Faust* (but not
only in those poems) assembled their doctrinal convictions, their
exhortations and warnings, together with the music of their
feelings. There resulted two works of a highly composite and, in
their essence, powerfully inharmonious nature. One of them was
in external appearance well-nigh geometrical. It recounted a
journey into the three realms of the world beyond, each developed
in thirty-three cantos in tercets, the whole being preceded by an
introductory canto to bring the total number to a hundred. The
other poem was careless even of any such external unity. In each
work, the component elements are now interinvolved, now held
separate or in contrast with one another. Yet they are among the
most majestic works of the human spirit. There has arisen therefore,
among the interpreters, the so-called problem of the "unity" of
these works: does it lie in one of the elements (if so, in which) or
in a synthesis of all elements? In view of the nature of the two
works the problem was bound to arise, but, expressed in these
terms, it was also bound to be insoluble. The right terms for
putting and resolving the problem would be these: to remember
the origin of the two works, to keep clearly in mind the concept of
poetry and of non-poetry, and to distinguish, in each work, the
poetry from the structure; but at the same time to remember that
spirits so energetic as Dante and Goethe, not only in the realm of
poetry but in that of the intellect and that of morals also, did not
resort, like others who were poets and solely poets, to the use of
plots or patterns of no intrinsic value, but took patterns which
were vitally important to them, distinct from, yet conjoined
with their poetry, and nourishing it, in a dialectic and energetic

unity. In these cases, then, the pattern cannot be a matter of indifference to us in our efforts to understand the personalities of Dante and of Goethe, nor yet in our efforts to understand the features of their poetry. Yet in a sense they too, like all structure, remain indifferent: it is not in these patterns that we can hear the voice of the poet.

[1936]

VIII

LOVE POETRY AND HEROIC POETRY

THE poetry of love and the poetry of heroism (also known as virile, ethical, religious, or sublime poetry) are commonly distinguished from one another in a way which can raise no objection as long as the proceeding is recognized to be merely empirical, classificatory, indicative; suitable, for example, for fixing roughly the different features of the love poet Petrarch and of the ethico-religious poet Dante.

But if for such an empirical classification one should attempt to claim strict precision and absolute value, trouble would begin. It would impair the steadiness and unity of poetry to introduce a qualititative subdivision. So this will be avoided. But then one will feel the need to abase (or even annul) one of the two poetries in the name of the other; to consider one of the two true and genuine, the other impure and artificial.

The most frequent choice is not to deny heroic poetry in the name of love poetry (though there are many readers who in their hearts respond only to love poetry, even if they bend the knee formally to the other), but, as is the inclination of theorists and philosophers, to despise or merely tolerate love poetry while exalting, as poetry in the truest and most ideal sense, the poetry of heroism.

Such was the doctrine clearly and vigorously proclaimed by Giordano Bruno.[1] With an anticipation of Schopenhauer's much advertised view Bruno condemned the cult of Woman, who, he said, "with a Circean enchantment, serving the ends of procreation, offers us a deceptive beauty", and deserves honour and love only for that pleasure which she gives and for that service which she performs – therewith Bruno openly and directly questioned the poetic fame of Petrarch who, he said, "having no gifts for a nobler task, nursed that melancholy in order nevertheless to display his ingenuity by committing to the canvas a portrayal of the motions

1. In the dedication of the *Eroici Furori* to Sidney.

of a vulgar, animal, and bestial love pursued with pertinacity" – a task of the same order as the verses composed by others in praise of the donkey, the fly, the beetle.

The injustice of this charge, the error from which it arises, can be fully comprehended only if one takes some piece of poetry which passes for heroic, ethical, religious, or in some other way sublime, and with rapt attention submits oneself to the full effects of its force. Only let us be sure that it is true poetry. If such it is, then certainly, contrary to a muddled notion arising out of an illicit interchange or contamination and confusion of the ethical with the aesthetic and poetic sphere, we shall not find this poetry to constitute a practical resolution, a moral volition abstractly fixed in the moment of its triumph over passion, over the sensible element ("vulgar, animal, bestial", as Bruno calls it), but shall find it to be intuition and contemplation of life, of life in its intangible entirety, in the process of its intrinsic and necessary oppositions which give it continuity, unity, reality. A rectitude, heroism, religious dedication which is not concretely human, not a leave-taking of love for a higher love with a return of the first love and a renewed leave-taking, not a wrestling embracement with its own equally human opposite, can belong neither to reality nor to poetic imagery. We need not think immediately of such heroes as those of the Italian epics of chivalry, untainted warriors, utterly steadfast in the faith, yet at the same time captives and slaves of love, or of Tasso's Tancreds and Rinaldos. Stretching the limits of that sphere which is commonly denominated the sphere of love, let us rightly understand by this word the entire sensible and affective element, all that which binds us to earth and breathes desire, trepidation, pleasure, yearning, melancholy in the bosom which aspires to the sublime and for a moment attains it. Recall the Greek heroes shut inside the great horse, hearing their names called by Helen and seeming to hear the voices of their wives from far away till they began to answer and would have emerged had not Ulysses restrained them. Recall Manzoni's Frankish heroes, crossing the Alps, keeping vigil at arms in the cold nights, but remembering always the pleasant mansions left behind them, and

cherishing in their hearts the warmth of remembered colloquies
of love. The poetry which sublimates earthly affections towards
the divine is at one and the same time the poetry of those affections,
living and present even when left behind, alive in the love of the
divine which cannot be love unless it partakes of the earthly, unless
the God is made flesh. On the other side, where ever is to be found
a love poem which, if it is true poetry, does not contain ethical
and religious elements, the yearning for the infinite and the eternal,
sadness for that which passes and dies, the obscure sense of sin
with the need to redeem and to raise oneself and the loved creature
to a heaven of purity, the vain and sorrowful striving to throw
down that barrier which needs must separate the souls of the
lovers, lying as it does in the very nature of creature love, in the
insuperable finitude of that love – and then, through conflicts,
troubles, and torments, joy, hope, and despair, wild desire and the
restraint and modesty which veils and reins it, a refinement and
ennoblement of the mind, its education for the heroism of a
renunciation for the sake of a better gain, its transcendence of the
human in order to achieve a wider, fuller, deeper humanity? Who
does not feel such a travail in the lyrics of that "dear deep master
of love", Petrarch? Who does not feel that there lies his poetry,
the poetry of love?

And so, it has often been thought and said, not without reason,
that the principal, indeed the only subject of poetry is love. But
also not without reason it has been thought and said that on the
contrary poetry's one true subject is the ideal, the infinite, God.
The two statements are compatible, indeed they can, when need
be, correct each other and join together. For the sake of such
unity lovers and cultivators of poetry are rightly wont to reject
the pretensions of an imposed morality to be required of poetry
in addition to that morality which it carries in itself, in its essence
as poetry. Such an imposed morality would destroy the spontaneous moral aspiration of poetry for the sake of an arid and abstract
moral doctrine.

It will be well to add a warning that when we speak of love
poetry these two words retain that imprint of nobility which

common ways of thought attribute to them. Thanks to this, love poetry takes distance from and defends itself against other manifestations, passional or artistically literary, which threaten to annex it in virtue of an apparent similarity of argument. In the common judgement which is the basis of classifications and in the terminologies which reflect them, those verses which are called erotic, gallant, sensual, anacreontic, madrigalesque, Arcadian, Metastasian, or marked by other terms to denote their "light" and "fugitive" quality, are indeed almost by their own nature discriminated from love poetry, which is not light or fugitive, but poised and steady, not darting hither and thither like a butterfly, but rising in flight like a dove or an eagle, whereas in those other gay literary compositions there is neither intimacy nor therefore intensity, and to please and be pleased is the guiding aim. Equally there is felt to be something repugnant about allowing into the neighbourhood of love poetry any lascivious, lustful, libidinous expressions and descriptions. These indeed have for their dominant note not gaiety – they are unsmiling, unlaughing – and they are not airily light but grossly heavy, and though, having their breeding and resting ground among sharp tormenting pricks, there hangs around them the haunting image of destruction, dissolution, death, yet they do not attain to human seriousness and dignity, they are unlit by the light of the ideal, unengaged in the struggle and spiritual process of dying into new life.

As in the definition of love, so in the case of the concept of the libidinous it is well to stretch the usual boundaries beyond the customary exclusive reference to the sexual sphere. Logically we should term libidinous whatever seeks to substitute for the moral drama of the soul the sham drama, tragedy, epic, or lyric of an unbalanced sensuality, closed within itself, unable to rise above itself, seeking desperately its own solution in itself, even should the maniac who undertakes this impossible task flee from Aphrodite like the chaste Hippolytus and be a sexual ascetic. Lust is not that alone which seems to hold the primacy in such a sphere, being linked, as Bruno says, to the naturality of procreation; there is lust of war and blood, of adventure and games of hazard, of stimulants and drugs of all sorts, it being lust whenever a man loses his liberty, attaches himself spasmodically to beings or particular objects of whatever sort, putting a fetish and idol in the place of the divine and the universal which shines in each particular thing and surpasses each. The obscene, which is the open and extreme manifestation of lust, is (it has been said) unpoetic because it has no truth in it, but in greater or lesser measure all expressions, in prose or in verse, painting, or music, which partake of the libidinous, are void of truth, caught up in the convulsion of delirious activity or madness. As such, they may indeed manifest themselves as in a high degree energizing, exciting, alarming. They may call for the devoted and anxious attention of the philosopher, the close inspection of the man of learning, for whom they rank as "human documents"; but these are not titles for celebration by the human heart in its delight in pure form, nor for the spontaneous exclamation "Beautiful!", and therefore the aesthetic judgement pronounces a verdict against them. And if upon this condemnation there is ever to supervene an act of pardon, the first step must be that the moral soul of man, aroused in all its fullness and integrity, shall confront these expressions in a mood of strict seriousness, shall in thoughtful piety envelop and thrust them back to the very confines of its being, and there allow them no other function but to serve as a stimulus for counteraction, for its own development and enrichment. Thereby out of a drama which lacked all true dramatic quality, because it lacked contrast and catharsis, there will be elicited a spiritual drama, and from the basis of a dark lust there will arise the imposing edifice of a poetical masterpiece, be it Dante's episode of the drama of Rimini or the Shakespearian tragedy of Antony and Cleopatra.

Here the dialectic of poetry is found obeying its own law in harmony with the dialectic of the moral conscience. This conscience never relaxes its sway, but perpetually keeps watch and ward over against the libidinous tumults of sensuality in all its various diverse, opposite, or mutually exclusive manifestations. Of such a watch and ward we may take as symbolic the historical cases of early civilizations fortifying and exercising themselves for higher ends by a severe sexual ethic. And when a deceptive doctrine purported to negotiate between the conscience and its enemy, to bring them to terms and to operations of mutual advantage, that doctrine earned and has retained the opprobrious description of laxism or jesuitry. Suspicion also extends to the sublimations of sensual and passionate love under colour of the Platonic or romantic ideologies of love. These, when they have outlived their first naivety, tend to degenerate into easy-going illusion and hypocrisy. On the other hand the moral conscience, like poetry, is anti-ascetic, seeing ascetic rigidity as a foolish attempt to terminate by a final tearing up of the roots, a struggle which the conscience on the contrary accepts and pursues: a struggle rendered fruitful just because there is here no annulment of sensible motions and affections. The conscience accepts and fights this battle, undaunted by incidental defeats and falls, which pains and blushes convert into an experience by which the will and freedom receive strengthening nourishment. As long as this continual correction and enrichment of experience is occurring, morality is basically sound. The loss of such basic health, the breath of disease and death, arise only with a denial of God, a pact with the devil, an idealization of lust, and the search, in its multiple and deceptive appearances, of the infinite, of infinite satisfaction in insatiable pleasure and indulgence, of the highest liberty in the basest servitude. When this ideal and the attitude which it inspires come to growth in and possession of a soul, or operating with a wider radius become habitual in a society or in certain social classes, then there is decadence, of which, indeed, the sole true distinguishing character is the origin which we have just traced for it.

The fact that "decadentism" has been so much talked of from the middle of the last century up to our times, is no mere fruit of literary fancy, but indicates a real state of mind, testifying to a profound travail in the modern conscience. But this travail is necessary for the formation or rather the establishment of a new faith to take over and to develop in greater purity and power the legacy of the old religions. This moral decadentism is matched by a pseudo-aesthetic production which is not love poetry (inseparable as this is from heroic and ethical and religious poetry), and is thus not in its essence poetry at all, even when it disguises itself and seeks to pass as such, or offers its impressionistic and sensual droolings as rapt contemplation of the cosmos and act of worship. By whom or how shall this literature of decadence be restrained and itself be consigned to decadence? It will happen just as it does when in the life of a society the moral conscience awakens and religious energies are reborn. So too in the aesthetic sphere there will arise men of poetic genius who, with the purity of their poetry, their strong and lively imagery, their rich passion elevated to a harmonious serenity, will drive out of the field those petty loveless, joyless, and thoughtless trailers in the dust, collectors of imaginous and verbal minutiae, rapt admirers of their own strained efforts which they glorify under the description of pure poetry.

[1936]

IX

ON A REFORMATION IN
THE HISTORY OF ART AND LETTERS

THE history of literature and art, for which it would be well to use, if tradition allowed it, a one-word description, such as either history of "art" or history of "poetry", has now reached a stage in its elaboration of critical principles at which an important self-reformation is called for, if its energies are to be restored and are to serve for a more speedy and assured progress in the future. Like all serious reformations this one should not be sudden and violent, but should issue from a deepened awareness of itself, its own true nature, and go towards an enhanced boldness in casting off methods of treatment which are inappropriate to that nature, deriving from confusions and prejudices.

For some years I have steadily worked to that end, pointing out contradictions which are implicit in the methods now in use, and both outlining the theory of those which should replace them, and giving, so far as I could, examples of such methods in practice. The persuasion that this problem is of great importance for our intellectual life leads me to turn to it again, in the hope of being able to expound it briefly in the appropriate terms, while also throwing light upon some neglected aspects of it.

By reformation is meant something more than a mere correction of particular details – in fact, a change in the totality or in the dominant feature of an existent form; that is to say in what is at present vital in such a form. There would be no point in promoting the reformation of what has already been reformed, or the replacement of that which has already been replaced by what it is now intended to subject, in its turn, to criticism. The form or type or ideal of literary or art history against which I am now pitting my arguments is not, then, the scholarly, the biographical, the rhetorical, or the academic, for these are types which only the ignorant can suppose to be at present actively cultivated in the world of learning. It is, on the contrary, the sociological form of the history of art and letters, together with other extra-aesthetic forms, against which I am launching my criticism.

It is true that there are anticipations of this sort of sociological history (as of all the other sorts of idealistic and romantic doctrine) in the brilliant suggestions of Vico's *Scienza Nuova*, indeed there is something of the sort even in the pages of ancient historians like Velleius Paterculus and the author of *De Oratoribus*. But the doctrine took formal shape in the hands of a school of writers at the turn of the eighteenth and the nineteenth centuries. It was then that almost all the schemes which are still in circulation were initiated or elaborated. Then it was that for the first time artistic development was envisaged as differentiated into two great epochs, that of Greek and that of Christian art; or alternatively into three, the oriental, the classical, and the romantic; or yet again into recurrent cycles of spontaneous or reflective, primitive or learned, naive or sentimental, popular or literary poetry; or finally in a combination of epochs or cycles composed into what was called a "spiral" pattern. These epochs and cycles were sometimes considered as being all of equivalent value, but more often as degrees of perfection or progress, or even of imperfection and regression. Accordingly art was sometimes delineated in a series of positive forms each perfect in itself, sometimes in a series in which each term is enriched and completed by the succeeding, sometimes in a series of cumulative degenerations from an original plenitude. At the conclusion of each of these series there remained a query about the future of art. This would lead, as the case might be, to a programme for the art of the ensuing phase, which, it was supposed, must issue forth as a necessary sequel to that of the foregoing phase; or to a prospectus of the more perfect art destined to absorb and sublimate the precedent; or to the indication of some form of the spirit, whether a spiritual, a philosophic, a religious, or a practical form, in which it was foreseen that art itself, in its universality, would become dissolved, therewith ceasing to play a part in civilization. In that age, thanks to the novel emphasis upon the national principle, the practice began of composing, along with general literary-artistic histories for all mankind, histories of the same sort limited to a single nation. The national histories were no longer viewed as entering into the general history as particular chapters or epochs, with a beginning, a duration, and a final end, but as being somehow independent of the general literary-artistic history of mankind, each with a perpetually enduring character of its own, though subject in the course of centuries to phases of grandeur, decadence, and recovery. There is no need in an essay which does not profess to relate the history of modern artistic and literary criticism to enumerate here the works in which the above-mentioned views were propounded. A reminder will suffice of such works as, in Germany, Schiller's treatise *On Naive and Sentimental Poetry* (the parent of innumerable histories and systems: indeed it has not yet wholly lost its potency) and Friedrich Schlegel's *History of Ancient and Modern Literature*, together with the historical part of Hegel's *Aesthetic*; in France Chateaubriand's *Genius of Christianity*, Madame de Staël's *De la Littérature considérée dans ses rapports avec les institutions sociales*, and other works; in Italy, Vico's poetic and "Homeric" doctrine, and his teachings on the reappearance of the same order of wisdom in Dante in the Middle Ages and De Sanctis' *History of Literature*. As to the speculations on what is to become of art in a future stage, it suffices to mention Hegel's theory of the disappearance of art in the intellectually mature modern age, Mazzini's and Wagner's respective views on the future of the drama and the opera. I need not go into the continuation of these schemes and speculations in the positivist period or their persistence up to the present time, for I have done so elsewhere[1] and anyway the signs are easy to see.

There is an unfortunately widespread disposition to treat all systems of ideas, methods, and intellectual ideals against which one reacts, as being so many illusions, deviations, or perversions of the human spirit, due to some external cause, some disaster, the mischievous authority of a sophistical thinker, the ill-starred prevalence of some misguided nation. Here we shall certainly not follow that example. We will on the contrary keep faith with the

---

1. *Teoria e Storia della Storiografia*, 6th edn., Bari, 1948, Pt. II, Ch. VII.

fundamental canon that a doctrine should be valued not by the measure of successive but by that of preceding doctrine. The form of historical composition which we now have under critical consideration not only, when viewed in this light, displays a positive and enduring merit and substance, but the merit appears so conspicuous, the substance so precious, that one is tempted to celebrate, even with a hint of inevitable exaggeration, the age which gave birth to it as the age which created literary and art history, we of a succeeding age being no longer creators and founders, but at best enlargers and reformers and transformers of the heritage. The creators were Vico and Herder, Winckelmann and Schiller, Chateaubriand and Madame de Staël, Schlegel and Hegel, with the other historians and philosophers of the said proto-romantic and romantic epoch.

It was indeed their merit that works of art and poetry ceased almost for the first time to be mere objects of learned and antiquarian annotation, or of dogmatic and arbitrary judgement, and were felt and viewed as living spiritual values, each in the setting of the time and the society in which it came into being. Criticism doffed its dusty and pedantic robe, laid aside its frigid and scolding manner, smiled kindly on the works to be judged, discerning and savouring their substantial beauty and making light of partial and secondary defects. Madame de Staël was delighted when she heard a lecture by Wilhelm Schlegel in Vienna, describing him as "un critique éloquent comme un orateur, et qui, loin de s'acharner aux défauts, éternel aliment de la médiocrité jalouse, cherchait seulement à faire revivre le génie créateur". In other words, it was then that criticism, ceasing to be erudite and dogmatic, became historical, became in fact the history of poetry and art, and so, like all history, and in contradistinction to arbitrary individualistic opinion, not negative but affirmative. This was so great an acquisition, and remains for us such a solid possession, as to oblige us at the very least to observe towards those critics the code which they themselves introduced, recounting in the first place what they meritoriously achieved and not what by reason of shortcomings they either never attempted or failed to complete.

Their shortcoming, it would be easy to demonstrate, was common to all the philosophy and historical composition of their time. This was finalistic, but the finalism was as yet extrinsic or transcendental. The Aesthetic of the time both promoted and was affected by this way of thought. At times it endeavoured to distinguish the intellectual and practical forms of the spirit from the artistic form, but then fell back into a confounding of art with these. However, this too I have set forth elsewhere, and accordingly need now do no more than inspect the logical and anti-logical implications of the error in a limited field.

In such critical schemes as those mentioned above, the assignment of single works of art in the scheme presupposed that they should be compared with each other, and certain general characteristics inferred from the comparison. It is thus, for example, that the idea is arrived at of a harmonious and contented disposition towards the external world which is then called the naive disposition proper to a certain group of poets, or, to take another case, the idea of the disposition which sorrows and yearns towards lost peace and happiness, the so-called sentimental disposition proper to another group of poets. Another such characteristic is the "lutte terrible de la chair et de l'esprit" which, according to Chateaubriand, produces the "grands effets dramatiques" of Christianity and Christian poetry; or the particular conception of the divine which differentiates the modern from the ancient poets. In the same way the critics arrived at the determination of the greater or lesser impact and radiation of literature on the life of the peoples, its greater or lesser degree of "nationality", as Friedrich Schlegel put it. Similarly De Sanctis assessed the variations in zeal or indifference shown in regard to politics and religion in the respective epochs of Italian literature. There were those also who, with attention fixed upon the externals of the various works of art, pointed to the prevalence in certain communities and certain centuries of the epic poem, in others of the drama, or of music, or of the visual arts; nor were schemes lacking for the delineation, on the basis of historical and cultural divergences, for example the contrast between Protestantism and Catholicism, of the opposition in content and in attitude between Germanic and Neo-Latin art. Such painstaking analyses of the products of art from many points of view has its own due place and importance. Moreover, it constituted another of those advances in historical method which the age that we are now celebrating accomplished. Yet this advance did not particular-ly concern the field of art and poetry but rather concerned the other sorts of history. In fact it was for the elucidation of the customs, moralities, philosophies, religious cults, ways of thought and feeling and conduct of the various peoples and ages, that recourse was now had, more than ever before, to artistic and poetic expression, those documents so warm with life. Just because they were used as documents, these historical and artistic expressions had ceased to be the subject and had become merely the medium and instrument of historical construction. At the very outset of any such enquiry one leaves the field of literary and artistic history for other historical fields. Such work will redound to the benefit of the history of philosophical methods and ideas, of moral conflicts and social institutions. It will constitute a chapter in the history of philosophy, civilization, politics, but it will no longer be history of poetry and art as such. This statement can be checked by observing how excellently mediocre or wretched or even bogus works of art often serve for documentation, often, in fact, by reason of their greater nearness to practical life and to intellectual abstractions, much better than brilliant or supreme works of art.

There is an objection which is bound to be made, yet could be ignored because a moment's thought suffices to show its logical absurdity, were it not implicit in the thought underlying a school of the history of the visual arts now enjoying considerable celebri-ty. The objection is this. The catalogue here set forth of the various sorts of analysis and general characterization of works of art included the cases of characterization by their philosophical, moral, social, and institutional features, but omitted the really important case which is that of an attempted or an achieved characterization by features (common to the works of art) of a purely artistic quality. The school in question aspires, in fact, to construct a history of painting as pure painting, recognizing only pictorial values, disregarding all material content, meaning by this images and expressions. It would be a history of artistic processes or styles showing how, for example, one painter propounded a problem, another came near to solving it, a third skirted it without noticing it, a fourth got still nearer, a fifth actually grasped and resolved it, and then a sixth (dear me!) let it slip again. What could be – at all events at first sight – more general and more dialectical and at the same time more purely artistic than a history on such lines? On the same model there has already been an attempt to build a history of pure poetry the subject of which would be not the mind or soul of the poets but rhythms, modulations, intonations, elevations, pauses, and such aesthetic quintessences. But in truth it is never possible to abstract from works of art any general characteristics other than those pertaining to their matter, that is, not artistic but logical and practical characteristics. For the very act of abstraction dissipates and destroys the individuality of works of art, and indeed the art as art. General aesthetic characters such as are mentioned in this connexion are either something that just does not exist, or, if they exist, they are in themselves material and extraneous to art, and this is made clear by the figure which the painters and the poets mentioned in the attempted historical compositions of this sort come to cut, the figure of inventors, perfectors, or careless inheritors of the devices in question – in a word, solvers of intellectual and mechanical problems.

Now there would be no harm whatever in works of art being put frankly to sole use as documents for incorporation in histories of philosophy, of civilization, of politics, or even of technical achievement, provided always that such histories gave themselves out for what they really were. The trouble arises when these histories are described, as is the custom, as histories of literature and art, promising what they do not then maintain. And in reality, they continually oscillate between the pursuit of a philosophic moral and social enquiry, and that of an artistic enquiry. And in that way they rouse two expectations and disappoint them both. For whoever seeks in such writings an adequate presentation, a concrete understanding of the poets and artists to which they refer, receives in answer something inadequate and abstract, something more and at the same time something less than the true reality of the poet, painter, sculptor, or architect in question. Something less, because every artistic impression in its own way embraces totality in its particularity, the extratemporal in its temporality, and thus comprehends the universal, whereas, in the writings in question, poet and artist are commonly expounded as expressions of something limited and transitory, a philosophic problem, a moral necessity, a political programme of some community or epoch, and thus lose both their individuality and their universality, or rather, that divine character as creators which is nothing else than their capacity to merge all practical limitations, all intellectual particularities, in the serenity of contemplation. But also something more, for philosophy, politics, morals, religion, and all the other preoccupations of an artist's age or nation, are indeed in the poet or artist, but are in him so perfectly fused with all other things, with history and the universal life, that whenever any of these is, in an account of his work, picked out and designated as a particular inclination, there is thereby attributed to him something more than he really conceived or desired, or could have conceived and desired.

The forcing of artists into such non-aesthetic schemes of interpretation rouses on the part of the artists, and of men of taste and intuition, and even of those who have a plain feeling for reality, protestations of such daily frequency, that no demonstration is required. The protesters are a veritable chorus, whose utterances sometimes take a rigorously logical form, as in the still unceasing arguments against philosophism and sociologism. Amidst that chorus let me pick out one utterance, one voice, that of Leo Tolstoi, who, conversing with a French visitor in 1901, in answer to some remarks on the history of the novel, said: "Don't talk to me of the evolution of the novel. Don't tell me that Stendhal explains Balzac and that Balzac explains Flaubert. These are fantasies of the critics. I like your French critics, they are the only ones that I read. Their essays are exquisitely composed. But I cannot accept their ideas on the Stendhal-Balzac-Flaubert succession. Genius does not succeed to genius in that manner. Each one is always independent." Tolstoi was quite right.

What I am now expounding: the contrast between a defective form of history and the as yet unsatisfied demand for another form, or, otherwise described, the contrast between certain already established types of history (civil, political, philosophical) and another type which is still in the formative stage (literary-artistic history), which latter is sometimes distinguished from but sometimes confounded with the former; this contrast has often been twisted into an antinomy between art and history. Starting from one or another of various standpoints, and in varying tones of voice, it has been said that history should look after the biography and the various vicissitudes of the artist, but that Aesthetics should have sole charge of the criticism of his works. (I have seen this argument repeated in the latest book of Professor Cohen, *Estetica del puro sentimento*.) Another version is this: the praise or blame accorded to works for their beauty or ugliness is a matter of taste. It is only the individual and social causes which concurred in bringing the works into existence that can be enquired into by severe and scientific thought. And yet another version is: that great works of art do indeed call for the work of aesthetic criticism, but mediocre, secondary, and altogether humble works can be dealt with by literary history. Finally, there are philologians who would have art criticism and art history kept entirely distinct and separate.

But we, after acclaiming the merit, the permanent gain for which we are for ever indebted to the Romantic critics, in the shape of their demolition of the old anti-historical, dogmatic, rhetorical, arbitrary criticism, and their healthy identification of art criticism with art history, cannot now follow the lead of the above-mentioned separatists, who show so much uncertainty in the concepts which they use and such ignorance of the history of those concepts, that history which gives the surest key for understanding their present status and future development. Our part should be, on the contrary, to search for the new shape of the history of art and letters which could satisfy what the old shape failed to satisfy; and if this shape already exists, in a growing or at least an embryonic condition, to determine its presence and to promote its growth and reinforcement, instead of hindering these.

The histories of art and letters of the Romantic and idealistic school include not only that sociological, non-artistic historical treatment which we have censured, but also, commingled with this, something which is authentic art history. Were there not such a commingling our censures would be uncalled for: the contradiction which gives rise to them would not exist. Those writers were, almost all of them, great lovers and experts of poetry and of every form of art, enthusiastic spirits, hearts well acquainted with the most various and profound stirrings, delicate fancies aware of the gradations and the poetic vitality of imagery. It was therefore easy for them, in obedience to their moral and philosophic urges, or to the dictates of some intellectual scheme, to present Dante as the compendium of the mediaeval conception of the world, Cervantes as the mocking gravedigger of the feudal and chivalric society, Shakespeare as the Dante of spiritual liberty and of the growing power of England. Yet when they set to and dealt with these poets and their works in detail, Dante appeared to them both mediaeval and non-mediaeval, Cervantes as the satirist but also the wistful exalter of chivalry, Shakespeare as the poet of the universe. In fact they saw Dante, Cervantes, and Shakespeare as Dante, Cervantes, and Shakespeare. Hence the great efficacy of their historical and critical writings on the interpretation of art, the sense and feeling and judgement of art. Even today we treasure their writings as containing almost all of the best and most pertinent thought concerning the artists of antiquity, the Middle Ages, modernity; and by comparison with theirs, the critical and historical writings of the succeeding age seem rather jejune. Zeal for art and for the right understanding of art reached the highest point in De Sanctis' History of Italian Literature: this, indeed, at the time of its publication, and for long after, was judged to be merely a collection of essays on single great writers. That judgement, were it correct, we should consider in this case as a tribute to the merits of De Sanctis, and not as a pointer to his limitations. But it is not altogether correct. His history is really a brilliant and powerful sketch of the political, moral, and intellectual history of the Italian people as reflected in its poetry and literature. Yet the characteristics of single writers are usually indicated by him in such a lively manner, their individuality so well portrayed, with such exquisite aesthetic judgement, that the non-aesthetic scheme which De Sanctis used as a frame recedes from our attention.

Such is, indeed, the approach which must be recommended as the only valid method for the historian of art and letters: the study of the characteristic in a single artist, the study of his personality and his work, which are really one and the same. Of such characterization we possess many excellent examples. It is arrived at not as a determination of static or scientific data according to the method of natural science, but by genetic and historical enquiry issuing forth into a delineation of the personality and works of the artist in their development. For while it is impossible to absorb and to relive the experience of a work of art without a certain historical culture, varying, of course, from case to case (the indispensableness of such a cultural basis is now recognized by all reflective and reasonable people), it is equally certain that a work of art cannot be rendered in mental terms, cannot be intellectually comprehended and criticized, otherwise than by achieving awareness of its internal dialectic. For example: it will be shown how a given artist began by imitating existing art, whether near to him or far from him in time, sympathetic or unsympathetic or even antipathetic to his temperament. In these imitations (it will be shown) he will proceed all the more clumsily and incoherently by reason of the energy of his own temperament, until, becoming aware of his difference from those others, he finds himself and rises to the height of an original production. It will be shown how another artist in his youthful years joyfully poured forth the inspiration bestowed upon him already perfect, as by the bounty of nature. But then he soon exhausted his vein, and it was of no avail that he sought every device for perpetuating his first successes, imitating and caricaturing himself, or imitating and striving to outdo others, until he relapsed into silence or found some other line of work as a critic, scholar, or politician. Of another it will be told how at first he seemed to want to make his mark in the world as a practical man, orator, reformer, or apostle. But experience shows that these were merely whims: passing through a series of excitements, disturbances, and disappointments the man finally settles down and finds his peace in aesthetic creation, but *tantae molis erat* to bring this to light. If these and similar examples are not historical processes, if the mind which elucidates them is not engaged in the composition of history, then I really do not know what history and its composition may be. And if the history of poetry and art consists in something other than developing, detailing, and colouring these dramas of the creators of art and poetry, then I ask what may be the meaning of art and poetry.

That the characterization of the single poet or artist is a more spontaneous and appropriate way of approach than the elaboration of an abstractly general history of art and letters is increasingly confirmed in practice by the arrangement and method of textbooks in these times. In the course of a century the essay and the monograph have become increasingly common media of critical and historical exposition, while sociological or general histories of art and letters have been on the decline. Indeed there would be still less of these in circulation were not many of them compiled for use in schools, or for the education of the unlearned, or for reference and aid to memory, lacking any true intellectual inspiration or originality: it were much better that they should frankly be called handbooks or manuals. It is true that conformably to certain industrial ways of thought which have crept into intellectual life, there is an expectation (but it is as vain as Noah's expectation of the return of the raven) of a new history of national art and letters, or of a new history of international artistic time-periods, or indeed of a new universal art history, to be generated out of the multiplicity of such essays and monographs. But in truth the romantic ideal of a general, national, or universal history now survives solely as an abstract ideal. It is to the essays and monographs that the reader turns, or he treats the general histories as compilations of various essays and monographs, or else uses them simply as handbooks. We see that authors spend the best of their energies in writing essays and monographs while deferring to future times the execution of cherished projects of grandiose general histories. Or if they do manage to get down to these, they shake them off as soon as possible and return to the composition of essays and monographs. It is well known that the most renowned critics of the past century were, almost to a man, renowned as writers of essays.

Even in the circles which maintain the tradition of sociological or otherwise non-aesthetic art history, the cumbersome and unsatisfying character of such compositions is often recognized. In the exposition of works under headings of classes and groups, it is continually necessary to refer to works which constitute exceptions to the arrangement, references which detract from the dignity of the scheme, as when certain geniuses are designated as "irregular" or "anachronistic" in their period or place. I will not dwell on this, but it will be worth while, as we have already mentioned the theory, so-called, of pure pictorial values, to recall the very fruitful concept developed by others (Fiedler, for example) of the discontinuous and fragmentary (or as it could be better termed, individual) character of artistic series; also the argument of the Vienna school of Worringer and others against the idea of a linear evolution and against the corresponding confusion between technical advances and artistic creations. The authors of these schools, if they follow up their own thoughts, will themselves gradually abandon history of the sociological type for the history of individualization.

Accordingly, both our critique of method and also the natural trend of things which, as Vico monumentally pronounces, "have neither ease nor capacity to endure outside their natural condition", point to the same conclusion. On the one side it is time to revise the conceptions of the history of art and letters to accord with the theory of aesthetics: on the other side to recognize accomplished fact, pronouncing that the truly logical form of such history is that which sets itself to characterize the single artist and his work. The corresponding didactic form is that of the essay and the monograph. The reformation of which I have spoken would therefore consist simply in the substitution of an individualizing history for the history in terms of general concepts practised by the romantic and old-style idealists, or rather the liberation of the individualizing from the shell of the generalizing mode, within which it first came to life, but afterwards suffered constriction.

The objection which can be made to my own ideal and to the censure which I have pronounced against the sort of history of art and letters which we have been considering is this. The censure, it will be said, may throw useful light upon difficulties which have to be dealt with, and the ideal may have its usefulness as a stimulus to accurate preparatory enquiry concerning the personality of artists and the features of their work. But this does not do away with the need for a general history (in which care will be taken, however, to liberate this from the perils implicit in such history as hitherto known). It is indeed incontestable that in a truly critical and philosophical exposition the single must be enframed in the total, the multiple must be seen in the one. It seems accordingly that an infinite series of individual characterizations by way of essay and monograph in which the single is detached from the whole, the multiple from the one, the historical work from the unity of history, the plant from the soil, must lack the hallmark of criticism, of philosophy. Whence there will arise the demand that the series of individual characterizations should be put through a further mental process in order to obtain from them and to assemble together the implicit nexus; and out of these a picture will take shape of the development of letters and the arts, nation by nation, epoch by epoch, or in humanity as a whole.

Before examining the justice of this charge which can be and is levelled at my theory, that it impugns the unity of science, let us first make it quite clear that the demand which we have just mentioned is at this, as at a previous stage, impossible and absurd. If we succeed in doing this, then it will be evident that the championship of the unity of science, in the name of which we are bidden to perform the impossible, is fallacious, because it presents that unity in a false and fantastic guise, or alternatively, if it rightly understands the meaning of such unity, yet fails to see it actually at work.

The absurdity of any attempt to solder together the various characterizations in order to make of them a general history has been already firmly established by the demonstration that whenever common characters are discerned in the matter of artistic works (and their form, when it is abstracted and materialized as "style", is itself matter), such a discernment of shared character is without aesthetic significance, and the shared character in virtue of which the common description is bestowed cannot be aesthetic. What serves as foundation for the common description will be, then, some extra-aesthetic set of characteristics. The conjunction will have for its medium not, so to speak, a physiological connecting tissue, but an artificial tissue sustaining the various characteristics. Or we might compare it with a wall on which a series of pictures are hung. Such in fact is the usual practice in such works. The treatment of the characteristics of the single poets and artists is preceded or periodically interrupted by observations on political events, philosophical movements, customs and fashions, religious and moral controversies of the times in which the poets lived. Far from achieving the much desired and exalted scientific unity, there is a loss even of such modest unity as was previously present. Blocks of history are piled serially on top of one another, and although into such arrangements there may enter a literary ability which masks from the imaginative eye the breaches of continuity, the interlying gaps in the discourse, the intellectual eye always perceives these. The sociological historians of art and letters not infrequently utter more or less involuntary confessions as to the impossibility of procuring a genuine fusion of elements in their works, or as to the artificial and empirical nature of the combinations between them. Emiliani Giudici said that the "historical observations" contained in the works of his predecessors produced upon him the effect of "page proofs of different works bound up by chance in a volume of literary history". Haym said that literary history is primarily concerned with the variations of the "ideas" of a nation, but that it was impossible to pursue the logical working out of these, it being necessary to take account of "individuals" with their temperaments, feelings, and personal creations. Gaspary, in his history of Italian literature, took pains to water down his "genres" with doses of "personalities". In a well-known German encyclopaedia (representative, as such books are, of established and popularized opinion), I read that literary history "is distinguished from other historical disciplines because while reciting a historical development it provides to an exceptional extent an analysis and criticism of single facts, and gives much attention to the psychological characteristics of individuals".

Such dualisms, trialisms, or heaping together of still more numerous disparate elements is, however, the least disadvantage of the method. The serious harm comes when out of a natural desire and keenness for coherence and logical fusion, the history of art and letters becomes entangled with one of the other sorts of history, political, philosophical, or moral, for example, so as to lose its own character. The Romantics were doomed to fall into this fault in the composition of their literary histories, but saved themselves in practice, up to a point, by dint of the possession of a sound taste and a lively sense of art; but never entirely. Even in a historian so admirably endowed with the sense of reality, so disdainful of abstractions and subtleties, so keen to seize upon and to illustrate the features of the artist as De Sanctis, I have sometimes had to remark a surrender to various faulty judgements which derived from the pattern of moral and political development in which he presented the Italian poets. I am bound here to limit myself to noticing such errors derivative from the methods employed, as not even severely disciplined minds were able to avoid. It would need too much time to point out the effects of partisan passions which, filtering through the pseudo-evolutionary pattern into works of artistic and literary history, used to give these a deliberate flavour of political partisanship, neo-Guelf, neo-Ghibelline, conservative or liberal as the case might be; and in our days (fortunately not in Italy) are wont to confer the barbarous quality of nationalism and racialism.

23

The impossibility of meeting the demand for a unitary treatment of artistic and literary history should not really afford any disappointment, for the unity which it is impossible to achieve is an imaginary unity, as fantastic and fallacious as the *infinitum imaginationis* criticized by the philosophers. True and concrete unity is by contrast that which we are always able to discern in the individual characterizations, the single essays and monographs. For as in every work of art the whole universe and all history is present in singular form, so the critic when he comprehends the work of art comprehends in it the whole universe, all history in that singular form. The contemporaries, kindred spirits, counterparts of the poet, his more or less partial and more or less remote forerunners, the moral and intellectual life of his time and of the nearer or more distant times in whose womb it was prepared – all of this is explicitly or implicitly present to our spirit when we study the dialectic of a single artistic personality. We cannot, of course, while studying such a single personality simultaneously attend to another or some others or all others each for its own sake. But such an incapacity for ubiquity which the psychologists call "narrowness of the threshold of consciousness" they ought rather to call the supreme energy of the human spirit, thanks to which it sinks itself in the object that interests it at the moment and will turn aside for no distraction, because in the single it finds all that which concerns it, in fact finds nothing less than the All.

This is the right occasion to dissipate that other erroneous notion already referred to, concerning the difference between the history of art and letters and history of other sorts, namely that the other history achieves a treatment of its subject in terms of general development, but the history of art and letters confines itself to treating of it in terms of individualities. (And sometimes this is viewed as a mark of inferior potency, sometimes as a mark of superior attractiveness in this sort of history.) But in truth histories of all sorts always treat of particular and individual acts, of some definite doctrine, or tradition, institution, or political event. Each has its proper theme, circumscribed and individuated, particular and not general, for as Machiavelli acutely remarked the sole value of history lies in "what it particularly describes". The false view that some histories have a general and others a particular subject arises out of an optical illusion, as I might almost term it. Histories of art and letters usually offer as their background an image of some moral or intellectual situation, or the like, and against this they review a multitude of works of art. To a superficial view, these latter seem to constitute multiplicity and particularity, by contrast with the background which constitutes unity and generality. But from another point of view the inverse conclusion could be drawn. Consider a commentary on a poem in which diverse historical observations on words, myths, usages, events, biographical details, and so on are appended to each stanza. Unity, organicity, constancy, generality will now appear to be present in the work of art, while multiplicity and particularity will pertain to the other sorts of history. The truth is that histories of all sorts are individual and universal, and are the one as much as the other. All of them posit the particular and all of them lead the particular towards the unity of the Whole. The theory of a differential character in the history of art and letters is mistaken, then, when referring to the methodic form. It may have some substance when, on the contrary, it refers to the particular content of the different sorts of history, and would amount, in the present context, to a reminder that art is art and not criticism, rationalization, system.

I have reviewed the justifying and favourable conditions which have made the way plain for a reformation in the history of art and letters in the direction of individualization. They are a growing precision as to the concept of art, and a spontaneous critical spirit which encourages the production of essays and monographs while discouraging that of general histories. Should I now go on to enumerate also the influences which continue to impede such a development, I should have to adduce unfavourable conditions and objections such as the following. On the one hand a persistent confusion of art with practical-moral life and with philosophic thought makes for the consideration of poets and other artists as mere mouthpieces and witnesses of practical or intellectual movements, or as practical, reasoning, theoretical agents, requiring treatment as such in so-called general, that is to say civil, political, and philosophical history and the like. On the other side a mistaken idea of science occasions the attribution of a scientific character not to the labours of critical research, but to the arrangement of facts in a unifying perspective; and while denying this character to the investigation of particular problems thrown up by various human interests (and these are always problems of an aesthetic or philosophic or moral or similar order, problems apt therefore for treatment in the history of these various spheres), attributes it, on the contrary, to the panoramic, summary, encyclopaedic compositions which attempt to reproduce things, or the totality of things, but in fact reproduce nothing but our incoherent and dead abstractions.

The insistence upon the rights of the philosophy and history of art over against other sorts of philosophy and history are in no sense a denial of these others, but only a rejection of usurpations occasionally attempted by them. In the same way, a reaffirmation of the true quality of knowledge and criticism is not intended to deny rights of existence to those prospectuses, panoramas, summaries, encyclopaedias, and other instruments of which we all make use when in need of some necessary information or bird's-eye view of an historical region into which we purpose to enter. What needs to be emphasized is that critical knowledge consists wholly in the theoretical problem. The arrangements of which we have been speaking have their own problems, but purely of a practical nature, and any claim made for them that they furnish a faithful or complete copy or reproduction of the facts is altogether imaginary. Let the authors of these compilations be reassured. The reformation of the history of art and letters of which I have been speaking is not intended to do them out of a living in the pursuit of which they are useful to ourselves also, but simply to discover the means of satisfying a need which they, in their preoccupation with other purposes, can neither satisfy nor feel.

[1917]

X

CRITICISM AND HISTORY
OF THE FIGURATIVE ARTS: THE PRESENT PHASE

In Italy, as well as in some other countries, the notion is again gaining ground that painting and each of the other arts with which the criticism and history of the figurative arts have to do, have their own respective and particular foundations in virtue of which they are intrinsically different from poetry, and therefore each one needs its own special form of critical and historical treatment and methodology.

My teaching is directly opposite. I uphold the unity of the arts and regard the division between one art and another as being of an outward and non-aesthetic order; and this teaching of mine is based upon the critical examination of physical and naturalistic illusions implicit in the theory of distinct arts, which is shown to be self-contradictory. It would seem reasonable, then, to ask that the present resurrection of the old theory should be presented in the same speculative-historical manner, with the same degree of theoretical and scientific precision, so that one might have an orderly argument to contend with. I might indeed insist upon this, and pending satisfaction I might well refuse to discuss with an opponent operating on a lower level. Sometimes, however, it is an intellectual duty to go out and encounter the adversary wherever he may be, especially when, as in the present case, we have to do with keen and purposive minds, exceedingly expert in the affairs of those arts to which they have devoted their attention.

It is not my fault, then, if I have to take up their assertion of the peculiar nature of poetry, and of each of the other figurative arts, in all the bareness with which they themselves present it. There are, it is true, some hints of a theory intended to supplant the antiquated teaching of Lessing to be found in writers like Walter Pater. But not much help could be got from a teaching so illogical that, on the one hand, it asserts that each art has its own special order of impressions and its own untranslatable charm, but at the same time says that all art tends to something other than itself, namely "towards the condition of music". (In other words it reaffirms the principle of the unity and identity of the arts in the illogical form of a monstrous tendency and effort of each one of them to approach a goal outside the range of its own nature.)

Since, then, no opportunity is offered of testing the logical process by which this assertion is supported, for the signs of such a process are either very feeble or altogether wanting, we cannot proceed otherwise than by observing the facts which have suggested the assertion, the ends towards which it moves, the motives behind it, and the results stemming from it. These seem to me to be very clearly displayed in the writings of these new critics and historians, among whom I will mention as one of the latest and boldest Roberto Longhi, who in virtue of his extensive knowledge of art, and above all of his *temperamentvoll* literary style, is at the present moment a notable influence in the world of Italian art history.

And to speak first of the motive: this is, in itself, a legitimate one, springing, in Longhi, from a just feeling that in painting and the other figurative arts what should be sought out, enjoyed, understood, is the sole artistic element, the aesthetic form, not the many-sided matter which has been resolved and overcome in the form. This leads to his denunciation of philosophical, symbolical, historical interpretations of painting, as also of passional and rhetorical interpretations. If, standing before a picture, one bethinks oneself of the ideas suggested in it, or of the history which it records, or feels a stirring of pleasure or an impulse to action, such as were indeed present to the painter as material precedents for his work, or elements afloat in his mind, one has not arrived at the contemplation of the painting as painting, as art; one has not received, or has ceased to receive, aesthetic impression.

But in this there is nothing peculiar to painting. Just the same happens in the case of poetry which is customarily contrasted with that of painting. We critics and historians of poetry have just the same struggle against the unintelligent who look for edification, narrative, hidden meanings, or material thrills, and have to be reminded all the time that not these, but the form, the lyrical quality, the rhythm are what make the poem (even should it be a long novel or a complex drama), that is to say something which is either more or less than those other things, something which differs from philosophic utterance in being intuitional; from perception or historical judgement in falling short of the distinction of the real from the unreal (or we may equally say in passing beyond that distinction); from practical excitement in falling short of or passing beyond the practical urge, which it depicts, but in the depiction draws it forth out of its own limits and instils into it the eternal drama of the world. That differentiation which the old theorists of aesthetics used to draw between the imitative arts (such as sculpture, painting, poetry) and the non-imitative (such as architecture and music) now makes us smile, for the very possibility of there being non-imitative arts raises the suspicion that no art is ever "imitative". In other words, suitable to our present argument, there is no support for the differentiation of painting from poetry to be found in the theoretical basis of these arts. That basis is the same, and gives rise to the same arguments. We thus actually find in these an additional demonstration of the unity of the arts.

However, the modern critics and historians of whom we are speaking fail to grasp this identity. And so, instead of searching as they should for pure aestheticity in pictorial art (that aestheticity which an external analysis fallaciously divides into poetic, pictorial, sculptorial, musical, and architectural art, and so forth), and instead of seeking out in each individual painting the aesthetic and spiritual individuality pertaining to it, they set forth on a blind and fruitless search for aesthetic character, not in the works themselves, but in the external condition which apparently differentiates pictorial from poetic works as a whole. What by these efforts they in fact succeed in grasping, is not painting or art, not an aesthetic act, but lines, colours, tonality, lights and shades, *chiaroscuro*, *sfumato*, and so on. According to them, in these would reside the reality, the sole true reality of painting. Yet even in this mistaken assertion they do but repeat a mistake which crops up identically in the case of poetry. For poetry too has often been said to reside in sensuous language, metaphors, figures, metres, though nowadays the talk is of stylistic and rhythmic processes – a mere change of formula. The mistake in either case arises from hotly pursuing and superstitiously clinging to apparent form, so that they find themselves at the last embracing not that pure form which in aesthetics is one and the same with content, content-form, but, instead, an abstract form; an error to which rhetoric, however subtle and exquisite, always succumbs.

There is in the history of Aesthetics a philosopher who pre-eminently represents this abstract formalism – Herbart. His view was that the beauty of art, like all other beauty, is wholly accounted for by simple formal relations: in poetry, those of thought; in painting, of lines and colours; in sculpture, of con-tours; in music, of tones. All else than these he regarded as something extraneous to pure aestheticity, and relegated it to the sphere of content, of the various and the accidental which excites interest. He inveighed ceaselessly against those who seek in one art the perfection proper to another, those who "regard music as a sort of poetry, painting as poetry, poetry as a higher plastic art and plastic art as a sort of aesthetic philosophy". But it is well known that no aesthetic school was ever so unproductive as that of Herbart: it never obtained any grip on the concrete reality of art. This does not mean that the austere German formalist was not prompted in his philosophy by a basically sound thought. He was contending against the pseudo-intellectual or realistic aesthetics of the Concept or Idea, and against the aesthetics of sentiment and passion. He was moved by irritation against those critics who, when they approach the work of art, "let the object fade out", giving themselves over to emotion or falling into ecstasies and trances, those "dangerous admirers", he said, "who in despite of the classic calm with which true artists place upon their products the seal of vigilant care and meditation, introduce into those measured and carefully patterned works their own infinite yearn-ing for felicity, seeming to wish to break them up and re-create them with their interpretation in order to distill anew the supposed revelation of a higher spirit which they themselves have introduced there". I often recall and repeat with full agreement one among others of his dicta about how the "cold judgement of the man of understanding", concerning himself exclusively with form, un-hesitatingly describes as "ugly" works which the common run of argumentative or sentimental humanity praises as marvellous.

Herbart's aesthetic theory was of a piece with his whole plur-alistic, anti-relativist, mathematicizing philosophy, and thus in conflict with the conception of reality as spirituality and pro-ductivity. Those who knowingly or unknowingly, with or without the same underlying conceptions, now offer a similar doctrine to that of Herbart, enter into a similar conflict. No more than he did, can they explain what function in the spirit is fulfilled by the supposed blending and enjoyment of pure or abstract formal relations, or to which "faculty" (to use scholastic language) such a proceeding should be referred, and with what manner of at-tachment and co-operation with the other theoretical and practical faculties. When we are talking of painting and the figurative arts there is indeed an easy temptation, often yielded to, that of assign-ing the enjoyment of the forms to one of the so-called "senses" of man, the "eye". I will not insult these modern critics and historians by attributing to them any such crude transference of ideas from physiological and sense studies. I think that they are as well convinced as I am that the physiologically defined eye and pleasure of the eye have nothing at all to do with painting or any art. From the angle of sense or of practical life pleasure of the eye might denote the feeling we have when we withdraw from excessive and weari-some glare into the protection of shade, or alternatively our cheerful relief in issuing from oppressive darkness into the daylight. But that is quite different from the altogether diverse joy which we have from a painting or a sculpture. These critics when they speak of the eye evidently mean, like Herbart, not a material and physiological but a "spiritual" eye, an eye not practical but theo-retical, dreamful, fanciful. The only objection here is that such an eye is simply a metaphor standing for the spirit as a whole, or anyway for the spirit as intuition. As a matter of fact a painting is seen, not with the eye, but with the whole strength of the spirit in that special formal disposition which is called lyrical intuition or aesthetic image.

No less metaphorical are, in aesthetics, the lines, colours, tones, shadows, lights, and other definitions of physical origin. All these are metaphors, metonyms, synecdoches to designate the motions of the soul. Here, however, we must steer clear of the misunderstanding and error which would treat lines, colours, and other such conventional elements as signs or symbols of feelings which they are employed to convey. For that would open up again a dualism between the sign and the thing signified, and thus a gap between content and form. That is not what we mean by describing lines, colours, and the rest as metaphors. On the contrary we mean to say, in a literal sense, that the sentiments themselves are really lined, coloured, shaded, illuminated, and are all one with those forms, the apparent distinction from the forms arising out of a counterposing of the abstractions of psychology to the abstractions of physics, so as to break in twain the single reality of concrete spiritual production, which is all soul just because it is all body. And we must at the same time dissipate another illusion, the illusion that each one of those lines, colours, and the rest could ever be present without one of the others, in fact without the whole range of such things, without reality as a whole. It happens in painting just as in linguistic expression: all the feelings enter into it though all are surpassed and idealized in the image of fancy. In this image practical sensation and experience have ceased to vibrate, nevertheless it includes the whole of life, for it is only by an abstraction that we can think of one portion or one aspect of life being given without the others. Vain, therefore, must be any attempt to link up particular orders of representation with particular orders of physical concepts corresponding in their turn to particular orders of sensation, as Lessing and others tried to do. Not only are the two sets of orders, once they have been counterposed, thereafter wholly unadjustable to one another, but, which is the point of substance, art is concrete reality in which each always contains all.

If that is true (and there could be no denying it save by way of a substitution of abstract, broken, irrationalized reality for concrete reality), it must follow that the critic and historian of painting and of the other figurative arts has the same task to perform as the critic and historian of poetry. The business of each is to penetrate rationally, not, indeed, the state of mind of the artist as a man, but the state of mind expressed in the work of art, which is called its inspiration or lyricity. This should need no arguing, for if the painter is an artist and not merely a mechanical combiner of lines and colours as a game or pastime, if his artisthood as a painter grows from the roots of his manhood and his works are human acts, then he must have been inspired and guided to take up his brushes and to paint his canvases by a feeling; and it is to this inspiring feeling that the critic, retracing not the technical process, far less the personal and practical biography of the artist, but the creative process, must make his way, resolving the intellectual problems to which this creative process has at each stage given rise.

It may be objected that in the pursuit of that goal the critic may be seduced by the abstract subject of the painting or by images which arise out of his own imagination, not that of the artist; or that he may lose his way amid more or less allegorical discussions. True enough, but in so doing the critic does, as we say, lose his way, thus ceasing to be a good critic. And for that matter the same accidents occur with equal frequency in the criticism of poetry. In either case there are needed a varied and lively historical culture, quick and delicate feeling, acute understanding, with which to sense the effective inspiration of the artist in its originality, its multiple relations, its eternal humanity, its particular and individual historical tone. Fromentin said rightly that such a task calls for *à la fois un historien, un penseur et un artiste* (that is, the complex mental cast of the critic). But difficult though the achievement may be, and rare as good and fine things always are, it does nevertheless occur, as can be seen in many pages of Fromentin himself, of Baudelaire, of Pater, and more brokenly along the whole course of the criticism and history of the figurative arts in its widening stream from the nineteenth century to the present day, and indeed in the books of these very critics of the school here under consideration, though they profess to do something quite different and indeed opposite.

But these critics and historians have another contention which they emphasize still more strongly. It seems to them to be very weighty and it wins much approval from the many who find it persuasive. This is, that criticism as we ourselves conceive it replaces the well determined lines and colours of painting by spiritual categories. Hoping to explain painting, it in fact annihilates it. Yes. But wait a moment. Criticism acts in just the same way towards poetry, substituting concepts for the individuality of rhythms, metres, images. So doing, in the one and the other case it performs its rightful function, for this transition from fancy to thought, from intuition to concept, is precisely the end of criticism. Not to want this transition is not to want criticism at all. But it is contradictory to desire criticism while at the same time claiming the right to hinder its movement and its attention to its task. And in fact these modern critics themselves do in their works replace the lines and colours and suchlike individual determinations by the "concepts" of these things, analysing and reasoning, or even, when they are neither analysing nor reasoning, expressing their own impressions in words which are not, after all, lines and colours. I have more than once confuted the extravagant notion of an art criticism entering into competition with the art, seeking to re-express it in a new medium. I will therefore merely record a wise observation made sixty years ago by Jakob Burckhardt about the descriptions which were then current of works of plastic art: "Were it possible to say in words that which is deepest in a work of art, the art would be rendered superfluous. The work in question had just as well remained unconstructed, unsculpted, unpainted." (For my part I should extend the saying by adding in reference to poetry, "unwritten".)

Should we accept what I will call the Herbartian fallacy of a pure or abstract pictorial form, void of spiritual content, what sort of a history of art could we then proceed to build on that foundation? Evidently, a history of artistic processes – I will call them artistic and not technical because I think that these modern critic-historians may rightly protest against being saddled with that confusion. They show an appreciation of the distinction between art and technics, due possibly, in some degree, to the ideas which I myself advanced and upheld some years ago when bent upon repairing the sophistry and confusion incidental to the novel idolization of "technique". The error of the present critics is a different one. Where it lies may be discovered fairly easily if we do but recall that artistic processes or styles are abstractions taken from single and concrete works of art. Consequently the history of art which these critics have in mind is – from the point of view of art – a history of abstractions. For these authors, instead of devoting their entire attention to single works of art and artistic personalities, discerning and patiently interpreting their subtle and delicate inwardness, and fixing their historical and individual outline, turn aside to explore the features common to a plurality of works of art. By this method they may at best (that is, if they do not exhaust themselves in sterile comparisons and annotations) succeed in tracing certain general trends in the feeling or, as Wölfflin has it, the *Stimmung* of various epochs and periods, reflected in the works of art, but not in fixing these works themselves in their individuality and originality. Their achievement will thus be to discern something not properly aesthetic, but cultural and practical.

Let us take as an eminent example the discourse on the History of Italian Art given by Lionello Venturi at the University of Turin in 1915. Venturi, who on other occasions has come near to practising the pure form of criticism which we ourselves uphold, has on this occasion, as he himself testifies, yielded to the fascination of the ideas of Longhi and Berenson. Thus Venturi enquires what "position" should be assigned to Italy in the figurative arts, a question which it would be worthwhile pausing to ban just as we banned a similar question from the history of poetry. There is a geography of Italy, and, if you will, there are Italian politics, culture, usages, but there is, strictly speaking, no Italian poetry or painting. Art is in itself always individual and universal, and

accordingly supra-national. Venturi, however, instead of banning
the question, gives it this new shape: which, if any, new style
did Italy create? Now according to him, when Italian civilization
embarked upon art, almost the whole world of art had already
been created. The pure plastic style was Greek, the plastic-archi-
tectural was Roman, the linear-architectural was Gothic, colour
was the creation of the Asiatics, and for Italy there was no other
field left free for invention save pictorial style, and in this, in fact,
Italy registered her chief achievements. In Italy, and particularly
in Venice, a "perfect fusion" of colour with plasticity was achieved
with the help of the new element, the "tone". Venturi writes:
"Giorgione maintained harmony between the tonal system and
the intensity of each single colour in a strange, exceptional balance,
which could not last and never reappeared, because the logical
consequence of the tonal principle was the prevalence of the effect
of light and shade. In fact Titian gradually reduced the colour
range of his palette until in the last years of his life his imagination
arrived at effects of light and shade, meeting in fusion and friction,
as though fairy fires were to flame suddenly in the night. But the
motion that was to give chromatic character to the whole effect
remained: for light eternally vibrates even where a form becomes
concrete. But when interest in the form reawoke, and static
constructive effect ousted the desire of motion from its pre-
eminence, this sufficed to retranslate light and shade into chiaroscuro. In fact Michelangelo da Caravaggio pursued tone to the
logical conclusion of its path, and destroyed the colour which had
given birth to the tone, in order to return to pure plastic effect."

Now Venturi himself ends by making it clear that the above
description of a cycle of development, assuming always that it
describes some reality, is the description, not of an aesthetic, but of
an ethical occurrence: for he represents this as a synthesis of the
Asiatic and the European spirit, the spirit of mystical, dreamful,
and accordingly chromatic Asia with that of intellectual, practical,
and accordingly plastic Europe; and the "perfect fusion of colour
with plasticity" he equates with the "perfect fusion between the
mediaeval and the Graeco-Roman world, Asia and Europe, the

ethereal and the solid, movement and staticity". And, in the same manner, Longhi, outlining in an essay those two grand eras, the linear and the chromatic, ends by identifying the former with the philosophical and gnoseological era of metaphysics, intellectualism, and exclusive humanism, the latter (surpassing and embracing the former) with the era of "nature organized in the spirit as creative actuality". In the same manner, others, instead of giving us the history of paintings and of the soul of the artist, give us a fanciful cultural history reflecting attitudes which were customary in the old-fashioned teachings of the philosophy of history.

A history of this sort should logically eschew all discrimination of aesthetic values and disvalues. For having reduced Art to being a mere document of certain mental and moral tendencies, it could track these down almost equally well in works good, bad, or indifferent. Just as those critics and historians, analysing the Baroque painting of the seventeenth century, can trace anticipations of modern or modernistic or futuristic painting, so I myself, years ago, studying Italian lyrical poetry of the same century, was able to point to fashions, images, verse forms, prosodies, sonnet structures, which anticipated the "picturesque" of the Romantics, and even the inventions and experiments of Baudelaire, Mallarmé, and other "exceptional" artists. Nevertheless, to my judgement, those in whom I espied those psychological curiosities were quite clearly minor poets or poetasters. By contrast, among the present critics and historians of painting, students of styles and narrators of the *fabula de lineis et coloribus*, there prevails a strong disposition, now veiled but now frankly displayed, to write up or write down the artists they study. They plainly display, for example, their dislike of Raphael, Leonardo, and also Michelangelo, by contrast with their warm liking and admiration for the "colourists" and some of the hitherto less known and less admired Baroque painters. With them, the "history of pure lyrism" becomes a sheer "transvaluation of all pictorial values", though the best try to impose on themselves some measure and carefulness in the enterprise.

This was worth observing, because it throws light upon some

other motives, this time psychological and passional rather than logical, which were at work in the formation and promotion of the new school: motives of sympathy and expectation in regard to the impressionistic, cubist, futurist, in a single word decadent fashions in present-day art. Viewed generally, as a style, this sort of art, whether in the realm of painting, of poetry, or any other, is characterized by an unbalanced attention to immediate and haphazard objects of the senses, which it seeks to unify and to idealize by dint of suggestions, symbols, hints, and other intellectualistic devices. It accordingly teaches and encourages its admirers to view the art of the past also with the same criterion of sensual value ("pure outpouring"), and in virtue of this to sift, to condemn, to praise. This psychological motive has operated powerfully with the new Italian critics and historians, but there is another motive which at least at the outset largely actuated an authoritative foreign promoter of the school, Bernard Berenson, namely the need felt by the expert in attributions, who when the aids to identification of the authorship of paintings offered him by Morelli and other elaborators of evidence fail him, and written documents give no reliable information, feels he must turn to the exploration and elucidation of "styles". In any case the frank prejudice and partisanship exhibited by the school in its distribution of merit and blame to the painters and other artists with whom it has dealt, show sufficiently well that for want of a doctrine urging them to seek out the real and intrinsic value of art, the critics in question have left the field open to individual preferences, favouritisms, likes and dislikes, in all shades of arbitrariness and exaggeration.

There is no other way of preventing such abuses and of obtaining a greater strictness and severity in the study of the figurative arts, than to give an increasingly "philosophical" character to art criticism and history. The time has passed when it used to be discussed whether the "laity" as well as painters themselves had a right to discuss and to appraise painting. Anyone who in our days raises the question anew and opts for the exclusive right of the painter, can be answered with the observation that the critique of painting being a critique and not an act of painting, is by that very token the business of the non-painter, the laity. If the painters want to move over to the side of criticism, where they will be made most welcome, they will cease at that moment to be painters and become laymen, that is, reflective and reasoning persons, while on the other side, when painting is under discussion, even the laity have to become, in a sense, painters, potential painters. (In the same way the critic of poetry must always be a potential poet.) But literary culture and learning is not the whole equipment that we must insist upon the critic exhibiting. We must go the whole way in observing and affirming that the line of development, the law of progress, for art criticism, is willy-nilly that of philosophy. Perhaps the uncertainty and weakness of art criticism and history results from the lack here of any such great philosophical critics as have given form and strength to the history of literature and poetry; critics like De Sanctis, who were responsive to aesthetic impressions, but at the same time versed in the precise and delicate knowledge of men's hearts, feelings, lives, and in the discussions of art. Instead of such men of full-blooded nature and robust intellect, painting and the other figurative arts have more frequently attracted the attention of amateurs, collectors, artists, scholars, eccentrics, and dealers, incapable of dedicating themselves, as true critics should do, to a serious and conscientiously truthful understanding of works of art in the simple and serious human terms proper to them.

The rapid disappearance in these times, specially in Italy and Germany, of the division and the barriers of mutual misunderstanding and antipathy between students of Art and students of Aesthetics, is an indication that there is a deep-seated and logical need, of demonstrable importance in our time, for an ever more genuine and complete spiritualization of artistic interpretation, for its emancipation from formulae of sense and from rationalism, and for the union of art criticism with philosophy. A further such indication is the frequent appearance of essays and treatises on the methodology of art history. Of these works it must be said that they lack a specific argument, for there is nothing whatever to say about method which would not apply equally to the study of painting and to that of any other sort of work of art. Nevertheless they do, for all their empirical and eclectic formulation, signalize the gradual advance of the historians and critics of art from a rudimentary and haphazard philosophy to one that is richer, more conscious and elaborate. Only a few art historians will attain to the higher elaborations and most stringent formulations of such a philosophy, maybe not more than three, two, or just one; but that will be enough to ensure that these new truths, propounded by a few writers, will be transmitted in more popular form, in the guise of results rather than of processes, of examples rather than of theories, to a wider circle, winning for that branch of studies the philosophical character which has already been won for others.

Evidence to confirm that the law and the line of development for art criticism and history is essentially philosophical can be found in studies devoted to the history of such criticism and history. Some twenty years ago I urged the need for such studies, took measures to promote them, and myself furnished some examples. And I am glad to see that now essays, and indeed more than one attempt at a somewhat general and comprehensive treatment of the argument, have appeared in Italy, France, and Germany, and the Italian works have been particularly praiseworthy.[1] The study of these works will make it clear that the problems which were during the centuries raised, formulated, or solved in the course of the centuries by the critics of painting were substantially the same which arose in the criticism of poetry, while sometimes the two criticisms followed the lead one of the other, or were even practised jointly. It will also make clear how the various periods

---

1. Besides the essays and reviews by Gargiulo which appeared in *La Critica* (vols. IV-VIII, 1906-1909) I will mention among recent publications L. VENTURI, *La critica d'arte in Italia durante i secoli XIV e XV* (in *Arte*, XX, 1917); G. VESCO, *L. B. Alberti e la critica d'arte in sul principio del Rinascimento* (ibid., XXII, 1919); L. VENTURI, *La critica e l'arte di Leonardo da Vinci* (Bologna, 1919); L. LOPRESTI, *Marco Boschini, scrittore d'arte del secolo XVII* (*Arte*, XXII, 1919); M. PITTALUGA, *Eug. Fromentin e le origini della moderna critica d'arte* (ibid., XX-XXI, 1917-18), in which the whole development from the Renaissance to the nineteenth century is discussed; and A. RECCHI, *C. Baudelaire critico d'arte* (ibid., XXI, 1918).

and schools of art criticism were directly or indirectly, consciously or unconsciously, subordinate to the various philosophical schools and epochs: those of the mystical doctrine of Aesthetics, of the Aesthetic of the Idea, the formalistic, hedonistic, and moralistic aesthetic doctrines; or indeed to the more general teachings of dualism, materialism, positivism, and so forth. There is nothing surprising in this. The categories and dialectical moments of thought are what they are. He who pronounces judgements or makes affirmations may move from one category to another, from one moment to another, from a more primitive to a richer concept, but he will never be able to evade the law of mind and operate outside its range, outside philosophy. It will be the worse for him if he feels this necessity to be a heavy and constraining yoke, for it will mean that he has not learned to make a virtue of necessity, to dominate his thoughts by Thought, thus converting constraint into liberty.

I will not enlarge upon the last point. In one of my essays[1] I have already proved and illustrated the dependence of literary criticism upon philosophic thought, and I will leave it to whoever will undertake the task to demonstrate the applicability of that truth also to the criticism of the figurative arts. It would not be hard to illustrate the analogy in the processes of the two orders of criticism by studying such concepts as those of "the imitation of nature" (in literary criticism sometimes called also "lifelikeness"), "the appropriate", "rules", the respective ends of "pleasure", "morality", "edification", "sociality"; and so too the contrast between "design" and "colour" (matched often in the case of poetic criticism by that between the "naive" and the "sentimental" or the "classical" and the "Romantic"), the delineation of the "characteristic" and the "expressive" (which in both orders of criticism were long used in a psychological or naturalistic sense to describe expressive and characteristic features, figures, actions, and words), and so forth. Analogous historical interpretations are also given of the respective development of the figurative arts and of poetry, sometimes on

1. See *Nuovi Saggi di Estetica*, 3rd edn., Bari, 1948, 201-215.

the basis of an ideal studied in its beginnings, its perfection, and its decadence; sometimes in terms of sociology, where poetry and art remain engulfed, sometimes in terms of climate, race, and other natural conditions, with an unperceived loss of their character as spiritual creations. There is also, in both fields, an analogy in the relation between criticism and learning, criticism and philology. In the criticism of the figurative arts, as in that of poetry, mere biographical or otherwise incidental scholarship has sometimes overwhelmed and suffocated critical intelligence. It is only because of accidental conditions prevailing in the pictorial tradition of certain ages, that the special form of scholarship which exerts itself to excogitate "attributions" appears to be peculiar to the criticism of the figurative arts. In reality the same is found also in the criticism of poetry and all other arts, though maybe in smaller bulk.

What, then, of the present moment? In its best exponents, art criticism like literary criticism has now reached a firm awareness of its own character as history, and not mere scholarship, and of the consequent need to utilize the accumulated material of scholarship simply as instrumentality of interpretation, and, where it cannot so serve, to discard it as useless and irrelevant. The progress of philosophic thought has been an increasing safeguard against the error of conceiving the product of art in the manner of deterministic and naturalistic theory: Taine and Spencer have lost their persuasiveness. The concept of art itself has been freed from misplaced intellectual, moral, and utilitarian presuppositions, and criticism has thus been enabled to seek, in art, nothing other than art. The progress and advance here spoken of are attested by the very school of art history which we have been criticizing. This school is at one with ourselves in what it rejects. It does not seek to return to the past, it does not wish to identify itself with self-centred erudition, naturalism or positivism, intellectualism or moralism. As we literary critics are learning to do ever better in our approach to poetry, so this school seeks in the works of art their artistic soul, the eternal yet various and individual lyricism of the human soul. It is true that the mistake of confounding together

pure form and abstract form, and of allowing its own strict principles to become infected by sympathy for certain present-day
strivings of artists, leads the school towards and sometimes plunges
it in the peril of a renewed evolutionism and naturalism, and even
into that illicit way of judging works of art by their conformity to
models which is the essence of academicism (it makes no difference that the academicians should term themselves futurists).
And then the overlooking of personalities in the zeal to observe
the development of styles seems to impede, instead of duly as-
sisting, that work which has already been done or is in course of
execution for poetry, and should also be pressed on in the domain
of painting and the figurative arts: the sifting of the true and
brilliant artistic personalities (few in number both in poetry and in
the other arts) from the host of imitators, plagiarists, mechanical
handymen, pictorial entertainers who paint and sculpt for the occasion or on commission, and not because they feel an inner urge,
pseudo-intellectual authors of "new art", framers of programmes,
founders of schools, morbid amateurs of sensations and oddities,
one and all of them offering plenty of material to the historian of
culture, but little or nothing to the true history of art. These
dangers and errors and defects are, however, the imperfect and
immature aspect of what we will call the "stylistic" school, and
do not efface that progressive value which we have recognized in
it. These modern critics and historians of the figurative arts should
overcome them by following the example of the critics of poetry,
widening their mind, culture, energies in order to acquire clear and
full awareness of the truth that in addition to painting and the
other figurative arts there is all the rest of art, universal art, without
which painting is not truly intelligible but takes on the air of a
monstrosity of the life of the senses. And beyond and behind art
there is the human spirit in the richness of its forms and in its
dialectical unity, without which art itself is not intelligible. Finally,
beyond and behind present-day or recent art, and also beyond all
that art which may, according to personal preference, be regarded
as beginning with Rembrandt or Giorgione or whom you will,
there is the painting of all times and all peoples, chromatic or

non-chromatic as you choose to call it, which cannot be thrown out of the door, for fear lest in the ensuing rough-and-tumble it might be not art, but a criticism unequal to its task, which found the door slammed against it.

[1919]

XI

THE CONCEPT OF ALLEGORY

WHEN one appears to have indicated with all possible clearness where the crucial point of a question lies, one is always rather taken aback to find that no attention whatever has been given to one's remarks, and the other party is carrying on comfortably with his preceding superficial considerations. It is thus that I myself, after carefully thinking over and defining the non-aesthetic nature of allegory, and from this deducing how the allegorical must necessarily be extraneous to the poetry of Dante (as it must be to any poetry),[1] am somewhat taken aback to hear voices from various quarters replying to me: Allegory is a form of expression of equal standing with all the others, and like any other may be used now with good and now with bad effect, according to the capacity and the more or less happy disposition of the poet.

But the matter cannot be disposed of in these all too simple terms. And so I must repeat my previous demonstration, adding certain historical illustrations. However, I will invert the order of my remarks so that I may begin by rebutting the opinion which I have just quoted (I fear that I cannot accord it so serious a description as an "objection").

When Allegory is described as a form of expression of equal standing with all the others, this amounts to saying that it is one of those many forms which were once taught as distinctions in the discipline of Rhetoric, and are still largely so taught in our schools. But it is well known that when subjected to philosophic criticism and brought out of abstraction into concreteness, these distinctions appear as infinite individuations of the one and only poetic form.

Now the crux of the argument is this: Is or is not Allegory a form of expression? I flattered myself that I had demonstrated that it is not.

Anyone with a feeling or memory for literature might be expected to have a vague sense or presentiment, even if not yet a clear and

1. See my *Poesia di Dante*, 6th edn. (Bari, 1948), esp. pp. 20-24.

distinct awareness, of this. He would remember the aversion always shown for allegory in modern aesthetics and criticism, an aversion which is not shown towards such other figures and tropes of Rhetoric as metonymy, apostrophe, hypotyposis. Hegel called Allegory *frostig und kahl*, cold and bald product of the intellect rather than of the concrete intuition and the deep feeling of the fancy; devoid of inner seriousness, prosaic, far removed from art.[1] Vischer saw in allegory the complete dissolution of the original relation between idea and image, an index either of artistic decay or artistic immaturity, inorganic in character and, as he remarked satirically, enveloped in mysteriousness (*Geheimnissthuerei*), but lacking the depth of mystery (*Geheimniss*).[2] I do not wish to pile up quotations and need only mention the unremitting polemic of our De Sanctis against allegorism. "Allegorical poetry is tedious poetry" is his counterpart to the saying, "Political poetry is bad poetry".

We admit the existence of allegory in the rhetorical sense such as that spoken of by Quintilian and other ancient rhetors, and moderns like De Colonia and Blair: that "*inversio [quae] aut aliud verbis, aliud sensu ostendit, aut etiam interim contrarium*" (Quintilian) – in the second of these cases it was called irony –[3] or as Blair termed it, "prolonged metaphor".[4] Of allegory in this sense an example in Cicero is: *Equidem ceteras tempestates et procellas in illis dumtaxat fluctibus contionum semper Miloni putavi esse subeundas*; in Terence: *Suo sibi gladio hunc jugulo*;[5] in Horace the whole Ode to the Ship, which is a simple, affecting poetical image.[6] But it is

1. *Vorles. über Aesthetik*, I, 499-501.
2. *Aesthetik*, III, 467-71.
3. *Inst. Or.*, VII, 6, 44.
4. *Lectures on Rhetoric and Belles Lettres* (London, 1823), pp. 158-9.
5. Specimens from the texts of the Rhetors can be found in R. VOLKMANN, *Die Rhetorik der Griechen und Römer* (Leipzig, 1885), pp. 429-33.
6. "Der nüchterne Verstand sieht das Vaterland, das Bürgerwut zerrissen, schweren Gefahren eines neuen Bürgerkrieges ausgesetzt. Des Dichters Aug', in schönem Wahnsinn rollend, schaut es im Bilde eines prachtvollen Schifferbaues, der, ein halbes Wrack, schwerlich lange den Fluten Widerstand leisten wird. Die einzelnen Züge dieses Bildes mit entsprechenden Vorgängen im Staatsleben in Verbindung zu bringen, daran hat er als ein

not this rhetorical allegory, which the rhetors attempt to distinguish in practice from "simile" or "metaphor" in general, that arouses for us difficulties in Dante and other poets. It is not this which has rightly been viewed askance by modern Aesthetics and criticism, or requires a special investigation and the framing of a special concept.

The tradition of allegory in the real sense is to be found in the history, not of rhetoric, but of philosophy; and the enquiry may begin with a recollection of the reproaches of the first Greek philosophers against the poets, when Pythagoras, Xenophanes, and Heraclitus, anticipating Plato, found fault with the Homeric poems. As an historian of Greek critical literature observes, poetry with its fables was wellnigh succumbing to the assaults of the philosophers when there appeared men of good will eager to rescue it. Since these apologists could not save the letter of Homer, they interpreted him in a manner calculated to satisfy both parties to the quarrel. "*On chercha sous les vers du poète un sens différent du sens vulgaire, un sous-sens* (ὑπόνοια) *comme dit le grec avec une précision difficile à réproduire en français: c'est ce qui plus tard s'appela l'allégoire, mot inconnu aux plus anciens philosophes*".[1] What Theagenes of Rhegium, Anaxagoras, Stesimbrotus of Thasos, Metrodorus of Lampsacos, and the Stoics, especially, did in antiquity, was repeated, as is well known, with great effect from the beginning of and all through the Middle Ages, with the design of reconciling the new religion with the pagan authors. Thus originated the doctrine of the "four senses".[2] The allegory of which we have to speak is not, then, the *inversio* of the rhetoricians, but the *hyponoia* of the philosophers.

As already remarked, modern criticism and aesthetics had already

---

Dichter von Gottes Gnaden nicht gedacht. Daran hat nur der gelehrte Verstand ein müssiges Interesse . . ." (W. GEBHARDI, *Ein ästhetischer Kommentar zu den lyrischen Dichtungen des Horaz*, Paderborn u. Münster, 1885, p. 86).

1. EGGER, *Essai sur l'histoire de la Critique chez les Grecs* (Paris, 1886), pp. 96-102.

2. See the exposition in COMPARETTI, *Virgilio nel Medioevo* (2nd edn., Florence, 1896), I, p. 139 seqq.

widely signalized the incompatibility of this sort of allegory or hyponoia with poetry and art. They had further hinted at and described, though not clearly, its peculiar nature, terming it a product of the *Verstand* or "intellect" and not of the "fancy", and because "inorganic", therefore "mechanical". But the process of allegory had still not been fully explored: it had merely been excluded from the aesthetic circle as an artificial or rudely immature expression, or at the utmost apparently recognized in its true character and assigned to a cold origin described as "intellect" or "abstraction". This merely tentative criticism did not cut off the evil at the root, and could not preclude a new plea for the legitimacy of allegory, whether as an enrichment or heightening of the intuition by the intellect, or as a particular form of expression. For these reasons I thought it incumbent upon me not to stop short with a mere negation and rejection of allegory, but to work out more thoroughly what it is in itself, in its positivity, its proper function, expecting that I should, with this, throw full light upon that incompatibility of allegory with art which had previously been glimpsed and affirmed rather than proved. It was thus that I arrived (and was, I think, the first to do so),[1] at the definition of allegory as a practical act, a sort of code (and as such, obviously practical in character), a cryptography using spoken or figured images instead of letters and ciphers, but not on that account essentially different from any other. Starting from that definition I constructed the laws of allegory and explained how when no authentic interpretation or declaration has been provided by the author, when no fixed system of cryptograms together with the key to the same is at hand, then the deciphering of allegorical works is a desperate enterprise, never getting beyond conjecture, or at most attaining to some greater or lesser degree of probability.

1. Home (in *Elements of Criticism*, 1762-65, London, 1824, p. 351) notices the deep difference between metaphor and allegory and compares the latter to hieroglyph, but he pursued no further this sudden insight. Sulzer (*Allgemeine Theorie der schönen Künste*, Leipzig, 1792, I, 95) retorts perhaps directly to Home: "Man muss sie nicht mit der Bildersprache verwechseln, die durch willkürliche Zeichen spricht. Dieser wollen wir den Namen der Hieroglyphen zueignen . . .".

As already observed, allegory took its rise in Greek antiquity, and took on a new lease of life, as an interpretative technique, in the Middle Ages. Borgognoni (in some singularly penetrating and sensible pages on the allegorical element in Dante, ignored, perhaps just because they are so penetrating, by the Dante specialists)[1] remarks that "the allegorical system followed by the learned men of the Middle Ages was a system of hermeneutics rather than of inventive exercise. It was the established presumption that in poetical works it was both possible and a duty to discover a progression of high moral and spiritual significances. But I do not believe that (save for some cases of personification and myth) anyone in the true and classical Middle Ages ever believed that such significances should be the guiding lights of the artist in his creative activity. This was an application to the works of profane artists, of the system in vogue since the fifth century for the study of the Bible, according to which the facts narrated in its books were made to bear moral and mystical significances in keeping with the new religion." Quite correct: and yet the distinction between the process of the artist and that of the allegorist needs to be still more strongly and clearly expounded. It must be recognized that this mode of interpretation, this reading of allegorical meanings, of second and third and fourth senses into what was written, was in effect the very act whereby the allegory was invented and composed. Moreover, this composition of allegorical cryptograms neither was nor is the sole work of readers and commentators of poetical works, but also the work of the poets themselves, who after composing their poems, were pleased to allegorize them (as they still do) by attributing ulterior meanings to that which they had freely composed with the unambiguous meaning of poetry. The allegorization effected by the poet himself is usually an extrinsic afterthought, and, as such, harmless. Not but what (as Borgognoni himself admits) there may be cases where the poet sets to work to compose his poem with an allegorical intention already in his mind, intending, that is, to create a fanciful complex

1. *Scelta di scritti danteschi*, ed. R. Truffi (Città di Castello, 1897), p. 124 seqq.

having value simultaneously as a poem and as a secret code for the conveyance of certain religious, moral, political, historical, or other concepts. And that is certainly (as Borgognoni says in accord with modern Aesthetics and criticism as a whole) "a proceeding which is intimately hostile to, indeed prohibitive of art, whose independence and free development it denies and necessarily prevents". The effects would be disastrous were it not in fact "impossible" thus to serve two masters. For in fact what happens is what I have described on a previous occasion: either the poet forgets his intentions in the warmth of his fancy, and yields himself up to his poetic inspiration (only afterwards, when all is done, will he return to comment allegorically on his accomplished work), or else he keeps butting in with his intentional plan into his poetical inspiration, breaking the aesthetic coherence of this, and producing a complex which is not poetry but, for what it is worth, just cryptography. These, naturally, are two extreme and typical cases. Between them lie various middling and mixed cases. For there are brilliant poets who in some scattered blemishes exhibit traces of the allegorism that was in their minds when they set to work, and there are allegorists who exhibit scattered passages of lively representation, gleams of bright poetry.

(As an aside, let me mention that analogous cases are found in historical composition. A critical historical recital may be rendered allegorical, by utilization for a moralizing or rhetorical purpose. In this case the historical work itself remains uncontaminated. Alternatively such a purpose may penetrate into the historical work itself, infecting it, rendering it tendentious history, that is not history at all but oratorical writing. And there are many gradations between such extremes.)

All this confirms my conclusion that the aesthetic critic when dealing with allegory which aspires to take the place of poetry, should have one care and one only: to reject it as he rejects any other poetic void or ugliness. There is usually no call for him to try and unravel the allegory, for attention cannot be given in the same act of inspection to both allegory and poetry, those mutual exclusives. In the particular case of Dante, just because he is one of the greatest human poetic geniuses, the allegory lies almost always on the surface, and only very rarely impinges on the poetry. If the impacts appear to be frequent, even continuous, the fault is with the commentators who have loaded the wings of poetry with allegorical implications.

As a task having nothing to do with aesthetic criticism there remains that of unravelling the allegory for its own sake, deciphering the code. This occupation is the delight or preoccupation of many, or anyway of many Dante specialists. I have never denied, nor would wish now to be so ungracious as to deny, that such enquiries, when they have some probability to go on, have their own little intriguing interest. But here we may appropriately cite a passage at the beginning of Plato's Phaedrus in which Socrates, invited to give an opinion on the topographical myth of Boreas and Orithye, recalls the naturalistic explanations which had been or could be offered by acute persons, but declares that he for his part will make no contribution to them, for, said he, if he once set himself to explain Boreas and Orithye, he would have to go on to explain the forms of the Hippocentaurs, the Chimaera, the Gorgons, the horses of Pegasus, and all this would take too much time, and impede fulfilment of the Delphic oracle's injunction "Know thyself", and along with the Self such angry or benign forms as those of the Typhon, which are nothing else than the self. – To speak plainly, I for my part leave such enquiries and disputes to anyone who has time to waste, or who, as Dante puts it, having little knowledge feels little distress at the loss of time.

[1922]

XII

FOLK POETRY AND POETS' POETRY

In the abundant literature dealing with popular or folk poetry admissions abound that while "folk poetry" is easily talked of, and it is not hard to agree on what works the description covers, yet it is very difficult (1)[1] to "define" it. Is it not better, it is then suggested, to go ahead without seeking a definition, thus sparing much headscratching?

For all that, the attempt is not abandoned to define folk poetry at the very least by contrasting it with the poetry of poets, the poetry of literary artists. Folk poetry, it is said, by contrast with poets' poetry, is anonymous, improvised, springs from the people, that is from the humble ranks of peasants and shepherds, originates and spreads itself collectively, is passed on by word of mouth, is always undergoing change, and so on and so on. (2) But such descriptions lack any method or consistency. Folk poetry is not always anonymous, nor has the other always an author's name attached to it. Improvisation, or rapidity of composition, is not the mark of one or of the other, nor yet is a slow deliberate rate of composition. It is not only the humbler ranks who compose folk poetry, nor the higher ranks alone who produce cultured and sophisticated poems. No poem can have a collective origin: a personal poet's work is indispensable at the birth of a poem. Poetry of every sort can or does spread through the society of its place of origin, and more or less far afield. Transmission by word of mouth was the rule for complex literary poems in times when writing was little practised. It serves even today for the circulation of epigrams and satirical sayings of anything but popular origin and character, which it is preferred not to commit to writing. As to the "fluidity" supposedly characterizing folk poetry, what is meant is simply the incessant imitation, adaptation, modification which happens equally to literary poetry at the hands of authors, copyists, publishers, interpreters, and other conveyors. (3) Even if all or

1. Figures in brackets refer to notes at the end of the chapter (pp. 393-6).

some of all those descriptions of folk poetry were to the point, they would in any case cover only external characters and would thus be useless for the definition of a quality of poetry. For such a definition could not be (like the descriptions already mentioned) drawn from external circumstances, but would have to penetrate to the interior. It would have to be not, so to speak, philological, but psychological.

There are, in fact, other definitions attempted on more psychological lines. It is said that folk poetry is impersonal or general, indifferent to or lacking in technique, unhistorical (that is, not assignable to any historical phase), asynthetic, expressed in propositions not built into sentence form, or in verses not composed in a chain of stanzas, or composed in imperfect stanzas, or in episodes through which there runs no connecting story, or in successions of scenes lacking the link of drama, and so on. (4) Some of these latter descriptions do indeed point to genuine and characteristic features in the thing described, yet they do not bring this into a clear light, and when formulated in this manner are easily confuted. For one might retort that all poetry is both personal and impersonal, personal in that its content is the passion of a human heart, but impersonal in that this passion, becoming poetry, must have surpassed and overcome itself in the universally human. Accordingly poetry can never reside in the abstraction or type, yet any poetry may become typical for whoever generalizes its content. On the other hand, no poetry is ever void of technique, even in the sense in which the word is here used to indicate formal precedent, discipline, school. Nay, it might even be said that folk poetry, disposing of a small number of patterns, and repeating these, is outstandingly technical. And then, there is no poetry outside of history, and as to the supposed asynthetic character of folk poetry, if synthesis were lacking all would be lacking, for there is no act of the human spirit that is not synthetic. If the syntheses of folk poetry are genuine syntheses, yet different from the syntheses of literary poetry, the right proceeding is to investigate and locate the quality of this differentiation in folk poetry, not to deny that the synthesis is there.

Naturally, the difference whose quality is sought out cannot be absolute or pertain to the essence, because there are no categories in poetry, that which is poetry being purely and simply poetry. Here too then the temptation of violating unity must be resisted. Let it be remarked that the contrast between *Volkslied* and *Kunstlied* was primarily proclaimed by that same people which invented the contrasting pairs "classical and romantic", "Latin and Germanic", and others of the same order, a conceptual corruption of the pure aesthetic judgement. (5) It is not to be denied that there is beautiful folk poetry and unbeautiful (non-poetic) folk poetry, just as poets' poetry can be beautiful or unbeautiful; and folk poetry can be as ugly, awkward, facetious, mechanical as the other, and includes also no less abundance and variety of gnomic, admonitory, anecdotic, playful verse which is not and does not pretend to be poetry properly so called. (6) Nor, when folk poetry is poetry, is it distinguishable from literary poetry: its modes are enthralling and delightful. (7) The difference to be investigated and the resultant definition will have to be, then, as already said, merely psychological, a difference not of essence but of tendency or stress. Within this limit, it may be useful to the ends of criticism.

By way of introduction we may consider the analogy with other spheres of spiritual life in which a cognate psychological difference is found. We will at once recall, in the intellectual sphere, how "common sense" (8)[1] is distinguished from critical and systematic thought, without any intention of asserting that there could be a common sense wholly uncritical and unsystematic, or a critical and systematic thought wanting in common sense. Nevertheless it is clear that common sense is that attitude of the intellect which effortlessly asserts obvious truths, whereas critical and systematic thought takes up matters of doubt, struggles and wrestles with them, overcomes them, and, with often painful effort and unravelling of complications, proclaims its truths. Which truths often seem the very same as those proclaimed by common sense, yet they are not the same, for they carry a weight which is absent

---

1. Italian *buon senso*, which, like the French *bon sens*, signifies an elevated form of common sense. (Translator)

from the pronouncement of common sense, in that they sum up a great number of judgements which common sense never bothered itself to formulate, carry in themselves the results of a long process, and are forearmed against the emergence or re-emergence of doubts against which common sense was unprepared (and common sense may never have experienced them, but could not prevent them from raising their head, nor find any means of safety except to take flight, that is, to shut itself in itself). The linguistic monument of common sense is to be found in popular literature, and is built up of proverbs, and of what is called the wisdom of the ages, the wisdom of the world, so often praised for its utterly solid soundness, but no one, even when quoting such proverbial wisdom with approval, will ever mistake its maxims for the works of criticism, learning, philosophy, with their series of enquiries, discussions, treatises, systems.(9) Many philosophical discussions may be aptly concluded with the quotation of some old and familiar saying or proverb, but this, precisely because it is placed at the conclusion of the discussion, no longer bears merely its old and familiar sense.

In the practical sphere, a difference is recognized between the natural insight of the child or the peasant, and the insight of the trained man. In morals, we distinguish between sheer innocence, which scarcely lights upon evil, hardly knows of its existence, does good naturally as though knowing of no other course, and is itself a bright and happy goodness; and, on the other hand, a forearmed and forearmed goodness, aware of the passions and their perils, having measured these, struggled against them, mustered strength to subdue them. Such goodness is ever watchful and is austere rather than happy. But the distinction here, once again, is not absolute. There is really no natural goodness that has never experienced or been stung by evil, nor is there any goodness so austere and effortfully acquired as to have wholly lost the element of innocent, natural goodness. All the same the two attitudes are differentiated, and all can see which of them prevails or dominates in any given character. *Beati sunt possidentes*: true enough, but we give our admiration to those who work and achieve, fight and win.

25

Now popular or folk poetry is the analogue in the aesthetic sphere of common sense in the intellectual and wide-eyed innocence in the moral. It expresses emotions which have no immediate background and precedent of arduous thought and passion, but simple feelings which receive a correspondingly simple form. The poetry of great poets excites and stirs in us vast stores of memories, experiences, thoughts, multiple feelings, and ever finer shades of feeling. Folk poetry makes no such ample circling and wheeling flight towards the goal, but speeds straight for it. The words and rhythms in which folk poetry takes its shape are fully adequate for its aims, just as the words and rhythms proper to high poetry, charged with suggestions peculiar to it alone, are adequate for its own aims. For an example, take the celebrated popular stanza on the turtle-dove that has lost its mate, and compare this with the words expressive of almost the same image, which Tommaseo puts in the heart of Matilda of Canossa, bereft of her mate, pining for love. It will be seen that there is here no contrast between a greater and a lesser artistic perfection. The contrast is, that behind the popular verse lies the simple experience of the desolate restlessness of widowhood, but behind the other the whole agitation of the senses and mysticism of the Dalmatian poet.

The popular octave thus describes the misery of the dove that has lost its mate and now drinks alone in the stream, abandons the choirs of birds on the flowery branch, beats its wings, lamenting, on its breast:

> La tortora, che ha perso la compagna,
> fa una vita molto dolorosa:
> va in un fiumicello e vi si bagna,
> e beve di quell'acqua torbidosa;
> cogli altri uccelli non ci s'accompagna,
> sugli alberi fioriti non si posa;
> si batte con le ali sopra il cuore:
> – Povera me, c'ho perso lo mio amore!

Tommaseo's Matilda found no relief in sighs, but like a forlorn bird lamented to God, the pain unsilenced in her heart:

> *Né mai dal chiuso petto si partìo*
> *il sospiro dell'anima solinga;*
> *e per la notte lamentava a Dio,*
> *quale su' tetti passera raminga . . .*
> *. . . Ancóra, o padre, ancóra*
> *l'acuto grido del mio cor non tace! . . .*

The tone of feeling, rhythm, word-stuff of these last verses mark a depth by the side of which the popular verse seems to be but on the surface of things. But the popular verse is no more superficial than the other: in it, too, there is a vibration of feeling, and it is deeply human.

Such is the character of all the folk poetry that comes easily to mind. In the Tuscan *stornello*

> *Fior d'erbe amare!*
> *Se il capezzale lo potesse dire,*
> *oh quanti pianti potrebbe contare!*

what else is there but desolate weeping by night, the face pressed down on the pillow, for a sorrow which is just any sorrow, sorrow viewed simply as sorrow. – There is another folk song which echoes the answer which so pleased Alceste in the *vieille chanson* of *ma mie, le roi Henri, Paris sa grande ville*; the singer would keep his love though the Pope should offer him all Rome in its stead:

> *Se il papa mi donasse tutta Roma,*
> *e mi dicesse: – Lascia andar chi t'ama –*
> *io gli direi di no, Sacra Corona.*

There is nothing here save the eternal "no" with which man rejects the proposal that he should give up what stands highest in his heart, what he has come to live and breathe for, and has no equivalent in anything else, and is thus priceless. – Again, a lover has quarrelled with his mistress and thinks he has broken with her, but in a little while the name returns to his mind with all its old charm, and he dreams of and hastens on the reconciliation and the renewal of his love:

> *Nel passar per la vetta di quel monte,*
> *al tuo bel nome mi venne pensato;*
> *mi messi in ginocchioni a mani gionte*

e di lasciarti mi parve peccato;
mi messi in ginocchioni in sulla via:
ritorni il nostro amor com'era pria!

Goethe took pleasure in bright imaginations of girls with their
longings, their ruses and caprices, their anxieties, their throbbing
hearts: he served up these miniature portraits and scenes with a
smile of indulgent irony. But in the folksong the image emerges
unassisted, yet radiating the grace of such girlish desire and expectation (the girl too young for a lover tells what kind of song she
would sing were she not so small, and had she but, like the elders,
a lover for herself):

Son piccinina, e volete che canti?
Queste più grandi l'averan per male.
Tutte quest'altre ci hanno i loro amanti;
sotto di me non ci vorranno stare.
*   Ma, se lo avessi lo mio amante anch'io,*
vorrei cantare e dire il fatto mio!
*   Se ce lo avessi lo mio amante ancora,*
vorrei cantare e dir la mia canzona!

Greuze painted his famous *La cruche cassée*, now at the Louvre,
with a mixture of the innocent and the vicious, the moralistic and
the sensual, typical of all his painting and in general of his age. But
the same transparent symbol, untainted by corrupt and over-
refined eroticism, expressive simply of the fear and bewilderment
brought on by the event, together with a tragicomic apprehension
of the impending wrath of Mamma, is given us in an Italian lay
of the sixteenth century.

Meschina me, che ho rotta la langella,
alla fontana la me s'è spezzata:
trista la sfortunata sorte mia!
Mo saccio, mo saccio, mo saccio,
mo saccio che m'occide mamma mia!

A poor woman of Naples sings a lullaby for her child, invoking
the Saint who gives sleep, Saint Nicholas of Bari whose church is
near the Dogana:

Santo Nicola mio della Dogana,
con l'acqua tua li malati sani;

> *e sani li malati poverelli,*
> *e sonno porti sotto lo mantello . . .*

And she seems to see the good Saint, answering her prayer: he leaves heaven and draws near to the child and makes ready to immerse him in sleep by knocking on his forehead one of his balls of gold. The mother who has invoked this magic yet watches in vigilant anxiety for the result:

> *Vieni, palluccia d'oro, e dàgli in fronte,*
> *dagliela in fronte, e non me gli far male . . .*

We are still within the range of the simplest feelings, but these are caught on the wing and poetically expressed. There is much beauty in that fear of the Saint himself, that raising of the voice and stretching of the hand to protect the child even against him. – And here is the woman whose anxiety for her lover gone to the wars is also a motherly sentiment: –

> *Giovanottini che andate alla guerra,*
> *tenete conto del mio innamorato.*
> *Badate che non pòsi l'arme in terra,*
> *perché alla guerra non c'è mai più stato.*
> *Non me lo fate dormire al sereno:*
> *è tanto gentilin che verrà meno.*
> *Non me lo fate dormire alla luna:*
> *è tanto gentilin, me lo consuma.*

This is war seen through the eyes of a woman, taking its significance from the thought that now there will be nobody to take care of her young man in all the little ways in which she used to do so.

Here is a song of quite different feeling, celebrating the most elementary vitality; an old song, for I have found it in collections of the late seventeenth century, of the impetuous expansion of physical energies in their prime:

> *Tanta ho una fame che mi mangerei*
> *Napoli attorniata di panelle;*
> *tanta ho una sete che mi beverei*
> *Castellamare con le fontanelle;*
> *tanto è il mio passo che camminerei*
> *Carotto, Pozzopiano e Tresaelle;*

tanto è il mio sonno che mi dormirei
cinquecent'anni con nennella bella!

To appreciate also in the case of this song (in which the singer would like to eat all Naples, drink the fountains, sleep five hundred years) what differentiates it from literary poetry, it would suffice to recall similar expressions of gaily exuberant energy in the works of refined poets, where we should always find the sense close at hand of something higher, holding the gaiety within bounds, tempering it with humour, or opening up a vista of wicked and perilous inebriation; or some such complications.

I will close this little collection of examples, drawn, as I said, from my own memory rather than from laborious research, by citing three lines of a veritably grim and balefully mocking character, lines from a ballad sung in a village of the Basilicata in 1799 on the occasion of a semi-political and semi-brigandish encounter in which a man of the other side was caught and killed in spite of all the precautions that he had taken. It is the dead man who is made to speak and to relate the vanity of all the precautions taken ("mother made me breeches of cloth") when he came up against so astute and victoriously powerful an enemy ("when the blow fell, I went all cold"):

Mamma mi fece le calze di tela,
ed io me le imbottii di canavaccio,
eppure freddo, allo colpo, mi feci! (10)

Here there is no doubt a great efficacy in the images expressing the mockery and the tragedy, sprung from an elemental human delight in savagery.

We shall now no longer, after thus defining it, be led to confound folk poetry with other types of poetry with which it has sometimes been identified or confounded. It is not "primitive" poetry in the usual meaning of a poetry poor in intellectuality but rich in sensibility and fancy; nor yet the poetry of a "puerile" or "childlike" art corresponding to the disposition and mentality of the child (as contrasted with the disposition and mentality of the simple, the elemental). It is not vernacular poetry, though the expressions of dialect often well fit it: for dialect may be and sometimes is the vehicle for the ways of thought of the educated, and for literary poetry. But our definition enables us to see why folk poetry has been variously felt to be impersonal, typical, generic, non-technical, non-historical, all of these being indistinct approximations to the character which we have assigned to it, and by the light of which the approximations should be interpreted so as to reveal the sense in which they are true. Thus "impersonal" must signify not that the expressions of folk poetry are not personal, but that they are not so strongly diversified as in the poetry of the poets, where the personality of these is illustrated in prolonged compositions. It is for the same reason that folk poems are felt to be "typical" or "generic" and not individual. In the same way it is not true that they lack technique, that is, are not linked to a certain artistic tradition, but only that the tradition to which the poets' poems are linked is by comparison much more substantial. Folk poems are certainly not outside of history: those of the Christian peoples have different accents from those of Greek or Roman antiquity. Yet history means culture, and a cultural specification and diversification is lacking in folk poetry, hence its preference for dialect rather than for the strongly historicized ways of speech of the courtly and cultivated world. Folk poems are, in their way, synthetic, but not with that synthesis of multiple feelings and great contrasts which is found in the poems and dramas, and even the short lyrics, of the poets. (11) The almost constant combination of folk poems, but not of literary poems, with the singing voice and with instrumental music is explained by the consideration of the elementarity of folk poetry. (12)

Our psychological definition which sees the essential mark of folk poetry in a disposition of mind or a "tone" of feeling and expression, forbids us to identify folk poetry with the poetry of the so-called people, or of other such extrinsically and materially delimited milieux. There is plenty of folk poetry to be found under the guise and in the purlieus of literary poetry, and in the so-called sphere of popular or semi-popular art there is to be found not merely literary art, but artifice. The true distinction can be established only on the ideal plane, and by intrinsic standards. It may be very true that folk poetry usually flourishes in the popular class, yet not only in that, for its tone may be discerned wherever there are minds so disposed, which is far from being only in popular circles or on the part of men of the people. Anyway it is well known that much folk poetry is the work of educated or semi-educated men and very little is the product of ignorant working people (as to which ignorance much might be said and many distinctions drawn). Now for the "tone" in question to make itself heard, it is but necessary that certain men, however well educated, should have remained in a state of simple and naive feeling about life or some aspects of life, or should from time to time fall back into that state. In the same way there are men of high critical intelligence who in some ways remain simple-minded, trusting to common sense, and there are men of great practical experience who are in some ways childishly innocent. What is impossible is that having lost our innocence and won in its place another resource, we should behave innocently for example, after exercising ourselves in criticism and philosophy, take our ways of thought from proverbs; or having wholly replaced the tone of folk poetry by that of literary poetry, turn back and resume the folk tone. (13) Therefore it is that the poets, when they have applied themselves to folk poetry or something approaching it, can, if one looks closely at such work (always provided that the result has been something beautiful and vital, and not, as so often, cold and tedious), be seen to have taken up certain elements, motives, forms of folk poetry, but either deepening them in the process or letting some sort of irony play upon them, with the consequence that this apparent folk poetry turns out to be highly refined poetry. Critics have said that "all folk poetry tends to become work of the poetic art". (14) It is not, however, folk poetry that exhibits this tendency. As poetry, it is self-satisfied and independent. It is the Spirit which needs must pass from the one tone to the other, and sometimes back again to the former. It is a mere scholarly illusion to think to find summed up in the great works of poetic art the small and scattered creations of the popular Muse, which in truth only exist as small and scattered, having their own "tone" and not a different tone which has got the better of theirs, and which, even when it seems to offer them a welcome and a permanence, has in fact extinguished them, in the very act of animating their appearances, which it resuscitates, with a new soul. (15)

[1929]

Translator's Note: – It was impossible, by reason of other connotations of the words in English, to translate the title of this essay literally as "Popular Poetry and Art Poetry". Of the two sorts of poetry discussed in the essay, it has been found necessary to render *Poesia popolare* generally as folk poetry, but sometimes also as popular poetry, and *Poesia d'arte* variously as poets' poetry, literary poetry, or works of the poetic art.

(1) For example A. D'ANCONA, *La poesia popolare italiana* (2nd edn., Leghorn, 1906), p. 363: "'*Poesia popolare*' is an easy enough phrase, but the genre which it denotes is hard to define." But Goethe wrote as early as 1822 concerning the *Spanische Romanzen*: "Man spricht so oft den Namen *Volkslieder* aus und weiss nicht immer ganz deutlich, was man sich dabei denken soll" (*Werke*, Stuttgart, 1840, XXXIII, 342).

(2) It is unnecessary to supply quotations to illustrate the use of these descriptions which are to be found, separately or together, in all treatises about folk poetry. Suffice it to mention in connexion with the last of the list, that STEINTHAL gave special prominence to it in his essay on *Epos* (in *Zeitschrift für Völkerpsychologie und Sprachwissenschaft*, Vol. V, 1868, pp. 1-57). Folk poetry, he said, is a *nomen actionis*, there being in reality no such thing as a *Volksgedicht* but only a *Volksdichten*, no *Volksepos* but only a *Volksepik*. COMPARETTI, in an essay on *Poesia popolare* (*Rassegna settimanale*, 1878, II, 45-47), assigns to folk poetry "certain forms which, created and kept alive by the people, are always, essentially, and in all circumstances popular", such being the *stornello, strambotto, canzone*: to wit, certain literary or even metrical genres.

(3) MENÉNDEZ PIDAL, in *El Romancero, Teorias y investigaciones* (Madrid, undated, but 1928), p. 38 etc., draws a distinction between 'strictly popular, poetry' (which he defines as 'that which becomes popular'), and traditional poetry which the people accepts, reproduces with emotion and imagination, and more or less reforms and refashions, as happens not only to oral but also to written traditional poetry, witness the case of the French epic and of the *Chanson de Roland* itself, and their elaboration through the series of codices in which they have been transmitted. This amounts to eliminating all substantial differentiation between so-called "popular" and "individual" poetry, though Menéndez Pidal feels that there must be a difference underlying the ill-formulated distinction drawn and upheld by several generations of scholars.

(4) Once again I refrain from piling up quotations, but see HEGEL, *Vorlesungen über die Aesthetik*, Hotho's edn. (Berlin 1838), pp. 435-40, concerning folk poetry; also the comments of VISCHER, *Aesthethik oder Wissenschaft des schönen* (Reutlingen and Leipzig, 1946, etc.), specially III, 90, 990, 1147, 1194, 1356-8; and Carrière, *Aesthetik* (3rd edn., Leipzig, 1885), II, 535-9.

(5) In this connexion Goethe wrote as follows on the unity of all poetry, in an essay of 1825 (*Dainos*): "Es kommt mir bei stiller Betrachtung sehr oft wundersam vor, dass man die Volkslieder so sehr anstaunt und sie so hoch erhebt. Es giebt nur *eine* Poesie, die echte, wahre; alles andere ist nur Annäherung und Schein. Das poetische Talent ist dem Bauer so gut gegeben, als dem Ritter. Es kommt mir darauf an, ob Jeder seinen Zustand ergreift und ihn nach Würden behandelt, und da haben denn die einfachsten Verhältnisse die grössten Vortheile; daher denn auch die höhern, gebildeten Stände meistens wieder, insofern sie zur Dichtung wenden, die Natur in ihrer Einfalt aufsuchen" (*Werke*, ed. cit., XXXIII, 341).

(6) There are even series of words and songs having an almost exclusively physiological purpose, e.g to regulate work, wherein lies the partial truth of the investigation of BÜCHER, *Arbeit und Rhythmus* (4th edn., Leipzig-Berlin, 1909).

(7) I analysed some exquisite Italian folksongs in *Critica* IX (1911), now printed in *Conversazioni critiche*, 3rd edn., Bari, 1942, II, 245-50. I called then for a selection to be made, on aesthetic lines, from the vast mass of Italian folksongs collected by the folklorists. My hope has not been wholly disappointed. See the anthology of religious folk poetry by Toschi, and my review of it in *Critica*, XXI (1923), 102-4, reprinted in *Conversazioni critiche*, Bari, 1932, III, 266-9.

(8) DESCARTES, *Discours de la méthode*, I, 1: "La puissance de bien juger et distinguer le vrai d'avec le faux, qui est proprement ce qu'on nomme le bon sens ou la raison, est naturellement égale en tous les hommes."

(9) A persistently returning illusion is illustrated in these well-known words of Tommaseo: "If we could collect and group under certain headings all the proverbs of Italy, of all peoples, of all ages, with all the variants in language, images, concepts, the result would be, after the Bible, the weightiest of all books of Thought."

(10) To assist easy understanding, I have given here an Italian shape to the dialect poems.

(11) The theory of folk poetry and literary poetry given by HEGEL in the already cited work, points broadly, on the basis of a distinction between people (or nation), and individual, towards the truth of the matter: "Obschon sich im Volksliede die koncentrirteste Innigkeit des Gemüths aussprechen kann, so ist es dennoch nicht ein einzelnes Individuum, welches sich darin auch mit seiner subjektiven Eigenthümlichkeit künstlerischer Darstellung

kenntlich macht; sondern nur eine Volksempfindung, die das Individuum
ganz und voll in sich trägt, insofern es für sich selbst noch kein von der
Nation und deren Daseyn und Interessen abgelöstes, inneres Vorstellen und
Empfinden hat. Als Voraussetzung für solche ungetrennte Einheit ist ein
Zustand nothwendig, in welchem die selbstständige Reflexion und Bildung
noch nicht erwacht ist, so dass nun also der Dichter ein als Subjekt zurücktre-
tendes blosses Organ wird, vermittelst dessen sich das nationale Leben in
seiner lyrischen Empfindung und Anschauungsweise äussert. Diese unmit-
telbare Ursprünglichkeit giebt dem Volksliede allerdings eine reflexionslose
Frische kerniger Gedrungenheit und schlagender Wahrheit, die oft von der
grössten Wirkung ist, aber es erhält dadurch zugleich auch leicht etwas
Fragmentarisches, Abgerissenes, und einen Mangel an Explikation, der bis
zur Unklarheit fortgehen kann. Die Empfindung versteckt sich tief, und
kann und will nicht zum vollständigen Aussprechen kommen. Ausserdem
fehlt dem ganzen Standpunkte gemäss, obschon die Form im allgemeinen
vollständig lyrischer d. h. subjektiver Art ist, dennoch, wie gesagt, das
Subjekt, das diese Form und deren Inhalt als Eigenthum gerade seines
Herzens und Geistes, und als Produkt seiner Kunstbildung ausspricht." "Das
Volkslied singt sich gleichsam unmittelbar wie ein Naturlaut aus dem Herzen
heraus; die freie Kunst aber ist sich ihrer selbst bewusst, sie verlangt ein
Wissen und Wollen dessen, was sie producirt, und bedarf einer Bildung
zu diesem Wissen, so wie einer zur Vollendung durchgeübten Virtuosität
des Hervorbringens." "In diesem Extreme aber darf jener Satz nicht aufge-
fasst werden, sondern er ist nur in dem Sinne richtig, dass die subjektive
Phantasie und Kunst eben um der selbstständigen Subjektivität willen, die
ihr Princip ausmacht, für ihre wahre Vollendung auch das freie ausgebildete
Selbstbewusstsein des Vorstellens wie der künstlerischen Thätigkeit zur
Voraussetzung und Grundlage haben müsse."

(12) This last, just observation I owe to V. SANTOLI, *Nuove questioni di
poesia popolare* (Turin, 1930; *Pallante*, f. 5), pp. 38-39.

(13) This is the reason for the distaste aroused by that pseudo-folk poetry
which was cultivated, principally in Germany (but by reflection in Italy and
also elsewhere). One may recall Heine's satire upon it in the first book of
the *Romantische Schule*, culminating in the comparison with the woman in
the tale, who, to regain youth, drank a great draught of magic *elixir*, of
which the proper dose was a single drop and found herself turning to a tiny
babe! Heine had his doubts even about the best or skilfullest products of
this sort of art: "So schön auch die Tieck'sche *Genofeva* ist, so habe ich doch
weit lieber da alte, zu Koln am Rhein sehr schlecht gedruckte Volksbuch
mit seinen schlechten Holzschnitten, worauf aber gar rührend zu schauen
ist, wie die arme nackte Pfalzgräfin nur ihre langen Haare zur keuschen
Bedeckung hat und ihren kleinen Schmerzenreich an den Zitzen einer
mitleidigen Hirschkuh saugen lässt" (op. cit., book II).

(14) "The popular lyric is always striving to become art-poetry." Thus I
find summed up in the manual of GAYLEY-KURTZ, *Methods and Materials of*

Literary Criticism (Boston, 1920), p. 135, the conclusions of an essay of L. JA-
COBOWSKI (1896) which I have not seen.

(15) Not to complicate the exposition, I have spoken here only of "poetry";
but it is clear that the psychological distinction of the two tones is to be
found in all the other forms of art, and the same criterion is valid for popular
painting, popular music, and so on. If I myself do not, later, extend the
argument so as to embrace these other cases, I hope that someone else will.

XIII

LITERARY COMPOSITION IN DIALECT

ITS SEVENTEENTH-CENTURY ORIGIN
AND ITS PLACE IN HISTORY

In the seventeenth century the use by literary artists of dialect for literary composition became for the first time the fashion, and had a great vogue all over Italy. I do not think that this fact has been adequately noticed in our literary and cultural histories. It calls for critical comment.

Truth to tell there was someone who in the middle of the last century noticed the fact and observed that it implied a problem. This was Giuseppe Ferrari, who, however, as he so often did, went on to propose such an extravagant solution that the net effect was the contrary of his intention: both fact and problem were put aside and forgotten. In an essay published in the *Revue des Deux Mondes* for 1839-40[1] Ferrari reviewed with copious but inexact erudition the works published in dialect in the various regions of Italy from the end of the sixteenth to the beginning of the nineteenth century, interpreting the origin, growth, and luxuriance of that literature as a deep and highly significant popular and regional reaction against the courtly and national literature: one of many manifestations of the particular historical drama of the Italians, caught up in the antinomy between federalism and unity. A national literature (so ran the argument) had been forcibly imposed, the example spreading from Florence to the other cities. Everywhere it demonstrated its courtly and aristocratic character, annulling local traditions, scorning local autonomies; whence its failure to percolate down to the peoples who spoke different dialects corresponding to different ethnic origins, and stuck to their respective customs and cherished divergent and particular

---

1. Issues of June 1 1839 and Jan. 15 1840; reprinted in Italian with some additional comments in G. FERRARI, *Opuscoli politici e letterarî ora per la prima volta tradotti* (Capolago, tip. Elvetica, 1852), pp. 431-545.

aspirations. The progress of the national literature was therefore observed askance and resentfully tolerated. But its prevalence was absolute and seemingly unchallenged in the great age which lasted from Dante to Ariosto and Tasso, from the fourteenth to the sixteenth century, while at that time the dialect literatures, despised and repressed, struggled on in raw poverty. But when the national literature was close upon exhaustion and began to lose prestige, its power wavered, and the adversary, waiting in ambush, collected its strength and raised the standard of rebellion, until in every city of Italy dialect poets arose who in their natural tongues celebrated the various ways of feeling and of life of the regions and the localities, with all their inwardly cherished fancy and pathos, and their imaginative aspirations. And in doing so they made use of the surviving relics of the great literary age. It was an insurrection, a retribution of the wrongs of tyranny, and it flamed up with the strongest and most widespread violence in the outlying parts of Italy, in the South and the Islands, Naples and Palermo, and in the North, Milan and Venice, where the penetration of the Florentine literature had been most difficult, while the movement was less definite and less impetuous in Central Italy. Observing this dialect literature, one is charmed at so much liberty of figures and attitudes, such spirit, abandon, folly, picturesqueness. One turns away in distaste from Italy and her national literature and one feels "tempted to enter into confederation with those undisciplined but ingenious and cleverly resourceful dialects". One becomes aware of the disadvantageous situation of the Italian language, a language without a capital city, spoken perhaps by "less than one in twelve" of the Italians. One becomes aware too of the problematical and seemingly almost desperate condition of the Italian nationality: perhaps neither the language nor the nationality are soundly and authentically real. The general, Italian element did, it is true, enjoy a sort of restoration around 1860 with the help of the French triumph over the Spanish influence, which had been on the side of the dialects. But the difference has not been composed, nor is the struggle over.

On the foregoing fervid or perfervid historical thesis of Ferrari, another Italian then also living in France and contributing to French publications proceeded to throw cold water: Guglielmo Libri, who published his remarks in the *Journal des Savants*.[1] Libri observed that the circumstance which Ferrari had found so singular and peculiar to Italy was in truth general, for the dialects, in spite of all difficulties, maintain their existence and produce works of art everywhere, in France and England no less than in Italy. As to the superiority which Ferrari attributed to the dialects over the Italian language, nobody had ever thought of recognizing this in the times when Italy was made up of competitive or mutually hostile communes and States, and it would certainly not be recognized now, in mid-nineteenth century, when the efforts of all were tending to bring about a fusion. But although Libri's answer was reasonable, yet in refuting the paradox of Ferrari it tended to bury the problem which had just been raised of the significance of the literature in question in Italy.[2] I believe that further enquiry would have led to a conclusion directly opposed to Ferrari's, namely (to state in advance the view which will here be propounded) the view that literary composition in the dialects was not an uprising against the national spirit, but a contribution to the formation and consolidation of that spirit.

Compositions of literary art in dialect differ in the following manner from the naive or spontaneous utterance in dialect. The latter either precedes the development of a national literature (in which case the word 'dialect' is barely appropriate for want of a correlative contrasting term), or else (and here the word 'dialect' is truly justified) it proceeds alongside of it, having its own law, as in the common conversation of ordinary people, in repartee,

---

1. For 1839, pp. 668-81. Ferrari replied with a brochure: *Deux lettres à MM. les rédacteurs du Journal des savants sur un article de M. Libri* (undated, but in fact Paris, 1840), which appeared in Italian in the Milan *Politecnico*, I, 1839, vol. II, pp. 324-43.

2. A few hints were contained in CARDUCCI, *Dello svolgimento della letter. nazionale*, and also in *Parini minore* (*Opere*, I, 168-9, XIII, 90-1), echoing Ferrari's theory. Camerini retorted in *Nuovi profili letterarî* (Milan, 1875), II, 310.

anecdotes, legends, satirical and moral verses, and the other vehicles which common people construct for their particular uses and requirements of expression. The ancient or exceedingly ancient "monuments" of Italian vulgar speech dating from before the prevalence of Florentine literature, or from societies still little affected by its influence, all those relics of Sicilian, Neapolitan, Lombard, Venetian prose and poetry, represent the "dialect" literatures which cannot be properly so described, since each might have become a national literature had the history of Italy developed differently, had the Kingdoms of Sicily and Naples, the Republic of Venice, the Commune of Milan formed autonomous cultural centres as did, in the Iberian peninsula, Portugal and to some extent Catalonia. In contrast stand the fables, songs, and other products which the folk psychologists collect from the customary oral (less frequently written) tradition, and which constitute what is more properly termed spontaneous or also "folk" dialect literature: a literature which is not, and could not be, exempt from all influence of the cultured and national literature, but expresses the way of life of the common people, or some way that is habitual with them, or sometimes one which has a wider range, as witness the former and still current custom among educated people in some regions of Italy, of addressing each other in dialect.

Different from both of these is the reflex or sophisticated dialect literature which presupposes as its origin and point of reference the national literature. Ferrari was quite right when he remarked that this had its flowering time when the national literature had already three centuries of splendid and glorious life behind it. He was wrong, or exaggerated, when he represented this as a circumstance peculiar to Italy, for the same was happening in the case of all reflex dialect literatures. Where he was completely fanciful was in finding the motive of the spate of dialect compositions in a spirit of rancour, revolt, vengeance, acrimony against the prevalence of the national literature, poised in expectation for the moment when this should display weariness and weakness and so become an easy victim of an assault.

It cannot, it is true, be denied that a few or more than a few of the dialect writers can be found proclaiming that the Bolognese or Neapolitan or some other Italian way of speech is as good as or better than the speech of Tuscany, claims which reflect affection for the native city or (more often) contrariness and paradoxicality: in any case they are never altogether serious. Banchieri, who made the claim for the Bolognese language in 1626, wrote also in Italian. Cortese, who among the Neapolitans boasted of the local language's merits most roundly, composed verses also in the Italian of Tuscany and was even an Academician of the Crusca. His friend Basile, author of *Cunto de li cunti* and of *Muse napolitane*, was a professional writer of Tuscan verse, editor and commentator of poets of the Tuscan school. Both were popular with and praised by such Tuscan writers as Lippi and Redi. Far from the effective or principal incentive to literary composition in the dialect having been a desire to dethrone and to replace the national literature, it was the desire to complete the work of this latter. National literature was seen not as the foe to the dialect, but as its model.

There were things that could not be well said except in dialect: only dialect could well render certain manners and fashions in sensibility, in imagination, in expression; certain tones and forms of amorous, satirical or burlesque poetry. The Italian comedy-writers of the sixteenth century, Tuscans or others, soon felt the need of resorting to dialect for the part of the vain and boastful Neapolitan gentleman, and other similar representatives of social classes, professions, trades, just as it resorted to Spanish for the swaggering and swashbuckling "Captain Matamoros", to German for the mercenary "Lanzo", Slovene for the "Stradioto", Latin for the Pedant. Later on there grew up from the roots of classical comedy, but with the aid of new elements, the *Commedia dell' Arte* with those masks that introduced into the performance all sorts of dialects and shades of dialect, foreign languages, mixed idioms and argots. At the same time love songs, expressing love in its most elementary and general form, were preferred in the utterance of the Sicilian ("ciciliane") or the Neapolitan ("villanelle napoletane"). In the natural course of development there followed poems illus-

26

trative of folk ways, those, for example, of the Micchi Passari or Neapolitan *guappi* (bullies), those of the Mei Patacca or "cutthroats of the Roman region", those of the *vaiasse* or bondwomen; with other prose narratives of farce and fable, dramas of fisherfolk, of Neapolitan, Milanese, or Venetian street life, or for that matter of Tuscan life, for the Tuscan speech too could take on the popular tone of dialect. By this time the epic, chivalric, and tragic kinds of poetry, and the higher love lyric, and also the tale having for its plot the play of passion or of character, were represented by classical works in the national literature. Yet by the side of these major and of some minor tones of expression, suitably voiced in the national literature, there were other minor tones which only literary compositions in the dialects could express.

No doubt the literature of the dialects was enriched considerably by other elements besides those originating in the poetic and artistic tendency just described. In the seventeenth century there was a craze for the new and the strange which encouraged the introduction of curious and uncouth dialect vocables into verse and prose compositions for the sake of their unexpectedness and the astonishment with which they were heard. The steady and growing addiction of the learned academies to literary exercises, and the slothfulness which encouraged some to adopt literary forms which, at least in appearance, required less scholarship and exposed the writer to less stringent criticism, were also partly accountable. Such non-poetical considerations lie behind the spate of translations into the dialects beginning at the end of the sixteenth and becoming still more abundant in the two succeeding centuries: translations of classical poems beginning with Ariosto's *Furioso* and Tasso's *Gerusalemme* and not sparing the *Aeneid*, the *Iliad*, Virgil's Eclogues, and even Dante's *Divine Comedy*. And the same is true of a vast quantity of poems, idylls, lyrics, dramas. There is no reason for their composition in dialect, indeed none for their composition at all, except the above described literary trifling. Still, such a lack of poetic seriousness, such mere academicism and laxity, should not be charged entirely to the account of dialect literature as such. Most of those superfluities which encumber the national literature of the same period had similar utilitarian origins. Indeed, the works of clear and deep inspiration are always and everywhere few and far between. The rest is just literature, or rather bad literature.

Granted this, it is easy enough to justify my affirmation that the development of the literature of the dialects in seventeenth-century Italy, far from being directed against national unification, was, on the contrary, contributory to unification. It did not aim to resist or to replace a national literature which was then revered, accepted, and cultivated in all quarters. On the contrary it took the national literature as its model for compositions which introduced into the national life those voices which had previously been unheard, or rather inarticulate. National unity (and such is the very nature of unity) is never complete and static. It is always an unceasing travail of unification, seeking out and drawing to itself as nourishment and enrichment all the varieties and the contrasts which arise out of them, rather than shunning them.

The truth of this affirmation is shown by the warm welcome which the compositions in each dialect found in the other regions of Italy, not excluding Florence, which, according to the opposite view, ought to have felt outraged. In the same way those stage characters for whom the comedy writers had written their parts in the various dialects (*Diversi Linguaggi* is actually the title of a comedy of Verucci) had been warmly welcomed everywhere. Indeed it was a certain Niccolò Villani from Pistoia, almost a Florentine, who first collected and displayed samples of all these dialect effusions, Sicilian, Neapolitan, Venetian, Paduan, Brescian, Bergamask, Veronese, Friulan, Modenese, Genoese, Sabine or Norcian, and so on.[1] Everywhere praises were bestowed on such compositions as charming and witty in the extreme. Moralists, satirists, and humorists joyfully bedecked their pamphlets with dialect quotations. And so in the seventeenth century Carlo Goldoni succeeded with his comedies (as Caravia, Veniero, Varotari,

---

1. *Ragionamento dell'Accademico Aldeano sopra la poesia giocosa de' Greci, de' Latini e de' Toscani* (Venice, 1634), specially pp. 70-1, 74-9, 88-97.

Boschini had never done with their poems and lyrics) in familiarizing all Italy with the Venetian dialect, giving it a status which it never afterwards lost, while Giovanni Meli, also succeeding where his forerunners Antonio Veneziano and Rau had failed, won admiration and acceptance for the Sicilian dialect with his poetry in which the conventional world of the Arcadians achieved renewal and refreshment. If other dialects and other compositions failed to win an equivalent applause and admiration, this was because the compositions were of small or no value. And if sometimes blame was cast upon dialect literature, it was never upon that literature as a whole or for reasons applicable to the whole of it. It was, for instance, levelled by some readers against certain aspects of that output of dialect translations and parodies of classical poems, an output originating in easy-going literary leisure and unrefined jollity. The easy-going welcomed it, and with them some people with an expert taste in recondite vocabulary and striking metaphor, but others were understandably moved to horror by what they regarded as a profanation of high and noble works. When Tasso's epic appeared in a translation into the Bologna dialect, and shortly after into that of Bergamo, the Tasso enthusiast Foppa (as is related by Panciatichi): "was like to go out of his mind, thinking it shameful to debase the majesty of a great poet with absurd buffoonery of that sort".[1] Later, Pietro Giordani protested against the cultivation of the dialects, those copper coins necessary for the use of the common people in their petty transactions, so unlike the precious metal of the Italian language current in high affairs:[2] but breadth of view in such a matter was not to be expected from Giordani. In our own time there has been at least one expression of boredom and contempt for dialect compositions, by a writer[3] who affirmed that dialect literature, "even in its most serious and honourable, high and dignified manifestations, is by its nature, its inborn necessities, debarred from ever attaining

1. *Scritti varî* (Florence, 1856), p. 247 (letter of 1647).
2. In a review of 1816 of a reprint of Balestrieri's Milanese poems.
3. Pietro Mastri, *La malerba dialettale* (in *Su per l'erta*, critical notes on contemporary literature, Bologna, 1903, pp. 303-26).

the level of the literature which finds in the Italian language its most natural and legitimate expression". He added that the inclination to cultivate dialect and to give it importance "denotes a perversion of taste", a triumph of "mediocrity" if not of "vulgarity", leading in the long run to "barbarization". As to these last strictures, we have already remarked that the art of dialect is beautiful only when it is necessary and not arbitrary, as could indeed be said of all forms of art, there being none which may not in some cases denote perversion of taste, barbarization, an excuse for mediocrity and triviality. As to the limits of the field in which the literary use of dialect is permissible, we may indeed fix these in a rough-and-ready way on the basis of our own observation, but it would be altogether wrong to try and restrain the divine providence from permitting (as has sometimes happened) that dialect should sometimes be the vehicle of expression for a profound pathos and an elevated sentiment.

Turning back now to an historical consideration of the social circumstances favourable or otherwise to the cultivation of literary art in dialect, one may notice a period of loss of interest and neglect during the climax of the Italian Risorgimento. All interest was then concentrated upon political and moral issues, philosophic and religious thought, which tended to restrain the fancy and its expression from straying outside the ambit of the national and unionist cause, which was at one and the same time the European and international cause. This precluded attention to things regional and local. The great dialect poet who was then discovering his powers, the Roman Belli, was untouched by the influences of the Risorgimento and cultivated the muse of the Roman dialect in isolation. The comic dialect stage (for example Altavilla's Neapolitan comedies) hardly went beyond the range of slapstick and the topical. Only the Piedmontese comic stage, in the decade of the fifties, was sometimes a vehicle of civil education. The old dialect literature was at that time neglected and almost forgotten. Liberal and patriotic circles showed such distaste for it that the Poerio-Imbriani family, though Neapolitans, were ignorant of the ancestral dialect, and one of them who wanted to study Race Psychology, set himself to learn it by grammatical methods, like a foreign or dead language.[1] On the other hand folk literature, quite a different matter from literary composition in dialect, excited a sudden and progressive enthusiasm, drawing its origin from Romanticism, the love of the primitive and unsophisticated. The search for these objects of fanciful admiration was pursued wherever they were or seemed likely to be found. If it led sometimes into the field of dialect literature that was quite accidental and betokened no interest in local autonomies. It was simply that men hoped to find in dialect writings the primitive and the simple as they found them in the *Nibelungenlied* or the Spanish lays. It was then that Tommaseo collected the songs of Tuscany, Corsica, Illyria, and Greece, and published his commentary on them.

For further demonstration that literary composition in the dialects served the ends of national unification, it suffices to see what happened when unity was achieved, Italy had a capital, a Parliament, a civil service, national schools, and a press, and all the components of the resurgent nation could converse and understand each other easily from one end of the peninsula to the other. In those first years of unity a solution was even found for that age-old problem of the Italian language. After being yet once again raised and discussed between Manzoni and his opponents in the traditional terms, it became obsolete and forgotten by dint merely of the actual writing and speaking of the language, which created and re-created itself, as it had always done, in disregard of the conflicting views of grammarians and lexicographers. Now it was just at that moment that dialect literature picked up and regained popularity all over Italy. It was then that Belli's work became posthumously famous and beloved, raising up imitators in other regions and also in his own Rome, including Pascarella, the greatest of them all; poetic voices like that of Di Giacomo lent themselves to the love lyric, songs of sorrow, pathetic and tragic drama; the short story and novel were furnished copiously not only with regional and local lore, but also with dialect phrases and echoes, by

1. See CROCE, *Una famiglia di patrioti*, 3rd edn., Bari, 1949, p. 32.

Verga, Serao, Fogazzaro, and many others; whereupon the ancient and effete Accademia della Crusca, lacking the energy to complete its Dictionary of the Italian Language, proposed publishing, in accordance with the spirit of the times, dictionaries of the various dialects. What had happened? Was it that just when Italy was united the spirit of local autonomy burst forth more vigorous and untamed than ever? Was there war and rebellion such as the fanciful Ferrari described? Not at all. What had happened was that the regions had chosen that vehicle of dialect literature, among others, for improving their acquaintance with one another, in just the same way that the conclusion of the separate existence of the Italian States called forth on every side research students and historical societies eager to investigate their documents and records. Once again, then, the process was one not of disagreement and falling asunder, but of unification, and the accompanying feelings were those, not of discord and antipathy, but of concord and sympathy. As had already happened in the seventeenth century, the dialect compositions of each region were welcomed in all the others, and such worthy figures as Pascarella and Di Giacomo were acclaimed as being, despite their use of the dialect and the disadvantages which that sometimes entailed, Italian poets.

As to the position at the present day, there were signs of weariness in the years just before 1914, but now there seems to be a positive distaste and dislike for dialect literature. The war and its after-effects have drawn Italy back into the vortex of international life, and in the various parts and various parties of Italy the thoughts and feelings and expressions are such as accord with the moment. The decadence of the old regional centres, already very marked after 1880, has lately proceeded apace, so that one is tempted now to speak no longer of decadence but of disappearance. Will they regain strength in some new guise in a more or less near future? Will the Muse of dialect learn once more to sing with feeling or to recount with wit, and so be once more welcomed and celebrated? These questions ask for no vain predictions in answer. They are meant simply as a reminder of the function which the exercise of the literary art in dialect has borne in Italy and might bear again, in certain circumstances, in the future; a reminder, also, of the reasons for the first rich output of dialect literature in the seventeenth century.[1]

[1926]

1. More recently W. TH. ELWERT (in Herrig's *Archiv*, 1939, vols. LXXV-LXXVI) has taken up this question again, accepting my two contentions: that the literary literature of dialect is to be distinguished from the natural literature of dialect, and that the former cannot come into being save in relation to a literature in the national language, a national literature. But he demurs at accepting my retort to Ferrari to the effect that the literary use of dialect was not a rebellious proceeding on the part of the various regions of Italy against the literature of Tuscan origin which had come to prevail, but on the contrary a process of enhanced kinship and spiritual unification. Elwert objects that the conditions in which the literature came into being were not the same throughout the four centuries from the sixteenth to the twentieth. And this is obvious, but it does not enter into the present question, which is exclusively concerned with the function actually borne by dialect literature in reference to national literature, whether, that is, one of rebellion or one of co-operation. Since nobody, not even the fanciful and paradoxical Ferrari, ever thought that dialect literature was capable of supplanting national literature once this had come into existence, the answer must be that dialect literature necessarily contributed to national literature a supplement drawn from the various regions and dialects, thereby contributing to the enrichment of the community of Italian life. See review in *Critica*, XL, 217.

XIV

THE BAROQUE

"The Baroque Age", "Baroque painting", and such terms are now in common use. Under one word are grouped things of the most various quality, painters who are genuine painters and painters who are flashy and false, true poets and pseudo-poets, and so on. "Fine Baroque" and similar complimentary descriptions are handed out, with the effect of giving a positive value to this concept, or an alternatingly positive and negative value. It would be absurd to protest against such use of a linguistic term, but the use renders it particularly necessary to clarify the concepts, going back to their origin.

Investigation of these origins shows that the word and concept of "Baroque" were invented as terms of disapproval, to denote not a period of cultural history or a form of art, but a type of perversion, of artistic ugliness. In my view they need to be retained or restored in this sense, when used on the level of strict and systematic thought, and the logical definition should be more carefully elaborated.

There seems to be no doubt that the origin of the word "Baroque" lies in one of those artificial mnemonic terms applied in mediaeval logic to the various figures of the syllogism. Among those terms (*Barbara*, *Celarent*, and the rest), two, at least in Italy, caught on far more than the others, namely *Barbara*, because it was the first of the list, and then, for some reason, *Baroco*, the term for the fourth mode of the second figure. Why should *Baroco* have won this prominence? It was no odder than the others, nor was the mode which it designated any more complicated. Perhaps it was because of the alliteration with *Barbara*. We find Caro writing in his *Apologia*: "If these syllogisms are correct, then *baroco* and *barbara* and all those others are just so many sugar-buns." As the movement against Aristotelian and scholastic traditions grew, such terms drawn from the disputations of the schools became increasingly unpopular and contempt was shown for the pedantic and uncouth mode of reasoning by affixing to it that one of the two well-known terms which appeared the more bizarre, and also had no meaning as a word. A bad piece of reasoning thus came to be called an "argomento in baroco". In the *Rime burlesche* of Giovan-francesco Ferrari, published in 1570, the pedant who with his show of learning succeeds in making the master of the houses where he teaches look foolish, does so in "baricoco":

> *E con qualche argomento in baricoco*
> *far restare il messere un bel castrone.*[1]

In the *Viaggio in Colonia* of Antonio Abbondanti, dated 1627, the well-known sophism according to which salted meat, by encouraging you to drink, quenches your thirst, is called an argument "in baroco":

> *Egli in baroco un argomento fino*
> *formò, dicendo: — per cavar la sete*
> *convien bere e ribere del buon vino.*
> *Carne salata non dà mai la meta*
> *nel bere e nel ribere; onde — ecco l'ergo —*
> *ch'avvien che la salsiccia pur dissete.*[2]

In the satire on pleasure, *Lussuria*, of Azzolini, of the same date, Jupiter thinks poorly of a syllogism "though it is in barocco" . . .

> *Rispose Giove: — Orsù troppo cammina*
> *tal sillogismo, sebbene è in barocco . . .*[3]

The dictionary of the Accademia della Crusca cites another example, less obvious and later in date, from Megalotti at the end of the seventeenth century: "Remember, before three post days are passed, we shall begin to get news of the decisions of the friars, their arguments in barocco, with what Brother So-and-so said

1. Venice, 1570, Chapter 42, 88.

2. *Viaggio in Colonia,* "pleasant chapters" by ANTONIO ABBONDANTI of Imola (Venice, Baba, 1627), p. 21. Incidentally the argument in question was not in *baroco*, in which the first premiss has to be a universal negative, the second a particular negative, and the conclusion a particular negative (as: Every P is T; some S are not T; therefore some S are not P).

3. See *Raccolta dei poeti satirici italiani* (reprinted Turin, 1853) II. 19.

and what Brother Such-and-such answered."[1] This sort of reference is easily found in the following centuries (compare Casti's "ragioni barocche" and Pananti's "idee barocche"[2]) down to the present day. Now from the use of "baroque" to describe absurd, exaggerated, pompous, fallacious manners of reasoning, to using it for some or all of the manifestations of art in the seventeenth century, the transition was swift, and probably dates from the middle of the eighteenth century, the time of the neo-classical revival, and maybe in France earlier than in Italy. The *Encyclopédie* notes and defines this use of the word, though applied only to architecture: "Baroque, adjectif en architecture, est une nuance de bizarre. Il en est, si l'on veut, le raffinement, ou, s'il était possible de le dire, l'abus,... il en est le superlatif. L'idée du baroque entraîne avec soi celle du ridicule poussé à l'excès. Borromini a donné les plus grands modèles de bizarrerie et Guarini peut passer pour le maître du baroque."[3] And in Italy Francesco Milizia wrote similarly in his *Dizionario delle belle arti del disegno*:[4] "Barocco is the superlative of the bizarre, the excess of the ridiculous. Borromini was wildly extravagant, but the work of Guarini, Pozzi, and Marchione in the sacristy of Saint Peter's is baroque."[5]

1. *Lettere familiari* (Florence, 1769), I, 74.
2. There are examples given in dictionaries: "Il étoit bien baroque de faire succéder" (Saint-Simon quoted by Littré). Marquis Carraciolo, Neapolitan Ambassador to Turin writes to Tanucci: "Oh quanti discorsi barocchi sono usciti fuori su tal soggetto" (Feb. 28 1763).
3. Quoted by WÖLFFLIN, *Renaissance und Barock* (Munich, 1888), p. 10. He says wrongly that the word was unknown to Milizia. (In later editions he says that the *Encyclopédie* ignores the word "Baroque" in the sense familiar to us, assigning the quotation here given to QUATREMÈRE DE QUINCY, *Dictionnaire historique de l'architecture*, 1795-1825, while he recognizes that Milizia uses the word in the present current sense.) WEISBACH in his recent *Barock als Stilphänomen* (in *Deutsche Vierteljahrschrift für Literaturwissensch.*, II, 1925, pp. 225-56) recalls the use of the word in a letter of De Brosses of 1739 (ed. Colomb, II, 119-20), in a passage which, as was then customary, brackets the baroque with the *gothique* – the matter would merit investigation in the interests of a better understanding of "Gothic" but this is not the place. For Weisbach see my review in *Critica* XXIII, now reprinted in *Convers. Critiche*, III, Bari, 1932, 150-53.
4. Bassano, 1797, I, 90. Baldinucci in his dictionary of the previous century ignores the term.
5. Against this more obvious and better documented derivation, etymo-

Whatever conclusion we reach about the etymology of the word, there can be no doubt that the concept of "baroque" was evolved by art critics to denote the form of artistic bad taste which characterized a great part of the architecture and also of the sculpture and painting of the seventeenth century, and is indeed all of one sort with the expressions "bad taste", "literary plague", and "delirium", used to condemn the prevailing style of poetry and prose of the seventeenth century, for which then the nineteenth invented the still current description "secentismo". Indeed "baroque" is so much all of one sort as to be identical with these. It has long been usual to talk of Baroque and the baroque tendency in literature, so describing writers like Marini, Achillini, Battista, Artale, and such use of the word is to be encouraged, for it pins down the identity of the artistic failing as found both in poetry and in the other arts, and also spares us such awkward paradoxes as discovering *secentismo*, the disease of the seventeenth century, in writers of the fifteenth, or of the decline of the Roman empire, or even, as has been done, in the fathers of the Church.

Baroque, then, is a sort of artistic ugliness, and, as such, is in no sense artistic but quite the contrary. It is something other than art, which has adopted the air and name of art, occupying and usurping art's place. This something, which will not obey the law of artistic coherency, but violates or cheats it, must evidently obey another law, which can only be that of whim, comfort, caprice, a law of utility or hedonism, we may call it which we will. Baroque, then, like every sort of ugliness in art, has its basis in a practical need of some sort which may be of varying shape and origin, but in cases like that now under consideration will be nothing more than the demand for and the enjoyment of the

logists cling to that from *barrueco* or *berrueco*, Spanish for the imperfectly rounded pearl called in Italian "scaramazza". But the Spaniards call the style *barroco*, not *barrueco*. Littré derives *barrueco* itself in the sense of "pearl" from the scholastic term, but Diez relates it to the Italian *verruca* (blister), Körting amuses himself with constructing a "bis-rocca". — Tommaseo-Bellini, who began by accepting the proper derivation, could not rest satisfied, but produced a Greek βάρος, a low Latin *barridus*, the verb παρα-κόπτω (to be delirious), and so forth.

agreeable, in disregard of all else, indeed in contrast with art itself.

Now, to distinguish the Baroque from other sorts of ugliness, of contrariety to art, we must first consider what sort of hedonistic satisfaction is that which the Baroque affords. But here we must observe that an enquiry of this sort can lead to no more than an empirical classification, for the modes of pleasure are infinitely various, infinitely shaded and graded. And these various classes or types of pleasure catered for by the unbeautiful are not mutually exclusive but often commingled, and sometimes one leads on to another, as Manzoni observed when introducing that imaginary "anonymous" author who managed to write a prose "at once rough and finicky".

Honestly, it is no very difficult task to point out the characteristic of the Baroque as distinguished from the "academic", the "senti-mental", the "melting", and suchlike. The Baroque substitutes for poetic truth and the charm which it inspires, the shock of the unexpected, the astounding, which excites, amazes, and pleases in virtue of the thrill which it communicates. The task is not difficult because, as is well known, this characteristic was proclaimed as the end in view by the literary men of the school. The chief of them, Marino, assigned to the poet the procurement of wonderment, *maraviglia*, advising anyone incapable of being astounding to "andare alla striglia", to take a groom's job. Other quotations would be easy, but superfluous. And there were, even at the time, those who pointed out the difference between the pure and ideal emotion belonging to poetry, and this unpoetic emotionalism, accusing the "modern poets" of "erring gravely . . . in their pathetic passages, . . . using recondite conceits and shows of wit becoming to the unfeeling and not to the impassioned, so that it is small wonder if they fail to grip and impassion the reader". And we read that "Tasso stumbled in this way sometimes", while Marino "fell disgracefully".[1] The extreme limits of amazingness were attained by poets of the seventeenth century like Artale with his extravagant sonnets, Lodovico Leporeo with his "leporeambics"

1. *Considerationi di messer Fagiano* (N. Villani) *sopra la seconda parte dell'Oc-chiale del cav. Stigliani* (Venezia, 1631), pp. 20-1.

and his "curious rhymed prose", and, marvel of marvels, his lines in which every word rhymed, for example:

> Cinthia, se mài con gli occhi gài sincèri
> tuoi lusinghièri, e dolci mi rimìri,
> gioie m'inspìri, e gli egri miei pensièri
> ergi ai sentièri degli Empirei giri . . .[1]

and so too in a rhyming prose celebration of the architecture of Borromini: ". . . tutti edificij costrutti a beneficij de' Regi dagli artefici de' Pontefici egregi, tra' quali più principali io celébro sul Tebro, tra quanti io conosca modellanti con novità e soprafino ingegno e pellegrino disegno, e all'età nostra, nell'Alma Città Tosca tener la palma del migliore inventore il signore Francesco Borromino, conforme le norme del pensiero vitruviesco e vicino all'eccellenza della di lui intelligenza nella costruzione e ristaurazione di Delúbri degli Insúbri" and so on.[2] For such stylistic prowess Leporeo was celebrated as "ingenium peregrinum et floridum" to whom the tribute could be paid, "nihil scribit vulgare".[3]

The same substitution of the realistically breathtaking for the tender heart-beats and contemplative raptures of art, is signalled by the historians of the arts in Baroque sculpture, painting, and architecture. Old Cicognara described the features of this sculpture, the undulating lines, studied countenances, emphasized muscles, perpetual peaceless motion, coquettishly outstretched necks, self-consciously charming gestures, affectedly mobile arms, curved fingers, one thigh thrust too much forward and one leg forcibly doubled up, luxuriantly rendered flesh, exquisitely worked hair and nails, and, besides these particulars of the human body, delicately sculptured trees and leaves. Cicognara went on to say: "No sculptor of the seventeenth century portrayed the affections,

1. *Leporeambi nominali di* LODOVICO LEPOREO *alle Dame et Accademie italiane* (s. l. a., ma Roma, 1682).

2. *Prosa rimata curiosa ritrovata da* LODOVICO LEPOREO. *Amico corporeo dei prosatori primari verseggiatori volgari scrittori singolari* (Rome, Stamperia della R. C. apostolica, 1652).

3. Thus Father Caramuel, one of the great technicians of this stuff, in his *Metametrica* (Rome, 1663).

while twelfth and thirteenth century carvers produced works full of affection."[1] Burckhardt writes of the "false dramatic liveliness" then introduced into sculpture and painting, with the result that the shallower and more superficial was the sentiment, the more agitated were the draperies, into the preposterous folds of which was translated the false drama.[2] He tells of architects composing in a perpetual *fortissimo*, accompanying columns, half-columns, and pilasters with a filling of half-pilasters, one-third pilasters, one-quarter pilasters, on every hand, with corresponding interruptions and protuberances of the entire entablature and in some cases also of the ground-story, seeking to enchant the eye with sheer display, the architectural members themselves dancing about, the roof lines breaking away to curve and quake in all directions.[3] Riegl expresses the perplexity which anyone now feels who approaches these productions as works of art: "A figure is praying, and in this act moves its limbs convulsively. Why these agitations? To us they seem pointless, incomprehensible. The figure's robe is violently inflated as though by a hurricane. Once again, we ask, why? Nearby is a tree whose leaves hang quietly. Why does the hurricane inflate the robe but not move the leaves?"[4] The fact is that the coherency properly belonging to the poetic and artistic images has been scrapped in favour of a coherent incoherency, or of a coherency aimed at the single purpose of producing, no matter how, feelings of surprise and astonishment. It is related that the famous soprano Farinello, unadulterated product of a seventeenth-century musical education, was singing bravura-wise to Emperor Charles VI, when the monarch, who was accompanying him on the harpsichord, stopped, and said almost paternally, "These great runs and passages of yours that never come to an end, these wonderful ventures, rouse astonishment and admiration, but they fail to touch the heart. You could more easily rouse feeling if

1. *Storia della scultura*, 2nd edn., VI, 69-72.
2. *Cicerone*, 6th edn., II, 483.
3. Ibid., II, 280-1.
4. A. RIEGL, *Die Entstehung der Barockkunst in Rom* (2nd edn., Vienna, 1923, pp. 2-3).

you could sometimes be simpler and more expressive." In fact the monarch, a man of taste, repeated the same criticism which we have quoted from a critic of Marino's poetry a century earlier.

There is no need to proceed with a demonstration of the obvious, namely that the Baroque is precisely this game, this infatuation for the amazing. The few and casual quotations already cited show it quite sufficiently. Whereas other forms of the unbeautiful are sometimes arresting, exciting, disquieting, the Baroque, for all its agitation and surface warmth, ends by producing the effect of coldness, and, for all the multitude of images which it brings on the scene and combines together, of emptiness. It is a further consequence of its nature that it seems at times to pass abruptly from the most subtle intellectualism to the most crass imitative realism in its representations. The Baroque, unable to win to its uses the poetic image which is at the same time spirit and body, feeling and figure, ideal and sensible, can but exercise itself with antitheses and other relations between empty concepts, in an effort to make a show of ideality and spirituality; or alternatively note down and reproduce the material and external features of things, making a display of extraordinary plastic energy and realistic boldness. But realism of that sort is intellectualistic, and spiritualism of that sort is materialistic. In the face of certain sculptures, paintings, and poems of the Baroque school, it is impossible not to feel that the representation of the loathsome, the dreadful, the bloody, or for that matter simply of the commonplace and plebeian, is undertaken solely in order to awaken admiration for the boldness and skill which has reproduced what others would never have thought of using as matter for art. The representation is a description, a description accomplished with *bravura*. Let me recall that often quoted passage of Father Orchi with the comparison of the confession of penitents with washing of clothes. In prolonged detail he recalls, piece by piece, the work of the washerwoman: ". . . elbows bared, loins girt, she takes the dirty garment, goes down on her knees by the waterside . . . (and so on for many lines and then) . . . with four wringings, three shakings, two sousings, and one twist, she brings it forth again neater and cleaner than ever". Even the comical and ridiculous is given such an emphasis of ultracomicality and supersmilingness that it ends by being as frigid as are the Baroque's depictions of passion and heroism. Straight hearty humour goes together with seriousness of feeling and a freedom of mind ascending to the summits of calm.

The examination of individual Baroque poems or paintings gives occasion to illustrate the absence of poetical and artistic coherency in the various parts, the various shapes, by contrast with a coherency for practical, utilitarian ends which, as already remarked, will be found present. Yet the error of supposing that certain types of form, when abstracted from single works of art, are always characteristic of the Baroque, always indicative of its presence, should be avoided. Such an error of formalism was committed by the Italian critic who adduced as an example of the Baroque such a mystical expression as the following from the pen of Saint Catherine of Siena: "Where was it that the sweet and loving Word taught us this doctrine? On the pulpit of the most Holy Cross. And finally he washed the face of our soul with his precious blood." Despite the apparent similarity of metaphors, this is really the very opposite style from that of the Baroque preacher with his laundry-confessional. The German critics who confound the antitheses of the Baroque writers with those of such mystics, contemporary with the Baroque, as Jacob Böhme or Angelus Silesius, err similarly.[1] There are writers outside Italy who used to be cited as affording clear evidence that Baroque was not just an Italian speciality, writers in whom, however, are to be found seriousness, enthusiasm, simplicity – I am thinking of Du Bartas – and whose

---

1. F. STRICH, *Der lyrische Stil des 17. Jahrhunderts* (in *Abhandlungen zur deutschen Literaturgeschichte* in honour of F. Muncker, Munich, 1916), pp. 29-33, where these among other verses of A. Silesius are cited as Baroque:

> *Ich weiss nicht was ich bin, ich bin nicht was ich weiss:*
> *Ein Ding und nicht ein Ding: ein Tüpfchen und ein Kreis.*

> *Gott selber, wenn er dir will leben, muss er sterben:*
> *Wie denkst du ohne Tod sein Leben zu ererben?*

27

metaphor- and epithet-laden versification denotes, not emptiness of heart and rhetorical frivolity, but a rhetorical verve in line, it is true, with his own and his age's inclinations. Góngora, so fresh and racy a writer in his early period, indeed in much of his work, arrived at certain forms of expression, not by the same route as Marino, but rather led on by the zest of artistic refinement, the ideal of a recondite poetry for adepts, which sometimes attained effects of strange beauty with a sort of enchanted rendering of a literary mythology superinduced upon natural objects. What matters more is the critical formalism which pretends to see close relations between the Baroque and the Romantic tendencies, in reality so different. For Romanticism does not feign agitation, it is genuinely agitated. It does not hunt down and industriously collect images and words to provoke wonder, but desires the image and the language of art to be the immediate outpouring of sentiment. This is its aesthetic fault. I doubt, for example, whether Faguet's favourite thesis on French Romanticism, not of the year 1830, but of 1630, is based upon observation of the inner character of what he writes about. His starting point is, in fact, the supposition that Romantic literature is that in which ". . . la sensibilité, l'imagination, le caprice et la fantaisie prédominent sur le goût de la vérité et de la mesure . . .; où le culte de l'antiquité et de la tradition disparaît . . . où l'inspiration des littératures étrangères est plus complaisamment accueillie que celle des littératures antiques".[1] But this is a definition of Romanticism by external characteristics, which leads Faguet by dint of comparison with external characteristics found present in the works of many French writers between 1610 and 1660, to extend to all the common description of Romantic. On this showing Corneille himself is dubbed "essentiellement un poète romantique"; nay, "le plus grand des poètes romantiques de France" because "il était exagéreur et avait le sens du grand et la passion de peindre en bien et en mal plus grand que nature", loving "l'invraisemblance" and preferring "l'imagination" to "vérité".[2] But that alleged Romanticism, so ill-defined as to

1. *Petite histoire de la littérature française*, pp. 100-1.
2. Ibid., p. 157.

include without reserve the great Corneille, least romantic of authors, poet of the reflective and resolute will, was nothing else than the Baroque, as Faguet could have learned from one of his alleged Romantics, Cyrano de Bergerac. Cyrano said of the "pointe" or witticism: "La pointe est l'agréable jeu de l'esprit, et merveilleux en ce point qu'il réduit tout sur le pied nécessaire à ses agréments sans avoir égard à leur propre substance .... Toujours on a bien fait, pourvu qu'on ait bien dit. On ne pèse pas les choses pourvu qu'elles brillent."[1] Baroquism consists in this Baroque spirit, not in abstractly fixed, but really fluctuating forms, which, in their variety of concrete manifestation may indeed incarnate the Baroque, but may, on the contrary, incarnate something different, or very different, or even totally contrary to the Baroque.

Understood in the general terms which we have held to in the foregoing, the Baroque is to be found in every place and time, now more and now less in evidence. It is an aesthetic vice, but also a human vice, universal and perpetual, as such vices always are, at the very least as potential perils. In the same way it has been possible to construct a generically human or psychological concept of the Romantic, and in terms of this to discover Romanticism now here, now there, among all peoples and in all epochs. The presence of the Baroque, as is well known, has been studied particularly in the artists and poets of decadence, notably of the Roman literary decadence, in Lucan, Statius, Persius, Martial, Juvenal, and so forth. These poets furnished the argument for a fine if somewhat tendentious book by Nisard, for there was in it an implied reproof to the French literature of his time.[2] A similar comparison has been enlisted in heated polemics about modern Italian literature, specially the poetry of D'Annunzio, and other literature of the most recent period. I am not saying that such parallels are improper or pointless, indeed I admit that they have a certain usefulness, as their spontaneous recurrence attests. But there seems to me to be far more usefulness in employing the

1. Ibid., p. 117-18.
2. *Études sur les poètes latins de la décadence* (Paris, 1834).

concepts both of the Romantic and of the Baroque in an historical and not merely a psychological sense, applying them to that which directly occasioned the coining and minting of the word in question, that is to say, in the case of Baroque, to that artistic perversion which is characterized by the longing for astonishment, and which was observed in Europe approximately from the later sixteenth to the end of the seventeenth century.

A closer definition of the historical concept of the Baroque, with a more accurate fixation of its character or characters, is not possible, otherwise than by way of direct knowledge and experience of these as found in the works of the Baroque type which were produced at the period in question. We have already dismissed as fallacious the proceeding of abstracting and classifying certain external forms as has been attempted, for example, in studies of the metaphors, comparisons, and other stylistic methods of Marino. But with knowledge and direct experience the historical concept of the Baroque becomes filled in with various and particular images, and thus a living possession of the critical spirit.

It is important to employ the concepts of the Baroque and the Romantic as historical concepts, precisely because this dispels the temptation of falling into the generic, and so into the insignificant and finally the erroneous, with an obliteration of the outline, the proper and individual characteristic of the works taken into consideration. Granted that in French or Italian or Spanish literature of the seventeenth century there may have been, in the generic sense previously indicated, certain Romantic manifestations, yet the works in question were in their inner essence different from the Romantic works of the nineteenth century if only because between the two there had passed two more centuries of human striving and spiritual struggle. Similarly, as I remarked in another connexion,[1] the Baroque characteristics which can be observed in D'Annunzio, all his resemblances to Marino and others of the seventeenth century, cannot alter the fact that a D'Annunzio could only come into being after Romanticism, *Verismo*, the Parnasse,

1. *Saggi sulla letteratura italiana del seicento*, 3rd edn., Bari, 1948, pp. 405-8.

the Nietzsche movement, and other such spiritual events which, since they occurred in the nineteenth century, were certainly not precedents for Marino.

At this point it is impossible to avoid disappointing those who are always enquiring into the "cause" of facts and shrink from declaring themselves satisfied until they have received such a causal indication – so that in fact they are never satisfied. Their disappointment will be occasioned this time by our replying to them that really and truly there is no "cause" of the Baroque. The Baroque, understood in the psychological or generically human sense, has no cause, because there is no cause assignable to human error, unless it be the *virtus dormitiva*, the sinful nature of man itself. And the Baroque understood as an historical concept has no cause because the "cause" is just the fact itself in the manner of its coming about, as can be seen from an examination of all such "causes" as have ever been excogitated. Not one of them stands up to the first critical prod. According to some of the more prudent enquirers, Humanism and the imitation of the antique were the cause of the Baroque, but they furnish no demonstration that these causes had by logical necessity to produce that effect. Others say the cause was Jesuitism, adding that *Secentismo* or Baroquism is nothing else but "Jesuitism in Art".[1] But there is no apparent reason why the Jesuits, defending the Catholic Church, educating men with their Spiritual Exercises, governing souls with their accommodating casuistry, terrifying them with depictions of the pains of hell or alluring them with depictions of the joys of heaven, needed to express themselves in the Baroque wise rather than, as in fact many of them did, and as became their habit with the decline of the Baroque fashion,[2] in plain and simple

1. Thus SETTEMBRINI in *Storia della letteratura italiana*, II, 235 seqq., and many others repeated the same.

2. Weisbach in his book *Der Barock als Kunst der Gegenreformation* (Berlin, Cassirer, 1921) attempts to demonstrate that in the art of the Baroque age the ideas of the Counter-reformation and the Jesuits are more or less prevalent, which may be true, but is off the point here. In his Preface, Weisbach recalls the result of researches by Braun, who studied the churches of the Jesuits in Belgium, Spain, and Germany: namely that there never was strictly a Jesuit

wise. Yet another cause assigned is the greedy pursuit of novelty. But to propound this means either to forget that men are always pursuing novelty, new life, or else to understand by pursuit of novelty the particular sense of a pursuit of false newness, in which case the assignment of the cause is a mere tautology.[1] Another alleged "cause" is: "Ermüdung des Formgefühls", exhaustion of the feeling of form, whereby this blunted feeling comes to require irritants and stimulants,[2] but this, which differs little from the preceding formula, is another tautology, for it merely describes the condition of aridity or artistic emptiness which pertains essentially to the Baroque as to any sort of pseudo-art. Let us not trouble ourselves with a multitude of other proffered causes, including that of the disease to which the poet Fracastoro lent a name when he celebrated it in his *Syphilis*, the disease which, spreading throughout Europe in the sixteenth century, is by some alleged to have finally brought on a spiritual and intellectual weakening which in an unexplained way revealed itself in the Baroque style. If, as these critical notes show, the seekers after causes have not yet been satisfied, I have no hope for my part of satisfying them. For to the question why between the ends of the sixteenth and seventeenth centuries Europe erred so conspicuously against good taste, and produced so much Baroque output, I should be inclined to reply, out of respect for the liberty of the human spirit, that the human spirit thus acted but of a desire so to act, and what happened was what pleased the spirit.

It is asking a different question to enquire where was the centre from which Baroque exercised its influence, which was the people which originated the Baroque fashion. This is a reasonable question provided that we eschew ethnological fancies such as attribute unchanging qualities to given peoples and races, and such naive

style. The observation of WÖLFFLIN (op. cit., pp. 61-73) to the effect that in Baroque art there prevails the gravity, indeed the heaviness, which corresponds to the social behaviours and manners of that age, is also irrelevant here.

1. For this and other such arguments compare my already quoted *Saggi sulla letteratura italiana del Seicento*, 3rd edn., Bari, 1948, introduction.

2. This is the view advanced by Göller: see WÖLFFLIN, op. cit., p. 61.

notions as that some one people or group of peoples has the office of corruptor, while others have that of the innocents who are corrupted. The Baroque was a manifestation of the European spirit in the age in question, and in a certain sense belonged to Europe as a whole, although in its origination and dissemination one or more peoples were first and foremost. Italian scholars of the eighteenth century, spurred on by patriotic zeal, competed with no less patriotic Spanish scholars in accusing each other's nations of responsibility for Baroque bad taste. Other countries also entered the lists, and the Italians reminded the French of Du Bartas, the English of Lyly. This sort of nationalism or misplaced love of country is extant even at the present time. The zealous patriots might more suitably have argued in an opposite sense, for from what country would the rest of Europe have taken on the fashion of the Baroque, what country was in a position to set the example or impose the mode, if not the country of greatest culture and civilization, the country from which Europe first received manufactures, industries, trade, institutions, geographical discoveries and technical inventions, and now, similarly, was receiving arts and sciences, literature and poetry, forms of conversation, entertainment, and ceremonial? Such a country in the sixteenth century and for some time after was Italy, with which was associated, in respect of some departments of culture and manners, and with the aid of the penetration of Spanish political power, Spain. The Spanish confuters of those Italian controversialists' contentions might thus well have chosen to concur and agree with them. In any case, for better or for worse, the Baroque style was essentially the Italian style. As such it was repudiated by the first who, in the literary field, rebelled against it, the French rationalist critics, and as such it was implicitly recognized by all the amateurs and purchasers of artistic production up to the end, not merely of the seventeenth, but almost of the eighteenth century, considering Italy, as they did, as the principal furnisher of court painters, sculptors, architects, musicians, and poets.

If the Baroque is truly not an artistic or poetic but a practical characteristic, whether of single works or, as is still more the case, of the joint productive enterprise known as the "school" or "mode" (and such enterprises have in themselves a practical character), then the history of art and poetry should deal with it, not in positive, but in negative terms, as a denial or limitation of art and poetry in the true sense. There is no great harm in continuing to talk about Baroque art and the Baroque age, provided it be never forgotten that strictly speaking what is art is never Baroque, and what is Baroque is never art. To me it seems that recent attempts to give value and prominence to so-called Baroque art by holding special exhibitions, have, by reaction, restored and confirmed the proper valuation, dispelling certain illusory attributions of greatness and solidity to the works in question. The practice of fixing concepts of particular ways of understanding the poetry and art of one or another given age, and making such concepts serve as standards of judgement, appointing, as it were, special tribunals for the art affairs of single ages, is destructive of any serious feeling for art and the history of art: for the one and eternal court of justice in these matters is the one and eternal concept of art. The history of poetry and art accordingly should search the Baroque age for genuine, non-Baroque art and poetry, and will be able to recognize these even if sometimes on the surface or in part they bear traces of the prevailing fashion, and even if they always take for granted and reflect its existence. It will so be possible to differentiate between on the one hand the main body and general type of Italian poetry from Tasso to Alfieri, in which the Baroque perversion has become constitutional, the disease has reached to the bone, serious and deep inspiration has almost disappeared, and nothing lively remains save a certain sensual impressionism with its attendant frivolity, witticisms, and irony; and, on the other hand, the contemporary English, French, and even Spanish poetry (for in this latter, in the seventeenth century, there ran a fresh streamlet of popular inspiration beneath all the flowers and foliage of rhetoric) in which the malady was not much worse than accidental and occasional. Where there was spiritual health, much the same could be said of the age's poetry, as Voltaire said of the absurd eloquence, the "faux goût" in expression, of Cardinal

Richelieu, which, however, "n'ôtait rien au génie du ministre".[1]
The one country where the poetic art fell into conditions no better
than or possibly worse than those in Italy – yet somewhat different from them, although Germany had copiously imitated
Italy – was Germany, which seemed altogether exhausted by the
effort of giving birth to the Reformation, the first step towards
the dissolution of the Catholic and confessional system of thought.
Italy was less thoroughly exhausted by the effort of giving birth,
with the Renaissance, to the first outlines of modern civilization.
But in both countries there was an absence of high poetic genius,
while in both there were to be found poetic gifts of a minor and
fragmentary order, green leaves, vigorous shoots, flourishing
among the withered or diseased foliage. Likewise in painting and
the other arts the critic will seek out from among the crowd of
facile, excessive, overloaded and overheated performers of that
century and a half, such personalities or souls as, even though but
half formed, and albeit few in number and feeble, can alone afford
him matter for his appreciation.

However, it would be somewhat inequitable to see in the Baroque of Italy nothing else but bad taste, and not at the same time an
exercise in style, a development of rhetoric, a refinement and
initiation into the secrets of art, of which a large part of Europe
then had need if it was to emancipate itself from mediaeval habits
and to launch forth into modern poetry, prose, and art, not to see
also in it, in fact, that literary and artistic education which Italy
copiously supplied to France and England, Spain and Germany,
not only in the shape of books of poetry and prose, but also by
sending forth its language masters, court poets, painters, architects,
choirmasters, singers, and players to those countries. This was a
final service which old Italy rendered to the culture of Europe in
what are considered the centuries of her decadence, a service which
has not been properly investigated by historians, or has been seen
under a false light and treated with a wholly misplaced contempt.
Foreigners easily forgot the services rendered, and dismissed those

1. *Essai sur les mœurs*, Ch. 176.

Italian visitors as "sonneteers", adventurers, charlatans, buffoons. And the Italian historians kept an embarrassed silence about them because they did not fit into the class of "national heroes" demanded by the public of later times.

But the craze for the Baroque throughout Europe, and above all in Italy, in what we call the Baroque Age, was perhaps beneficial also in another way. In the life of the individual there are tendencies to evil of which he can liberate himself only when they come to a head and in so doing print themselves on the memory as a warning. And it is so too in the lives of peoples and of the human race. If later generations, indeed we ourselves, feel distaste and dislike for those bloated forms, those clever tricks which were intended to rouse our astonishment, and for all those overloaded and complex metaphors and antitheses and witticisms, ready to discern in them and to denounce or mock at such *Secentismo*, *Barocchismo*, *Concettismo*, or whatever name we apply to the abuse, it is surely due to that Age's having taken upon itself, and expiated, all the possible sins of this kind, that we for our part are able to display such clarity of judgement and definiteness of pronouncement. The Baroque Age, then, even in its sheerly Baroque aspect, was not a useless experience.

[1935]

XV

THE "AESTHETICA" OF BAUMGARTEN

For more than twenty years I had searched the booksellers' catalogues and their shelves for a copy of the very rare *Aesthetica* of Baumgarten, a work which I had in my time read and studied in a copy procured on loan from a German library, but greatly desired to possess among my own books, as being the first in which this name of Aesthetics was used to designate the studies to which I had devoted much of my intellectual life. I had quite dismissed the hope from my mind, when some weeks ago, most unexpectedly, one of the booksellers who had my request on his records announced that he could, for the price of so many Swiss francs, provide me with a fine copy of both parts of the work (which it is particularly hard to find together). I wrote at once to close with the offer, and for some days waited, fearing a slip 'twixt cup and lip. But the book arrived, the copy was really a fine one, almost unused, the two duodecimo volumes having a pretty eighteenth-century binding in white parchment sewn with pale-pink thread and the title in gold lettering. I turned them over and over in my hands and contemplated them with delight.

After some thirty-two years I was observing, with an agreeable return of youthful impressions and memories, the frontispiece which I knew so well: "*AESTHETICA* | *scripsit* | Alexand. Gottlieb | Baumgarten | *Prof. Philosophiae* | *Traiecti cis Viadrum* | *Impens. Joannis Christiani Kleyb* | c | ɔc | ccl" and in the second volume "*AESTHETICORUM* | *Pars altera* | *scripsit*" etc., as in the first save for the date, which in this is 1758. The second little volume is half the size of the first, the first running from page 1 to 400, not including Preface and Contents, the second from 401 to 600. The pages of the second had been printed shortly after those of the first, that is about 1750, but the author fell sick and could not supply the concluding part of the manuscript. After eight years of illness (that slow consumption which ended his life before he was fifty years old) he had despaired of ever resuming work and terminating the book, and had allowed the publisher to put what was already printed, though incomplete, on the market, with a brief note of explanation which he himself composed: "Si quis tamen superes" (thus runs the pathetic yet dignified conclusion of the note), "amice lector, qui me curas, qui me nosti, qui me amas denique, disce fortunam ex aliis, ex me, qui jam octavum in annum per ambages aegritudinum circumerro, quae videantur inextricabiles, quam necessarium sit, maturius bene cogitandis optimis assuefieri. Quid enim agerem, uti nunc sum, pro virili hoc agere nescius, profecto, nescio."

So I began to spell out again the stately opening paragraphs of the book, engraved long since on my memory: first and foremost that which describes the new Science: "AESTHETICA (theoria liberalium artium, gnoseologia inferior, ars pulcre cogitandi, ars analogi rationis) est scientia cognitionis sensitivae." Paragraph 14 fixes the intrinsic end of this sensitive knowledge: "Aesthetices finis est perfectio cognitionis sensitivae qua talis. Haec autem est pulcritudo. Et cavenda eiusdem, qua talis, imperfectio. Haec autem est deformitas." Smilingly I re-read those objections which had been advanced against the philosopher as he took upon himself to elaborate this new science, together with his parries and retorts. "Indigna philosophis et infra horizontem eorum esse posita sensitiva, phantasmata, fabulas affectuum perturbationes, etc." Reply: "Philosophus homo est inter homines, neque bene tantam humanae cognitionis partem alienam a se putat" (§ 6). Another objection: "Facultates inferiores, caro, debellandae potius sunt quam excitandae et confirmandae." Reply: "Imperium in facultates inferiores poscitur, non tyrannis" (§ 12). This was like old music, returning to charm my ear. This Latin of Baumgarten's, which, as his hearers recorded, he illustrated in lively German, with wit and grace, is often epigraphic, but usually harsh, knotty, and involved. A faint echo of his oral style still reaches us in the pages of a lecture notebook of one of his pupils which, preserved with his other papers in the library of Berlin, has now been printed as an appendix to a doctorate thesis (B. Poppe, *A. M. Baumgarten, Seine Bedeutung und Stellung*, etc., Borna-Leipzig, 1907). Whereas in his

Latin work Baumgarten retorted to the charge that aesthetic knowledge, sensitive and confused, by contrast with logical and distinct knowledge, is a "confusio mater erroris", in these terms: "Sed conditio sine qua non, inveniendae veritatis, ubi natura non facit saltum ex obscuritate in distinctionem" (§ 7), when teaching orally he phrased his retort in quips and witticisms: "Our opponents say that confusion is the mother of errors. Let us follow up the metaphor: a mother cannot go on childbearing for ever, so confusion will not go on breeding errors for ever." He passed in review all the stimulants of the *impetus* or poetic inspiration and exaltation, including the virtue of the draughts drawn from the clear fountain of Aganippe and other waters celebrated in myth, adding: "Since our ordinary water fails to produce these effects wine is usually recommended" (§§ 85-86). Sometimes he summed up his thought in pleasant little rhymes, for example, this one concerning the six characters which aesthetic knowledge, or poetry, ought to possess: "Reichtum, Adel, Wahrheit, Licht, Gründlichkeit und Leben, Wer das meiner Einsicht gibt, hat mir viel gegeben" (§ 22). Elsewhere he recounted anecdotes like that of the ready and magnificent liberality of the Spanish Ambassador at the imperial court, Count Montijo (§ 286). He counselled his Germans to take French models, just as Horace had counselled Greek models for the Romans, because he considered that Germany and France were at that time in a relation like that of Rome and Greece (§ 56). He could not deny that those French writers who enjoyed pensions and incomes, that is leisure, were far better off than the Germans who for the most part cultivated learning "um des Brotswillen", for bread (§ 84). To affirmations of the superiority of logical over aesthetic or poetic knowledge he replied (§ 8) reasonably and quietly enough in his textbook, but in his oral lesson he could not, philosopher as he was, refrain from holding up for reproof what so often underlies the haughty attitude of philosophic and ratiocinative utterance, with its contempt for what is fine, complex, and sensible: "the slapdash manner of the idle man who wants to learn a couple of definitions by memory and to be spared further trouble". He had the highest regard for his rank and dignity as a

Professor. Thus shortly before his death, asked how he wished to be buried, he answered *je akademischer je besser* (the more academically the better). Yet he had no reverence for the traditional figure of the philosopher. "When the philosopher is represented as a rock of which the upper half is in the clouds, where a notice says 'Non perturbatur in alto', this amounts to forgetting his humanity, as if the Stoics and their sages were not by now ridiculous" (§ 6).

Son of a Pastor who preached in a garrison church, born into a family of theologians and educated with the utmost strictness, a man of ardent religious faith whose bearing of his sufferings ('Serenitas animi est demonstratio demonstrationum,' he used to repeat to himself in sickness) and peaceful death were related by his biographer Meier (Halle, 1763) almost in the style of the edifying recital of a saint's life, Baumgarten was not on that account any less earnest and bold an investigator of truth. He was one of those countless scholars, modest in their academic way of life, but persevering and courageous, of whom Emmanuel Kant was one: founders of the spiritual greatness of Germany. Thus despite the opposition prevailing between Pietism and the Wolffian philosophy, Baumgarten did not hesitate to recognize the great merit of the latter; and again, despite his adherence to Wolff, he saw what was deepest in Leibniz and had been ignored by Wolff. And though his bent was all for analysis and system, he saw the great and fundamental importance of poetry and took this for the object of analysis and scientific systematization. The retorts to those who wished to forbid the philosopher to handle such light or low or slippery material now make us smile, but at the time they betokened more than ordinary courage, for they ran counter to age-old habits invested with solemn dignity, and were altogether against the powerful currents of the times. It was to this courage that we owe the announcement, I had almost said the "proclamation", of the new autonomous Science of Aesthetics, having for its function the grouping and unifying and arranging of the many scattered doctrines concerning poetry and the arts.

Let us be quite clear that inventing and naming a new science by empirically rearranging certain classes of cognitions constitutes no contribution to thought. We have seen many more or less ill-judged constructions of this sort, especially by "positivists" of the second half of the nineteenth century. But to discern and fix a truly original principle, referring to it concepts which previously appeared to be divided or contrasting, and were certainly until then rudely or immaturely expressed, thereby lighting up in all its extension a sphere of the life of the spirit, is something very different, an achievement which has occurred only at long intervals in the course of centuries and of millennia. Baumgarten was not perhaps the man of genius who accomplishes this by his own unaided efforts, but, to use a rather homely figure, he was the man who gave a good and timely push to the cart and set it going on its route. Since the beginning of the sixteenth century, efforts had been more or less consciously made to develop an autonomous science of poetry, or Aesthetics, after the Poetics of Aristotle had been rediscovered and investigated mainly by Italian scholars. Thanks to them, in the seventeenth century, a new mental attitude developed towards these problems, manifested in a number of new concepts and words which then came into use, such as: genius and ingeniosity, judgement "without argument", or taste, the fancy, the first impressions neither true nor false, sentiment, and so forth. And now, at the beginning of the eighteenth century, the times were ripe. From various quarters, under various guises, and with varying depth of insight, the new science made its appearance. One such source was Leibniz and his school, who fixed their attention on the "petites perceptions", the "perceptions confuses, dont on ne saurait se rendre raison", the field of "le goût, distingué de l'entendement", a field different from that of the intellect. Another source was Vico, with his discovery of a "poetic logic" and his view that the fancy, as opposed to the intellect, is the primitive and eternal origin of poetry. And then there were the sensitives, the amateurs of art impatient with all scholastic rules, like Du Bos, who referred the criticism of poetry to the sentiment; Gravina, Muratori, Calepio, and other such Italians who in their various ways asserted the claims of the fancy, and had for their counterparts and pupils the Swiss Bodmer and Breitinger. There was Bilfinger, who went so far as to ask for a new "organon of feeling and imagination" to stand beside the logical organon of Aristotle. But it was Baumgarten who first uttered the name, then new, of "Aesthetica" which has remained, first of all in his *Meditationes philosophicae de nonnullis ad poëma pertinentibus*, which was his Doctor's thesis at the University of Halle in 1735 when he was in his twenty-first year, then in the lectures which he held on the subject at the University of Frankfurt on the Oder in 1742. Although his friend and pupil Meier, who first edited and arranged and published in German Baumgarten's lectures, gave to these the less unusual description of "Fundamental Principles of all Sciences of the Beautiful", Baumgarten entitled his own treatise, which he began to publish in 1750: "Aesthetica". Thereby he indicated that general science which the ancients had not known and which had not found its place in Aristotle's triple pattern of the organs of knowledge as Logic, Rhetoric, and Poetic. For indeed "If I am to think sensitively in the mode of beauty, why am I to do so solely in prose and verse? What of painting and music?" And then, Rhetoric is at most a subdivision, which, juxtaposed to Poetic, proves to be largely the duplicate of this. "Aesthetic should be more general: it should say what is applicable to all beauty, and should apply general rules to each beauty" (*Vorles.* § 1). Baumgarten was, then, an inventor, though in the manner and within the limits that have been stated. We shall agree with Thomas Abbt, who in 1765 wrote a "Life and Character of A. G. Baumgarten" shortly after his death (and I possess a copy also of that rare little volume, printed at Halle), that: "those acquainted with the argument know well that the name of Baumgarten is in virtue of this branch of learning to be included among those of inventors of the second rank (*Erfinder von der zwoten Ordnung*)" and that "in the future the honour to which he has well-established rights will be accorded to him". Baumgarten understood also that a philosophical science of this sort was needful for the criticism of literary works, since it must take for its starting point philosophically established criterions "nisi velit in diiudicandis pulcre cogitatis, dictis, scriptis, disputare de meris gustibus" (§ 5); adding that "the commentator, in order to present the true sense of writers, and to present it fully, has need of the aesthetic cognition" (*Vorles.* § 4). Even if Baumgarten had gone on to give an erroneous determination of the property of poetry, he would still have the merit of the insight, presentiment, or guess with which he affirmed that poetry has about it an originality in view of which there must be assigned to it an independent position and a corresponding science; and the merit of having driven this home by conferring upon the said science an appropriate name which endured.

But actually Baumgarten, by dint, once again, of gathering together and fusing thought from many quarters and from the tradition of a series of precedent enquiries, did more than that. He identified the aesthetic sphere as a theoretic sphere which, within the realm of the theoretic, was ideally anterior to the logical or intellectual sphere. "Logic may, as theory, be regarded as the elder sister of Aesthetic, but in practice (*Ausübung*) Aesthetic is the elder of the two." In this way he entered into that more genuinely modern current of philosophy which did not stop short at the enumeration and description of the various "faculties of the soul", but saw these in a genetic series, or as his great Neapolitan contemporary would have put it, as "eternal ideal history". Baumgarten's establishment of the aesthetic sphere as *cognitio*, and more precisely as *cognitio sensitiva*, anterior to the distinct or logical cognition, was important in that with more or less coherency and awareness of implications it destroyed the basis of the pedagogic theory of poetry and art which had viewed these as posterior to the logical activity, works of art being regarded as a means whereby the wise man or philosopher, either himself or by the instructions which he gave to the producer, procured that the one and only recognized *cognitio*, logical cognition, should be dressed up in a guise alluring to the feelings and the senses. But poetry is not born as a consequence of the logical. It is born precedently to the logical. It is not an allurement to the senses but a *cognitio*. This implication of Baumgarten's doctrine explains the fierce opposition against him on the part of numerous followers of the old intellectualistic theory of poetry. All of them accused him of debasing poetry to the level of the sensual. "According to these advocates of Aesthetics (said the critic Riedel), a composition is poetical in proportion to the degree of sensibility and of the fantastic that has gone into it. People of that sort, professing ideas so perilous about poetry, should not set themselves up as judges." "No, for heaven's sake no!", exclaimed another, Quistorp. "Nothing for the intellect, nothing at all! Everything, first and last, for the senses and the imagination! And now here is what you are wanting, Aesthetics, the newly invented depiction of souls!" And old Gottsched said mockingly: "Wait a little and you will see that painting will begin to appeal to the nose and the palate." In that circle of conventional thinkers, Baumgarten was regarded as a veritable "Nicola-ite", one of those heretics (it is uncertain whether they ever really existed) who stood between Christianity and Paganism, with an indulgent attitude in erotic matters, or one of those priests (who certainly existed), who in the eleventh century, resisting Popes Stephen IX and Gregory VII, insisted upon a right to the joys of marriage. There thus broke out what has been called the Aesthetic War, *der aesthetische Krieg*, about which we have a fairly detailed narrative from the pen of that same Professor Bergmann who recently exhausted my patience with his extravagant philosophy of history based upon sexuality and looking forward to a rebirth of humanity modelled upon the community life of wasps and ants, and balanced on the maternal or matriarchal principle,[1] but who twenty years ago was able to think like a sane member of Christendom (see Chapter XII of his book *Begründung der deutschen Aesthetik durch A. G. Baumgarten und G. F. Meier*, Leipzig, 1911). The champion of the rights of the Aesthetic Science was the aforesaid Meier, whom his opponents, in their venomous moments, called "the Frankfurt Professor Baumgarten's monkey in Halle", while in less crude and more alert moments they mocked him with ironic admiration of his deeds of chivalry in defence of the splendour and honour of the new Goddess, Aesthetic, who had won his loyalty:

1. In *Critica*, xxx, 138-40; now in *Conversazioni critiche*, v, Bari, 1939, 298-301.

Kein Ritter griff so schnell zum Speere,
Wenn seiner Göttin Reiz und Ehre
Ein Rittersmann in Zweifel zog.

Baumgarten left his friend, who was more engaged than himself in the literary life of the times, and better able to conduct controversies in print, to cope with all this. He thanked him for coming to his defence spontaneously, unasked and uninstructed, ("me non rogante, me non mandante"); but for his own part, while holding fast and firm in his own doctrine, he disdained to reply, or merely observed dryly that he stuck to his theory and his teaching that poetry is *oratio sensitiva perfecta*, and that those hostile critics had distorted the adjective *perfecta* into an adverb *perfecte* which they then misread as equivalent to *omnino*, thereby foisting upon him the opinion that poetry is *omnino sensitiva*. Worse still, he said, they had taken *sensitiva* in the vulgar sense of things gross and sensual, "turpiuscule vel etiam obscenius dicta per jocum". They were fighting, then, against ghosts of their own raising (see the preface to the third edition of the *Metaphysica*). Baumgarten, in affirming the unlogical or as he put it "non-distinct" character of poetry, had no notion of denying that distinct thoughts, of the intellectual order, were to be found in poetry. As he explained in his lectures: "We call Aesthetics a science of sensitive cognition, but not on the grounds that in poetry all is sensible and nothing is distinct (logical). The grounds of our contention are, not this, but: that poetry's principal or determining motives (*die Hauptbegriffe*) are always sensible, whereas discourse in which the motives (*Hauptbegriffe*) are logical is called logical and scientific. In sensible discourse, the distinct concepts are concealed (*versteckt*). It is not that beauty resides in confusion: it resides in the development of the confused representation towards beauty" (§ 17). We feel that there is here almost an anticipation of the saying of De Sanctis that in poetry the concepts (which must of course be there, if in truth the spirit is fully present in every one of its forms) have been "sunk and abandoned" in the form, that is in the images and the fancy.

We ourselves today are nothing if not upholders of this definition of Baumgarten which seemed to Herder the best ever
pronounced, truly a classical definition of poetry – "oratio sensitiva perfecta" – against the sensualists who regard poetry as an
instrument of miscellaneous pleasure or indulgence, of noisy
futuristic fun and games or of spasmodic delectation in decadent
verbal or phonic refinements; also against the histrions of the
sublime, who would make of poetry the town cryer to announce
and communicate to all peoples their high cogitations on the nature of man and the world, on life and the other life, on humanity's
duties or expectations, and suchlike mysteries; and then also
against the sentimentalists who would use poetry as an outlet for
their passions of all kinds, and other such people. Against all of
these we in our modern formulations maintain that poetry is
"perfectio cognitionis sensitivae qua talis" and that this sort of
perfection is "pulcritudo" or beauty. But how many are equal to
the appreciation of this "point de maturité", as La Bruyère would
have termed it? The poet, the true poet, the poet of genius, is,
as history shows and as is perhaps natural, a rarity, but neither is it
to be believed that those who open their hearts worthily to poetry
(swoons and raptures of admiration are no proof whatever of such
worthiness) are many in number. That fusion of pain and joy, of
agitation and calm, that joy which is streaked with pain, that calm
which knows that it has been all agitation and that the agitation
still lives on, restrained by itself, comes only where there is a
collectedness of the mind, an inner elevation and purification,
which never happens with the lower generality of men, and with
the many happens only feebly or fleetingly: only with the few
does it happen fully and freely, giving rise to a spiritual attitude
and capacity. Whoever enters into the aesthetic sphere, said Baumgarten to his pupils, must have a great heart, *"muss ein grosses Herz
haben"* (§ 45). And for sure, as Friedrich Schiller rightly observed,
the aesthetic elevation is intimately conjoined to the moral elevation and spills over into this. Finally it must be said that far
fewer than is generally supposed are those philosophers who have
a correct and a profound understanding of the virtue and office of

poetry "qua talis". Nor does the approval which is widely expressed for certain conclusions of the aesthetic science give grounds for presuming that a veritable understanding exists; for what is expressed, if it is not merely what Leibniz called "psittacism", is but a superficial and indolent acquiescence.

However, when we consider the sort of poetry of which Baumgarten had knowledge (the poetry of ancient Rome and that of the eighteenth century), and the nature of his criticism, we feel inclined to think that he arrived at his theory not so much by the path of experience as by that of systematic ratiocination, so that the theory presented itself as an abstract deduction lacking the inspiration of a correlative induction. We may indeed make this assertion, provided we mean it as no more than a psychological description, and do not carry it too far. For productive thought must really always be composed of both ratiocination and experience, both deduction and induction. Baumgarten may have had little enough true knowledge of true poetry, yet what he had and acquired and divined was sufficient for him to be able to fix his clear definition of poetry and to keep it firm against attempts to confute it. Much the same happened some time after with Emmanuel Kant, whose knowledge of poetry and art was little different in quality or in scope from that of Baumgarten; this did not prevent him from conceiving his Critique of Judgement, in which he once and for all traced certain essential characteristics of beauty. He who is not a philosopher born may live in the midst of a reality offering the richest incentives, not converting these into experiences, and still less rising from them to concepts and theories. He lives amid them without taking them in and comprehending them. But the philosophical mind may need no more than some occasional hint of reality to lead him to the discovery of new aspects of the universal.

However, Baumgarten's major contribution to Aesthetics, namely that definition and plain pronouncement, marked the limit of his possibilities. He was not able to think out and work out the details without becoming, in the stress of the effort, drawn back or drawn forth into ways of error, or entangled, helplessly strug-

gling, in a labyrinth. How was that? What was the obstacle in his
further path which he could neither beat down nor circumvent?

It was, perhaps, the conception accepted by the school to which
he belonged, which Leibniz termed *lex continui* and summed up in
the phrase: *natura non facit saltus*: the conception, that is, of a
development of the spirit and of reality by a progression of merely
quantitative differences. Let us consider those three orders of
perceptiones – the obscure, the confused, and the distinct – which
Leibniz distinguished, deriving them in some degree from the
scholastic, and particularly the Scotist system of which he was a
keen student. Let us remember that distinct perceptions were given
forth by Leibniz and his pupils as the domain of logic, science,
judgement; confused perceptions as the domain of poetry, fancy,
taste; obscure perceptions, the lowest grade, as the region lying
beneath the level even of confused cognition, for this, though not
distinct, is nevertheless clear, whereas the obscure are truly so,
lacking all figure and expression. (The word "confused" is mis-
leading to us with our present use of the term, and we may help
ourselves to a better understanding by mentally translating it into
"indistinct" or "non-intellectual".) Now what, to our present eyes,
after over two centuries of further analysis and systematization,
do these three sorts of perception, recalled and reconsidered, represent? They appear surely as three distinct forms of consciousness, the "obscure" corresponding to practical passionality or sentiment, or something of that kind; the "confused though clear" to
pure intuitive knowledge, or fancy; the "clear and distinct" to
knowledge of the intellectual, critical, philosophical order: in
fact to Thought. These are three forms from the one to the other
of which there is no gradual transition, for a sentiment, no matter
how richly and intensely developed, remains always a sentiment,
and never becomes an intuition; an intuition, however ample,
never becomes a concept, a judgement, but remains always a
poetic phantasm. The transition from the one to the other is not
by quantitative grades but by implication and dialectic, not by
summation but by crisis, not (to use terms of biology) evolutionary
but epigenetic. But Leibniz and his disciples conceived it as quanti-

tative, gradual, evolutionary (*perceptio minime obscura, perceptio minime clara, obscurior, clarior, aequaliter clara* etc.: see the *Metaphysica* of Baumgarten, 528-32), holding that the obscure, confused, and distinct perceptions formed a single scale along which, passing first from the more to the less obscure, you proceeded onwards to the less clear and thence to the more clear, and from this to the less distinct and so on to the more distinct, the whole passage thus reaching from the *regnum tenebrarum* at one extreme to the *regnum lucis* at other, the one Positive Form towards which the whole process worked being the "distinctio" or logical-intellective form.

Now such a conception of the relation between the various forms of perception or consciousness, and that quite other conception of Aesthetics as an independent science, and of the poetic knowledge as anterior to the logical and having its proper *perfectio* in *pulcritudo*, were substantially discordant. Inevitably, either the former was bound to confute and dissolve the latter, strangling the newborn science of Aesthetics in its cradle, or else this last was bound, in the development of its activity, to induce a profound correction and transformation of the concept of consciousness, its forms and their mode of operation. This last was what by dint of prolonged efforts ultimately came about but, for the time being, aspirations did not reach so far, and the contradiction remained, though necessarily a source of discomfort from which vain efforts were made to find an issue. This can be seen in the case of Baumgarten, who strives repeatedly but vainly (and particularly in the sections of his works dealing with *veritas aesthetica* and *verisimilitudo*) to assert a form of truth which should be at one and the same time (as called for by the abstract monist or quantitative-gradualist conception) identical with logical truth (though imperfect), and also perfect with a perfection of its own, and beautiful with the light called beauty. Baumgarten's device for attaining some sort of tranquillity amid these contradictions came to him (as I think certainly, although he does not say so expressly and is not aware of it) from the formulae of Rhetoric, which, being a practical operation, aims not at the discovery and affirmation of the truth but at persuasion and mental suggestion, its *perfectio* and its standard of discrimination being seen to lie in efficacious pursuit of those aims; for which reason it rejects truth when this is unpersuasive and accepts untruth provided it be persuasive. Thanks to this more or less conscious assimilation to rhetoric, aesthetic truth is by Baumgarten presented as that assertion, whether true or false, which the reader of poetry, according to the particular conditions of culture in which he finds himself (seasons, locations, and other circumstances), accepts as true; the important matter being that such "truth" shall be neither *supra* nor *infra* but *intra horizontem aestheticum* and that its "falsity" should not be discernible within the said horizon. The false must be *verisimile* or *splendide mendax* and the true must not be *falsisimile* (a word coined by Baumgarten in his § 489) or, as Dante puts it "quel ver che ha faccia di menzogna". But such an assimilation of aesthetic truth to the truth or rather the non-truth of rhetoric, offends the poetic conscience in its sureness that the charm of beauty is not a trap set for credulity to tumble into; and it offends the moral conscience which cannot accept falsehood into the circle of the true, nor accord to it even the slightest indulgence. Baumgarten feels the force of both these reproaches. It is above all by the second that he is pricked, as can be seen from his insistent harping upon his distinctions and explanations, a sure sign of discontent, and from the objections which he addresses to himself anticipating those of his opponents and readers, and answering them not triumphantly but with evident embarrassment. Thus on one occasion he interrupts himself sharply and warningly: "Quid autem illud est ambiguitatis? Nunc falsa conceduntur, nunc denuo dissuadentur aesthetico? Dic sententiam explicite." And then he can do no more than repeat himself: "Uti dixi hucusque non sine necessariis determinationibus, ita pergam" (§ 471). But this is not the worst. On one occasion he seems to hear a voice preaching and storming against himself: "Quousque tandem abutere patientia nostra? quamdiu nos etiam furor iste tuus eludet? Quem ad finem sese effraenata jactabit audacia? Tune vero, magister veritatis logicae et ethicae publice constitus, mendacia commendas, velut aliquando splendida, et falsa veris miscere, tamquam operam maximopere nobilem?" He attempts to save his face: "Sed sedatis animis, boni viri, revertamur ad nostrum, quod vos nonnunquam male habet, phlegma philosophicum. De salute Graeciae res non agitur" (§ 478). In both Baumgarten and Meier certain absurdities too palpable to be mentioned result from the mistaking of oratorical effect for poetic truth; what must, however, be mentioned is their preposterous theory of aesthetic concepts, judgements, and syllogisms – a wild mistransference of operations belonging to the *cognitio distincta*, precisely in virtue of its distinctness, to the sphere of *cognitio confusa*, which had already once been propounded and developed by ingenious Italian rhetorician, of the seventeenth century. And the same inability to maintain a clear distinction between poetic and intellective truth underlay Baumgarten's intention of including in his Aesthetics a discussion on the means of safeguarding and maximizing the accuracy of the senses by the use of microscopes, telescopes, barometers, thermometers, megaphones, and similar instruments.[1]

1. Yes, among the confusions of Baumgarten's thought there is a hint of this muddle between the theory of poetry or aesthetics and the theory of induction. But the assertion which some have made that Baumgarten's principles and general line of thought should have required him to develop his theory of *cognitio sensitiva* into a theory of induction, is a betrayal of his best thought, that thought which won him a place in the history of philosophy. I stated as much in my *Estetica* (6th edn., pp. 235-6), and I cannot concur with A. Baeumler who, in *Kants Kritik der Urteilskraft: ihre Geschichte und Systematik*, I, Halle, 1923, pp. 168 seqq., undertakes to "purify Baumgarten in the opposite sense" to mine. I cannot accept either his confutation of my statement that the German critics executed what I called a betrayal of Baumgarten's thought. Baeumler says that the only critics who took such a line were Ritter, Zimmermann, and Schmidt. That is to say "only" one of the greatest German historians of philosophy (Ritter), the greatest historian of Aesthetics (Zimmermann), and the author of the best monograph then existing about Baumgarten (Schmidt). In 1900, when I was writing, these were the chief authorities on Baumgarten. — No doubt, Baumgarten's interest in induction, as in everything concerning the sensible, the particular, the individual, is connected with the wider drift of modern thought towards the concrete which includes both the formation of the physical and natural sciences and also the formation of the aesthetic science. But the point here at issue is the different one, that *cognitio sensitiva sive aesthetica* is not the observation and experiment of the natural sciences, but belongs to a different order of processes of enquiry.

Nevertheless Baumgarten has a paragraph (525) in which, after listening once again to those objections and reproofs ("has certe fictiones concedes esse mendacia: cur itaque definis, illustras, distinguis et analogica saltim commendare videris?") and after retorting to them (in traditional style) that he despaired of disaccustoming people from making use of false beliefs, he seems to be suddenly assailed by a doubt suggested by certain words of Saint Augustine. He suspects that Augustine has seen the point better than he himself ("forsan tamen S. Augustinus me felicior est"). The words of the Saint which had so struck him were these: "Non omne quod fingimus mendacium est; sed quando id fingimus quod nihil significat, tunc est mendacium. Quum autem fictio nostra refertur ad aliquam significationem, non est mendacium sed aliqua figura veritatis ... Fictio quae ad aliquam veritatem refertur, figura est; quae non refertur, mendacium." (See this passage in *Quaestionum Evangeliorum libri duo*, II, 51, Migne's edition, part 2, page 1362.) They had struck him, yet he had not rightly understood them, as appears from the explanations which he furnishes in the paragraph in question and in the corresponding passage of the *Vorlesungen*. They afforded him no guidance towards a different conception of *veritas aesthetica* as a truth not of logic but of expression, an expression not of judgements but of feelings. They were the less able to do so in that he himself clung obstinately to the fusty distinction between sensitive knowledge and sensitive expression, between content without expression and expression available for application to the content. Thus both Baumgarten and Meier habitually divided Aesthetics into *heuristica* (invention), *methodologia* (disposition), and *semiotica* (expression), never suspecting, either of them, that the three are *unum et idem* and consist, really, in the last of the three, in pure expression.

It would have been necessary for Baumgarten, if he was going to treat aesthetic truth seriously as "prelogical", and poetry as *oratio sensitiva perfecta*, and fully to justify such a solemn affirmation to his own, rather than to others' satisfaction, that he should have extirpated and destroyed every notion or trace of a notion that the truth of poetry is a "minor logical truth". Such an extirpation and destruction was but the natural consequence of the proclamation of the philosophical and autonomous science of poetry. Yet it fitted ill with the metaphysical or cosmological premiss of that Leibnizian philosophy of which the said science itself was an outcome. The case called for a double simultaneous performance: the banishing of that premiss and its replacement by another, with a deeper penetration into the peculiar quality of aesthetic truth. Only some time later, after long labours, successive attempts, failures, and part failures, did the achievement come. Let us, although in philosophy every particular problem is general, and every general problem correspondingly particular, limit our attention more or less to the particular aesthetic problem. The first great step should have been, and ultimately was, the ever so difficult one of denying the division, in the aesthetic sphere, between content and form, the significant and the signified, intuition and expression. Such a division has its use in the more complex logical sphere, the sphere of "prose", where it is an aid to the distinction of logical process from expressive process, thought from the affective tone of thought, concept or judgement from language. There is, of course, no greater or clearer mark of aesthetic crudity, immaturity, stupidity, than the question often heard in regard to a poem, picture, or musical composition: What does it mean? What is there to be learnt from it? Aesthetic education, that is, the part of education which has for its object the training of taste, consists precisely in conveying that poetry has no meaning outside of itself, means nothing but itself, what it says in its images and its rhythm. In the same way, in the field of theory, the struggle of the "aesthetic" against the "anaesthetic" philosopher, of the few philosophers who are aware of the quality of art against the larger number who have never cultivated that awareness or are naturally precluded from entering into it, is a struggle to advertise the sublime "insignificance", from the intellectual and practical point of view, of poetry, art, beauty, and to procure the inclusion of this "insignificance" among the categories of the spirit. All of this was at last accomplished (so far as it is licit ever to speak of accomplishment in philosophy and in life itself) when the doctrine of poetry as pure form and pure intuition, and as identity of intuition and expression, came to be formulated.

The achievement, by dint of keen struggle, of such a formulation, liberating us once and for all from the logic, concept, or philosophy which seeks to meddle with the business of poetry, producing, directing, and restraining this to fit its own standards, is at one and the same time the starting point for the further question, as to the nature of poetry. This is a question not as to poetry's content (that content coincides with form, as intuition coincides with expression) but as to its material: the question what is the condition, the antecedent, the spiritual form which, when poetry makes its presence felt, lapses to the status of matter. And at this stage it becomes clear that the antecedent, the material in question, is what in everyday language is called passion or feeling, which is as much as to say the practical world which takes its general appearance from inclinations or desires. Baumgarten had an inkling of this when in his lectures he spoke of the "language of the heart" proper to the poet, and of the longings (*Begierde*) which he feels in himself and stirs up in others, and of his urge towards the future (*Zukunft*), his construction of possible worlds (§ 36). But in all this there is much confusion. The formulation of the principle of the lyrical quality of all art, of the immanence of the lyrical character in pure intuition; the consequent endorsement of the claim of art to provide a catharsis for the passions, not by way of a flight from these, but by way of their elevation into the theoretical sphere, in which the violence of their agitation becomes restrained, commuted and converted into musical stresses and resolutions, into living harmony – all this had to wait upon more stringent labours.

But once clearness is achieved regarding this new point, once the world of passion or practice has been established as the antecedent and material stage upon which art follows as its contemplative transfiguration, we can without further risk of straying or losing ourselves take up the other problem of the universal character of art. For that transfiguration and catharsis is at the same time a liberation from the onesidedness and particularism of praxis, an integration of particular feeling in the wholeness of all feeling, and of the individual in the cosmos. An ancient doctrine that poetry and philosophy are twin routes towards the Absolute here finds its proper scope in a corrected and limited version. Baumgarten himself saw objective or metaphysical truth "nunc obversari intellectui potissimum in spiritu, dum est in distincte perceptis ab eodem, LOGICAM STRICTAM DICTAM, nunc obversari analogo rationis et facultatibus cognoscendi inferioribus, vel unice, vel potissimum, AESTHETICAM" (§ 424). But Baumgarten, and others after him, located the full and true, objective or metaphysical reality on the yonder side of the Spirit, how or where it is hard to understand, while on the hither side he placed two mirrors to reflect it, one of them somewhat veiled, yet still luminous in the interstices of the mist ("confused but clear") – and this was art – the other bright and limpid ("clear and distinct") – and this was philosophy. The two mirrors jointly stood as *veritas subjectiva* or *veritas aesthetico-logica* over against the first and objective truth (§ 427). For us, on the contrary, the notion of a mirroring no longer arises, because for us the something supposedly mirrored, the reality beyond the spirit, is a ghost which has vanished, and the supposed mirrors are themselves realities or functions of the one reality. They are for us not a pair of parallels, logic and the sensitive analogue of logic, but two necessary forms of the Spirit to be developed dialectically within its unity.

We have just been sketching in its main features the course taken by Aesthetics and philosophic thought from Baumgarten up to our own stage of mastery of general philosophic concepts and of the special concepts of art which constitute our new or modern Aesthetics. Now what is all this business of ours about if not the care of an estate which we have, for sure, tended and improved (and are still doing so), but which in the first place we had to inherit? Is it possible to understand in their inwardness those concepts, and all the other doctrines of modern Aesthetics, without knowing how they came into existence, what were the conditions and obstacles they came up against, how they have been transformed, limited, broadened? I myself, having, in my distrust for the facile theories of the beautiful and the artistic then pouring forth from the presses, dutifully run through all the varieties of literature on the subject before undertaking my revision of the theory, then did everything I could to rouse attention to the history of Aesthetics, but I must say that these particular strenuous efforts of mine had scant success. My theories undoubtedly have been successful; I have been and am much listened to; but my counsel to look backwards, to win acquaintance with the long line of thinkers who had preceded me in my meditations and enquiries about art, to love and venerate those who helped on powerfully the advancement of these ideas, to observe with sympathy the efforts, though frustrated, of others, has been wholly ignored and neglected. The blame for such indifference is not mine. Truly I have never been ungrateful towards those from whom I have learned, witness the excellent Baumgarten whose *Meditationes* I, a disciple far removed in time and place, piously reprinted *meis impensis* as an elegant booklet in Naples in 1900. I put a few copies on sale, but there was not a single buyer, and I ended by handing round the whole edition as gifts to friends, nor, I believe, did a single one of the recipients read his copy. Since then I have over and over again tried to persuade German scholars and publishers – including Meiner of Leipzig, publisher of the *Philosophische Bibliothek* – to reprint, with an adequate commentary, the excellent man's *Aesthetica*, only always to get the answer that *duo vel nemo* would buy the book. I should have made up my mind to have it reprinted here, at Bari in Italy, profiting once again by the magnanimity of my friend Laterza, had not your country, my excellent Baumgarten, had not, that is, the successor of King Frederick William I who transplanted you from Halle to the University of Frankfurt on Oder and of King Frederick the Second whom you celebrated in a copy of Latin verses which you wrote and recited on taking up your Professorship, unleashed a war; which war was followed by all kinds of consequences including a world economic crisis, affecting publishers among others. And though like Faust I am *immer strebend* (and hope accordingly to be *erlöst*), yet the time is coming when I shall have to say to myself with Petrarch: "Hide it no longer from thyself, thou'rt old!", So I have now ceased to hope for that reprint, of which I hoped to be the editor.[1]

To return now to the substance of this discourse. When my exhortations and incitements to the study of the history of Aesthetics, and other similar studies, has met with resistance, I have undoubtedly been obliged to recognize how that union of philosophy and history permitting, the frequent leaps from the one to the other, which long practice and training had made me consider easy and almost natural, is far from easy and natural, and will, on the contrary, always remain possible for the few only. In the present case, I consider to be particularly instructive the study of the Aesthetics of the eighteenth century, when the prehistory of this science ended and its history began. The first century of this history (I mean, roughly, that which begins with Gravina and Vico in Italy, the Swiss school and Baumgarten in Germany, and reaches as far as Kant, Schiller, Herder, Humboldt, and Goethe) displays the problems, theories, and chains of argument with a freshness, ingenuousness, clarity, transparency which in the following century were largely missing. The latter century made use often enough of ready-made concepts, worn-out phrases. There was an abundant crop of *epigoni*, and in the sphere of Aesthetics I should not hesitate to describe even Schelling and Hegel, not to mention their ponderous disciples.

I should particularly recommend a bath of history as beneficial for the midwifery of contemporary philosophical pregnancies. The use of such baths might greatly reduce the incidence of those very frequent abortions which are the new aesthetic theories being brought forth in Italy in these latter years. Not one of these has been a live birth no matter how much noise the parents have made about them. Do they think that mere noise can bring the stillborn to life? The cure here suggested might set to rights the brains of

1. However, Laterza did not cease to think of it, and four years later, on the occasion of my seventieth birthday, he reprinted the *Aesthetica*, the text being edited by Prof. Tommaso Fiore, while I added, finally, some historical and bibliographical notes.

some who have brains (the prime condition, certainly, for the efficacy of a brain cure). Others, no doubt, would continue to do exactly what they do now, being incapable of anything different or better. Perhaps, alongside of the frivolous improvisers, there might arise a select body of scholars, conscientious and methodical workers, in the field of Aesthetics. If they had the humility and the vigour to read your works, old Baumgarten, that would be enough to confute and dispel a good deal of their cloudy thinking. Lend an ear for a moment to their nonsense. Here are some who want to promote a sort of Aesthetics which shall, according to their heart's desire, be "empirical", divorced from any philosophical system. *You* can easily drive home to them how Aesthetics came into the world at one and the same time for the better understanding of art, and also to meet the requirements of system by bridging the gap between *perceptiones obscurae* and *perceptiones distinctae*. It was born as a thoroughly philosophic science and can only live as such. Then there are others who imagine, much in the same way, that there are in Aesthetics "empirical" truths which can be transported from one system to another very much as bricks and stones can be shifted at pleasure into one or another edifice or pattern. You could bring home to them the personal experience of your own lasting inability to fit the aesthetic and "prelogical" knowledge, bright with its own perfection and beauty, such as you had conceived in your theory, with the *lex continui* of the Leibnizian system which you accepted. You could not do so, because what you had conceived was not an empirical truth, but was a philosopheme, which called for a new principle, a new systemization. Then here are yet others who accuse your Aesthetics and all those which, like it, have taken poetry's proper and distinguishing quality for their point of departure, of "cowardice", by which they mean failure to grasp the deep concept that art is philosophy or religion or prophecy or moral leadership of mankind, with a consequent lapse into a sheerly sensualist doctrine. These you will be in a position to mock as you mocked their predecessors in your own times, of whom you said that they, less skilled than youthful philosophic neophytes (*philosophorum ipsi pueri*) mistake *perfecta* for *omnino*, mistake divine poetic innocence and half-witted foolery for one another, and their own vain poetasters' presumption for poetic inspiration. Next on the list is a ponderous panlogist, one who, long accustomed to proclaim as sole reality the sole and eternal act of thought, and to loll happily in that vacuous vision, seems all of a sudden seized with satyriasis, and runs about crying that art is not representation, knowledge, and catharsis of feeling, but is feeling in itself, feeling, *cupiditas*, need to be satisfied, pleasure to be enjoyed, vengeance to be prepared, plot to be woven, crime to be excogitated, and so forth; what answer will this fellow receive from you who rightly thought that even love, when it wholly possesses and ravages the soul, is incompatible with poetry? About love and lovers your words were these: "Misere quod omnes eripit sensus ipsis, nam simul suam Lesbiam adspiciunt, nihil est super illis." You knew that poetry begins to come to birth where there is a gazing from afar, an unsatisfied desire, a dreaming and fancying: "quando autem absentis angiportum perambularunt, clausam januam fenestrasque vacuas salutantes, subito se in montes et lucos ex urbe removent, ibique suum naturae miraculum procul vident dulce ridens, dulce loquens audiunt, fingunt, scribunt, canunt, psallunt, pingunt" (§ 87). But then that same proclaimer of untamed feeling continues to keep in his pocket his stale panlogism, and is ready to pull it out and declare that the feeling in itself, the art in itself, of which he had spoken, is abstract and unreal, nothing else being real save the logical thought which thinks this. You will then be able to comfort him by bringing to his notice what he does not know or has never thought of: "ex nocte per auroram meridies" (§ 7); you will pity him because he, in the incivility of his mind and soul, in his total aesthetic obtusity, seems to know nothing else save thick darkness and blinding noon, and fancies that he can join them together in a repulsive embrace; he knows nothing of the dawn which stands between the two, between, that is, the agitations of the feelings, and the discriminations of philosophy. He does not know the transition from the one to the other which is Dawn, Poetry.

29

As for myself, old teacher, you can still today teach me something: you can teach me to strengthen myself in a feeling which was not natural to me, was indeed unknown to me almost throughout my life, but of which, alas, I have now had to learn the sharp savour (and little it would have mattered if I had only had to learn this in regard to this business of Aesthetics and literature). I mean the feeling which made you pray never to have leisure enough to reply to assailants like those you saw before you ("ne mihi tantum usque otii concedat quod per litigia hujus furfuris, quando mihi moventur, terere, delapidare, perdere liceat" – *Metaphysica*, Preface, 3rd edn.) – a feeling which though I have had to arm myself with it, I leave unnamed.

[1932]

XVI

INTRODUCTION TO THE AESTHETICS
OF THE EIGHTEENTH CENTURY

Eighteenth-century Aesthetics are dominated by the enquiry into and the discussion of the theory of taste. Of this there is material or bibliographical evidence in the succession of treatises, essays, notes, observations, dissertations on the subject appearing from the end of the seventeenth right up to the end of the eighteenth century. They bore the names of Dacier, Bellegarde, Bouhours, Rollin, Seran de la Tour, Trublet, Formey, Bitaubé, Marmontel, and (at a higher level) Montesquieu, Voltaire, d'Alembert, among the French; Addison, Hume, Gerard, Home, Burke, Priestley, Blair, Beattie, Percival, Reid, Alison, among the English; Muratori, Trevisano, Calepio, Pagano, Corniani, among the Italians; Tomasio, J. U. König, Bodmer, J. A. Schlegel, Wegelin, Heyne, Herz, Eberhard, J. C. König, Szerdahely (a Hungarian offshoot of the German school), and Emmanuel Kant among the Germans, the last and greatest of whom wrote the *Critique of Judgement*, devoted mainly to criticism of the aesthetic judgement or "taste". And the foregoing list of names is far from being an exhaustive catalogue. The word "taste", transferred from the sense of the palate to serve in a metaphorical sense, came to enjoy an unexampled popularity, though the metaphor was not entirely new.[1] Interest in the problems which arose concerning taste was of the liveliest, though the solutions offered were controversial and tortuous. Seran de la Tour was among those who commented:

1. The aforementioned Hungarian Georg Szerdahely remarked: ". . . ista hominis facultas sentiendi pulcrum et turpe dicitur Gustus, non penitus novo, sed magis usitato nomine: constat enim mihi, hac eadem intelligentia loquutos aliquando fuisse Graecos Latinosque veteres, metaphora a Gustu palati facta. Modus iste loquendi tunc erat infrequens, deinde penitus cecidit jacuitque, dum tandem ab hominibus antiquae originis et spiritus suscitaretur et illa hominis proprietas facundo hoc Laconismo cognominaretur. Jam modo nomen illud gentium praecipuarum civitate est donatum, habetque sensum non adscititium sed proprium . . ." (*Imago Aesthetices seu doctrina Boni Gustus breviter delineata*, Budae, 1780, p. 8).

"Il n'est point de société dans laquelle on ne parle du goût; rien de plus commun que les conceptions sur ce sujet: chacun alors s'empresse de dire ce qu'il en pense; mais à peine s'est on arrêté à une proposition pour en expliquer l'idée, que la contradiction suit immédiatement l'assertion."[1]

We must now look carefully into what the nature of this problem was, and clearly define it. And we may start by observing that it was simply the new form of the very ancient problem "What is the beautiful?", first raised by the sophists, attempted on various lines by the Hellenic philosophers, lingering on in the pages of the fathers of the Church and the scholastics, and taken up afresh by the Platonists and Aristotelians of the sixteenth century.

The problem had from great antiquity been ill set as one of a research into the character or characters of beautiful objects, natural or artificial, their beauty being thus conceived as external to the spirit of man: this made a satisfying solution impossible. The tentative and unsatisfying debate in the *Hippias Major* could be taken as symbolic of a discussion which dragged on for many centuries.

But even in its new form the problem was, despite all appearances, ill set. The question was no more 'What is the beautiful?' but 'What is taste?' The error in the setting was once again of the same order. Taste was taken to be the pleasure which is felt in the presence of certain objects. Now that this was just pleasure in general was not admitted: neither was it admitted that the pleasure in question was the same as the pleasure to which the good, the true, or the useful gives rise. (Had such admissions been allowed, the problem itself would never have arisen.) Thus the problem of the nature of the pleasure of taste inevitably took on the aspect of the old and traditional problem, asking what was the character or characters of objects which produce such pleasure. Treatises directly devoted to the nature of the beautiful, and sometimes proclaiming that enquiry on their title-page, were rare but not

1. *L'Art de sentir et de juger en matière de goût*, new edn., revised by M. ROL-LAND (Strasbourg, 1790. First edn. 1762).

unknown (it suffices to recall Crousaz, André, and Hogarth); but practically all the treatises on taste in fact end up with a theory of the beautiful, of natural and artificial beauty, essential and arbitrary beauty, intellectual and moral, visual and audible beauty, beauty of bodies and spirits and deity, and so on. Even Kant's theory culminated in this manner with his well-known distinctions between 'detached' and 'adherent' (as well, of course, as between natural and artificial beauty). And Beauty, in Kant's theory, is ultimately a symbol of morality.[1]

It was, for sure, both significant and important that the enquiry into the pleasure of taste, that is into a motion of the psyche, now held the place of honour, and that in this range of thought as well as in others, men had moved on from Ontology to Psychology, or rather from Physic and Metaphysic to the Philosophy of the Spirit, conformably to the tendency of modern philosophy since Descartes. That was the right way, the only way to be followed straight forward, the only way aiming at no goal outside itself but affording a point of arrival and a point of departure wherever you stood. But the enquiry into the philosophy of the aesthetic spirit, though eagerly undertaken, was checked by the principle which had been assumed at the outset: the principle of pleasure or of the pleasure of taste, propounded not as an active form, but as a passive moment (passive, it is true, not in itself, but in respect of the aesthetic spirit) and incapable, by reason of such passivity, of determining the character of the aesthetic spirit. At that level at which pleasure constitutes elementary spiritual activity, organic or economic, all spiritual activity is reduced to a single rank. To seek to use pleasure as a touchstone of spiritual activities is, if the fanciful image be allowed, rather like trying to distinguish the various tribes of the fish world by referring to the water in which all of them live, move, and have their being.[2] Hence the

1. The natural transition from one enquiry to the other seems to be symbolized by the title and subtitle of Hogarth's book: *The Analysis of Beauty, written with a view of fixing the fluctuating ideas of taste.*

2. It may be useful, for greater clearness, to recall here that according to the theory which I have propounded and upheld elsewhere, pleasure and pain belong directly to the most elementary form of praxis, which I call

454 THE PHILOSOPHY OF ART AND LANGUAGE

impossibility of getting decisively beyond the hopeless enquiry into the essence of beautiful objects, of things objectively or physically or metaphysically beautiful.

There is a sort of record or solemn monument of the unceasing urge and, at the same time, the abiding impotence of the century in question to attain a theory of the aesthetic spirit: it is the concept which at that time received doctrinal embodiment and the dignity of a spiritual category – the concept of the Sentiment. The concept was no doubt helped into existence also by unsatisfied strivings in the spheres of moral philosophy and the theory of knowledge. But the chief contribution was certainly made in the sphere of enquiries of an aesthetic order into taste and beauty: enquiries which were more directly responsible for the erection of Sentiment into a third spiritual form side by side with, or in between, the form of Knowledge and the form of Will. The concept of Sentiment (called by the German writers *Gefühl* or sometimes *Empfindniss* when it was desired to distinguish between *Empfindung* on the more theoretical side, and *Empfindniss* as closer akin to the Will),[1] conceived as the third form, is in truth an organization of

vital, hedonistic, utilitarian, or economic, constituting the dialectic of this. (In Spinoza's terms, pleasure is *transitio a minore ad majorem perfectionem*.) Now in virtue of the unity of the Spirit, the other forms of activity (moral, logical, aesthetic) and their correlative dialectics respectively of good and evil, true and false, beautiful and ugly, are in necessary correspondence with pleasure and pain, for which reason the latter are said to "accompany" them. And in fact they do accompany every form of activity, in that whether we be performing an act of judgement or a work of art or an ethical deed, what we are doing will always be an act of vitality. But this accompaniment is not, as has sometimes been argued, a relation of the psychic to the physical, of the spirit to the natural organism. It is on the contrary a process inside the Spirit to which the so-called natural organism itself also belongs as a spiritual entity. It is right to describe the alternation of pleasure and pain as "passive" only when regarding it as response to other activity, yet the response itself is not passive but active. The dialectical conception of pleasure and pain entirely eliminates the old problems as to the priority of the one or the other of these related terms.

1. F. J. ESCHENBURG, *Entwurf einer Theorie und Litteratur der schönen Wissenschaften* (new improved edn., Berlin-Stettin, 1789): "Von dem was wir gewöhnlich Empfindung (*Sensation*) nennen, oder von der blossen Wahrnehmung des auf uns wirkenden Gegenstandes und des dadurch auf unsre

this confusion and absurdity, an oscillation between the two distinct forms, or else something secondary and passive raised to coequal rank with the active forms. Historians of philosophy have erred in ascribing to the psychologists and philosophers of the eighteenth century the merit of discovering the new spiritual category. The alleged discovery was really an adventure into which they plunged and in which they entangled themselves just because they failed to "discover" that which they were really seeking. The adventure, it is true, was not sterile, but was something quite different from the attainment of a new explanatory principle.

Yet viewed from another angle those enquiries into taste, while missing their intended aim, deserve praise, great praise, for the observations and thoughts of permanent value to which they gave rise on the way. Beneath those ill-set problems, beneath the fallacious crust, there were real problems making their presence felt. The disquisitions of antiquity and of the Middle Ages and the Renaissance concerning the Beautiful had also had such a value and served a purpose, even if only that of upholding, amid unavoidable oscillations, the concept that besides the values of intellectual truth, moral goodness, private convenience, there was a further value neither to be reduced to any single one nor to be resolved into all of these taken together. This was the beautiful, some of the characters of which, such as its relation to contemplation and to these senses which were held to be pre-eminently contemplative, and the unity which beauty confers upon the various without abolishing variety itself (nay, stimulating variety by inducing harmony within it), they had remarked and recorded.

But far more fruitful than those anticipations were the enquiries of the eighteenth century into Taste, with their gradual outlining of a spiritual sphere belonging neither to the intellect nor to practice. The assertion by those earlier thinkers of a *pulchrum* having its place alongside of the *verum* and the *bonum* was now repeated with a deeper significance as the discernment of a "sense of order and proportion", a "moral sense" which is the sense of the beautiful

Vorstellungskraft gemachten sinnlichen Eindrucks, lässt sich noch das Empfindniss (*Sentiment*) unterscheiden" (§ 11).

and the good, an "inner sense", discovered by Shaftesbury, Hutcheson, and others, indwelling in the human spirit. But rather
than those, it was the term "Sentiment" which prevailed in the
end: it indicated as yet in a dim and uncertain manner – but this
sufficed to forbid its denial and oblivion – the sphere of the aesthetic. The general tendency of all those writers was contrary to
the old saying "de gustibus non disputandum": this saying, indeed,
when transferred and applied to the business of the beautiful,
amounted to a denial and mockery of the reality of the aesthetic,
reducing it to an arbitrary play of the senses and the individual
fancy, or, as we would now put it, to the sway of the hedonistic
and utilitarian form. More or less successfully, by dint of various
devices and at the cost of various contradictions, those enquirers
and essayists upheld the rationality or absoluteness of taste, as a
perfectly legitimate and indeed obligatory subject of disputation
in terms of its own criterion.[1]

It was their merit also to have observed the difference between
the pleasure of taste and the pleasure of the excitement of the
senses, how the former has a character of disinterestedness, that is,
has no reference to utility; how it pursues no aim, this being the
proper quality of a unity in variety which is its own aim, being
that particular synthesis which is accomplished by beauty which
Hemsterhuis, here confounding, however, synthetic power with
rapidity in time, defined as "that which affords the greatest number
of ideas in the shortest time". And so too Burke, who seems little
of a philosopher, very much of an empiricist, and as an empirical
psychologist drawn to the physiological, lays down, in excellently
philosophical wise, the disinterestedness of the aesthetic pleasure,

---

1. For example GERARD (*Essai sur le goût*, French translation, Paris, 1766,
p. 241): "On dit communément qu'il ne faut pas disputer des goûts. Cette
maxime est vraie si par goût on entend le palais, qui rebute certains aliments
et qui en aime d'autres . . . Mais la maxime est fausse et pernicieuse, lorsque
on l'applique à ce goût intellectuel qui a les arts et les sciences pour objets.
Comme ces objets ont des charmes réels, de même il y a un bon goût qui les
apperçoit réellement et un mauvais goût qui ne les apperçoit point; et il y
a certaines méthodes dont on peut se servir pour corriger ces défauts de
l'esprit qui corrompent le goût."

just as he distinguishes the aesthetic criterion from the criterion of "fitness", and from the criterion of the perfection of a thing in reference to its end; and proclaims the wholly contemplative "love" which pertains to beauty by contrast with the "desire" which pertains to the affections of the senses in quest of acts of possession.

All these are among the propositions elaborated by the eighteenth-century theorists of taste and of the beautiful, including the invention of a third spiritual form, "Sentiment", concerned with beauty and the aesthetic, which flow together into Kant's *Critique of Judgement*. This work, when analysed in its single parts, as has been undertaken by scholars recently, seems to contain nothing or next to nothing that was new:[1] and yet it is all new, and has caused all those precedent treatises which Kant knew and utilized to fall into oblivion. The newness consists in the critical and philosophical vigour with which Kant works up and elevates that confused and fluctuating mass into powerful concepts and systematicity. With good reason did Heydenreich, a follower of Kant and an aestheticist of some merit, shortly after the appearance of the *Critique of Judgement* celebrate the new glory of German philosophy which had now introduced the "critical method" also into the field of the theory of taste, until lately (he said) occupied in part by the "dogmatic" philosophers, but for the greater part by the empiricists of the English school: the critical method, combining speculation with experiment, had corrected the errors of either side.[2] Kant's provisional conclusion, following upon that succession of tentative efforts, forms part of a general process which I have described elsewhere – the process by which modern thought

1. See the research work of O. SCHLAPP, *Kants Lehre vom Genie und die Entstehung der K. d. U.* (Göttingen, 1901), and those more recent of BAEUMLER, *Kants Kritik der Urteilskraft, Ihre Geschichte und Systematik* (Halle, 1923), and CASSIRER, *Die Philosophie der Aufklärung* (Tübingen, Mohr, 1932), and others.

2. See the preface, and more especially the appendix (vol. I, 185-197) to his translation of one of these empiricists: ARCHIBALD ALISON, *Ueber den Geschmack, dessen Natur und Grundsätze, verdeutscht und mit Anmerkungen und Abhandlungen begleitet* von K. H. HEYDENREICH (Leipzig, Weygand, 1792).

has gradually filled up the gap that antiquity on the one hand,
Christian thought on the other, opened between the rational and
the sensible, morality and life.[1] It is indeed one of the most conspicuous episodes in that long and various mental travail.

Nevertheless, in the *Critique of Judgement* there remains a certain
amount of material which never passed through the critical process, a certain amount that has been empirically piled up, residues
taken over directly from earlier writers. Of such an order is the
dualistic treatment of the beautiful and the sublime, taken by
Kant mainly from Burke. Burke drew a contrast between the
Beautiful, which was for him social and sociable sentiment, love
and sympathy for the small and the delicate, and the Sublime,
which demands the great and the imposing, being a pleasure in
painful and fearful stirrings when one is immune from any practical effects, safe from any attendant losses. There remain, moreover,
in Kant's work, or there arise afresh in it, some contradictions to
which no solution is given, at least in the form in which they are
propounded – for example the exclusion of every interest, end, or
concept from the pleasure of the beautiful is upheld side by side
with the conclusion that the beautiful is a symbol of morality.
This contradiction was at once observed by Kant's opponent
Herder.[2]

More than these aspects and problems, what most calls for attention in the *Critique of Judgement* both as it took shape itself and
as it summed up all the precedent eighteenth-century enquiries into
taste, is that the truths about the aesthetic, about beauty, which it
affirms, were arrived at indirectly, by the hidden force of the
effective aesthetic conscience triumphing over the faulty setting of
the problem: they are therefore somewhat scattered and not con-

1. See in this volume the essay: 'The Worldly Pair of Sciences', pp. 749-62.
2. "Da es vorher nach vier kategorischen Momenten ohne Begriff und
Interesse, ohne Vorstellung des Zwecks u. f. nicht nur allgemein gefallen
musste, sondern sogleich vom Schönen hinabsank, sobald man an Güte
dachte; jetzt im letzten Paragraph des Werks wird das Schöne ein Symbol
des Guten, des Sittlichen sogar, und zwar alles Schöne: schöne Formen,
schöne Kleider, schöne Farben, schöne Gebäude" (*Kalligone. Vom Ange-
nehmen und Schönen*, Leipzig, Hartknoch, 1800, III, 259-60).

centrated upon the fact which it was desired to explain, not fully identified with it. It would not be over-frivolous to fit the characters of the aesthetic pleasure as summed up and fixed by Kant into a riddle of this sort – What is that thing which pleases without conceiving, and without practical advantage, is purposive without an aim, yet is an object of universal pleasure? If it is neither intellectual truth nor moral goodness nor economic advantage, what is it?

We now know the answer to the riddle and can answer "It is Poetry, or, more generally, art." But Kant did not say or really know this. For him the answer was not art. And it was not art for those eighteenth-century theorists of taste who, if they theorized about beauty, usually kept their theory of Beauty and their theory of Art quite distinct, or made of the latter a sequel treating of Beauty imitated or imitative Beauty. Art was certainly not the answer for Kant, who conceived of Art as a beauty adhering to a concept, a joint production of the intellect and the imagination, and viewed poetic genius itself as a sort of play of those joint forces.

Such a view was one of the inevitable consequences of having made of pleasure, even in the limited sense of pleasure of the taste, the basis of the enquiry – something, that is to say, which must be, in the sense already indicated, not active and productive but passive.[1] A research starting from an enquiry into pleasure could at the utmost make its way by surreptitious, fragmentary, and winding routes to the concept of poetry and art. But the enquiry into the production of poetry and art was the high road in the required direction; it offered a transition first to taste, and then to the explanation of that which was believed to lie outside the range of poetry and art, but was felt to be, and indeed was, beauty; not something external but a creation of the human fancy, for such are the things or rather images which are commonly given the description of natural beauty.

1. Hence the dissatisfaction felt by Kant's followers and the problem set for such men as Schiller, Humboldt, and Körner of discovering, as they put it, an "objective" definition of Beauty by way of complement to that of Kant.

An enquiry into the nature of poetry and art on these lines had been in course for centuries, constituting a scientific tradition which might be termed Aristotelian, as having its principal origin in the Poetic and Rhetoric of Aristotle. It was a tradition parallel to that of the enquiry into Beauty, remaining essentially distinct and detached from this, even when at times it seemed to be linked and involved with it. It was in this enquiry into poetry that Aesthetics in the stricter sense was present and coming to birth, and were it not for the afore-mentioned preconceptions that were entertained of a primacy of the ideas of Beauty and Pleasure, it would seem strange that the historians of Aesthetics have either ignored, or given very much of a back place to the tradition of this enquiry: for example, Zimmermann, among others, leaps straight from Plotinus in the third century after Christ to the eighteenth century, marking the intervening centuries as "eine grosse Lücke" in the history of Aesthetics,[1] that is, a gap in which there falls, totally ignored, all that keen work on the theory of poetry, literature, and art, which began with Aristotle and the other essayists of antiquity, and was concluded in the Renaissance and the seventeenth and eighteenth centuries, principally in Italy, but also in France, Spain, and elsewhere. The conception of taste, of "judgement without argument", had its origin in seventeenth-century Italy,[2] to describe the act of criticizing poetry; the concept of *ingenium* or *genius* came into being at the same time to denote, by contradistinction from the intellect, the productive faculty of poetry. The "Sublime" was a product of the same tradition, derived from the highly valued and much studied treatise going by the

---

1. *Geschichte der Aesthetik als philosophischer Wissenschaft*, p. 147.
2. The usual attribution of it to the Spaniard Gracián is incorrect. I have already remarked in *Estetica* (9th edn., Bari, 1950, p. 209) that Gracián uses this word not in connexion with the beautiful and with art, but in con-nexion with the practical sphere. Both before and after him the Italians, whether using that word or another, individuated a special aesthetic power or faculty of judgement unaccompanied by logical argument, to use the very clear definition of Zuccolo in 1623. See my new enquiries into the history of aesthetic concepts in Italy in the seventeenth century in *Storia dell'età barocca in Italia*, 2nd edn., Bari, 1946, pp. 161-210, 217-32.

name of Longinus,[1] where it was clearly and unmistakably used to denote what was, in the last resort, simply the "excellence" of artistic expression, its "beauty". This early critic was endowed with the most delicate sensibility in regard to it.[2]

In the eighteenth century this theory of poetry and art failed to rouse general interest, nor did the studies devoted to it compare in volume and prominence with those devoted to the other theory. On the other hand, its professors made powerful efforts to deepen its philosophical tone, and to attain systematicity. It should suffice to recall that doctrine of poetry or poetic logic which Vico proclaimed in his *Scienza Nuova*, a logic of language and poetry of which he made use to interpret Homer and Dante;[3] and then, that doctrine of *cognitio sensitiva* or *Aesthetica* which some decades later Baumgarten raised to the rank of a special science.[4] But it

1. Concerning the authorship and date of the *De Sublimitate* see the recent important enquiries of ROSTAGNI, *Il Sublime nella storia dell'Estetica antica* in *Annali della R. Scuola Normale sup. di Pisa*, s. II, vol. II, 1933).

2. See, for example, how, in reference to a poem of Sappho, he observes that the things said in it are the things that all lovers say, but that the excellence is given by the choice of the high lights (ἡ λῆψις ... τῶν ἄκρων) and their union (ἡ εἰς ταὐτὸ συναίρεσις). *De Subl.*, 10.

3. Even now most of the German historians of Aesthetics (Baeumler, Cassirer, and the rest) continue to ignore or to rule out Vico, on the grounds that the Germans did not know him or come under his influence. None the less Vico lived and thought, and the history of his thought does not coincide with the vicissitudes of his influences on Germans or others.

4. E. BERGMANN (*Ernst Plattner und die Kunstphilosophie des 18. Jahrh.*, Leipzig, 1913), basing himself on an unpublished course of Aesthetics held by Plattner at Leipzig in 1777, maintains that Plattner accomplished a veritable revolution and was the first to create the science of art, passing beyond the passive view of taste, to which Baumgarten remained bound, to an insight and conviction concerning the active moment of art. But the *cognitio sensitiva* of which Baumgarten had treated was not primarily the knowledge or judgement of the products of sensitive cognition, but rather the act of knowing itself, and the accomplishment of that act. Hence HERDER (*Von Baumgartens Denkart in seinen Schriften*, in *Sämmtliche Werke*, ed. Suphan, XXXII, 178-92) eulogized the author of the *Aesthetica* for having brought poetry back to her "Mutter und Freundin, die menschliche Seele", and drawn thence his definition. Plattner, emphasizing more than Baumgarten that passional and sentimental moment which finds expression in poetry, yet saw in this sphere "an obscurely felt rather than distinctly apprehended effort to scrutinize the mystery of the world and of the human being", thus

fell to neither of these thinkers to be followed by worthy disciples or continuers, able to develop or add to their new and fruitful teachings, or to link them up with the more detailed work of critics and art lovers among whom the sense of art was attaining a fuller maturity.

Of the two, the German Professor and pioneer teacher had, it is true, more than a few disciples, imitators, and popularizers; but these were disciples and popularizers who for the most part misunderstood his thought, rendered it shallow. They changed and corrupted the *oratio sensitiva perfecta*, that definition of poetry with which Baumgarten had assigned to the "confused or sensitive knowledge" a proper and autonomous "perfection", sometimes into a "representation of sensible perfection", sometimes into "sensible representation of perfection", so that *cognitio poetica* or *sensitiva* ended by taking on the aspect of an intellective cognition of a lower order or diminished scope, as can be seen in Meier, and more clearly in Mengs, Mendelssohn, and others.[1]

When Kant in the *Critique of Judgement* set out to rebut the theory of "renowned philosophers" that "beauty is nothing else

maintaining the Baumgartenian dualism of the confused and the distinct mode of apprehending reality. This does not impair Plattner's real merit, which needed recording, illustrating, and indeed insisting upon, since ZIMMERMANN (*Gesch. der Aesthetik*, p. 204), citing without its context a page from some lectures published by a pupil in 1836, had quite misled students as to the nature of Plattner's theories (see p. 290 in the historical section of my *Estetica*, 9th edn., also Bergmann's lucid and convincing interpretation of the said page in op. cit., p. 179). Plattner's views, never put into book form or published, had no direct influence on the aesthetic enquiries and discussions of his time. Bergmann tries to demonstrate an indirect influence on Moritz, Goethe, and Jean Paul. That Baumgarten belonged to a different tradition from that of the theorists of taste transpires even from some remarks of Baeumler, who seeks to show him as belonging to that tradition: "Baumgarten hat für das Geschmacksproblem im engeren Sinne nicht viel Interesse bezeigt" (op. cit., p. 87).

1. MENDELSSOHN, *Ueber die Hauptgrundsätze der schönen Künste und Wissenschaften* (quoted by Zimmermann, p. 181), says plainly: "ist die Erkenntniss der Vollkommenheit sinnlich, so wird sie Schönheit genannt, . . . die verständliche Vollkommenheit erleuchtet die Seele und befriedigt ihren ursprünglichen Trieb nach bündigen Vorstellungen. Wenn sie aber die Triebfeder des Begehrungsvermögens in Bewegung setzen soll, so muss sie sich in eine Schönheit verwandeln . . .".

but perfection understood confusedly", retorting that the confused knowledge of perfection is itself an intellectual knowledge, or any way no more different from this than the judgement of the common man differs from that of the philosopher,[1] he was certainly right, but his retort was aimed at Wolff and the misunderstandings which had arisen among Baumgarten's pupils, not against Baumgarten, who said no such thing but always meant the *perfectio* to be understood of the *cognitio sensitiva qua talis*, even if he did not wholly avoid a relapse into intellectualistic interpretation in regard to sensible representation of the distinct concept.[2] This slip by Kant would not have much importance were it not a proof that he did not know or failed to understand the concept of poetry contained in Baumgarten's systematic work, just as he did not know or failed to penetrate the similar concept of poetry and language which was gaining ground here and there among the early German Romantics (not to mention Vico). Kant, therefore, just like the theorists of taste and the writers of Baumgartenian derivation (among them Riedel, who anticipated the Kantian tripartition of the faculties and the linking of beauty with senti-

1. *Kritik der Urteilskraft*, § 15.
2. ZIMMERMANN, op. cit., pp. 60-61, says that for Baumgarten beauty is "sinnlich erkannte Vollkommenheit"; but neither these words nor this concept are to be found in *Aesthetica* §§ 15-16, to which he refers the reader; the term used there is *"perfectiones cognitionis sensitivae"*. VON STEIN (*Die Entstehung der neueren Aesthetik*, Stuttgart, Cotta, 1886, p. 358, rightly remarks that if Kant intends to refer to Baumgarten, then he had misunderstood him. So too SOMMER (*Grundzüge einer Geschichte der deutschen Psychologie und Aesthetik von Wolff-Baumgarten bis Kant-Schiller* (Würzburg, 1892), p. 345. Perhaps Baeumler's explanation (op. cit., pp. 113-19), to the effect that Kant knew the remarks in the *Metaphysica* in which Baumgarten appeared to abide by the Wolffian definitions on this point, and knew the works of Meier and Mendelssohn but had perhaps never read or properly taken heed of the *Aesthetica*, is the right one. However that be, the Kantian misunderstanding or misreference reappears, in aggravated form, in all or almost all the later works on Aesthetics as a stereotyped confutation of Baumgarten's doctrine, for example, ROSENKRANZ, *Aesthetik des Hässlichen* (Königsberg, 1853), p. 11: "in der Baumgarten'schen Aesthetica des vorigen Jahrhunderts der Begriff der Vollkommenheit mit dem der Schönheit identisch genommen ist. Allein, Vollkommenheit ist ein Begriff, der mit dem der Schönheit nicht direkt zusammenhängt", etc.

ment), neither understood nor even glimpsed the pregnant value
for the speculative development of the philosophy of the spirit of
Baumgarten's concept of a *cognitio sensitiva* distinct from and
anterior to the *intellectiva*, or indeed that of the whole sphere of the
Wolffian *facultates inferiores* or the Leibnizian *petites perceptions*.
Instead of using this to render more organically complex and
concrete the ancient bipartition of theory and praxis, knowledge
and will, he resorted to the expedient of postulating the third
sphere of "sentiment", receptacle of the ununderstood.[1]

There was, indeed, nobody save only Schleiermacher, among
the post-Kantian aesthetic theorists, who was interested in attending to that true cell of aesthetic activity on which the eye of
Baumgarten had lighted, and which Vico had more deeply considered, while some other thinkers had just espied it. And for that
very reason Schleiermacher remained without influence. It is true
that among these post-Kantian aestheticians the persistence of such
a man as Herbart in basing himself in eighteenth-century wise on
the critique of taste, and in seeking, by way of formal and pseudo-
formal terminology, an objective concept of the beautiful, was in
contrast with the behaviour of the majority who banished the
argument on taste and the beautiful, and transferred the centre of
their attention to Art, thereby in some measure causing a fusion
between Aesthetics and the Philosophy of Art. In some measure,
but not altogether, and not in an intimate union: for more or less

1. The difficulty was appreciated by some writers of the times, and in this
connexion there should be noted a passage of MEINERS, *Revision der Philosophie*,
p. 226 seqq., which I find quoted in the well-informed book of K. H. Po-
LITZ, *Die Aesthetik für gebildete Leser* (Leipzig, Hinrichs, 1807, I, 22-23), which
I here reproduce: "In der Aesthetik ist die Hauptquelle unserer Kenntnisse
noch streitig. Ebenso zweifelhaft ist es bisher ob die aesthetischen Begriffe
zu dem Foro der bis jetzt von den Philosophen entdeckten Kräften oder
einer eignen von den Griechen und Römern nicht wahrgenommen Fähigkeit
gehören. Es giebt Männer die einen angebornen Geschmack des Schönen
und Guten verteidigen, und dabei unsere Idee von Schönheit u.s.w. als
etwas ganz Relatives ansehen. Umgekehrt sieht man wieder unveränderliche
Ideale des Schönen und Guten von solchen behaupten, die den Geschmack
für eigentümliche Kraft halten. So lange diese Punkte unausgemacht bleiben,
scheint die Aesthetik in die Form einer Wissenschaft nicht gebracht werden
zu können."

distinct from that theory of art, albeit commingled with it, there remained a "Callologia" or Metaphysic of the Beautiful, and a doctrine of natural beauty and the beauty of natural objects. Awareness that the one object of Aesthetics is Art, that no beauty has reality outside Art, that therefore no Callology independent of or parallel with the philosophy of Art can ever be admissible, was lacking. Even when in the second part of the nineteenth century psychological or empirical systems of Aesthetics replaced the previous philosophical or metaphysical systems, the new sort of treatise continued to embrace parallel theories of the Beautiful and theories of Art, held together only by their imperspicuousness. Such a dualism is anyhow ineradicable in the ever-recurring manifestations of the *Aesthetica vulgaris*.

It was only in Italy, early in the present century, that this dualism was resolved with a full understanding of what was being done, and an Aesthetic was constituted as Philosophy of Poetry, Fancy, Language, Art, Pure Intuition, and Expression. This philosophy gave first place to, indeed gave place to nothing else except, the productive process, illustrating beauty as this process itself in its free deployment, and referring to this process the so-called beauties of nature which are not natural facts but are also themselves spiritual acts. Consequently nobody in Italy, not even the Scholastics and neo-Scholastics (and this is saying much) now occupies himself with the composition of theories of objective beauty, because in the mental field the place of such theories has been captured by others which have cancelled the traces of the previous occupant.

In Germany, on the contrary, mainly because of a deadlock into which art history has fallen, the need was felt to elaborate a doctrine for the elucidation of its guiding concepts and criteria.

But in Germany, while on the one hand the need has been felt for the elaboration of a doctrine to elucidate the guiding concepts and criteria of the history of Art, which had come up against unmanageable perplexities, the problem of the relation of this new science of art (*Kunstwissenschaft*) with the old theory of the Beautiful has been tackled in the crudest and most superficial

30

manner, by keeping Art for the science of art, and Beauty for Aesthetics, as though the great question were not precisely that of the relation between concept of beauty and concept of art, and as though the handing over of the former to new "specialists", so as to limit one's attention solely to the latter, were a way of understanding this in the full light of truth. The ultimate root of the error lies in the false conception that a non-philosophic or purely "scientific" treatment (*Kunstwissenschaft*) of an ideal category is possible.[1]

So slow and difficult is the advance of thought, that there are still periodical hold-ups and entanglements in that false setting of the problem of the beautiful, which gave so much labour to the philosophy of antiquity and to the Aesthetics of the eighteenth century.

[1933]

1. Regarding this school of a separate *Kunstwissenschaft*, see what I wrote as long ago as 1911 in my essay on Fiedler (in *Nuovi saggi di estetica*, 3rd edn., Bari, and specially pp. 240-1) and so in 1915 concerning a book by Utitz (in *Conversazioni critiche*, I, 3rd edn., Bari, 1942, 20-22); compare also a recent booklet by the same Utitz, *Geschichte der Aesthetik* (Berlin, 1932), pp. 70-73, where he expresses himself more doubtfully and prudently. Baeumler, in a work which remained unfinished (*Aesthetik*, München-Berlin, 1934), attempts to record separately the history of the two problems of Art and of the Beautiful, but seems not to understand the relation between them and their substantial identity.

XVII

THE AESTHETICS OF F. SCHLEIERMACHER

W HEN many years ago I was working on the preparation of my history of Aesthetics, I knew nothing of the aesthetic theories of Schleiermacher. No author, major or minor, had recommended them as deserving my attention. But as I perused the pages of Zimmermann and Hartmann, in which they were treated roughly and even rudely, I was able to divine from those words of abuse, and from the few textual quotations from Schleiermacher which accompanied these, that he must have made important pronouncements which those critics had not understood. I therefore procured his lectures on Aesthetics, in the original and never reprinted edition of 1842, then still stocked by the German booksellers,[1] which I read, and at once understood their singular importance, so that I assigned to Schleiermacher, in my history of that branch of learning, a very conspicuous place.

But, in Germany, not even those who like Haym and Dilthey had devoted special study to the life and the thought of Schleiermacher had ever taken any account of his Aesthetics; nor, after I had drawn attention to these teachings, did Schleiermacher's compatriots begin to show an interest in them. This is attested by a fervent admirer who has recently arisen in Germany; after remarking upon the neglect and the disapproval with which the teachings had been steadily treated, he observes that "the one critic who has tried to do justice to Schleiermacher's Aesthetics is a foreign scholar". It must, he adds, be attributed to B. Croce as a special merit, that he has sought to defend those teachings against the unmeasured attacks of Zimmermann and Hartmann, dedicating to them an entire chapter.[2]

1. FRIEDRICH SCHLEIERMACHER, *Vorlesungen über die Aesthetik*, aus Schleiermachers handschriftlichem Nachlasse und aus nachgeschriebenen Heften herausgegeben von Dr. Carl Lommatzsch (Berlin, Reimer, 1842).
2. RUDOLF ODEBRECHT, *Schleiermachers System der Aesthetik*, Grundlegung und problemgeschichtliche Sendung (Berlin, Junker u. Dünnhaupt, 1931),

Now Schleiermacher's lectures are from the literary point of view most uninvitingly presented and developed. Far from displaying a thought that has achieved all-round maturity and a capacity for clear and harmonious exposition, they reveal the process of a mind groping to find its way through perplexities, indeed scarcely ever getting beyond the stage which properly should precede that of literary execution. But I was attracted by the complete opposition of the teachings to those which had, in Germany, prevailed with Schelling, Hegel, and their numerous disciples. All these, instead of patiently searching into the difficult problems of the proper office of art, its genesis and its connexion with the other forms of the spirit, took over from current ways of thought a concept of art that was showy, superficial, syncretic, contradictory. By this instrumentality they strove to give art a place in the pattern of their philosophical systems. Now they exalted art to the topmost peak of the spirit, as the true organ of truth or the beatific condition, now, on the contrary, they abased art to the rank of a provisional and transitory manifestation, doomed to disappear when the evolution of history should have attained a higher and final stage. That manner of treating the problem, however exalted the speculative vein of some of those philosophers, struck me as unsubtle, and decidedly inappropriate to the theme under discussion, and I attached myself instead to another tradition, I mean the one which, on the basis of the Aristotelian Poetics, arose in Italy in the sixteenth and continued with increasing purposefulness and awareness in the seventeenth century, culminating in the concepts of Vico's *Scienza Nuova* concerning Poetry, while in Germany it was pursued more or less by Leibniz, and his school, and especially by Baumgarten, and then by Hamann and Herder. Schleiermacher, with singular earnestness and understanding, renewed and extended those enquiries into the unlogical or prelogical form of cognition, attaching himself not to those who were mistakenly resuscitating a sort of aesthetic Plotinism, but to these latter men of the eighteenth century, and his recent critic and

p. 2. See also the information contained in Odebrecht's introduction to the *Aesthetik,* quoted later.

editor opportunely recalls that his teacher at Halle had been an offshoot of the Baumgarten school of Aesthetics, Eberhard.[1] And Schleiermacher himself was aware enough of the place he was filling in the development of the aesthetic science. For he gives,[2] in the historical notes serving as an introduction to his lectures on Aesthetics, great importance to the Leibniz-Wolffian school, reckons Kant to be akin to those who regarded Aesthetics as a counterpart (*Seitenstück*) to Logic, praised Schiller for shifting attention from the phase of taste to that of productive spontaneity, and, as to the Hegelian system, observes with astonishment the exalted situation in which this places art, but reserves his own judgement about this on the grounds that it is difficult to pronounce an historical judgement upon that which, in reality, is still in course of occurrence. Schleiermacher, instead of seeking art in that sublime sphere of the higher world or the absolute spirit, in the supposed company of religion, where it is said to be, jointly with religion, subject solely to philosophy, seeks and discovers art in that less hieratic guise in which it had appeared to the Leibnizians and to Baumgarten, namely in the place (*Ort*) of the "non-organic" (meaning non-practical) activities, the cognitive and theoretical. Among these, he finds art to be the mode of cognition analogous and opposed to the scientific mode, this last being the cognition of "selfness" (*Selbigkeit*) while art's mode is the cognition of "difference", or of the proper and individual (*Eigentümlichkeit*).

Now this system of Schleiermacher's may be blamed for exhibiting a classificatory static character, in that the two cognitive forms which it distinguishes from one another are not subsequently conjoined by degrees of speculation and dialectical process. Equally it may be objected that his concept of scientific-philosophic knowledge refers this to a universal as yet in the abstract stage, whereas the true and concrete universal is both individual and at the same time historical; in view of which it would be more correct to say that the distinction between universal and individual

1. See Odebrecht's introduction to his edn. of the *Aesthetik*, pp. viii-xii, xxii.
2. In Lommatzsch's edn. pp. 1-17.

does not arise in the aesthetic and artistic act, but does arise in the logical and philosophical act, where indeed there is (Schleiermacher sometimes says) a relation of antithesis (*Gegensatz*) between them. What may be considered a more serious fault on the part of Schleiermacher, more directly affecting his aesthetic teaching, is his attribution of the production and criticism of art not to man as man, or pure spirit, but to man as belonging to this or that national cycle. Such an opinion would tend to destroy the ideal character of art, abasing it to the rank of a practical business corresponding to the peculiar requirements of the racial or traditional groups to which men belong. As in Schleiermacher's time, so too today, and in an aggravated degree, a great many Germans (I will not say the German people) indulge in and take for granted the blasphemously anti-spiritual nationalization of universal human values, so that this point in Schleiermacher's Aesthetics has won for him approval and praise. Yet be it recalled to his honour that the national character of art was understood by him in a far from absolute, indeed highly empirical manner; or rather, he qualified the affirmation almost out of existence.[1] But in any case, these various deviations fail to impair Schleiermacher's successful delineation of the field of Aesthetics as that of a knowledge prior to logical knowledge.

As the basis for his closer definition of the aesthetic form of knowledge, he takes "immediate self-knowledge", which, according to his express observation, is not knowledge of the ego or self-consciousness, this being the thought which conceives constancy through the diversity of moments, but is, on the contrary, "the very diversity of the moments", is, in other words, life itself in the throb of living, ceaseless alternation of pleasure and pain.

Does Art, then, consist in this immediacy of consciousness, throb of life, gush of feeling? Schleiermacher takes care not to

1. ". . . denn sonst würde daraus folgen, dass durchaus nur Kunstwerke zwischen Gliedern desselben Volkes verständlich wären. Das wird niemand zugeben. Nun aber wird jeder gestehen, dass ein griechisches Kunstwerk nicht so affizieren kann, wie es die Griechen affizierte" (*Aesthetik*, ed. Odebrecht, pp. 88-91). The last observation is at the same time trite and trivial.

identify art with pathos or feeling, as indelicate and inartistic critics in our own times as well as his are disposed to do. Yet he remains aware that without the throb and pathos of life Art would lack its material. For Art originates with the conferment of form upon this material (or, what comes to the same, the conferment of theoretical form upon that which previously had passional and practical form), introducing nexus, order, proportion, unity, outline, in the flux of pains and pleasures, in virtue of an act of *Besinnung*, self-recollection, which we would describe as "contemplative synthesis". This recollection is not that mere brake and control upon the transports of joy and grief which distinguishes the well-bred from the unbred man, but is a mastery over the agitation of the passions by the creation of an image to endow this with measure and rhythm. Gesticulation is transformed into mimicry, or natural mimicry (sometimes called by Schleiermacher *natürlicher Ausdruck*) yields to the mimicry which is art, or, quite simply, to Art, which is, in this sense, all mimicry. Art is a dream, but a waking dream (*der wachende Traum des Künstlers*), whereas the dream which is really dreamed belongs to the immediacy of experienced life.

The new editor of the *Aesthetics*, Odebrecht, considers this exposition of the thought of Schleiermacher, contained in the course of lectures published by Lommatzsch in 1842, and thence extracted and illustrated by myself, to be an inferior popularization, when compared with what he considers Schleiermacher's true Aesthetics "in correct, unfalsified, and systematic form". This is to be found, according to Odebrecht, not in the lectures of 1832–33 but in those of 1819 and 1825 on which, especially on the latter, his own new edition is based.[1] I beg to offer the opinion that Odebrecht here indulges in that excessive zeal that discoverers and editors often show for the texts and documents which they have, usefully and laudably, made available. For in fact the lectures of 1832–33

---

1. FRIEDRICH SCHLEIERMACHER, *Aesthetik*. Im Auftrage der preussischen Akademie der Wissenschaften und der Literatur-Archiv-Gesellschaft z. Berlin nach den bisher unveröffentlichen Urschriften zum ersten Male herausgegeben von R. Odebrecht (Berlin und Leipzig, De Gruyter, 1931).

472 THE PHILOSOPHY OF ART AND LANGUAGE

provide the final form of Schleiermacher's thought upon the subject in question, the fruit of a further seven years of enquiry and meditation, devoted to the preparation of a system of Aesthetics, and Lommatzsch, who was, I believe, Schleiermacher's son-in-law, thoroughly informed about his intentions and projects, chose to publish the later rather than the earlier set of lectures, which he certainly knew about. I cannot agree with Odebrecht that the exclusion from the lectures of 1832-33 of the previously used term *Gefühl*[1] (sentiment) is a sign of degeneration or coarsening of the thought. What, after all, was the significance of this term in Schleiermacher's philosophy? Rather than for a particular form, did it not stand for a neutral point between Knowing and Willing, for the unity of the Spirit at its apex, which is its full reality? If this was its function – and this would explain its close relationship with the concept of religion – clearly it could not serve as the premiss to the doctrine of Aesthetics; for the premiss of this is life in its simplicity and immediacy, the material ready for the *Besinnung* to remould into aesthetic form by the conferment of rhythm. If however "sentiment" stood precisely for such immediacy of life or of self-consciousness, as it undoubtedly did in Schleiermacher's earlier lectures,[2] this would set up a duplication in terminology, harmless and indeed perhaps convenient and telling in the case of other philosophers, but very confusing in that of Schleiermacher, who had given "sentiment" a markedly different sense in his system. Now since Odebrecht himself holds that Schleiermacher deliberately excludes the term from his last lectures,[3] it is to be presumed that this was due to a recognition of the logical impropriety of retaining it. And finally, I confess that I am

1. Odebrecht, in his introduction, p. xxiv, and in the monograph quoted, pp. 50-55.
2. "Das eine ist das Element des Wissens, das andere ist das, wodurch das Eigentümliche unseres Wissens sich ebenso im Bewusstsein realisiert wie das Gemeinsame in Wissen. So gewiss nun jenes Gebiet des Wissens ist, ist auch dieses das Gebiet der Kunst, und nun in diesem Sinne können wir sagen, dass, indem wir dies Gefühl nennen, alle Kunst vom Gefühl ausgeht" (*Aesthetik*, ed. Odebrecht, p. 48).
3. "Es scheint fast als sei er (der Ausdruck Gefühl) absichtlich vermieden worden" (introd. cit., p. xxiv).

not much grieved by the omission in the 1832-33 lectures of the description of the particular process of artistic production found in the earlier ones, the process being in these described as beginning with excitation, or sentiment, whence arises *Stimmung* or soul-weather, then *freies Spiel der Phantasie*, free play of the fancy, due to purify and determine itself in the *Urbild* or original image, the final stage being the *Ausbildung*, the accomplishment and refinement of the image.[1] Now all these are psychological, not speculative distinctions; they do not distinguish genuine spiritual moments one from the other, but simply sort out empirically observed gradations. For instance, the statement that Art springs not directly from the sentiment, but from the *Stimmung* which is a "moderation of the excitation",[2] may rouse the retort that this moderation (*Mässigung*) is either itself a rhythmicization and enfigurement of pathos, in which case Art has already come into active being, or else is something not to be understood unless perhaps as a passage from one to another tone of feeling, from the more to the less agitated, always within the practical sphere of experienced life. That Schleiermacher, in his last course of lectures, let drop these psychological and empirical distinctions is to be attributed not to the exigencies of popularization (popularizers as a matter of fact usually rejoice in this sort of psychological pabulum), but, on the contrary, to that sort of speculative simplification which deepens the understanding.

There follows by inference, upon Schleiermacher's wholly spiritual concept of the artistic activity (activity which, with an act of *Besinnung* or new synthesis, imposes rhythm, and therewith order and unity, so accomplishing the aesthetic mediation of the immediate self-consciousness), the conclusion that the real work of art consists entirely in the internal image, *das innere Bild*, and that whatever, without pertaining to this, becomes united with it, must be a secondary adjunct, pertaining to another sphere, comparable with the vocabulary or script serving for the communication (*Mittheilung*) of thought. Once again, from the point of view

1. *Aesthetik*, ed. Odebrecht, pp. 48-52 and passim.
2. Ibid., pp. 106-7.

of speculative theory, we may and must qualify our assent, for the adjective "internal" arises out of a dualism (external/internal) that has no place in strict philosophical concreteness, the image being, concretely speaking, equally internal and external, psychic and physical, as much intuition as expression, indeed requiring to be expressed in order to be intuited, just as physical life is the necessary condition of the psychic. Schleiermacher could never disengage himself from a more or less Spinozian dualism holding apart Thought and Extension, Spirit and Nature. And yet, just as before, when we disregard unresolved general difficulties of this sort, we cannot but accept the substance of Schleiermacher's thought. The effective tendency of this was really to distinguish between expression and "communication", between the theoretical moment and the practical moment in the artistic process. No doubt the two concepts were not altogether clear to him and sometimes he subtracts from the "internal" image something which is essential to its concreteness as an image, as when he seems to want to relegate to externality (or communication) the versification of poetry;[1] or when he contends that the conception may be perfect without the external expression corresponding to it[2] – at the very least, such distinctions should have been accompanied by a theoretical explanation which Schleiermacher did not provide. Not but what Schleiermacher has always a lively sense of the difficulties besetting him, and every intention of recognizing and coping with them, rather than getting round them. For example Schleiermacher attempts a solution of the question, ignored by all other writers on aesthetics, why it is that not all original images, not all *Urbilder*, take on the character of Art. He tries to answer it by emphasizing the social aspect: "Only some of them discover a connexion with the external world," he says (meaning, a connexion with the desire of other people who will "commission" a work of art); the others fail to discover it; but he adds the warning that the work of art derives, not its origin, but only its overt occasion from the demand of others.[3] But this solution is incomplete

1. Ed. Lommatzsch, p. 196.   2. Ibid., p. 219.   3. Odebrecht's edn., pp. 84-85.

for the reason that, as already observed, no clear distinction has been drawn between the expression and the communication, nor yet, consequently, between two meanings of the question which is asked. In the first and fundamental meaning the query concerns that labour by dint of which the Spirit brings those images which are for it, in the circumstances, the most important and urgent, to intuitive and expressive perfection, but relegates the others to the background or to temporary oblivion, or to expectancy of some new operation. Now Society does indeed exercise a stimulus which may be expectant and inviting towards the work of art, although it may be, on the contrary, negative. (The history of poetry and art sometimes records how the artist has sung, painted, or sculpted in defiance of the society around him, keeping true to himself alone, or at the utmost turning an eye of hope towards the society of the future.) In the other and more obvious meaning, the question relates to the existence of the practical conditions necessary if the artist is to be able to fresco a wall, build a house, commit his poem to writing or to the printing press, put his drama in the mouths of actors on a stage.

Thanks to his firm grasp of the "interior" character of Art, or, in other words, for this was his deeper meaning, of Art's wholly theoretical spirituality, Schleiermacher was able to dismiss outright the whole range of empty discussions about "beauty of nature" or "natural beauty". But the same awareness, and the placing of art wholly in the image, outside the range of the physical means of communication, should logically have led him to deny all value and meaning to the distinction between the particular arts, for this distinction is altogether built upon an involvement in those material means of communication. In reality the image which lives in the spirit is poetry, music, painting, sculpture, architecture, high and low relief, and so forth, all at once. The artist produces it as a Whole, a sonorous, lined, coloured, moulded Whole, and as such the artistic understanding receives and re-experiences it. It is no help to say, like Schleiermacher,[1] that in

1. For example, Lommatzsch's edn., p. 152.

the internal image there is already a tendency towards this or that definite sensible type, for this indisputable remark simply means that every work has its own sensible form, and that every work of art is thus differentiated from every other; and not that poetry is differentiated from music, painting, sculpture, and so on, in such a way that the sphere of artistic representations available for each art may be defined. (From its chief representative, I once coined a description of this traditional error as "the Lessing error".)[1]

Nevertheless, a considerable part of Schleiermacher's lectures on Aesthetics is taken up with enquiry into the differences between the particular arts; and instead of duly following up his general and philosophical explanation with a history of poetry and of the other arts (as elsewhere in his system he follows up Physics with Natural History and Ethics with Politico-Moral History), he propounds a classification or rather a wearisome sequence of attempted classifications. It seems to me that his recent examiner and editor finds in this the highlight of Schleiermacher's Aesthetics![2] I too consider this part of the work to be important, but for a different and opposite reason, namely for the objective irony which pervades it, whence the more the author attempts to define any one art as against another, the more does he find the one in the other, and the more he sets forth to follow the divergent ways of the distinctions, the more is he led back to the single common centre. For Schleiermacher was an attentive, subtle, and high-principled critic, whose mind was not to be charmed or cheated

1. As this doctrine of the unity of Art, as opposed to that of the spheres of the particular arts, which I proposed and expounded in my *Tesi di estetica* of 1900, and have since then never abjured, is from time to time attacked, though seldom with any more valid arms than those of vociferation, it may be useful to propose it afresh in the terms used by Gabriele D'Annunzio in 1907, in commenting upon a page of the fourteenth-century writer Arrigo Simintendi: "Here verily the word is three-dimensional. And here it may be seen how all the arts, when they develop maximum expressive energy, show themselves simply as that 'rhythmic unity' which abolishes the material means. It is art that gives quality to the material, and not the other way round. As the word rids itself of inconsistency, so bronze rids itself of fixity. The static image and the dynamic image are solely the creations of two orders of pure rhythm" (*Le faville del maglio*, II, Milan, 1928, pp. 239-40).

2. Odebrecht, introduction, as quoted, p. 172.

either by the grossly imaginous and cumbrous distinctions which were good enough for other writers on Aesthetics, or by those which he himself thought out and tried out, demolishing them with criticism almost at the same moment that he set them up.

One or two examples will suffice to illustrate his operations in the rôle of philosophic brother of the Danaids. He conceives that, among the arts, there must be a fundamental division between those which issue directly from self-awareness and are therefore rightly artless (*kunstlos*), such as mimicry and music, and those others which issue from awareness of objects (*gegenständliche Bewusstsein*), such as the figurative arts and poetry; but then he observes that the content of both series is the same, save that overtly and in external appearance "the one is richer than the other".[1] In truth the position of that first series would conflict with his principle which makes art consist in an overcoming of the immediate consciousness. He also remarks that, as in languages there is the interjection, so in poetry there are forms which can be called immediate in that they lack any representation of objects, as do mimicry and music. But this is true of them "in differing measures and grades". Thus the immediate forms in poetry press onwards and "provide a bridge towards reflection".[2] Schleiermacher attempts to differentiate painting from sculpture, saying that the former may represent various species and individuals simultaneously, the latter only single figures. But then he remembers that sculpture too produces "groups", yet qualifies the qualification with the remark that it can do so only within close limits.[3] He tries out another distinction: sculpture interests itself solely in the living or animal side of figures, while painting is more interested in their ethical side. But then he has to recognize that sculpture, too, expresses the ethical side.[4] So he attempts yet another differentiation: sculpture is concerned solely with the figure, while painting is concerned also and most essentially with light and its effects. But then he has to recognize that sculpture is not unconcerned with light; for if it represents the body in its independence,

1. Lommatzsch edn., p. 127.
2. Ibid., p. 156.   3. Ibid., pp. 175-76.   4. Ibid., p. 136.

this is only its prevailing tendency (*mehr*), not its absolute character. Moreover, when sculpture produces groups, it cannot prevent the single figures from partaking in certain arrangements of light, even if this be not the prime concern of the sculptor; while for sculpture in relief light is so important, that this sort of sculpture must be considered a "transition to painting". The object of sculpture is pure form, the earth viewed in its independence, and that of painting is the earth viewed in relation with the cosmic system, and accordingly in a setting of light;[1] but between the one and the other there is room for movement, not clear-cut distinction; indeed it is difficult to conceive the earth unattached to the cosmic system.

The distinction between the figurative arts and poetry is for Schleiermacher this: the image (*Bild*) is the property of the former, and the representation (*Vorstellung*) that of the latter. Yet he has to recognize that the representation can never stand detached from the image, nor the image from the language expressing it. The two therefore go together, though on different levels, and are not to be severed, because they are inwardly the same thing.[2] We will ignore such other distinctions as those of the "poeticity of poetry" and the "picturesque of painting", the former of which passes over into painting and the latter into poetry;[3] likewise the differentiation of sculpture from architecture which Schleiermacher explains by a prevalence (*Ueberwiegen*) of corporeal forms in the former and of mathematical forms in the latter;[4] the distinction of architecture from gardening;[5] and finally that of the lyric, which is musical, from the epic and dramatic which are imaginous, which is once again not absolute but a matter of "more or less", since musicality seeps into the epic and the dramatic, and imaginousness into the lyrical.[6] Schleiermacher sometimes acknowledges with something between bewilderment and resignation: "My intention was to separate and here we are, quite on the contrary, at the conclusion of a review of the arts in a relation which unites them together."[7]

---

1. Ibid., p. 137.   2. Ibid., pp. 139-40, 148-49.   3. Ibid., p. 143.   4. Ibid., p. 155.   5. Ibid., pp. 129-30.   6. Ibid., pp. 648, 660-61.   7. Ibid., p. 143.

Sometimes, however, he aims at an effective "reunion",[1] that ill-famed and absurd sort of "reunion of the arts" which follows upon a precedent mistaken separation of them. (As if they were not, by their nature, already united, always one and the same.) But once he admits that in the innerness of each art is always to be found the same thing, because the differences lie in "the variety of vital functions pertaining to the organism" – are, in other words, extra-aesthetic.[2]

There is thus in Schleiermacher an exemplary and instructive confusion and contradiction about what he says of the problem of the unity and distinction of the arts. But his argument is quite clear when he proceeds to propound the proposition that there is no other difference between works of art than "the perfection of the art itself", and so no other aesthetic value than the form, and no other object of judgement than the achievement, non-achievement, total or partial, perfect or approximate achievement of this. Careless of the appearance of paradox, he declares that a poem and an epigram, a picture and an arabesque, provided they are artistically perfect, are aesthetically of the same value and not to be compared with one another: when, as is usual, a writer of poems is rated above a writer of epigrams, and a painter of pictures above a painter of arabesques, the comparison is really (he says) between the social grades of persons, and has no reference to the purely aesthetic element. Schleiermacher is accordingly one for whom all labels are alien to art. He dismisses "religious" art along with convivial (*gesellig*) art; and so too lascivious, erotic, and playful art.[3] If he concedes that art is *Spiel*, this means only that it is not labour, not practical activity.[4] The concept of artistic value as "the perfection of the art itself" satisfies him, and leaves him free from the need for another concept, or anyway for another word, the word "beautiful". This he seems inclined to

1. Ibid., p. 167: "Das Höchste ist eine Vereinigung aller Künste zu einer gemeinschaftlichen Leistung".
2. Ibid., pp. 217-18.
3. Odebrecht's edn., pp. 65-74.
4. Ibid., p. 80.

480 PHILOSOPHY OF ART AND LANGUAGE

banish from Aesthetics along with "sublime" and the various
other partners commonly linked with them.[1] But if he had investigated the long and various history of the word "beautiful" he
would have found in it substantially nothing else than the designation or symbol of artistic perfection itself. Truth to tell, had there
not been this impelling sense of the need to establish and to define
the sphere of art, then the idea of the beautiful would not have
haunted men's minds so insistently. Aesthetics, then, should not
neglect this idea, but receive and resolve it in itself. As I have said
elsewhere,[2] the solution upon which certain German theorists
have hit, of demanding the construction of a science or philosophy
of art, while reserving the study of the "beautiful" for a different
science, which could perhaps retain the description "Aesthetics",
falls to the ground because there is no other room for a science of
philosophical character dealing with the "beautiful". Unless indeed
one should fall back upon a "descriptive psychology" busying
itself with classifying and illustrating all the innumerable pseudo-
aesthetic concepts which make their pompous appearance in
treatises of Aesthetics – for instance in Hartmann's *Philosophy of
the Beautiful* – adding to these, as is only fair, the others which are
ranged in Rosenkranz's *Aesthetics of Ugliness*. Such a psychology,
once those concepts were ridded of the improper philosophical
envelopes in which it was customary to wrap them, would
amount to little else than a series of definitions of dictionary type.

Schleiermacher fails to attain an acceptable solution of the problem of language, indeed what he does attain is a sheer absurdity.
Yet few have felt as keenly as he the problem of the nature of
language. A presupposition which he did not question prevented
him from arriving at the truth, although in the desperate tension
of his enquiry he seemed almost to touch it. This mistaken presupposition, which Schleiermacher shared with many other philosophers of his day, was to the effect that language consisted of
two elements, the musical and the logical. But this did not enable
him to explain poetry. It is obviously erroneous, though it would

1. Lommatzsch edn., pp. 140-42.
2. See the foregoing chapter in the present volume, pp. 465-66.

at first seem inevitable, to assign the logical element in languages to prose and the musical element to poetry. For the musical element, though essential to poetry, by no means makes up the whole of it, and yet the logical element certainly does not come in to fill the gap. If the composition of poetry includes something more than music but does not include logic, what is the other element? What is there in poetry besides euphony of language? What is the mysterious Something, *Etwas*? The representations furnished by poetry are sensible and individual representations. But language, considered as pure sound, would be incapable of such representations, while language considered as logicity working in terms of the antithesis between the individual and the universal has no rational standing in respect of the sensible representation of the individual.[1] Yet the poet, by means of words, accomplishes the miracle: he accomplishes it in virtue of his mastery of the use of language, enabling him to constrain language to perform something beyond its natural potentiality, and out of the expression of the universal and general he wrests the representation of the individual and the particular. This conclusion (which however absurd Bergson and others have revived in our own day) is the absurdity which one might expect when one entertains the absurd notion of a mastery operating in defiance of nature, a logicity which under violence and duress annihilates itself and gives birth to a sensibility which was never in its own womb. But we must ask ourselves what better conclusion than this absurdity could ever be achieved by submitting to criticism that mistaken presupposition as to the two supposed elements of language, an original (*ursprünglich*) logicity and a musicality somehow compounded with it? For that matter what, better than this absurdity, could serve as an introduction to the true theory, in which the nature of language is not logical but fanciful, and consequently (since the fancy is its own self-expression) language is all one with sounds, tones, lines, colours, and so forth, to mention the various classes of language, phonic, plastic, musical, and so forth which it is customary to

1. Lommatzsch edn., pp. 642-48.

distinguish (but only empirically)? An advance in this direction
was undertaken, not without natural hesitations and oscillations
and contradictions,[1] by Vico, Hamann, Herder, Humboldt, and
some others; but Hegel was too much in the grip of logicism to
partake in it, and Schleiermacher ignored and neglected the enquiries and speculations of those thinkers. And yet, if he could not
advance along the path, his critical flair led him repeatedly up to it.

As was incidentally observed before, Schleiermacher, if he was
to win a greater harmony and a superior unity for his aesthetic
concepts, needed to overcome the dualism or Spinozism to which,
on the contrary, he clung, with unfavourable consequences that
can be observed in some of his aesthetic theories. Notable among
such faults is the correspondency and parallelism which he institutes between nature and art, whereby nature is seen as producing
according to certain types and schemes, and art has these same
types and schemes as the basis of its own operations. Not only, on
this basis, are the figures of art required, if they are not to be
condemned as empty or untrue, to illustrate in the individual the
race (*Gattung*,) but the scheme or type should be represented more
purely in the individual as portrayed by art than in natural objects,
in which the scheme is often masked, disfigured, mutilated.[2] Thus
Schleiermacher finds himself unwittingly brought back to the
theory of the "imitation of nature", indeed to that of the "idealizing imitation of nature", wholly repugnant to his own fundamental
concept of art as the rhythmic expression of immediate consciousness.

Thinkers are not to be judged on the persistence in them of
obsolete theory, or on the contradictions into which they run, but
on their setting and solving of new problems, their definition of
new concepts. Schleiermacher presented more than a few new

1. Humboldt himself, for example, in his dissertation on *Hermann und
Dorothea*, § 12, had not got beyond regarding language as an instrument
originally forged for the use of the intellect, which poetry required to
elaborate and to transform to make it apt for the purposes of the fancy.
That is, he adhered to the theory criticized above.

2. Lommatzsch edn., pp. 106-7, 146-47, 149.

problems and concepts to modern philosophy, not only in his ethical but also in his aesthetic enquiries, neither of which, and least of all the second, have been accorded by students of philosophy the high credit which they deserve.

[1933]

XVIII

ROBERT VISCHER AND THE AESTHETIC
CONTEMPLATION OF NATURE

In my discussion of the Aesthetics of the *Einfühlung* doctrine I
have deliberately said nothing of the man, Robert Vischer, who is
considered its original author in virtue of his dissertation of 1872:
Ueber das optische Formgefühl.[1] The use of that technical term is
due to him, moreover, and he believed it to be of his own coining,
but later discovered an earlier case of its use in a page of Herder.[2]

Robert Vischer was a son of the celebrated writer on Aesthetics,
Friedrich Theodor. Robert devoted himself to the history of the
figurative arts, and deserves a special and eminent place among
the writers of the last quarter of the nineteenth century. During
his formative period the positivist or philological school was at
its zenith. It permeated, among other studies, those of the art
historians, displaying a fiercely antiphilosophical and anti-aesthetic
animus. But Robert Vischer, though working along lines of
painstaking scholarship and investigating art in its dependence
upon historical conditions, never forgot that the criticism and
history of art consists ultimately of aesthetic problems. He was
thus able, in 1886, to prefix to a volume of studies in the history of
art a dedication to his own father expressing his clear awareness
that "in zealously pursuing specialized historical researches he had
not sought to demolish the bridge between his own and his father's
sphere of thought".[3] In his first monograph, the ample *Luca
Signorelli and the Italian Renaissance*,[4] which remains the principal

1. Now reprinted together with two other essays: *Der ästhetische Akt und die
reine Form* (1874) and *Ueber ästhetische Naturbetrachtung* (1890), in the small
volume: *Drei Schriften zum ästhetischen Formproblem* (Halle, Niemeyer,
1927).

2. *Drei Schriften*, etc., p. 77.

3. See p. ix of the preface to *Studien zur Kunstgeschichte* (Stuttgart, Bonz,
1886).

4. *Luca Signorelli und die italienische Renaissance, eine kunsthistorische Mono-
graphie* (Leipzig, Veit, 1879).

work in existence regarding this painter, he perhaps dwells excessively on the importance of the local, political, and traditional
conditions, the tyrants, the warriors, the quarrelling families, the
monkish asceticism of Umbria amid which Signorelli's art developed; the impressions which he received from the Papal Court
of Rome, from the Humanists and the Epicureans, and the various
artistic influences which he underwent. Yet the emphasis on all
this does not prevent the author from returning to the central
consideration, the artist's bold and powerful temperament and
character, rich in capacity for inner contrasts; nor from essaying
a complex and complicated study of the character of *terribilità*
in Italian art, that "aweful" character which was so marked in
Signorelli. But in the essay on Raphael included in the *Studien*
Vischer comments upon the shift of interest since the earlier
generation of Rumohr, Schnaase, and such art historians, thanks
to which in his own generation it was not, as with them, the *logos*
or *pneuma* of Raphael which received attention, but the particulars
of his life, the chronological order of his works, his technique.[1] He
for his part will investigate the characteristics of the art of Raphael,
the "objectivity" and harmony commonly attributed to him,
which are in truth merely predicates indicating something that
remains mysterious, a fundamental potency in him, a special, rare,
and well-ordered disposition of spiritual faculties reflecting a world
of exalted blessedness.[2] In similar wise Vischer deals with the art of
Giotto and Dürer and many works of the Middle Ages. He has
a particularly valuable brief work on Rubens,[3] in which he altogether shakes off his preoccupation with determining conditions,
and indeed confutes the alleged correspondency between Rubens'
figures and the population Flanders, saying that it is rare to see
in Flanders "the heavy frame of the male or the plump country-
woman of such calibre as he introduces into his pictures: however
excellent the models which he obtained, he must have created the

1. *Studien*, p. 91.
2. *Studien*, pp. 125-27.
3. *Peter Paul Rubens*, ein Büchlein für unzünftige Kunstfreunde (Berlin,
Cassirer, 1904).

type of his images for himself". He must, that is, have created them from the fundamental motive of his own fancy, the potent surging vitality finding its form in those figures throbbing with force and seeming in each throb to be pursuing pleasure or combat: they glorify the flesh, animal nature, but (rather than in heroic or profound vein) in Bacchic playfulness, decoratively, in an exploding orgy of colour. Vischer enjoyed discussing this interpretation with Fromentin and Julius Lange, two of the keenest judges of art in Europe in the second half of the nineteenth century. And in Robert Vischer's rules of method there are such laudable ideas at work as an aversion for those literary descriptions which art critics are apt to furnish of the works of painters, forgetting that these think their thoughts "in soulful forms",[1] while the critics think theirs in words.

These observations upon Robert Vischer's lively and serious experience and understanding of art would suffice to justify my detaching him from the main body of the aestheticists of *Einfühlung*, one and all more or less ignorant of art, even, or especially, when they expressly loaded themselves with borrowed and unintegrated information about it. However, the problem of *Einfühlung* itself affords a more direct and definite motive for the detachment. Robert Vischer meant by *Einfühlung* a critical and speculative research, but this was by the others debased to something superficial and trivial, to a psychological research sometimes puffed out with some arbitrary metaphysical digression. He himself was well aware of the difference, holding himself at a significant distance from his dubious scholars, but the difference was explicitly affirmed and proved by a friend of his later years, Glockner, who made it clear that Vischer's problem was unpsychological (*unpsychologisch*) and transcendental in character.[2]

In what then did this problem really consist? It certainly did not

1. In the preface to the work on Signorelli, p. vi seqq.
2. HERMANN GLOCKNER, *Friederich Theodor Vischer und das neunzehnte Jahrhundert*, Berlin, Junker und Dünnhaupt, 1932); which includes (pp. 168-269) a virtual monograph entitled: *Robert Vischer und die Krisis der Geisteswissenschaften im letzten Drittel des neunzehnten Jahrhunderts*: see esp. pp. 243-49.

consist in tracking down and announcing a concept to serve as the explicatory principle of art: indeed at no time did he ever make use of his theoretical formulas in his various works on art history. His particular problem was the different one of finding a possible and a correct explanation of what is called the beauty of natural things, the beautiful in nature; or in other terms, how we attain to the so-called aesthetic contemplation of nature, and the corresponding pleasure. This pleasure must, as everyone sees, be quite clearly distinguished from the practical pleasure afforded by nature when we enjoy a pleasant, sunny spring day, or something of that sort. For unlike this, it is a pleasure of contemplation.

Historically, Robert Vischer's problem links on to the final thoughts of his father on aesthetic questions. Friedrich Theodor Vischer had started by utilizing the fanciful and cumbrous dialectic current among the disciples of Hegel, to provide an apparent solution for the problem of the beautiful in nature by introducing one of those customary triads which to us of the present day have the appearance of having been excogitated for the sheer display of ingenuity. The first moment, or thesis, in this triad of the world of art was natural beauty, which is objective because it lacks the subjectiveness of fantasy. The second moment, or antithesis, is the fantasy, which wants objectivity. The third moment, or synthesis, is Art, in which the two deficiencies are mutually made good, the result being subjective-objective all at once. Later, however, the sense of the truth prevailed with the elder Vischer. He saw that the ample and particularized list that he had provided of the various classes of natural beauties, and also of human and historical beauties, had resulted simply from surveying things now with the painter's, now with the sculptor's, now with the poet's eye; that is, surveying them with the fantasy. He therefore corrected himself and expressly resolved the beauty of nature into the beauty of the fantasy. His original triad fell to pieces and he made no attempt to replace it with another, but contented himself with dividing Aesthetics into a first general part treating of the beautiful in itself and the fundamental concepts, and a second part which dealt with the realizations of the beautiful, imperfect in the aesthetic sphere of nature and perfect in the artistic sphere. What, he asked himself, are the particular works of the fantasy which we call natural beauties, singular unions of a natural shape with a spiritual content? They are not unions of outer with inner, thought with object, sentiment with image, attained by the mediation of reflective thought. Yet neither are they immediate and total fusions, as is the case with the fetishes of natural religions, which are at the same time natural objects and divinities. F. T. Vischer developed the theory that they are symbols, that is unions unlit by reflective thought, dim, yet not blind and superstitious, but always accompanied by an awareness of a comparison that has been instituted, a correspondency that has been discovered, between inner and outer, real and unreal for us at the same time, illusions which are experienced, yet not on that account mistaken for reality. As he himself wrote: "I call this an inner feeling of the image and the content, a deep, dark, certain, intimate and yet free feeling, which by contrast with the unfree feeling of religion might be called a clear-dark feeling, if this word were not itself over-imaginous."[1] Thus the elder Vischer had arrived at the terms *Zusammenfühlen* and *Hineinfühlen* which were forerunners of the more successful *Einfühlung* adopted by the son.

Robert Vischer's chosen task was nothing else than to unravel the difficulties involved in explaining the origin of these "symbols", as his father termed them, this perception of nature as animated, animated by something similar to our human feeling, indeed by something that is all one with it.[2] There was, at hand, a rather frivolous explanation, accepted by some of the aestheticists of *Einfühlung*, which he at once rejected: the so-called "association of ideas", really quite irrelevant to the matter in question, since what required to be explained was the image in itself, not its possible relations with other images, thoughts, or ideas.[3] How now

1. See *Kritik meiner Aesthetik* in *Kritische Gänge*, N. F., Heft v (Stuttgart, Cotta, 1867), especially pp. 139-45.
2. I hold to the final expression of his thought: *Ueber aesthetische Naturbetrachtung* (1890, in *Drei Schriften* etc., pp. 55-56), it being unnecessary here to follow the detailed modification of his thought in successive phases.
3. Ibid., p. 6.

does the fusion of our personality with the image, so that the two become one, come about? Certainly a profound relation subsists between Spirit and Nature, both having been born out of the same original womb (*Urschoss*), Nature as the lowest grade of the Spirit and the Spirit as the acme of Nature. Therefore it is that Nature can not only be investigated intellectually but also contemplated aesthetically. And yet, despite that bond, the division persists, and this persistence both of the bond and of the division constitutes the torment. Even on the level of sense, in the vision which we have of things, the physical excitement of light is transmuted into a spiritual excitement, the external qualities are interchanged with the qualities of our sentiment, while in the motor function, the motion of the glancing eye upon the object seems to be a movement and liveliness of the object itself. On the higher level of *Einfühlung* transposition occurs in another mode, whereby the inner sense embraces, let us say, a tree, passes over into the tree's vegetable expansiveness, and then, as it retreats from that inwardness back to its own outwardness, feels the character of the tree's woody configuration: stiffens, stretches, and trembles, and feels the air with the tip of the tree's twigs. The life of things thus turns to life in the soul: "the valley opens wide", "the stream glides", "the soil revives", and so on; while life in the soul turns to the life of things: Nature appears as peace, joy, suffering, heaviness, sadness, anguish, desolation, love, and grief. It does not suffice to say that we, with our fantasy, transport our soul into Nature, we must turn our attention to that which renders possible such a "transport", as it is called (but it is not really such); to the fact that our body, and accordingly our countenance and our voice, has a capacity of spiritual expression, and it is this property and activity which is contemplated in the aspects of Nature. The elder Vischer had drawn attention to this important point when he remarked that "every spiritual act is explicated and at the same time reflected in determinate vibrations and inscrutable modifications of the nerves, in such wise that thereby the image of the act obtains a representation and that in the very hidden intimacy of the organism there takes place a symbolic reproduction (*Abbilden*). The external appearances which operate upon us in so remarkable a manner that they cause us to introduce into them the dispositions of our soul, owe it to this inward image to serve as its representation and objective manifestation. The presumed disposition of the nerves in the so-called vibrations is met by the corresponding phenomenon in nature, which excites it to action, strengthens it, confirms it, and with it the spiritual movement which is mirrored in it".[1] But in the younger as in the elder Vischer all this is a gleam of insight rather than a well controlled theory. The process is seen within a veil of mystery. The elder does in fact speak of the "mystery" of this "secret writing" (Geheimschrift).[2] The younger concludes that "the content of a landscape is our own being, but immersed in the unknown being of Nature", and again: "In the outwardness of Nature even our knowledge of ourselves disappears for, in the aesthetic act, Nature and fantasy operate in the most intimate fusion." At the end of the enquiry or meditation we find ourselves then back at the starting point, the enigma of Nature. "The appearance of life in Nature, remains, as Nature remains, a mystery" (ein Geheimniss).

Both the elder and the younger Vischer, it is clear, held to the traditional conception (continued by German idealism) of Spirit and Nature as two entities or distinct forms of being, and their way of getting beyond this dualism was not that of critical thought, but that of a fallacious dialectic procuring unification in a transcendent principle, God, the Absolute, the Idea, or however it might be termed. Given an abstract spirit and an abstract Nature, the aesthetic image, in the view of these thinkers, was produced by the coming together of these two factors, the cause being both in ourselves and in Nature.[3] The consequence was, as already observed, an inevitable renunciation of the problem as insoluble, a surrender to the antagonist. Even at that point where both father and son seem closest to achieving unity and identity, the point at which

1. *Kritische Gänge*, loc. cit., p. 143.
2. Ibid.
3. "Die Ursache dieser Wirkung kann nicht nur in uns, sie muss auch in der Natur liegen" etc. (R. VISCHER, op. cit., p. 25).

the spiritual act is considered in its corporeal vibration, they do not overcome the dualism, for there too they take for granted the subsistence of two different things, as it were a text and a translation, and the elder Vischer was inclined to call in the aid of Psychology and Physiology, had he not despaired of attaining, even by that, the desired solution.[1] But we have overcome that dualism; we know that a spirit without body is just as empty and absurd as a body without a spirit; that will without effective action is not will, and action without will is equally not action; that intuition without expression is something as unreal as expression without intuition. And so we take good care not to divide in twain the single act, lest when once this unity was broken we should have to strive vainly to re-establish a unity out of duplication, risking shipwreck in an unhallowed mystery engendered by abstraction and shallow thought. Robert Vischer recalls on one occasion the youthful saying of Goethe that genius has "the smell and the sense of the earth" (*Erdgeruch und Erdgefühl*)[2] a saying which is no mere metaphor but a philosophical hint that should be taken in the strictest sense.

By a fortunate contradiction, the elder Vischer, modifying his own theory, had recognized that so-called natural beauty is itself a beauty of the fantasy, which amounted to proclaiming the abolition of the category of the beautiful in Nature. This true conclusion he then, however, proceeded to compromise by drawing a distinction between a beauty which he called pure "aesthetic" beauty, pertaining to the fantasy in nature, and an "artistic" beauty, which was that of fantasy as art. If natural beauty is – as he says – the work of the fantasy, yet this is inefficacious until it is rendered concrete in expression, that is, in art; and natural beauty is substantially and inevitably artistic beauty. The spirit can evoke a landscape and enjoy it as beauty, only by giving corporeal form to an intuition, eliciting and gathering, with that very act, out of

1. "Es liegt noch ein Geheimniss, dass die Physiologie aufzuklären hätte, wenn jener Punkt, wo Seele und Nervencentrum Eines sind, uns nicht in ein undurchdringliches Dunkel gehüllt wäre" (*Kritische Gänge*, loc. cit., pp. 142-43).

2. Ibid., p. 59.

the things in the environment the forms, lines, lights, and colours which are the concreteness of that intuition. The proceeding is not different from that of the painter who conveys on his canvas some artistic intuition that he has formed. The elder Vischer, after affirming that the ideal or aesthetic intuition in a certain sense kills (*tödtet*) the object in its practical value, the material in this process suffering destruction by the form, observes opportunely that "the common way of expressing aesthetic pleasure at a landscape is to remark that it is just like a picture".[1] Robert Vischer, no less rightly, observed how in the process of imitative contemplation of Nature, as he called it, or *Einfühlung*, the whole acquires a dominion over the parts; he observed too the impulse towards rhythmical utterance (*Trieb der Rhythmisierung*), and towards the deliberate elimination of the extraneous and disturbing elements (*abwägende Ausscheidung des Fremdartigen und Störenden*).[2]

Now if there is a difference between so-called natural beauty and so-called artistic beauty (and there certainly is, although it relates to the externals and not to the inwardness of beauty), the origin of it should be sought not in a supposed deficiency of the expressive or artistic moment in the former, by contrast with its presence in the latter, but altogether elsewhere, namely in the practical moment which follows the aesthetic act and has a finality which is not aesthetic but practical, pertaining to the economic form of the spirit. Those modifications of the given reality which serve to perpetuate, that is, to reproduce the expressions (and every practical action is synonymous with such a "modification of given reality"), pertain to this form. Such modifications, viewed naturalistically, and classified accordingly, take on the name of "beautiful things", in a material sense: such are the painted canvas or panel, the sculpted marble, the acoustic sequences of sounds and tones, and so on. These material things are the instruments of practical acts, not of aesthetic acts. For these latter cannot be reproduced save in virtue of a sympathy in poetic fancy. Where this is wanting, these things are in no way superior to any of the

1. *Kritische Gänge,* loc. cit., p. 53.
2. *Drei Schriften,* p. 75.

other things that are seen, touched, heard. And not all the forms of
art that are created, not every aesthetic intuition-expression, are
followed by the production of such instruments for reproduction
and communication. There are poems and pictures which blaze up
in the spirit which creates them, projected into words and lines
and colours, but are then extinguished without apparent trace.
Artistic visions of so-called natural beauty are among these. The
consensus of aesthetic admiration which is accorded to certain
places or figures and persons is to some extent, though the extent
varies, illusory, being unrooted in any constancy of work created
by genius, such work as is kept alive or rather kept susceptible to
revival, by technical skill. Such a consensus, when closely examined, proves to consist of a series of individual intuition-ex-
pressions, precariously held together by a link not of identity,
but always of mere similitude. It is for this reason that discussion
on whether this or that natural object is beautiful or ugly, or on
which parts are beautiful and which ugly, is the sort of discussion
that one avoids or cuts short, or wearies of because it leads to no
conclusion; in strong contrast to the discussions about those things
which men stamp, as it were, with the seal of an individual and
unmistakable form created by themselves. There is a criticism of
works of art, but there is no criticism of natural beauty so-called,
though this too is a creation of the human spirit.

Robert Vischer's *Einfühlung* is defined by Glockner as a "mixed
irrational product". He praises the enquiry which led to it as "a
first important attempt on the basis of a wide experience to conceive
philosophically the higher synthesis, as known in the history of
German idealism".[1] And indeed, even if the positive result was
scanty, the effort which led to it was serious, and accordingly
instructive and profitable. And another product of Robert Vischer's thought was also profitable: the attention which he gave
to the formative process of dream-images, and to the careful
studies of K. A. Scherner on the subject.[2] But here too, perhaps,
the positive result was bound to be scanty, because those images

1. Op. cit., p. 236.
2. *Leben des Traums* (Berlin, 1861).

which, in dreams, are induced by psychological or physiological stimuli, have a practical character, for they are wanting in the very constituent of the aesthetic act, the conferment of rhythm upon images, the contemplative surpassment.[1]

[1934]

---

1. See in this connexion my *Conversazioni critiche*, Series III, Bari, 1932, 29-31. Vischer's two essays on *Raphael* and *Rubens* have on my advice now been made available in the Italian translation of Elena Craveri Croce (Bari, 1945).

IV

THE THEORY OF HISTORY

I

HISTORY, CHRONICLE, AND PSEUDO-HISTORY

I

"CONTEMPORARY History" is a description commonly given to the history of some period regarded as very recent, be it the last half-century, decade, year, month, day, or even hour or minute. In strictness, however, we should reserve the expression for a history arising immediately out of the act that one is performing, the consciousness of the act itself: for example, the history which I am relating of myself in virtue of composing these present sentences, in other words the thought going into this composition and inseparable from it. The use of the word "contemporary" is here correct. The history in question is, like every spiritual act, outside time, neither "before" nor "after" but taking shape "at the very time" of the act, and distinguished from it not chronologically, but only ideally. The history which we call "non-contemporary", or "past", is by the same token a history which finds its history ready-made and shapen, and assumes the function of judging that history, equally if it is thousands of years, or less than one hour, old.

On closer consideration, however, we discover this ready-made and shapen history, this "non-contemporary" or "past" history, when it has a real significance and is not just empty talk, to be quite as much "contemporary" and indeed in no way different from that previously described. The important condition is in either case that the fact of which the history is related must vibrate in the mind of the historian, or to put the matter in the professional language of historians, there must be intelligible documents. That a tale is told, or various tales told, about the fact, so that the tale and the fact become united or mingled, means simply that the fact takes on an additional richness, and not, in any way, that it loses its importance as that which is indispensably required to be present. It means that narrations or judgements have themselves now become facts, "documents" requiring to be interpreted and judged. History is never based upon narrations but always upon documents – it may be upon narrations reduced to the status of documents, and used as such. Contemporary history springs directly out of life, but "non-contemporary" history also springs directly out of life. For evidently it is only some concern of present life that can spur us to enquire into a past fact, and such a fact, when identified with some concern of present life, is a present and not a past concern. This is recalled, in varying manners, by any number of working maxims current among historians, and accounts for the popularity, if not indeed for the deeper meaning of the somewhat trite saying that history is *magistra vitae*.

I have quoted these historians' maxims in order to remove any note of paradox from the proposition that "all true history is contemporary history". The rightness of that proposition is promptly confirmed by reference to the reality of historical composition, and can be abundantly and clearly exemplified from this. However, it is necessary to avoid the mistake of lumping together the writings of historians in general, or of certain groups of them, and then, with an eye upon some abstract man, perhaps ourselves abstractly considered, asking where is the present interest that acts to stimulate the writing or the reading of such works, for example, histories of the Peloponnesian or Mithridatic wars, of Mexican art or of Arabian philosophy. For me myself, at the present moment, there is no such interest, and therefore for me, at this moment, those histories are not histories at all, but at the most mere titles of historical works. But they have been or will be histories in the minds which have worked upon them or will work upon them, and in my own mind, at such times as I have pondered or will ponder them, shaping them to my own spiritual needs. But turning now our attention to real history, historical thought as it is conceived and in the act of its conception, we shall soon recognize that this is fully identical with the most personal and contemporary of histories. When the cultural development, I will not say of myself (for this would be saying too much, and perhaps erroneously), but of my historical moment, opens up to me the problem of Greek civilization, Platonic philosophy, or some particular phase of Attic behaviour, then that problem is as closely bound up in my being as the history of some business deal upon which I am engaged, or of some love-affair of mine, or peril overhanging me. I investigate it with the same anxiety and suffer the same sense of disquiet until I manage to solve it. The life of Hellas is, in the case in point, present in myself. It rouses, attracts, or torments me like the image of my competitor, or of the woman I love, or the dear child for whose safety I tremble. Likewise with the wars of Mithridates, Mexican art, and other such examples.

If, then, contemporaneity is not the characteristic of a particular class of histories (except in empirical classifications which are quite legitimate in their own place), but unfailingly characterizes all history, then the relation of history to life must be envisaged as a relation of unity, not indeed of abstract identity, but of a synthetic unity which both distinguishes and unites the terms. In the light of this, to speak of a history in the absence of documents will seem as fanciful as to speak of the existence of something while asserting the absence of a necessary condition for its existence. A history unrelated to its documentation would be unverifiable. But since the reality of history lies in its verifiable character, and a narration such as is needed, to incarnate an historical judgement, can only rank as an historical narration in so far as it critically expounds the document (a process of intuition and reflection, awareness and self-awareness), it is clear that such a history, void of meaning or truth, would not be history at all. How could a history of painting be composed by one who did not see or enjoy the works of which he proposed to illustrate the origins critically? And how could such a history be intelligible to one who lacked the artistic experience which the narrator counted upon in his readers? How could there be a history of philosophy without the works or at least fragments of the works of the philosophers? Or the history of a sentiment or style (say, Christian humility or chivalric honour) without a potential, or more truly speaking without an actual renewal of the experience of those particular states of mind?

But once the indissoluble nexus of life and thought has been established, doubts as to the certainty and the usefulness of history vanish suddenly and entirely, so that it is hardly possible any more to recall them. How could a present product of our spirit be uncertain? How could knowledge which solves a problem emerging from the heart of life be useless?

II

But can the nexus of document and narration, of life and history, ever be broken? An affirmative answer has been provided in the mention which we have made of histories of which the documents have been lost, or, taking the more general and fundamental case, of which the documents are not alive in our mind. It has already been implicitly recognized that each one of us is at some time or other in this situation as regards some or other part of history. The history of ancient Greek painting is generally speaking for the most part a history without documents, and so are the histories which we read of peoples whose precise place of residence, prevailing thoughts and feelings, and individual achievements we do not know. Likewise the histories of literatures and philosophies of which we have not the texts (or if we have them in our hands and gaze upon them with our eyes, we yet lack the power to penetrate their inner significance, whether for want of subsidiary knowledge, or for incompatibility of temperament, or by reason of inattention on our part).

In these cases the nexus has been broken, and since the history was nothing else but that nexus, what remains is not history, or can only be called history in the same way that a corpse is referred to as a man. That, however, does not mean that what remains is nothing, any more than a corpse is nothing. Indeed if it were nothing, we might as well have said that the nexus is indissoluble, for "nothing" is never an effectual element. But if it is not nothing, if it is something, what is this narration without a document?

A History of Ancient Greek Painting, as given in the traditional accounts which have come down to us or have been built up on

their basis by modern scholars, will be found to consist in a series
of names (Apollodorus, Polygnotus, Zeuxis, Apelles, etc.) encrust-
ed with biographical anecdotes, a series of subjects of painting
(the Burning of Troy, Battle of the Amazons, Battle of Marathon,
Helen, Achilles, Calumny, etc.) sometimes described in considerable detail, and a series of expressions of more or less accentuated
praise or blame, all these names, anecdotes, subjects, and judgements being ranged roughly in chronological order. But the
names of the painters, where there is no direct knowledge of the
works, are empty names, the anecdotes too are empty, and empty
are the descriptions of subjects, the approving or disapproving
judgements, and empty too the chronological order, for pure
mathematics has no power to express a real development which
we cannot conceive in thought for lack of the constituent elements.
If those verbal formulae say anything at all, this is because of the
notions of ancient painting which we derive from fragments,
secondary works, copies, or analogous works of art in other
media, or in poetry. Apart from the little that we know in that
way, the history of ancient Greek painting is just a tissue of vain
words.

Or we may correct this last to the description "words void of
determinate content". For we would not deny that by uttering
the name of a painter, we turn our thought to some painter, to a
painter, indeed, who is also an Athenian. And with the words
"Battle" and "Helen" we turn our thought to a battle, indeed a
battle fought by hoplites, or to a fair woman, who may be like
one of those familiar figures of Greek sculpture. All the same,
we are left to choose which of innumerable possible facts we shall
let those names evoke. Hence their content is indeterminate, and
accordingly empty.

All histories detached like this from their living documents are
in the same way empty narrations, and being empty, lack truth.
Did there or did there not truly exist a painter named Polygnotus,
and did he paint in the Poecile at Athens a portrait of Miltiades?
It will be said that this is true, because one or more of those who
knew him and saw the painting bear witness to its existence. But

we ought to say that it was true indeed for this or that witness, but for us is neither true nor false, or (the same thing) is true only according to the testimony of those witnesses, that is for an extrinsic reason, whereas intrinsic reasons are always needed for truth. Since that proposition is not true (being neither true nor false), by the same token it is not useful. Where there is nothing, the king loses his rights, and where the elements of a problem are lacking, not only the possibility of solving it but the effective will and need to resolve it are lacking, so that the recital of all that empty information is utterly useless for the reality of our lives. Life is present, but that history which has become reduced to an empty narration is past, and at the present moment (if not absolutely, καθ' αὐτό) irrevocably past.

There remain the empty words, and these are sounds, or graphic signs standing for sounds, which are held together and in existence, not by an act of thought (if they could be thought they would soon cease to be empty), but by an act of will which reckons upon some advantage from the persistence of the words, for all their total or partial emptiness. Mere narration, then, is never anything more than a complex of empty words or formulae asserted by an act of the will.

With this definition we have at last hit upon the long desired distinction between history and chronicle. Our previous search for this was vain because we tried to find the distinction in a difference in the quality of the facts which history and chronicle respectively took for their object, attributing for example to chronicle the recording of individual and to history the recording of general facts, or to chronicle private and to history public facts. (Really, of course, the general is individual and vice versa, the public is private and vice versa.) Or to history there have been assigned important and memorable facts, to chronicle unimportant facts. (Really, of course, the importance of facts is always relative to our own momentary situation – for a man plagued by a mosquito the evolutions of this little creature are certainly more important than the expeditions of Xerxes.) Evidently even in these fallacious distinctions there is an element of good sense which aims at differentiating history as that which is interesting from chronicle as that which is not interesting (that which is general, or big, being considered interesting by contrast with what is particular or small). There is some propriety also in the other often quoted differentiations, as when history is said to be tightly welded while chronicle is disconnected, history to have a logical and chronicle a merely chronological order, history a function of penetrating into the inwardness of events while chronicle sticks to the outer surface, and so forth. But these are metaphorical rather than conceptual differentiations, and except where metaphors are limited to serving as mere expressive form for thought, what they achieve at one moment gets lost at the next. The truth is that chronicle and history cannot be distinguished as two forms of mutually complementary or superior and inferior history, but must be viewed as two different spiritual attitudes. History is live history, chronicle is dead history, history is contemporary, chronicle is past, history is an act of thought, chronicle is an act of will. All history becomes chronicle when it is no longer present to the thinking mind, but is merely recorded in the abstract words which were once concrete and expressive. The history of philosophy itself, when written by or read by the unphilosophic, is chronicle, while the entries of the monk of Cassino who recorded, for example, "*1001. Beatus Dominicus migravit ad Christum. 1002. Hoc anno venerunt Saraceni super Capuam. 1004. Terremotus ingens hunc montem exagitavit etc.*", which we should be inclined now to peruse simply as chronicle, are history, for these facts were living for the monk, who wept for the departure of Blessed Dominic, was appalled at the human and natural scourges which descended upon his countryside, and in the succession of events espied the hand of God. Yet that history may have been handled as mere chronicle by the monk, if he copied down the mere formulae without keeping the content present to his mind, intent solely upon not letting those records perish but passing them on to those who, after his time, would inhabit the Abbey of Montecassino.

The discovery of the true distinction between chronicle and history, the formal and thus truly real distinction, not only exempts us from the laborious and sterile pursuit of material, that is to say fanciful distinctions, but enables us also to dismiss a very common opinion that chronicle is anterior to history. As the ancient grammarian Marius Victorinus phrases it in often repeated and generalized and universalized words, *"Primo Annales fuere, post Historiae factae sunt"* (Annales being chronicle). But our enquiry into the character, and therewith the origin, of the two operations shows the opposite. First comes History and then Chronicle, first the living, then the corpse. To seek an origin for History in Chronicle would be like seeking the source of life in the dead body which is a residue of life, just as Chronicle is a residue of History.

III

History which has become detached from the living document, and turned to Chronicle, is no longer a spiritual act but is a thing, a complex of sounds and other signs. But the document detached from life is also just a thing, a complex of sounds and other signs, as for example the sounds and letters which served for the communication, once upon a time, of a law; the lines traced in marble to portray a god, expressing a religious sentiment; the heap of bones which at one time served the organism of a man or an animal.

Now do these things, empty narrations and lifeless documents, exist? In one sense they do not exist, for what is external and outside the spirit does not exist. We have already learned that chronicle exists as an empty narration just in so far as the spirit produces and consolidates it by an act of will – such an act necessarily comporting a new act of awareness and of thought – an act of will which abstracts the sound from the thought in which the sound had its certainty and concreteness. Similarly those lifeless documents exist in so far as they are manifestations of a new life, just as a lifeless body is also, in reality, a process of vital creation, for all the appearance of decomposition and death by contrast with a particular form of life. Just as we continue to describe as "narrations" those empty sounds which once incorporated the thought of a history, for memory's sake, so we continue to think of those manifestations of new life as residues of the life which was there before and has now really been extinguished.

This chain of deductions puts us in a position to take account of a division, insisted upon by certain modern methodologists, of historical sources into narrations and documents, or as is often said into traditions and relics or residues (*Ueberbleibsel, Ueberreste*). This division is irrational for the purposes of empirical practice, and may indeed be taken as a typical example of the inopportune introduction of speculative thought in such practice. It is so irrational that there is never any possibility of distinguishing between the two things desired to be distinguished. An empty "narration", considered as a thing, is just like any other thing which is described as a "document". Moreover, where the distinction is upheld, there at once arises the further difficulty that history now has to be based upon two different orders of data, as if with one foot on land and the other in the stream. In other words there are two parallel authorities one of which continually refers enquiries to the other. When an escape is sought from the inconvenience of this parallelism by defining the relation between the two kinds of sources, then either this relation is seen as a superiority of one over the other, with which the distinction vanishes since the superior form embraces and annuls the inferior, or there must be postulated a third form in which the other two are unified yet at the same time distinguished, which is another way of denying their existence within the abstract conditions in question. It seems to me, accordingly, significant that the division between narrations and documents has not been taken up by methodologists of the most thoroughly empirical school, who will not entangle themselves in these sorts of subtleties, resting content with such classifications of historical sources as the written and the symbolic, while on the contrary the division in question was emphasized by Droysen, an historian with a strong disposition for philosophy, in his *Elements of Historics*, and has been popular with other methodologists in Germany, where thanks to the rich national philosophic tradition there are many such hybrid empiricists of the type known in our Latin countries as "pedants" or "systemists". True enough, there is some pedantry in such intrusions of philosophic reasoning, but for all the contradictions which it brings in its wake the intrusion is salutary indeed. For does it not rouse the mind from its empirical slumber, and reveal the presence of spiritual acts where men supposed that there were merely things? – And thus it shows relation and unity at work where the terms of an irreconcilable dualism seemed to confront one another. The division of historical sources into narrations and documents, the attribution of a superior rank to documents, with narrations retained as a subordinate but indispensable element, constitute a sort of mythology or allegory, an imaginous representation of the relations of life and thought, document and criticism, in historical enquiry.

It is document and criticism, life and thought, that are the real sources of history, the two elements of the historic synthesis. But they are not precedent to history, that is to the synthesis, in the way that we think of fountains as standing in their places before one arrives with his vessel to draw water from them. No: the sources are within the history itself, within the synthesis, constituent of it and constituted by it. The idea of a history having its sources external to itself is another image which we must efface, like the image of history following upon a precedent chronicle. The two fallacious images in fact end by coinciding. The sources, viewed in the empirical manner as external things, are, just like chronicle, which is a class of those things, not precedent but subsequent to history. It would fare ill with history if she waited for her birth upon elements which can only follow in her wake, external things. One thing leads to another thing, not to thought, and history, were it born of things, would be a thing, that inexistent thing of which we have already spoken.

All the same, there must be a reason for the seeming anteriority of chronicle and the seeming externality of sources in respect of history. The human spirit preserves the mortal remains of history, the empty narrations, the chronicles, and the human spirit likewise gathers up the traces of past life, relics and documents, maintaining them as far as possible unchanged, and when change sets in restoring them to the original condition. What is the purpose of these acts of will devoted to preserving the empty, the dead? Is it perhaps [in Foscolo's expression] the illusion and the vanity which would retain man, after his extinction, at the threshold of the nether powers, by the construction of resting places for the dead, sepulchres? But sepulchres are not vanity and illusion, they are the product of a moral act symbolically affirming the immortality of the work of individuals who, though dead, live in our memory and will live on in the memory of the future. And thus that transcription of empty narrations, gathering together of dead documents, is an act of life performed in the service of life. A time will come when they will help us to reproduce more richly in our spirit the history of the past, summoning it into the present.

For dead history lives again, and past history becomes present, as and when the development of life calls for it. The Romans and Greeks lay in their tombs until at the Renaissance the new maturity of the human spirit reawoke them. The primitive, unrefined, and barbarian forms of civilization lay forgotten or almost disregarded until the new phase of the European spirit known as the Romantic or Restoration movement discovered a "sympathy" with them, that is to say, recognized them as presently interesting to itself. Much of history which for us now is chronicle, many documents now mute for us, will be traversed by new vibrations of life, and will become once again eloquent.

The origins of such a re-animation are altogether inward. No wealth of documents or narrations can bring them about. On the contrary the re-animation itself gathers in its wake or projects forward masses of documents and narrations which would otherwise remain dispersed, inert. There can be no understanding whatever of the effective process of historical thought unless one starts from the principle that the spirit itself is history, makes history at every moment, and is at the same time the result of all foregoing history, so that the spirit is the carrier of its own history which is all one with itself. To forget one aspect of history and to remember another is the very rhythm of the life of the spirit which operates by self-determination and individualization, perpetually undoing such determinations and individualizations in order to create others of richer composition. One might say that the spirit would relive its own history without the aid of those external things called narrations and documents. But those external things are instruments which it shapes for itself, preparatory acts which it accomplishes, in order to bring about the vital inner summons. And in this process these things come to resolve themselves. To such ends does the spirit celebrate and jealously guard the "memories of the past".

What each of us constantly does, noting down in his diary dates or private business memoranda ("chronicles") or putting away in a drawer ribbons and pressed flowers (may I be allowed these references to touching pieties as an example of the collection of "documents"?), is done on a larger scale, as it were on behalf of society as a whole, by a class of workers called philologians, or speaking in more detail by scholars when they collect testimonies and narrations, by archivists and archaeologists when they collect documents and monuments. And the places where they keep these objects, the "white and silent houses of the dead", are called libraries, archives, museums. Who can think ill of the scholars, the archivists, the archaeologists who perform this necessary, and therefore useful and important, duty? All the same there is sometimes a tendency to smile at them and pity them. Sometimes indeed they themselves lead us on to smiles and amusement at their expense by their naive pretension of holding history under lock and key, and of ability to unseal at will, for thirsty humanity, the "sources". Whereas history is in us all and the sources are in our heart. Our heart and it alone is the melting pot in which the *certain* is converted into the *true*, and then philology, married to philosophy, produces history.

[1937]

IN PRAISE OF INDIVIDUALITY
AND AGAINST "UNIVERSAL HISTORY"
AND FAKE UNIVERSALS IN GENERAL

I

In a number of current academic writings it is stated, not without expressions of disapproval and protest, that I have proclaimed my disbelief in "universal history". But the under-informed informers in question, from ignorance or failure to penetrate my thought, omit to mention that I have really endeavoured to demonstrate that all universal history, in so far as it is really history, or in those parts which exhibit historical verve, is always particular history, while particular history, when and where it really is history, is always universal history. The one enshrines the universe in the particular, the other refers the particular to the universe. And this mental process is not two things, but one single thing.

What I have indeed ruled out is that vulgar sort of universal history which would atone for lack of an effective universality of thought by a universality of matter, of things, embracing all the facts that have been related as occurring in all the continents of the earth. But this in any case is a universality that cannot be realized in this form, there being no justification for the delimitation of history from pre-history, of human from non-human history, or for that matter of history on this planet from history on other stars or planets. Furthermore, the accumulation of all events in a single mass is a desperate enterprise, while the distinction between historical and non-historical events is arbitrary. In practice, this sort of universal history is just an aggregate or piling together of a certain number of chronicles, not perhaps without an admixture of duly elaborated histories, the whole going to form a bulky *Chronica Mundi* the scheme and contents of which will vary from age to age. In our age, for example, the scheme of the four monarchies, *de quatuor imperiis*, which so long held the field, is

out of fashion. The modest intellectual standing of such compilations or "histories" is well shown by the fact that responsibility is
taken for them increasingly not by authors, but by publishers,
who commission them and farm them out, having seldom at their
disposal a worker capable, we will not say of the requisite width
and depth of thought, which are not really required, but of the
sheer effort of carrying so huge a load. Accordingly they hire
teams of workers to share out the work among them. It sometimes
happens that among these there are one or two writers marked out
by historical inspiration and thought, and the chapter or section
or volume contributed by them will stand out, differentiating
itself as a misfit in such company. These collections having, in
their general scheme (and usually also in their single parts) no
historical problem at issue and therefore presenting no thought
engaged upon solving it, serve principally to flatter the innocent
ambition of worthy citizens to possess the whole history of the
world well packed and arranged along a single bookshelf, but
they are seldom suitable for impassioned reading and still less do
they serve to awaken any sort of historical sense in the reader,
who, if he works his way through them, will probably end with a
sense of boredom and disappointment.

After showing in this way what universal history in practice
boils down to – anyone may verify the plain truth of this – we
might well say no more, and dismiss it as an exercise of no interest
or significance. But from this we are withheld by noting that
this universal history, which is neither true nor false but just lifeless,
gives rise to and furnishes the material for an important cultural
formation. Important, we say, because it expresses an aspiration
and a reaching out towards something better than a mere chroni-
cler's compilation, and still more because it is the form of an
error which persistently haunts and misleads historical thought,
though at the same time, as errors do, it calls into being a mental
resistance and induces the mind to explore and discover more
thoroughly the true nature of historical thought. The error in
question is the Philosophy of History, in other words the aforesaid
universal history, but philosophically elaborated.

The spirit of man cannot put up with the inorganic and unthink-able, cannot find rest in that material unity, that accumulation which remains no less chaotic in its essence even when a superficial order is imposed upon it. At times the authors of universal histories are themselves disquieted. Without renouncing their method, they yet seek among the facts a unifying fact, for example the centrality of Europe in the history of the world. Or if like Ranke they perceive that this is insufficient, they define universal history as the history of those peoples who have developed by interaction upon one another – an evidently inadequate definition. In reality there is no fact unifying the other facts, nor will it avail to stretch out to the physical sun of Copernicus or Galileo, or the mystical sun of Campanella. There is nothing for it save to climb or take flight towards "the One that moveth the sun and the other stars", not a fact, but God. And such a flight is undertaken by the philo-sophers of history, no matter though they may use for God the names of Idea, Spirit, Matter, or whatever other ideal notion it may be. But like Icarus these flyers tumble to earth in perplexity, for what is needed here is not to fly but to think, to conceive reality, and in the first place to unwind patiently and bravely the web of abstractions woven into the chronicles and universal histories, or let us say, to break the ice and discover the running water under it. They, on the contrary, maintain superstitiously those abstractions, classifications, and divisions, those *idola theatri*, petrified by a long tradition, enriching or varying them with others of the same sort, as Orient and Occident; Sumerians, Babylonians, Assyrians, Indians, Persians, Egyptians, and Romans; Early Times, Antiquity, Middle Ages, Modernity; and so forth. And they profess to give to these strings of abstractions a higher philosophic value, raising them to be divinities of the second order, or indeed of the order of God himself, who, it would seem, instead of creating the concrete and individual thoughts and actions of men, toyed with these abstractions which men have devised for their own use.

All this is called "discovering the meaning of history", a sort of chase outside or above history for the meaning which history already has in itself, in its essential reality and truth, in the operations of every thinking mind, indeed in every vital activity, for this is never unaccompanied by a self-awareness which is its own history. An absurd situation results. On the one side we are shown an outer or exoteric history, "history as the historians write it", as we are told somewhat contemptuously, and on the other side what purports to be an inner or esoteric interpretation, the privileged task of the philosopher.

Now whether he is aware of this or not, the philosopher in question will find ready to his hand, and will make use of, the process of allegory. (The first great era of the Philosophy of History, the Middle Ages, was in fact much given to allegory.) However, the philosophy of history is distinguished from allegory (which is a sort of hieroglyphic exhibiting no logical relation, but only a semantic relation, between the symbol and the thing signified), in that it converts the allegorical relation into a real relation. Introducing allegory, it makes of it a super-history which imparts the motion to history, a hidden hand which in some incomprehensible manner guides visible reality. The manner is incomprehensible, because when fact and the Reason for fact are separated from one another, and the Reason is moved into a sphere of transcendence, a dualism arises which so long as those terms are used it will never be possible to resolve.

Now since the second term in the dual relation, Reason, which supposedly provides the meaning of the allegory, is not engendered out of the matter under examination by an act of thought, it follows that this term must be imported ready-made from some other quarter, in fact from a theoretical conviction formed and cherished by the philosopher, or from some belief to which he holds. It may accordingly be true or it may be false, it may be logical or it may be a product of the imagination heated by love, hatred, or other affections. It may be theoretical and systematic and it may be mythical. It may for example take the form of this proposition: "The Spirit passes through a circle which carries it from the fancy to the reason, from the reason to practical operations, and thence, by way of the pathos of these operations, full-circle back to the fancy"; or of this other: "Pure being, abstract Being, engenders its contrary Not-Being, or nothing, and by the negation of this negation, regains itself as concrete being". These either are true propositions, or may here conveniently be regarded as such. But the proposition may instead be one which we view or here choose to view as untrue, as for example: "Humanity, divided into classes, passes through three stages of purely economic life, which is the reality behind all religious, poetical, scientific, political, and moral appearances, and at last resolves itself into a classless society"; "History consists in a contrast between peoples and races, one of which is privileged and chosen to dominate and guide all the others". Or in place of these propositions there may stand a confessional belief, as in the universal histories composed by churchmen, or a pessimistic conviction held by men who view human affairs despairingly – the pessimist-dialectician Hartmann exercised himself along that line – or a conviction of irrationalism as displayed by some who gloat in imagination over the accidental and irrational in history, and advertise this without noticing that they are advertising their own poverty. But be the propositions in question true or false, they all become equally untrue when they are twisted and bent into the guise of historical facts and events; when the categories of thought, instead of serving to bring concrete judgement to bear upon the intuitions, are themselves erected into thinking and judging organs, producers of mental monstrosities, hybrids incapable of generating truth, but projecting a foam of abstract phantoms and phantom abstracts. Such is the intrinsic logical vice of every sort of philosophy of the already philosophic, and thus of every Philosophy of History, whatever its particular forms and illusory appearances and whatever high concepts and noble aspirations may have penetrated and mingled in it. We read of the prime importance of the moral significance which Christianity imparted to history by the construction of its philosophy of history.[1] But what was really important was the wonderful way in which Christianity refined and

1. E. g. see WINDELBAND, *Lehrbuch der Geschichte der Philosophie*, ed. Heimsoeth (Tübingen, 1935), par. 21, pp. 213-25.

33

deepened the moral conscience and the religious character of that conscience, when it established a new principle to operate through the centuries as it still operates in us, as a perpetual power of redemption. This was important, and not the philosophy of history that was constructed upon it and became for long ages the model of similar erroneous constructions, now all in ruins and requiring final demolition and clearance.

Another consequence of the jumbling of philosophic categories with intuitions, so that, as suggested above, each contaminates the other, is the tendency to a closed system exhibited by all the philosophies of history. Either they treat the course of history as it has unfolded heretofore as being now concluded, having reached its final point, or else – and the difference is only apparent – they deduce logically how history is to run in the future, and illustrate its course, thus offering what is really not a picture of the future but of the present past, since there can be no effective thought about that which is to be done, or will happen, but only about that which has been done, has happened. In the philosophies of history not only does the total course of history appear as finished and concluded, but also its events and periods, one and all, are rendered fixed and static in the guise of judgements that have been let fall, one after another, by God, or the Idea, or generally speaking by historical necessity, so that our part is simply to bow low and obey – as though in the reality of becoming there could ever be any point that was not moving, any judgement to be accepted and not to be disputed in the most various ways, any total victory or any total defeat, any present that does not carry the whole past on its back and the future in its womb. The false idea of historical necessity is certainly enervating for moral activity, but what is worse is that it breeds a deleterious sophism which is most often pronounced in times of political upheaval, and eagerly seized upon by those who in the words of an old poet of ours "know not how to embrace adverse fortune lovingly". Unable to love adversity, to nurse it in their bosom, these "wretched folk" are always ready to commit it to a speedy interment, hypocritically bowing to the will of God which they use as a cloak to cover their own private convenience and advantage. But the only sort of historical necessity is the necessity which impels the historian, the logical necessity which bids him to understand the past as it was, neither praising it nor blaming it where praise and blame are out of place. The practical law which impels to action is nothing else than liberty, and between liberty and the necessity of truth there is no conflict, the latter being the eternal correlative, the other aspect, as it were, the theoretical aspect of Liberty.

Transcendence, as it appears in the Philosophy of History, is the same as any other Transcendence, identical with that which appeared in the Philosophy of Nature, flowering and withering with, indeed in unison with, that twin. Like every transcendence it takes two forms, that of myth and that of metaphysic – and the two are not strictly distinguishable because all metaphysic smacks somewhat of myth, containing a representative element, while all myth smacks somewhat of metaphysic, thanks to a logical element in it which differentiates it from pure poetic fancy, whereby it has this character of myth. Yet the two are distinguishable in some degree, even if not in strict logic, in a manner corresponding to the distinction between religion and theology, while if the latter couple be regarded jointly as a single form the two former are distinct from this also, and each is opposed by Criticism, or Philosophy. It may be mentioned that these three forms have themselves been worked into the schemes of the Philosophy of History, in the guise of three historical epochs of humanity (as readers of Turgot and Comte will remember): the theological, the metaphysical, and the critical or scientific. But such epochs are not in truth historical but ideal and eternal, living and present in every act of thought. For thought is perpetually emerging from its struggle against the mythical and the metaphysical, strengthened and refreshed in its critical energy.

II

The nature of the above-described process of philosophizing *upon* history (that is, upon universal history reduced to the level of compilations and chronicles), instead of philosophizing *in* history, may be illustrated without a laborious exposition of all its various manifestations and forms which have, for that matter, been well summarized in various special works. It suffices to pause for reflection upon the most famous and certainly most weighty of all the writings of this sort, Hegel's *Philosophy of History*, the work of a philosophic genius who was also endowed with an acute historical vision.

Hegel's starting point was the conviction that the work of the historians, ancient and modern, had never, in any of its branches or sub-branches, attained the form of truth, as he undertook to show in the review with which he prefaced his own work. He first distinguishes two types of historical writing, the *ursprüngliche* (original) and the *reflektierende* (reflective). The former, which is exemplified in the works of Herodotus, Thucydides, Xenophon, Polybius, and Caesar in antiquity, Guicciardini, the Cardinal de Retz, and Frederick II in the modern age, is history recounted by the narrators of contemporary events which they witnessed or took part in, so that they cannot rise above the facts narrated. The second, which looks beyond the present, is divided into four sub-types: 1. "general" histories, compilations of information from various sources on the affairs of a people, a country, or the whole world, for instance those of Livy, or Diodorus Siculus, in antiquity, and Johann Müller in modern times; 2. "pragmatic" histories, which accompany the narration with moral and political reflections, for which the example is once again Müller; 3. "critical" histories, which examine the truth and credibility of the "historical tradition" and have, like Niebuhr's work, the character of a "history of histories", and finally, 4. "special" histories of art, religion, science, law, navigation, and so forth, which in a certain sense mark the transition to "philosophical universal history". This is a strange list – an enumeration (rather than a dialectical phenomenology of their errors) of what Hegel seems to regard as the historical abortions which are all that any historian of those who have not risen to the third and one true type of historical writing, the "Philosophy of History", can produce. What, however, is wanting in the above list is precisely genuine history, that history which, because pondered and understood, is intrinsically philosophical, and is to be found in all the truly historical parts of the books recalled by him and of others not recalled by him. This history, which is in its nature philosophical, does not glory in that epithet, unlike the so-called "philosophy of history" or the "philosophic history", which needlessly and tendentiously boasts the epithet, while it does not ponder history but overshoots it without noticing that it does so, and comes back to history only for the purpose of graciously supplying it with a reality alien to history, a "super-history" as we here term it.

The structure which Hegel traces for his super-history (which presupposes and exploits the work of the historians as a sort of inferior drudgery that can be used to serve higher ends) is founded upon the doctrine of the gradual development of liberty as e-nunciated in his Philosophy of the Spirit. In the first degree of this graduality, which corresponds to childhood, one man alone is free and is obeyed by all others, patriarchally, as his children and subordinates. In the second degree, corresponding to youth, naive faith and obedience is discarded and true liberty is attained, but it is still a liberty shorn of substance. In the third degree, corresponding to manhood, the individual has his own ends, but pursues them only by putting himself at the service of the generality, the State, whence arises a contrast between the personalities of single men and the obligation towards the generality. In the fourth degree, for which the counterpart should be old age – and Hegel cannot but pronounce this metaphor, but forthwith withdraws it – the subjective spirit becomes reconciled to the objective, is perfectly free, and possesses substantial liberty. The working out of the scheme of the Philosophy of History comports the demonstration that "experience" – the facts contained in the books of the historians but by them left void of thought[1] – must and do correspond to the foregoing *a priori*.

It is possible, in explicating the philosophy of the spirit, to give

---

1. *Vorlesungen über d. Philosophie der Geschichte*, ed. Lasson, pp. 135-37.

a plausible sense to this doctrine of the degrees of liberty, interpreting them as dialectical moments of a single concept (for instance
the subjection of individual to individual as thesis, the liberty of
individuals deploying their strength or even spontaneously serving
a general cause of their own choice as antithesis, and true, full
liberty which is at the same moment submission to the ideal, as
synthesis). Perhaps that was, more or less, the theoretical purport
of Hegel's thought. But to detach these moments, to attribute to
them the character of historical epochs and to attribute conceptual
precision to the epochs – this was to substitute a mythology for
the truth of historical development, that is for the concept which,
in opposition to the dualism and contrast between history and
reason prevailing in the mind and the conduct of the men of the
sixteenth century, had come to affirm the unity of reason and
history, the rationality of the real and the reality of the rational.
Those are the words used by Hegel himself in a solemn statement
of doctrine, but Hegel fell from his own high level and weakened
his doctrine in the illustrations which he gave of it,[1] just as he
also cheapened and squeezed and distorted the genuine concept of
development which he had inferred by conceiving it – under the
influence of traditional religious patterns – in the form of a development towards a final goal, along which the Idea realizes
itself in the history of the world, passing from the "in itself" to
the "for itself" and thus attaining its own end. Hegel said that
without a goal for history to work towards, development would
have degenerated into mere "change" or mere "quantitative" and
not "qualitative" increase,[2] whereas in truth historical thought has
no room either for quantity, which pertains to the physico-mathematical sciences, or for quality for its own sake, which pertains to
ponderings upon the categories and their omnipresent eternal
circle, but only for the critical universal-individual which discerns
the one in the diverse. Having taken this wrong turning, Hegel,
instead of allowing the historical judgement and meditative history

1. For this see my *Saggio sullo Hegel*, 3rd edn., pp. 156-58, and *Ultimi
Saggi*, pp. 238-39.
2. Ed. Lasson, pp. 129-38.

to develop out of the pure categories and the categoreal moments, proceeded to operate with pseudo-categories, that is with a ready-made and presupposed doctrine serving in his hands as an instrument to procure illusory severances and combinations and express the philosophical characteristics of the facts – but not of the facts known to living experience, to intuition, for what Hegel here calls "experience" is simply the body of universal history as he accepted it, with little modification, in the traditional patterns. Thus he retains the comfortable old divisions between prehistory and history, between the history of the civilized peoples and the undeveloped or soon arrested history of the uncivilized peoples, for he rightly rejected the notion of a primitive age of high wisdom and spotless morality, a terrestrial paradise, which some of his philosophical contemporaries retained or resurrected. But Hegel severed the primitive or prehistoric age from historical times with a clean conceptual cut, as being devoid of knowledge of the State and therefore wanting in any history[1] worth remembering or recording – just as if, seeing that thought is judgement and judgement is historical judgement, there could possibly be thinking beings who did not in their way make history, and as if such beings could possibly live in neighbourhood without having some such notion of the State as the native Africans themselves must have (though Hegel excluded Africa from the purview of history for its alleged ignorance of that idea). He retains the other customary division between the history of the East and of the West, to which latter he aggregates the new Europeanized American world. But this division also he invests with conceptual rigour, his East not being the geographical relative East because, says Hegel, although the earth is a sphere, history does not revolve on itself, but has a particular East, that is Asia, where just as the external and physical sun rises to set in the West, there likewise arises the more nobly bright internal sun of self-consciousness.[2] Hegel retains as actors on his stage and as historical individualities the currently classified peoples of ancient and of modern times, and if in the

1. Ed. Lasson, pp. 138-46.
2. Ed. cit., pp. 232-33.

course of the eighteenth century these had been given a spiritual guise as *esprits des peuples* or *Völkergeister*, Hegel actually gives them a logical guise as personifications of speculative categories. He assigns each people to one category and one only. When it has fulfilled its relevant mission it must die. No people may appear a second time in the drama of history, for to appear a second time it would have to change its animating category, and thus become a different people.[1] Hegel retains the six-thousand-year period of the manuals of universal history as the span of history and assigns to the years of this period the task of ripening the spirit to the attainment of the concept of itself – a task to which they apply themselves with all their resources.[2] Along this course the dialectic of the conceptualized peoples unfolds itself. In China we find man really becoming something only after his death. In India we find man spiritually and vitally dead, whelmed and drowned in Brahma. In Persia there is a dawning of light in the spirit, and the particularity of single men rises to major importance, yet it is their natural heritage that ranks as absolute. In Egypt there is a kind of fermentation, a liberation from that immersion in nature. But it is only in the West, in that first brilliance of the West that is called Greece, that the single elements of the spirit of the East fuse into a concrete unity, the spirit of man becomes something on its own account, the particularity and formality of the Egyptians is superseded in the phase of objectivity, and individuals being now bound together in the general form of the Fatherland, the subject finds himself ethically equipped with his rights and is free in himself.[3] Such is the course of the transition from East to West, and like to it are all the other transitions, including the already-mentioned general and fundamental movement of the East, where one only is free, towards Greece and Rome, where many are free, and the ulterior movement towards the Christian-Germanic world in which all are free, and which is the conclusion of the whole metaphysical historical *fabula*.

Hegel's allusion to the German people as the only one capable of

1. Ed. cit., p. 165.   2. Ed. cit., pp. 148-63.   3. Ed. cit., p. 511.

settling the conflict which Christianity provoked between feelings and existence, Church and State,[1] serves to call attention to the way in which the mythological element, present in Hegel's as in all other Philosophies and Metaphysics of History, is infected by a passional and private current which in Hegel's case reflects not, as with Kant in his *Idea of a Universal History in the Cosmopolitan Sense*, the passion of universal humanity as felt by one aspiring for the great confederation of the nations, the state of States, guarantor of the rights of all men, but the private passion of a single people or race. Even a recent commentator on Hegel's *Philosophy of History*, who esteems it as, in its own sphere, "the most powerful and invincible product of the human mind", cannot but admit that in the last resort it is to be "admired and exalted as nothing less than the myth of the Christian-Germanic soul, one of the profoundest of all myths".[2] How different from Vico! Vico too in a part of his work fell into the same error of historicizing the categories of his profound philosophy of the spirit, and framed the theory of historic cycles according to which the ideal moments become empirical epochs. (Hence Vico was precluded from embracing the idea of perpetual progress, which is the very definition of the spirit in its perpetual outdistancing of itself.) But Vico, with his stern respect for philosophic dignity, and his noble impartiality, did not allow his vision of history to become contaminated by private and passional tendencies, nor yet by the "puffed-up vanity of nations", which he contemned. Humanist that he was, he did not people the void with corporeal shapes of his mental categories, but introduced these into the fullness of historical reality, exaggerating somewhat the features of this, but not reshaping it to suit abstract patterns. The universal history traced by Hegel is like a drama written around the shadowy impersonations of doctrines imagined by him, but there is more than imagination in Vico's depiction of the change from the savage but pregnant early ages

1. Ed. cit., p. 748.
2. See K. Leese, *Die Geschichtsphilosophie Hegels, auf Grund der neu erschlossenen Quellen untersucht und dargestellt* (Berlin, 1922), p. 312.

of man to the civilization of Greece and Rome, the conversion of this civilization into a new savagery, no less pregnant and, as he said, no less "generous", the Middle Ages, and then the grand emergence from this to the new civilization of the Renaissance. It is on this pattern that historians have continued and still continue to work, though they are now inclined to assign a larger part or even a directing function, in their depiction of the barbaric Middle Ages, to the enduringly active tradition of the ancient Graeco-Roman civilization which lived on in Christianity, and then, gaining energy and authority with the humanistic movement, finally determined the crisis and dissolution of the mediaeval conception of the world.

In Hegel's Philosophy of History we may also observe what we have noticed as being the logical tendency of the Philosophy of History to deny or to depress the concept and sentiment of liberty and the moral life, although the intention had been to raise this to the rank of the supreme principle. Since this is a tendency implicit in the very form of this kind of doctrine it would be a mistake, when inspecting the work of Hegel, to seek its prime and principal origin in his personal character, that is in his quality of an obedient Prussian subject and functionary who neither understood nor loved the European Liberal movement of his times, and clung fast to the bureaucratic and administrative monarchy in whose shadow certain free institutions or privileges of the Middle Ages had been permitted to continue a languid existence. Nor need we discern a contempt for morality in Hegel's famous theory of "historical men", "great men", "heroes", those whom he terms "agents of the spirit of the world", not to be judged, he says, by the moral criterion because "the history of the world moves in a sphere higher than that of morality".[1] For the pages in question, which are among the warmest and liveliest that he wrote, really contain only the expression of a thoroughly justified *indignatio* against the arrogant stupidity of the typical school-master who casts moralizing aspersions and blame upon the actors in history instead of pay-

1. Ed. cit., pp. 74-84 and cf. 153-54.

ing attention to the work created by them. Only it must be admitted that from time to time, in his theoretical demonstrations, Hegel's imagination ran away with him, causing him to draw distinctions between great men and small men, and apparently to accord moral privileges to the former which he denied to the latter, while he stresses too much the connexion of achievements with single individuals. The achievement of individuals certainly impresses the attention and the memory, but the achievements of men are really accomplished jointly by these individuals and by all the other spirits who participate whether by seconding or withstanding their efforts, and whether great or small, near or remote. For all alike bring their contribution and leave their mark. Where Hegel does injure the idea and conception of morality is in the exaltation of the *victrix causa* at the expense of the *victa*, from which the first would seem to be real and the second unreal, the first solar light and the second shadows dispelled by this, the second dead, and the first alone living on in ulterior history. In truth, both are equally alive and dead, for contrary to the erroneous view of Hegel and of all the other practitioners of the philosophy of history, there is no final goal of history and consequently no question altogether finished and done with and ready for pigeonholing. Every single event bears the comment "To be continued". The dislike which Hegel and other German historians who learned from him or thought like him showed for Cato of Utica[1] (Cato, whom Dante chose, though no Christian, to take a place in the Christian story and whom Campanella placed alongside of Socrates and Christ),[2] is noteworthy in the light of the fact that Cato has kept his place in history as a living example no less than Caesar. For if Caesar by means of the foundation of the Empire kept Rome living for a fresh term (I think it was Mommsen who once described this achievement as a sort of administration of a bank-

---

1. Particularly in the essay *Die Verfassung Deutschlands* (1802) in *Schriften zur Politik und Rechtsphilosophie*, ed. Lasson, pp. 113-14.

2.   *Contro sofisti Socrate sagace,*
       Contro tiranni venne Caton giusto,
       Contro ipocriti Cristo, eterna face.

rupt estate),[1] Cato, through all the centuries, has been his counterpart, and has always been there to reconstruct in men's minds, and in their actions and deeds, the conditions of liberty.[2]

III

A foretaste of the Philosophy of History was afforded in the Messianic conceptions of the Jews and in the cosmologies of the East. But it took a clear and striking shape for the first time with the coming of Christianity, especially in the writings of the Fathers of the Church, a shape which was substantially preserved in later non-ecclesiastical versions. (We will not here mention the variations introduced by certain mediaeval thinkers or visionaries like Gioacchino di Fiore.) In the Renaissance, there was a return to a non-mythological history of the sort practised by the Greeks and the Romans which gradually digested new orders of ideas including, towards the end, those of Rationalism and the Enlightenment. The Philosophy of History was relegated accordingly to ecclesiastical circles, both Catholic and Reformed, and was ignored by

1. For that matter, Hegel himself attributes to the age of the Roman Empire a negative character of decadence and despotism, placing the new positive and progressive element in Christianity.

2. Let me recall if only in a footnote the criticism of Engels in his *Ludwig Feuerbach und der Ausgang der klassischen deutschen Philosophie*, Stuttgart, 1882, where he says that the Hegelian doctrine, by justifiying and at the same time negating what had already happened, was conservative on the one hand and revolutionary on the other, for it could be appealed to both by Prussian semifeudalism and also by the Proletariat in its ascent towards the abolition of the State, and communism. However, Engels himself was not exempt from that logical fault into which Hegel and all the philosophers of history fell, that of forgetting real humanity in favour of solid blocks of accomplished facts, serving really as disguises for philosophical categories. Hence Engels' own deduction of the future course of events which was to resolve history into a super-historic realm of liberty, founded by the proletariat. Engels did not notice that this was the same method as that by which Hegel and the other philosophers of history had been led to establish a climax and conclusion for history – though Hegel himself was sometimes upset at the sight of what his logic had led him to, and made efforts to loosen the chains which he had so energetically forged.

secular historians who found no motive for taking issue with what in no way arrogantly challenged or disputed their conception and handling of historical narration. Vico himself took no account of it, and in the elaboration of his work, so rich both in speculative thought and in historical clarity, he had recourse to some pre-Christian conceptions which he developed in greater depth. The eighteenth century, when it spoke of "Philosophy of History", meant nothing more than a history narrated in the spirit of the Enlightenment and the Reformation, with appropriate comments.

But the above-described indifference of the historians towards the surviving tradition of the Philosophy of History changed to violent repudiation and mockery when in Germany, where that mediaeval tradition had lingered on longer than elsewhere in the universities, it was seized upon by the post-Kantian idealists and the Romantics, and, gaining great prestige and favour as an intellectual fashion, was worked up, finally, into the Hegelian scheme which as we have seen spurned every other type of historical writing, ancient or modern, and proclaimed as the sole authoritative and truth-revealing history a sort of history of which, according to Hegel, the historians had no notion, never having risen to the required altitude of vision. In Hegel's own work, fortified though this was by wide historical reading, and abounding in fresh and sound judgements, which repay study even today, there was all too much, both in the imaginous general scheme and in the compendiums of historical fact which were subordinated in it to the pattern of pre-established metaphysical categories, which could not but horrify precise and anxiously cautious historians. But much greater extravagances were to be found in other schemes of the same school, both those which were oddly swathed in the likeness of biblical and oriental Christian legend, and those which affected an entirely different and novel character of rationalist or illuministic type, pointing to apocalypses of a humanitarian pattern. We may rapidly and sporadically recall some of these extravagances. Friedrich Schlegel envisaged the history of the world as a fall from a primitive age of innocence and high wisdom into irreligion and impiety by dint of the warfare between the sons of Seth and the sons of Cain. Görres, on similar lines, articulated history into ages corresponding to the six Mosaic days (incidentally he made Christianity typify the morning hours and the Islamic religion the evening hours). History according to Schelling began with a primitive and immobile age of monotheism, then lapsed into polytheism, a fall into evil, an Iliad, and finally an Odyssey standing for the return of humanity to God. In the same way, with variations in the imaginous pattern, the other minor philosophers traced their schemes. Somewhat differently, though preserving the notion of a primitive age of innocence in which man was reasonable by nature and by instinct, Fichte recounted that the second age, one of lost innocence and of sin, in which reason took the shape solely of authority, had been followed by a third age (Fichte's own) in which all was sin and even authority was worthless. Krause started with an initial age of innocence budding beneath the influence of nature and of God, passing into an age of growth and youthfulness. Both of them completed their systematic historical patterns with a deduction as to the ages of the future; Fichte delineated a fourth age, "of Science", to be followed by a fifth and final "of Art", in which reason would wear the vesture of beauty; Krause a great age of the perfection of the human race in the complete and harmonious development of all its faculties, and the exercise of full dominion over Nature and itself. In this age, all single human societies would unite into one collective individuality. And there were other prophecies of similar type. In these, the characteristics of the epochs and the peoples were delineated in ever more astonishing and naive fashion. Thus, according to some of these philosophies of history, the ancient world is the real or natural side of history, and its relation to the modern world, which is the ideal and spiritual side, corresponds with that of nature to spirit, finite to infinite. Again, we learn that the principle of the ancient world is sensation and that of the modern world intellect, and that the peoples are distinguished by the prevalence in each of them of one particular faculty, thus, of rationality in the Chinese, of imagination in the Indians, penetrating intuition in

the Egyptians, will in the Jews, and so on through lists of characteristics which defy attention, so that it is best to yield to impatience
and boredom and to refer the reader to the old volume of Professor
Flint, who anthologized and passed in review these ambitious and
extravagant constructions. Of recent revivals of this sort of argument there is no need to take account.

The antagonism, indignation and mockery of those historians
who worked on the basis of documents and citations, and were
not always mere chroniclers and men of erudition, but sometimes
had keen insight into substantial problems, thanks to a spontaneous
though perhaps unsystematic philosophical vision, did not of
itself suffice to chase away and confute the new pretensions of this
Philosophy of History with its specious claim to elicit the truth of
history, by applying to experience an *a priori* (which *a priori*,
moreover, was not the pure and plastic *a priori* of the categories,
but a metaphysicized and mythologized variant). An adequate
confutation could be furnished only when the debate had been
carried on to the ground of logic and methodology, or of philosophy in the stricter sense, where the error could be analysed,
traced to its origin, and exhibited as dialectically unmasked. But
the young philosophers of the time were the Positivists, who by
censuring not only the Philosophy of History but Philosophy
itself rendered themselves helpless. For metaphysical idealism they
substituted a no less metaphysical naturalism. Ignorant of the lessons of Kant as to immanent finality, they revived a mechanistic
determinism, thereby ruining not only the Philosophy of History
but history itself, which they strove to resolve, by violence and
compression, into an impossible natural science, while clamping
upon it a system of abstract classifications called "sociology".
This, even today, numbers its devotees, some of whom even
believe in the possibility of utilizing it to discover a law of historical occurrence with a reliable applicability to the ages of the
future.

Both the Philosophy of History, and the Historical Determinism
which followed upon its heels, require, for their confutation, a
searching enquiry into the nature of the act of thought which

generates an historical proposition, that is, into an act which we
are at every moment performing, but which is performed on a
great scale and at a great depth by true historians, or let us say by
historians in their true moments. Such a searching enquiry brings
forth the doctrine of the ideal contemporaneousness of every
work of historical thought, or, otherwise expressed, the doctrine
of the birth of the historical act from the matrix of a practically
individuated need to operate, or to prepare an operation, in order
to issue out of a given situation. Thence the need to know that
situation, the situation of ourselves in the world that surrounds us,
and therewith the world itself, the forces at play in it. According
to this doctrine every historical affirmation is limited, and thereby
rendered possible, by the need out of which it springs, and it is
not given to jump outside these limits without tumbling into the
void (the void may be masked or splendidly veiled to give the
illusion of solidity, but that will not prevent the painful disillusionment of a helpless collapse). The historical judgement is
always the answer to a question thrown up by life for the engendering of new life. Once what was required to be known is known,
and light has been thrown upon what was in shadow, there is
nothing more to ask. The light has shed its gleam and now is the
time to operate. Before another historical question can be asked
and answered, a new situation and a new need must have taken
shape. Histories unstimulated and undirected by practical problems may exhibit fancifulness and argumentation, not serious
historical thought.

It is for sure mere fancifulness and argumentation when the
Philosophy of History undertakes a philosophical elaboration of
those answers [to problems] which are already philosophical,
since they include the knowledge of those categories of the spirit
which have their dwelling and are to be found solely in concrete
historical judgement. And this is the moment to recall our inverse
and complementary judgement that all philosophy has its dwelling
exclusively in history and as history, and that philosophy and
history coincide and are identical. Hegel glimpsed or scented this
truth, but then at once lost track of it when he got the notion of

"applying" a ready-made philosophy, void of history, to a ready-made history, void of philosophy. Those who now say or believe that the doctrine here formulated of the identity of history and philosophy is simply a repetition of what Hegel said, have either failed to ponder the works of Hegel and the works illustrating the modern doctrine, or they grossly fail to discern the difference between phrases which may sound alike but get their meaning from different historical and cultural situations. Let this be said once and for all, not to vaunt a claim of originality, but to assist in the understanding of the concepts in question.

There can be no ulterior philosophic elaboration of the propositions and discussions of history which are already philosophic. There is, however, a work to be done in respect of them which is not a work of thought or philosophy but commits to memory the numerous historical affirmations which we have made and now possess, and arranges them in classes whereby the particular and individual are transformed into the general and collective. This is an operation upon which all are continuously engaged, and which the historians properly so called practise and adapt for their own purposes. In doing so they are more or less clearly and definitely aware of what they are about, and this awareness is deliberately studied by the specialists in historical method. It is an awareness that the value of these classifications is not cognitive but instrumental, and consists in their susceptibility for retranslation, as and when required, back into the original individual propositions which alone ever were and still are cognitive acts. On the other hand it is true that the builder of such convenient classes sometimes forgets his purpose, and thoughtlessly – though it may be only a moment before he recovers himself – slips or feels himself drawn into treating them as knowledge, falling thus into the net which he himself had spun with another intent. More often it happens that with distress and irritation he sees them being misunderstood and misused by others who have found and received them already made at his hands, these delicate instruments, of which he himself well knows the use and the scope, what treatment they can bear and at what point they will break, but which

34

he sees others snatching and brandishing like hatchets, waving and hitting wildly, thus cutting and rending and defacing the reality of history. But however that may be, it is this forgetfulness and lapse of awareness that gives the psychological impulse for the creation of the abusively conceptualized representations which then serve as the scattered elements for the construction or reconstruction of the deplorable Philosophy of History.

What more natural than that one should arrange a number of the historical propositions that we possess under the headings of histories of Italy, France, Germany, Greece, ancient Rome, Persia, Japan? Those historical propositions, being propositions of truth, belong not to the domain of nations and States but to the realm of truth. Yet none the less it serves a useful purpose to group them together and bring them to the attention of the intelligent who well know that what they will read under these headings will always be the drama of the one and only humanity. For the unintelligent, however, the characters of the peoples, delineated for certain limited purposes, take on a rigid, exclusive, and static guise, becoming transformed from abstractions of the intellect into metaphysical entities. Thus transformed, and personified, they stand ready to act their parts for the Philosophy of History, which engages them for various roles in its metaphysical or mythological drama, in the way that we have already illustrated.

It is also very natural that in expounding the formation of certain institutions, moral attitudes, ideas, we should arrange them under periods or epochs, labelling each of these with an indication of some moment in the spiritual formation, so that we talk of Greece which created the eternal models of beauty, of Rome the parent of law, of the ascetic and transcendent Middle Age, the Renaissance which exalted the value of earthly life, the eighteenth century which sharpened the blade of reforming and revolutionary rationalism. But in the mind's eye we never lose sight of the fact that these are signposts amid the problems upon which we are engaged, and not realities, the sole reality being our spirit which produces and understands them. But these necessary and well-devised indications can also be turned into the pawns on a metaphysical chessboard, when by establishing sequences and contrapositions and dialectical relations between them we illude ourselves that we have embraced the whole story of the world, having, in reality, merely experienced a trait in the history of our own mind. To the naive and childish eye of the inexpert these mere convenient labels end by appearing to be "objective" realities, and the Greeks are envisaged as perpetually engaged upon creating or admiring plastic or poetic beauty, the Romans as perpetually austere, the Germans always lusting for battle, destruction, and booty, the Italians of the Renaissance untroubled by melancholy or the sense of sin, wholly preoccupied with the discovery of nature and the cult of art, the French of the eighteenth century always in a reasoning and logical frame of mind. (One recalls how the witty Princess Matilde once jokingly asked Doctor Gebhart, to his surprise and confusion, how it was that in the times of the Greeks and Romans, in classical antiquity, there was nothing but sun and blue sky and holidays and "il ne pleuvait jamais"!)

Following a similar pattern peoples and epochs are classified as equivalent to certain spheres of spiritual production in order to designate the character of the art or philosophy of an age or of a people. Hence come the descriptions of the French mind as intellectualistic, the English as empirical, and idealism is said to correspond with that of the Germans, naturalism with that of the Greeks, and spiritualism with the modern age; or again, poetry and art in the classical form is ascribed to Italy, art of a ponderous and conflict-ridden order to Germany, eloquence is given as the character of the poetry of France, and so on. But when the temptation arises, as it often must, to convert these formulas, so useful for certain occasions, into realities, it is necessary immediately to get the better of this by recollecting that the collective and general, being an abstraction, is not art, philosophy, or life, and that the only reality is this or that thought, poem, political event, or moral creation. "There is nothing new in history" and "Everything is always new in history" are not two propositions but the single proposition of the universal-individual or individual-universal which excludes the presence or intrusion as a middle term of the common or general, *das Allgemeine*, an extraneous formation of what we have called practical or instrumental character.

There are other cases in which the proposed divisions, and the ascription to them of reality, have an origin not directly in historical affirmations but in sentimental and practical inclinations. It was thus that there emerged in the heretical movements of the Middle Ages and in the great Lutheran rebellion the idea of a primitive Church, depository of a simple faith, without priestly orders, riches, or political interests, a model to which men should return; or again, in the tumultuous and passionate agitation of the Romantics, the idea of a serene Hellas, or a Middle Age all devotion and chivalry. These projections of states of mind were mistaken for historical realities, and belief in them became an impediment to the understanding of the facts in question and necessitated the work of critics and adversaries for the recovery of a right perspective. Finally, what is the "modern art", "modern philosophy", "modern life", "modern ideal" of which everyone talks and of which we too, being articulate men, must needs talk? Is modern art something outside of ourselves or is it not rather – speaking of it with all modesty and humility but also with pride and assertiveness according to our state of feeling – the art which each one of us creates or loves, and accounts it new because it is beautiful, and beauty is necessarily fresh and new, different from the already existing, a new-born bud – in a word, of the prèsent moment, "modern"? We must speak in the same vein of that philosophy, life, ideal, which, being ours, we adorn with splendid images, metaphors, hyperboles, and in so adorning it risk detaching it from us, depriving ourselves of the best or the whole of ourselves in order to place it in a Beyond, an objective or metaphysical reality, where our present enemy, the Philosophy of History, will seize upon it, make it a pawn, one in the series of pawns which she has amassed or reshapen, and will place it at the head or tail of the procession to symbolize that it is those others, and not we ourselves, that have generated it, and those others that stand to demonstrate its necessity, truth, beauty, nobility – as if there could in truth be any generation or demonstration of that which realizes itself, in a blaze of perpetual renascence, proving its necessity by the very fact of its existence!

IV

This bringing down to earth of all the customary concepts of historical enquiry – the characters of peoples and of epochs, the separation of primitive from civilized peoples, of pre-history from the history of peoples without history and again from that of the historic peoples, of Eastern from Western civilization – all of which we have reduced to the ranks as mere empirical distinctions, aids to narrative serving a different purpose from the pursuit of that which alone is real and true; this radical negation of the grand synthesis of the events of the world which is offered in the brilliantly variegated patterns of Universal History, but is by us irreverently considered a *species sine cerebro*; this requirement which we have imposed that all serious and effective historical understanding must be simply a vision and judgement of the single and individual facts which one by one the mind and the spirit grasp and penetrate and render intimately familiar to themselves; all this induces in those who are new to our disciplines a sort of alarm and bewilderment, as though they were being asked to renounce a great treasure which they formerly possessed, and to content themselves with a few scattered and elusive gleams of truth. Is this, then, the historical knowledge which claims to be the highest and indeed the only genuine knowledge of reality that there is? Must the Spirit of Man, then, vainly sighing for liberation in the wide open air, vainly striving and longing to embrace the utterly unattainable All, remain imprisoned in this Platonic cavern from which the sunshine can but be glimpsed in patches?

Such questionings may indeed be painful and disconsolate, yet it is not too difficult to assuage them by a simple educative device which is calculated to dispel the gloomy oppression that had settled upon us. Let the distressed enquirer consider what we do, what happens to us, when we read poetry. Obviously we cannot simultaneously read more than one poem, for should we want to read

two at a time we would read none. One would distract us from
the other, one would kill the other. We do not mourn this as a
privation, on the contrary, as in a love suit, we joyously concentrate
on the one object, reading attentively every word and beat of the
poem, surmounting any difficulties which we encounter in this or
that part, re-reading in order better to fix in the mind a passage
or a verse and thus to gather up into ourselves its inspiration and
form, and finally to pause in the enjoyment of a full satisfaction.
Then, indeed, we pass on from that poem to another, to a new
world, a new love, different from the other but equal to it in its
demand for our full attention. From Homer we pass to Virgil,
from Dante to Shakespeare, and these, with the other poems that
we read and make our own, will not have been ours in vain, for
of them, as of all our aesthetic, intellectual, and moral experience,
our living and operating personality will be composed. Others
will in like wise read all or some of the pages we have read, and
make them their own, and also other pages which we have not
read because we have not come across them or they were unwritten
or unknown in our times; and the experience of those others like
our own will be both full and partial, will be intensive and at the
same time limited in extent, for extent must always be limited.
But who ever would exchange those single and individual poems,
be they few or many, that we have enjoyed or understood, for
the imaginary totality of poetry in its infinite and ever new manifestations? Who would wish to embrace a cloud? Doubtless there
are some who pine and sigh for the possession of that abstraction, a
Pure Uttermost Beauty, disdaining the petty business of creating
or re-creating and enjoying a single particular and determined
poem. We know what to think of them. There are also excellent
people who have a sort of knowledge of the universal poetry of
all peoples and epochs, but get this knowledge from the outside,
from hearsay, from exact information about the content of poems,
as befits scholarly librarians or cataloguers, but have never perhaps
intimately savoured a single poem. One smiles at such people, as
I did, if I may recall a youthful memory, when a friend, an excellent and meritorious scholar to whom I gave a dissertation in

which I had recalled a forgotten work of a forgotten seventeenth-century author, told me with touching delight how pleased he was with himself for not having omitted that author's name from a literary history. He had not weighed or read or even seen the book, but he had come across its title and had mentioned it along with other books in his learned compilation. Such in the last resort must be the history, whether described as universal history or by some variant name, of those who set forth to comprehend in its scope many, very many, or, as it is imagined, all the facts pertaining to its sphere, all materially classed and enumerated. But these will be titles without content, facts that are no facts, because their individual character, which is all one with their genesis and their history, will not be visible.

Now each of our single historical judgements carries within it, by implication, all the others that we have formed precedently, drawing its origin and strength from them, and these judgements of ours have received and never cease to receive into themselves the content of other men's judgements, subjecting them to critical selection, and this process increases and multiplies perpetually, in us and in all, whence there is born what is called the historical culture of a society or an epoch, which is no less of a reality for being, like all reality, in conflict with itself and in motion. But this reality of historical culture has always as its sole living and eternal source individual judgements formed in individual situations, communicating with each other, conflicting, supplying each other's deficiencies, attaining harmony, and then out of this harmony engendering a new and beneficial discordance. To seek harmonious truth elsewhere than in this eternal vital process, to believe that one has found it for example in some pontifical authority, or in some revelation from on high (even from the high heaven of some metaphysic like the Philosophy of History) is to drive a miserable bargain like that purchase recalled by Lichtenberg of a fine knife which had neither handle nor blade. That harmonious truth in which we all participate is born out of the truth which the individual presents to himself, is the defin-ition of the freedom of thought and the demonstration of its spiritual necessity for the intellectual advancement of mankind.

Implicitly we have at the same time got the better of another occasion of dismay, appeased another anguish, namely the suspicion lest our summons to the particular situation of the individual, our advice to avoid distractions and give heed single-mindedly to overcoming and freeing oneself from that situation by means of historical truth, by dint of one's own decision and action, may not conceal and favour a kind of egoism, or at the least egotism, and the cult of the prosaic utilitarian maxim "Each for himself and God for all". But the act to which we summon each man, the decision and action of each several one of us, constitute like each one's utterance of truth an action which is instrinsically moral, and accordingly super-individual, universal, linking and co-operating with the moral action of all men to form the "work of all", society, civilization. Thus an individual in some given sphere or epoch will hold the mastery over others with their own approval and aid, by dint of his own energy and capacity, like Pericles, who as Thucydides says was both moved by the free people of Athens and moved them, a prince in a democracy, and Cavour, who sometimes seemed to be king, parliament, and ministry in his own person, and was indeed all these because they lived and worked in him. What such men obtained spontaneously could surely never be obtained by such as seek to regulate and uniformize the world from on high, teaching it how to live properly and peaceably and faultlessly, as though the world were a babe in its nurse's arms or a boy undergoing a mistaken training in the performance of certain tricks and efforts on lines more suited to a riding horse or draught animal. Undeniably men's actions include evil-doing, but what else is evil but the vital impulse, necessary as the material and the implement of action? Man could not pit his own strength in action were there not this strength which sometimes responds but sometimes resists the yoke and compels that other strength to fight and to engage more strenuously in order to have the mastery. What were life without death? What were beauty without the unbeautiful, truth without error, the useful without the useless, good without evil, pleasure without grief?

Can a regulation from on high chase evil from the world, that is break the mainspring of life, destroying simultaneously physiological vitality and morality? What is mistaken for egoism or egotism is the eternal and fruitful struggle of good against evil, the motive power of individual and social progress. This is the definition of political and moral liberty, just as the individual origin of truth was found to be the definition of the liberty of thought.

It is in our present passion, our truth, our will and action that the whole of reality lies, and outside this circle of the Spirit there is nothing. The universe draws itself together into this circle, or rather it is the universe, as those who love, whatever the object of their love may be, know and testify in their words and songs. We have mentioned Progress. Like other forms and moments of the Spirit Progress is by the Abstractionists transferred into an external world and is sought where it can never be found, in something due to occur once and for all, or perhaps destined never to happen. But Progress in its full and genuine truth is our progress, the progress of the world in us and with us, in perpetual and therefore interminable realization. Who is there that does not feel this progress in every good and useful work that he accomplishes, in every beauty that he creates, who does not feel and rejoice to feel the world living and going ahead albeit amid griefs, disasters, and ruins? Where is the need or want or idea or reality of any other progress? Our own individual act is all that counts, and in it, like the giant of the fable, we touch firm ground and gain new strength. When in our labours alongside of others, in the family, the community, the country, the nation, disagreements, misunderstandings arise between ourselves and the others, and painful crises, we do not sacrifice our individual consciences to the others, but shoulder our part on our own, face opposition on every side, comforting ourselves with the splendid words of the poets, and thus in a more worthy manner we renew our links with family, country, nation, humanity, and co-operate with them in a hidden and salutary manner. For in our own personality we discover universality, God who inspires us, guides us, upholds us, God whose glory we serve. This perpetual redemption, perpetual salvation of himself which the individual effects within himself, this is a definition like those previous definitions that we have found of the liberty of thought and of action. It is the definition of the religious life.

[1943]

HISTORY AS AUTOBIOGRAPHY AND VICE VERSA

Among the types of "source" which history students are advised in handbooks of historical method to treat with the greatest distrust, there figures prominently the autobiography, said to be a source for novels rather than for history. Such manuals, however, do not afford more than rather rough indications, and remembering this we may put up with the condemnation of autobiographies as a warning against rash use of certain types of record. But looking into the question more accurately we will find that the type in question, which is distinguished by a merely external and literary difference from the diary, the letter, and other vehicles for the narration of personal vicissitudes, embraces not only what are in effect (as the manuals complain) novels, that is to say, agreeable combinations of the imagination for titillating and entertaining the feelings, but also – singly or commingled – agitations and outbursts of the affections, loves and hatreds, joys and pains, desolation and despair, and then also cleverly devised attacks and defences in the cause of self-love and vanity and other individual interests, and finally, what most concerns us here, perfect creations of historical thought.

These latter alone, in whatever context they are found, truly merit the description of autobiography, which should mean the delineation and valuation and recital of one's own past life, which is nothing other than the action that one has accomplished, the work that one has done, an action and a work that are personal only in the sense of having been performed in total collaboration with the Whole. At every moment of our life, at every pause in our action, autobiographical reflection arises, whenever some obscurity besets us and forces us to strive for light, to acquire a consciousness and understanding of what one has done, of what has happened. The literary species of autobiography corresponds to this perpetual ideal phase.

However, when we compare autobiography in the sense that

we have said – the true sense – with what is called history, it seems to exhibit an historical imperfection for two reasons. Firstly because the conception or the recital of a man concerning his own work simplifies the subject, imposing upon the reality a fanciful purity of outline, while often there is a more or less unconscious replacement of real facts by phantoms suggested by that sort of mythology which men build up around themselves, or by reading back the knowledge of later events into former, or by mistaking results for the fruit of intentions. All of this, it is said, is proved by the documents which are subsequently found and which refute the recital of the autobiographer or rectify it. The second reason alleged is that the criterion by which the facts narrated are interpreted and judged, fails to fulfil the requirement of history that it should rise above the mind of the author or part-author of the facts.

Well, let us begin by examining the second reason. In truth, the autobiographer does rise above his own mind of the past in virtue of his mind of the present. He looks upon his own work from the vantage-point of the new situation in which he stands, just like any other historian. And his new point of view will in the future be further superseded by himself in the future, or by others, from a still higher and more commanding point of vantage. As to the first reason, the historian in general, no less than the autobiographer, has to simplify, to give emphasis to the main lines of an event, and this is not a fanciful but an intellectual proceeding. The autobiographer is no worse off than the ordinary historians in respect of inaccuracies in his work which new documents that come to light or a re-examination of existing documents will reveal, thus opening the way for amendments or amplifications. And the accusation of attributing intentions by the light of subsequent consequences is often levelled by short-sighted readers against what are really keen-sighted interpretations of the course and nature of an event or a travail the origin of which is in fact rendered clearer by its outcome.

All this shows us that an autobiography is a fully ranking historical composition, like any other. But we must go on to acknowledge and confess the inverse truth that all true history is always autobiography. What difference is there between a deed which is called mine and any other deed which I am moved to re-enact in myself, tracing out its history? Surely that deed of "mine" is simply referred to me as a man and as such it is both mine and not mine, for it pertains also to other men. And by thinking upon it I detach it from myself, objectivize it, and if I wish once more to attach it to my practical self I cannot – I must instead perform another deed, enter into another total collaboration with the Whole. And this too will be subject to the same fate, becoming an object of thought, recognized as the deed of the Whole and not of myself. Conversely, what is called the work of others, for example the *Oedipus Rex* of Sophocles, Aristotle's definition of the relation of matter to form, the victory of the Greek Polis over the Eastern world, is mine and yet not mine, is part of my humanity as it concretely is, having historically become so. Those works do not belong to Sophocles, Aristotle, the Greek peoples, but to whoever rediscovers them in himself and relives them. It was thus that Montaigne said of a concept labelled as Plato's that this opinion was no more "according to Plato" than "according to Montaigne", since the two thought alike.

If, then, an autobiography is the history of our works, all the other histories of the works of mankind which all belong to us are also substantially autobiographical. Nay, it is the greater or lesser intimacy or autobiographical insight into works or historical events that gives us the measure of the excellence of a historical view or study.

[1941]

IV

THE EXAMINATION OF CONSCIENCE
AS HISTORICALLY UNREAL BUT MORALLY REAL

It might seem a scandalous disregard of the grave and painful seriousness of our self-examinations, our scrutinies of the conscience, our repeated attempts to discover in certainty and in truth what our conduct has been, and what our errors and faults, that we should propose to relegate to the poetical intuition the knowledge that we have of our feelings in our past life and actions. Is self-examination, then, a vain and desperate enterprise, not to be commended? But how could we desist from a proceeding which we feel to be natural and necessary? How extirpate and renounce a function if to do so would at the same time be to damp down our energy, break our impetus, invalidate our moral conscience?

To answer this objection and remove this doubt the first thing to be pointed out is this: the purpose of self-examination, in the terms in which it is proposed to us, is unattainable. The examination cannot be conducted upon our direct experience, but only upon certain traces of this which seem to remain when the experience has vanished, being absorbed in the event, the accomplished fact. These traces are called "memories" of ourselves or of others. But what else are memories, even our own, than attestations of our own individuality to ourselves? As mere attestations, they will necessarily be fragmentary and abstract assertions, wanting in definite sense, lacking that fullness and intimacy of truth which could only be found in the whole that fuses the parts, the whole in which those feelings were both realized and denied. To give life to these memories there must needs intervene tendencies and needs of our own, and images aroused and elaborated by these. Thereby the memories will be rendered lively, lively but not truthful, lively with practical and not with theoretical life. We know that some men are said to have "happy temperaments". They bear the load of their past without the smallest scruple, remorse, or shame. It has been unkindly said that women in particular have a wonderful capacity for cancelling from their mind anything in the past that could upset them, bring blushes, or cause embarrassment. At the opposite extreme are the scrupulous who in everything that they have done sense an impurity, and are odious and abominable in their own sight. There are ascetics who after long penitential severities die in a dreadful delirium, their eyes fixed wildly upon inevitable hell fires. Who can ever tell the one or the other or tell anyone at all what really, in just measure and without exaggeration in either direction, have been their true faults and merits? The exaggeration in the one or the other direction arises out of people's present action, and is a function of this, and could only cease if they abstained from action, that is, from living.

However, if there can be no cessation, resolution, or composition on the plane of a theoretical pursuit of the truth, there is a cessation on the plane of practical action, when the frivolous man is forced out of his frivolity, and the scrupulous man is likewise forced to discipline his scruples, to desist from an enquiry that can get nowhere, to castigate his egoistic imagination of individual perfection, to act, and, it may be, to redeem himself in action.

The examination of the conscience of which we appeared to be denying or disputing the propriety, retains, then, its validity, and is not touched by our criticism which, while it strikes at an illusion masquerading as history, does not strike at a quite unillusory moral reality. The "examination" is not really an examination but a cautious and alert mustering and marshalling of the forces of the will, holding them back and spurring them on, knowing those forces only as much as serves for bringing them into action, acting altogether in the present because the "past" with which it concerns itself is not the past judged historically for its own sake but a past which is passionally experienced. It is a past seen in the light of what we have become or are becoming and treated as something which satisfies us (and therefore we would maintain it), or alternatively as something which gives us remorse (and therefore we would fain cancel it from reality). But

if it gives us present remorse, it did not do so at the moment when
we performed the action. We could never have performed that
had our mind not been momentarily made up and at peace in
itself and sure of what we were doing. In this practical and moral
proceeding, and the debates in which it is enveloped, the images
certainly take their colours from the past, but they take their
vitality from the hopes and fears, the trusts and distrusts of the
present, and its virtue is not cognitive, historical, but educational,
practical. What matters it if I was strong and good in the past,
seeing that the past is past, and it is *now* that matters? But it is
important that I should consider myself to have been strong and
good if this image expresses my will to be so now. What matters
it, again, if I did not really commit the errors and faults of which
I now conjure up accusing images, if these accusing images represent my will not to fall into such errors? The halt which the
moral conscience itself from time to time calls when self-examination goes too far, can only be explained when we understand that
this is not a silencing of enquiry into the truth, but a limiting of
the imagination in a process which serves the needs of the moral
conscience up to a point, but beyond that point is harmful and
must be stilled.

And all this is in part true also of the proceedings of the law
courts (the real law courts, by contrast with the metaphorical
court of conscience): the enquiries into fact in those courts proceed
on similar lines though there is a dissimilarity arising out of the
circumstance that here the issue is legal and not moral. The enquiries of the courts are not enquiries into genuine historical truth.
On the other hand they are also not images and symbols of real
processes. They belong to that inferior order of history or pseudo-
history which is founded upon evidence. It is useful to recall that
the "historical critique of evidence" was prepared and anticipated
by the procedure of the courts and the rules which these established
for computing the comparative value and the psychology, or
authority, of witnesses. The likeness to the proceedings of the
conscience lies in this: the enquiries are conducted solely for the
purpose of discovering a basis for the application of law, so that

the true purpose of them is to maintain the continuity of law for the advantage of human societies. Accordingly the basis may be not a fact which is supposed really to have happened, but a presumption.[1] "Let the just man perish provided the guilty do not escape" is a sentiment put by the poet in the mouth of a tyrant. But detached from its context and understood as a general principle it sums up the purpose of the law in the courts, which is the purpose of maintaining itself, and thereby alone fulfilling its particular usefulness. The fact that the mind of a judge is different from the mind of an historian, that the judge's activity is not in itself of a moral character, in no way detracts from the reality and necessity of what takes place in the courts.

[1941]

1. On this matter see the excellent remarks of P. CALAMANDREI, *Il Giudice e lo storico* (Milan, 1939).

V

HISTORY AS THE HISTORY OF LIBERTY

I

THE HISTORICAL CHARACTER OF WRITTEN HISTORY

The critic of historical writings faces the same (or similar) difficulties as the critic of poetry. In either case, there are critics who simply do not know where to begin, and never succeed in finding the thread which could link the book to their own mind. Others tackle the task with the use of altogether unsuitable and arbitrary criterions, self-contradictory in their eclectic variety. Only a few bring a right judgement to bear, conformable to the works under criticism. In Italy, for sure, these are not so few as they were, but when I think back to my youth between 1880 and 1900 it seems to me that the criticism and history of historical writing was even more deficient than the criticism and history of poetry. It consisted in superficial and external studies concerning the historian's studies, his career, his reliability, and so on. Almost the only work which, in its relevant parts, could have set an example and given a better lead, De Sanctis' *History of Italian Literature*, was itself wrongly interpreted and misvalued and indeed quite discredited.

Historical writing is not to be judged as literature, or "eloquence", in the spirit of the old Humanists who when they had time on their hands translated Horace or, alternatively, penned an historical commentary on some event or episode of no moment whatever to themselves, but which they viewed as a frame suitable for a noble and elegant covering. The Abbé Vertot, to someone who offered him evidence to enable him to correct his account of a siege, remarked "Mon siège est fait" – he had written his literary page. Paul-Louis Courier was of opinion that "toutes ces sottises qu'on appelle l'histoire ne peuvent valoir quelque chose qu'avec les ornements du goût", and that it was quite legitimate to make Pompey win the Battle of Pharsalia "si cela pouvait arrondir tant soit peu la phrase". And no doubt it is to be desired and required that history shall be written in a good style, but just as literary style is often found unaccompanied by historical thought, so historical thought, though expressed in a poor or outworn style, will maintain its virtue as thought.

Historical writing is equally not to be judged by the greater or smaller abundance and precision of the information that it conveys. For evidently there are abundant and precise catalogues of information which right at the first glance we feel not to constitute history, while there are books which convey little information, or perhaps even a heap of incorrect and legendary and fabulous information, but are rich in historical understanding – we need but mention the *Scienza Nuova* of Vico. Catalogues of information can be termed chronicles, records, memorials, or annals, but not histories. Even when they are judiciously compiled, so that each single item is referred to a source, that is, to attentively sifted evidence, they can never by any manner of means, so long as they remain on their own level, get beyond the surface of the source and the evidence, so that these will be reported as things that are heard or related, and can never become truth for us, truth which we elicit from our own inner experience. It is no doubt desirable that the information included in historical writing should be carefully verified, if only to deprive the pedants of an objection which they disingenuously but effectively level against works of vigorous historical thought. Moreover, precision is a moral duty. None the less precision and historical value are different in idea and in fact. They can and do exist separately. The brass of the chroniclers, or even the highly polished metal of the philologians, will always be something very different from the gold of the historians.

Furthermore, an historical writing is never to be judged by the degree of its impact on the imagination, its power to move and excite, to edify or to intrigue and amuse, for these effects are obtained also by dramas and novels, and are not necessary in a historical work, which may be comparatively cold, difficult, and laborious, and may (as has been said also of the purest and greatest poetry) at first reading, or for average readers, be tedious. Those watchful custodians of the sacred patriotic and religious flame who compose histories "for the use of (French, German, Catholic,

Protestant, or whatever it may be) families", full of heroic gestures, pious acts, edifying examples, and on lower planes the cultivators and compilers of anecdotal books suitable for the dreamers of adventures and of passionate love-affairs, have at all times produced literary works that have been called histories and been taken for such, but are really instruments of sensation and excitement, displeasing to intellects engaged in enquiry for the truth (Polybius in his day aimed shafts at the rhetoricians who dressed history in the weeds of tragedy) and altogether different from those works in which severity of thought, not pathetic imagining or moralization, sets the tone.

An historical writing is to be judged solely for its historical quality just as a poem is for its poetical quality. Historical quality may be identified with an activity of comprehension and intelligence, stimulated by some need in the practical sphere which cannot realize itself in action until first the doubts and obscurities and semblances which stand in the way are chased aside by the setting and resolution of a theoretical problem – an act of thought. It is the urgency of a need in the practical sphere that provides the origin for this, be it a moral need to know where one stands in order that inspiration, activity, the good life may spring forth, or a sheerly economic need to decide where advantage lies, or an aesthetic need to master the significance of a word, an allusion, a state of mind, in order to enter into full communion and enjoyment of a poetical work, or an intellectual need, such as the need to arrive at a solution of a scientific question by correcting and completing an inadequate and therefore perplexing view of its terms. What is called the knowledge of the "real situation" refers to the process of reality as it has hitherto developed, and is thus called historical. All the histories of all times and peoples originated in that manner, and here it is that histories still have their origin: in newly formed needs and the corresponding new obscurities which envelop them. We cannot understand the histories of other men and other times unless we can bring back to life in ourselves the needs which they arose to satisfy, nor will posterity be able on any other terms to understand our history. Often the historical quality of a book will for us be dead and inert, matter for mere literary appreciation or learned reference or entertainment. But then the new experiences which come to us, the new needs arising in us, of a sudden come into connexion and coincidence with those of other times, and bring them back to life, much as is said to happen to certain images of Christ and the Madonna, which allegedly exuded red blood when wounded by blasphemous and sinful words or deeds. All learning, all historical culture, in its specific elaboration and endeavour, relates to the general need for maintaining and promoting the civilization, the activity, of human society. Wherever that impulse is weak, historical culture is at a minimum, as we see with the peoples of the Orient. When there is a sudden rupture or suspension in the progression of a civilization, as in Europe in the early Middle Ages, historical writing dries up and coarsens along with the society to which it belongs.

II

THE TRUTH IN HISTORICAL WRITING

The practical need which underlies all historical judgement confers upon every history the character of "contemporary history", for however (even exceedingly) remote the facts contained in it may be in the chronological sense, the history is really always responsive to the present need, the present situation, into which those events convey their reverberations. Say, for example, that I stand between accepting or evading an act of expiation, and in order to make up my mind I collect my thoughts to understand what this institution or sentiment of expiation is, how it arose, was transformed, assumed a purely moral significance. In this process the scapegoat of the Jews, the various magic rites of primitive peoples are part of the drama being played out presently in my soul. If I directly or indirectly relate their history, I am relating the history of my own situation.

And as the present condition of my soul constitutes the material, so also it constitutes the document, the living and internal document, of the historical judgement. What historians commonly call documents, whether written or sculpted or drawn or held in gramophone records or indeed in natural objects such as bones or fossils, have no virtue as documents, and are not documents, save in so far as they rouse and stabilize in me the memory of states of mind that are in myself. In all other respects they are just ink, paint, paper, metal or shellac disks, and so on, without any psychic efficacy. If I have not in myself, at least dormant, the sentiment of Christian charity or of salvation by faith, or chivalric honour, or Jacobin radicalism, or reverence for old tradition, it will avail nothing for me to cast my eye on the pages of the Gospels or the Pauline epistles, the Carolingian epic or the speeches in the National Convention, the lyrics, dramas, or novels which expressed the homesickness of the nineteenth century for the Middle Ages. Man is a microcosm, not indeed in a naturalistic sense but in an historical sense. He is a compendium of universal history. And what investigators specially term "documents" may be recognized as playing but a small part in the total of documentation, when we think how we continually rely upon such documents as the language which we speak, familiar customs, semi-instinctive intuitions and reasonings, experiences which we have as it were taken into our very organism. Certainly, in default of the special "documents", some of our historical reconstructions would be more or much more difficult. But without these other and more general documents they would be wholly impossible, as we see when one of us emerges from a disease with loss of memory and change of nature, as though making his way as a novice and a stranger into the world where he formerly belonged. Here we may turn aside to remark that it was a half-perception of the truth that history is not given to us from outside but lives in ourselves, that helped to lead the philosophers of the Romantic age, like Fichte, into their mistaken theorizing as to a construction of history by means of sheer abstract logic, unaided by any documentation, though some of them, like Hegel, then contradicted themselves by imposing a synthesis from without, thus forcing the supposed *a priori* to join hands with a supposed *a posteriori* (the document) entering from the other side of the stage.

A practical need, and the state of mind expressing it, is then the necessary but merely crude material of historical writing. Now historical knowledge, by the mere fact of being knowledge, must be something other than a "reproduction" or "copy" of such a state of mind, if only because a useless duplication would be alien from the Spirit, which never creates uselessness. We can see now the vanity of the unrealizable programmes of some historical writers (their actual performances are something quite different) which promise the presentation of life as lived in its immediacy. On the contrary, historical writing has to rise above life as lived, in order to present it in the form of knowledge. At the utmost, these writers may be doing something other than what they profess. Believing themselves historians, they may tend to work up the raw passion of life into poetry. Now it is true that passional material always has to be more or less rapidly passed through the sphere of the poetic fancy (poetry, in the specific sense, being the result of a deliberate halt and sojourn in that sphere), yet none the less historical writing is not poetical but intellectual. Historical thought not only, like poetry, stamps universality upon the image, but it further links the image to the universal intellectually, in the distinguishing and unifying operations of the judgement.

Abstractly, the judgement is analysed into the two elements of subject and predicate, intuition and conceptual category, but concretely the two elements are a unity, in the indivisible truth of which the truth of history has its being. It is therefore mistaken, or at any rate a merely picturesque and logically inexact judgement, to diagnose the success or failure of a work of history as lying either in the perfection or imperfection of one element alone, or in the effectual or ineffectual combination of both – for example, in the liveliness or weakness of the image and the precision or imprecision of the criterion. For it is impossible that the image should be historically lively and the interpretative criterion mistaken, and equally impossible that the criterion should be strong and correct while the image is faded and dead. Uncertainty and confusion in either must also involve the other.

Books are, it is true, sometimes commended for the efficacy and truthfulness of their narrations of fact, while at the same time they are blamed for a deficiency in deeply meditated and firmly held directing ideas; or it may be complained that in them the categories of mind are confounded with general representations or classifications, the latter being brought in to qualify and explain the facts although they themselves are really groups of facts requiring qualification and explanation. But if that narration of fact had really been so efficaciously truthful as was said, it could not but have corrected the criterions and eliminated the false categories. Whenever it seems that in the same work excellent expositions of fact go together with mistaken concepts, a closer inspection will reveal that the book contains, juxtaposed or intertwined, two different histories informed by two different philosophies, one old and conventional, ill conceived and ill meditated, the other fresh and uninhibited, well conceived. When the book exhibits a clear and firm criterion, which is none the less abstract and one-sided, the resulting forced explanations will be matched by forced illustrations, resembling puppets pulled by a string or worked by a spring. The historical works of the "historical materialists" afford an example. The men whom those authors portray are as inhuman as their theory, which errs against the fullness and dignity of the spirit.

By contrast, in those historical expositions in which the criterions used do measure up to the facts to be interpreted, a single life circulates through the whole, and the images are as clear and persuasive as the concepts are limpid and convincing. Facts and theory dominate each other reciprocally.

The criticism of works of history properly consists in delivering judgement as to whether a given historical relation is full or empty, whether it harbours at its heart a practical need which brings it in touch with the seriousness of real life; and in discerning where, in the given work, the intellectual element is fused with the intuitive and where it is not, in other words where the historical judgement is operative and where it is not operative.

III

THE UNITY OF AN HISTORICAL COMPOSITION

It is the problem which is stated, and which in the act of state-ment is resolved, by the historical judgement, that confers unity on an historical composition. This unity is, then, of a wholly logical character. A problem can be and is linked with many other particular problems, but inasmuch as all of these are gathered together and unified in the single problem chosen for treatment, the logical unity persists.

The literary form in which the historical composition clothes itself, does, no doubt, find room also for a new and non-logical element, correlated to the practical need which has stimulated the historical thought, and in turn by this transformed and shapen into a direction or ideal of action. And this element, with its own bias, makes itself felt in the language, the "style". But this af-fective element, since it enters at a later stage, must, in order to preserve the unity, the literary unity, of tone, subordinate itself to the earlier element (in the way that particular problems have to be subordinated to general problems in a logical unity). Hence all agree in regarding it as literary bad taste when a work of history is penned in the style of a speech, sermon, satire, or other rhetorical composition, instead of observing a critical-expository tone such as can rise above and repress, yet at the same time embody and reveal the passionate and rhetorical element. Thus great historical compositions, if they are great literary works, express at one and the same time, not stridently and confusedly, but harmoniously and without confusion, both the mind and the temperament of their authors, both a strength of thought which nothing can distract from attention to the truth, and also the warmth of feeling.

The logical unity of an historical work is not exhibited by the many books described as "history" which have their unity not in a problem but in a thing, or rather in an image. Such are the histories of nations, peoples, lands, towns, lakes, seas, or of some single individual or group of individuals. (Of course these remarks do not apply when such images are merely used as titles for books in order to give an innocent indication or label notifying the scope of the book's contents. They do apply when the images really constitute the argument of the book.) The nature of their theme, if coherently pursued, precludes such books from being histories. They may be chronicles arranged in a pattern around the image, or they may, when the poetic spirit takes charge of the material, be poetry, with a reversion (and this may be a *felix culpa*) from history to the epic, which is sometimes said to be the womb of history. But if, as usually happens, they are not coherently developed, then such books will be a medley or ringing of the changes upon various themes, mixing historical thought with fantasy like Michelet's History of France (to quote a single and in its way notable example from among so many), in which the fanciful idolization of France as a physical, intellectual, and moral person with her own genius and mission in the world, able to be interrogated in her past and present for the purpose of shedding light upon her future, is undoubtedly varied and accompanied by keen and original historical judgements arising out of the moral and political problems to which Michelet unmistakably devoted a deep, noble, and lifelong attention.

The harm begins when such works are sought to be rendered coherent even while they maintain their incoherency, because then they do a worse offence to logic than was committed in the lyrical asides which we have been describing, when at all events they did not drag logic on to the floor and force her to dance and sing. But now we have to watch fruitless contortions executed in a vain endeavour to impose logical unity where there can be none, and executed this time not by poeticizing spirits failing to rank as single-minded cultivators of history, but by rhetorical and sophistical authors who hammer out the theoretical "concept" of France, Germany, Spain, England, Russia, Switzerland, Belgium – all these really being particular and transient things, and as such not concepts to be defined, but facts, matter of history, requiring themselves to be discerned and interpreted in the light of the eternal conceptual categories. No more needs to be said about this, for here in Italy we have quite recently been plagued by a shapeless dispute about "the unity of the history of Italy", in which Italy was handled as a material thing.

Bad as this is, there is a worse case still to be mentioned, namely when Things are interpreted as having a substantial existence, that is to say as having the sort of reality and value which lies solely in the actions performed by the spirit, its political and moral, scientific and artistic works – for of these, and not of the things which are mere abstractions and have no development, does history treat and conduct explorations. When Things are substantialized and the spirit, with clipped wings, is materially compounded in them, then of necessity they assume an equivocal air, offer themselves as media for all the morbid and the monstrous dregs of the lowest layers of human nature, for lust, the instinct of prey, violence, ferocity, cruelty, and in the wake of these contempt of life, accidie, desire of dissolution, everything which man, in rising to spiritual activity, presses and holds down with his foot, being here liberated, invited to expand, foully admired and cherished.

In our days, these morbid and monstrous histories of monstrous and morbid things can take the form of "nationalist" or "racial" histories when the theme is a group of such things, or of "biographies" (appropriately termed *vies romancées*, in recognition of their unhistorical character) when it is one single individual thing. Nationalistic histories are not to be confounded with those "national histories" which (when they are not true and genuine histories upon which the national label has been fixed for mere convenience) are found to be collections of information about some single people, chronicles of its life, books of edification and exhortation, or, maybe, poetry. They are on the contrary dark and stupid exaltations of something like the "Lombardic scent" (but it might equally well be "Germanic", "Aryan", "Semitic scent") which our Carlo Troya spoke of when discussing the Lombards in Italy: something which *bene olet* for the nostrils of some folk, and of which there is nothing further really to be said, yet it is celebrated as something altogether marvellous and unique, something between the bestial and the divine, object of a frantic passion and a mystical cult. Everyone knows what a mass of literature (and of what sort) all this gives rise to at the present time in Germany, and scarcely anywhere else.

Biography of the better sort will be found to come under one or other of the four definitory headings explained above. The recollections of the life of an individual rank as chronicle; reflections and exhortations, praise and blame, will rank as eloquence in the broad sense; a biography may really belong to the sphere of poetry; or finally, when an individual life is pondered and weighed exclusively in respect to the work which it has achieved or is performing (work which none the less cannot be exclusively ascribed to that individual, work which surpasses him), then in that case biography is in no way to be distinguished from any other sort of history, from which it will not even differ in its dominant literary tone. But the *vie romancée* cannot and will not be classed in any of these four orders. It is something quite different, moreover, from the good old historical novels in which an historical judgement used to be translated into the recital of imaginary events calculated to illustrate and popularize it. What the *vie romancée* sets out to do is to present the "essence" of a given individuality, not, for example, the poetry and thought of Dante but what we might call his "Dantehood", not the religious and political action of Luther, but "Lutherhood", not Napoleon in the history of the world, but the world shrunken and distorted to a "Napoleonity", and so forth. These extravagances we could well ignore, did not a pathological appetite for morbid complexities of the psyche, detached from the productive process in which alone they have a significance and bear a reference to truth, prized and admired in themselves, confer importance upon them. The more ingenious of such biographies receive nourishment from such impure sources, and thereby gain a certain originality, but most of them are absurdities.

IV

"NECESSITY" IN HISTORY

When judgement is brought to bear upon a fact, the fact is taken as it is and not as it might otherwise have been. As the old logicians put it, the judgement is ruled by the principle of identity and contradiction, and therefore affirms a logical necessity. This is all that is meant by "historical necessity", the notion of which has been viewed with so much suspicion and has even been the target for rebellious assaults, by those who supposed that historical necessity was a denial of human liberty, whereas in truth it only denies logical absurdity. This will be clearer if we recall that historical necessity has to be affirmed and continually reaffirmed in order to exclude from history the "conditional" which has no rightful place there; not, of course, the grammatical conditional, the "if" clause which can be used without a qualm, nor yet that "if" which is employed to elicit from an historical event a warning or counsel of general or abstract character, not properly belonging to history, as when we say that *if* in July 1914 the statesmen of Germany and other countries had controlled their nerves, then war would not have broken out. This sort of "if" is sometimes useful for underlining the importance of certain decisive acts, and stimulating a sense of responsibility. What is forbidden is not this, but the historical and logical, or rather anti-historical and illogical "if". Such an "if" arbitrarily divides the single course of history into necessary facts and accidental facts (it must do so, for if all facts were considered accidental, history would remain solidly one; for "All facts are accidental" would mean nothing different from "All facts are necessary"). Under the sign of this "if" one fact in a narrative is graded as necessary and another one as accidental, and the second is mentally eliminated in order to espy how the first would have developed along its own lines if it had not been disturbed by the second. This is a game which all of us in moments of distraction or idleness indulge in, when we muse on the way our life might have turned out if we had not met a certain person (as we did) or not committed a fault (which we did), cheerfully treating ourselves, in these meditations, as though we were the necessary and stable element, it simply not occurring to us, in this game, to provide for the transformation of this self of ours which is, at the moment of thinking, what it is, with all its experiences and regrets and fancies, just because we did meet that person and did commit that fault. For if we went on to such a full exploration of reality the game would soon be up. The popular scorn for "wisdom after the event" stands as a reproof against such daydreaming fallacies. When the attempt is made to play this sort of game on the field of history, where it is thoroughly out of place, the effect is too wearisome to be long maintained. It took a philosopher, a very abstract philosopher, Renouvier, to write a whole book (*Uchronie*) on the theme "le développement de la civilisation européenne tel qu'il n'a pas été, tel qu'il aurait pu être" in the conviction that the political victory of Christianity in the West was a contingent fact which might not have taken place had there but been a small but momentous difference in the course of events at the end of the reign of Marcus Aurelius and a variation in the fortunes of Commodus, Pertinax, and Albinus!

We must distinguish two other meanings which are also given to "historical necessity", and which stand for mistaken ideas, from this term as taken in the logical significance of which we have been speaking, and which is the characteristic of a thought that is conscious of its responsibility and will not run after distracting trifles. The first of these rejected meanings is that there is necessity in history because the preceding facts in the series entail the succeeding facts in a chain of cause and effect. We cannot too strongly stress this simple and fundamental, but for minds bewitched by naturalism and positivism still somewhat elusive truth: that the concept of cause (of course the "concept" and not the "word" which belongs to ordinary conversational usage) is and must remain alien from history, having been born in the realm of the natural sciences and having there its office. In practice, nobody has ever been able to recount any historical event by the balancing of effects with causes. At best it has been possible to make a display of "scientific" learning by clamping upon a recital constructed according to the different method proper to history the improper nomenclature of causality. The deterministic bent of mind may also reflect itself in a forlorn and pessimistic style of treatment such as is only natural when history, instead of appearing as the work of man, requiring to be carried forward and renewed in action, seems to descend upon him like a shower of dislodged stones tumbling from a mountain peak into a valley and crushing him as they fall.

The other mistaken meaning of historical necessity is sometimes equivocally introduced with the observation that there is a logic in history too – as if there could possibly not be a logic in history if mankind is logical and ponders history, as we have seen that he does do, logically. But "logic" in the observation in question means something quite other than logical quality: it means an alleged design or programme ruling the beginning, the development, and the end of history, the historian's task then being that of discovering this hidden master-pattern, this true and final explanation, behind the appearances of the facts. Often have the philosophers excogitated such a design, eliciting it from the concepts of the Idea or the Spirit, or, in just the same way, from that of Matter. But Idea, Spirit, or Matter were always just various disguises for the Transcendent God, who alone could conceive such a design and impose it upon mankind and see that it was carried out. It is always best to strip away the disguises and to consider this view of historical necessity primarily in its simplest and nudest form. Tommaso Campanella in his sonnets, with no intention of satire or mockery, wrote of the *comico fatal libro*, libretto of the comedy of fate, and of the "scenario", drawing these comparisons from the stage directions which he saw used by the theatrical directors of the players of the *Commedia dell'Arte*, for assigning the parts and controlling the performance. Abbé Galiani, for his part, drew his simile from the game played by the holder of marked dice, *dés pipés*. Once again we may say that history has never really been narrated according to such a prescription. Its advocates revealed their helplessness as to method by actually demanding that the enquiry should bring to light a pattern not contained in the evidence and the documents, which must therefore, absurdly, be discovered by some other means. In practice, at one moment they used the evidence as a symbol and at another moment as a superfluous adornment of that declaration of their political, religious, philosophic, or other beliefs, inclinations, hopes, fears, which they dignified with the description of history. The Transcendent God, just like causality, is alien to human history: if He were, history could not be, history being her own Dionysus of the Mysteries, her own "Christus Patiens" working for redemption from sin.

When we have eliminated the dual error as to necessity in history, we have also banished the derivatory concept of a foreknowledge of the future. Usually it was only the last act in a divine programme (the coming of Antichrist, the End of the World, the Last Judgement) that was revealed, but all else that stretched between the present and that last act stood written in the book of Providence, of which some page might from time to time be revealed to a pious soul. Similarly, in the system of causality, the chain of cause and effect stretched forward and calculation could arrive at its future links. In practice, the attempt to foresee was laid aside in the first case with a pious reference to the inscrutable divine will, in the second case with a confession of bewilderment at the gigantic complexity of the actors involved, (and here the faithful naturalist followed the example of Zola, the naturalistic novelist of the Rougon-Macquart family, who after tracing the family tree in all its branches and ramifications exemplifying the workings of the law of heredity, when he came to the place allotted to an unborn child could only mark it with the ironical and unanswerable question: "Quel sera-t-il?"). All the same, this urge, to know history in advance, remains habitual with many readers and its satisfaction is by many writers judged to be required by their dignity. The result is, as we have said, a procession of images lacking any substance save that of the personal fears and terrors, or hopes, of their authors.

The defenders of human liberty ought to offer a firm resistance to the lures of both the causal and the transcendent necessity, instead, as they so often do, of tilting against the logical necessity of historical thought, which is the very condition of liberty.

V

THE EXHAUSTIVE QUALITY OF HISTORICAL KNOWLEDGE

It is insufficient to say that history is historical judgement. We must go on to say that all judgement is historical judgement, is, in fact, history. Judgement being a relation of subject to predicate, the subject, that is to say the fact which in the given case is being judged, must always be a historical fact, a becoming, an evolving process, since immobile facts are not to be found or even conceived in the world of reality. Even the commonest perception, being an exercise of judgement (if it were not this it would not be perception, but mere blind and dumb sensation), must be historical judgement – as for example the perception that the object before my foot is a pebble which will not fly away like a sparrow at the sound of my step but must be pushed aside by my foot or stick, for in truth the pebble is an evolving process which resists the action of dissolving forces, or yields to them by slow stages, and my judgement relates to an aspect of the history of that process.

But we must press on still further and face up to the ulterior inference that historical judgement is not one order of knowledge but is knowledge itself, the form which totally occupies and fills the cognitive field, leaving room for no other.

All concrete knowledge must, in fact, share the nature of historical judgement in being inseparable from life, from action, that is, in being a suspended or expectant moment of this, answering the need, as we have said, for eliminating an obstacle encountered in some obscuration of that situation in which life, action, has to find its determinate and particular way of issue. Knowledge for the sake of knowledge not only lacks that sublime and aristocratic character which some impute to it (it is in fact typified by the silly pastimes of the idle, and by the silliness of all of us in idle moments), but is actually impossible, for where the practical stimulus fails there is neither matter for nor purpose in knowledge. The intellectuals who advocate the detachment of the artist or the thinker from the world around him, his deliberate withdrawal from "vulgar" practical disputes, unwittingly prescribe something that is not, as they believe, salutary, but mortal to the intellect. A paradisal existence, without work or travail or obstacles to be surmounted, would be an existence without thought, every incentive to thought having fallen away, and even without contemplation, for active and poetic contemplation contains in itself a world of practical struggles and affections.

It is not difficult to demonstrate that so-called natural science, together with its complement and instrument the mathematics, is based upon the practical necessities of living, and devoted to their satisfaction. This thesis was emphatically propounded by the great herald Francis Bacon on the threshold of modern times. But at what point in its process does natural science perform this useful office, thus becoming truly and properly knowledge? Certainly not while it is formulating abstractions, building up classes, establishing "laws", which is to say relations between classes, giving a mathematical shape to these laws, and so on. All those works may be called outworks, designed to protect knowledge that has already been won, or to help in winning more, but they are not cognitive acts. It is possible to possess on one's library shelves or stored in the memory all the lore of medicine, all the species and subspecies of disease with their symptoms, and yet, to quote Montaigne, to possess "bien Galien mais nullement le malade", and there is a like absence of any knowledge of history in one who possesses one or other of the innumerable universal histories, and has furnished his memory from it, an absence which persists until at a given moment under the stimulus of events that learning shakes off its stiff immobility and there emerges thought, thinking out a situation, political or otherwise. In just the same way the medical expert, until he reaches the point of confronting a patient and divining and understanding what is wrong with the patient, that particular patient, in the conditions peculiar to him at that juncture, will possess no knowledge, and when that moment comes he will know, not the abstract scheme of an illness, but the concrete and individual reality of the illness. The natural sciences have their starting point in individual cases which the mind does not yet understand or does not fully understand, and they perform the long and complicated process of their labours in order to bring back a trained mind to proximity with individual cases, and to leave it in direct communication with them so that it may form its own judgement.

The theory that all genuine knowledge is historical knowledge is not, then, in any true sense in contrast with natural science, for this, like history, does its work in the world, the humble world. The theory is in contrast with that philosophy, or, more accurately, that traditional idea of philosophy which has its eyes turned to heaven and thence obtains – or awaits – the supreme truth. This division of earth and heaven, this dualistic conception of a reality transcending reality, a metaphysical beyond the physical, this contemplation of the concept in isolation from the judgement, is what gives to such philosophy a character that is always the same no matter what be the term which it uses to designate the transcendent reality, God or Matter, Idea or Will, provided always that this be presumed to stand above or in contrast with an inferior or merely phenomenal reality.

But historical thought has played rather a cruel game with this respectable transcendent philosophy, just as it has done with its sister, transcendent religion, of which the philosophy is indeed the theological form or rationalization. It has *historicized* it, interpreting all its concepts, doctrines, disputations, and for that matter its despairing scepticisms as historical facts, historical affirmations, arising out of certain needs which are thereby in part satisfied but in part left unsatisfied. And thus justice has been done, and an honourable epitaph inscribed, as was justly due to a way of thought that had so long dominated and at the same time served the ends of human society.

It may be said that with this historical criticism of transcendent philosophy, death has come to philosophy itself viewed as an autonomous activity, for its pretension to autonomy was based upon its metaphysical character. What has taken its place is not another philosophy but History, or, in equally correct terms, philosophy as identified with history or history as identified with philosophy – Philosophy-History in fact, having as its principle the identity of the universal and the individual, of intellect and intuition, and rejecting as arbitrary or illegitimate any separation of the two elements which are really one. History has long been treated as the humblest form of knowledge, and philosophy as the most exalted, but now, by a singular inversion, history seems not only to get ahead but actually to chase philosophy right off the field. However, that "history" which was relegated to the lowest place was not really history, but chronicle or erudition, it worked from the outside, building upon evidence, whereas this history which has now been promoted to such high rank is historical thought, the single and integral form of knowledge. When the old metaphysical philosophy purposed to hold out a helping hand to history, to elevate it from its lowliness, the hand was really held out not to history but to chronicle. And since that philosophy's own metaphysical character forbade an attempt to elevate chronicle into true history, all that happened was the superimposition of a "philosophy of history", that is, as already described, a sort of forecast or pre-elaboration of a divine programme which it should be the business of "history" to copy as a draughtsman with more or less success copies a model. The "Philosophy of History" – in this just like the Myth – was the effect of a mental impotence, or, as Vico called it, "myopia of the mind".

No doubt among the various types of instructive literature there exists one consisting of productions which are considered to be philosophical without being historical, because they seem to revolve around abstract concepts purged of any intuitive element. But in reality, if such works are more than empty elaborations, if they contain full and concrete judgements, then the intuitive element must be present in them, though invisible to the crude inspection of those who will only recognize it when tricked out in the trappings of chronicle and learning. It must needs be present, because whatever philosophic formulas are propounded come in answer to the need for light upon particular historical conditions, and are in turn correspondingly rendered intelligible by these. In fact, to take an example very close at hand, the methodology which I am here propounding cannot be truly understood without a reference, which I usually leave merely implicit, to the political, moral, and intellectual conditions of our times, which they help to describe and to diagnose.

What, then, should become of the specialists or professors of philosophy whose function it seems to be to counterbalance the philologians or learned quasi-historians, offsetting the series of crude facts which these latter offer as history, with a series of abstract ideas? (Truly, this is to buttress one ignorance with another ignorance, a very useless proceeding.) The philosophers in question are the natural conservators of transcendent philosophy. Even when, verbally, they proclaim the unity of philosophy and history, in practice they deny it, or at the utmost they descend from time to time from their higher world in order to pronounce some faded generalization or historical falsehood. But as and when the sense of history grows sharper and the historical mode of thought becomes more widespread, then the historian-philologians will have to be invited on their side to confine themselves to the useful work of philology pure and simple, while the professional philosophers may be politely thanked and dismissed, on the grounds that philosophy has now discovered on the heights of historical composition the conditions of life and activity which they could not provide. Theirs was a philosophizing in the cold, unstimulated by passion and interests, lacking any particular cue from the occasion. But Goethe said that all genuine poetry is "occasional" poetry, and it is no less true that all serious historical composition and philosophy must be "occasional", the cue which thence arises for poetry being passional, while for history-philosophy it is moral and practical.

THE CATEGORIES OF HISTORY AND THE FORMS OF THE SPIRIT

The argument against transcendence has by some been carried beyond its rightful range, and has led them to deny the distinction between the categories of the judgement, and to regard these too as being a transcendence. The categories, it has been said, are all one with the judgement, and are enriched and changed in each single judgement, so that there are as many categories as there are judgements, that is, an infinite number.

But the distinction of the categories from each other has really nothing to do with a "transcendence" of these in respect of the judgement. It is, on the contrary, internal to the judgement itself, performed by the judgement as its self-actuation. It is imposs-ible to judge otherwise than by distinguishing. We distinguish *a* by its quality as distinct from the quality of *b*, that is to say, ac-cording to categories. It would be a strange sort of judgement which did not qualify the act *a* as an act of truth, the act *b* as an act of beauty, the act *c* as an act of political sagacity, the act *d* as an act of moral sacrifice, and so on, but instead of drawing such distinctions merely pointed to an intuition of *a*, *b*, *c* etc. as being severally different. This may adequately serve the needs of the fancy, but not those of the mind. And the categories do not change, even if by 'change' be understood 'enrichment', for they are themselves the operators of change. If the principle of change itself changed, there would be an end to motion. Not the eternal categories but our concepts of the categories are changed and enriched, as they come to absorb ever new mental experiences, with the result, for example, that our concept of the logical act is much more subtle and more elaborate than that of Socrates or Aristotle, and yet these concepts, the richer or the poorer, would not be concepts of the logical act were not the category of logic constant and discoverable in all of them.

Where the line of argument which we are now criticizing shows clearly that it has been pushed beyond its proper range, is in its incapacity to give an account of that impulse of truth which there must be, and which needs to be brought to the light, in the error of transcendentism, inasmuch as behind such errors there lurks always an impulse of truth. In this case it consisted in the motive of holding firm in the flux of reality the criterion of the spiritual values (good, true, just, etc.) each in its own character and in opposition to its own opposite (evil, false, unjust, etc.), and of protecting them against the confusions and negations to which the carelessness of sensebound men exposed them. The error of transcendentism consisted in the attempt to detach them from that flux and to locate them in a superior sphere, transcending reality, thereby providing for the logical problem a solution pertaining merely to the world of fancy. Yet as a protest against sensism and hedonism the motive was serviceable to intellectual and general spiritual health, and despite the error it has operated beneficially at various points in the history of ideas. It was beneficial, in the first place, when Socrates pitted against the Sophists his definitions and then those ideas which Plato transferred to a sphere above the skies. A recent instance is the recourse of the severe educationalist Herbart in Germany to a similar defence against the perversions of dialectic and of historical thought effected not so much (though somewhat) by Hegel himself as by the Hegelian school, perversions which seemed to undermine the seriousness of moral life by the extreme fluidity and flexibility of its concepts, and the seriousness of thought by its compromises and easy change of sides. Herbart's reaction, like all reactions, went too far: it separated concepts from representations, marking off their outlines so sharply as to enclose each in itself, without possibility of deduction or relation. Yet that distinction, though dearly bought at the price of a proclamation of the transcendence of values in respect of facts, was something better than the mixed pudding of representations and concepts, concepts pure and concepts empirical, which some now seek to reintroduce into philosophic thought, perhaps without clearly knowing what they are advocating, and without understanding the great loss which it would involve of the hardly – won results of philosophic criticism, which is always at once conservative and revolutionary.

Any rational coherence that there may seem to be in such demands results from the fact that the abstract unitary philosophy of which they are the expression does not really try out its propositions in the interpretation of particular facts, in particular, and precise judgements, in concrete thought, needful for relating the history of the various activities of mankind. If it did, they would quickly fall to pieces. The writers in question find it easier and more prudent, when positively obliged to utter some historical narration, to introduce surreptitiously the distinctions which they deny in their methodology, or else to use them, but to declare them merely empirical, much as the Moslem envoy of the Grand Sultan to Charles Bourbon's Court in Naples used to drink plenteous champagne at banquets while calling it, and insisting upon it being called (so I have read in a diplomatic document of that time) "lemonade". May I be forgiven this parallel which, however unbecoming to philosophic gravity, undoubtedly fits the case.

VII

DISTINCTION OF ACTION AND THOUGHT

Certain philosophers have strangely supposed that the interests of an integral and pure immanentism required (as though immanentism belonged properly to the Kingdom of Darkness) a general blowing out of the lights. No wonder that these have gone about combating and scoring imaginary victories over even that original and fundamental distinction which the common sense of humanity has always established and observed, and the schools of philosophy have always respected – the distinction between knowing and willing, between thought and action.

The argument rests on that basic sophism which consists in using one and the same term in two different acceptations, and, having proved a thesis in respect of one, in causing it to apply equally to the very different other one. Now there is a lesson which is the upshot of all modern philosophy, from Descartes to Vico,

Kant, Hegel, and the thinkers of the present day. It is, that thought is as active as action, and not just a copy or an impression of a reality thereby making itself known; so that the business of thought is to frame and to resolve problems, and not passively to receive portions of reality, thought being thus not something outside of life but a function of life. The sophism which we have denounced is this. Thought and will, it says, being both active, are indistinguishable, and the distinction drawn between them (such is the disingenuous allegation) is that same erroneous distinction which used to be drawn between the activity of the will and the passivity of thought. But this is a sophism, and as such is without validity. The ancient distinction between knowledge and will, thought and action, remains intact.

Yet while intact in substance this distinction is now notably corrected and deepened. Previously, it had been conceived in the light of a juxtaposition, parallelism, or divergence of two faculties of the soul, and it was customary to claim an absolute precedence for one or other, either for the faculty of knowing, or for the faculty of will and practical action. But in truth if without knowing there can be no *praxis*, no less is *praxis*, as we have already shown, necessary and indispensable for knowing. In the circular conception of the Spirit there is no call for a prior absolute and a posterior dependent upon this, for in the circle the first is always becoming last and the last first. In such circularity lies the true unity and identity of the spirit with itself, self-nourishing and self-advancing. This is the organic and speculative and dialectical unity, by contrast with the other sort of unity which can only be lifeless, mechanical, and mathematical.

Could this absurd and naive attempt to cancel the distinction between the two moments of the spirit succeed, the result would be simply to destroy thought and action. Thought, if identified with the will and its ends, would cease to be the creator of truth. It would develop a bias and bend towards falsehood. But will and action, if unillumined by the truth, would become mere passional and morbid agitation and convulsion. This does not happen, because it would be contrary to the nature of things and the life of the spirit, which is for ever resisting the wiles with which practical interests seek to cut across and deflect the logic of truth, and for ever labouring to convert passional blindness into enlightened will and action. For this reason there need be no fear that the order of things will collapse and the world come to an end.

But if there is no fear of that, yet we must not let ourselves presume that the theory which sets out to destroy the distinction (or rather the unity in distinction) of knowing and acting can be dismissed as idle academic chatter. On the contrary it is stimulated and greatly encouraged by the notorious distempers of our times, or those reaching a peak of virulence in our times. Look around and listen to the voices which ring loud in the intellectual and artistic, religious and political circles, indeed in every section of society today, and you will encounter everywhere exhibitions of indifference and irreverence for critical thought and truth, an activism strong indeed in its forceful impetuosity, but devoid of ideal light. If in some cases these voices issue in nothing more substantial than an inferior literature, in other cases one may observe how easily the proclaimers of the static identity of thought and action, after mortifying in themselves the keen vigilance of interior clarity and distinction, go on to assume in public life an attitude of sophism and rhetoric which suits their private ends. Thus are recruited the ranks of those "clercs" whose "trahison" a French writer some years ago felt moved to single out for denunciation. A bad theory and a bad conscience generate one another, support one another, and finally tumble over each other.

VIII

HISTORICAL COMPOSITION AS A LIBERATION FROM HISTORY

It might have been expected that social maladies like those described above, together with others more or less similar, would have been subjected to a careful and profound analysis, and that after determination of the origin and nature of the infection they would have been subjected to a cure, or at the very least placed in some sort of ideal isolation ward to prevent infection of the still uncontaminated. But instead of that, it is the custom to level accusations against historical thought or "Historicism", holding these responsible for disseminating the diseases by dint of "promoting fatalism, dissolving the absolute values, sanctifying the past, accepting the crude brutality of matter of fact, applauding violence, commanding quietism, withholding assent from the creative forces, thus weakening their impetus, blunting the sense of duty, inducing inertia and lazy compromises!". All these charges have their own names in the sphere of morality, names such as pusill-animity, failure of the will, lack of moral sense, idolization of the past, timid conservatism, cowardice veiling the conscience with consciously insincere pretexts such as the appeal to historical necessity in circumstances which call for resolution and action according to moral necessity, and so forth. Although one or other of these failings is indeed sometimes found in writers of histories, as in men of all sorts (we may mention Hegel, whose social conservatism and obsequiousness to the throne, be it considered a sin or a peccadillo, has gained celebrity from the mere fact of his greatness as a thinker and historian), yet this has nothing whatever to do with historical thought as such. On the contrary historical thought, if it enters into the matter, corrects such deviations.

We are products of the past and live immersed in a past which envelops us on every side. How can we advance towards new life, how create new activity, save by taking leave of the past, rising superior to it? But if we are enveloped in the past, if the past is, in fact, ourselves, then how can we rise superior to it? There is only one route, that of thought, which does not break the link with the past but grows upward out of it in an ideal growth, and converts it into knowledge. We must look the past in the face, or, discarding metaphors, we will say that we must reduce it to a mental problem and resolve it into a new proposition of truth which will form the ideal premiss for new action, new life. Such is our daily behaviour when, instead of folding up under the checks and blows that we have received, or blushing and pining over the faults we have committed, we examine what has happened, probe into its origin, follow the course of its history, and having made up our minds, then, following our intimate inspiration, we determine what we had best do or ought to do, and set about doing it with a good heart. That is how mankind always behaves in respect of its great and varied past. Goethe once said that the composition of histories is a way of unburdening ourselves of the past. Historical thought grasps the past to turn it to use, and transfigures it into its object, and thus the composition of history is our liberation from history.

But a strange mental obscuration may prevent us from seeing that history fulfils this cathartic office just like poetry, only that while poetry liberates us from passion, history liberates us from servitude to accomplished fact, the past. Still stranger is that intellectual bedazzlement which causes the thought that opens to us the gate of the prison in which without it we should remain incarcerated, to be mistaken for the gaoler. Historians, not to be confounded either with the monkish compilers of chronicles and *res gestae*, or with the scholarly collectors of narrations and documents who zealously extract from them the news of well-attested facts (nor yet with the half-baked compilers of school textbooks), have always been men of varied activity, predisposed to ponder over the situations that have arisen, in order to get the better of them and to help others to get the better of them by tackling new tasks. Such men were politicians who have written political histories, philosophers who have written histories of philosophy, artistic spirits bent upon attaining an appreciation of works of art through an understanding of the history of art, men of great civil and moral fervour who have turned sternly critical eyes upon the history of human civilization. Ages pregnant with reforms and changes are ages which give much attention to the past, both to that past from which they wish to cut loose, and to that past on to which they wish to re-attach their threads in order to continue the weaving of the web. Ages which are custom-bound, in their slowness and heaviness prefer fables and novels to histories, or indeed reduce history to the rank of a fable or novel. In the same way men who shut themselves up in a private circle of affections or of economic interests, ignore what has happened and is happening

in the wide world, recognizing no other history than the unventi-
lated history of their own circle.

IX

HISTORY AS PREMISS OF THE STRUGGLE OF VALUES

The opponents of historiography, or "anti-historicists" as they
dare to term themselves, not only blame history for protracting
the burdensomeness of the past by preserving its memory (whereas they themselves exalt the happiness of the peoples which have
had no past or have forgotten it), but they blame history still
more for merely, as they say, recounting the facts instead of passing judgement upon them as it should properly do.

It will seem extraordinary that such a charge can be levelled,
seeing that the affirmations of history are judgements *par excellence*, indeed the only sort of judgement whose existence is known.
For a book of history consists in a woven web of narrations and
judgements, it being impossible to narrate without distinguishing
qualities, judging, diagnosing one fact as being of a political,
another of a religious, yet another of an intellectual nature, and so
on. There is a well-known formula of Ranke: "Expound things as
they really happened." But Ranke either neglected to say, or
presumed it to be understood, that it is impossible to expound
things without qualifying them, and that is judging them, because,
following the basic principle of logic, the predicate of existence is
indissolubly united with the predicate of quality.[1]

What these people find fault with is not that history omits the
act of judgement, the one true judgement, the act of thought, but
that it omits to pronounce eulogies or condemnations in the name
of certain ideal ends which they desire to defend, to sustain, to
cause to triumph by hauling up before them, as though before a
court, men of the past, to answer for their actions and to receive
either a reward or a merited imputation of wickedness, vice,
foolishness, incapacity, or whatever it may be. In this connexion

1. See the demonstration in my *Logica*, Part I, Sec. 2, Chapter 5, and compare what I say about RANKE in *La Storia*, 3rd edn., Bari, 1939, pp. 75-92.

it is often forgotten that the existing courts of law, or of moral opinion, deal with things of the present, with men who are alive, active, and dangerous. There is no small difference. And the men of the past were already answerable to the courts of their own time, and cannot be acquitted or condemned twice. They are not answerable to any new court, because, as men of the past, who have entered into the past and are as such the objects, exclusively, of history, they are subject to no judgement except that which penetrates into the spirit of their work, and understands them. It understands them, but contrary to the saying *Tout comprendre c'est tout pardonner*, it does not at the same time pardon them because they have passed beyond the range of rigour or clemency as well as beyond that of blame or praise. By general agreement, those who while engaged in narrating history take pains to administer justice, pronouncing sentences or acquittals under the impression that such is the business of history (whose 'court' they suppose to be literally a court of justice), are considered to be lacking in the historical sense – and no less so though one of them should bear the name of Alessandro Manzoni. We cannot read such judgements without feeling mildly vexed at the incongruity and vanity of them, much as one would at seeing somebody beating up an immobile and inexpressive statue. "Caesar is guilty because he deprived Rome of freedom" is a condemnatory sentence which, however austerely or solemnly mouthed, can in no way affect Caesar and is meaningless for us who take our stand on the level of history, where the individual ceases to appear as one who must choose his own course of action, and appears instead as one who has executed the task which the course of events and his own internal calling assigned to him – and this is what it behoves us to understand. Caesar handcuffed and dragged before a pseudo-historical tribunal, branded as guilty and sentenced to a punishment which he must serve it is not quite clear where or how, leaves us altogether cold, whereas the mind is at once interested and stimulated if the historian, not passing sentence but just judging, explains how the passage was effected from Rome's restless republican oligarchy and civil wars and relaxed awareness of political liberty, to the Empire, which lasted for many centuries, and performed its own task and bequeathed it to the centuries to come, so that it still lives on in our thoughts and in a great part of our institutions.

Only the historical judgement which frees the spirit from the grip of the past and remains untouched and unspotted by party rivalries, attentive and alert against their force and their wiles and their traps, defending its own neutrality and limiting its own operation to the providing of light in answer to requests, only this judgement it is that renders possible the formation of a practical purpose, thereby opening the way to the processes of action, and so to the oppositions in which action is necessarily involved, the opposition of good to evil, of utility to the disadvantageous, beauty to ugliness, truth to falsehood, in a word value to disvalue. And in that field, where they rightly belong, we rightly hearken to the pronouncements of agreements and repudiations, praise and blame, utterances which are described as judgements but are not really judgements. They are not really judgements, and the need has accordingly been felt in philosophy to distinguish them from the true judgements in which the value of anything is identical with its existence, to distinguish them as "value judgements", in which things are assessed for what they are worth in their contrast with worthlessness. And it would truly be better to describe them simply as "expressions of feeling". Among such expressions there are those concerning the content of history, thanks to which the men and the deeds of the past are elevated to serve as symbols of what is loved or detested in the present, symbols of liberty or tyranny, noble virtue or egoism, sanctity or diabolic perfidy, strength or feebleness, high intelligence or stupidity – whence our love for Jesus and Socrates, our admiration for Alexander and Napoleon, our horror of Judas, hatred of Pope Alexander VI and Philip II, and alternating partisanship for Caesar and Pompey. These are wholly natural sentiments. Maybe they need to be toned down and subdued in our history books in the interest of good taste and logical unity, yet they must inevitably colour our language, and there is no call for blame when they reveal something of our nature which it was impossible for us to conceal. We need never blush on that account, unless the loves we reveal are sordid, the hatreds unworthy. For all that, these are not historical judgements, and still less are they the purpose of history, as the judicial school of historians, the Tacitean stylists, the emulators of the manner, but not of the mind, of Augustine, imagined. Necessary as they are in the sphere of action, and unfailingly present in the tones of every spoken or written incitement or self-incitement to action, yet they are at variance with the logic of historical composition, which cannot admit that either persons or deeds should be wholly pure, and rejects the enquiries in question as irrelevant and therefore insoluble. And indeed, what man possessed of any modesty can bear to hear himself or any action of his described as "good", without feeling forthwith a twinge of remorse, as if he would be guilty of an offence against the sanctity of truth if some protest or disclaimer did not spring to his lips?

What then is the reason of this useless yet apparently agreeable transposition of the "value judgements" from the field of the present, where they serve a purpose, to the representation of the past, where they not only get in the way, but distract attention from the object of enquiry? The answer may be found, perhaps, in that weak sort of vanity which, far removed from the perils and efforts of real contests, dissembles its own nature by delivering fierce verbal attacks against those who cannot rise out of their tombs to retort. Old-fashioned scribes, adulators of the powerful men of the day, were always ready and eager to sermonize severely against the personages of history, from the high chair of their own austere and incorruptible dignity as historians. (But if perchance those personages found champions among the living men of power, keen to uphold the reputation of the dead as a support for their own reputation, then the scribe quickly changed his note.) It is much to be wished that this old-fashioned sort of historical writer, so well suited to servile times, may not reappear in our present and, as we like to hope, not servile days. But a judicial school of historical writers is so much in demand that we must reckon upon strong favour for a resurrected "judicial" school: and indeed, the wish may be father to the deed.

X

HISTORY AS ACTION

Thus we pass from historical composition, which unburdens us of past life, to history as present life, new history. In this new sphere the categories, which went to form judgements, no longer act as the predicates of subjects, but act as forces promoting action. We here use action in the widest possible sense, to embrace action useful or moral, artistic or poetic, and any other sort of action that there may be, not excluding the action of composing philosophies, histories, or rather history-philosophy, which is at once the history of past thought and the assertion of present thought, new philosophy, which in due · course will itself become the object of historical narrations.

Such being the spheres of action, of human activity, to these there correspond the fundamental and original forms of historical composition; political or economic history; history of civilization, morals, or religion; history of art; history of thought or philosophy. Some uneasiness is often expressed as to this distinction of four forms of history, but the distinctions were not discovered or excogitated by a single philosopher, even if one philosopher has particularly concerned himself with improving the definition of the distinctions. On the contrary they were formed by the mind of mankind, which has never employed other distinctions than these, or something which could be subsumed or resolved into these, any more than it appears ever to have pronounced names of values other than the beautiful, the true, the useful, the good, and their transparent synonyms. Should anyone discover or wish to propose any others let him come forward with them. But quite apart from the authority of mankind – which may indeed be questioned, but not lightly questioned – there arises also this difficulty. It would not suffice to add another category or some other categories, as though the present four were a numerical series susceptible of being sporadically prolonged as such series are. No, the new categories would have to be worked in and

37

linked up by a new systematic and dialectical elaboration, and arranged in a new and invariable order of ideal succession (ideal, not in the sense of 'abstract' but in differentiation from the temporal or chronological order for which it is sometimes foolishly mistaken). To retort that the categories are innumerable and infinite just as the particular actions and judgements are innumerable and infinite is, as we have seen, not a philosophical solution but a mere renunciation of judgement, of thought, and also (since action must always be specifically qualitative) of action.

But in any case, no matter how many or of what sort these may be, all of these spheres of activity must be animated by the principle of liberty, synonymous with activity or spirituality, and by definition perpetually life-creating. A forced, mechanical, compulsory, or externally regulated creativity is something never seen or even conceived, in fact a senseless piece of phrasing.

Another synonym of this same activity is the perpetual enrichment and perpetual forward growth of spirituality out of itself, in such manner that nothing of the created is lost or becomes static – in a word, perpetual progress. Decadence is indeed a legitimate and current word when used in reference to certain sorts of ideals or achievements which are dear to us (though all too often its use serves simply to swell the tedious lamentations of those on whose mouth there is always a "pejor avis", a "nequior", or a "vitiosior"). But in the absolute sense, in history, there is no decadence which is not also a formation or preparation of new life, that is, progress.

The concept of progress has, however, often been called into question, mocked and scorned, and never more loudly than today. But the doubt, scorn, and mockery were really addressed not to the exalted spiritual law of progress, which satire and scepticism could never reach up to, but to certain comfortable illusions of comfort-loving and illusion-loving folk given to quietly floating on calm waters in preference to arduous navigation through winds and waves, given, that is to say, to imagining an "age of progress" due to continue, and to offer hospitality, for ever and ever, without interruption or disturbance – a reduction of eternal spiritual progress to the dimensions of a particular age, society, and way of living, which would materialize it and paralyse its movement. Progress in the true sense has nothing to do with the crude pursuit of pleasure and happiness, in fact it could equally well be viewed (did one so choose) as a progress towards ever deeper and more complex human suffering.

Another attitude, seemingly different from the foregoing but in truth amounting to much the same, is that of the people who in order to spare themselves and the human race the pains and losses incidental to conflict, seek ever to blunt the edges of disputes, to resolve them by way of compromise and mutual concession, to establish perpetual peace in this or that part of life, or in life as a whole. But men like Leo X and Luther are more vivid in history than such a man as Erasmus, whose idyllic ideal of abstention from theological quarrels, of reasonableness and simple goodness, came into good repute only a couple of centuries later, when the great theological struggles of his time had reached the limit of exhaustion, affording a breathing-space for humanity and tolerance, though in reality, on the soil well and advantageously worked by the religious disputants, new and not less vast and fierce struggles were ripening.

Certain transcendentist and religious views, which look upon history and the world as a condition of grief and pain, to be cured and changed only in another world, quite naturally and coherently deny progress, because they deny life itself. But the attempted amalgamation of the concept of progress with that of a final and paradisal condition, and of life considered as activity with life considered as staticity, or non-life, is an incoherent proceeding on the part of certain philosophical schools much under the influence of religious myth and theology. The most important and representative of countless such attempted combinations is that made in the philosophy which has outstandingly contributed to the historical view of reality, to the interpretation of life as a synthesis of opposites, and of 'being' as a 'becoming': the Hegelian philosophy. Contradicting and corrupting its own principles, this philosophy proceeds to describe the stages and the course of the

progress of thought up to a culminating point where becoming
ceases, giving way to the philosophy of the Idea beyond which
there is no passing. It describes similarly the course of religion
and of art, up to the point of their immersion in the same philosophy, where both obtain their quietus. And it traces universal
history up to a crowning conclusion in the Germanic world, 'the
world of full liberty', and in the Prussian State, regarded as the
highest and final political form. But the version most current in
our own times is that of historical materialism, the invention of
the post-Hegelian Karl Marx, who describes human history in its
progress from the slave economy of antiquity and the serf economy
of the Middle Ages up to the modern economy of capitalism or
wage-labour, all of these bound by the iron yoke of necessity
until, thanks to a new and dialectical progress signalized by the
negation of the negation, history is seen now to be on the brink
of entering into its final and perfect stage, a Communistic economy
which is to set up the reign of liberty on earth. The Hegelian
conception has not only been confuted by philosophic criticism,
but has been thoroughly exploded and discredited by the actual
course of history, which in the course of a century has overleaped
all the bounds that were set for it. The human mind has set itself
problems which Hegel never thought of, poetry has continued to
produce works of beauty, while the Prussian State has been unable
to stand up to the free states which it so much despised, and now
no longer exists, even as a sentimental aspiration, on the territory
of Prussia. The Marxist version, with its clumsy Economic Absolute
replacing the Hegelian Idea, and supposedly pulling the strings
of events, has been explicitly or implicitly confuted by the whole
of subsequent critical thought, economic, historical, and philosophical, while in the sphere of facts it is belied by the actual performances of the Communist system (and the more widespread
or general this becomes, the more resounding will be the *démenti*),
there being not a glimmer of the promised reign of liberty, but,
on the contrary, side by side with old and enduring tensions,
new tensions, and a violent compression of all the forms of intellectual and aesthetic, as well as political life, preparing the soil for

still other conflicts. The disappointment has been such that it has
been necessary to call to the rescue the illusion that what has not
yet been done will be done hereafter – whence the witty remark
that in Russia the verb is always conjugated in the future.

Very properly, then, the idea of a progress which somewhere
stops short at a point of satisfaction and happy attainment, has
been held to clash with that of the infinite progress of the infinite
spirit which perpetually generates and overcomes new contrasts.
But it will be well not to yield to the mistaken impression that the
latter progress signifies therefore either a continuous reduction of
men's accomplishments to futility, or a race painfully run towards
an unattainable goal. For if in this conception of progress everything passes away, everything is by the same token preserved. And
if mankind is inexhaustible, and has always a task in front of it,
and every accomplishment is followed by doubt and dissatisfaction
and the call for a new accomplishment, yet accomplishment, from
time to time, is really possessed and enjoyed, and what had seemed
be the anxious rush of life turns out to be in reality a succession of
resting-places, of satisfactions immanent in dissatisfaction, of fleeting moments which pause for the delight of the contemplator.
This is most clearly demonstrated by art and poetry, inexhaustibly
creative of ever new forms, creations which present themselves
in a bloom of strength and beauty like deities in some calm
Olympus. The historian, moved as he is by an impulse of attention
to the future even while with an artist's eye he surveys the past,
sees in this light the works of mankind in every field, at one and
the same time imperfect and perfect, transient and abiding.

XI

THE MORAL ACTIVITY

What is the end of moral activity? Let us suppose that the
theological doctrine that it is obedience to the commands imposed
personally by a God has been rejected, and let us further suppose
that the doctrine of the pessimists or life-deniers, who place it in
the mortification of the will to live, culminating in an ascetic

extinction, a lure to universal suicide, has been converted to its opposite: we may then say that the end of morality is the promotion of life. "Long live the creators of life" was Goethe's poetic invocation.

But life is promoted by all the forms of spiritual activity, with their respective works of truth, beauty, and practical utility. Thanks to them, reality is contemplated and comprehended, the earth is covered by the operations of agriculture and industry, families are bred, states are founded, wars fought, blood shed, victories won, and progress realized. What has morality to add to these accomplishments of the beautiful, the true, and the variously useful or advantageous? The answer may be "good works". But concretely good works will necessarily be works of beauty, or of truth, or of utility. Morality itself, in order to attain a self-realization in practice, converts itself into passion, will, and utility, becoming the philosopher's thought, the artist's fashioning, the farmer's or manual labourer's hard effort, or again, breeding of children, pursuit of politics and war, wielding of limbs and weapons. It will be said that into all such works morality injects an intention, namely the moral or non-utilitarian intention. But it is a vicious circle that we should seek to define morality by the intention and the intention by morality, and leaves our problem in an indeterminate condition which was, in fact, skilfully exploited by the Jesuits for the support of their highly immoral "direction of the intention". At the opposite extreme, the utilitarians have pointed to the absence of any external mark of identification upon "good" as opposed to merely "useful" works, as supporting their negation of an original character in morality, which they identify with utility.

Morality is simply the struggle against evil. Were there no evil there would be no call for morality. Evil is what continually threatens the unity of life, and therewith spiritual freedom, and the good is the continual restoration and safeguarding of that unity, and therewith of that freedom.

Good and evil, the struggle between them, the triumph of the good and the ensuing recovery of the antagonist ready to threaten new danger, these are not the effects of the irruption of some force extraneous to life, as portrayed in the mythological representations of a tempting and seducing demon. They are in life, or rather they are life itself, for life – to use the vocabulary of natural science – requires a specialization of functions inside the single organism, which may be expressed philosophically by saying that life perpetually displays distinction in its forms, and unification in the circle of those forms. Now just as in any organism there is a tendency to disorganization, health being that balancing of the unbalanced which dominates and contains the malady, so each special form is carried on by its own special character, its individuality, and the necessary impetus of its operations, towards totality, thrusting itself still forward when it ought to be withdrawing after accomplishing its own function. This thrust, this exuberance, would destroy the unity of the spirit, would indeed be self-destructive, did not the competition of the other forms, pressing forward each in its turn in the same manner, provide a rein and a brake. The question *why* the process runs its course in this way, or the notion that it might run in a different way, without struggle, without exhausting transitions, without perils, stoppages, deviations, and entanglements in evil, would have as little sense as the question why "yes" has "no" for a counterpart, or the notion of a pure and no-less yes, or a life that should not contain death and have to overcome death at every moment. Well, that action which keeps the single activities within their own bounds, stimulates them to perform their own function and that alone, impedes thereby the relapse of the spirit into disunity, and guarantees freedom, is the action which faces and fights evil in all its forms and grades, and is called moral activity.

This is the key to an understanding of the moral activity which on the one hand executes no task particular to itself and on the other hand attends to them all, ruling and tempering the work of the artist and the philosopher no less than that of the farmer, the manufacturer, the paterfamilias, politician, and soldier, respecting all these works in their autonomy and strengthening that autonomy by keeping each within its due bounds. How foolish, then, is the presumption of moralists who wish to moralize poetry, or the pursuit of knowledge, or the economic activity by interfering with their nature, when morality, on the contrary, moralizes them by giving each free scope to unfold that nature. For the same reason what the man of taste feels to be ugly, or the man of truth false, or the man of business to be inconsequent and therefore unprofitable and damaging, figures in their consciences as an evil for which they reproach themselves and feel remorse, so that the belief that theoretical errors and ugliness in art have their root in moral evil is philosophically profound.

It now also becomes clear why among the forms of historical composition one has always appeared as history *par excellence*, history of histories. For while histories of art, philosophy, and various sorts of economic activity have been considered special histories, the history of the State in its character as the ethical state of society, the rule of life, or the history of Civilization, which, being less narrowly political, less imperfectly mirrors the moral life, has been marked out as history true and proper, history as contrasted with mere histories. The various schools of "Philosophy of History" were on one side designed as attempts at this sort of moral history, which the present writer, coining an expression which has found favour and passed into common use, designated as "ethico-political history", a term itself conveying that morality is not identical with politics or utility, or with any of the other forms of human activity, but includes them all, and converts them, even while they pursue their own several ends, into ethical action.

Ethico-political history, then, does not stand above the other histories, or absorb them into itself, but penetrating all of them, receives from them its own concreteness (as for that matter each of the forms does from all the others). There is a solidarity in human life which forbids the thinker or the artist to cut the link which binds him to the other forms of activity by placing himself above or beyond them or in their stead, whereas it is from them that he draws vital draughts. Likewise the Saint may not move in a sphere removed from the cares of the world, otherwise his sanctity will become a luxury and will reveal the lineaments of egotism. That disdain which the artist sometimes shows for the concerns of men of action, and they for his concerns, or the gentle-hearted man for those who struggle fiercely on the political stage, indicates narrowness rather than superiority. It is at best a sort of occupational disease, a *morbus opificum*. This solidarity of life itself has as a consequence the solidarity of the various histories, each of which in turn emerges from the others and re-immerses itself in them.

XII

HISTORY AS THE HISTORY OF LIBERTY

That History is the History of Liberty is a famous saying of Hegel repeated by word of mouth and made known to all Europe by Cousin, Michelet, and other French writers. For Hegel and his listeners the meaning was that which we have already criticized, namely that history treats of the birth of liberty, its growth, its full-grownness and static continuance in that definitive stage, incapable of further developments ("the Orient, the classical world, the Germanic world – freedom for one, freedom for some, freedom for all"). The same expression is here repeated with a different purpose and content, not assigning to history the theme of the formation of a liberty which once was not and one day will be, but affirming that liberty is the eternal informer and the subject indeed of all history.

As such, liberty is on the one hand the explicatory principle of the course of history, and on the other hand it is the moral ideal of mankind.

In these days we are perpetually hearing in accents either of rejoicing, or of honest resignation, or of tearful despair that liberty has now taken wing from the world, that the ideal of liberty has set on the horizon of history, a sunset without the promise of a dawn. Those who speak and write and publish such things must be pardoned according to the manner of Jesus, "for they know not what they say". If they knew, if they reflected, they would see that to proclaim the death of liberty is to proclaim the death of life, the breaking of its mainspring. As to what ideal has been substituted or could be substituted for that of liberty, they would have great difficulty, if asked, in telling us; they would indeed, once and again, perceive that there is no other to equal it, none other to make the heart of man beat at the thought of being man, none which could better answer the law of life itself. For life is history, and needs an ideal to provide for the acceptance and honouring of liberty, and its enablement to produce works on an ever higher level.

Quite obviously, in offering such demonstrative propositions as a reply to the legions of those who think or at any rate speak otherwise, one is saying things which will occasion a smile or a quip at the expense of the philosopher who, like a man newly arrived from another planet, seems unaware of what reality is, blind and deaf to its hard features and voice and summonses. Not to linger unduly upon the contemporary collapse in many countries, and the growing disposition in many others for a collapse of those liberal ordinances which were the grand and seemingly imperishable achievement of the nineteenth century, is it not obvious that all history displays a mounting succession of oppressions, barbarian invasions, sackings, tyrannies both profane and ecclesiastical, national wars, civil wars, persecutions, exiles, executions, which are merely punctuated by brief spells of restless, unsure, and disorderly liberty, brief flashes of a happiness never much more than espied at a distance? In the light of this spectacle, to say that history is the history of liberty sounds either ironical or, if seriously meant, just foolish.

The office of philosophy is not, however, to let itself be shouted down by the version of reality conjured up by the afflicted or abandoned imagination, but, by chasing away such imaginings, to interpret reality. In such enquiries and elucidations philosophy, remembering how a man who enslaves another awakens the other's self-awareness and fits him for liberty, quietly accepts the alternation of epochs of greater and lesser liberty – the more established and unquestioned the liberal ordinances are, the more do they tend to become mere habit, with loss of vigilant self-awareness and resourcefulness for defence. Thus there will come one of the relapses described by Vico, the return of something thought to have been banished from the world once and for all, and this "recourse" will open the way for a new "course" in history. Such was the case with the democracies and republics of Greece in the fourth century and Rome in the first before Christ, when liberty survived in their institutional forms but not in the mind and custom of men, and then died out in the forms themselves. Thus does it happen that one who has failed to help himself or to respond to good advice is at last abandoned to learn a harsh lesson in the school of life. Or the philosopher will contemplate Italy, exhausted and undone, laid by barbarian hands, still decked in her imperial vesture, in the tomb, but then, as the poet says, rising to new life as the agile mariner of the Republics of the Adriatic and the Tyrrhenian. Or he will recall how the absolute monarchs quashed the liberties of barons and clergy, liberties that had become privileges, imposing upon all alike a rule exercised by their own officials with the backing of their own armies, thus preparing the way for a much wider and more effective participation of the peoples in political liberty. Or he will recall Napoleon, another destroyer of a liberty which retained no more than a name and an appearance. He annulled the name and the appearance as well, levelling the peoples under his sceptre, but leaving those same peoples hungry for liberty, better aware of what liberty is, and on the alert to erect free institutions as they did, soon afterwards, throughout Europe. But even in gloomier and heavier seasons, the philosopher perceives how liberty found a voice in the verses of poets and the pages of thinkers, as the proud and solitary inspiration of certain men resistant to the influence of the world around them, like that friend in seventeenth-century grand-ducal Siena, that "most liberal spirit" born in "dire prison" and abiding like a "sleeping lion" for whom Alfieri composed his dialogue of *Virtù sconosciuta*. In all times, the propitious as well as the adverse, Liberty is clear and strong and self-aware only in the minds of the few – the few, but it is they who alone have historical importance, just as it is only the few who really attend to the great philosophers, great poets, great men in whatever line of work, even though crowds acclaim them and deify them, ready to abandon them at any moment for other idols, other objects for their acclamations, their natural disposition to display adulation and servility under any flag and any motto. Taught, then, by experience and meditation, the philosopher will think and say to himself that if in times of liberal complexion one may have the pleasant illusion of belonging to a great company, and in illiberal times the opposite and disagreeable illusion of being almost or quite alone, the pessimistic illusion may well be as illusory as the optimistic. The conclusion of these and many other similar ponderings will be that history is not an idyll, but neither is it a "tragedy of horrors". It is a drama in which all the actors, all the members of the chorus, are, in the Aristotelian sense, "middling", guilty and guiltless, compounded of good and evil – and yet the directing thought of history is always the good, with the evil serving for a stimulus, and the work of history is the perpetual and in the long run ever successful effort of liberty to re-establish the social and political conditions for a more intense liberty. The quickest demonstration of the impossibility that liberty should live otherwise than in danger and as a combatant, is the horror which we feel of the immense and more than mortal tedium that would belong to a world of uncontrasted freedom, a world rid of all menaces and oppressions. We cannot bear to imagine it.

What then are we to say of the sufferings for the loss of liberty, the invocations, the disappointed hopes, the words of love and of fury uttered by men in certain junctures and ages of history? We have already indicated, in a similar connexion, what they are. They are not philosophic or historical truths, but neither are they errors or dreams. They are motions of the moral conscience, history in the making.

[1937]

VI

PROGRESS AS STATE OF MIND
AND PROGRESS AS PHILOSOPHIC CONCEPT

In present-day "topical talk" we often hear repudiations of faith in progress, backed up by mention of the civilizations which once led a splendid life and then perished, sometimes leaving no trace or scarcely a trace behind them. And concern is shown lest civilization is going to be found always running this course of ascent and descent, and signs are adduced to indicate a decadence already in course.

When such things are said with the air of an announcement or virtual discovery of a new truth, a thoughtful man may be left wondering at this air of wonderment, and asking the announcer what on earth were his thoughts when in time past he read in so many books the tale of the passing of empires, of destructions and losses of all sorts; the tale of how, on the tracks of the most refined and delicate civilizations, there reappeared and flourished the crudest wildness and savagery, the most fearful ferocity; the tale of the exceeding slowness with which men laboured to produce the conditions of their survival, and of the catastrophes which marked the great epochs of this planet. How indeed was it ever possible for men to imbibe from such lessons a faith in peaceful and even and irresistible progress, such as for a time they commonly cherished in their imaginations?

The present-day repudiation of faith in progress is, in fact, not a judgement that has matured in the serene temples of thought, but an aggrieved and angry reaction of men's feelings on observing the decline or weakening of an agreeable belief into which others, or we ourselves, had led our society, the belief that the world we lived in was firmly established, and that however things might change, or whatever contests might arise, there would anyway never be a return to the inferior conditions of other remote or recent times, and that nothing substantial or fundamental could possibly be lost, nor mankind in general depart from civilized feelings and practices which had now become second nature.

Now neither Graeco-Roman antiquity, nor the Middle Ages, nor yet in any large measure the first centuries of the modern age – the age which largely restored the culture of antiquity yet was aware of its own merits, and no longer bowed down by an exclusive reverence for the old – was subject to the illusion of which we are speaking. The first to do so was really the eighteenth century, the century of the shadow-dispersing enlightenment which believed itself destined to conduct mankind from that moment along the path of self-perfection, perfection, that is, of its rational being. But the revolution in France, which was at first greeted as the opening of a new and peaceful and reasonable social epoch, turned to tragedy, and the ensuing military dictatorship renewed the imperial idea with its attendant policy of *debellare superbos*, and accordingly, after this dual cycle had been watched and experienced, faith in progress was renewed in a less naive manner, it being now recognized that there must always be struggles among men, though at the same time the liberal system, with its discovery of methods for regulating and abating conflict so as to obviate the need for revolutions and wars, or anyway to render them less violent, gave grounds for confidence. The conception of "universal history" had crystallized. A new school of history, which although drawing its origins from romantic, sentimental, and backward-yearning inclinations yet attained a novel depth, filled in the gap that had been left between Antiquity and the Renaissance, recognizing a progressive character in the Middle Age, that age which was both new and ancient, both Christian and Roman, the formative age of the individual nations. Such was the basis for the theory of an assured progress, and for the faith felt in this. It was almost wholly forgotten that the so-called "universal history" which ran so continuous a course was essentially the European history of some centuries or tens of centuries, limited both spatially and temporally. Thus in the nineteenth century the great illusion arose and prevailed that the societies of mankind had now found their way on to the King's

Highway of history, and that with all this civilization history itself had become civilized. Colonial adventures and conquests were justified as aspects of a European civilization which had found this way of promoting world civilization.

Out of these dreams (as we are often told) mankind was rudely awakened by the pistol shots at Sarajevo in 1914, and by the ensuing rush of events which like unleashed furies, breaking their bounds, fell headlong on the world, exciting wars and revolutions, spectacles of horror surpassing those of the barbarous ages, because facilitated by civilization's technical achievements. Nor after three and a half decades do the Furies seem wearied. Nay, they promise far more powerful and wonderful spectacles in coming times. What wonder if a denial of faith in progress follows upon these events which have certainly taught no new lessons to those who had already meditated upon the soul and history of man, but have been a good *actio oratoria*, or object lesson, to drive them home into the mind of all those others who were resting in the fools' paradise which lasted on into the second decade of our century? The demonstration was a costly one, but it was certainly efficacious, indeed perhaps all too efficacious in replacing the almost frivolous sense of security by an equally extreme discomfort, distrust, and timidity, which in itself brings on or promotes the ills that are feared. The customary comparison with physical ailments, of which the doctor makes a diagnosis and indicates the inevitable course, is not altogether correct, for social and political evils leave much room for the goodwill of men, who can think out and adopt the means for coping with them, as well as for the action of great men who reveal themselves in the hour of disaster and stand out as leaders of the others in the cause of general safety. In any case, to defend one's own faith and to spend one's own forces for it is a manner of conquering in despite of death, for thereby the ideal is preserved intact and is handed on to new generations, new combatants. All of which is clear and obvious, but it was well to recall it as an antidote to the moral pessimism which often follows upon the fading of illusions. Pessimism is always noxious because it leads nowhere and seeks to derange the firm laws of life, life which is not a pastime but a labour, not pleasure-seeking but ethical.

Now if progress, in the sense here expounded, is simply a mental condition of satisfaction, faith, or hope in respect of the present or the future of the world or of the society to which one belongs, a pleasant but in the long run not a safe illusion; and if, further, every time that this has been translated into an historical law, as in the eighteenth-century *Essais sur le progrès* or the nineteenth-century Philosophies of History of idealist or positivist inspiration, it has been found fallacious both as a law and as a fact, how comes it that the concept of progress as a law of the spirit and of history constantly recurs? This happens because, in its modern, logical, and rigorous interpretation, progress is nothing other than the rhythm of the spirit itself, sole criterion for explaining and understanding history, sole possible and desirable orientation for the moral life. For what is the reality of the spirit and of history? It is a continuous unfolding and intertwining of acts which are the works that men accomplish, be they philosophical concepts, poetic creations, or deeds of practical utility, of beneficence, of religion, but in any case works and not feelings, commotions, enjoyments, or sufferings. The individual coincides perfectly with these works, so perfectly as to leave no remainder, for we cannot call the accompaniment of pleasure and pain, happiness and unhappiness, which is merely the reflection of effort, inseparable from effort, incapable in itself of serving as a lure or of providing a conclusion, we cannot call this a remainder. The only question put to the individual concerns what that individual did and stood for, not what pleasure or pain ensued. Now how does an act take place? In the first place a mind must receive into itself and reconstruct in thought the (historical) situation in which the individual comes to be placed; next, on the basis of this recognition, the individual work is introduced and produces change, innovation; and one's work is only serious, is only a work in the full sense, when it accomplishes that modification and innovation, thereby realizing a progress, and offering to oneself, one's contemporaries, and posterity a new and richer historical situation, on which they will work in their turn. Thus we enquire into the progress undergone by philosophical thought through the labours of Socrates, Plato, Aristotle, Vico, Kant, or Hegel, and through the bequest left by them not to inert and passive heirs, but to active heirs who will be co-operators, like themselves, in the reality which is the history of the world. And we ask ourselves what action was fulfilled by Pericles or Caesar, Saint Paul, Luther, or Calvin, or again what distinctive human note was sounded uniquely in the poems of Homer, Dante, or Shakespeare, or in the sculpture of Pheidias or of Michelangelo, and so forth. Antonio Labriola, when he had renounced the anti-historical attitude of Herbart, and taken up again with the orthodox historicism of the Hegelians, refurbished, however, by historical materialism, wrote that history is the "mistress of us men" and that "we are lived, as it were, by history", but this was an attribution to historical conditions of a prevalence or governance over the work of man, and his intrinsic liberty, in which alone progress is located and able to be understood. History is always the history of progressions, never of retrogressions, and herein lies its greatest efficacy, the maintenance of an awareness of everything that the human race has acquired, as premiss of new acquisitions. Retrogressions and decadences, though as already said they have a meaning for our feelings, as occasions of displeasure, are definitely out of place in history, because, for history, such times are seen to be engaged in efforts, experiments, and tests upon new stuff of life apt for new works, new progressions, which could not have been accomplished or even conceived without an interlude which in itself is not a subject of history but a lamentable or shameful entry in the chronicles. All men in their various modes are conjoined in the work of making history, and are responsible for history. What matters it if for a longer or shorter time some truth or institution or art that has once been thought, founded, expressed, lies neglected and ignored? They exist in the world, and in due course the conditions will occur for them to become efficacious. Their means of communication are not just those that are visible for any eager and resourceful observer, there are also hidden communications which alone explain the callings,

38

dispositions, capacities to which men are born. In a deeply inspired poetic epistle to his friend Gino Capponi the poet Tommaseo says that "our life is a seamless robe" so tightly woven that one thread cannot be extracted without ruining the whole, and continues: "In every moment of our lowly life, there lies some deep and infinite virtue, seed of immortal health: the good you do in secret hours may render happy and more noble some distant alien people, or the last descendant of a race to you unknown." Such is the universality of man, living in the universal spirit, and in the immortal spirit's truly immortal immortality. Can it be imagined that the heroes of old times survive only as described by Plutarch? No, they are at work as cosmic forces, generating new heroes in the mysterious "realm of the mothers". When, in the words of the poet, such men stood undismayed while ruin fell upon them, what was this undismay if not the tension of their moral will in the act of contributing to the world an imperishable force of which it is impossible to imagine the annihilation. (Reality, we well understand, changes and grows, but it cannot be annihilated.)

The progress which is achieved in work is the only joy worthy of man, an austere but reliable joy, fed not by imagination and illusion but by certainty and possession, not projected into a desired future but fully gathered and accomplished in the actual present, yet such that man may always renew it and in a certain sense make his enjoyment continuous by making his life a working life.

[1947]

HISTORY PREPARES ACTION WITHOUT DETERMINING IT

I⊤ must by now be clear that the relation between historiography and practical activity, historical knowledge and action, is that of a link, but not a causal or deterministic link. Action is preceded by an act of knowledge, solution of a particular theoretical difficulty, removal of a veil from the face of reality – and yet, as action, it springs exclusively from an original and personal inspiration of purely practical quality and aptitude. There is no way of arriving at this by means of a concept of "knowledge of what to do", for knowledge is always of things done, never of things to do. Such words in fact either mean nothing or else they designate something which is already not a knowing but a doing. For all its correspondence with the historical vision which precedes and conditions it, action is always clearly enough a new and different proceeding, which in due time will itself constitute the material for a new and different historical vision. We may say, then, that history stands to practical action as a preparation, but not as a determination.

We are reminded of the theory of poetry and art, in which a similar relation was found between aesthetic contemplation and practical action, it being made clear that art prepares the human soul by purifying it from passion, and refining it, but in no way determines it to proceed along any particular line, for if it did so it would be no longer (or not yet) art, or poetry, but the play of practical passion. Such a relation to practice is, then, not true simply of art, or simply of history, but equally of all the theoretical forms. To arrive at action, it is necessary first to leave the world of poetry, of fancy, for that of history, judgement, but then there is a further stage, lying beyond history, which, however, would not take the form that it does save for the preceding historical stage. Thus too the new poetry of a poet who has prepared himself by long study of earlier poetry has an altogether new and sometimes seemingly opposite appearance, and yet is linked to that earlier poetry, and without the preceding discipline would not be what it is.[1]

This disposes of the objection that because historical knowledge neither removes nor modifies the obligation that each one has of looking after his own interests by deciding, determining, and executing what it is his duty and advantage to do, therefore history is, from the practical point of view, useless. (From the same commonsense point of view poetry would also be "useless".) But it should be made quite clear that the above-described usefulness of history as a mental preparation for action has nothing whatever to do with what at first sight seems a thoroughly sensible and is certainly a widespread notion, namely that the purpose of historical knowledge of reality is to supply an exact description of the situation in which we stand in order to indicate in accordance with this what modes of action are suitable for protecting, reinforcing, correcting, and remedying that situation. In this picture the historian takes on an appearance like that of a doctor who diagnoses an organism and prescribes such a regime as may be expected to keep it in good order, or such medicines as may expel the elements of disease.

This would be all very well if the work of history in fact consisted in the maintenance of social equilibrium and the elimination of disturbances to the balance. But since, on the contrary, history is concerned with the perpetual creation of new life and the formation of new and ever different equilibria, the figure of the doctor is not at all an apt analogy. An actor on the stage of history must in every one of his acts illustrate both conservation and revolution, constancy and change, conservation being the necessary basis for revolution and constancy for change. Every politician worthy of the name embraces these two attitudes which are not parallel or co-ordinated but each subject to the other. There are no exceptions, not even such men as are commonly marked out as diametrical opponents, conservative and revolutionary, not even those who take the extremest and most combative attitudes. For what conservative does not seek to innovate in

1. See *La Poesia*, 5th edn. (Bari, 1946), IV, 1.

order to preserve the existing in a more secure way, that is, in a way different from that in time past, and what revolutionary does not seek to preserve institutions or specializations which are necessary for his work, or does not, as the work proceeds, try to ground it in institutions or specializations which he seeks to preserve? It is true that the division of labour and social specialization call into existence professionals or experts in the maintenance of equilibria, but such people, as is known, are not called politicians, but administrators, or technicians, to use a term applied to those who watch over and adjust machines of whatever sort it may be, economic machines, social, national, or physiological machines, in which last case they receive the name of doctors. The substitution of technicians for politicians, in fact as well as in argument, the crucial importance often given to these "experts" in matters which really require the insight, resolution, and daring of politicians, and the inevitable effect of this confusion shown in the schematic character of the measures taken, the dangerous delays, the drift of affairs, have often been marked as signs of a reduced mental and political vitality in the nations of today.

The most helpful example of a man in whom we may study this attitude as of a technician or medical man towards historical reality, with the consequence of a one-sided and fallacious historical vision and an inability to reach practical decisions, is afforded by Taine, in regard to whom we have also the advantage of the widespread celebrity of his work as a philosopher, man of letters, historian, and dispenser of high political counsels grounded upon history. For Taine's is an example that everyone remembers.

Now that the cloud of admiration in which his own age enveloped that supposedly original and deep and vigorous thinker has dispersed, it is perhaps time to perceive clearly that he did not advance the critical method in a single one of the various studies into which he launched. He neither reinforced any previously discovered truth, nor discovered any new one. He sowed no new seeds. Instead he put many paradoxes and contradictions into circulation. It is mournful, it is distressing, to have to reach this conclusion in view of Taine's noble character and earnest labours.

It is much like the judgement that we sometimes have to pass on the copious and elaborate output of estimable men who dedicated themselves to art and poetry, without getting art and poetry to bestow any favour on them, for all the great show of originality that they put up. Taine was never blessed in his work by the refreshing winds of truth, he was driven forward by the tyranny of an idol which he called "Science", and which to his eyes took on the semblance of the medical man, more especially of the alienist and the specialist in women's diseases charged with attendance upon the hysterical and deranged patients of the Salpêtrière (which Taine himself had frequented). The whole world, in fact, took on for him the appearance of a sort of Salpêtrière, and humanity that of a *fou* or *malade*, in whom sanity could occur only by accident, or a *gorille féroce et lubrique* whom civilization cannot educate intimately, but only tames and weakens. Taine wrote about philosophy, and rapidly, with the air of one flicking away a fly, got rid of Kant and the a priori synthesis, that is to say, of the spirit of modern philosophy. He read Hegel and proclaimed himself a Hegelian, without suspecting that Hegel was a Kantian who had carried Kant further, and that the Hegelian idea was a more developed form of the a priori synthesis and of the dialectic contained therein. Therefore what Taine liked in Hegel was the external shell, and he amalgamated Hegel with Condillac. Perception was for him an *"hallucination vraie"* which accidentally finds a counterpart in an external reality. He figured that he would apply the experimental method to philosophy; while to history, which, he considered, had barely begun to rest upon solid foundations (thanks to his own work,[1] he proposed applying the classificatory methods of the natural sciences. As such an application was in practice impossible despite all his efforts, which like all similar efforts past or to come were doomed to vanity, all that he could do was to introduce into the problems of philosophy and history a metaphysical and naturalistic premiss. He drew fantastic pictures of an "historical reality" determined by geographical and

---

1. *Correspond.*, IV, 130.

racial conditions, circumstances, and moments, and by *facultés maîtresses* and other mythological entities. Why this historical reality should move and change instead of staying fixed and firm was not explained. In short, a tangle of logical errors in which Taine lingered contentedly untravailed by self-criticism. At the beginning of his career he was a critic and historian of art and poetry, but he pinned these down in series of classifications appropriate to the natural sciences, identifying poetry and art, in their history, with the practical sentiments and their realization, and setting himself, in his *Histoire de la littérature anglaise*, the task of arriving at a *définition générale de l'esprit anglais*. Practical and ethical life, too, he converted into a series of psychological, or more often physiological and pathological schemes. A French critic said of him that for all his literary history he had never understood what a verse was, and in truth he had no inkling as to the poetical quality of a poem. He was much respected in the universities, and admired by the journalists who repeated but did not understand his formulae, but by his absurd pronouncements on art he pricked such an artist as Henri Becque into rebellion and irreverence. Taine really belongs not to the history of thought, philosophy, criticism, historiography, but to that of cultural movements and fashions. He is an outstanding representative of the craze for the natural sciences and specially for medicine which for fully forty years engaged the life of Europe in futile attempts to remodel the whole of culture on a naturalistic pattern. The aspiration for an "experimental" philosophy, a historiography reduced to the level of botany and zoology, has as counterpart the equally absurd notion entertained by Émile Zola of "the experimental novel". The two men, the two minds were of the same order, powerful like great machines, but machine-like also in their intricacy and monotonous rhythm, lacking altogether a delicate touch or an effortless abandon.

Like Renan and other French writers Taine was recalled by the disasters of 1870-71 to his responsibilities and duties as a citizen. But his historical and political notions were too peculiar to admit of him performing any really useful service to his country. The famous preface of 1875 to his *Origines de la France contemporaine* deserves to remain famous, but only as a naive confession of political ineptitude. In it he recalled that as a twenty-one-year-old voter in 1849 it was his business to register a vote for some list of fifteen or twenty deputies, and to make a choice among the most varied political doctrines, republican and monarchical, democratic and conservative, Socialist and Bonapartist. How should he set about it? The motive that was good enough for others was not good enough for him. He wanted to vote according to conscience, not according to preference (much as though one should decide to take a wife in disregard of inclination and preference, basing oneself on knowledge, which would certainly get one nowhere on the way towards marriage). And he observed, rather scandalized, but with interest and surprise, how his fellow-citizens, disregarding his inhibition, his loud and seemingly forceful preliminary objection, calmly went off and voted. Yet he had made clear to them that *dix millions d'ignorances ne font pas un savoir*. But the mistake was his, and not of those who went off to vote according to their preferences, for those preferences were desires, impulses, needs, yes, and imaginations, illusions, from all of which the web of human actions is spun, the story of mankind composed, and from which issue the new forms of life, and those errors which are fruitful. Whereas from Taine's abstractions nothing came forth, and his practical resolution, left in a voluntary suspense awaiting the pronouncement of science, was doomed to remain suspended for ever, science being unable to answer a question which is not a scientific problem but a summons to practical resolution.

With his habitual want of self-criticism Taine never paused to criticize the question which he had put to himself. Starting from dogmatic assumptions he spun out the web of his arguments to the culminating conclusion that the social and political form in which any people may *entrer et rester* is determined by its character and its past and ought therefore to be shaped *jusque dans ses moindres traits, aux traits vivants auxquels on l'applique*, and that therefore in order to be able to choose a constitution appropriate for France, it is first necessary to know the reality of contemporary

France, and accordingly, since the present is the consequence of past history, to trace the process of its formation. And this, to be scientific, was a research to be conducted *en naturaliste* with the same perfect objectivity and indifference as *devant les metamorphoses d'un insecte* – the very opposite, evidently, of the method followed by genuine historians who, by participating and taking sides in history in the making, acquire by this very passion the mental strength to dominate the first passion in order to understand history, and even when they attain understanding, continue passionately to participate. The historical enquiry which Taine proposed to carry out was an empty one, empty like the purpose which he assigned to the ideal politician of his imaginings: *diminuer ou du moins ne pas augmenter la somme totale, actuelle et future de la souffrance humaine,*[1] as though suffering were a body susceptible of quantitative measurement and not something which men are always ready to face in whatever form for the sake of an enterprise of love. Taine endeavoured to make good this emptiness by the fulfilment of long labours calculated to produce their effect in a distant future. The book he worked at with the design of prescribing a remedy for the malady of France was to have the character of a *consultation de médecins,* and he foretold that the patient would take a long time about accepting the doctors' advice, and even then would sometimes behave unwisely and incur relapses. But first of all the doctors would have to come to an agreement, which, however, they are sure to do since the moral sciences have now abandoned the a priori method. For, in future, political ideas, endorsed by the united Academies of Moral Sciences and of Inscriptions, will filter down through the universities and the

1. See a letter to Lemaître in *Correspond.*, IV, 236. Taine's disciple Paul Bourget, as was lately recalled by his successor in the Académie Française, when envisaging the contemporary condition of France, also "se considérait comme un médecin qui étudie un corps de malade et qui veut établir d'abord un diagnostique perspicace. Si le corps avait été bien portant, il n'aurait pas eu besoin de s'occuper de lui, mais, devant les maux qui assaillent de toutes parts ce grand individu social, tourmenté par la fièvre et ne sachant où trouver le repos, il s'efforçait désespérément de remonter aux sources des souffrances et de leur chercher un remède."

thoughtful public just as the theory of electricity descends from the Academy of Sciences. Maybe in a century the approved political ideas will penetrate the Parliament and the Government, and politics will be as scientific as surgery and medicine.[1]

Taine's history of the old regime, the Revolution, and the Empire is accordingly the story of a malady, namely of the *esprit classique* of the rationalistic age, the Enlightenment. We need not now resort to a critical exposition in order to demonstrate that if rationalism (which is one of the imperishable forms and necessary forces of the human spirit, and, in another context, is the description of a highly vigorous and successful era in the life of Europe) is to be treated as a malady, there can be no right understanding of the history of civilization in its unfolding, the histories of the centuries before and of the century after the eighteenth. Taine's interpretation of the French Revolution has been too often criticized already. All that is necessary here is to inspect the practical consequences that he arrived at after his long and laborious enquiry into the relevant historical documents.

Some notion is given in the editor's preface to the last volume of the uncompleted work. Very naturally, Taine's way of conceiving the relation between theory and practice, history and politics, aroused expectations of practical proposals from his pen. It seemed (as with the analogous case of Ranke in Germany) that the country could turn to him for advice on this or that situation, this or that project of reform. But poor Taine evaded such requests and insistences, with a modesty that was commendable, but which put the "Science" for which he had made unsubstantiated claims of efficacy in rather a poor light. "*Je ne suis qu'un médecin consultant*", he used to protest. "*Sur cette question spéciale je n'ai pas de détails suffisants; je ne suis pas assez au courant des circonstances qui varient au jour le jour.*" Recognizing that there was no general principle from which to deduce a series of reforms, he limited himself to advising against resort to simple solutions: one should, he said, feel one's way, adapt oneself, accept the irregular and the incomplete.[2] This was no

1. See a letter of 1848 in *Correspond.*, IV, 45-46.
2. See vol. VI, pp. XIII-XIV.

doubt prudent counsel, but it was either too generic to be useful or else was particular and unilateral to the point of indicating preference for one method and one party against the other method and the other party, in fact one of those *préférences* which he had set out to avoid as being illicit and dangerous. It was, in fact, a confession of bankruptcy on the part of the medical and pharmaceutical view of history and politics of which Taine had been the spokesman and the vainly strenuous champion.

[1938]

VIII

THE OLD AND THE MODERN IDEA
OF PHILOSOPHY

The relation of identity which has now been established between philosophy and the historian's work modifies the common notion of the former far more radically than of the latter.

After history has clearly distinguished its character from that of anecdotal writing, and has further asserted itself as the product not of feeling and fancy but of thought, it still allows the anecdotic art to perform its useful and necessary function in its own field. But philosophy, after identifying itself with historical composition, historical thought, wholly rules out and annuls the notion of a philosophy outside or above history. Having become, in fact, the conscience of history it can no more be separated from it than the moral conscience can be separated from moral action or the aesthetic conscience from artistic creation or, as the textbooks put it, taste from genius. Even after such a definition has been given of philosophy as my own ("the methodology of historical composition") it needs still to be recalled that the methodology would be abstract if it did not coincide with the interpretation of the facts, did not continually renew itself and find its development in line with the understanding of them. The differentiation between philosophy and history thus remains merely a practical or scholastic convenience. No philosophical problem can be resolved unless it is propounded and developed with reference to the facts which occasioned its arising. Without an understanding of them it cannot itself be understood, but remains abstract, giving occasion for those insoluble and interminable disputes which occur so frequently among the philosophic schoolmen as to appear to be the element in which they naturally have their being, carrying them idly and vainly up and down, hither and thither, in a perpetual motion which, however, always leaves them exactly where they were. If philosophy has been the target for a particular sort of mockery such as has never invested mathematics, or physics, or other natural sciences, or even history, there must be a reason for this, and the reason is just what we have said. To historicize philosophy, if we do it seriously, means to make philosophy respected and, if you will, feared.

The notion of a philosophy above and outside history is often disguised as a distinction between "supreme", "universal", "eternal", "major" problems of thought, and "minor", "inferior", "particular", "contingent" problems, albeit the former set of problems appears now under a different guise, no longer as concerning God and immortality etc., but as concerning the relation between knowing and being, problems of gnoseology and phenomenology. And different also, at different times, is the relation presumed to lie between the former and the latter, these being at one time considered as empirical, non-philosophical, and at another as insoluble save for a prior and underlying resolution of the former. If sometimes, in these disputes, there is a flash of truth, this either means that good sense refuses to be ignored, and raises its voice, or that almost unconsciously the debate finds a real meaning and a possibility of solution for its problem in the particulars of history.

Something similar happens in regard to the so-called inferior, particular, and contingent problems which, if no philosophic light comes to shine upon them, or if they are left to await one final illumination from philosophy at a culminating moment which never gets any nearer, lose their outlines, fall into confusion, and become matter for all kinds of arbitrary solution based on mere feeling and imagination, until somebody decides to help things out by some philosophic reasoning which may be rather less grandiloquent than that of the "sublime" philosophers, but will be serious and critical and therefore not sterile. This is how there arise various special theories in the different fields of history, theories which often have a much greater speculative value than those of the scholastic and insipid "sublime" philosophy. It behoves us to encourage a double and convergent change of mind, whereby the specialists may raise themselves to the level of philosophy, while the generic philosophers may shake loose of the "major" problems sufficiently to cope with those "minor" problems in which the major have their being and sole possibility of being tracked down and solved. But it will be best not to indulge in extravagant hopes, for what is needful is the discovery of the virtuous mean, that point of excellence which, as Aristotle knew, is the highest and hardest to attain. In other words the philosopher-historian and the historian-philosopher will ever be a rarity, a restricted aristocracy.

A deplorable consequence of regarding philosophy as standing outside and above history and dedicated solely to the "supreme" problems, is that those who deal in these last claim to exercise a function as directors and reformers of society and the State. Historical philosophy, or philosophical history, is modest, because it is for ever leading men to face up to reality, and then, after causing them to accomplish a catharsis in the truth, leaving them free to seek and to find their duty and to act accordingly. But the other kind of philosophy is emboldened by the memory of its theological and ecclesiastical origin, or perhaps simply puts on an air of boldness in performing exaggerated evolutions in the void from which it is always vainly struggling to emerge. The practical courses which it enjoins may be noble, or nobly intentioned, or ignoble, as when Auguste Comte bids his followers to *réorganiser la société*, or Karl Marx bids his to revolutionize and to rationalize social life, or yet other thinkers counsel the use of philosophic method to hold the peoples in servitude. The incongruity does not vary with the quality of the aims. It may be that great minds, the authors of new philosophical conceptions, have sometimes usurped a function which did not properly belong to them, deducing arbitrary programmes from their abstract philosophy, but if so that is the dead and perished part of their work.

With the resolution of philosophy into history (whether this be regarded as a fact or as an aspiration) it may be said that "philosophy is dead". But speaking more rightly, since that which appears to be overtaken by death is something that was never really alive, let us say that it is an old, outdated idea of philosophy that is dying, and yielding its place to a new idea sprung from the deepest thought of the modern world. We mean of course that it is dying ideally, for materially it will continue to drag out an existence like so much else that is ideally superannuated, and will serve to maintain on the stage of the world in the humble status of one among the many crafts, a craft of philosophy. But in its true essence philosophy can no more than poetry be a mere craft.

[1938]

IX

THE HISTORICISM OF HEGEL
AND THE NEW HISTORICISM

Hegel's merits as the thinker who imparted an historical character to philosophy and a vigorous impulse to the historical studies which attained such a pre-eminence of honour in the nineteenth century are outstanding. On the other hand he and his school have been regarded with great suspicion by the historians, who have charged them with forced, arbitrary, and unilateral proceedings. The two judgements upon Hegel, seemingly contradictory, are both justified, and can both be embraced by a single mind, if it is ready to ponder, sift, and conciliate them.

The deep historical significance of the Hegelian philosophy lies in the dialectic which sweeps away all the abstract distinctions and oppositions of classificatory logic, which when transported out of conversational language or the language of the natural sciences (or of naturalistically designed textbooks of the moral sciences) into the field of historical thought, turn out to be specially fitted to prevent an understanding and to involve the mind in insoluble enigmas. Under the application of such discriminations as those between Being and Appearance, Substance and Accident, Ideal and Real, Rational and Irrational, Positive and Negative, Good and Evil, Something and Nothing, and so forth, History either has the air of being abandoned to the caprices of the irrational because the rational is not of this world, or the air of a mixture of rationality and irrationality, a succession of sporadic facts, resistant in its very nature to the operations of thought. It is the Dialectic that re-establishes concreteness in place of abstractness. For on the one hand it reunites what the abstract or scientific intellect divided for its own ends, and on the other hand it turns the negative into the inmost spring of Becoming, of progress, which proceeds by the steps of thesis, antithesis, and new thesis, or synthesis. Thereby it deepens and defines in a previously unknown manner that concept of development which is the central concept of History.

This is a logical principle or "discovery" to be placed alongside of the other great discovery or principle enunciated a century earlier by Vico, when in opposition to Descartes and the mathematicizing and anti-historical early Rationalism of his times, he pronounced that one knows only that which one does: accordingly men, in that they make their own history, have of it an intrinsic and real knowledge, different from the knowledge of the mathematician who knows only those fictions which he himself makes for his own use. Hegel was not informed about Vico's principle, and showed no cognizance of it, though it is really the necessary premiss for viewing historical development as susceptible of understanding.

If we subject to enquiry those rigorous rules of method which Hegel enunciates in the course of his historical writings, we shall see that they all lead back to the dialectical concept of method. Thus in his history of philosophy he rejects the method practised by Brucker and the rest, of addressing to the philosophers of the past questions such as they could not possibly answer, being not fixed and eternal questions, but questions conditioned by the circumstances of later and more complex ages with previously unknown spiritual needs. Similarly he refused to try and translate, explain, or justify popular religious beliefs in terms of the concepts of free thought,[1] or to introduce into the interpretation of history "influences" or even "reciprocal action", while he insisted, on the contrary, on the unity of the spirit which is entirely present in each of the various forms of any one age.[2] Then again, he insistently recalled that there are no "dead philosophies" but only dead philosophers, dead as mortal men, and that whatever has once been thought is eternal and not a transient something, and that events are not only committed to the sanctuary of memory but are present and alive as when they were brought about, and constitute the very essence of the spirit, and so on.[3] We might say that for

1. *System und Geschichte der Philosophie*, ed. Hoffmeister (Leipzig, Meiner, 1940), pp. 62-73.
2. Op. cit., pp. 141-48.
3. Op. cit., pp. 70-71.

39

him dialectic was not simply theory but something which he lived out in the unity of his mental and practical life, showing a steady interest in contemporary happenings which is rare among the major as well as among the common or garden philosophers, who usually shelter themselves with *fuge rumores* for their motto. Hence the depth and truthfulness, the ever challenging and thought-stimulating character of his interpretations of philosophical, religious, artistic, political and moral history.

There is, however, another aspect of Hegel's work which justifies the dissatisfaction and disapproval of the historians. Hegel was incapable of working out to its conclusion his dialectical principle. Had he done so, along rigorously critical lines, it must needs have brought him to the position of an absolute immanentism, an absolute humanism and historicism. But Hegel was strongly committed both to the patterns of ancient and especially of the neo-Platonic philosophy, and also to those religious and theological traditions which Lutheranism and Protestantism (supported, in this field, throughout the seventeenth century by the lingering scholastic and metaphysical schools of Spain)[1] had preserved and cultivated in the German universities. These patterns and traditions had been more than a match for the rationalism of the Enlightenment, incapable of deep critical thought and for that matter itself positing a sort of intellectualistic transcendence in the enlightening and supra-historical *Raison*.[2] The forces of the new dialectic were too young and immature to get the better of that transcendentist and theological inclination. They sufficed

1. On the recent researches on this forgotten strand of German philosophy see ESCHWEILER: *Die Philosophie der spanischen Spätscholastik auf den deutschen Universitäten des 17. Jahrh.* (Münster, 1928); LEWALTER: *Spanisch-jesuitische und deutsch-lutherische Metaphysik des 17. Jahrh., ein Beitrag zur Geschichte der iberisch-deutsche Kulturbeziehungen und zur Vorgeschichte des deutschen Idealismus* (Hamburg, 1935); M. WUNDT, *Die Schulmetaphysik des 17. Jahrh.* (Tübingen, 1939) and see my reviews in *Critica*, XXIX, 63-65, XXXVI, 66-67, XXXVIII, 166-67 (reprinted in *Conversazioni critiche*, IV, 26-29, and *Pagine sparse*, ed. Ricciardi, III, 327-29).

2. In addition to my remarks in *Teoria e storia della storiografia*, 4th edn., pp. 224-27, read the acute essay of Carl C. BECKER, *The Heavenly City of the Eighteenth Century Philosophers* (New Haven, Yale University Press, 1932).

to liberate Hegel from what he called "the metaphysic of the intellect", but not from the metaphysic of *Vernunft*, "Idea", or "Mind", which, under whichever term it was known, was equally conceived in the trancendentist manner.

That this should have happened with Hegel can astonish and outrage only those who have never meditated upon the arduous course of his thought and his slow advance along it. Vico, also, after conceiving the life of the spirit as "an ideal eternal history, basis of the particular histories which run their course in time", went some way towards erecting this principle into a transcendent principle, as a result of which, instead of finding it operative in its entirety in every single one of the acts of men (which are always acts of an eternal ideal history wholly coincident with themselves), he envisaged a history of empirically severed epochs, assumed by him to correspond with the single moments of the ideal process. Vico thus impaired the reality of history by depriving it of the individual character of its development and so of its growth and advancement out of itself, that is, of its perpetual "progress" (the word came into use in the eighteenth century).[1] In consequence Vico, who as a European, an Italian, and a Neapolitan, strongly alive to and aware of the value of poetry, the critical function of thought, the energy which creates political States, the ethical conscience which by its operations civilizes them, appeared nevertheless, on one side of his work, to cut down his vision of reality to match the oriental idea of the circle and of the "courses and recourses", uttering a pessimistic *nil sub sole novum*, and appeared on the other hand to subject the drama of history to a law of natural immutability, corresponding to those of Copernican or Newtonian physico-mathematical science, of which the final upshot was once again pessimism.

Hegel's shortcoming was similar, but far more serious and extensive. Instead of handling the dialectical principle, which it is his glory to have introduced into logic and history, with critical caution, he abused it. In the first place he rationalized, and did not

1. This is the critical point of Vico on the "courses and recourses" expressed in my *Filosofia di G. B. Vico*.

really liquidate, the mythical conception of a God, creator of nature and of man in his image and likeness. Next he depicted the Idea as it "resolves" to issue forth from itself and to become other than itself in the world of nature, and then returns to itself in the human world, of man and his history. With such imaginative and arbitrary proceedings Hegel dialecticized all the distinctions of philosophy, treating them as abstract theses requiring to be raised to the level of truth by synthesis with their opposites. He went further and similarly dialecticized (in other words he retained and raised to the level of truth, but by a summary conferment upon them of a meaning and an office for which they were unsuited) the concepts of the natural and physical sciences, and the merely classificatory discriminations used in the moral sciences, nay, even the actions and events of history.[1] Very naturally, then, the historians, the naturalists, and the philosophers themselves rose in protest against the usurpations of the dialectic, all the more so when in the Hegelian school this method, which had never prevented Hegel himself from radiating truth on every hand, became thoroughly mechanical and dull.

No doubt Hegel, too, affirmed the unity and identity of philosophy with historiography, and it is irrelevant here that he explicitly affirmed this unity and identity only in regard to the history of philosophy. For since in Hegel's view Thought is the force which produces all reality,[2] the formula which he used in fact identified all history with the history of thought, or philosophy, and the abstract relation which he posits between "History of Philosophy" and "Philosophy of History" is perfectly coherent. But his way of arriving at this identification was to refine the empirically distinguished epochs of history into philosophical categories, and to coarsen the categories of philosophy into historical epochs, whereby philosophy and the history of philosophy

1. This criticism I elaborated particularly in my essay of the year 1906 *Ciò che è vivo e ciò che è morto della filosofia di Hegel*.
2. "Das Denken ist das Innerste von Allem, das ἡγεμονικόν." "Der konkrete Gedanke, näher ausgedrückt, ist der Begriff, und noch weiter bestimmt ist die Idee. Die Idee ist der Begriff insofern er sich realisiert." (*System und Geschichte*, cit., pp. 97-99.)

came to coincide, and philosophy traversed, in its temporal development through the centuries, its logical or ideal cycle. In the same way political history came to coincide with the various forms of liberty and with their logical succession (liberty of the "one", the "several", and the "all", having as their correlatives the three great epochs of Oriental, Graeco-Roman, and Christian-Germanic history) and had thus the additional character of a theory of liberty in its logical and educational progressions. To be noticed here is Hegel's conversion into philosophic categories of the wholly empirical concept of "peoples", "nations", and "races", and of the *Völkerseelen*, national souls, which were made to incarnate – in political history – the successive grades of liberty, in such wise that each of the peoples having played its part finally retired from the stage of history. All this, however, is not an identification of philosophy with history, but a sterile attempt to resolve history into an abstractly conceived philosophy, having for result a corruption and maiming on both sides. Through the illicit interchange of roles the philosophic categories lose their ideal quality, and the intuitions lose their corporeality. Hence arises in the (Hegelian) history of philosophy the impossible concept of a Thought which acquires its categories one by one in the course of time,[1] whereas Thought, like the Spirit as a whole, is always entire in every one of its acts, and in its self-distinction, which is not a self-division but is the eternal Becoming and life of the Universe. And there arises analogously in political history the impossible concept of a liberty which instead of being the principle of all moral development, at work in everything that is done, must instead construct itself stage by stage, passing through the successive phases of being a liberty for one, for some, and finally for all.

---

1. In the *Encyclopaedia*, Par. 384, Hegel writes: "The Absolute is the Spirit: this is the highest definition of the Absolute. To discover this definition, to understand its meaning and content has been as it were the absolute aim of every culture and every philosophy, the goal of the efforts of every religion and every science: this impulse alone explains the history of the world." [Croce here quotes his own translation from the Introduction to the *Philosophy of the Spirit* – Translator.]

The consequence of this faulty proceeding is that the history of philosophy, after attaining in the highest category the full understanding of itself as Idea, becomes fixed in a definitive philosophy, so that in fact (no matter how much Hegel and his school may seek, discordantly, to deny it) thought must needs come to an end and die, since it can only not die by developing perpetually, while the history of humanity, having similarly reached its peak in the Germanic branch of mankind, superior in its political institutions to the peoples which did not profit by the Lutheran Reformation, and now enjoying full consciousness of liberty, must needs come to a pause for want of anything more to do. For there was not even a provision, as in Vico's arrangement, for the recommencing of the cycle, nor again is there any evidence that Hegel, like Tommaso Campanella, was under the incubus of "an instant ending to all human things", an imminent termination of the world process. Thus the historians' protestations against Hegel's doctrine were justified in reason and were very often, thanks to the inadequate, inexact, and one-sided versions which he gave of this or that human achievement or action, justified also in detail. But over and above this, the human mind itself raised a more general protest against his implicit affirmation that philosophy and art would come to an end, and still more against his explicit theory that art and poetry had now concluded the century-old task of manifesting the Idea in sensible form, handing it over now to the definitive performer of the function, Philosophy, after which it remained only for art and poetry to die.[1]

Not only did Hegel's very bold attempt to resolve history into abstract philosophy and the historical epochs into categories fail in its object, but Hegel himself bore witness to the failure. Firstly history remained for him entangled in the outwardness of time (time and space are for Hegel general determinations of the "Idea" outside itself – that is, they belong to "nature"). Now time and space are not external but are internal in the spirit itself, constructions of the spirit. Secondly he was unable to maintain a strict

1. On this point, which I brought out particularly in a discussion with Dr. Bosanquet, see my essay included in *Ultimi Saggi*, pp. 147-60.

speculative significance for his great notion that the real is the rational and the rational the real, but had to allow the accidental and irrational to linger on alongside of the rational, and had to excogitate the sophism of a true rational in conflict with an untrue rational. Thirdly he was obliged to have recourse to the same sort of sophism when facing the spectacle of the irregularity of the world of nature, which he crudely explained by the "impotence of nature to actuate the Idea"!

Kant (as I have elsewhere commented), when he equated thought with the act of judging, and defined judgement as the unity of category and intuition, unconsciously established the principle of the identification of philosophy and history, and put an end to all speculation on the abstract concept, so that, forerunning and indeed outrunning Robespierre he "decapitated" (the witticism is Heine's and our Carducci put it into verse) not a mere king, but "God", that is the transcendent God. Hegel, however, failed to draw the inescapable conclusion deriving from Kant's reformation of the theory of judgement, and rebuilt a philosophy of the mind or Idea, reintroducing, against his better inspiration, a dualism between spirit and nature, mediated by the transcendent Idea issuing forth from and turning back into itself. Consciously or otherwise, Kant was altogether quit of religion, and entirely taken up with *Kritik*. Hegel remained within the ambit of the religions, as shown not so much by his proclamation of Christianity as "absolute religion" or his flirtations with Protestantism as by his offering an equivalent of mythology and of transcendent religion in his System.

The new Historicism accepts, extends, deepens, and applies Vico's principle that men know only that which they do (consequently all that they know is their own history which they made themselves), and Hegel's principle of a dialectical development proceeding by conservation, on the one hand, and on the other hand by the replacing of that which is surpassed. But not less than these two principles the new Historicism grasps firmly and extends and deepens and fecundates and integrates with them also the Kantian theory of judgement. But it rejects, first and foremost, the so-

called "philosophy of History", regarding it as at best a mythological or "symbolical" foreshadowing of Historicism's own doctrine.
It denies along with all other philosophical a prioris the a priori
knowledge of history in any of its parts. It admits no historical
proposition purporting to elucidate the "document", that is life
as it has been experienced, such life being itself, in truth the crowning or rather the fundamental document of all documents. Historians truly deserving the name cannot protest against this method
in the way that was justified in the case of the Fichtian, Schellingian, and Hegelian teachings which subjected sober reality to
the transcendence of the pure and abstract category. But neither
have the men of philological scholarship any right to put up an
opposition unless indeed forsaking the purity of their calling as
collectors and verifiers of documents, they give themselves airs,
as often happens, and offer their services as inferior historians,
imagining that they possess a whole when they only possess
abstracted bits and pieces of non-organic material on which they
endeavour by the labours of the imagination to confer an apparent unity. The historians have all the less a motive for protest
in that the philosophers themselves, meeting them halfway, have
noted and recognized the historical character of their own philosophizing, renouncing their naive and illusory belief in supra-
historical definitions which – if there is any truth in them at all –
are found on a thorough inspection to be Historically determined
forms of thought.

There is a charge which was not without some reason levelled
against the old Historicism, and is now levelled against the new.
It is the complaint of the moral conscience that the accomplished
fact was invested as it were with the dignity and office of moral
law, or, popularly expressed, that success, regardless of its quality,
was hallowed and came to take the place of the intimate moral
criterion. And undoubtedly this theoretical error, this blunted
moral sensibility, was indeed present or apparent in the philosophical writings in question, either as a reflection from the conservative or reactionary inclinations of their authors, or for some
other reason which led to a worship of strength in itself, the heavy

hand, or violence, as the highest power in the real world. Yet even when, quite differently, such philosophers (as can be recorded to the honour of the Italian Hegelians) were in no way servile towards existing might, nor worshippers of success, nor lovers of tyranny, but warm and sincere advocates and promoters of all the works of freedom and education, a suspicion continued to hover around them on account of their Historicism. The logical upshot of their doctrine, even if not explicitly or complacently formulated, was felt to be the compression of the liberty of men under an imaginary necessity born of a confusion of identity between the respect due to truth (whence the recognition of what has happened just as it did happen as being part of our world and of ourselves) and the dignity of the moral conscience (which is for ever creating new facts and so renewing the world and ourselves). That this, however undesired, should have been the upshot, was inevitable, because a Thought which had interrupted the continuity of life at a certain point and found now no way of re-attachment and of resumed progression, resorted to the expedient of restoring the Transcendent if not under one set of appearances then under another: as for instance the domination either of a God or else of an Idea standing fixed and immobile above the world and enforcing one or another of the particular and transient forms of history. Now human activity requires to be enlightened by a thought both critical and objective and fully and religiously observant of the past, which it has to explain as it really happened and not as it may oscillate in the view of an impassioned imagination. And it has no less need of the moral conscience, which is the ever returning inspiration of its free practical action, or in other words, of each one's ever new and concrete personal duty. It needs both these wings and cannot sacrifice one for the sake of the other without the supposed beneficiary also becoming weakened and exhausted.

There is no such thing as a "factual situation" fixed once for all, for the moral conscience. The function of this last is to restore that which appeared to be definitive to an undefinitive condition – for no definitiveness is more than a moment in eternal process and progress, just as no truth is definitive in an absolute sense since the new conditions of life which are perpetually being created, and the criticism aroused by these, dissolve the definitiveness when they exert pressure to complete it, to enrich it, and to replace it with a new and once more definitive-indefinitive truth. The reluctance ordinarily shown in accepting these obvious truths and real propositions is what should properly be considered surprising, and the strange accompanying fear which is really a frightened shrinking from life's own perpetual outstripping of itself and from the unpausing progression of thought beyond every point of arrival. But our wonderment turns to a smile when we recall that it is ever the habit of the plebeian, and of the plebeian always lurking in each one of us, to dream of the end of troubles, of peace in a definitive and delightful leisure – it is a dream which never ceases to recur. The philosophers themselves, being human, have yielded to this dream, seeking or imagining that they have discovered the perfect republic, the truth of truths, the surpassing of the world in a world above.

And finally, there was some justification or pretext for suspicions that the old Hegelian or Idealistic Historicism converted man, the individual, into a passive or indifferent instrument of the Idea, or of Providence, weaving the plot of history behind his back and using him for their own ends. But when our present-day "Existentialists", having apparently only just discovered the existence of the driving force and the travail of vitality, proclaim their great astonishment and absorbed interest (for my part as a constant reader of drama and lyric poetry I have never been unaware of it, indeed I accorded it great prominence in my theoretical exposition of the philosophy of the spirit) and proceed to repeat criticism of the above-mentioned sort at the expense of the new historicism, then one cannot repress a certain irritation. For by this time it can surely be expected that all should recognize that there is no dividing line having on one side of it the spirit, on the other side man, on one side a providence, on the other a puppet which providence moves by a string, on one side a universal and on the other an individual, but there is only the spirit, providence, the universal, which is nothing else but the life by which we live, the logic of this life, the concreteness of universal in individuality, and therefore there is no Fate weighing upon men unless they choose to give the name Fate to their own liberty.

[1942]

X

THE HISTORICAL MATERIALISM OF MARX
AND HIS ALLEGED PROMOTION OF COMMUNISM
FROM UTOPIA TO SCIENCE

I THINK that I have shown clearly enough that Marx, while he may have successfully dressed up the Idea of Hegel in a materialistic or rather an economic garb, introduced no speculative or logical improvement into the Hegelian system whatever. He accepted in its entirety the inferior and antiquated part of that sytem, of theological origin, and practically ignored the rest of it. In other words he accepted just what modern philosophic criticism, on the strength of over a century of Hegelian controversies and mental experiments, has rejected, after diagnosing the initial error which the powerful Hegelian system had failed to expel and had instead embraced and permitted to operate deleteriously within it.

I will now attempt to match that demonstration with another, namely to show that Marx's boast, repeated by innumerable scholars of his, that he promoted Communism "from a Utopia to a Science" was an illusion, originating in Marx's own already mentioned uncritical acceptance of the logical and historical scheme of Hegel. I will show that the claim is in any case quite unfounded, because Marx was, and remained, in his innermost mind, a Utopian.

What exactly is a "Utopia"? The saying goes that the Utopia of today will be the history of tomorrow", and in this sense a Utopia means simply the outline of a possibility which cannot today be actuated for want of the needful conditions, but which will or may meet with such conditions in the future. Utopia, however, should properly mean that which is *nowhere*, that which, in another manner of speaking, is "outside of history", of any history, of any historical conditions, and which negates history, which is movement, the dialectic of opposites, by tending to a static fixity. Every attempt to expel the opposites from history is vain, and every conception in which the opposites are suppressed is contradictory and empty, or Utopian.

Now Communism, which seeks to overcome all forms of social inequality and to abolish the inequality itself, just as Hegel's Absolute Spirit was to overcome all forms of mental travail and, at the pure peak of its achievement, to abolish travail itself, is a Utopian conception, because were it attained reality would no longer be *living*, just as at Hegel's peak the spirit would no longer be *thinking*.

Marx remained with his mind halted in a Utopia, the then recently born and popular Utopia devised by Owen, Saint-Simon, Fourier, Cabet, and their like, men much admired and always defended by Marx, and defended at his behest also by Engels,[1] though Marx asked indulgence for these men in that owing to the still immature development of capitalism in their day they had not, as he said, substituted for the "arm of criticism" the "critique of arms" (in other words they had not converted criticism into a material weapon). True, on this point he did not care to commit himself too explicitly, but did his best to evade all embarrassing questions about the character and constitution of the new society which was to arise after the suicidal victory of the proletariat, that class which was to compass the death of all the classes, dying itself into the bargain. He resorted sometimes to the usual quips of those who are cornered with awkward questions, as when he said that he refused to compose menus for the Cafés of the future. One can easily infer the unreal character of this new society, this *neue Menschheit*, new humanity, due to spring forth out of the *rücksichtslose Kritik alles Bestehenden*, ruthless criticism of all that is existant (these are terms used by Marx from 1843 onwards), from his affirmations that in such a society the State would be abolished, there would be neither civil nor penal law, and no dissension between individuals or groups, because the free development of each would be the condition for the free development of all – in a word, there would be Paradise on earth, in

1. See Engels' well-known book, written with the help of Marx, *Dührings Umwälzung der Wissenschaft* (3rd edn., Stuttgart, 1894), pp. 274-86.

which man would be liberated from the sweat of his brow and
the anguish of his heart. The coincidence of these affirmations
with the naivest reveries of the present-day anarchists will be
noted, but it is perhaps more relevant to note the precedents to be
found among the Utopians of the early nineteenth century, Saint-
Simon with his notion of a technical government in replacement
of political governments, and more particularly Fourier, who had
discovered in the social world that attraction *qui vient de Dieu* by
contrast with the constriction of Kantian duty *qui vient des hommes*:
that same attraction (he said) which Newton had discovered at
work among the planets, *l'attraction passionnée* in its various forms,
among which room was not wanting for *l'attraction papillonne*,
each individual in the new society being at liberty to choose the
occupations most pleasing to himself, twenty different ones if he
will. Whoever cares may track down the traces of these notions of
Fourier in the writings of Marx in his formative period and in the
Deutsche Ideologie of 1845-46 (a youthful work in which Marx and
Engels, as a matter of fact, fixed once and for all their historico-
philosophical standpoint). He will read how, contrary to the existing necessity of a division of labour, in a Communist society
which regulates general production there will be no need of
specialists, and the individual will be able to do different jobs at
different times of the day, a huntsman's in the morning, a fisherman's in the afternoon, a shepherd's in the evening, and if he likes,
that of a critic of cooking in the home, without needing, unless he
desires, to become a huntsman, fisherman, or shepherd.[1] If I
understand rightly, this is precisely an illustration of the *passion
papillonne* celebrated by Fourier.

Well, if the basis of Marx's thought remained that of the
Utopians,[2] wherein did he distinguish himself from them and

1. Cf. MARX-ENGELS, *Über historischen Materialismus*, ein Quellenbuch, ed.
H. Duncker (Berlin, 1930), pp. 71-72.
2. That this basis was taken over unchanged by the only Italian Marxist
who seriously pondered and assimilated Marx, Antonio Labriola, I have
already previously pointed out (cf. *Materialismo storico ed economia marxistica*,
8th edn., Bari, 1946, pp. 305-6 n.). Labriola has it that in the Communistic
Society "organized so as to afford to everyone the means of self-perfection",

actually procure himself the illusion of having advanced from
Utopia to Science? Certainly not merely because he had banished
the method of persuasion, propaganda, and personal example
which had been proclaimed and practised by the Utopian Communists, and had returned to the tradition of Babeuf and the later
and then contemporary manner of Blanqui. The function of
violence was indeed admitted by Marx, but only as a midwifery
which brings the mature foetus to birth. Violence, for him, executes the sentence which history has already pronounced upon
the outdated. Marx's concept was founded upon a scheme of
philosophy borrowed and imitated from the Hegelian original,
simply borrowed so far as concerns the succession of epochs logically derived from each other, but imitated with variations in so far
as Marx's historical epochs are distinguished, not, like Hegel's, by
differing grades of liberty, but by economic grades, and in so far
as the protagonist is no longer the Germanic civilization but the
proletariat, destined to bury the bourgeoisie just as this had in its
day buried feudalism, and as the feudal serf economy had once
buried the slave economy of antiquity. It is this metaphysical
construction of theological origin, this system of a priori discernment of the future (which Labriola tried to render respectable
under the name of "morphological forecasts"), this inferior Hegelism to which Marx and his henchman Engels declared the
German proletariat to be heir,[1] that Marx understood when he
spoke of "Science", and it was thanks to this "Science" (really

after the "removal of all those impediments to the free development of each
one . . . which now differentiate classes and individuals" each one comes
to find "in the measure of the needs of society the measure of what for
him is feasible and requisite to do" and adapt himself thereto "not through
external constraint" etc etc.; and the antinomy between best and worst,
the opposition between rights and duties, will fade out, because each one
will provide according to his strength and will receive according to his needs,
naturally; and penal law will largely become obsolete, and there will be no
call for religious sanctions, etc., etc. See his *Discorrendo di socialismo e di filosofia*, 2nd edn., pp. 101-2.
1. The ideas developed much later by Engels in his essay on Feuerbach
are already contained in Marx's *Critique of Hegel's Philosophy of Right*,
published in 1844.

metaphysics of the deepest dye) that Marx imagined he had
established Communism on a firm foundation and was entitled
to describe it as "scientific" by contrast with the foregoing
"Utopian" variety. In his view Communism was not a social form
that had once existed and must now be regained, nor yet, even,
an ideal to be realized. It was the effective movement, *die wirkliche
Bewegung*, which history accomplishes by its own indwelling
logic.[1] Marx was always very rigorous and meticulous in criticizing
and opposing every attempt to jump one of the transitional grades
of which he had deduced the necessity. Above all he opposed the
impetuous and anachronistic revolutionarism which at that time
refused to ally itself with bourgeois radicalism or to back this up
in its demands for the liberal institutions necessary for the perfection of the bourgeoisie, the perfection itself being the prerequisite
for its overthrow by the proletariat. Equally did Marx condemn
the impatience of those who would not wait for the proletariat
to attain the ripe vigour and awareness necessary for it to become
the ready and capable successor of the bourgeoisie and creator of
the new society. Marx thus took on the air of a moderate and a
conservative by comparison with those who like the Bakuninists
were always ready for the fray. Yet in this he was not really a
conservative or moderate, but if anything a pedantic devotee of
the old Hegelian logic and metaphysic of history. Mazzini was
mistaken in the well-known judgement passed upon Marx that
he was lacking in "deep philosophic convictions". The convictions were, in their way, deep, and were held tenaciously, but
they were of the quality that I have described.

History, however, moves in freedom, little recking of the
schemes devised not by the thoughtful but by the imaginative to
cover its future manifestations, their rhythm, and their tempo.
Marx, in the course of his forty years of political activity, paid the
price of many disappointments for having built up in the Communist Manifesto the illusion of an imminent catastrophe and
collapse of the bourgeoisie, a rapid jump from the realm of

1. *Über historischen Materialismus*, cit., p. 72. (I quote this because I have at
this moment no access to Rjazanov's edition.)

Necessity to the realm of Liberty, or into a quasi-Fourierist Paradise of attraction and harmony. I will not here repeat or summarize the history of his political activity from his first association with Communistic groups and associations, and his editorship of the *Neue Rheinische Zeitung* followed by his share in the German insurrectionary movements of 1848 and 1849, up to the foundation and subsequent dissolution of the International, and the programmes of Gotha and Eisenach. It can be read in many books.[1] I will only remark that more than once he lapsed from the way of thought of the old Hegelian dialectic into a causalistic or determinist mode, as when he expected a repetition of the general revolutions of 1848, regarded by him as an effect of the great economic crisis which had preceded that political crisis. Vainly he awaited a repetition of similar effects from a fresh series of world economic crises. In later years both Marx and Engels were hard put to it to patch up the patterns of historical materialism so as to match, in some degree, the reality of events in the years after 1848.

It may be worth while to reopen here a much debated question that has been variously answered. Marx's theory of surplus work and surplus value and of the profit derived from unpaid labour has sometimes been judged to have no connexion with ethics, at other times to be a moralizing doctrine. The best answer is, perhaps, that Marx arrived at the doctrine in question, so alien to the nature of economic science, and for that reason now forgotten, by way of a simple objective comparison between two different types of property institutions, the individualist and the collectivist. Although this comparison was in itself drawn in terms of economics and sociology, the motive was no doubt moralistic, namely to formulate and to bring home against capitalism the charge of dishonest exploitation of the workman's labour, thereby rounding off the doctrine of historical materialism with a conclusion of a moral complexion.[2] In any case, *Das Kapital* was planned and composed by Marx after he had already worked out,

1. For example O. Maenchen-Helfen and B. Nicolajevski, *Karl Marx* (Paris, Gallimard, 1937).

2. *Materialismo storico ed economia marxistica*, ed. cit., pp. 109-111.

without any reference to such a theory of the origin of profit, the materialist conception of history.

This doctrine was as mistaken, in economics, as the doctrine of historical materialism in the field of historical theory, but both of them had and in part still have much efficacy in the field of rhetoric or propaganda, where things said do not need to be true, but to be stimulating to the imagination and exciting to the mind. It sufficed that, according to his own prescription, the arm of criticism should become "materialized", should become the creed of the roughest elements, and thereby be transfigured into the "critique of arms". For this reason in my youthful book on Marx, of over fifty years ago, while I depreciated Marx as a thinker, I admired his political gifts as a revolutionary and saluted him by the appellation "Machiavelli of the proletariat", implying a parallelism with Machiavelli the counsellor and stimulator of the princes in the cause of the unity and independence of Italy.[1] I am now less than ever inclined to underrate his efficacy in the history of our times. He has not, indeed, brought into existence the new Communist society, because no man and no effort could avail to convert a Utopia into a fact, but he certainly contributed to bringing about that great event which was the Russian revolution, and the agitations and revolutions which it brought or is now bringing in its train in other countries. Possibly Karl Marx would be astounded if he could see what has in fact taken place in Russia and elsewhere under the standard of his name and teachings. Perhaps, even, he

---

1. Marx was aware of the carpingly moralistic quality of his style but could not remedy this, because, though he did not know it, it was an inevitable reflection of the non-scientific or semi-scientific investigations out of which *Das Kapital* was born, not without an implicit distortion of the economic sense of "value". Marx tried to justify himself in the preface to the first edition, which, however, makes the contradiction inherent in the book only the more glaring: "A final word to obviate misunderstandings: doubtless I portray the capitalist and the landowner in no rosy light. But I am concerned with persons only as personifications of economic categories, carriers of certain relations and class interests. Least of any can my theory, which describes the development of the economic formation of society, hold the individual responsible for relations of which he is socially the offspring, though he too may be able subjectively to raise himself above them." (4th edn., Hamburg, 1890, p. viii.)

would be grieved, for he undoubtedly dreamed the dream (at least in his youthful years) of a perfect society, so perfect that for its sake, notwithstanding the ontological argument of Anselm, the predicate of existence was left lacking from that perfection. A believer's enthusiasm and ardour, an apostle's unshakeable endurance, strong enough to inspire the dedication of a whole life of poverty and suffering to the attempted realization of the dream, can be denied neither to Marx nor to his faithful and worthy friend Engels.

The indignation which I feel is not directed against Marx, obliged though I am to refute his theories when propounded as truth; nor yet, quite obviously, against Russia, though that country, following its destiny, offers us, not a Communism to redeem mankind, but that same menace of Panslavism which was proffered by the Tsars and from which the classical lands of Europe seek repair, seeing in it their own death and the death of civilization; nor yet, just as obviously, against the workmen who like every other social class seek to better themselves, though this particular method has not obtained and cannot ever obtain for them either economic welfare or an impossible real equality; nor yet, finally, against "Socialism", so-called to distinguish it from Communism, the twin of Liberalism, with its active and beneficent record in the whole nineteenth century. Not to these is my indignation directed, but to those disastrous "intellectuals", those Italian or other professors who for years on end took no heed of Marxism, but now have had their heads turned and exert themselves to celebrate, inculcate, and dispense this doctrine in their fallacious writings, because success seems to them to have crowned and garlanded it in Russia. Of all the countries of Europe, Russia has the scantiest traditions of thought and intellectual method, the poorest experience and training in this spiritual sphere. Marx himself never dreamed that Russia could be the first country to create a society in correspondence with his dreams, assigning this role, if to any country, to that which stood in the industrial vanguard, England, while to his native Germany he attributed seniority in the development of the type of science which he himself cultivated. As long ago as 1829 the Russian Peter Chadaief diagnosed the indwelling mental weakness of his own nation, which he explained by its century-long isolation from Graeco-Roman and Renaissance culture, and even from the logical teaching of the mediaeval Scholastics: "Où sont nos sages, où sont nos penseurs? Qui est-ce qui a jamais pensé pour nous? Solitaires dans le monde nous n'avons rien donné au monde, nous n'avons rien appris au monde, nous n'avons pas versé une seule idée dans la masse des idées humaines, nous n'avons en rien contribué au progrès de l'esprit humain, et tout ce qui nous est revenu de ce progrès, nous l'avons défiguré".[1] But now come our professors and pile up upon the texts of Marx and Engels, of which their knowledge is scanty, a further heap of manuals and catechisms (one wonders whether their knowledge of even these is direct and discriminating), the work of minds alien and hostile to speculative and historical and critical research, capable and stalwart politicians, no doubt, like Lenin and his successor Stalin (the much more cultivated Trotzki they never quote); and no doubt soon they will be similarly quoting the learned views of Vishinsky, Molotov, and Marshal Timoshenko. Such are the fruits of the vanity, frivolity, truckling to fashion, opportunism, and stupidity of Professors (not quite all), and particularly Professors of Philosophy whom long experience has taught me to regard as incorrigible – but for that very reason attention must be drawn in order that they may be known for what they are, and not allowed to waste the time of people engaged upon conscientious study of the truth.

[1947]

1. *Lettres sur la philosophie de l'histoire*: in *Oeuvres choisies* of Pierre Chadaief, first published by Fr. Gagarin S. J. (Paris, Leipzig, Frankfurt, 1862), pp. 23, 26, 27.

XI

OF HISTORICAL CULTURE, SCIENCE, ACTION, AND RELIGION

Having now reached an understanding that in historical thought poetry and philosophy, intuition and category, attain their synthesis, the latest and the fullest form of knowledge, we cannot but press on to the further conclusion that the culture which is founded in philosophic and historical thought, this carefully trained harmony and unity of the theoretical spirit, is what alone is properly called Culture, the only true and entire, "humanistic" or "human" culture.[1] This living culture, even while holding fast to its constant principle, articulates and diversifies itself in the most various personifications, in the poet, the philosopher, the scientist, the man of action, nay in each man who passes under any of these names, since each has his particular sphere of experience and his particular practical problems. But where the intimate link with historical culture is weakened or broken, the most exalted poet, the deepest philosopher, the most learned scientist, the stoutest man of action will exhibit greater or lesser blemishes of rawness, of inculture, and will fail to protect his work from perceptible deleterious effects in style and to some extent in substance. True enough, as I once wrote when defending Goethe against over-emphatic charges of deficiency in historical sense and political indifference, "the foolish mind is then most incoherent and empty when it gives itself great airs of coherency and fullness, but genius has its own hidden routes of communication and union",[2] routes which ensure or permit the reopening of vitally necessary relations. This should be remembered when judging individual cases.

Historical culture, which deserves the description "religious" since it is an intimate raising of the mind to the thought of God, opens to us the vision of the world and of the self in a perpetual

1. See "Humanism and Historicism" (in *La Storia*, 4th edn., Bari, 1943, pp. 311-17).
2. *Goethe*, 4th edn., Bari, 1946, 2nd part, p. 119, note.

becoming, unpunctuated by any terminal point on which the eyes can be fixed or by any halting-place where one may linger. At every instant a world dies and we die with it, a world is born and we are reborn with it. Of this the poets sing, the philosophers reason, and history tells the tale to the mind. Every attempt to arrest the ineluctable Becoming in the world and in ourselves is a contradiction of the life which we live and which alone we truly wish to live, a loud utterance, maybe, of mere words, but void of thought. On the other hand, there can be no comfort in an idle contemplation of universal becoming. On the contrary we must break our ease, act practically, act without pause. It is not only Lucan's Caesar but every man when he is most truly himself, and least subject to illusion, who *nil actum credit, dum quid superest agendum*, and the *quid* in fact always *superest*, is always pushing and inciting. But then, how is it ever possible to act on a ground that is for ever moving under our feet? Step by step, we can never tell which way or with what velocity it will move next. Is this not enough to make us despair of our strongest and best pondered intentions, to fear for every attempt we make to realize them?

In pained perplexity we call for help, and the consoler, the helper, is Science, Science to which we have continual recourse as to one that can marshal shifting reality into classes and laws, by conferring a knowledge which, as Bacon opined, is a technique for facilitating action, for easing the business of living. And Science in this context means not only physico-mathematical or other "natural" sciences, but all those mental disciplines which perform a similar office in the field of psychology, in the arts of prudence, of economic and political conduct, and so forth, all of which busy themselves with classifying human actions, formulating regularities and rules, quantifying and calculating according to their own lights, one and all bringing us the benefit of their assistance in our practical operations. Just as the geologist informs the engineer about the weight and resistance of his materials and the farm expert informs the peasant about seeds and rotations, the zoologist enlightens the cattle-raiser, so political science, economics, and tactics provide information for statesmen, industrialists, financiers, soldiers, enabling them, with an exactitude varying from case to case, to arrive at the highly necessary and highly desired "foresight" by which they may determine their actions. The benefit that Science has in this way conferred, and confers, upon working mankind is so immense that it is not surprising if in some moments of history, as in the second half of the nineteenth century, people looked to science for a complete redemption from the pains, evils, and insanities which afflict mankind, while the scientist often affected the air of a priest or secular wonder-worker, and the parasite Superstition found a new and lush source of nourishment in the tree of Science.

Yet, however potent the spells of this sort of magic of the intellect, however effective its injunctions to ever evolving and ever revolving reality to desist from sudden leaps, to reveal, in obedience to experimentation, its intentions, life programmes, or "laws", whereby the undisciplined "history" of things, shot through with surprise, exchanges its name and its appearance for that of a disciplined "nature" in which the surprises are neither too big nor too frequent and continuous, yet Science, for all its great and ever progressing achievements and "discoveries", can never succeed as once used to be proudly claimed in "predetermining" practical action. That in present conditions Science cannot always be ready on the spot with the means to satisfy our demands is, of course, readily allowed by the scientists. But on the other hand many people fail to grasp from a theoretical point of view (though all must feel it) that strictly speaking Science never does and never can attain to the predetermination of action, that there must on the contrary always remain a gulf fixed between scientific foresight and the accomplishment of an act (such accomplishment never being the mechanical fulfilment of a generic prior plan, but always the invention of new action for a new and individual situation), and that perplexity, of greater or lesser intensity and bearableness, must always persist and reappear even where the certainty and security seemed greatest, so that it is always necessary at a certain point to make up the mind to an action lying not so much outside as beyond the classifications of Science, an action not formally scientific but actively practical. Many people neither understand nor agree to this theory, but surely all ought to see it clearly since there is no one who does not know the inevitable and painful necessity of daring. In actual fact, since the mind simply must be made up, everyone ends by acting outside and beyond the limits of his knowledge. But what, then, is the spring of their action, what demiurge or mediator intervenes to bridge the seemingly unbridgeable, the gap between the theoretical and the practical world which even Science cannot overcome, though Science has at hand such a wealth of instruments and apparatus of unquestionable usefulness for the man of action? All this is as fuel, but whence comes the spark to start the conflagration?

If we recall the pages of history, the biographies of men of action, we meet on every hand this original resolving force, this demiurge and mediator, this spring, this spark, and we feel all the diverse yet linked feelings which its presence arouses, feelings of courage and trepidation, hope and resignation, will to victory and austere preparation for possible defeat, readiness to play a game that will be both dangerous and sublime, the eye remaining fixed always upon something which instils confidence and confers assurance, excites reverence, compels devotion, and requires dignity in humility. One hears once again those words which in the course of history sounded so variously, with such diversity of images and forms – the *alea* or dice that must be cast, the *audacia* which alone can compel fortune, the "Providence" in which one must trust, the "Will of God", the dread "Summons of God" to the soul, or then again the "inspiration" that is obeyed, the "daemon" impelling to an action which one would never have expected to be called upon or to be able to do, the "necessity" which encompasses us and draws us on, the "sacrifice" of the self accepted for the sake of saving the "better self", the "dying in order to live", and so many other phrases and figures which recall to us the great moments of human history, their epic and tragic heroes. The solemnity of such memories confirms and throws into brilliant relief the existence of the mysterious force which works in men's actions and resolutions. Yet this is no less to be recognized in the ordinary affairs of daily life which are a tissue of resolutions and actions requiring and exciting (on a small scale, if you will) those same concepts and words which in other circumstances were so majestic and striking. This too is history, and has its heroes, commonly spoken of as the modest, stay-at-home "heroes of duty", silently sustaining and winning their battles, well knowing how to sacrifice themselves and to die. Each of us in his family and social life knows and honours such heroes who often enough are heroines, wives, mothers, daughters, sisters whose modesty would shrink from accepting a description which is in the strictest sense a true one.

The name of the force of whose interventions we are continually aware must never be pronounced in vain, yet at this point it must be pronounced, albeit without emphasis, because an incredible blindness of soul, ignobility of thought, deficiency of poetic feeling which are far from peculiar to our times, indeed are the bane of all times, are disposed to confer upon it the pitying or disapproving description of "irrational" or "unlogical", base blasphemy of the devotees of superficial logic and arid ratiocination against the very fountain of all rationality, *la Somma Sapienza e il Primo Amore*: for from such manipulators of the severed bones of the created, the creating Spirit, "Highest Wisdom and First Love", remains wholly hidden. Hence derives not only the theoretical impoverishment of a debased thought and philosophy, but moral harm, mortification of courage and of the will through the slackness and timidity which it promotes, the ignorance in which it leaves men concerning the divine in themselves, the habit which it induces of waiting and watching until observation and a more or less scientific knowledge shall have given a prior guarantee of the success of the enterprise to be undertaken, with the result – since such a guarantee can never be forthcoming – of a continuance in idleness, inaction, or wrong action.

The detailed description here given of the process of action, firstly of its preparation in historical culture, next of its equipment with the instruments provided by scientific investigation, finally of the original, irreplaceable, and decisive issuing forth of the act from inspiration and from moral courage, should surely have precluded any mistaken notion that our doctrine culminates in an exaltation, approval, and recommendation of the improvisations of pseudo-genius, the activism of brainless adventurers. Such a conclusion would constitute not a rectification of the poltroonery which we have here criticized, but a diametrical opposite, and such opposites, as is known, converge in their final effects. But if our doctrine is so misunderstood, this would be a mistake worthy of men who, while they confer upon God the appellation of Ir-rational or Non-logical, will no less naturally confound a scrupul-ous and religious exertion to fulfil the behest of conscience in a resolute pursuit of the good, however dangerous the path, with a frenzied and witless pursuit of sheer doing for doing's sake.

[1939]

V

ECONOMICS AND ETHICS

I

ON THE POLITICAL SENSE

THE mention of "political sense" brings to the mind the notion of a sense of fitness, opportunity, reality, suitability of means to an end, and so forth. Those who work and judge the work of others in the light of such notions are considered to possess the political sense. Those who act otherwise are considered, no matter how highly moral their purposes, or how noble the ideals by which they are fired, to lack it.

Since this is the view constantly taken in daily life, it is unreasonable to object to a statement that political action is simply action directed by a sense of utility, and directed towards useful ends, to be considered in itself neither moral nor immoral. What none the less occasions repugnance particularly against this last proposition, is an unwitting confusion which is often made between the concept of the useful and that of the egotistic. Yet Aristotle himself warned us not to confound love of self with wrong love of self, while the whole development of modern thought, in the various sciences having for their object the practical activity of man, insists upon this distinction and rehabilitates the concept of utility.

This confusion has on the one hand blurred the demarcation between politics and morals, thereby impeding or weakening the serious valuation of politics. And on the other hand, since the living reality of politics cannot possibly be overlooked, it has led to the habit of treating mere politics as something in which it is impossible to help getting involved, though it often has a more or less immoral character. A dualism is thus set up between political action and moral action. And this gives rise both to the vulgar judgement that politics is a necessary evil (some philosophers have enthroned this vulgar judgement at the apex of their sublime speculations, treating politics and the State as a provisional expedient relative to a transitory phase of human existence) and also to all those illogical propositions which affirm that one must some-

times do ill in the service of the good, that the right end justifies
the immoral means, that private morality is one thing and public
morality another, that you cannot help dirtying your hands in
politics, that faith has to be broken and crimes committed when
the interest of the State demands it. These are illogical propositions, for our human conscience persists in proclaiming that it is
in no case whatever permissible to break faith or commit crimes,
that there is not one morality for the home and another for the
market-place, that one cannot do ill in order to procure the good,
as if good and ill were merchandise to be bartered, that hands
must always be kept clean, that the quality of means and of ends
must be homogeneous. One would be disposed to call them not
only illogical but disgraceful, until one remembers that they have
been found on the lips of men like Frederick of Prussia and Camil-
lo di Cavour, as an expression of the honest distress which is felt
when one has to commit actions that one sees to be rationally
necessary, without being able to square them with the doctrinal
scheme that one professes. It happens that the authors of such
actions afterwards in their own persons disclaim them, either
heaping blame painfully on themselves, or putting the whole
responsibility on God, who placed them in a quandary in which
they could not act otherwise. But the truth is that if in the clear
light of the moral conscience one has decided that it is necessary
to perform such an action (necessary not, of course, for the satisfaction of a private thirst for power or some other such ambition or
passion, or because such is one's crude and vicious habit, but for
the execution of a sacred trust, the strengthening or revival of
one's country), then the action is not a breach of faith, a murder,
or any other sort of scoundrelism or wickedness. In the same way
the "magnanimous lie" of which Tasso speaks, by the mere fact
of being "magnanimous", could not be, save by poetic metaphor,
a lie.

Political action is useful action. Indeed these two concepts are
co-extensive, so that it will never be possible to point to any
character which could distinguish the political as a sphere within
the sphere of the useful. Political ability is required for governing

a State or leading a party, but so it is for running a family, for conducting affairs of love and friendship, indeed for utilizing the services of animals and even for dealing with things, if these be regarded as subject to laws and somehow (for instance in the way suggested by Campanella) having life and feelings. In our talk of politics and of political actions we mean then simply to turn attention to groups of facts which commonly stand out with exceptional prominence and give rise to enquiry and discussion more than others. But we could not trace a logical limit to these groups within the infinite range of the works of utility. We must be content with the general notion conveyed by the word "politics", and fortunately that will suffice for our needs.

For the customary attempted definition of political actions as those, among practical and utilitarian actions, which pertain to the life of the State, break down with the difficulty of defining the State. What is the State? Simply a succession of useful actions on the part of a group of individuals, or of reciprocal actions between those individuals. There is nothing in this to distinguish it from any other such process of activity by another group or indeed by an individual, for every individual lives, not in isolation, but in some form of social relationship. It avails nothing to define the State as a complex of institutions or laws, for there is no social group, no individual, without institutions and life-habits, or unsubjected to norms and laws. Strictly speaking, every form of life partakes in this sense of the nature of the State. When we talk of the State as something specific we are therefore simply relying on the general notion which that word conjures up.

The concept of the State, then, cannot help us to trace a special sphere of political actions within the general sphere of utility. Still less can the State be conceived as an entity having a life of its own beyond or above individuals, to be set over against all single actions. Here we have one of those tricks by which metaphorical language so often misleads the unreflecting, while rhetoric completes the delusion. The State, like the Good, the True, the Beautiful, decked out with capital letters, is hoisted into the heights as a shining star. Hence we have absurd discussions on what the Good, the True, and the Beautiful are in themselves, objectively, absurd theorizings upon the manner of men's comportment in regard to those fixed ideas, their imitation and actuation, or betrayal and rejection of them. All of which doctrine ends in a dissatisfaction from which there is no issue save by a return to the awareness that there is no True, but only the thinking mind, no Good, but only the moral will, no Beautiful, but just poetic and artistic activity, no State, but just political actions. For that matter the word "State", which was given its political significance by the Italians of the Renaissance, seems almost a verbal contradiction, with its suggestion of something "static" in a sphere – that of political life – which is dynamic like all life, or, better worded, is spiritually dialectical. Undoubtedly, as said above, the word "State" is intended to designate the complex of institutions, customs, and laws which regulate actions, and more particularly the complex of fundamental and constitutional laws. But we must observe in the first place that the laws themselves are simply actions by individuals, the effectuation and continuous maintenance of certain volitions concerning more or less general tendencies which it is deemed useful to encourage. (This is an argument to be further developed in the chapters on the theory of law.) And in the second place we must observe that since these tendencies can only be abstractly indicated by the laws, they cannot be put into effect by mere obedience or imitation on the part of individuals. No! The effectuation of the tendencies is in fact the very process of their creation, and the laws are a mere material element which cannot enter into the formal synthesis. We can put this more simply as follows. The laws are indeed important, but far more important is the manner of their observance, the effective behaviour of men. It is well known that laws, in the course of their interpretation and execution, are adapted, improved, in fact changed. For this very reason, it is impossible to admit in pure theory, in pure enquiry after truth, a distinction which is habitually made in political teaching and debate, where it has a great but purely practical importance, the distinction between the State and the Government. If one seeks the concrete, and not mere abstractions, the State is simply the Government and has its whole being in this. Outside the uninterrupted chain of governmental activity there remains simply the hypostasis of the abstract requirement of this activity, the presumption that the laws have a real and stable content other than the actions which are performed by their light, or in their shadow.

What we have just enunciated is one of those "perilous truths", rightly so termed because they can easily be utilized to defend or to justify reprehensible deeds and inclinations. The critical theory according to which Grammar is not a body of truth but consists of abstractions and arbitrary propositions might thus be hailed by the schoolboy with no taste for grammar, whereas the proper reading of that theory is that grammar has to be learned because it is useful, and its use of abstractions is designed precisely to promote its usefulness. The abstract nature of the laws, the fact that the State becomes concrete solely in the Government, does not mean at all that institutions, customs, laws are to be disregarded or despised, or that government should proceed on a day to day or hour to hour basis, with ephemeral and *ad hoc* laws, and in the absence of any real difference between normality and revolution (normal life being itself a continual revolution) that revolutionary acts can properly be performed at any moment. Inferences of this sort are just pleasant sophisms, based, as sophisms always are, on a play of words, a concealed passage from one type of argument to another. Laws are abstract, but there never has been and never can be any getting along without laws. Rightly the laws are revered, in Aristotle's phrase, as "intelligence void of appetite", acts of will which the individual himself in creating them pledges himself not to disturb with his interests and his cravings. Everyone demands laws, stable laws, in order to be able to conduct his life in the oncoming times, making a plan which will indeed suffer variation from the course of events but will not be without its efficacy. A relative stability of the laws is what is called "peace", and is desired by all men who are intent upon their work. Institutions, laws, habits, make up the power and attraction of tradition and of the past, and governments unfounded upon any right, but simply upon fact, fail to root themselves, or do so only slowly and with difficulty. The ancient peoples had a particular reverence for lawmakers as the founders and reformers of States. For warriors and diplomatists represent the power of action in the present, the salvation of States from danger and ruin, their victories and conquests. But legislators represent the conservation and accumulation of such benefits in the future under the guarantee of institutions. Polemics and satire against legal "bigotry", against "vestal virgins" of the institutions, may sometimes be a useful corrective to a superstitious timidity in handling the affairs of the State. There is often associated with this a polemic against the formal school of jurists, designed to discredit the pedantry and superficiality of those who fasten on to an abstract element and refuse to recognize the reality of the movement of history, the changes which have occurred and cannot be undone. But at least equally deserving of reproof, and perhaps more so, are those who lack the sense of tradition, continuity, legality. They may be men of good will, but the good that they do is inevitably shifting and shallow, being based simply upon the reckonings of the single individual. Those others might be rightly charged with deficiency in political sense, but these are certainly lacking in juridical sense, which is a form or a special aspect of the political sense taken in its integrity.

An objection to the resolution of the reality of the State into that of the reality of political actions, and to the resolution, in their turn, of political actions into useful actions, would seem to be presented by the widely received doctrine that the origin and the constitution of the State lie in Force. This at first sight seems the direct contrary, or at least something very different, from our concept of utility or economic fitness. Nor has there been lacking an attempted eclectic combination of the two supposedly opposite or diverse concepts, whereby force or violence was placed at the origin of States, but utilitarian fitness in their life and development. This gives us occasion to remark that the "birth" or "origin" which is at issue in this and similar researches is nowise an historical fact but signifies the origin, the birth, the eternal nature, indeed the very idea of the State. This puts out of court any historical distinction between origin and development, first age and later age of the State. Man, as the ancients knew and said, is by nature a social or political being, and the State (to speak in modern terms) is not a fact but a spiritual category. Moreover, the idea of Force should not be limited to what is suggested by crude images like that of seizing someone by the neck, bending his spine, holding him prostrate, and so forth, but should be thought out in its full significance as truly including the whole human and spiritual force of man, the shrewdness of the mind along with the strength of the limbs, foresight and prudence along with courage and boldness, gentleness with severity, innocence with perspicacity and indeed cunning, the virtue of beauty with the beauty of virtue.

If the concept of force be thus rightly understood, it becomes evidently impossible to imagine force distributed among a multitude of men in such wise that one or a few have it and the others lack it, or that some have more of it and others less, so that the former get the better of the latter and dominate them. The distribution of force is not quantitative but qualitative. It takes the form of a variety of aptitudes, capacities, virtues. Each of these seeks its complement in the others, each has need of the others, each may impose upon the others, threatening them with the withdrawal of its own required contribution, bringing pressure upon them. The upshot of these various pressures is an agreement upon a way of living, a reciprocal consent. The dilemma whether the State rests upon force or upon consent, the enquiry whether only a State based upon consent or also a State based upon force can be legitimate, are of a piece with the above-mentioned distinction between State and Government. Force and consent are correlative terms in politics: where there is one, the other cannot be lacking. It will be objected that the consent in question will, then, be "forced consent". But all consent is forced, more or less forced, but still forced. It necessarily arises from the "force" of certain facts, and is therefore "conditioned". If the condition of fact changes, then the consent, naturally, is withdrawn, debate and struggle supervene, and a new consent is based upon the new condition. There is no political formation that can elude this pattern. In the most liberal of States and in the most oppressive tyrannies there is always consent and the consent is always forced, conditioned, and mutable. Were it otherwise, the State and the life of the State would themselves disappear.

Let us translate the terms of this relation with other words, and call "authority" all that which represents the moment of force (premisses, threats, rewards, and penalties), and "liberty" all that which represents the moment of spontaneity and consent. We shall have to say that in every State, authority and liberty are inseparable, as is shown in the case of despotism and of liberalism when these are carried to extremes. Liberty hammers away against authority, yet needs authority, and without it would itself disappear. Authority represses liberty, yet sustains or resuscitates it, for without it authority itself would disappear. Rightly we exalt liberty. What other word wins a warmer and dearer response in the human breast? Love is perhaps the one word that exerts an equal power, and in a certain sense the two words have one and the same content, for liberty like love is life in expansion, in self-enjoyment, life in all its forms which each one feels in his own way, life in the infinite variety and in the individuality of dispositions and activities which compose the universe. By liberty we here mean nothing else than the joy of action, the joy of living, the *naturalis facultas ejus quod cuique facere libet,* and not that isolated moral liberty which frigid moralists are wont to espy or to put in its place, to the extent of distorting even the frank and free abandon of Romeo and Juliet to match their "moral liberty". But it is proper to celebrate also authority, order, rule, the sacrifice which each one must make for the advantage of every other one, and all for all; and which is a communication of power on the part of each to each, and all to all. The word "liberty" lights up the mind, the word "authority" renders it serious and severe. The respective celebrators of force or authority, and of consent or liberty, forget that the opposite term is always included as a correlative in the one which they seek to celebrate exclusively. That is their error: the practical politician ends by agreeing with Joseph de Maistre that to the people one should preach the advantages of authority and to the rulers those of liberty.

No doubt the arguments for liberty against authority or for authority against liberty, for the principle of consent against that of force, or vice versa, and those also for the State against the Government, often contain "in a glass darkly" important considerations. But these concern historical and contingent situations and concern the feelings and interests of the citizens of a given State at a given time. It results from philosophical immaturity, or sometimes from the deliberate design of statesmen or from controversial zeal, that such considerations are puffed up into the guise of supreme concepts, or anyway of inferences and deductions from supreme concepts, so that sheer political issues appear in the colours of speculative thought. Questions of where sovereignty resides, in what person or persons it is vested where the State has this or that form, may well have a practical importance and meaning. On the other hand in pure theory there can be no such location of sovereignty and the questions cannot arise. Of course as long as it is supposed that force is a homogeneous substance distributed in varying quantities among those who compose a State, it is quite logical to define sovereignty as the possession of force or of prevailing force, and to seek out where this possession lies in the various forms of States. But once that inexact notion has been superseded by the conception that force is qualitatively various, it can no less logically be concluded that in any State each one is turn by turn sovereign and subject, monarchs included. For not a few kings have lamented that the liberty enjoyed by the humblest, by those who possess nothing, have no ambition, are indifferent to praise or blame (like the "Pulcinelle" in the second part of Faust) is denied to themselves. Viewed as a relation sovereignty pertains to none of the single terms but to the relation itself. The effort to get beyond this, to locate sovereignty in something which surpasses and masters the relation, may indeed induce a pronouncement that the sovereign is God, "from whom is all power", or the Idea, or History. The meaningless question is here

transformed into one that has meaning. If, now, sovereignty is
found to be present in every part of the relation, but not confined
to any one ("nec cubat in ulla"), evidently the classification of
States according to the persons exercising authority in them, and
first and foremost the celebrated threefold formula of monarchy,
aristocracy, and democracy, must be denied any speculative value.
The latter formula has, still as a matter of fact, a philosophical
sense, not concerned with the location of sovereignty but with
the distinction of three moments which occur in all political life:
the co-operation of all, the taking counsel of the few (notables or
aristocrats), and the decisive resolution of the one. In this sense the
triple formula refers not to the differing forms of States but to the
organic composition of any State whatever – the State, in fact.

The political theories which we have dismissed because of their
unilateral character had at all events the countervailing merit of
being founded upon some one real aspect or moment which it
was their business to emphasize loudly in circumstances where this
tended to be forgotten or denied. But there is one political theory
which has not even this merit, being founded upon no aspect of the
political relation; and none the less it is the theory which boasts
the greatest number of adherents. It is the theory which, rather
than "democratic" or "Jacobin" (words susceptible of misunderstanding), we will call by its rightful name "equalitarian". The
democratic theory which stands for a tendency to give a greater
weight to the mass, the people, the plebs, in political debate and
decision, is in fact necessarily empirical, a matter of more or of less.
Jacobinism might be a better term, but it brings to mind a practical
measure of recourse to compulsion and violence in order to put
into application an abstract ideal, and we call "Jacobin" not only
the democratic extremist but all those, including extreme conservatives and aristocrats, who exercise such compulsion and violence, seldom for long or to much good effect. The democratic
argument may or may not in the given circumstances be meritorious, while Jacobinism will surely in no circumstances be meritorious, but neither of these is intrinsically impossible and absurd.
But the equalitarian theory is intrinsically impossible and absurd.

It presupposes the equality of individuals and founds States upon the basis of this equality, the very idea of which is unthinkable save in the form of an autarky, a self-sufficiency, leaving each equal to the other thanks to none having to ask the other for anything. Such an equality not only could not serve as basis for the State, but would be a signal of the superfluity of the State, each individual being, in such an hypothesis, a State in himself. Even a "contract" is unthinkable between these self-sufficients, for it is diversity, the origin of reciprocal rights and duties, which gives occasion for contracts. For the State to come into being in such conditions some *Deus ex machina* would have to make his appearance. Beings unequal to and dissimilar from the others would have to fall from the sky or somehow become severed from the rest, and with this the hypothesis and the theory itself would come to nought. Certainly, just like those other theories, this one has had and has and may in the future have efficacy as the myth which stands for certain economic and moral trends and requirements. Nor will we deny that a subordinate theory derived from it, the theory of majority rule, has value as a practical instrument and as a symbol of the practically possible at a given moment. But on the level of political science it is totally false, and when it is taken as a standard of judgement for political thought it leads the mind into insuperable difficulties and loss of direction. In this theory the idea of "equality" is reinforced by those of "liberty" and "fraternity", but in an altogether empty and therefore arbitrary sense, which explains how men of lively political and historical sense have come to pronounce curses against those noble words, and in hatred of them to figure as partisans of a crude and distorted "force", mercilessly chaffing the believers in these trite formulae and those who hawk them about for the use of nincompoops. What in fact can be more idiotic than to predicate "liberty" and "fraternity" of a string of cold, smooth and equal billiard balls? It is here fitting to remark that the equalitarian theory, which has no logical standing in the relations of politics, has its rightful origin in mathematical and mechanical constructions which are inapplicable in the field of life. In fact, although it is an error which crops up afresh in all times, its greatest vogue was in the century dominated by mechanical discoveries.

Equalitarianism, it might be supposed, represents the last depth of political disorientation and obtuseness. Yet there is a still lower phase resulting from the spasms of heart and mind induced by the theory. In fact the theory promises respect for equality and for the abstract freedom of equality, but promptly breaks the promise, because every elaboration of the theory, every inference from it, every attempt to put it into application compromises the equality and restrains the liberty if only (as ingeniously proposed by Rousseau) in order "to compel men to be free". The championship of the principle of equality and liberty then has to be handed over to the partisans of egoarchy or anarchy, the doctrine which alone promises men full and entire enjoyment of liberty, albeit at the cost of a total upheaval of judgement on the whole historical development up to our present times, with a transference of admiration from social to antisocial personages. But this theory, engendered in the womb of the equalitarian theory, is a daughter who takes vengeance on the mother, a critique and irony, a *reductio ad absurdum* at the expense of equalitarianism by a theory which itself likewise lacks all right to be called a political theory since it denies the very object which a political theory should explain.

[1924]

II

THE STATE AND THE ETHICAL PRINCIPLE

POLITICAL action, in the pursuit of some determinate end, turns everything into means for that end, everything, including in a certain sense even morals and religion, that is to say the religious and moral feelings and institutions. The starting point is always particular to the individual case. The human beings in question are what they are, and their particular ideas, preconceptions, good or bad dispositions, virtues, defects, constitute the material with which and on which one has to work. There is no question of exchanging it for something preferable. If the only way to induce them to join forces, to come to an agreement, is to flatter their illusions and vanities, to appeal to their most superstitious and puerile beliefs, like the miracle of Saint Januarius, or to their shallowest ideas or interpretations of ideas, such as liberty, equality, fraternity, and the other so-called "principles of 1789" (big realities in the realm of passion, however valueless they may be in the field of theory), then this must be done. There is nothing scandalous about this. Every form of human activity when it puts forth its full effort enlists the force of all the others, appropriating and utilizing their products. One might just as well cry scandal because the poet appropriates thoughts, feelings, joy, grief, good and ill, to use them all as winged images, material for poetry.

But there is another reason in our case for not crying scandal. Poetry, sheer poetry, does not void the spirit or the world of reflexion, criticism, and science, but on the contrary prepares the way for them and virtually invites them on to the scene. And just so does political activity, sheer politics, not destroy morality but give birth to it – morality which is then the surpassing and the accomplishment of politics. There is not, in reality, a closed and isolated sphere of self-sufficient political or economic activity. There is simply the process of spiritual activity in which the perpetual self-assertion of utility is followed by the perpetual resolution of utility into morality.

The ethical spirit finds in politics both the premiss for its own activity, and the instrument for this. Politics are for it like a body which it fills with new life and uses for its own ends. There is no moral life without precedent economic and political life, or, as the ancients said, "vivere" comes first and then "bene vivere". But equally there can be no moral life which is not also economic and political life, no soul without a body. The moral man cannot act out his morality save in political works, in accordance with the logic of politics. A historian has commented upon two letters written by Saint Bernard almost at the same time, in the course of his lively and eventful campaign for the Curia against King Ruggiero of Sicily, containing opposite statements. "This", says the historian, "was politic, but the policy was not that of a Saint." One must retort that this is exactly what it was, the policy of a Saint who in the pursuit of saintly ends made himself thoroughly at home with the only real means at his disposal, political means. Did not the Protestant Reformation, which so effectually promoted the recovery of moral sincerity and intimacy, necessarily use political methods from the very outset, and learn them from its Jesuit adversaries, great masters of political doctrine and method?

It is the non-moral character of politics, the anteriority of politics to morality, which marks its special role and enables it to serve as an instrument of moral life. But the sphere of politics is neither isolated nor self-sufficient. The fact that it has its own special quality must not be misconceived and twisted into a theory of, as it were, virgin birth for politics, with the corollary that there could be a politician wholly void of moral conscience (which would be like admitting that a statesman need not be a man). The speciality of politics sprouts from the tree of unity, of human nature. It is one moment in a spiritual circle. For let us consider. Could a poet who had no experience of feelings, of morality, of thought, could such a frigid, dull, and deficient poet be a poet at all? Is not poetry for sure the expression of a personality, and is not the full development of the man therefore the prime condition for a poetic creation? Do we not laugh at would-be poets who think to attain to poetry by stylistic efforts and metrical devices and jottings of whatever they happen to see or hear, and do we not bid them return far back to the roots of being, there to cultivate a heart and a mind? The case would be just the same with a politician who lacked moral experience and a moral conscience. Not only could he not persist in his work, nor bring to it the devotion due to a serious calling, but he could not even achieve the management of other men by dint of exploiting their moral sentiments. To him, lacking the experience of such feelings, their psychology would be a closed book. He would not even succeed in being a "cynical politician".

However, when we enter into the ethical sphere, it is no longer simply this moral and human experience, indispensable to the politician, that is in question. We have left the political sphere behind us, we breathe the air of the moral life in which politics is no longer an end but a means. The moral man is the *vir bonus agendi peritus*; his moral education has need to be accompanied by a political education and by the observance and exercise of the practical virtues like prudence, wariness, patience, boldness.

With the advance from the merely political to the ethical level the word "State" itself takes on a new significance. It now no longer stands for the purely utilitarian relation, the synthesis of force and consent, of authority and liberty, but has become an incarnation of the human ethos, the Ethical or Cultural State as it is sometimes called. Together with the word "State" the words "authority" and "sovereignty" also take on a new significance, connoting the authority and sovereignty of duty and the moral ideal. "Liberty" also now comes to mean moral liberty, necessarily identical with that duty and that moral ideal, and "consent" betokens an ethical approval and homage rendered to "force", but to a force which is the force of good, and is no longer a more or less forced consent, but one full and entire. Fear gives way to love, or, in theological terms, "the Law" to "grace". Even the word "equality" gets a new meaning, referring no longer to mathematical equality but to the Christian equality in God, whose children we all, high and low, are, in the consciousness of our common humanity and our common rights. In the light of this character, exemplified by the elevation in meaning of these and similar words, the ethical State will not tolerate other forms of association above itself or on a level: all must be subordinate or else denied and annulled. When the Church confronted the State and overshadowed it, the Church was the real ethical State, and when the earthly State took up the struggle against the Church it did not rest until it had embraced the Church within its own being, considering itself as the one true Church and trustee of a more perfect morality.

From this point of view, the exaltation of the State initiated by Hegel in the classical period of German philosophy, and echoed later by Spaventa in Italy (where it still enters a good deal into school teaching), might seem to be blameless, though rather superfluous. Since the State was identified with the moral life as its concrete manifestation, it was quite a natural proceeding to elevate it to the altitude of Kant's moral law, and to recommend it as a proper object for the same sort of reverence and veneration. But those doctrinaires had committed, and are still committing, an error in envisaging moral life in the inadequate form of politics and the State.

In the simple and political sense the State, as we know, is one and the same thing as the Government. It consists in a relation of force and consent, and those who will not accept this relation and intend to change it are viewed and treated as foes. They are, as the case may be, called traitors, rebels, conspirators, or undesirables. They are put to death, imprisoned, exiled, or persecuted and punished in other ways. The necessary instinct of self-preservation in the political order, that is in this relation of force and consent, brings it about that free and unruly spirits, and even men of critical and thoughtful mind who considering things by the light of eternity never judge merely by the standard of existing and present things, are watched and suspected. By alternating threats with flattery, the governors manage to make friends among these men, or to entice them to their side, and regimes of the most different descriptions have their "men of letters", now called intellectuals, who, as may well be imagined, when they manage to submit to and serve the State, and to produce theories and poems useful for the ends of the State, prove to be intellectuals of some-what coarse grain. The poet of poets has placed in the mouth of a politician words to fit the case of the men of finer race and tem-per, the untameable, the tormentors and disturbers of themselves and of others: "He thinks too much: such men are dangerous." And a formula coined by a theorist runs: "Omnis philosophia, cum ad communem hominum cogitandi facultatem revocet, ab optimatibus non injuria sibi existimatur perniciosa."

But moral life holds in its embrace, along with the governors and conservatives, the opponents of governments, the revolutionaries. The latter it holds perhaps in a closer embrace, because these are the men who more particularly open up the ways of the future and stimulate the advancement of human societies. Morality condemns none save those who have not yet attained the moral level, and often praises, admires, loves, celebrates those despised and rejected by governments, the condemned and the conquered, who thus become canonized as the martyrs of the Idea. In the eyes of morality, every man of good will serves the cause of culture and progress in his own fashion, entering into the harmony which resolves all discords.

Where morality is conceived as the "ethical State", and this in turn is identified with the political State or just "the State", the idea gains ground (and the theorists of the school do not shun formulating it) that concrete morality resides in the governors, in their act of governing, and that their opponents are to be consid-ered as foes to the moral Act, meriting not merely punishment according to or exceeding the rigour of the law (as is or at any rate may seem reasonable), but also a lofty moral condemnation. This is so to speak a "governmental" conception of morality. As it was first formulated in the days when Hegel felt impelled to take up the cudgels against the whimsicalities and romantic vanity of the so-called "fine and sensitive souls", by praising the good citizen rather than the genius and the hero, there was a partial justification for it in the circumstances, and for the rest it was accounted for by the personal conservatism of Hegel with his great admiration for the Prussian State of the Restoration. But it is hard to see why it should still at the present time be cultivated with the fervour now shown by the writers of the school, ecstatically bowing down before the sublime image of the State. These inebriated exaltations, this Bacchic delirium in favour of State and Government, should not distract us from keeping in mind what the State really is: a narrow and elementary form of practical life from the limitations of which moral life bursts forth on every side in flowing and fruitful streams, streams so fruitful, indeed, that they continually provoke the unmaking and remaking of politics and the State, forcing them to reconstitute themselves in conformity with moral requirements.

[1924]

III

MACHIAVELLI AND VICO

THE name of Machiavelli has become a sort of symbol of stark politics. It is a name which without question signalizes a great crisis in the development of this science. Antiquity, of course, was not without some notion of the distinction and antinomy between politics and ethics, as is shown by the mere fact of their treatment as two different branches of learning, while discussions on such subjects as just and unjust law, natural and conventional law, or again, force and justice, testified to a recognition of the antinomy and the emergence of a problem relating to it. But the antinomy never became spectacular, or constituted the kernel of researches and meditations. Nor yet did this happen in the long centuries of prevalence of Christian thought, for the contrast between the *Civitas Dei* and the *Civitas Terrena*, and later that between the Church and the Empire, found a solution in the doctrine of the dual powers instituted by God, or in that of the supremacy of Church over Empire, or of Empire over Church, and was thus prevented from issuing into a sharp speculative dispute. Yet beyond doubt Christian thought, in which scrutiny of the moral conscience looms so large, by sensitizing this conscience was preparing an inevitable explosion. Niccolò Machiavelli is held to be a highly typical figure of the Italian Renaissance; but it would be well to bring him into some relation with the Reformation, that is with the general urge which in his age was so lively, inside as well as outside Italy, to know the human being and to explore the problem of the soul.

It is a commonplace that Machiavelli discovered the necessity and the autonomy of politics, of politics which lies beyond moral good and evil, or rather, on the hither side of them, and has its own laws against which it is vain to rebel, nor can politics itself be exorcized or chased out of the world with holy water. This is the idea which pervades all Machiavelli's work, and though it is not formulated with the didactic and scholastic precision which is often taken for the hall-mark of philosophy, and is indeed frequently presented by him with a disturbing accompaniment of images which waver between political virtue and the pursuit of power by means of crime, yet it must be considered a profoundly philosophic concept, the true and proper foundation of a philosophy of politics.

What is often not recognized is the sharp bitterness of the language in which Machiavelli couches this assertion of the nature of politics and the necessity of the political science. "If all men were good", he says, then these precepts themselves "would not be good". But men are in fact "ungrateful, changeable, fleers from perils, eager for gain"; so that it is more urgent to get oneself feared than to get oneself loved, and then, when fear has been ensured, one may, if possible, try to win love as well. It is necessary to learn "a essere non buoni", to act without goodness. You must break faith when that is in your interest, for, if not, others would break faith with you; you must undo the man who is awaiting his opportunity to undo you. Machiavelli's longing is for an unattainable society of good and pure men; he dreams that such there had been in times long past, and meanwhile he prefers the wilder folk of the Swiss mountains and of Germany to the more civilized Italians, French, and Spaniards, who (it was then the great hour of Spain) are "the pest of the world". On reading the horrors recounted in history, says Machiavelli with a shudder, "whoever is born of human flesh and blood will feel horror at the example of evil times and will be consumed with immense desire to follow that of good times". In the presence of such clear testimony of a strict and sorrowful moral sensibility it seems astonishing that there should have been so much talk about the immorality of Machiavelli. But then the common herd identifies morality with unctuous sermonizing and bigoted hypocrisy. By contrast with Machiavelli, Guicciardini exhibits no such painful and melancholy preoccupation. Guicciardini in considering the "unkindness" of men displays merely a mild contempt for them, and shakes down quite comfortably to seek his "private advantage", his *particolare*, in the much decried world. If this *particolare* had not involved him in serving the Medicean Popes, he would have loved Martin Luther "more than myself", in the hope that the rebellious friar would lay low the ecclesiastical State and put an end to the "wicked tyranny of the priests". Guicciardini was concerned with men of a different temper from man as he appears in the pages of Machiavelli.

Moreover, Machiavelli seems to be wracked by mental conflict concerning this Politics of which he has discovered the autonomous workings. At one moment it seems to him an odious doom to have to dirty his hands in dealings with the impure. At another moment it seems to him a most sublime calling, to lay and strengthen the foundations of that great institution, the State. Often enough he speaks of this in tones of religious gravity, as when he recalls the saying that for the good of the State one must be ready to lose not only one's good fame but the salvation of one's soul. And again, he looks back with scarcely concealed longing to the time when pagan religion placed the supreme good in the honour of this world, and exalted men high in human glory, praising the great of heart, the stout of arm, the virtues whereby man attains the summit of strength, by contrast with the Christian religion which points the way to the truth of the other world, contemning this world, praising an abject lowliness, assigning the highest rank to mere contemplators, and prizing suffering above energy. Is Politics divine or human? Machiavelli delights in the image of the Centaur, the beautiful invention of the poets which bridges humanity and animality. His Prince is partly man and partly beast of prey. And lest there should be any doubt as to the purity of the human element, it is to the animal element that he ascribes the force of the mind, the Prince's cunning, as partaking at once of the nature of the fox and of the lion. For the lion is helpless when ensnared, the fox does not defend himself against wolves, and only an unskilful ruler would wish in all circumstances to play the part of the lion. The art and science of politics, sheer politics, brought to perfection by the Italians, were for Machiavelli a matter for pride, and when the Cardinal de Rohan said to him that the Italians were ignorant of warfare, Machiavelli answered that the French were ignorant of statecraft.

Who was it that that took up the thought of Machiavelli and carried it to a further conclusion? Not the "Machiavellians" who enlarged upon his maxims and illustrations in their treatises on the Raison d'État, often interlarding the maxims with moralizing observations of no value. Nor yet the "Anti-Machiavellians", with their claim to combine and identify politics with morality, and their schemes for States founded upon the pure dictates of goodness and justice. Nor yet the eclectics who produced parallel theories of morals and politics, and in these, instead of working out the antinomies, blurred them, treating them as regrettable contrasts which are, in fact, part of the experience of life, but occur by mere accident. The true continuers of Machiavelli were none of those schools, but were in the first place certain thinkers who strove to expound the concepts of prudence, of wariness, of what in general they called political virtue, without either confounding this with moral virtue, or treating these two as opposites. Among such writers of the seventeenth century we may mention Zuccolo. As continuers of Machiavelli are to be considered also certain powerful intelligences which saw beyond the wariness and shrewdness of the individual as these were delinated by Machiavelli, to the truth of the divine work of Providence. Such a mind was Tommaso Campanella.[1] But the veritable and worthy successor of Machiavelli whose powerful mind brought together and fruitfully married the immortal thought of the Florentine Secretary and the scattered wisdom of his critics was another Italian, Vico, who had no great love for Machiavelli, yet, being in reality filled with his spirit, clarified and purified this, integrating Machiavelli's conception of politics and of history, solving its puzzles, tempering its pessimism. The two great Italians can truly stand together as a symbol of the whole philosophy of politics in its basic idea.

In the thought of Vico, politics, force, the creative energy of States becomes viewed as a moment of the human spirit and of

1. For the period between Machiavelli and Vico see my account of the Italian political theorists of the seventeenth century in *Storia dell'Età Barocca in Italia*, 2nd edition, Bari, 1946, part I, chapter 2, and see also chapter 6.

the life of societies, an eternal moment, the moment of *certainty*, upon which there for ever follows, in the development of the dialectical pattern, the moment of *truth*, of fully fledged reason, of justice and morality, in fact of ethical life. The symbol of the Centaur is now no longer valid. What seemed to be the bestial part of man is now found to be, like the other part, human, to be in fact the first form of will and action, the necessary premiss to any other form. Without passion, force, authority, there can be no human ascent. The strongest of men are the best, and it is from the hard rule of the strong that there emerge mild and civilized societies in contrast with the rule of the strong – and yet this "generous barbarism" has been the condition of their own emergence. And in that barbarism they must from time to time be plunged back to recover themselves, just as Machiavelli said that States must from time to time be recalled to their principles (this was a generalization from a maxim current among Florentine politicians that every five years the State should be "taken in hand again" so as to "instil into men that terror and fear which they felt at the first taking of the State"). Machiavelli, discoursing of the art of statecraft, takes on a religious tone, but Vico does not hesitate to speak of the "divinity of force". And just as Machiavelli found "the mountain-dwellers among whom there is no civilization" better material for the touch of the statesman's hand, for (he said) "a sculptor can better draw a fine statue out of virgin marble than out of that upon which others have worked rudely", so Vico discerned with approval a more vigorous political vitality among the barbarian peoples, who therefore are better fitted to found new States, whereas over-civilized and corrupt peoples cannot be reformed, just as misshapen and broken statuary can only be thrown back into the melting-pot to serve for new work. The hardness and the insidiousness which necessarily characterize politics, recognized and advocated by Machiavelli though sometimes against the moral grain, are by Vico developed as an inherent part in the human drama, for ever in course of creation and re-creation. Vico sees them in a double perspective as real good and apparent evil, for the good appears evil when viewed from the

level of a higher good that has issued forth and arisen out of its
own womb. And distress yields to a contemplation of rational
necessity and to the feeling of trust in the Providence which
governs human affairs.

We may say that Machiavelli was an unconscious exponent of
the doctrine of Vico, and Vico an unwilling exponent of that of
Machiavelli. Their common doctrine is not, indeed, to be found
neatly formulated in their respective pages. It has to be inferred
both from conceptions scattered through their works and also
from their judgements, inclinations, sympathies, dislikes. It can
be tracked down by the expert eye which has followed the course
of thought and of life in later times and therefore, to use a manner
of speaking, understands what it was that they were aiming at
better than they did themselves.

[1924]

IV

THE PHILOSOPHY OF ECONOMY
AND THE "SCIENCE OF ECONOMICS"

WHAT rationality required, observation has now fully confirmed: there is at work a practical form of the Spirit which we have called the utilitarian or economic form, and it is right that there should correspond to this an Economics, or Philosophy of Economy. But though our demonstration seems irrefutable, it will not be fully persuasive as long as one important point is left unexplored, the relation between the Philosophy of Economy as we have outlined it, and the Science of Economics.

This science, which has taken various forms and names, from "political" or "national" to "pure" or "mathematical", was foreshadowed in antiquity, but it is in the last few centuries that it has been mainly built up, and it is now exceedingly flourishing. Economists have often recalled with pleasure how Hegel in his day[1] praised Economics as "a science which does great honour to thought by its discovery of laws working in a mass of accidental occurrences". Is its object the same as that of our Philosophy of Economy? If so, how does it arrive at concepts so different from those which we ourselves illustrate? Or is it an empirical science? And in that case whence does it gain the rigorous character which seems to raise it above mere empiricism and to let it enounce truths that are not merely empirical? Two rigorous sciences cannot surely both busy themselves with the same object. And yet there do seem to be two, and this perplexing, puzzling duplicity seems to arise out of our enunciation of a Philosophy of Economy or an Economics which is not the Science of Economics.

If we investigate men's economic actions with a mind free of preconceptions, if we track them down and fix them in their pure and full reality, we do not succeed in establishing a single one of

1. *Phil. d. Rechts*, Par. 189, *Zus.*

those concepts and laws which the Science of Economics lays down and insists upon. Each individual is different at each instant of his life, in his wants and his actions which are always new and fresh and incomparable with the other wants and actions of others or of himself at another moment. Say that A yesterday spent sevenpence to buy a loaf of bread and today once again spends sevenpence for the same purchase, it does not follow from this that the sevenpence of yesterday were identical with those of today, or the bread the same, or A's need the same today as yesterday, or the expenditure of effort involved in his action the same on both days. Say now that B also spends sevenpence for a loaf, B's action is different from A's just as A's of today differs from A's of yesterday. If we lead the economist on to this ground of reality (or rather into this Heraclitean stream in which the hands cannot twice be dipped in the same water), the economist will feel impotent in the absence of any foothold on which to begin basing any one of his theories. An economic theorem proclaims: The value of a commodity depends on the quantity of it, and of all other commodities, available in the market. But what is a commodity? Bread, for example, or wine? In reality there is no abstract bread or wine but a particular piece of bread, a particular glass of wine, a particular individual who to eat the one or drink the other would, according to the circumstances, give a whole treasure or nothing at all. The law of Gossen, a basic law in economic theory, has it that any satisfaction whatever, if prolonged over a period of time, diminishes and finally disappears. But what are these satisfactions which are prolonged, and diminish, and disappear? Reality knows nothing but actions which take on a different tone with every shift in circumstance, every change in the operating individual. The difference is qualitative, not quantitative. A eats the sevenpenny loaf, and in swallowing the second or tenth or last mouthful experiences a pleasure not less than that of the first mouthful, but different. The last was, in its way, as necessary as the first, for without it he would have been cheated either of his normal satisfaction, or of the fulfilment of his routine or his fancy. That economic man seeks the maximum of satisfaction with the minimum of effort is the primal economic doctrine, but not even that superlatively general and simple principle accords with reality. In order to save twopence on the price of an article offered at ten shillings, A will haggle for an hour, thus gaining the maximum satisfaction by the minimum means then at his disposal. To show off, B will light his cigar with a five-pound note, thus gaining in his own way the maximum satisfaction that he desired with the minimum means at his disposal, namely the hilarious destruction of a banknote. If this is how things are, it is not maxima and minima, but individual ends and respective appropriate means, that come into question, in other words, seeing that ends and means are really all one, individually differing actions.

In considering these infinitely various actions we may abstract in greater or smaller measure from their differences, and thus construct a series of types or classificatory concepts and of empirical laws so as to impose a uniformity within certain limits upon that which is not uniform. It is by this proceeding that we obtain the concepts of bread, of the consumption of bread, of successive 'doses' of bread and of other objects for exchange with bread, and so forth. This means abandoning concrete reality, concrete knowledge, in favour of a feigned reality excogitated for certain mental purposes. If the Science of Economics consisted solely in the fixation of a series of types and laws of the sort described above, it could be numbered among the descriptive empirical sciences, and it would for us, in our present research, suffice to refer back to what has already been said about the relations of the Philosophy of Practice with the art of practical description, classification, rules, casuistry. But the Science of Economics is not simply descriptive, it cannot be summed up in the pattern: "Goods belong to the classes a, b, c, d, e, etc., and class a is exchangeable with class b in the proportion of one to three, class b is exchangeable with class c in the proportion one to five etc." Such a pattern necessarily implies approximateness, averageness, the "more or less" so. The classes are approximately those of the preceding pattern, exchanges are made on the average in the stated proportions, things today are more or less thus and tomorrow will be a bit more or a bit less so. But by contrast the propositions of the Science of Economics are rigorous and necessary, like Ricardo's law: "When lands of differing fertility are put under cultivation, all the owners except the owner of the least fertile land will receive, in addition to the absolute rent, a differential rent"; or Gresham's law: "Bad money drives good out of circulation". In fact it is inconceivable that lands of differing fertility, all under cultivation, should not command a differential rent. It may be said that the State may confiscate the differential rent, or the owner may by bad cultivation squander it, but this does not impair the solidity of the proposition. Nor is it conceivable that along with inconvertible paper money, the volume of which depresses the value of the monetary unit below the metal content of good money, such good money, in the shape of gold coins, should circulate freely and be taken at the same valuation as the paper unit. Some witless possessor of a golden hoard may indeed, while the bad money is in circulation at a discount, agree to exchange his gold freely for paper, but a sensible fellow will put the gold in his strongbox, and the economic law describes the dictates of reason, not the irrationality of the witless. These propositions of the Science of Economics, like all the others, are in fact not descriptions but theorems.

The word "theorem" at once conjures up notions of mathematics. And what else, indeed, can the Science of Economics, whose propositions are neither philosophical nor historical, nor yet merely naturalistic, be unless a mathematical discipline? In fact it shows the marks of a mathematical character, not indeed those of pure mathematics, arithmetic, algebra, or calculus, but those of applied mathematics, using as the basis of its calculation concepts taken from the real world which by contrast with the formal character of number have a material character. The Science of Economics is nothing else but the application of mathematics to the concept of volition or action. It does not, however, examine the nature of volition or action, but applies calculation to certain determinated human actions in order to get a rapid view of the inevitable resulting configurations and consequences.

No wonder then if by the standard of truth the theorems or laws of the Science of Economics prove all to be tautologies on the one hand, arbitrary determinations on the other. Ricardo's law concerning the rent of lands of differing fertility is simply the definition of difference of fertility in lands. Gresham's law about bad money is simply the definition of bad money. The law "every customs barrier destroys wealth" and the law "demand for products is not demand for labour" are mere definitions of customs barriers, and of the demand for goods and for labour. It could equally well be shown that all these laws are arbitrary, for the concepts of lands, customs duties, goods, money, and so forth are arbitrary, and the laws take on a character of necessity only when these arbitrary concepts have been postulated. The same could be demonstrated of any geometrical theorem, for equally arbitrary and tautological are the theorems that the area of a quadrilateral equals the base multiplied by the height, or that the sum of the squares on the hypotenuse is equal to the sum of the squares on the other two sides. Yet geometry none the less remains geometry, with all its virtues, without the aid of which we could not have built the house in which we live, nor measured our planet or the other stars which circle around us or around which we circle. Similarly without those schemes of economics we could not find our way in empirical reality, but would suffer what was suffered when economic science was in its infancy: measures would be taken by governments which would accentuate in the highest degree the ills which they were intended to remedy, like the economic and financial ordinances and proclamations of the Spanish regimes in Lombardy and Naples in the seventeenth century, which are remembered as classical examples, one might say, of that sort of absurdity. And still today astute interests profiting by public ignorance manage to gain acceptance for ruinous measures on the plea of public necessity, dressing up their proposals to appear advantageous, or advantageous in a different way from what might truly be pleaded on their behalf. Thus high tariffs are demanded as a means of accelerating the slow progress of industry, when they really lead to the growth of artificial and spurious industries at the expense of the spontaneous and legitimate.

The special form of applied mathematics practised in the Science of Economics has often been compared with the proceedings of Mechanics, and the "economic man" of the former with the "material point" of the latter, and Economics has been described as "a sort of Mechanics" or simply as Mechanics. And naturally so, for Mechanics consists simply in schemes of calculation on the basis of a reality which in the eye of philosophy is spirituality, but is transformed into force or a system of forces for the purpose of calculation. Economics, on its side, carves out from the flow of volitions certain groups which it simplifies and stiffens into the scheme of "economic man", the laws of "least effort", and so forth. In the light of this mechanizing procedure there is a certain naivety about the questions sometimes put, why Economics does not deal also with ethical, aesthetic, or logical facts, or as to the best way for bringing these into its sphere. The Science of Economics deals with the concept of will or action which it renders abstract and quantitative. Now the ethical facts are, precisely, will and action. But since the Science of Economics dispenses with qualitative distinctions, not even investigating what qualitatively distinguishes the economic act which is its special object, quite evidently it could not throw the ethical facts into relief by distinguishing them from the economic facts and developing that distinction. It presupposes a lumping together of these two orders of facts, and in a certain sense the whole body of them are already and indifferently included in its sphere. Aesthetic and logical facts, in the sense of representations and thoughts, elude all economic calculation, but when regarded as partaking within the unity of the Spirit of the character of volitions, then they too are lumped in indifferently with the others in the sphere of the Science of Economics.

Being intrinsically quantitative, this Science is none the less so when it eschews arithmetical and algebraical symbols, and differentiates itself thereby from Mathematical Economics in the stricter sense. The advice tendered in the name of philosophic or historical schools that Economics should correct its abstract and arbitrary character by becoming historical and philosophical or "psychological" is bad advice. If Economics cannot enounce the universal truths of philosophy nor the particular truths of history, neither can philosophy and history perform the smallest act of calculation. Economics has no eye for the truth, but they have no strong arm with which to check and dominate the flood of facts which threaten to overwhelm man and, if unchecked, would prevent him even from winning awareness of them. The tendency shown by Economics to develop as Pure Economics, laying aside its attention to practical questions (which partake of the character of historical questions), is a sound one.

But Economics, as a science of mathematical character, but not a branch of pure mathematics, since it presupposes certain material data, harbours other enemies in its own bosom. The material data can be multiplied infinitely, giving rise to infinite economic propositions, each distinct from every other. The data can also be marshalled into groups, simplified, and unified in a process culminating in an unqualified "x". Where the former tendency prevails the result is what has been called economic empiricism, an unwieldy assemblage of unconnected propositions. Where the latter prevails, we reach the pattern of a supreme generalization in which sometimes no sign whatever remains of the human action originally envisaged, a pattern which becomes indistinguishable from those of Mechanics or indeed of arithmetic, algebra, calculus. Economic Science is properly by its nature bound to be both abstract and empirical and to connect and unify its isolated propositions. But it must no more lose sight of distinction than of unity, each being necessary. There are two methods which from different angles are equally useless for the calculation of economic consequences. One proceeds exclusively from the generality of the science, the other from its particularity. The first views all the facts as a single fact, the second all the facts as diverse, uncoordinated, unlinked by similarities or by chains of dependence. In what measure the generalities and the particularities should respectively be expounded in economic treatises has been much discussed, but this is a question of sheer expository and educational expediency, to be resolved only case by case, in line with the teacher's needs. It would be quite arbitrary to try and limit Economics to this or that degree of abstractness, allowing it, for example, to treat of "material goods" or wealth, but not of services, or allowing it to develop capital as a concept distinct from land and human labour, but forbidding it to fuse these three concepts into one. Any unification and any differentiation may prove useful, and those who thunder against the abstractions of economists are themselves but half-hearted abstractionists.

Those who are versed in economic studies must have recognized in the ideas expounded above the logical considerations underlying the history of the Science of Economics, with its division into schools, its controversies, setbacks, triumphs, and progress. The quantitative character of the Science is clearly indicated in its earliest documents, the enquiries of Aristotle into price and value in the *Politics* and *Ethics*, and can be discerned also in the rare observations on such topics by mediaeval and Renaissance writers. The economists, even when not using mathematical terminology, have always developed their deeper arguments as mathematicians, for instance, in the Italian eighteenth century, Galiani, Genovesi, and Verri. The greatest Italian economists of the nineteenth century, Francesco Ferrara, was a mathematician. The economic principle, one and the same thing as the excogitation of economic man, was formulated by the head of the Physiocrats, Quesnay, and although the denomination "Political Economy" proposed by Montchrétien in 1615 in the long run prevailed, it was sometimes challenged as the description of the new branch of learning by that of "Social Arithmetic". The progress of the science took not only the form of the discovery of new economic theorems, but also that of the linking and unification of those previously treated in isolation: material and immaterial goods, cost of production and rarity, net product and gross product, agrarian and non-agrarian rent, production, distribution, and circulation of wealth, laws of economics and of finance, social and individual economics, value in use and value in exchange. It has been possible also to bring into the scheme of traditional and orthodox economic teachings those of Marx, which seemed revolutionary, but were simply patterns applicable to a particular case, inferred from the comparison of different types of economic order.[1]

The Science of Economics has to consolidate its status not only by withstanding the exaggerations of empiricism, but also by eluding the threats of the so-called historical school. This school, on the plea of the infinite variety of historical facts, refused to recognize abstract schemes in the Science. A sharp campaign had to be conducted against this historical school, in which Menger and others of the Austrian school distinguished themselves. The proclamation of the character of Economics as a pure science by Cairnes was the result of another campaign against the excessive political character of economic studies. A confusion between abstract and concrete, and within the sphere of the concrete between the economic and the ethic, led to repeated demands specially by the German economists of the "ethical school" and by Catholic economists everywhere, for an economic science based upon ethics, which in turn gave rise to a reaction in the opposite sense in the shape of an economics based on sheer egotism (this extreme attitude is represented by the treatise of Pantaleoni). There have been no comparable threats to economics from the side of philosophy, for among the many errors of recent times, with their great harvest of economic research, this one has not been numbered.

Now, thanks to the work of Jevons and other Englishmen, of Gossen, of the Italians of the school of Ferrara and of the Austrians, the Science of Economics has attained complexity and simplicity at one and the same time, by dint of applications, extensions, and reductions. Continuing on these lines it may become better ordered and clearer, but organic it can never become, for its nature as a quantitative branch of learning, as applied mathematics, in which postulates and definitions can never be anything else but atomistic, forbid it to develop organically on the basis of a single principle, like a philosophic science.

It may here be worth remarking, to crown these observations,

1. See B. CROCE, *Materialismo storico ed economia marxistica*, Critical Essay (1900; 7th edition, Bari, Laterza, 1944).

that the interpretation of the words of Hegel quoted above as an expression of admiration for the degree of truth attained by Economics, as though Hegel had meant to say that the Science of Economics did honour to the speculative reason, could only arise where there was ignorance of Hegelian gnoseology and terminology. Hegel actually said that Economics does honour to the thought which lays down laws and determines facts, that is to the "intellect" whose abstractive and arbitrary character he denounces throughout his philosophy. He thereby confirmed that this is no true or philosophic science, but a descriptive and quantitative branch of learning, developed with much exactness and elegance. His praise, then, itself implied a limitation which we have set out to illustrate and justify, showing how this science is constructed, and offering the complement and contrast of an Economy or Philosophy of Economy.

[1909]

V

THE ECONOMIC CHARACTER OF LAW

LAW A CREATION OF THE INDIVIDUAL

LAW is an act of will having as its content a series or class of actions. With this definition we forthwith banish from the concept of law one characteristic which is often treated as essential to it, namely that law must be "social". We thereby extend the concept of law to embrace the sphere of the isolated individual. But to guard against misunderstandings on this important point we will remark that "society" has an empirical meaning and also a philosophical meaning. Law is not "social" in the empirical sense, but it must not and cannot be regarded as devoid of social character in the philosophical sense. Reality is a togetherness of unity and multiplicity, and an individual can only be conceived in relation to other individuals: the relationship of individuals is what gives efficacy to the process of reality. Without multiplicity there could be neither knowledge nor action, nor yet art, thought, utility, or morality. An isolated individual severed from the reality which he constitutes and which constitutes him, would be an abstraction, an absurdity. The concept we have in mind is not, however, absurd when used controversially to rebut a false concept. The individual is here viewed not as absolutely isolated, but isolated relatively to certain contingent conditions falsely supposed to be essential. It is the use of the term "society" that is here abstract and unreal. "Society" has as one of its meanings a multiplicity of beings of the same species, but this introduction of the naturalistic concept of "belonging to the same species" obviously at once confers an arbitrary character. Were this empirical sameness of species lacking, society, real society, would not on that account be lacking too. In a multitude of men a man may fail to encounter his own kind, and will behave as though those men did not exist, yet even in that case he will live in society with beings commonly called natural or supernatural, his dog, his horse, the plants, the earth, the dead, God. Though consigned to solitude, cut off from the fellow-members of his species, yet those other forms of society, his communion with reality, will never fail to enable him to pursue his life of contemplation, thought, action, morality. To understand the spirit in its universality, it is necessary to disregard whatever is contingent, and society in its empirical meaning is something contingent from which the concept of the isolated individual, isolated from the *societas hominum* but not from the *societas entium*, reality, assists us to free ourselves. Hence the great services that this concept has rendered to Logic, Aesthetics, and particularly to Economics, which began to develop on philosophical lines only when it learned to treat economic facts as occurrences arising internally in the individual prior to their translation into the lives of so-called "societies". Thus there was formed the concept of the isolated economy. And correspondingly Economics, Aesthetics, Ethics, in fact the whole range of philosophic sciences and enquiries, lost their true character and purity when a crude sociology plunged back into the flux of social contingency the universals which philosophers had painstakingly cleansed from those accretions in order to contemplate them in their simplicity. In defining law as a formation belonging not only to societies, but also to the isolated individual, the idea was simply to draw attention to the concept of true society, which is reality in its entireness, and to eliminate the lure and confusion of accidental circumstances.

No great effort is required to conjure up cases of individuals fixing laws for themselves, carrying them out, modifying them, offering themselves rewards, and threatening punishments. We need not evoke the excellent Robinson Crusoe, so frequently called upon by the economists. Without the effort of conceiving ourselves cast on a desert isle with only a bag of flour and a Bible, we can simply take a look at everyday life where examples of individual legislation are offered in inexhaustible number in the shape of rules or programmes of life. Who can carry on without such programmes? Who does not lay down for himself the undertaking of certain actions and the avoidance of certain others?

From early youth we begin making laws for ourselves in this manner, and through all succeeding ages this internal legislative activity continues, to be terminated only at death. A man may say for example: I will follow the calling of a landowner, and every year from June to November I will live in the country, but from December to February I will live in town, and from March to May I will travel for pleasure and improvement. Any such programme will take its shape and its details in line with the varying conditions and openings that are given. Individual laws are devised concerning behaviour in respect of religion, the family, marriage, friends, the State, the Church, and even concerning this or that other individual, for, as has been remarked and explained in the Logic, an individual, when conceived as a fixed entity, becomes a concept, an abstraction, group, series, class. It would not be difficult to draw up a comparison between individual laws and programmes and "social" laws. One could amuse oneself by discovering in the individual constitutional settlements, laws, regulations, decrees, temporary provisions, contracts, by-laws, and all the other sorts of legal instruments which have application in society. In what way do the programmes of the individual differ from the laws of society? Are not the laws programmes, and the programmes laws?

We put the question, not to express a doubt that this is so, but to underline a fact which to us seems to stand four-square against any attempt to contradict it. Yet it may be and commonly is objected that one great difference distinguishes individual laws from the laws of society and the State: the latter impose a constraint and the former do not. It is for that reason that the latter are truly laws and the former only programmes. But an objection in these terms can carry no weight. In our survey of the Philosophy of Practice as a whole and in its parts, never have we encountered, in our examination of the will and of actions, this "constraint" (except in the negative sense of a deficiency of will and action). No action can ever be constrained; every action is free, because the Spirit is freedom itself; and while in given circumstances an action which was aspired for may not eventuate, a constrained action is

43

inconceivable, a contradiction in terms. Is this belied by the facts? Let us look at the facts directly and without preconceptions, and to avoid all possibility of misunderstanding let us take an extreme case. Say that by the law of an atrocious despot, enforced by a cut-throat police force, a tribe of men are commanded to sacrifice their firstborn sons to a God in whom the despot believes and the tribe does not. Are the men to whom the will of the tyrant is communicated constrained to execute it? What threat can make a man say yes when he wishes to say no? The tribe will rebel, take up arms, disperse the tyrant's satellites, kill him or reduce him to impotence, and in this event the law will have no force of constraint. But even in the opposite event, if they do not rebel at the risk of their lives, or prefer to defer the rebellion to a more propitious moment, and meanwhile bow to the despot's will and hand over their children for slaughter, they will have suffered no constraint, they will have freely chosen to preserve their lives at the cost of those of their children, or to sacrifice some of these in order to gain time to prepare a rebellion with a chance of success. Social laws, then, are sometimes observed and sometimes violated, but in either case freely. Violation may be requited by a so-called penalty, when the legislator having imposed a certain class of actions takes certain determined measures against those who will not comply, and wills a further class of actions designed to facilitate the previous class, the penalty being a new state of affairs presented to the individual with the design of inducing him to change his previous course of action, which however he still remains free to do or not to do. To avoid the penalty or its repetition he may now freely decide to obey the law, yet he may also still freely rebel against it, as before.

There is no compulsion in individual laws, and equally none in social laws. Conversely obedience to and rebellion against individual laws, and the procedure of rewards and punishments under these, occur just as in the case of social laws. Returning to the previous example, the individual who adopted the plan of living as a landowner may come to feel a strong bent for the arts or for music, and cease to take pleasure in what formerly attracted him, the proximity of mother earth, harvests and vintages, things which previously appealed to him as suited to his condition, the ideal life for him, but now have become tedious and boring. If he is an earnest man, not one who chops and changes the whole time, not the individual equivalent of those peoples who in mid-November change the laws passed in October, piling reform upon reform and revolution upon revolution, he will examine the situation in which he finds himself, and may come to the conclusion that his new inclinations are just a fancy, not in line with his true vocation, and that his original plan must stand. There will then be a conflict in his mind between that plan and his new rebellious wishes. Maybe he will then sometimes betray his plan to yield to the blandishments of his artistic or musical interests. But since this will be a violation of his individual law, and force must be on the side of the law, the disobedience will be followed by particular measures such as throwing away the paintbrushes or violin, or even renunciation of customary indulgence in artistic pursuits in the hours of leisure, such as previously he allowed himself, but now finds to have become perilous. In other words, when there has been violation of his law, the individual imposes upon himself toils and renunciations which are in the fullest sense acts of self-punishment. Take the other case, analogous to what happened in the sphere of social law. The individual may find that he is overwhelmed by artistic or musical enthusiasm to the point that his first plan, his first individual law, seems never to have reflected, or anyway no longer to reflect, his true and profound inclinations. Therefore he will rebel against his previous law and destroy its traces in himself, just as in the other example the people destroyed the law of the despot, attacking, imprisoning, or killing its author.

Programmes, plans, or individual laws are, then, laws, and since this concept thus embraces the isolated individual no less than society, evidently a "social" character is not essential to the concept of law. On the contrary, the only laws that have real existence are the individual laws, and there can thus be no question of treating individual and social laws as two forms of the general

concept of law unless "individual" and "society" be both taken in
an empirical sense, outside the range of philosophical thought. But
taking the term "individual" in its philosophical sense, as meaning
the concrete and individualized Spirit, it is clear that the so-called
social laws must themselves be translated into individual laws, for
to observe a law it is necessary to make it one's own, to individual-
ize it, and to rebel against a law it is necessary to expel it from
one's own personality in which it improperly sought to introduce
itself or to linger.

The negation of a social character in the concept of law liberates
philosophy from a series of problems and related theories dependent
upon that supposed character. Chiefmost among these is the
distinction drawn between political and juridical laws on the one
hand, and merely social laws on the other, and within the class of
juridical laws between those of public and those of private jurisprudence, between civil and penal laws, between national and
international laws, between laws properly so called and regulations, and so forth. If the concept of social laws is itself empirical,
all derivative distinctions and sub-distinctions which are proposed
must be likewise empirical, and it becomes impossible to defend
one such distinction against another, or to correct those already
made and to propose others. An examination of any one of those
distinctions at once reveals their lack of philosophical foundation.
A distinction has been drawn between juridical or political laws
and merely social laws on the grounds that the former are com-
pulsive and the latter merely conventional, but, as has been shown,
compulsion is equally out of the question in both, while if all
that is meant is that a penalty is attached to violation of the former,
this is the case in merely social laws just as much as in juridical
laws. The "juridical" law against counterfeiting money can be
violated only at the risk of a prison sentence. The "social" law
that a salutation has to be acknowledged is violated at the risk of
designation as an ill-bred fellow and of consequent exclusion from
respectable circles. Is there any essential difference between the
two sorts of law? An attempt has been made to differentiate them
by saying that juridical laws are promulgated by a supreme power

which watches over the observance of them, and social laws by particular groups of individuals. But that supreme power is certainly not vested in a super-individual dominating individuals. It is vested in individuals. If that is true, its authority and power is neither more nor less than that of the individuals who compose it. In other words, those juridical laws are the laws of a group empirically considered to be peculiarly close-knit and strong, but these laws are effective only in so far as the individuals in the group spontaneously observe them, considering it advantageous to do so. Monarchs who believed themselves exceedingly strong have often been taught to think otherwise by events which have shown them, in direct and disagreeable fashion, that strength lay not in their persons or titles, but in a universal consent. When this failed their power failed, or shrank to a gesture of impotent and almost ridiculous command. Laws which seemed excellent remain unapplied, because they meet with a tacit general resistance, or are said to be out of touch with the times, a fact which should in itself suffice to bring home the inseparability of "State" and "Society". The State is not an entity but a mobile complex of all sorts of relations between individuals. There may be good reason for roughly delimiting this complex and endowing it with the attributes of existence to distinguish it from other complexes, indeed there is no doubt about this, and we leave it to the jurists to think out these and similar opportune though fictitious distinctions, which are by no means to be dismissed as irrational. We must only recall with insistence that what is fictitious is fictitious, and therefore refrain from elaborating it in terms of reality, piling up volume upon volume of laboured philosophical argument. For such argument would be void of effect, though the practical distinctions in question are by no means, in their own sphere, similarly void. Our point of view is not that of the jurist but that of the philosopher, and since the philosopher is precluded from framing or using practical or empirical distinctions, it behoves us to include in the single category of law along with the English Magna Charta the statutes of the Sicilian "Mafia" and the Neapolitan "Camorra", and along with the *Regula Monachorum* of the Order of Saint

Benedict the rules of that Spendthrifts' Brigade celebrated in the sonnets of Folgore da San Gemignano and Cene della Chitarra, and recalled also by Dante, or again, along with the ecclesiastical and military codes, that "droit parisien" which one of Balzac's characters studied for three years in the blue boudoir of one lady and the pink boudoir of another, and which, though never publicly mentioned, forms (according to the great novelist) "une haute jurisprudence sociale, qui, bien apprise et bien pratiquée, mène à tout".[1] Among laws we will even include those literary and artistic codes prescribing the production of works having this or that sort of subject-matter or arrangement, for example, of dramas conforming to the rule of an arrangement in five acts or in three parts for performance on successive days; of novels conforming to the rule of not exceeding four or five hundred pages of a given format; of monumental statues conforming to the requirement that they must either be in the nude or in heroic vesture. Evidently, anyone who violates such codes may (and at the present moment does) find himself blackballed by the academies of "good taste", and may for that very reason be warmly welcomed by the counter-academies of the bohemians, just as the serving of a prison sentence is a qualification for reception into certain criminal fraternities.

These examples, deliberately chosen for their exceptional and outrageous character, well illustrate how the concept of law must for the purposes of philosophic elaboration be taken in its full logical range. There is a curious sort of coyness which deems it below the dignity of philosophy to enter into certain arguments, and is thereby led to restrict arbitrarily, and so to distort, certain philosophical concepts. The concept of Law, in particular, has been wrapped up in a tradition of solemnity and has from this derived associations which require to be dispelled. Unless this is done there is no way even of obtaining an insight into the nature and efficacity of those unwritten and unalterable laws of the Gods which Antigone championed against the decrees of men, or of

---

1. Balzac, *Le Père Goriot* (Paris, Calmann Lévy, 1891), p. 85.

those Lacedaemonian sentences in obedience to which the Three Hundred fell at Thermopylae; or of those laws of the fatherland which with irresistible authority enjoined Socrates to remain in prison at the moment when his friends were counselling and facilitating a flight.

Life is made up of little and even trivial actions, and of great and even sublime actions, or rather of a close web of perpetually various actions. It is foolishness to try and cut the web into pieces, to cast some aside as inferior and to fix attention solely upon some fairer specimens, for with this cutting and ripping the web itself will have ceased to exist.

II

THE CONSTITUENT ELEMENTS OF LAW:
CRITIQUE OF PERMISSIVE LAW AND OF NATURAL RIGHTS

After eliminating improper restrictions and empirical divisions from the concept of law, attention may be redirected to the character which we have said to be apt for defining that concept, and with this we are in a position to distinguish laws from other spiritual formations with which they are often confounded by reason of metaphors and of overlapping terms in current speech. Laws, we have said, are acts of will concerning classes of actions. In the absence either of volition or of classification there can be no law except by an extension of language or by metaphor.

Absence of volition is the reason why the so-called laws of nature or of natural science are not laws but mere statements of relations between empirical concepts, or simple rules. Thus it is said to be a law in natural science, and more precisely in physics, that platinum melts at 1773 degrees C., and it is said to be a grammatical law that, in Greek, masculine nouns of the first declension have a genitive in ου (save for exceptions which arise under both the laws in question). But these are about as much laws as the king of spades is a king, and students of the history of ideas know that the denomination "law" was introduced by the Stoics as a metaphor taken from the world of politics in which it originated and applied to the world of nature. We have already pointed out that empirical concepts and rules can be given the literary form of the imperative, as, for example: "If you wish to melt platinum, heat it to 1773 degrees", or: "If you wish to speak Greek, inflect the masculine nouns of the first declension with ου for the genitive case." But the literary form has no bearing on the nature of the matter, and those "imperatives" are "hypothetical imperatives", that is false imperatives, improper laws. Until someone – it may be myself – makes me speak Greek or open a laboratory where platinum is melted, the grammatical and physical laws in question will remain mere schemes, instruments of cognition which have not yet become instruments of action. The jurist who fixes types and rules is not the legislator, and only the legislator, who with one of his hands grasps the sword, can endow the jurist's mental products with the character of laws.

Now we already know that empirical concepts, schemes, and rules are the product of an act of will, not merely the will which is implicit in the activity of thinking, but a particular sort of will which out of representations and concepts fashions a mixed product that is neither representation nor concept and, although it is irrational by the standard of pure theory, yet fulfils a due function in the economy of the spirit. But Law, in its proper sense, is an act of will which presupposes the previous act of will whereby pseudo-concepts or classificatory concepts are fashioned. For it is a volition having as its object a class of objects. It is impossible to command the speaking of Greek in conformity with grammatical rules, or the melting of platinum in conformity with physical rules, until those rules have been established. And here we may discern with extreme clearness the gulf between the two orders of spiritual formation which is apt to be clouded and obscured in a confusion between the two orders, when relations between classes are cast into the literary shape of the imperative, so as to become rules. The difference is recognizable in this simple manner: a rule can be translated into the establishment of a class. Thus: "If you wish to melt platinum, heat it to 1773 degrees" says neither more nor less than "Platinum melts at 1773 degrees".

(The identity of the two propositions has already been demonstrated.) On the contrary, the law "In every city there is to be opened a physical laboratory for the melting of platinum" cannot by any means be translated out of the imperative into the indicative mood.

Absence of volition, then, disqualifies the "laws" of the natural sciences, but other spiritual formations which are commonly described and regarded as "laws" are disqualified not by absence of volition but by absence of classification. Such is the case with "economic law", "moral law", and indirectly also with the "laws" of logic and aesthetics. The moral law says: "Thou shalt will the universal", or in other words, "Will the good, the useful, the true, the beautiful". In itself, viewed in its own reality and not in its theoretical presentation as the concept of itself, this is a volition. But the object of this volition is the spirit itself, which has being and existence just in so far as it wills and affirms itself. Its object, then, is a form or universal, whereas laws, properly defined, have always to do with something material which is at the same time not sheerly individual, a generality, a class and not an idea. The universal laws, better termed Principles, are the Spirit itself, the producer, whereas what are properly called laws are a special product of the Spirit. The former are not laws in the same sense as the latter.

It is once again absence of classification, of generalization that precludes us from describing a single and individual act of will as law. My resolve at this moment not to rise from my chair, not to go forward and warmly greet the friend who has just looked in to interrupt my work at this ill-chosen moment – this is an act of will, not a law. But an interior act of will consisting in the purpose or programme of always remaining seated and behaving coolly towards friends who dropped in in the morning hours, so as to give them to understand that such visits upset my work and must be discontinued unless they wish to suffer the penalty of a cold reception from their friend – that would be law.

By recognizing the general and not universal character of the contents of laws, and their quality of contingency, not of necessity, we can attain to a solution of certain celebrated controversies

which previously balked our attempts to settle them or to demonstrate the settlement. First of all, the controversy whether
permissive laws are conceivable, and whether the old formula
that law *aut jubet aut vetat aut permittit* is valid. It is generally
admitted that law *aut jubet aut vetat*, and that the only sense in
which it can permit is by the removal of a previous prohibition,
that is the total or partial abrogation of another law. But in
reality the law, being an act of will, purely and simply *jubet*: to
command is to will: to order the opening of a physical laboratory
in every city is to will that this should be done. Now since
every affirmative will necessarily implies a negative will (affirmation being inseparable from negation), every command must
always be viewed as being at the same time a prohibition, every
jubeo a *veto*, the question whether it be given the verbal form of
command or prohibition, positive or negative, being of no importance. That there should be alongside of the commanding or
prohibitory laws also permissive laws, is inconceivable, not because
laws do not accord permissions, but because permissiveness is
already implied in that which is imperative or prohibitory: every
jubeo or *veto* is a *permitto*. There is no permissiveness about principles, or universal volitions, for there is nothing that lies outside
their scope. But a single volition, by its self-affirmation, does not
exclude the affirmation of other and infinite volitions, since what
is single can never have universal range. The laws are volitions
of classes of acts. They prescribe series of acts of greater or lesser
width but always within insuperable limits, so that any law always
refrains from willing (that is from commanding or from prohibiting) all the other actions and classes of actions which can or could
become objects of the will: from its point of view they remain
permitted. All the laws that have ever been promulgated up to a
certain moment, taken all together, cannot attain the fullness of
the universal, and though fresh laws be heaped one upon the
other and distinguished, refined, subtilized in a frantic attempt to
cover all cases, the result will be a *progressus in infinitum*, not the full
exhaustion of the inexhaustible. In other words, outside of law and
of the laws there will always remain that which is optional, al-

lowed, indifferent, faculty or right, or whatever word be used to express the concept which is the counterpart of command, prohibition, duty. The contrast between the two concepts indicates the finite nature of law, which necessitates that when a determined faculty or option or right is cancelled by a new law, when something previously indifferent is differentiated, from the soil of the new law there must always spring up anew the optional and indifferent, faculty and right.

Another character arising out of the contingent character of the laws is their mutability. The laws are mutable, whereas principles (or "laws" of universal content) are immutable, ever available to serve as form for the most varied historical material. Since actual conditions are constantly changing, new laws have to be continually made to supplement the old which require correction, modification, or even abolition. This can be seen both in programmes for individual life and in those programmes which are called social or political laws. The variety of ways in which laws can be changed is one of those questions which does not concern us, for from the standpoint of philosophy there is never more than one such way: the production of new law by free will operating in new conditions. What is called an "involuntary" change is just a formula to describe certain voluntary changes which occur with less solemnity than certain others. (But the solemnity of the human will performing its function will even in those cases not be lacking.) It is not for the philosopher to decide whether in the practical field conservation or revolution is the fundamental concept. Every conservative is, for the philosopher, at the same time an effective revolutionary in that he is continually adapting the law which he wishes to conserve to new circumstances, and every revolutionary is at the same time a conservative, being constrained to take for his point of departure certain laws which he maintains at least provisionally while engaged in changing certain others and replacing those by new laws which he then intends to conserve. Revolution for Revolution's sake, the cult of the Goddess Revolution, is madness no less mad for having been attempted in history. It ends, like all mad projects, in suicide, when the revolution proceeds to revolutionize itself and turns into reaction. The distinction by which revolutionaries and conservatives are counterposed to each other is merely empirical: its meaning has to be sought in the particular historical circumstances which gave rise to it. Cavour was a conservative in regard to certain problems and a revolutionary in regard to others, and indeed the Mazzinians regarded him as a conservative, the legitimists and clericals as a revolutionary. Robespierre ranked as a revolutionary for the Girondins and even at the last stage for the "moderate" Danton, as he had come to regard himself. But in the eyes of Hébert and Chaumette he was a conservative, the enemy of the free development of the "rights of man".

There is a contradiction also in the concept of an eternal code, an ultimate or model legislation, a system of universal rights, variously described as rational or natural or whatever it might be. Natural right, universal legislation, an eternal code which claims to fix that which is transient, offends against the principle of the mutability of laws, which is itself a necessary consequence of the contingent and historical character of their content. If natural law could fulfil its pretensions, if God permitted the business of Reality to be administered according to the abstract notions of writers and professors, then the formation and application of the Eternal Code would once and for all arrest Development, put a stop to History, terminate Life, undo Reality.

This end of all things does not come about because although contradiction is possible in discourse, it is impossible in concrete actuality: God, that is to say Reality, stands in the way of its realization. So-called Natural Law, whenever it has come on to the ground of concrete actuality, has fluctuatingly included two different orders of facts, neither having anything to do with its first pretensions. In the first place, under the description of Rational or Natural Law there have been advanced proposals for new laws seemingly better than the old and good by comparison with the degree of badness now found to pertain to the old. The old, then, were viewed as unnatural and irrational, the new as rational and natural. Just as those of erotic and passionate temperament at each new falling in love, untaught by previous experience, proclaim in full seriousness that the new love will be definitive, constant, and eternal, so men when they create new laws easily succumb to the illusion that the new, unlike those which they have replaced, will never change, forgetting that the old were in their day young and (as the old carnival song had it) "were the delight of many men". Those "natural" laws are historical, those "eternal" laws are transitory, like all the others. The character of "natural" and "eternal" law has at some times and places been ascribed to religious toleration, free trade, private property, constitutional monarchy, and at other times and places to the extirpation of infidels, commercial protectionism, Communism, the republican form of the State, and anarchy.

The second order of facts which have been entitled "Natural Law" correspond to an attempt to surpass the contingent and transitory character of juridical concepts and to reach to the principles of the Philosophy of Practice, those principles which are eternal and immutable, but purely formal, and therefore not laws. Treatises on "Natural Law" pursuing this aim are really simply treatises on Ethics, and sometimes very good ones. If in such treatises the ethical teaching is accompanied by descriptive detail leading up to proposals for social, juridical, and political reforms, the result is a medley of the two orders of facts which we have distinguished, philosophical facts and single cases. But "natural law" is nowhere to be found in either part, being itself a logical and real contradiction.

In our days, thanks to the enhancement of historical sense, the very names as well as the elaborations of Natural Law and the Eternal Code have almost wholly lost their old prestige. But illegitimate problems rooted in that contradictory concept, or illegitimate methods of expounding problems which are legitimate when expounded in their true terms, still persist. An example of the former sort of persisting illegitimacy is the theory of the Natural Rights of Man, which pretends to distinguish between the rights which belong to man by nature and those which derive from historical contingency. Among the former there are enumerated such rights as the right to life, liberty, work, family existence, and among the latter the rights which are written in the constitution of some country or in some set of contracts. But man outside society, which here means the same as outside history, man as an abstract spirit, has no right of any sort except to be a spirit. The lists of natural rights are either tautologous, merely repeating that man as a spirit has the right (and duty) to develop his existence as a spirit (which, as a living man, he cannot in any case help but do), or else they are arbitrary rationalizations of historical contingencies, the "right to work", for example, was the slogan of the workers of the *ateliers nationaux* in 1848, and previously that of the insurgents of Lyon, while the "right of untrammelled property" was the slogan of the bourgeoisie in their agitation against feudal restrictions, and has now once again become the slogan of the same bourgeoisie in their resistance to the socialist movement.

Examples of the second sort of erroneous persistence may be found in arguments used for assailing or defending social and political institutions, when, instead of these being assailed as irrational or defended as rational in regard to the given historical circumstances, they are assailed as being incompatible with the true notion of rights or with the true notion of the particular institution in question, or defended as being compatible with these, that is on what are properly termed "abstract grounds". Thus the reformer will uphold the right of women to the local or the parliamentary vote by reasoning that women form part of the State and have general and particular interests which need to be upheld directly, and not through the intervention of males, whose interests are sometimes constrasting. The conservative will totally reject this reasoning by adducing the proper range of women's concern, which is, he says, confined by the law of nature to within the family. The reformer will uphold divorce as the necessary complement of marriage, on the grounds that where spiritual harmony fails all other links should cease. The conservative condemns divorce as contrary to the very nature of marriage, and degrading it to the level of concubinage or "free love". Other instances could be multiplied. When such arguments and counter-arguments are in the air, who is going to say that Natural Law has disappeared from the scene? The proposal of woman's suffrage may be a serious or a ridiculous one, according to when and where it is made. Divorce may be a highly moral or a profoundly immoral institution, according to time and place, for only narrowness and ignorance could regard peoples who practise divorce or some relation between the sexes different from our customs as living outside the pale of humanity or in a permanent condition of immorality. And similarly with peoples which at present deny or in the future may extend the suffrage to women. Not even polygamy and free concubinage can be regarded as immoral, irrational, and unnatural, seeing that it was regarded as a legitimate institution in certain times and places, nay, whatever be the repugnance of civilized European hearts and stomachs to the idea, the same must be said of cannibalism, for it will surely be agreed, if one makes the necessary mental effort, that among the man-eaters there were men who enjoyed a perfectly clear conscience while they devoured their fellow-man, this they did as calmly as we now devour a roast chicken, without any feeling of hatred for the chicken, but knowing that, at any rate at the present moment, that is the way of life. Those accusers who rashly base their arguments on an imaginary rational law do not remember a page of Cornelius Nepos which they probably had to translate at school. It deserves quoting. "Expertes litterarum Graecarum nihil rectum nisi quod ipsorum moribus conveniat, putabunt. Hi, si didicerint non eadem omnibus esse honesta atque turpia, SED OMNIA MAJORUM INSTITUTIS JUDICARI, non admirabuntur nos in Graiorum virtutibus exponendis mores eorum secutos. Neque enim Cimoni fuit turpe, Atheniensium summo viro, sororem germanam habere in matrimonio, quippe quum ejus cives eodem uterentur instituto: at id quidem nostris moribus nefas habetur. Laudi in Graecia ducitur adolescentulis quam plurimos habere amatores. Nulla Lacedaemoni tam est nobilis vidua quae non ad scenam eat mercede conducta . . ." etcetera.[1] This reminds us that there is nothing

1. *Vitae excell. imper.*, Preface.

specially modern about the unreasoning condemnation of morals which happen to be different from our own, or about the reasonable recognition that there is a variety in morals.

III

THE UNREALITY OF LAW AND THE REALITY OF ITS EXECUTION – THE SIGNIFICANCE OF LAW IN THE PRACTICAL SPIRIT

The willing of a class of actions (thus we have defined law) is the willing of an abstraction. But "to will an abstraction" is as much as to say "to will abstractly", and this cannot really be willing at all, for willing is necessarily concrete, in a determined situation, with a volitional synthesis corresponding to the situation, leading immediately to action, in fact having itself the character of effective action. It seems then that the volition which is law should be described as a pretended volition, contradictory in being void of a unique and determined situation, ineffectual because arising from the unsure soil of an abstract concept, in fact a volition which is not willed, an act of will not real but unreal.

And such indeed it is. What is really willed is not the law, but the single act which is performed "under the law", the execution of the law. It is the single volition which alone is put into effect, the execution of the law is the one volition which is really willed and put into operation. The law has been framed, and life continues with its incessant flow of new problems. Some of these do not enter into the scope of the law and find a solution according to the universal principles of practical philosophy, economic and ethical. Others come within its scope, and in that case the law has to be implemented unless indeed it be held the wiser course to change it, to flout it, or to try and quietly undermine and invalidate it.

But even in situations within the scope of the law, when it is a question of acting in accordance with it, of "executing" or "applying" it, the law is unreal. Once again we must beware of words and metaphors and consider things in their directness. Direct consideration demonstrates that the particular situations of a volition and an action can never be foreseen by a law, and that it is therefore impossible to act according to law, to execute and apply it. The real event is always a surprise, an event that happens once and for all, and is known only in its occurrence, so that each new event requires a new measure, like a new dress for a new body. The measure of the law, being abstract, oscillates between universal and individual, and has the virtue of neither the one nor the other. "Put the law into effect" – that is the programme of a pedant in life, just as it is the programme of a pedant in art to "apply" the rules of the art. The true artist obediently follows the guidance of his aesthetic conscience, and the practical man follows the inspiration of his practical genius. The "single act" performed in execution and observance of the law really observes not the law but the practical and ethical principle, and observes it by individualization of it. A man who has his memory full of laws composed or accepted by himself, when he comes to the point of action makes a humble obeisance to the laws but follows his own good sense.

The law in Italy and some other countries requires men on reaching twenty years of age to register at an office and to perform military service for a certain period. Let us overlook the possibility that those called up for service might rebel, take over the Government of the country, abolish the law of conscription, and re-establish a law of voluntary service. Let us overlook the other and not wholly imaginary case that the conscripts might violate the law by taking refuge beyond the frontiers, hiding in an underground retreat (like the heroes of Father Bresciani's novels), or following the Tolstoyan precept of non-resistance to evil, suffering imprisonment sooner than service at arms. Let us, instead, take the case of the law-abiding citizen who becomes a soldier in order not to go to prison, or of the loyal one who recognizes his duty to serve his country. Either one of these, in presenting himself at regimental headquarters, is evidently not obeying the voice of the law, that mere *flatus vocis*, but obeying his utilitarian or else his moral conscience. But what steps will he now take to fulfil the law which requires him to perform military service in precisely such and such a manner? Each individual has his own

44

temperament, gifts, physical strength, and each one will perform his service in a way that is all his own, different from the way of others. It will be a difference not just of better or worse, of fulfilling the law more or less thoroughly, but of the manner of performance even when all are putting an equal diligence and zeal into it. On the parade ground it may seem that all are performing the same movement, but in reality each is moving differently from the other. When the column marches across the ground each man seems to be marching like the others, but in reality, even in the Prussian Army, each marches in his own way. To the quick and distant glance there seems to be uniformity, to the closer inspection there is diversity of form. Could one perform the experiment of putting side by side a regiment of today and a regiment of fifty years ago, without any change in the meanwhile in the parade regulations, arms, uniforms, and so on, the difference would at once strike the eye, a difference enhanced by changes in the general atmosphere, the level of instruction and manners, diet and housing. We cannot perform this experiment across a lapse of time, but we can observe the comparative application of the same army regulations in two different populations. The effect is that of a single book written in two different languages, which aesthetically must be considered as two different books. (The poet Giusti translated out of his native Florentine into Milanese dialect, or Porta translated from Milanese into Florentine, are no longer Porta and Giusti but two new poets.)

The impossibility of applying the law, of incarnating it in facts, the necessity of operating case by case as historical circumstances require, is the real basis of the radical conclusion reached by some people in different ages and places that laws are useless and should be dispensed with. If in the final resort it is single action that counts, and decision and execution lie with the single individual, what boots it to entangle the actors in strings and knots which at the moment of action they must needs burst asunder? Why spend all that care and anxiety on shaping instruments which at the crucial moment will be thrown aside to allow bare hands to tackle the task? With such reasoning the ideal has sometimes been

advanced of a society without laws in which each performs his
task through sheer love of the work – such was the theory of
Fournier's "Harmonics" and of many Utopian Anarchists. Another
cherished dream is that of the absolute and paternal government
of the good old times conducted by a benevolent despot who being
unshackled by the provisions of law could deal with every case as
the goodness of his heart suggested to him. To cite some less wild
and more realistic examples, it has been suggested that the judge
should frame the law as he goes along, to suit the case, should
in fact cease to be a judge – having no law to apply he could
not strictly speaking pronounce a verdict – and become a free
conciliator and moral reformer. Or at least, it has been suggested,
he should sweep aside juridical fictions and judge according to the
particular reality of the case. These are, for sure, theories which
will not hold water, not even the last mentioned, which has an air
of sweet reasonableness. For the so-called "juridical fiction" is part
and parcel of the law, and is present even when seemingly absent.
For it is always a fiction to include a concrete case in an abstract
category. But it has been a mistaken retort to these erroneous
doctrines when the upholders of the utility of the laws have proclaimed that law admits of no individual solutions, since it requires
rigid obedience. The retort is mistaken because what one might
call "legitimate" individuality, evasion, and breach are a permanent element in the facts, implicit in the very nature of law. The
objectors and the upholders are, then, equally wrong, the former
in decrying the laws as useless, the latter in attributing to them an
impossible utility. No doubt as in many other discussions of
ostensibly philosophical character, such arguments often conceal
some practical and political point of contention, and if wrong on
one level are right on another, with right and wrong bafflingly
distributed on both sides. Those who protest against Law are
often really protesting against an excess of legislation, or rightly
asking that the judge should be less bound to a pedantic or mechanical routine than he often is. Those who exalt Law are often
withstanding revolutionaries who seek to abolish certain laws of
crucial importance for civil progress, or who tend to discredit

all the laws in order to induce a chaotic agitation in which society would lack all rule and guidance. All this, however, is extraneous to the philosophical problem which is our present business.

Had the upholders of the utility of the law been content with one of those commonsense arguments which always win the day even though they be not logically rigorous, they would have pointed out how at every point of human history there arises a demand for laws, order, justice, the State: "Better a bad Government than none at all. Better a steady abiding in inferior laws than a mad chase after better and still better laws with all the unsettlement that brings." Or from another point of view: "God preserve us from brilliant despots, inspired judges, tribunals overflowing with equity." Such are the voices that resound through history. For the sake of legality hundreds of battles have been fought, rivers of blood have flowed, the weariness of litigation is sustained day after day, and energy is poured out in a way which superficial intelligences, but they only, are able to regard as waste of time and trouble. In truth no effort made for the maintenance of one's right is wasted, and none is more sacred, for at the same time it upholds the offended majesty of the law, the Right of all. Those who argue against the laws can do so with a light heart because they are surrounded, protected, and kept alive by the laws. Should law begin to waver and topple over they would soon find their arguments and their chatter dying on their lips like those of Dante's shepherd struck dumb at the sudden appearance of the wolf eyeing him in the wood.

> In quella guisa che talor, veduto
> da la lupa nel bosco, il pastor suole:
> come spirito e senso abbia perduto,
> gli muoion ne la lingua le parole.

And they would rush to reconstitute the laws, no matter whether good or bad, in order to regain security, to recapture some peace and quiet, that peace and quiet which is necessary even for academic declamation against the laws.

However, abandoning such commonsense considerations and passing to philosophic argument, we must make it still more clear that the utility of law resides not in its effectuation, which is impossible, for nothing can be put into effect save the single act of the single actor, but in the fact that the volition and execution of the single act usually is helped on by an initial attention to a generality of which the single act is a particular example, a class of which it is a component. It is much the same proceeding as that by which in taking aim one first observes the region around the target. The law is not a real and effectual volition but an unmistakably imperfect and contradictory volition. But this it is just because it is preparatory to the perfect and synthetic volition. Law, the volition of an abstract, is not a real volition but a help to real volition. To use a hackneyed comparison, scaffolding is an aid to the construction of the house, and the fact that it is thereafter demolished in nowise means that it was useless for the purpose in hand.

We can here once again descry a precise analogy between the constitution of the practical and the theoretical spirit. In the latter, also, we meet with theoretical formations which are not really such, but exhibit internal contradictions, positing representations which act as universals, and universals which are representative, arbitrary formations requiring the will to command that which it cannot command. For representations and concepts do not follow upon but precede the volition, the practical act, and therefore cannot really be commanded by the will. But we know that those feigned concepts, those schemes, those laws which are not laws, those falsities which being self-confessed are not false, in fact sustain the memory and assist thought to find its way in the colourful variety of life which it penetrates and suffuses. They are not truly thoughts, yet they help us to think. They are not truly imaginations, but they help us to imagine. The philosopher normally lingers over the pseudo-concepts in order to rise above them to the universals. The artist, too, ponders over them, in order to discover beneath them the individuality, the lively and ingenuous intuition, which is what he seeks. And the same pseudo-concepts, having become objects of volition and been turned from schemes into laws, fulfil an analogous office in the practical spirit, enabling the will to wish in a certain direction where it will hit upon the purposeful action which is always an individuated action.

No less important is another aspect of the analogy. Pseudo-concepts would be impossible if reality did not include, along with the dissimilar, the similar, which is not indeed the universal-necessary, but is the general, or so to speak a not so contingent contingency, a not so variable, relatively constant, variety. The arbitrariness of pseudo-concepts lies not in a positing of the similar where there is dissimilarity, but in a rigidifying of that variable which is only relatively constant, so as to make of it something absolutely constant, converting similarity into identity. The practical spirit, which creates reality, has need to create not only the dissimilar but also the similar, and not only that which lasts an instant but also that which lasts more or less unchanged for a year, a century, a thousand or a million years, and not only the individual but also the species, not only the great man but also the people, not only the actions done once and for all, but also those which recur in similar though not identical repetitions. This is the office performed by the laws which constitute "social order", indeed cosmic order. But in any case it is an order that is only relative and includes in itself instability, a rectilinear figure which in reality, examined closely, proves to be made up itself of curves. Hence it is necessary to frame the laws and at the same time, while observing them as best one may, to violate them in the execution.

Our characterization of the law as an unreal volition which none the less serves to help and prepare real volition, throws light upon a concept that in the course of our exposition of the essence and operation of the act of will we rejected, namely the concept of a plan, design, or model pertaining to the practical activity, by "executing" a pre-established design by which practical activity (according to the view we have rejected) realizes itself. We, on the contrary, demonstrated that the design and the execution of the design are in reality all one, and that if man operates by constantly changing his design, this is because he changes the reality which is the basis of his action. Neither in the Philosophy of

Practice in general, nor in Ethics in particular, is there any room for the concept of a pre-established design. True, in Ethics there is a distinction between the universal and the merely individual action, but no less true is it that the universal can exist concretely only as embodied and individuated, as this or that single good action. The ethical universal is not a design and cannot be desired in itself, unindividuated, just as falling in love is with a particular person and not with love abstractly considered. But the concept of a design established precedently to action and executed by means of the action, despite and because of its having no proper place in Economic and Ethical Philosophy, must have its legitimate significance in some other order of facts, whence it has been introduced here. Otherwise it could never have been thought of and applied erroneously. We have now seen that this meaning fits the case of law. Laws are, in fact, plans or designs which are actuated, or more properly speaking are not actuated, by the operating individual.

IV

THE CONFUSION BETWEEN LAWS AND PRACTICAL PRINCIPLES:
CRITIQUE OF LEGALISM IN THE PHILOSOPHY OF PRACTICE
AND OF THE JESUITICAL MORALITY

Nothing, perhaps, better illustrates the genuine nature of the laws better than an examination of the grave errors which have crept into the Philosophy of Practice through failure to appreciate the character of these mental formations (the laws) as nothing more than a helpful device; and through confusion between the laws and the practical principles to each of which there has been wrongly attributed the character of the other.

In our daily life we are for ever surrounded and supported by laws, laws without number, though at any given instant of limited number. The Ten Commandments still bid us: "Thou shalt not take the name of God in vain" – "Honour thy father and thy mother" – "Thou shalt not steal" – "Thou shalt do no murder" – "Thou shalt not covet thy neighbour's house, nor his wife, nor his manservant, maidservant, ox, ass nor anything that is his . . ." and so forth. The ten or hundred commandments of prudence on their side enjoin: "Don't make too many enemies" – "Mind your own business" – "Make yourself agreeable to the more powerful" – "Strike before you are struck" – and so on. The multitude and detail of these laws easily lead to the false notion that the whole complex of them suffices to regulate our utilitarian and moral life, and that practical principles can be replaced or fully represented by a Decalogue or a Code functioning as the true regulator of life.

But the Decalogue, the Code, the *Corpus Juris*, however ample, detailed, and subtle, can as we know never suffice to cover the infinity of actions arising out of infinitely various factual situations. Every law brings in its trail, as the inevitable shadow thrown by its light, the mass of indiscriminate actions, those to which the law is irrelevant, the unforbidden, the permissible, the right and faculty of doing or not doing. It follows inexorably that if the practical principles are conceived as a succession or complex of laws, there must then be attached to these the concept of what is not merely *legally* optional but *practically* indifferent.

Let us see how this works out. At every instant of life we find ourselves facing situations of fact to which our laws either have no applicability at all, or only a very approximate applicability such as we have already described, and thus at every instant of life we lack the guidance of law and stand faced by the undifferentiated, the indifferent. The practical man knows or feels very well that the laws are a simple device and provisional exercise, falling short of action. He knows and feels that he must each time meet the situation of fact, perceive it in its originality, and produce his own action as an original act. But a man who has embraced the legal conception of practical activity, and has abandoned practical principles as useless or, as he supposes, inexistent, now that he finds himself let down also by the laws in which he had trusted too greatly, has no other guidance left but that of his own arbitrary whim. But that which is arbitrary is not guidance, it is lack of guidance, not action but inaction, contradictory action, not activity but passivity, not prudence and morality but imprudence and immorality.

The legalistic conception of the practical principles tends thus to bring about the death of the practical, replacing activity by passivity, good by evil. Setting out to determine exactly the true concept of liberty, it arrives at the arbitrary, which is the very contrary of liberty.

It may here be pointed out that this moral legalism, on which the attention of critics has been centred, is only one particular case of general practical legalism (the general case has hitherto escaped attention). The reason for the neglect of the general in favour of the particular is to be found in the habitual failure of philosophers to recognize the economic form in its autonomy. But from the examples which we have chosen it is clear that legalism is an error which invades the Economic no less than the Ethical form. In both it introduces the philosophic absurdity of the "practically indifferent". Even a man lacking, perhaps momentarily, a moral conscience, supposing he should look to the laws for guidance in his practical conduct, would lose his utilitarian bearings and fall into the arbitrary, to the ruin of his own individuality. To take the usual example, if I make it a law of health not to drink wine, but then find myself all of a sudden in a physiological condition that calls for a glass of wine to speed the heart and give me the strength of which I have need, why then, if in my blind faith I forget that the law is relative, not absolute, and that the only absolute law is to do at a given moment what is at that moment advantageous, clearly in reasoning and acting in that way I am substituting for prudence superstition, the arbitrary, and am working to my own disadvantage.

Ethical and Economic Philosophy must sternly exclude the concept of the morally or practically indifferent, which whenever it creeps into their doctrine spreads a subtle corruption. In the true field of Practice, occupied by these philosophies, there can be no room for an option which is not at the same time an obligation, for a right which is not at the same time a duty, for an absence of compulsion which is not at the same time a prohibition, for a permission which is not convertible into a command. Πάντα ἔξεστιν, ἀλλ' οὐ πάντα συμφέρει, said Saint Paul (Corinthians I. 10, 23) in obscure and haunting words which have given rise to so much disputation, and we may interpret this "All things are licit for us but we claim no licence": everything can and must be elaborated by the will and must receive the form of liberty. To eliminate wholly this parasitic concept it is necessary to penetrate to the region of the concept of legalism in the general philosophy of practice, to show, as we have done, how it originates in confusion between principles and laws.

The upholders of Rigorism have been aware of the perils and disasters into which the theory of Ethics tends to slip and have accordingly joined issue with the school of the Laxists, the theorists of the "morally indifferent". But in vain – for as long as both contestants stuck to the ground of legalism, both were right and both were wrong, Pharisees and Sadducees, Jansenists and Molinists. The Rigorists fastened desperately upon the law, refusing to admit that it could possibly be doubtful so as to leave room for the morally indifferent. The law, they said, was certain. But in truth the law can never be either doubtful or certain. For since it concerns itself with empirical concepts it never defines anything exactly, and therefore cannot be certain. Yet since its object is not concrete action, but only the preparation of concrete action, the question of defining the indefinable does not arise, so that neither is the law uncertain or doubtful. It eludes these categories of doubtfulness and certainty. The Rigorists found the morally indifferent obstinately cropping up afresh, and could not extirpate it. They might give the advice to take that course of action which was the more painful and distasteful, but this too was a recourse to the arbitrary, the evil. On the other side the Laxists could extend to whatever width they chose the field of the morally indifferent, adducing the dubieties of the law, its impotence as a practical principle. But since they did not recognize any practical principle having a form different from law, they were obliged to have recourse to law for some sort of guidance and direction in life. Not finding this in the law itself they had to locate it in the authority of the interpreters of the law, and where the interpretations differed in a weighted valuation of the respective authorities, such as the rule laid down by Theodosius II for the quotation of the Roman jurists. But since two or three or four or a hundred authorities when they are uncertain are really no better than one equally uncertain authority, the conclusion of the matter was that any authority was good enough to justify an action. Probabilism, far from being a contradiction of legalism, is its logical consequence. If it is an authority that has to decide, why should the authority of one among persons who are all estimable and trustworthy weigh for more than that of another? Why rank Papinian above Paul or Ulpian? Villalobos holds that a priest who has committed mortal sin cannot celebrate mass the same day, but Sánchez holds that he can. Why then should a priest who finds himself in that condition follow Villalobos rather than Sánchez? True, making a blind choice between Sánchez and Villalobos he falls into the noose of the arbitrary, but the arbitrary is enmeshed with legalism, and the more he struggles to escape the tighter he is held.

The legalistic doctrine of the sphere of practice affords the basis for a much reprobated moral theory which we will term the theory of Jesuitry, not because it is peculiar to the Jesuit order or to Catholicism, but in deference to the most conspicuous and most accomplished literary exposition of such a theory so far recorded in history. The Jesuitic moral theory is that which admits the possibility of cheating the ethical law by the exercise of reason.

Cheating or getting round the law is of course an everyday occurrence which in itself is neither moral nor immoral, being one of the many methods employed in the social struggle, sometimes in a good cause and not properly deserving the description of cheating. A law considered to be unjust should be opposed openly, but if the imposer of the unjust law, or he who promoted it for his own interest, has drafted it faultily so as to admit of an interpretation which eliminates or reduces the injustice, then it is only natural that the opponent should profit by that error, if only to discredit the law and constrain society to discuss it afresh. Who does not applaud Portia's trick to save the life of the noble Antonio against Shylock? Shylock, that *ferox animus*, has indeed found some praise as a symbol of the tenacity with which rights of any sort should be upheld, but Portia will always receive praise from the elect as an appealing characterization of a well-devised rebellion against an unjust law.

But what is completely irrational, yet seems to be admitted by the Jesuitic morality, is cheating of oneself, in this case cheating of one's own moral conscience. To cheat one's conscience, to rebel against it with force or craft, this is indeed contradiction, the arbitrary, evil. No doubt sometimes we strive to silence the inner voice which warns us, the Socratic daemon, the guardian angel. This happens in the utilitarian no less than in the moral sphere, as when in yielding to some harmful indulgence which we had resolved to eschew, we try hard to tell ourselves that there is something different about this particular case. We try, but we do not really succeed. We may for an instant dim our conscience, but we cannot extinguish it totally and permanently. The very effort to do so rekindles it.

The Jesuitic morality cannot be regarded as a derivation from simple ethical legalism. Legalism gives rise to the contradictions which we have already expounded. It generates the morally indifferent and at the same time suppresses it and, having suppressed it, resuscitates it only to suppress it again, and so on, in a sterile alternation, to all infinity. But it never sanctions a cheat. Never does simple legalism afford a justification for pretending, when one wills a determined action, that is, when one has formed a determined intention, that on the contrary one wills a different action or has formed a different intention, the pretence known as "direction of the intention". The intention is what it is, and cannot be directed at pleasure. There can never be any justification for holding to the letter of the moral law with the deliberate intention of violating its spirit.

What the Jesuitic morality tends towards becomes ever clearer, however, if we conceive of it as a confluence of legalism in the sphere of practice with theological utilitarianism, in other words, when not only is morality viewed as a sequence or complex of legislative definitions, but these laws are held to be the product of the arbitrary whim of a God. As such, they are not in themselves moral and are not observed for their intrinsic rational necessity, but simply as the lesser evil, for fear of something worse or for hope of future advantage. In that case, between Man and the Divine Legislator there is a deep implacable contest, the contest of the weak against the mighty, in which the weak finds his strength in cunning and follows the tactics of deceit. Hence the dominating concept of the Jesuitical morality: to gain all possible ground at the expense of moral or divine laws, to render the least possible measure of fulfilment of their commands, and then, when summoned for a reckoning at the confessional or at the last judgement, to argue around the law with interpretations showing that what one did fell within the field of the optional, the permitted. God forbids man to kill man; but does he mean to forbid this act when its motive is the glory of God, and when the hand of the killer is as it were the hand of God himself? Surely not – and therefore it will be permissible for the Jesuit to kill or send to his death his Jansenist opponent, who by publicizing the defects of the Holy Company which is the army of God on earth, harms the divine interests. That killing will be not merely permissible, but an act of duty. And what if one should wish to kill the adversary, not out of zeal for the divine glory, but on account of his harmfulness to the personal and immoral interests of the Jesuit? This too is permissible, provided that, although animated by personal hatred, at the moment of killing one turns aside from the real motive and directs the intention to the glory of God, thus justifying the means by the end.

Such is the monstrous logical product of the marriage of legalism with theological utilitarianism, and such is the essence of the Jesuitical morality, *horrendi carminis*, object of universal horror and loathing. We call it a logical (or illogical) product in order once again to make it clear that we are here considering nothing else save theories, and offering a critique of these alone. In practice, Jesuit morality was often much better than it was in theory. Even Father Caramuel, the author of the considerations on the right

of the Jesuit to kill a Jansenist, must have been a good enough man
at heart, for after managing to twist the moral law into giving an
affirmative answer to his question, he yielded to softness of heart,
gave a new twist to his twist, and concluded negatively that the
Jansenists *occidi non possunt quia nocere non potuerunt*, are not to be
killed because they are poor devils as incapable, he said, of obscur-
ing the splendour of the Company, as the owl of hiding the light
of the sun.[1] And Saint Alfonso dei Liguori, often in our days cited
as an example of that degraded morality, when he came to the
task of dishing up the usual repugnant casuistries in respect of the
sixth and ninth commandments, felt the strong distaste which one
would expect from the gentleman and man of breeding that he
was, at the necessity of expounding Ethics according to that
tradition. In protestation he exclaimed: "Nunc aegre materiam
illam tractandam aggredimur, cujus vel solum nomen hominum
mentes inficit. Det mihi veniam, quaeso, castus lector . . . Utinam
brevius . . . aut obscurius explicare me potuissem! Oro studiosos
ut . . . eo tempore saepius mentem ad Deum elevent et Virgini
immaculatae se commendent, ne dum aliorum animas Deo student
acquirere, ipsi suarum detrimentum patiantur."[2] If "Jesuitry" came
to have the connotation of moral corruption, the fault lay, more
than in the theories, in the type of education practised by the
Order, an education tending to depression and servility, to the
reduction of man to the condition of a *senis baculus*, docile and
passive instrument in other men's hands. And the fault lay in the
confusion of consciences which that type of education not only
permitted but encouraged concerning the real motives of actions,
thanks to the drugging of the ethical will with sophisms, devotional
enticements *aisées à pratiquer* for the easier opening of the gates of
Paradise, and *chemins de velours* to serve as a comfortable way of
access to heaven. Philosophically, Rigorists and Laxists stand on
the same level, yet in fact the Rigorists were usually austere and
energetic souls with a strong sense of the genuine character of
morality, on which side the Laxists were often deficient and at

1. Pascal, *Prov.*, I, 7.
2. *Theol. Moralis*, 7th edition, Bassano, 1778, I, p. 178.

fault. On the other hand it must in justice be said that the Laxists also had some merit and perceived a truth, for in turning their attention to the complications of reality and of human life they unconsciously, in their distorted doctrines, pointed to the necessity of an Ethics which should be less abstract and less out of tune with human reality.

[1909]

VI

THE PRINCIPLE, THE IDEAL, AND THE THEORY
OF LIBERTY

It is admitted and recognized on all sides that during and after the Great War of 1914-18 the sentiment and ideal of liberty were seriously shaken and impaired in the world. Not only have liberal institutions in many countries where they seemed to stand four-square tumbled to the ground, but on every hand there is a coolness, a distrust, a detachment in respect of that ideal, which seems no longer to be able to inspire the heart or inform the will of men.

It should, however, be no less obvious that the alleged decadence of the liberal idea, the "crisis" which some describe as having overtaken it, is a strange sort of decadence or crisis in that it is unillumined by any sign of a new ideal being at hand to replace the old ideal and put it out of court; and equally there is no sign of any new sort of settlement to take the place of that which has been demolished and defaced. The liberal ideal is a moral ideal of humanity and civilization, and a new and victorious ideal ought to present itself as the ideal of a new, more vigorous, more profound humanity and civilization. But that is certainly not the aspect of the one party which, in practice, offers its candidature for the succession, the party of regimentation, of constraint, which, whether exercised in the name of a race, or of the State, or of the dictatorship of the proletariat, or whatever the idol may be, is devoid of moral character, of creative force for the development of civil and human life. All that it possesses is a potential capacity to widen the range of material life for some at the expense of the material life of others. Constraint can, no doubt, fell to the earth with a powerful blow, and so reduce to silence, one who seeks the solution of a mathematical problem, but none will claim that the silence thus obtained represents a solution for the problem. All that has been achieved is that a man is lying prone on the ground while the problem remains in suspense pending its solution by a mathematician. This illustrates the sterility of regimes founded upon the exercise of constraint, or, as it is politely termed "authority", in the fields of thought, science, art, social habit, human relations. Under them, whatever continues to flourish and reproduce itself in various branches is owed to the persistence and survival of liberal inspirations and engrained habits, which, however, in course of time fail for lack of nourishment and by the natural decease of the bearers of the tradition. Meanwhile, not one of the formulas purporting to express new ideals is capable of being upheld in methodical debate, or of finding justification in critical thought and interpretation of history, in fact, of holding its own in quiet and careful and attentive discussion. Each is therefore reduced to a mechanical repetition of formless phrases, supported not by any sort of argument but by the utterance of threats. Amid all this din of arms and shouting, this scorn and mockery, the ideal of liberty remains substantially untouched and invulnerable. It could be dissolved and superseded only by the influence of another and more worthy ideal, and of such an ideal even the notion eludes us.

The inference from the experience of our present time will be that the crisis is not a crisis of a particular ideal (like, say, that which once overcame the ancient *polis* when the ideal of empire took its place, or the feudal system when it was outshone by absolute monarchy), but a crisis of ideals as such, a dispersal and corruption and loss of that moral enthusiasm which ennobles the life of the individual and exalts that of mankind, signalizing its great epochs. Why and how this crisis should have come about we can learn from history, and especially from history subsequent to 1870, when the deeds and words and spirit of Bismarck, and the theory and action of Marxist Socialism, combined to discredit the ideal of liberty. Even while retaining and profiting by liberal institutions, the peoples were caught up in a material and economic way of life. This aspect of the historical period has been duly described in another place. If I were to attempt here to summarize briefly the significance of this historical development, not yet completed and perhaps now passing through its gravest and most perilous phase, I would place it in the anguish and travail of the attempt being made to give shape to a new religious faith for humanity or for the civilized nations, at a moment when the ancient religions have lost their strength but the religion of liberty has not only not yet been translated into the form of common sense and popular opinion, as is needful even if some mythical trappings have to be brought into service for the purpose, but has not even attained an intellectual development among the educated classes capable of forfending the assaults and the wiles of opponents.

There is no reason in all this for losing courage or abandoning oneself to a pessimism which can only be contradictory and inconclusive, nor for settling down miserably to the expectation of a series of centuries of barbarism, in the spirit of the visions and predictions of some apocalyptic writers of our times, whose theories, like all works of the imagination, point to something abstractly possible but devoid of any certainty. One should keep up one's courage, in the first place because it is the duty of man to work and fight, and in the second place because human society has passed through other ages of moral weariness and choking materialism, and has always emerged from them through a spontaneous rekindling of enthusiasm and ideals, a return of spiritual springtime, the word and example of religious and apostolic genius which in due course, whether quickly or slowly, gains the assent of the peoples.

Meanwhile the task for men of study and thought like ourselves is to uphold and to enrich the precise concept of liberty and to construct the philosophic theory of it. This is the contribution which can properly be expected from us to the work of restoring and reviving the liberal ideal and way of life. The necessity and the importance of this concept may meet with some sceptical smiles. There will be quoting from the poet to the effect that the tree of theory is grey while the tree of life is green: in other words, concept and argument do not produce passion and force of will which alone have practical efficacy. But this division between thought and action, as though the two were indifferent to each other and not mutually conditioned, disappears under the glance of a penetrating eye. In live and concrete spiritual reality the two terms are perfectly united. In the act of thought there is at the same time an act of will, for thought is brought to birth solely by a moral stimulus, by grief, anguish, and the need to remove an obstacle from the flow of life, and what it leads to always is a new disposition of will, a new behaviour, a new mode of action in the practical field. A thinker who does not suffer his problem or live his thought is no thinker but a rhetorician, a repeater of formulas which were once thoughts in the past or in the minds of others. If it has rarely or never happened that a thinker was at the same time a statesman or captain or party leader or popular agitator, this is because of the technical specialization of human activities each of which, however, though working in its own special range, has always an eye to the whole. The labour of speculative thought does not remain closed in its own range but seeks there the energy required for working in the wider world, and accomplishes this not only by the communication of the logical process to others who receive it and can thus more rapidly cover the same intellectual ground and make it their own, but also, and above all, thanks to the conversion, in the minds of the many, of reasoned argument into self-evident truth, common sayings, proverbs, divested of all theoretical apparatus and transmuted into articles of faith, a sure guide for the soul. Thus are formed the intellectual and directing classes without which no human society has ever been able to live, whose vigour is the measure of the vigour of a society. As for the other class, great or overwhelming in number, which barely concerns itself with the problems of public and moral life, not pursuing these with heart and mind, but simply registering the alternating satisfaction or dissatisfaction of its own particular needs – the so-called "masses" to whom romantic demagogues ascribe mysterious and magic virtues and pay their homage – it is not to be hoped that the truths discovered by thinkers, and passed by them into the common cultural heritage, should easily penetrate into minds so little sensitive to ideal motives. But it is necessary to bestir ourselves to educate this class with a view, in the first place, to its providing an ever richer flow of new and fresh recruits for the directing class, as members of it and co-operators with it, and in the second place with a view to attaining a progressively harmonious relation with it. Unless and until that happens, and in the measure that it does not happen, it must be treated with politic measures suitable to the case, to prevent it from encompassing the work of society, of civilization, in ruin. For ruin and upheaval of this sort have happened more than once in the course of history. Yet always, with greater or lesser difficulty, in longer or shorter time, the overthrown barriers have been re-erected and the stream been reconducted to its normal course.

The philosophic theory of liberty, for greater clearness and fullness of exposition, distinguishes three aspects or grades. The first of these is Liberty as the Creative Force of History, history's true and proper subject, so that with a slight variation of meaning we can repeat with Hegel that history is the history of liberty. In fact, whatever man does he does freely, whether his deeds be actions or political institutions or religious conceptions or scientific theories or creations of poetry and art or technical inventions and schemes for the expansion of wealth and power. Non-liberty, we have remarked, is sterile. Its illusory works have the character of what in poetry and the arts are called imitations or artificial manipulation such as dish up existing poetry and painting perhaps in bizarre and tasteless combinations, but are unable to produce anything really new and original. They lack aesthetic reality and are therefore left aside by the art critic and historian. Similarly all acts which are accomplished against the grain, however much they may serve the ends of individual security, nourishment, or convenience, are allotted to the physiological sphere and not to the moral and civil sphere to which they belong only in appearance. The times which bear the mark of a suppression of freedom enter into history only by virtue of the fact that there never can be and never is an absolute oppression, a total suffocation. Indeed the very violence with which liberty is crushed gives rise to reactions of various sorts. In such a situation we will see works of liberty in progress, with the favour and support of the oppressors themselves; not that these desire any such thing, quite the contrary, but being obliged to procure certain aids and services in order to keep their social and political system running at all, such as the assistance of doctors, engineers, jurists, administrators, scientists, writers, and finding that there is no mechanical means of producing men with such qualifications, they are obliged to let them develop and conduct their professions in some degree of freedom. We see also the efforts and the deeds of the oppressed, the opposition, which, whether openly or clandestinely and silently, will always in some way be present, and to some extent constitutes an element of refreshment, of relief, in the dry and bitter season, and sows seeds of other things to come, in the fullness of time. Were it not so, the times of which we are speaking would be altogether sterile, seasons of death and not of life, or at all events not of human life, empty intervals in the course of history, a notion which thought refuses to embrace, and which is belied by the greater or smaller output which "times of oppression" have, in spite of everything, produced, and still more by the luxuriant flowering which always marks the end of such an age, and must in some sense have been present in the preceding historical conditions. The historian observes and judges from a point of view other than that of the men who are passionately engaged in the struggle, both those who believe that they have demolished liberty and those in the opposite camp who mourn the death of liberty and seek to compass a resurrection. The historian knows that what is at stake in the struggle can never be the death or life of liberty (for liberty is in reality humanity's own struggle with itself). What is at stake is a more or a less, a slower or a quicker rhythm, and the creeds pitted against each other are phantasms and illusions, symbols of the parts which each have to play and to sustain.

The second aspect or grade is that in which liberty is viewed no longer as the moving or Creative Force of History, but as a Practical Ideal aiming at the creation of a maximum condition of liberty in human society, by the overthrow of tyrannies and oppressions and the establishment of customs, institutes, and laws tending to guarantee such a condition. A thorough scrutiny of this ideal will reveal that it is neither different nor distinguishable in any way from moral conscience and action, and further that all the moral virtues, all the definitions given in ethics, which place the end or purpose of conduct in respect for the person of others, in the good of the universal, in the enrichment of spiritual life, in the unceasing betterment of the world, or whatever it may be, ultimately resolve themselves into the conscience, the will to liberty. For in the last resort these virtues and ends are to be identified with the desire that liberty shall triumph against all contrarieties and impediments, so as to develop its life-creating force. When we minister to the sick, soothing or mitigating their pains, we do so in order to regain for society a source of energy, of liberty. When we educate children, the purpose is to shape beings capable of looking after themselves freely and autonomously. When we uphold the just against the unjust, the true against the false, we do so because injustice and falsehood are a succumbing to passions, to mental inertia, whereas truth and justice are acts of liberty. We can now see how misplaced are the fear and horror which some feel at the mention of a recognition of full and unlimited liberty to be enjoyed by mankind. Their thoughts run at once to the misuse which will be made of it by the ill-intentioned or criminal, by the feeble-minded and by children. They forget that these cases are guarded against or provided for by the criticism and moral vigilance of society, by the punitive apparatus of the State, by the existence of asylums, reformatories, prisons, schools, and so on, and they fail to see that the talk of the necessity of liberty is concerned solely with the necessity for easing the path of those who are neither ill-intentioned nor criminal, nor yet immature and inexpert, but for that very reason have an activity to be put into effect, whereas those others succumb to the passivity of bestial impulse, madness, puerility, ignorance, or whatever it may be. It ought to be perfectly clear that it is only in reference to the former that all obstacles to free activity are described as harmful to human society.

We have now seen that the liberal ideal coincides with the human conscience. Accordingly it is found in some form or other, and in some degree, in all ages, so that it is improper to regard it as an historical fact, born at a certain moment, with a certain span of life, and destined like all historical facts to fade and die. It is true that the liberal ideal is commonly described as a wholly modern formation having its origins in the seventeenth and its great flowering in the nineteenth century. But properly speaking what came into existence in that period was not the sentiment and ideal of liberty, but an acquired consciousness of the essential character of liberty, of its value as a supreme principle. That had in earlier ages been hindered by the reigning notions of the transcendent and the laws and prohibitions connected therewith and imposed from on high, which on every hand constrained and limited and inhibited men, often by dint of persecutions and torture applied by the men of one creed to another (by Catholics to Evangelicals, Evangelicals to Catholics, and so on). As the wars of religion drew to a close, the hour struck for the sentiment of tolerance. It came gradually to be seen as a better proceeding not to suppress the ideas of nonconformists but to let them argue things out with the other side. And that liberty, in turn, served to introduce all the others, until finally the principle at the centre of them all became apparent. That guiding principle was the affirmation of a higher and more complex ideal which in full flood overwhelmed the creeds of the Transcendent, passing beyond them, shedding light and warmth, forming the soul of modern man which is different from that of mediaeval or of antique humanity – a pure movement of liberation of which nothing whatever is understood by historical materialists, and others in their wake, who think to explain it by the formation in the same age of capitalism, industry, free trade, and a social class termed the bourgeoisie: in a word, by an economic fact. Nor is it much better understood by the help of a purely psychological pattern of derivation from the Calvinistic idea of vocation or mission, such as some have endeavoured to trace. This awareness and desire of liberty as the supreme and fundamental good, which worked so powerfully in the generations of 1830, 1848, and 1860, and seemed a perpetual possession of the human spirit, is what we have described as appearing to have lost its strength and vitality to some extent everywhere in the present-day world.

The third aspect or grade of liberty that has to be recalled here is the elaboration of the force and ideal of liberty into a Philosophical Concept framed in a general conception of reality which can define and justify it. This implies an intimate union of the theory of liberty with the history of philosophy upon the developments of which it has depended and depends. During the long reign of metaphysical and transcendent philosophy, the concept of liberty as the law of life and of history could not find its due place, and was hard put to it to gain admission. Even when awareness of liberty became intense, this took place in the field of sentiment and action rather than in that of thought.

What, then, was required, in order that a philosophy might reflect and support that ideal? It was required that the practical negation of the transcendent should become a logical negation, that philosophy should be conceived as absolute immanentism, immanentism of the spirit, as contrasted with naturalism and materialism or with a dualism of spirit and nature, absolute spiritualism. And since the spirit is the dialectic of distinctions and oppositions, a perpetual growing beyond its own range, a perpetual progress, this spiritualism must be also absolute historicism. Now such a philosophical conception was very remote from the mentality of the country in which the ideal of liberty had its first and noblest success, becoming incarnated in institutions and customs which served as a most efficacious example for other peoples – England. The prevailing philosophy in England was, and continued to be for some two centuries, empiricist, sensist, utilitarian, with a corresponding agnosticism and possibilism in religion. Hence the eldest daughter of liberty was for a long time the least well equipped to provide a philosophical illustration of her own ideal and practice. The truth of this remark can be tested by reopening the famous *Essay on Liberty* of John Stuart Mill, in which the author's sincere liberal faith finds an undignified and debased exposition in terms of the concepts of well-being and happiness, foresight and opportunity, together with the concept of a human imperfection which (so long as it lasts) is said to make it advisable to leave the field free for the most different tendencies, for con-

trasting opinions, for individual characters, but always only so
long as no harm results to third parties and so on. The erroneous
belief that liberalism is identical with utilitarian individualism, or
"atomism" in Hegelian terminology, and that it degrades the
State to be the instrument of the hedonism of the individual, is a
consequence of such feeble reasonings. Liberalism might, perhaps,
be more properly identified with a moral individualism which
treats the State as the means and instrument to a higher life, and
in doing so requires that the citizen should be devoted and serviceable to the State, and ready if need be to give his life for it. But
that sort of theorization belongs to a stage at which the concept
of the individual has not yet been critically elaborated. It still
substantializes the individual as a monad or naturalizes the individual as a physical person who has to be respected and guaranteed, instead of resolving the individual into the individuality of
doing, of action, that is to say into the concreteness of the universal.
Moreover, a laxity of moral notions, a superficiality in current
historical conceptions, encouraged indulgence in the roseate
theories of progressism, the notion that with the invention of
elections, parliaments, and the free Press, a royal way, a *chemin de
velours*, had been discovered to enable an indefinite continuance in
the accumulation of conveniences, wealth, and power, the enlargement of culture and the refinement of a brilliant civilization, with
no more hard and cruel conflicts and devastations, no more wars
or revolutions, no risk of relapses into inferior forms of politics
and social intercourse, but only gentle agitations susceptible of
being quietly solved by means of discussion and agreements. On
the contrary, the moral ideal requires incessant effort and vigilance,
continuous regaining by grief and labour of the heritage bequeathed
by our fathers. And the course of history, the "education of the
human race" as Lessing called it, moves along rough paths and
alongside of precipices, with leaps and bounds, tumbles and injuries
and deaths. It does not lead to any final condition of immobile
felicity, and no more can it discover and put into use a gentle,
safe, and wholly reliable route of progress. The very worst ever
known in the past may present itself afresh, though in novel

conditions, so that the overcoming of it will constitute a new and higher achievement. The epic of history, in fact, is nearer to being tragical than to being idyllic. Not to have meditated this truth, but to have indulged in fatuous and dangerous optimism, is the principal reason for the present pessimism and faint-heartedness whereby in the face of difficulties which were only to be expected, since they are of the essence of the rhythm of individual life and history as a whole, resort is had not to the shedding of illusions and the renouncement of frivolity but to an abandonment of the ideal itself. And the abandonment of the ideal leaves room for a sort of stupefaction in which men fall prey to the forces which rage around them.

On the other hand, in Germany, where philosophic thought embodied in grandiose systems had advanced far beyond the doctrines of sensism, hedonism, utilitarianism, empiricism, and associationism, there persisted, in the core of the new and original ideas, metaphysical and theological elements which subjected the ideal of liberty to pre-established historical patterns, while in the political sphere the thin and dubious tradition of liberty in the life of Germany, the dimness of the sentiment of liberty, the readiness of men to subject themselves to authority, caused the idea of liberty to be overwhelmed by the idea of the State, a personified abstraction tricked out with the attributes and attitudes of a Jewish divinity. There was a happier conjunction of historical thought with liberty in the French Restoration and July Monarchy, but France lacked powerful philosophic minds who might have drawn the many threads together into a firm speculative knot. Nor yet was there a systematic elaboration of the idea of liberty as a speculative principle in Italy, in which country the most conspicuous and authoritative party in the Risorgimento period combined Catholicism with Liberalism, while the other freedom-loving parties held to the abstractions of eighteenth-century rationalism. The new Italian schools of philosophy either remained within the sphere of Catholic presumptions and ways of thought, or accepted the concepts of German idealism and the associated worship of the State. Still worse was the position when in the second half of the nineteenth century, under the influence of Darwinism and Evolutionism, it became the fashion in the countries with a flourishing liberal tradition to justify the liberal ideal by concepts of sheer animality, the struggle for existence and the survival of the fittest, with the result that the dialectic of thesis, antithesis, and synthesis, and the theory of alternating triumphs and defeats, and the upward advance from one solution to another, all of which liberalism had included in its spiritual vision of life, were cleared away to make room for a fierce imagery of wild beasts of different races clawing and devouring and destroying each other.

The limitations and defects of a theory need not prevent the thing which is the subject of the theory from prospering and flourishing where its own vital force is sufficiently vigorous. We see beautiful poems and paintings and sculptures produced by men whose views upon art are arbitrary, conventional, and old-fashioned. We see admirable moral actions wrought in all simplicity by men who profess a crude materialism or utilitarianism. No doubt this conjunction of discordant thought and action in one soul betokens an incoherency, a contrast. But it is out of such incoherency and contrast that coherency and harmony have to come into being. It is not astonishing, then, that the powerful and fruitful impetus of Liberalism in England and Europe in the nineteenth century, which laid low the absolutist governments, freed the peoples from foreign domination, united them in great States, and gave rise to lively exchanges, intellectual, moral, aesthetic, as well as economic, between the nations, rested content or put up with some such formulations of the theory of liberty as those which we have just mentioned. Such a man as Cavour was so deeply and religiously inspired by the idea of liberty that his words and deeds seem almost of themselves to constitute a living and sufficient theory. But that could not still suffice when conduct began to lose its clarity, to vacillate, to become indefinite, and when action weakened or yielded, forswearing its ideal and following the courses which at first it condemned; and meanwhile false concepts, judgements, histories crowded in to celebrate irreverently the "death" of liberty and to dictate an infamous epitaph. When that has happened, it is no longer possible to do without a truly adequate theory of liberty which, pending the recovery of energy in the active field, meanwhile makes a beginning in the theoretical field by dissipating the murky mist and restoring mental clarity. At such a time, if there is little or no liberty elsewhere, in the mind of the thinker the weaving of the tissue of liberty must begin anew.

While thinking out anew the problem of liberty, reconstructing or constructing the foundations of the theory of liberty, it is possible as we go along to correct some erroneous notions which very directly impair the life of our own times. One of these is the dimness which still surrounds the relation between moral liberalism and the doctrine of economic freedom. The latter is not a consequence of the former, but stands to it as matter stands to form. For the purposes of the moral conscience, economic life figures as mere material, and on that level of materiality stand all the proposed economic systems, *laisser-faire*, protectionism, monopolism, planned and rationalized economies, self-sufficiency. No one of these can claim the distinction of a moral character, for one and all have a merely economic character and each can in given historical circumstances be adopted or rejected by the moral will. No doubt, given the division of labour, free enterprise and free trade is a wonderful stimulus to the production of wealth. None the less this policy is abandoned in circumstances such as those of war (inter-State warfare being only a special case of a more general sort of war situation), and this of itself shows that there is nothing absolute about it. The same is true of a capitalistic, Communistic, or any other system of ownership. These must of necessity be variable and cannot possibly be identified with a programme for general and permanent wealth and welfare. And such a programme would not only be utopian in character, but would have nothing to do with morality. Ethics cannot and does not concern itself with that impossibility, individual or general welfare, but solely with the aspiration for higher things, the *excelsius*.[1]

1. See my *Etica e Politica*, 3rd edn., 1945, pp. 316-20: *Liberalismo e Liberismo*.

There would be a similar impropriety in introducing here notions of cause and effect, seeking (like some theorists) an external basis for moral and civil freedom in the precedent fact of a system of free economic enterprise. On the contrary, even where such a system is adopted as being more advantageous than the alternatives, what determines and executes such a choice is moral and civil liberty, and it is this that provides the basis and justification for the economic ordinance in question.

There is another theoretical error which is advanced this time not by the advocates of free enterprise but by the Communists. This is the distinction drawn by the latter between juridical or "formal" liberty, and actual or "real" liberty. The former, it is said, was conceded to the peoples in consequence of the Revolution of 1789, and rendered illusory and empty by being thus separated from the second. Indeed, worse still, it was cunningly exploited to frustrate the agitation and demand for the second. But closer attention reveals that juridical, formal liberty is in fact liberty pure and simple, true and proper, in all its purity as a moral principle. It is the only liberty there is. The other sort of "liberty" is a type of economic organization, and more precisely the much invoked Communistic organization of equality. The frightful confusion by which the Historical Materialists have lumped the two liberties together in a single concept demonstrates the crassness of the contribution of that school to questions of moral and spiritual life. No doubt on the purely economic level the Communistic ideal is one among those which in given conditions are possible or plausible, and according to those conditions more or less capable of being upheld for a certain time. But for the reasons already given the assertion that this type of economic system (which is wrongly labelled the system of "equality" and "justice") is by contrast with the free enterprise type truly the foundation of liberty, must be rejected. Liberty stands in no special relation to either one or the other type of system. It reviews them all, and from time to time adopts or annuls any one of them according as they help or hinder its grand purpose of the enrichment of spiritual life. Those who insist upon asserting a false relation between liberty and the type of economic order must necessarily resort to the flouting of liberty and consent and the establishment of their economic order by recourse to violence. In accordance with the noted principle that 'the same arts which do gain a State, must it maintain', they cannot but uphold their system by violence and the repression of liberty, actuating what they call justice by denying the first and most elementary justice, the respect of the moral personality of men. What we are here remarking is rationally evident and thus has no need to be verified by evidence, though clear and indisputable evidence is in fact provided by the "dictatorships of the proletariat" of our own days which are quite unable to produce liberty, however much they may write about it in their constitutions, and quite unable to shake off the dictatorial character, which is in reality their own character. The true relation is in the present as in the former case this: liberty comes first, and is fundamental, and liberty, without any preconceived notions, picks out, approves, and authorizes one or another type of economic organization which in the particular given historical circumstances appears as morally healthier and by the same token economically more advantageous. That pair of "surviving Goddesses, Justice and Liberty", celebrated by our poet Carducci, may well be cut down to a single Goddess, Liberty, that is to say the Moral Conscience, who in virtue of her own character is the arbiter of justice.

We may here mention also a third erroneous concept, derived this time not from the rivalry of economic systems but from the strictly political field, the field of political conduct: a concept summed up in the phrase "non-intervention" and carrying a suggestion of liberal prestige, as standing for the liberty of the single peoples to resolve their internal disputes by debate and if necessary, indeed, by civil war. The phrase and the accompanying notions have reference to something of undeniable weight, namely the prime duty of Governments to safeguard the life and prosperity of the particular State entrusted to them, and to consider the affairs of other States under the sole light of the hopes and threats, advantages and harms which may result for their own State from them.

The memory of the crusades, so idealistic in their deceptive appearance, so different in reality, the memory also of certain Catholic crusades foolishly launched by Habsburg Spain, and of those wars of religion which ravaged and bathed in blood the countries of Europe only to end not with the victory of one or the other Church but with a reaffirmation of the principle *cujus regio illius religio*, followed by a great wave of rationalism, illuminism, and an inner decay of both Catholicism and Protestantism – these and similar experiences left a quite natural repugnance for ideological policy and the exercise of "international morality". But however that may be, yet it must be made perfectly clear that non-intervention is a matter of expediency, of political necessity, not of liberal method. States, as such, are unable to promote the liberty of other States except when by doing so they promote their own advantage, making of the affairs of those other States not a moral issue but an issue of power politics. No doubt it is much to be desired that the rulers of the various States should come to consider as politically advantageous for these the extension of liberty among the peoples, and should favour the birth of such liberty and become increasingly aware of the danger which States organized upon different principles represent for the world, danger which it is their duty to observe.[1] *Proximus ardet Ucalegon*: the flame licks the neighbouring timber and threatens to spread. And yet, they must never overstep their own limits and assume the direct role of creators of liberty. That belongs solely to religious spirits like those which animated and filled the history of the Risorgimento in Italy, and ended by shaping the policy of Ministers to their own ends and converting their own demands into political necessity and advantage.[2]

As to the theory of liberty, it is well to note here that it is mistaken to seek for such a theory in the juridical formulations of free institutions and guarantees of liberty. The usefulness and

1. See Omodeo's review of Fisher's *History of Europe* in *La Critica*, xxxvi, 1938, p. 53 seqq.
2. See once again in *Etica e Politica*, pp. 345-49, the essay *Giustizia Internazionale*.

importance of such juridical argument is not denied. But it consists in the historical content of the concrete and weighty political requirements which they bring up for discussion and which find an expression and an affirmation in them; not in any definition of the concept of liberty, for such a definition can only be philosophical, not juridical. The moral assent which is given to certain institutions is not given to their abstract form, which is rightly the object of the jurist's attention, but to their practical efficacy in given times and places, circumstances and situations, which though it may last for a long time, is always in the nature of things conditional and transitional. What may appear to be juridically perfect contrivances to guarantee liberty are liable to be in practice instruments for the suppression of liberty, and vice versa. Montesquieu, who worked so hard on these problems,[1] and formulated the famous theory of the three powers, the executive, the legislative, and the judiciary, which serve to check each other, but being forced by the motion of events to move, end by necessarily moving in harmony with one another, could not successfully argue that this institutional mechanism served to generate and maintain liberty and to prevent servitude. For where the free mind is lacking, no institution can avail, and where the free mind is present, the most varied institutions can in due time and place render good service. Concrete liberal institutions are the *ad hoc* products of political genius inspired by liberty, or, what comes to the same, of liberal genius equipped with political prudence. To keep this genius alive in a people is the supreme duty, but it must not be imagined that the majority of men can cultivate it consciously. To do so requires depth of feeling and a power of intellectual synthesis found only in the ranks of the élite, who are devoted to the ideal.

Considered in this aspect, then, liberty is wholly a question of the disposition of minds fired to fervour and love. We cannot but feel deeply concerned and distressed, therefore, at the scant interest, if any at all, shown for the idea of liberty and for its safeguarding

1. *Esprit des Lois*, I, II.

in the present-day literature of philosophy, and no differently in narrative, dramatic, and historical literature, in strong contrast to what happened in the first half of the nineteenth century and should be happening at the present moment when our heritage from that time is suffering grave injury and risks being totally lost. Philosophy and history, indifferent to the distresses and alarms of those who love this sacred treasure, turn their present attention to other and abstruser questions, or else, submitting to the influence of dark appetites and restless sensation, contribute to the general coarsening and dulling of wits. It is this state of affairs that has led me, for what my thoughts and capacities are worth, to revive the theme of liberty in my philosophical and historical writings of the last twenty years. In the course of those labours, I have come to realize the defective condition of the theory of liberty, which in the day of trial proved to be too lightly armed and too easy a target for the enemy. At the conclusion of this brief sketch of some of what seem to me to be the fundamental features of this theory, I must declare that the argument has such manifold aspects and is involved with such numerous and weighty problems of life and history as to require the energy and keen attention of many minds which will not, I trust, fall short of this high duty.

[1939]

VII

NOTES ON MORALS

I

"SINS OF THOUGHT"

"SINS of Thought" is one of those improper expressions, which may indeed convey something real and may be perfectly legitimate in current language, but if taken literally by reading into the words the concepts of which they are abstract signs reveal themselves as contradictory, showing that the form of words itself betokens an inadequate analysis, understanding, and distinction of the content. What in fact can "sinning in thought" mean? How is it possible when thinking to sin? How can thought, the health-giving flow of truth, be sinful? All the same "sins of thought" are really sins, great or small, and this is because they are motions of the will, and, indeed, are sometimes called by the more proper description of "sins of desire".

However, this explanation is so far from solving the difficulty that this now confronts us in a yet stronger shape. How can there be "sins of desire"? "Desire" is in itself "sin": for, as we know, it is opposite to the will, and finds its place in the acts of the will as something that has been restrained and left behind. Sin, in the shape of desire, is with us all the time. Moral man, when he acts morally or displays his acquired moral habit, is always, each time, in the position of the Saint struggling against a demonic tempter, or of the Archangel straining to subdue the dragon, or, if one will, of the Virgin who bruises the serpent with her heel, calmly – yet bruise it she does, and holds it down by direct contact. Elsewhere I have remarked (I think) that unless all the evil of the world (all the desires) were somehow in us, we could not understand evil, we would lack the sympathy necessary for re-creating in ourselves the wicked or perverse characters of a drama or a novel. The dialectic of life would leave us cold and unconcerned.

"Sins of desire", then, though it has over "sins of thought" the advantage of referring the matter in question to the practical sphere, is itself an inexact expression. "Sins of desire" are not just desire but are a group or particular class of sins. We may take as an example that of the wife who at the sickbed of an odious husband does not, indeed, neglect a due care for the patient, but all the same cherishes in her breast the idea that death will perhaps rid her of the tormentor. Another example: a candidate for a post observes with pleasure that misfortune has overtaken his rival, though he has not himself had any hand in this. Now what examples like these refer to is not the dialectical moment of desire, but something beyond that, an action. Every one of the positive motions of our will, even should it find no exteriorization in what are commonly considered to be acts and actions, is in fact in some manner actualized, be it only by producing modifications in ourselves which in due course produce their effects. For example, acts which appear to be mere wanderings of the fancy have the effect of making us perform our duty coldly, and what is done coldly is done ill, without enthusiasm, without inventiveness, and thus without the efficacy which it might have had.

Herein lies the wrongdoing of those who say: "We are doing our duty, only let us desire what we like." Their indulgent dream of desires unbanished, unchecked, marks a falling short of duty. Banished and checked, such a dream invigorates and sharpens the will, but, indulged in, it enfeebles this. The way to Hell is paved with good intentions, thanks to which incipient adulterers, as is well known, always set out with the intention of a purely spiritual relation of soul to soul. It is so with all those who indulge themselves in various ways, and then come to suffer the penalty of the indulgence. The moral man heeds the scruples of his conscience in regard to any "sin of desire", and likewise charges them up against others.

Yet there are cases when such an indulgence of fancy seems really and truly to be a moral desire. Don Rodrigo (in the *Promessi Sposi*) threatens and terrorizes a whole district: the plague carries him off: has not the plague effected a good riddance? Has it not been like a broom, sweeping away bad rubbish, permitting the accession of Rodrigo's kind and Christian heir, with a programme of making good his predecessor's crimes? How should not the announcement of that death be received with rejoicing, and since what is received with joy may well be embraced as an object of desire, how should it not have been desired and prayed for? But that fine moralist Manzoni sees to it that the only one of his characters to feel and express that sentiment of joy should be the morally incorrigible Don Abbondio. In fact, to say that in such cases what is desired is the triumph of the good is false. What is really desired is that one should oneself be spared a pain, a labour, a vexation, an effort. Really, then, the longing is egoistic. Don Abbondio wished Don Rodrigo and his like out of the world in order to shirk occasions of duty such as he had so often neglected. Any other judgement on this case will lead back to the error of a distinction between means and end, and will leave us defenceless against a way of thought which, starting with the admission of "sins of desire", will end by applauding the commission of criminal acts.

It is therefore that when some favourable circumstance occurs for an individual outside the range of his own will, he will, if he is a man of fine feeling, discern that the joy which he might feel would be a wrongful joy, and will dismiss it from him. Nor will he, like a hypocrite, display satisfaction at the spectacle of some "judgement of heaven". On the contrary a man of fine feeling will speak and act in such a manner as to show himself willing, were it possible (or had it been possible), to undo the misfortune of another which had redounded to his own advantage, to forgo the fillip thereby given to his own cause, to resume bravely the struggle against the vanished obstacles and difficulties. But men of coarse feeling, with minds confined to economic and juridical considerations, satisfied with an outward observance and careless of inner motions, give themselves up to such wrongful joy. The strong and pure mind, wholly absorbed in its task, disregards the outcome of events, knowing that these are never really good or bad, favourable or unfavourable, but simply set new conditions for new action.

[1915]

II

TELLING THE TRUTH

Lying is the particular bugbear of moralists, and truly it is more displeasing than other forms of evil, in the same way that cowardice is more displeasing than violence, and calculating egoism than egoistic passion and fury. It betokens not only an impoverished moral sense but an impoverished will.

Since lying is to be numbered among the worst moral faults, it is needful to define it carefully, to understand it well, in order not to confound it with something else which does not call for censure. If the two are confounded, the reproof may miss its aim and lose its efficacy. Fortunately the moral sense is highly refined and does not make the sort of mistakes which overtake abstract doctrinaires.

Theoretical confusion would certainly arise were one to define lying as not telling the truth. Such a definition would call for too many valid exceptions. It is impossible not to agree that in many cases it is neither possible nor right to tell the truth, so that if we held by that definition it would be necessary to admit – in defiance of logic and of feeling – that in many cases it was permissible to lie.

That it is admissible and even a duty not to tell the truth in the course of a struggle (for example, when defending oneself against a bandit) is notorious and undisputed. And the same applies to cases where there is no struggle, the classic one being when a revelation of his true condition to a patient would further worsen it. In all such cases conscience tells us that there is here no question of lying, that what we are doing is not merely innocent, but is our duty.

Conversely everyone knows that telling the truth may constitute an offence against the moral conscience, as we see in the case of malicious purveyors of true information, people who torment us with revelations, enemies who have the sharpest of eyes for discovering our weak points and wounding us. But all of these "tell the truth". Indeed we can gather up the truth which falls from their envenomed lips and turn it to our own advantage. *Salus ex inimicis*, we are benefited by our foes, the saying has it. Unintended benefit redounds to us from people whom we do not hesitate to describe and to dismiss as men of ill will.

Well then, when should one "tell the truth" and when should one not? And what constitutes lying?

It will be best first to give heed to another question which is often neglected: What is the meaning of "telling the truth", or communicating what is true to other people?

If one comes to think of it, as soon as we have thought the truth we have said it, said it to ourselves, because thought and language are indissoluble. But when it comes to saying it to others the matter becomes difficult, desperately difficult. Truth is not a merchandise to be passed from one to another, it is thought itself in the act of thinking. And how is that to be communicated?

The fact is, we never communicate the truth. All we do, in our intercourse with others, is to devise and employ a series or complex of stimuli in order to put others in a condition to match up to our frame of mind, to rethink the truth which we ourselves thought. Why, we do not "tell the truth" even when addressing a learned society, academy, or college class. We do not tell it, because we can do nothing more than devise and utter sounds calculated to facilitate or bring on effects external to ourselves.

If this is how matters stand, the problem of communicating with others, speaking with others, is not one of telling or not telling the truth, but one of acting upon others in order that they may act. Among the necessary methods of such an operation there has to be included the giving of guidance for the thinking or rethinking of truth, but the prime and permanent purpose will be to enhance, to modify, or to improve the life of the other.

The fulfilment of this purpose is procured by evoking for the other images which convey a vital impulse. The general form of the operation might be termed oratory, the "art of stirring the feelings", as the old rhetoricians called it. For speech-making is its most explicit form. It is an art which from the days of Plato to those of Kant has often been censured for "not telling the truth", but the fault has never lain with the art, it has lain rather with the narrow views of philosophers who failed to explore its deeper character and its true office.

It is natural and proper that a military leader haranguing troops before launching them into the battle does not dwell upon the possibility, likelihood, or near certainty, as it may seem to him while making the speech, of a disastrous outcome of the engagement, nor upon images of pain, death, dishonour, corpses abandoned to the wolves and vultures, but upon the splendour of the combative effort, the joy of victory which will not fail to crown it, the advantages which will follow, and perhaps the prospects of booty.

The oratorical art follows the opposite process from that of art properly so called. Art proceeds from life to images, oratory proceeds from images to life. When the images produced by art are used as means, art yields to oratory, and the field becomes open for discussions upon edifying and upon corrupting art – a perfectly good distinction except that what is in question should now no longer be called "art" since it has become "oratory".

What the orator does on more or less solemn occasions, each of us does the whole time in his talk with others, which is always turned to that same end of influencing the attitude of others towards ourselves, or towards something else, in what seems to us a desirable way. Everyone all the time uses imagery drawn from the unreal to replace or to soften the images of the real where these would have a harmful effect. It would be only too easy to give examples, so I will merely observe that a play like Ibsen's *Wild Duck* and still more the *Praise of Folly* of old Erasmus contains them in abundance, should anyone need them.

The fact that men in this way continually influence each other by means of unreal images has led many to pronounce that "Life is a Lie" or, more mildly, that "Life is Illusion". There are some who inveigh against the lie of life and yearn for the moment when they will leave it behind them and cleanse themselves from the stain, albeit in the Stygian waters. Others, those of mild disposition, sing the praises of kindly Illusion, last deity left to men. But in fact there is no question of illusion and none of a lie, there is simply Life, life in its spontaneity intent upon obtaining incitements for its own continuation and growth. Suppose that for some years I have believed that there stood at my side a faithful Achates or a faithful Penelope, and that my reliance upon the fidelity of friend or wife, my delight in that affection, my certainty that they would stand by me in misfortune, has been my comfort and repair, my incentive to labour at my task. I have been happy in life and work. But say that now of a sudden I perceive that friend and wife were not at all what I had imagined or been caused by them to imagine. I perceive this, and I suffer. But how can this present grief detract from my past joy, from the work that has been accomplished, the service that has been rendered to the ends of life? Was I living in a delusion? A delusion is such at the moment in which it is felt, that is, in my supposed case, now. But then, in the past it was not delusion and it was not truth: it was my feeling of confidence and strength. To the deceiver I can now utter the philosophic verse: "Not thee I loved, but the Goddess once alive, and now dead, in my heart", the Goddess who is Life. Well, the dream has collapsed, the hope has fallen to dust, and now what remains unless to recreate it or to construct another? And how shall I construct another? By scientific methods? What scientific method will ever teach me to put my trust in this or that person, to regard a given condition of life as safely assured, the roof over my head as proof against danger of collapse, the bosom upon which I lean as a firm support? I shall have to proceed as before, create or receive from the words of others images of life, and so live. I shall have to say, as in fact we do say: "It behoves me to believe."

The distinction between lying and oratory is, then, clear. Life requires an alternation of truth (historic truth) and of vital images (oratorical incitements), the latter not less than the former. The liar is not he who suggests vital images, but he who fails to bring forward historical truth when it is necessary. He who brings it forward when it is not beneficial is worse than a liar, a villain – for with a single word, a syllable of "truth", one may sometimes kill a man. And he who suggests consoling images when they are of no avail but are, on the contrary, harmful, is a flatterer, an adulator. When is it, then, that historical truth or vital images are to be disallowed? When, instead of promoting a moral benefit, they are designed to promote a merely utilitarian gain for the speaker, be he a bearer of truth or of lies.

Historical truth and vital images are, in fact, to use a trite comparison, drugs that can serve either the ends of health or the ends of poisoning ourselves and our neighbour. Equally culpable is he who fails to administer the drug when it is needed, and he who administers it when its effect is poisonous.

III

DELIGHT IN EVIL

"Delight in Evil", perversity, villainy, is something that strikes the imagination in the liveliest way, and provides one of the most effective arguments in favour of the existence of a positive tendency to evil in man, and thus in favour of the reality of evil as a force corresponding to the opposed force of goodness, and of the fact of ineffaceable original sin, with its consequence of an insoluble moral dualism, giving some colour to the Manichaean theory. "No less firmly than I believe in the existence of my soul", wrote Edgar Allan Poe in "The Black Cat", "I believe that perversity is one of the primitive impulses of the human heart, one of the faculties or primary indivisible sentiments which constitute the character of man."

A first and milder form of delight in evil is what is often called the pleasure of forbidden fruit. Experience tells us that to forbid something is to render it enticing.[1] Despairing of being able to pluck out the final root of this pleasure, or anyway wishing to save the bitter effort that it would cost, people sometimes adopt the device of removing the prohibition, permitting the previously forbidden, thereby succeeding in diminishing the heat of certain

---

1. "Oh, would virtue had been forbidden! We should then have proved all virtuous, for 'tis our blood to love what we are forbidden" (from the *Yorkshire Tragedy*, an English play of the Shakespearian age).

appetites, lessening the charm of seductive imagination, and momentarily obtaining an abatement of the ill-effects of the tendency, though such a remedy far from repressing the tendency actually encourages it. This is a mode of proceeding most often tried upon children, young people, and women, a method which in default of any other and more refined manner of exercising restraint may be imposed by the circumstances. It is perhaps because of the many prohibitions which surround it, parental, legal, and penal, that love, love in its naturalness, its cumulative sharpness and strength and the spicy quality of the satisfaction of its urge, as of a pleasure won by combat or guile, has seemed to some moralists to be a passion having its deep root in the delight in evil. Among these moralists I will number Baudelaire, who has expressed this thought in prose and also in verses of deep inspiration and powerful style.[1]

Let us, however, think over this business of the pleasure of forbidden fruit and see whether our rapid conclusion that it points to an original impulse towards evil can really be maintained. We will see that "delight in evil" owes its description simply to a verbal formula which is in use for describing such experiences, a formula which instead of defining in positive terms defines in negative terms, and instead of portraying plain reality in itself, portrays it with reference to morality and stains it with images of immorality, with moral reproofs. For what we are speaking of is really simply the pleasure of surmounting an obstacle, all the livelier for whatever painful trials may have lain in the path. What is there "evil" in that? Does not the same pleasure follow upon a stout effort to obtain some truth or to achieve any other noble

1.   . . . *Qui donc devant l'amour ose parler d'enfer?*

Maudit soit à jamais le rêveur inutile,
Qui voulut le premier, dans sa stupidité,
S'éprenant d'un problème insoluble et stérile,
Aux choses de l'amour mêler l'honnêteté!

Celui qui veut unir dans un accord mystique
L'ombre avec la chaleur, la nuit avec le jour,
Ne chauffera jamais son corps paralytique
À ce rouge soleil que l'on nomme l'amour!

(From *Delphine et Hippolyte*, poems suppressed by order of the Court.)

end? Is it not generally agreed that men of strong temper despise easy problems and embrace those that are difficult, that men of vigorous morality are exalted and contented when they are called upon to sustain great and severe trials, while in the mediocrity of every-day life their strength wanes and perishes for want of a commensurate purpose?[1]

But the following objection will be made. The feeling in question would indeed be innocent were not the obstacle which is overcome by the enjoyers of forbidden fruit the moral law itself. The pleasure in question is a "delight in evil" because there is rejoicing over the violation of the moral law. – We answer that the morality which is in this case represented in the form of a law, imposed by an outside authority, Society, or God, is for that very reason not morality but brute fact, external obstacle, against which the liberty of the individual comes up and rejoices to get the better of it. Were the obstacle not a frigid and external law but the moral conscience, a law which the individual sets for himself, offering to it a spontaneous obedience, it would be impossible to rebel against it and to rejoice at the rebellion. Or the rebellion and the rejoicing would result solely from a momentary obscuration of the conscience, a descent to a lower level, quickly followed by remorse. In fact once the moral conscience has awoken, once the law has become an inner law, once duty has become love, the rein which previously was ineffectual will become effectual, the lower and narrower urge will yield to the higher and fuller, dense and wicked voluptuarism to spiritual harmony and beauty. In this field the removal of prohibitions is sometimes of some service as an educative measure (for men, not for women or children), enabling the liberty of the individual, which was at odds not really with morality but with the external and oppressive form of the law, to discover itself spontaneously.

However, the taste of forbidden fruit is not what is considered delight in evil *par excellence*. Nor can we fully identify with this last that pleasure in another's pain which is called the joy of

---

1. "Marcet sine adversario virtus" – Seneca.

revenge. Indeed this is the place for confuting or explaining a common psychological error, by means of a denial which we here make that there can ever be, strictly speaking, pleasure at another's pleasure, or pain at another's pain. The pleasure and pain of an individual are, as such, absolutely incommunicable, it being an absurd idea that one individual should pass into the being of another, one moment of reality be a different moment of the same reality. Pleasure at another's pleasure, pain at another's pain, are our own pleasure and pain, felt for motives of our own, just as the pleasure of parents at the matrimonial happiness of their children is certainly something different from the honeymoon bliss of the children in question. In the pleasure which we feel at the pain suffered by another there is, then, always a motive of our own which is something other than the other's suffering. In the case of vengeance, it is the actuation of the utilitarian form of justice, the resort to a kind of economic calculus according to which, by causing pain to him who has caused pain to us, we think we can force him to refrain from inflicting more pain on us, or else by rejoicing over the circumstance which has brought pain to him who pained us, we win the feeling of having God, Luck, or the course of events on our side, almost as our ally. So that even in revenge we rejoice not in the other's ill but in our own advantage. It is only when we have risen above such utilitarian vengeance to the level where punishment is inflicted for moral motives, and inspires no longer a mere satisfaction at the strengthening of our personal advantage, but the very different satisfaction at the strengthening of the moral order itself, that, by comparison with this last, vengeance seems something wrong and wicked, an un-balanced satisfaction of our individual purposes. At that level of the conscience, blame falls not only upon him who takes vengeance, but, as we have demonstrated, in another connexion, on whoever out of negligence, vanity, or individual luxury condones the crime or offence, and lets it go unpunished.

But delight in evil, in its pure and classical form, is usually identified not with the savour of forbidden fruit, nor with that of vengeance, but with a rejoicing in the hurt and harm that befalls

another, a disinterested rejoicing in that for its own sake. Thus
Schopenhauer, describing the various types of anti-moral incentive,
distinguishes between egoism and malevolence, the former of
which treats another's hurt as a means, while the latter treats it as
an end. And egoism, he says, even in the shape of envy, is human,
but delight in evil is diabolic. In reality there is nothing in the life
of the spirit that is disinterested, that is to say purposeless and irrational. The good, too, is in its way interested, and so is that
wicked delight. And the distinction between that delight and
egoism is as superficial as all other such distinctions propounded
in Schopenhauer's Ethics. Delight in another's hurt, which is no
concern of ours, in fact signalizes the advantage to ourselves of
an enhanced relative strength through the mere fact of the weakening of others. In this way a farmer or trader gains by the other's
poor harvest or commercial failure because either it brings him
some advantage or at the very least spares him from relapsing
to a competitive position below the average. Thus La Rochefou-
cauld unkindly says that one feels some pleasure at a friend's
misfortune because one may perhaps by aiding and comforting
him put up the value of one's own friendliness, one's own person.
Even when delight in harm to others seems to be wholly objective,
aesthetic, as it were, unaccompanied by any obvious advantage to
us, indeed involving us in some disadvantage, if we examine the
matter down to the roots we will always find there an individual
interest, which may be the gratification of some sensual or imaginous appetite for sensation, variety, extraordinary spectacles, unusual
pleasure, purposes, that is to say, which taken in themselves are
neither moral nor immoral but simply useful to the life of the
individual or a single moment of that life – and constitute accordingly not a delight in evil but a delight in what on the
economic or utilitarian level is good.[1]

1. *Non quia vexari quemquam est jucunda voluptas,*
    Sed quibus ipse malis careas, ea cernere suave est.
                                            LUCRETIUS.

In Boccaccio, *Decameron*, x, 3, Nathan says to Mithridanes, who had come to
kill him because he could not bear to be outclassed by him in liberality:

These considerations serve to demonstrate the absurdity which is entailed in the concept of "delight in evil", an absurdity, one may say, displayed in the words themselves, because evil, when it is really evil, felt as such, is pain and not delight, and if it is not felt as evil it is not evil. If there were really in the Spirit a faculty of evil, we should have to discover what is its field of action, it being impossible that any spiritual force should be suppressed or left unsatisfied. The average or vulgar respectable man, thanks to this false philosophy, arranges in fact to maintain alongside of the more spacious field assigned to virtue, a closed orchard available for vice. But men of nobler temper, who abhor mediocrity, disdain such petty compromises and follow a logic in the grand style, either plunging into the excesses of untamed individuality, or else valiantly labouring to subdue all these to the service of a dominating moral activity. Sometimes the two extremes seem to meet or to alternate in one individual, and thus we encounter such characters as the gifted wastrel, the magnanimous pervert, the honourable "bad lot". In other cases one side gains strength from the other as shown in the *corruptio optimi pessima* and in the conversion of great sinners who become great saints.

[1918]

IV

THE "PLEASURES OF THE IMAGINATION"

Time was (in the eighteenth century) that many aesthetic philosophers engaged in the difficult problem of finding a proper place in the system of the spirit for the Fancy, confounded the "pleasures of the imagination" with the pleasure of art, and the frequent debates on these pleasures culminated in well-known didactic poems in the English and French languages. Our own

"My son, there is no need to ask or to grant pardon for your intention, whether you call it wicked or by whatever name you choose. For your motive was not hatred but the desire to be judged better." I do not know why one of the commentators chooses to describe this philosophical remark upon the psychological genesis of crime as "sophistry".

century also has had experience of this identification and confusion, thanks to the aesthetic theory of "apparent feelings" which was first sketched by Kirchmann and taken up by the somewhat obtuse metaphysician of the Unconscious, Eduard von Hartmann. Kirchmann, though he lived in the nineteenth century, thought largely on the lines of the eighteenth century and the Sensualist school.

This theory exhibits a confusion. For, if we adopt the old language of philosophy, the pleasures of the imagination relate to "matter" and the pleasure of art relates to "form." In more modern terms, what is called form in art is nothing else than the contemplative attitude of the spirit, while what is called matter is, in itself, the practical play of the passions. The pleasure of art is of theoretical origin, the "pleasures of the imagination" are of a directly practical origin.

The truth of this is testified by what was already in antiquity noted and commented upon with surprise: that in art things are pleasing which outside art are displeasing and painful (the lowest animals, and corpses, said Aristotle, while Boileau cites *"le serpent"* and *"le monstre odieux"*). In the pleasures of the imagination, on the contrary, pleasure depends upon the image which is summoned up or composed being itself agreeable, serviceable as an instrument of pleasure. Not indeed of sheer unmixed pleasure, which is a mere abstraction, nor yet of a more or less uniform, placid, idyllic pleasure, but of a feeling which through a variety of adventures and travails makes always for a pleasurable conclusion. (Images of voluptuous pain, leading up sometimes to the joy of martyrdom itself, are thus savoured in the imagination.) For this reason I myself have steadily classed those theories which develop the encounter with and defeat of ugliness (once the subject of elaborate systematic works of philosophy and still cherished by second-rate academic aestheticians in Germany and elsewhere) as being not aesthetic theories at all, but hedonistic theories, fallacious and harmful in the field of aesthetics. Where those theories depict any genuine psychic process, it is the process of the "pleasure of the imagination", not "the pleasure of artistic creation". For the same reason I have rejected the theory of "apparent feelings", unless these feelings be so understood that the pleasure in them is seen to derive wholly from the "appearance" itself, from the value of the appearance, that is from the artistic form. In the pleasure of the appearance, the actor is Man as a universal. In the pleasure of the matter of the appearance, the actor is man as an individual, with his particular interests, inclinations, and likings. In the former pleasure there is equal enjoyment of the sublime, the comic, the mild, the fierce, the austere, the voluptuous, all belonging to the sheer spectacle of humanity: in the latter nothing counts save what serves particular private requirements. It is of course quite obvious that the images of genuine art can be and are brought into service among the pleasures of the imagination, and this is the basis for the educationalist's concern as to what books should be encouraged and what disallowed, what pictures should be shown and what kept out of sight of boys and girls, because as the pupils do not approach these with a perfect concentration upon truth or aesthetic value, they may receive from them either help or hindrance to their moral formation. The distinction which we have drawn gains strength from this example.

The pleasures of the imagination, then, belong to the sphere of practice, yet it is well to give another warning against identifying them with the undertones of fantasy which accompany volitions, representations which reflect the unfolding of the will against a shifting background of hopes and fears, love and hatred. What constitutes and determines these latter is the quality of the volition itself, the end towards which the will tends. But in the case of the pleasures of the imagination the pleasure and satisfaction obtained by means of the imagination directly constitute the end. The "pleasures of the imagination" are thus not the feeling pertaining to activity in general, but are a case of hedonistic or utilitarian activity. It is similarly mistaken to class these as "play", for play is not an activity but is the alternation and variety of the activities of life, each of which can represent a relief and rest from any other.

What the pleasures of the imagination are is this: they are needs which do not or will not find their satisfaction in a certain form of reality, yet will not renounce the achievement of some sort of satisfaction and reality. They therefore obtain satisfaction through imagination. It would seem simpler and tidier to repress outright these needs which will not or cannot attain satisfaction. But they are so lively and urgent that it would in the circumstances be exceedingly laborious and painful, if indeed possible, to repress them forcibly, and it therefore appears a better arrangement for them to fulfil their cycle in the imagination. An illuminating comparison can be made with the process of diseases which we cannot immediately surmount but must leave to run their course and to be gradually overcome by the vital powers. Meanwhile we use drugs to diminish their force. The pleasures in question, then, are not imaginary, ineffective, fictitious, unreal, but are quite real and effective, as is proved by their physical, or as the language of a dualistic philosophy has it, psycho-physical manifestations. The proceeding of Kirchmann and Hartmann, the theorists of "apparent feelings", in assigning to them a lower intensity than that of the real feelings, is quite arbitrary. They might equally well be said to have a higher intensity, the fact being that they are qualitatively different. The notion that they are of the same quality, but of inferior intensity as compared with the "real" ones, is the origin of the much remarked and deplored disappointment which follows when long-cherished dreams are realized. This disappointment is spared only to him who knows that dream, which is in its own way real, is dream, and conveys the gratification of dream, while reality is real and produces the different gratification of reality. Knowing this, he will follow the wise advice of the poet of *Il Vendemmiatore*, "enjoying" the present, "hoping" the future, and thus "winning a doubled joy".

Be it noted that we have spoken of needs which cannot or will not find an issue in the sphere of so-called reality. In fact it is unlikely that the dreamers would always realize their dreams if only they could. This is the case even with love fancies. It is well known that there are women whom one likes to love in imagination but has no desire to love otherwise. A fierce imaginative hatred involving imaginary beatings, hidings, floorings, and killings of

47

an adversary on whom the dreamer would not inflict the slightest injury if he had him in his hands is exceedingly common. A contrast has commonly been observed, indeed, between what is pleasing in the imagination and what is attempted and realized in reality. Fierce natures like to cherish peaceful imaginations, and the corrupt indulge in dreams of innocence, as if to compensate for what they have renounced in their active lives, while men of spotless life harbour in dream the worst of their own natures, which they have as it were expelled from their lives into the dustbin. Strictly speaking, by this process neither do the former improve nor do the latter deteriorate. Their desire and their will stand firm, and the process of imagination is circumscribed and runs its course without entanglement with the effective will. Here there is no question of a nursing and cherishing of desires, which might deserve moral condemnation or reproof, but rather of a self-liberation from desires. The fierce or dissolute man returns from his virtuous dream refreshed and reinforced for the pursuit of his ferocity, his dissoluteness.

None the less it is a fact that men feel a certain shamefacedness about giving themselves up to the delights of the imagination, particularly men of ripe experience, sobered by acquaintance with the duties and the obligations of life, by contrast with boys, and especially girls, for whom the travails of the imagination are a matter of great importance, are drama, romance, tragedy, source of despair and of consolation, are, in fact, what they call "the ideal", with a rather absurd employment of that philosophical term. Even peoples are sometimes distinguished and graded by the degree of their absorption in dream, and excessive lingering in dreams and delights of the imagination, promoted sometimes by artificial methods, has been considered a sign of the inferiority of the East compared with the relatively undreaming but thoughtful and active West. But the sense of shame can easily be explained with the aid of the comparison with disease and the therapy which lets it run its course. No one is proud or pleased about his own sufferings and miseries, or the time taken up by attending to and alleviating them. In the light of the same comparison we can understand the blame which attaches to those who instead of taking steps to remove as far as possible the conditions which sometimes necessitate explosions of rage or amorous daydreamings about Prince Charming or the Ideal Woman, make a habit of the malady and of the remedy. Hence too the judgement of the common man who despises those peoples and individuals who devise means to intensify this sterile sort of life, wasting their energies upon the soporific and benumbing divagations of the imagination.

[1918]

V

THE BARRIER BETWEEN MINDS

We constantly hear complaints that arguments are vain, because at the end each one keeps the opinion which he had at the beginning. And since written and printed books are but the transposition of arguments on to a broader and less personal stage, doubts have also been expressed as to the efficacy of books for modifying ideas and opinions. The view that they are in fact useless has been advanced with the utmost elegance of persuasiveness and irony in two poetical epistles of Goethe.

But the fact that everyone labours to argue and many work hard at writing books might seem on the other hand to be a strong indication that arguments and books are not useless, otherwise there could never be so much labour expended on them. And this suggests the alternative question whether what is vain may not be that idea derived from mechanics or maybe chemistry, that one man's thought flows into another's thought in such wise as to sunder its elements, purify it, recompose it, or otherwise induce modifications in it. This idea is far from the reality, and serves to encourage these complaints that argument and books fail to achieve anything.

The image in question does not rightly portray what happens in an argument between man and man, nor yet what happens in the simpler case between teacher and pupil, or even between a tutor and some quite small child. The learner is never a *tabula rasa*, for evidently on whatever side the teacher approaches him he finds something already formed, ideas and tendencies or, more accurately speaking, problems which are not the teacher's problems. For the teacher can only have his own problems and give the solution of those. The pupil accordingly takes from the master as much as is useful to himself, cognate to his own ideas and tendencies, and rejects the rest. Or rather, if he is a diligent and respectful pupil he does not reject this altogether, but without fully digesting it in his brain and mind he commits it to memory as to a provisional store whence it may gradually slip away altogether, or it may in due course serve some good end. The time will come when the pupil's new problems will grow to more or less of a likeness with those of which the master gave the solution, and that is the moment for those words, hitherto mute, to speak, and they will be the scholar's own words. Was the tuition, then, in vain? It seems, on the contrary, that it was doubly useful, the first time when it both negatively and positively reinforced the personality of the scholar, and the second time when it gave him additional aid. The tuition will have been useless only from the point of view of one who looked for the pupil to become a duplicate of the master (that is, who desired something useless in itself).

But let us forget the case of school and think once more of argument in general. Why, in a discussion, should I accept the ideas of my fellow-disputant and opponent however just they may be? I have my problems, and these are not his problems, not even when it seems that we are discussing the same problem. For each of us understands it in his own way, refers it to his own experiences, links it with his other thoughts. Therefore each of us is broaching a different problem. In the discussion he will think that I am intent upon understanding what he says. But in truth I am intent only upon understanding myself better, and nothing is therefore more natural than that I should come out of the discussion more than ever firmly rooted in my own conviction. Even should he shake me, leave me without words to reply, disturb me, he is not disturbing me in my problem but is inciting me to formulate other problems which at that moment are beginning to assail me (that is the disturbance) and will in any case be my problems, not his. If this is true of my response to him, it is equally true of his to me, always presuming that we are both discussing in order to utter truth, and not, as often happens, in a spirit of obstinacy or under the influence of some petty or malign passion, if, in fact, we are saying something more than empty words. Given this condition, each of us will recognize the other's right. Everyone knows the dissatisfaction that one feels when a disputant, after the first few exchanges, meekly yields to our argument. We are dissatisfied because we suspect that the opponent whom we have so easily converted has not thoroughly understood the argument. If he did, he would put up a struggle, and even if he ended by agreeing with us, that is, by arriving at a problem and consequently a solution so close to ours as to pass for identical, he could only do this after a lapse of time, an interval of thinking the thing over by himself with the help of new experiences and incitements. As in the case of the school lesson, there is no question of the discussion being useless or useful solely in that it makes us think out our own thoughts more clearly and forces us to frame and phrase it exactly. There is a further utility, but that is for the future and not the present, it concerns other problems which we will take up, not those which we have already resolved, and it will take effect in the shaping of our personality, and not in the achievement of an impossible unison with other individuals, for such uniformity between individuals is impossible.

The destiny of solitary thinkers, uncomprehended in their own time, meeting with no other response to their words but scorn and mockery, has been deemed matter of tragedy. Sad too has been accounted the dilemma of every man of keen and vigorous mind who must either mutilate himself in order to find companionship in his intellectual life, or if he gives free rein to his genius must put up with solitude and seek comfort in the thought of the appraisers and disciples who will give heed to him long after his death. Truly there is no dilemma here, for he cannot but choose the second alternative. But although it is broadly true that he who goes farthest forward and rises to the greatest heights must endure the greater solitude (in other words problems like his own, or analogous or very close to them, are going to take shape only in course of time, so that only later will there be a movement of agreement with him), yet we are all lonely, being all individuals, that is to say diversities, and our agreement with each other is always a disagreement, our understanding always a misunderstanding. If sadness were the necessary fruit of loneliness, not only the great and the very great, but every one of us, however modest, must needs partake of the sadness, for each of us has his own originality, cannot fuse with or be fused in others.

And it would be no consolation to consider that, while each one with sure intent sought truth in his own range, and each fulfilled the good as required by his own particular conditions and temperament, yet all alike were afloat on the great ocean of being. For that feeling of sadness results from the thought of our reciprocal solitude, of our debarment from mutual penetration, of the necessity that each should go forward by the side of the others, hemmed in by the others, interfering and interfered with, but in the deeper sense unknown and unknowing, a stranger among strangers. Is there then no way of breaking these barriers, of penetrating into the impenetrable? For sure there is, and we use it the whole time, when we desist from the attitude of disputation and assume that of hearkening to the adversary and understanding him, and he thus ceases to figure for us as the hostile opponent of our thought and becomes its object. And our problem then becomes the problem of understanding him, not the problem of a moment ago, but another problem, no longer "theoretical" but "historical", or to use more correct language no longer the one-sided history of ourselves but the history of ourselves and of the other taken together, the true history which is both the necessary preface and the conclusion to any argument.

It is to history as the peacemaker and consoler that the great unrecognized have always appealed, confiding that history in its course would not only give factual proof of the truth of their ideas, but would accord to these an express and conscious recognition. This is the historical attitude which makes it possible for us to welcome our adversaries into our own being, sometimes as dear but still youthful brothers, sometimes as fathers and ancestors outdated but still venerable, sometimes as children for whose inexperience one must be indulgent, noting that their fresh outlook on things, due to that very inexperience, often allows them to perceive new aspects of them. Even these historical judgements can never win complete agreement, nor do they wholly liberate us from our solitude, indeed the wider and more comprehensive our mind is, the better the understanding and the warmer the welcome that we give to others, assigning to them their due places, the smaller is the company or indeed the more absolute is the solitude in which we find ourselves. If we understood everything, took account of all, and gave to each single one his just place, we should become God, all-understanding and incomprehensible to all. But that cannot be, and for that reason God – an individual who is no individual, an unlimited and abstract individual – is a being of the imagination. But the loneliness of superiority is not sad, is not solitude of the sort that we have been considering. Far from that, it is the very definition of that spiritual communion the law of which is a progressive detachment from particular and single attitudes for the sake of achieving a better union with them in the universal mode. And it is tolerance – not that ignoble tolerance which puts up with what it detests because it just has to, or lets all opinions pass because it is indifferent to all – but a tolerance removing the barriers between thought and thought, arranging and linking them in patterns of development, and thus bringing them to a unity.

[1918]

VI

GRACE AND FREE WILL

As in a mirror I look back at my past life, my work. What of them belongs to me? What in them can I in full honesty call my own? If some thought that has arisen in me seemed to myself and to others something gained for truth, the way it arose in me was by a sort of illumination in the mind, and now that I better understand its character and implications and retrace the history of its genesis, I see that it was the logical and necessary consequence of work conducted in the past by other minds, of century-long debates in which the part played by opponents has been as efficacious as that played by proponents. It is as though the idea in question had entered into me of its own accord, my mind being simply the stage or theatre for this appearance. If I recall an action of which I am glad, I feel I should be foolish to attribute the merit of it to myself, for when I performed it some power had awoken in my breast which carried me to it, overturning all obstacles if there were any, while if on that occasion, as on other occasions, that power which directed and sustained me had been lacking, I could not myself have generated it. The action in question, then, like the thought, performed itself in me rather than being performed by me, necessarily so, because Reality, or the Spirit if we call it so, had need of this in the logic of its development. If anyone praises me, I cannot enjoy the praise without a certain uneasiness and embarrassment, as if the reward were offered on the basis of faulty information, so that I should be doing wrong to accept it. On the other hand, people sometimes blame my mistakes and bad conduct, and I myself recognize that I have made certain mistakes and behaved badly in certain ways. When I look into the origin and character of these, I do not, for sure, try to excuse them on the plea of circumstance, for circumstance can never mechanically determine mistakes and wrong actions, and therefore can never excuse them. But all the same I have to recognize that if I had not uttered those errors, committed those faults, then my best truth would never have been born (for it drew nourishment from the experience of those errors), nor would my best action have been performed (for it was remorse and revulsion from evil that improved and strengthened me). That error and wrongdoing, then, were necessary and in a certain sense good, and they belong not to me but to the author of evil and of good, the Spirit that develops and grows in such ways, the Providence that so ordains, and follows therein its logic of contraries which is known as dialectic. Grace descended upon me at certain moments, while at other moments Providence withheld grace, letting me err and sin in order to prepare new material and conditions for my work (which is the work of Providence).

Necessity and dialectics, Grace and Providence, bring about the dissolution not only of the concepts of free will and responsibility, but of that of the individual as an entity, a reality. The place of this last is taken by the clearly distinct concept of the individuality of the action in its enactment, having its own quality that can never be confounded with that of other actions. Such an individuality is the very definition of the true and effective universality which is not abstract but concrete. And quaint indeed must seem the desire of immortality for an essence or individual soul in another life, when we cannot attribute to it even in this life the qualities of reality and existence. For what we find before us are individuated thoughts and actions, not individuals, and we find always the universal at work on the creation, dissolution, and replacement of individualities, but never do we find individuals and the universal facing each other like two realities.

So that is how things are – and yet, they are not like that and do not seem like that. For as soon as I desist from sheer self-contemplation, to plunge again into active and practical life, of a sudden whatever had been dissolved and convicted of nullity reintegrates itself and arises in restored energy and dignity. I find myself to be once again an individual, endowed with free will, responsible for my actions, worthy of praise or condemnation, attached to my individuality and my life and – as long as I live it – unable to think of it as other than immortal. And thus I banish from its presence the intimations of mortality which would impair and weaken it, I throw forth ahead of it the prospect of an infinite continuation, that hope of living which never quits life, not even at the last breath which is itself an act of living, not of dying. All that, too, is rational and necessary, necessary for "physiological" life and for the higher spiritual life, for work in the field of practice and in the field of theory, for deeds of utilitarian or of moral

import. That justification which in my contemplations, my meditations, I found for my errors and my wrong actions, at the point
which we have now reached is of no avail at all, for the fact
remains that those errors are painful to remember, those wrong
actions sear my soul, and I would fain never have uttered them,
never have committed them, would fain expunge them from
reality were that possible, and since it is not possible I writhe, and
from my anguish the only relief is a temporary forgetfulness that
comes with engagement in other thoughts, other actions, while
the only cure comes with a return to the task in a better spirit,
with a resolve to make good misspoken words by a better utterance, and ill deeds by better deeds. And, by the same token, I
no longer disclaim the truth which I have thought or the good
which I have done. Far from severing it from myself I claim it and
embrace it as my own, take pleasure in the memory of it, draw
from it a confidence that my further performance will be worthy
of the preceding, and the present such as may befit the past. And
if anyone would dispute my deserts I run to the defence and rebut
the injustice and even, as the saying is, *sumo superbiam*.

At first sight there seems to be in this alternation of attitudes a
flagrant, insuperable contradiction. But deeper consideration will
show that we are in the presence simply of the alternation of
thought with action, of theory with practice, two categories of
the Spirit and of Reality which exist each for the other's sake, and
by dint of distinction and opposition resolve themselves into that
one and only conceivable unity which is the eternal process of
unification. When we contemplate and meditate, what else do
we than seek the truth, weigh in thought the history of ourselves,
of others, of the human race, of the world – in a word, History?
And action is the creation of the history which we thus think.
Truth is only in thought. Action is not truth, and does not affirm
truths, for what appear to be truths affirmed in action are never
anything else than conditions and instruments of action, action
in its concreteness. Therefore attempts to found truths unknown
to the theoretical reason upon the "practical reason" are vain. The
"truths" in question are undoubtedly unknown to the theoretical

reason just because they are not truths at all. Otherwise we should have to confer that title upon the imaginations of men and women in love about their lovers, which for us are imaginations, but for them are the solidest reality. We all know that such imaginations cannot be dispelled by any critical process, but only by the cessation of love, of which they are part and parcel. It is equally mistaken, and is morally pernicious, to introduce the theoretical attitude into the field of practice, shirking the necessity for action, for the utterance of non-theoretical judgements of "practice" or "value" (such utterance being itself action), on the plea that Grace is withheld and that Providence is unwilling. In the performance of his tasks the individual must act as though he were his own grace and providence, must compel these to serve him, or to use less paradoxical language must make himself worthy of them by his own deeds and efforts.

My purpose in here calling attention to the dual aspect of theory and of practice within the unity of the life of the Spirit was not to restate this surely indisputable conclusion, but rather to raise the question whether the age-long theological controversy of Grace and Free Will could not be expounded with much gain in clearness and simplicity by viewing it as ultimately signalizing a collision and transposition between two points of view, the theoretical-historical and the practical-moral. Thus we might say that as historians we always take up the point of view of Grace, Providence, and Justification by Faith, whereas as makers of history, practical men, we take up that of Free Will, Responsibility, Justification by Works. And this, for the aforesaid reason, is not a dualism. In the history of that controversy there has always been noted the presence of a tension between such approximate and contingent terms as mysticism in contrast with activism, religion in contrast with the practical life, Christianity in contrast with Catholicism or Jesuitism, and a corresponding pull between the opposed but in different circumstances equally legitimate demands for a greater austerity for a greater measure of accommodation, accompanied by complicated psychological considerations of the need for easy-going concessions, for dull and unenquiring acquiescence, or for energetic action. In the hands of the opposing parties of theologians, the contrast hardened into an insoluble dualism, for instead of seeking a solution on lines of immanence and dialectic, able to do justice to both aspects and to their unity, the theologians sought an abstract and transcendental solution, and were thus forced either to deny Providence and Grace or to deny Free Will, or rather, as in fact happened, to make a combination of the two by picking and choosing, compromising, subtilizing, and resorting to meaningless terms. However, beneath the surface of those theological disputations, there lurked the speculative problem which was what really gave them their allurement and rendered them fruitful for philosophy. Philosophy may seem to have turned aside from them, but the truth is that thanks to nourishment received from them, philosophic travail on these questions is now stilled.

[1929]

VIII

THE WORLDLY PAIR OF SCIENCES: AESTHETIC AND ECONOMIC

I

SPIRIT AND SENSE

In conspicuous distinction from the Middle Ages, the modern age accords great prominence to the political and economic aspects, and to the highly variegated artistic aspects of life.

Not of course that the economic and political, or the artistic aspects, were absent in the Middle Ages, but they were less prominent. No individual can live without those two spiritual organs, and no age, no matter how barbaric or primitive. And the age in question was marked by some strong manifestations in the sphere of art and poetry. All that it is wished here to emphasize is that taking mediaeval society as a whole it was not upon these aspects that the accent fell. For a preliminary and almost intuitive confirmation of this it suffices to take a glance at such mediaeval buildings as survive. The buildings or ruins of the high Middle Age, in particular, consist of churches and monasteries and castles, by contrast with the modern age's display of factories, markets, bourses, banks, parliamentary and ministerial buildings, and of museums, picture galleries, exhibitions, theatres, schools, and so on. Further confirmation is provided by a rapid glance at the poetry, literature, and art of the Middle Ages, consisting in the main of works of edification and exhortation, of narratives and allegories, and only to a minor extent of personal and lyrical compositions. The politics of the age, when they went beyond the provision of elementary necessities for sustenance and defence, were devoted to ultramundane ends, as in the crusades for the conquest of the sepulchre of Christ, and the disputes between Church and Empire. Mediaeval economics had relapsed into the "natural" stage, almost without specialized industry and exchange. A revolution began when the Italian Communes, and the great Norman and Swabian monarchs, began to pursue national and

State policies, deliberately devoted to the promotion of prosperity and culture. Then the arts and the trades revived, and their expansion at first went side by side with the ultramundane programmes, but at times outran them. At last, with the Renaissance and the Reformation, two movements which appeared to be contrasting but were in fact complementary (for the Renaissance, while seeking for Graeco-Roman antiquity, fell upon reality and nature, while the Reformation, while seeking for Gospel Christianity, fell upon free thought and criticism), the modern age was ushered in. It is such differences in accent and rhythm which perpetuate the distinction and opposition which our histories place between Middle Ages and modernity, needful for high-lighting these differences. For wrong though it would be to treat those differences as marking clean cuts, seeing that in historical thought we should treat them only as signs which appear and disappear, shine and fade out, in the continuous unity of history, yet they do serve to enable us to follow the profound drama of human history in its passage, now gradual, now revolutionary, from Middle Age to modernity. If those differences be erased, or reduced to unimportance, or again, if the values in question be confused, then the Middle Ages will disappear from history, or else the modern age will be reduced to the rank of a Middle Age in the depreciatory sense of an age of spiritual poverty, which is how already reactionary historians and ascetically religious minds are inclined to judge it.

A heightened intensity of political and economic activity and also of various sorts of artistic activity in the first centuries of the modern age had its theoretical counterpart in the development of two new fields of thought and study, the politico-economic (for we here view politics and economics within the framework of their substantial philosophical identity) and the aesthetic (or philosophy of art). These two sciences were all but unknown to mediaeval philosophy, which in the practical sphere recognized nothing save morality, and so, when faced with political and economic problems, and unable to evade them, solved them in terms of moral formulae, while in the theoretic sphere it recognized nothing save logic, and reduced poetry and art to serve as instruments for the interpretation and diffusion of sacred truths. Then, of a sudden, at the Renaissance, the political science or Science of States sprang into vigorous being, closely followed by the lore of the Arts of Prudence, and then somewhat later by the teachings of Economy, which were elaborated in firm laws and rules in the eighteenth century though still stopping short of a full philosophical awareness. Distinctions were now drawn between law and morality and attention was turned to the human passions and to the problem arising out of them;[1] and meanwhile the Renaissance itself revived enquiry into the concepts of poetry, the figurative arts, architecture, and music. There was a search for a common foundation underlying all these, and a delineation of the faculties that operated in the creation of all the arts, which enquiry reached a first objective also in the eighteenth century, with the discovery of the original nature of the new principle, and the constitution of an autonomous science to which was given the new name of Aesthetics. No more, of course, than in any other sphere of knowledge could doctrinal systems of Aesthetics be laid down once and for all, but there was a tracing of the directions along which work then began and still continues, and the need for and potentiality of such directions was felt then and is still felt.

The two new sciences had a radically anti-ascetic, anti-transcendental, worldly and secular character. But neither was this observed and affirmed and set forth by the modernizing spirits who cultivated the new sciences, nor were these sciences rejected and rebutted by the antiquated and traditionalist spirits who, had they discerned that character, should have taken arms against them. On the contrary they tolerated them or even joined in cultivating them, under the influence of the needs and demands of their times. The one case in which there was a reaction and a sustained controversy and attempt to vanquish one of these sciences, or rather a part of one of them – the polemic against Politics or the

1. For historical notes on these apparently dissociated but in reality intimately connected developments, see my *Filosofia della Pratica*, 6th edn., Bari, 1950, passim.

"Reason of State" – consisted not in an attempt to dismiss the new science in itself, but rather to oppose the harsh and nude form in which it was presented by Machiavelli and his school, the authors of the opposition being themselves more or less men of politics, who took steps to combine the new with the old in an eclectic union, one of those unions in which, really, it is never the new that is tempered but always the old which little by little is corroded and falls away. Indeed the anti-Machiavellist Jesuit Fathers, out to defend the Catholic Church by modern methods, took to Machiavellianism so heartily that they introduced it where the author of the system would never have done, namely in the sphere of pure ethics. In the same way the Jesuits made a certain contribution to the formation of modern Aesthetics when, in their schools of humanistic rhetoric, they advanced or appropriated the theories of the sensuous, of the imagination, of the fancy, of the mental gifts or genius, and of the judgement of the senses or good taste. In the later and worldlier Catholic Church there was no repetition of Savonarola's bonfire of vanities. The Economic Science, particularly in its first unphilosophical shape as "Political Arithmetic", was far from rousing scandal or suspicion. Only later, with the spread of doctrines of extreme competitive individualism, was there from time to time some talk of moralizing Economics and of a resuscitation of the *justum pretium* dear to the tradition of Thomas Aquinas. If indeed in either camp there had then been awareness of the nature of the two sciences, it would be unnecessary and superfluous to illustrate it now. But I believe that the present observations are not superfluous because they arise out of the full awareness to which a movement can only reach when it has plenty of history behind it, and can be embraced as a whole, and seen in relation to its counterpart, the movement out of which and in opposition to which it originated. Such awareness is not general even today. For my part, when I have met learned priests, starry-eyed monks, and other devout people who had rashly taken up and played with the concepts of modern aesthetics, I have warned them: "Look out, you are trafficking with the devil." I say the devil, because I remember that Friedrich Schelling, meditat-

ing on the origin of languages in all the vigour of their irreducible
individuality, defined them as "diabolic" or "satanic", an idea
which the grammarian D'Ovidio found extravagant – and true
enough, it is somewhat outside of the mere scholar's range.

What, then, when all is said and done, is the function of these
two sciences? Briefly, it is to give a theoretical justification, and,
by dint of definition and systematic consideration, the rank of a
positive and creative form of the Spirit, to what was called
"sense" – sense, which in the Middle Ages had been viewed with
suspicion if not actually banned and exorcized, but which the
modern age, in its practical proceedings, was rehabilitating. Now
"sense" had two associated but distinct meanings, firstly, that which
in knowledge is not logical and ratiocinative, but sensible and
intuitive; and, secondly, that which in practical activity is not in
itself moral and dutiful but pursued because liked and desired,
useful and pleasurable. Consequently, the doctrine which rehabili-
tated sense developed on the one hand into a logic of the senses or
poetic logic, science of pure intuitive knowledge or Aesthetic,
and on the other hand into a logic of the pleasurable or useful,
Economic in the widest sense, and all this was nothing more nor
less than a theoretical and philosophical "redemption of the flesh",
as it is called, a redemption of life as life, of earthly love in all its
aspects. Of course, this justification of "sense" implied at the same
time its spiritualization. For sense was transferred thereby from its
situation as extraneous to spirituality, opposed to it like a dangerous and insidious and greedy and for ever utterly irreconcilable
enemy, to a situation inside the spirit, where its function was
spiritual (though with a particular quality of spirituality), and
where its operation and its value would be found indispensable for
full and healthy spiritual life. But if sense, being received into this
more elevated sphere, was thereby spiritualized, the spirit became
correspondingly merged in sense, or more properly speaking it
recovered its integrity and harmony, and was relieved of the pains
which had derived from the mutilation of some of its essential
and needful aspects. Logic and Ethics came down to earth from
the overworld to which they had been relegated. Logic emerged

48

from the scholastic and formalistic phase to become enquiring, experimental, and inductive. Ethics renounced the character of a transcendental legislation and became moral sentiment or conscience. And the enmity previously shown by Ethics for the passions and for the objects of desire turned to a friendly view of these, sometimes severe, sometimes indulgent, but in any case not aiming at their eradication from the human heart, but at their elevation and purification, for the strengthening of moral life and action itself. All the principal concepts of modern philosophy are closely bound up with the two new sciences. Without them the intellectualistic Logic of the Abstract Universal could never have been challenged by the Speculative or Dialectical Logic of the Universal Concrete, which was so much influenced by the analogy of art or poetry with thought, that for a time there was a disposition to view art as the major and one adequate organ of truth. Nor yet without them could History have been raised above its condition as a mere chronicle or record of events or as mere *opus oratorium*, tuition by means of exemplars or cautionary morals to point the tale, to recognition as the very idea of Philosophy in its plenitude and its operative phase. Nor, finally, without the two new sciences would it be possible to complete the circle of the conception of reality as Immanence.

The expert in the history of philosophy can fill in this sketch of one aspect of its history in the modern age with innumerable details. It would be most instructive to recall the protests that have been occasioned or revived by each attempt to maintain or to resurrect the mediaeval disclaimer of the two sciences, or to renew, albeit in forms shaped or clothed by modern thought, the separation between spirit and sense. As examples we may cite Vico's championship of historical thought against the rationalism of Descartes, Galileo's argument against the Aristotelians, Schiller's protest against the residue of rigour and asceticism remaining in the ethics of Kant, the rebellion of the Romantic aesthetes against the frigidities of classicism, the criticism levelled against the Conceptual school of Aesthetics (even when the "concept" was watered down to an "idea") by the Expressionist school, and so on. Such, indeed, is the perpetual inspiration of those philosophies which spring from the fertile soil of life, experience, poetry, in contrast with the bloodless academic and school philosophy which dwells in a world from which passion and fancy are banished, and has a weakness for the abstractions of formal logic and ethics. However, this is not the place for developing that argument further. Meanwhile it must always be remembered that the triumph of a way of thought never signifies the triumph of a definitely fixed truth or system of such truths, but means only the determination of a direction for future movement, in the course of which the old and already surmounted difficulties are to be remembered, and new difficulties, which will never fail to crop up, are to be faced and solved.

II

SPIRIT AND NATURE

The question which must here be developed is this: what is the contribution (to which we have referred) of the two modern and worldly sciences towards the closing of the circle of immanence? This will give us occasion to pause over the most weighty of those dualisms which have impeded and still impede the closing of the circle, to wit the dualism of spirit and nature.

More than a dualism, this is a tangle of dualisms which must be unravelled one by one. The first of these finds its origin and support and continual recrudescence in a popular belief, and it consists precisely in the supposition of two different orders of reality, two different worlds as it were, as for example a "world of man" and a "world of nature", the latter of which would include all other beings, from animals to stones; or else it may be a world of the "conscious" and one of the "unconscious", or of "life" and "mechanism", or however else the two worlds are to be fixed and constituted. This dualism, though grounded not in thought but in the imagination, has proved singularly tough, so tough, in fact, that critical thought, which cannot properly accept any dualism, instead of criticizing and annulling it forthwith, started off by keeping it in existence while at the same time attempting to interpret it thanks to a spiritualization of nature, the second term. But the attempt is rooted in contradiction and can only end with a fresh recourse to the imagination. This takes place even in the earliest and most naive attempt along those lines, the Renaissance Philosophy of Nature, decked-out luxuriant mythology of Pythagorean symbols, personifications, animisms. It is yet more clearly apparent in the Nature Philosophy of the idealistic and Romantic movement, which, however, from the very beginning, encountered a reasoned opposition from Fichte and others. (Fichte termed it *Schwärmerei*, day-dreaming.) Philosophies of this latter school took as their starting point the concept of that which is "other" than the spirit, intrinsic otherness, the absolute unconscious (as though the absolutely unconscious could be conceived), and thereby they confirmed the initial and fundamental dualism. But then, by treating this "other" or "unconscious" as "estranged reason" or "petrified thought", thereby shouldering the duty of penetrating and reconstructing the unconscious or estranged dialectic, they supposed themselves to have got the better of it. It little matters whether the dialectic in question was developed along the lines of Schelling, by degrees, or those of Hegel, by triads. The method remained substantially the same, relying upon metaphor and imaginous analogy, whether nature was expounded with the categories of the spirit or with the more restricted categories of the logos. Those philosophies have been controverted, not only and not primarily by logical refutation, but rather by the comic quality found in their remembered or pretended sayings, such as "the diamond is a pebble attaining self-consciousness", or "the hurricane is a fever of nature". Like the Nature Philosophies of the Renaissance, with which they had affinities and historical links, those of the Romantic Age sometimes harboured thoughts and hopes of rediscovering and applying a magical art.

But the very basis of these constructions is removed, and the problem of nature given a different turn, by a development of the theory of knowledge which has gradually brought awareness that there are not two orders of reality or two worlds, one spiritual and the other material or natural, one governed by purpose, the other subject to causality, one living and the other mechanical, but that there is on the contrary one compact unseverable reality which can be, as occasion requires, expounded by means of the concepts of spirit, life, and purpose, or by means of those of matter, cause, mechanism. The double order of reality and the duality of worlds is seen to be but a fanciful projection of a twofold operation of the human spirit, so far removed from reality that not only may animals, vegetables, minerals and stones, but along with these also man himself, with his feelings, thoughts, actions, works, and history, be envisaged and expounded schematically, naturalistically, mechanically, deterministically, as is in fact the proceeding of the many natural sciences which find their material in the life of the spirit, from the sort of experimental zoology which is termed experimental psychology, to the sort of physics which studies the phonetic laws of languages. However, this teaching of a twofold form available for the exposition of the real, if understood as positing a duality of modes of thought, one mode concerned with purpose and the other with cause, would, while dissipating the phantom of nature as before described, threaten to impair also the concept of spirit. For the one and unique reality, being viewed alternately in two diverse modes, would undergo two modes of distortion and would be unthinkable and unknowable in itself. To escape from this impasse there is no other way available than that of attributing to one only of these two ways, and recognizing as belonging to it alone, genuine thought and truth, attributing to the other what has been called an "economic", that is a merely practical and instrumental function. This has been effected by the modern criticism of the sciences which has been led willy-nilly, and despite all lingering in the untenable halfway houses of intuitionism and phenomenism, to the discovery of a logical necessity for affirming and confirming the unique truth of speculative thought and of the absolute spiritualist conception of reality as history; and it has been led to the demonstration that whatever knowledge of truth is contained in the natural sciences is historical knowledge. There is, in our days, an ever increasing emphasis upon concrete, individual, and historical reality in the study of so-called Nature.[1]

There is, however, also another significance in the dualism of spirit and nature, and the foregoing theoretical dissolution and resolution of the concept of nature does not fully meet the case of this. We may deny the claim of nature to constitute an order of reality, a particular world, but nature seems to reappear as that something within the spirit itself which thought finds to be present as its object, making for a dualism of subject and object. What in fact is the object, the object in itself, differentiated from the subject, if it is not the returning ghost of the unconscious, the non-spiritual, the material, in fact of that Nature which critical thought failed to dissolve, or only partially and momentarily dissolved, whence its prompt resuscitation by the imagination, and reappearance in a new guise? This is in fact so. And the consequence is that the efforts made to reabsorb this object are no less vain than the aforesaid proceedings of the philosophies of nature. They turn out to be tautologies or puns, as when there is pressed upon us a duality which is the unity of the subject-object relation. They announce the terms of the problem without resolving it. Or they try to *escamoter* the object, causing it to disappear and then to reappear as fact contrasted with act (that is, as nature contrasted with spirit), or as past contrasted with present (new temporal metaphors for nature and spirit), and suchlike metaphysical sublimities. Meanwhile the dissolution of the alleged reality of mechanical nature which we have already effected if it forces us to conclude that the object cannot be this same non-existent nature, does not tell us what this something which the thinking mind takes to be the object of thought actually is. This failure leaves the door open for the reappearance of the ghost of nature. Logically, the object cannot but be itself also Spirit, but surely not that mode of

1. See the notes of DE RUGGIERO in *Critica*, on contemporary philosophy. The English physicist EDDINGTON in *The Nature of the Physical World* (Cambridge, 1927) has humorously illustrated the contrast between the living observation of reality and lifeless schematizations: "A pig may be most familiar to us in the form of rashers, but the unstratified pig is a simpler object to the biologist who wishes to understand how the animal functions."

the spirit which is thought, thought whose function is that of subject and not of object. What mode, then, can it be? It is those two philosophic sciences which we have described as peculiarly modern, one referring to *praxis* in its dynamism and passionality, the other to the exercises of the fancy, which offer us the data required for solving the problem. They reveal that the object is nothing other than that passional life, those stimuli, impulses, pleasure and pain, the various and multiple commotion, in fact, which forms the material of intuition or fancy, and through the agency of this, of reflection and thought.[1] The consequence of this conception will be an abandonment of the old scholastic definition of truth as *adaequatio rei et intellectus* (for the *res* as such does not exist) and its substitution, if anything, by the formula *adaequatio praxeos et intellectus* – but the notion of *adaequatio* must of course be considered metaphorical. That "nature" should be identified with the practical cycle of desires, appetites, cravings, satisfactions, and reawakening wants, with the concomitant movements of pleasure and pain, was an idea which flashed upon the philosophers Fichte and Schelling, and provided the theme for the work of Schopenhauer. But those thinkers, above all Schopenhauer, conceived metaphysically of the Will, placing this outside of the Spirit, qualifying it as 'blind', and treating thought and representation as a *posterius*, in much the same way that Hegel conceived metaphysically of the Logos, placing it at the basis of nature and the spirit, and other much lesser thinkers similarly exalted other forms of the spirit, Frohschammer, for example, the Fancy, and Hartmann the Unconscious. But the Will should, on the contrary, be conceived of as, inside the spirit, a particular form or category of the spirit itself, and as the most elementary of the practical forms, that in which the higher practical form, the ethical, perpetually translates and incarnates itself, while thought and

---

1. I reached this conclusion some twenty-five years ago in my *Philosophy of the Spirit*, by way of Aesthetics and the Logic of History and of a critical return to the traditions of classical Idealism. It has been reached along other lines by Dewey. See the essay on him by De Ruggiero in *Critica*, XXIX, 341-57, esp. 345-6.

fancy themselves find in it their outer shape as word and expression, and in this operation make acquaintance with the practical experiences of feeling of all sorts, and of the opposed poles of pleasure and pain. Thought, even when it is pondering and criticizing the thoughts of others and tracing their history, is intent not upon thought but upon the practical life of thought, for thought is always the thinking subject and never the object of thought. How, for example, can we think a thought of Emmanuel Kant otherwise than by thinking of that man in his creative process, effortfully taut and intent, with his experiences, affections, doubts, enquiries, and means for satisfying these; how otherwise, in fact, than by reflecting upon him as practically engaged, no matter how much the practicality may have been concerned with the activity of thinking? And why should we reflect upon that practical engagement of Kant unless it were to resolve our own mental problem by means of it, and not of the thought of Kant in thinking of that act?

However, even when we have thus still more drastically expelled nature out of the subject-object relation, we have still not wholly come to an end of the series of dualisms or seen the last of that ghost. For back it comes, and worries and plagues us, like some heavy influence irrupting into our spiritual life to sunder it apart, pushing our will in the direction of evil, our mind in the direction of error. *La nature: voilà l'ennemie*: that material, mechanical, deterministic nature which stands in opposition to the ends, the ideals, the liberty of the spirit, that Schopenhauerian Will, acknowledged as nature, source of pain and evil which, notwithstanding all that Schopenhauer may say, we cannot extinguish in ourselves by a renunciation of the will which would be itself an act of will, nor by ascetic practices which are themselves an endless series of volitions. However, if we have never discovered a nature outside the spirit, we cannot possibly conceive of a nature ranged against the spirit. If evil and error are in the spirit they cannot be nature. And what then are they? As already shown in regard to the object, they cannot be a form of the spirit, for in that case they would have a positive and not a negative character, and would be goodness and truth, not evil and error, whereas evil and error we see to be painfully negative. Nor, however, can they be mere appearance or illusion, for were they so then the struggle against evil and error would be void of seriousness, a mere pretence of struggle, or at most a delirium. But that struggle is terribly serious and real. The only solution is that evil and error must have both characters in itself. It must be a positive which assumes the likeness of a negative in the stress of its passage from that first positive form to the form of a higher positivity, in which process the stress and the struggle are truly serious. And we must say that evil will be not that positivity which has been left behind, but a falling back towards it after it has been left behind, a falling back which partakes of the contradictory, and accordingly also of the painful and shameful, because once something has been left behind there is no returning to it in the earlier condition, which we may term that of naivety and innocence, but only in the altered condition of remorse. But now, is there in the sphere of the practical spirit a positive of inferior grade and another of superior grade? We are helped once again by the science of the useful, the agreeable, the *quod mihi placet*, of the affections and passions and tendencies which in ordinary talk are actually termed "natural", and which the science in question displays as the elementary and general form of praxis. This form is distinguished from the higher, ethical form, but without being directly opposed to it. Such opposition arises only when the moral man is born out of the utilitarian man, and there is a passage from actions of personal utility to actions of duty, involving a breach which in its course gives rise to the various phenomena of evil, the fleeting and rapidly surmounted temptation, the partial backsliding, and that which seems to be total and precipitous; the repining over a small fault and the terrible remorse for a great sin; courageous resolution, wavering, the plunge to disaster, and then once again recovery, renewal, redemption. Evil, then, is the torment of falling back (without really falling back), from morality to mere "natural" utility, which, though a lesser good than the other, is none the less, taken in itself, a good and not an evil, a positive and not a negative. Those who mistakenly persist in denying the spiritual form of utility, recognizing only the moral form of the practical spirit, are, one fears, animated not by an excessively vigorous moral conscience, but, on the contrary, by one that is too weak, vacuous, and soft, since they take away from morality its combative character or leave it in a mere sham combat with its own shadows. But the concept of the pleasurable or useful, offered by the economic form, not only keeps for it this combatant character, but gives it a possibility of victory which would be ruled out if evil, instead of arising in ourselves as a crisis in our effort of growth and elevation, impinged brutally upon our spirit like a wedge driven into it by some uncontrolled extra-spiritual force, nature or matter.

Thus these two peculiarly modern sciences, Aesthetics and Economics, provide a conciliation of spirit and sense, free the spirit from the incubus of an external nature, spiritualize the object for the subject, interiorize the struggle of good against evil, and, excluding the transcendent, clear the stage for absolute immanence. They are the two sciences which are in a special sense worldly. One who for many years has cultivated them and found in them much illumination for his spiritual life may be allowed, as he draws towards the end of it, to pen this little celebration of them.

[1931]

IX

ORIGINAL SIN

Pages justly to be called "sublime" are those in which Vico described the awakening of moral awareness in mankind in its savage condition, in the "bestioni umani" as he called them, when the blaze of lightning suggested to them the idea of God: and other such pages by other writers who have movingly described the origin of thought and language. But for all their sublimity they do not match the measure of the life of the Spirit, in which there are no chronological befores and afters, but only priority and posteriority of concepts in their ideal order. Thus spiritually speaking there are not first of all savage human giants and then afterwards morally aware human beings, but there are men in whom both characters live, for the spirit is all of one piece, not made up of different pieces.

In the single yet multiple nature of the Spirit, that opposition which arises out of the distinction of the Forms, and is called the struggle of Good and Evil, originates and extinguishes itself. Therefore man can never become sheer good or sheer evil. A man may vanquish this or that particular evil in himself but no one will ever be able to vanquish Evil as such. Whoever sets out to do so is on the way to madness, for this would be an attempt to live in contrast with the law of life. The unity of life in its goodness and badness is that genuine "original sin" which cannot be redeemed even though Gods or Sons of God shed their blood for this: unless haply beyond the one life which we know and can alone conceive.

No doubt, when we observe the extreme examples of good and wicked men whom we can observe in the moral field, we do appear to espy a clear distinction between the two. But a hidden voice in the breast of every one of us forbids us to gloss over the faltering or failing nature of man. Everyone feels in himself the wild beast (to call it "animal nature" might be to malign the animals). Each hears this beast raging and roaring, and in the exercise of his own moral virtue endeavours to draw off the wild thing into fields where it can vent itself harmlessly or not too harmfully. In the last resort there is at disposal the land of dreams, where without actual sin desires can be cherished such as no one would acknowledge, scarcely even to himself. Whoever is (as Hamlet said of himself in part praise and part blame, almost as though ashamed of it) "indifferent honest", consents to give play to the vital force in himself which would not be strong at all if it did not tend to be headstrong. The philosopher observes that this force should be governed but not trodden down, for were it tyrannically tamed and subdued there is risk that it would be rendered incapable not only of evil but also of good, and the moral perfection attained would be a death of morality by starvation of material. In all this we see why men of serious nature hate to be praised, for they feel that in accepting the praise they are giving countenance to a social untruth.

We see too in art, that we could never re-create in ourselves or have a comprehension of those beings which art offers for our contemplation, unless we could enter into their passions, and that in art all perfect beings are considered to be conventional figures, as are also all demoniac beings, whereas our feelings go out to those whom old Aristotle called "middling", that is human beings in whom we can recognize ourselves.

But history opens up to us quite a different view – I mean genuine history of the sort which does not track down the faults of men but strives to tell what man has achieved. This sort of history is not about the sins of men but about the actions by dint of which, with hard labour, man has created all the nobility, utility, truth, and beauty that there is in the world. Thus art is said to speak to our heart and history to our reason.

Yes, but if we thus reaffirm the impurity of man, what comfort can we ever have in a life such that even the fulfilment of duty, with the surrenders which this requires, will never afford us the full satisfaction of our own purity, but will, on the contrary, sharpen our insight into the incompleteness of every man. With this we come round again to the question: "Is life worth living?" – a petty question, as we immediately feel, without being able at once to explain the pettiness. Well, the explanation can be found, and the question, which is basically eudaemonistic, can be all the more easily rejected in that it refers to an unattainable satisfaction. It will be a further foolishness on the part of this eudaemonism to try and construct a calculus of pleasures and pains apt on the one hand to comfort us and on the other hand to dismay us in regard to the worthwhileness of life. For obviously no pleasure, however intense, can atone to us for any pain. Each pleasure, each pain, is enclosed in itself. Yet on the level of the moral conscience we will rediscover a full acceptance of life, because life is not for us a sort of theatre outside the entrance of which we may ask ourselves whether or not to go in and enjoy the play. We are, on the contrary, born into it already bound by ties of feeling and duty towards the lives of other people and towards the things in it. From these we will reap joy and grief, but it will not be the joys that will persuade us to accept life, or the pains that will dissuade us from accepting it. This will be the work of life itself, and the sole comfort remaining to us at the hour of our departure will be that of having served life to the best of our ability.

[1950]

VI

ESSAYS IN CRITICISM
AND LITERARY HISTORY

I

HOMER IN THE CRITICISM OF ANTIQUITY

In the last chapter of his *Poetics*, Aristotle discusses whether the mimesis of the epic poets or that of the tragic poets be the better, and his answer is that tragedy is better in that it is more condensed and has a firmer unity than the lengthy and variegated epic poem, from any one example of which the material for several tragedies could be extracted. Aristotle even terms the epic ὑδαρή (diluted poetry). This conclusion, although it results from the inspection and comparison of two literary genres, none the less expresses a correct idea which in modern terms might be described as that of the relation between non-poetical and poetical motifs, the former of which bulk larger, on the whole, in epic than in tragic poetry. Aristotle expressly calls attention to the distinction between the accidental satisfactions which may be furnished by a poetical work, and the satisfaction which derives solely from its poetic quality. Aristotle and the other Greek writers when they speak of the epic are thinking essentially of the Homeric poems, and it must be allowed that in the *Iliad* (though Aristotle reckoned the *Iliad* and the *Odyssey* to exhibit an almost perfect unity by comparison with the other epics) the structure and the poetry are divorced to a degree which was one of the chief incentives to the philological dissections and argumentations which went under the name of "the Homeric question". Variety and diversity, however, is a character, often deliberate, of all composite works. The informative parts of the *Iliad*, like the catalogue of the ships, can only possibly be ascribed to non-poetical motives and to the structural requirements of the work; and so also the all too numerous and monotonous accounts of battles and duels, which delighted the insatiable amateurs of warlike episodes and prowess, and those who wanted to hear celebrated the names of persons, families, places, and native cities; and, again, half-playful episodes like the quarrels, misunderstandings, intrigues, threats, and fears of the Gods, which gave light relief to hearers caught up too tensely in the horror of the description of all those battles, mutilations, and massacres.

In this respect the *Iliad* set the model for the epic poems of ancient and modern literature, for Virgil, Tasso and his imitators, and such tardy cultivators of the epic as Voltaire. The model was sometimes simplified and sometimes complicated by the influence exercised also by the *Odyssey*. And sometimes, without the need for a model at all, other works, to meet similar requirements of the public, displayed similar features.

The poetry of a work is not, of course, to be sought for in its structure, but floats above this, like a plant which blossoms and flowers overtopping the wall that supports its tendrils. Or we may say that it lies not in the series of variations which break up a melody, but in the melody which is continually being broken and resumed, and not in the plot but in the accents with which the plot is recounted, the lyrical inpouring, the soul-drama which every veritable lyric accent portrays, the deep and stern drama of the tragedy of life itself. In the *Iliad* the poetry is so great and so abundant that in antiquity, alongside of the judgement that the epic is inferior to tragedy and therefore Homer inferior to the tragic poets, there ran the apparently, but only apparently contradictory judgement that the work of Homer is itself "tragic", as when Plato in the *Theaetetus* and the *Republic* called the *Iliad* a "tragedy" and Homer "prince of Tragedy", while the philosopher Polemon in a saying recorded by Diogenes Laertius calls Homer "the Sophocles of the epic" and Sophocles "the Homer of tragedians". Nor indeed was the link between Homeric poetry and the ensuing development of the tragedy ever overlooked.

The much-praised "serenity", "objectivity", "humanity" of Homer are in fact just this tragic sense of life, rendered in his own tones and colours, but such as really lies in the heart of all genuine poetry. He is objective because as a poet he takes no sides, as between Greeks and Trojans, but lets courage and fear, ardour and discouragement, boldness and despair cross and recross the lines, seeing Greeks and Trojans equally at the mercy of fate and the Gods "tamed by the hard goad of Zeus". Nor does he side with his own particular heroes, but takes account also of their unheroic lapses, their rashness, rage, weaknesses, faint-heartedness, cowardly thoughts, flights, so that not one of them is blameless. Pure and uncontaminated heroes, all of a piece, are to Homer unknown. Nor does he feel bound by any respect for the Gods, accepting them as they were conceived in popular religion, exercising varied and capricious powers, but no wiser or better than the humans beside and against whom they contested. ("Homer", the author of the *Treatise on the Sublime* said, "can at will make Gods of men and men of Gods.") Now inhumanity goes with a taking of sides in such manner that men appear to other men no longer as fellow beings but as obstacles to be overcome, forces to be subdued; and in forgetfulness of the common tragedy nothing is remembered but the present battle of one against the other, for the attainment of our ends by the defeat of his, or for the triumph of the just cause against the unjust. Homer, taking no sides, never hardens his heart, but shows pity and the understanding which comes from the heart, hearkening and attending to the simplest and lowliest affections. Achilles weeps, and so displays his love for Briseis who has been reft from him. Briseis utters the sad distress of a woman torn from freedom and marriage into slavery, together with the hope of better things inspired in her by the kindly Patroclus. Agamemnon well knows the failings of Menelaus but feels a tender and paternal responsibility towards this younger brother; and if he is unjust to Achilles, he confesses this fault to old Nestor. Hector blames Paris, yet treats him with indulgence, and Paris, knowing his own failings, shows the humility proper to a weak and vain man, and promises to try and behave better, but then fails, or perhaps never even tries. Helen, Helen of the long robe, queen among women, blames and despises and curses herself as a "shameless bitch", bowed under the load of the Gods' fatal gift of beauty, making of her an instrument of woe and ruin in their hands, and she is caught in a suspense of the will, incapable of resistance or responsibility, so that Priam and Hector and the other men of great mind and soul who on her account suffer the fierce buffetings of war do not condemn her, for in their heart they have forgiven her and treat her with a sort of religious reverence and protect her with chivalrous devotion. The culminating poetic masterpieces inspired by this sense of humanity are the great scenes of the leave-taking of Hector from Andromache and that meeting of Priam with Achilles when the two marvel at and admire each other and together give way to tears and lamentation.

Even in the most savage episodes of the *Iliad*, like the killing of young Lycaon by Achilles, this sense of humanity, tragic humanity, is present. In Achilles there is at one and the same time an enraged and murderous and pitilessly mocking human beast of prey, and a man who judges himself and life and yields to its law and accepts his own fate of death. Hatred, vengeance, fury at being unable to deal out to the enemy anything worse than the death which will shortly be at hand for him also, find utterance in a frightful sarcasm addressed to the youth pleading to be spared, and whom in cruel mockery he calls "friend" and "dear one" (φίλος); exhorting him as though seriously wishing to persuade him, thing of small importance as he is, to yield himself willingly to a death which is of such small import compared with the deaths of those already killed and about to be killed, including the killer himself – soon to fall in a similar death – who might now but does not spare the boy for whom that matter of small importance is nothing less than the infinity of life. At those words the boy stands still as though spellbound, while the other slays him and shouts insults over the body of the fallen, primitive expressions of unsated delight in vengeance. In this fierce scene are combined pity for the boy and pity of a different order for Achilles himself as we see him caught in his bestial and palpitating rage, rushing fatally towards his own as well as the other's destruction. Homer is objective, not indifferent, a tragedian, not a miserable and despairing pessimist, for what comes uppermost in his feeling, and rounds it off, is the idea of the heroic will. His heroes know that soon they must dry their tears and get on with their work in life, since destiny has shaped the soul of man for suffering, Zeus having determined that they should fight on from youth to extreme age, falling dead one after another; and like Achilles, they prefer a short life of travail and war, with victory closely followed by their own death, to a long life of peace and quiet. A renunciation, a desertion from life, an escape, a withdrawal to a strifeless world beyond this world, is never counselled or sighed for by Homer. Yet Homer knows a world beyond, one which is included in the world itself, that of fame, glory, the song of the poets, one's name on the lips of men and women, one's memory in their hearts. This is what the great Hector and the great Achilles, on the brink of death, see blossoming above their blood and anguish, a new life arising from the peace of the tomb, the immortality for which man ever aspires and without which he could not indefatigably pursue his task. The tragic sense is in Homer crowned by heroism and immortality, and thereby raised to the serenity of poetry. Homer is celebrated as the teacher of the Greek peoples, but he is the teacher of all the peoples of humanity, for with the first conspicuous poetical creation that was ever seen in the world he afforded, by the virtue of his poetry, a true ethical and religious vision of life. The very coming into existence of his poem was an implied and tacit lesson on the character of poetry which is light, clearness, *claritas*. For poetry may be difficult but it must always be clear in its depths.

The distinction between structure and poetry, I believe, clears up many puzzles about the *Iliad*. And another problem much exercising the critics and historians, the problem of the difference between the *Iliad* and the *Odyssey*, may, I think, receive light from another criterion which, not unknown to antiquity, has been elaborated and fixed by modern aesthetics. This is the distinction between poetry and literature, or more particularly between poetry wild and poetry tamed, genuine "lyrical" or "tragic" poetry, and agreeable, charming poetry which we must pronounce, in the teeth of traditional judgements and use of words, to be not truly and rootedly genuine poetry, for all the fine features, including poetical features, which it may embrace and adapt.

A distinction on these lines between the characters of the *Iliad* and the *Odyssey* is also drawn by the critics of antiquity. This, I am convinced, is the substance, or at all events the unconscious trend, of the observations of the pseudo-Longinus, author of the *Treatise on the Sublime*. But for want of formulas to denote such aesthetic distinctions, he could express it only in a different way, adducing a metaphorical contrast between the age of maturity and that of decline, the midday sun and the setting sun. There is, however, no reason whatever for taking the *Odyssey* for the work of an old man rather than that of a man in his prime or indeed in his youth, or one in weariness and decline rather than in the full maturity of his faculties, and the real difference of the two poems is indicated in the remark of the same Greek critic that in the *Odyssey*, by contrast with the *Iliad*, the dramatic gives way to the narrative, the poem, being pervaded by delight in fairy-tales, stories, and discourse, lacking the steady sublimity, strength of passion, persuasive energy, wealth of images found in the *Iliad*, and sometimes depicting ordinary life somewhat in the style of the comedian. It has been left to our times to produce an argument, like that of the Homeric specialist Drerup, in support of a poetic superiority in the *Odyssey*. "The Odyssey", writes Drerup, "with its fanciful and colourful depictions, with its eternally youthful celebration of conjugal fidelity and of final reunion after long separation, touches us moderns more closely than the bloody series of battles of the *Iliad*." And he finds the *Iliad* dense and heavy, relieved only by the meeting of Achilles with Priam and by Hector's leave-taking. But for the most part modern criticism, also, attributes a lower poetic rank to the *Odyssey*, finding it more rationally developed and ordered, less archaic and more modern, that is more studied, its art being more sapient and refined, its style less plastic and its colours less bright. It utters the poetry of the intimate feelings, the domestic affections, rather than of heroism and tragedy. It reflects a more sane and conscious morality, and even takes on at times a moralizing tone. In it the gods are treated with greater respect than in the *Iliad* and altogether the *Odyssey* has the nature more of a fable and novel than of an epic or a tragedy. Such are the typical judgements of modern critics. And in truth the personages of the *Odyssey*, Ulysses equally with Penelope, and even the charming Nausicaa, are comparatively wanting in intensity and depth, indeed have no great need for them, the tone and purpose of the poem being different from those of the *Iliad*.

All these observations, for which appropriate quotations could be cited in a more elaborate analysis of the problem, lead of themselves to the conclusion that the difference between the two poems lies not in a difference of poetic rank but in a difference of nature. The *Odyssey* is indeed a work of art, but the impetus of poetry has, in the *Odyssey*, ceased to pervade the work. The *Iliad* is the ancestor of all great modern poetry. The *Odyssey* is the admirable ancestor of the literature of travel and adventure, of long separations and dispersions, of desired and achieved reunions, of all that excites and interests the imagination without all too strongly engaging the heart and the mind. We have wished, in these pages, to indicate that the best judges of art and poetry in antiquity were themselves not unaware of this.

[1940]

II

TERENCE

THE Roman critics discerned as a weakness in Terence his lack of the power, or virtue, of comedy. This adverse opinion is found in some celebrated verses attributed to Caesar,[1] and is perhaps the reason why the grammarian Volcatius Sedigitus, in drawing up a hierarchy of the comic poets, assigned to Terence only the sixth place, Caecilius getting the first and Plautus the second. The author of these verses deplored the fact that because in him comic power[2] was not superadded (*adjuncta*) to his verses, sweet or delicate (*lenibus*) as they were, therefore Terence was held of little account (*despectus*) and could not equal the Greeks, remaining a *dimidiatus Menander*. And because none the less Terence inspired in him sympathy and affection he sighed: "*Atque utinam*", and lamented: "*Unum hoc maceror et doleo tibi deesse, Terenti.*" But how can one love a poet while feeling that something substantial is missing in him? Is not that which we admire in a poet precisely that which is essential, the soul, the poetry, which is either there or not there? That *purus sermo* and *lenitas* in his composition, was it not the manifestation of the poetry itself, in the appropriate and necessary

---

1. They have recently been ascribed instead to Cicero. See HERMANN in *Musée belge*, XXXIV, 243 seqq.; G. DE SANCTIS in *Riv. di filol. classica*, N. S., X (1932), pp. 330-331; FERRARINO in *Studi ital. di filol. class.*, Florence (1939), pp. 51-58; but, on the other side, with strong arguments, G. PERROTTA, in the same *Studi* etc., pp. 111-25.

2. It makes little difference if as in the modern editions a comma is put after *vis* and the word *comica* is attached to *virtus*. The sense in either case is that the power of comedy is denied to Terence. But I must wholly reject the interpretation that what is denied to him is power in general, and that accordingly "Terence failed to stir the affections deeply" (TAMAGNI-D'O-VIDIO, *Storia della letter. latina*, p. 331), or as Leo (*Gesch. d. röm. Liter.*, I, Berlin, 1913, pp. 253-54) puts it: "Terence is a half-Menander: he has a taste for the good word but his agreeable style lacks strength and therefore he is inferior in expressive quality to the Greek comedy." For my part I feel a certain reluctance against making Caesar contradict himself so flatly (Terence a mere cultivator of the right word, a poet who touches the heart yet lacks poetic force, etc.).

tone? But if that which was found lacking in him was not an essential, but an "adjunct", something whose presence or absence was equally possible, why lament so much over its absence? Why call the poet of one's affections a "half man", which is as much as to say a eunuch?[1]

Not one of the many who have quoted those verses seems to me to have asked these reasonable questions. Whoever had done so could not perhaps have found any answer except this, which rises out of the root of the matter, namely that the author of the verses was caught up in the theory of the "genres tranchés", the clear-cut poetical genres, according to which comedy was no comedy unless it was comic and mirth-provoking. But this theory conflicted painfully with the author's own feelings, and while he would not sacrifice the theory, neither would he fully sacrifice his feelings, whence the inner contradiction in the judgement contained in the verse. It was very similarly that Francesco De Sanctis felt the power of Machiavelli's *Mandragola*, but in view of Machiavelli's abstention from working up a gaily confidential atmosphere around the plot and the characters, treating them rather with an air of disgust and detachment, De Sanctis concluded that the work was an artistic failure because it was not a comedy. But if in fact it were a tragedy where would the harm be? (So I myself once enquired.[2]) And no more would there be any harm if Terence's comedy were not comedy but something else. Surely there is nothing strange about such a suggestion, now that the links between Euripides' tragedies and the New Comedy have so often been recognized and stressed. One finds in some literary histories a similarity traced between the comedy of Terence and the "bourgeois" comedy of the sixteenth century,[3] as indeed was recognized at the time by an Italian writer, Signorelli, who in the

---

1. I cannot think how Prof. EDW. E. RAND of Harvard University can write "Jules César...l'appelle un autre Ménandre, si j'interprète correctement cette fameuse phrase: *dimidiate Menander*" (*Térence et l'esprit comique*, in *Revue des cours et conférences*, 15 June 1935, p. 393).

2. *Poesia popolare e poesia d'arte* (2nd edition, Bari, 1946), p. 247 seqq.

3. See among others PICHON, *Hist. de la littér. latine* (Paris, 1903, 3rd edn., p. 81).

Hecyra found "an excellent model for tender comedy such as calls for a poet of sensitive and delicate heart. This sort of comedy", he added, "has across the Alps degenerated into an unpersuasive and halting *comédie larmoyante*."[1] But perhaps these comparisons across the centuries are better avoided lest one fall into the way of infecting the spontaneous and naive sentiment of the Roman poet (a sentiment not lacking in Roman restraint) with the *sensiblerie* of the Enlightenment.

Terence was still more adversely judged by critics and historians of the nineteenth century. Roman comedy, indeed Roman poetry in general, and together with this the comedy of the Italian Renaissance, and other art forms of that epoch, were despised as unoriginal because evidently modelled upon Greek comedy. As though the art of a later age were not always, in one way or another, based upon what went before! The critics and historians in question did not altogether deny this, but in their view the Roman poets ought to have based themselves on such indigenous traditions as the Atellan mimes (described by Valerius Maximus as *genus delectationis italica severitate temperatum*), and the Renaissance Italians should have sought their basis in the religious plays, so rich in profane and comic elements, and the popular farces. By so doing both would have been in line with the Romantic theory of the organic and autochthonous development of literature and of everything else, a theory which in its zeal for nice explanations of the facts seemed to require the facts to fall in with its own view of how they should have come about. If they erred against nature by failing to do so, all the worse for them, and they were duly arraigned and punished. The only thing would have been to tell Plautus and Terence to their faces that they must refrain from reading those seductive authors Menander, Diphilus, and Apollodorus, and to tell Bibbiena and Machiavelli not to read the two Romans but to fix their attention on strolling players and the actors of the sacred confraternities, on the Macci, the Pappi, the Bucconi, the Dossenni. They of course would have shrugged their

1. PIETRO NAPOLI SIGNORELLI, *Storia critica dei teatri antichi e moderni* (Naples edition, 1813, III, 154 seqq. A first succinct edition appeared in 1771).

shoulders at this preposterous proposal that they should drop the works which spoke to their mind and feelings and artistic sense and abase themselves to bear company with popular and plebeian mimes whose very existence they had forgotten.

This false idea of originality which clamours for an art unrelated to the art which went before it, for a purely national or purely provincial art, is now rarely found in the criticism and history of modern literatures, but it persists or at least lingers on in regard to ancient literature, without heed for the results of the long and now antiquated discussions of other times on the independence of French from Greek tragedy and so on.[1]

The other adverse judgement levelled against Terence suggests that the pleasure he gives us, the reputation he enjoys, are all due to our having no access to the Greek originals from which he more or less freely translated. If ever the ignorance is made good by the discovery of those originals, then, it is suggested, the pleasure will cease, the borrowed glory will slip away. Well, let us for argument's sake assume that the dramas of Terence are just translations, very fine translations, no doubt, exquisitely phrased in pure Latin. Why should the discovery of the originals impair their reputation? The Greek text of Homer is known but this does not render Vincenzo Monti's Italian version of the *Iliad* less admirable, it being beautiful in itself as well as a medium serving the needs of those unable to read Homer himself. Shakespeare's English text is known to the Germans, but Schlegel's German translation remains a classic. Beautiful translations are always the work of some poetic spirit who embraces the original and warms

---

1. "Permit me to smile when people say, What a great man was Racine to have created *Phèdre*! But Racine took this character from Euripides and confesses it. Not only this, but he took it also, and still more, from Seneca. The third scene of the first act is almost all Euripides: her declaration of love comes from Seneca, so too the jealousy scene. Why, Racine borrowed not only the situations but the images, the thoughts, the sentiments. All of which goes to show just nothing at all. Racine remains as far as ever removed from an unskilled patchwork playwright. Accusers of Racine, you have before you all nature, all works of art. I give you licence to imitate, to borrow from right and left. Take up your pens. Emulate Racine. You see, the pen falls from your hand." Thus De Sanctis in his essay on *Phèdre*, in 1856.

it with his own life.[1] Why should the fact that Terence's "translations" stand to some extent in lieu of the lost Greek comedies be
viewed as a weakness and detract from their merit? August
Wilhelm Schlegel, with his cultivated dislike or Romantic prejudice
against everything Roman and Italian, in his lectures on dramatic
poetry made no more than a bare and disdainful allusion to
Plautus and Terence ("no creative artists"),[2] but spread himself on
the Greek comedy, forgoing mention of the two authors still
living in their works in order to treat of authors whose works are
non-existent (in Schlegel's time much less of them had been

1. On this account I cannot rest satisfied with Jachmann's dual measure for
judging the artistic value of translations, by determining first of all how
difficult the original is in respect of content, language, metre, and secondly
what beneficial enrichment and refinement is brought into the translator's
own language by the translation in question (see his article on Terence in
the new edition of PAULY-WISSOWA, *Encykl. der klass. Altertumswissenschaft*,
1934, p. 625). These no doubt are criterions of a cultural order, of use in
the history of the international circulation of literary works, and the history
of the language, but are insignificant from the point of view of art. The
fundamental condition for a beautiful translation is that the translator himself should be a poetical spirit who brings to the work a tone of feeling able,
to some extent, to stand in lieu of that of the original poet, untranslatable
in its fullness and uniqueness. See my *Poesia*, 4th edn., Bari, 1946, pp. 100-104.

2. *Vorlesungen über dramatische Kunst und Literatur*, Amoretti's edition, I,
171. More inexorable in his presentation of Terence as a mere translator, and
so necessarily inferior to his originals, is the acute and learned Jachmann.
In the article quoted he allows him no other than the technical merit of
contaminatio (p. 629) and while admitting the beauty of his style, accounts
for this as "Atticism", the consequence of having "tief eingefühlt" himself
in the dramatic school of Menander. But the explanation is inadequate.
The basis of a literary judgement must be a keen feeling for the work of the
poetic author, a capacity to recapture its character and tone: but that would
not suffice for a lively re-creation of the work in another language, another
form. For this latter there is needed a poetic disposition in the "translator"
himself, whose work will always to some extent differ from the original
(as I have pointed out). There is a certain unfaithfulness in beautiful translations; they are "falsely fair". I feel some doubt also about the customary
notion of "nachschaffen" or "nachbilden", accepted also by Jachmann, for
the prefix "nach" to my mind negates the "schaffen" and "bilden". In conversation a distinction may be made between a "gestaltender" and a "repro-
duzierende Dichter", but this will not pass muster in serious criticism, for
the poet is always, as such, though with variety of tones, "gestaltend" and
"produzierend".

discovered than now). But numberless are the blunders of critics who, when discoursing of art, often forget the subject of their discourse. One almost blushes to recall them and to confute them. For example the charge is blunderingly laid against Terence that the dramas which pass under his name are really by Scipio or Laelius, or by one of the two in collaboration with Terence. Antiquity too had its "Baconians", the sort of people who would attribute Shakespeare's dramas to the most unpoetical of lords of his time if thereby they could wrest them from the poor actor, "sweet William". In antiquity such people wished to strip the wreath of Apollo from the brow of an African, a slave, a freedman, and the initiated whispered it around that this wreath properly belonged to illustrious personages who, disdaining or blushing to appear before the public as theatrical authors, had brought in some poor fellow of their acquaintance to stand for them. That Terence's comedies should be the fruit of a collaboration must seem unlikely to anyone who appreciates what style is. But even were it so, and even if the author's name has been deliberately falsified, what has that to do with a judgement on poetry?[1] Are we giving marks to Terence in an examination or competition, and trying to make sure that his answers have not been cribbed from another candidate? Professors, when they engage in criticism, find it difficult to drop the attitude of the examiner. This accounts for a certain suspicion and disapproval shown by them towards Terence.

So I have for the sake of argument accepted the worst that the critics can or could bring against the works of Terence – that they are translations and not written by Terence – and I have shown that it has no significance for the appreciation and judgement of the works themselves as poetry. That does not mean that I myself think they are straight translations from Greek originals. Terence, of course, himself says that he took this or that comedy from Menander or another Greek. The old stage directions

1. See my former summary observations on the tedious and empty disputes concerning the crypto-author of the Shakespearian dramas (in my *Ariosto, Shakespeare e Corneille*, 4th edn., Bari, 1950, p. 75 seqq.).

confirm this and name the other Greek, Apollodorus. The approved and required method in the Roman theatre was to take the schemes or frames of the Greek comedies and to keep their location in Greece. In fact, to judge from Terence's apologies, it seems to have been considered improper to fuse two or more of these well-known schemes together,[1] though once one was adopted great liberty was allowed in tacitly recasting it, introducing variations, and extra episodes and personages.[2] However, what matters for us is not the frame, but the embroidery, not the argument or fable, but the flow of poetry infused in it. This was understood during the many centuries of European literature in which the word "imitation" had a significance, at the same time humble and noble, as the acceptance of a traditional outline to serve as a frame to support the embroidery, the creation of beauty.

But in later times the philologians, untrained for the judgement of art, if not actually deaf to poetry, gave great and primary importance to the canvas, and ended by glorifying the weaving of the canvas itself with the scientific-sounding but in this context unscientific term of "technique". So nowadays, instead of enquiring after poetry, they pronounce judgement and allot retribution on the good or bad technique of the work, with an air of knowing the job, which, since we are here discussing drama, would mean being expert stage-managers or actor-managers, with a sound knowledge of theatrical continuity and effect. It was therefore inevitable, when some papyrus discoveries brought to light several long fragments of Menander and a good part of one of his comedies, that they should soon weigh up and pass judgement that the "technique" of Menander was superior to that of Terence, whom they regard as little better than a bungler.[3] Be

1. See F. NENCINI, *De Terentio eiusque fontibus* (Liburni, Giusti, 1891), p. 5: "Terenti aetatis tale fuisse ingenium, ut ad captandum spectatorum favorem poetae Graecorum fidos faterentur interpretes."
2. For Terence, see LEO, op. cit., pp. 238-48.
3. G. CAPOVILLA, *Menandro*, Milan, 1924, pp. 338-39, in comparing the *Hecyra* with the *Epitrepontes* reproaches Terence with "feeble technical devices". G. COPPOLA, in his edition of the *Comedies of Menander*, Critical Text and Comment (Turin, 1927, p. 163), pursuing the same comparison

that as it may (and personally I feel this also to be a prejudiced assessment), the point is that the canvas or technique in poetry is a secondary matter. I will here enlist the assertion of this simple truth, so hard to put across to the stiff minds of the philologians, made by Michel de Montaigne in reference precisely to Terence. Montaigne had a great affection for the Roman comic poet, calling him "admirable à représenter au vif les mouvements de l'âme et la condition de nos mœurs". Montaigne had little use for those whose interest lay and was centred in the plot, the accidents, the complications, the diverting adventures. "Il en va de mon aucteur tout au contraire: les perfections et beautez de sa façon de dire nous font perdre l'appetit de son subject: sa gentillesse et sa mignardise nous retiennent partout; il est partout si plaisant, *liquidus puroque simillimus amni*, et nous remplit tant l'âme de ses graces que nous en oublions celles de sa fable".[1] As Montaigne says, we forget it, or rather we take no heed of it. What does it matter to us that the usual slave, the Know-all or Think-of-all, produces the usual shrewd devices for getting cash for the young master and hoodwinking the old? What does it matter that the sweetheart turns out to be a daughter of the old man's friend and marriage supplies a happy ending? Our eye follows something which arises out of this tale and leaves it behind and dances above it.

affirms that the Roman author "in order better to get the somewhat lame thread of the drama moving (!!!) emphasizes a detail of the most trivial and unpleasant sort (!)" thereby "provoking the inefficacy of the third act", and consequently Terence, or the Greek imitator whom he took for his model, "imitated Menander very poorly, managing to suppress the truly dramatic parts while needlessly heightening the colour of the insignificant scenes". Very differently was the *Hecyra* judged by an old "technician of the stage", truly expert in the theatre of all the ages, and himself a writer of comedies, the already quoted Napoli Signorelli: "The opening point is most happily chosen and the passions are handled admirably. There are in this play neither tangled skeins, nor tortuous tricks by slaves, nor buffooneries, showing that the true pleasure of the theatre can arise from something quite different. The characters are all good, not with the imaginary goodness of moral treatises, or the heroic goodness appropriate to tragedy, but with that ordinary goodness which guards a man from serious fault without precluding some weaknesses." (*Storia Critica*, as quoted, III, 176 seqq.)

1. *Essais*, II, 10.

Moreover, it is improbable that Terence's plays are mere or even free translations of Greek plays, with at the most some well-conceived changes of detail, but having no originality save that poetic quality which always pertains to the work of the artistic translator or adaptor, and without which he could not accomplish it.[1] But the scholars wish to deny Terence the authorship even of the changes of detail. Where the sources relate that a given character or scene was introduced by Terence, they reply that these are too fine and masterly to be flour from the mill of Terence, and that the old commentator must have made a mistake or has been misunderstood or his text meddled with, since those sections also are certainly by Menander or some other Greek comediographer overlooked by the commentator.[2] This seems to me, I confess, arguing in a vicious circle. In any case the fact is that Terence and Plautus had before them more or less the same models: and what a difference divides their two temperaments and respective dramatic output![3] In the plays of Terence there is

1. SUETONIUS, in the *Vita P. Terentii*, recalls: "Adelphorum principium Varro etiam praefert principio Menandri." Donatus in his commentary notes in one place that Terence did "melius quam Menander", and in another that he composed εὑρητικῶς, inventively, and so on. That Terence in general aimed at a "closer lifelikeness" is the opinion of Cupaiuolo in his edition of the *Adelphoi* (Rome-Milan, 1904), p. LXXXI.

2. To cite only one, the most authoritative, of these scholars, Jachmann on page 632 of the article quoted writes regarding the first scene of the *Andria*, which is missing from both the comedies of Menander, used by Terence, that this must be copied from "an irgendein attisches Muster"; and on pp. 635-37 Jachmann says that the scene with Antiphon in the *Eunuchus* cannot have been, as Donatus says, invented and admirably worked up by Terence, who was a mere translator and not an original mind. Pasquali (*Studî italiani di filologia classica*, vol. XIII, 1936, No. 2, pp. 117-27) defends the authenticity of the text of Donatus against Jachmann, who here too showed the soundness of his taste, by arguing that artistically the addition in question is not worth much, and that even poor old Terence, borrowing here and there, could have written it.

3. Montaigne, in the essay already quoted, says: "J'estime que les anciens avoient encore plus à se plaindre de ceulx qui apparioient Plaute à Térence (celuy-ci sent bien mieulx son gentilhomme) que Lucrèce à Virgile." (It must be mentioned that Montaigne entertained the belief that Terentius was a pseudonym of Scipio or Laelius: *Essais*, I, 39.) I myself dislike drawing parallels and will refrain from comparing the two Roman comedy writers

a unity of feeling, a steady and coherent personality, an artistic
chastity and nobility, a shyness about leaving his own range and
breaking or straying into those of others. Translators, on the
contrary, are usually versatile, and in this versatility display their
artistic sensitiveness and their prowess. Why did Terence compose
only "sex comoedias"? Probably because "son verre n'était pas
grand mais il buvait dans son verre". The tale, so often foolishly
repeated, originating in the misreading of a page of Suetonius,
that after publishing his six comedies, Terence went on a trip to
Greece where he translated and adapted no fewer than a hundred
and eight comedies of Menander, but was shipwrecked and died
of grief for the loss of the *novas fabulas* among his baggage, might
smack of mockery at the smallness of his literary output. But the
relation of Terence to Menander may be other than the modern
grammarians suppose. The right idea may be that which is perhaps suggested in a well-known passage of Saint Jerome, who
knew and valued both authors, and advised enquiring students to
accept as the four standards of poetical style Homer and Virgil,
Menander and Terence,[1] a hint, maybe, that as Virgil stands
to Homer so – in the other couple, for whom, as Petrarch

so as to make one superior to the other, or each superior in certain respects,
but will quote a specimen of such current comparisons from a good en-
cyclopedia: "Von Plautus zeichnet sich Terentius durch kunstgerechte An-
lage und Eleganz der Sprache aus, steht ihm aber an Kraft und Witz nach,
wie er auch hinter der lebendigen Komik seines Vorbildes Menanders
zurückblieb." But I think it cannot be gainsaid that Plautus is principally
strong in caricature, the portrayal of the grotesque, the laughable. All his
work, including the many serious reflections occurring in it, the human
touches of which he shows himself a master, fits in and harmonizes with
that, though he could also turn out a comedy for "white nights" like the
Captivi, and one of pathetic adventure like the *Rudens*. "He renders all the
affections ludicrous without offending their nature", said Gravina most
happily in his *Ragion Poetica* (1709), ch. 24. In any case the character of the
two authors is conspicuously diverse, and so is their treatment of Greek
originals, as is generally recognized. See LEO, op. cit., pp. 246-48, 250-51.

1. In the epistle LVIII *ad Paulinum* (Migne's edition, 1, 322-23): "Romani
duces imitentur Camillos, Fabricios, Regulos, Scipiones. Philosophi pro-
ponant sibi Pythagoram, Socratem, Platonem, Aristotelem. Poetae aemu-
lentur Homerum, Virgilium, Menandrum, Terentium. Historici . . .".

remarked,[1] the "altitudo stili" of the epic does not obtain – Terence stands to Menander.

In truth, the increased but by no means voluminous stock which we now have of Menander's writings is far from confirming the view of Terence as being merely a graceful and gifted translator. Rather, it serves to emphasize the differing features of the lively, impetuous, smiling Greek, so agreeable and witty, though he can also be warm-hearted and pathetic as with Glycera and the soldier of the *Perikeiromene* and Abrotonon and Carisio of the *Epitrepontes*; and on the other hand of Terence, with his deep humanity and feeling, not easily moved to mirth and laughter.[2] Maybe further discoveries of other Menander plays, permitting a fuller valuation of Menander's personality, will indicate a closer connexion between the two authors, but at this moment I do not think that there is ground for going beyond what was already known because recounted by Terence himself: that Terence took some plots from Menander.[3] The copious literature, still piling up, which busies itself with cataloguing all the scenes which he took from Menander, with the changes and adaptations which he introduced, is altogether conjectural and sterile, and, frankly, seems to me just so much scholarly raving. If *tantus amor* spurs on the scholars to acquire knowledge of this sort (as though there were not already

1. See *Vita Terentii excerpta de dictis F. P.* (reprinted in Hague edition, 1726).

2. Quite differently does Croiset, with the usual bias against Terence, define the difference: "Une comédie de Ménandre n'est pas du tout une simple série de dialogues finement nuancés où se reflèteraient des sentiments toujours tempérés" etc. (*Ménandre*, in *Revue des Deux Mondes*, 15 April 1909, p. 817).

3. That the recent Menander discoveries do not encourage the view that Terence's plays are mere translations from Menander has been widely admitted, but the inference has been drawn that if Terence did not copy Menander he must have copied other Greeks. "Grâce aux papyres récemment découverts, nous voyons aujourd'hui s'accentuer les différences, qui, d'après les témoignages des anciens eux-mêmes, distinguaient Térence de Ménandre. Mais en quelles proportions les caractères que nous croyons lui être propres ont-ils été développés par la lecture des poètes secondaires, de Diphile et d'Apollodore en particulier?" G. LAFAYE, *Le Modèle de Térence dans l'Hecyra*, in *Revue de philologie*, XL, 1916, p. 30.

an excess of it in regard to other poets, and very little of it – as has
been found – of any use for the interpretation of the poets),
then on with the business of digging up more papyri, and meanwhile, a little patience!

Still less does the comparative study of the new fragments
authorize conclusions as to a superiority of Menander as a true
poet over Terence as a mere man of letters, or of Menander as a
creative mind over Terence as a mechanical mind. Or is one to
try and take seriously the absurd pastime in which the philological
scholars, taking on the air of philosophers, and thus degenerating
into bad philosophers, have begun to indulge with such zeal and
pleasure, the game of supposing that the discussion of certain
moral, political, or other concepts underlies the poets's works,
constituting what is with heavy emphasis called their "problems"?
By such devices a German scholar[1] showed the gulf which divides
an "artist of genius" like Menander and a "clever comedy writer"
like Terence,[2] or rather, (since even this rank was denied to him)
Terence's immediate model Apollodorus of Karystos. Just think
of it: Menander in the *Epitrepontes* felt and propounded, according
to this scholar, the moral problem of the duty of chastity for the
male, equally with the female, before marriage. This tremendous
and sublime problem Terence-Apollodorus threw aside for the
petty pleasure of changing the scene and resolving a "technical
problem".[3] Our Italian Pasquali,[4] hotly pursuing the German, put
the essential greatness of Menander in this self-revelation in the
Epitrepontes as a "thinker absorbed in problems of social ethics"[5]
including a problem such as that of pre-matrimonial male chastity
which is "eminently modern, Kantian, Ibsenic";[6] and although

1. K. Stavenhagen, *Menandros Epitrepontes und Apollodoros Hecyra* in
Hermes, xlv (1910), pp. 564-82.
2. Thus Pasquali, *Perché s'intenda l'arte di Menandro*, in *Atene e Roma*,
xx (1917), 178 n.
3. "Die Freude am technischen Problem hat zur Umgestaltung der *Epitrepontes* geführt" (Stavenhagen, op. cit., p. 581).
4. G. Pasquali, in the article quoted, xx (1917), p. 177 seqq., xxi (1918),
p. 21 seqq.
5. The same, xxi, 15.
6. The same, xx, 184-85.

Menander "did not actually solve it" (alas, he sighs, it has not even yet been solved),[1] yet, we are told, he was able to develop it in the way that Ibsen would have done, which Pasquali proceeds to divine and describe.[2] In reality, this problem belongs not to the Kant of philosophy, but if at all to the Kant of the casuistic exercises, and the mental atmosphere of this problem is lacking in Ibsen. (Nora in the *Doll's House* has nothing to do with the case.) Where it is found is in such an abstract and insipid moralist as Björnson, whose drama on the subject (*The Glove* of 1883) Pasquali should, if necessary, have called in to support his odd thesis. It would be superfluous here to explain once again that the existence of a conceptual problem (moral, political, or otherwise) so far from confirming the presence confirms the absence of poetry:[3] and in any case not only is the problem in question not enunciated in Menander's comedy, but the particular case cited by the German scholar and his Italian follower does not arise. What Carisio reproaches himself with is a fault quite different from that of not having retained the flower of chastity to offer to his bride.[4]

I have confuted these distorted judgements which it is now fashionable to pile up against the art of Terence, in the interests of truth and logic. In the same way the preceding objections and reserves which I expressed on the theory that Terence was a mere translator are the fruit of a methodic doubt and critical caution. Yet once again I will be prepared for the sake of argument to admit the improbable hypothesis that the six comedies attributed to Terence are simple translations from Greek comedies. For that is not the point. Translations or originals, these six comedies are

1. "A general solution of that problem, while society remains in its present condition, is impossible, for the only theoretically (?) acceptable one, the obligation of complete chastity until marriage for both sexes, conflicts too strongly with the nature of the male" (xx, 185).

2. xx, 185-86.

3. This is surely very elementary, but as it needs constant recalling, I will this time quote some words of the poet Grillparzer in 1816: "No poet on earth has ever created a masterpiece by starting with a general idea" (*Werke*, 4th edition, xiv, 7).

4. "You gird at the unwilful distress of a woman: I will show how yourself you fell likewise" (Coppola's edition, vv. 608-9, Jensen's edn., vv. 530-31).

present and expressive and they reveal to us the soul of a poet having his own accent, his own music, his own prevailing feeling. The reader of poetry asks the critic to remove the obstacles and help him to enjoy the poetry; that, and nothing else. Other questions, even if they are sensible and soluble, yet since they relate to something outside and apart from the poetical work, do not meet the reader's need, but on the contrary overlook it, and are therefore tiresome or at least otiose. I suggest that after so much irrelevant comment it is time to tackle that which alone is relevant. It is time, after lingering so long with his scholarly commentators, to turn directly to himself, and to learn from him his "dominating feeling", which fortunately is something very dear and precious – human goodness. The human goodness in question can be more closely described as one which is well aware of human weaknesses, but would rather trace and observe the spontaneous awakening and development of the finer affections, thereby placing bounds upon those which are less noble and pure, so as to offset them and elude their dominance.

The first and most obvious example of this is the manner of his treatment of the shameless wench, the "meretrix mala" of the other comic dramatists. Terence never shows this character as totally and utterly "mala". With him, she always exhibits some inclination to good and generous behaviour, some disposition or longing for virtue, some feeling of humility regarding her position. Terence seems not to believe that a human being can be radically wicked, and seems unwilling to exclude any one of them from the pale of humanity.

Thus we hear of the young Chrysis migrating from Andros to Athens under the spur of need and neglect at home. She has no thought or desire of vice, indeed at first she lives by the hard work of spinning and weaving. Then she yields to the temptations which beset youth and beauty where the helps and hindrances of family and social links are lacking. She yields to the lure of pleasure and sinks gradually to the position of a courtesan. But she still arouses feelings of friendship and strong affection, and when near to death she is in a position to call on a young man who is like a brother to her, and to entrust a young girl whom she has treated as a sister to his faith and honour, placing her hand in his as in that of a husband, friend, brother, father, in fact as the representative of all institutions and moral relations. The young man, who was never her lover, follows her bier weeping with the others, and his father too, responding to these marks of gentleness which he sees with pleasure in his son, joins in the mourning.

Bacchis, in the *Hecyra*, had been warmly loved by young Pamphilus. But Pamphilus, at his father's orders, marries against his own will. He leaves his bride untouched, with the firm intention of restoring her as a virgin to her parents, and he continues his amour with the other. The lover, now that she no longer has the young man all to herself, becomes ill-tempered and overbearing, so that by contrast the gentle yieldingness of the bride wins him over, and little by little he shifts his love and ends by dropping Bacchis. But the bewildered relatives, at the height of the painful and hopeless tension between the young husband and wife, suspect that Pamphilus is still in the sway of his old mistress. Pamphilus' father proceeds to question her and is ready to pass on to threats. But Bacchis takes no malevolent pleasure in the troubles of the young couple and their families, harbours no vengeful feelings against the lover who has left her or the bride who is the cause of this, but says truthfully that Pamphilus is no longer visiting her. The father asks her to repeat this to his womenfolk, and she, who is no better than she should be, feels a mingled pride and shyness at being required to appear before a bride who must necessarily look on her with hostility, in a respectable house which in itself is a reproach and humiliation for her; and she knows that no other girl in her position would do it. But her good heart prevails, and a sort of natural honesty, and she goes. As luck will have it, at the encounter she is able to produce evidence which, much better than her own statement, cuts the knot and allays the painful tension between the young husband and wife. And great is her joy.

> *Quantam obtuli adventu meo laetitiam Pamphilo hodie!*
> *Quot commodas res attuli! Quot autem ademi curas!*

Gnatum ei restituo, paene qui harum ipsiusque opera periit:
uxorem, quam nunquam ratus posthac se habiturum, reddo:
qua re suspectus suo patri et Phidippo fuit, exolui . . .

She rejoices and congratulates herself upon being the one chosen to dispel such great troubles, to bring about so much joy in a family which certainly did not expect this from her. At this point one of those excellent scholars who cannot admire one poet without running down another, affirms that Bacchis is "much inferior" to Abrotonon in the *Epitrepontes*, whom Terence must have had in mind, because Bacchis "talks too much of her generosity, laying on an excessive air of modesty", particularly in the verses just quoted, whereas Abrotonon "who felt that she had served as a decoy for herself, instead of indulging in self-praise, works out her plans carefully and proceeds to put them into action without talking too much about herself."[1] Here there are misstatements of fact, for if Abrotonon had quickly lost the affections of Carisios, Bacchis, too, after repeated declarations of love and a long attachment had been abandoned by Pamphilus. And if Bacchis is pleased with what she has done, but neither asks nor expects a reward, Abrotonon had in mind the reward of winning her freedom. Nor is it possible to point to a passage in which Bacchis "lays on an excessive air of modesty" and at the same time "talks too much of her own generosity". The satisfaction which she shows, even if she wears it a little bit like a halo, becomes her well, for the poet never claimed to be depicting a woman of exquisite fineness and austere perfection. Let us, however, ignore these details. The point is that poetically the two characters are quite different. Abrotonon is a poor creature, a little *cocotte* usually down on her luck, who cannot herself make out how Carisios came to pick her up, and comically complains that he does not even want her company at meals and has already left her in "unmarried purity" for as long as three days. She is also a good creature who makes haste and takes pains to discover whether the exposed child is or is not the son of Carisios, and who was its mother. All this she does and says pleasantly, shrewdly, and amus-

[1]. CAPOVILLA, op. cit., p. 339.

ingly. What has this to do with Bacchis? Bacchis refuses to be like
the other courtesans with their cold crude selfishness, their hatred
and vengefulness against anyone who has escaped from their
clutches and is no longer any use to them. Her behaviour at that
meeting, I think, has no need to be judged by these moralizing
scholarly gentlemen, for it had already been fittingly judged and
understood and felt by young Pamphilus in his expression of
warm gratitude and tenderness when after her saving action she
comes up to him with a plain greeting.

O Bacchis, mea Bacchis, servatrix mea!

He calls her "his" Bacchis, "his" in a different sense from before,
"his" as she now speaks to his heart; his old feeling for her being
restored and purified, and changed in its quality and savour. The
words which they now exchange are not those of the former
lovers, but of two beings who have been raised on to another
plane. He still finds in her the charm that renders her delightful to
look at and speak with wherever it may be, while she still admires
in him the manners and the mind which make of him the most
charming young man in the world. And she wants him to be
happy in his new condition and affectionately recommends him to
be good to his wife, who well deserves this "Recte amasti, Pam-
phile, uxorem tuam". The wife, whom she has just seen for the
first time strikes her as most charming, "perliberalis". The two
leave their common past behind them and find each other on a
new and higher level in the present.

There is a similar kindly disposition, at bottom, in Bacchis'
girl friend Philotis, who, though amazed and outraged by Pamphilus' desertion of Bacchis, rejects the lesson inferred by the old
hag that girls should feel no pity for any man; but should despoil
them, mutilate them, injure them all, not excepting anyone,
when they hold them in their power. What, asks Philotis "eximium
neminem habeam?" – not even one of them? And to the old
woman's repeated arguments she objects again. "Tamen pol
eandem injuriumst esse omnibus", as if to say that one could not
and should not be as vindictive as that.

The other Bacchis (the character in the *Heautontimorumenos*) is shown as a courtesan in the full display and zeal of one greedily pursuing her business interests. Yet she too feels the need to explain to young Antiphila, who is on her way to meet her bridegroom, that she behaves like this not out of sheer viciousness but because she is caught up helplessly in the logic of her situation. "Nam expedit bonas esse vobis: nos quibuscum est res, non sinunt." It is the selfishness of the male, she means, which brings this about, seeking nothing else but voluptuous beauty and turning the back when this fades. And Thais in the *Eunuchus*, Thais whose name thanks to Dante has come in the Italian language to designate the most shrewish sort of whore, is in Terence just one of those who follow the iron logic of the life to which they have given themselves, and think and provide against future woes. But she is not a bad woman. Thais, in her way, feels affectionately for young Phaedria, and if she courts the soldier, it is because she expects to win from him the gift of a young slave whom she hopes to restore to the bosom of her family and thus to gain for herself some goodwill to console her solitude in the city. I recall how in the expurgated text of Terence (that of Monsignor Bindi) which I was given at school the episode of Bacchis' success in getting herself by that means received into the household and home of Laches "in clientelam et fidem", contrary to good family morality, received a pained comment on the lines that the "corruption of those pagan times" could alone excuse Terence. The good Monsignor Bindi had already transformed Phaedria and Thraso into two suitors for "the hand of Thais", which Phaedria had the good luck to obtain! For all that Monsignor Bindi understood and enjoyed his Terence much more sensibly than many modern scholars.

In view of this handling of the figure of the courtesan in the Terentian plays I cannot help wondering that these eminent scholars have missed the occasion for congratulating not of course Terence (that mere "santo pequeño"), but Menander, on the discovery and exploration of the "problem" of the "redemption" of the fallen woman, foreshadowing a favourite theme of the

French Romantics. As a matter of fact they have not wholly overlooked this, and let us hope that they will follow it up with their customary intuitive penetration into broad issues and delicacy of interpretation of particulars. Thus Lafaye says that Terentius-Apollodorus "semble avoir voulu, comme les romantiques, ra-jeunir les types traditionnels en leur prêtant des sentiments con-traires à l'idée que l'on se faisait géneralement: de là la bonne cour-tisane, fine, sensible, désintéressée".[1] According to this critic Terence was unconventional for love of novelty, not, then, in a Romantic but at most in a Baroque spirit. For the Romantics were drawn to paradoxical characterizations by the spirit of revolt against society with its conventions and laws. But in truth it was neither the spirit of revolt nor a Baroque love of the amazing and the bizarre that guided the straightforward and delicate Terence.

Naturalness, indulgence, goodness of heart pervade other scenes and other characters also in the plays of Terence. Nowhere in the pages of Giovanni Boccaccio – eager expert though he was in all the paths which natural love finds for surmounting hindrances, winning its ends by the subtlest tricks and eluding all precautions – is there any such humane moral atmosphere as in the first scene of the *Andria*. The father has very sensibly decided that the best way of deterring young Pamphilus from getting into mischief is to leave him entirely free; and observing him in his youthful oc-cupations and amusements, his delight in horses and hunting, his interests too in philosophers and their disputations, and his social activities, is delighted to see him behaving temperately and tactful-ly, surrounded by popularity and affection. The father observes that he also frequents the house of Chrysis, joining in talks and supper-parties but without committing himself or scorching him-

---

1. Article quoted, p. 19: but the reference to the ἑταῖραι χρησταί of Me-nander based upon PLUTARCH, *Quaest. Conviv.* 8, 3, does not match the case or provide evidence that Menander handled the character of the courtesan with feeling. For all that is there said is that the *hetairai* and mistresses are either impudent and insolent and in that case are punished and deserted by the young men: or else are honest and affectionate, in which case a legitimate father is found for them or the young men are allowed to linger on in their attachment.

self with the flames of love. The father is pleased with this too, for his son's and his own sake, and when he sees the boy distressed at the death of this woman, he approves of that proper sentiment and joins respectfully in his grief and tears. But at the funeral he sees among the other women one that he does not know, a pretty, shy, attractive girl, who they tell him is the dead woman's sister. This is somewhat of a shock. A veil drops from his mind, there is a flash of comedy in this dissipation of a comfortable illusion, leaving him surprised, but at the same time seriously concerned. Tut-tut – so that is at the root of the affair, is it:

> Attat, hoc illud est,
> hinc illae lacrimae, haec illast misericordia!

The two young persons' love soon after reveals itself infallibly without any need of words from them or from others when, as the flames lick the pyre and the girl ventures too close, Pamphilus, greatly alarmed,

> adcurrit: mediam mulierem complectitur:
> "Mea Glycerium" inquit "quid agis? quor te is perditum?"
> Tum illa, ut consuetum facile amorem cerneres
> rejecit se in eum flens quam familiariter.

Four verses which are a picture in themselves, a poem of inconsolable grief, of watchful loving care, as the woman gives way to her feelings and seeks and finds comforting protection from the man she loves.[1] The youth is worthy of this trusting abandon, he feels the responsibility which falls on him for this girl who has given herself to him, whom if he were to throw aside in order to

[1] The only observation inspired by this wonderful scene in the mind of the scholars is that according to an inference from the commentary of Donatus Terence here converted a dialogue which in the Greek original took place between the old man and his wife into one between the old man and the freedman formerly his slave, thereby disturbing the technical balance of the comedy (see, for example, LEO, op. cit., I, 338-39). Another scholar, Jacoby, with what I can only term a "perverse" keenness of insight, arrived at the discovery, for which he was praised, that Terence "introduced the freedman as a manner of showing his own gratitude (as a freed slave) to his former masters". (P. FOSSATARO in Riv. di fil. classica, XLIII, 1914, p. 453.)

fulfil the marriage arranged for him by his father, he would not
only consign to utter despair, but would expose her to corruption in the corrupt world, so that for his fault that innocent
and charming nature would be ruined:

> *Hem, egone istuc conari queam?*
> *Egon propter me suam decipi miseram sinam,*
> *quae mihi suom animum atque omnem vitam credidit,*
> *quam ego animo egregie caram pro uxore habuerim!*
> *Bene et pudice eius doctum atque eductum sinam*
> *coactum egestate ingenium inmutarier?*

The vow made to the dying Chrysis was sacred, and he will not
loosen his grip upon that hand which she placed in his, and which
he gripped as he swore the oath.

Quite a different note of passion is portrayed in young Phaedria
(in the *Eunuchus*), a passion without ethical content, all feeling and
desire, greedy and violent, steadily persistent, however badly the
woman behaves and however much he himself tries to free himself
from the coils. Phaedria and Thais, one may say, are on the same
level. Parmeno sums up his situation for him, and tells him what
to do:

> *Quid agas? nisi ut te redimas captum quam queas*
> *minumo: si nequeas paululo, at quantum queas:*
> *et ne te adflictes . . .*

Thais tries to compromise between her preference for him and
her own needs and ambitions which require her to give some
satisfaction also to the other man, the rich soldier who was formerly her lover. In her words there is a resignation bordering upon
melancholy:

> *Ne crucia te, obsecro, anime mi, Phaedria.*
> *Non pol, quo quemquam plus amem aut plus diligam,*
> *eo feci: sed ita erat res, faciundum fuit.*

And Phaedria ends by acquiescing, in order not to have to sever
relations with the woman, only begging and insisting that he is
not to be kept waiting more than two days, during which he goes
off to his farm, but cannot stay there more than an hour or two
before he is back in the town hanging round Thais. Once again

Parmeno cannot resist philosophic reflections on the oddity of poor mankind, and sees no remedy:

Di boni, quid hoc morbist? adeon homines inmutarier
ex amore, ut non cognoscas eundem esse! Hoc nemo fuit
minus ineptus, magis severus quisquam, nec magis continens . . .

Phaedria, that is to say, was not a blind and crude slave of the senses, but a man who had fallen into a net and was struggling in it and simply drawing it tighter. For the moment he was in the sway of an inebriation which one day, however, would be dissolved.

In the same spirit (I use this expression advisedly, for surely those pretended eulogies of a poet, be it Terence, Menander, or any other, for depicting "daily life as it really is in itself" or for "competing with nature and beating her at her own game" are quite senseless), in the same spirit, I say, the dramatist delineates the passionate old man Menedemus (in the *Heautontimorumenos*), that father who cannot forgive himself for having by his strictness caused his son to go off on military service, and now himself works furiously on the land, anxiously avoiding the slightest pleasure or relaxation, for that would seem to him time stolen from the son whom his behaviour had thrown into the fatigues and harshness of military life. The contrast in the educational methods of the two fathers in the *Adelphoi* is not, as some moralizing commentators would have it, designed to inculcate the lesson of avoidance of extremes, but serves to illustrate and to express wonderment at the variety of human conduct and its unforeseeable consequences. Terence really does not know what to think of the two respective methods and takes sides for neither, least of all for a schoolmaster's synthesis of the two. Demea, who has seen his strict methods frustrated in the outcome, proceeds to adopt the opposite method which he previously denounced and opposed, but does so in a mood of angry exasperation as if wishing it to do its worst, and to end in disaster. He violently exaggerates the easy-going methods of his brother, punishing him by forcing him also to practise his indulgence on a new and widened scale, and

making him reel with the mounting measure of his liberalities.
He wishes thereby to demonstrate to him that the praise and the
advantages which he has hitherto enjoyed were not won *ex aequo
et bono*, but simply by yielding to the interests and passions of
others. War-weary, he drops the reins and spurs his horse to a
precipitous and disorderly gallop, but all the time he clings to the
opinion that his method was the right one and will have to come
into its own again. On the other side the indulgent brother does
not really cease to believe in his method, or consent to forswear it.
There is no question, then, of a "problem" or an educational programme, but simply of a clash of temperaments and feelings, and
a tangle of chances, eluding all educational theory.

Alongside of the contrast between the two father-brothers, the
two mothers are shown in the *Hecyra* as placed in different circumstances, indeed, calling for different attitudes, but equally
disposed for self-effacing maternal sacrifice, one for her son and the
other for her daughter. This harmonious correspondence between
the minds of two mothers has astonishingly been dubbed a mere
"duplication", and more or less blamed on the usual presumption
that Terence must always and in everything be inferior to the
great Menander.[1] The unfortunate Philumena, too, innocent victim who confides the secret of her shame to the mother only,
concealing it from husband and father, must, it seems, be judged
inferior to Pamphila of the *Epitrepontes*. But in truth these girls and
brides of the Terentian comedies are delineated in their innocency
with delicate simplicity. I will end this brief series of illustrations
of Terence's handling of the human affections with a reference to
the parasite in the *Eunuchus*, so different a figure from the cut-
and-dried caricatures of the other comic writers (Ergasilus in the
Captivi of Plautus, for example). He is as amusing as a Casanova
when he sets forth his guiding principle that fools are sent into the

1. "The plot of the *Hecyra* works out on its own lines though somewhat
haltingly with the duplicated relations between Sostrata-Laches and Myr-
rhina-Phidippus. The two husbands grumble at their wives with an excessive
symmetry, though it is true that the characters of the wives are different,
with many points of contact in their difference . . ." (CAPOVILLA, op. cit.,
pp. 339-40).

world solely for the benefit of clever fellows. Since the world
contains such a soldier as Thraso, living on boasts, longing to be
recognized as brave, far-sighted, clever, brilliant, why not at his
side a Gnatho to humour him and so make a living for himself?
There can be no question of altering him, changing him for the
better. The utmost that would be possible would be to leave this
rich soil uncultivated, unharvested, for someone else to exploit,
and that would be a pity. So Gnatho follows up the soldier's
boasts with approval, applause, epigrams, confirmations and corol-
laries of what he says, laughs at the quips which Thraso thinks
must be amusing, bears with endless repetitions of the soldier's
exploits, asks to have them repeated as though he had forgotten
the details and would love to hear them again. But Thraso is also
the poor fellow who, however much he is wronged and fooled,
cannot give up Thais, but creeps back to her and as usual recalls
the example of his peers in heroism. "Qui minus quam Hercules
servivit Omphalae?" Gnatho approves: "Exemplum placet."
Gnatho's masterpiece as a knowing and competent man of the
world is when he gets the warrior, and himself too, accepted into
the new combine formed by Phaedria and Thais, by dint of the
prudent counsel that Thais is too extravagant to be kept by one
man and that since a partner must be found none could be better
than this rich spendthrift fool who is already on the spot. Even
Thraso and Gnatho are not villains, they are poor devils who get
on as best they can. True, Pasquali complains that Terence has
spoiled the delicate delineation of Thais by Menander (in a comedy
which is lost so that no one can say what that delineation was:[1] a
new proof of the abounding but peculiar imagination of the
scholars). He spoiled it, according to Pasquali, in this last scene
"quite unworthy of the charming creature (Thais)" and thereby,
"though he may not have offended the majority of the spectators,
he certainly must have offended the more refined even of his

---

1. Unless this be the Thais, not surely so very charming, alluded to by
Propertius (IV, 5, vv. 43-44: "mundi Thais pretiosa Menandri. Cum ferit
astutos comica moecha Getas", where "pretiosa" means able to sell herself at
a high price.

contemporary readers", for the scene was a contradiction "not only by logical but by psychological and artistic" standards, and "Terence's *Eunuch* thus ends on a note of disharmony".[1] If Dante treated poor Thais with unmeasured contempt, Pasquali seems to have become captivated by her wiles and to have forgotten, as amorous dreamers do, what she really was and what she is shown to be by the words of Phaedria and Parmeno and in her own words to them. On the other hand Pasquali also displays an erudite moral zeal blind to the feelings which, in all their gradations and complications and interplay, are the stuff of life and the stuff of poetry too, which is free of such scruples and niceties. Whatever the unknown Thais of Menander's unknown comedy may have been like, Terence's Thais is quite all right as she is, and excites our human understanding and compassion.

These are the mainsprings of the poetry of Terence's comedies, among which the palm used to be given to the *Eunuchus*, so full of life and with a good deal more of that comic and sometimes farcical element in it than in the other comedies, where this is slight or almost wanting. Perhaps it would be better to give the first place to the *Hecyra*, followed by the *Eunuchus*, the *Andria*, the *Adelphoi*, the *Heautontimorumenos*, and last, because having more the character of a mere comedy of intrigue, the *Phormio*.

Thanks to the kindly feeling which he shows in observing and depicting human life, and an occasional touch of something like Christian charity – and by no means, therefore, simply for his excellent Latin – Terence had his warm admirers in antiquity[2] and

---

1. In the already quoted *Studî ital. di filol. class.*, p. 129.
2. According to Leo, Terence's success was that of a writer for writers: "Doch gab es Kreise, denen das feine terenzische Wesen zusagte; es waren die literarisch Interessierten, und diese waren zahlreich geworden, auch in den obersten Schichten der römischen Gesellschaft. Hier dauerte seine Wirkung fort, und wurde stärker mit dem Wachsen des literarischen Interesses" (op. cit., p. 257). The judgement of Varro on the three Roman comic authors has been too much simplified by Leo (p. 237), who takes it in the superficial sense that Terence not only initiated the "inventions" of Menander, but strove to emulate him also in the "determination of the characters". Varro's passage, in which there is no mention of Menander, can bear the common-sense interpretation that Caecilius exceeded the others

was among the most read Roman authors in the Middle Ages, and was as dear to Petrarch as afterwards to Montaigne, Erasmus, and Carlo Borromeo, and for his mildness and suavity and artistic clarity seemed almost the Virgil of the Roman comic theatre. In later times familiarity with him, as with all Latin authors, has declined, with the particular assistance in his case of the depreciatory attitude of the professional scholars. But whoever reopens his pages will find his attraction undiminished, and will forget the passage of the centuries.

[1936]

in the plot or action ("in argumentis"), Plautus in lively dialogue ("in sermonibus"), and Terence in the characters ("in ethesin") or, as it would now be better phrased, in the portrayal of feeling.

III

VIRGIL

MANY times has the conduct of Aeneas towards the Carthaginian Queen been decried, stigmatized, blamed, condemned. There exists a veritable anti-Aeneas literature, which some student might well collect and set in the frame of an essay.[1] There is of course a comparable movement of dislike for other more or less unpleasant characters in poetry, the drama, and the novel, such as the cruel Creon, the perfidious Iago, the traitor Bireno, whom good souls would wish in no way to resemble, while there is a converse movement of ready affection for the martyr Antigone, the slandered Desdemona, deserted Olimpia, and even for that headstrong but great-souled Othello. These feelings have been dismissed as morbid romanticism, but they and the judgements which accompany them really spring from the sound roots of an unspoiled humanity.

This quite natural distaste for Virgil's Trojan hero, the man Aeneas, has, perhaps not surprisingly, but, as I shall show, quite unjustifiably, been sometimes converted into censure of the poet Virgil. Commentators and critics complain that much less poetic force has gone into his depiction of Aeneas than into that of Dido. Dido, they say, is alive and real, Aeneas on the contrary is abstract, cold, stylized, monotonous, primitive, and deliberately archaic. The poet, they add, should have used his lights and his shadows to give us a more tender and feeling and distraught and delicate Aeneas to match the woman he loved. Aeneas should have shown more pain for the separation, and not have been made to talk in that subtle, argumentative, self-justifying, and sometimes even

---

1. I confess that I myself, aged sixteen, threw my little stone at Aeneas, in a school essay, subsequently printed in a literary journal, which I am flattered but somewhat astonished to see now included in the body of "Virgilian literature", and quoted and discussed, for example, in the copious critical compilation of C. BUSCAROLI, *Il libro di Didone*, text with interleaved translation followed by an ample explanatory and aesthetic commentary, Milan, 1932.

coarse and brutal way, nor made to resort to secret methods and wiles. Reading these censures, one almost expects the commentators and critics themselves to phrase those laments which Virgil should have drawn from the breast of Aeneas, those harrowed and mournful words which should have been on Aeneas' lips, and we must thank them for refraining from providing such amendments and poetical improvements.

A parallel error would be the misuse, as criticism of Sophocles, Shakespeare, or Ariosto, of the rebellion of our feelings and consciences against Creon, Iago, and Bireno or blaming a painter for placing shadow or a black spot there where it is required for the harmony of his picture. In the fourth and sixth books of the *Aeneid* Aeneas is admirably juxtaposed to Dido and shows up just as Virgil wanted him, small-minded, unpleasant, contemptible. It was not, of course, with the critical intellect that he wanted Aeneas to appear like that. On the intellectual level, in fact, he perhaps desired and believed the opposite, and considered his hero to be forgiven and justified. The desire in question belonged to Virgil's deeper being, his creative poetic will, which is all that matters and all that concerns us. That desire sprang from his inspiration, the inspiration (in the Dido episode) of love, love which in its imperious force *omnia vincit*, seizing hold of a noble being, a high-souled and upright woman, and causing her to disregard all other obligations and duties, and to hearken solely to the new duty, the new law to which she has become subjected in religious obedience, forgetful of reputation and glory, disposed – for love's sake – to humble supplications, ready even for death. In that realm of love Dido is the heroine, and Aeneas is (that feeble thing) a man in love who is unequal to love – no strong Hippolytus rejoicing in the fatigues of the chase and resistant to Venus, but a weakling who, without knowing quite how, has had his foot caught in the amorous snare, and as soon as other and for him more pressing interests beckon, turns his mind to disentangling himself with little heed for the consequences. In poetry as in life anger and contempt fall upon such men in such situations. Maybe Maria Mancini did not really pronounce the words of anger and reproach attributed to her when she was constrained to take leave of young Louis XIV and his court – "Vous m'aimez, vous êtes roi, et je pars!". But the legend is accurate by the logic of love. An all-powerful King who does not feel the obligation of placing his omnipotence at the service of his love, to make it triumph over every prosaic obstacle – what a King, what a man! It takes a woman like Racine's Bérénice, in love, but only up to a point (the point where political interests which she recognizes to be more important supervene), to meet such a situation with ready resignation. To the lover who frigidly eludes her appeal for help Emma Bovary retorts: "Mais moi, j'aurais tout donné, j'aurais travaillé de mes mains, j'aurais mendié sur les routes, pour un sourire, pour un regard, pour t'entendre dire merci." Ibsen's women revealing their long torments and rising above their own natures utter as it were hieratic condemnations of the man who has killed their soul, the artist who has sacrificed them to his art, the man of affairs who has sacrificed them to his ambition. And those of Baudelaire, in the frenzy of love, pour contemptuous reproaches on the fool, the useless dreamer who would temper that sublime delirium with moral precepts and contaminate it with extraneous elements, but

> *ne chauffera jamais son corps paralytique*
> *à ce rouge soleil que l'on nomme l'amour.*

This verse seems not merely to describe but boldly to define the failure of the faint amorist.

Aeneas belongs to this order of men who in love play the part which in war and the clash of arms is played by cowards and deserters. Virgil, of course, does not side against him, indeed he makes some show of defending him and putting a good appearance upon him. But the poet who is uppermost in Virgil, following the inexorable logic of poetry, far from sparing him depicts him in action and in speech just as befits his case. In the beginnings and development of Dido's love Aeneas stands by passively. It is not he but Dido who *caeco carpitur igni*, the flame invading her marrows and a wound gaping in her bosom. She lives wholly in her love for him, and he just lets himself be loved, and in the hospitable city enjoys the restfulness and pleasure of such a love after so many buffetings by sea and land. And when the command of Jove, that is the temporarily neglected purpose of reaching Italy, requires his departure, his quick decision is lightly clouded not by the vision of pain in the features of the loved woman, but rather by that of the *dulces terras* which he will now have to leave. Egoist that he is, to the point of naivety, and all wrapped up in the great enterprise which he is destined to accomplish, there is not so much as the stirring of a struggle of the passions in his heart, he being incapable of this, for he does not love and has never really loved. His problem is just now to get clear without peril and with the least trouble for himself and his men, and how to break his decision to Dido:

> *Heu quid agat? Quo nunc reginam ambire furentem*
> *audeat adfatu? Quae prima exordia sumat?*

On this all his worry is concentrated:

> *Atque animum nunc huc celerem, nunc dividit illuc,*
> *in partisque rapit varias perque omnia versat.*

And the best he can think of is to conceal the preparations for the departure and to wait for a good moment to tell the Queen. In this he does not wholly succeed, for if he is careful and cautious the Queen has the quick perception of the loving:

> *At regina dolos (quis fallere possit amantem?)*
> *praesensit . . .*

and therefore he is forced to embark on the conversation which he hoped to elude or defer, and which on Dido's side is a despairing and hopeless recourse to memories, reproaches, supplications, in the grandeur of an explosion of the affections, and on Aeneas' side an evasion, an avoidance of her glance, a muttering of things either commonplace ("always he will remember her and the kindness shown to him"), or discourteous ("we are not linked by marriage"), or stupid ("why does she seek to hold him back from reaching Italy, the promised heritage of his son?"). He seems hardly to have noticed that the world includes not only Italy and his son's heritage, but love, the power of unpardoning love, which hitherto supported him in the guise of a keen devotion, but now confronts him in its terrible anguish, its rebellion against the threat of desolation and death. The woman in love suddenly sees clearly, a veil has fallen from her eyes:

> *Nam quid dissimulo aut quae me ad majora reservo?*
> *Num fletu ingemuit nostro? num lumina flexit?*
> *num lacrimas victus dedit aut miseratus amantem est?*

All that Aeneas can manage is to assume a polite air of grief on his side also, to make a show of feeling himself the pangs of a great love, of wishing to console the suffering woman and not knowing how, of wanting to speak kindly to her, but all the time he is trying to speed up the departure in order to cut short his embarrassment and vexation:

> *At pius Aeneas, quamquam lenire dolorem*
> *solando cupit et dictis avertere curas,*
> *multa gemens magnoque animum labefactus amore,*
> *iussa tamen divûm exsequitur classemque revisit . . .*

And in this he steadfastly persists: "Mens immota manet, lacrimae volvuntur inanes . . .", until the moment that the sails swell in the wind for the departure which the Queen witnesses at dawn, from the roof of her house, and in the fading view of the ships reads the signal of her own death. She has nothing left to do in the place, formerly so full of tasks and hopes, where she had built a splendid new city, now turned for her into an uninhabitable desert:

> *Vixi, et quem dederat cursum Fortuna peregi,*
> *et nunc magna mei sub terras ibit imago . . .*

The episode of Dido has been so often correctly analysed, and recently in Italian critical literature with so much delicacy by Fiore, Mocchino, Bignone, and others, that it would be quite superfluous to illustrate yet again its poetical beauties and artistic perfection.[1] Nor have one or two quite minor jarring notes, such

---

1. A measure of the depth to which the criticism of ancient literature had sunk in Italy before recovering in the last twenty years is afforded by an

as the forced emphasis in Dido's complaint to the man who is deserting her that no pledge remains of her love ("si quis mihi parvulus aula luderet Aeneas"), been overlooked by sensitive and alert critics like Mocchino. But for my purposes it suffices to have called attention to the delineation of Aeneas as a man incapable of love – artistically no less a triumph than that of the passionate queen.

This delineation has its climax and seal in the wonderful scene of Aeneas' encounter with Dido in the great forest, when Aeneas shrinks to yet smaller and feebler stature, while Dido gains height in the grandeur of her grief and disdain. He speaks to her and she will not look at him but keeps silence, and when he has finished, instead of answering turns her back on him and repairs to the shade of her first husband. Never was Aeneas so petty and foolish and maladroit as in what he says to try and placate her and make peace. "Never would he have thought that she would take her life." In fact he measured her passion by his own loveless heart. "He had left her not of his own will but by command of the Gods." As if that command could have any force or weight for a heart in love. "Qui donc devant l'amour ose parler d'enfer?" Who in such a case would dare speak of the Gods? Dido, different though she be from the mad women who speak those words, yet in this is at one with them.

> Talibus Aeneas ardentem et torva tuentem
> lenibat dictis animum lacrimasque ciebat.

essay on Dido published by Valmaggi, a Turin university professor (published in *Rivista di filologia classica*, xxv, 1897), on the lines, said the author (p. 51), of "scientific and experimental aesthetics". The inspiration of the episode is there described as "by no means that of passionate love" but "political and religious": the passion is said to be on the side of Aeneas and not of Dido, who "is introduced solely as a foil to Aeneas", while she displays no love and not even "the sentiment of love in its fineness and entirety", and she "does not fall for Aeneas on account of any notable physical (!) or moral gift . . . but solely by the wish and the direct intervention of the deity"; and all this is confirmed by the fact that when meeting Aeneas in Hades she shows no sign of still loving him despite the injuries received, as she should have done, "for the poets have always imagined love to be eternal".

> *Illa solo fixos oculos aversa tenebat,*
> *nec magis incepto voltum sermone movetur,*
> *quam si dura silex aut stet Marpesia cautes.*
> *Tandem corripuit sese atque inimica refugit*
> *in nemus umbriferum, coniunx ubi pristinus illi*
> *respondet curis aequatque Sychaeus amorem.*

That is the love that's pure, that is the love that's true, in which alone the wounded and embittered heart, smothering its tremendous passion, not oblivious of the past but able to transmute its anguish into the languor of melancholy, may be somewhat soothed.

I have hinted that the censures heaped upon Virgil for his delineation of Aeneas in the Dido episode, though mistaken, are not without an element of justification, lying elsewhere, however, than in this perfectly harmonious episode. What is discordant and inharmonious is the depiction of Aeneas, the hero of the poem, who after long wars and travails successfully conveys and settles his Trojans in Italy, laying the foundation of the greatness of Rome. Why needed this hero to irrupt perfidiously and destructively into the affairs of the heart of a most noble woman, why had he to become entangled in a mellay of the passions playing the part of him who rewards love with desertion, and devotion with despair and death? Why must he cut the poor figure that we have recalled? Had he only held off from the intrigue of love he would not have fallen short of love's requirement (the pacific citizen who has no taste for the clash of arms, and stands aside from conflict, is neither a coward nor a deserter). Enough that he should have followed the advice of the Venetian girl Zulietta to Jean Jacques Rousseau to "attend to his mathematics and keep away from women", that is, in Aeneas' case, stuck to his heroic exploits and left Dido in peace. It was certainly a poetic error to involve Aeneas in that relation; nor could this be made good by introducing the "will of the gods", for if that will may be held to justify or explain an action in life, it cannot expunge an artistic error once committed, any more than it can make a false verse sound well or an ill-matched colour appear harmonious. Virgil did what he could to repair the artistic error; perhaps the last scene which we have recalled was designed deliberately for this. But with what effect? A commentator writes: "En le mettant de nouveau en présence de Didon, il est probable que Virgile a voulu effacer l'impression désagréable que laisse au IV livre la dureté de son héros et lui prêter enfin les sentiments tendres que nous avons jusqu'ici vaine-ment attendu de lui. Il s'y est assez mal pris, Énée se montrant aussi maladroit qu'au IV livre. Ce qui est certain c'est qu'il s'est proposé, et ceci est assez piquant, de donner une contrepartie à la fameuse scène de rupture, c'est à dire en attribuant cette fois à Énée la tendresse, à Didon l'insensibilité inflexible."[1] But what fails is Virgil's intention to restore coherency to the structure of his poem and to the hero around whom it is built, and not his poetry, which is here altogether successful and sublime. And let it be well under-stood that it is Aeneas, not the poet, who is "maladroit", for Aeneas is depicted according to his deserts in that situation into which he had floundered helplessly. None the less the artistic error which we feel, and which Virgil does not make good, is amply atoned for by this episode of Dido, this tragedy of amorous passion which the heart and fancy of Virgil had conceived and which he then found no better means of inserting in the poem that he was composing than by the commission of that error, ex-ploiting his hero in the role of the character required to serve as a foil, a contrast in inferiority, to Dido. And perhaps without this device that tragedy would have been laid aside and never complet-ed and preserved for us. The contradiction which deranges and upsets the figure of Aeneas, and his mission, is thus handsomely compensated; and moreover in itself it is unimportant, for the poetic reader can and does in fact disregard it. The exploitation of the character of Aeneas gives to the poetic story of Dido its coherency and truth, without deleterious effects for the poetry which surrounds Aeneas himself in the last night of Troy or at his meeting with King Evander in the wooded spot where Rome is destined to arise. But it is necessary to keep the one Aeneas

1. A. CARTAULT, *L'art de Virgile dans l'Énéide* (Paris, 1926), pp. 456-57.

distinct and apart from the other, and not to strive to harmonize them by over-subtle interpretations, at the cost of tedium and a loss of poetic enjoyment. To my mind abstractions of this sort are not difficult to perform and are often desirable and necessary for the reader of poetical works. Others, however, feel them to be in some way not only difficult but positively improper and wrong, and instead of resorting to them there is a hunt by such critics for a harmony and unity where this does not exist – a source, as I am always pointing out, of many laborious and absurd interpretations in the particular cases of the *Divina Commedia* and of *Faust*.

[1938]

IV

JESUS AND THE WOMAN TAKEN IN ADULTERY
(Gospel of St. John, 8. 2-11)

THERE is general agreement that the story of the woman taken in adultery is an interpolation in the Johannine Gospel: the critics have pointed out the signs which lead to that presumption. According to Loisy the episode was excluded from the synoptic Gospels because "le fait avait quelque chose d'un peu choquant pour le sens chrétien, la rencontre du Christ avec la femme adultère, et son attitude indulgente, paraissant de nature à compromettre son prestige devant les non-croyants, juifs et païens, et même aux yeux des frères: surtout la discipline ecclésiastique s'arrangeait mal d'un tel exemple".[1] It was included in the non-canonical Gospels, certainly in that of the Hebrews and perhaps in that of Peter, and Papias knew it and quoted it. Thus little by little it made its way into the recognized Gospels and retained its place there.[2]

Investigation to determine whether the story had an authentic historical origin in some deed, some saying, of Jesus, or whether, more probably, it originated in the sphere of doctrine as the answer to a casuistic enquiry into the moral status of those zealots and guardians of the law who promote and execute punishments for crimes such as those of which they themselves are guilty, would be pointless. Whatever its origin, the writer who drew upon tradition or shaped the episode in his imagination, or who moulded it into its still surviving form, was an artist. Let us re-read it.[3]

And early in the morning he came again into the temple, and all the people came unto him; and he sat down and taught them.

And the scribes and Pharisees brought unto him a woman taken in adultery; and when they had set her in the midst,

---

1. A. LOISY, *Le quatrième Évangile* (2nd edition, Paris, Nourry, 1921), p. 280.
2. Ibidem.
3. Translator's Note: Croce in his text quotes "the old and classic Italian translation of Giovanni Diodati". We here quote the English Authorized Version.

They say unto him, Master, this woman was taken in adultery, in the very act. Now Moses in the law commanded us, that such should be stoned, but what sayest thou?

This they said, tempting him, that they might have to accuse him. But Jesus stooped down, and with his finger wrote on the ground, as though he heard them not.

So when they continued asking him, he lifted up himself and said unto them, He that is without sin among you, let him first cast a stone at her.

And again he stooped down, and wrote on the ground.

And they which heard it, being convicted by their own conscience, went out one by one, beginning at the eldest, even unto the last: and Jesus was left alone, and the woman standing in the midst.

When Jesus had lifted up himself, and saw none but the woman, he said unto her, Woman, where are those thine accusers? Hath no man condemned thee?

She said, No man, Lord. And Jesus said unto her, Neither do I condemn thee; go, and sin no more.

For a right understanding of these lines it is first of all needful to dismiss the notion that the narration contains a doctrinal proposition and demonstration. Still less is it to be read as affording the resolution of a case in law. Adjudication on cases never can rise to the full rank of a judgement or doctrine, but must always have about it a certain abstractness and indetermination leaving room for the varying emphasis of particular feelings and the corresponding elaborations of the imagination. As an example of the mistakes to which any attempt to construe the sentence of Jesus as a doctrinal pronouncement must inevitably lead, that of the illustrious Loisy may serve once and for all. He writes: "Mis en demeure de s'expliquer, le Christ s'abstient de résoudre le cas directement, mais il pose lui-même à ses auditeurs un cas moral qu'ils devront examiner dans leur conscience d'accusateurs avant de pousser plus loin l'affaire dont ils s'occupent. Si l'on faisait application rigoureuse et générale de ce principe, il n'y aurait aucun crime dont la société pût poursuivre le châtiment. Mais la réponse est censée avoir été ce qu'il fallait pour se débarrasser d'importuns en leur signifiant que leur question n'était pas à poser par eux. Et si la conclusion de l'histoire n'est pas d'une très grande vraisemblance, elle ne manque pas de piquant."[1] Disappointing and almost offensive here is the subjection of a poetic masterpiece to the analysis of the absurd

1. Op. cit., p. 284.

consequences of a logical and rigorous application of the judgement in which it culminates (and such an application could not be avoided if it is regarded as a doctrinal utterance). Worse still is it to have the behaviour of Jesus reduced to the level of a clever method for getting rid of some tedious and vexatious arguers by covering them with embarrassment and confusion. Worst of all is it to have this noble, moving piece of drama described and actually praised as "piquant".

No, there is no question here of an ethical or juridical theory, and all too facile would be the criticism which points out the necessity and the majesty of the law (Aristotle's "dispassionate intelligence"), which must be observed just because it is the law, the foundation of all human society. The question here is of something which eludes criticism, and is as important as is respect for the law, an inner process, a mode of feeling, a deepening of the moral conscience, thanks to which the guilt and impurity that there is in every man, however pure and righteous, the remorse which everyone must feel in himself, the danger which everyone feels for ever pressing in upon him, is made living and present as it was not before. Centuries after, the awareness that was then kindled found expression in the half-sarcastic and half-despairing utterance of the Shakespearian hero: "I am myself indifferent honest, but yet I could accuse me of such things that it were better my mother had not borne me." Such motions and commotions of the heart do not make for the elaboration of theories, but for the creation of life itself, of the new Christian life, stern and pitiful, humble and exalted, rich in experiences known little or not at all to the antique moralists, never afterwards extinguished and now built into our modern consciousness. Jesus, Paul, and the others who accompanied and followed them were not investigators, definers, demonstrators of ethical concepts, but creators of an ethos, a morality, and as such are above all to be historically observed and contemplated: and this character is alone the inspiration of the author of the episode of Jesus and the woman taken in adultery.

Behold the scribes and the Pharisees, observers of the law with a fanatical fidelity which is the very cement of their faction or party. Here they come, triumphing in the trap which they have set for Jesus and his doctrine, driving him with their interrogations into the dilemma of either openly denying the authority of the law, or withdrawing, in frightened embarrassment, from his well-known position. In front of them they drive a woman, a human creature, suddenly snatched from a voluptuous abandonment to face a dire threat and probably a cruel punishment, surrounded by the men of her race who have become for her accusers, judges, executors of the law, executioners. There she stands, dazed with shame and terror, seeing no way of escape, resigned, perhaps, to her inevitable lot. And all this, which we hear and see, she expresses simply by her silence, her renouncement of any defence or prayer or lament, helpless as she is in the grip of those in whose hands lies her fate. Jesus, leaning down to draw characters in the dust, interrupted in his meditation by that crowd and by the noisy violence of the scene which has burst upon him, is also at first silent, and listening, as it seems, with but half his attention, continues to write. He has well understood the mean purpose of these men, to score a doctrinal victory over him whose feeling and thought is so alien to themselves, ignorant as they are of the problems which travail him, the light of truth and goodness aflame in him. For the purpose of such a victory, they drag forth one of their own kind, a being of flesh and of feeling, one hallowed by the imminence of punishment and death, but for them as it were a senseless instrument of demonstration; and they are all ready to utilize her for a brilliant display of distinctions, syllogism, quotations, as though playing at cards, heedless of her sufferings which do not touch them and are in any case of no account in their eyes compared with their party interests and scholastic disputations. How to answer them? What does the meaning and obligation of an article of the law signify beside the really present and urgent moral case constituted by their stupid wickedness, or wicked stupidity, which in its keen readiness annuls any sense of their own unworthiness, any memory of man's single sinful and pitiful nature? What importance can the fault of this weak woman have when weighed against their own presumptuous and eager cruelty? As they press, Jesus at last stands up and utters not an answer to that question of theirs which, however legitimate in other circumstances, is for him irrelevant and to be dismissed, but a brief and solemn saying of emotive, not logical character, compelling them to look inwards into the depth of their own hearts, to recollect themselves and be ashamed. Then he sits again and resumes writing, having said and done all that was called for by the occasion, leaving no need for further discussion or comment. The effect of his word is instantaneous. Not one of these fierce and argumentative accusers protests. Words fail them, one and all, for at that moment all have looked into their hearts, and a stern sentiment such as cannot be eluded or ignored weighs upon their minds; and not one finds any better course than to break away and depart, first the older, with their greater load of experience and sin, and then, one by one, the younger.

Jesus meanwhile remains, in apparent aloofness, absorbed once more in meditation. When he looks up again the scene is empty save for the woman whom they had dragged there tumultuously, now free and alone. Jesus, as though returning after an absence, asks her what has happened meanwhile, and she answers in plain and humble and timid language, still bewildered by the storm that has passed over her, too much astounded by the sudden and unexpected reversal of the situation for any sort of demonstration of joy or gratitude, and seeming still to be awaiting a decision of her fate. She, too, perhaps has experienced a revulsion, and Jesus does not condemn her, that is, he utters no reproof but looks to her continuing life and, bidding her sin no more, says all that he can and should say.

The purely human and poetic character of this materially small but greatly moving drama occasioned some difficulty for its acceptance into the canonical scriptures, but for centuries, and still today, it has stirred souls with that magical power of poetry which can admonish without resort to admonitions, teach without resort to instruction, reveal to men the deepest recesses and most delicate fibres of their humanity. The great Italian painters of the

Renaissance, and others unnumbered, have taken it for a theme. But no poet has ventured to rewrite or revise the words, to change in any way the action of the scene or the features of the characters, for the words, the attitudes, the features, are perfect.

[1939]

V

DANTE'S POETRY: ITS CHARACTER AND UNITY

THIS excursion through the three canticles of the Divine Comedy[1] naturally makes no absurd pretension to have summed up the entire poetical content of the poem, or described it in all its parts, but has simply named the various peaks and shifting formations in that immense mountain range, with the intent of furnishing precise and particular indications to the reader of Dante so that the characteristic spirit of the poet (which for us constitutes the true unity of his work) may not elude attention as a vague and empty generalization.

What, then, is this spirit of Dante, this ethos and pathos of the *Comedy*, this "tonality" that is so special to it? To put the matter briefly, it is a sentiment of the world, founded upon a firm faith and a sure judgement, animated by a robust will. Of reality, Dante has a knowledge which no perplexity impairs or divides or weakens. It is a knowledge of reality in which the mysterious is reduced to just that residue – intrinsic in the conception itself – before which one must bow humbly, the mystery of creation, of providence and the divine will, which reveals itself only in the vision of God, in the heavenly beatitude. And to Dante it seemed perhaps that in the mystic raptures which he experienced or imagined, even that mystery tended to become clear. But such mystic awareness, in his poetry, could necessarily only be rendered in negative terms, as a relation of experience of ineffable things. With no less sureness does Dante judge the various human affections, ever fully aware which actions are to be approved and furthered, which to be condemned and repressed for the true and worthy ends of life; and his will does not waver or slide between contrasting ideals, nor is it torn by contradictory desires. Such discords and stresses as we find in his ideas and his standpoints are implicit in the things themselves, the material of future historical

1. In my book on *The Poetry of Dante* this chapter follows upon the three which treat in detail of the *Divine Comedy*.

development, but in him they are present only as undeveloped germs, extraneous to his own compact and unitary mind, his firm faith and steadfast conduct, his sureness in thought and action. Within this robust intellectual and moral framework, then, vibrates the sentiment of the world, unsurpassably various and complex, as felt by a spirit who has on all sides observed and experimented and meditated, and is fully aware of 'human vice and valour', not superficially or at second hand, but through individual experience of those affections in himself, in the activities of life and in lively sympathy and imagination. The intellectual and ethical pattern contains and orders this seething material; wholly subduing and enchaining it like a powerful opponent who, even when subdued and bound down, yet with powerful muscles contends grandly and magnificently against his bonds.

It is this spiritual attitude which the many alternative definitions of the character of Dante's poetry to be found in the pages of critics and interpreters have in mind and seek to track down and to determine. How could any eye miss something so real and effectual and obvious? Truth will out – or at very least will proclaim its presence with patches of light. If these critical formulas are so often strained and inadequate, that is because they either make use of unsuitable concepts or have recourse to metaphor or go astray in abstractions and catalogues of abstractions. It is commonly said, for example, that Dante portrays not what is happening but what happened, not the present but the past; but what else lies in that abstruse distinction, or in the observations from which it springs, if not the fact that in Dante all the affections are contained and bound down by a general thought, a steadfast will, which surpasses each particular? But the dynamic representation of a force which surmounts and subdues another force is really, like all poetry, the representation of what happens, not of what has happened, of a motion, not of a stillness. It is said that Dante is supremely objective, but no poetry is ever objective, and Dante is supremely subjective, always himself, Dante; so that here "objectivity" must be a vague metaphor to designate the undisturbedness, unbrokenness of his conception of the world, the clear-cut quality of his thought, the decisiveness of his volition, and the resulting precise contours of his delineations. It is often noted as a characteristic of Dante that he annuls distances in time and diversities in manners, ranging the men and the events of all epochs on a single stage. But this means merely that Dante measured the ways of the world in all centuries and circumstances by a single steady measure, a definite standard of truth and goodness, projecting the image of the transient upon the screen of the eternal. To the form of Dante's work writers attribute the characters of intensity, precision, concision, and so forth, nor is it doubtful that one who dominates strong passions by the force of his will expresses himself vigorously, intensely, and by dint of scrutinizing and understanding those passions gains precision, and by disregard of petty detail concision. Yet simply to count up characteristics in this way is to rest content with the surface. Another description of Dante is as a "sculptural" and not a "depictive" poet, and sure enough if sculpture here stands for the manly, vigorous, robust, resolute wielding of hammer and chisel by contrast with the relaxed action of the painter wielding (as Leonardo said) the "featherweight brush", Dante can well be termed sculptor, not painter, for there need be no quarrel with a choice of images, though they be logically and critically valueless in the same way that the comparison of Dante with Michelangelo is valueless. There is a well-known sentence in the *Ottimo Comento*: "I who write this have heard Dante say that never for the sake of rhyme did he say something different from what he meant to say, but that very often in his verses he made words say something different from what they were by other poets used to say." *Verba sequuntur*, and if they do not follow quickly they are dragged along by force, as Montaigne added. Again, affirmations that the character and unity of Dante's poem are wholly comprised in that metre of the *terza rima*, so vehement and yet so calm, which grips, ranges, and disciplines the song of the poet, this is true and yet not true, like so many of those now fashionable attempts (specially in regard to the visual arts) to locate an artistic essence in an abstractly defined form. No doubt it is only with his use of this metre that

Dante displays himself as the poet of the *Divine Comedy*, and he expresses the drama of his soul altogether in and through this metre, and the *terza rima* was certainly not – as has been suggested – excogitated and selected by him as an allegorical reflection of the Trinity, or if such a notion crossed his mind this could only be as an addition or aid to the incentive which he already felt in himself, the spontaneous urge of his expressive fancy, intimately united with the threefold verse. United, that is to say, not with this metre considered generically, but with Dante's own sort of *terza rima*, kneaded from the elements of his own language, syntax, style, scanned with that inflection and accent which marks it off from the similar metre of other poets. This obvious consideration makes it clear that the metrical pattern cannot be adduced as the determining feature of the poem unless by it there is implied the whole ethos and pathos, intonation or tonality, of the *Comedy*, in fact the spirit of Dante.

This, according to the universally current idea of Dante, is an austere spirit, and we have already said as much above, for austere he needs must be, and much experienced in sorrow, who checks and dominates his passions. Yet the notion of a Dante for ever frowning in his wrath, the frequent harping upon his melancholy, misanthropy, pessimism, can be pushed too far, and there is justification for an attempt, such as has been made in these pages, to correct and soften some of the lines of that traditional and conventional portrait. For all those features in Dante which struck his contemporaries and passed into legend, for all the justice which there may be recognized in Boccaccio's record of his "thoughtful and melancholy" aspect, the poem itself leaves us no doubt but that Dante's mind held a wealth and variety of interests which shifted between modernity and antiquity, between present experience and suffering and learned or scholastic consolations, while his sentiments, ranging from the violent and sublime to the gentle and tender and even the wittily sparkling, were no less rich and various. And then – he was a poet; and in his exile wanderings through Italy his was not an eye restricted to the inspection of things political and moral from that special standpoint, but ranged over the whole field of vision, delighting in what it saw, responding with admiration to the beautiful and with sympathy to the spectacle of the humble. He was, as well as a poet, in a special sense an artist, ever studious of art and of art theory, and proudly enthusiastic about the *bello stile*, or fine manner, and he took an exceeding pleasure in language, in the living word which thought, in a divinely creative spasm, engenders as its own incarnation, rightly fitting, appropriate, sensuous. There was in Dante's mind, then, far more variety of feelings and above all far more happiness than is commonly thought, though feelings and happiness compatible with his austerity, and thereby tempered and coloured.

On the ethos and pathos of Dante, and on its intellectual and practical implications, argument frequently arises both in Italy and abroad, taking the shape of an enquiry whether the spirit of Dante is or is not "modern". Put more precisely and clearly the question is whether Dante can or cannot be taken by us moderns as a master and guide in spiritual life, in the pursuit of political and moral ideals, and in all other matters. Truth to tell, all great men are guides to life, but none can be sole guide, for each of them is a moment of history, and the true guide is history as a whole, not merely the history which we continually re-create, but above all that which at every instant we ourselves create. The *Divine Comedy* is eternal in its poetic form, but as regards its material it is conditioned by the historical moment in which it came into existence, the particularity of which has here already been indicated. Attention to that historical setting will suffice to let us discern what there is in Dante which was absent until he arose, and what, on the other hand, is not and never was to be found in Dante, but was a later formation. We shall thereby be able to subtract from his portrait certain shades and hues which have been abusively inserted in it.

The Middle Age, with its fierce asceticism and its high-spirited zestful warfare, that earlier and crude Middle Age, could not find a place in Dante. There is perhaps no great poem which is so void as his of the passion of war for its own sake, with its commotions, risks, efforts, triumphs, adventures. The epic of the

822   ESSAYS IN CRITICISM AND LITERARY HISTORY

Middle Age, the Carolingian cycle, does but echo faintly in some allusive stanza. Asceticism is replaced by a firm faith fortified by reason and doctrine, and the zeal of the citizen replaces the zeal of the soldier. That is to say, things which were out-of-date were replaced by the things which really characterized Dante's age, Dante's Italy, or which, to put it at the least, characterized his own mentality and were the object of his own continuous and intense interest, his own human passion. I have often shown my aversion for the attribution of ethnic characters to poets, but I will go so far as to say in answer to the description of Dante as "Germanic" (for which German critics are not alone and not primarily responsible), that if by this term is understood a suggestion of mystic, ascetic, and warlike motives in Dante, then the attribution is quite wrong and should be substituted by Italian, Latin, or some such contrary. There is in the *Fantasie* of Giovanni Berchet a finely conceived scene in which Italians and Germans meet at Constance to deliberate upon conditions of peace. Well, in such a scene Dante would not stand among the "blond folk", the helmeted and mail-coated barons "flashing a message from the days of yore", but in the group of those men in long plain capes "with dark and piercing eyes for sole adornment".

Something else to be avoided is an over-close comparison of Dante with Shakespeare, the first poet in the ensuing history of European poetry to match him in rank. Shakespeare represents, or rather is, another epoch of the human spirit, in which Dante's conception of the world had been overthrown. The shadow of mystery now once again lay athwart that brightness which had thrown light even upon the necessity of mystery, and a perplexity of mind and soul such as Dante had not known, or had soon dominated, now set the tone.[1] As to the Romantics of a still later age what shall we say? Their infinity, their dream, were not the infinity and dream of Dante, nor their style his *bello stile*, nor was their sentiment of nature akin to that of the poet in whom Grimm actually denied the existence of such a sentiment. Their feeling for life,

1. See my study of Shakespeare in *Ariosto, Shakespeare e Corneille* (4th edn., Bari, 1950).

in fact, was the opposite to his, and whoever reads or declaims Dante in the Romantic manner misconstrues and betrays him. If we take "Germanic" this time to stand for "Nineteenth-Century Romantic" we may say that Dante was no more Romantically than he was mediaevally Germanic. Had he known the heroes of Romanticism, the Werthers, Obermanns, Renés, and the rest of that pale crew, he would perhaps have located them in the "black mire" among the despairing *accidiosi*. He was doubtless not without experience of this hopeless state of mind which in the Romantic period underwent a special elaboration and cultivation, and became widespread and the object of admiration and worship, but is not really particular to any time. Dante himself, perhaps, was in his youth the victim of that affliction, and like the Romantic heroes, let melancholy, hopelessness, accidie drive him into dissipations. Such may be the meaning of the sonnet addressed to him by his friend Cavalcanti in reproof of the "wretched life" in which he was "settled", of the "craven soul" and "tedious spirit" which had come to possess him. But in any case he soon emerged from that bewilderment and relegated it among his experiences, as he did likewise with those boiling amorous passions of which his biographers tell us, to make them the material of the episode of Francesca. There is no sentimentalism whatever in the *Divine Comedy*, only the joy and grief and pride and courage of living, held in check by moral conscience, but sustained and animated by high hope.

Such, in rapidly sketched outline, is the authentic image of Dante to be discerned in his own work. But it is necessary to insist once again, in conclusion, that this image which usefully differentiates Dante from other poets and thus helps us to understand and appreciate his work, has about it something cramping and prosaic until it is placed in its setting and resolved into the great stream of the poetry itself, the incomparable poetry which cannot be forced into any frame or labelled as belonging to any class, but soars at large in the cosmos. Hence our delight in Dante's rhythms and words, even the slightest and least emphasized, enveloped as they all are in that charm, whether it be that Dante in mythological language tells us of Dawn, "old Tithon's paramour", issuing forth from "her dear friend's arms", or that he calls snow "the white sister", or whatever it may be. This, the essential, cannot be described by any other characteristic than the universal character of poetry, and thus considered Dante is no longer Dante in his finite individuality but is the voice of wonderment and of stirred feeling with which the soul of man ever responds to the perpetual creation of the world. At this point all differences fade, and we hear only that eternal and sublime refrain, of which the ultimate accent is the same in all the great poets and artists, ever new, ever old, hearkened to with perennially fresh excitement and joy, the accent of unqualified poetry. To those who spoke in such divine or rather deeply human tones there once used to be given the name of genius: and Dante was a Genius.

[1920]

THE LAST CANTO OF THE PARADISE

Dᴀɴᴛᴇ – as all will surely now agree – had a different notion of poetry from ours. What for us is the whole of poetry he regarded as the "fine raiment" or "fair style" (the "decorative" as contrasted with the "illustrative" element); the substance lying for him in scientific concepts and moral intentions, an idea which guided him in the composition of his sacred poem. This, of course, does not at all mean that if he had taken our own more correct view of poetry, he would thereby have surmounted certain impediments and dangers and become a freer and a better poet. Ideas, correct or otherwise, are without efficacy in respect of poetic creation which, in its virtues or its failings, may be equally accompanied either by correct or by incorrect ideas. However, it does mean this, that we should consider his poetry not in the light of his own idea, which as part and parcel of the whole mediaeval system of aesthetics and philosophy has been critically surpassed, but by the light of our own which we hold to be true or at any rate more helpful for the understanding.

From this point of view we are obliged to distinguish the poetic tones of Dante's poem from those which basically are not poetic, and this is something which rouses resentment in the inexpert and the thoughtless, giving the cue for facile exaltations of the unity and integrity of Dante, rhetorical denunciations of the mutilations and cuts which we are supposed to be effecting, as though a critic were a butcher or a surgeon severing pieces of flesh, and not just a discerning thinker, and as though discernment were out of place, or unnecessary, in one treating of Dante.

Must we stick to the customary valuation of the last canto of the poem? Here is a passage from Del Lungo's essay on it. "In what other work have the ponderous intricacies of scholastic theology ever been pressed into service and dominated so as to produce the charm of poetry as here in this ascent to the peak, in wonder and in awe, recollection and piercing endeavour, confidence and misgiving, submission in the very act of victory, humility as of one defeated at the very moment of triumph? Invocations, exclamations, protestations of the inadequacy of language for the theme, preface and accompany the supreme delineation which cannot, however, be more than an adumbration of that which in itself, for all the might of the human word, must remain ineffable. But Dante takes up the challenge, even though his words can but drown the final notes of the immortal canto in that ineffability."[1] For all the sincere respect which I feel for the scholarship of the late Del Lungo, I must say that this is rhetoric and not criticism. Next, I look at the essay of Pistelli, and in the first pages find, not without a point of irony (Pistelli appeals to the authority of "antiquated aesthetic theory", making it his boast to know and observe no other), a blunt rejection of the distinction which I am in the habit of making between structure and poetry, on the grounds that "the bare shape of the building has its artistic importance also, even if it does not yet display the reliefs and mosaics and pictures with which it will later be adorned",[2] and here I am obliged to say that words like this display something between failure to understand and a deliberate refusal to understand because the mind is bent upon another purpose, that of contradicting and showing up the person one contradicts as an object of ready mirth for the ignorant and the indifferent.

No doubt whatever but that the final canto corresponds admirably to the purpose of the poem, such as it is. Dante set out to depict the *visio divinae essentiae* which affords the *perfecta beatitudo hominis* as the proper and actual conclusion of the journey through the three realms of the Beyond.

Philosophically speaking, such a vision is inconceivable. It implies but fails to satisfy an ambition to "see" that which can only be "thought", that which humanity has always thought and always thinks; indeed it might be said that the whole business of man has always been and always is to think it, pur-

1. *Il canto XXXIII del "Paradiso"* (Florence, 1913), p. 24.
2. *Il canto XXXIII del "Paradiso"*, new and corrected edition (1922), p. 9; cf. p. 45.

suing in all its thoughts the theme of the divine essence, the *rerum natura*, the eternal spirit. The philosophers who, not content with thought, have placed above thought the notion of an "intellectual intuition" (in other words precisely a *visio essentiae*), have either under such a name signified the concreteness of thought (thought being always at the same time an intuiting which arises out of the intuition and permeates it), or else, instead of rising, as they supposed, to a higher level, they have sunk below the level of thought. The mystics, who reckon to attain that essence without thought, are either thinkers without knowing or wishing it, or else mere gatherers of impressions or of spasms of the feelings and the senses. Poets cannot conceive that essence for the obvious reason that poets' knowledge is not of ideas or of externalized things, but simply of their own feelings. Goethe, when he thought of the Mothers, the Generating Ideas, decided finally not to describe Faust's visit to their realm, limiting himself to expressing in negative form the aspiration towards that which is approachable by no passage, responsive to no prayer, and the infinite extension of its domain where a man finds nothing familiar and no foothold.

> Nichts wirst du sehn in ewig leerer Ferne,
> Den Schritt nicht hören den du thust,
> Nichts Festes finden, wo du ruhst.[1]

And although Faust, despite Mephistopheles' warning, would "seek in that Nought the All", nothing more comes of it than that, Mephistopheles indicates a scene of novel mythology, the occasion for a novel irony – the labour of the Mothers around the fuming cauldron:

> Bei seinem Schein wirst du die Mütter sehn;
> Die einen sitzen, andre stehn und gehn,
> Wie's eben kommt. Gestaltung, Umgestaltung,
> Des ewigen Sinnes ewige Unterhaltung:
> Umschwebt von Bildern aller Kreatur,
> Sie sehn dich nicht, denn Schemen sehn sie nur.[2]

1. "Nothing wilt thou see in the ever void distance; wilt not hear thy own step, find nothing firm whereon to rest."
2. In the glimmering thou wilt see the Mothers, some seated, others standing

If philosophy, for reasons of logic, denies to man the vision of the divine essence, this is denied to the Christian also by his faith, which requires that before attaining to this he must have left this mortal life and ascended to the realm of the blessed, to Paradise. Dante, not wishing that this conclusion should be lacking in the relation of his journey, and finding himself precluded by faith as well as logic from doctrinally expounding – by the method which had served him in handling philosophical and theological concepts – what is in its nature not doctrinal, but an intuitive act, had only one way open to him: to recount how by grace the vision of God had been conceded to him, and to declare the impossibility of relating it in conceptually valid language.

And this way he pursues in this last canto with all that mastery of word and verse which he has progressively attained in the course of the three canticles and which in the *Paradise* exhibits its freedom and power as never before. Saint Bernard prays to the Virgin to obtain from God the privilege, for Dante, of beholding the beatific vision, and Beatrice and the other blessed ones join in the prayer, so that the Madonna assents and obtains this grace. And Dante is admitted to see – but this "seeing" is something which transcends the human word – an immensity and intensity which the memory cannot register. Yet he hopes that he may be empowered to relate and to render intelligible some part of it or some faint idea; but in the attempt all that he can achieve is to repeat in various modes that what he saw was beyond telling, so that he recounts not what he saw but what he should have seen, the programme, so to speak, in lieu of the ineffable performance, the unity of all the parts of the universe, the substance, the accidents, the property, the universal form of the nexus; and when he strives to say something at least of what he directly saw, of his contemplation and ocular perception of nothing less than the

and moving as it may be. Forming and transforming, the eternal pastime of eternal mind, amid thronging shapes of all creatures. But thyself they will not see, for they see nothing but Schemes."

Compare verses 6222 and following, 6246 and following, 6256, 6285 and following.

Divine Trinity, the summit of theological and metaphysical thought, he describes instead three circles of diverse colour occupying the same space, the second a reflection from the first, glowing with a human likeness, and the third like unto fire: wherewith Dante once again exclaims that word and voice fail him for such a thought, and that what was granted to him by grace was a lightning vision which contented his mind only for an instant.

After adding my tribute to the deserved admiration which is felt for this final scene in the great journey, this last chapter in Dante's message, may I be allowed still to observe, with all moderation, that what we have admired is a lesson, a lesson on an exalted theme, magnificently developed on the highest level of style, but still a lesson conducted according to the technique of teaching. And having paid my tribute to this lesson, may I be permitted to disregard it when seeking, elsewhere than in this admirable didacticism, the poetry which Dante (a great poet, though the literary commentators seem often to forget it) uttered in this very canto? Or are we to be given only the choice between drinking or drowning, the choice between assigning to poetry what pertains to instruction or renouncing the search for poetry in this canto on the grounds that everything there has to be placed on the same level as what we have spoken about, and in no way distinguished from it?

Professor Cosmo,[1] who has recently commented on the last canto of the *Divine Comedy* with exceptional prudence and discernment (for example he has rightly denied that Dante figures in it as a mystic and a follower of Saint Bonaventura), has indeed recognized that the poetry of the canto does not lie in the delineation of the beatific vision and in Dante's relation of it. Seeking this poetry elsewhere, Cosmo locates it "in the sentiment with which Dante approaches those concepts which are for him the supporting foundations of his whole spiritual world", so that "if the reader does not succeed in seeing the truths which Dante

1. *L'ultima ascesa*, an introduction to the *Paradiso* (Bari, 1936), pp. 399-407.

discovers, he sees and feels the spiritual development whereby Dante stage by stage attains to them; and this suffices for the creation of poetry".

Here, I think, we are on the right path, for what else can and should be asked of a poet than that he should, by expressing the motions of his soul, the fullness of his feelings and sufferings, raise them to the level of beauty?

Yes, but where is it in this canto that Dante really expresses his sentiment? Not in the many verses (two thirds or more of the entire canto) in which he strives to utter while protesting that he cannot utter, for these are plainly a sequel to his theological exposition, continuing it up to the point where theology has to deny itself, having reached to the inscrutable and ineffable. Indeed if we lost sight of this deliberate intention of Dante the theologian to round off his recital with the necessary warning that at this point theological demonstration has reached its limit and thus he can speak no more, we would risk seeing him in the light of a schoolmaster who had forgotten the argument of his lesson and was beating about the bush to maintain his prestige with the students by emphatic gesturing and enthusiastic declamation.

The poetic reader, however, knows very well where it is in this canto that Dante really expresses his feelings – in three terzains which alone stand out and outshine all the remainder:

> Qual è colui che somniando vede,
> e dopo il sogno la passione impressa
> rimane, e l'altro alla mente non riede;
>   cotal son io, ché quasi tutta cessa
> mia visione, ed ancor mi distilla
> nel cuor lo dolce che nacque da essa.
>   Così la neve al sol si dissigilla,
> così al vento nelle foglie lievi
> si perdea la sentenza di Sibilla.

This is the lyric cry of a man who has long been enveloped in a dream of singular delight and joy, composed maybe of contradictory, absurd, and chaotic shapes such as the intellectual memory could not retain, but leaving behind it a penetrating recollection of pleasure and well-being to outlast the image which induced it.

"Ed ancor mi distilla" – the last drops continue to fall of that joy
which had rained down so abundantly – "lo dolce" – that sort of
delight which mildly permeates the organism and soothes and
harmonizes it. Whatever the content of the dream may have been
the recollection of that joy is an abiding possession. The content
has evaporated, melted like snow in sunshine, scattering (and
with this stately image Dante once again exalts the mystery revealed to him but now again lost from sight) like those answers
which the Sybil wrote upon the leaves that were scattered to the
wind. It has vanished – yet it had been a reality, a possession, like
the paradise lost which man treasures in the depths of his heart,
pining for it and failing to find it and knowing that it is to be
found nowhere. Yet whenever he seems to recollect it and to
glimpse some feature of it, the stimulus reawakens, though dimly,
and the memory becomes clearer:

> La forma universal di questo nodo
> credo ch'io vidi, perché più di largo,
> dicendo questo, mi sento ch'io godo.

And now I seem to hear the "Dantists" remark sarcastically that
for me the wonderful final canto, viewed as poetry, shrinks to
three or four terzains and a simile. On the matter of measurement
I might answer like the Abbé Galiani when he was shown a sonnet
whose lines, as printed, were of exactly equal length and all bad,
that poetry is not to be computed with a tape-measure. Poetry,
like the divine grace of which Dante speaks, is a lightning flash
upon the mind. And as to the simile, poetry is always comparison,
similitude, expressing the supersensible by the sensible, the eternal
by the transient, humanity by the individual, and it is thanks to
this that such comparisons can be translated into prose and used
in scientific discourse to illustrate the meaning of concepts. However, this is no place to extemporize a theory of similes, all the
more since everyone must agree that one of the finest features of
the great poetry of Dante lies in these similes, which in themselves
are veritable lyrical utterances.

There is in the canto another passage which is dear to me; this is not the stylized prayer of Saint Bernard to the Virgin (which Cristoforo Lantini assigns to the "deliberative order" of discourse), but the conclusion of the prayer, when the good old Saint who has taken Dante under his protection, praying on his behalf to the Virgin in the full assembly of the Blessèd, ends by drawing her attention to the attitude of those blessèd ones who have joined in with his prayer:

> *Vedi Beatrice con quanti beati*
> *per li miei prieghi ti chiudon le mani.*

It is a scene as from a Giotto fresco: all the Blessèd, with one accord, raise their joined hands in the fervour of their desire, so humble and simple. And it culminates in the figure of the Virgin who, without speaking, signifies assent by the look of her eyes which have visibly approved and concurred in a prayer so conformable to her own benign and compassionate heart:

> *Gli occhi da Dio diletti e venerati,*
> *fissi nell'orator, ne dimostrâro*
> *quanto i devoti prieghi le son grati.*

There follows the intercession of the Virgin with God, intensely expressive because mediated by the eyes alone, those eyes which with incomparable clearness look upon the divine power and without need for words are at once understood:

> *Indi all'eterno lume si drizzâro,*
> *nel qual non si de' creder che s'invii*
> *per creatura l'occhio tanto chiaro.*

Herewith the grace sought for is conceded, and Bernard, who has been watching and aiding and guiding Dante like a kindly father, now as with paternal delight in the good fortune of a son performs his last office of directing his eyes to the vision of God:

> *Bernardo m'accennava e sorridea,*
> *perch'io guardassi in suso . . .*

It is like a family rejoicing in which all join, showing in their various actions their pleasure at the long desired and long awaited happiness which has at last befallen the one dear to them all.

Poetry springs forth from the mind of Dante even when least to be expected. He wishes to say that an instant sufficed to submerge his vision in the abyss of oblivion, and he expresses this somewhat elaborately with a mediaeval display of mythological learning:

> Un punto solo m'è maggior letargo,
> che venticinque secoli all'impresa,
> che fe' Nettuno ammirar l'ombra d'Argo.

Yes, but what a vision that last line opens up, of the ship Argo, the first ever to be launched and to cleave the waters, observed with wonder by Neptune as he feels the shadow upon his transparency. Here the first ship is espied by the god who recognizes an unprecedented violation of his realm, and not, as in the fragment of the tragedy of Accius, by an ignorant shepherd astounded to see "tanta moles" which "labitur fremebunda", pushing aside the waters with a great noise;[1] or as in Catullus' ode, by the Nereids flocking around "monstrum admirantes" and inflaming the sailors with their voluptuous nudity – a pretty touch in the Alexandrine manner.

And see how the poet gives dramatic expression to the concentration of the meditating mind, the inner flame which feeds and is itself fed by the ardour of the meditation:

> Così la mente mia, tutta sospesa,
> mirava fissa, immobile ed attenta,
> e sempre di mirar faceasi accesa.

Such are the delights, the illicit, forbidden delights enjoyed by one who sacrilegiously breaks up Dante into bits and pieces: delights unknown, of course, to the chaste and pious critics who insist upon having their Dante whole!

For my part I can only wish them, in the words of Leopardi, "Pace e vecchiezza il ciel consenta". They deserve both rewards, peace and old age, for I see they are intent upon economizing all effort, whether of brain or of nerve.

[1938]

---

1. See the fragment in *Scaenicae Romanorum poësis fragmenta*, Ribbeck's edn., I, 187-88.

53

VII

PETRARCH

THE DREAM OF LOVE OUTLASTING PASSION

Tutta la mia fiorita e verde etade
passava; e 'ntiepidir sentia già 'l foco
ch'arse il mio core; et era giunto al loco
ove scende la vita, ch'alfin cade.
  Già incominciava a prender securtade
la mia cara nemica a poco a poco
de' suoi sospetti, e rivolgeva in gioco
mie pene acerbe sua dolce onestade.
  Presso era il tempo dove Amor si scontra
con Castitate, et agli amanti è dato
sedersi insieme e dir che lor incontra.
  Morte ebbe invidia al mio felice stato,
anzi a la speme; e féglisi a l'incontra
a mezza via, come nemico armato.

More than once amid the travails of his long passion Francesco
Petrarca had turned his thoughts to this imagination of the end
of the green season and of the oncoming of autumn and winter
for himself and his love; and for an instant he had stilled the
impetuosities of the present in such a contemplation of the contrasting image of that future. He had thought upon this for the
first time at the height of his unsatisfied longings in the sonnet "Se
la mia vita", in which, foreshadowing how the years would in due
course ravage the still youthful Laura, it seemed to him that he
would then have the hardihood, the *baldanza*, to tell her of his
long travails, seeing that the season would then be *contrario ai bei
desiri*, unpropitious to gallant desires; and that from her he might
in response to the revelation receive *alcun soccorso di tardi sospiri*,
the comfort of belated sighs. In delicate and indeed barely hinted
form, this "unpropitious" and this "comfort", which is no comfort
because "belated", suggest the melancholy and the regret which
she would then feel for the unaccepted and frustrated offer of so
much love. The tone is that of elegiac premonition, something
far distant from the "covert desire and dexterous insinuation

that Laura should not tarry too long in taking pity on him"
recorded in the commentary of Carducci, who here let himself be
misled by excessive deference for the interpretation and judgement of the inexpert Muratori, inexpert, that is, in matters of love
and poetry. One of the ways of misinterpreting a poem is to read
into it that which may have been present in the circumstances of
its origin, but which the soul of the poet puts aside or will not
utter, not perhaps even to itself; and thus to convert the innocent
images of poetry into calculated means to an end.[1]

But now, as the autumnal season wore on, the thought of
Laura's fading youth, and of his own entry into the age of stilled
desires, of tamed affections, of self-reining grief and pleasure, of
readier resignation, took on a new colour and inspired in him an
unwonted mildness. The sun of life sets, but the sunset has its own
beauty, bringing something which youth did not know, and making good in one place what is being lost in another. There is no
sheer relapse into emptiness, coldness, loss of love which is the very
pulse of life. The flame dies down, but the warmth still inhabits
the soul. The woman once loved in the heyday of beauty and the
heat of the senses is still loved. The image which sprang from the
heart and took strength from the fancy is now poised beyond the
range of physical detail, being idealized, "seen with the eyes of
love", and is thus untouched by bodily change, survives through
it, retains its charm, so long as something still remains of the loved
creature, so long as she lives and breathes. The enchantment is not
broken as happens when one love is eclipsed by another, or by
the dedication of a soul to sanctity or heroism in disdain and
forgetfulness of earthly affections: it continues and exercises its
old magic power, but in novel conditions, for the sensible and
animal accompaniment of love has abated its lustfulness, removed
its weight, and thereby the higher moral and intellectual faculties
have become freed and invigorated. Thus it is given to look back

1. The above-mentioned interpretation has been further degraded by
commentators who have drawn a comparison with two frivolous sonnets
of Boccaccio ("L'alta speranza" and "S'egli advien mai") and with Bembo's
very shallow sonnet ("O superba, o crudele").

and to meditate the past without a breach in the continuity of feeling, to say frankly without concealment or pretence what one really felt and thought and desired, to confess and even to smile at one's own errors and follies, to confess that the dictates of reason were reasonable and the rigid command of virtue beneficial, to be indulgent to oneself and to others, to show a human pity for mankind, not excluding one's own self or the other creature of flesh and blood to whom one has brought suffering and who has suffered, and who is now before our eyes in the light of a new mildness, our companion on that journey of love and grief. The two lovers now appear like two convalescents recovering from that disease which is the fever of life itself. They exchange and compare impressions of what they have been through, and often the same word comes to both lips, the same surprise, sorrowful and mild, overcomes them. It is like a brief lingering upon the threshold before final departure, and to the imagination it seems that in this way after so many harsh labours and painful agitations love, with its animal passions subdued, but its better and humanly nobler aspect safe and sound, has preserved its integrity.

This season of tranquillity which Petrarch had spied from afar and then seen approaching ever nearer, is now denied him by the event of Laura's death. The verses which we have recorded tell of the unfolding of that hope, of the passing of the green and flowering age, the subsidence of fierce passion, the advancing of life on that decline which ends with envelopment in the shadow of death, and tell at the same time how the loved one was already ceasing from her suspicious and defensive waywardness and meeting his show of love with some kindly word of wit, some quiet pleasantry. And the verses go on to describe the approach of the expected moment of conciliation and release, figured in the encounter and engagement of Love with Chastity, not here two allegorical abstractions, but two real currents of feeling formerly divergent and contrasting, now reconciled and complementary. The two lovers appear not as one eluding the other, one far removed from the other, or one in humble supplication while the other remains haughty and aloof, but seated quietly side by side discoursing of their concerns as if taking counsel and making plans, after so much storm and stress, for the ordering of the brief time that remains.

This long cherished and familiar dream was so dear to the poet's heart, and so cruel was its frustration, that twice he harked back to it in two other sonnets which have been mistakenly dismissed as mere literary exercises for the display of ability in saying the same things with different words, whereas in truth (as another critic has rightly seen)[1] they spring from a need to go further in defining and specifying his feeling towards the vision of that tranquillity which he had anticipated, that renunciation without renouncing, which should have been the transition to a new rhythm of life. In the two quatrains and the first terzain of the second sonnet he resumes the sorrowful plaint against that death which had interrupted the developing process of assuagement and placation.

> Tempo era omai da trovar pace o triegua
> di tanta guerra, et erane in via forse;
> se non ch'e' lieti passi indietro torse
> chi le disuguaglianze nostre adegua.
>
> Ché, come nebbia al vento si dilegua
> così sua vita subito trascorse
> quella che già co' begli occhi mi scòrse;
> et or conven che col penser la segua.
>
> Poco aveva a 'ndugiar, che gli anni e 'l pelo
> cangiavano i costumi, onde sospetto
> non fôra il ragionar del mio mal seco.

The final terzain strives to shed a livelier colour on the scene:

> Con che onesti sospiri l'avrei detto
> le mie lunghe fatiche, ch'or dal cielo
> vede, son certo, e duolsene ancor meco!

But this sonnet, certainly inferior to the first, evidently did not satisfy Petrarch, for he took up the theme in a third, closer to the first, which adds further touches to the scene of the two lovers seated in converse together.

---

1. R. GIANI, L'amore nel "Canzoniere" di Francesco Petrarca (Turin, Bocca, 1917), pp. 230-233.

> *Tranquillo porto avea mostrato Amore*
> *A la mia lunga e torbida tempesta,*
> *fra gli anni de la età matura onesta*
> *che i vizî spoglia, e vertù veste e onore.*
>   *Già traluceva a' begli occhi il mio core*
> *e l'alta fede non più lor molesta.*
> *Ahi, Morte ria, come a schiantar se' presta*
> *il frutto di molt'anni in sì poche ore!*
>   *Pur vivendo, veniasi ove deposto*
> *in quelle caste orecchie avrei, parlando,*
> *de' miei dolci pensier l'antiqua soma;*
>   *et ella avrebbe a me forse risposto*
> *qualche santa parola, sospirando,*
> *cangiati i volti e l'una e l'altra coma.*

Wonderful is the last terzain, the deep-felt melancholy of Laura's answer, the group of the two lovers who have felt the arid blast of the wind of time, and sit, pale of aspect and grey-headed, but still lovers.

In the *Trionfo della Morte* there is more of this sweet converse which never really happened, as where the poet tells of Laura visiting him in his dreams, and relating what had been in her mind while she was on the earth; how the same flame burned in her too, and how she "feared its perilous sparks" and therefore armed herself with cold aloofness for the sake of their good repute, and how often she had to feign anger when she felt desire mounting in him, but had mild looks and words for him when she saw him aggrieved and despairing. "Teco era il cor; a me gli occhi raccolsi."

Such would indeed have been the argument of their converse had it taken place. But Laura in the *Trionfo della Morte* is no longer the faded and aged Laura, at once saint and sinner, a mortal of the earth. She has been transferred to heaven, and the terzains of the poem are prolix by contrast with the sober beauty of the sonnets.[1] Thus in the poetry of Petrarch the much longed for redemption of passion by the play of memory, of regret, of kindly reconsecration of love remains unachieved, an imagination, not an experience.

1. See DE SANCTIS, *Saggio sul Petrarca*, ed. Croce (Naples, 1907), pp. 286-8.

But had the experience been achieved, would it not have proved to be a fleeting instant, eternal indeed thanks to its intensity, but still an instant, rather than a new phase? More than a change of season in the life of love, would it not have marked a farewell to life itself, with its never to be subdued torments? Can it be conceived that a thrill of sweetness and melancholy should give rise to a placid way of life, the sort of sleepy comradeship enjoyed by two aged lovers, something like the tremulous idyll of Baucis and Philemon, recalled in this connexion by De Sanctis?[1] Surely this notion is incompatible with the note of sorrowfulness running through all this imagination, with its lingering upon Laura's *santa parola*, the rapt or holy word rounded off with a sigh? For sure, an inept comparison can impair the truth of a poem.

There is in Flaubert's novel *Éducation Sentimentale* a description of the condition of love when it has lost its glow and is emitting the last sparks. This is at the end of the novel, when Madame Arnoux, many years after, visits Frédéric who had loved and been loved by her, but been denied the enjoyment of love. She comes suddenly to his study, "à la nuit tombante", and he receives her with joyous excitement. "Dans la pénombre du crépuscule, il n'apercevait que ses yeux sous la voilette de dentelle noire qui masquait sa figure." For a long while they smile at each other without breaking silence. Then they ask questions, recount what has happened since their last meetings, recall the details of these. Like Laura she tells how she feared to be carried away and overwhelmed by passion. "J'avais peur! Oui . . . peur de vous . . . de moi!" She roams round the room, looking at the furniture, the ornaments, the portraits. Then she wants to take a stroll with him, on his arm, and, walking, they talk of their love, how strong it was on either side – "sans nous appartenir, pourtant", sighs he, and she answers, "cela vaut peut-être mieux", and she tells how she had come to see that he loved her and of her anxiety and delight in his passion and his reticence. Hearing this, "il ne regretta rien. Ses souffrances d'autrefois étaient payées". They return indoors, Ma-

1. Ibid., pp. 237-8.

dame Arnoux removes her hat, and "la lampe, posée sur une console, éclaira ses cheveux blancs". This is for him like a blow on the chest, but he dissembles, sits at her knees, takes her hands, and tells her fervently all that he had not been able to say before, and she listens to this outpouring addressed to the woman that she no longer is. In the intimacy of this talk, the nearness of their bodies, the old desire awakens in him, furious, violent. "Cependant il sentait quelque chose d'inexprimable, une répulsion et comme l'effroi d'un inceste." She was a woman, but she had been raised by him to an ideal, and now he could not bring himself to "dégrader son idéal". He breaks away, rolls a cigarette. The clock strikes eleven, in a quarter of an hour she must go. "Tous les deux ne trouvaient plus rien à se dire. Il y a un moment, dans les séparations, où la personne aimée n'est déjà plus avec vous." She rises and says goodbye. "Je ne vous reverrai jamais! C'était ma dernière démarche de femme. Mon âme ne vous quittera pas. Que toutes les bénédictions du ciel soient sur vous." Before leaving she asks for scissors, undoes her hair and cuts a long tress. "Gardez-les! adieu." From the window he watches her call a carriage and drive away. "Et ce fut tout."

I have told the story in broad outline with the help of a few selected phrases. But these pages of Flaubert, judged by the standard of beauty, deserve to stand alongside of the exquisite lyrics of Petrarch, are, in fact, under the guise of a narrative, a kind of lyric, perfect in its own way. I take pleasure in insisting upon this at a time when it is fashionable to run down the poet-novelist and at the same time to fall into ecstasies over the so-called pure or quintessential lyric, usually a laboured compost of poor and disconnected sense-impressions and abstract designs. But lyricism is a delicate flower which opens under the sun of poetry on no other soil than that of the human heart.

[1937]

VIII

THE POETICAL QUALITY OF BOCCACCIO

Recent Italian criticism has progressively reached the correct conclusion that Boccaccio in his prose works, above all in the *Decameron*, is a poetic and not a prosaic writer. Whether or not authentic, the quip attributed to Salviati that Boccaccio *non fece mai verso che avesse verso nel verso* has a good deal of truth about it: Boccaccio's real verse was indeed in his prose. This is not, be it noted, "poetical prose" of the hybrid type sometimes so described, but quite simply poetry, a poet's song, difficult though it be to analyse its metres or classify them according to the metrical rules which for that matter are always inadequate measures of poetry. How could one designate as prose the writings of one so innocent of the critical, argumentative, or didactic vein as Boccaccio, so wholly given up to the utterance of sense and fancy? How can it be imagined that his musical periods would gain by being shorn of their rhythm, their upward and downward beats, the so-called inversions, the dying falls, and so forth, and rendered smooth and crisp and even? One might as well turn Dante's terzains, Ariosto's octaves, and Foscolo's blank verse into prose, an exercise now discarded even in schools. And certain long speeches placed in the mouths of Boccaccio's characters are not to be comprehended by the standards of ordinary conversation, which would indeed require them to be more rapid and various and broken up into question and answer. Their tone and purpose is only to be understood by standards akin to those of epic and dramatic poetry.

For centuries they were judged otherwise. Boccaccio's prose was dubbed artificial and was accused of bad influence upon later prose-writers. This was in part the reflection of an insensibility to poetic value, and of a confusion between poetry and prose. Given these, the charge was natural, for poetry is certainly not a good model for prose, the two being quite different. In justice, however, it must be acknowledged that the traditional judgement has something more than this to support it. In the abundant writings of

Boccaccio we meet not only the seeming prose which is really poetry, but also that other sort of prose – "rhetorical", "literary", or "humanistic" – derived from the study of Cicero and the ancients, and from love of mythology and ornate trappings: a prose which is not like that other prose, inwardly expressive of poetic feeling, but accepted and entertained in its ready-made elegance. This humanistic prose is what we chiefly meet in some of the minor works like the *Filocolo* and the *Ameto*, and here and there in other works, even in the *Decameron*; and it was this alone which lent itself to cultivation and imitation, for what is poetic, like all else that is individual and original, cannot be imitated but can only give rise to diversity. There was some justification, then, for the protests raised against this second sort of Boccaccian prose by writers who jibbed at heavy stateliness in their enthusiasm for a homely and spontaneous fashion, and in later times for all those anti-academic spirits, rationalists, polemists, propagandists, who wanted things and not words, fruit and not leafage, and in still later times for the school of Manzoni and others who demanded a literature suitable for educating the Italian people in clarity of thought and modest, simple modes of language. But once their purpose had been more or less attained, that sort of judgement on Boccaccio and on his bad influence lost significance and has now been almost forgotten, though not officially reversed. Yet even so, while recognizing some justification for the reproaches delivered against Boccaccism from that educational standpoint, it is necessary to urge a certain respect even for the humanistic and rhetorical prose of Boccaccio and others, a certain attention to the value and utility which they had. This style (and the same could be said of "Petrarchism") was a useful training in complexity and refinement of language, and served at different times as a corrective to the slipshod prose of the eighteenth century and to the prose of the Romantic school with its "sobbing periods", so much detested by Puoti and similar purists, and finally to the excesses of the Manzonian "bourgeois" prose itself, against which Carducci promoted a reaction.

Still, whatever we may think about the value of the humanistic and rhetorical prose of Boccaccio, we must not confound it with that real and great and clear prose of his which is poetry, a confusion into which even De Sanctis sometimes fell in his analysis of Boccaccio's sentence construction, and in such quips as the well-known one that "Boccaccio has the mind of a Plautus and the style of a Cicero".

Now if Boccaccio is a poet, there is another judgement upon him, springing from the nineteenth-century envisagement of the history of poetry as an ethical and social history, or as a close parallel to this latter history, which should not be allowed to stand, and is, in fact, in course of elimination. Once again we will take our formulation of this judgement from its best and most authoritative spokesman, De Sanctis. De Sanctis figures Boccaccio as the opposite of Dante, the adversary of the Middle Age, the representative of a sensuality, a comedy, a satire, ousting the deep and sincere life of the feelings, and so a symbolic figure of the new Italy which persisted from the Renaissance to the beginnings of the Risorgimento, the Italy which dozed in a voluptuous idyll, mocked merrily at all things sacred and profane, and took no heed for anything else.

Even were that a proper assessment of the spiritual life of Italy over a period of three or four centuries (in fact such an account is highly exaggerated and conventionalized), the view of Boccaccio which it implies can only be supported by the evidence of one or two of his ideas and attitudes. But such is not the essential Boccaccio, who on the contrary is a poet. To be a poet means always to rise from the level of practical inclinations to that of a full humanity, in which sensuality and laughter themselves undergo a transformation into something greater. Boccaccio had not passed through the moral and intellectual experiences of the Dante whom perhaps he so loved and revered just because Dante was so different and in a certain sense stood so much higher. Boccaccio was not marked out as a man of faith, ideals, and striving (whether religious, ethical, or political); he did not plumb the deeper struggles of a soul seeking its perfection or of the will straining to perform its duty. His were above all the youthful experiences of the ardent lover, convinced of the invincible might of love in the human breast, and at the same time those of the contemplator of human follies who respects those who are prudent and clever enough to turn these to their own ends, and takes pleasure in their wiliness and wit. Yet, rising above the level of these experiences to that of poetry, he could not but attain to the touching vision of human affections in general, suffering as well as delight, wonder as well as gaiety. On the poetic level there is in fact nothing more to say about the contrast between Boccaccio and Dante than that the one was not the other, any more than he was some third poet. It seems very obvious, but such things have to be repeated as a protection against "odious" comparisons and the distortions to which they give rise.

Let us examine one of those tales of Boccaccio which are accounted sensual and lascivious, the tale of the nightingale, the tale of Messer Lizio da Valbona and of his daughter. This daughter of Lizio's old age was guarded with all jealous care by the affectionate father and the mother, but she hits it off with a fine young man who comes to the house, and in order to procure a meeting with this beau she conceives the device of feigning to fret and toss in the hot nights in her little chamber, and asks to be allowed to sleep on the adjoining terrace in the cool air where she can hear also the sweet song of the nightingale. The father's resistance is overcome partly by the indulgent plea of the mother, the stratagem is put into effect, and the bold young man climbs up to the terrace and lingers so long with the girl that the rising sun finds them asleep in each other's arms. The father, coming to see how the girl has slept, draws back the curtain and sees the amorous spectacle, but instead of giving way to anger quietly calls his wife and resignedly points to the scene. Then, waking them up, he makes the two take the marriage oath in his presence and then leaves them happy on the couch which has become an improvised marriage-bed. Where in this tale is the luscious sensuality and lasciviousness which, if one is looking for a comparison, can certainly be found in the French variant of the same story told in the appendix to the *Contes* of La Fontaine? Boccaccio's poem breathes a smiling sensitiveness to that love which, by hook or crook, always wins its way, overcomes all obstacles, gives a little girl the advantage in a trial of wits with two elderly and experienced people who have done their utmost to conjure precisely that peril. The father is stern, irritable, and impatient with his tricksy daughter, but once the accomplished fact has demonstrated rudely that nothing could tame the untamable, he does not lose his temper but seems almost to have foreseen the event, which thus comes to lack any outrageous or astounding character. He simply takes the step which is required to regularize the triumph of instinct over regimentation. Up to that point his function was that of father, guardian, tutor, but now he must just play the man who has known and not forgotten the reality of men's feelings and passions. The young couple are in startled confusion, the girl ashamed of the situation in which she has been discovered, the youth conscious of his betrayal of the trust of the friendly father, and fearing punishment. But neither would have been disobedient and deceitful or done any harm had not love carried them away, they themselves hardly know how. What Messer Lizio says when he calls his wife to observe the spectacle and draws attention to the attitude of the sleeping daughter is humorous in the extreme, a comical comment upon himself and his daughter, an effusion of comprehension and kindliness. So at least anyone must feel who gives himself up to the music of Boccaccio's style and imagination instead of lingering crudely upon material details.

Let us look at just one other example, a tale reckoned among his most satirical, a sort of foretaste of Voltaire, the tale of Ser Ciappelletto. Where, in this, are to be found blatant and wounding shafts against the monks, the business of canonization, or the credulity of believers? For that matter laughter, caricature, and farce are all lacking in it. The scoundrel himself and the merchant who entrusts him with a business enterprise and the two usurers who give him hospitality all behave, according to their respective lights, reasonably and purposefully. So too does the friar, "a man of years, of devout and righteous conduct, well versed in the scriptures, a venerable man", who is called in to hear the scoundrel's last confession, and questions the "penitent" diligently and scrupulously, indeed with a certain breadth of view which is quite unfanatical. If he is hoodwinked, so in the circumstances would anyone else have been unless Ser Ciappelletto had happened to run into a confessor as brilliant, naughty, and bad as himself, who might have spotted his type by signs overlooked by others. All our attention is concentrated upon Ser Ciappelletto, who whatever may be said of him from the moral viewpoint is in himself a wonderful human or, if one will, demonic force (the demon himself, after all, is human); wonderful in his power of observation, inference, and deduction, wonderful in his artistry as he imagines or plays a part, compelling the onlooker's sympathy. All his life he must have been thoroughly exploring the mentality of friars and confessors, attentively noting how they talk and how they must be talked to to win their confidence, memorizing the choicest and aptest expressions of contrition, fervour, devotion, and piety! "God has sent me this trial", "God, who has given me the strength . . .", "That true and veritable body of Christ", "The Saviour who redeemed me by his precious blood" – why should he have noted and treasured these phrases, meaningless and useless for himself, unless in the spirit of an artist stocking the imagination and the memory? It is the whim of an artist, who enjoys doing what he can do well, and does it primarily just for his own exclusive pleasure, even if he quite likes having a small audience to admire his rhetorical prowess, it is this whim, and not any concern for the interest of his hosts, a matter of total indifference to him, which makes him so ready with a plan to save their face. He is not a scoffer eager to display his impiety and to offend God yet once again in the most outrageous of manners, like certain atheists who behave as though they were personal enemies of God, challenging him with defiance and raillery. Ser Ciappelletto is wholly indifferent to God, uninterested in him, careless whether he does or does not exist. For him it is men who exist, and he himself who knows how to handle them, cozen them, ruin them, make a mockery or plaything of them, despising them all the time. Alive and healthy he had done all this in the way of business, now on his deathbed he would do it by another and final mode of trickery, by dying in the odour of sanctity. *Qualis artifex pereo,* Ser Ciappelletto could say, like Nero, but in his mouth there would be no regret, only the gay assertion of his triumphant power. The poet Boccaccio thrills again to the art of Ser Ciappelletto, watching him with tense and unflagging admiration. What does he admire so much? It is, as we have said, that human force of intelligence, experience, imagination, will, expressiveness, that unique sublimation of the wariness and wiliness which had always interested him so greatly. And for all the black character that he attributes to Ser Ciappelletto, he makes friends with him and brings us to the same sentiment so that we take leave of him not with a shudder but with a smile as for a brilliant oddity, and we have an inkling that God himself would smile and show clemency so as not to lose such an artist from the circle of his heavenly court, and not to encourage the opinion voiced in the Renaissance that good company was only to be enjoyed in hell. The tale, from beginning to end, is factual, fluent, animated, free of argument, but pervaded by the feelings of admiration and astonishment. The periods are veritable strophes. Take for example this which falls from the lips of the penitent:

"Disse allora ser Ciappelletto: — Oimè, padre mio, che dite voi? La mamma mia dolce, che mi portò in corpo nove mesi il dì e la notte, e portommi in collo più di cento volte, troppo feci male a bestemmiarla, e troppo è gran peccato; e se voi non pregate Iddio per me, egli non mi sarà perdonato." (Then spake Ciappelletto: — Alack, father, what sayest thou? My dear mother that bore me in her body nine months day and night, and after that more than an hundred times upon her shoulders — too wicked was I to curse her, too great a sin it is. Pray God for me, else it can never be forgiven.)

There is a different tone in those strophes which render the active life of the hero:

"Egli, essendo notaio, aveva grandissima vergogna quando uno de' suoi strumenti (come che pochi ne facesse) fosse altro che falso trovato: de' quali tanti avrebbe fatti, di quanti fosse richiesto, e quel-

li più volentieri in dono che alcun altro grandemente salariato. Te-
stimonianze false con sommo diletto diceva, richiesto e non richiesto . . ." (As a man of law, it shamed him greatly when one of his
deeds (it happened but seldom) was found not to be falsely drawn.
False deeds he would draw as many as they asked him for, and
gave them for the asking more readily than at a great price. For
false witness, he was ever ready to bear it, asked or unasked . . .)

Of a similar and comparable inspiration to this, but drawn with
a somewhat coarser and less attentive art, is the figure of Margutte,
in Luigi Pulci's *Morgante Maggiore* – Margutte, loaded with the
vices of Turk and Greek, indeed with all those known to the
region of hell, seventy-seven mortal sins and venial sins unnumbered, whom the very human Morgant nevertheless mourns on his
death because of his agreeableness, his *piacevolezza*.

The atmosphere of these tales, which are customarily considered
merely sensual and satirical, is, then, in truth much wider and
freer, and having shown this it is hardly necessary for our purposes
to go over the well-trodden ground of the situations, affections,
sentiments, outside the range of the sensual and the comic, which
enliven the *Decameron* and also parts of other works of Boccaccio,
particularly the *Filostrato* and the *Fiammetta* – agonizing adventures,
sacrifices inspired by love in no narrow sense of this word,
displays of loyalty and generosity, resolute confrontations of
death. Nor need we pass in review the variety of Boccaccio's
characters, the undulation of his style, the colourful depiction not
only of personages in their stillness or motion, but also of natural
scenes of earth and land, forests, countrysides frost-bound or sun-
baked, storms, shipwrecks, desert isles, or again lonely city alleys
where strange things happen of nights. For that matter we will
not repeat the saying that the *Decameron* contains the "whole
human comedy", for that is a merely emphatic and, really, shallow statement. Still less will we describe the *Decameron* as "the
mirror of the daily life of that time", this being as untrue of Boccaccio's work as of any other poem. The poets are not "mirrors",
least of all mirrors of extraneous circumstances. What, on the
contrary, we will recall with insistence is that Boccaccio like every

other individual poet works upon a restricted material, and that while his spirit is open to that which is high, noble, generous, lamentable, and tragic, he has his own way of embracing these feelings, that of a man whose feet are firmly on the ground, one not given to renunciations, who regards the war of extermination waged by the spirit against the flesh as foolish and monstrous. When Ghismonda's love is discovered by her father, and she knows that Guiscardo has been captured and believes him already lost to her, tears well in her eyes and she would fain break into lamentation, but she proudly masters her weakness: "with wondrous strength she calmed her features, and ere making any petition for herself, resolved in her own mind to die, believing her Guiscardo already dead". And she addresses her father, firmly and quietly, but with feeling, showing herself a woman of intelligence and decision, but still also a woman of flesh and blood not afraid of hinting at the rightful importance for herself of her amorous desire. Indeed in one breath she affirms this natural right and also the prudence and measure and carefulness of her conduct. Her father, on hearing her, esteems the "greatness of mind" of his daughter. Such are all or almost all the heroines of love and death whom Boccaccio brings on his stage. On the other hand Boccaccio, as we have said, ignores the stern travails of the moral and religious conscience. He likes to conceive of virtue in its noble and carefree aspect, in the magnificence and stateliness of the chivalric ideal, carried to its extreme in extraordinary events and situations, in surprising and incredible actions. And this, one may remark, should modify the customary judgement which sees Boccaccio in complete contrast with the Middle Age, for on the contrary in the early poems and romances and also in the *Decameron* the motives of mediaeval chivalry bulk large. The chivalric ideal was shortly to become in Italy matter for mockery, but Boccaccio did not herald that development. It is alleged that Boccaccio, so concrete and realistic in his depictions of sensual passion and comedy, becomes abstract, exaggerated, and conventional when he passes on to treat of the sublimity of virtue in another sense. But this is not so, nor does it suffice to adduce the tale of Griselda or that of Natan and Mitridanes, or portions of this, for against these one may throw into the scale those of Messer Torello and the Saladin, of the Count of Anguersa, Madonna Beritola, Federico degli Alberighi, and others like them. All that need be said is that even in the *Decameron* a detailed examination shows us that not all is equally strong and vivid, or inspired with equal warmth. In any case a Boccaccio shorn of his ideal of chivalric magnificence – that ideal which was the counterpart of his assertion of sensual joy and of his observation of the comic, and thus restored the balance of a complete view of life, at once real and ideal – would be only a half Boccaccio.

[1931]

IX

ARIOSTO

At the touch of that harmony which welled from the depth of the poet's nature, the variously graded hierarchy of the sentiments native to Ariosto underwent a first transformation.[1] They ceased to be autonomous, they became subordinate to a single mastery, they were no longer wholes but parts, no longer motives but occasions, no longer ends but instrumentalities. Perishing, they transmitted their vitality to a new life.

The magic power which accomplished that prodigy was a tone of expression, it was in fact that disengaged, light, infinitely various, ever charming tone which the old critics termed Ariosto's "confidential air", accounting it as one of the "properties" of his "style". And it is in this that his style wholly consists; indeed, since the style is nothing else than the expression and the very soul of a poet, this was the essential Ariosto in his harmonious poetizing.

The reduction and destruction of the sentiments under the impact of the expressive tone is palpable in the prefaces of the single cantos, in the argumentative asides, the incidental observations, the coming back to the point, the choice of vocabulary, the sentence structure, but above all in those similes, which form pictures in themselves, designed not to reinforce the stress of feeling but to relax it, and in the sudden interruption with which the poet truncates his narratives sometimes at the most dramatic moment, leaping with agility to some other recital of a different and often altogether opposite nature. So much is palpable, can be prosaically isolated and analysed. But this is only a small feature of the impalpable whole which runs like a subtle fluid, not to be grasped by the apparatus of learning, but only as soul known by soul.

This tone is also to be identified with the often noted and named but never well defined Ariostean irony, which has eluded

1. These sentiments were described in the fourth chapter of my essay on Ariosto in *Ariosto, Shakespeare e Corneille*.

definition by being often taken for a sort of playfulness or mockery similar or identical to that sometimes employed by the poet in his contemplation of chivalric personages and their adventures. But thus to define it would be to restrict its range and coarsen its character. It should always be kept in mind that this irony does not invest certain sentiments, for example the chivalric and the religious, and spare others, but invests all equally, and is thus not an idle game but something much loftier, pertaining purely to art and poetry, the victory of the fundamental motive over all the others.

All the sentiments, the sublime and the playful, the tender and the strong, the outpourings of the heart and the devisings of the intelligence, the love talk and the laudatory catalogues of names, the descriptions of battles and the words of wit, all are equally abased and equally raised up again in the enveloping irony. On the newly levelled ground there arises the miracle of the Ariostean octave, alive with a life of its own; an octave which is most inadequately described as "smiling", unless smile be said in an ideal sense, as the manifestation of a life free and harmonious, balanced and energetic, pulsating richly through the veins and finding repose in this very pulsation. These octaves have the corporeal quality sometimes of flowering girlhood, sometimes rather of a well-formed and supple limbed masculine youthfulness which troubles not to display its muscular prowess because every attitude and gesture proclaims this. – Olimpia, after many vicissitudes, and a long and stormy sea journey, lands with her lover on a wild desert island:

> Il travaglio del mare e la paura,
> che tenuta alcun dì l'aveano desta;
> il ritrovarsi al lito ora sicura,
> lontana da rumor, ne la foresta;
> e che nessun pensier, nessuna cura,
> poi che 'l suo amante ha seco, la molesta;
> fûr cagion ch'ebbe Olimpia sì gran sonno,
> che gli orsi e i ghiri aver maggior non ponno.

Here all the reasons for the deep sleep of Olimpia are accurately set forth; but all that is clearly secondary to the intimate sentiment conveyed by the octave which seems to take pleasure in itself, and really does take such pleasure in the resolution of a movement, a becoming, into its accomplishment. – Again, Bradamante and Marfisa, joining forces, vainly hunt King Agramante, to kill him:

> Come due belle e generose parde
> che fuor del lascio sien di pari uscite,
> poscia ch'i cervi o le capre gagliarde
> indarno aver si veggano seguite,
> vergognandosi quasi che fûr tarde,
> sdegnose se ne tornano e pentite;
> così tornâr le due donzelle, quando
> videro il Pagan salvo, sospirando.

The same process here, and the same result. But these are to be observed even where there appears to be nothing of intrinsic interest in the material, but only, it may be, a conventional notion or a complimentary phrase by way of courtly homage or expression of friendship and esteem. To say of a fair lady, "In every act she appears a Goddess come down from heaven", is a commonplace. But Ariosto gives this such a turn and a rhythm that one feels the Goddess majestically descending amid the wonder and reverence of witnesses and rivals – truly, a little drama:

> Julia Gonzaga, che dovunque il piede
> volge, e dovunque i sereni occhi gira,
> non pur ogn'altra di beltà le cede,
> ma, come scesa dal ciel Dea, l'ammira ...

To assemble a mere string of names of admired persons, varying the bare succession at most with an obvious play of words, is even more commonplace, but Ariosto arranges the names of the contemporary painters as though in a Parnassus, placing the greatest of them in a special niche and managing by sheer mastery of stress and accentuation to make each of the names resound as if full of life and meaning:

> E quei che fûro a' nostri dì, o sono ora,
> Leonardo, Andrea Mantegna, Gian Bellino,
> duo Dossi, e quel ch'a par sculpe e colora,
> Michel, più che mortal, Angel divino ...

The "sentences" or judgements of Ariosto were by De Sanctis regarded as "obvious", "not deep or original", and others have added "banal" and even "contradictory". But they are judgements of Ariosto, matter not for thought, but for song:

> Oh gran contrasto in giovenil pensiero,
> desir di laude, ed impeto d'amore!
> Né, chi più vaglia, ancor si trova il vero,
> ché resta or questo or quel superïore . . .

Even in those risky passages where another writer would have plunged into sheer lasciviousness, Ariosto manages at one and the same time to reduce and to refashion his argument, for example in Ricciardetto's adventure with Fiordispina:

> Non rumor di tamburi o suon di trombe
> furon principio all'amoroso assalto;
> ma baci, ch'imitavan le colombe,
> davan segno or di gire, or di fare alto . . .

Ariosto's irony, like to the eye of God surveying the motions of his creation, whole and entire, seems to love it equally in all its parts, the good and the bad, the vast and the minute, man and the grain of sand, because all of it is his handiwork, and in it he heeds nothing else than the motion itself, the eternal dialectic, the rhythm and the harmony. The meaning of "irony" has here shifted from the common use of the word to that which the followers of Fichte, the Romantics, gave to it. And we would be glad to use it in this sense to explain the nature of Ariosto's inspiration, had not those thinkers and men of letters gone on to confound irony with so called "humourism", an attitude of oddity and extravagance, disturbing and destructive to art. The critical judgement which we propose lies on the contrary altogether within the sphere of art, within which Ariosto himself steadily remained, never straying weakly in the direction of would-be humour and extravagance, but displaying the irony of an artist aware of his own strength. This perhaps is why Ariosto was never much appreciated by the streaming-haired Romantics, who preferred Rabelais or even Carlo Gozzi.

To disarm the whole hierarchy of sentiments, to level them

down all equally, to deprive all objects of their autonomy, of
their particular life and soul – this amounts to converting the
world of the spirit into a world of nature: an unreal world
which exists only by virtue of our positing it. In a certain sense
the whole world becomes for Ariosto "nature", a lined and coloured surface, shining but unsubstantial. With the keen observation
of a descriptive naturalist he scans the objects in all their features,
and not, like other artists of genius, with exclusive attention to
one feature which for them is important. With him there is no
passionate impatience, no casting aside of the irrelevant. His
portrait of Saint John might seem to smack of smiling irreverence:

> che 'l manto ha rosso e bianca la gonnella,
> che l'un può al latte, l'altro al minio opporre;
> i crini ha bianchi e bianca la mascella
> di folta barba ch'al petto discorre . . .

But the same method serves him for depicting the beauteous
Olimpia, forgetful of her chastity, which might have suggested a
different choice of features or still more appropriately some hint of
covering veils:

> Le bellezze d'Olimpia eran di quelle
> che son più rare; e non la fronte sola,
> gli occhi, e le guancie, e le chiome avea belle,
> la bocca, il naso, gli omeri e la gola . . .

And it serves him even for the single-hearted and courageous
Medoro, whose youthful heroism might seem to call for less
attention to his flourishing young person and more to the indications of his bravery and devotion:

> Medoro avea la guancia colorita,
> e bianca e grata ne la età novella . . .

The ever recurring portraiture of the characters and description of
the setting in which they are discovered, with the accompanying
scenes of animal life and reports of natural phenomena, make up
the more obvious and palpable side of this process of converting
the human world into a world of nature. We will refrain here from
statistics, if only because a German scholar has with intolerable

and cloying conscientiousness enumerated the depictions, the similes, and the metaphors of Ariosto in a heavy volume.

It has been wrongly inferred from this apparent naturalization
or objectivization (which as we have shown has really a profoundly
subjective character) that the quality of Ariosto, his form, is that
of the cold and indifferent observer, entirely concentrated upon
things. And this diagnosis has linked Ariosto with his contemporary Machiavelli, of whom it is conventionally said that he conducted
an acute investigation into history and politics, described their
process, formulated their laws, and uttered his own conclusions
in the inexorable objectivity and scientific coldness of his prose.
In a certain rather strained sense it is true that both the prose-
writer and the poet in their diverse fields and for different purposes
destroyed a pre-existing spiritual content – in Machiavelli's case
it was the mediaeval religious conception of history and politics –
by their naturalism. But such a summing up of Machiavelli, the
thinker who pored over the facts and illuminated them with a
fresh intellectual vigour, the writer who used the vehicle of a
cold style to express his stern passion, is really no better than a
vivid stroke of description, just as it is by no more than a metaphor
that Ariosto is summed up as naturalistic and objective, seeing
that in truth his naturalism was a step towards a new spiritualism,
a creation of spiritual forms of harmony.

We shall do well, however, in correspondence with our own
conclusions, to withdraw the customary tribute paid to Ariosto
either for his epic quality, that epic nobility and glamour so much
praised by Galileo, and by other critics, both ancient and modern, or for the alleged admirable coherency of his characters.
For how could there be, in the *Orlando Furioso,* an epic quality
when its author not only lacked the ethical sentiments proper to
epic poetry, but proceeded to dissolve in harmony and irony
even such scraps of the epic tradition as he might, somewhat du-
biously, seem to have inherited? How could there be found, in
this poem, characters in any true sense, if in art the characters of
the personages can only be the various, diverse, and contrasting
notes of the poet's soul, incarnated in creatures which seem to live

their own individual lives, but in truth live all with the same life
variously distributed among them, sparks from one central flame?
It is a gross error of critical approach to think of the characters as
living on their own account, as though they could continue their
life outside the work of art to which they belong, equally and
conjointly with the strophes, the verses, and the words. In the
Orlando Furioso, where the passionate sentiments are all subdued
and muted, we find not characters but outlined and tinted figures,
without depth or relief: and the features are generic or typical
rather than individual. The various knights are all much of a
piece, differentiated only by their goodness or badness, courtesy
or rudeness, or by some external and accidental attribute, if not
simply by their names. The women in the same way are differentiated as amorous or perfidious, as virtuous and content with a
single love, or dissolute and perverse, or else by the diversity of
their adventures or the names they boast. Much the same goes for
the episodes and descriptions (the madness of Orlando is scarcely
if at all individualized, but merely typical, and only by way of
fulsome compliment could it ever have been compared with the
madness of King Lear), and the same, again, for the delineation
of landscapes, palaces, gardens, and other objects. Even the coherence of the characters in the very crude sense of a conformity
to established type has sometimes rightly been found wanting,
for these personages often play fast and loose with their own
characteristics as and when required by their adventures, or rather
the exigences of their author.

These observations are not pointless, since the demand for objectively shaped and coherent characters has led not only to
eulogies of Ariosto on the part of those who have thought that
he supplied them, but also to equally unfounded censures on the
part of those who have missed them. Thus De Sanctis on one
occasion pronounced Ariosto's feminine creations to be inferior
to those of Dante, Shakespeare, and Goethe. The comparison is an
impossible one. Angelica, Olimpia, and Isabella most certainly
lack the passional intensity of Francesca, Desdemona, and Gretchen, but the latter lack the harmonious octaves in which Ariosto's

women enjoy their activity and their repose, indeed their very existence. Or rather, neither of these groups lacks anything except by the standard of a misguided criticism, for no real deficiency or poetic contradiction is involved in these apparent shortcomings. De Sanctis further found the sentiment of nature to be lacking in Ariosto, and charged this as a deficiency; but, as the great teacher De Sanctis himself used to say, the sentiment of nature arises not from nature, but from the attitudes of the spirit of man, the sense of comfort, melancholy, or religious terror which man himself infuses into nature and then discovers it where he has placed it. But these attitudes, in their differentiation, were incompatible with the fundamental attitude of Ariosto himself, and if they had strayed into his poem, sounding some note of sentiment, this would quickly have been felt as discordant and anomalous. Another objectivist critic, Lessing, deemed Ariosto's depiction of the beauties of Alcina to have badly overstepped the limits of poetry. De Sanctis retorted that what Lessing blamed, the material quality of the description, was in this context the very quintessence of the poetry, for the beauties of the witch Alcina, being a fraudulent disguise, called for a material description. The charge was unjust, but the retort, though highly ingenious, was also not quite justified, for as we have seen Ariosto's mode of description is always like that, whether he be delineating a true beauty like Olimpia or a false beauty like Alcina. The true answer surely is that it is quite vain to look for rapid, energetic portrayals, live likenesses, in Ariosto. Such portraits fixed with a stroke or two of the brush are the product of a way of feeling which Ariosto either could not command, or suppressed in himself. Those *occhi ridenti e fuggitivi*, the shyly smiling eyes which wholly fix Leopardi's Silvia, or the *doux sourire amoureux et souffrant* which fix De Vigny's soul-mate in the *Maison du Berger*, are in the range of those poets, and not of Ariosto.

There are two mistaken ways of reading the *Orlando Furioso*. The first is to set forth as though one were reading a well-phrased book of high moral inspiration, like the *Promessi Sposi*, pursuing through all its portions the workings of a serious process of the

human affections which circulates throughout the whole, inform-
ing and shaping even its smallest details. The second is the method
suitable for reading such a work as *Faust*, that is to say works in
which the general composition, being determined more or less by
intellectual considerations, does not wholly match the poetical
inspiration of its several parts, so that the poetical parts have to
be distinguished from the unpoetical bridges or links, and the
reader, if poetically sensitive, hurries through the latter in order
to linger with delight over the former. The *Orlando Furioso* is as
free as any work of human imperfection could be from the
unevenness of this second order of works. It is a work of even
composition, yet it lacks the particular form of passionate seriousness which pervades the former order and inspires portions of
the latter. It has to be read, therefore, in a third way. The reader
must follow the details of the tales and the descriptions, but look
beyond them to a content which is always the same, yet clothes
itself in ever novel shapes, and attracts us by the simultaneity of
this sameness and this inexhaustible variety.

As may be seen, this judgement endorses and yet rectifies the
judgement which, it may be said, has accompanied the *Orlando
Furioso* from the moment of its first appearance, the judgement
that it is a work devoid of seriousness, light, gay, pleasant, frivolous. Cardinal Sadoleto in the authorization which he gave in the
name of Leo X for publication of the edition of 1516 described
it as composed *ludicro more*, though he added – perhaps translating
words of the poet himself – *longo tamen studio et cogitatione multisque
vigiliis confectum*. Bernardo Tasso, Trissino, Speroni, and other
such grave and pedantic persons did not fail to blame Ariosto for
framing his poem for the sole end of entertainment. And Boileau
termed it a mere collection of *fables comiques*, Sulzer a "poem
designed purely for entertainment, unguided by reason", Home
"unbridled and extravagant", riddled with interruptions and tedious through its excessive variety. Even today the school manuals
often draw up a sort of balance-sheet in which such assets as the
perfection of the octave, the liveliness of the narration, the agility,
are weighed against such liabilities as lack of deep feeling, light

without warmth, inability to stir the heart. One may agree with this, subject to the remark that the authors of such judgements see and note everything which is on the level of their eyes but do not lift their eyes upwards to the outstanding virtue thanks to which Ariosto's frivolity discovers itself as a deep and rare seriousness, the deep commotion of a heart which in its rare and subtle gentleness is somewhat aloof from those commotions which are ordinarily considered to belong to life and reality.

Aloof, not sundered or alien or indifferent. Resuming and developing the analysis we have already begun, it is well to utter a warning against a facile misinterpretation of the "destruction" which is procured by the mood and the irony of Ariosto. This is not a total destruction and annihilation, but a destruction in the philosophic sense which implies also conservation. Were it otherwise, what would be the use of the variegated material and affective content of the poem which we have passed in review? As Don Ferrante in the *Promessi Sposi* would have put it: Are the stars in heaven just fixed there like pins in a pin-cushion? A total indifference of the feelings, a lack of content, may lie at the root of other men's rhetoric, but not, for sure, of the poetry of Ariosto. Let us not confound rouge plastered upon dead cheeks with a rosy blush which adorns the living. From indifference springs the soft and verbal musicality of the *Adone*, not the octave of the *Orlando Furioso*. From indifference sprang also (I quote once again that old enthusiast for Ariosto, Giraldi Cintio, with his distinction between the "facility" of Ariosto and the "sweet sound void of sentiment" of other poets) those eight hundred stanzas of one of Giraldi's contemporaries which, he says "seemed to have been gathered from the flowery meads of poetry, so full of grace did they appear as one passed from one to another, but taken all together were so empty of sense that they seemed sprung, rather, from the soil of childishness", for their author had been "solely intent upon the delight which springs from the glamour and choice of words, and had wholly neglected the dignity and value which springs from judgement".

If Ariosto, in the act of composing his poem, had not passionately embraced, in all their due variety as already described, the materials entering into his poem, then there would simply have been no impetus, enthusiasm, thought, or emphasis, for him to temper and subdue to the harmonious set of his own soul. He would have come cold to his poetic task, and true poetry can never be conceived in coldness. Coldness, I think, characterized the origin of those five cantos which he suppressed and replaced by others. In these one recognizes everywhere of course Ariosto's usual adroit touch in the descriptions and the transitions, and they contain all the usual Ariostean elements – tales of war, chivalric adventures, love stories (the love of Penticone for the wife of Ottone, and of Astolfo for the wife of Gismondo), satirical stories (the foundation of the city of Medea and the sexual law which she there imposed), astounding inventions (the knights imprisoned in the body of the whale where they have bedroom, kitchen, and dining hall) and copious moral and political reflections (on jealousy, ambition, and against unjust masters and mercenary troops). Nevertheless we feel that Ariosto wrote them at an unfortunate moment, not in the full vein of poetry, but somewhat against the grain, and without the necessary engagement and warmth. Even in the (canonical) *Orlando Furioso* are there not passages where he languishes? Not, it would seem, in the forty cantos of the first edition, the work of his twelve-year-long poetic springtime, but surely in the later additions all of which, as might be shown, are of merely intellectual origin, and are therefore, except for the episode of Olimpia, little loved or read. The clearest sign of merely intellectual elaboration is in the long-delayed conclusion of the poem, with the double betrothal of Bradamante and the competition in courtesy between Leone and Ruggiero. Here the tone occasionally becomes positively pedestrian. And behold, the philological scholars, straying into the realm of critical appraisal, have hit upon these very episodes, where Ariosto's genius languishes, and upon the five cantos where it stumbles and misses its aim, as showing evidence of an Ariosto advancing on the way of progress, becoming "serious", and stretching out a hand (could it be believed?) to Torquato Tasso!

For readers who find the formulae of philosophy distasteful or
difficult, the process of "destruction" may be rendered more comprehensible by a comparison with a proceeding used by painters.
In their technical language a colour is said to be "veiled" when it
is not erased, but toned down. All the sentiments which enter
into the scheme of Ariosto's poem are evenly toned down, so that
they preserve not only their distinct appearances but also their
reciprocal relations and proportions. In the "clear and transparent
mirror" or the "bright and tranquil crystal" of the octaves they are
dimmed like "pearls on a milky brow", but their variety is unim-
paired, and their lustre is still proportionate to the strength with
which they possessed the mind of the poet. The comic, the sublime,
the voluptuous, the reflective, and every other sentiment, reduced
but at the same time restored, remains its own self. Sometimes the
poetry reaches a limit in passing beyond which Ariosto would lose
his own tone, but close though he approaches to this limit he
never crosses it. We all know by heart the most bestirred passages
and verses in the *Orlando Furioso*, when Medoro, surrounded by
the attackers, wheels round like a lathe, taking cover from the
trees and never for a moment losing touch with the person of his
master, and Zerbino, on the point of killing him, looks on his
fine features and is halted by compassion. Another such passage
shows Zerbino on the point of death seized by despair at having
to leave his Isabella to the mercy of unknown men, while she melts
into tears and utters sweet vows of eternal fidelity; and yet
another tells of Fiordiligi hearing or rather divining the news of
the death of her husband . . . As one repeats such verses there is
always a catch at the throat, a beginning of tears. Recall Fiordiligi's
spasm of presentiment:

> *E questa novità d'aver timore*
> *le fa tremar di doppia tema il core.*

The dreadful news comes: Astolfo and Sansonetto, the two
friends with her in her retreat, conceal it for some hours, then
decide to approach her to prepare her for the disaster which has
overtaken her:

> *Tosto ch'entraro, e ch'ella loro il viso*
> *vide di gaudio in tal vittoria privo,*
> *senz'altro annunzio sa, senz'altro avviso,*
> *che Brandimarte suo non è più vivo . . .*

The images and the rhythm convey the tremor that overcomes the poor darling, one feels the wrench and then the abrupt plunge into the black abyss of desolation. There is another moment in the same tale when grief seems to engender fresh grief in a crescendo. It is the moment when Orlando makes his expected entry into the temple where they are celebrating the funeral of Brandimarte Orlando, his friend, his companion, and the witness of his death:

> *Levossi, al ritornar del Paladino,*
> *maggiore il grido e raddoppiossi il pianto . . .*

De Sanctis, when he came upon such scenes and words in his lectures on the *Orlando Furioso*, used to say to his pupils: "You see that Ariosto had a heart indeed." But even in those cases he went on to insist truly: "Ariosto never carries his situations to the point of agony", for to do so would have been to violate the tone of his poem. And De Sanctis showed how Ariosto utilized interruptions, charming similes, reflections, adornments of style, to check the mounting flow of agonizing grief. Altogether too exacting in their demand for something excessive and undue are those critics who are irked by the octaves which celebrate the name of Isabella, as that chosen by God to adorn for ever after the most lovely, gentle, courteous, wise, and chaste women (a compliment to the Marchioness of Mantua, Isabella d'Este). They do not understand that those stanzas, and the "Depart in peace" which precedes them ("Vattene in pace, alma beata"), closing the episode of Isabella's sacrifice of her own life to keep faith to Zerbino, together with the whole tale of the drunken rage of Rodomonte and the preceding semi-comic scene of the holy hermit who "like a skilled helmsman" steers Isabella along the path of chastity, and who zealously prepares "a fine and grand repast of spiritual food", whereupon Rodomonte seizes him by the neck and sends him hurtling three miles deep into the sea, are all words and fancies expressly designed to procure that the death of Isabella shall not plunge the *Orlando Furioso* into an atmosphere of tragedy with an accompanying tragic catharsis. For the *Orlando Furioso* brings with it all the time that harmonious catharsis which we have now sufficiently illustrated.

Ariosto's elaboration of his sentimental and passional material – accomplished despite and indeed thanks to the reduction to which he subjects it – and the colourful variety, the so human character, which thereby come to inform the poem, caused us at the very outset of this analysis to make this much clear: we define Ariosto as the poet of harmony, but thereby indicate only the dominant accent of his work. He is the poet of Harmony and also of something else, the poet of the harmony attained in a particular realm of feeling. In fact the harmony achieved by Ariosto is not generic but altogether his own.

[1918]

X

TORQUATO TASSO

My reply to the customary regrets that "tragedy" was either wholly wanting or very weakly represented in sixteenth-century Italy – upon which alleged deficiency there have been directed various subtle enquiries, leading to an explanation in terms either of the Italian temperament, or of the character of the times, or of some other such abstraction – has been simply to point to the tragic poetry and art which there was in that period, and first and foremost to that of the *Gerusalemme Liberata*. For if the tragic lies in the sudden issue of vital impulse and delight into grief and death, so that they find therein nobility, purification, and redemption, we must surely give the title of tragedian to the creator of Argante, the warrior who, as he sallies forth to the supreme trial, embraces in pensive melancholy the city that he has striven to defend but which is now doomed; and of Soliman, who, seeing in the heat of the battle one of his comrades suddenly struck down by the sure hand of Rinaldo, stops short confounded, irresolute, neither fighting nor fleeing; and passively, silently, submits to the death fate had in store for him; and of Clorinda, forgetting her ferocity in a Christian death; and of the witch Armida, for whom the desires she kindles and the passions she arouses are a game until in that game she herself is assailed by passion and learns in love for the first time what it is to suffer desperately; and then also of Tancredi, Erminia, and the other heroes and heroines of the poem.

Consider Clorinda, whose life has been all a warlike frenzy, Clorinda contemptuous from childhood of women's concerns, exercising her body, donning armour, hunting the bear and the lion when there are no men to fight, for ever victoriously felling her foes and proudly seeking fame and renown in arms. Nothing can distract her from that compelling ideal, that incessant rage to be duelling and fighting. And now she is making ready for an enterprise more perilous than any before. The old serving man who reared her and has ever been at her side endeavours to dissuade her. At last he determines to reveal what he had always kept from her: the secret of her origin and condition. Clorinda, at this announcement, lifts her eye in rapt attention. She listens and learns that her parents were Christians and that a Holy Warrior has always watched over her and that appearing to him in dreams he has often commanded him to baptize her, and has even now appeared to announce at one and the same time her imminent conversion and her death. Now the old man remains stricken by fear and by doubt of the faith in which he himself has reared her. She too, stricken by the same alarm, waits irresolute, but only for a moment. Then, chasing away the disturbing alien suggestion, she renews her pagan vows and her choice of that way of life, and sets forth upon the enterprise she had undertaken.

But doubt had for a moment touched her, and nothing ever passes without leaving a trace in the mind. Together with Argante she sallies forth from the besieged city, performs the appointed task of setting fire to the great tower, and with her companion withdraws fighting. But just as she is making for the city she turns to pursue and kill an enemy who had sought to strike her, and thus by error she is left outside the walls when the gate closes. Alone in the press of the enemy she feels that she is lost:

> Ma poi che intepidì la mente irata
> nel sangue del nemico, e in sé rivenne,
> vide chiuse le porte, e intorniata
> sé da' nemici; e morta allor si tenne.

Dismay besets her heart, just as doubt, instigated by Arsete, had previously beset her: "Perhaps this is the true faith!"; but the dismay too lasts but a few moments, nor is there any panic. Seeing that no one has noticed her, she thinks there might be safety in the general confusion, so she goes round the city in order to attempt a re-entry by another gate. But Tancredi has seen her, followed her, and deemed her a warrior truly worthy of personal combat. This is one of the most poetic moments in the story:

Va girando colei l'alpestre cima
verso altra porta, ove d'entrar dispone.
Segue egli impetuoso; onde, assai prima
che giunga, in guisa avvien che d'armi suone,
ch'ella si volge e grida — O tu, che porte,
che corri sì? — Risponde: — Guerra e morte.

That clash of arms which she had heard before she sighted the enemy, was the sound of doom. Her question: "Why this speed? What will you?" feigns ignorance, but she knew in her soul the answer before Tancredi spoke it.

For "the fatal hour" has come to terminate "duly" the life of Clorinda, that blind whirlpool of a life that has surged from battle to battle, exploit to exploit, slaughter to slaughter, and which cannot bring her at the end to any other fitting conclusion but the sharp stroke of death – so mad a course needs must end in collision or a headlong fall into the abyss.

How strongly Tasso felt the pathos of this tale of a wellnigh successful escape giving way to the imminence of an inescapable death, is shown by his having, in the revised version of the poem, the *Gerusalemme Conquistata*, worked out the episode afresh, with additional details, and with the conferment of a graver and deeper significance, by linking it up with the new episode of a dream of Clorinda's to match the dream of her old servant. In this dream she had seen a vast foliage arising to touch the sky and to cover the whole earth with fronds of cypress and cedar and palm, together with a clear, sweet, fresh fountain rousing a longing in her to bathe in the purifying waters. While she lingered hesitatingly, a giant advanced to fight her and overcome her, and she, on the point of death, seemed to repent and to seek grace.[1]

She seeks safety at the other gate of Jerusalem, the "Sheep Gate", and behold, there she sees or seems to see the reality corresponding to the fountain and the frondage seen in the dream:

giunge in prima
dove da l'ale aperte alto dragone
chiara acqua sparge entro marmorea conca,

1. *Conquistata*, XV, 41-47.

> *onde la via non l'è rinchiusa e tronca.*
>   *Del gran torrente 'l mormorar dappresso*
> *ella sentiva; e 'n su l'ombrosa sponda*
> *vide, o veder credea, palma e cipresso*
> *e d'umil cedro ancor la verde fronda.*[1]

At the same instant she feels the onrush of her fated slayer:

> *Turbossi; e di sua morte udiva il messo,*
> *che fea d'armi sonar la via profonda:*
> *a cui si volse, e disse . . .*

Tasso was following a genuine artistic inspiration in developing and deepening this episode, as the continuation shows. Better it would have been if he could have worked out and composed this in his poetical springtime, for in the *Conquistata* the lines are unclear and the colouring discordant, and the effort is too apparent. Even so, the final touches portraying the emotion of Clorinda as she sees realized the prophetic forebodings of her dream, and her acceptance, in a deepening conviction of its tragic import, of the message of the clash of arms coming up from the road below, are beautiful.

In the meanwhile, emotion and presentiment are still checked and mastered by the manner of feeling and of action habitual to her. She answers defiance with defiance and fights on in fierce fury with every arm and every limb at close quarters through the night. Nor is there any change on her part when both the combatants, wounded, weary, and breathless, pause for rest and by a kind of common impulse peer at each other through their visors. In the pale dawn – for now

> *(già de l'ultima stella il raggio langue*
> *al primo albor ch'è in orïente acceso)*

– surely some gentleness should dawn also in the fighters, their mind should rise for a moment above their mortal combat. But such a feeling, such a thought, arises in the man, not in the woman. Clorinda rejects them with redoubled ferocity. The ingrained harshness will not be thrown off: in her mounting rage there is

1. *Conquistata*, xv, 65-66.

something of a headlong rush into the doom of death. She stubbornly refuses the petition of Tancredi to know the identity of the brave foe who will either defeat him or be defeated by him; nay, she gives a deliberately insolent and provocative answer, reminding the crusader, lest perchance he had forgotten it, of the injurious defiance she had just wrought against the Christian army:

> *ma, chiunque io mi sia, tu innanzi vedi*
> *un di quei due che la gran torre accese.*

After which, it would come naturally that she should die in the same spirit as her companion Argante, whose last words and gestures have been described as "fierce, proud, and dreadful", or like Suliman, whose dying had been in every respect "grand and haughty". But no: for as she is pierced and laid low and near to death there comes uppermost and is revealed in her a sensitive and delicate, weak and humble creature piteously lamenting. Once already she had of a sudden revealed her womanhood in mid-battlefield, when the foeman's sword had knocked the helmet from her head:

> *e le chiome dorate al vento sparse*
> *giovane donna in mezzo al campo apparse.*

But that revelation of golden-haired beauty served then but to throw into relief the prodigy of her warlike boldness and bravery. Now, with Tancred's sword planted in her breast, the womanhood is all revealed: beneath the armour appears the sign of an habitual elegance, a gold-broidered garment, soft and light, sustaining her breast, but now bathed in flowing blood:

> *e la vesta, che d'òr vago trapunta*
> *le mammelle stringea tenera e leve,*
> *l'empie d'un caldo fiume . . .*

The heroine gives way to the "pierced virgin", who as she fails and falls utters with "voice distressed" her last words softly, sweetly, sobbing.

What has come about? It has come about that the deep primal soul in her, already apparent in the nobility and generosity of certain contrasting characteristics in her warlike way of life, has at the near approach of death at last blossomed, introducing an utter novelty in her every feeling, thought, act, word, and very tone of speech. Death and death alone had the power thus to sober her, and Clorinda, who until then had seen the world solely as a field for wonderful deeds of strength amidst plaudits and celebrations of fame, now at last, when ready to leave it, sees into the depth and fullness of its human aspect, sees it as pain, as love meriting not disdain but pity, as pardon, conciliation, surpassment of the transient in the eternal.

Tasso clothes this conversion in the trappings of belief in the miraculous intervention of God and the magic virtue of the holy water which washes away all sin and gives assurance of heavenly bliss, from which we might infer lessons and judgements concerning the elaborately mechanical devotionalism, claiming Tasso's allegiance, of Counter-Reformation Catholicism. But the beliefs in question must here be considered exclusively as providing a symbolism for the moral crisis, the human feeling, the pacification achieved in the sphere of a human sublimation into purity. A more pertinent observation for the aesthetic critic would be to note a certain hastiness or abruptness in the crisis. The poet himself seems to feel this, for he has recourse to the rather unhappy remedy of a gloss contained in four lines, which the reader usually tries to overlook,[1] and a still more evident sign of this it is that, after himself sitting in judgement on his work, he introduced in the revised version, the *Conquistata*, that long preparation by way of dream, mysterious confirmations, and presentiment of fate, to temper the suddenness of the transformation.

The catharsis of the tragedy takes place in the sweetness of dawn, the silence of the countryside, in which nothing can be heard save the hidden murmur of a brook:

---

1. "... disse le parole estreme; / Parole ch'a lei novo un spirto ditta, / Spirto di fè, di carità, di speme; / Virtù ch'or Dio le infonde, e se rubella / In vita fu, la vuole in morte ancella" (Stanza 65, vv. 5-8).

Poco quindi lontan nel sen del monte
scaturia mormorando un picciol rio;

– the brook to which Tancredi runs to fetch water in the helmet for the christening of the dying one, who is the woman of his love, pierced unwittingly by him in the disguise of that same helmet. Already his heart had been rendered sensitive by the words of mutual pardon, sought and granted, the request of baptism, the sound of that voice; but now a presentiment of something tremendous seizes upon him bodily, in mystic sympathy, before even it finds a way to his mind. As he approaches and bends to release the dying head from its helmet:

tremar sentì la man, mentre la fronte
non conosciuta ancor sciolse e scoprio ...

The dying one is wholly possessed now by the new idea that has dawned for her, the new sweetness filling her breast absorbs her, and when she sees before her the man who had loved her but in whom she had ever seen only the armed enemy, giver or receiver of death, ignored in every other respect, she now desires at last to leave him with a kind word. But she has no strength to speak, and can only extend her hand – the "naked" hand (no longer armed) of a woman, the "cold" hand of the dying – and with that act she yields to death:

e la man nuda e fredda alzando verso
il cavaliero, in vece di parole
gli dà pegno di pace. In questa forma
passa la bella donna, e par che dorma.

Not the lightest hint of amorous affection is here admitted: every individual earthly attachment, even the relation of love, is dissolved and surpassed. Clorinda has never been subdued by love in her lifetime, and even in her death knows love only in the act of rising above it and taking distance from it. That subsequently Tasso exhibits Clorinda looking down from heaven upon Tancredi, grateful for the rite of baptism which has saved her soul, and assuring him that she returns "as much love as to creatures may be giv'n", is just a Petrarchesque afterthought.

I have been trying to bring out the intrinsically human character of the Clorinda conversion scene because there seems still to be room for warning and advice against the treatment of poets as representatives of religions, systems, historical epochs, and so forth rather than, as is alone legitimate, of poetry. The warning here is not to make of Torquato Tasso a spokesman for the Counter-Reformation.[1]

Consider, now, another place in the poem, the story of the shriven, pardoned, penitent Rinaldo who, taught by the hermit Piero, makes his way at dawn to the Mount of Olives. Here he fulfils his vigil, kneels, prays, and God grants him a sign of grace, causing the dew-drops to shine on his garments and turn them to an appearance of whiteness. But it is not in this ritual that we feel the poetry of the scene to lie: it lies in the youth who has just broken loose from an amorous bondage, and now plunges at dawn into the freshness and purity of nature, amid valleys and mountains:

> Era ne la stagion ch'anco non cede
> libero ogni confin la notte al giorno,
> ma l'orïente rosseggiar si vede,
> ed anco è il ciel d'alcuna stella adorno;
> quando ei drizzò vêr l'Oliveto il piede,
> con gli occhi alzati contemplando intorno
> quinci notturne e quinci mattutine
> bellezze incorruttibili e divine.

In that fresh delight the man's soul seems to be washed clean; the beauties of the celestial vault, to his admiring and unaccustomed eye, appear constant and eternal by contrast with the unsteady and fugitive beauties of mortal creatures. These were human, but they are divine. And yet... And yet the seemingly higher beauty, as soon as the divine-demonic force of desire and love,

---

1. Nor yet, of course, by the same token a spokesman for the Renaissance, a "last voice of the Renaissance", as in a recent book (L. TONELLI, *Torquato Tasso*, Turin, 1935, pp. 33, 35) I am charged with doing. But that error – it would indeed be an error – I did not commit, for in the passage quoted by my censor Tasso is called "the last voice of Italy", and rightly so from the viewpoint in question there, namely that of the Baroque Age. No spokesman, then, either of the "Renaissance" or of the "Counter-Reformation"!

love's delight and torment, confronts it, appears feeble, languid, cold. At that moment those "sweet looks and features of Armida", which are later to appear to him in the enchantments of the wood, come somehow to his mind and his thoughts are bewildered:

> Fra sé stesso pensava: — Oh quante belle
> luci il tempio celeste in sé raguna!
> Ha il suo gran carro il dì; l'aurate stelle
> spiega la notte e l'argentata luna:
> ma non è chi vagheggi o questa o quelle;
> e miriam noi torbida luce e bruna,
> ch'un girar d'occhi, un balenar di riso
> scopre in breve confin di fragil viso.

He is astonished, and finds no answer to his self-questioning. The mystery remains unsolved, and even while he admires the splendour of moon and stars and sun he feels the peril, as he has already felt the pain of the contrast. How potent a small fragile human creature can be over against the wide heaven! How intense by the measure of the pale light is the "dark troublous light" of a glance from a flashing dark eye, a brilliant smile! What infinite fascination there is in the small features doomed though they be to death and dissolution!

Rinaldo breaks loose from Armida and dominates his passion not in virtue of a religious ethic symbolized in the purity of mountains and sky, but by the triumph of a human power over a human power, the victory of "reason" over "sense" – reason, whose message flashes forth from the polished shield placed before him as a mirror by Ubaldo, arousing shame and anger against himself ("anger the warlike minister of reason") for having sunk into that life of ease and luxury. The lure of love is not destroyed by the religious or moralizing revulsion. It is, indeed, indestructible, and when one believes or asserts that it has been destroyed, that is the beginning of a desperate debate that can end only in ascetic madness or in hypocrisy. But it can indeed be controlled, reined in, confined to its own limits, by dint of action, of the creativity proper to men, of "reason": whence the superior pity and indulgence and indeed amusement with which the creative man of art, thought, politics, beneficence, observes the affairs of love. But such control and superiority do not betoken incomprehension or aversion, indifference or harshness, as may be seen in Tasso's Rinaldo, for he, though detached from Armida, nevertheless remains linked to her. Brought to her presence he feels shame, almost like a child, for the obligation under which Reason has placed and places him of proving false to all the pledges and promises previously, in the heat of passion, profusely tendered, rejecting her who was hitherto his absolute, recognized, obediently served mistress.

> Ei lei non mira; e, se pur mira, il guardo
> volge furtivo e vergognoso e tardo.

But when she has then heaped reproaches on him, saying and doing all that she possibly could not to lose him at all, or not altogether, Reason, resolve, the duty of returning to his companions forbids the return of the old passion. Yet:

> v'entra pietade in quella vece almeno
> pur compagna d'amor, benché pudica,
> e lui commuove in guisa tal ch'a freno
> può ritener le lacrime a fatica.

With words of affection he manages to calm and comfort her, he confesses himself the partner of her error and tries to draw her too out of it with him, and to establish with her a new and higher relation of devotion and protection, based upon what is still for him a sacred memory.

> Fra le care memorie ed onorate
> mi sarai ne le gioie e negli affanni;
> sarò tuo cavalier, quanto concede
> la guerra d'Asia e con l'onor la fede.

Nor does he depart from that profession despite her rage and the mad plans of vengeance – vengeance is still love – which she cherishes. On his side, too, the pity is still streaked with restrained but unforgotten love.

Love, as pain and renunciation, appears variously in the persons of Rinaldo and Tancredi, Armida and Erminia. De Sanctis, who had the excuse of the youthful Romanticism and Byronism which he never wholly shook off, was unjust in his appraisal of Tasso's women when he called Armida "far-fetched", Erminia "insignificant", Clorinda "sullen and cold". He was severe especially about Sophronia, who went against his whole theory of how woman should be portrayed in art – her poetic character would depend, he considered, upon her yielding to the passion of love. Sophronia De Sanctis dismisses as "stiff, all of a piece, an artificial and solitary figure collocated in an ill-fitting world, whence the exaggeration in her religious tirades". Again he judges her "an offspring of the brain, a Christian conception streaked with pagan and platonic reminiscence", a "heroine and martyr of the faith", in whom however "the ecstasies and ardours of a saint are wanting". From the first to the last word of Tasso's portrayal De Sanctis finds her inharmonious, from "a virgin, she, of ripe virginity" to the deplorable "Since they shall not together die, she'll not refuse to live together".[1]

Truly speaking, this "of ripe virginity" is not a clumsy euphemism for "old maid", but means no longer unripe, fit for marriage, and would not have been misunderstood by one who remembered Horace's "matura virgo": at the most Tasso might have been reproached for a latinism. But it happens that when one forms a dislike for a poet one ends by taking offence the whole time on every occasion. Thus Galileo, a fanatical Ariosto enthusiast, could not stomach the dissimilar art of Tasso, and when he came upon Sophronia described as withdrawing her eyes and passing out of the house veiled, he protested that this was ungracefully written – she had not cast her eyes into the street in such a manner as to have to withdraw them! Galileo's comment was really excessive even if Tasso was in this case less happy than Petrarch in a similar description of a severe withdrawnness. To return to "Since they shall not together die she'll not refuse...", surely Sophronia, hitherto wholly absorbed in her heroic dreams, thoughtless of ever loving or being loved, careless of her "high beauty", living

1. "Vergine di già matura verginità" ... "Ella non schiva, poi che seco non muor, che seco viva."

away from the world in the almost cloistral solitude of her house, could not, on the instant that a youth unknown to her heart or her fancy offered either to die for her or to die with her, wholly change her manner, character, tone, bearing, voice. Surely it was her part not to change them at all, to remain just what she was and what in facing the tests she had proved that she could be. She accepts the youth because it is conformable to reason and humanity that she should accept him for her husband. She will bear him kindly company, which in itself is a great and unhoped for felicity. Later she may come to love him, but for the moment she cannot and must not. The figure of Sophronia, the strong woman, ready to sacrifice herself, ready to risk death, as she has done, for her people, cannot be reduced and sunk into the drama of a girl settling her affair of the heart by a final yielding to love. In the tragedy of Sophronia, the drama of her admirer Olindo is just an incident, and is resolved on that level.

Is Sophronia an unreal being? She is not an unhistorical being, at all events. One of those, in the pages of history, who played just such a part was Charlotte Corday, and there was, too, an Olindo in the case. He was Adam Lux, the young deputy for Mainz, an ardent republican who, on the day that Charlotte Corday was condemned and sent to her death, saw and followed her, and, inflamed by her heroism, shouted that she was greater than Brutus. When in his turn he too was seized and condemned, he was able to declare: "At last I can die for Charlotte Corday".[1] We have an anticipation of the French heroine even in the detail of her sudden pallor (as is reported) at the sight of the engine of death. In Sophronia's case:

> Ella si tace; e in lei non sbigottito,
> ma pur commosso alquanto è il petto forte;
> e smarrisce il bel volto in un colore
> che non è pallidezza, ma candore.

So much for history. In poetry, of which we are talking here, the reality of Sophronia is the reality of the soul of Torquato Tasso,

1. See, among many, CHÉRON DE VILLIERS, *Charlotte de Corday* (Paris, 1865), pp. 412-23.

who, now as Tancredi, now as Olindo, loved desperately the
woman who has no love for love, a fair warrior like Clorinda, a
woman of high beauty but high and royal thoughts like Sophronia,
a woman exceeding in stature the man, or at all events the lover.
This too is a link between love (love which is always the dream of
the unattainable) and pain.

[1937]

XI

CERVANTES

W<small>ITH</small> rapt attention, curiosity, and wonder, we watch, in the first pages of the book, the birth, growth, irresistible development, and finally the issue into practical resolution of the ideal of the Knight Errant in the person of the country gentleman of the Mancha: we see the good Alonso Quijada indulging a taste for chivalric romance, then gradually suffering a change, a reformation, an elevation to heroism, as he pursues that fascinating study. Next he is devising and planning his action, cleaning and fixing the arms needful for such noble exercise, choosing his name as a warrior and that of the lady of his thoughts. He can no longer now stay idly weaving his fancies, he must be up and doing, for the troubled world awaits and urges on his labour of charity and justice. And soon, unnoticed by his own people, there he goes one morning throwing off the peaceful habits of years, leaping to horse, and riding across country:

> Y así, sin dar parte a persona alguna de su intención, e sin que nadie le viese, una mañana antes del día (que era uno de los calurosos del mes de julio) se armó de todas sus armas, subió sobre Rocinante, puesta su mal compuesta celada, embrazó su adarga, tomó su lanza, y per la puerta falsa de un corral salió al campo, con grandísimo contento y alborozo de ver con cuanta facilidad había dado principio a su buen deseo. Mas apenas se vió en el campo, cuando le asaltó un pensamiento terrible . . .

The terrible thought was a twinge of conscience at the want of an investiture for the duty he means to perform. He had never been dubbed knight. Hence his first adventure at the inn which he takes for a noble castle, with the host whom he takes for a valiant knight, and the *mozas del partido* to whom he pays court as to fine ladies; an extraordinary and yet quite natural adventure, at once complicated and simple, to be followed by others of the same natural and spontaneous character.

The narrator's art is barely noticed; men, deeds, and things seem to move of their own accord in the tale, and for this *Don Quixote* is commonly described as being from cover to cover a "living" book. But critical thought cannot rest satisfied with a metaphor like this, albeit a metaphor of recognized poetic beauty: for poetry is not life, it is feeling exalted to fantasy. The task for critical thought is to distinguish what feeling it is which is particularly represented in the person and the adventures of Don Quixote.

There is nothing recondite about it: anyone can grasp and define the guiding spirit of the book while they read it: it is the feeling which they discover in their own heart. This is the feeling of sympathy, a word which in our old Italian dictionaries used to be defined as "reciprocal inclination or similarity of disposition, will, and affection"; as much as to say recognition of worth in the person for whom the sympathy is felt, of something corresponding to what we ourselves love, cultivate, aspire to, or at least desire and honour. Where love and ideals are wanting, sympathy is scanty or absent. "Sympathy" must not here be confounded with "compassion" (though the words are etymologically analogous) – compassion means that which we extend to the pains and miseries of mankind regardless of the presence or absence of merit in the sufferer, and surely no one has thought or could think of offending Don Quixote by suggesting that he excites compassion in his madness, misadventures, rough-and-tumbles, sore wounds. No, what he excites is sympathy.

In fact we find Don Quixote continually winning assurances of this from the folk he moves among. If on some occasions he runs into people who rudely or thoughtlessly or wantonly misjudge and mock and maltreat him, the better sort always take to him. First to wish him well is that peasant of his own village whom he has summoned to accompany him. The lust of wealth and power with which he has enflamed Sancho Panza from time to time is eclipsed and overcome by love, admiration, and veneration for his master. Sancho is actually possessed by the sentiment of honour, honour which would be violated if he broke the link between them; and thus, when he has demurred at following him on a second expedition and sees him resigned to seeking another squire, he suddenly yields, and in tears offers his services again, declaring himself incapable of ingratitude and desertion, and half comically, half earnestly says that he must not blot the reputation of his family "que ya sabe todo el mundo, y especialmente mi pueblo, quién fueron los Panzas de quien yo desciendo" (ii. 7). Similarly, when on another occasion Don Quixote scolds him, he feels utterly ashamed of himself, declaring that he only needs a tail to be a complete ass and that the master had better give it to him, and like that he'll serve him as long as he has breath. Even more unanimously than the other characters in the book, its readers loved and still love Don Quixote from the moment of his appearance on the literary scene, calling him "delightful" and "ingenious". Then, later, in the days of nineteenth-century Romanticism, they addressed to him tender words of affection such as Byron's in some famous stanzas of Don Juan.

In those stanzas, indeed, feeling for Don Quixote is pushed to the extreme length of wrathful indignation at the smiles which surround him, whereas a smiling sympathy, a perfectly fused sympathetic smile, is just what he calls for. The smile never dispels admiration for the nobility of his character and the rightness of his judgements: these not only remain intact, but are heightened in their effect by the aura of comicality. Even when a wild beast, a lion, which he intrepidly challenges and attacks, evades him and cheats his ebullient heroism by treating him as a child or imbecile and quietly re-entering his cage, this fails to render him foolish or despicable in that scene.[1] For Don Quixote had indeed defied and faced the lion, and it was not his doing if the tremendous conflict failed to materialize. Comical, but heroical!

Truth to tell, this synthesis of the serious and the absurd, of imaginative faintness and fervour, gainsaying and eager acceptance, lies in the human soul itself. There can be no will, no deed, without hope, and no hope without belief in the reality of things hoped for, whence every man, however wise he may seem and

---

1. "Hasta aquí llegó el extremo de su jamás vista locura. Pero el generoso leon, más comedido que arrogante, no haciendo caso de niñerías ni de bravatas, después de haber mirado a una y otra parte, como se ha dicho, volvió las espaldas y enseñó sus traseras partes a Don Quijote, y con gran flema y remanso se volvió a echar en la jaula" (ii, 17).

be, is wholly encompassed in illusions. When, on the completion of his action, his accomplishment, he sees that they are illusions, he must, if he is to go on acting and living, desire them all over again and radiate others like them into the future. Byron, in his verses, said that Socrates too was a Don Quixote, the Quixote of wisdom: but then every one of us is in his own way the Quixote of something, like him illuded, like him – who was so prudent and sensible, so worthy of unfeigned esteem and unqualified admiration in other matters – in some respects a bit mad. All of us from time to time pay the penalty for having believed, trusted, dreamed. We call this disappointment, disillusionment, reawakening. It is the price we pay for our life, though it be as noble, austere, skilful, cautious as any may be. The man moved wholly by pure and abstract reason is a puppet contrived by pedants – pedants who are themselves Quixotes of a sort – and the puppet cannot move. What, then, is to be done? The disappointment, the awakening, the pain must in their due hour be accepted, and when the moment has come for calm contemplation, the human comedy-tragedy must be seen in some mirror like that of *Don Quixote*, to be wept over and smiled at. At another hour, the hour for philosophic thought, the task will be to appreciate the logical process in which all this figures as necessary.

Don Quixote too requires illusion. Without it his life would be idle and empty. He wants it so keenly and fixedly that experiences and demonstrations, however hard and clear, fail to rouse him. So do the commonsense warnings of Sancho ever at his side. The need and the will to be deceived suggest and furnish ever fresh explanations and motives of persistence. At one moment or another we may almost seem to catch him deliberately deceiving himself: for example when after trying out the helmet which he has fashioned for himself, and finding that at the first stroke of the sword it falls to pieces, he carefully remakes it, but refrains from another test, taking it confidently as it is.[1] One just glimpses the

---

1. . . . y no dejó de parecerle mal la facilidad, con que la había hecho pedazos y, por asegurarse deste peligro, la tornó a hacer de nuevo, poniéndole

intention of self-deceit in such moments of feeble cunning when we shut an eye on our own proceedings. But beyond the appearances, in the very midst of the illusions, lies the true reality, the ideal which makes us live and work, suffer and die for it. Here we sometimes encounter despair: here we sometimes rise to the sublimity of suffering and of the heroic will. This last is the case with Don Quixote when, having been vanquished, unhorsed, and thrown to the ground by the Knight of the White Moon, and required by the victor to confess that his lady was not the fairest on earth:

> molido y aturdido, sin alzarse la visera, como si hablara dentro de una tumba, con voz debilitada y enferma dijo: – Dulcinea del Toboso es la más hermosa mujer del mundo, y yo el más desdichado caballero de la tierra, y no es bien que mi flaqueza defraude esta verdad; aprieta, caballero, la lanza y quítame la vida, pues me has quitado la honra! (II, 64.)

At that point of the story the smile has faded into invisibility. More often it hovers near at hand without disturbing the words and deeds of Don Quixote. One example suffices: the beautiful scene of the meeting with the goatherds who invite the Knight to share their rustic repast, seating him on an overturned trough. After the meal, taking a handful of dried acorns for the object of his thoughts, he opens his mind to all the trite observations he has ever read in novels and poems about acorns and the golden age. It is a flow of exclamations and reminiscences:

> Dichosa edad y siglos dichosos aquellos a quien los antiguos pusieron nombre de dorados, y no porqué en ellos el oro, que en esta nuestra edad de hierro tanto se estima, se alcanzase en aquella venturosa sin fatiga alguna, sino porque entonces los que en ella vivían ignoraban estas dos palabras de tuyo y mío. Eran en aquella santa edad todas las cosas comunes: a nadie le era necesario para alcanzar su ordinario sustento tomar otro trabajo que alzar la mano, y alcanzarle de las robustas encinas, que liberalmente les estaban convidando con su dulce e sazonado fruto. Las claras fuentes y corrientes ríos en magnífica abundancia sabrosas y transparentes aguas les ofrecían . . .

unas barras de hierro por de dentro, de tal manera que él quedó satisfecho de su fortaleza y, sin querer hacer nueva experiencia della, la diputó y tuvo por celada finísima de encaje" (I, I).

All these trite tales he recites with a full conviction, a pious fervour, an accent as of one who knows and can teach and advise others. He goes on to tell of the bees who in hollow tree-trunks formed their republics and tendered their sweet honey to anyone who stretched a hand for it; of the cork trees which provided a roof for the hut; of the earth which bore fruits spontaneously without being stabbed by the plough; of peace, concord, harmony among all men; of milkmaids, fair and innocent, dressed only with the scanty garments needed for modesty, garlanded just with hops and ivy; of love-declarations expressed in simple language, free of fraud and malice, trickery and violence; and of a justice that used never to be abused for the sake of favours or interests. He went on to recount how that golden age became lost to the world, and the Knights Errant then appeared to defend virgins, to protect widows, help the orphans and the needy, and how he himself was one of those champions.

> *Desta orden soy yo, hermanos cabreros, a quien agradezco el gasajo y buen acogimiento que haceis a mi y a mi escudero: que aunque por ley natural están todos los que viven obligados a favorecer a los caballeros andantes, todavía por saber que sin saber vosotros esta obligación me acogistes y regalastes, es razón que con la voluntad a mi posible os agradezca la vuestra.*

The goatherds, we are told, listened in silence to the long discourse, and the peroration and conclusion addressed particularly to themselves – "sin respondelle palabras, embobados y suspensos le estuvieron escuchando". They, at that moment, constituted Don Quixote's illusion, "his brothers". The reality lay in the sacred zeal which inflamed him and fed on the illusion.

Of course *Don Quixote* does not keep continuously that high level of representation and poetry. Cervantes was a man of letters and meant to compose a work of entertainment, and so, for ornament and variety, introduced a good deal of extraneous matter. He also added to the first a second part, containing excellent passages but others where the tale degenerates into farce. Goethe, in one of his verdicts which are so full of point and also so much to the point, said to Chancellor Müller in 1819: "As long as the hero builds up illusions he is romantic, but when he simply is mocked and put upon, then we lose interest."[1] The brilliant Cervantes – it is just this that charms us – was not fully aware of his own genius, of the poetic world he was creating. A more sophisticated artist, or one of a more sophisticated age, would have presented it in a more compact unity, but Cervantes compounded with it passages of the merely amusing, sometimes, but not always, good of their kind.

It was as a satire of chivalry that *Don Quixote* was first classified by the critics, though its readers were really delighted by its deeper, less evident qualities. The Romantic age understood its human character and poetical essence. It would have been well not indeed to stop short at that point, but to use that understanding and judgement as a basis for particular interpretations and further necessary elucidations. Instead of which a certain *decepta aviditas* has, as so often happens, in stretching for the glittering reflection, dropped the real bone into the water. That is to say, books have appeared which show no reverence for the simplicity and single-mindedness of this work of genius, which is much to be deplored. The irreverence takes a double form: first the use of Cervantes' work as a text or pretext for conceits, concepts, and precepts in the way that preachers have made and make use of biblical texts – the practice could well be left to the preachers, or rather they too should be encouraged to adopt a more serious style. Secondly: the working up into conceptual form of the substance of the book itself, regarding it as figurative or allegorical reflection of philosophical positions, concerning the relation of ideal to real, imaginative to historical, rational to irrational, and so forth. The commentators have even discovered in *Don Quixote* an actualization of the researches of the Italian Aristotelians into the ninth book of the philosopher's *Poetics* (said to have been followed attentively by Cervantes when he was a soldier in Italy), relating to their divergent inferences as to the differences between philosophy, poetry, and history; or alternatively the actualization of the Platonic-Augustinian philosophy, and so forth. I shall not

1. *Unterhaltungen mit dem Kanzler Friedrich von Müller*, ed. by C. A. H. Burckhardt (2nd. ed., Stuttgart, 1898), p. 34.

pause to expound all this (it would be tedious) or to confute it (it would be too easy). And indeed, if nationalistic Spaniards have gone in particularly for the former abusive mode of interpretation while pretentious Italians have joined in the second, we have nevertheless had some Italian writers on the right line, such as Delogu in his book on Cervantes. I must add that even some highly superior works of interpretation like that of Americo Castro on the thought of Cervantes in its connexion with the Italian and Spanish Renaissance need to be taken with reserve, not for any doubt about the reality of such a live cultural influence upon Cervantes, but because, as I have already said, Cervantes as a poet could really feel no other influence than that of universal and eternal humanity.[1]

[1939]

1. My friend Castro, while agreeing with me that the matter of poetry is not things but the feelings of the poet, writes "yo añadiría y *las ideas*" (*El pensamiento de Cervantes*, Madrid, 1925, p. 19). But no! It is wrong thus to add ideas, for these, in so far as they are ideas, are the business of philosophers, not poets. If it be explained that what is meant is ideas which have turned into feelings, evidently the reference is no longer to ideas but solely to feelings. This was the sense of my own statement, which will not suffer an addition that is in contradiction to it, even if, as in this case, suggested with amiable intentions.

XII

SHAKESPEARE

I

THE PRACTICAL AND THE POETIC PERSONALITY

IT may seem unnecessary, but it is better forthwith to give warning that the proper object of the aesthetic critic's and historian's study is not the practical but the poetic personality of Shakespeare, the character and development, not of Shakespeare's life, but of his art.

Not that one would wish to ban that natural curiosity which enquires what sort of men those were in daily life whom we admire as poets, thinkers, scientists, although this often leads to disappointment, because the life behind the artist's, philosopher's, or scientist's work is sometimes of slight interest or none at all (sometimes, however, it does repay study). In the case of Shakespeare it would certainly be gratifying to be able to remove the veil of mystery which seems to cloak him: to know what were the passions, the mental and moral trials through which he passed, and above all what he thought of himself, whether, as seemed to those who rediscovered him some centuries later, he really had little idea of the greatness of his genius and work, and for what reason, if any, he neglected to have his plays printed and exposed them to the risk of being lost to posterity. Was this in him the innocence and naivety of a poet or the proud indifference of a man who, wholly satisfied with the greatness of his work, might disdain worldly applause and the mirage of glory? Or was it sheer indolence? Was the neglect, again, casual or deliberate? Did he, as some guess, think that his works, born for the theatre, would live on in the theatre, where his fellow-actors would have seen to it that they were treated as he would have wished and as they deserved? But all these enquiries, it is clear, relate to the biography, not to the artistic history of Shakespeare. This last gives rise to quite different enquiries.

The two sets of enquiries are not, of course, wholly unrelated. Their very difference constitutes a superior relation between them.

If the aesthetic critic and historian could know in detail the chronology, circumstances, authorship, composition, recompositions, adaptations, and collaborations attendant upon Shakespeare's dramas seeing the light, undoubtedly some profit would derive from this for his own study of them. He would not have to puzzle over certain interpretations, to ponder in some perplexity over certain extravagances, incongruities, inequalities, wondering whether they are aesthetic errors or artistic forms of an intricate, not easily grasped internal coherency. But that is absolutely all that he would gain, and it would be offset by a temptation to attribute more than their proper value to external circumstances. In the last resort, in any case, the critic's judgement must rest upon intrinsic reasons of aesthetic import arising spontaneously out of the work under criticism. And the chronology which he will have to trace will be not a real or material, but an ideal and aesthetic chronology at best roughly coinciding with the other, but sometimes sharply diverging from it. If the authenticity of the works were well established, the critic would escape all such errors as calling Shakespeare the author of works or parts of works by Greene, say, or Marlowe, or giving the name of another author or an ascription of anonymity to works effectively by him. But such errors of naming are in reality already corrected by the underlying understanding that it is the poetical personality of Shakespeare, not the biographical and practical, that interests the critic, so that he can face with serenity the danger – no real danger and in any case highly improbable – of assigning to the symbol Shakespeare a work of which it can really be said that it springs from the same fount of inspiration as, or one very like to, Shakespeare's, and of equal value with the best of his works; or of adding to the various poor and inferior works assigned to that author yet another one. For the name, as used by the critic, betokens, not some title to property, but a differentiation of aesthetic quality and values.

As I have remarked, these things bear repeating firstly because a tacit and tenacious but erroneous conviction that practical and poetic history are one and the same thing, or else some ignorance as to their true relation, underlies the vast and mainly sterile labours which make up the bulk of Shakespearian scholarship. This like almost all nineteenth-century scholarship is unconsciously swayed by romantic ideas of a mystic and naturalistic unity. No wonder that among the early exponents of blended aesthetics and biography we find Emerson, and among the most notable contemporary exponents, Brandes. The purpose of those labours is in fact to plot a precise chronology, to track down biographical occasions, explain allusions, discover intentions, and thus (such is the hope) to arrive at a full knowledge of the Shakespearian poetry. It is the same hope that indirectly and distantly beckons on the many enquirers eager to show their acumen in solving puzzles or turning out academic theses and dissertations. But unfortunately the traditions and documents bearing on the life of Shakespeare are few, and all of them, nearly, refer to fortuitous or unimportant particulars. Letters, confessions, diaries of the man, or authentic and copious information about him are lacking. Almost every year some new Life of Shakespeare is published, but it is time to acknowledge and to accept clearly that a life of Shakespeare cannot be written, but only at best a vague and fragmentary biographical chronicle serving rather to express the anxiety of grateful posterity to possess at least some shadow of a biography than truly to satisfy the needs of knowledge. Because of this lack of documents the learned literature in question consists almost wholly in an ever growing accumulation of guesses, each in greater or lesser degree confuting or challenging or varying another, but all alike in their inability to furnish truth. A glance at any Shakespearian bulletin shows references (regarding the Sonnets) to the "Southampton theory", "Pembroke theory", and so on, that is, to conjectures that one of those noblemen was the "W. H." of the printer's dedication, other notions being that he was a musician William Hughes, or William Harvey, third husband of Lord Southampton's mother, or the bookseller William Hall, or a pure fiction, or "William Himself" jocularly invoked by the poet. There are also the theories as to the identity of the Dark Lady of the Sonnets, the "Fitton theory" (Mary Fitton, a lady-in-waiting), the "Davenant theory" (the mother of the poet Davenant, of which man Shakespeare himself was according to a tradition the father), with other theories as that she was the French wife of the printer Field, or just an imaginary and conventional personage of the world of the Petrarchesque Elizabethan sonneteers. One critic has the hardihood to state that he spent fifteen years of enquiry and meditation on the Davenant theory.

A crop of conjectures similar to that which has grown round the biographical information supposedly concealed in the Sonnets relates to Shakespeare's own marriage, his relations with his wife, the affairs of his family, and his professional activities. Then there are the puzzles about authorship: whether *Titus Andronicus* is an original work or one patched up by Shakespeare, whether *Henry VI* is wholly his, partly his, or merely revised and added to by him; which pieces of *Henry VIII* and *Pericles* are his, which Fletcher's or some other's; whether *Timon* was completed by him from someone else's sketch or the other way round; whether and how far a *Hamlet* by Kyd or another poet entered into the composition of *Hamlet*; whether some of the "apocryphal" plays like *Arden of Feversham* and *Edward III* ought to be ranked as canonical. The difficulties are equal and the conjectures equally numerous about the chronology of the plays. Some assign the *Midsummer Night's Dream* to 1590, others to 1595; *Julius Caesar* is assigned to 1603 or alternatively 1599, *Cymbeline* to 1605 or 1611, *Troilus and Cressida* to 1599 or 1603 or again 1609, while there is a theory that it was composed in three pieces successively in 1592, 1606, or 1607, with additions by outside hands. *The Tempest* is by most assigned to 1611, but others claim it for some years earlier, while the first version of *Hamlet*, according to some contentions, dates not from 1602, but from 1592-1594. From this multitude of conjectures the dubious indications of stylistic and metrical analysis afford no escape. But the sole use of conjectures is to aid discovery by stimulating the pursuit and interpretation of documents from which certainty may be inferred. Otherwise they are vacuous and vain. Even if they led to certainty they would not necessarily provide or identify the terms for the solution of the problems of

Shakespearian poetic criticism. But if they cannot be converted into the coin of certainty they are no better than drifting products of the imagination, unfit even for use in the attempts at a piecemeal Shakespearian biography or chronicle. The more cautious spirits, desirous of saying something about the life and character of Shakespeare without more than a minimum draft upon fancies and hypotheses, have been reduced to retailing a string of generic assertions to the effect that Shakespeare was good, honest, polite, helpful, prudent, laborious, free-and-easy, cheerful, and so on, all of which entirely fails to fix the outline of an individual personality.

Most of these writers, however, give currency to the unlikeliest conjectures as ascertained facts. Passing from conjecture to conjecture and from assertion to assertion, they serve up as "The Life of Shakespeare" a mere romance, one, moreover, which is invariably too colourless to have artistic value. Materials for the construction of these romances are greedily snatched out of the poet's works, on the grounds that (as the author of one of these tedious romances puts it) it is impossible that a man should have left behind him over three dozen plays and poems without providing the means to extract from them his life-story, experiences, and personality. And in a sense this is true. But it is true not of the practical and biographical but of the poetic life, experience, and personality of the author of those plays and poems. There would be an exception if in the poems there had been intercalated passages – they would of necessity be prosaic and not poetic passages – of crudely informative and biographical content. Shakespeare does nothing of the sort. Where this is lacking, there will be no way of approach through the poetic to the practical, for the relation between the two is not deterministic, as between causes and effects, but creative, as between form and matter, and accordingly incalculable. A real feeling, at the moment when it is sublimated into poetry, is thereby uprooted out of its real and practical soil, and rendered serviceable to the composition of a world of dreams, one of the infinite possible worlds. It will be as vain to seek therein the reality of that feeling as to seek the drop of water fallen into the ocean and transformed out of recognition by the vastness and pressure of the ocean itself. One is tempted to recall, as a warning, a strophe in one of Shakespeare's own sonnets in which he addresses his friend upon their friendship:

> Nay, if you read this line, remember not
> The hand that writ it; for I love you so,
> That I in your sweet thoughts would be forgot,
> If thinking on me then should make you woe. (Sonnet LXXI)

When, then, shall we say when we read in Brandes' book (which I here quote because it has been so widely read) that Richard III, the deformed crookback who regards himself as pre-eminent in mind, stands for Shakespeare himself, doomed to the despised life of the actor though proudly aware of his genius; and that Prince Arthur in the play of *King John* commemorates a son whom the poet lost when composing the drama; that the scapegrace bachelorhood of Henry V is that of Shakespeare himself in his first London years, that Brutus in the play of *Julius Caesar* reflects Essex and Southampton, the poet's protectors and unlucky conspirators against the queen; that Coriolanus, contemptuous of praise, betokens Shakespeare himself in the attitude which it behoved him to adopt towards public and critics; that King Lear's bitterness over ingratitude is the poet's own for the ingratitude which he felt on the part of colleagues, managers, and pupils; that Shakespeare (nothing less), though accustomed to compose in the early morning, must have written that dreadful tragedy by night; and many other fantastications of the same order? Why, we shall say that they call neither for endorsement nor for confutation, but simply for recognition as irresponsible and accordingly quite uninteresting conjectures.

We may say the same of another book, that of Harris, which has excited attention. In this, on the basis of an examination of his poems and plays, Shakespeare is found to be sensual, a neuropath, almost an erotomaniac, weak-willed, and throughout his life fascinated and dominated by a dark, wayward, faithless woman, Mary Fitton, this being the key to his saddest tragedies and to the mystery of his last years when he withdrew to Stratford, not to enjoy the peace of the country like some *fœnerator Appius*, but sick in body and mind to seek comfort for his miseries, or rather to prepare for a death which was not long in coming.

A particular effort has been made to correlate the composition of the great tragedies with the course of the poet's life and with public events in England. There may or may not be truth in these confrontations. Shakespeare may have been an active and emotional participant in the affairs mentioned or may on the contrary have remained a calm spectator of tempests from the seashore, moved only by *Scheingefühle*, the sense of appearances and dreams, as the psychologists call a tone of feeling which is found in artists. There is not the slightest value, either, in the conjectural identification of models for some of his characters, some contemporary adventurer for Shylock; the Emperor Rudolph II, a dabbler in science and magic, for Prospero – for the relation between the model and what the artist creates is, once again, one of incommensurability. When reading Shakespeare, or, indeed, any other poet, one may of course feel that some words spoken by a character have the ring of a reminiscence of some feeling or experience of the author himself, as when (in *Cymbeline*) Posthumus exclaims: "... Could I find out the woman's part in me, for there's no motion that tends to vice in man but I affirm it is the woman's part", or again Thersites (in *Troilus and Cressida*): "Lechery, lechery, still wars and lechery; nothing else holds fashion: a burning devil take them". Some have similarly felt the mark of a personal memory in Dante's scene of Francesca – the reading and the surrender. Yes, one may think and suspect so, but such thought and suspicion has no further consequence. Nor may any sure inference be drawn from a few passages in which the poet appears to interrupt the even flow and aesthetic consequentiality of his work in order to bring out – by an undue stress – some realistic and practical mood of his own. Even granting that there are some such passages in Shakespeare, it remains doubtful in his case (as in other poets' cases) whether that improper emphasis springs from overwhelming, overbrimming feeling or from some other accidental cause.

The poetical and the biographical are sufficiently unrelated to justify us in forbearing to express amazement and indignation over the "Baconian Theory", which has it that "Shakespeare's" plays are really by Francis Bacon, and the similar more recent hypotheses that they are by Roger, fifth Earl of Rutland, Rutland in co-operation with Southampton, or even an association of dramatic authors (Chettle, Heywood, Webster etc.) with Bacon to give a final touch, or finally (the latest such discovery) by William Stanley, sixth Earl of Derby. To these hypotheses a thousand or perhaps considerably more volumes, brochures, and articles have been devoted. Extravagant as they must indeed seem to trained and cautious scholars, they have at least the merit of (in some wise) administering an involuntary ironic comment upon pure scholarship and its abuse of conjectures. Let it even be conceded that in the rather limited mind of the philosopher Bacon there would be room for the far greater mind of our poet: even then nothing more would have been discovered and proved than the occurrence of a marvel, a sport, a monstrosity of nature, while the aesthetic problem would remain untouched. For the dramas would still be the same, King Lear would weep and inveigh, Othello would be torn with rage, Hamlet would debate and waver in the face of circumstances and his destined duty all in the same way as before, and over them all, as before, would lie the veil of eternity.

All this is scholarship gone astray, by contrast with a scholarship deserving of our gratitude for the work it has done in providing for us, with artistic discrimination, the best possible texts of Shakespeare's works, and interpreting his language and historical references. But the scholarship which has gone astray, whether or no it achieves some biographical end, distracts attention from the real task of aesthetic criticism, indeed it employs biography, imaginary or authentic, to confound and darken the artistic vision. What is art and what is merely documentation it confounds together, and transports into the realm of art the results or supposed results of its inspection of documents. It breaks up the serenity of the work of art into fumings and ravings, fearful or ferocious spasms, shows of sentimental rapture or frantic lust. In the case of poets whose biography is well documented it is well known that we have to force ourselves to consign these to oblivion if we are to enjoy their art in its ideal quality, that is to say, in its truth. Poets and artists have always felt resentment and distaste for the idle gossips who probed into their private lives and drew upon these for the framing of artistic judgements. This, in fact, is the reason why it is often said that contemporaries are not good judges, nor yet an artist's neighbours or fellow-citizens, and that a prophet goes unhonoured among his own people in his own place. That very disadvantage in which we stand as regards the biography of Shakespeare has a compensating advantage to balance it: the contemplation of his work on the ideal level suffers less obstruction. But this advantage is lost by the conjectural critics who, like the mule of Galeazzo Florimonte in the celebrated sonnet of Berni, fabricate boulders in order to knock up against them. In the above-mentioned book of Brandes, and also in that of the more inventive and subtle Harris, one may note just such a submersion of Shakespeare's art beneath material psychological detail. This has with Brandes such results for his rating of the poet's works as the treatment of *King Lear* and *Timon of Athens* as two equally ranking instances of misanthropy on account of ingratitude. Indeed, Brandes makes a disvalue out of artistic value. For where all his extravagant methods do not avail to reduce a drama to a psychological document, Brandes is ready, as in the case of *Macbeth*, to dismiss that masterpiece as "uninteresting" because "one cannot feel in it the heartbeat of Shakespeare"; of that Shakespeare, to wit, whom Brandes imagines as taken up with certain practical purposes and interests. The same abuse occurs when the attempt is made to interpret art in terms of some so-called "picture of the society of the age", introducing considerations which, like those of the poet's personal biography, are alien to the argument and occasions of distraction. (And such attempts usually display the same ignorance of history.) It is thus that Taine, having decided for himself that the Elizabethan English were "des bêtes sauvages", described the drama of that age as a reproduction "sans choix" of "les laideurs, les bassesses, les horreurs, les détails crus, les moeurs déréglées et féroces" of the times in question. Shakespeare's style was accordingly "un composé d'expressions forcenées". In fact, reading the well-known pages of his *Histoire de la littérature anglaise*, you hardly know whether it is poets or murderers of whom the tale is unfolded, artistic stresses and harmonies or swordsmens' violent affrays. Let us set against all these distorted portrayals of a Shakespeare wailing and whistling in the wind of the savage passions of his times or exhibiting in wrath, loathing, and bitter sarcasm the lacerations of his own infirm mind, that contrary judgement of Goethe, who argued to Eckermann that the Shakespearian dramas were the work "of a man in perfect physical and mental health". Healthy and strong and free he must certainly have been when bringing into existence his poetry: for such are the qualities of poetry. Though quieter in tone, the same deterministic error pertains to all attempts to make the figures and actions of the dramas hinge upon the political and social events of the times, such as the defeat of the Armada, the conspiracy of Essex, the death of Elizabeth, the accession of James, geographical discoveries and colonial expeditions, the clash with the Puritans, and so forth; or to co-ordinate Shakespeare's poetic output with the books he read, Holinshed's chronicles, the Italian tales, Plutarch's Lives, Montaigne's essays (Chasles and others have recently correlated his later and greater poetic inspiration with his readings of Montaigne); or with the conditions of the English theatre of his day, the various tastes of the spectators in the dear and the cheap seats (Rümelin's "realistic" criticism stresses these last considerations).

To sum up: Poetry must indeed be interpreted historically, but the history in question must be relevant and pertinent, not extraneous or linked with it solely by the sort of connexion which there is between a man and that which he passes by or sheds from himself or casts off as being harmful or useless or – which comes to the same thing – already used to the limit of its usefulness.

[1919]

XIII

SHAKESPEARE'S TRAGEDY OF THE WILL

There is tragedy in the conflict between the will to good and the will to evil, but there is also a sort of tragedy of the will in itself, sometimes precedent and sometimes successive to that other tragedy. It may be that the will, instead of disciplining and exploiting the passions, surrenders itself to their impetus. It may be that the will, while seeking the good, remains doubtful and dissatisfied as to the goodness of the choice. Or lastly, it may be that the will cannot choose a way, any way, to follow, knows not what to think of itself and the world, and churns away in the void.

The first of these conditions is commonly characterized by pleasure, pleasure which gradually extends its sway over a mind, drugging and drowsing the will, dispersing its forces, vapourizing it. Thinking upon that enchantment of delight and perdition, one becomes aware of the image of death suggesting itself in all naturalness. For that enchantment is death indeed; not, maybe, physical death, but certainly inner and moral death, death of the spirit; and without the spirit man is but a decaying corpse. It is from the violent sense of the allurement and tyrannical might of pleasure and from horror at its efficacy to induce abjection, dissolution, and death, that the tragedy of *Antony and Cleopatra* draws its inspiration.

Embraces and amorous languors, music and perfume, glitter of gold and velvet, brilliance of lights and depth of shadows, enjoyment now ecstatic and now frantic, make up its world. The sovereign of this world is Cleopatra, hunter for pleasure, giver of pleasure, spreading around her and among all who come near her the tang and frenzied itch for pleasure, herself giving the example and the incitement and conferring upon the orgy a royal and almost mystical character. One of the Romans plunging into that world of hers says, marvelling at her demonic or divine power:

Age cannot wither her, nor custom stale
Her infinite variety: other women cloy

> *The appetites they feed: but she makes hungry*
> *When most she satisfies. For vilest things*
> *Become themselves in her, that the holy priests*
> *Bless her when she is riggish . . .*

Cleopatra calls for songs and minstrelsy that she may melt into the flow of the music with an intenser pleasure:

> *Give me some music; music, moody food*
> *Of us that trade in love . . .*

She knows well how to play with men, by crossing them and by moving them, and tells the messenger she sends to Antony:

> *. . . If you find him sad,*
> *Say I am dancing; if in mirth,*
> *Report that I am sudden sick . . .*

In her words sensual charm rings out in all its fierceness:

> *. . . there is gold, and here*
> *My bluest veins to kiss, a hand that kings*
> *Have lipped, and trembled kissing.*

Whoever is near her follows her in that mad pace of living. Look at her two attendants joking with the soothsayer on their loves and future marriages and manner of death: listen to the first words of Charmian, festive and amorously flirtatious: "Lord Alexas, sweet Alexas, most anything Alexas, . . . where's the soothsayer that you praised so to the queen? Oh that I knew this husband which you say must charge his horns with garlands."

Antony is lured and carried away on that sharp stream of pleasure. Drunk with pleasure, the rest of the world, the real workaday world, seems to him heavy, prosaic, contemptible, tasteless. The name of Rome itself has no more authority for him:

> *Let Rome in Tiber melt, and the wide arch*
> *Of the ranged empire fall! Here is my space.*
> *Kingdoms are clay, our dungy earth alike*
> *Feeds man as beast . . .*

and clasping Cleopatra he has the feeling that they two form a pair such as can ennoble life, life which apart from that has no meaning.

57

This is not the sentiment of love but, once again, of pleasure. Cleopatra loves pleasure and caprice, and power which gives access to both of them. She loves Antony too as a part of her pleasures and caprices and as her instrument of power. She works hard to keep him bounden to her, when he strays she fights to regain him, but her eye is always on other things which are as necessary to her, indeed more necessary, and to keep which, if the necessity should arise, she would sacrifice him. Neither does Antony love her. Clearsightedly he recognizes her for what she is, inveighs against her, and then, without forgiving her, takes her again in his arms. "Fall not a tear," he bids her (who has lost him the battle against Octavian), "give me a kiss: even this repays me." The end of love is the union of two beings in an objective purpose, a moral agreement: but here we are outside morality, outside the will itself, in the engulfing whirlpool.

Of the two, it is Antony who is played out and vanquished, Antony who has known and experienced the life of labour which now in his madness he despises; has known war, the struggle of politics, the governance of States, the fleeting caress of victory and glory. More than once he has tried to rediscover the link with his past and to advance towards a future. Ethical discernment has not failed him, he sees Cleopatra as she really is, he bows reverently to the memory of the dead Fulvia and treats his new wife Octavia, whom he does not love and whom he will abandon, with all respect. For a brief moment he stages a return to the old world, mixes in political affairs, makes deals with colleagues and rivals, and seems to have slipped the chains that had held him. But the effort cannot be sustained, the chain falls back on him, with an ever weakening reluctance he yields to that destiny which favours Octavian, the loveless, cold, firm-willed Octavian. Ill-fortune besets the man of pleasure at every step; those around him see his aspect changing, see him as no longer the man he was, as one conceiving small, almost ridiculous notions, vain ambitions. And they are led to reflect that men's minds are but a part of their fortunes, that externals determine the shape of the inner man. He himself feels an inward flux, and compares himself with the changing form of mists which a breath dispels, like water falling into water. But the man in this state of dissolution was once great and still displays flashes of greatness in bold, soldierly action, great words, generous impulses. With his generosity he shames Eno-barbus, who had deserted him and now kills himself in his shame, and Antony still holds others around him, ready to die for him, by the feeling he inspires. Cleopatra is superior – or inferior – to this. She has never sought or wished any life save that of pleasure and wantonness, and in her heady abandon there is still logic, will, coherency. She is coherent too, in her suicide, evading death in the prisons of Rome, the humiliations and mockeries of an enemy triumph: she elects instead a death savouring of a royal pleasure. And linked with her in the same death fall her women attendants, for whom she is the goddess and queen of a pleasure that spurns "this vile world", the life not worth living when it is no longer lovely and glittering. Charmian before giving herself death utters the last farewell to her mistress:

> . . . *Downy windows, close;*
> *And golden Phoebus never be beheld*
> *Of eyes again so royal. Your crown's awry,*
> *I'll mend it and then play.*

[1919]

XIV

BEAUMARCHAIS

CHERUBINO AND THE COUNTESS

WHAT a poetic masterpiece they form, Cherubino and the Countess, in *The Marriage of Figaro*! Every attitude, retort, sigh, or murmur in that love relation has a wonderful delicacy and felicity. The drama is slight but impassioned, impetuous and headstrong for all its controlled reserve, its whole theme springing from the heat of the senses and of the fancy in the boy and the scarcely conscious yielding of the woman to an invitation which she would not listen to and yet ardently accepts and welcomes. This seems to lead to nothing, but in fact it leads to the experience of an amorous passion in which two souls receive the marks of renunciation, memories, regrets, longings that will never cease. Cherubino is not, as is usually said, just the youth awakening to the first awareness of Woman and of the transports of love: his is the heightened amorous temperament, for which the highest ideal and vital principle is the love of love; he is bold, brave, and generous – how otherwise could he serve his ideal were he not ready for every encounter, were he not chivalrously blameless, were he on the contrary timid and vacillating in his own eyes first, and then in those of the lady to whom he looks up as "belle et noble", "imposante", too exalted to be desired – and yet desired? See how without a moment's hesitation he leaps from the castle to avoid compromising her, runs eagerly to pick up the ribbon she has dropped and clasps it in his fist, challenging any man to attempt to wrest it from him, half unsheathes his sword against the Count, his colonel, to insist upon satisfaction for the offence of a pungent remark. (The offence, as soon as uttered, loses its outline in the reality of the situation.) On her side the Countess, no longer loved by her husband, who runs after other women and is jealous, for mere reasons of pride of what she does, tries indeed to bring the Count back to reason and his duty but knows in her hidden heart that she no longer loves him, though she had married him for love. She is aware of the secret ardour of the boy and feels in herself a disturbance which is at the same time a motion of unaccustomed pleasure. Love besets her in a different situation and shape from those known to her as a girl. She dreams, and her dream has a quality of sinfulness which both repels and attracts her. At one moment she sternly combats the passion which she must condemn and ought to suppress – however dear to her the anxious devotion with which it is urged. But at another moment she deliberately incites it. Now she would hide even from herself the nature of her feeling, feigning that it is one of compassion for the "malheureux enfant", but now again she recognizes it frankly and marvels at the change which has come over her in that she has those feelings. She will not yield, and is thus free of outward guilt, but at heart she has yielded and has incurred inward guilt. Don Basilio has cunningly imagined and foreseen what was brewing; the Count has had occasion for suspicion and is all on edge to make sure and to exact a penalty; only Suzon, the faithful, quick-witted, experienced lady's maid, has fully divined and understood, and therefore protects and assists the two in their developing passion. She has no clear, deliberate purpose but takes sides with a woman's instinct for the intrigue of love against legal and conventional duty. The Countess, agitated and breathless, awaits Cherubino in order, she says, to scold him severely, but Suzon suggests to her to make him – when he comes – sing a melancholy love song which he renders very prettily; and when the Countess then murmurs: "Mais c'est qu'en vérité mes cheveux sont dans un désordre", she smiles at her: "Je n'ai qu'à reprendre ces deux boucles; Madame le grondera bien mieux." At this the lady collects her dignity, knits her brow, and asks: "Qu'est-ce que vous dites donc, mademoiselle?"; but the smile or rather the tiny arrow which has caught her off her guard has done its work. Suzon has read clear in her soul, and is helping her, has already begun to help her, in her whole-hearted transport of abandonment to that wild and charming boy – nay, Suzon herself stays toying with that folly, not asking herself whether she will be able to stop and withdraw at a certain moment or will pursue the charming perilous adventure to the end.

(It seems to be my fate that every motion of aesthetic admiration which I feel must be followed or accompanied by a critical disgust. I have opened the "standard work" on Beaumarchais, the two big volumes of L. de Loménie's *Beaumarchais et son temps* (2nd edn., Paris, 1858), to see what is said there about the *Mariage de Figaro* and I find the illustrious French academician, in face of this miracle of humanity and art, curling his lip in mortification or perhaps displeasure: "Cette création de Chérubin est-elle bien vraie? ... Est-ce bien là une personification exacte de la puberté en général chez les jeunes gens, non seulement de treize ans, mais même de quinze et seize?" and he insists upon reminding us that "même au dixhuitième siècle on comprenait assez bien tout ce qui se mêle de sentiment délicat et élevé aux premières ardeurs de l'adolescence, pour accueillir avec transport un autre Chérubin qui apparaît, je crois, la même année que celui de Beaumarchais, et qui en est comme la contrepartie", that is to say the somewhat stylized Paul of *Paul et Virginie*. And with a sigh of satisfaction at the memory of that model of purity and every other virtue he concludes: "Voilà bien le souffle moral, qui tempère en les épurant les premières agitations des sens dans un adolescent à la fois plus naturel et plus intéressant que Chérubin." Comment would be superfluous: it would consist in those words which Flaubert was wont to use upon professors and academicians: "du moment qu'ils se mêlent de l'art", suitable enough on the lips of him, a fellow-Frenchman and a contemporary, but not on mine.)

Beaumarchais did not produce a literary masterpiece like this at his first shot. He began with the dramas *Eugénie* and *Les deux amis*, which give no hint of such capacity. They are moralizing pieces on error and repentance, extreme goodness and perfectly virtuous conduct. "Ah! Dieu! Que de vertus!" remarks Monsieur de Saint-Albin in admiration at the more than virtuous conclusion of the second play: the exclamation may stand with emphasis on the tedium, however, rather than the admirability of the plot. There was in Beaumarchais a moralist, a social critic and controversialist who needs must have his say, and not only could not do so poetically, but checked the fresh and clear poetry which strove to issue forth from another and more hidden side of Beaumarchais. This began, perhaps, to find its way to utterance when, in his celebrated self-defence in the Goëzman affair against the young woman's accusations, he gradually passed from those triumphant vindications which left her nothing to stand upon, to a direct glance at her – a glance of human understanding. "Eh, quel homme assez dur se défendrait de la douce compassion qu'inspire un trop faible ennemi, poussé dans l'arène par la cruauté de ceux qui n'ont pas le courage de s'y présenter eux-mêmes? Qui peut voir sans s'adoucir une jeune femme jetée entre les hommes et forcée par l'acharnement des uns de se mettre aux prises avec les autres; s'égarer dans ses fuites, s'embarrasser dans ses réponses; sentir qu'elle en rougit, et rougir encore plus de dépit de ne pouvoir s'en empêcher." At first he had played with this adversary like a cat with a mouse, but now he draws in his claws and plays harmlessly, indulgent and almost sympathetic towards that feminine vanity and levity – Oh so vain! Oh so light! which is charming like the childlike in the child. He says so in one of his interrogations in the Court. "Quoi qu'il en soit, vous voulez absolument une interpellation avant de nous quitter? Il faut vous satisfaire. Je vous interpelle, donc, Madame, de nous dire à l'instant, sans réfléchir et sans y être préparée, pourquoi vous accusez dans tous vos interrogatoires être agée de trente ans, quand votre visage, qui vous contredit, n'en montre que dix-huit?" The intention may have been mockery but as mere words these could not but sound flattering, stimulating to her ready imagination, which at once conjured up as truth the self-portrait that she cherished in her desires. In fact (so he continues): "malgré la colère que vous en montrez aujourd'hui, avouez-le, Madame, cette *atrocité* vous offensa si peu que, prenant votre éventail et votre manteau, vous me priâtes de vous donner la main pour rejoindre votre voiture; sans y chercher d'autre conséquence je vous la présentai poliment, lorsque M. Frémin, le meilleur des hommes, mais le plus inexorable des greffiers, nous fit apercevoir que nous ne devions pas descendre du Palais ensemble avec cet air d'intelligence peu décent pour l'occasion. Alors vous saluant de nouveau, je vous dis: – Eh bien, Madame, suis-je aussi *atroce* qu'on a voulu vous le faire entendre? – Eh bien, vous êtes au moins bien malin. – Laissez donc, Madame, les injures grossières aux hommes, elles gâtent toujours la jolie bouche des femmes. – Un doux sourire, à ce compliment, rendit à la vôtre la forme agréable que l'humeur avait altéré et nous nous quittâmes." Thus recounting, Beaumarchais rose above the legal squabble, above accusers and calumniators, to the heights of an artist's enjoyment.

Gaiety triumphed altogether over the moral and satirical veins in the *Barbier de Séville*, intended by Beaumarchais as "une pièce amusante et sans fatigue" – his censurers said a "farce" and he rectified "une espèce d'imbroglio". The story is of a girl who by cunning and boldness succeeds in eluding the oppression of her harsh and watchful guardian and takes the bridegroom of her choice: an *andante allegro* from beginning to end, with much wit and delicacy in its dialogue and imagery, witness the celebrated refrain of Don Basilio on the theme of calumny: "D'abord un bruit léger, rasant le sol comme hirondelle avant l'orage, *pianissimo*, murmure et file, et sème en courant le trait empoisonné . . ." – a hymn of praise to Calumny, sung by a skilled practitioner thereof who has long considered its especial quality, the scope of its insinuating, gradual influence, and can describe it so as to arouse admiration as for any other masterly work of man or spectacle of the prime power of nature. Liveliest of all are the actions and words of Figaro, a character on whom there has been much discussion. Scholars have recognized in him the last theatrical representative of the "slave" personage in Graeco-Roman comedy. Historians and sociologists have spied in him the long downtrodden Plebs rising to look its masters in the face and to judge them pending the moment for a revolution: and a line of ancestors has been sought for this Figaro, thus conceived. There is some truth in both observations, but a truth which concerns the history of theatrical plots and of social transformations, not aesthetic truth, and not the part played by the Figaro character in the *Barbier* and still more in the second comedy of the *Mariage*. This part is rather to be compared to that of the Mephistopheles of Faust – they are alike in their uninhibited cleverness in every part they have to play, in every turn of affairs that comes to plague themselves or others – Mephistopheles (and like him, Figaro) is always on the spot, lively, acute, and highly audible.

In the *Mariage*, in particular, the character of Figaro is so prominent, and his satirical shafts aimed at aristocracy, magistracy, and the world of politics come so thick and fast, that one gets the impression that he is the chief personage in the comedy. And so perhaps he is – in the comedy. But not in the poetry. In this the charming figures of the Countess and Cherubino take the lead, and here Beaumarchais is at the height of his humanity. In the remainder of the play he shows himself agreeably satirical and amusing when, indeed, he does not display yet a third vein as the tearful, sentimental moralist, which happens when he suddenly raises the absurd and shifty Marcellina to self-display as an exemplar of the vice of which society renders her guilty, declaiming with emphasis: "Hommes plus qu'ingrats, qui flétrissez par le mépris les jouets de vos passions, vos victimes! C'est vous qu'il faut punir des erreurs de notre jeunesse..." The reader remarks at once how out of place this is, but Beaumarchais did not: he thought the scene in question was a fine contribution to the educational and civil stage, "dirigeant l'attention publique sur les vrais fauteurs du désordre où l'on entraine sans pitié toutes les jeunes filles du peuple douées d'une jolie figure". Fortunately Figaro appears again to retransform the tearful drama into light comedy: having been discovered to be the offspring of Bartolo, who was pursuing him for debt, and of Marcellina, who had wheedled a loan out of him and was insisting on fulfilment of his written promise to marry her. Figaro, who had only just escaped from being forced by legal sanctions to repeat the horrible experience of Oedipus, breaks out, half angry and half amused at the judge still discoursing to him of justice: "Elle allait me faire une belle sottise, la justice! Après que j'ai manqué pour ces maudits cent écus, d'assommer vingt fois Monsieur, qui se trouve aujourd'hui mon père! Mais puisque le ciel

a sauvé ma vertu de ses dangers, mon père, agréez mes excuses . . .
Et vous, ma mère, embrassez-moi . . . le plus maternellement que
vous pourrez."

However the author judged this comedy, celebrated in the
years just before the French Revolution for its passionately interesting polemical aspects, his heart was certainly not with the
protagonist Figaro but with those two secondary persons suggested to him by his Muse in a moment of rare felicity. He will
have asked himself, one feels, what had happened to them in
later life, as one does about real persons, and it must have been
thus that he came to put their subsequent adventures on the stage.
What then happened to them? It happened that Cherubino became
an officer, went to the wars, returned unexpectedly one night,
still on fire with love, to the castle where the Countess was alone,
the Count having departed on a distant journey. In that solitude
Cherubino's love triumphed. And a child was born. The Countess
felt that she had been taken by surprise, indeed by force, and in
letting Cherubino know of this shattering event and of the terrible
position in which it left her towards her husband, she forbade him
ever to try and see her again. Cherubino answered by sending her
back her letter, the portrait which he had drawn of her, and a
lock of her hair that he had carried: he told her that since he
might not see her again and life had become hateful, he would seek
to lose it by volunteering for an attack; and a postscript to the
letter said that he had done this and now lay mortally wounded
and asked only, with these farewell words, not to be forgotten.
The years pass: the Count has understood what had happened,
knows that the child is not his, will not forgive his wife her
infidelity, harbours designs of vengeance against her and the child
illicitly bearing his name. One day he comes across the box in
which the Countess kept those last relics of her lover, and with
feelings of hatred and anger opens her anguished and despairing
letter. But then those feelings give way to one of mild compassion.
"Ce n'est point là non plus l'écrit d'un méchant homme! Un
malheureux égarement . . . Je me sens déchiré." The two spouses,
human beings who have erred and suffered like all others in the

course of their lives, and are by now ageing and disposed to indulgence and pity, now find their way, through a series of strange
occurrences and complicated reconsiderations, to a conciliation,
giving rise to a new and purer affection. As though to seal the
mutual pardon the son of the Countess and Cherubino marries the
girl he loves, who is the daughter of the Count by another woman.
"O mes enfants," the Count exclaims, "il vient un âge où les
honnêtes gens se pardonnent leurs torts, leurs anciennes faiblesses,
et font succéder un doux attachement aux passions orageuses qui
les avaient trop désunis! . . ." But here we become aware of the
first Beaumarchais with his emphatic sentimentality, the Beaumarchais of the tearful comedies of which the *Mère coupable*, with
its elaborations of the plots of wickedness against goodness and
innocence leading up to the triumph of these last, gives the full
measure. No doubt the theme of a fault committed in the high
heat of passion, and of mutual indulgence and pardon in the evening of life, can afford food for the fancy, but treated in this superficially theatrical manner it remains abstract and sterile. By the
side of its brilliant forerunner the "Mère coupable" can but confirm
the old Spanish saying about the sequels to much-applauded
works, "nunca segundas partes fueron buenas". But though
worthless as art, the *Mère coupable* remains a singular testimony to
the prolonged vibration, in the soul of Beaumarchais, of those two
creatures of burning and perilous passion who one day came to
him enveloped in a bright vision of smiling poetry: Cherubino
and the Countess.

[1937]

XV

GOETHE

WAGNER THE PEDANT

I CONFESS to a weakness for Wagner, the *famulus*, Doctor Faust's assistant. I enjoy his naive and limitless faith in learning, his honest aim to be a serious student, his simple straightness, unaffected modesty, unfailing deference and gratitude to his exalted master. I feel for him in his inclination for quiet handling of parchments, his hatred of crowds, noise, and hurdygurdies, and of promenades and excursions, to which he so greatly prefers the evening retreat into his own little room with its books and his pen, to read and think and make notes. I cannot bring myself to blame his little weaknesses, which amount merely to the aspiration one day to deserve the applause of society as a savant and a wise counsellor. I have not the heart to reproach him with his way of invariably judging and reasoning with the phrases and the maxims of moderation. How can you reproach a man with the very mainspring of his life and activities?

Maddening, though unintentionally, Wagner certainly is to those of altogether opposite spirit: the sight of placid and contented sanity is always intolerable to the neuropath and that of prosaic felicity to one tossed amid gales and tempests of passion. He is often intolerable to Faust himself – at times his expression, his voice, positively frighten the master, who speaks to him exclusively in tones of impatience, tedium, sarcasm. There is really no conversation between them: Wagner never understands what is said, nor does Faust ever hope to make such a man do so. Faust simply takes the occasion to discharge his resentment against the universal lie, and against himself: Wagner is absorbed in trying to enrich his treasury of knowledge and wisdom, culled from the lips of the Master. Devotedly he drinks in his words: but not one of the concepts which they express reaches his brain to any effect: those wise saws interpose too solid a barrier. Faust pursues his feverish inner monologue interrupted only by foolish phrases of rejoinder from the gaping Wagner, veritable stings and goads to the stirring, striving, struggling Professor. But the great man's cutting, contemptuous retorts seem to the pupil once again masterpieces of learning – *so gelehrt* – which instead of confounding him re-excite his admiration.

Wagner does not and indeed cannot remark Faust's open scorn, sarcasm, contempt, for he cannot conceive that his own virtuous ideal of learning and mental recollectedness can have an absurd side, while reverence for the great man at whose side his good luck has placed him submerges and annuls in him the self-respect which would have rendered him sensitive to the reproaches. But one would like to say to him: "Quite right, old fellow, to stick to your simple dignity and affectionate devotion, listening in humility and not feeling at all hurt. Faust is a philosopher and a man and his wrath against you is purely intellectual. Mind what you are about, all the same, should you marry; for if instead of one of the timid silent creatures that Jean Paul often bestows on his learned fools, you should choose for wife a Faust in skirts, a Titaness or Valkyrie, you will be exposed not just to such smart philosophic slaps in the face, but to a rain of dislike, hatred, nausea, such as you really do not deserve. This is the fate of that colleague of yours the diligent historical scholar Tessmann who will conceive the fine notion of marrying Hedda Gabler!"[1]

Many a critic has hit on a parallel between the Faust-Wagner and the Quixote-Sancho couple, but in truth Faust has nothing in him of Don Quixote and Wagner very little of Sancho Panza. If anyone, it is Wagner who has something of the Don Quixote about him: he is a Quixote of the old learning. For Wagner's ideal is precisely the Humanistic ideal conjoined with the Baconian:

---

1. HEDDA: Tessman, my friend, is a specialist.
   BRACK: Quite so.
   HEDDA: Specialists do not make amusing travelling companions, at all events not for long.
   BRACK: Not even a specialist . . . whom one loves?
   HEDDA: For God's sake don't use that disgusting word.

(IBSEN, *Hedda Gabler*, II, I)

to pore admiringly over ancient histories; to draw from them prudential maxims and rules, political and moral; to search through the laws of nature to discover their social utility. It was an ideal already in course of dissolution in Goethe's time, by reason of a prevailing scepticism concerning naturalistic, abstract methods, and a scorn for arid erudition and rules of conduct. In its place there was being or would soon be cultivated a renewal of the old Augustinian zeal to *redire in se ipsum*, to explore the human mind and soul, and a new sentiment of the religious wonder of history, a new insurgent and heroic ethic. Of such an intellectual development, though surging all around him and shaking his own master to the depths, Wagner had not the slightest inkling. He remains chivalrously faithful to an out-of-date science, conceives the highest good to lie in possession of a library rich in codices and parchments, a cabinet replete with natural curiosities and observational or experimental instruments, a medical art laying down written rules for the way to kill the patient, and – in order that one may oneself cut a figure in the world – an acquired skill in the exercise of persuasion and of the rhetorical *actio*. Insatiable desires, vertiginous dreams of the superman are disturbances which he, blessedly, has never experienced, although as he amiably remarks he too has "sometimes hours of fancy free", very much as Don Quixote found himself now and then in the real world of his niece and his serving-maid.

The pleasure that never fails when one reaches the place in *Faust* where Wagner enters on the scene seems to me to be equalled only by the fury which seizes upon Wagner's master at the same point.[1] The character who takes the stage is comical – and what a worthy entrance does he make! Faust is still warmly thrilling in the

---

1.   *O Tod! ich kenn's — das ist mein Famulus —*
           Es wird mein schönstes Gluck zunichte!
           Dass diese Fülle der Gesichte
           Der trockne Schleicher stören muss!

('Sdeath! I am sure that's my assistant! – An end to my fairest happiness! Ah that the sapless bore needs must destroy this plenitude of vision!) Translator's Note: In the original of this essay, Croce gives his own loosely metrical Italian version of the extracts.

intensity of the contact he has taken in his brief, intense colloquy
with the Spirit of the Earth, so quick to respond and then to
disappear. Wagner, who had heard voices, believed, in his simplicity, that the master was declaiming a Greek tragedy, and now
asks to be allowed to profit by this lesson in declamation. The
entrance itself, and subsequently each interchange in the two
conversations between Wagner and Faust, is a marvel of brilliant
naturalness, perfect fusion of the serious and the comic. Not that
the character of the pedant was new to literature – who can forget
the satirical sketches by Erasmus of the rusty scholastic disputants,
or those of the Ciceronian Humanists in Italian seventeenth-
century comedy, or those outdated but fanatical Aristotelians
lampooned in the controversial writings of Bruno and Galileo?
Yet those depictions were, as said, satirical, they belonged to the
negative form of criticism developed with witty eloquence, and
producing at best caricatures – not poetry. Sometimes, poetry is
just brushed, but not sought or taken up, as in Bruno's figure of
Polihimnio, "... a Jupiter who from his high observatory observes
and considers the life of other men, subject as they are to such
errors, calamities, miseries, fruitless fatigues", whereas, "he alone
is happy, leads a celestial life contemplating his own divinity in
an anthology, dictionary, Calepino, lexicon, cornucopia, Nizzolio,
or what not". But Goethe, like a true poet, has no use for satires,
encomiums, sheer black and sheer white, he cares only for the
game of lights and shadows, knows only mankind in its humility
or its grandeur as the case may be. The pedant, mocked by the
controversialists of the sixteenth century, loaded by the comedians
with every sort of insult (ultimately, poor patient brute, with the
attributes of thieves and pederasts), turned, in Goethe's hands, to
an idyllic and most virtuous creature, who could even be interesting and moving. The good and the bad character, the virtuous and
the vicious, the wise and the foolish – what are these but abstractions, as these terms, taken in isolation, are themselves abstract?
From the point of view of Aesthetics it may indeed be proclaimed
that perfectly good and virtuous characters are not poetical, but
then it must be added and explained that neither are perfectly bad

and vicious characters, not because virtue and vice are inartistic, because perfection in either of these two directions, taken in isolation from the other, proves, when represented, to be something dead, an abstraction. Now who could ever say which of the two, Faust or Wagner, was in the right? Who could say that the wrong lay wholly in the double limitations of Wagner's mind (his cult of learning reduced not only life but learning itself to aridity) or in the double limitlessness of Faust, wildly striving to join and to sum up in a single act life, learning, and pleasure? Goethe's Wagner, the human-hearted pedant, suits admirably the modern feeling for the unity of contraries, the indivisibility of the human spirit. In his particularity he has had a long and various and honourable line of successors, among the latest of whom have been some of Anatole France's light vignettes – for instance Silvestre Bonnard, member of the Institute, who before giving himself over to the labour of protecting and marrying off nice girls, himself "with magnanimous ardour" labours away at ancient parchments from which modest efforts he awaits an outcome "somehow mysterious, vague, and sublime".

Wagner is sentimental and warm-blooded in his affection to the point of having to address his master in lyrical tones, not with the sublime lyricism of Faust's own winged language, but with an idyllic lyricism which is at times quietly contented, at times heaves a sigh:

> Wie anders tragen uns die Geistesfreuden
> Von Buch zu Buch, von Blatt zu Blatt!
> Da werden Winternächte hold und schön,
> Ein selig Leben wärmet alle Glieder,
> Und ach! entrollst du gar ein würdig Pergamen,
> So steigt der ganze Himmel zu dir nieder.

Here is another sigh:

> Wie schwer sind nicht die Mittel zu erwerben,
> Durch die man zu den Quellen steigt!
> Und eh' man nur den halben Weg erreicht,
> Muss wohl ein armer Teufel sterben.

His delight lies in savorous contemplation of the images of glory, scholarly glory:

Welch ein Gefühl musst du, o grosser Mann,
Bei der Verehrung dieser Menge haben!
O glücklich, wer von seinen Gaben
Solch einen Vorteil ziehen kann!
Der Vater zeigt dich seinem Knaben,
Ein jeder fragt und drängt und eilt,
Der Fiedel stockt, der Tänzer weilt.
Du gehst, in Reihen stehen sie,
Die Mützen fliegen in die Höh',
Und wenig fehlt, so beugten sich die Knie,
Als käm das Venerabile.

In the scansion of these verses the rapt but somehow subdued air of one tasting a mystic joy, primed at the same time with noble envy, comes to life: we can see the ecstatic air with which Wagner utters them, we can follow the modulations of a voice well trained in rhetoric, in these apostrophes, exclamations, emphatic descriptions.

Let us not forget in this idyll the poodle that takes to following Faust, just a dog with nothing particular about it to Wagner, yet, since the master seems to take an interest in it, calling for some show of benevolence on the pupil's side, an aphorism, a gracious compliment seeming somehow to raise it to the level of their companionship, and of the academic world:

Dem Hunde, wenn er gut gezogen,
Wird selbst ein weiser Mann gewogen.
Ja, deine Gunst verdient er ganz und gar,
Er, der Studenten trefflicher Skolar.

The well-characterized, lifelike Wagner of the first two scenes does not altogether lose his artistic liveliness even among the allegories, caprices, and oddities of the second part, in the scene of the Homunculus. The commentators have written many subtle observations upon these, to small effect, it would seem, because the very need for subtle interpretations betokens the failure of the recital to speak for itself, the non-coincidence of idea (if idea there be) with form. Even so, Wagner, now "Dr. Wagner", celebrated occupant of a professorial chair, with a dense crowd of students drinking in his words, and a *famulus* of his own named Nicodemus, comes before us as one whose head has not been turned by success, faithfully venerating the memory of the old master and patron who had suddenly disappeared in a way he could never understand. He keeps Faust's study unchanged, his hood still hanging on the nail ready for his return, in which Wagner still hopes and trusts. Nicodemus remarks that Wagner will never let his own name be mentioned even lightly in rivalry with that of Faust, the sublime: "Modesty is his chosen part." And, when, after hearing himself called by that delightful affectionate abbreviation of "Father" by the Homunculus emerging from his distillations, he sees his creature turn straight to Mephistopheles in full understanding with him, and hears him announce his immediate departure, in company with his two companions, for the Pharsalian fields, poor Wagner, feeling himself abandoned, breaks forth in anguish: "And what of me?" "You", answers mockingly the young offspring of science, "must stay here to do things of great importance. You will not fail to reach a glorious destination. Farewell." Wagner resigns himself, but not without emotion:

> *Leb wohl! Das drückt das Herz mir nieder.*
> *Ich fürchte schon, ich seh' dich niemals wieder.*

Even amid the coldness of these allegories Wagner's eyes are bright with human tears.

[1918]

XVI

GOETHE

GOETHE's notions about the immortality of the soul must not be allowed to dominate the scene (in *Faust*, Part II) where the chorus of Helen's handmaidens are rendered, in dissolution of their beings, back to nature. Not but what these notions do indeed make their appearance there, nor should we ignore this. Goethe felt altogether certain of immortality, and this certainty was founded for him principally on the consideration that we cannot do without it (*dass wir nicht es entbehren können*). He said this also to Eckermann, explaining to him that he drew his conviction from the concept of activity, because "if I ceaselessly labour to achieve my end, it is Nature's duty to assign me another form of existence so that I may continue to labour". He added, however, that "we are not all of us immortal in the same way" and that "to figure in the future as a great Entelechy, you needs must really be one".[1] This idea of what has been called "aristocratic" immortality has been advanced from time to time and can be found in the literature of the subject. We find it in Italy, for example, in the dissertation written in 1868 by Marianna Florenzi, once the friend of the romantic King Ludwig I of Bavaria, and frequenter of old Schelling, and then, in later life, active in philosophical labours.[2] Marianna Florenzi, setting herself the question "whether all souls can lay claim to immortality or only some privileged souls", believed there to be an unanswerable case for the view that "there are inferior souls in which the animal and material part is preponderant. These feel no need for immortality . . . but remain heavy and coarse, enslaved to the senses, dominated by vices, and having no other craving but to satisfy these." She added that "immortality being due to man as a free and independent person",

1. *Gespräche mit Eckermann*, Feb. 4th and Sept. 1st 1829.
2. *Dell'immortalità dell'anima umana*, Essay by Marchesa Marianna Florenzi Waddington (Florence, Le Monnier, 1869).

those only are worthy of it who by dint of their own activity and by the effect of their own development, elevate themselves to the status of moral persons.[1] These thoughts and rationalizations, common to Goethe and to the famous Italian beauty (she was niece to the still more famous beauty Cornelia Martinetti, celebrated in Foscolo's *Grazie*: her own effigy is still a brilliant item in the series of paintings of female beauties in the Munich Hofburg),[2] can hardly be held to confirm what is commonly understood by immortality – the survival, as substance, of the abstract individual. When we have eliminated the factor of the merely imagined, what remains, in these notions, of real thought does but affirm the immortality of human work which works on for ever proportionately to the magnitude and conformably to the quality of its origin and its development. The good Eckermann, thrilled and stirred by the doctrine imparted to him, told Goethe that "this more than any other incites to noble actions": and indeed he who wholly or for the most part lacks that idea of immortality and the sense of responsibility which goes with it, and thus in effect says to himself: "après moi le déluge", will turn out to be correspondingly devoid of real moral earnestness.

Goethe was very pleased when he conceived the notion of using his theory about immortality for the scene on which he was engaged in the second part of *Faust*, portraying the chorus of Helen's handmaidens as "unwilling to descend to the lower regions, but desiring to dissolve into the elements on the cheerful surface of the earth".[3]

They were creatures of sense and instinct, those girls, like the many young girls and maidens whose doings and secret stirrings and unspoken or half-spoken words Goethe had interpreted and divined in their several measures, portraying with love and indulgence, and the warmth of an affectionate smile, those pretty narrow-browed creatures. These handmaids had been Helen's house-

1. Ibid., pp. 39-41. On this essay see the remark of Fiorentino in his commemoration of the authoress (*Scritti varî*, Naples, 1870, pp. 413-14).
2. For this lady see E. CORTI, *Ludwig I von Bayern* (Munich, 1937).
3. *Gespräche*, cit., Jan. 25 1827.

hold companions in Troy. After the tremendous Fall they had accompanied her back to Sparta: at the gates of the palace there, when the Queen, at sight of the home of her youth, had been overwhelmed by tragic memories and the fatality of her beauty, they for their part remained unstirred, unafraid, unable to understand how beauty and its fascination could possibly be occasion for lamentation. Soon their fleeting interest was attracted to the treasure stored in the palace, especially the *mundus muliebris* therein, overjoyed to think that Helen would now take possession of it, and they would be admiring "beauty in rivalry with gold and pearls and jewels". In their light thoughtlessness the girls cannot enter into the mind of their exalted queen; they can only seek to envelop her in glittering optimism as they pit their *joie-de-vivre* against her distress.

But now Mephistopheles, in his disguise as Phorcis, amuses himself teasing them. How well he knows them in their girlish, flirtatious, sensual shamelessness, this "brood born in war, grown up amid ruins, mad for men, seducers and seduced, unmanners of soldiers and citizens". He taunts and mocks them still when Helen praises their faithfulness in service; beside her, the swan of beauty, he finds them to be a brood of greedy geese flapping their impoverished wings. The girls cannot stand it and one after another leaves the chorus, not without some sharp thrust at Mephistopheles, returned by him in kind: "How hideous is ugliness by the side of beauty" – "How stupid, by the side of intelligence, is stupidity!"

This duet or rather, as such an alternation was termed in Greek tragedy, stichomythia, has been by at least one commentator combed for all the hints which might lie embedded in its tangles. He has explained that Mephistopheles, desiring to disturb the realm of beauty, over which he, the ugly one, has no power, disguises himself as a moralist, and with a moralist's reproof ("never yet did beauty and modesty go together") provokes the girls to insolent retorts whereby they themselves, issuing forth out of the realm of beauty, become ugly.[1] But really

---

1. H. RICKERT, *Goethes Faust*, Tübingen, 1932, pp. 364-5.

there is no more in it than a lifelike squabble between a group of wenches set on exploiting their youth and looks for enjoyment without care or repining, and an experienced *coureur* amusing himself with teasing them into vociferation, telling them to their faces (or nozzles) truths which make them scream, truths they want to hide from themselves and everyone, telling these with exaggeration and injustice in that, just to madden the ladies, their light lasciviousness is treated as deep corruption and wickedness.

It amuses Mephistopheles not only thus to anger and provoke them, but also to frighten them. So after announcing to Helen the death which awaits her in the impending solemn sacrifice, when the shocked and startled girls ask what will happen to them, he answers with the coldness of gloating cruelty: "She will die a noble death, but you are going to hang and dance like dead thrushes all in a row from the beam of the roof." This is altogether too much for their game spirit, their repartee; words fail them. The chorus leader speaks now for them all, asking pardon for their behaviour, witless (*hirnlos*) girls that they are. Then the unfortunates pursue their lamentation: "O most venerable of the Fates, wisest Sybil, keep closed the golden shears, proclaim for us light and safety, we who already feel ourselves hanging, dangling, swinging. How dreadful for our little limbs that want rather to dance and then fall resting on a darling bosom."

Some commentators have found these verses inappropriately close to farce, but truly their tone is, for a more skilled taste, most charming, sympathetic, indeed humane. Vanity remains vain even amid the images and the affairs of death. Ann Boleyn, the day before her execution, talking to her gaoler the Governor of the Tower of London, said: "I heard say the executioner was very good, and I have a little neck", and putting her hands round it she laughed very heartily. The night before the execution she was heard to "jazer le plus playsemment du monde", among other things chatting about the name the ballad-writers would give her – perhaps "Reine Anne sans teste"; "et disant tels propoz se mit à rire si très fort qu'onques ne fust oui telle chose, bien sachant toutefois qu'elle mourrait lendemain sans nul remède".[1] In much the same way now the girls of the chorus, forgetting altogether the jests, cracks, insults they have been exchanging, proceed to supplicate Phorkias (Mephistopheles) to show them a way of escape from the doom of death:

> Speak, tell us quickly, how are we to escape the dreadful odious knots drawn threateningly around our necks: already poor wretches we feel we can no longer breathe, we shall suffocate unless you, O Rhea, high mother of all Gods, take pity on us.

Mephistopheles, who so well knows their flightiness and incapacity for reflection, deems it necessary to ask them even in that extremity whether they will have the patience to listen to a rather long speech. "Patience we have enough and to spare, for while we listen we can go on living," the girls exclaim in chorus.

Mephistopheles has opened to them a prospect of safety in the fortress of Faust and his warriors; he has hinted at halls opening out one beyond the other "boundless, vast as the world", "where you can dance". At once their minds return to the accustomed images of gaiety and pleasure: "And partners too?" "Splendid partners – ranks of blond-curled striplings fresh and fragrant. Paris alone when he pressed the Queen so close was not less fragrant." Poised helplessly between joy and fear the girls line up to approach the castle of Faust. Their leader finds it necessary to preach a little sermon:

> Pressing and foolish girls, image indeed of the feminine! Slaves of the moment, playthings of changeful weather, of luck and doom, unable to meet either with calm mind. Each of you shouting down the other and by the others herself held down, save only when in joy or grief you laugh or shriek in unison. Now silence! Wait and hear what our lady in her high wisdom will decree for herself and all of us.

In the castle the sight of the squires and pages thrills them wildly: hungrily they watch those graceful movements, those golden curls on peerless brows, those cheeks pink like peach-down, for

1. The Governor's letter to Thomas Cromwell is dated May 18th 1536 and the envoy Chapuis' letter to Granvela June 6th. Given in Friedmann, *Lady Anne Boleyn* (Paris, 1903), II, 330, and Sergeant, *The Life of Anne Boleyn* (London, 1924), p. 294.

which their mouths water ("*gern biss' ich hinein*"). And when Helen with her hand pledges her troth to Faust, they nod and comment that they being all virtual captives after their great disasters, it needs must happen so.

> *Women, men-loving, cannot be choosers, only knowers: as occasion determines, they make free of their soft charms now to some fair-headed shepherd, now to a dark and hairy faun with equal right.*

And made as they are for kisses and embraces, frail creatures of flesh – so the poet has portrayed them in all the scenes of the third act, what can they do when Helen has disappeared and Panthalis summons them to follow their queen to Hades, to the throne of the Inscrutable, with sober steps as would beseem faithful handmaidens? This is how they answer:

> *Queens are welcome everywhere: in Hades too they stand aloft among their peers, close by Persephone's side. But how shall we others pass our time, in a scene of thickly growing asphodel, by tall poplars and fruitless willows? Are we to screech displeasingly like bats, we ghostly ones?*

That is to say: in stern Hades they would suffer tedium, and they would fain not go there. Their leader alone is of another mind: she burns with desire to follow her queen – and it is not merit alone, but also faithfulness that can fortify one. Turning therefore to the girls she cries to them: "Whoever has won no renown, desired no nobility, belongs to the elements: betake you therefore to them."

But that is just their desire: nature would return to nature. "Behold us restored to the light of day, no longer – well we feel and know it – as persons. But to Hades we shall never return. Nature eternally living has full rights over us, and we over Nature."

And now this resolution accomplishes itself for four groups each of which sings the celebration of those particular tendencies and affinities in virtue of which they go to their new place in the new life, one turning to Dryads, or nymphs of the trees, a second to Oreads, nymphs of the mountains, a third to Naiads, nymphs of the springs, and the fourth to nymphs of the vines. In these lyrics the tone is brisk and zestful as beseems creatures who have chosen the manner of their dissolution and fulfil it cheerfully, passing from a human life of joy and smiles to the similarly joyous and sportive life of nature. What do they lose by the change? Consciousness, perhaps? But they had so little of it, they were already so largely nature. They will continue as before both enjoying and giving enjoyment with their changeful bestowal of delights mingled with alternating caprice, whim, intoxication, rapture.

I find it hard to explain how the critics, coming upon these fresh and vivacious representations and upon the witty, charming art which pervades the second part of Faust, prove so insensitive, and set about deforming them into allegories, concepts, and artificial intellectualisms. This is indeed what the Latin adage calls exchanging *pro thesauro carbones*: it gives us, instead of the treasure of the poetry of Wolfgang Goethe, the coals of the critics' own mental dryness and poverty.

[1933]

XVII

FOSCOLO

THE case for Ugo Foscolo's recognition as a European man and writer is somewhat easier to plead – being supported to some extent by accepted judgements and recognitions – than that for Vittorio Alfieri. Only by dint of considerable effort can Alfieri be detached from the narrow frame of his Italian renown as the political apostle of the national Risorgimento and as the literary man credited with having given to Italian literature the one thing which it lacked – tragedy – and be presented in his true colours as a European writer and an extreme individualist, or, as some now crudely put it, a libertarian or anarchist. Ugo Foscolo, too, has remained unknown to the European world of letters in the complexity of his personality and in his principal works. For on the strength of the book by which he became known and was studied outside Italy in his own time, the juvenile *Jacopo Ortis*, still today appearing in new translations and editions, he has been grouped with the pre-Romantic and proto-Romantic devotees of sadness, despair, suicide; while the poem *I Sepolcri* is docketed by scholars and critics in the series of poetic productions of England, France, and Germany at that time on the subject of tombs and cemeteries. During the years of his sojourn in England, Foscolo's critical essays were published by the best English reviews. And the late Giuseppe Manacorda in a recent study of Foscolo's poetry recalls continually, not as models imitated by Foscolo or authors studied by him, but as kindred spirits linked to him in time and in spiritual background, Hölderlin, Novalis, Tieck, Heinse, Goethe, Rousseau, Chénier, and many others. We would not of course deny that Foscolo, even more than Alfieri, communicated a strong impulse to national Italian sentiment, thereby justifying a view that the Italian patriots of the nineteenth century were Foscolo's offspring, in the same way that he himself descended from Alfieri, whose name, he said, he loved and honoured to the point of idolatry. Indeed Foscolo's action in this field might be described as without any parallel, since he operated upon Mazzini and through the words of Mazzini upon the younger generation. However, the use to which a people puts its poets and writers does not suffice to fix their own intimate character and significance.

Foscolo's was a grim view of the world: he felt and believed in the pressure of an unknown and violent force upon him, that force which pushes men into the world, into the sunlight, and obliges them to live "life's fitful fever"; then, inexorably, casts them down into the gloom of death and oblivion. The thought of death was with him dominant and wellnigh predominant, and like a Shakespearian character he chose to be familiar from youth onwards with death, not only in its aspect as oncoming destiny, but in the form it takes when invoked and desired, as suicide, the way out to be held ever open. Such a mood and outlook if no further defined might give rise to the most varied types of conduct, asceticism or cynicism, grim renunciation or frivolous enjoyment, activity or inactivity, embittered withdrawal or fervent and assiduous effort and exercise. For Foscolo it could only give rise to this last, making him sensitive, energetic, poised for expansion and action, open to generous impulse. Foscolo's case well illustrates the relation of life to philosophy, life offering itself, its experience, to thought, and receiving back the offering in a clearer, stronger form. By dint of courage and intellect, in the gathering gloom of that unknown and alien and so therefore materialistic force, Foscolo was able to espy a light, to find firm ground from which to recapture spontaneity, autonomy, liberty. What matter if this liberty came for him in the throb of "pleasure" or "pain"; or if he gave the name "tedium" to the not-being and not-doing, the negative dialectical pole in the forward-moving process, a tedium conducive to action? Or, again, what matter if he called "illusions" the ideals of beauty, virtue, friendship, country, humanity? In the very act of so calling them he admitted them in practice and asserted them in theory, paying homage to them and owning their necessity. From this derived his life as citizen, soldier, artist, scholar, friend, lover, a life which he proudly ever felt and claimed to be high and worthy and intrinsically righteous, as all the youth of Risorgimento Italy felt with him, and all those too who know something about human worth and how it is commingled with human failings. What if fault-finding, gossipy dunces have often assailed it with their moralizing ineptitudes? We may well ignore them.

This is not the place to recount or even swiftly sketch the life story of Foscolo as citizen and soldier, or to repeat the stylized yet wholly just summing-up of Cattaneo, that when Foscolo could do nothing else for Italy he created for her a new institution – that of exile – which would be of the highest efficacy in time to come. Nor will I say much of Foscolo's work as thinker and critic, though to do so would give me an opportunity to air my favourite notion that we should cease to track down the history of philosophy solely in the works of professional philosophers, many of whom, mere scholars and thesis-writers and compilers of systems, are much less important than non-professional thinkers who have things to say, not just words to utter. No doubt Foscolo's speculative ideas were of the agnostic and materialistic order: important as they were for his conduct and his politics, they were objectively without much importance or originality. They marked his philosophical limit, the darkness encircling and hemming him in. But then Socrates too gave up his meditations on nature and the cosmos, but produced some notoriously philosophical work which has been efficacious through the centuries. I mean to say that Foscolo, though he limited his enquiries to the sphere of the human soul, and disclaimed any attempt to mount to the origin of things, gave forth lively, fertile thoughts on man, art, politics, morals, history, religion.

In this range too he belonged to the European culture of his time at the highest level, so that in thinking of him the representative names of that spiritual epoch come to one's lips. In his view of poetry and of literary criticism and history he ranks among those who rediscovered a deeper outlook: he was indeed one of the very first to take advantage of the teachings of Vico a century earlier. He was fully aware of the intimate link binding poetry to life, and he disputed the capacity of those who, however learned in the rules and models of art, had never felt human passions in their breast, never thrown themselves into the clash of wills, feared, suffered, loved, and hated, to produce or to pass judgement upon poetry. Invective against the academicals, the armchair scholars and the "cloistered race", the schoolmen of old Italy, runs right through his pages, and his own argument for the historical interpretation of poetry is that true poetry, having taken its sustenance from the feelings and passions of men of various ages, cannot be understood save by reference to these. In this respect then he was, in the best sense, a Romantic, an admirer before all of the "primitive poet". But at the same time he was a Classic, disliking what he called the sentimental, often artificial taint of the modern writers and admiring the naturalness of the ancients who "described things as they saw them without swelling them out to suit jaded tastes". At the head and forefront of art he put "harmony". The style which he admired was the energetic, concentrated, sober style of the Greek authors by contrast with the easy fluent modern French style which "dilutes a thought into ten sentences". When the Romantics aired their theory of "national" and "historic" drama, he objected that poetry is in no way tied to "national subjects" and has no use for historical exactitude. Very strong in Foscolo was the sense of poetic form – not meaning by this the outward conformity to models and rules – and the sense of great poetry, and he was therefore able to take a fresh view of Dante and the other masters of poetry, and to recognize that much which the literary men of his time called poetry was nothing of the sort, Italy having remained almost bereft of poetry for two centuries despite the quantities of verse composed between the lifetime of Tasso and Alfieri. The function which he assigned to poetry and the arts was that of heightening the tone of life and human awareness of it, as an inward catharsis, one might say, an "aesthetic education". His theories and critical works no doubt exhibit imperfections, waverings, deficiencies, but the broad outlines, as here described, are unmistakable.

The same may be said of his other theories, particularly of the thought which he unflinchingly and positively professed that the sole reality lay in motion, agitation, feeling, action. In this he showed himself fully possessed by the spirit of the new age which sees salvation in the doing of deeds, and happiness in the creation which is close to and joined with pain. Accordingly, agnostic and pessimist and virtual materialist that he was, he yet by a significant contradiction was an assertor of the historical – not, indeed, of historical learning and anecdotes and examples but of objective and substantial history. And he summoned the Italians to historical study, which, he urged, should, like poetry and poetical criticism, be taken out of the hands of friars and academicians and cultivated in human fashion and with serious understanding of what was written about. Of this he himself gave the example. In politics he disdained to captivate the ear of the credulous multitude which gives its trust to the purveyors of easy promises, choosing instead to repeat the stern truths of Machiavelli and Hobbes, confirmed to him by his reading of history and by daily experience. He urged the Italians to military service as "the sole hope for our country" and made them ashamed of the wordy denunciations with which they masked their leisurely sloth. He did not oppose the Napoleonic regime for the reason that, whatever one might think of it, it was shaking the Italians out of that sloth of centuries into agitation and action, whereas he was hostile to that of Austria, which tended to soothe and hypnotize. Contrary to the Epicureans and other philosophical sects he held fast to the duty of participation in the affairs of country and state, and literature itself had for him a political character since he could not conceive of health in one part of social life and not also in the whole organism. Nor was it on doctrinaire utilitarian grounds that he justified these practical and political concepts, as might appear from his acceptance of certain philosophical concepts; for he felt "compassion" stirring in the depths of the human soul, and also (with Vico) "bashfulness". Nor was he an "atheist": amid his errors and his severe trials he found support, as he says, in "conscience" and "God".

Were there no more to relate of Foscolo than what we have here said of his personal life and critical and political writings he would rank as a great man: the educator of manful oncoming generations, the restorer of principles of ethics and aesthetics, founder in Italy of the new literary criticism. But he was a poet, the pure poet of few verses but those few perfect and eternal. Even his prose reveals his poetic temper, especially in the early works, where – while lending colour and strength – it will not allow the prose to take its ease and find its balance as prose, and sometimes even disturbs the arrangement and logical proportions of the treatises such as the inaugural lecture on the functions of literature. Once he observed this clash of talents in himself and wrote in a letter: "I believe that this fashion of prose-writing comes from weeks of thinking out and warmly cherishing my thoughts and chanting them verse-wise to myself in phrases quite different from those of prose." He added that "the Greeks and Latins were more prudent than ourselves for they opted absolutely for one or the other and did not try as we do to do business in both the trades of prose and verse". As to this, Europe knew Foscolo and still knows him primarily in his juvenile work *Jacopo Ortis*, where this hybrid style is most evident. As an expression of the author and his times it is a notable work, and, far from being a mere literary imitation, it contains a choice pick of Foscolo's thoughts and sentiments in early life under the semblance of an imitation. But this world of thought and feeling it presents in too immediate and realistic a manner, often in strident tones, emphatic and rhetorical. This was the verdict of the Italian critics from the moment of the book's appearance, when the veteran Bettinelli remarked on the excessive tension of feeling and style, the effort displayed in order to interest and to move the reader. It may be well to adduce some passages to illustrate the relation of Foscolo's *Jacopo Ortis* to his later works. The themes of his poems are all anticipated in this book, and, for one, the desire for remembrance and for love beyond and at the tomb. Thus we read: "I am comforted by the thought that I may be mourned . . . my burial place will be moistened by thy tears and those of that heavenly maiden. For who ever consigned to eternal forgetfulness this pleasing anxious being? Who ever looked for the last time upon the sun's rays, bade farewell for ever to nature, relinquished his joys, hopes, illusions, even griefs, nor cast one longing look behind, nor uttered one sigh? Our dear friends, surviving us, are part of us. Some pious drops the closing eye requires: it is dear to our heart that the newly dead should be borne on loving shoulders and that on some fond breast should be outpoured the last sigh. Even from the tomb the voice of nature cries, and the cry vanquishes the silence and darkness of the tomb."[1] Without any doubt Foscolo really lived in a state of feeling such as this and was as people say "sincere". But it was so far only a generic sincerity, unable at the moment of expression to hit upon a spontaneous and beautiful form. And since form and content are one, the sincerity itself was rendered imperfect. In the passage quoted, instead of directly depicting the commotion in his breast, Foscolo has recourse to rhetorical argument, reinforced by two interrogations, in order to demonstrate what has no need for demonstration, and there is in the words and the phrasing an overswollen sentiment (as in "some pious drops", "heavenly maiden", etc.) which he cannot maintain, so that here and there (as with "newly dead") the prosaic peeps through. But when the same thought reappears in *I Sepolcri*, word and rhythm are spiritualized, the link across the tomb is given by "corrispondenza di amorosi sensi" and the breeze bends a tree which is "di fiori odorata arbore amica", which affords to the ashes the refreshment of "molli ombre", and the loved one prays, the lonely wayfarer hears the sigh, when "from the tomb the voice of nature cries". And somewhat further on in *Ortis* he writes: "Oh Lorenzo, often I lie down on the banks of the Lake of the Five Sources, and I feel on cheek and beard the caress of the breezes as they ripple the grass and refresh the flowers and wrinkle the clear lake waters. And can you believe it, I fantasticate delightfully that the Nymphs appear to me, naked and dancing, rose-wreathed, and in their company I summon Love and the Muses, and from out the loud and foaming waterfalls I see emerging, breast-high with hair dripping on their dewy shoulders and with

1. Translator's Note: The English reader will recognize what Croce maybe did not, that part of this passage adapts with scarcely a change verses from Gray's *Elegy*, and accordingly these have been used in the translation.

gladsome eye, the Naiads, friendly guardians of the sources . . ."
That "can you believe it" betrays the author's recognition that he
had not really experienced that hallucination, but was striving to
render in narrative and emphatic form a fanciful desire, of wholly
poetic nature, and requiring a finer and wholly poetic form such
as it received in some of the many such portrayals which we
admire in the *Grazie*, for example when the "amorose Nereidi
oceanine" rise from the waters "a mezzo il petto ignude" and
crowd round the Goddess Venus "a fior dell'immensa onda rag-
giante".

We have said little of Foscolo's poems. The two tragedies that
he must needs compose by force of that attraction which theatrical
realism, the prospect of the crowded house, seems to exert even
upon great poets – it symbolizes somehow the other and greater
theatre which they are to command in the hearts of generations
of men, but sometimes it betrays them into superficiality and
forms which do not correspond to their true inspiration – are better left unconsidered, together with the miscellany of juvenile
verses rejected by the poet but tastelessly included as "Poems" by
the editors, and certain later satires and rhymes poorly conceived
and seldom finished. The truly authentic Poems of Foscolo amount
only to fourteen sonnets (not all excellent), two odes, one or two
brief pieces in loose hendecasyllables, the *Sepolcri* and the fragments
of the *Grazie*. The last two should be studied with awareness of
the didactic character recognized by Foscolo as pertaining to the
poet, derived by him maybe from Vico's notion of the "primitive
poet" who instructs in matters of religion and society, and leading
to a certain interpolation of precept in the exalted poetry of the
Sepolcri. This same element prevented the *Grazie* from ever getting
beyond a tentative and fragmentary composition. Present-day
Italian literary criticism has coped admirably with these few poems.
I will mention only the recent works of Donadoni and Manacorda
and the acute study of Citanna, works agreeable, I feel sure, to the
spirit of Foscolo, representing the latest and maturest form of that
very type of criticism, at one and the same time historical and
artistic, which he conceived and first encouraged in Italy. There

would be no point in repeating over again such admirably ex- ecuted analyses, nor would discussion of some unresolved ques- tions of detail be in place here, where the design is to mark down the general character of this poetry of Foscolo's which among the manifestations of his soul was the most intense, for, as he once said in description of his great poetic projects, "in them, there wells up in fullness and originality, without external aid, that liquid aether which lives in every man" and of which "nature and heaven" had assigned to him his part.

Four fundamental motives can be discerned in them: Death, the consummation of all grief; Heroism, the affirmation of virtue in human will; Beauty, which affords breath to pleasure; Fancy or Art which rescues human feelings from death and with a perfume of eternity renders them immortal. In these poems the four motives are now conjoined, but now one will seem to rise into dominance over the others, yet all are still present and active or felt to be near. And in truth those motives are inseparable, forming the single motive of life in its direct reality unadulterated by other-worldly conceptions, in its fullness as Love and Grief, Death and Im- mortality. Whatever is unbalanced, whatever is merely particular, is here effaced. Where does Foscolo exhibit the horror, the spasms of horror in the face of death, a horror of desperate rebellion, found in so many Romantics and pre-Romantics? With him, death is mirrored and delineated in the grateful image of evening, the falling shades in which his warlike agitation turns to quiet and gentleness. The earnest acceptance of death rings through the whole poem of the *Sepolcri*. Nor, on the other hand, is death ever felt by him in the character of a dimming, or snuffing out, or extinction, of the vigour of the affections. He celebrates the heroes of thought and action, shows delight in beauty and pleasure, depicts the features and movements of women, landscapes, natural spectacles, and celebrates the virtue of poetry in words and accents which come only to one who accepts in his heart all human pas- sions, gives himself to them without reserve, labours with them and in them. His verse has the beauty of this passionate disposition for grief, for joy, for love, and thereby seems to acquire the quality of a charming living person, roundedly supple, harmonious in utterance, engaging in every gesture. Those images of his are no frigid material, no product of thought for thought's sake, no memory of past struggles, but living and present drama settling into shape even as it develops. The final impression is one, not of detachment from life, but of enhanced love of life as thought, action, pleasure, and preparedness for death trusting to the loving remembrance of surviving friends and the hearts of the poets.

Foscolo is "classical" not in virtue of his fine Graeco-Latin scholarship or his feeling for antique mythology, but for this complete singleness of feeling. And that places him among the greatest poets of the nineteenth century. Let us examine two specimens of his work, the Ode to Luigia Pallavicini composed in 1799 when the poet was twenty-one, and the fragments of the *Grazie* composed in his highest maturity and published posthumously. Some think that there lingers in the ode a touch of eighteenth-century gallantry and frivolity and that in the *Grazie* there lurks an anticipation of that sensual dilettantism which came out fully in the Italian and other poets of the late nineteenth century. But neither suspicion, for all the appearances, is true. The Ode too is a hymn to beauty, the charming, amiable, voluptuous beauty which spoke to his senses and his fancy. Here reigns the lovely woman, queen of hearts, and is recalled as she appeared in elegant society, imparting an unwonted fragrance to the air when, in her lively dancing, rebellious curls fell on her rosy arm, a charming impediment to be prettily shaken away. The poet still hears the pleasing tones of her voice, still carries in memory the smiles and acts and gestures, the words expressing and inviting love. His fancy is filled with antique images of beauty, it glows with the bright figures of the Hellenic goddesses; he recalls their deeds and adventures, and into that ideal world he brings his fair Ligurian, not in frivolous gallantry, but because those divine images of beauty are really revived and set in motion by the women he meets and admires and loves in the world: of such idolizations, exaltations, dreams, his love is made up. But that beauty had been almost spoiled, or perhaps truly spoiled: the fair one had been thrown and dragged along the stony beach by a shying horse, and now she lies, pale and exhausted, reading from the expressions of the doctors "some flattering hope of pristine beauty saved". There is something childlike and moving in this woman's trepidation – a woman never wholly ceases to be a child. The poet senses the instant of fear and hope and as to a child addresses his loving sympathy and consolation. He conjures up for her a sequence of brilliant mythological pictures to flatter her, maybe, with noble comparisons, or to liven her hopes with tales of health recovered and beauty triumphant. Amidst these comes a conventional imprecation ("Accursed he who first...") against whoever encouraged ladies to mount the horse, "exposing beauty to new risks". There is a smiling tone in all these comfortable words, but the smile is less superficial than first it seems, because the poet knows that beauty must find an end in trouble, age, and death, but (thinks he) I render it eternal, "in breathing deathless soul" (as he later says in the *Grazie*) "into the shapes I paint". The fair one, whatever be in store for her, smiles already in the pages of this Ode which tells the catastrophe, and pretends to promise the material restoration, of her beauty. And thus to all time she will smile on in her ever verdant youth. Far from echoing eighteenth-century gallantry, the Ode is closely akin to the following Ode "To his Mistress Restored to Health", which in another manner portrays the same feelings and repeats the magical-poetical process whereby imperishable life is created.

Likewise in the *Grazie*, in what are materially called the fragments of the unfinished poem, there is nothing whatever of that fragmentary dilettantism which ranges over surfaces, rejoices in its own virtuosity, and is as rich to the eye as it is poor to the soul. In vain will such a defect be sought in the descriptions of Zacynthus fragrant with orange and cedar, or of Galileo's Bellosguardo where as the astronomer spied the stars from his hill the night-long noise of silver waters between the poplar-lined banks of Arno distracted him:

> *e il disviava*
> *col notturno rumor l'acqua remota*

che sotto ai pioppi delle rive d'Arno
furtiva e argentea gli volava al guardo;

or in the visions of Venus bestowing favours upon the Graces
while the Nereids sigh towards them, of blue-eyed Pallas ruling
her virgin choir, of Psyche, silently weaving her loom, repeating
only to herself the story of her passion as the pattern swells upon
the cloth; or again in the evocations of the harp-player sending
forth harmony into the valleys so that as she pauses, "still the hills
can hear it", or of that dancer from whose bodily grace and
smiling mouth music issues forth – "some act, some grace, some
motion brings sudden loveliness into her eyes" – or of the swan
"sailing on snow-pure wings", or so many others. In the smile of
the Graces human grief and piety is commingled – and so upon the
woven fabric worked for them there is shown the warrior's dream
at dawn, when he sees the anguished countenances of his father
and mother, and then awakening, and seeing his prisoners before
him, sighs deeply. Nay but all humanity is present at every point
even in those verses where the charm of beauty and pleasure seems
uncontrasted. For there too love is seen promising joy but bringing tears: "Gioia promette e manda pianto amore". In the *Grazie*
too the classic line is steadily respected. The affections have that
verecondia, that restraint, which Foscolo deemed to be the necessary condition of love – as it is also the necessary condition of true
poetry.

[1922]

XVIII

STENDHAL

I BELIEVE that Sainte-Beuve, usually so judicious, was quite wrong when he diagnosed the following defect in Stendhal as novelist: "He came to the novel from critical writing bringing with him certain anterior and preconceived ideas", as a consequence of which (Sainte-Beuve continues) Stendhal's characters are "not living beings but ingeniously constructed automatons in which at every movement you can discern the spring inserted by the craftsman and worked from without".

Take the last point first. If this were true, how could one explain the fascination of those novels of his which, once read, stay in the mind – the characters, actions, sayings which will not be forgotten but go on arousing dreams and reflections in us? Surely characters which were constructed by critical effort would not hold fast like this but would fall straight away from the mind or stand frigidly propped up, unable to excite us in any way. Whereas Julien Sorel, Fabrizio del Dongo, Madame de Rênal, Matilde de la Mole, the Duchess of Sanseverina, Count Mosca, Julien's serial seduction of his mistresses, his tutorship at the Rênals', his withdrawal to the seminary, the night visit which wrenches Madame Rênal from her religious compunction and fervour, and then again the presence of Fabrizio at Waterloo, his love scenes with Marietta, his imprisonment in the castle of Parma, to cite just a few of Stendhal's characters, episodes, and scenes, have about them an unexpectedness which is the mark of life. I do not assert this on the mere testimony of my own taste or that of those who think like myself or those to whom I might appeal as unprejudiced readers: surely everyone can see and know the growing attraction exerted by Stendhal, the very great influence upon the late literature of the last century and that of the present day, the curiosity aroused by any newly discovered page of his, any anecdote about his life. It may be just a matter of fashion but fashion's favours are not conceded without some objective reason.

And now for the first point. Wherever are to be found those "ideas" which Stendhal is alleged to utilize for the construction of his novels, those "two or three ideas", as the critic puts it, "which he believes to be correct and above all stimulating, and trots out at every turn"? The allusion may very likely be to the "energy", "passion", "utility" much spoken of in those tales, but from the reading of any of them, nay from this very remark of Sainte-Beuve, one may quickly discover that they are not Stendhal's ideas but his sentiments, loves, fancies. I will never weary of repeating that a writer's "ideas" – or philosophic endowment – are the equivalent of his critical and systematic mind (critical, in taking account of difficulties and objections; systematic, in linking various propositions together and reducing them to a unity) and though something which is neither critical nor systematic may take on the appearance of an idea, it will be in truth a sentiment. The labour which has been abundantly devoted to Stendhal's philosophy of practice and politics, and to his judgements and characterizations concerning famous persons or nations (notably the Italian), seems to me to have been all wasted. The substance of his critical works, his topographies and treatises on painting and literature, seems to me the same as that of his novels. Whether as novelist or as historian he depicts the Italy of his dream, or rather, his dream in the guise of Italy. (So naturally the "Professors" venturing into aesthetic criticism condemn the *Chartreuse de Parme* as depicting an Italy which never existed, least of all in 1830.) It is irrelevant that Stendhal occasionally, or even abundantly, notes down real facts and observes aspects of reality, for those facts and aspects are incorporated into a whole of an aesthetic and not a critical order.

No, Stendhal was not a theorist of energy, passion, efficiency, but one enamoured and obsessed with them. His disposition was the very opposite of the unpoetical – it was highly propitious for artistic creation. A close comprehension of his art requires an understanding of just what his "enamoured" attitude was. It has already been in some degree indicated. His was a nature not in itself energetic, practical, passionate, but enamoured of those

936 ESSAYS IN CRITICISM AND LITERARY HISTORY

modes – enamoured, that is to say, of something generic, of mere
forms wanting a concrete determination.

Passion, efficiency, energy – to these he eagerly aspired. But
what is their content? He cherished no political ideals or ambitions
of reform or reconstruction. Even his precious Napoleon became
for him quite un-Napoleonic, a pure and simple "Professor of
Energy". Moreover, while the grand purposes of humanity failed
to arouse him, it is not to be supposed that personal desires of a
strictly utilitarian sort for wealth and power as means for pleasure
and satisfaction did so any more. His ideal has quite wrongly been
equated with that of Casanova (whose memoirs Stendhal was for a
time believed to have composed). Casanova knew exactly what he
wanted. He was, in his way, a man of purpose, bent upon hoodwinking simpletons and gathering flowers and fruit in the garden
of Cythera. These inclinations and their indulgence he described
in his autobiography with perfect coherence and in the liveliest
colours. Of this there is no hint in Stendhal, and his equal want of
real utilitarian and of ethical urges spelt inability to feel with deep
passion of any sort. The passions, in fact, make their appearance
with him as distraction, experiment, pastime, and he amuses himself with them when he ought, it would seem, to be wholly
plunged in them. And though he talks so much of love, and so
much admires its warm, resolute pursuit and the unconditional
lovemaking of the Italians, yet love is never really uppermost
with him, colouring his thoughts and feelings as with genuinely
amorous temperaments.

Call it as you will, formal or generic, Stendhal's ideal is moreover
confused and contradictory. He seems to conceive of no other sort
of energy or passion than that which ministers to the inclinations
of the individual, but he assigns to these a grandeur and an heroic
quality found only in the higher dedications of energy. Sometimes
he seems to be aware of the difference between energy and passion,
and he makes his Fabrizio remark that "un être à demi stupide,
mais attentif, mais prudent tous les jours, goûte très souvent le
plaisir de triompher des hommes à imagination". But for the most
part he represents as identical or co-operative the two qualities

which are in truth mutually opposed, since true energy is nothing else than the resolution of the passion into the will, or otherwise said the domination of passion by the will: when energy accepts in greater or lesser degree to be directed by passion, it becomes correspondingly weakened and finally turns into its own contrary, a want of energy, a weakness. Stendhal was thus one of the first or perhaps the very first to frame that false but oft repeated judgement that the truly energetic characters are to be found among criminals, gaolbirds, convicts (those in the prisons of Civitavecchia, he used to say, when he was Consul at that port). His fictional characters are delineated by reference to two basic types, that of the high ecclesiastic, cold, calculating, dissembling, tenacious, unswerving from his purpose, and that of the man of inflammable imagination, liable to be blinded by anger, dragged along by the lust of vengeance to use of the sword or pistol, thereby losing in an instant the fruit of long endeavours. These two types Stendhal combines in a single individual in both of his two principal personages, Julien Sorel and Fabrizio del Dongo, both launched on high ecclesiastical careers, both absurdly and inopportunely prone to violence and bloodshed.

Bearing in mind the ideal which is Stendhal's source of inspiration – the ideal of an ungenuine heroism, an empty energy or passion – we may make a clean sweep of the censures commonly directed against the structures of his novels, and, to begin with, of that levelled by a critic of good sense, Émile Faguet, against *Le rouge et le noir*, praising the early and middle part in which the plot is developed, but finding the resolution of this fortuitous, and thus trivial and false. Faguet says that Stendhal should have made his choice between the only two logical modes in which the plot could have been resolved: "either Julien should have married Matilde with her father's consent, and have gradually become an aristocrat of great pride and harshness towards the humble folk; or he should have married her in despite of her father and carried her off to the slums to join him in constituting a couple of envious, bitter, rebellious misfits". But either of these resolutions would have required in the author an ethico-social feeling which Stendhal wholly lacked. Only so could he have either made of Julien a sort of anticipation of Rabagas, or described the perversion and corruption or an energy devoid of morality. This would have been to write a different novel altogether, for either such resolution would have necessitated a different premiss, a different development of the plot, a different style.

It would appear rather less fanciful to argue that since the inspiration of Stendhal is an abstract and contradictory ideal, this should have been illustrated, not in positive and serious narrations, but in some negative and satirical representation as of a Don Quixote charged with empty volition. Such a suggestion could find some support in many passages in the novels as they stand, which seem to verge upon irony. There is something decidedly ironic and quixotic about the way that Stendhal's heroes, Julien and Fabrizio, took Napoleon for an historical and literary model much as Don Quixote himself chose Sir Amadis or Sir Esplandiàn. Julien is perpetually gazing at the portrait of Napoleon, poring over his *Memorials of Saint Helena*, and on marking a small success in one of his essays in seduction he discovers "à force de songer aux victoires de Napoléon" what there is new in his own achievement. "Oui, j'ai gagné une bataille – se dit-il – mais il faut en profiter, il faut écraser l'orgueil de ce fier gentilhomme pendant qu'il est en retraite. C'est là Napoléon tout pur." And on another similar occasion: "Il faut – se dit-il – que je tienne un journal de siège: autrement j'oublierais mes attaques." And so too Fabrizio with this invocation and pledge: "O roi d'Italie, cette fidélité que tant d'autres t'ont jurée de ton vivant, je te la garderai après ta mort." Matilde de la Mole too has her forerunner – she models herself upon the personality and the life story of her ancestor Boniface de la Mole, in whom she sees typified the amorous energy of the age of the Renaissance. (We may see in him the other face of Stendhal's two-sided historical devotion for Napoleon and for the Italian or quasi-Italian sixteenth century with its loves and its bloodshed.) Matilde's love for Julien is itself an imitation which continues right up to the culminating episode, the acceptance of the severed head from the hands of the executioner into her own hands, as Margaret of Valois, *la Reine Margot*, similarly bore away the head of her own similarly decapitated lover. And the author notes: "Cette idée la transportait dans les plus beaux temps du siècle de Charles IX et de Henri III."

This insistence upon *grands exploits* and upon the strict sense of *devoir* evinced by Julien in his inglorious little affairs sounds like irony, and ironical in the same way seem to be Fabrizio's unending enquiries, while in pursuit of love, whether what he is or has been experiencing is love, yes, and even the magnificent episode of Waterloo in which details and incidents seem one and all to throw into contrast dreams and daily life, ideal and real, poetry and prose, so that in this connexion also Fabrizio wonders whether he is experiencing the real thing: "Have I really been present at a battle – at the battle of Waterloo?" And one might go on to the conclusion that the intimate and objective sense of Stendhal's novels is irony, and that their failing lies not, as Sainte-Beuve argued, in their construction out of the stuff of criticism, but conversely in their uncritical construction, that is, in the fact that the irony is unclear and is arbitrarily repressed or contradicted by the author, who fails to leave to the objects of his narration the requisite freedom of movement whereby they could have followed out their own tendency to the pattern of comedy. But we cannot be satisfied with this interpretation either. It postulates a Stendhal other than he was and other than in his times he could have been, a counter-Stendhal, such as only we in our times, after a century of Stendhal-Beylism, of rhetorical energy-worship, might imagine. Nor are those passages which seem to be ironical really so except in virtue of the logical and ethical judgement which we pass on them. Taken in themselves, in their own contexts, they are perfectly serious. At the utmost Stendhal is a Don Quixote out to tell his tale, never discovering the sublime and extraordinary which he seeks, but taking many a tumble into the grotesque – and heedless of doing so.

Stendhal's novels are not, as Faguet would have it, susceptible of correction by changing this or that part of them. A change of tone means the introduction of a wholly different mental attitude: but much as a parody requires the work parodied, so that altered form would need the form as it is. No! Ill-balanced, abrupt, and inconsecutive as the composition of the novels seems to be, on a closer view they are seen to be just of the natural and proper shape to express Stendhal's ideal.

Seriousness, not irony, characterizes this ideal, but not the seriousness of morality or passionate feeling, only the seriousness, already indicated, of a troubled and contradictious craving for grandeur, energy, passion. Stendhal, portraying himself in all his books, but most thoroughly in the two major novels, whose heroes Julien Sorel and Fabrizio del Dongo are really one and the same character presented in two times, two settings, or rather just against two different decorative backgrounds, was simply portraying that measureless craving. But this being purely selfish or self-centred, lacking an object of passion, switching and swinging from one to the other pole, from calculated effort to wild impulse, from Machiavellian priestliness to Romantic gun-and-swordsmanship, there could be no exemplifying it in any purposeful, meaningful, logical action: it had to be left free – this craving – to reflect itself in a romance more adventurous than the romances of adventure. For while in these, amid shifting scenes, the hero himself remains stable, in the Stendhalian romance the hero himself is continually heading off in this or that direction and displaying abrupt, unexpected mobilities. But since Stendhal's own mentality was genuine and not frigidly worked up to match a preconceived formula, his characters for all the strangeness of the fiction attain and maintain that liveliness which only a true stirring of the artistic fancy can communicate.

The real hero is Stendhal himself, with his sublime yet ridiculous furore for passion and energy, his sudden heats and chills, his somehow split mind with one side acting and the other observing the process of action, one side imagining and thinking and the other criticizing the thought and the imagination: a psychic condition which is nowadays treated as a nervous disease, and is certainly inharmonious and divided.

Thus, observe Stendhal in his character as Julien, with Madame de Rênal – at last – in his arms:

Au lieu d'être attentif aux transports qu'il faisait naître, et aux remords qui en relevaient la vivacité, l'idée du devoir ne cessa jamais d'être présente à ses yeux. Il craignait un remords affreux et un ridicule éternel, s'il s'écartait du modèle idéal qu'il se proposait de suivre. En un mot, ce qui faisait de Julien un être supérieur fut précisément ce qui l'empêcha de goûter le bonheur qui se plaçait sous ses pas.

And again in the scene where by dint of coldness he reconquers Matilde:

Ses bras se raidirent, tant l'effort imposé par la politique était pénible. — Je ne dois pas même me permettre de presser contre mon cœur ce corps souple et charmant, ou elle me méprise et me maltraite . . .

And yet again:

— Ah! qu'elle m'aime huit jours, huit jours seulement, — se disait tout bas Julien, — et j'en mourrai de bonheur. Que m'importe l'avenir, que m'importe la vie? Et ce bonheur divin peut commencer en cet instant si je veux, il ne dépend que de moi! —
Mathilde le vit pensif.
— Je suis donc tout à fait indigne de vous, — dit-elle en lui prenant la main. Julien l'embrassa, mais à l'instant la main de fer du devoir saisit son cœur. — Si elle voit combien je l'adore, je la perds . . .

In all this self-watching and weighing, does or does not passion truly subsist? Elsewhere in the recital of the affair with Matilde he says:

À la vérité, ces transports étaient un peu voulus. L'amour passionné était encore plutôt un modèle qu'on imitait qu'une réalité.

Fabrizio, we have already remarked, cannot conclude whether he is or is not in love:

Mais n'est-ce pas une chose bien plaisante — se disait-il quelquefois — que je ne sois pas susceptible de cette préoccupation exclusive et passionnée qu'ils appellent de l'amour? Parmi les liaisons que le hasard m'a données à Novare ou à Naples, ai-je jamais rencontré de femme dont la présence, même dans les premiers jours, fut pour moi préférable à une promenade sur un joli cheval inconnu? Ce qu'on appelle amour, — ajoutait-il — serait-ce donc encore un mensonge? J'aime sans doute, comme j'ai bon appétit à six heures! Serait-ce cette propension quelque peu vulgaire dont ces menteurs auraient fait l'amour d'Othello, l'amour de Tancrède? Ou bien faut-il croire que je suis organisé autrement que les autres hommes? Mon âme manquerait d'une passion, pourquoi cela? Ce serait une singulière destinée!

It is a combination of this doubt with the pleasure or *amusement* of defying the wrath of her friend "dont la mine était plus terrible que celle d'un ancien tambour-majeur" which alone incites him to eye and to court the fair songstress Fausta. "Serait-ce enfin de l'amour?" he wonders: and Fausta, sensing the strangeness of his feelings, regards him with a sort of fear. He for his part "n'était plus retenu que par un reste d'espoir d'arriver à sentir ce qu'on appelle *de l'amour*; mais souvent il s'ennuyait".

It is ennui, subtle boredom, that in fact circulates in the veins of the Stendhalian hero. Therefore his actions are never so casual as when he most desires them to be calculated. Fabrizio fights his unworthy adversary Giletti, who has assaulted him: but why does he go on to kill him?

> *Le combat semblait se ralentir un peu; les coups ne se suivaient plus avec la même rapidité, lorsque Fabrice se dit: — À la douleur que je ressens au visage, il faut qu'il m'ait défiguré. — Saisi de rage à cette idée, il sauta sur son ennemi la pointe du couteau de chasse en avant . . .*

From amidst his various essays in love and in politics, secular and ecclesiastical, he is summoned by the Archbishop, who names him his Vicar, thus opening the prospects of a career in the prelacy. Does he really much desire that?

> *Fabrice courut au palais archiépiscopal: il y fut simple et modeste, c'était un ton qu'il prenait avec trop de facilité; au contraire, il avait besoin d'efforts pour jouer le grand seigneur. Tout en écoutant les récits un peu longs de monseigneur Landriani, il se disait: — Aurais-je dû tirer un coup de pistolet au valet de chambre qui tenait par la bride le cheval maigre? — Sa raison lui disait oui, mais son cœur ne pouvait s'accoutumer à l'image sanglante du beau jeune homme tombant de cheval défiguré.*
> *— Cette prison où j'allais m'engloutir, si le cheval eût bronché, était-elle la prison dont je suis menacé par tant de présages? —*
> *Cette question était de la dernière importance pour lui, et l'archevêque fut content de son air de profonde attention.*

While in prison Fabrizio learns one day of the death of his father and breaks into irrepressible grief:

> *Les juges sortis, Fabrice pleura encore beaucoup, puis il se dit: — Suis-je hypocrite? il me semblait que je ne l'aimais point.*

He is somewhat stirred by the commencement of his amour
with young Clelia, as Julien was by that with Madame de Rênal.
But here it is the woman rather than the man who is impassioned.
There are some exquisite touches:

> Le huitième jour de la prison de Fabrice, elle eut un bien grand sujet de honte:
> elle regardait fixement, et absorbée dans ses tristes pensées, l'abat-jour qui cachait la
> fenêtre du prisonnier; ce jour-là il n'avait encore donné aucun signe de présence.
> Tout à coup un petit morceau d'abat-jour, plus grand que la main, fut retiré par lui;
> il la regarda d'un air gai, et elle vit ses yeux qui la saluaient. Elle ne put soutenir
> cette épreuve inattendue, elle se retourna rapidement vers ses oiseaux et se mit à les
> soigner; mais elle tremblait au point qu'elle versait l'eau qu'elle leur distribuait, et
> Fabrice pouvait voir parfaitement son émotion; elle ne put supporter cette situation,
> et prit le parti de se sauver en courant.

Now Fabrizio finds the charm exercised upon him for years by
his beauteous and stately and brilliant relative, the Duchess of
Sanseverina, fading in the light of the girlish image which begins
to haunt him. But has it faded for ever?

> Une nuit Fabrice vint à penser un peu sérieusement à sa tante: il fut étonné, il
> eut peine à reconnaître son image; le souvenir qu'il conservait d'elle avait totalement
> changé; pour lui, à cette heure, elle avait cinquante ans.

In just such revelations of himself with all his aimless aspirations,
all the involuntary ironies arising therefrom, the illusions and the
disillusions, the coherency and the incoherency, stands the strength
and the beauty of Stendhal's art. It is his successful way of never
professing to be more than he really was, a victim of nervous
disease, but a victim who could achieve a cure by the clarity with
which he recounted his case. Had he been a sick man at the level
of art, he would have had to resort like more than one more recent
sufferer to the employment of an elaborate or "artistic" style;
instead of which he was able to rest content with that workaday
conversational style, simple and unjewelled, for which his model
was, as he said and as is well known, the prose of the Napoleonic
Civil Code.

[1919]

XIX

IBSEN

IBSEN'S heroes and heroines are one and all tensely expectant; consumed with craving for the extraordinary, the intense, the sublime, the unattainable, contemptuous of any sort or degree of quiet happiness and virtuous resignedness to one's imperfections. Consider how Hedda Gabler mocks and despises her hard-working, good-natured, second-rate husband and his aunts, poor old dears. She cannot endure the slightest reference to home life, children, or duties of any sort. Infidelities and illicit amours too she rejects as things common and vulgar, yet in such things she feels herself becoming enveloped. She looks around, and is taken with mortal tedium, because, ready as she is to dare any and every way, she seeks in vain in the world "something free and brave, something lit by a ray of absolute beauty". The soul of Ellida, fluid as the sea, is turning ever seawards, yearning for her birthplace and for that unknown and perhaps criminal man from the sea who one day had approached and talked with her and become linked to her by the throwing of betrothal-rings into the waves. Nora in eight married years had awaited patiently that "wonder" which alone could give sense and savour to the monotonous course of ordinary happenings, her marriage, her children, her social relations. And since to help her husband to overcome a weakness she has once secretly committed a small fraud, her heart beats at the thought that were this discovered he would at once throw himself forward to take the blame in her place, gladly sacrificing for the woman who had erred for love of him everything that he holds dear, prosperity, position, reputation, honour. Rebecca West penetrates into the severely pious and traditional old family home of the Rosmers, intent to use the glamour of her person and her art to seize upon the last of the line and make him the instrument of her own career as a combatant for freedom and progress against the old ideas. Rita marries Allmers in order to possess him wholly, in jealousy of her sister, of his studies, and even of their child – the force of her grasping passion frightens even herself.

What of the men? Solness would fain be the one and only builder of churches, houses, towers, suppressing all others or enlisting them as aids and instruments, and suspecting every younger man who might push forward to oust him. He attempts the "impossible", that is – in defiance of his constitutional dizziness – to mount the pinnacle of the soaring tower that he has built and to place upon it the inaugural wreath. Rubek, to create works of art, has turned his back on life, but then, a prey to miserable drunkenness, torments himself with what he has missed. Borkmann's dream was to appropriate by dint of his banking operations all the sources of power, capturing the treasures of the soil, the mountain, the forest, the sea, in order to render thousands upon thousands of men happy and content. In his advance to power he slips, falls into the clutches of the law, is gaoled, spurned, isolated, yet he does not give up, but waits day by day for a summons and an entreaty by the people that he should return to lead them. Of different stuff is the dream of Gregor Werle: it is to destroy the lies, hypocrisies, illusions on which men ignobly rest their head as on a downy cushion, and to found a new life of pardon, mutual help, and redemption upon the basis of truth unwaveringly displayed and scrutinized.

All these examples come from Ibsen's later, mature period. But the inspiration of the earlier dramas is not different: between the works of the two periods there is a great difference in form and in artistic power but not in substance. A clear artistic development can be traced in Ibsen, but not a clear intellectual or sentimental development, nor can one discern the marks of deep conversions or changes. Would-be narrators of his mental history have found it impossible to convey a feeling of motion, because young, mature, or old, Ibsen's spirit was ever the same with its enduring unchanging thirst for the extraordinary and the sublime. Already in an early work we find Peer Gynt ranging round, as he puts it, to realize "his Gyntian self... the crowd of desires, cravings, passions, the ocean of fancies, pretences, rights", all of which "swells his breast and gives him life to live". And already Brant is obsessed by the idea of duty for duty's sake, the more than Kantian duty which is so pitiless and cruel for him who embraces it; "All or Nothing" Brant, who in the sweeping strength of his character draws Agnes away from the man who loves her, inspires her with his own hard faith, lets her son die and then herself die for the faith's sake, and treads down every personal feeling of his own but leaves ever intact his higher self, his inexorable will, his "all or nothing". In an even earlier play, *The Pretenders*, the protagonist, King Haakon, may be a *pius Aeneas* refashioned to fit Ibsen's direct or indirect knowledge of the German-style philosophy of history, but around the King stand wildly passionate, frantically possessive characters, Duke Skule and particularly the terrible Bishop Nicholas. In *The Love Comedy* we have the poet Falke with his ideal of a love which, overthrowing every obstacle, *omnia vincit* in a great campaign against lies and hypocrisy. In the very dissimilar *Northman's Expedition*, the pathos of all the principal characters (expecially of Hjordis, who is Hedda Gabler in barbaric form and setting – that is in the form and setting which really becomes her) is nevertheless the same.

The one and only satisfaction into which this urge for the extraordinary and the sublime can ever issue is one of self-destruction, of tragedy. Circumstantial reality, the meanness and ignobility of other men, the laws, society – all these bar the way, and so too, which is worse, do the defects of the heroes themselves, their past faults and present weaknesses, the hindrance which rises up out of the depth of the soul. Indeed perhaps these two orders of obstacles are really all one, and all of the second sort, for Ibsen dimly recognizes that if his hero fails to act upon society he cannot be superior to it, cannot even be equal to it. The fault which lies in Peer Gynt is evident, but it is present too in Brant, who rejects all worldly prudence and then, after for some time drawing the crowds, is abandoned by all, and left alone on the mountainside. He hears then a ghost calling to him: "Die, the world has no need for thee!" and feels that Jesus eludes him like a word which eludes memory. And when at last he summons heaven to tell him whether for salvation the firm, unshakable will suffices, the answer which he hears is that God is the God of Love. And so it is with all of them – all are likewise guilty. Solness has achieved his own glory sowing grief and unhappiness all around and sinning not in deed but at least in the vehemence of a sinful desire which presses upon the course of events. Borkmann, to attain supremacy, breaks away from the woman who had loved him and whom he had loved, and fans the flame alight in a sister soul. So too Rubek has espied in a woman just the outline for a sculpture, overlooking the being of flesh and blood within the outline, the woman who loved him as a man, and who, rejected or neglected, is burnt out with passion or survives as a mere ghost. Gregor Werle, arrogant reformer and ideologue, grabs at the delicate texture of life, pulls out fragments here and there to eliminate deceptions, rends the whole thing to pieces and instead of bringing redemption and purification brings death with every touch of his hand. Hedda Gabler passes from deeds of spite to crimes and more crimes, and when she believes that she has illumined the world with one ray of absolute beauty, a "beautiful death", finds that what she had really devised and compassed was a death of the most miserable and sordid type – by a stomach wound in a prostitute's lodging. Ellida breaks her plighted troth to the mysterious suitor to marry another who rescues her from misery and desertion: she has preferred prosaic comfort to her poetic idol. Nora has let herself be dressed and played with like a doll and has idly daydreamed about a "wonderful" time coming: she has neglected to cultivate in herself human personality with its rights and duties, never making the requisite effort to know herself and others. Rita, throwing herself into the very frenzy of love in her selfish desire for sole possession of Allmers, has twice, in deed and in thought, despised and neglected her own child and has lost him, and with him has lost the sympathy of Allmers and weakened the force and fervour of his original love. Rebecca has allowed the love which she has conceived for Rosmer to affect the course of her calculating ambition. For love she has caused his wife to die, and when she remains alone with him and in his spiritual vicinity she has gradually yielded to the honesty, the pure moral force, which radiates from him. But

now she can no longer love him either impurely – for she herself
has been purged – nor purely, for the load which she bears on her
conscience. She has shut herself off from both sorts of happiness,
the sharp troubled happiness of sense and the gentle happiness of
the heart.

Some among these and other characters of Ibsen's find a way of
escape in a renunciation of their frantic desire. For example Ellida,
the Woman from the Sea, by her own free decision refuses to
follow the mysterious man who has returned to fetch her, and
thus finds peace and a return to the rhythm of normal life. The
Allmers couple, parents of the little Eyolf who, as they feel, perished
by drowning through their fault, resolve to lead a new life dedicated to the succour of the abandoned. Nora, leaving husband and
children, withdraws to try and understand, as she had never attempted to do, something about herself and the real world. Consul
Bernick, in the *Pillars of Society*, publicly confesses his guilt and
achieves an exalted expiation by courting civil extinction. That
ill-omened moralist Gregor Werle, and Madame Alving who for
legality's and respectability's sake put up with her dissolute husband and whitewashed his memory, are by contrast left inconsolable, the former in presence of the spectacle of a broken family
from which all mutual trust and affection has departed and of the
poor dead girl, who had refused to go on living without the affection of her putative father; the latter with her son, heir to the
father's disease, who has made her swear to free him by the
administration of poison from oncoming insanity. Such desolation, harbinger of death, is not, however, typical of Ibsen's characters. Most of these do not linger in the expectation of death, but
march forth resolutely towards it. Brant climbs his mountain
anew, and while he prays the Lord for enlightenment on his attempted task, an avalanche destroys him. Peer Gynt, having
reached the end of his wanderings and adventures and failed to
realize his Ego, can only bow his head to the bosom of Solveigh –
the eternal feminine, his Gretchen as it were, who has always been
waiting for him – in death. Solness climbs his tower to garland it:
in the very act he yields to vertigo, falls, and is destroyed. Hedda

Gabler, having driven to suicide Lowborg, the one man who had
afforded her a taste of the extraordinary and could, she hoped,
thrill her with a "beautiful death", wakes to the fact that her secret
design has been understood by another man who is watching her
with lustful intent. She kills herself. Borkmann and Rubek allow
themselves to be quietly led to death by the women they have
abandoned. Hand in hand they throw themselves in the river.
Rebecca West, by loving, has purged herself of the very right to
love. Rosmer now loves her, but can share with her nothing but
death, and in death makes her his wife. Thus is the expectation of
the sublime always cheated, whether it take the satanic and sensual
or the divine and ethical shape. For a sensual passion collides with
the conscience, an ethical passion embodies a present or a past
offence of the conscience against itself.

This is indeed the poetry of despair: not just of pessimism for
the fading of pleasure and the transience of life, but of the awareness that men have that they can never achieve the ends which
their nature commits them to attempting or desiring to attempt.
Yes, Ibsen stands fixed in this mood: the incidents and the symbols
change, but at the end, as at the beginning, all is repining and
frustration. Other great poets become close and familiar to us,
but Ibsen never leaves his heights to show love for the simple
things that we love, an imperfect love, as ours is, compounded of
joy and suffering. He looks out upon all through a glass of unique
colour that he never replaces with the plain or varied glass which
the rest of us hold to our eye. However, if his psychological attitude
remains ever the same, his art, we repeat, develops and grows
towards perfection. At the outset, Ibsen employed traditional
forms, the historical drama for which the Romantics gave him a
model, and the philosophical, humorous, ironic drama of the
same school, with the examples before him of Schiller, Goethe,
and Byron, and their imitators in Scandinavia, who were much
influenced by the Germans. *Peer Gynt* follows the mode of the
second part of *Faust* and falls into its very stylistic difficulties and
defects, *Brant* consists in a ceaseless flow of weighty but all too
wordy eloquence, while *The Comedy of Love* and *The League of*

Youth are not far removed from the French comedy "à thèse". True, there are hints throughout of the lion's claw, specially in *The Claimants* but also in *Peer Gynt*, in which the scenes of the Trolls and of the mother's death are justly famed, and admirable is the priest's pronouncement at the grave of the man "whose hand had but four fingers". So too in *Brant*: what severe liveliness there is in the hero's presentation and utterance, what wild grief in that of his Agnes who has lost her son and dare not blame the man who let the boy die in order to keep his pledge. There are depths from time to time in *The League of Youth*, while one of the secondary characters in this play, Selma, clearly foreshadows Nora in *A Doll's House*. A detailed study of Ibsen reveals ever more of such hints and signs, and throws additional light on the singleness of his inspiration. Nevertheless it is only after 1875 that Ibsen discovers his own original form, particularly in *A Doll's House* and *Ghosts*, and the process of perfection continues its course and reaches its final purity in the series beginning in 1883 with *The Wild Duck* and *Rosmersholm*. This last is, in my opinion, the masterpiece. It might seem that this is just the moment when he becomes fully disconsolate and despairing: yet this he has always been. But certainly he now enters into fuller possession of his hopeless despair by dint not of a moral development, but rather of a deepened art, a clearer insight into his own feeling. Such insight, such awareness had been inadequate in *Peer Gynt*, moulded on the extravagant satirical and jocose style of the second part of *Faust*, inadequate also in *Brant*: in this latter play the protagonist is moulded to serious, heroic stature, yet, before the catastrophe breaks, his action supplies an unintentional criticism of his conception and character, a chink in his armour. This is a fault rarely committed by Ibsen in any later drama, perhaps, indeed, only in *The Enemy of the People*, where one is left doubtful whether Dr. Stockmann is delineated as hero or fanatic, a deep or a dull character, sublime or grotesque. In the fullness of his powers Ibsen can delineate at one stroke the zeal for the extraordinary, the sinfulness which corrodes it, the renunciation, desolation, death which await it – all together, all in his own form.

This is the form constituted by a sort of impassioned, inconclusive monologue, dramatic just because inconclusive, divided, fought over. Apart from some verses, Ibsen wrote nothing but drama: drama came to him spontaneously, naturally, necessarily. His dramatic creations are moments and phases of his own spirit, that spirit wholly absorbed in the craving for a felicity attainable only in the attainment of the sublime, the extraordinary, but sensitive and uncompromising, at the same time, in its awareness of responsibility and guilt. How could they then possibly overcome obstacles, realize their own vital ideal, mould a life around them to their heart's desire, or take up harmonious attitudes, in a smoothly lit prospect, exhibiting the rounded definiteness of figures moving towards action, revealing only in action what they are or what they can and will reveal of themselves? Rather than this, Ibsen's creations are souls engaged in confession, suffering because their confession is not yet concluded, penetrating, divining, understanding each other while still unconfessed, discovering themselves in the light of heaven of which they are not yet worthy, but which already shines upon them as upon souls in purgatory. Hence these dialogues in which they seem to be at work trying to understand themselves, and those sudden bold rendings of interposed veils. "Let us talk frankly, let us no more lie," says Rita to her husband. Allmers proceeds to set forth to her his decision to throw up his scientific work and attend wholly to the crippled child. To which Rita, who has seen into him more deeply than he knew or desired, replies: "But not because you love the child." "Why, then?" "Because you have been consumed with self-mistrust, because you began to doubt your vocation for a great task." "You noticed that?" (He makes no attempt to defend himself, he seems to have known it already.) Both of them have inveighed against the dwellers round the lake for not risking their lives to save little Eyolf from drowning. But when calm returns to them and their judgement on themselves and others takes firm shape, then to her husband, still repeating the same things, she turns and asks softly: "But Alfred, are you sure we would ourselves have taken the risk?" "Don't think of doubting it!" he replies painfully, trying to change the subject. And she: "We too are mortals." These creatures of Ibsen's say out loud what most of us say only to ourselves, and that too softly and rarely, so that it is more like a murmur within us which we bend our ear to hear. They are priests one to the other and not only for the receiving of confessions but for the giving of comfort, encouragement, aid.

RITA
(slowly)
For sure, some change is befalling me – what a painful sensation.

ALLMERS

Painful?

RITA

Yes, some sort of birth.

ALLMERS
Yes indeed – or a resurrection, a passage to higher life.

RITA
(gazing forward hesitantly)
Yes, but it's the loss of happiness, all of life's happiness.

ALLMERS
In this, the loss is itself the gain.

RITA
(keenly)
Words, words! In the last resort we are just poor dwellers on this earth.

ALLMERS
We have some kinship too with sky and sea, Rita.

The closing scenes of *Rosmersholm* express the climax of such an interpenetration and fusion of souls, renouncing happiness, purifying themselves, renouncing life itself.

When Ibsen's art, as the saying is, "conquered" at last the indifference of the public, and warm admirers, fanatical partisans, interpreters and imitators flocked around forming a "school" eager to distinguish itself from all those which had gone before or been in the running beside it, then this art became dubbed "the problematic art", and celebrated for its peculiarity of posing moral and social problems instead of either providing ready-made solutions and stock ideals like the French comedies "à thèse", or else realistically depicting loves, hatreds, passions, actions. The difference was noted with approval, but this did not extend to the proclamation of a "problematic art". Problems are the domain of the thinker, and Ibsen, for all his rich observation and keen perception of mental turmoil, is far from being a thinker. And this was well for him, for had he been a thinker his whole world of passionate feeling would have suddenly perished in the draught of critical intelligence, even more quickly and totally than did Goethe's wealth of youthful sentiment under the influence of a Goethe turned into a gently smiling sage. And then again – how could such unvarying storm and disorder be accorded the description of problem, and mental problem at that? True enough Ibsen does from time to time incline to set himself problems, but the sort of problems which the history of ethics shows never to have been solved and which logic finds to be insoluble: problems of moral casuistry. In *A Doll's House* is the husband in the right? Surely not, he is an egotist. The wife, then? She lacks a conscience. Then is the husband in the wrong? How can he be seeing that he observes the law and the code of honour? The wife? After all, she tried to save her husband from falling ill and dying. Or take again *John Gabriel Borkmann*. Was it Borkmann himself who was in the right when in the service of what he believed to be his appointed mission he cast off the woman who loved him? He had killed a soul. Was it then the woman? But she had no right to expect happiness for herself at the cost of depriving thousands of the happiness they might have known, and their loss of an improved social level. Was Borkmann then in the wrong? Yet he had sacrificed in the first place himself, his heart, for he too was in love. Was the woman in the wrong? She could not possibly suffocate her close and urgent need for happiness and spiritual redemption (for him as well as for her) for the sake of the distant and problematic happiness of multitudes yet unborn and nameless. But small wonder that these insoluble problems added to the popularity of the drama especially with the somewhat uncritical female sex, and above all with the least critical of all intelligences, those of the feminists. To such a point, indeed, did these, under the influence of the plays, make themselves tiresome and hateful with their psychological and moralizing or antimoralizing comments that, as has been recounted, certain Scandinavian families put on their dinner-party invitations: "No talk about *A Doll's House* please". Ibsen himself dabbled in casuistry, but not overmuch, forewarned by his sense of art. When an English critic, visiting him, put it to him that in his work the ideas must have preceded the dramatizations, Ibsen, quite rightly I think, denied this, and I judge to be also quite correct what the critic further reports: that "from Ibsen's statements this at least emerged, that there occurred a phase in his compositions at which they might as easily have developed into critical treatises as into drama". No doubt: but then in fact they did not turn into critical treatises, and Ibsen never wrote a page of didactic prose. They always turned into dramas because always, from their very first germination, they had been dramas and his had been the soul of a dramatic poet.

For this reason his creations are not cold-blooded animals, not, as one of them describes himself, cold fish, such as are the mere personifications of abstract ideas. On the contrary they desire and suffer, utter wild cries, words of trembling emotion, solemn declarations. Hedda Gabler, throwing to the flames the manuscript composed – with the help of another woman's attentions – by the one man she herself is attracted and drawn to, uncertain whether in love or hatred, cries out in ferocious exaltation: "There goes your child, fair curly-head, the child you bore to Eybert Lowborg!" ... Irene, meeting once again, years later, the sculptor Rubek who had used her as model for his great work, with sad gentleness reproaches him, as they talk over the old times: she tells him what was the greatest gift she really gave him: "I gave you my soul, my soul in the pride of life and youth . . . and then I was left empty at the breast, I had lost my soul, I had given you that gift, Arnold, and I was dead." Ella Rentheim, hearing from Borkmann, now old and almost insane, how though loving her he had made up his mind to leave her, passes sentence upon him, pronouncing judgement as though raised above him and indeed above herself too, like an independent power: yet in that very act she is the impassioned incarnation of a femininity worshipping itself: "Do you understand? You put out the fire of love in me. The Bible tells of a mysterious, unpardonable sin. Until today those words were incomprehensible to me. Now I understand them. That capital sin, unpardonable, is putting out the flame of love in a human creature." The poet furnishes these creatures with lineaments, gestures, clothing, full reality, because for him they are real and not patterns of thought. Borkmann, dignified, fine-featured, keen-eyed, with grizzled curly hair and beard, dwells alone, apart from his family, on an upper story, pacing up and down all day in his black coat of old-fashioned cut, going over the past and awaiting, more stubbornly than ever, the future. Hedda Gabler has "distinguished bearing, pale complexion, calm cool looks, light chestnut hair", and she appears to us in her home, "in elegant day dress, rather voluminous". Beside her stands the very different figure of her husband; "cheerful, stoutish, fair hair and beard, wearing spectacles, a bit shabby". One by one they are thus depicted for us, yet Ibsen's dramas, for all their plastic poetical-ness, are worked out with a simplicity which sometimes strikes us as naive. With so expert an artist this betokens, not poverty and impotence, but deliberate neglect of externals. Nor yet are the symbols which serve him as images and lyrical analogues signs of poverty or impotence – the tower from which Solness will fall, the Alving asylum which will go up in flames, the wild duck which flounders and fattens in the attic of the Ekdal house, forget-ting sea and sky. For this art of courageous and chaste avowal, this almost religious art, the style and the naive proceedings of the primitive are suitable: Ibsen, sure of his strength, has recourse to them, and in this deliberate simplicity exhibits that strength.

[1921]

XX

CARDUCCI

"ERA UN GIORNO DI FESTA . . ."

CARDUCCI'S poem has points in common with certain "impressions" related by Heinrich Heine of visits paid to Catholic churches in a vein of curiosity. Bonardi[1] has pointed them out, and no doubt they are there, but whatever Carducci took from Heine he completely transformed. The sly hints and mocking humour of Heine are turned by Carducci into a serious theme stirring him to a higher poetry. There is something here, then, of Heine, but only on the cultural, not the poetic plane. In Carducci's verse a different and higher spirit prevails.

The Lombard church entered by the poet exhibits its ancient, simple architecture: a religious solemnity is being celebrated. Yet natural life, everyday life, is close at hand, pressing and penetrating, and the sunshine breaks in:

> *Era un giorno di festa, e luglio ardea*
> *basso in un'afa di nuvole bianche:*
> *ne la chiesa lombarda il dì scendea*
> *per le bifori giallo in su le panche.*

Uninhibited like the sun the crowd in the adjoining piazza breaks in too, invading the church with the noise of the cattle-market and the fair, the music and the songs:

> *Da la porta arcuata, che i leoni*
> *millenni di granito ama carcar,*
> *il rumor de la piazza e le canzoni*
> *e i muggiti veniano in fra gli altar.*

(Incidentally I have seen this verse which makes the doorway "love" its load of stone lions censured as stiff and forced, but it stands for some such Latin as Horace's *amat janua limen*: Carducci's verse is never far apart from "i latini suoi", his Latins, any more than is Ariosto's: in this poem too there breathes Latin sobriety.)

---

1. *Heine e Carducci* (Florence, 1907), reprint from *Rivista di lett. ted.*, I, 10-12.

This natural life, this life of human feeling, compels the poet's attention and moves his heart. The religious rite does not engage his feelings and is dismissed curtly:

> La messa era cantata, ed i boati
> de l'organo chiamavano il Signore . . .

and without a break of syntax he proceeds:

> in fondo de la chiesa due soldati
> guardavan fisi ne l'altar maggiore.

Here the presence of the soldiers stands grammatically on the same level as what preceded, but it is the two soldiers who stand out, because the homesickness bespoken by their earnest gaze is felt and harvested by the poet who therefore gives it an importance which he withholds from the sacred aspect of the rite:

> Tra quella festa di candele accese,
> tra quella pompa di broccati e d'òr,
> ei pensavan la chiesa del paese
> nel mese di Maria piena di fior.

And so too, in his inclination to understand and to embrace the poor, sorrowful, wistful, unsated soul of mankind, the poet espies in a corner of the church that other figure which he will now hymn and render dominant in the whole picture, till she absorbs it altogether and inspires the poet's fancy to the pattern of the whole lyric:

> Sotto la volta d'una bruna arcata,
> in tra due rosse colonnette snelle,
> stava la bella donna inginocchiata,
> giunte le mani, senza guanti, belle.

Who she is the poet neither says nor seems to know or to want to know. For him there is simply, in that act, the beauty of a woman in prayer: and what else could be the object of that prayer, so earnest, with clasped hands, but love? In the two soldiers the poet had felt and responded to the tremor of their simple feelings, and now, in this woman, equally unnamed and unknown, he feels the travail of a pang of love.

Whatever touch he gives to this woman's figure, concerns

wholly her aspect as he continues to watch her at prayer, a prayer
which reaches its highest climax and resolution when she lifts
towards the altar a face bright with tears, poised in hope and expectation of help:

> Umido a la piumata ombra del nero
> cappello il nero sguardo luccicò . . .

She is a young lady of the late nineteenth century, as the large hat
with its feathers half hiding the face shows. She is dressed with
customary elegance, but within she is all agitation, all pitiless and
tormenting passion. I confess that I cannot follow my friend the
acute critic G. Citanna[1] in his observation that in these verses the
blackness of the eye and of the hat "cancel each other out rather
than heighten their respective value", being "set in counterposition and fused on the same tonic level without any gradations".
To me it seems that the poet, in his keen direction of sympathy
upon the psychic drama before his eyes, has indeed differentiated
and graduated the rival blacks, the heavy fixed black of the hat,
the moist and shining black of the eye flashing forth:

> e in un lampo di fede il suo mistero
> quel fior di giovinezza a Dio mandò.

I dissent from the same critic's censure upon "flower of youth" as
"abstract" and upon "mystery" as being, he says, too great and
ponderous a word and thus in this setting inadequate and inexpressive. But the words which depict the passion of love are never too
great or too weighty for one who in that passion feels life and
death and sums up in it the universe (the "mystery" in the poem
is "her mystery", "il suo mistero"). "Flower of youth" is no
abstraction but renders the almost fatherly sympathy of the poet
watching the young woman in her plight of love. I cannot think
that in this poem a greater "intimacy" (as the critic seems to
desire), let alone a direct show of passion would be at all suitable.
Love is here inspected from outside, in the person, the attitudes,
the bloom of beauty and youth in another, and thus seen is

---

1. *Il romanticismo e la poesia italiana* (Bari, 1935), 265-67.

understood, pitied, soothed – love, ever reawakening love, decreed by nature.

At the sight of this worshipper in her sweet trouble and parched
desire, there awakens in the mind of the poet, that is, of Giosue
Carducci, steeped in the images of history and the rhythms of
Italian poesy, the memory of an age-old poetry in which love
and religion were purely and simply at one. On the lady's "uplift-
ed eyes" he weaves a psychological interpretation, sweetly fanciful,
akin to those projections of invisible spiritual processes into the
visible world dear to the mediaeval artists of the *dolce stil nuovo*:

> *Io vidi, come un dì Guido vedea,*
> *uscir da quei levati occhi una stella,*
> *e da i labbri, che a pena ella movea,*
> *un'alata figura d'angelella.*
>   *La stella tremolando un lume pio*
> *sorridea, sorridea, non so a che;*
> *salia la supplicante angela a Dio,*
> *chiamando in atti: — Signor mio, mercé.*

An old-time way of thought and imagination, idealizing a present
and actual state of feeling, conferring on it a sort of legitimacy or
chrism, this is the fresh tribute which the man of fine literary
taste and range brings to the throbbing beauty beneath his eye.
Carducci's art is rich with the fine flower of culture and, without
awareness of this, not to be understood. But this play of fancy in
which he has almost deliberately involved himself, this illustration
or suspension of the narrative with its abatement of poetic tension,
soon gives way again to a reassertion of the real and the natural:

> *Si volse il prete a dire: Ite . . .*

Here again the religious rite is mentioned in purely material and
indifferent detail and there is a hint of unconcern, if not actual
dislike, in the description of the officiant as "the priest".

> *. . . Potente*
> *ruppe il sole a le nubi sormontando,*
> *e incoronò d'un'iride scendente*
> *la bella donna che sorgea pregando.*

What an admirable stanza! With what strength of line it brings together in a single sentence, almost, the act of the officiant, the radiant and triumphal invasion of the sunlight, the woman rising from her knees with the last words of prayer still on her lips to receive, unknowingly, this halo of sunshine. And what a celebrative note there sounds in this spectacle of the sun, of sympathetic nature, taking pleasure, as it were, in this fair creature, paying homage to her with a crown of shifting colours and brilliances.

The painted Saints too, inside the church, play their part in this human drama, the Virgin Mother joins and seems to sum it up:

> *Corse tra le figure bizantine*
> *vermiglio un riso come di pudor;*
> *ma la Madonna le pupille chine*
> *tenea su 'l figlio e mormorava: – Amor.*

The Madonna, the mother's heart, knows that love though struggled against has to be accepted, as all of life, spirit and sense, blameful-blameless, bittersweet as Petrarch said, has to be accepted.[1]

In this poem the charm of beauty and love prevail together with unsated desire and inseparably conjoined grief.

[1940]

---

1. In confirmation of the above remarks on the points of contact between Carducci's poem and Heine's narrative, see Heine's page on his visit to the church of Trent in *Reise von München nach Genua*, Chap. xv: "Here one prays, dreams, and commits sins of thought; the Madonnas signal forgivingly from their niches, with fellow-feeling if any pretty faces are scored with forbidden thoughts. In every corner there is a brown place for shedding sins off one's conscience" etc. Heine goes on to make merry over a lady confessing a long string of sins to a young friar. The narrator sees only, greedily, the fair one's hand. Bringing this page into relation with Carducci's poem, even in a note, goes against the grain — it seems a profanation, or worse. The page should be read at another time when in a mood for broad jokes. To think that critics are or were in the habit of adducing such merely cultural precedents, pertaining solely to the material side, as "sources" of poems!

XXI

LATE D'ANNUNZIO

As "late" works of D'Annunzio may be classed those after 1904, that is after the composition of the volume entitled *Alcione* and of *La figlia di Iorio*, the last to exhibit some sort of originality. What followed were works which repeated or exaggerated the old themes, the old forms, the old devices: literary exercises of a routine order, the writer being by now incapable of anything else.

To the pre-war decade belong the tragedies *La fiaccola sotto il moggio* ("The Light beneath the Bushel", 1905), *Più che l'amore* ("More than Love", 1906), *La nave* ("The Ship", 1908), *Fedra* (1909), *Parisina* (1913) with music by Mascagni, and in French *Le Martyre de Saint Sébastien* (1911), *La Pisanelle ou la Mort parfumée* (1912), *Le Chèvrefeuille* (1913: Italian version entitled "Il Ferro"); further, the novels *Forse che sì forse che no* ("Perhaps yes, perhaps no", 1910) and parts of the series *Leda senza cigno* ("Leda without Swan", 1913); also, in verse, *Le canzoni d'oltremare* ("Songs of Overseas", 1911), and in prose *La vita di Cola di Rienzo* together with *Proemio* (1905) and *Contemplazione della Morte* (1912).

It would serve no purpose to scrutinize these works for their shortcomings and badness. Contemporary criticism has dealt with them destructively, indeed they pass criticism on themselves, so naked is the artifice of their composition, needing no definition beyond the indication of the works themselves. Wantonness, incest, sadism, ferocity, cruelty, delinquency, and a toying with the memories of ancient Greek tragedy and mediaeval mysteries are the means used in a vain attempt to excite violent and troublous moods. But for all the magnificence of the stylistic devices the end is not achieved. The magnificence, instead of reinforcing such feelings, weakens them, by trifling with them for mere literary effect. As usually happens with D'Annunzio, feelings supposedly heroic are contaminated with the aforesaid, as for example in *La nave*, *Più che l'amore*, and even *Canzoni d'oltremare*; feelings supposedly of affection and kindness are submerged by the sensuality which steadily prevails and dictates to the author, forcing him to delineate not persons but bodies, and not even idealized bodies but bodies heavily fleshy, radiating attraction for the senses but also that disgust and recoil which flesh does sometimes excite. These works contain occasional "Beauties of D'Annunzio" but even these special pages are but repetitions of exhausted forms brought under the false light streaming from a central, all-embracing falsity.

All this was well known and undisputed in the year 1914, four years after D'Annunzio had left Italy to reside in France, where in virtue of a sensuality investing his very gift of language – it was with the ear of sense that he heard words and so was impelled to take sensual possession and to make sensual use of them – he proceeded to write tragedies and other so-called dramas in both modern and archaic French.[1] Serra, in the fine, witty, and at the same time truthful account, which he penned at that time, of the condition of Italian literature,[2] unhesitatingly described D'Annunzio as an exhausted writer now devoid of personality, having become "a sort of sample of a language, an aesthetic attitude, a stylized mechanical heroism available for all uses". The last works, according to Serra, had shown up the artifice in all its nakedness, "dispelling almost instantaneously his halo of illusion and prestige". And Serra, exemplifying his judgement, continued:

> He [D'Annunzio] has quietly pitched his tent in Babylon, and set up shop there, ready to execute all orders whatsoever: to produce literary articles or if occasion demands nationalist rhymes for the Corriere della sera, to turn out librettos for Mascagni, ballets for the Russian corps, mysteries and dramas or what-will-you, for Italy or for France, for the oratory, the theatre, the cinema, it being now all one to him and all exhibited quite indifferently: the clichés are known to all, the themes used up and exhausted in the utter monotony of these products for

1. For D'Annunzio's use of archaic French see the essay by G. CONTINI in *Letteratura*, I, pp. 12-19, Florence, 1937: *Vita macaronica del francese dannunziano*.
2. *Le lettere* (Rome, 1914, reprinted with additions in *Opere*, Rome, 1920), 52-57.

the market. We are being invited to a sale – the contents of every drawer in the shop are included.

Here are more of Serra's observations:

> Consider this style compounded of the measured, spicy classicism of the French nationalists and of the huge, unrhythmically panting utterance of Claudel with adjuncts of old dactylic and tragic scansion; consider these verses of antique style and modern stress – they are the fruit, not of the efforts, but rather of the indifference of the mechanic for whom all metals, all materials are good enough for his press – he collects and fires whatever scraps he finds to hand, left over from his former work, the drawing-room mysticism and decadent Latin in his Saint Sebastian, the palaces and paintings of Ferrara in Parisina, the Levant of the Crusades and some mariners' lore in Pisanella. Remnants of Forse che sì reappear in Il Ferro. Everything he uses, careless altogether whence he takes it and from what pretended diversity of ideals; anything is good enough to serve for the usual clichés of lust flowering in blood, of innocent ecstasy exuding from lust, of heroism and incest, the invariable conclusion of these literary artifices.

And yet this exhausted artist, with no poetry left in him (though still trying to work himself up and to excite others by the provocative force of imagery), retained in his armoury of rousing imaginations certain ones which were not indeed qualitatively different from the others, but were of a different material order: imaginations of war, which took on the colour of nationalistic patriotism, accompanied by much greed of adventure, destruction, rapine, bloodshed, such as filled his dreams already along with the other cravings aforesaid. Having departed to France for purely private reasons, it had amused him to strike an attitude as an "exile" from home, on a level with those great exiles who on foreign soil had worked for the creation of the new Italy. He was, it seemed, awaiting the advent of an Italy worthy of himself, author of *La nave*, pioneer enthusiast for the virtues of aeronautics (had he not himself coined an Italian word "velivoli" for the new flying machines?). From French territory he delivered hymns of celebration and triumph on the outbreak of Italy's war for Libya, directing his tirades verbally against the Turks, but really and substantially against the Austrians. Then came the European war to provide him with the outlets and the scope for action which he longed for. He was selected as the orator to deliver that commemorative celebration of Garibaldi's exploit with the Thousand, which heralded Italy's entry into the war. And soon he passed from political action in favour of Italy's intervention, to military service and departure for the front.

Thus began a six years' period (1915-21) in which the man who had for a quarter century been one of Italy's most brilliant artists, and then for a further ten years an indefatigable literary craftsman, broke into Italian political history as a combatant, an inspirer of combatants, an inventor and executor of bold enterprises, the culmination being his occupation of Fiume against the decisions of the governments of both hemispheres – an occupation on behalf of Italy which he protracted against the decisions of the treaty-makers and the will of the Italian Government itself, which was compelled to drive him out by force. This is no place, in an essay of poetic and literary criticism, to recount or pass judgement upon these deeds. What properly belongs here is, however, a mention of the efficacity of his rhetoric in the cause of war, for this derived not solely from the example he gave personally, but also from his prestige and skill as a man of letters and stylist, greatly superior to others as an intoxicating speechmaker even when become incapable of poetry. Nor is this all, for his success was owed also to intelligence, shrewdness, and sense of the due moment. After the rout of Caporetto he addressed a gathering of officers of all arms as follows: "Ours not to ask what has happened: useless for us would be such knowledge. At first some would fain have lost consciousness in order to know nothing of that horror, worse than the darkness of desperation, worse than a despairing death." But then, striking a note of hope: "If shame there was, it will be washed away. If there was infamy, it will be avenged. The spirit is already at work upon the brute mass rousing it from its misery." How well he found accents to move the hearts of the seventeen-year-olds summoned in 1917 to drive back the invader: "Only yesterday you were children with a mother to smooth your hair, put the lamp on your desk, turn down the sheets. From that you have been called away by the summons which must be followed, and all at once you were breathing a new air, that of the heights. You were caught up: and now you can understand better than from any fable the meaning of transfiguration and rapture. This is the moment of understanding, the moment, above all others, of the spirit."[1] In these talks to soldiers and simple folk the artful phrasing that was elsewhere shallow became efficacious. We ought to include in his best rhetorical performances, as a rhetoric of action and gesture, his flight with eight aeroplanes over Vienna, not to spread fear and fury with bombs, but to drop "a tricolour greeting in the three colours of liberty" in the spirit of Italian humanity. The signal seemed to proclaim victory and an end to war, with a new era of peace among the peoples heralded by Italy.

Yet neither during nor after the war did D'Annunzio revive as a writer. He might write of warlike exploits and deaths in battle, he might mourn lost friends, but the sentences were never pure from physical and carnal obsession. In cruel and acrid terms they illuminated the hateful and material features – never the inner life of thought and feeling. A troublous riot of sensations and images generated the *Nocturne*, a book composed as he lay in the dark with shaded eyes to recover from an injury to the eye, and designed to give outer shape to the countless visual impressions passing before him "with a definiteness of form and pungency of detail which vastly heightened the pathetic intensity". The *Faville del maglio* ("Sparks from the Anvil") of 1924-8 are mainly autobiographical. When he sought lyrical elevation he resorted – which was nothing new for him and reflected French models – to forms of divine prayer and Franciscan praise, filling out these with the usual multitudinous adumbrations of whatever objects his eye rested upon.

D'Annunzio's final phase, his last thirty years and more, that is to say, seems to me to offer little scope to the critic who is not content with reiterating the obvious. Any critical problem which remains to be solved is more likely to concern the value and significance of his best work, which may be said to start with *Canto*

1. See *La riscossa*, speeches published by the Government Press Office, Milan, 1918.

novo or even some pages of *Primo vere* and to end with such works as *Alcione* and *Figlia di Iorio*.

Criticism at the beginning of this century found its most urgent and indeed inescapable preliminary problem, in dealing with D'Annunzio, to be the sorting out of a confusion (due in part to careless and superficial reading, in part to the author's deliberate craft) between the genuine and the bogus parts of his work, between the D'Annunzio who was really expressing himself and that imaginary, counterfeit D'Annunzio who so readily assumed the masks of a poet of goodness or piety, expiation or high tragedy, superhumanism, heroism, or gospel-utterance. For it was this bogus D'Annunzio who more than the real D'Annunzio won belief and praise and the flattery of imitation. But once the required surgical operation had been successfully performed, its results were lasting, for never again did the critics ascribe value or significance to the pseudo-D'Annunzio, author of projects and programmes: when he continued along this false line they were prepared in advance and could not be deceived. The very outlet which D'Annunzio as projector and programmatist discovered in the realities of war so that he could actually give vent to those tendencies in a partly beneficial way, served but further to mark off the limits of D'Annunzio as a genuine artist.

These limits were by the writer of the present notes defined in 1903 as those of a "dilettante of sensation" (limits, it was added, within which D'Annunzio was strongly entrenched and insuperable). Certain critics have subsequently sought to modify this definition but I hold to it as the simplest and truest. The discernment of this character was not an invention of mine, it had already been mooted by various readers and critics.[1] It is mine only in that I selected it from among others and gave it preference as the basis of interpretation of D'Annunzio's works. One of the most responsible and attentive of recent critics, Francesco Flora, author of a critical monograph on the poet[2] and of an admirable critical

1. See Flora's contribution to *Leonardo*, Florence, July 1923, where he makes some just observations.

2. Ricciardi, Naples, 1926.

commentary on D'Annunzio's *Laudi*,[1] offers the alternative delineation of a D'Annunzio carried away by lascivious excess, by
a "constitutional lasciviousness", impairing a great part of his work
by perverting it into a rhetorical means towards concupiscence.
In other parts, however, according to Flora, the poet rises superior
to this into a serene, airy lyricism. I myself question this diagnosis
of a fierce lustfulness: what I find in him is rather detachment and
curiosity, pursuit and savouring of experiences, not that whirlwind
which seizes upon the lustful as in Dante's *Inferno*, not the delirium, anguish, fixation, folly belonging to that state of mind and
its expression: I do not find in him the signs of the erotomane.
I am equally unconvinced about that wrestling match between
lust and lyricism allegedly played out with varying fortunes in
D'Annunzio's work, nor can I accept that picture of an inferior
D'Annunzio employing rhetoric to the ends of lust. The only
inferior D'Annunzio I recognize is the one who seeks to evade his
own limits by feigning spiritual interests which can never be his:
likewise a rhetorical D'Annunzio I know – the one whose appearance signals the moments of weariness, mannerism, decadence
in the artist. Flora's psychological delineation seems to me better
to fit Gustave Flaubert, who was the author of *Tentations* and
Salammbô on the one hand, and of *Madame Bovary* and *Éducation
sentimentale* on the other.[2] It does not fit D'Annunzio, who never
emerges from the world of sense, but is at home there, cultivating
and governing this realm of his, drawing from it all the delights
he wants, including the delights of cruelty which seem to offer him
a singular enjoyment.

It was, I think, a proper conclusion worthy of retention, to
ascribe D'Annunzio's best art to this inspiration, and to discard all
that work in which he vainly laid claim to a higher inspiration.
Such was the conclusion reached thirty years ago. Perhaps it rather
overvalued the best work of D'Annunzio, a natural consequence
of the great effort put forth to segregate it from the inferior work

1. Mondadori, Milan, 1934.
2. On Flaubert's two aspects see my *Poesia e non poesia* (4th edn., Bari,
1946), pp. 260-72.

which infected and sometimes smothered it. And then too little attention was given to the character and origin of the poetry: a natural fault, because things have to be done by stages, and this was a further problem properly to be tackled only when the preceding problem had come fully to the surface of consciousness.

The ulterior problem for the critic of D'Annunzio's poetry is this. By common agreement there is a lack of "humanity" even in the best of it. This seems quite undeniable. All his work attests it, and indeed much of what has been discerned and rejected as false is simply a failed attempt to achieve this "humanity" through the medium of the human tragedy of terror and pity. The failure underlines the fact of the lack and of the limit. This limit is most evident in certain pages in which the quality of the argument seems to promise an irresistible appeal to the heart: yet the author, who sees and describes the scene with amazing clarity and perfection, watches it impassively, with but a heightened curiosity of the senses. Take for example the episode in *Trionfo della Morte* when the mother of the drowned boy, desperate and distraught with grief, hastens to the scene and raises her lament:

> *In the shadow of the rocks, over against the white sheet shaped to the stiff form of the corpse, the mother uttered her plaint in the form hallowed by all the past and present grief of her race. It seemed that the lament would never end.*

In *La figlia di Iorio*, a pretty little piece unjustly handled by many critics, the sensual and sanguinary background seems to be relieved by goodness, purity, and the generous, expiatory sacrifice. But these are introduced in fairy tale style, which, if it excludes the falsity of tone of some other similar attempts by D'Annunzio, leaves them without solidity: if anything in the play is solid it is that background which impresses itself so strongly as to involve the whole work in the climax of the voluptuous death in the consuming flame. A perfectly clear tone, a response to sheer and simple feeling, is perhaps to be found only in some early compositions from the time before he had, simultaneously, perfected his technique and exhausted his vein. Flora, who rightly observes that D'Annunzio wholly lacks the sense of sin while correlatively

his art is devoid of "cordiality", "domestic intimacy", "friendliness", has not hesitated to translate "non-humanity" into the positive term of animality or bestiality. "If a beast or a tree were to
express itself, it would be in the D'Annunzian manner. Humanity
in this art is nature: the colours, odours, tastes, sounds of things
as they are humanly digested, and not the thoughts and feelings
which a man forms, are here transcribed into a symbolic music. If
Man is God coming to consciousness in us, then D'Annunzio is
nature coming to consciousness – a beast, one might say, conscious
of nature."[1] For that matter all can see the consistency of D'Annunzio's culture, one in which all the *humaniora*, History, Philosophy, Religion, even the higher Poetry, are missing.

Now if in all solemnity we proclaim this absence of humanity
and presence of bestiality in D'Annunzio (in justice to those very
humane beasts the dogs and those highly spiritual beings the birds
we must observe that the use of the words is metaphorical), we
must perforce deny him any intimately poetical quality, for what
else is poetry but humanity? Can "nature", can a beast, acquire
consciousness without becoming aware of a limit, thereby passing
beyond this into humanity? It avails nothing to hail D'Annunzio
as a great poet "lacking inwardness" or as a great "lyrical landscapist" (according to the view of Gargiulo in his finely observant
and discriminating book).[2] Inwardness and humanity are necessary to the painter and the landscapist, for it is the soul, not the eye,
which paints. Flora noticed this difficulty and the need there was
to resolve it and to reconcile the denial to D'Annunzio of needful
qualities with the affirmation of value in his best work. So he
proclaimed that humanity, totality, cosmic feeling could after all
be ascribed to D'Annunzio, but not in the elect form displayed
by other poets: rather, in a form special to himself, in which the
distinction of spirit and nature fades, the spirit becomes concrete in
nature, whereby the poet achieves, like other poets, a conjunction
and harmony with the All. He adds that in the charge of want of
humanity levelled against him there lurks "the shadow of the old

1. FLORA, op. cit., p. 219.
2. ALFREDO GARGIULO, *Gabriele d'Annunzio* (Perrella, Naples, 1912).

transcendent, the shadow of the old Creator, the problem of the sense of eternity outside physical time" and other irrelevancies.

There is no complaint to be made against this judgement as regards its critical method, nor would there be as regards its content, were not the "humanity" which is found to be lacking in D'Annunzio one and the same thing as the harmony with the All, with the life of the Cosmos, lack of which is lack of the life of the Spirit. There are other poets who are strongly, almost wholly, absorbed in the senses, in mere vitality, in pleasure and pain, yet they redeem themselves in poetry through sheer suffering and its expression, whereby the animal is resolved into the man, the natural is spiritualized, or, to use my own philosophical terms, the lower stage of the spirit is dialectically surpassed in the higher stages. With D'Annunzio this never happens. Never, touching one string, does he awaken the whole human harmony to life. Frequently he wins our admiration for his artistic skill, but he never transports us by rising above himself and so raising us above ourselves.

That characterization of him as the "dilettante" here again proves useful, though some would have us discard it. For the dilettante of vital sensation would quite evidently be incapable of surrendering to that rapture of the universal which is the mystery of poetry. He could not shuffle off the interested hedonistic attitude which would check his self-surrender to the full contemplation of the mystery of life. This accounts for the character of D'Annunzio's composition, from which there is never absent a certain self-satisfaction: the artist is aware, and makes the reader aware, of his skill and flourish, and the words he uses are continually reminding us of the fact of language and dictionary. The Odes of the book *Alcione*, his best artistic achievement, are admirable but never altogether convincing or spiritually satisfying. How should we not admire *Versilia* in its celebration of fresh fruit and foliage, young flesh and blood, through the songful medium of a woman's prayers and promises and invitations and yieldings? But even this poem is (though but lightly) shackled to the tyranny of dilettantism. How should one not greatly admire the ode on the death of a stag, *La morte del cervo*, unsurpassed and almost unrivalled in its marvellous conversion of lines, colours, odours, motions, sounds, savours, into well-shapen phrase and syllable, rhythm and metre? Yet this composition does not only display but also at the same time explicitly declares the skill of the crafts-man who has moulded "in Corinthian bronze" – that is in the wealth of the Italian vocabulary possessed by him – "what his bright eyes saw". With the Centaur, man and beast, the poet's "soul surcharged with drafts of antique power" does indeed throb. But this is an exercise of rare and frantic pleasure rather than a true rapture finding its culmination and release in the joy of song.

And so, for all its luxuriant appearance, the world of D'An-nunzio conveys a sense of poverty, the poverty of a Midas, if you will, condemned to convert into the gold of sensation whatever he touches. Hence what is called the "monotony" of his art. Now poetry is never really monotonous, even when a poet remains for ever within his own range of feeling or his own hierarchy of feel-ing, presenting it variously. But with D'Annunzio we have the repetition of the same proceeding, the same game, the same elaborate or indeed subtle tricks, with little poetic charm. The critics have accordingly attempted to rehabilitate this poetry by attributing to it recondite meanings and elaborate reasonings. In this connexion I would recommend that the *cliché*, originated, I think, by Borgese, but used by pretty well all critics, that D'An-nunzio created "new myths", should be discarded. "Myths" are not objects of artistic creation, but formations thrown up in the course of men's intellectual experience: concepts still clouded or infected by imagery, signs not of the power but of the "poverty" of the human mind in its immaturity, as the first great thinker to formu-late a theory of them pronounced. D'Annunzio's myths are not concepts or even would-be concepts: they are mere representations of the desire and life of the senses, or at most what old-fashioned rhetoric used to call "personifications".

As soon as D'Annunzio's art began to receive wide attention, its similarity to that of the Italian decadence, the Baroque school, the school of Marino, was observed: a many-sided and far from superficial likeness which I will not here illustrate, having done so elsewhere.[1] Elsewhere I have also remarked upon the monotony, the propensity towards mere game-playing and the resort to extraneous artifice in the seventeenth-century artistic appeal to the senses.[2] Not only should D'Annunzio be denied any comparison with the great, severe, austere poets, but he should not be compared either with those, like Tasso, and Foscolo in his *Grazie*, in whom there is a hot vein of sensuality and eroticism. For these poets lift themselves to the level of the heroic and religious drama of mankind whence D'Annunzio remains absent. A comparison with them could only emphasize his essential poetic aridity. He will remain a notable symbol of decadent art – common opinion (*vox populi vox Dei*) has already pronounced this judgement.

[1935]

1. *Saggi sulla letteratura italiana del seicento*, 3rd edn., Bari, 1948, pp. 405-8.
2. *Storia dell'età barocca in Italia*, 2nd edn., Bari, 1946, p. 324.

VII
MORAL AND POLITICAL HISTORY

I

THE SIXTEENTH-CENTURY CRISIS IN ITALY:
LINKS BETWEEN RENAISSANCE AND
RISORGIMENTO

THE historical method of causalism or determinism, which refers events to this or that particular fact materialistically conceived (and so equally incapable of generating or accounting for reality) is always to be avoided, and no less than elsewhere in a historical enquiry into the Italian Decadence and the subsequent Risorgimento. The right method is to take account solely of the living historical process, the spiritual process for which the fact is the revelation of its own reason.

Various "causes" have been adduced to "explain" the Italian sixteenth-century crisis, singly or jointly, and to these some credence is still generally accorded. First and foremost, the failure to fashion Italy into a single State, on the model of the large States then coming into existence, is held accountable. But the formation of a great and potent Spanish State did not save Spain from crisis and internal decadence, nor did multiplicity of small States debar the Swiss Republics or the Low Countries from contributing as they did to the civil and religious renovation of Europe, or hinder the Germans from accomplishing the Reformation and then in the eighteenth century adding stature to the thought of Europe. A preference for having one or for having several political centres in a country can really only be decided in regard to circumstances. As these vary, the one or the other may be more or less fitted to the requirements of public life and the promotion of human progress. In the nineteenth century political unity was felt to be absolutely necessary for the sake of freedom and civilization, and so, first of all in the form of federal unity and then in the form of the unified State, it was ardently advocated and after sustained efforts achieved. But in the sixteenth century such unity was neither practical politics nor an ideal aspiration. And the same must be said of the other "Cause" usually linked to the foregoing – the loss of national independence and the establishment of foreign domination and hegemony. According to circumstances such an inclusion within a plurinational political unit, or even the submission to a foreign hegemony, may be either advantageous or the reverse. If it had been truly felt to be harmful, odious, intolerable, Italy would have revolted in the same way that the Low Countries revolted against the same power, or that Italy did against Austria later on in the Restoration period.

The theory of these two "causes", historically quite invalid, was the fruit of the passions of the Risorgimento. The spirit of that age, neglecting, in its forward flight, any penetration into the real spiritual condition of the sixteenth century, made use of the events of this century for the weaving of romances, dramas, poems suggestive of its own ideals, and wrote its histories in the same manner. And alongside of these two "causes" there appeared another emphatically propagated myth: according to which the "cause" lay in the loss of liberty in fifteenth-century Italy through the extinction of the mediaeval communes, particularly the outstanding commune of Florence; out of which theory sprang the celebrated romances and tragedies of Guerrazzi, D'Azeglio, Niccolini, with many others, and histories written in the same key. True enough, liberty is something essential in the life of a people and for the judgement which we pass on this. But in saying this we have in mind the liberty which is intimately present in men's moral endeavour, continually shaping its own forms, creating them ever anew, in face of a political problem which unceasingly changes with changing conditions. In the sixteenth century no genuine political problem could arise in regard to mediaeval communal liberties, for these had been overwhelmed two centuries earlier by frank or concealed despotisms, surviving only in one or two institutions or customs shorn of their original significance and incapable of reanimation or development. No doubt the strictures of Guicciardini and Vettori upon the wellwishers and defenders of those liberties – judged by them to be men interested only in the profit or glory to be got out of participation in public affairs, and not in the least in freedom – are misplaced: there were among them generous characters with a love and disinterested desire of the beauty of liberty. But such characters were never lacking; even in the ages of the most supine servitude there were to be found devoted admirers of figures and episodes of Graeco-Roman history, of unhistoric and idealized versions of Harmodius and Brutus. The point is that there was no sign, in the sixteenth century, of men actively inspired to a real struggle in the real conditions of the moment, with dedicated minds and hearts. Even the die-hard champions of Florentine liberty, all of them – as their writings show – desirous of oligarchic conservative republics on the model of Venice, such as were later realized also in Genoa and Lucca, stayed inactive for want of such dedication. With hardly an exception and including the noblest and most intelligent of them, Segni, Varchi, Adriani, Jacopo Nardi himself, they finally came to terms with Cosimo dei Medici and having no other hope accepted the new regime in Florence as the best available or the least bad. The final struggle and fall of the Republic of Florence left behind it no sacred memories to vouch for a future restoration of liberty. We learn from Segni that the commotions and protests of the Florentine exiles in Naples in the presence of Charles V occasioned mere laughter and mirth in Italy. It was much the same when Perugia, inspired by republican memories, took arms against the Pope. The history of the mediaeval communes of Italy, far from being celebrated in epic strains, was usually observed with pity or abuse, and finally in the next century served as material for burlesque poems. Among the historians, even those who had personally played a part as citizens defending the Florentine Republic, when they came to treat of Florentine liberty in their books, could recall only the negative aspect, the succession of delusions provoked by a liberty never truly realized or enjoyed.

Yet another "cause" explanatory of the Italian crisis was advanced more than once in a similar process of deduction by naive devotees of foreign history. The argument now was that since the European peoples which have been pre-eminent in power and civilization were those same that had embraced the doctrines of

Calvin and Luther, therefore Italy should also have embraced them, and the willing or unwilling failure to do so was a great misfortune. And certainly this matter of religious reformation is essential and vital, but it is not to be equated with the acceptance of a certain model, the discharge of a certain routine. There are many modes of religious renewal and maybe the one just mentioned did not fit the intellectual and cultural level attained by Italy – it was in fact poorly esteemed by such great minds and supremely free spirits as Giordano Bruno.

The Renaissance, setting high value upon earthly life, had shown some indifference to the heaven which for so long had held the Middle Ages in rapt attention. Yet it was not an irreligious but a religious movement, in spite of, or rather because of, its rational, its seriously rational bent. For, as in these days it is good to re-member, reason is the eternal principle which rules and regulates and guides ever upwards the life of man, and religions are in their living elements, their fruitful speculations, their affirmations, no-thing else but lights of reason radiating through mythical frames which reason will end by discarding so as to shine undisguised. If the Renaissance did not at the outset deliver a revolutionary at-tack upon the sphere which passes for being in a special sense re-ligious, yet it could not pause and slumber in that sort of detach-ment and indifference, but needs must in its scrupulous devotion to reason go on to treat all of reason's problems, taking in too the related problems of the ethical conscience, of liberty, politics, history, all the modes of the realization of the divine in the world. All of these were involved in the summons which had been ut-tered for a religious reformation.

Strong evidence that Italy, of all the countries of Europe, was nearest to the development of the rationalism of the Renaissance into a rational religious reformation, lies in the fact that as soon as the idea of such a reformation became known through contact either with Luther's Germany or with Spanish mysticism ferment-ing under the influence of Erasmus, it was readily welcomed above all in the circles of the Humanists and in cultivated society. A still better proof is that in Italy the idea took a radical form, speeding from negation to negation, destroying in its course not merely the Catholic Church but all the Christian myths, the divinity of Jesus, the Trinity, the immortality of the soul, and so forth. The Italian adherents of the Reformation, exiles in Protestant lands, often aroused astonishment, concern, and suspicion by their uncompromising rationalism, complaints, for instance, that "the Italians, finding the Church of Rome begin to pall, would stand for no religion at all". They were numbered among the boldest and least hesitant innovators in those countries, encouraging and nourishing the idea of Natural Religion and the closely allied idea of Toleration – a first stage towards that Religion of Reason that was to ripen later.

But how came this movement, so pregnant with promise, to a halt in Italy, so that there the thoughts which had just been aroused were dissipated, and the spirit of Italy, losing its impetus and enthusiasm, was turned back upon itself, and renouncing all effort humbled itself before the Church of Rome, turning to small occupations and distractions? For in the second half of the century we discern on every hand a torpor with which goes a new manner in life, in literature, in thought, greatly different from the swift alacrity of the early sixteen-hundreds. We can make no answer without retracing the line of thought which leads to the aforesaid empty enumeration of "causes". Or alternatively one will give an answer which merely repeats the content of the question, as when one says that the attempt itself was premature, for want of the required support and through defect of circumstances, or that the Renaissance was an aristocratic and not a popular movement, wherefore the religious stirrings which went with it never or hardly ever penetrated to the common people, for which reasons the Renaissance permitted the seeds of *renovatio* and of inner freedom that it inherited from the Middle Ages to wither, and itself degenerated into mere formalism and outwardness.

It is the business, no easy one, of history to ascertain and to qualify, that is, to know what has happened – and to abstain from entanglement in pointless enquiries. What has already been said defines what the crisis and decadence of Italy in the sixteenth century really amounted to: an arrested development, a suspension of the deepening of the rational enquiry already in process, an inadequate receptiveness for those evangelical and Pauline inspirations and suggestions emanating from the religious Reformation, which were available for reshaping and for reduction to a purer form. Here and there the attempt had been made. Savonarola's narrowly moralistic and ascetic experiment left dogmas and orthodoxy untouched, and took no account of a progress achieved, from the level of which it was impossible for Italian civilization to step down. Francesco Burlamacchi in Tuscany conceived the scheme of an alliance between the new religious current and the cause of freedom, viewing these, however, simply as two political forces capable of being conjoined. There was nothing in this of the true reforming spirit. And later on Paolo Sarpi, the intrepid adversary of the Court of Rome, neither himself undertook nor encouraged the undertaking of a decisive step by Venice – had he done so, it would have been too late, for the heroic and militant early age of Protestantism was then at an end.

But the working out of what was implicit in the Italian Renaissance was a logical necessity which European civilization in the long run had to take over and pursue, as can be seen in the history of the century and a half which ran from the evangelical revolution of the first half of the fifteenth to the new rationalism of the second half of the seventeenth century. The inner and directing virtue then at work was all the time that rational principle which the Renaissance had affirmed against the transcendent principle of the Middle Ages. It was this same Renaissance which, conserving as the chiefmost and the most truly rational achievement of the Reformation its reassertion of the moral conscience against the sacramental and casuistic code of the Catholic Church, went on to disencumber Protestantism from the mediaeval archaism which still enveloped it, from the irrational absorption in the Book, the Bible, and so brought it to the stage of an enlightened theologism, while at the same time by the action of this same Renaissance, the mythical conceptions of predestination, incarnation, trinity were being converted into pure philosophical ideas, and the inclination

and recurring suggestion of codified asceticism was warded off by
the approval and free play accorded as expressions and instruments
of civilization to healthy economics, politics, literature, and science.
And sometimes the work of the Renaissance was accomplished, not
within the circle of religious interests, but by a frontal assault
upon these from outside, aimed at demolishing dogmas and superstitions. Novel intellectual positions were established by the com-
paigns of the anti-trinitarians, the Arminians, Socinians, advocates
of natural religion, natural rights, or the social contract. By such
controversies in sheerly intellectual terms the advance of reason,
its elevation and its deepening, was speeded on. And in the narrowly political field the modern type of kingdom took shape,
freed from the residues of feudal variety and mediaeval particularism, and in its wake the form of State which accords toleration
in matters of religion. The first glimmerings of political liberalism
meanwhile were sensible in the demand for freedom of thought
and its public expression, wherein was recognized the supreme
value of living thought in a living human civilization.

But in all this deployment of European energies – no straight
and simple process, but one full of complications and setbacks if
only for the engagement of peoples far less advanced in civilization
than the Italians of the sixteenth century, and entailing long wars
and revolutionary struggles – Italy's part was apparently small,
being restricted to the work of the last but not unworthy inheritors and representatives of the Renaissance, the exiled children
of Italy and their descendants in foreign lands where they kept
alive both name and memory. And sometimes, in the next age,
Italy looked forth like a disinterested spectator upon that great
and fervent scene of European history, as though murmuring, in
Manzoni's words: "I was not there." For this reason the century
and a half in question bear with us the description of "the Italian
Decadence".

It is a term which, provided we remember the merely approximate sense which is all that we can prudently allow to the
notion of "decadence", we may well employ. The failure or
weakening of an ideal always spells what is called decadence. And

here it should be noted that by ideal is not meant just any image or conception for which one may fight and die. Were this meant, then any fanaticism, inebriation, or blind passion could fill the book. No! We mean an inherent effective and efficacious moral ideal, a life-enhancing and therefore freedom-promoting ideal, such as alone can sustain human strength. The historian, as the morally alert man, feels and marks down the incidence of the accent of liberty in the situations of history, undeceived by fallacious appearances, undeluded by strange or harsh fashions assumed by liberty, or by what looks like and is not liberty, or by what looks like the contradiction but is really the envelope of liberty. In the late centuries of the Roman Empire the accent of liberty and spiritual progress marked the Galilaean sect, not the governing Emperors and high officials nor the Roman Stoics dreaming of the old republican institutions and conspiring, nay spilling or taking their own lives for that cause. And so in the Italy of the Counter-Reformation and the Spanish domination liberty and progress lay not with the brave Italian soldiers and captains who fought for the King of Spain on all the battlefields of Europe, Africa, and America, or with the obedient and zealous clergy who stood up to the heretics and often suffered martyrdom. Admirable and heroic as they were in their persons and in the discharge of their responsibilities when rendering spotless service to their faiths and oaths, they were yet not creators of the future but representatives of the past. The age was an age of Italian decadence because by the side of many unflagging upholders of the past, Italy could muster very few apostles of the future, and those few scattered and perplexed.

It is worth remarking how after the last mild utterances, in counsel or in print, of the last Florentine Republicans, there was an end to all elevated political publication. Under this term we cannot class all the memoirs, pamphlets, or long books composed to support the cause of the Church, the Princes, the oligarchies, written, that is, in defence of purely particular interests, unillumined by any ideal point of reference, nor yet general invocations of the name of Italy or exhortations to rise and expel the foreigner and re-create a great and glorious Italy, because these, though much praised and admired by men of letters even at the present day, were simply literature, and not political writing such as of itself amounts to concrete political activity. The political maxims proffered were simply counsels of cunning, unlit even by that poetic vision, which had been alive in Machiavelli, of the man of cunning and violence strong enough to throw out the foreigners and to unite Italy as a powerful State. The day of the citizen was over, that of the courtier had arrived; the disposition for ruling and governing had given way to that for rendering service with private profit; prudence and the wiles and dissemblings suggested by it formed now the capital virtue, and manuals giving instruction *de re aulica* or on how to serve at court poured from the press. Historical writing switched its attention to military and diplomatic concerns: for the internal struggles which Machiavelli had used for his argument in preference to the narration of wars and political intrigues had died down. Rare indeed were the flashes of ideal inspiration brightening the pages of the historians and political essayists – now and then some lament, some longing, some utterance of indignation and rebellion was too strong to be suppressed. Alone the solitary Tommaso Campanella gave his message, and that too in the form only of a Utopia, the *City of the Sun*, delineating the reduction of the human race to unity, equality, and uniformity in a world about to come to its end with a dissolution into the Godhead.

Small wonder, then, that the histories of those centuries of Italian life were a mere recital and depiction of cowardice, stupidity, melancholy, horror, ill relieved by an occasional mocking laugh or ironic smile. But the office of history is to record and to interpret what humanity creatively achieves – institutions, sciences, systems, the positive and not the negative, doing not undoing, construction and not demolition. Were there nothing positive and constructive in an age there would be no history to write about it for "where there is nothing the King himself loses his rights".

But in truth even in the ages of decadence the ideal never wholly loses its sway. Not only are flashes and streaks to be discerned in single individuals but the ideal force, albeit not strong enough to animate life as a whole, yet invests certain parts, preserving past achievement, here and there enlarging its bounds, accomplishing things good and true, preparing the material for a general recovery and renewal of progress. No doubt such sparse and disconnected labours are meanwhile liable to be themselves caught up and merged in the general decadence, but on the other hand so much as can evade this and can hold out will exert a healing influence, much as in an organism the undiseased parts may succumb to the disease, but may on the other hand assist the slow recovery of the diseased. Sometimes their healing efficacy is attested by the half-conscious distrust which their presence is seen to have aroused, (like that of Caesar for the lean and pale Cassius), by the warnings administered and the hostility shown or put into effect against those who on the face of it seemed to be performing harmless specialized tasks.

In such a spirit should we enquire into the age of Italian Decadence and in such a spirit did I in fact compose my History of the Baroque Age, thereby drawing the criticism (but I esteemed it to be praise) that in the seventeenth century I had given weight not to the average and typical but to attitudes and works already fore-shadowing those of the following two centuries. I expounded the extent to which the rationalism of the Renaissance was still oper-ative, and was, indeed, widening its scope, most conspicuously in the physical and natural sciences, but also in certain ranges of speculation on human conduct, for instance in the recognition of a rightful and in no way perverse liberation of the concept of prudence and policy from that of morality, or in the place given to the ideas of fancy and taste in the theory of poetry and art, or once again, in the domain of humanistic culture, in an enlarged knowledge and appreciation of Greek and Roman history and of heroic antiquity which the Jesuits too had to admit into their programmes of studies, recognizing sensibly that there could be no return for society, or even for the Church, to the institutions and manners of the Middle Ages. The main thread was indeed

broken but this did not prevent the continued weaving of subsidiary threads, albeit lacking the knot that should hold them together,
and so left loosely hanging. And turning from the range of
theory to that of practice it can be seen that the monarchical and
princely governments did much to unify and equalize rights and
usages, and to raise, upon the decline of the old baronial class
which had now become a mere court aristocracy, an active and
intelligent class which would later take on a function of direction,
and was indeed already providing agents and ministers for the
direction of the affairs of the States, it being impossible to get on
without employing "capacity", while its employment is always
the first step towards giving it an established place and putting it
in the way of future advances.

All the same, Italy between the mid-sixteenth and the end-
seventeenth century gives the impression of a country not really
alive, not alive on that spiritual level where energies converge in
hope and confidence upon a light shining ahead. Other-worldli-
ness pervaded the mind of Italy, and the pious practices enjoined
to keep the devout continually attentive to the images of death
and dissolution and to the salvation of their own souls were reflected in an oppressive pessimism – too oppressive to be shaken
off personally by the wonderful speculative genius who now
emerged from the culture of the sixteen-hundreds and in a unique
degree brought together the multiple traditions of the Renaissance and the fruit of the labours of the new age, to all of which
he gave a new shape in correspondence with his own original
conceptions of the human mind and of human history. All the
future affirmations of the nineteenth century were foreseen or
glimpsed by him, save only the idea of a humanity perpetually
outgrowing its limitations: and so his profound view of historical
development as the unceasing rhythm of the spirit remained
unmatched by the complementary thought of "progress", that is
of the uniqueness of the course of history, to such a point that, for
all his profession of Catholicism, he failed to recognize the uniqueness even of such an event as the rise of Christianity. And so, from
the Christian vision of an accomplished act of redemption and of

a Church defending and preaching the new imperishable faith, Giambattista Vico fell back into the oriental conception of historical cycles with a naturalistic law taking the place of the development of the religious-ethical drama of human history.

Vico's contemporary, Pietro Giannone, cannot be placed on quite the same intellectual level. Yet if Vico stands for the highest achievement of philosophy in the stricter sense in continuance of the intellectual development of the Renaissance, Giannone is the voice of the soul of Italy recovering integrity, retempering the morality of the Renaissance, resuming here too an interrupted task. The conditions, of course, had meanwhile changed, the wars of religion now lay behind and the new principle of toleration was everywhere prevalent, as developed by Descartes and other philosophers of the century, nor may the contribution of the last Italian thinkers, the great Bruno and the great Campanella, be forgotten. Giannone found his opportunity and his place of combat in the resistance of the modern State to the persistent usurpations and unabated pretensions of the Church of Rome – for the newly established absolute monarchies throughout Italy, at first more feared than respected but later subtly differentiated from and contrasted by political writers with tyrannical dominations (being praised as the rule of "the good prince"), became instruments of secularism, of progress, and indirectly of that liberty which vainly a century and a half earlier men had sought to restore and to embalm in the forms of the mediaeval Republics. In the service of that cause and with an eye upon the work done by the monarchy in France, Giannone's feelings warmed towards the Austrian dynasty now following the Spanish on the throne of Naples, and still greater was his fervour when in Carlo di Borbone his motherland obtained a King of its own. But Giannone was the author of the *Triregno* as well as of the *Storia civile*, and in that renewed attention to the religious problem and in the solution which Giannone gave to it we can see a revived concern with rationalism and with the spiritual urges such as in the Italian Renaissance had been awoken with and by means of the Reformation. Now it happened to Giannone in the course of his exile (an exile similar to that of the Italian Reformers of the fifteen-hundreds, ending too, like theirs, in the martyrdom of a long imprisonment and death in prison) to be brought to Geneva, where so many memories remained of the thought and the labours and accomplishments of his forerunners. Among other families he found there the descendants of Francesco Burlamacchi. One and all they had applied themselves to the essential though modified and intensified fulfilment of their ancestors' resolve to seek Italian liberty by the long and arduous method of religious renewal rather than through political combinations. And a century later another descendant of the exiles, Sismondi, was with his famous work of history to recall to the memory and the heart of the Italians the glorious liberties of their Communes and the fate which had befallen them in the sixteenth century and the ensuing crisis of Italian power and civilization in the age of the Counter-Reformation. And in so doing he would sting them with a silent reproof and add strength to the already stirring Risorgimento.

The first beginnings of this Risorgimento came in the age of Giannone, not only in the region of his birthplace, but throughout Italy, with varying modes and speeds but thenceforth without interruption. And Italy, re-entering European history, passed through all Europe's phases, from that of anti-Papal and laicist monarchy, by way of reforming monarchy, Jacobinism, democratic Republics, to the demand for liberal constitutions pressed in the teeth of a foreign power desirous of maintaining on Italian soil the old absolutist way of government with the new Ultramontane exaggerations. At last, with the triumph of the liberal conception, there was reached one of those ideal conclusions which cannot be (and in this case was not) surpassed in any ulterior advance, being such as hold within themselves the unlimited possibility of innovation, development, advance, and indeed themselves supply the requisite formula for this. When the liberal order comes up against entangling obstacles, or forces of compression, these, however important and significant, do not confront it as a new and rival ideal, but simply as retardations and vicissitudes in the course of the one and only ideal, invincible in having for its aim no static satisfaction but the fervour of work and of the struggle for higher modes of life.

When the movement of the Risorgimento, as above described, read back into the past its own loves and hatreds, this had the effect not only of inserting a hiatus between Renaissance and Risorgimento, but of mutually estranging the two ages. And so the latter, seeking its own historical precedents, found them more easily in the Middle Ages and the Communes, regarding the Renaissance as the age of Italian paganism and materialism, of a lettered and rhetorical sensualism against which it was the duty of the new Italians to react. My main aim in this essay has been to show that the Risorgimento was in truth the continuation of the Renaissance in its rational and religious theme: the interposition of the age of decadence does not therefore betoken disconnection and decadence of a complete nature.

[1939]

II

ITALIAN CULTURE AGAINST
SPANISH BARBARISM

THE Italians had come to regard the Spaniards as their inferiors in many intellectual and ethical concerns. This must be recalled if one is to understand the astonishment and then the humiliation which overtook them when hordes of Spaniards worked their way up from Sicily, originally in order to withstand the invasions and ravages of the French, and to assist in liberating the Italians from this "Gaulish" outrage, but then, when in a few years they had again vanquished these Frenchmen, to establish their own dominion over the Italian lands. We can hear the astonishment and the grief echoing in those verses in which Ariosto points to Africa as Spain's nearer and more rightful object of attack instead of afflicted and miserable Italy:

> Non hai tu, Spagna, l'Africa vicina,
> che t'ha via più di questa Italia offesa?
> E pur, per dar travaglio alla meschina,
> lasci la prima tua sì bella impresa.[1]

Leader of the Spanish enterprise was Gonzalo of Córdova, the so-called "Grand Captain",[2] whose fame had reached Italy first in the various tales of the taking of Granada. Then he had come to the kingdom of Naples with a handful of men to aid young King Ferrantino against Charles VIII's Frenchmen and had also freed Ostia for the benefit of the Holy See, after which, triumphantly received in Rome, he was awarded that decoration of the Rose which the Popes conferred each year upon some one conspicuous

---

1. *Orlando Furioso*, XVII, 76.
2. First so named by the Italians. See *Breve parte de las hazañas del excelente nombrado Gran Capitán*, contained in MARTINEZ DE LA ROSA, *Obras completas* (Paris, 1844), III, 113. See also *Cronicas del Gran Capitán*, edited by Rodriguez Villa, in *Nueva biblioteca de autores españoles*, vol. X (Madrid, 1908), which includes also *Las dos conquistas del reino de Nápoles* (first published Saragossa, 1554).

figure of Christendom.[1] In summer 1501 he again moved into the Kingdom, this time through Calabria, against the French, and next year occupied Atripalda, hoisting there, as was immediately known in Naples,[2] "the King of Spain's flag". In the next phase he appeared to give way before the preponderant French, retreating on Apulia; but in April 1503 he received reinforcements from Spain, and on the 28th of the month won the great battle of Cerignola. On May 13 he occupied Naples, on December 29 gave battle on the Garigliano, and on January 3 1504 received the surrender of Gaeta, which marked the completion of the conquest of the Kingdom.

A Spanish song in celebration of the fall of Gaeta expressed the proud consciousness and at the same time the new indomitable might of Spain:

> *Gaeta nos es subjeta,*
> *y si quiere el Capitán,*
> *tambien lo será Milán.*
> *Si el poderoso Señor,*
> *rey de los cielos y tierra,*
> *quiere hacer esta guerra,*
> *¿ quien será defendedor?*
> *Si su favor dá favor*
> *a nuestro gran Capitán,*
> *los franceses ¿ qué haran?*
> *Los poderosos Leones,*
> *reyes de muy grand estado,*
> *descuiden de su cuydado,*
> *descansen sus corazones;*
> *passadas son sus passiones,*
> *y de bien en bien irán,*
> *que todo lo ganarán . . .[3]*

Of Alonso Hernández, a clerkly personage in Rome at the time of the Borgias, we have already recalled the *Historia parthenopea*, the poem composed in honour of the Grand Captain. In his wretched

1. GUICCIARDINI, l. 1, cf. GREGOROVIUS, *History of the City of Rome*, VII, 460.

2. PASSARO, *Giornali*, p. 129.

3. BARBIERI, *Cancionero musical de los siglos XV y XVI* (Madrid, 1890), No. 340, p. 172.

verses Hernández too exhibited the great pride of the Spanish sovereigns, warriors, and whole people. The Catholic Kings he proclaimed to be the greatest in Spain since the Moorish invasion, and never before had there been such agreement between kings and subjects, "y aquestas son cosas de alto texidas" – such is the high ruling of divine providence. The Grand Captain, father of the fatherland, Spanish luminary radiant over Latium ("luzero de España que el Latio ha lumbrado"), has displayed to the world what the Spaniards are worth when pitted against the erstwhile famous power of France, showing that there are powerful forces in the great West, forces of Spain and the Spaniards, able to down the French and to refute the vain opinion that they are entitled to rule the world. Mockingly he adds that devout persons are wont to bring gifts and offerings to various shrines, to Santiago, Loreto, Rome, but that France knows only the battlefields of the Grand Captain, to whom she offers men, horses, guns. The Spanish people have the virtue of dominators. The French are no doubt brave but the Spaniards surpass them in endurance, ready to win or to die:

> Yspanos ardientes y muy animosos,
> reinando la colera con malenconía,
> los quales aquellos dan tal osadía,
> que mueren o acaban sus hechos famosos.

When the fight begins they seem tardy and slack, but little by little they take fire until they achieve the most dreadful climax of violence. They are further prudent, temperate, faithful in any trial, loyal to ancient usages:

> Antiguas paternas han ynstituciones,
> que padres a hijos las bien enseñaron,
> los unos con otros después praticaron,
> y hazen de aquellas sus observaciones . . .

Ready of hand, quick of mind, above all else they hate to beg, seeking their fortune with the sword and with their labours:

> Y fuera d'España vy alguno partir
> que un rreal solo apenas lo lleva,
> y va hasta Roma haziendo tal prueva,
> que nunca le falta comer y vestir.

The Spaniards honour women, they are courteous:

> Y siguen de niños tan noble criança,
> mas no por lisonja ny otro color.

Splendid is the life of the great ones of Castile, who make a practice of sending their sons to serve for some time as pages in other great households to learn virtue and the point of honour:

> virtud y doctrina, y mejor conoscer
> en quan sotil pena consiste la honrra,
> y ansí, desde pajes, esquiven deshonrra
> y presto la huyan sin les enpecer.

All the same this poet, so warmly praising and celebrating the usages of those great Castilians, being himself a resident in Italy, at home in the atmosphere of culture and learning, cannot refrain here from a word of blame for the small Spanish esteem of letters:

> En solo una cosa no han advertencia,
> y desto me spanto, no quieren hazer;
> no ponen sus hijos dotrina aprender,
> y han en las letras muy gran negligencia . . .

Not even this last qualification had been thought necessary by another and slightly earlier Spanish writer – about as good an historian as Hernández was a good poet. Friar Fabricio Gauberte de Vagad published in 1499 at Saragossa his *Corónica de Aragón*, a childish enough work criticized by the Spaniards themselves (perhaps chiefly on account of the narrowly Aragonese viewpoint), but very significant as a manifestation of Spanish feeling as a whole at that time.[1] It is the more remarkable because Gauberte wrote by order of the Deputies of the Kingdom of Aragon and his work was examined by those "tan egregios magníficos y famosos doctores" Gonçalo Garcia de Sancta Maria, "lugarteniente

---

1. A copy of this very rare book is preserved among the incunabula of the University of Cagliari library. By permission of the Ministry of Education I was able to study it at Naples. Bibliographic details are available in Gallardo, *Ensayo*, IV, 850-51. An adverse judgement on Gauberte is given by "el bachiller Juan de Molina" in his *Crónica antigua de Aragón*, printed at Valencia in 1524, which is translated from the work of Lucio Marineo. There is a copy in the National Library of Naples. I quoted the criticism in *Giorn. stor. d. lett. ital.*, XXIII, 403-5.

de justicia de Aragón", and Gaspare Manete, while we are told
that the Catholic King manifested his approval by ordering "que
añadiessen en el salario que assignado me hovieran que diessen
algo más, porqué según que le agradara mucho más se le mereçía
de quanto ellos assignaran". One may overlook the fantastic history which Gauberte gives of the ancient Spaniards who before
the times of the Greeks and the Romans "ya por immortal fama
arreavan toda la Europa", while their king Hesperus "sojuzgó
primero la Italia y Hesperia como a España de su nombre la
llamó", events of which memory had faded because of the negligence of the Spanish and the shamelessness of the Greek and Roman writers; one may overlook also the panegyric of Spain
which following the convention of popular celebrations of towns
and cities vaunts the superiority of Spain over all other lands for
natural advantages, air, farm products, domestic animals, sea and
river fish, and exuberance of products generously poured forth
towards other lands. But we must take note of the parallel often
drawn by Gauberte between Spain and Italy, greatly to the advantage of Spain. The Spaniards, he says, are gentle knights, and
not, like the Italians, greedy shopkeepers: "la gente de acá toda
refuye y anda muy léxos de las tristes ganancias, partidos, interesses
y mercadurías de Italia, que allá todo se vende bien como acá todo
se dá; la gente de acá toda sabe más a la corte que a la tierra y al
trato, toda está puesta más en cavalleria, en honrra y esfuerço,
que en officios de manos, más en criança, fidalgía y nobleza, que la
gente comun en Alemaña y Francia, que los más son officiales y
viven de sus artes, todos salen a varones acá, y varones de honor".
Not only the men of Spain, but the women of Spain too are
worthier than those of Italy, and for a reason somewhat astonishing in the mouth of the monk of Saint Bernard, professed scion of
the monastery of Santa Maria de Santa Fé – that the Spanish
women are not "cold" like the Italians'. This strange praise for the
Spanish is, however, the premiss to yet another charge against the
Italians; "y ahun fasta las damas de Hespaña en dexar de ser frías,
como son las de Ytalia, y en saber festejar y ser mucho más dulces
que no las de allá: no sé si lo calle, más razon no lo sufre: detienen

los hombres tan de amores vencidos, que les fazen dexar y poner en olvido los tan pavorosos y crimenes fieros que allá se platican". As to political power, the tone of his discourse can well be imagined: Spain confers on the world not only the products of its soil, its noble steeds, but also men capable of controlling the destinies of the peoples, chiefs spiritual and temporal, popes, emperors, kings. Pope Alexander was Spanish, and Emperor Maximilian, the greatest knight of the age, son of the daughter of the King of Portugal and Eleonora of Aragon, was Spanish too. To Italy Spain made a gift of the magnanimous Alfonso, who taught the Italians the previously unknown virtues of courtesy and magnificence: "para que mejor la instruyesse y enseñasse cerca de la magnificencia y de la virtud más real y famosa que es la dadivosa grandeza, cortesia y criança, que de antes ni sabian los principes de Ytalia del recibir tan magnificamente las embaxadas, ni menos del mesurado festejar de estrangeros, quanto después han deprendido del serenissimo festejador soberano y magnanimo rey don Alfonso". And if (Gauberte observes defensively) it be remarked that Alfonso's successor in Naples, Ferrante, was a bastard, let this teach the world what stuff even the bastards of a Spanish King are made of. Then Spain is the true bulwark of Christendom against the peril overhanging Europe: the Africans, "toda la morisma", fear Spain and Spain only: the great exploit of Africa would be an accomplished fact had not Italy called in the French and France descended into Italy: "si la siempre discorde y tan zenzillosa Ytalia no zizañara y sembrara discordias, no procurara su perdimiento y estrago, fasta llamar su enemigo y ponerlo en su casa. O maldito el desatiento cruel y de la Ytalia que le llamó y del rey de Francia, quel tal seguió para tanto perdimiento y daño de toda la Christiandad . . .".[1]

Such was the attitude of the Spaniards, conscious of their power, drunken with their good fortune, flaunting their strength and valour over against the Italians, vaunting the superiority of their own people and creating for them a pre-history or legend. Not in

[1]. I have reproduced longer extracts from Gauberte's chronicle in *Rassegna pugliese*, XII (1895), pp. 38-41.

that political posture had the Spaniards at an earlier time taken a
foothold in Sicily when called there by the Sicilians themselves,
in their rebellion against the French, as heirs of the Swabian power,
nor was it thus that later on they had come to Naples with King
Alfonso, called to play a part in the affairs of the Kingdom in
virtue of his adoption by the second Giovanna and supported by
some of the barons. New also was the cultural attitude. The Italians
had been accustomed to seeing the Spaniards in the posture of
admirers and disciples, indeed humble disciples – it was thus that
King Alfonso and many gentlemen, prelates, and scholars from
Spain had presented themselves, eager to learn good letters and
Latin from the Italians, to shake off barbaric uncouthness, to pass
sometimes from the calling of arms to those of poetry and learning.
Your ancestor came to Italy as a fierce warrior (Pontano told
Girolamo Borgia in verse), but your pleasures are now not those
of a follower of Mars but of a cultivator of the Muses:

> Sirisium, Borgi, domus est tua, quam rigat amnis
> Siris in Herculeis advena littoribus.
> His consedit avus, terra devectus Ibera,
> quem procul a patria Martis abegit amor.
> Te nec bella iuvant, nec te iuvat aereus ensis,
> parta nec hostili praeda cruore placet[1] . . .

Of a certain Don Juan from Saguntia another Humanist writes
that Rome so refined him, "ita expolivit", that "in Hispano corpore
Romanum pectus ostendet, suorumque dignitatem omni virtute
consequatur".[2] Refined and Italianized in like manner were Spaniards bearing such names as Avalos, Guevara, Cabanilla, Milá,
Díaz Garlón, ornaments of the Alfonsine and Pontanian Academies.[3] It is off the point to argue for the thesis of a tenacious
retention of Spanish character and customs by Spanish immigrants

---

1. *Eridani*, II, 20 (*Carmina*, ed. Soldati, II, 384). "Sirisium" in verse one is
Senise in Basilicata; see CROCE, *Vite di avventure, di fede, e di passione*, 2nd
edition, Bari, 1947, pp. 304-5.

2. PETRI GRAVINAE panormitani *Epistolae atque orationes* (Naples, 1599),
p. 169 (letters written in the early fifteen-hundreds).

3. See *Biografie degli accad. alfonsini detti poi pontaniani* by MINIO RICCI
(undated, but really Naples, 1875).

resisting the influence of Italian culture, from such an example as
Ferrante d'Avalos, Marquis of Pescara, said by Giovio to have
talked Spanish and read Spanish books of chivalry as a child in
Naples.[1] The Avalos had been among the first families to accept
Italian ways, and Ferrante's father, Alfonso d'Avalos, was according to Giovio himself "a thorough hater of Spanish wits".[2] If
young Ferrante, left an orphan, was bred as a Spaniard among
Spaniards and proclaimed himself one of their race, the Italians
considered him almost a traitor and the event fell precisely in the
high tide of Spanish fortunes in Italy.

Such triumphant airs on the part of the conquering and domineering Spanish people, together with the admiration aroused by
the spectacle of such power and with the imitation and flattery
which such circumstances bring on, filled Italy in those early
years with the renown and record of the Catholic Kings and their
Grand Captain, and with the manners, conventions, fashions,
language, and moral standards of Spain, some good and some bad,
but all of them deemed good because pertaining to the victors
and really or supposedly sources of their strength and triumph.
The already existing Spanish influences in Italy, especially in
Naples and Rome, recovered and expanded in those early years
of the century, and Spain seemed to be invading Italy, not only
with her arms, but with the disturbing imprint of her national
spirit upon Italy's own tradition, morality, and very culture.

Naturally enough the exponents of this culture were roused to
wrath and attempted to withstand an invasion which was in their
eyes barbarian – as indeed it was, though also in Vico's approbat-
ory sense of "noble barbarism". Naturally they inveighed against
the reinforced resurrection of the Middle Ages against the culture
of antiquity and Humanism on the hallowed ground of Italy.
Among the many documents attesting this reaction, such as the
sentences of Pontano and others already quoted, outstanding for
its warmth of feeling and abundance and variety of particulars,

1. GOTHEIN, *Die Kulturentwicklung Süd Italiens*, Breslau, 1886, p. 406.
2. *La vita del Marchese di Pescara*, in *Vite di XIX huom. ill.*, translated by
Domenichini (Venice, 1559), 180.

is the little treatise in Latin of the South Italian Humanist Antonio de Ferrariis (known from his birthplace Galatone in the province of Otranto as Il Galateo):[1] the treatise *De educatione*, which was published only long afterwards in 1865, and was then warmly praised as a manual of morals and pedagogy. Its appearance gave rise to speculations that the celebrated treatise *Il Galateo* of Monsignor della Casa had been taken from the author of *De educatione*.[2] What passed unnoticed was the character and historical significance of *De educatione* itself.[3]

"Il Galateo", then about sixty years old, had lived much of his life in Naples[4] and in close contact with the Spaniards at that court. He had learned Spanish and got to know the principal works of the Spanish poets, observing Spanish characteristics and tendencies from the steadily Italian point of view of an heir and guardian of the civilization of his own home. In the wars which had bled the Kingdom he had indeed espoused the Aragonese against the French cause,[5] but "Aragonese" meant for him "Italian" and "Neapolitan" fidelity to the Neapolitanized dynasty descended from King Alfonso. Well can we understand his pain and perplexity at the interference of the Spaniards of Spain in the affairs of Naples. The pretext had been to bring aid to the related dynasty

1. First published in *Scritti inediti e rari di diversi autori trovati nella prov. di Otranto* by F. Casotti; reprinted with an Italian translation in Vol. II of *Collana di scrittori di Terra d'Otranto* (Lecce, 1867), from which I take the following quotations. For other bibliographical information see my note in *Giorn. stor. d. lett. ital.*, XXIII, 394-97.

2. The title of della Casa's book, as is now known for certain, was derived from the latinized form of the name of Galeazzo Florimonte.

3. Gothein, already quoted, makes good use of the testimonies of Il Galateo to colour his account of the Renaissance in South Italy, but all he knows of him are the epistles published in vol. VIII of Mai's *Spicilegium* and the dialogue *Heremita* which Gothein believes to be unpublished, though really it was published in the already quoted *Collana* (Vol. XXII).

4. On Il Galateo see in addition to the monograph of A. DE FABRIZIO, *Antonio de Ferrariis Galateo, pensatore e moralista del Rinascimento* (Trani, Vecchi e C., 1908), the sketch I have given of his character and works in *Poeti e scrittori del pieno e del tardo Rinascimento* (Bari, 1945), vol. I, and for the bibliography see ALDA CROCE, *Contributo a un'edizione delle opere di Antonio Galateo* (Naples, 1937, extracted from *Arch. stor. per le prov. napol.*, vol. LXII).

5. *De educatione*, p. 141.

on the throne of Naples, but the real game was to gain the mastery at the expense of these and to yoke the country to Spain. The behaviour of the Catholic King had been such as to embarrass even the Spanish apologists.[1] But many still imagined that he would restore the throne of Naples to the young son of King Frederick, Ferrante, Duke of Calabria, whom at that time he was holding in Spain. They did not appreciate that it was (in the words of Guicciardini) "vain to expect in our century the magnanimous restitution of a great kingdom".[2] Il Galateo was one of those who clung to this belief that the young Duke would in due course return to Naples to wield with firm hand the sceptre of old King Ferrante. He only feared lest this youth born in Italy but reared in Spain should, amid so much boisterousness of the Spaniards, change into a thorough Spaniard before his return.

His father, King Ferrante, had given him as tutors the Count of Potenza and the Humanist Crisostomo Colonna, to the delight of Galateo, who around 1500 had composed an epistle to testify full aproval of these excellent preceptors.[3] Colonna was present with his pupil at the defence of Taranto in 1501, and when, after the capture of the city by Consalvo in 1501, the Duke of Calabria was shipped to Spain, he went with him. Galateo, who bore him a strong affection, revealed to him his own fears and hopes, and imparted warnings and exhortations, in a new and lengthy epistle written between the last months of 1504 and the first of 1505.[4] This became a short treatise, in fact the *De educatione* of which we

1. Gauberte, writing in 1499, says of Frederick, who was then reigning in Naples, "que de mano de rey de Castilla y de Aragón espera para siempre posseerle". Hernández, a spectator of this rape, proffers the embarrassed affirmation that the Catholic Kings "han ellos avido algun desplazer Del rey don Fedrique e lo deven hazer, Y alégale causas que causa traya" (*Hist. parthenop.*, Bk. 11).

2. *Storia d'Italia*, Bk. VI.

3. This is the second of those published by Mai in the *Spicilegium*, where may also be found (VIII, 511) verses by Pontano on Crisostomo and the Count of Potenza, "nostros queis licet educare reges". On Colonna see G. AUGELUZZI, *Intorno alla vita e alle opere di Crisostomo Colonna da Caggiano, pontaniano accademico* (Naples, 1856). Galateo addressed several letters to him.

4. I myself fixed these dates in *Giorn. stor. d. lett. ital.*, XXIII, 398.

are speaking.[1] That this was written in a moment of great stress is
shown by the disorder of the composition, the abundant digressions and repetitions, but also the warmth of the style expressing
the lively and anxious concern of the writer. Too long had his
patience already been tried by the triumphant exhibitionism and
boastfulness of the Spaniards, when to rouse him to yet greater
indignation and irritation, nay to a demonic rage, there came into
his hands, while he was composing his epistle, Gauberte's *Corónica
de Aragón*,[2] against the author of which he let fly such varied
contumelies as "insanus quidam, nescio cujus ordinis aut pecoris
monachus; Gothus aut Poenus aut proselytus, profanus, barbarus
hostis Italiae; chronistes major ipse (sic enim se ipsum, sed ego
cornisten appello) celtiber; bestia, vitio gentis, arrogantissima;
tam ineruditus quam inflatus superbia gothica" and so forth. The
book had already been in existence for some years without receiving a condign answer, no doubt because it was not in Latin but in
Spanish, a language which not all of Il Galateo's compatriots had
mastered like himself.[3]

The scheme of the epistle may be briefly described as a comparative review of methods of education, ancient and modern,
concluding in favour of the Italian, and the purpose needs no
further description than the exhortation addressed to Colonna as
tutor to the young Prince: "Italum accepisti, Italum redde, non
Hispanum.[4] The picture of the Spanish way of life given by
Galateo – not without a running commentary of expressions of

1. In the two manuscripts inspected by me (Bibl. Naz. V. F. 68, and Bibl.
Brancacciana, VI. A. 11) the title is simply *Galateus medicus ad Chrisostomum
de educatione*.
2. "Insolens et insanus nescio cuius armenti monachus cogit me insanire,
et ea quae non erant propositi mei, proferre. Occurrit mihi, antequam epi-
stolam signarem, illa insana bellua; non potui me continere, quin responde-
rem, nec ignoro responsionem meam illi honori futuram" (p. 122). Both
printed editions of *De educatione* mistakenly give the author of the *Corónica*
as Gambertus instead of Gaubertus.
3. "Si latine scripsisset, nam non omnes ut Galateus, inter Hispanos ver-
satus, linguam hispanicam noverunt, multos haberet qui temeritati, inscitiae,
et ingratitudini eius obsisterent" (p. 132).
4. p. 137.

repugnance, resentment, and horror – is worth closer examination. What he stresses as the dominant and central feature of the Spanish (particularly by contrast with the Italian) way of life is, as already indicated, the contempt for "letters", that is for culture, ostentatiously affected by Spaniards and French alike. Gauberte in his panegyrics of the Kings of Aragon notes complacently that they were all illiterate: the Spanish nobles considered literacy unsuitable for the class of hidalgos;[1] knowledge of Latin they esteemed a base and peasant accomplishment, but "algaravia" or the mouthing of harsh Saracenic (Arab) aspirates from the depth of the throat they greatly approved as appropriate to a "fidalgus et palatinus" – nobleman and courtier – and a "galanus" – man of gallantry.[2] Rejecting the fine Latin calligraphy of the Renaissance, they likewise clung to what they called the "Gothic" script of long strokes, covering their paper with baffling obelisks, anchors, and hooks, which when he first saw them Galateo took to be Phoenician characters from the early age of mankind, and could never get to decipher.[3] With what ingratitude towards Rome, which had civilized ancient Spain and ennobled the Spanish with Latin blood, did they boast themselves descended from the Goths! And Goths they really were, sprung from Scythia, all save a few who had preserved the sacred seed of Rome, these being the truly illustrious men of Spain such as, in recent times, Villena, Juan de Mena, Lucena, protesters against vainglorious Spanish ignorance. Other exceptions among the Spaniards known to Galateo were the brave Captain Diego Mendoza, of Iberian, not Gothic ancestry,[4] and Nuñez Docampo, keeper of the Castel dell'Ovo in Naples,[5] who had

1. pp. 129, 133-34.
2. pp. 131, 134, 136, 137. — Il Galateo's is the earliest or one of the earliest assertions of an Arabic origin for the Spanish guttural sounds, a theory long entertained but now quite discarded: see Gröber's *Grundriss*, I, 400.
3. p. 134.
4. This is the Diego Mendoza in whose house La Motte spoke those insults against the Italians which led to the "Challenge of Barletta" (see GALATEO, *De pugna tredecim equitum* in *Coll.*, II, 261).
5. The custody of the castle had been committed to him by the Grand Captain, see CANTALICIO, *De bis recepta Parthenope*, l. II. For Docampo compare YRIARTE, *César Borgia*, Paris, Rothschild, 1889, II, 209, 228-29.

entrusted his children to Pietro Summonte, disciple of Pontano, in order that when the time came they might return home to Spain with a knowledge of letters and an Italian education.[1] For which modesty Galateo felt for Docampo a boundless affection: by contrast most of Docampo's compatriots were tireless boasters of their own merits,[2] not sparing the Italians in their "donayres" or sharp sallies ("in suis dicteriis quae donaria dicunt").[3] Their idea was to give the Italians a telling example of what magnificence, the courtly and gallant life, are – those Italians whom they regarded as unimaginative shopkeepers, because (as Galateo put it from the opposed point of view) they were sober, serious, and intent upon intelligent accomplishment. To the Italian ideal they opposed the Spanish ideal of the Castilian grandees, infected as this was in many respects with Oriental luxury and obstinately maintained Arab characteristics. In regard to which our author calls attention first and foremost to the over-delicate diet with elaborately sauced and scented dishes such as the "white dishes" or blancmanges ("alba fercula"), more like unguents than meats, the meticulously ordained basting of game, sprinkling of salt, spreading of tablecloths, offering of drinking-vessels.[4] In converse with women, then, what an endless to-do of gallantries, what long and empty chatterings, what perpetual visitations of young and old, with song and music, by night and also by day, to the doorways of the fair.[5] Hence the womanish paraphernalia applied to men's bodies – scents and unguents, gloves, bared breasts, rings, bracelets, chains, and for elderly men wigs, dyed hair, rouge.[6] Night is turned to day, but they sleep through the morning.[7] Hence too the phrases of adulation,[8] the fashion and value set upon witticisms,

1. pp. 110-11, 129, 134-35.
2. pp. 132, 155.
3. pp. 130-31.
4. pp. 140, 141-44.
5. pp. 120-21, 146-47.
6. pp. 121, 147, 162-63. Marullo too in *De principum institutione* (composed 1496, published in *Poetae tres elegantissimi*, Paris, 1582, f. 102 *t*) alludes to the Spanish women's pastes and cosmetics: "quique emollire venenis corpus, et Hispanae pellem de more maritae quaerat?".
7. p. 145.   8. p. 165.

sallies, gags, pleasantries or "ledorias" ("hispanos lepores, blanditias argultulas, scommata, ledorias").[1] They go in much for money wagers:[2] and as for games of chivalry Galateo thought highly of their "stick game" on hearsay before he saw it, but when he saw it thought little of it (perhaps through ignorance of feats of arms): it seemed to consist in raucous Arabic cries, scarves, turbans, "you follow, I fly", "I follow, you fly", pressing of shields on shoulders instead of breasts as should be, in fact an enactment of cowardly flight and unmanly pursuit, a thoroughly Moorish business.[3] What of their poetry? Would anyone dare to compare it with Dante's and Petrarch's, especially the latter's great Ode to Italy? What figure did the "Spanish Homer" Juan de Mena cut beside Petrarch? With his *Coronación*, better termed "Cornication", to which some-one of Córdova had furnished a commentary. By comparison with the Italian poets these Spanish rhymesters deserved rather to be called "copulators", indeed the Spaniards did call them in their language "copleadores".[4] Effeminate, languorous, plaintive, sad was their music.[5] But the full measure of the coarseness and primitiveness of Spanish ways was to be seen in the contrast of the Spanish with the Italian methods of education. Grandees of Spain and ordinary knights alike sent their sons to be brought up in noble or knightly houses much inferior to their own degree. There they were used as servants and left to consort with the boys, the "rapazes" – veritable "rapaces" in the Latin sense, or rascals to speak plainly. Thereby they became, the Spaniards thought, more patient of fatigue, more cunning, subtle, ready, witty, politic and bold, but they certainly did not turn out more wise, respectful, modest, honourable, for this was education fit for a Davus, not for a Pamphilus.[6] It was said to be regarded as a success in upbringing that the pupil should be skilled in hoodwinking and good at whisking away or purloining an object, that he should have a stock of witticisms ready for all comers, be able to

1. p. 138.   2. p. 151.   3. p. 155.   4. p. 154.   5. p. 152.
6. pp. 132-33. However, Tansillo (*Balia*, 1) later praised the Spanish ladies in another respect, specially the Galicians, for feeding their own offspring and being ready to do the same to help other ladies of their own rank.

wheedle money for gaming purposes and have the art of accepting as gifts things not seriously offered as such: all this was called
"desenvolturas". Spain was thus proving the ruin of Italy. Italian
ill-luck had indeed stemmed from the Spanish Popes, from that
ironically misnamed Callixtus who, once enthroned, at once began
to do injury to the line of his protector Alfonso, and would have
devastated Italy had not death halted him, to Alexander or Rodrigo
his nephew who carried his uncle's plans into full execution,
bringing on to Italian soil first the French and then the French
together with the Spaniards.[1] Few as were the Spanish soldiers
planted on the Kingdom, seven thousand in all, veterans as they
were of wars of hatred and extermination against the revivers
or habitual practitioners of piracy in the Mediterranean, infidels
or Spaniards or Catalans as the case might be, these few were
enough to bring impoverishment, giving rise to the proverb:
"Where the Spanish heel treads no grass grows."[2] This, however,
was as nothing compared with the corruption they had brought
or were bringing in, thereby ruining the old Italian morality. The
Spaniards were given to boasting much of all they had taught the
Italians since their arrival. Would to God that their ships had never
reached the coasts of Italy! For what was it that they had taught?
Not letters, the art of war, laws, navigation, commerce, painting,
sculpture, agriculture, or any other of the works of civilization;
but usury, theft, piracy, slavery at sea, games, seductions, light
loves, the trade of murder, soft croonings of dismal songs, Arab
dishes, hypocrisy, soft luxurious beds, ointment and scents, elaborate table-manners and suchlike nonsense, things worthy of themselves, being like all barbarians both wanton and cruel. The French
first and then the Spaniards had introduced into Italy, especially
Naples, pomp and fussiness of attire and other bad habits, and
since their arrival there had been a great increase in gaming and
fraud.[3] Unmentionable vices which Gauberte had the hardihood

1. pp. 112-14.
2. pp. 164-65., cf. 177-78.
3. pp. 117, 123-25, 151.

to ascribe to the Italians had really come in with the Aragonese.[1]
And elsewhere our author says that it was through the "Western"
influence that Italy learned the ways of adulation, the mode of
address in the plural, the employment for mortal men of the titles
of Majesty and Highness, and of Lordship for just anyone, together
with hand-kissing and foot-kissing or humble and obedient service
as the mode of concluding letters, with all other such flattering
excesses.[2] Other Spanish inventions were the multiplicity of duels,
with all the niceties of their ritual; the challenge "a las armas" for
every minor little infraction or observation, calling in the "King
at Arms" with vain and childish forms of challenge and challenger,
flight and concealment, sending and receiving of letters according
to the sense or rather nonsense of the code, one to have choice of
field, the other of arms as laid down in certain rules, work of the
devil, with all that heraldic foolishness of sable and vert spun out
subtly by Kings at Arms, Carnival Kings, Kings of the Martinmas
bean, or what you will.[3] Spaniards and other foreigners had brought
in the mode for foreign words which together with the rising
fashion of Tuscanism was driving out Latin, with the result (says
our author) that "it seems a fine thing fitting a man for business
and the court to know French and Castilian, and I can hardly but
say that he who thinks so well of knowing foreign languages and
so poorly and cheaply of knowing Latin remains ignorant of the
Gospel but knows the rhymes and ballads of thereabouts as if he
had lived in those countries": and no doubt he himself, for thinking and talking and writing otherwise, would seem to the devotees
of those throaty songs a very simple, graceless fellow.[4]

Thus did Galateo consign French and Spaniards, but principally
Spaniards, to perdition, repeating the witticism that God made the

1. pp. 121-22: "Pudet dicere, sed dicam, quia verum est: ante adventum
Aragonensium nulli in aula procerum huius regni pueri venales erant aut
custoditi; incognitum erat illud vitium ante adventum exterorum.
2. *Esposiz. del Paternoster*, part 2, in *Collana*, XVIII, 79.
3. *Esposiz. del Paternoster*, pp. 25-26. Whoever found the bean in the cake
used to be proclaimed king of the feast. For this appellation see MENÉNDEZ
PIDAL, *Poesía juglaresca y juglares* (Madrid, 1924), pp. 281-82.
4. *Esposiz. del Paternoster*, part I, pp. 149-50, part II, p. 101.

other races from good oil, but these two from the dregs He found
left over;[1] while he exalted Italy to the skies, especially the city of
Venice, that model of the ancient Italian freedom in which the
national spirit still breathed vigorously, the one hope of a better
future.[2] Yet, as he terminated this arraignment worthy of Juvenal,
one doubt persisted in his mind. He must, he said, answer a tacit
objection raised against him. These Spaniards or Goths, with
their uncouth ways and all those vices, had nevertheless got the
better of other peoples, including the civilized Italians.[3] To our
modern impartiality this would clearly indicate that our author,
while duly noting the defects and vices of barbarism, had failed
to notice the corresponding virtue of an untamed youthful vigour.
Galateo, however, gets out of this with an answer taken, he says,
from his own medical experience: he had often seen intemperate
men who refused to follow doctors' orders emerge safe from
deadly diseases while others who were temperate and obedient
died. This meant, not that disease was anything else but disease,
but that capricious fortune sometimes intervened to help and to
save. Morally speaking, such a recovery, such a victory, gave no
ground for celebrations. Rightly the Carthaginians held it for a
capital crime to have won a battle by faulty methods and leadership.[4] A clever enough answer, but a light and shallow one, and
meanwhile the mad Spaniards were trampling on the wise Italians,
the frivolous and corrupt were triumphing over the serious and
moral people. Young Ferrante, Duke of Calabria, returned to
Italy no more, but some years later his tutor Crisostomo Colonna
returned alone, and we find him acting as tutor to an Italian princess, Bona Sforza.[5] The last scion of the royal house of Naples
remained prisoner of the Aragonese of Spain. It was in vain that
by an irony of fate Filippetto Coppola, son of that Count of Sarno
who had been beheaded for planning the Barons' conspiracy
against old King Ferrante, now lost his own life in a vain attempt to
help young Ferrante to break his captivity and attempt the

1. *De educatione*, pp. 134-35.   2. p. 127.   3. p. 155.   4. p. 156.
5. AUGELUZZI, op. cit., p. 15, and cf. Galateo's own Epistle *Ad illustrem
dominam Bonam Sfortiam* (in *Collana*, III, 139).

recovery of Naples.[1] The young man, reverting to the Spanish
origins of his family, and surrounded by a Spanish Court, married
the widow of the Catholic King and died half a century later in
Valencia, where his memory is preserved at the monastery of Saint
Sebastian which he founded.[2]

Galateo himself, six years after the composition of his invectives
in De educatione, began to view things differently, with resignation,
calm, and even a ray of hope. Forgetting about the caprices of
fortune, he resumed another train of thought from the same
epistle, the theory of the succession of the kingdoms – a gloomy
theory, to start with, for if the dominion of Rome was the Kingdom of Iron, that of the Spaniards could only be the Kingdom of
Mire, last and worst of men that they were, recalling Saint Paul's
"Ii sunt in quos fines saeculorum devenerunt".[3] But in 1510,[4]
under the impact of the new victories of Ferdinand the Catholic
on the shores of Africa and of the stirring news of journeys and
discoveries accomplished by Spaniards and Portuguese, he could
no longer persist in his view of the victorious destiny of Spain as
sheer disaster. After all, every other people had had its turn in
history, the Easterners, the Greeks, the Carthaginians, the Romans,
Goths, Lombards, Franks, Germans. Only the Spaniards had so
far never had one: "soli Hispani hucusque vicissitudinem non
habuerunt." Yet they had always, when serving others, such as the
Carthaginians and Romans, been considered most doughty soldiers. Now, under King Ferdinand, who had swept away from
Spain the last vestiges of Arab dominion, and had trained them
well in arms and in the observance of just laws, they had advanced

---

1. SUMMONTE, Historia di Napoli, III, 455-57, and for the Duke of Calabria
CARACCIOLO, De varietate fortunae, ed. Gravier, p. 89, also references in my
essay Isabella del Balzo, regina di Napoli (in Storie e leggende napoletane, 4th
edn., Bari, 1948).

2. For a description of the society around the Duke of Calabria in Valencia
see the Libro intitulado El Cortesano of LUIS MILÁN (reprinted in Coleccion de
libros raros o curiosos, VII, Madrid, 1874).

3. De educatione, pp. 104, 163.

4. Ad Catholicum regem Ferdinandum (in Collana, III, 105-16), and see the
remarks of GOTHEIN, op. cit., pp. 418-19.

to the first post on the stage of the world ("te regnante, caput orbis erit"). Italy, coveted by the Turks and not without experience already of infidel invasions, would, like all the rest of Christendom, win profit and safety from the Spaniards. O Spaniards, he now exhorted them, hear the words of one who is no prophet but no ill-wisher. "Ne perdite, Hispani, occasionem; venere vestra tempora", "Do not miss the occasion: your times have come". But the task requires, he added, that you match your fortune with virtue, and show yourselves gentle as well as strong.

Of the same mind was Sannazzaro on his return from the voluntary French exile into which he had followed his King Frederick. It is said that when the Grand Captain desired to visit the antiquities of the Phlegraean Fields and chose for a guide Sannazzaro, they set forth together from Castelnuovo discoursing of the greatness and victories and power of Spain. But when they reached the cave of Posillipo the poet adroitly changed the argument, saying: "My lord, having talked of the fair fortunes of Spain it is time that we spoke of the great destinies of Rome, for which, if it be your pleasure, this cave offers an excellent occasion." Whereupon he went over the memorable events of Rome and Italy as mistress of the world and "while the Grand Captain listened intently, touched on the various events which had befallen the Kingdoms, observing that while formerly the Spanish nation had been in captivity, now, under different influences of Heaven, it was enjoying an age of glorious domination".[1]

Spain had won, and the Italian political thinkers, Machiavelli and Guicciardini, explained the victory as the reward of Spanish ability.[2] The Humanists resigned themselves, while the political thinkers contented themselves, for the time being, with detached and objective examination of the facts. Or at the utmost, like the poet-politician Machiavelli, they dreamed of Italy regaining that skill at arms which so well served the Spaniards and other peoples, and of an Italian Prince who should employ the arts of Ferdinand

1. G. B. Crispo, *Vita di Giacopo Sannazzaro* (Rome, 1593), pp. 21-23.
2. See *Il Principe*, chapters III, XVI, XXI, and Guicciardini, *La Legazione di Spagna* of 1512-13 (in Vol. VI of the *Opere inedite*).

the Catholic in the interests of divided, inharmonious, subdued Italy. As to the Italian people, the little men and the masses, they too resigned themselves to mutterings or imprecations that "God had turned Spaniard".[1]

(1894-1915)

1. "Havite dicto che Dio è partiale o spagnolo?" is one of the blasphemies listed for the examination of penitents in the *Speculum confessariorum* (1525) of Fra Matteo Corradone (reprinted in Venice, 1543, by Bern. de Viano, folio 8).

III

THE CHARACTER OF SPANISH CULTURE

Wᴇ should distinguish sharply between the sort of influence which Spanish literature and culture had (as has often been said) upon the culture of Italy, and the very different sort of influence exerted by the French and English cultures in the eighteenth century, and somewhat later by the philosophy and poetry of Germany. These last radiated an influence comparable with that which the Italian culture of the Renaissance had shed throughout Europe in an earlier age. That is to say, these cultures were, turn by turn, representative and symbolic of new concepts and new ideals, progressive human mentalities, of humanism, rationalism, the Enlightenment, liberalism, romanticism, historicism. By contrast the Spanish culture neither furnished a new idea nor opened up a new spiritual avenue. It would be impossible to give such a description to the reorganized and politically reinforced Catholicism of the Counter-Reformation of which the Spaniards were leading authors and constant champions, nor could it be any better applied to the mediaeval idea of chivalry and adventure which stayed with them longer than with other peoples and even gave its special mark to their colonial action in America, at a time when elsewhere in Europe (and even by reflection in Spain itself) that idea was retreating under the impact of developing needs and habits and standards. The life of chivalry, inspiring so much Spanish poetry, especially of the dramatic order, was just then beginning to be more than a warm and regretful memory, fit for celebration in poetry but also in conventional literature: as everyone knows, the critical, ironical, humorous genius of Cervantes took fire from those admiring and regretful memories. And the only legacy left by the triumph in Spain and the partial or only momentarily complete prevalence in Italy of the ideas and the moral attitudes of the Counter-Reformation[1] was to link Italy

---

1. Among others who have remarked that the mental constriction and intimidation was less in Italy than in Spain, though there too not entirely

with Spain in the role of exponents of reaction and obscurantism assigned to them by the historians. Now far from being a promotion of culture, this role constitutes an impediment to the development of culture. Therefore it is that the general character of Spanish culture exhibits a very different aspect from that of the other cultures which have earlier or later radiated an influence in Europe.

Now Thought and Philosophy are the balance and the instrument by which a culture exhibits its power, so we may sum up our previous remarks in the statement that Spanish culture was wanting in thought and philosophy, or, what amounts to the same thing, that it rested upon a mode of thought which was antiquated even though lately patched up and powerfully supported. This comes out clearly in an argument sustained some fifty years ago, but insufficiently remembered, by Menéndez Pelayo and other Spanish savants who claimed, contrary to the denials or rather the "ignorance" of certain modern critics, that there was indeed a Spanish thought and Spanish philosophy.[1] Menéndez y Pelayo himself laboured to reconstruct the tradition of this Spanish thought and to illustrate its sempiternal vigour. Apart from asserting that in antiquity and the Middle Ages Spain could boast three philosophical schools, going by the names of Seneca, Averröes, and Maimonides (as to which all too many doubts could be raised), Menéndez claimed the existence of three further schools in modern times, to which he gave the names of Lully, Vives, and Suárez. But what fruitful seeds came into modern philosophy from Raymond Lully's *Ars magna* and *Arbor scientiae* no labours can avail to establish – unless it be recalled that Giordano Bruno, in the various unco-ordinated experiments of a period when he was still moving amid outworn ideas, set store by those arid

the result of oppression and violence, but partly of a free consent, may be mentioned CANOVAS DEL CASTILLO, *Historia della decadencia de España* (published by him, Madrid, 1854, as a continuation of the *Historia general de España* of Mariana), II, 26.

1. See the three volumes of MARCELINO MENÉNDEZ Y PELAYO, *La ciencia española* (*Polémicas, proyectos y bibliografía*), with introduction by Gumersindo Laverde Ruiz (3rd edn., Madrid, 1887).

exercises in methodology, and with him others who were busy upon the arts of memorization and combination, and logical machines. Luis Vives, without doubt, has his importance in the history of the critical overhaul of the Aristotelian system accomplished by the Italian Humanist school, and so too the attempt of Fox Morcillo among others to reconcile Aristotle with Plato are of interest, though neither decisive nor original, and likewise the scepticism of Sanchez in his *Quod nihil scitur*: all of them derivations from the Renaissance philosophy and not advances beyond it in the way that the works of Bacon and Galileo and Descartes certainly were. It is to Italian thought that we should assign also the Spanish authors of treatises on the art of politics and calculations, rhetoric and the poetic and artistic faculties. Clever and lively as these authors might be in their treatment of detail, or great stylists like Gracián, they were not original in their premisses or procedure, nor were they progressive in their line of enquiry. The incidental foreshadowings of the theory of natural law discoverable in Suárez, Mariana, and De Soto are too particular to confer originality upon the culture in question: they cannot be said to have exhibited a fundamentally novel approach. Moreover their outward and occasional teaching of the doctrine of natural law from a Catholic and Jesuit standpoint had for its counterpart a similar but truly modern teaching derived from the extreme Protestant and rationalist field of ideas which largely inspired the political judgement and the reforming movements of Europe in the next age, and still exerts an influence. The truth of the matter was involuntarily admitted by one of those who were associated with Menéndez y Pelayo in this argument. It was Pidal who acknowledged that in a certain sense the existence of a Spanish philosophy might be denied since "the only truly important characteristic note common to almost all our philosophers and our systems is the note of Catholicism".[1] And in fact Leibniz by "Spanish philosophy" meant simply the "scholastic" philosophy which was still much in evidence in his time. Now the promoters

1. op. cit., II, p. LI.

of this argument, seeking a tradition to justify the attribution of a Spanish character to a modern and alien philosophy, had much in mind that process of nationalization which Galluppi, Rosmini, and Gioberti had promoted in Italy in the nineteenth century, when they accepted modern and alien (especially German) ways of thought, but gave them a "national colouring" in virtue of which our Italian writers cut the figure of "interpreters and reanimators of the ancient wisdom of their own country".[1] But as to that, these Italians, when they looked back on their past, could genuinely discover in Bruno, Campanella, Galileo, and Vico the forerunners of modern philosophy, so that the Italian thinkers of the Risorgimento soon moved on from their initial Catholic or neo-Guelph standpoint to the conception of a modern and European yet Italian thought, which after being repressed and oppressed by the Catholic Church was now regaining liberty. And in its new freedom (so they were able to feel) it was following the same path as an alien and non-Catholic thought, a sort of younger and in some respects more fortunately placed brother to the Italian philosophy. By contrast those Spaniards who laboured to harmonize modern thought and traditional Spanish thought were neither willing nor able to proceed in the same manner, for want of any real justification in the history of their philosophy.

The total or partial want of philosophical originality and of a fresh moral and religious outlook accounts for the failure of Spanish poetry and art, though productive of many graceful and vigorous works in a popular vein, and some poetic masterpieces, to make a deep impression on the culture of Italy. Art and poetry, indeed, cannot in virtue of aesthetic beauty and of the enchanting and uplifting character which by right belongs to them, operate directly upon the quality of culture. They cannot do so for the very reason that they turn attention away from what is practical and contingent, as has, or should have, been known, ever since the time of Schiller, by the theorists of Aesthetics. We describe this as the "non-determining" character or non-

1. op. cit., I, pp. XIX, XLVII.

practicality of Art. The influence which poetry and art, and especially literature and the rhetorical forms of art, exert upon culture
and the life of society can only come from their subject-matter or
rather the states of mind which that subject-matter suggests or
instils, the new spiritual attitudes which it promotes. But of these
the origin (and also the consequences) lie in the world of Thought.
For example, from the thought of the Enlightenment and the
humanitarians originated a literature which on the one hand
displayed satire against the present and the past, and on the other
hand was marked by *sensiblerie*; while from idealist and historicist
thought came a literature marked by reverence and idolization
of the distant past, with religious self-questioning and aspiration
towards great deeds and high sacrifice. And what was the subject-
matter or raw material of the Spanish poetry and art if not the
rigid and fanatical Catholicism of the *autos*, the *vidas de santos*,
and so forth, together with the sentiments of honour, fealty, and
warlike prowess according to the lights of mediaeval chivalry?
But these fell upon a ground, in Italy, where similar sentiments
already lay inert and fallow: sometimes, maybe, rousing these to
new life, but more often failing altogether to stir or to stimulate.
Nor was the "realism" of the Spanish picaresque novel anything
new for an Italy possessed of Boccaccio and Pulci and their like
and their successors. There was no fresh inspiration here. Spanish
realism, in this and other forms, amounted simply to a particular
sort of workaday comedy and humour.[1] People read and enjoyed
Don Quixote as a witty, graceful, mirth-provoking tale, unsuspect-
ing that it had beneath the surface a deep poetic meaning surpassing
the critical and satirical intentions of its author himself. This was
to be discovered by the Romantics, thanks to the wistful affection
for the past which they brought to its study, and their broad
experience of the dreams and sufferings of humanity. It was they
too who communicated to Europe an enraptured feeling for
chivalric Spain, Arab and Christian, with its vast passions of love,

1. See in this connexion the penetrating analysis by VOSSLER in *Realismus in
der spanischen Dichtung der Blütezeit*, in the Acts of the Bavarian Academy
of Sciences, Munich, 1926.

honour, and vengeance. *Don Quixote* did not even purge Italy of the literature of chivalry, for this continued for quite a while, discarding perhaps the names of Amadís and Esplendián, but offering tales of love and adventure like *Calloandro* among many others which were eagerly read, being finally displaced only by the vogue of the English and French sentimental and bourgeois novel of the eighteenth century.

Anyone used to examining old libraries and book collections may well be led spontaneously to suspect that Spanish works of literature roused little interest in seventeenth-century Italy, by noticing how rarely one comes across them and in what small numbers – which seems surprising after all that has been written about the overwhelming of Italy at that time by Spanish literary influence. What a difference from the vast number of French books or translations found in the most modest public or private Italian library of that century. The same suspicion is aroused by the frequency of the incitements addressed to scholars to explore the influence of Spanish culture in Italy at that time in order to lay bare the secret springs of life in sixteenth-century Italy. There would be no need for this if the influence in question had been noticeable, and therefore publicly remarked and recorded, like that of French literature. In any case the required researches have now been pretty thoroughly made; let us consider what they have revealed.[1]

In the Renaissance and the early sixteenth century there had been a fashion for singing "coplas" and light Spanish ditties. And in much the same way in the seventeenth century Italians read and sometimes imitated the verses of Góngora, Lope de Vega, and others who were themselves imitators of the Italian lyrical style. In the sixteenth century there had been reading of the Amadís tales

1. See my book *La Spagna nella vita italiana durante la Rinascenza* (4th edn., Bari, 1949) and for the seventeenth century, besides remarks in my *Saggi sulla letteratura italiana del seicento* (3rd edn., Bari, 1948), also those in *Problemi di estetica* (4th edn., Bari, 1949), *Teatri di Napoli* (4th edn., Bari, 1947), and in some detail in *Nuovi saggi sulla lett. ital. del seicento* (2nd edn., Bari, 1949), pp. 225-250. The researches of Farinelli, Mele, and others are there quoted.

of chivalry, and in the seventeenth century Italians read the picaresque novels and *Don Quixote*, while for over half a century Spanish drama was translated and imitated; for use, however, only in courtly or popular entertainment, scarcely penetrating the higher literary circles. In a different range, but one not wholly remote from the theatre, or at all events from the theatrical, especially the sacred and edifying theatre, popularity was won in Italy by the Spanish preachers who carried to extremes the customary technique or the pulpit, introducing the fashion of so-called "preachable concepts". There was also, in each century, a more intimate influence exerted, not on the imagination, but on the heart of the reader: in the sixteenth century the writings of Valdés stirred and heartened the Italian reformers, and in the next century the Italian Catholics received similar comfort from the mystical writings of Saint Teresa, Saint John of the Cross, and also Molinos, whose "Guía espiritual" was, however, soon declared heretical. Upon the minds of students of theology and moral casuistry influence was exerted by such men as Suárez, Mariana, Escobedo, Caramuel, and suchlike major dispensers of Catholic science, or more properly of anti-science, or at the best a science that was retrograde and reactionary. As to the practical example given in social conduct, the Spaniards may have helped to establish a firmer military and political sentiment in Italy, and to win credit for an art of government hedged about by reserves and mysteries, but on the other hand they encouraged among the Italians that cult of the grandiose, the ceremonious, the elaborately sensitive, which for ever retained the description of "spagnolismo".

All of this, and the rest that could be added, amounts to something not indeed negligible, but apt to confirm the argument advanced and illustrated above. Spanish culture does not characterize any distinct phase in the history of Europe as it presents itself for ideal assessment, and accordingly represents no such phase in regard to Italy. And so when the "philosophers of history" fell to assessing the parts played by the single peoples in the march of civilization, following the theory whereby the "Völkergeister", spirits of the peoples, had been called each one to play its part in the history of the whole, that is of the Modern Spirit, the Italian and the French, the English and the German, were recognized as having done so, but not the Spanish people, despite its prolonged challenge to other peoples for the political hegemony of Europe. It must in conclusion be emphasized that the theory of the "Völkergeister" only matched a restricted experience of history, being applicable neither to the Christian civilization of the Middle Ages nor yet to the European history of the nineteenth century. Still less does it seem likely to fit the future if in the future we are going to see not an alternation of national hegemonies but a more harmonious co-operation within the cultural, economic, and political unity of Europe.

[1926]

IV

GENEVA AND CALVINISM

It would be hard to imagine two cities more different than the one which Galeazzo Caracciolo had left behind him and the one in which he now came to reside.[1] Naples then had, except for Paris, the largest city population in Europe,[2] and teemed with a proud nobility housed in splendid palaces. Its boundaries, already enlarged by the Kings of the Aragonese dynasty, had been further widened by the Viceroy Toledo, and, favoured by the peace imposed by the Spanish power, Naples could now display at ease its abundant literature and poetry and cultivation of the arts. Pageant and feast, sound and colour flourished in the mild Neapolitan winter and the blazing summer, fanned, however, by sea breezes. Consider by contrast little Geneva with its few thousands of citizens modestly and poorly housed, having at a distance of a league or half a league on every hand the boundaries of foreign and perhaps, like the Dukes of Savoy, hostile lords, so that vigilance against surprises might never be relaxed; having too (no doubt) its own natural beauty in the setting of hill and plain, near to the great river and the well-stocked lake, with attractive islands and Mont Blanc in view, but exposed to piercing blasts from the mountains and the cold draughts from Rhône and Arve, so different from the warm caress of South Italian breezes.

It was not many years since Geneva, small as it was, had displayed a way of life similar enough to that of South Italy. It had been

---

1. These pages are taken from an Essay in which Croce recounts at length how Galeazzo Caracciolo, firstborn of the Marquis of Vico, left Naples and his beloved wife and children in order to have freedom to profess the reformed religion which he had embraced with ardour: and thus he became a conspicuous figure in Geneva (Editor's note).

2. "Ducentamilia civium capita pro comperto habetur, qui numerus a nulla Europae civitate praeter Lutetiam superatur", wrote the Genoese Umberto Foglietta in *De laudibus urbis Neapolis* in the mid-sixteenth century.

not only a Catholic but an ecclesiastical city, governed by a
Bishop who in the good old days had more than once been seen at
the head of his armed cavalry. Thirty-two Canons headed by a
Provost had occupied their rightful stalls, side by side with eleven
chaplains called "Maccabees" from the name of their chapel, and
there had been seven cures of souls and parishes, those of Holy
Cross by Saint Peter, New Saint Mary, Saint Germain, Saint Mary
Magdalen, Saint Gervais, Saint Léger, and Saint Victor. Of convents there had been five in all, two Franciscan, one Dominican,
one Augustinian and one Cluniac house, places of cheerful and
easy living as attested by the troop of concubines and their swarm-
ing offspring. Famous relics, a portion of the brain of Saint Peter,
and an arm of Saint Anthony, to swear an oath by which was a
tremendous matter, were venerated at Geneva. They were a
pleasure-loving race, the Genevans of those days, frequenters of
taverns where the wine flowed freely, knowing the comfort of
warm baths, eager attendants at the mystery plays staged with
actors of both sexes and also at the farces on moral themes and in
the comic style. The city's environs were pleasant and cheerful
and there was much easy coming and going. But all of this had
been utterly changed in the course of a few years. The suburbs
were now divided from the town, for military reasons, by a broad
belt of fortifications, friars and nuns had been driven out, their
convents demolished or converted to other uses, sacred paintings
had been whitewashed, statues smashed, altars for the Mass
smashed and their pieces used for profane purposes, among others
for the floor of the place of execution where the first to die was
moreover a priest. The relics of the Saints, foremost among them
the brain of Saint Peter and the arm of Saint Anthony, had been
thrown into the River Rhône. Only four out of the seven churches
remained, stripped and despoiled: those of Saint Peter, Saint
Germain, and the Magdalen in the upper and that of Saint Gervais
in the lower city: and in these neither ringing of bells nor organ
tones nor elaborate music was now to be heard, nor vestments,
candles, and lamps to be seen – the audible and visible beauty of the
catholic liturgy, dear to the poetic sense, was gone, now that these

Churches had been "thoroughly purged of all that was idolatrous".[1] Taverns and bath-houses were closed, the wild women of the quarter "porta pulchrarum filiarum" banished, the stage suppressed, likewise all gambling, cosmetics and other "munditiae" forbidden to the womenfolk, holidays limited to Sundays and these devoted strictly to worship, and the former dwellers in the outskirts crowded into the narrow lodgings of the city. And for ten years before Caracciolo's arrival immigration of French, Italian, Spanish, Flemish, and other foreigners had aggravated the crush and was changing the nature of the population and filling the old city with new tones of voice and ways of speech.[2]

The city had asserted its political independence both of the Bishop and of the Duke of Savoy who had before, not without rivalry, divided the sway. It had become a Republic with its three assemblies or councils, those of the two hundred, the sixty, and the twenty respectively, and with its Syndics. But the civil power was flanked by an ecclesiastical power owing it no allegiance, represented by pastors examined and chosen by ministers and acting through the Consistory in which the pastors sat together with twelve elders from the three councils, two from the twenty, four from the sixty, and six from the two hundred.[3] The civil and

1. From Ochino's description of the city in one of his Geneva sermons on his arrival in 1541: see BERNARDINO OCHINO, of Siena, Sermons, 1st part, 10th sermon.

2. A most lively and entertaining account of the declericalization and domestic upheaval of the city is given by ANTHOINE FROMMENT, Les actes et gestes merveilleux de la Cité de Genève nouvellement convertie à l'Évangile, Revilliod, Geneva, 1854. Fromment lived through these events. See especially XXXII-VII and LXIV. To redress the balance see also the moving account of a Poor Clare nun, Jeanne de Jussy, on the events which befell the convent of her order, at Bourg-de-Four, and the migration of the nuns to the Duke of Savoy's domains, in Le Levain du Calvinisme, about which there appeared an article by J. P. FERRIER in the Journal de Genève of August 28 1935. See also Les Chroniques de Genève by MICHEL ROSET, ed. Fazy, Geneva, 1894, and Relazione di Ginevra by CARDOINO, among the MSS. of the Naples National Library, X, folio 1; further, the 3rd vol. of DOUMERGUE's Jean Calvin, Lausanne, 1905, describing the city in Calvin's time. For Geneva before Calvin see J.B.G. GALIFFE, Genève historique et archéologique, Geneva, 1869.

3. See E. CHOISY, La théocratie à Genève au temps de Calvin (Geneva, Eggimann, n. d., but 1896).

ecclesiastical powers acted in agreement, sometimes the one and sometimes the other prevailing: at the time we are speaking of the ecclesiastical, dominated by the strong will of Calvin, prevailed. On the gates of the city stood letters signifying the name of Jesus Christ:[1] not only in later times, but even then, much in Geneva recalled what Savonarola had intended for Florence when he proclaimed Jesus Lord of the city – but he had failed to realize this theocratic project both because Florence was Florence and because he himself was not Calvin. Calvin, after being once driven away by the antagonism of a large part of the population, had returned to Geneva and gained the upper hand against the "libertines" or party of tradition. He was now administering the final blow from which the defeated partisans of the old ways and of an easy life on this earth were not to recover. He had pitilessly chastised the nonconformists of every shade, and the very year before Caracciolo's arrival there had been instituted by ordinance of the ministers an annual visitation of all households to interrogate all men and women concerning the faith and to distinguish the right-thinking from the unsubmissive and also from the ignorant.[2]

Such was the outward aspect of Geneva at that moment – and to the outer eye how immeasurably finer and richer had been the aspect of the city he was leaving. But to the inner eye there might appear in the small and troubled and closely pressed city signs of a deep invigoration, of impetuous renewal, active in the present but still more promising for the future, a spiritual wealth, in fact, which by comparison revealed the hidden poverty behind the gorgeousness of the other city, marking the difference between appearance and reality, the pretence and the genuineness of living strength.

That same independence which the Italian Communes had won for themselves from feudal lords and emperors in the Middle Ages, Geneva had now asserted for itself in a later age. The independence of the Italian cities was won by a spiritual struggle engaging the forces of culture, of industry and trade, of constitu-

1. ROSET, *Chron.*, cit., bk IV, c. 61.
2. Ibid. v. 27.

tional and political reform, nor did this lack some religious motives, as shown by the activity of heretical movements and of
Franciscanism. Yet in the main it brought no break with traditional
religion, and although, in thought and deed, this struggle prepared
the way for a new view of life and a new faith, it held off from a
direct struggle against the old faith, a direct religious reformation.
But in Geneva the movement for political independence fused
with that for a thorough religious reformation – political and
ecclesiastical independence were two causes rendering each other
aid and succour. Geneva could not submit anew to the ducal rule
of Savoy because it had embraced the Reformation, and it clung
all the more strongly to the Reformation because it did not wish
to fall back under that rule. Geneva therefore defended itself with
tough heroism year after year, unmasking conspiracies, suffering
territorial devastations, answering arms with arms, up to the
moment of the great triumph of that December night of 1602,
shameful for the Savoy Duke, when the citizens of Geneva over-
tipped the ladders up which in time of peace the ducal soldiery,
egged on by Jesuit confessors praising the enterprise and promising
eternal glory, were feloniously climbing.

The fusion of the causes of political independence and religious
reform had consequences transcending the affairs of the little city
itself: it rendered possible the formation in the heart of Europe of
an asylum or refuge to which the victims of religious persecution
could repair from all other lands, a centre of discipline and learning, propaganda and evangelization – a "Rome of the Gospel"
over against the Rome of the Popes. The question why Geneva
and not (at all events in the same measure) any other reformed and
independent city fulfilled this function is not to be answered,
really, by geographical, linguistic, or other external considerations,
but by recalling that Geneva in those times meant Calvin. Therefore the refuge of Geneva was the seat of the doctrine and discipline
laid down by Calvin.

Which doctrine and discipline looks at first sight like the replacement of one church, one Pope, one system of dogma, with
another church, Pope, and system of dogma: for the place of a

way of thinking guided entirely by its own internal logic and rejecting all premisses not framed by itself, was here taken by a book, the Bible, this Bible being interpreted in a particular manner, the manner of Calvin himself. Calvin was inexorable against the advocacy of a free criticism, for example against Sebastiano Castellione, who observed and proclaimed that the *Song of Songs* is a collection of love songs; inexorable, too, against those proclaiming dogmas other than his own. But such a phase of conservatism was indispensable after the accomplishment of so great a revolution as the destruction of the Papal authority and the rupture of the ecclesiastical unity of Europe, when an anarchy of opinions seemed to be threatening such as would endanger all that had been won and might pulverize the Reformation itself, yielding place to a reaction towards a new and more oppressive sort of idolatry. The followers of Calvin were appalled at the possible consequences of freedom of judgement, "l'incertitude de toute la parole de Dieu" as a contemporary and fellow-citizen in Geneva, writing of Castellione, put it.[1] There is no escaping the fact that the burning of Servet at the stake had the approval of the greatest, the conscientiously responsible Reformers. It was by the restriction or suppression of freedom that Calvin then safeguarded the very life and future prospects of freedom. For if the Bible was substituted for the Pope and the Church, nevertheless it was not those things, but a book requiring interpretation. And Calvin was one of its interpreters, one, in that time, enjoying in the highest degree that almost absolute authority which men of learning and philosophers exert for a shorter or a longer time upon their disciples. But he was, like all thinkers, mortal and transient, and his place would in due course be taken by new interpreters, progressively emancipated from tradition, and in the last resort by free-thinkers. Why now should the fate of Servet offend our human feelings far more than the many burnings decreed by the Holy Office in Rome and in other Catholic countries? The reason is evidently that the things done by the Church of Rome we judge to have

1. ROSET, op. cit., IV, 69.

been wholly conformable to its institutions, while Calvin's deed we judge by the measure of the freedom and toleration which were implicit in the movement of the Reformation and came to development and strength in subsequent centuries. In indulging these feelings we are no doubt misdirecting our judgement and offending against historical objectivity, for we overlook the fact that freedom and toleration came to grow on that very stem whose roots Calvin preserved by the severities of which that against Servet is an example. Similarly superficial is our spontaneous applause for the Socinians and tolerationists of that age who rebelled against the putting to death of the unorthodox, but were little listened to or followed and impotent to change or mitigate the laws. The fact that we now hail them as our forerunners shows that in their own day they were premature: we have no right to adjudicate upon what it was possible at that time to do, and right to do, from the point of view of that which was then impracticable and so left undone.

The Calvinist Church in Geneva maintained an oppressive vigilance and censorship over the whole range of the lives of the citizens, prohibiting with severity and prescribing in detail just like, elsewhere, the Church of Rome. Indeed the Calvinistic oppression was the more vexatious because springing from a more fanatical spirit, taking its model rather from the Old Testament and the prophets, and more thorough-going in its execution within a narrower ambit in which nothing could elude the eye of the pastor or the ear of the informer. But there was this great difference: the oppression of the Church of Rome, where and when it was able to be directly or indirectly exerted with its full weight, was designed to stabilize the past, and in so doing it mortified intelligences and temperaments, encouraging the propensity to a servile and calculating manner of life, instead of building up new energies for the future. By contrast the Calvinistic discipline (superior in this also to the Lutheran, because this held the inner life and the life of politics and the State divided as in separate departments) stimulated a new moral seriousness; steeled the characters of men; spurred them on to an activity which was understood as the accomplishment by each one in his own sphere of a divinely assigned mission; interpreted the attainment of prosperity through a man's work as a sign of divine grace; and acted upon the modern and secular world with an efficacious mediation now recognized by the critics and historians who are investigating this activity in its great variety and wide ramifications. The new moral seriousness contributed to the independence of Holland, the free institutions of England, the development of the American colonies into the United States: it promoted on every hand culture, industry, trade, political constructiveness, free thought, even, and in the last resort through the Calvinist who was Jean Jacques Rousseau it prepared the way for modern Kantian ethics. Geneva for some time paid the price of all this fine work by languishing beneath the censorship of its consistory. But then Geneva too broke out of the swaddling-clothes and grew in strength to maturity and liberty. There was something in the attitudes which first the Genevan "libertines" and then the "Socinians" had maintained, but what they too had to contribute could be recognized only at the end of the testing time of Calvinist severity – in their own day they were anachronistic and therefore had to succumb for a while and bide their time.

More than all else, the theology of Calvin appeared archaic with its stiff assertion and defence of the divine Trinity. How much more full of light are the arguments of the anti-Trinitarians who assailed him, forerunners of the rationalist and intellectualist criticism. Not that any great effort was really needed in such an assault, seeing that it sufficed (as Hegel once remarked)[1] to count one, two, three, as laid down in arithmetic, in order to reach the conclusion that one cannot be two and three. Now the thought of the trinity or triad is one of the most ancient human intuitions, traceable in the most varied religions and systems of ideas. It renders in more or less mythological form the need which is felt for the speculative concept, not of unity or multiplicity in the abstract, but of the one which is multiple and the multiple which

1. *Vorlesungen über die Philosophie der Religion*, edit. Marheineke (Berlin, 1840), II, 237.

is one, and it points to a logic which can give satisfaction as being not over-scholastic and static, but dialectical and dynamic. The Catholic Church had taken in trust the deep concept of the divine Trinity, and Calvin had the merit of preserving it outside that Church. For this indirectly attaches him to modern philosophy, whereas Servet and the Socinians originated no deep philosophical speculation, save perhaps in a negative manner by giving occasion for the defence and development and deeper understanding of the concept and logic of the Trinity.

Even more archaic, and ferocious in its archaism, appears the Calvinistic doctrine of predestination, for election or for damnation, which God makes of his own will *ab aeterno*, dividing mankind into the two classes of the elect and the reprobate. The easy-going mentality of our times once again sympathizes, not perhaps with the post-Tridentine and Jesuitic eclectic theology, but at all events with the anti-predestinationists who upheld against the doctrine of the divine election of individuals, and the concession of grace to single persons, the doctrine of a general concession of grace to all men. Yet the myth of predestination according to the voluntary choice of a God contained once again the germ of a great thought, indeed the very idea of history which, in its course, condemns and destroys individuals, generations, and peoples, and then from the hecatombs brings forth by the agency of great men, or of the elect, those ideal values of thought, beauty, and moral worth that live for ever. History, that is to say, happens not for the sake of the salvation or felicity of individuals, but, as Calvin would say, *ad majorem Dei gloriam*. It was necessary to rid this thought of its mythological and theological coating in order to exhibit it as truth, and this was the work of the philosophy of a later age and of its theory of history, according to which election and reprobation, victory and defeat, were not arbitrarily decreed by a transcendent God but were the immanent operation of the Spirit in its actualization. The opponents of predestination were really the forerunners of the historians of the Enlightenment in their application of the criterion of *ratio ratiocinans*, and in politics of democracy with its equalizing and levelling tendencies. To these we will not deny importance or wealth of historical consequences, although taken in themselves they smack of the onesided and the over-simple. By comparison, the doctrine of predestination points to something of more weight and width, nothing less than the principle of free competition for the election and the prevalence of the best: the principle, that is, of equality before the law, but not material equality between individuals, the consequence of which would be a standstill of human history. From Calvinism and its concept of predestination, Liberalism derives its austerity, its opposition both to the popular and to the aristocratic, its combination of longsufferingness and buoyancy, humility and daring.

For the reasons which we have here set forth summarily and without lingering over special aspects, John Calvin deserved for all his harshness and narrowness the faithful and devoted followers ready for any sacrifice in the defence and advancement of his Reformation whom he did in fact have with him in his day. Among these was that Neapolitan gentleman who in June 1551 knocked for admittance at the gates of Geneva.

[1933]

V

ITALIAN DECADENCE

The Italian Decadence of the age which runs from the middle of the sixteenth to the beginning of the eighteenth century was seen by our historians of the generation of the Risorgimento as moral decadence, feebleness, egoism, in a word blameworthy deficiency. This judgement later gave way to others which adduced the harmful consequences of the change in the Eastern trade routes and other such shifts in the world situation, resulting in impoverishment, gradual decline in political power, and so in culture, learning, art, and so on.

These latter explanations are in their way instructive, and no doubt the men of the Risorgimento were excessively moralizing and naive, not to say rhetorical and sermonizing, in the explanation which they offered. Yet perhaps what they said was more to the point. For the ever shifting winds of fortune are one thing and the will and work of men is another, and human history is the history of man's laborious efforts to adjust himself to new conditions and thereby to adjust the conditions to himself, so as to be able to put his heart into utilizing them and living worthily. Maybe one who has lived in affluence must live instead in poverty, one who has worked on a great scale must work on a small scale, and this will not be decadence, just as no man who from a condition of glory returns or "falls" to a condition of obscurity will feel this to be a decay unless he be innerly decayed. Quite rightly among the old-fashioned exemplars of virtue there was numbered Cincinnatus, who returned from military commands and victories to his plough. Where the spirits remain high, there is always the latent possibility of a recall to commands and to victories when the way of the world comes round to offering or more truly to imposing an opportunity. This is as true for peoples as it is for individuals, and none should be advised to be great, but only to be strict, or at most to stand prepared. Thinking much upon past glories, and desiring them back, like cherishing vast designs instead of simply maintaining an inner readiness for whatever may come, is a distraction from the salutary task of the present moment, the mark of a small mind, a real decadence. And such was the case in the Italy of that time, where there was much idle indulgence in thoughts of past glory and in hopes of its miraculous restoration. Never were there more invitations and salutations addressed to this or that new Augustus or new Scipio. The Risorgimento writers were well advised not only to make an end of these imaginary grandeurs but to emphasize the difference between glory and virtue, culture and civilization, vigour and display. And just as in poetry they awoke a preference for the brief lyric rather than the cumbrous composition, and for "popular" rather than learned and rhetorical poetry, so in recounting the history of Italy they stirred up enthusiasm for the primitive assertions of liberty, the birth of the Communes, the little "rural Commune" celebrated tenderly and loftily in the verses of Carducci.

As historians they diagnosed the character of the Italian decadence and blameworthiness – want or weakness of patriotism. There should be no difficulty about accepting this conclusion, like the rest, if the *Patria*, object of patriotism, be rightly understood as symbol or synecdoche. For deep and serious love of country embraces love of family, mankind, and God, the cult of truth, the zeal for what is good, unflagging effort in every field of work. Philosophy has taught that "Nulla virtus solitaria", and it has been only in our own days that men have attempted to isolate the virtues in solitude with the notion of an abstract "Patria" floating aloft, and for that very reason thought compatible with savagery, greed, violence, crime. In the age of decadence it was not only Italian patriotism with its political and military adjuncts which decayed, but with it the life of religion, the morality of society and the home, thought, learning, even style and language. For style became windy and swollen, language impure and sterile, that is generic and inaccurate.

We will say then – for better clarity – that it was not simply patriotism or the spirit of citizenship which had weakened in the Italians, but moral zeal in all its warmth and width. Was it a total failure that occurred? We cannot say that, if only because we owe some respect, some gratitude, to our ancestors of a few generations ago. Had the failure been total, Italy would have perished – and Italy did not perish. Moral zeal came nearer, perhaps, to suffering a visible eclipse in Tuscany and Florence, the erstwhile centre of the great moral intellectual and artistic accomplishment and the great historical effort of Italy at the moment of transition from the Middle to the Modern Age – Florence which had stood for the true Italy at that moment but then, after the brief brilliance of the last attempted defence of the Republic, had languidly submitted to the Medici rule, to political forms without substance. Florence, which had been the first to mock at the rigmarole of chivalry, now created orders of knighthood and decorations, gave itself up the composition of grammars and vocabularies and to pretensions of linguistic excellence, and having formerly cherished the robust virtues of a Dante, a Machiavelli, a Michelangelo, turned to the cultivation of correctness and temperance, not to say frigidity and pusillanimity. Elsewhere in Italy the decline was more gradual, for example in Venice, which could still mount warlike offensives and defensives and where the struggle for political power and spiritual keenness was still awake, as shown in the resistance to the schemes of the Papacy. Venice, at the dawn of the seventeenth century still favoured freedom of scientific enquiry and lived in the atmosphere of an ecclesiastical if not a religious reformation. There was a part of Italy where, far from declining, the moral zeal of which we are speaking was just coming into being – in Piedmont, thanks to the rule of the Savoys. It must be recollected that a people is not something given, but something that evolves, it does not exist naturally, but comes into existence through spiritual guidance, by dint of effort upon effort. It is said that the North-West Italians had military virtues wanting elsewhere in the peninsula: as against this, when Emmanuel Philibert, engaged in creating his army, issued steel helmets to the Alpini, he found that the good mountaineers took them home to use as saucepans. There was yet another part of Italy in which signs were plainly given that popular vigour was unabated, thus in the upheavals of Naples and Sicily. Here too there were signs of intellectual novelty in the meditations of the South Italian philosophers. Decadence was ever more rife, yet there was some shedding of defunct and pedantic matter, and the literary history of the times displays a kind of barbarian invasion into the domains of the petrified and bloodless literature on the Tuscan model. There is something of this already in Tasso's poetry, which so displeased the Florentine literary world and even the young Galileo, and much more of it in Marino (dubbed "the poet of Naples" by a Tuscan satirist), and his school. And the same may be said of the new architecture, sculpture, and poetry of the time: indeed the art first of Venice, then of Bologna and Naples, prevailed over that of Tuscany. But Tuscany itself was at the same time delivering its latest vigorous intellectual affirmation, its forward-looking mathematics and physics and natural science: for side by side with the academies of the merely wordy and the circles of the literary voluptuaries stood Galileo and his school. Meanwhile, irrespectively of separate sovereignties and regional differences, all Italy necessarily maintained a certain standard of attention to immediate daily problems of local government and justice, of social service in the form of charity, of religious observance heightened by the increased formalities of the cult. There was even a general aspiration towards a higher form of national life. It was not possible for Italy to evade subjugation by the Spanish power, to demand national independence, but at least from time to time and in various Italian quarters attempts were made to play off France against Spain, and the Guelph-Ghibelline contest gave occasion for a rivalry of Spanish and French fashions of dress throughout the peninsula. At certain hopeful moments, even, some Italian power would attract expectant attention, as when in the first half of the seventeenth century there were for some time hopes that the policy of Piedmont would find its way to an alliance with the still independent Italian State of Venice. And since, to use Alfieri's expression, the human plant grows healthily in Italy, and since furthermore the ancient culture of the country did not wither away but continued to put forth its fruits, despite the want of freshening and strengthening spiritual influences, good specimens of humanity were to be found flourishing on every hand. When they found no suitable conditions or tasks in their native land their energies spilled over into other lands. And so, small though the part of Italy might be in the European events of the seventeenth century, the part of the individual Italian was great, were he a military leader or engineer (it was Italian engineers who constructed the siege-works of Antwerp and La Rochelle), a politician, or a technician in any field. Or he might also be a man of intellect and faith, for Italians contributed in an important measure not only to the Reformation movement but also, most conspicuously, and in correspondence with what is finest in the Italian character and mind, to the formation of modern Rationalism and the cause of religious toleration.

Yet though such qualifications are rightly insisted upon by a historian of seventeenth-century Italy desirous of narrating justly and resistant to the conventional atmosphere of desolation and gloom spun around the period, it remains true that, generally speaking, moral zeal dried up, and Italy was decidedly abased by comparison with the other countries of high culture. Everywhere in Europe, if only by a contagion from Italy and Spain, there were to be found in that epoch such characteristics as Counter-Reformation, Jesuitry, delight in titles, competitive ceremonialism, the cult of duelling, bad taste, the Baroque, academic vacuity, and scientific pedantry. But elsewhere, in opposition to these things, or too deep to be disturbed by them, a vigorous life was in motion, new forms in politics, a new science, a new literature were coming into being. In Italy, on the contrary, those characteristics were unchallenged or prevailed, and in this respect not even Spain, but perhaps only Germany, was worse off than Italy. As the saying is, Italy was then fatigued and resting from this fatigue – a fine and solicitous metaphor indicating that she was at all events not dead and done for. Indeed it may be something more than a metaphor, since in its way it confutes all who seek for a cause or causes of moral events. The confutation lies in the reminder that there is no cause for decadence save that peoples succumb to fatigue and by one means or another (sometimes by way of malady or crisis) they win for themselves repose.

And additional though scarcely necessary proof that the decadence in question was a decay of moral zeal and of the keen experiments, researches, conflicts, anxieties, joys, griefs, laborious efforts which go with it, can be gained by looking at the picture from a point of view which we will not go so far as to call sceptical, pessimistic, quietistic, but which, devoted to transcendental religion, tends to consider as vanities all mundane ardours for politics, science, or the like, considering the observance of religion and obedience to the Church as the sole test of a healthy and useful life. Viewed in this light the very notion of an Italian decadence comes to nought, reproof gives way to praise and dislike to sympathy. In fact when the historians of the reactionary school speak out their mind to the full they proclaim this "decadence" to be an imaginary thing unfairly invented by heretics and liberals. In much the same way Dupanloup at a later date and in a celebrated discourse declared the ills of Italy to be "imaginary" and blamed Louis Napoleon's France for credulously giving ear to them and thus being drawn into war against Austria. Not dissimilarly the worshippers of transcendent Reason, those for whom passions, disputes, and wars rank as mere unreason and folly, have failed to discern decadence where we point to its presence. A suggestion of envy runs through certain depictions of eighteenth-century Italy, Voltaire's, for example, when he writes: "L'Italie était le pays le plus florissant d'Europe s'il n'était pas le plus puissant. On n'entendait plus parler de ces guerres étrangères qui l'avaient désolée depuis le règne du roi de France Charles VIII, ni de ces guerres intestines de principauté contre principauté et de ville contre ville: on ne voyait plus de ces conspirations autrefois si fréquentes. Naples, Venise, Rome, Florence attiraient les étrangers par leur magnificence et par la culture de tous les arts. Les plaisirs de l'esprit n'étaient encore bien connus que dans ce climat. La religion s'y montrait aux peuples sous un appareil imposant, nécessaire aux imaginations sensibles." Or again: "Les cérémonies de la religion, celles des préséances, les arts, les antiquités, les édifices, les jardins, la musique, les assemblées occupèrent le loisir des Romains, tandis que la guerre de trente ans ruina l'Allemagne, que le sang des peuples et du roi coulait en Angleterre, et que, bientôt après, la guerre civile de la Fronde désola la France."[1] Even today in such quarters the question can be heard, "Where then was the decadence? There was a way of life as good as any other, obeying its own laws: the character of decadence has been assigned to it by the arbitrary standard of outsiders, but in their despite it is a way of life which it is permissible to choose and cherish in preference to any other." Then there is a class of philosophers, "generic" philosophers, who go so far as to deny that there can be anything decadent or any periods of decadence. For according to them decadence is everywhere, in every act and deed, and there can be no progress which does not involve letting something fall and decay, just as there can be no living without dying. Since then, they say, decadence is in every life, it cannot ever give its particular character to any way of life: it is all just the way of the world. The answer to these people is that true enough the world goes its way, but there are possibilities that some people or some individual may be trodden under foot in the process or may incur exemplary punishment for not keeping up the pace. The world indeed moves on from life to life, but the Italian people might have perished as other peoples have perished. As to the supposed arbitrary standards issuing from our own minds, why, what is truly arbitrary is the standard applied by those critics themselves, namely the concept of a life of quietude and immobility such as never existed save as an empty longing, while the criterion of ethical zeal and purposeful energy, to which judgements of decadence refer, is a necessary one, relative to the reality of life as it has always been, to our feeling as men. Those profuse praises for the eighteenth-century life of peace and pleasure are just poets' fancies. That talk of an Italy all diversions and smiles, smiling at everything and everybody, herself included, is mere conventional chatter. If you look at the documents you will not find that calm

1. *Essai sur les mœurs*, chapters 183, 185.

and gaiety, but you will be tempted rather to say that Italy had lost the faculty of healthy laughter necessary for the health of the spirit, and was trying to make up for it artificially with burlesque rhymes, academic witticisms, mock-heroic poems with more punning than pleasantry.

No doubt the Italians were unaware, or little and seldom aware, of the fact of their decadence. They considered themselves highly civilized by comparison with the dwellers north of the Alps, and these for their part still admired Italian learning, capacity, ability, deftness in all skills and arts, and when in need used to call for the help of Italians. And as happens in such cases the reputation of the Italians for some time outlasted their usefulness. Italian historians who were no longer of the great Florentine school received commissions from foreign potentates, and their works together with many other books and booklets of little or no value, as well as many novels of which the titles have been forgotten by all except learned specialists, were translated out of the Italian into all other tongues. Our versifiers, usurping the name of poets, were invited to foreign courts, and others of our products, good or bad, made their way in the world, confirming the impression of Italy as a lively and productive country.

Towards the end of the seventeenth century the foreigners somewhat suddenly discovered and proclaimed that Italy had decayed, that Italian poetry was brilliant but insincere, Italian science frivolous and wordy.[1] The French made the discovery about literature, the circles inspired by free Holland made it about science. Almost at the same moment, though to the tune of certain angry denials which did but confirm the truth of the charge, the Italians themselves began to feel their decadence and the more sincere and conscientious plucked up the courage to acknowledge

1. De Segrais wrote these verses to Ménage, who was leaving for Italy:

> Ah! ce n'est plus dans ces beaux lieux
> peuplés jadis de Demy-Dieux,
> qu'on trouve la haute science;
> malgré son triste aveuglement
> la présomptueuse Ignorance
> y triomphe superbement.

it. So now the event was accompanied by awareness of the event, the process, reaching its conclusion, was accompanied by a clear vision of the outline which had thitherto been masked by incidents and appearances. It was then precisely that Italy began to recover. Decadence, from being a form of life, became a spur to life. Albeit slowly and painfully the pulse quickened.

The quickening did not immediately take the form of a national uprising against the foreigner for the recovery of popular liberties. At that time no man of sense would have conceived a design so far removed from the realities set by the relations between the European powers and the development of political institutions. Nor was there, to begin with, as a direct manifestation of recovery, any lively interest in the economic and juridical problems of the community. What happened to begin with was a revolution in literature and style – it would be too much to say a poetic revolution. "Arcadia" – later so much mocked and despised – began to stir, and a simpler, less pretentious manner of composition was sought. Scholasticism, Aristotelianism, crude beliefs of all sorts were dropped in favour of observational science and mathematics and Cartesian philosophy. Research started into the past history of Italy and, for the first time, into the history of Italian literature. All this constituted the beginning of a moral revival. For just as a condition of decadence had invested, as we saw, all the activities of life, so now a resumption of progress, however partial in appearance, spread, as always, without limit to its scope and into the very roots. The most important indication of all was that the Italians began to study foreign, especially French and English, books with a modest intention to learn from them, though not without some rightful rebuttals of foreign insolence and scorn. What more than all this could have been done? While Italy was "resting", other countries had forged ahead. It was now necessary to rise from that rest and to make up lost ground. Thus ends the story of Italian decadence – and begins the story of the Italian Risorgimento, which truly starts, not in 1815, as the textbooks have it, but – dawningly – around 1670.

[1925]

VI

THE MORAL LIFE
OF SEVENTEENTH-CENTURY ITALY

A CERTAIN misunderstanding is quite likely to arise – let us be on the look-out for it – as a consequence of our shifting the so-called Italian Decadence on to the plane of morals rather than that of economic and politico-institutional changes. Now changes of this last sort can only be of significance as indications of social decadence when they affect the moral life of a community – hence our proceeding. But to come to the misunderstanding. It is commonly imagined that there are in man and in human societies two different and opposed "elements" (or some such term), the good and the bad. In certain ages the "bad" is deemed to overcome and destroy the "good", society thus falling prey to some demon, either one shamelessly rapacious or one subtly seductive and corrupting. From this view derives the interpretation of history which is read by pessimistically and morosely inclined people into the events of all ages and nations, no doubt, but in special and frequent measure into those of the country and the age which we are now considering. How often has the moral life of Italy from the second half of the sixteenth until almost the end of the seventeenth century been luridly depicted as a succession of turpitudes: with lordlings at the head of gangs of bravos and assassins, henchmen and armed ruffians, heaping up crimes and outrages; with nobles and barons receiving servile honour from their inferiors and rendering no less servile honours to their higher lords, and these in turn cringing to the Kings of France or Spain, the Emperor or the Pope; with multiplication of absurd ceremonies and competitions; with the common people cowed and barbarized by want, ignorance, and immorality; with luxury, display, and conceit counterfeiting the wealth and culture that were not what they had been; with hypocritical and superstitious religion dominating each and all; and then, like judgements from heaven, those dreadful pestilences, earthquakes, ruinous wars, rebellions to be subdued only by savage reprisals.

Such accounts have enjoyed much popularity. The taste for the horrific prevails also among readers of histories. And because the depictions in question are of a sort to assist summary and slapdash judgements they flatter the lazy mind. Intelligent people, however, see through them in two ways. For first of all they observe that collecting instances of crimes, degeneracies, misfortunes, ignoble, stupid, and insane actions does not amount to understanding the historical truth about an age, since collections of this sort can be accumulated more or less in respect of all epochs, and are indeed habitually offered as history by the expedient of omitting to relate or perhaps to investigate the other side of things – what is normal, regular, sane, good principle and practice, all of which may indeed lie hidden somewhat out of sight. Chroniclers, reporters of sensational events students, of criminal records, satirists, and slanderers are what they are, but they are not investigators or judges of history. Secondly (and here too the objection raised by the intelligent is justified) the conditions of the times you are enquiring into should always be recalled. Our present ways are not to be taken as the measure of past ages, which must, on the contrary, be viewed in relation to their own setting and precedents. Under such inspection much which at first sight seems wholly bad takes on another colour or at all events displays certain aspects not previously observed. If one were provisionally to adopt this image of two elements or forces grappling in conflict, one would have to conclude that the good element needs must have had the better of the other albeit after sustaining fierce aggressions, for otherwise the society itself would have disintegrated. But in truth the conception of the two elements is itself fallacious, and the question whether a given age or a given people possessed a greater or a lesser endowment of moral goodness than some other is often asked, but being ill-constructed cannot be answered.

Serious historical enquiry into the moral life of a people or an age needs must turn its eye upon the ideals which that people or that age formed and elaborated. It was upon that virtue which develops and enlivens ideals that we were pointing our enquiry when we said that in Italy in the times which we are considering there was a decline and decay of moral zeal. We will not now – for these reasons – embark upon one of the usual arbitrary or sentimental, one-sided, and superficial surveys of the moral habits and customs of our period. We will instead of this treat the morals as they should always be treated in history, as the effect of an ideal. Where the ideal is inferior so will the morals be, where the ideal is breaking down the morals will break down too. Or sometimes we may have to treat an ideal as an obstacle against which another ideal was pressing so as to overcome or change it. Finally we may be envisaging the inception of a new mode or tendency of conduct in which new ideals become manifest. Only by this method can we pass beyond the sphere of the anecdote to that of the logic of history and deliver judgements instead of just reporting our feelings.

Italy's loss of intellectual originality and of the pure vein of poetry and art was quite certainly accompanied by loss of the power to forge fresh ethical ideals, and there is a restricted sense in which the last loss lay at the root of the others and explains that weakness and incompleteness of the thought and the art of the seventeenth century which we have described. Now the new ideals then being tentatively developed in the European countries, on the ethical-religious side of things, can be roughly summed up under two headings, first that of a deepening of Christianity along the lines of Calvinism, Puritanism, and Jansenism, and secondly that of a rationalist urge in religion expressed firstly by the aspiration of discovering a natural or universal religion at the heart of every particular religion, and secondly, by the conception of a religion of reason having as its indispensable accompaniment toleration, or in other words confidence in the sure processes of critical thought. In politics the ideal was that of an absolute princedom or monarchy progressively getting the better of mediaeval decentralization of political power and concentrating this instead wholly in the management of the State, that is in the hands of the monarch and his ministers and the standing army supporting him. Meanwhile there could be discerned the outlines of new free institutions, not as a continuation of the mediaeval liberties, but as a product of the democratic conscience of certain branches of Protestantism, expecially the Calvinistic and its derivates, and in yet greater measure as the product of the rationalist and contractualist theories basic to the newly arising school of natural law. (For the most part this was for the time being finding only literary expression, but some practical applications there were too.) In economics the ideal was variously the colonization of lands in America, thriving trade, industry advancing with the advance of the positive sciences, finance capital outstripping that landed proprty which in the deep Middle Ages had so largely set its stamp upon Europe, with a correlative weakening of the old privileged nobility in the face of the rising commercial, industrial, and professional middle class.

All of these ideals received their first impetus in Europe principally from the Italy of the Communes and the principalities but also still earlier from the Italy of the Norman-Swabian monarchy. It was thus Italy which in the "pre-history" of modern times prevailingly set the political and economic and cultural pattern, without however continuing to contribute in any significant measure to the same process when it attained its full historical maturity. "Italy", and not the Italians: for the Italians as already remarked continued to influence actively the ideals and the realizations of Europe, contributing to the "History of the Italians outside Italy" to which Cesare Balbo would have called attention. But in its very nature this cannot be "Italian History" unless perhaps in the sense of echoing a past Italian age, or keeping alight a flame that was threatened with extinction in Italy. If from contemplation of the varied and vigorous life of those times in England, France, Holland, and Geneva and more sporadically elsewhere, we turn our attention back to the land of Italy, seeking out the way of life of the various Italian societies, we may indeed here and there discern at work processes like those apparent elsewhere, but in general we find nothing moving in politics, religion, or economics, no Calvinism or Jansenism, rationalism or school of natural law, no striving for national unity under an absolute ruler, no aspiration for human dignity and freedom, no trading and industrial enter-

prises, no personalities comparable to Richelieu, Mazarin, Cromwell, De Witt, Grotius, Milton, Arnauld, Pascal, Descartes,
Spinoza – at most, possibly, some rare spirit showing some affinity
of spirit and mind to such men.

Italy had become a conservative country resting on its laurels,
its old-time ideals and abilities. But these had lost their old vigour,
for there is no vigour without aptitude for development and
transformation, and the various Italian States had halted along
certain lines once marking a keen advance, but now not even
fully maintained and defended. Even that unificatory movement
of a sort which Spain had initiated in Italy by attaching to its
long-held island domains of Sicily and Sardinia also the whole
southern part of the peninsula, besides the important Lombard
province in the north, hung fire, and remained incomplete.
Philip II had not even brought off his attempt to round off the
work indirectly by drawing the Italian States into a confederation.
True, some pro-Spanish theorists did indeed affirm that Italy
constituted a confederation under the King of Spain, but the
facts did not closely correspond to the theory. Not only did
Venice hold out and resist absorption into the Spanish sphere, but
other princes and governments such as the Grand Dukes of Tuscany and the Dukes of Savoy, indeed even the Popes of Rome,
leaned from time to time towards France, in order to rescue by
such offsetting of the Spanish and the French powers what they
still called "the freedom of Italy", that is Italy's non-subjection,
directly or even indirectly, to a single power. "Spain" and "France"
were the recurrent symbols of a deliberate exercise in balance.
The peace of Câteau-Cambrésis seemed to have frozen the situation as between the Italian States: for over a century and a half
their frontiers remained substantially unchanged.

All the surviving Republics, large or small, from Venice and
Genoa to Lucca, though they might afford room for mild contests
between the old and the new nobility, terminable easily enough
without any train of revolutionary consequences or marked social
and political transformations, took on a strictly aristocratic or
oligarchic character. Contests of this sort, on the model of those

in the Republics and especially in Genoa, were also to be found in the non-republican States wherever institutions of the nobility and the people remained in existence, and where there was an older and a newer order of nobility, as in Naples. As in the Republics the effects were mild and they passed almost without a trace. The wise constitution of Venice was a matter of Italian pride, seen as a sublime monument of ancient Italian wisdom, the imperishable foundation of a new *urbs aeterna*, and was long studied and admired by the men of letters. But the Venetian Republic held together by force of inertia, or of tradition and habit, not by dint of flexibility or of a vigour adequate to command or keep up or cope with the requirements of the new times. There was no future for Venice and no hope of rebirth save by way of an extinction in favour of new and superior arrangements in line with modern ideas. Already these old States were dogged by the monarchies, Genoa for example by that of the Savoys as well as by the Spanish, which had tried to swallow it and had succeeded in taking it in tow, and by the French.

It was the age of absolute monarchy, and the rest of Italy conformed to what was becoming the rule throughout Europe, allowing this tendency to take its course without entering in any determinate and intentional manner into the process, or making any energetic Italian contribution in action or in art and poetry, but simply accepting it with a submission partaking of fearfulness. Had this been possible, the process would have met with a prolonged Italian resistance, both in Florence, where after the last attempt at an armed defence of the Republican tradition the spirit of freedom lingered on for decades among the exiles, and among the passionate cultivators of remoter and nearer history, and also in South Italy where the barony and the nobility were straining at the leash and the popular class too suffered from the harshness of the tightened monarchy. But in Naples and the other Spanish dominions royal absolutism was imposed by overwhelming foreign might and was visible in the shape of viceroys and foreign governors, and absolutism in Tuscany too owed its existence to the same forces which had implanted and upheld it. Absolutism was not

without its beneficial effects. It put an end to factions and fighting
and mutual persecution between the Communes – and we have
seen that the mock-heroic poets looked back upon the old period
of the Communes quite unsentimentally, indeed with cruel ridicule.
It checked the political individualism of the Barons and promoted
a more elevated and better grounded idea of the State. Such benefit
wrought to the cause of "peace and quiet" was recognized, and
the recognition stands at the root of the distinction often drawn,
in the political theory and controversy of the times, between
"monarch" and "tyrant". But only in the eighteenth century was a
certain social and national spirit instilled into the forms of monarchy: indeed in the reigns of the early Bourbons in Naples and
the early Lorraine princes in Tuscany this spirit was not merely
accepted, but warmly and hopefully applauded. In the smaller
ducal principalities of Mantua, Modena, and Parma, regimes
midway between the patriarchal and the despotic, political dead-
ends, had replaced the older governments. But in Piedmont and
the other domains of the Duke of Savoy the instalment of absolutism bore a different and unique character, for there the inhabitants
felt an age-old affection for their native dynasty whose return
they had loyally and hopefully awaited during the period of
foreign occupation by the troops of France and Spain. The prince
who achieved the Restoration and first assumed the kingly title,
Emmanuele Filiberto, suppressed or reduced the surviving mediaeval and feudal features in favour of better arrangements conducive to prosperity and the observance of order and justice, and
inspired his subjects with a sense that military glory was something
pertaining to the nation and to their own native place.

From time to time the establishment of absolute rule in Italy
encountered resistance and rebellion in the name of the traditional
liberties and privileges, notably in the mid-seventeenth century,
when simultaneously with outbreaks of this sort throughout
Europe there were risings in Naples, Palermo, and Messina. But
these were extreme convulsions of decrepit anachronisms, which,
far from moderating, positively pushed ahead the advance of
absolutism. In the single case of England a certain continuity was

preserved and the ancient assemblies there confronted and defeated royal absolutism, merging gradually into modern parliamentary and liberal arrangements. In all other countries, including Italy, mediaeval institutions like the surviving mediaeval Republics themselves had to meet with extinction in the embrace of the monarchies: later on, in the fullness of time, there would spring from the breast of these monarchies – containing implicitly a wider liberty than the old liberties guaranteed by charters and privileges and parliaments of barons and municipalities – representative institutions. Those uprisings therefore were conservative, indeed reactionary, rather than truly revolutionary in character.

And with the single exception of the Ducal State of the Savoys, which instead of standing perpetually on the defensive repeatedly took the offensive and actually gained in territory and in self-confidence, the various States of Italy exhibited a conservative, defensive, and so gradually declining posture in the international balance of power. The Savoy State took part in the Thirty Years' War for its own ends, unlike Venice, which declined to be lured by any promise of advantages, heeding only the defence of some relics of the Venetian Empire against the assaults of the Ottoman power. Valour and energy went into this defence, admirable courage and constancy, rewarded for a time by the recapture of the Peloponnese, but unable for more than a short while to avert imminent fate or to stop the gradual advance, now swift and now slow, of the enemy. Genoa quite early lost in Chios the last relic of its eastern possessions, yet fought a valiant war of defence against the encroaching Savoys and yielded only when Louis XIV sent the heavy guns of his fleet. Even so it was only the abandonment of Genoa by the Allies in the peace negotiations which forced upon the Republic the humiliating conditions of Versailles, a humiliation more dishonourable to the large and aggressive party to the contract, than to the small victim of oppression. The Grand Duchy of Tuscany vainly strove to acquire Corsica, Genoa's ever rebellious subject island destined to severance from Italy, nor did it ever succeed in annexing lands from the Spanish-garrisoned regions. And altogether Tuscany was of small account in the pol-

itics of Europe, although to some extent a participant in virtue
of the subsidies granted to the King of Spain and the Tuscan
regiments which sometimes fought in the wars of the Empire. The
Papacy had in the second half of the sixteenth century and for a
while later accumulated a vast spiritual power which it then found
to be gradually diminishing, but considered as a territorial State
it lacked a political soul and was without the capacity of expanding
by radiating a national and governmental attraction. Such a radiation had been attempted as recently as by Paul IV, and was
later on cherished as a dream, but no more than a dream, in certain
"neo-Guelph" cultivators of Utopias two centuries later. Spanish
Italy too was devoid of an inspiring principle, merely following
the lot of the monarchy of which it was a province: this was a
declining lot all through the century, which socially, economically,
and culturally became considerably worse than the lot of the
province itself. Also drawn into and held in the orbit of the
Spanish monarchy, Genoa pursued its own trading and banking
affairs but henceforth undertook no individual political exploits.
This virtual lack of vigour and political independence, indeed the
very fact of being small States in an age of wealth and growth for
the greater States, made it difficult for them to preserve what
might be preservable in their heritage or to seek out new op-
portunities opened up dramatically by the expansion of world
trade and by military events. Thus while Venice, Genoa, Tuscany,
whichever it might be, strained to preserve or recapture their
trade with the Turkish subject lands, reaching agreements with
the Sultans, at that very moment France or Spain would frustrate
the whole plan, forcing them to cut losses and to give up. The
trade of the West had already passed into the hands of the Flemings,
Dutch, English, and French, and in the American trade Italy could
have no part. The late fifteen-hundreds still witnessed a certain
stubborn defence of the Italian trading interests, and there were
plans for reviving industry and commerce. But in the next century
the once glorious wool manufactures almost wholly came to an
end in Venice, Lombardy, and Tuscany. In that century the population of Italy as a whole slowed down its rate of increase and

perhaps even declined. Almost the only advances to offset the
many declines were the founding of the new port of Leghorn by
the first Medici Grand Dukes, and Emmanuele Filiberto's economic
reforms in Tuscany.

The idea of Italy, of independent, free, great Italy, located
geographically in "that fair land which sea and Alps surround,
and Apennine divides . . .", and spiritually in the common language, literature, culture, memories of the far-off time of freedom
from foreign yokes and of an Italian equilibrium, if not as a unit
or even a confederation, yet anyway as a system of republics,
Communes, domains, monarchies – this idea hovered aloft, as it
were, high up above the small and feeble political ideas of the
various Italian States. Sometimes, for brief moments, it seemed to
be poised in men's view, as though it might descend into earthly
reality. But no! It remained in the condition of a vague and passive aspiration, nay more often a sentimental and passive nostalgia
for the past. For sharing a land and sharing historical origins does
not of itself suffice to bring about a movement or a political form:
for that it must be linked to concrete interests, appetite for greater
prosperity, wealth, and power, tendencies towards a higher way of
life. Tendencies of this sort, ultimately springing from lively
ethical and religious ideas (for example the late eighteenth-century
rationalist and democratic idea, or the nineteenth-century liberal
historical ideal) were simply not at work in our period: there was
indeed as yet no sign of them. And the political and economic
interests of the Italian lands did not converge, but in part actually
conflicted. If for a moment the Italian idea seemed to become
impregnated with energy, when the rhetoric and the verses of
Tassoni, Testi, and so many others rang out at the time of Carlo
Emmanuele I of Savoy's uprising against Spain, this was all just a
device of suasion and argument turned to the ends of the particular
policy of a particular State, indeed of a single man who in his
thirst for greatness and glory nursed the successive ambitions of
becoming Duke of Milan, Lord of Genoa, Count of Provence,
King of France, King of Bohemia, and Roman Emperor. The
desires for freedom and independence then expressed were in a

subsequent age idealized in conformity with subsequent aspirations. But when they were uttered they were not thought incompatible with acceptance of the rule of France in certain parts of Italy in replacement of or offsetting that of Spain, and they are properly explained only in the light of the momentary politics of that time. And thus they evaporated without leaving any tradition behind them. It is altogether mistaken to try and link up with them the national movement of later centuries which began afresh on quite different grounds and with different ideas. For the same reason a history of Italy in the seventeenth century – or equally in the preceding and still more in the next succeeding centuries – cannot be told as an organic narrative, in fact strictly speaking it is not a single history with one subject passing through a unique development, but is just the sum of the various richer or poorer histories of the various Italian centres of life and States.

But patriotic zeal, political foresight, military valour were not wanting within those narrow limits: we must see what there was of them in Venice, in the circle of its statesmen and admirals, in the Duchy of Savoy, among the ministers and the local militias, in the breasts of certain active and gallant dukes, or in Tuscany of wise Grand Dukes of the Medici dynasty, and in some of the Roman Popes. We must recall also the Neapolitan, Sicilian, and Lombard gentlemen who commanded regiments or armies by commission of their kings, that is the Kings of Spain; the State officials and municipal representatives who administered business and justice as best they could, sometimes with wisdom. The ordinary people themselves were not always without a share in such strivings for the public weal, witness the defence of Cuneo and other Piedmontese lands, the resistance of the Genoese to the Duke of Savoy's attempt on the Republic by means of the Della Torre conspiracy, the wars of Venice against the Turks and the revolts of Naples and Messina. In these not only did the old war-cries of "Saint George!" and "Saint Mark!" ring out rousingly after long torpor, but also those of "The Royal Republic of Naples!" and "our ancient liberties" (of the citizens of Messina). The only apostles and martyrs that the Italy of those days could muster were among the makers of those uprisings and revolutions. They were men who personally felt some passion, some faith, and risked and lost their lives for it. Lawyers or ordinary townsmen, they cherished anachronistic hopes, they served antiquated ideas, morals, and institutions, but serve them they did. Apostles and martyrs Italy had produced in the sixteenth century and would produce copiously and of a high and noble order at the Risorgimento. Meanwhile in the sixteen-hundreds there were but the aforesaid modest people and no others: for apostles and martyrs do not spring up where the mood is of idle and quiet resignation and where no ideal cause tempers the valour of its adherents. Among the writers of those times there were sometimes men of some spirit and generosity, but in such conditions they did not rise to apostolic fervour but sank into sighs and regrets, bitterness and satire. Among those who did risk their skin not all were men of faith and rectitude, some were but rebellious and turbulent spirits, or landed in disaster as more or less solitary conspirators moved by personal rancours or the purposes of groups and factions. The great currents of politics were dried up: those which were watering the ground of other nations did not spill over into Italy nor did any spring forth spontaneously from Italian soil.

Once again we are brought back to consider the inner life, the religious life as it had been stabilized and rendered uniform by the Catholicism of the Counter-Reformation. The Italian dissenters had retreated to refuges in Protestant countries and were in ever dwindling numbers joined by further dissenters who usually embraced Calvinism. Hopes of forming inside Italy – and precisely in Venice, rendered suitable by that Republic's sustained conflict with Pope Paul V and the Interdict, and by the greater facility there of contacts with the Protestant countries and the freedom of entry given to books of all sorts – a hearth and home of the Reformation came to naught when that conflict drew to a close. The Venetian journeys and interviews of Diodati failed of their purpose. Paolo Sarpi, though joining in the Protestant outcry against the Papacy, and though his followers included such bold spirits as Fra Fulgenzio, held back from the decisive step both from political prudence and by personal inclination. In the nobility and among the highly educated Protestantism was still favoured and sometimes secretly entertained as by Loredano, but the more resolute spirits, De Dominis and Biondi, emigrated, and later on Gregorio Leti. Other developments, such as the mysticism and quietism of Molinos in Rome (severely repressed), had merely episodic importance. Orthodoxy reigned undisturbed, and without need of such numerous burnings at the stake as had been necessary in the latter fifteen-hundreds. But this orthodoxy, conservative in character, was timid. It did not breathe fervent and expanding faith but – behind disguises – an inner weakness. It feared free discussion and indeed feared to become too fully conscious of its own reasonings, and was thus incapable of arousing speculative thought, bold conceptions of practical renovation, or any purposes or steps tending to such ends. Now the Catholic Church had carried out no small reformation in the sphere of clerical and monastic discipline, and in education, profiting, in self-defence, by the suggestions of its adversaries. But since it had decisively repulsed every attempt to lead the souls of men back to that grand test of loneliness in the sight of God and humility in the presence of the divine Grace, what was best in the Reformation found no way of entry, and Catholic Orthodoxy assumed permanently that legalistic imprint, that character of externalism which the Jesuits carried to a particular extreme. The good results of this sort of religious practice were limited, necessarily, to an unquestionable checking of the excesses of wickedness and immorality, with the promotion of pious works for other-worldly ends, and of charitable works for softening the woes of this world. Churches, convents, monasteries, pious foundations of all sorts were multiplied in Italy. To some small extent they served for instruction and education of children and humble people, for aid to the hospitals, rehabilitation of fallen women, ransoming of captives: to a much greater extent for ceremonial worship and for the shamming, empty life of the monks' and friars' communities. Orthodoxy weighed too heavily on the mind of all for there to be any clear understanding of the damage that was being done. The inverted social economy was

supinely accepted, the very voice of satire ceased to tease priests
and monks; only a few compassionate people spoke up for those
young girls who were reft by their parents away from the rights
and duties of motherhood to fulfil a sterile destiny of superstitious
devotion to which often they were really condemned for covert
motives of worldly advantage and profit. The morality resulting
from this religious pressure was equally humiliating and repugnant,
a morality of bigotry which the satirists of the times, from Soldani
to Menzini, made their target, especially in Tuscany, where it
flourished most odiously. But what was worse, because more
general, was the coarsening of the conscience by bargains struck
between good and evil, duty and advantage, God and the world,
bargains too with that secretly operating kind of utilitarianism
behind the veil of religious forms. The Italians of the previous
century had been dubbed "pupils of Machiavelli", now they were
considered instead to be "pupils of the Jesuits" (or simply of the
priests). The two descriptions were not really altogether separate:
both of them fail to take account (and should therefore be disclaimed) of the innumerable examples of deep idealism and disinterested enthusiasm for the true and the good offered by the
Italians during the long centuries of their history and confound the
religious and moral usage of a particular age and local situation
with the whole of Italian history. This does not mean that there
was no need to probe the problem of the inner character and
consequences of so-called Catholic morality. This is a general
problem which it is proper to touch upon in this place because
this is the context in which its reality and seriousness can best be
understood. Consider the crude juxtaposition and alternation, in
the artistic output of those times, of sensual, lascivious fleshliness
and of the fear of God and dread of Hell: this is but one aspect of
a heteronomous morality which knew not how to accept natural
reality and to spiritualize and elevate that which it accepted. Above
all there should be recalled what has been said already of the
incapacity of this morality to furnish the principle of activity which
modern society called for – an activity not to be limited to the
sphere of shrewd behaviour, dexterity, comfort, or of religious

observance and charity, but expanding into the sphere of ethics, politics, and culture to display its productive prowess in each one of them. Thus the orthodoxy of the Counter-Reformation second-ed and abetted the Italian decadence and was itself an orthodoxy of decadence. And in that heavy decadence not a few had recourse, when they sought a higher way of life, to the doctrine of the age of decadence in antiquity, to Stoicism as they found it presented in the classical literature with which they were so familiar. Profess-ing Stoicism, they used Epictetus and Seneca as their devotional manuals, and it is in the light of this sort of seventeenth-century Stoicism that we can understand the rather bitter indifference towards politics and all human passions displayed by our ancestors of recent generations, and by them termed "philosophic".

There was but one live source of intellectual and moral elevation and this did not then flow abundantly or spill over in a widening and fruitfully refreshing stream, yet it was, as we know, present: the fount of thought, criticism, culture, flowing quietly yet de-veloping great energy in the range of the positive sciences, echoed in accents of veritably religious enthusiasm. "He who looks up-wards to the highest attains himself to the highest degree: and the way to look upwards is to contemplate the great book of nature, the object of philosophy." Thus Galileo, celebrating the human mind, the inexhaustible inventive faculty of man. With its usual shrewdness the Catholic Church spotted the danger which lay in these critical and scientific speculations and hedged them around with every sort of impediment and obstacle – prohibition of books from beyond the Alps, that is from free and Protestant lands, censorship of books printed in Italy, trial and punishment of the men of science. The letters of Paolo Sarpi, though he lived in Venice, which was still open to international influences and indul-gent to men of learning, are full of laments about the curtain thrown round Italy. The political satirists ironically praised the Ottoman monarchy, which forbade the use of the printing press. Panciatichi, a man of letters who travelled to Paris in 1670, wrote in surprise mingled with envy: "Here there is the greatest freedom of all sorts, scholars from all nations and great abundance of books." Then and for a long time to come the only foreign literatures known in Italy were the Spanish and the French. The Spanish, far the better known, brought no fresh and modern ideas, but was in this respect even poorer than the Italian, while the less known literature of France was still in the phase of reflecting Italian influence. The Italian curtain was so tightly closed that the political and religious controversies and the rationalist philosophizing of other countries passed wholly unnoticed. Yet the germ of modernity could not be wholly rooted out by the precautionary repressions and educative discipline of the Jesuits, intent upon lulling and distracting the Italian intellect: it kept on throwing up new shoots. There was no way for it but to close an eye and give some toleration to research in the field of physics and natural science, especially as some of the princes favoured such activities and there were even churchmen who employed themselves in such things. The old school, which stood firm upon the authority of traditional texts, watched in alarm and dared not open its mouth. So Italy, with the work of her critics and scientists, contributed to the formation, at home and abroad, of a new and modern sort of religiosity, in which lay the beginnings of a better Italian future. And there was progress too in the spiritual unification of Italy, partly in consequence of the Spanish hegemony itself, which worked against municipal particularism, partly through spontaneous developments in literature and culture. The fact that at this stage, for the first time, there was a flowering throughout Italy of dialect poetry is to be interpreted, not as a fresh outbreak of municipalism, but as a further manifestation of a unity which was reinforced by the reciprocal study and mutual applause accorded by each region to the products of the others.

We are speaking not of the conscious efforts of men, but of inevitable developments. The moralist can find very little of interest in the biographies, autobiographies, and letters of the sixteen-hundreds. There is little in the lives of even the most famous of those poets and authors beyond the details of their subservience to the various courts, the protection they enjoyed, the hostilities they encountered in careers unglorified by any serious purpose, unlit by any faith laying claim to their combative energies: very different lives from those of the few heroic spirits like Campanella, Sarpi, Galileo, made up of irresistible vocations, studies, explorations, discoveries, sustained struggles, travails, hardships, for these last were lives similar in some respects to those of the missionaries and Saints of the Church, and on some sides higher than these. But that Italian society as a whole lived sluggishly and feebly, the fewness of biographies of intimately dramatic character well attests.

To foreigners arriving in Italy, this seemed a country of leisure which in some moods they would regard as enviably pleasant, in others as vile and unworthy. This last was the judgement of the keenest spirits among the Italians themselves, often expressed in outbursts of impatience against the leisured life of *serva Italia*, that home of gossip and petty backbiting, while elsewhere men were thinking, doing, fighting, shedding blood and winning laurels. In this atmosphere arose the proverb of the Italian *dolce far niente* (unthinkable in respect of the active Italy of the Communes and the Renaissance) and that of the *nazione festaiola*, the carnival country. These words are still current, partly through the inertia of tradition, partly because these failings of the Italians have themselves become traditional and persist and sometimes become virulent. It would however be absurd to take them at their literal meaning or to understand "leisure" in the sense of physical idleness. Physically the Italians worked as much as other people, perhaps more, the peasants and herdsmen in their harsh poverty, the artisans, the professional men, officials, scholars, in fact all such as always have to work to get a living and to discharge their duties: in fact in their way the nobles and the courtiers also worked hard to win posts and promotion. The leisure of which the foreigners perceived the effects and the aspects and of which the best Italians were ashamed was the aforesaid spiritual leisure, the failure of their thought and their will to strike out and to carry to a more advanced condition the whole system of social relations. All else was and should be viewed as the mere consequence of this failure.

We are now in a position to comment upon the way of life of

that age with more justice. The headstrong conduct of the nobles, their gangs of henchmen, their crimes which often passed unpunished by authority, their euphemistically termed "honourable excesses", were by no means unparalleled in other European countries, being natural effects of strenuous but uncompleted attempts to subdue the individualistic knights and barons in line with modern conditions. In Italy, where the barons had in some cases never been disciplined, in other cases had taken a new lease of life as a semi-Spanish order, the State, which ought to have reduced them to equality of conditions with its other subjects, was usually weaker than in other countries, obliged to compromise and even to connive to the great harm of discipline: its severity was shown, implacably, only in the repression of political unrest and innovation. The same, or much the same, conditions account for the spread of banditry, brigandage, and crimes of violence. The nobles, having lost the reality of political power, clung all the more tightly to the old forms of antique chivalry and the point of honour, whence the Italian (and still more the Spanish) scene appeared to be dominated by pageantry, pride of lineage, disdain, snobbishness, subtle and spasmodic attention to codes of behaviour, squabbles about precedence, challenges and duels, to the exclusion of any more serious aspects. All this pomp, ceremony, circumstance, and accompanying superstition admirably matched the character of Catholicism after the Council of Trent. The grand plan was to feed the visual and other senses, to work upon the imagination, since there could be no question of nourishing the heart, the mind, the poetic fancy. Accordingly spectacles of all sorts, sacred and profane, were multiplied, processions, catafalques, illuminations, firework displays, tourneys, bullfights, tilting matches, automatons, triumphal arches, pasteboard statues, shows and emblems, while moved by similar intent the academies echoed with Baroque verses and playful dissertations on futile or absurd themes. Women were virtually excluded from the entertainments of society. No more did the ladies of spirit, as in the previous century, take a part, nor yet, for that matter, the cultured courtesans, while the fair disputants of the drawing-rooms of the next age were still to come.

Ladies versed in letters – were it only in theological and ascetic letters – landed up in convents. Thus little by little did Italy's reputation for serious intellectual achievement decline, while from such activities as we have just described the Italians acquired a repute as most cunning actors, singers, composers, decorators, and versifiers, for which they were either praised as a "nation of artists" or despised as "charlatans and buffoons".

This way of life in some respects came to an end, in other respects continued in a more refined style, with the changes at the end of the seventeenth century which we have described. Thus the merely playful academicians yielded place to those interested in enquiry and discussion; the cultivators of a frantic and tumid Baroque to placid and simple "Arcadians", the violent and sanguinary attitude to the mild and gallant; taking the law into one's own and one's henchmen's hands to the respect of sovereignty; priestly and monkish ubiquity to challenging of the ecclesiastical power, a resolute resistance to its usurpations, and the cult of royal authority; and finally passive acquiescence in existing things to criticism and the demand for reform. It was symbolic of this change that people should give up dressing "Spanish style" in favour of "French style", and should acquire instead of the Spanish tongue the French tongue, which had meanwhile, thanks to Descartes and Boileau, become the language of "reason" and "good taste". A new principle had been established, a new spirit had arisen: the way and the tone of living changed accordingly.

[1928]

VII

ARCADIA[1]

"ARCADIA" – the name sometimes excites scorn and derision, sometimes evokes images of peace and of the gentle thoughts and diversions of a peaceful existence. I will not linger much over the first and for a long time frequent association, still widely current, of which Baretti may not have been the originator but was certainly the most wrathful and sarcastic exponent, followed in this by the many who have felt it their duty to display virile disdain for the "languid bleatings" of the Arcadians. By contrast, eighteenth-century Arcadia has roused and rouses sentimental affection, for example, to cite one name, most dear to me, of one of the few genuine poets of our time, Salvatore di Giacomo, amorous and melancholic, sad and impassioned, bitter and tragic spirit who like the dream of a lost earthly paradise ever treasured the memory of Arcadia, the light lyrics of Metastasio and the pretty powdered faces well set off with patches. And I must confess that I too feel a certain tenderness for Arcadia. It was for me like revisiting an old haunt of familiar delight when for the first time I visited the villa on the Janiculum, and on long summer holidays in Perugia my favourite walk was to the "Frontone", where once upon a time in a sort of amphitheatre framed by trees, beside a still standing arch, the Arcadian group of that city used to meet, with "Lucilla Neomenica" (the Marchioness Anna Antinori) as their chief ornament, among other figures of the best Perugian society. Often I glance at the garlands of verses which they printed for their parties and celebrations, like this now in my hand, entitled *The Shepherdesses of Arcady*, for the marriage of Ferdinando di Borbone, Duke of Parma, with Maria Amelia Archduchess of Austria in 1769. For frontispiece it has a charming engraving: framed amid close twining trees and foliage, an elegant young shepherdess leans upon a rocky throne blowing quietly into her horn: at her feet are three

1. Speech given in Rome on November 24 1945 at the Biblioteca Angelica, for the inauguration of the academic year 1945-46 at Arcadia.

representatives of her flock. I feel inclined to repeat the excellent Latin of your backward-harking, reactionary, untamed fellow Arcadian Diego Vitrioli: "O festivam voluptatem, pecoribus istis denegatam, quibus unica gothica barbaries sapit. Placidior tum erat in beata morum simplicitate respublica, neque inconditae plebis vociferationibus stupebat Italia." Vitrioli was much delighted to be received amid the laurels of the Bosco Parrasio "acclamante universo Arcadum coetu", and I too, a quarter of a century ago, received with pleasure my Arcadian's diploma, linking me to a pleasure of the past.

It would be no use trying to submit these sympathies and antipathies, this praise and blame, to methodic discussion, for they are not logical judgements but various and contrasting sentiments springing from various and contrasting inclinations. And their object is not the historically real Arcadia, but the idealization of the sentiments. So let whoever will detest or desire Arcadia, and in Frederick II of Prussia's words find his own way of beatitude: we will not object to either choice. How could one presume to bid Salvatore di Giacomo refrain from idolizing his ladies Violante, Isabel, Bettina, those countesses and noblewomen who plucked at the harp, fingered the spinet, sang their little pieces, and flirted with knights and abbés? What if, on close inspection, these were a bit silly and affected? But for that matter how could one get between a nobly austere professor and his duty of despising and denouncing those spiritless Arcadians? How explain to him that they were not spiritless at all, since in that great national academy there was included the best Italian society, with the scientists, the statesmen, the leading warriors of the time, and finally many who in the ensuing revolutionary age became champions, heroes, and martyrs of liberty: while the acclaimed shepherdesses of Arcady were often the mothers and first tutors of the patriots of Italy.

But coming now to our real business of discussing Arcadia as an historic reality the first question is what meaning and importance this institution had in the public life, literary and ethical, of Italy? To this question we have a ready and universally agreed answer. Arcadia was the reaction against the mode of the Baroque which had for over a century dominated Italian letters and behaviour, and this mode was routed thanks to a union of well-disposed intelligences from one end of Italy to the other, all intent upon substituting on every hand a serious and measured expression of feeling and thought for the Baroque cult of the "amazing", with its empty and artificial entwinement of images and swollen profusion.

We are, however, attending rather too exclusively to Italy. We should take a wider look at the general European movement of which Arcadian proceedings in Italy were but a single case and illustration. That movement in the intellectual sphere was Rationalism. During the seventeenth century it had carried the leadership of European culture away from Italy and over to France and England, whence it now returned to the country which had prepared the way for it with the brilliance of Humanism and the Renaissance and had furnished, as forerunners and initiators, those apostles of natural religion and of the natural law who went for this faith into exile from an Italy which meanwhile fell back under the oppression of absolutism and the Counter-Reformation. The first great speculative assertion of the movement was the philosophy of Descartes. Rationalism meant in practice war against everything that survived of mediaeval thought, institutions, and folkways, reforms in every department of life to meet the needs of the opening new age, and these reforms claimed rationality by contrast with a past which was deemed irrational. The Baroque mode which meanwhile dominated Italy, Spain, and Germany, but had manifestations also elsewhere including France and England, was nothing else but the continuation in utmost exaggeration of the elaboration and conventionality dear to the Middle Ages. (The habit of regarding these as barbaric led to the attribution to them of a spontaneity and simplicity beyond the truth, for barbarians in fact love to hang ornaments around themselves and set great store by the glitter of coloured beads.) There is a thread running right through from the mannerism of the Provençals and of Petrarch to that of the school of Marino, the poets of Baroque conceit, and it was against this that Rationalism proffered a simple,

orderly, and limpid style of writing, in which it was assisted by
Arcadia. Indeed, as some if not all of its adherents were aware,
Arcadia learned lessons from Descartes and played a more effective
part in preparing the modern age than was the case with Humanism
and Evangelical Reformism, and without abatements of energy
or changes of course. The Rationalism of which Arcadia was the
literary manifestation exercised a more profoundly beneficial influence in Italy than in France and England. In these countries it
marked a continuation and intensification of public progress already in action, but for Italy, after a hundred years of Counter-
Reformation, Jesuitism, abstention from public life, it marked the
crisis of decadence and the beginning of national resurgence, of
the "Risorgimento" which first showed itself in the spheres of the
reform of letters, developments of legal and economic theory, a
change in the State's outlook on the Church, the growth of civil
law, the introduction into governmental posts previously as good
as reserved for the privileged aristocracy of the class of educated
men. Arcadia was not, indeed, the originator of this new life, but
sprang from the same womb, and because of this kinship the most
intelligent and energetic society of the time from circles active in
public life was to be found amicably assembled in the Arcadian
haunts. It suffices to mention that Giambattista Vico adhered under
the name of Eufilo Terio, while in January 1787 Wolfgang Goethe,
already admired in Italian literary quarters as the author of the
passionately studied *Werther*, smilingly took his seat under the
names of "Megalio", a tribute to his greatness, and "Melpomenio",
because his eminence lay in the higher order of poetry. Among the
Neapolitan patriots of 1799 the heroic Eleonora de Fonseca Pimentel entered Arcadia as "Altidora Esperetusa".

The reformation of literary expression accomplished by Arcadia
cannot in a historical assessment be placed merely on the same
level as earlier or later linguistic and stylistic movements, such as
that of the Purists against what was neither pure nor precise, but
disagreeably slack and generic in eighteenth-century prose, or
that of the Romantics pitting their love of pathos and violent
colour against a bloodless classicism, or again the school of

Manzoni favouring a subdued tone and an everyday language in reaction from the overblown style of the academies, or finally that return to the rich and variegated tradition of Italian speech urged by Carducci against what he called the "Manzonianism of the Stenterellos". All these limited or occasional movements had their reason and momentary value, not to be compared, however, with the lasting and substantial victory which was won for the elementary notion that speech and the written word exist for the sake of expressing feelings and thoughts, not for making amusing and ingenious combinations or, as a contemporary critic of the Baroque put it, "mere noble buffoonery" ("noble" being here used for false conception of nobility). And against this victory there arose no reaction: it permanently purified the aesthetic judgement of the Italians, at least up to the present time, keeping them on the alert and suspicious in face of any renewal of the Baroque mode, whether, as in the time of my youth, in the shape of D'Annunzio's lushly sensual amateurism (how quickly the Italians got over their passion for him), or as more recently when imitating foreign models there was a vogue for "pure poetry" or deliberate "hermeticism" in prose or verse. Against such resuscitated Ludovico Leporeos one would fain call in the help of the original Arcadia and first and foremost of the most chaste and Hellenic "Opico Erimanteo" – Gian Vincenzo Gravina.

Now if this has been a right account of its history, why has there been and is there still so much scorn and disdain directed against Arcadia, as shown by the belittling use often made of its name? What justice lies in such a valuation? There must be some element of justice in a valuation which is itself part of history. And once this is properly understood, as it behoves us to understand it, should we acquiesce in it? The answer is that just because Arcadia caused streams, nay floods of verse to course through Italy, it became the symbol of the absence of poetry, of verses which are not poetry but usurp the place and the aspect of poetry. Naturally therefore Arcadia has been disliked, derided, and deprecated by champions standing in the ranks of the truly poetic – disliked in proportion to its diffusion.

This is an irrefutable fact. Arcadia did not create poetry and never produced a single poet of those who for the power and complexity of their work are called "great". There is, however, something more to the true story than that, and we have still to reach our judgement upon it. Arcadia was born and flourished in the age of rationalism as the manifestation and instrument of this movement: and the reason why true poetry was lacking and its place taken by verses of non-poetic intent in Arcadia was that this was the characteristic of the age itself, and its limitation. For this greatly progressive age, like all ages, all historical movements, indeed every work of man, had its historical limits. Each one is something in particular and by the same token is not something else: it is a *determinatio* comporting a corresponding *negatio*.

Where Reason is crowned Queen, there must be a fading out of myths, a rebellion against every affirmation made on the strength not of ratiocination, but of the inertia of traditional beliefs or of authoritarian dictation from without. There must be a perpetual reference back to the criticism of the thinking mind, with rejection of any revelation other than the self-revelation of the thinking mind and of all faith that has not become thought. But intellect, or ratiocinating reason, has here its own limit. For it accompanies and ever illuminates, but can never create the other forces which enter into the tissue of life, such forces being morality, which can result only from free moral inspiration; poetry, which, rising above love and grief, finds its repose in the calmness of beauty; and one must even add philosophy, which is not mere ratiocination, but requires the speculative faculty which alone can light upon and present and resolve spiritual problems and is, though not identical with, yet closely akin to the faculty of poetry. And so the century which followed upon the triumph of Rationalism and saw all in rationalistic terms was not poetic, nor yet in any true sense philosophical, as is obvious from consideration of the schools of sensism, materialism, empiricism which supplied its substitute for philosophy, and from the hedonistic and utilitarian character of its ethics, and indeed also from the very abuse it made of the word "philosophy", which it assigned to every sort of small and superficial reflection. By contrast that century was great in mathematics and physics, and cultivated even the moral sciences by the naturalistic method, thence deriving the precepts and formulas needful for programmes of political and social reform. Hence its rationalism was charged with being irreligious, or again anti-historical, or sceptical and irreverent towards the epic and tragic history of man. Right at the beginning of the century Vico discerned this character and traced in negative terms its inevitable future course. And it turned out as he foretold. The century devoted itself, not to the deepening, but to the popularization of knowledge, to compiling dictionaries and encyclopaedias. It was unpoetical and mathematicist, losing sight of the concrete in its keenness for the abstract. In vain did Vico invite his contemporaries to return to the researches and meditations of history, this and not outer nature being the true *regnum hominis*. It was only at the very end of the century that the speculative spirit arose, like a strong man shaking off an inebriation, and by the agency of Kant subjected physical and mathematical science to critical enquiry, demonstrated the ineffectuality of the intellectualistic logic when faced with the problems of reality, and reinstated moral conscience and spiritual beauty in the places whence they had been dislodged by the utilitarians and the aesthetic hedonists.

Meanwhile there were neither great philosophers nor great poets. Italy's last great poet had been Tasso, France's Racine, England's had been Shakespeare or at all events Milton, Spain's Cervantes and Lope de Vega, while Germany had as yet hardly appeared on the poetic stage. Poetic geniuses, it is true, follow upon each other at a distance of centuries or sometimes millenaries. But this century was notably defective even in the feeling for poetry. Thus learned researches and interpretations were concentrated on Dante's works (the Baroque century neglected to do even this), but the poetry was neither understood nor liked, and drew derision and contempt from men of renown. New editions of Shakespeare's works were initiated, but he was hardly better treated than Dante. Only at the end of the century, with the Romantic movement, did his direct influence upon the hearts and minds of men begin. The century brought to its fullness the "Homeric Question", a complex of problems of scholarship, but the most expert Homeric scholar in Italy – Cesarotti – not only translated Homer into prose and verse to fit the taste of the century, but deemed Ossian as invented by Macpherson – that Ossian who is now remembered simply as an example of the power of an illusion to rouse human devotion towards the non-existent – altogether superior to Homer. Keen judges of poetry were wanting. Of the major British critic, Samuel Johnson, it has been shrewdly said that he understood whole numbers but not fractions, and that he could only appreciate the prosaic element in poetry. And indeed the presentation of prose as the ideal for poetry, the praise of poetical works in the measure of their nearness to prose, are deliberate with Montesquieu, Fontenelle, Buffon, D'Alembert, and the basis of often repeated appreciations. Strange to say this was the moment when enquiries into the aesthetic pleasures and taste were being carefully pursued, and when the theory of Art and Beauty was receiving from the Leibnizian school the name of "Aesthetics", destined to widespread acceptance. But those enquiries, which were much bound up with the sensist and intellectualist conceptions, were unconnected with any love or knowledge of poetry in its clearness and intensity. Here Vico must once again be mentioned as an exception: he had a sublime theory of poetry which he found impersonated, sublimely, in Homer and Dante. The poet who pleased the critics of the times was on the contrary Horace, coupled with the modern Horace, Alexander Pope. Typical in this is Kant, whose singular insight and vigorous speculation enabled him to deliver correct and original views on the theory of taste, but to discourse upon art seemingly without any contact with poets or artists. Nor could he ever shake off the idea that art was a co-operation between the intellect and the imagination.

In a mental climate thus doubly alienated from poetry what could be the part of Arcadia? Simply to do what was then done in every part of Europe: to produce a clear and graceful pseudo-poetry in facile verse and rhyme, and in decorous blank metre.

This output was literary in character, partly erotic and gallant in
the phraseology of elegant conversation, partly gay or satirical,
partly didactic in its adornment of scientific and moral themes – a
last conventional echo of the Virgilian *Georgics*. There was also
the celebratory type of composition, "d'occasion" as it was rightly
called, serving various occasions, and one could add to this classification or further subdivide it. Other critics have analysed and
described all this pseudo-poetry and accounted for its difference
from true poetry by the prevalence in it not of the fancy but of
the intellect. I should like particularly to recall some fine pages in
Housman's 1933 lecture, *The Name and Nature of Poetry*. It is
unnecessary to repeat here or to enlarge upon these analyses. But
one injustice has been committed, erroneously, and as the result
of an error. As a retort to those who have been beguiled into
regarding this literature as poetry, and would fain praise it as such
or as one of the sorts of poetry, it may be well to affix the term
"pseudo-poetry". But this is just the denial of a quality, not a positive definition. The rebuttal of an incorrect description is no
reason for rebutting the thing incorrectly described. For be what
it may the thing is there, giving pleasure and having its own value,
on account of which it is admitted to rank as literature. Housman
too says that much of this literature is excellent, admirable, and
enjoyable. It may be called mere diversion and pastime, but as
such, finding its literary shape, it recognized and respected the
rules of art, the rules of beauty. For this it obtained legitimate applause and praise which we should not and will not withhold on
our own part. It is a sign of this that within its own compass we
distinguish what is fine literature and what is poor literature,
what succeeds and what fails, the better and the worse Arcadia.
Some well-known specialists in the poetry of the seventeen-
hundreds join in the accepted fashion of habitually referring to
Arcadia in tones of irony, of derisive pity, and this seems to me
tedious, unjust, and even rather stupid. It is not to be justified either
as a rejoinder or sanction for the presumption of the Arcadian
writers. They were not presumptuous, but often themselves explained what they wanted to do and would have done if they

could. Thus Annibale Mariotti, one of the Arcadians who met beneath the mild Umbrian skies at the Frontone in Perugia (he was indeed their leader, the Apollo at the head of their choir), shrank from the very temptation to attempt a poetry of rapture and ecstasy. Disclaiming, in certain hendecasyllables of his, such ethereal inspiration as might "lift me out of myself and let me see and speak only things high and new of bright imagination born", he asked the Muses to open for him "an easy path befitting my slow mind".

> Non io però fin dall'eteree sedi
> un foco agitator chiamo e desio
> che l'irritabil core ecciti a moti
> troppo vividi e spessi, e, per gli occulti
> del cerebro recessi arbitro errando,
> l'ordin vi turbi delle impresse forme,
> e me tolga a me stesso, ond'io non vegga
> e non parli che cose altère e nove,
> sol da un ardente immaginar create,
> tal ch'io me poco, ed altri non m'intenda.
> Piano sentier, qual si conviene al pigro
> debile ingegno mio, m'aprite, o Muse!

Carlo Innocenzo Frugoni, almost the highest master of the Arcadian poetry in Italy, for his part displayed an almost fierce sincerity in regard to himself. More than once when too much praised and loaded with honours he exclaimed: "Who am I? Just a versifier, and not a poet, which name, usurped by many, is deserved by only the few who had a heavenly mind and a tongue to utter great things." Yes, when we open these men's verse books we should do so with a kindlier and more intelligent approach, like that with which Eduard Mörike greeted the Anacreontic or Arcadian poet of Germany a century before, Brockes: "Lead me, old man, still through your rococo garden: its flowering growth is dewy, fresh, and perfumed still."

I shall be asked whether the distinction between true poetry and the eighteenth-century intellectualistic "poetry" is definite and absolute. Were there no poetic voices in Italy in the two centuries after Tasso? Well, what must always be absolute and definite is simply the criterion of judgement, without which we could not think at all. The facts, the history, are on the contrary always various and changeful, and nothing essential to the human mind is ever anywhere wholly wanting in it. And so, up and down the Arcadian century, poetic accents were to be heard now loudly and now softly, and the voices of antiquity also were heard again. But for great poetry Germany had to await Goethe, France Alfred de Vigny, Italy Alfieri and Foscolo. The understanding of poetry returned truly with the Romantic movement. It behoves us critics to discern the poetic tones even when they are rare, and for my small part I have not shirked the task but have found them not only in Metastasio, but in Rolli, Vittorelli, and Tommaso Crudeli, in Manfredi, and even in him whom Baretti termed the "cloying, flirtatious, over-sugared" Zappi, of whom there are poems that one must frankly call beautiful. I have also drawn attention to the more active presence in Italy of classically educated opponents of the light, unimaginative, and unfanciful style of poetry: though few and far between, they raised the rival standard of the Greek, Latin, and Italian antique. There is this also to be said. The Arcadian literature cannot be charged with neglecting form, indeed it took pains that the form should be smooth and correct, and debated the matter academically. But it was natural that it should fall for superficial and conventional modes of expression by the suggestion of the very arguments which it handled. It was not just chance, either, that the Arcadian century was the great age of the improviser, when great improvisers rose to a sort of monstrous rivalry with great poets and were even given the supposed due of the great poets – a laurel wreath on the Capitol. Very few, as always, were those who, though remaining intellectualistic and literary writers, were exquisite artists, makers of perfect verse. There was Boileau in France and Pope in England. Italy too had one such, to whom for moral and patriotic motives a higher rank may have been attributed than what was due to him: Giuseppe Parini, author of *Il Giorno*. Recent criticism has accorded him his rightful and still proud position. Parini, of whom Carducci said that he always kept "one foot in Arcadia", really belonged there altogether. He was a most accomplished maker of eighteenth-century poetry, poetry whether of love and intrigue or gnomic, didactic, satirical. Never did his verses shine forth with "piercing shafts of truth and grandeur" such as, in Parini's own words, Vittorio Alfieri conjured up "from those dark regions where the feelings reign". Nevertheless his merit was such that Arcadia should celebrate it as its own highest peak, and Parini remains a glory of Italian literature of the same order as Pope in the literature of England.

[1945]

VIII

INTRODUCTION TO THE HISTORY
OF EUROPE IN THE NINETEENTH CENTURY

I

THE RELIGION OF LIBERTY

THE Napoleonic adventure was over. The despotic genius had left the stage which he had been filling with his presence. His conquerors were agreeing or trying to agree and to co-operate for the replacement of the strongly managed but ever precarious imperial domination of the French nation over Europe with a stable arrangement, to which end old regimes were being restored and territorial possessions readjusted. At that moment the hopes of the peoples were high and demands rose on every side for independence and freedom. The more these were met with denial and repression, the more energetically and passionately they were renewed. The hopes blazed up afresh, the resolves hardened, as they encountered disappointment and defeat.

In such countries as Germany, Italy, Poland, Belgium, Greece, and the distant colonies of South America the oppressed nations were straining and heaving against their foreign dominators. There were agitations on the part of nations which were wholly or partly assigned to a forced union with States which had acquired them by conquest, treaty, or dynastic inheritance, and there were agitations against the enforced splintering of nations into a multiplicity of small States whereby they felt themselves hampered, enfeebled, and disqualified for the part they were entitled to play in the world, lowered in dignity by comparison with nations that were united and powerful. Furthermore, these and other nations were clamouring for guarantees of civil rights, for a share in administration and government to be exercised by new or revived representative bodies, for freedom of association, for promotion of the economic, social, or political purposes of private citizens, for freedom of the press to discuss ideas and interests, for "Constitutions", as they had come to be called. Where such constitutions had been granted as a concession, as in France, the demand was for guarantees of their permanence and widening of their scope, and where, as for example in England, representational government was in being as the result of a long and gradual formation, it was for the removal of some remaining liens and bondages and for a general speeding and rationalization to suit a brisker and more progressive manner of life.

The various peoples were sprung from different historical origins, were living in different conditions, with different mental dispositions and habits: and accordingly the aforesaid demands had a different order of importance, a different scope and intricacy and tone of urgency in the one or in the other country. In one what seemed most urgent was liberation from the foreign yoke or national unity; in another the attainment of constitutional instead of absolute government. In one country electoral reform and the extension of political eligibility was the need, in another an entirely new or remodelled representative system. In some countries civil equality and religious toleration were acquisitions already inherited from earlier generations, notably from the recent Revolutionary and Imperial transformations of Europe, so that what remained to be wrested was the admission of fresh social classes to the work of government. Elsewhere it was still necessary, as the first step, to combat the civil and political privileges of feudal classes, to eliminate servitudes, and to shake off burdens of ecclesiastical oppression. With all these differences in urgency and timing, the demands were all linked together and the attainment of one led to the pressure of another and, in the distance, of yet others to come. There was a word which summed up the entire number of them and expressed the spirit behind them: the word was "Liberty".

This was not a word new in history, or in literature and poetry, or for that matter in the rhetoric of letters and art. There had descended from Greece and Rome the memory of numberless heroes of liberty, with tales of the noble and tragic events in which life itself, however dear, had been sacrificed to a liberty still dearer to great hearts. The Christians, and all through history the Christian churches, had invoked liberty, so too the Communes struggling against Emperors and Kings, the feudal lords and barons also against Emperors and Kings, while the Emperors and Kings had claimed to be contending for liberty in resisting the lords, the barons, and the corporations which strove to usurp sovereign rights. Kingdoms, provinces, or cities, mindful of their own parliaments and charters and privileges, championed liberty against the absolute monarchies engaged with or without success in overthrowing such obstacles and limitations. Loss of liberty had always been considered a reason or a sign of decadence in the arts, the sciences, the economy, the morality of societies, whether that of Imperial Rome or that of Spanish and Papal Italy. And yet, just the other day, "Liberty" in company with "Equality" and "Fraternity" had like an earthquake shaken to ruin the structure of old France and of almost the whole of old Europe, the dreadful impression of which events had not yet passed away but seemed to have tarnished the charm and freshness of the ideal. And indeed the trinity of ideals in which "Liberty" was thus associated – "Reason's immovable and deathless triad", as the poet Vincenzo Monti hymned it – fell into discredit and wellnigh into odium. Liberty, however, detached from those companions, soon rose anew upon the horizon like a star of matchless brilliance. And the name of Liberty was uttered by the younger generations with the heartfelt admiration that goes out to a freshly discovered idea of vital importance for the understanding of past and present and for finding the way into the future.

For indeed the name of Liberty, ancient as it was, became filled with a new ideal content, and this was not only felt but was pondered by the men of that time, as is shown by the problem which they soon found themselves considering, what was the differentiating characteristic of the liberty of the moderns compared with that of the ancient Greeks and Romans and that of the Jacobins of the other day. Among the first to take up this problem were Sismondi and Benjamin Constant. Constant developed it in an address to the Paris Athenaeum in 1819. They were the first of many to do so up to our present times. There was a kernel of reality in the problem though the contrast was drawn with faulty crudeness between an ancient conception held by the Greeks and Romans and their supposed imitators the Jacobins, and that of the moderns; as though the present were not the resultant and latest consequence of the whole of history and as though the single flow of development could be thus broken by a static counterposition of old and new. Thus the enquiry which started from the assertion of that contrast tended to lose itself in abstractions, sundering the individual from the State, civil liberty from political liberty, liberty of the one individual from the liberty of all the other individuals limiting it; whereupon political liberty without civil liberty was assigned to the ancients, civil without political, or with only a subordinate degree of political, to the moderns; or, contrarily, attributing to the ancients a higher degree of liberty for the individual in relation to the State than that enjoyed by the moderns. Such faulty abstractions will always arise when Liberty is defined in terms of legal distinctions having a practical character and reference to particular impermanent institutions instead of to the superior and indeed supreme idea which embraces and surpasses all institutions.

The content of the concept of liberty being something which must be sought in its rightful historical location, that is in the history of "thought" or "philosophy", we can say that when the men of that time became aware that the content was somehow novel, their awareness was really of nothing less than a novelty in the mind and life of men. There was a new concept of humanity and the way ahead looked wider and more visible than ever before. This was no sudden or casual achievement of thought, no position attained by a leap or a swoop, but the reward of the secular labours of philosophical tests and conclusions. By dint of this, the distance had been progressively narrowed and the conflict progressively appeased between Heaven and Earth, God and World, Ideal and Real. Ideal quality had been recognized in the real and real quality in the ideal, and with this there was recognized the unbreakable unity, the identity of the two. But the history of thought and philosophy includes for us the whole of history, so-called civil, political, economic, or moral. They mutually sustain each other. The concept of liberty derived then not only from the history of Plato, Aristotle, Galileo, Descartes, Kant, but from the history of the Greek struggle against the barbarian world, Rome's civilizing Romanization of the barbarians, the Christian redemption, the Church's struggle against the Empire, the contests of the Italian and Flemish Communes in the Middle Ages, the Renaissance and the Reformation which signally vindicated the value of individuality, the one in point of efficacy and the other in point of morality; and then again from the history of the wars of religion, the English "Long Parliament", the championship of freedom of conscience by the religious sects in England, Holland, and the American colonies, the American proclamations of the Rights of Man, the further declaration which the French Revolution implemented so strikingly, and finally all the technical discoveries with the resulting transformation of methods of production. All these events and creative movements of history, with others, helped to form the new conception of reality and humanity, finding the law and the rule of all things in the things themselves, and finding God in the world. However, the last stage in the progression, then just accomplished, had been quite outstandingly decisive, indeed almost conclusive. In it the dissension between Reason and History, inflamed in the course of eighteenth-century Rationalism and the French Revolution, so that contempt and repudiation of History had come to be proclaimed in the name of Reason, was subjected to criticism. The criticism had been efficacious, and the dissension abated, thanks to the dialectical way of thought. This way of thought does not sunder the infinite from the finite or the positive from the negative, and therefore it had led to the meeting of the real and the rational in the new idea of History. The full meaning of Vico's saying that the Republic sought by Plato was nothing else than the course of human affairs could now be understood. Mankind no longer felt crushed by history and no longer rose in rebellion to assert its own rights against a history and a past that needed to be shaken off as shameful. Rather did mankind now see itself as the true and unwearying author of a world history which was like the mirror reflecting its own life. History seemed no longer devoid of spirituality and abandoned to blind forces, nor yet requiring to be underpinned and progressively redressed by extraneous forces, but manifestation and actualization of the Spirit, and so, since the Spirit is Liberty, the work of liberty. Yes, altogether the work of liberty, with liberty for its sole and eternal positivity, actualized solely in the forms of history and conferring a meaning upon these, thereby explaining and justifying in the only possible way the function of the negativity, that is of unfreedom with its succession of thwartings, oppressions, reactions, tyrannies, which in Vico's language look like tempests driving down, but are really winds of opportunity.

Such was the thought and philosophy of the age that was then beginning, one which sprang up and found its way everywhere and was on the lips of all, as witness the stanzas of the poets and the phrases of the men of action no less than the formulas of the professional philosophers. In its wake there might follow some debris of the past. In the manner of its presentation there might be incongruities. It might fall into contradictions. But it was the philosophy which went ahead and outdistanced all others. The marks of it may be found even in the works of its very adversaries, backward-looking, reactionary, clerical, Jesuitic. There is some irony in the fact that this new spiritual outlook took its name from the unlikeliest place, from Spain, the European country which had most of all closed its doors against modern philosophy and culture, remaining pre-eminently mediaeval and scholastic, clerical and absolutist. For it was Spain which dubbed the new way of thinking *liberal* by contrast with *servil*. And here it is well to emphasize what is so often overlooked, that the philosophy of an age is to be sought not solely in the works of its philosophers or the greatest among them, but must be gathered from all that age's manifestations. Indeed in the specialists, however great, of philosophical studies, it is sometimes not found at all or only dimly. For they are after all individuals who may do some work on the problems of their own times but then pass beyond to an anticipatory statement and resolution of problems which their own times are not yet aware of, or capable of fully grasping. And conversely because of the usual individual limitations they may fail to include in their systematic thought certain problems which their own times have stated and resolved. In their place they may have retained erroneous and antiquated thoughts. Great philosophers, like all sorts and conditions of men, have no specially reserved places in the van or the middle ranks or the rear of their contemporaries but are found sometimes in the one and sometimes in the other. The great philosophers of free Athens, fine flower of Athenian liberty, were not in their philosophizing abreast of the vital realities of their day, being too much put off by democratic agitations which offended their sense of harmony, and too much involved in naturalistic logic. But the case best fitted to be cited here will be that of Hegel, the greatest philosopher of the age now under consideration, the profoundest theorist of dialectics and history, the identifier of Liberty with the Spirit and the Spirit with Liberty. For all this he merited, because of certain inclinations and political conceptions, to be called *servil* rather than *liberal*. In this respect thinkers of less philosophical stature or even some of either sex who are not considered philosophical at all, such as Madame de Staël, stand much above him.

The conception of History as the history of liberty was necessarily matched in the sphere of conduct by the affirmation of liberty itself as the ethical ideal. It was the ideal, in fact, which had developed in close relation to the ponderings and stresses of civilization as a whole, passing, in modern times, from the conception of liberty as a complex of privileges to liberty seen as natural right, and from this envisagement as abstract natural right passing on to envisagement as spiritual liberty of the historically concrete personality. Thus developing, the ideal had become progressively coherent and healthy, with the approval of the parallel philosophical movement which held that the law of being must also be the law of right being. The ideal could be denied only by those who in one way or another still saw right being as something alien from being, according to the old tenets of transcendental philosophy, or by those who introduced this alienation into their argu-

ments without understanding what they were doing. Let us consider two types of objection that were manifested. It was objected
that the ethical ideal of liberty neither authorized nor itself promised to root out the evil that is in the world, and therefore, it was
said, this ideal is not ethical. What this overlooks is that if morality
were to root out the very idea of evil it would itself fade away,
since morality's sole vitality and reality consists in the struggle
against evil, and its sole glory. And again, it was objected that the
affirmation and acceptance of an ever renewed struggle meant the
denial to mankind of the peace, happiness, blessedness which is the
eternal human aspiration. Here what is overlooked is the very
greatness of the modern conversion of the sense of life from the
idyllic (and consequently elegiac) to the dramatic tone; from the
hedonistic (and consequently pessimistic) to the active and creative;
with liberty itself viewed as perpetual recapture and perpetual
liberation, perpetual battle in which no final victory is conceivable
because such a victory would mean the death of all the combatants,
that is, of all living beings. With this in mind it is easy to see the
insignificance of other objections which were at that time and
later and up to the present moment frequently repeated, as, for
example: that the ideal of liberty, in virtue of its very excellence,
is for the few, the elect, and not for the many, the mass, who have
need of impositions from on high, authority, chastisement. Such an
assertion is precisely parallel to one of which the absurdity is
obvious: that truth is for the few and that for the many non-truth,
error is needful – as though truth were not truth in virtue precisely
of its intrinsic capacity to expand, to enliven, to transform wherever, in developing conditions, it is able to arrive. Here is a still
more extravagant objection: that liberty is the rightful property of
certain peoples which in very special circumstances have evolved
it, for example of the insular English, or of noble-blooded strains
like the Germanic, which cultivated it in the culturelessness of
their forests. This is an argument which degrades spirit to the level
of matter and submits it to a mechanical determinism. And the
objection is furthermore belied by the facts. England, for example,
was in many respects a teacher, but also in many respects a learner

of liberal thought from the continental peoples. Germany for a long while forgot its sylvan liberty and idolized authority and subjection.

What was the ideal of the new generations? The answer was conveyed quite simply and without need of further precision by the word "liberty". Further elaborations would have merely dimmed the idea, whatever erroneous objections were raised by frigid and superficial people when in their surprise and mockery at what they considered an empty abstraction they asked ironically and sarcastically: "What is liberty? Liberty of whom and from what? Liberty to act how?" But the word was too inwardly infinite to suffer epithets or empirical exactitudes, which did not mean, however, that limits were not spontaneously set in its self-realization. It was indeed by such acts of liberty that the concept became particular and acquired a content. But the distinction often made between "singular" and "plural" liberty, liberty and liberties, proves to be a mere incompatibility of abstractions since "liberty" exists solely as "liberties". However, no particularization of liberty, no institution arising out of it, ever sums up and exhausts liberty, which it is impossible to define in juridical terms, that is in terms of institutions, and moreover cannot even be considered as linked with institutions by a logical necessity. For they are historical facts, and therefore are attached to or detached from the concept solely by a historical necessity.

We have broadly enumerated the political demands which at that time approximately constituted the historical embodiment of liberty – embodiment, one might say, in a fine and rejuvenated condition making for heartiness and heedlessness. Embodied spirituality, spiritualized embodiedness, significant solely in regard to the end towards which they tended, the end of a wider scope, a greater intensity and extension, for the life of Man. The idea of nationality took shape in opposition to the abstract humanitarianism of the eighteenth century and to the insensitiveness shown even by writers of the stature of Lessing, Goethe, and Schiller, towards the idea of people and native land, the indifference shown by their generations to foreign occupations. It tended to the advancement of

mankind in the concreteness of personality, whether the personality of single men or that of groups of men having common origins
and memories, habits and attitudes, in a word of nations historically existent and active or potentially active. There was nothing in
the idea of nationality necessarily inimical to the formation of ever
larger and more comprehensive national bodies, for "nation" is a
spiritual, historical, evolutionary concept, not, like "race", a statically scientific notion. Even when leadership or primacy was claimed
for this or that people, as by Fichte and others for the Germans,
Guizot and others for the French, Mazzini and others for the
Italians, and certain Poles or Slavs for Poland or the whole Slav
branch, the lesson taught was that the people in question had the
right and the duty of taking the lead as the standard-bearer guiding all the peoples to civilization, human perfection, spiritual
greatness. The German nationalists might say that the German
was a chosen people, but hastened to add that it was such in its
cosmopolitan, not its narrowly national character. Constitutions
and representative governments were intended to bring into the
labours and achievements of politics more capable and strong-
willed men and classes than those who had previously alone exercised these, and who would now have to meet the competition of
the newcomers. The free press offered the field for the exchange
of ideas, the clash and weighing-up of passions, the clarification
of situations. In its pages disputes and agreements were made
manifest: it was, as was pertinently observed, the medium whereby the Great States, Europe, and the whole World performed the
functions for which the small States of antiquity maintained their
Agora. The system of a parliament containing two great parties,
conservative and progressive, moderate and radical, Right and
Left, enjoyed a wide approval which revealed the disposition to
control the impetus of social change for the avoidance of revolutionary upheavals and bloodshed, the competition of interests
being rendered mild and humane. Local autonomies were defended
or demanded with keen sensitiveness against the centralizing and
absolute character first of the rule of the Revolution and of the
Empire, and then of the restored monarchies. It was feared that

centralization reducing all to a dead level would impoverish and desiccate the flow of life, when by contrast local autonomies would secure better administration and would better bring forward the political gifts of oncoming generations. Constitutional monarchies on the English model struck a balance between the excessive historicity of the absolute monarchies and the deficient historicity of the Republics. They were recommended as the only sort of Republic suitable to those times, for the old-style political theorists held that England's Government after the Glorious Revolution was Republican, not Monarchical. The revival of historical traditions was in every sphere inspired by the desire to assemble and preserve all that could continue to be useful, all that was not going to be dead wood, in the modern age or for the next stretch ahead: regional institutions and usages, the old nobility, peasant ways, naive religious beliefs. The throwing down of the barriers which were then hampering (or had once hampered) industry and trade was designed to stimulate individual inventiveness and pluck and competition, and to augment riches which, by whoever they were produced and owned, were still the riches of society as a whole and in one way or another, sooner or later, would always come round to serving the ends of society, its interests and its moral elevation. Those various demands, then, in the shapes and detailed forms which they took, converged all in the same sort of purposiveness.

Quite possibly, of course, or rather quite certainly, some or many of these liberal institutions, when in the course of history conditions ceased to call for them, would perish while others would become ineffective, inadequate, unsuitable. They would then have to be altered or even scrapped and replaced by others. But that is what happens to all the concerns of men: they live and die, change and recover, become merely mechanical and antiquated. But when this should happen to these institutions, the agent of change, readaptation, and consignment to the scrapheap would be once again Liberty, and the process would be one of Liberty finding a fresh and more youthful or more maturely robust embodiment. Thus it was altogether compatible with the strict and cautious logic of the central idea of liberalism that when the differences which had engendered the two-party system waned, this system should melt into a system of multiple groups formed provisionally to cope with particular problems; or that autonomous government should give way to a demand for centralized government in the interests of steadiness, or constitutional monarchies to Republics, or national States to States of plural nationality or to United States through the formation of a wider, for example European, national loyalty, or that economic *laisser-faire* should be tempered and more narrowly confined by industrial organization or nationalization of services. The earlier Liberal generations seldom envisaged such changes and sometimes or usually denied the possibility of them. But it was a possibility implicit in the principle which they proclaimed, and we who after more than a century of varied experience and mental effort can see it, should keep it in mind throughout our interpretation of that seedtime, indeed in our entire treatment we must see in the seed the plant due to grow from it and to give it the character of fertile seed, not sterile cell. There was also a possibility which gave rise to the novel envisagement by Goethe of progress not as a straight line, but as a spiral: the possibility that when dead wood had to be cut out this crisis of renewal would give occasion for reactions and for the triumph of various sorts of authoritarian regime over the liberal regimes for some period and over some area, greater or smaller. Yes, but even when and where this happened Liberty would continue to keep things moving and would in the long run re-emerge in wiser and stronger shape. And then, already at that time, what we have called the spiritualized embodiment of liberty was sometimes accompanied by an embodiment without spirituality, and therefore without health. The cult of nationality tended for some of its less balanced apostles to take on the colour of a materialistic pride and acquisitiveness, a grimly xenophobic racial excitability, and for such people the cult of history and the past would degenerate into stupid idolatry, and reverence for the religions into pseudo-religious revivalism, and so too attachment to existing institutions into a conservative timidity, respect for constitutional reforms into want of enterprise in making necessary modifications, economic competition into the protection of the selfish interests of this or that social group: and so on and so forth. Yet such weaknesses and fallibilities and presages of future troubles were inseparable from the true value of the demands then being advanced and of the institutions being called into existence. They could not rob the Liberal movement of its substantial nobility, its powerful ethical virtue, for these were crowned with poetry, armed with logic and learning, unwearied in action, ready for victory and power.

The deep seriousness of the Liberal ideal was attested by poets, thinkers, journalists, propagandists, apostles, martyrs gathered in great and growing numbers around its standards, and the comparative fewness and feebleness of those serving different ideals underlined the strength and victorious destiny of this one. The previously prevailing divorce of theory from practice, science from life, private from public concerns – as though it were ever possible to seek and discover truth without living in the pathos and experience and desire of truth in action, and as if man and citizen, individual and the society forming and formed by individuals could ever stand apart – was now recognized in theory for the token of decline and decadence which it had been, while facts also proved the wrongness of this divorce. The mere man of letters and philosophy, the inactive dreamer, the intellectual and rhetorician handling the images of the sublime, but evading the fatigue and danger of the duties suggested and required by those images, displaying instead servility and ceremonious adulation, had now become objects of scorn. Authors writing to command and living on the patronage of courts and governments, instead of awaiting the favour of the public and making a living on that sole basis, were contemned. What was admired was sincerity of profession, integrity of character, the matching of words with deeds. A new moral significance was given to the concept of personal dignity and to the sentiment of a true aristocracy, having its rules, its severities, its exclusivisms – an aristocracy that was now liberal, and thus purely spiritual. Hearts went out to the heroic figure of the poet-combatant, the intellectual ready to fight and die for his idea. Nor was such a figure just the product of heightened imagination or of edifying literature. He appeared in flesh and blood on the fields of battle and at the barricades in every part of Europe. There were thus "crusaders" as well as "missionaries" of Liberty.

After listing and contemplating these features of the Liberal ideal, there need be no hesitation about calling it a "Religion", for such it was from the point of view of an attention to what is essential and intrinsic in religions, a conception of reality and a related ethic, and of disregard for the mythological element, which in a secondary manner differentiates religions from philosophies. It was from the modern dialectical and historical thought that Liberalism drew its conception of reality and related ethic, and no more was needed to give it a religious character. Personifications, myths, legends, dogmas, rites, propitiations, expiations, priestly orders, pontifical vestments, and all that have nothing to do with the essence, and the particular religious bodies do wrong to isolate them and present them as indispensable features of religions, thus giving rise to the various artificial religions or "religions of the future" invented during the nineteenth century, only to fall one and all into well-merited ridicule. Meanwhile, unlike these copies and caricatures, Liberalism showed its religious essence in its own forms and institutions. The Liberal religion was not coldly and deliberately invented but came into being naturally, so much so that at first it trusted to being able to live alongside of the old religions as their companion, complement, and aid. The truth was that it stood over against them, but at the same time summed them up in itself and followed upon them. Together with the philosophical strains it drew in the religious strains of the recent and remote past. Beside Socrates it placed the human-divine redeemer Jesus. It felt in itself the experience of Paganism and Christianity, Catholicism, the Augustinian and the Calvinist and all other faiths, and thought to stand for their best purposes as the effort to render purer, deeper, more powerful the religious life of mankind. It therefore celebrated its own origin by no change in the calendar, no initiation of a new era severed from the past as

Christianity had done, and then Islamism, and then, in imitation, the National Convention, with a decree matching its abstract conception of liberty and reason – a decree which, remaining equally abstract in execution, was abolished only after it had been forgotten. Nevertheless the notion of a rebirth, a reborn age, found utterance on all sides as though saluting the "Third Age" or "Age of the Spirit" prophesied by Gioacchino da Fiore in the twelfth century, and now visible to the human society which had prepared and waited upon it.

II

OPPOSITION OF FAITHS

The religion of the new age found itself among and in the way of other competing and hostile religions which, though it had critically weighed them and, expressly or implicitly, got the better of them on that level, had nevertheless their own believers and were making converts, and thus stood out as significant historical realities corresponding to certain ideals which perpetually reappear on the scene.

First and foremost among these stood, by right if not in fact, the Church of Rome as the most logical and direct negation of the liberal idea. The Church of Rome was fully aware of this, and deliberately, as soon as Liberalism began to take shape, proclaimed its attitude in the shrill tones of syllabi, encyclicals, sermons, papal and sacerdotal admonitions; and, save for fleeting episodes or appearances suggesting the contrary, it pursued this opposition in all its practical operations so thoroughly as to be recognizable as the prototype or pure form of all the other oppositions to Liberalism; the one, moreover, whose implacable hatred best illustrates the religious character and rivalry of this last faith. For the liberal faith the end of life lies in life itself, duty consists in the increase and elevation of this life, and the method is free initiative and individual inventiveness. Catholicism retorted that the end of this life lies in a life beyond, for which it is mere preparation. The preparation is accomplished by fulfilling the duty of believing and doing what is ordered by a God in Heaven through his Vicar on earth and his Church. Now no doubt this other-worldly authoritarianism can exhibit a logical systematicity, a deductive coherency, superior to other similar conceptions, yet it is wanting in that logicality and coherency which can truly match reality. For if we observe the actions of the Catholic Church in history they are of two sorts. There are those which in fact are devoted to those same ends of civilization, knowledge, orderly conduct, political and ·social regulation, social accomplishment, human progress. This side of its activity is most plainly seen in the great age of the Church, when it had taken over a great part of the heritage of the ancient world and was defending the rights of conscience, freedom, and the life of the spirit against the barbarians and the materialistic overbearingness of emperors and kings. The other side is seen in actions performed when the Church had lost that function or lost the hegemony for which it gave an opportunity, and being hard pressed by the civilization which it had itself helped to bring into being, developed into the mere conservator of antiquated and defunct forms, and of rudeness, ignorance, superstition, spiritual oppression, becoming in its turn more or less materialistic. But the defence of this programme is not strong enough to withstand the assault of a History which is the history of liberty: it is defeated and forced to display its contradictions in the field of fact. The Renaissance (which was something quite other than an impossible attempt to return to pre-Christian antiquity) and the Reformation (something quite other than an equally impossible attempt to return to primitive Christianity) were each in its own way approaches to the modern conception of ideal and real, and they mark the inner decadence of Catholicism as spiritual power – a decadence that did not issue into a regeneration or suffer an arrest. Rather, it was rendered irremediable by the reaction of the Counter-Reformation. The body but not the soul of the old Church, its worldly power, not its sway over minds, were preserved, which was a political and not a religious achievement. Science and learning, the support and co-operation of which is a sign of superiority for any moral and political ideal, now abandoned the Catholic Church. All the original and creative minds, philosophers, naturalists, historians, men of learning, publicists, passed over or were pushed over to the other side, or at all events found welcome and the understanding of disciples on that side. And left to itself the Church could but restore the edifice of mediaeval scholasticism, introducing by force of circumstances or political calculation secondary variations, and appropriating as much from the science and culture of the non-Catholics as could serve for ornament without too clearly displaying its origin. The atmosphere had been rendered progressively unfavourable for Catholicism by the end of the wars of religion, the spread of the new idea of toleration, English Deism, the idea of the natural history of religions, Rationalism, Enlightenment, and the criticism of ecclesiastical and papal privilege and rights. And thus the French Revolution found the Church enfeebled and politically almost unarmed. Now it is true that out of the harm and distress inflicted by that Revolution, and the movements of resistance and rebellion against it, the Catholic Church won an unexpected measure of succour, in that political aid now came once again from States or classes suffering defeat or feeling themselves threatened or engaged in a struggle for self-defence, while sentimental support came from hearts seeking an escape from the stormy and arid present into pleasing and gentle imaginations of the past. The political aid, however, was purely political, that is, available only for compassing political ends: the sentimental aid arose from untrustworthy conditions of feeling, likely enough to vary or turn into the opposite as happens with mobile fancies and desires, and the Church quickly and pretty generally learned to mistrust them. Thought and Science continued to take a different path. It was as though the Church were stricken with sterility as a divine punishment for a sin against the Spirit, the spirit of sincerity. The most that Catholicism could boast was that amidst those storms and alarms support came from some doctrinaire controversialist of fanatically logical tendency within the system of his abstractions, some lover of extremisms and paradoxes. But here too the Church scented more to distrust than to rejoice over: for such supporters really breathed an alien air of perilous independence. It was above all else the work of the Catholic historians which, when compared with that of the Liberals, showed the poverty, nay triviality and puerility to which Catholic thought had been reduced. For while Liberal history set about reconstructing with intelligence and admiration the story of Christianity and the Church in the last centuries of the Empire and the Middle Ages and such aspects of modern times as the overseas missions and martyrdoms for the faith in far lands, the partisan history of the Catholics notoriously considered the whole tendency of modern history in the light of a horrible perversion, as authors answerable for which they arraigned such men as Luther, Calvin, Voltaire, Rousseau, and other "corruptors", together with the "Sect" which, according to this version, had by dint of a secretly woven web of deceits scored a temporary diabolic triumph – all this being, of course, not so much history as cautionary tales for children. But what worst of all threatened the Catholic position was the enemy's penetration right into the ranks of the Faithful, and moreover into the picked company of the most intellectually and morally distinguished among them. Such Catholics felt drawn to the causes of political liberty, national independence, the unification of peoples in national States, freedom of religious belief and freedom for the Church itself, the spread of culture and of technical and industrial improvements. And so too they felt drawn by agreement and sympathy to the work of the modern philosophers, writers, and poets, and they began to study and to interpret history – including the history of the Church which they loved chiefly as it had been down to the fifteenth century, not as it had been since then and in their own times – in a new fashion. This movement of approach and conciliation varied considerably in tone and composition from country to country. The spirit in some was different, almost opposed. It was known as Liberal Catholicism. But the emphasis was clearly on the former word. Liberalism, not Catholicism, was the gainer by the resolve of these Catholics to open the door and admit a liberal ferment into the old system. The Catholic Church stood on the alert and frowned upon Liberal Catholicism much as formerly upon Jansenism, of which, indeed, the new movement was in more than one way the successor, with a similar disposition in civil and political matters. But with its usual prudence and diplomacy the Church to the best of its possibilities avoided striking personally at certain of its individual supporters, such as writers of wide fame and popularity, sincere and highly esteemed Catholics, whose condemnation would have given offence and caused perplexity to believers.

For all these reasons the Catholic way of thought, with the doctrines which held it together and fortified it, did not on the level of ideas constitute a very serious opposition to Liberalism, as is best shown by Liberalism's renunciation, and as it were distaste for the idea, of a continuation of the assault upon Catholicism which had been launched in earlier centuries, both with armed force and with the weapon of the written word, wielded notably by Voltaire and the Encyclopaedists. Liberalism had entered upon the fruits of this struggle, and for this reason it would have seemed improper and pointless to pursue it. The work would be done by time. Indeed it would have been stupid and somewhat inhuman. For after all, though Voltaire and his friends had forgotten it, the old faith was one method of assuaging human suffering and grief and resolving the dreadful problem of life and death; a mythological method, no doubt, but not on that account to be rooted up violently or opprobriously turned to ridicule. It would also have been highly impolitic, since much of mankind knew and respected the duties of social life as a derivation from those beliefs, those comforts, those teachings, which thus stood at the base of the works and institutions of charity and providence, and of habits of order and discipline. It would be politic to assimilate and transform such entities gradually, not to sweep them away without knowing how to replace them or furnishing a substitute. The attitude towards Catholicism and the Church was in line with the impartiality, appreciation, respect, even reverence shown by the Liberals towards all things of the past, all things of yesterday. This did not mean, however, that Liberalism, in its awareness of its own historical origins, repudiated its link with Christianity. And

Christianity survived in the Catholic Church too, however utilitarian and materialist this had become. Where there were men of evangelical spirit they were felt to be sister souls meet for sympathy and heartfelt co-operation beyond all barriers of doctrine. In creative literature the figures of the good friar, good bishop, good parish priest, simple, honourable, courageous, heroic, became familiar: they were not less warmly depicted than the heroines, so fair and virtuous, or other secular heroes, though sometimes they were carefully placed in contrast with the clergy at large, the Church of Rome as a whole, or, above all, the figures of prelates and Jesuits. Severe vigilance and offensive measures were reserved to cope with a political Catholicism ever ready to support conservative and reactionary regimes, and well knowing how to stir up the masses in the countryside or elsewhere as during the Revolution and Empire it had in fact roused, and inspired with fanaticism, the peasants of the Vendée, the hosts of the "Santa Fede" and "Viva Maria" agitations, and the various Christian and Apostolic armies which had marched under its leadership. The times were now changed, but the peril of such demagogic agitations and outbreaks was not necessarily past, and meanwhile political Catholicism could and did exploit it to frighten off developments in the direction of liberty and civil progress. The struggle against political Catholicism, as contrasted with a struggle against Christianity or the Christian side of Catholicism, finally received the special denomination of a struggle against "Clericalism", a word either invented or put into wider circulation with a new sense around 1860. "Clericalism", "black Clericalism", and not Catholicism, was now said to be the enemy.

We need not here linger over the other Churches or religious Confessions, State Churches or Government-encouraged Churches which, after passing through a stage of Rationalism and Enlightenment, finally drew so near to idealist and historicist ways of thought, that the Church of Rome came to lump together Protestantism, Freemasonry, and Liberalism as being all one business. They stood at all events for a much less thorough opposition to Liberalism than the Catholic. Similarly less thorough, and at first sight merely technical and reflecting not a religious feeling but just political expediency, was the other opposition in the path of Liberalism, the object of its first and fiercest and most important assault. This was the opposition of the Absolute Monarchies (it is hardly necessary to take here into separate account the few and puny survivals of patrician and aristocratic government which in any case followed the same line). Yet every ideal must in the last resort rest upon a world-picture, and to that extent have a religious basis. Absolute Monarchy looked on the Kings as shepherds of the peoples, those flocks requiring to be led to pasture, to mating and breeding, and kept out of any harm's way which might come to them from heat and cold or from wolves and wild beasts. For Richelieu, minister of Louis XIII, the people were "mulets", and in the same spirit the philanthropic d'Argenson, Louis XV's minister, sought to create "une ménagerie d'hommes heureux". Metternich likewise opined that it was for princes alone to conduct the history of the peoples, and a certain Prussian minister of the Restoration period much in the same vein answered protests of the city of Elbing by declaring that the Government's measures were "beyond the limited comprehension of subjects". The religious basis here lay in the idea of the divine institution of the monarchy and priestly character of the early kings. (It makes no difference if many of its exponents were unbelieving sceptics.) When in the Middle Ages the Church and the Empire fell into conflict, the intellectuals of the Empire had never for a moment abandoned the theory of its divine institution, as can for example be seen from Dante's lore of the "Two Suns". Later on, Luther's doctrine had been no less obsequious towards the Princes and the State: the Lutheran derivation of the State from a divine order did much to invest it with a sanctity of which the results became deeply rooted in German thought and behaviour. For these reasons Absolutism – especially in the form it took in the France of Louis XIV – found its legal sanction in the theory of the divine right of Kings, while the Restoration sovereigns, induced thereto by the one among the victors of Napoleon who was most disposed towards ideology and mysticism, entered into the Holy Alliance in order – as the preamble to this declares – "comme délegués de la Providence" to govern "les branches d'une même famille" (that is, the peoples) by application of "les préceptes de la sainte religion", precepts, that is, of justice, charity, and peace. Prince Metternich to the words of his already quoted added that Kings were responsible for their actions "to God alone". Nevertheless it was not from this ideology that the absolute monarchies drew their strength. It had by this time long been dissipated by the political thinkers, and English and French revolutionaries had made a harsh end of it with the judgement and execution of Charles Stuart and Louis Capet. Nor from their shed blood had any fresh line of kings by divine right received a consecration. One of the least religious of men ever to rise to historical greatness (if indeed true greatness can ever be unaccompanied by the religious spirit, which is doubtful) had with but the slightest occasional recourse to the ideology in word and deed reshaped that very monarchy which in many respects, and signally in its Absolutism, had just served as a model for the monarchies of the Restoration. The Holy Alliance itself did not retain the religious aura intended for it by its chief designer: Kings and ministers utilized its machinery while they ironically smiled over the profession of faith which was its theoretical premiss, if they recalled it at all. What the Absolute Monarchies really drew their strength from was the merit of the services which, like the Catholic Church, they had rendered and were still rendering to civilization. For it was they that had overthrown feudalism, tamed the ecclesiastical power, put together great States out of a plurality of small ones, sometimes giving them a national or mainly national character, and had furthermore simplified and improved the administration, brought about an increase of wealth, defended the honour of the peoples and won glory for them, and in the period just before the Revolution and the Empire had of their own accord or by imitation or constraint finally abolished feudal privileges and customs, becoming what were known as "administrative monarchies". The taste for Republics had been weakened by the experience of the French Republic and the others which followed upon it, while the Empire had strength-

ened the system of monarchy. For it was shown that monarchies
were still capable of historical development, capable of satisfying
the demand of the peoples for a representation and a share in the
Government, capable of undertaking or effecting liberations and
political unifications, of leading nations to greatness and personify-
ing their aspirations. Liberalism therefore set about breathing its
spirit into these monarchies, thus signally proving its own ideal
aptitude for according future with past, new with old, and maintaining historical continuity to the avoidance of wasteful dispersal
of the institutional achievements and heritage of skills resulting
from past labours. The Holy Alliance which had come into being,
composed of absolute monarchies partly of dynastic and plurinational, partly of incompletely national character, was something very different from a Holy Alliance of free and independent
peoples. Hopes and promises cherished in their eager hearts by
many of the combatants against Napoleonic hegemony and despotism were belied and disregarded once the danger was over.
Almost everywhere the restored monarchies proceeded to arm
themselves for defence and offence against national patriotism,
and the Liberalism which shared its enthusiasm, that is against the
ally of yesterday. They were sustained by backward-looking forces
of reaction, courtiers, aristocrats and semi-feudal groups, hangers-
on of the Church, the lower populace of town and country, and
above all by the fact of being actually in possession, which counts
so much for any government. Side by side with those mentioned
there were, however, forces of a nobler quality upholding these
regimes: administrations and diplomacies of ancient tradition,
strong and glorious armies, skilled and devoted servants of the
State, century-old dynasties which seemed inseparable from the
peoples whose fortunes they had so long shared for better and
worse and were still providing princes of personal worth and
continuing prestige; conservative forces, no doubt, rooted in the
past, but not on that account such as could be left simply to wither
away and die. The problem was, how to persuade or to constrain
the absolute monarchies to emerge from the contradictions in
which they were enmeshed, to take the step from which they

shrank, to give up their obstinacy and to become constitutional. It was not practicable for them to seek the alternative course of a return to the enlightened monarchism of the eighteenth century or, as the aristocrats desired, to still earlier semi-feudal and oligarchic methods of rule. Too much had happened in the meanwhile. Nor yet could they resort to the methods of Napoleonic absolutism when they lacked that military and imperial dynamism which had rendered them attractive or tolerable, because cloaked in glory. They remained therefore with an awkward mixture of the old and the new on their hands, trying to hold things together by police measures, censorship, and severe repressions. Liberal Constitutionalism offered a way of preserving and at the same time renewing all that was worth preserving. Kings would surrender every vestige of their sacerdotal and pastoral character to become not precisely according to the eighteenth-century prescription "first of the servants of the State", but guarantors of the rights of the nation, poetic symbols of a living national history. There was no conflict between the "Grace of God" by which they had formerly held their investiture and the "Will of the People" which recalled them now to their thrones, for the acceptance of the past does not mean renunciation of the present or of future hopes.

We have seen that the sympathy of some Catholic and Absolute Monarchical elements with Liberalism – and the readiness of Liberalism to receive and absorb them – did not suffice to dissolve the essential mutual enmity of the systems. The same must be said in regard to yet another system and faith which seemed to merge with Liberalism or at least to become indissolubly linked with it: the democratic ideal. The Liberal and Democratic creeds not only found themselves joined in opposition to Clericalism and Absolutism, and so fighting on common ground, but were more positively associated in the demand for individual liberty, civil and political equality, popular sovereignty. But the identity of their demands was more apparent than real, for the meaning given by each to "individuality", "equality", and "sovereignty" was different. By the Democrats, individuals were seen as power-centres of equal value, to each of which should be assigned an equal range, or what was called "equality in fact". For the Liberals, individuals ranked as persons equal to one another only in their humanity, that is in an ideal and legal equality, a freedom to move and compete. The people was understood by the Liberals not as a summation of a number of equal powers, but as an organism differentially constituted from various and variously interrelated elements, complex, therefore, in its unity, comprising governed and governors, such governing classes being no closed castes but open and flexible, yet for all that not unnecessary organs of government. Sovereignty the Liberals saw as residing in the synthesis of the whole, not in the analytically distinguished parts. The ideal of the Democrats required a religion of quantity, mechanism, rational calculus, nature – the eighteenth-century faith. That of the Liberals required a religion of quality, activity, spirituality – the faith which had dawned with the nineteenth century. Here too, then, the contrast was one of religious faiths. Was the Democratic faith the earlier, and did the Liberal draw its origin therefrom? Why yes, in the general sense in which Liberalism was also derivative from Catholic theocracy and absolute monarchism. And we may recognize the derivation from Democracy also in a more special and immediate sense. There had been a progressive and dialectical growth of the modern Liberal thought out of the thought of the naturalists and rationalists. Galileo and Descartes had helped towards Kant and Hegel. And again, we have to recognize that everyone passes through a youthfully radical phase of negations and affirmations both of an equally abstract character. But once they had reached the level, these two faiths, one of them truly vital and the other a survival, faced each other (as they still do) in alternating friendship and enmity. The idealistic philosophy rejected the theory of Natural Law, Contractualism, Rousseau's social atomism and his "General Will" – that poor substitute for providential purpose and the design of history – nor would it accept the drawing of an opposition between State and Individual, which in the idealistic theory were the terms of a single indissoluble relation. On more strictly political ground, the Liberal movement had severed con-

nexions with the Democratic, which, in the extreme form of
Jacobinism, had carried the blind and insane pursuit of abstractions to the point of destroying the living physical tissues of the
social organism. This was not all. Jacobinism, supposing "the
People" to consist in one part, and that the least civilized, of the
people, the surging and impulsive and inorganic masses, and
exercising tyrannic power in the name of "the People", fell to carrying out the very opposite of its own design. Instead of opening
the way to equality and freedom, it opened it to a dead level of
slavery and dictatorship. The abhorrence for revolution felt at that
time and throughout the nineteenth century (itself so rich in revolutions) was essentially an abhorrence for the democratic and
Jacobin type of revolution, bloody in its spasmodic convulsions,
sterile in its grasping at the impossible, leading to collapse under a
despotism that would darken the mind and weaken the will. "The
Terror" inspired a terror which became one of the abiding sentiments of society. There were some who came to the support of
its methods, as the only ones which could have won the benefits
of the French Revolution and could win further benefits to come.
But they failed to convince, for other and more judicious thinkers
were able to expose this sophistry. Later on, indeed, by the action
of time and still more of tendentious palliations, the grimmer aspect
of the French Revolution could be relegated to the shade, while the
finer passions and actions which had accompanied it were brought
to light, but the time we are writing about was too close to those
events, there were too many testimonies and impressions of the
vulgar and prosaic reality of them still alive in men's minds, for
the Democratic ideal to derive strength and splendour from their
memory. Indeed this ideal had come badly out of the business,
forsworn on each and every hand. Of such old Jacobin protagonists
of the Revolution and promoters of the Terror as had survived,
many of the less unpractical had passed first into the service of
Napoleon and then into that of the Restoration Absolutisms, being
reckoned among the most resolute and inexorable executors of
the campaign against democracy and against liberty. (Did not the
most serene of poets observe that it were well to crucify every

fanatic at thirty years of age because whoever has put faith in illusions, when he sees through them, becomes a scoundrel?) There were some honest men who kept faith with their old illusions and lived on in a state of bewilderment, for ever gloomily turning over in their mind the errors, perfidies, accidents which had checked the advance of their pure and lovely ideal of Equality and Popular Sovereignty, just as it was seemingly about to attain realization and to become eternally valid for the beatitude of men. The word "Republic", as we have seen, was not beloved, having about it a shrillness or alternatively a crassness which were not savoured: yet some men, and some of the younger generation among them, still felt the charm of its venerable associations or of its rationalistic over-simplicity. At the moment, however, neither the Democratic nor the Republican cause counted for much. Liberalism, which represented a philosophical and political advance upon those positions, was able on the one hand to take advantage of the spontaneous aid offered by certain of the still faithful Democrats and Republicans, and on the other hand by keen vigilance to ensure that these allies did not, at some decisive or crucially changeful moment, compromise its gains by excesses or follies or disorders, or become the unintending and unconscious promoters of victorious counter-offensives from the Clerical and Absolutist side.

There existed, in those dawning years of the nineteenth century, yet another opposition to Liberalism, at that time only nascent, but destined soon to make its weight felt and to be progressively fierce and threatening. This was Communism, to use forthwith its most appropriate and classical name rather than that – somewhat muted in tone – of "Socialism", which gradually came to betoken something different, merging itself in Liberalism, Democratism, and even Catholicism. It will be well at this point to trace the lineaments of this movement. We have said that it was nascent at the moment which we are describing, for the old idea in question, as old as the history of mankind and repeatedly reappearing in the course of it, then took on a new form connected not with those fanciful utopias of the past, but with the conditions resulting in the world from the new philosophy and the new pursuits of human energy. In those older Communisms, including the eighteenth-century versions and even that of Babeuf with his "Conspiracy of the Equals", there had been persistent streaks of asceticism, motives of renunciation in favour of simple, primitive, inelegant ways of life, and of abhorrence of the town and longing for the rural way of life. By contrast the Communism which took the stage early in the nineteenth century accepted the mundane and immanentist conception of life with the same readiness as the Liberals, and like them advocated the extension of consumption, the perpetual increase of wealth, the promotion of science and technical inventions, machinery, and all the other apparatus of economic progress. In this sharing of objectives lay its affinity with Liberalism. Nor did the two clash so strongly as is commonly believed and has been thought by some authors, over the opposition between the Communist desire to socialize some or all of the means of production (to socialize all would really be a nonsensical aim) and the Liberal fidelity to the principle of sacrosanct private property and unlimited competition. It should by now be agreed that Liberalism and economic "Liberism" (the doctrine of free enterprise and trade) have indeed had common ground in the past and perhaps have still, but do not coincide. Their meeting has been only provisional and contingent, *"laisser-faire et laisser-passer"* being recognized as maxims valid in some circumstances, but invalid in others. Liberalism cannot make it a matter of principle to refuse to socialize or nationalize this or that branch of the means of production. Nor has it in practice always refused to do so – often it has instead agreed. Liberalism has opposed such steps only when in given circumstances they might tend to retard or diminish the output of wealth and instead of promoting an equally shared economic improvement might cause a deterioration which very likely would not be equally shared, thus not increasing the liberty of mankind, but restricting it and making for oppression, loss of civilization, decadence. For the only measure by which projects of reform can be judged is that of their liability to promote or to hamper life and liberty. "Property" itself correspondingly has two aspects and two meanings: sometimes it stands for a mere economic institution liable to be modified (and in fact frequently modified) in order to make it better serve the ends of moral and human personality, but at other times it stands for the needful instrument and form of this personality, the destruction or damaging of which brings with it destruction and damage to moral progress itself, and goes against "human nature".

It would be more accurate to say that such destruction offends the very duty and mission of man, which is not to enjoy comfort, but to re-create himself in ever higher forms, entering into the eternal poem of history – a task like that of the poet and artist. Communism itself after an early period in which it asked for its designs to be put into full realization by governments of scientists and technicians, or by the foundation of small model societies calculated to exercise an irresistible attraction by the display of an enchanting felicity, and after periodical returns to the methods of Democratic Jacobinism, plotting and planning violent upheavals and seizures of power, proclaimed that its own realization depended upon the course of history, presenting mankind with the dilemma that either the capitalistic system of private property must be maintained with a resulting decline and damage for economic wealth, or if it was desired to guarantee and to increase production, private property must be abolished. Communism held that this prognostication was confirmed by the succession of economic crises and destructions of wealth which – such was the Communist argument – with the attendant train of bankruptcies and disturbances represented the sole means for Capitalism to recover its balance. Now if this were really the situation and these the prospects, there could be no course for Liberalism save to endorse or to appropriate the Communist programme: the whole point was whether these things were really happening, or happening as tidily and quickly as the Communistic theorists argued. It was a question of experience, not of ideals. The conflict between Communism and Liberalism on the level of ideals, of religion, was of another order. It concerned the opposition between spiritual and material values, due to the essentially materialistic character of Communism, its deification of body, of matter. The preaching of its first apostles at the beginning of the nineteenth century was materialistic, although this philosophical description was only conferred upon it and found to suit it somewhat later on, and then not by its adversaries, but by its ablest theorist. Its principle is the notion that the economic form underlies and generates all the other forms of life and is alone real, the others being, in respect to it, mere derivations, appearances, or phenomenology. Now in a living philosophy of the Spirit economic activity takes its place as one which arises out of other activities and also leads up to others, and is thus itself one of the activities having a spiritual character. But when, torn out of such a system and isolated, it is set as a kind of stone foundation for the others, then it loses its spiritual and takes on a material character, from which aridity there can never spring up and flourish morality, religion, poetry, or philosophy – nor yet, in the long run, that economic life which calls for vital warmth, keen intelligence, strong feeling. The early nineteenth-century "Utopian" Communists were already noticeably indifferent to the life of the Spirit, all intent upon mechanical marvels, the advantages of industrial organization, the hope of a stable and happy condition of society as the result of economic reforms. Ignorant or careless about history, they soon set about falsifying it, giving out that Liberalism was the mere cloak of capitalist interests, that modern civilization was not a human but a class or bourgeois creation, and that the political struggle was a mere contest between economic classes, religions mere inventions for enslaving and drugging the common people, and philosophies conceptual constructions similarly reared for the defence of the exploiters – and much more such nonsense. Now a society modelled according to a materialistic thought of this sort could not but be a mechanical product, and since machines, unlike organic and spiritual beings, do not work of their own accord, but need someone to wind them up and check them, such a society would of necessity be regulated by a perpetual dictatorship obliging its components to move along certain marked curves, to profess certain beliefs and to hold aloof from others, to modify or suffocate their thoughts, desires, and wills. If such a society is not a community engaged in mortifying itself for the sake of the Kingdom of Heaven, it will be an army on the march for objectives known only to its dictatorial commanders, or a gang of slaves, possibly well fed and trained to erect astonishing pyramids. It will in any case lack that self-governance in virtue of which a society is a society. Labouring free from the complications but also without the inducements of competition it might perhaps multiply the products of the earth and of man's handiwork, but it would none the less impoverish the souls intended to be served by that wealth, and would in the long run dry up the true source of wealth, which is the liberty of the human spirit. Men would then become, according to Leonardo's saying, "channels for food". It is religious ideal, no doubt, but leading to a literal, not merely metaphorical *abêtissement*. Of course, the devil's never so black as he's painted, for example in the painting which we have had to execute in order to get to the bottom of his theory and his logic, and the consequences due to derive from it. Communism, as long as it is not in a position to fulfil that "renewal", which is really a demolition of human life, and has to stop short of installing its continuous unending tyranny, as long – that is – as it operates with censures and demands, and threats too, assailing the selfishness of private economic interests for the advantage of the community, supplying the social classes which stand outside political life with some sort of (mythical) political ideal, rousing them, teaching them discipline, and in a way educating them, so long is it displaying its virtuous side, and it would be ridiculous to seek to expel it or to desire its disappearance from the world. By contrast its guiding principle and its materialistic religion are properly to be expelled and annulled on the level of theory.

We have enumerated the various oppositions which Liberalism found in its path, ready formed or in embryo, in its own early career. Some of them later declined and almost disappeared, while others gained in solidity and strength, and yet other oppositions came into being and will have to be mentioned at a later moment, both because of their late emergence and also because they had not the same original character as the earlier, but were derivatory, eclectic, or of mixed type.

The fundamental oppositions which we have examined, those with which Liberalism's conflict was religious on the lines of *"mors tua vita mea"*, must not be confounded with the varieties embraced by Liberalism itself, or with the divergences and party differences which resulted from these. Such a variety was conformable with its own nature, indeed its nature – the rule of its game – was nothing else than such pursuit of good and prudent courses by the method of discussions, associations, counterassociations, persuasions, resolutions backed by this or that majority, making it clear what could be asked for and obtained in given but not unchangeable circumstances. By contrast what we have called the oppositions stood against and sought to overthrow the Liberal system itself. They were not to be overcome otherwise than by that method which is the only final recourse in politics, the *ultima ratio* of sheer force, in its necessary character as one of the realities implicit in every political act and situation; by the force of popular outbreaks and wars, armed vigilance, repression. By a singular misunderstanding some have described the liberal method as that of the "Unarmed Prophet", whereas without having to re-explore the theory of Liberalism and indeed of politics at large, we can observe by a glance at the facts that fiercer battles, more copious bloodshed, more obstinate contests, more ready and willing sacrifices have been engaged and offered for the Liberal idea than for any other. The charge of soft yieldingness alluded in truth to the essential characteristic of Liberalism which is its pride: it alluded to the law of Liberalism which is on the one hand to uphold even with force what we have called the rules of the game, but on the other hand to treat liberty as itself the rule of the game, implying respect for others' opinions, readiness to listen to the other side, to learn from it, and above all to get to know it well in order that the adversary may not conceal himself by concealing his thought and intentions. Thus wherever Liberalism was established, all the ideals, Catholic, Absolutist, Democratic, Communistic, were to have freedom of speech and propaganda, provided only and always that they did not overthrow the Liberal Constitution. In this manner their contradictions would be brought to light, while all the detailed demands compatible with legality, all the good and just proposals which from time to time should become associated with those ideals, or taken under their wing, would have had as good an opportunity of being realized as any other demand or proposal. The presence and alertness of such opponents would furthermore be a perpetual spur to lively and vigilant maintenance of the faith, like the heresies and sects in all religions. Liberalism had reason to be proud of this method, but there was also humility and modesty in it. Ideals may indeed on the theoretical level be classed as good or bad, superior or inferior. But men cannot be thus distinguished and contrasted. Each of them is a mixture in various proportions of true and false, high and low, spiritual and material, and any one, though he may call himself or boast of being reactionary, may when it comes to concrete action defend or radiate liberty, while one believing himself liberal may act inversely. Each in his own way makes a contribution, positive or negative, to the Good which makes use of these individuals and passes beyond them. Now it is between men that the effective struggle takes place. John Milton, writing his early and archaic formulations of modern liberty, said that he who suppresses a truth or a germ or possibility of truth does worse than the author of a physical murder for "he slays an immortality rather than a life". For the loss of a truth often costs mankind terrible disasters and the truth must be reacquired with unspeakable pain.

A philosophical system may reckon its own superiority by the capacity which it shows of receiving the truths of other systems into its own broader range, and thus dominating them, while at the same time it subjects their arbitrary and fanciful aspects to a revision, converting them into logical problems and solutions. The superiority of a moral and political ideal is shown when it similarly accepts, verifies, utilizes, and converts the values and the efforts of achievement put forth by the opposing ideals. The inferiority of those other ideals is shown by their incapacity to do anything of the sort, so that they can only meet opposition by a sterile and total rejection. The Liberal ideal did not shun this test, but submitted to it in full awareness, confident of passing well through it.

III

ROMANTICISM

Simultaneously with the birth and growth of Idealism and Liberalism there appears on the stage also Romanticism. The actors are often the same persons. It is by no mere chance that the Romantic movement is found springing up and expanding by the side of these others: the relation or series of relations between them which we shall now illustrate should never be forgotten.

There is a distinction which ought to be kept in mind, but has commonly been overlooked by the great multitudes of recent and present writers on and historians of Romanticism: if it is overlooked, there is bound to be a misdirection of adverse comment against certain meritorious spiritual manifestations, and of favourable comment towards others deserving of reproof. The resulting narrative will perforce be contradictory and confused. I mean the distinction between Romanticism in its theoretical and speculative aspects and Romanticism as sentimental and moral behaviour. For investigation of the underlying realities will show that the two were not only quite different, but actually opposed to each other.

Romanticism on the level of theory and speculation betokens argument, rebellion, and criticism directed against academicism in letters and intellectualism in philosophy, such as had come to prevail in the age of the Enlightenment. This sort of Romanticism reawoke sensibility for great and genuine poetry, explaining the process in the new science of "Aesthetics", or theory of the fantasy. It grasped the importance of spontaneity, passion, individuality, and assigned to these their place in ethics. It recognized and proclaimed the rights of the existent, the effective, in all their local and temporal variety, founding the modern way of writing history not as a contemptuous and derisive backward glance at earlier ages, but as comprehension of these in their formative contribution to the present and the future. This Romanticism furthermore restored and revived all the aspects of historical work, civil and political as well as religious, speculative, and artistic. Meanwhile it confined the naturalistic and mathematical sciences, and the mental methods appropriate to them, to operation within their proper limits, demonstrating their incapacity to resolve the antinomies encountered by the mind outside their range, and the necessity for them, therefore, to operate in the field of abstraction and isolation. Finally, this Romanticism sensed the active and combative savour of life and thus provided the theoretical premiss for Liberalism. And even its irrationalities were not merely wanton. Thus when sometimes it exalted sentiment and mystic rapture above all else, it did so in a justified revolt against abstract intellectualism, so that the irrational and impermanent utterance contained a nucleus of reasoned truth. Similarly in such ill-conceived experiments as the devising of a philosophy of history above all histories and of a philosophy of nature above the natural sciences, this Romanticism was influenced by the deep need for a history which should be at one and the same time philosophy, and for the concept of nature understood as development and historical process, discoverable at the base of all scientific classifications and conventions as the prime material upon which "scientists" in the narrower sense have to build. This Romanticism, then, far from exhibiting any contrast with the modern philosophy of Idealism or the Spiritual Absolute, is identical with this, or with some of its particular teachings. It is indeed an alternative name for this philosophy, and the use of it gives rise to mistakes and verbal paradoxes, as when, by naming the course of philosophy from Kant to Hegel "Romantic", we cause some to mistake this philosophy for a didactic form of Moral Romanticism.

This other Romanticism, moral and sentimental, operative in the practical field, belongs to a quite different sphere. The first or speculative Romanticism, bright (as we have shown) with truth, may at times have been judged excessive and temerarious, but it never fell into sickness, weakness, madness, and all attempts to confute its teachings failed and are still failing. The same cannot be said of the Romanticism which we now have to consider. A diseased character marked it from the very beginning, and it was steadily frowned upon by the moralists, though in varying tones of reproof, now indulgent and compassionate, now severe and satirical, and treated as being in need of a healing disintoxication. The very men to whom was chiefly due the merit of liberation from intellectualism, the principal authors of critical and speculative idealistic and Romantic thought, Goethe and Hegel, took this view of moral Romanticism, banning and blaming it as unhealthy and shameful. It was assuredly not to this Romanticism that the complimentary descriptions of "Protestantism in philosophic form" and "Liberalism in literature" were addressed. The gap between the two Romanticisms, in their conceptual essence, positive for one and negative for the other, is adumbrated also in the historical distinction which has become usual between the "first" and the "second" Romantic generations, the former a blossoming time and the latter a supervening decay and degeneration of Romanticism. But in truth the line of division is not so much one between persons and periods, but between intrinsic ideals. Still less reason is there to draw it between Latin sanity and German morbidity. The Germans may have been early and conspicuous sufferers from the moral malady, but the thinkers and moralists whose sane views were required to cure the malady were also primarily Germans. But these Germans, both the sufferers and the authors of the cure, were preceded and followed by non-Germans who shared in a malady of the modern age which respected no frontiers, or shared in the mental labours which the age, without distinction of nation, mustered in defence. And in fact the malady was dubbed, with impartiality as between the nations, *mal du siècle*.

The malady of the century has been wrongly although repeatedly diagnosed and expounded as the result of detachment from the age-old ancestral faith in which for so long men's feelings and desires had enjoyed an untroubled sureness. But this is not the truth. When an old faith is superseded by a new faith, this last engenders a warm enthusiasm which almost drowns the pain and regret felt at the abandonment and loss of the old. Already in the eighteenth century the educated and ruling classes of society had to a great extent cast aside Christianity without any resultant disease of the mind like the Romantic conflict: indeed the process occurred not without a sort of gaiety and contentment. Those violent rebels against the law and morals and mind of their times, the *Stürmer und Dränger*, who in some ways may rank as the first of the Romantics, in their impetuous negations and destructive outbursts gave a display of deranged strength rather than of perplexity and weakness. The fact was that moral Romanticism, the Romantic malady or malady of the century, had no grip on either the old or the new faith, neither on the traditions of the past nor on the rationality of the present religion, and accordingly no grip either upon the practical and moral standards which went with them. The malady was in fact a lack of faith exasperated by an anxiety to forge oneself a faith, but without the ability to do so or to rest content with any of those which were on offer, or to guide life and thought by their principles. And naturally so, for faith springs spontaneously and inevitably from hearing the voice of truth in our own soul: it cannot be conjured up by busy play of the will and the imagination.

The malady had more to do with the difficulty of getting a grip on the new faith and taking it for a rule of life than with detachment from the old faith. To realize and to put into effect this new faith required courage and manliness, the sacrifice of certain ancient comforts and flattering assurances no longer to be entertained, and moreover, on the part of anyone aspiring to understand and expound and stand up for his beliefs, it required experience, culture, and a well-trained mind. Men of robust mind and constitution were able to traverse individually, stage by stage, the distance from one faith to the other, emerging from the tempestuous inner experience into calmer waters. There were also those of clear and simple intelligence and straightforwardness who by the sheer light of goodness and virtue were enabled to embrace without complications the practical conclusions of the new outlook. This was not possible, however, for womanish, sentimental, incoherent, voluble spirits who egged themselves on to multiply doubts and difficulties which they were then unable to master, and courted perils which they then succumbed to. Unable to rediscover the natural centre which they had obscured by their scepticism, they gravitated from point to point, but no point could now serve as centre. They had broken the nexus of finite with infinite, of the sensuous with the ideal, and now in despair they identified the infinite with this or that finite, the ideal with this or that sensible. They had lost the true God and were fashioning idols only to destroy them again or see them fall to destruction. For the part cannot stand for the whole, the phantasm compounded of caprice and frenzy cannot take the place of clear and sustaining mental creation.

We accordingly find these womanish "Romantics" hankering after a return to the transcendental creed and the peace which it seemed to promise. They yearned to lay aside in silent renunciation the doubts and the anxieties of the thinking mind. They would embrace a code for the sake of the sheer release from personal responsibility in the solution of their inner conflicts which observance of a code would provide. Now the Catholic faith seemed to represent in the highest degree such transcendentalism in belief, such a fixed observance. Thus not only people of Catholic origin and upbringing but Protestants, Lutherans, or those born in more exotic faiths or no faith at all, were to be found returning or drawing towards the Roman faith, performing the official rites of conversion, and yet for all that never becoming thorough and genuine Catholics and never quite convincing the genuine Catholics of their sincerity. This Catholicism of the converts appealed too richly to the senses and the imagination, was too much excited about colours, music and singing, ancient Cathedrals, images of the Madonna and Saints; it worked itself up too easily into orgies of sin and tearful repentance; and on the ground of dogma, while proclaiming itself ultra-orthodox, it was not always correspondingly obedient to the Roman Pontiff's behests and policies, and varied its supposed or intended anti-Protestantism with frequent suggestions of the necessity of a new form or reform of essentially Catholic character but affording the possibility of an absorption of both Protestantism and Catholicism. But there were also outbreaks of anti-Catholic or anti-Christian passion in other quarters – or even among those of whom we have been speaking – with demands for a return to paganism and the supplanting of the Blessed Virgin by a Hellenic or Germanic-mediaeval Venus. Others, intrigued by the new studies of Eastern language and literature, interested themselves in ancient Eastern cults or new and bizarre mixtures of them, or in a revival of magic, while finally others plunged into a pantheistic nature-worship, abandoning themselves to the sensations which this seemed to offer and thus, they said, recovering the primitive religion of the Germanic races.

Side by side, or sometimes co-incarnate with such metaphysical and sacerdotal spirits, went those of a more erotic tinge, seeking their redemption in the love and the divinity of the beloved woman. This cult was not properly speaking a revival of the thirteenth-century motive of the school of Dante, nor of the theme of the Renaissance Platonists. It was the romantic religion of love characterized by the subtilization and sublimation of the senses. The object was not Woman, strong in her virtue and chastity, holding off the male lover and thus chastening him, for the betterment of his nature, and obliging him to purge his passion of all low and earthy desires until thus purified he can go forward with her to the supreme Beauty and Goodness which is God. The object was now, on the contrary, Woman as a creature, she too, of love and sense, made to suffer and die of love, an adorable being invested with a divinity the lure of which could alone give warmth and meaning to human life. Sometimes this creature of love would take on the majestic air of a priestess of the cult performing acts of initiation and worship. There was much pathos in the succession of raptures, inebriations, disappointments, despairs, but over all there re-emerged always the idea of the shape of Love, or of Woman, descending earthwards ever and anon to bestow a celestial nimbus on the fair or dark ringlets of some woman of flesh and blood.

At other times, or for other spirits, the play of fantasy chose ethical and political themes, themes of political fantasy, we will say, rather than of politics, for the Romantic malady could

70

hardly embrace real politics. The idea was to seek a faith and a beatitude in ways of life different from the present, usually by an attempted resuscitation of the past. Now the immediate past, the age of the *ancien régime*, stood out too clearly in memory, too precise in its contours to be idealized and solemnly sublimated. Therefore – and also by the attraction of the studies recently devoted to the better understanding of this period in the interests of a recovered sense of historical continuity – the Middle Ages were eagerly seized upon. Distance rendered them amenable. It was easy to mistake, in the glimmering light, shadows for substantial figures: paragons of fidelity, loyalty, purity, generosity were glimpsed, of mingled lawfulness and lawlessness; and then the alternation of the usual with the unexpected, of simple life in a small and peaceful vicinity with adventures in the vast and unknown and incalculable world. To this Religion of the Middle Ages we are indebted for the more or less academic restorations of ancient castles and cathedrals, for the pseudo-Gothic fashion that swept Europe, the pseudo-poetry which amateurishly revived the mediaeval epic forms, the morality plays and songs and entertaining literature about knights and tourneys, enamoured châtelaines and pages, minstrels and jesters, and then for the romantic masquerades, and even for some disguises which were fastened on to the ancient monarchies in their restored form, grotesquely resurrected emblems and habits and costumes rescued from antiquarian collections. Princes were among those bitten with this mode: the Prussian Prince, later King Frederick William IV, and King Ludwig I of Bavaria, who pursued it with some ability. But if that of the Middle Ages was the principal cult of this sort it was not the only one. By its side and sharing the honours there grew up the religion of the race or national strain, particularly of that one which a defective knowledge and meditation of history had made to appear the creator and dominator of the Middle Ages, the German. Its virtues were investigated and celebrated in every part of Europe (although historically it would have been far more to the point to rediscover the Roman basis of European unity and self-awareness). It was exalted as the young and pure element in the historical formation of Spain and Italy no less than France and England and, while it had become thin and corrupt in those countries, was supposed to have kept its youth and valour, available for a regeneration and Germanization of the world, in modern Germany. Less fortune attended the rival attempts of certain other alleged "pure strains" – Latin, Celtic, Iberian, Slav, to follow the example. And there were yet other cults of an ethico-political type which obtained a larger or smaller following, for example the belief in the return to nature and the countryside and simple peasant customs showing the inspiration of one of the chief forerunners of Romanticism, Rousseau, and in marked opposition to this the tempestuous, frenzied, titanic ideal which was a bequest from the movement of *Sturm und Drang*. But the cult which above all claims attention for the success of its appeal and the manifold branches that it threw out, was the "Aesthetic" cult, the idea that life should be lived in terms of passion, imagination, beauty, poetry, so different from the reality of life, which cannot be lived all on one level, but must pass from one to the other in a harmony of all its forms and accordingly abhors the pathological superimposition of a single form, such as the aesthetic, upon all the others which are, in their due function, equally important. The very nature of poetry, moreover, is resistent to that sort of "aestheticism". Poetry is the surmounting of action in cosmic contemplation, in which practical activity is suspended, albeit as a first step towards the renewal of activity. Romanticism, accordingly, by the damage which it wrought to life itself, also caused more or less damage to the poetic aspect, degrading it to a practical purpose, the immediate and convulsive expression of crude feeling in cries, shrieks, and delirium.

The aberrations we have been describing all sprang from perversion in the sense that they assigned to the particular, the contingent, the creature, the place due to the universal, the eternal, the creator. But in their variety and complexity and intricacy of sentimental appeal they afforded room also for perversions in the narrower sense, for inversions of ideals going far beyond mere exaggeration and substitution: for wanton lust cultivated as an ideal, for voluptuous entertainment of cruelty and horror, for pleasure in incest, Sadism, Satanism, and such monstrous and also stupid excesses. Such perversion is found or glimpsed in some even of the major poets and authors such as Chateaubriand, Byron, and Shelley, in whom fortunately it is seldom more than an incidental or evanescent blot on works of an altogether different order.

The "malady of the century" has frequently been investigated in the infinite variety of its grades and shades, sometimes well and sometimes less well: I need not therefore do more now than trace, as I have done, its origin and its relation to the philosophy and religion of Liberty. We have seen that the malady originated simply in failure to grasp firmly this philosophy and religion, while seizing, however, upon certain sides of them which were, in that very act, distorted, whence the sense of history was found degenerating into sentimentality for old times and the nostalgia of Restorationism; nationality was found degenerating into the fanatical adoration of the racial group; freedom into authoritarianism of the ego; and poetry as a life-value into a relation between life and poetry in which each tried to translate itself directly into the other. Yet even upon this version of Romanticism the Liberal faith exercised a great influence, sometimes (as should be remembered) pointing beyond it, sometimes restraining it, sometimes subjugating it. The sentimental malady endangered not only Liberalism, but every form of ideal aspiration and honest religious feeling, including those which stood against or deviated from Liberalism. Unsubdued, it would have disintegrated all of them, enfeebled and ruined all intellect and all purposefulness in sensuality, chaotic desire, headlong passion, idle fancy, capricious unrest. The danger throve on the weak resistance which it encountered, being in its moral essence a danger which is at all times present, but in the vastness and complexity of modern society swelling to greater dimensions and acquiring additional malignity from the exacerbation and debasement of society's internal struggles. In course of time it infected the wider ranges of art, philosophy, public feeling and behaviour and opinion, national and international, and, what was most glaring and hateful, it was given and proudly gave itself the appellation of "Decadentism". For this was nothing else than a heightened and worsened version of the old moral Romanticism whose notions it took over and applied still more basely and vulgarly.

But that was later. In the first decades of the eighteen-hundreds the religion of Liberty breathed youthful enthusiasm, and its very adversaries, the traditional religion, the traditional monarchy, and the Democratic movement for the Rights of Man, wore an air of dignity and majesty which was wanting in the contendents in later contests. The setting of moral Romanticism was a vigorous growth of hopes, purposes, generous efforts, hemming it in, putting it to the test, and often converting it towards good ends. The finest spirits of the age, involved as they were in its drama, were all, generally speaking, caught by the malady, but in them it had the character of growing-pains soon surmounted with an improvement in terms of experience, disciplined steadiness, widened human understanding. Among these were numbered the clearest-eyed and the severest critics of Romanticism like Goethe, already recalled, who called the poetry of the Romantics "hospital poetry", and advertised his dislike for the "sentimental folk" who when put to the test always fail and exhibit a small and ungenerous spirit, and Hegel, also already recalled, who most exhaustively analysed and caustically satirized the absurdities and vanities of the Romantics, holding up to them like a magic mirror the good shrewd prose of real life with its tireless efforts and physiological griefs and pleasures.

But of course a good many of the Romantics, lacking the mental energy to subdue and pacify the bewilderment which they had conjured up in their own breasts, or to consign it to oblivion in the resumption of a modest citizenly way of life, went to the bad, some by way of madness and physical suicide, others with moral suicide, abandoning themselves to dissoluteness or toying insincerely with a half-hearted and arid religious conformity, but most of them just idling and complaining in loneliness and boredom, like Byron's Manfred who passed his days "loathing our life" and might have been, as an onlooker says, a noble creature, but became instead a dreadful chaos, maze of lines confused. There were yet others, however, who though unable either to subdue or to forget the enemy, would yet not terminate or drag out their life ignominiously but, when the call to action or to resolution for action came, found firm ground in that ideal of Liberty of which they could neither master the theory nor take on the tone in their life, but which yet exercised some sway over them by its sheer beauty. Some of these, though in the unresolved confusion of their ideas they gave themselves for pessimists or for desperate victims of love betrayed and disappointed, or of intolerable listlessness and tedium, went off to fight and die for the cause of oppressed peoples or varied the succession of their romantic follies and breakdowns with robust patriotic and political action. The Romantic traits are strongly marked in almost all the men of the time, as shown in their lives and letters and as comes out unmistakably in their portraits – Romantic in their features, expressions, coiffure, pose, and habiliment. It might happen that in some countries where the active struggle for liberty was somewhat out of view, the Romantics (who as such were merely victims of their nerves and imagination, not bearers of a political aspiration) acquired the repute of being conservatives and reactionaries, such being the suggestion of their expressed likes and dislikes, their whims and their petulances. But where the struggle was lively and heartfelt, and the best intellects won over to Liberalism, Romanticism became almost a synonym for this, and the young Romantics were stalked as suspects by priests and police. Refractory spirits, they were judged likely to be engaged in conspiracies in the "sects" and liable to rise in arms whenever the occasion should present itself – and of this suspect character the signs were the exhibition of cosmic despair, universal mysticism, sudden fits of the sublime in love and heroism, plunges into desolation for the dream of unattainable beatitude, promenades beneath the friendly moon, Hamletic visits to cemeteries, Romantic pallor, Romantic beard and hair, Romantic everything.

A guiding thread for the history of Europe in the nineteenth century can be provided by nothing else save by the spiritual forces which we have watched as they came into being, fell into pattern, lined up, and encountered one another at the beginning of the century. They alone are of the requisite quality to animate the history of the religious and moral soul of the century by which those practical activities that in one or another way aim at progress in particular fields – political, military, administrative, diplomatic, agricultural, industrial, commercial, and so on – are informed, upheld, rectified, transformed. They all depend upon that spiritual direction. No doubt each can be considered in itself for the particular ends which it serves and can be placed as the principal subject at the centre of histories written from the military, diplomatic, bureaucratic, industrial, or other similar point of view, but not at the centre of the sort of history, the sort of historical survey, which interests men outside their own specializations, men in the fullness and height of their humanity.

This is real history, however much the name may be abused for what should at the most be called the chronicle of events ranged in chronological order. Occurrences may be investigated and traced right back to their genesis, but nothing more will ever be discovered than that they were the product of some precedent activity (maybe the activity of nature) or that they were themselves activities competing and conflicting with other simultaneous activities, all of which, so far as concerns the activity of which the history is being told, figure as its raw material or as the stimulus by which it takes its particular shape and development: without them it could no more have come into being than a mill could work without grist of some sort. Either one holds to this view of history or one will end by saying, with thinkers of low grade, that history is nothing else but the clash and intricacy of events, exhibiting sometimes "regular evolutions" and at other times "interrupted evolutions", when there has been disturbance or upheaval or flow in some unexpected direction, sideways or backwards, in reference to their previous direction. How illogical and how dispiriting, whereas real history always sounds a warlike note in respect of the struggle of life.

On the other hand it should by now be clear that historical determinism of any sort must be ruled out. We accordingly refrain from assigning the pre-eminence in our history (as writers are wont to do) to any such single event as the so-called industrial revolution, the wonders of technical progress, the new relationship between old Europe and the American lands, the formation of the modern colonial Empires and so forth. These are not factors but facts of history. Equally must we avoid giving such pre-eminence to one or the other of the series of spiritual factors, taken as independent or mutually limiting or even reciprocally affected entities. Doing so, we should slip into an idealistically disguised but still naturalistic determinism. For the forces which we have described above are not, in the interpretation and exposition we have given of them, properly speaking factors, nor are they a plurality, but a unity: or rather a unique process involving the self-affirmation of what we have called the "Religion of Liberty" through its struggles against the oppositions which duly and necessarily rose against it, and through the absorption of elements absorbed from those very oppositions or of new forms generated in the course of the victorious struggle bringing it an increase of strength and power of renewal. The process embraces likewise the enrichment of the oppositions by the absorption of new elements or re-arrangement of the old, whereby they too show a certain originality in attack and defence and hindering manoeuvres. In the stress of this struggle the Religion of Liberty is continually exposed to the Romantic malady in its changeful forms, but continually gets the better of it.

We may now ask ourselves whether this process worked itself out wholly in the nineteenth century, in such manner that looking back from the twentieth we may regard the division between them as not merely chronological, but also moral. Is the new century a moral entity with which there starts a new process, a new spiritual tendency? We can put the question this way. Did there arise at the end of the old or the beginning of the new century a new Religion, a real Religion broader and more powerful than the Religion of the nineteenth century, and destined therefore to surpass and replace it? This is the essential question raised by a narration of the history of Europe in our period. Willingly or unwillingly, knowingly or unknowingly, all the historical works and manuals devoted to this period revolve around this problem which some pose more clearly than others. My history is naturally not intended to demolish or replace those others as a whole or in detail. The attempt would be pointless. It suffices for me to recall those writings by allusion, which may even be tacit allusion. The events and successions of events which they relate are general knowledge. The task here will be to throw the problem into clearer light and relief by pursuing and exemplifying in detail the preceding exposition, showing, by the record of its successes and later encounters with opposition and variations upon its fundamental theme, how the Liberal Ideal performed its work, and with what fortunes. Our history is in fact the history of a War of the Spirit, which is really and truly entitled to the description of "The Great War".

[1931]

INDEX

Philodemus, 241
Philology: marriage of with philosophy produces history, 508; and the science of language, 254-6
Philosophy: arises from unforeseeable and necessary creative inspiration, 134; and art criticism, 372; no authority over poetry, 282; and culture, 1010; does not engender philosophy, 104; and history, oneness of (Hegel), 28, 29; is itself, not poetry, practice, or morality, 10; as methodology of history, 175; problem of, is knowledge of good, 100; unity of, with history, 185. *See also* History
Pichon, R., 777 n.
Pimentel, Eleonora de Fonseca, 1058
Pinturicchio, Bernardino Betti, 115
Pisistratus, 311
Pistelli, Ermenegildo, 826
Pittaluga, M., 370 n.
Plato, and Platonism, XLV, 5, 13, 16, 70, 199, 241, 296, 381, 541, 567, 593, 726, 1011, 1071; on Homer, 377, 770; value of poetry denied, 241
Plattner, Ernst, 461, 462 n.
Plautus, 776, 778, 780, 784, 798, 843
Plotinus, 209, 241, 460
Plutarch, 594, 794 n., 895
Poe, Edgar Allen, LIII, 729
Poetry: aesthetic and historic interpretation of, 314-15; antecedent to logic, 82; and art, 216-17; concreteness of, 306; its cosmic character, 220, 263, 280; efficacy of, in literature and civilization, 307; an expression of new language, 312; folk poetry, 382-93; founded on human personality, 221; heroic, 331-7; an historical fact, 314; is language in its genuineness, 287; and literature, 59, 296-308, 773; logic of (Vico), 244; love, 331-7; as lyrical intuition, 216; never objective, 818; phi-

losophy no authority over, 10, 282; and prose, 286, 304; structure and, relationship between, 328-30, 773. *See also* Art, Expression, Literature, Rhetoric
Polentone, Sicco, 115 n.
Political sense, the, 637-48
Politics: born with the Renaissance, 751; constitute an original force, 136; Machiavelli and philosophical concept of, 655-6; and morals, 637-8; political action is useful action, 638
Politz, K. H., 464 n.
Poliziano, 311
Polybius, 516, 548
Polygnotus, 501
Pontano, G., 995, 996, 998 n., 1001
Pope, Alexander, 21, 172, 1062, 1065-6
Poppe, B., 428
Porta, Carlo, 690
Positivism, L, 5, 24, 129, 191, 209, 527
Pozzi, Giovanni, 3
Pragmatism, 45
Prati, Giovanni, 3
Predestination, 1025-6
Problem: is one with its solution, 86
Problems, alleged or nominal, 87-91; are always individual, 740-2
Progress: concept of, ignored by Vico, 142; and decadence, 589; individual, validity of, 537; is limited and infinite, 581; as philosophical concept, 589-94; is rhythm of spirit, 592; as state of mind, 589-94; in work, only joy worthy of man, 594
Prose: Foscolo and, 927; as an ideal for poetry in 18th cent., 1062; ideal lies in restraint of the sign, 286; and mathematical symbolism, 286; opposed to poetry, 286
Proudhon, Pierre-Joseph, 217
Protestantism: and Catholicism, 1087; Croce's uncomplimentary references to, XLIII; and Hegel,

610; mediaeval archaism of, 980; use of political methods for moral ends, 650
Priestley, Joseph, 451
Probabilism, 699
Propertius, 304, 799 n.
Pulci, Luigi, 848, 1013
Puoti, Basilio, 842
Puritanism, 1038
Pythagoras, 209, 377

Quatremère de Quincy, Antoine-Chrysostome, 411 n.
Quesnay, François, 668
Quintilian, 288, 289, 291, 294, 299, 321, 376
Quistorp, Th. Johann, 434

Rabelais, François, 854
Racine, Jean, 779, 804, 1061
Ranke, Leopold, 511, 573, 602
Raphael, 367, 485
Radcliffe, Anne, 219, 292
Rand, Prof. Edward E., 777 n.
Rationalism: cultural importance of, in 17th-century England and France, 1057; during Reformation in Italy, 978-9; manifestation of, in Arcadia, 1058; religious nature of, 1039; of the Renaissance, 978
Rau, S., 404
Reason: destructive of myths, 1060; and History, dissension between, 1071; philosophers as martyrs of, 22; religion of, 979
Recchi, A., 370 n.
Redi, F., 401
Reformation: and Catholicism, 1082; complementary to the Renaissance, 750; Italians and, 1031; Machiavelli and, 655; originated in Humanism, 167
Reid, Thomas, 451
Rembrandt, 373
Rémy d'Auxerre, 112 n.
Renan, Ernest, 599
Renouvier, Carl, 558
Retz, Cardinal de, 516

Renaissance, the: and Catholicism, 1082; complementary to Reformation, 750; introduces political science, 751; links with Risorgimento, 975-88; and Middle Ages, 750; and Philosophy of Nature, 756; prepares way for Aesthetics, 751; its religious and rational character, 978
Rhetoric: and allegory, 376; Croce's enmity towards, 305; not a quality of art, 220-1; and Romantics, 299; vitiates concept of expression, 234
Ribbeck, Otto, 833 n.
Ricardo, David, 664-5
Ricci, Minio, 995 n.
Richelieu, Cardinal, 424-5, 1040
Rickert, H., 917 n.
Riedel, F. G., 434
Riegl, A., 415
Rigorism, and Rigorists, 698-702
Risorgimento, the: began about 1670 (Arcadia), 1035, 1058; and dialect literature, 406; and religion, 719. See also Arcadia, Renaissance
Ritter, H., 441
Rjazanov, D., 624 n.
Robertson, J. M., 244
Robespierre, Maximilien, 165-6, 615, 684
Rodriguez Villa, Antonio, 989 n.
Rohan, Cardinal de, 657
Rolland, M., 452 n.
Rolli, Paolo, 1065
Rollin, Charles, 451
Romanticism: and the Baroque, 418-20; and Catholicism, 1104; criticized by Goethe and Kant, 1109; and Middle Ages, 1106; moral and sentimental, 1101-2; and Mystery, 40-41; and Nature Philosophy, 756; non-Romanticism of Dante, 822-3; overcome by Religion of Liberty, 1112; premiss and synonym (almost) for Liberalism, 1110; revolt against

DATE DUE